Student's Thesaurus

Third Edition

MARC MCCUTCHEON

Viva Books

New Delhi | Mumbai | Chennai | Kolkata | Bengaluru | Hyderabad | Kochi | Guwahati

First Indian Edition 2010
Reprinted 2014, 2019

VIVA BOOKS PRIVATE LIMITED

- 4737/23 Ansari Road, Daryaganj, New Delhi 110 002
E-mail: vivadelhi@vivagroupindia.net, Tel. 42242200
- 76, Service Industries, Shirvane, Sector 1, Nerul, Navi Mumbai 400 706
E-mail: vivamumbai@vivagroupindia.net, Tel. 27721273, 27721274
- Megh Towers, Old No. 307, New No.165, Poonamallee High Road, Maduravoyal
Chennai 600 095, E-mail: vivachennai@vivagroupindia.net, Tel. 28290304, 28294241
- B-103, Jindal Towers, 21/1A/3 Darga Road, Kolkata 700 017
E-mail: vivakolkata@vivagroupindia.net, Tel. 22836381, 22816713
- 7, Sovereign Park Apartments, 56-58, K. R. Road, Basavanagudi, Bengaluru 560 004
E-mail: vivabangalore@vivagroupindia.net, Tel. 26607409, 26607410
- 101-102 Mughal Marc Apartments, 3-4-637 to 641, Narayanguda, Hyderabad 500 029
E-mail: vivahyderabad@vivagroupindia.net, Tel. 27564481, 27564482
- Beevi Towers, First Floor, SRM Road, Kaloor, Kochi 682 018, Kerala
E-mail: vivakochi@vivagroupindia.net, Tel: 0484-2403055, 2403056
- 232, GNB Road, Beside UCO Bank, Silpukhuri, Guwahati 781 003
E-mail: vivaguwahati@vivagroupindia.net, Tel: 0361-2666386

www.vivagroupindia.com

Published by arrangement with
Facts in File, Inc.
132 West 31st Street
New York 10001
USA

ISBN : 978-81-309-1362-9

Published by Vinod Vasishtha for Viva Books Private Limited, 4737/23, Ansari Road, New Delhi-110 002. Printed and bound by Anand Sons, Delhi.

Y0001

Student's Thesaurus

INTRODUCTION

Welcome to the greatly expanded third edition of *The Viva Student's Thesaurus*. We've added nearly 50,000 words of text to help you express yourself on paper and in speech, better than ever before.

WHAT IS A THESAURUS?

A thesaurus is a book that lists synonyms and antonyms. Synonyms are words that have the same or similar meanings, and they can often be substituted for each other. Antonyms, on the other hand, are words that have the opposite meanings. By way of example, *shy* and *bashful* are synonyms for *timid*, and *bold* and *assertive* are its antonyms.

WHY USE A THESAURUS?

A thesaurus is a valuable reference tool for improving your writing. But how can it be valuable to you? For starters, it can help you avoid overusing any particular word, thus making your conversation and writing more lively and interesting. As a case in point, the word *valuable* has been used twice in this paragraph. If it were to appear again, it would make the text too repetitive. As a substitute, a synonym, such as *important,* would be more appealing (*appealing,* by the way, is used here as a synonym for *interesting*).

There is another important way in which a thesaurus can be of value to you. If you know a word that is not quite right for your purposes, then a thesaurus should be able to provide a perfect alternative. For example, suppose you want to find the right word to describe a skinny friend but don't want to use *skinny* because it seems negative. You can look in this thesaurus and find substitutes, such as *thin* or *lean*.

HOW DO YOU USE THIS THESAURUS?

This thesaurus has been organized to be simple and easy to use. The word you are looking for is known as a primary entry, and you can find it listed in alphabetical order. A primary entry is presented in **bold** type. The part of speech that the primary entry is follows immediately in its abbreviated form in *italic* type.

Next is a list of synonyms and then a sample sentence illustrating how the primary entry word can be used. If the primary entry word can be used in more than one way, additional synonym lists follow. If there are any antonyms, they will appear at the end of the synonym lists.

This thesaurus has an extra vocabulary-building feature called *Word Search.* It lists words and terms *related* to the primary entry that are not synonyms of it. After locating synonyms for, say, *dog* (*canine, hound, mutt,* etc.), you may require some words to accurately *describe* a dog. A coat streaked with gray, for example, is said to be *grizzled.* The soles of a dog's feet are known as *pads*. The lower cheeks of a dog are its *chops*. With this fun but oh-so-useful feature, you will be able to make your writing more descriptive and precise.

A variety of abbreviations are used in this thesaurus—mainly referring to parts of speech. It is important to be familiar with them when using the thesaurus. Following is a list of the abbreviations used in this book:

adj. adjective
adv. adverb
ant. antonym
interj. interjection
n. noun
prep. preposition
vb. verb

This thesaurus lists thousands of the most commonly used words; however, you may be looking for a word that has not been included. Omissions occur when a word is judged to be too obscure to include or when there are no synonyms good enough to merit inclusion. For example, *alphabetize* means "to arrange in the order of the letters of the alphabet." But there are no other words that mean precisely the same thing, so *alphabetize* does not appear in this thesaurus. Finally, a word of caution is in order. In some of the synonym lists, you will find words that look like they cannot be substituted for the primary entry, or at least not in the accompanying sentence. This happens because there are very few words in the English language that are truly interchangeable. Synonyms of the primary word that will not work in the sample sentence are included because there are other situations and other sentences for which they may be just right. In general, synonyms most closely associated with the primary entry are listed first.

Now you know how to use this thesaurus. Keep it on your bookshelf next to your dictionary, for it should prove to be as essential.

A

abandon *vb.* **1.** desert, reject, forsake, drop, renounce. *Uncaring people abandon their friends in a crisis.* **2.** discontinue, abort, cease, stop, forgo. *A major avalanche forced the climbers to abandon their attempt on Mt. McKinley.* *–n.* **3.** gusto, dash, animation, verve. *Hip-hop dancers perform with abandon.* **Ant. 1.** keep, claim. **2.** continue, maintain. **3.** self-control, restraint, caution, moderation.

abandoned *adj.* **1.** shameless, wild, loose, immoral. *The playboy led an abandoned way of life.* **2.** vacant, deserted, unoccupied, neglected. *An abandoned building typically becomes a ruin.* **Ant. 1.** upright, moral, virtuous, chaste. **2.** occupied, maintained.

abandonment *n.* discontinuance, cessation, halt, stoppage. *The abandonment of the mission was caused by a defect in the rocket.* **Ant.** continuation, prolongation, extension.

abate *vb.* diminish, subside, lessen, weaken, decline, wane. *It was at least 48 hours before the rain began to abate.* **Ant.** increase, strengthen, intensify.

abbey *n.* monastery, convent, friary, priory. *The abbey is a refuge for those monks and nuns who seek to live an uncomplicated life.*

abbreviate *vb.* condense, shorten, contract, compress, reduce. *"Mister" is usually abbreviated as "Mr."* **Ant.** lengthen, extend, increase, expand, protract, prolong.

abbreviation *n.* condensation, shortening, abridgment, compression, reduction. *Virtually everyone knows the abbreviation for "Doctor."* **Ant.** expansion, enlargement, extension, increase.

WORD SEARCH

(Common abbreviations)
AC: *alternating current, air conditioning*
A.D.: *anno Domini, in the year of the Lord*
a.k.a.: *also known as*
a.m.: *ante meridiem* (before noon)
AM: *amplitude modulation*
anon.: *anonymous*
ASAP: *as soon as possible*
aux.: *auxiliary*
B.C.: *before Christ*
C: *Celsius, centigrade*
CEO: *chief executive officer*
cl.: *centiliter*
cm.: *centimeter*
co.: *company*
COD: *cash on delivery*
corp.: *corporation*
CPR: *cardiopulmonary resuscitation*
DA: *district attorney*
DOA: *dead on arrival*
Dr.: *Doctor*
ESP: *extrasensory perception*
etc.: *et cetera* (and so forth)
F: *Fahrenheit*
FM: *frequency modulation*
ft.: *foot*

FYI: *for your information*
g.: *gram*
GOP: *Grand Old Party*
hq.: *headquarters*
in.: *inch*
IQ: *intelligence quotient*
kg: *kilogram*
km: *kilometer*
l: *liter*
lb.: *pound*
mg.: *milligram*
ml.: *milliliter*
mm.: *millimeter*
mph: *miles per hour*
oz.: *ounce*
PC: *personal computer*
p.m.: *post meridiem* (after noon)
P.S.: *postscript*
RBI: *runs batted in*
rpm: *revolutions per minute*
RSVP: *repondez s'il vous plait* (please answer)
SOS: *save our ship/save our souls*
TBA: *to be announced*
UFO: *unidentified flying object*
VIP: *very important person*
VP: *vice president*

abdicate *vb.* resign, renounce, relinquish, abandon, vacate, surrender. *The rebels forced their king to abdicate his throne.*

abdomen *n.* stomach, belly, midsection, tummy, gut. *The boxer was punched in the abdomen.*

abduct *vb.* kidnap, shanghai, steal, grab, seize. *Terrorists abducted the ambassador.* **Ant.** free, release, return.

aberration *n.* abnormality, irregularity, oddity, anomaly, deviation, quirk. *Snow in July is an aberration.* **Ant.** norm, regularity.

abhor *vb.* loathe, detest, despise, hate, disdain, reject. *Vampires abhor garlic, crosses, sunlight, and—most of all—wooden stakes.* **Ant.** adore, love, admire, prize, cherish, treasure.

abhorrence *n.* loathing, repugnance, aversion, detestation, disgust, hatred. *Most people react with abhorrence to the thought of increased taxation.* **Ant.** approval, admiration, acceptance, endorsement.

abhorrent *adj.* revolting, nauseating, abominable, detestable, repugnant. *Cruelty to children is the worst kind of abhorrent conduct.* **Ant.** admirable, commendable, laudable, praiseworthy.

abide *vb.* **1.** remain, linger, stay, tarry. *Please don't hurry off, but abide here with me.* **2.** endure, tolerate, bear, suffer. *Many people can't abide the smell of cheap cigars.* **Ant. 1.** leave, depart, quit. **2.** reject, decline, spurn, oppose.

abiding *adj.* unshakable, firm, constant, lasting, enduring. *Honest people have abiding trust in others.* **Ant.** passing, momentary, temporary.

ability *n.* capability, competence, capacity, aptitude, skill, talent, qualification. *She has the ability to excel in graduate school.* **Ant.** inability, incapability, incompetence, inadequacy.

abject *adj.* **1.** wretched, hopeless, miserable, terrible, piteous. *His abject condition is the result of losing his job.* **2.** servile, cringing, groveling, subservient, spiritless. *The student's abject apology made little impression on her teacher.* **Ant. 1.** dignified, hopeful. **2.** assured, spirited, admirable.

ablaze *adj.* **1.** burning, blazing, flaming, flaring, aflame, afire. *The building was totally ablaze before anyone knew what was happening.* **2.** bright, shiny, aglow, luminous, radiant. *The boy was ablaze with love for the girl next door.* **Ant. 1.** extinguished. **2.** gloomy, somber, depressed, dispirited.

able *adj.* capable, qualified, competent, effective, proficient. *The personnel director was looking for able employees.* **Ant.** inept, unable, incapable, unqualified.

able-bodied *adj.* strong, fit, healthy, sound, strapping, athletic. *John was able-bodied enough to unload the entire truck by himself.* **Ant.** disabled, handicapped.

abnormal *adj.* odd, unusual, unnatural, irregular, extraordinary, uncommon. *The boy's abnormal behavior was a source of concern for his parents.* **Ant.** normal, common, ordinary, natural, usual, typical.

abnormality *n.* oddity, exception, irregularity, peculiarity, aberration. *Her only abnormality was putting ketchup on her ice cream.*

aboard *adj.* on board, topside, on deck. *When Gilligan came aboard, we knew we were trouble.*

abode *n.* home, house, residence, dwelling, habitation, quarters. *If I were rich, my abode would be a truly grand old castle.*

abolish *vb.* eliminate, negate, disallow, end, cancel, nullify, rescind, revoke. *The Emancipation Proclamation abolished slavery.* **Ant.** conserve, retain, establish, create, institute.

abolition *n.* ending, termination, elimination, eradication, repeal. *The abolition of slavery was long overdue.* **Ant.** establishment, start, creation.

A-bomb *n.* atomic bomb, nuclear bomb, thermonuclear bomb, weapon of mass destruction. *The A-bomb can unleash a staggering amount of power.*

See also NUCLEAR BOMB.

abominable *adj.* awful, horrible, nasty, loathsome, despicable, deplorable, atrocious. *Slavery was an abominable institution.* **Ant.** great, wonderful, commendable.

aboriginal *adj.* native, indigenous, endemic, original, primal, primitive. *The aboriginal people living on the island are actually transplanted Asians.*

aborigine *n.* native, indigene, first inhabitant, original settler, settler. *The aborigines lived there long before anyone else.* **Ant.** immigrant, new arrival, foreigner.

abort *vb.* cancel, terminate, abandon, halt, stop, cease. *A computer malfunction forced flight controllers to abort the shuttle launch.* **Ant.** conclude, complete, finish, achieve.

abortion *n.* miscarriage, termination, expulsion, infanticide, aborticide. *Unfortunately, Mary had a spontaneous abortion and lost the baby.*

about *adv.* **1.** almost, approximately, around, nearly. *It's about 93 million miles from the Earth to the Sun.* **2.** around, throughout, everywhere. *As the man walked through the dark cemetery, he kept looking carefully about.* –*prep.* **3.** concerning, regarding, involving. *The movie was about ghosts and goblins.*

above *prep.* **1.** over, beyond, past. *This book is not intended for people above the age of eighteen.* **2.** over, higher than. *Her name was above his on the list.* –*adv.* **3.** over, overhead. *His bedroom is on the floor above.* **Ant. 1–3.** under, below, beneath.

abracadabra *n.* incantation, invocation, charm, hocus pocus, mumbo jumbo. *The magician shouted "abracadabra" and some other invocation and the rabbit vanished.*

abrade *vb.* scrape, grate, scuff, scour, grind, erode, gouge, sand. *We were warned that the rough surface of the stone might abrade the table's finish.*

abrasion *n.* scratch, scrape, cut, chafe, irritation, scuff. *She fell and suffered an abrasion on her left hand.*

abrasive *adj.* harsh, annoying, irritating, unpleasant, grating, disagreeable, caustic. *Chalk makes an abrasive sound when it is scraped across a blackboard.* **Ant.** soothing, comforting, pleasant, agreeable.

abridged *adj.* condensed, shortened, reduced, compressed, abbreviated. *In order to save time, the student read an abridged version of the assigned book.* **Ant.** expanded, extended, increased, augmented.

abroad *adv.* **1.** overseas. *She spent a delightful summer vacation abroad.* **2.** astir, active, afoot, restless. *Ghosts are typically abroad after midnight.* **Ant. 1.** stateside. **2.** asleep, quiet, still.

abrupt *adj.* **1.** curt, blunt, rude, rough, gruff. *Abrupt responses often cause hurt feelings.* **2.** sudden, hasty, instantaneous, precipitous. *Careful drivers rarely have to make abrupt stops.* **3.** steep, sheer, vertical, perpendicular. *The cliff's face has an abrupt drop.* **Ant. 1.** polite, courteous, civil. **2.** gradual, unhurried, deliberate. **3.** gradual, slow, easy.

abscess *n.* swelling, inflammation, pus-filled sac, boil, pustule, fester. *Kate had a terrible abscess in her mouth that required immediate care.*

absence *n.* **1.** want, need, lack, deficiency, inadequacy, shortcoming. *Absence of effort will get you nowhere.* **2.** nonattendance, nonappearance. *Unexcused absences from work can result in dismissal.* **Ant. 1.** supply, abundance. **2.** presence, attendance, appearance.

absent *adj.* **1.** away, missing, truant, elsewhere. *My best friend was absent from school today.* **2.** absentminded, bemused, preoccupied, inattentive, distracted, oblivious, dreamy. *His absent look betrayed his lack of attention.* **Ant. 1.** present, available. **2.** attentive, alert, aware.

absent-minded *adj.* inattentive, oblivious, scatterbrained, forgetful, remote, dreamy. *He was so absent-minded, he often forgot to tie his shoes.* **Ant.** attentive, alert, aware.

absolute *adj.* complete, conclusive, perfect, whole, total, full, unqualified, unlimited. *The United States no longer has absolute domination of Olympic basketball.* **Ant.** restricted, partial, limited, incomplete, conditional.

absolutely *adv.* definitely, doubtlessly, completely, entirely, wholly, thoroughly. *I am absolutely certain he was the man I saw.* **Ant.** possibly, probably, somewhat.

absolve *vb.* exonerate, excuse, free, acquit, pardon, clear. *He thought he could absolve his guilt by sending her flowers.* **Ant.** charge, condemn.

absorb *vb.* **1.** assimilate, incorporate, digest, retain. *People with photographic memories absorb everything they read.* **2.** engross, preoccupy, captivate, enthrall, hold, engage, fascinate. *She was so absorbed in the computer game that she lost track of time.* **Ant. 1.** lose, eliminate. **2.** bore, distract.

absorbing *adj.* engrossing, interesting, fascinating, exciting, captivating, intriguing, thrilling. *Network television has a noticeable lack of absorbing shows.* **Ant.** boring, dull, tiresome, unexciting, uninteresting.

abstain *vb.* avoid, forgo, refrain, spurn, resist. *Many people abstain from drinking hard liquors.* **Ant.** indulge, revel, overdo.

abstinence *n.* forebearing, self-denial, celibacy, sobriety, temperance. *When it came to alcohol and tobacco, my grandmother practiced complete abstinence.* **Ant.** indulgence, splurging, extravagance.

abstract *adj.* **1.** hypothetical, theoretical, speculative, conceptual, ideal. *Scientists frequently deal with abstract questions.* –*n.* **2.** abridgment, condensation, synopsis, summary, extraction. *The conference speaker presented an abstract of his latest article.* **Ant. 1.** concrete, specific, practical. **2.** enlargement, expansion.

abstruse *adj.* abstract, recondite, esoteric, arcane, difficult, complex, unfathomable, deep. **Ant.** easy, simple, clear.

absurd *adj.* foolish, ridiculous, preposterous, laughable, irrational. *Parents frequently think their children's behavior is absurd.* **Ant.** reasonable, sensible, rational, logical.

absurdity *n.* foolishness, nonsense, craziness, silliness, idiocy, ridiculousness. *The audience enjoyed the comedian's absurdities.* **Ant.** sense, wisdom, reality.

abundance *n.* **1.** profusion, sufficiency, ampleness, excess, surplus. *The local library has an abundance of excellent books.* **2.** wealth, riches, prosperity. *Who wouldn't like to live in abundance?* **Ant. 1.** scarcity, lack, deficiency. **2.** poverty, destitution.

abundant *adj.* plentiful, ample, copious, rich, bountiful, bounteous. *Farmers are always hoping for abundant rainfall.* **Ant.** scarce, rare, meager, scant, insufficient.

abuse *vb.* **1.** insult, malign, slander, scold, berate, reproach. *A considerate employer will not verbally abuse his or her employees.* **2.** misuse, exploit, mishandle, misapply. *A good leader does not abuse her power.* **3.** hurt, harm, injure, mistreat. *To abuse an animal is unforgivable.* –*n.* **4.** misuse, mistreatment, cruelty, injury, harm, hurt. *Child abuse can never be condoned.* **5.** insults, scolding, berating, tirade. *An old-fashioned tongue-lashing is a kind of abuse that makes many people angry.* **Ant. 1.** praise, compliment. **2.** respect, honor, protect. **5.** praise.

abusive *adj.* insulting, offensive, offending, rude, contemptuous. *Considerate people try not to use abusive language.* **Ant.** respectful, complimentary, courteous, polite.

abut *vb.* border on, conjoin, adjoin, juxtapose. *Our backyard abuts that of the Smith family.*

abysmal *adj.* **1.** unfathomable, immeasurable, deep, bottomless. *They had reached a particularly abysmal section of the ocean.* **2.** bad, awful, terrible, wretched, lousy. *The team's performance on the field was abysmal.* **Ant. 1.** shallow, measurable, fathomable. **2.** excellent, good, great.

abyss *n.* chasm, pit, emptiness, nothingness, void. *On the brink of an abyss is not a good place to get sweaty hands.*

academia *n.* academe, world of scholarship, school, college, halls of ivy, intelligentsia. *Sherry had an unquenchable thirst for knowledge, so we knew she would thrive in academia.*

academic *adj.* **1.** scholarly, studious, scholastic, educational, pedantic. *He has no practical experience—his background is entirely academic.* **2.** hypothetical, conjectural, theoretical, speculative, moot, impractical. *Since she's now deceased, any discussion of how she should have spent her life is purely academic.* **Ant. 1.** uneducated, unschooled, unlearned. **2.** practical, realistic.

academy *n.* school, institute, institution, prep school, secondary school. *I'll be training to become a police officer at our local police academy.*

accede *vb.* consent, agree to, yield, acquiesce, give in. *We must never accede to the demands of terrorists.* **Ant.** refuse, fight, oppose.

accelerate *vb.* hasten, hurry, quicken, speed, expedite, rush. *The runner suddenly accelerated as she neared the finish line.* **Ant.** decelerate, slow, delay, retard, brake.

accelerator *n.* throttle, gas pedal, power control, speed control. *Joe punched the accelerator and we took off like a shot.*

accent *n.* **1.** emphasis, stress, accentuation. *In the word "wonderful," the accent is on the first syllable.* **2.** inflection, tone, intonation, pronunciation, enunciation. *He speaks with a foreign accent.* *–vb.* **3.** enhance, emphasize, stress, accentuate, highlight. *Fresh flowers accented the room's decor.* **Ant. 3.** underplay, minimize, underemphasize.

accept *vb.* **1.** receive, acquire, gain, obtain, take. *He was more than happy to accept the gift.* **2.** acknowledge, affirm, concur, approve, agree. *The hostess accepted her guest's explanation for his late arrival.* **3.** assume, acknowledge, endure, tolerate, submit. *He finally learned to accept his defeat.* **Ant. 1–2.** reject, refuse, resist. **3.** deny, repudiate, disavow.

acceptable *adj.* **1.** adequate, sufficient, tolerable, average, passable, fair. *A report card full of Cs may be acceptable, but it's definitely not outstanding.* **2.** satisfactory, suitable, worthy, fit, proper. *The editor thought the manuscript was acceptable.* **Ant. 1–2.** unacceptable, substandard, poor, unsatisfactory.

acceptance *n.* approval, recognition, endorsement, sanction, confirmation. *The appointed official has yet to gain public acceptance.* **Ant.** rejection, repudiation, scorning, spurning.

accepted *adj.* proper, approved, suitable, conventional, standard, customary, established. *Blue jeans are not the accepted mode of dress at formal weddings.* **Ant.** unsuitable, improper, unconventional.

access *n.* admittance, approach, entrance, entry, passage, route. *The president has access to the nation's top secrets.*

accessory *n.* **1.** addition, accompaniment, appendage, supplement, attachment, extension. *Most cars come with optional accessories.* **2.** accomplice, confederate, partner, coconspirator, assistant. *The bank teller was an unwitting accessory to the robbery.*

accident *n.* **1.** misfortune, mishap, calamity, misadventure, crash, collision. *Automobile accidents claim thousands of lives every year.* **2.** chance, luck, fortune, happenstance, fluke. *She made the discovery by accident.* **Ant. 2.** intent, intention, plan, design.

accidental *adj.* undesigned, unintended, unintentional, unplanned, unexpected, unforeseen. *Some of our most significant scientific discoveries have been accidental.* **Ant.** intended, planned, designed, expected, foreseen.

accidentally *adv.* unintentionally, unwittingly, haphazardly, fortuitously, by chance. *I accidentally slammed the door on my hand.* **Ant.** intentionally, by design, wittingly.

accident-prone *adj.* clumsy, inattentive, inept, bumbling, bungling, incautious. *His inattentiveness made him accident-prone.* **Ant.** cautious, safety-conscious, careful.

acclaim *n.* **1.** applause, honor, homage, praise, enthusiasm. *The best-selling author's new book was greeted with great acclaim.* *–vb.* **2.** commend, applaud, compliment, praise. *All the leading critics acclaimed her latest movie.* **Ant. 1.** condemnation, criticism. **2.** berate, denounce, criticize.

acclimate *vb.* adapt, accustom, adjust, condition, habituate, fit in. *It takes time to acclimate oneself to a foreign culture.*

accolade *n.* recognition, acclaim, award, prize, praise, honor, tribute. *The director won accolade upon accolade for his work on* Lord of the Rings.

accommodate *vb.* contain, hold, house, admit, include, lodge, shelter, quarter. *This classroom can accommodate twenty-five students.*

accommodating *adj.* solicitous, obliging, hospitable, helpful, gracious, eager to please. *The stranger was so accommodating, he even changed our flat tire for us.* **Ant.** unhelpful, ungracious, demanding.

accommodation *n.* **1.** solicitude, helpfulness, care, assistance, courtesy, kindness. *After we complained to the media about our permanently lost luggage, the airline bent over backwards to give us every accommodation.* **2.** housing, lodging, quarters, room, suite, shelter, berth. *The accommodation consisted of a grass hut and a hammock.* **Ant. 1.** snub, rejection, roadblock.

accompany *vb.* attend, escort, join, follow. *Mary's little lamb accompanied her everywhere.* **Ant.** desert, leave, abandon, forsake.

accomplice *n.* confederate, collaborator, cohort, helper, partner, associate. *The man's wife was his accomplice in crime.* **Ant.** opponent, adversary, rival, competitor.

accomplish *vb.* achieve, attain, reach, realize, fulfill, complete, finish, perform. *Charles Lindbergh accomplished his goal when he flew across the Atlantic.* **Ant.** fail, forsake, abort, attempt, neglect.

accomplished *adj.* **1.** skilled, masterly, expert, gifted, brilliant, talented, polished, experienced. *Laurence Olivier was an accomplished actor.* **2.** completed, established, proven, realized, accepted. *The control of polio is an accomplished fact.* **Ant. 1.** incompetent, amateurish. **2.** unproven, unestablished.

accomplishment *n.* **1.** achievement, attainment, triumph, victory, success. *Hillary's 1953 climb of Mt. Everest was a notable accomplishment.* **2.** skill, gift, talent, expertness, proficiency. *Learning to dance beautifully is just one of her many accomplishments.* **Ant. 1.** failure, mishap, disappointment. **2.** lack, deficiency.

accord *n.* **1.** agreement, harmony, concurrence, concord, tune, uniformity, conformity. *His views on disarmament are in accord with mine.* –*vb.* **2.** agree, conform, correspond, coincide, concur, match. *Her views on the environment accord with his.* **Ant. 1.** discord, conflict, difference. **2.** differ, disagree.

accordingly *adv.* therefore, consequently, hence, thus, then, ergo. *He spends all his time at a computer; accordingly, he doesn't have much of a social life.*

accordion *n.* concertina, (slang) squeezebox, (slang) groanbox, melodeon, instrument. *Who needs an electric guitar when you can get down with an accordion instead?*

accost *vb.* approach, greet, assail, hail, confront, address, call, assault. *The homeless man would always accost those who passed him on the street.* **Ant.** ignore, neglect, snub.

account *n.* **1.** story, report, description, explanation, narrative, tale. *The victim gave police a full account of the robbery.* **2.** importance, worth, significance, value, regard. *Since he has been known to lie, his explanation is of very little account.* **3.** record, register, invoice, bill, statement. *She owes almost $1,000 on her credit-card account.* –*vb.* **4.** explain, justify, rationalize, interpret, clarify. *Please account for your activities last night.* **Ant. 2.** insignificance, unimportance, worthlessness.

accountability *n.* responsibility, liability, obligation, culpability, duty. *If you're going to be a babysitter, you must accept a certain amount of accountability.*

accountable *adj.* responsible, liable, answerable, guilty, blameworthy. *The girl's parents held* *her accountable for damages to the family car.* **Ant.** unaccountable, unanswerable, blameless, innocent.

accountant *n.* bookkeeper, auditor, CPA, comptroller, (slang) number cruncher, (slang) bean counter, (slang) pencil pusher. *The accountant kept track of the company's finances.*

accounting *n.* record-keeping, bookkeeping, auditing, balancing the books. *He was good with figures so he decided to make accounting his career.*

WORD SEARCH

accounting period: *calendar year, fiscal year*
book of records: *ledger, daybook*
cheating on records to hide profits: (slang) *cooking the books*
computer program for organizing figures into columns: *spreadsheet*
correcting mistakes: *reconciling*
earnings yet to be received, entry of: *accrual, accounts receivable*
enter new figures into book: *log*
examination of records: *audit*
examiner of records: *auditor*
decreasing value over time: *depreciation*
increasing value over time: *appreciation*
losing money: *in the red*
making a profit: *in the black*
money owed: *accounts payable, liabilities*
profit after expenses: *net profit*
profit before expenses: *gross profit*
selling of equipment, property and other assets to raise cash: *liquidation*
tally of profit or loss, final: *bottom line*
valuable items and property: *assets*
withdrawal of funds: *draw*

accredit *vb.* sanction, certify, authorize, endorse, recognize, validate. *The board of directors plans to accredit the new academy just as soon as the testing of instructors is concluded.* **Ant.** reject, denounce, invalidate.

accrual *n.* growth, increase, accumulation, addition. *The annual accrual in my savings account was significant.* **Ant.** loss, decrease, decline.

accrue *vb.* grow, increase, accumulate, add up, expand. *Open an interest-bearing account and watch your money accrue.* **Ant.** decrease, diminish, shrink.

accumulate *vb.* collect, gather, amass, assemble, stockpile, hoard. *The collector accumulated an impressive quantity of rare coins.* **Ant.** decrease, diminish, lessen, disperse, scatter.

accuracy *n.* precision, correctness, exactness, preciseness, authenticity. *Teachers have to evaluate term papers for accuracy.* **Ant.** error, mistake, faultiness, inaccuracy.

accurate *adj.* correct, right, perfect, faultless, precise, true, reliable. *At the county fair, the weight-guesser's estimates were mostly accurate.* **Ant.** inaccurate, incorrect, wrong, mistaken, imperfect.

accusation *n.* allegation, charge, claim, complaint, assertion. *Your accusation is totally unfounded.*

accuse *vb.* blame, charge, implicate, incriminate, indict, reproach. *Don't be hasty and accuse someone before you have all the facts.* **Ant.** clear, acquit, absolve, exonerate.

accuser *n.* incriminator, finger-pointer, tattletale, informer, (slang) rat, (slang) fink. *The accuser claimed to have witnessed the crime firsthand.*

accustomed *adj.* **1.** habitual, ordinary, everyday, usual, common, regular, customary, conventional, routine. *For many people, fresh coffee in the morning is part of their accustomed behavior.* **2.** adapted, used to, familiar with. *After twenty years of marriage, the woman was accus-*

tomed to her husband's little quirks. **Ant. 1.** unfamiliar, strange, unusual. **2.** unfamiliar, unaccustomed.

ace *n.* expert, master, champion, (slang) crackerjack, (slang) whiz. *She was an absolute ace at chess.* **Ant.** amateur, beginner, incompetent.

ache *vb.* **1.** hurt, throb, smart, pain, suffer. *Even after all these weeks, my back still aches.* **2.** crave, yearn, desire, covet, want, need, suffer, agonize. *The young man's heart aches for love.* *–n.* **3.** pain, hurt, discomfort, soreness. *Some people see a doctor for every little ache.* **Ant. 3.** relief, comfort.

achieve *vb.* attain, reach, complete, accomplish, realize, fulfill, conclude. *The newspaper achieved its circulation goal.* **Ant.** fail, miss.

achievement *n.* attainment, accomplishment, fulfillment, realization, feat, deed. *Graduating from college is quite an achievement.* **Ant.** failure, disappointment, defeat.

Achilles' heel *n.* vulnerability, weakness, susceptibility, failure, handicap, chink in the armor. *Our basketball team's lack of height proved to be our Achilles' heel, as we lost the game to much taller opponents.* **Ant.** strength, power, potency.

acid *adj.* **1.** sour, tart, citrus, vinegarish, sharp, bitter. *Lemons and limes are known for their acid taste.* **2.** sarcastic, caustic, satirical, sardonic, bitting, acerbic. *The comedienne was known for her acid wit.* **Ant. 1.** sweet, sugary, saccharine. **2.** gentle, kind, mild, soft.

acknowledge *vb.* **1.** admit, allow, concede, accept, concur, recognize. *He was finally forced to acknowledge that he wasn't suited for college.* **2.** consider, deem, hold, agree, recognize. *Einstein is generally acknowledged to be one of the greatest scientists of all time.* **3.** accept, receive, respond, answer, recognize. *The young woman was unwilling to acknowledge the boy's interest in her.* **Ant. 1.** refuse, refute, deny. **2–3.** ignore, neglect, overlook.

acknowledgment *n.* **1.** admission, confession, concession, disclosure. *His acknowledgment of guilt made an investigation unnecessary.* **2.** credit, recognition, attention, notice. *Most people like to receive acknowledgment for their efforts.* **Ant. 1.** denial, refusal, rejection, disavowal.

acne *n.* pimples, (slang) zits, pustules, blemishes, skin inflammation, pockmarks, blackheads. *He had a terrible case of facial acne.*

acoustics *n.* sound qualities, noise properties, sound transmission, echoes. *The acoustics in the auditorium were excellent for the concert.*

acquaint *vb.* **1.** introduce, meet, present. *Are the two of you acquainted?* **2.** inform, advise, notify, familiarize, divulge, reveal. *Are you acquainted with the facts of the case?* **Ant. 2.** withhold, conceal, hide, retain.

acquaintance *n.* **1.** familiarity, experience, awareness, knowledge, appreciation. *She has a considerable acquaintance with contemporary theater.* **2.** colleague, associate, companion, comrade. *Most people have lots of acquaintances but only a few close friends.* **Ant. 1.** ignorance, inexperience, unawareness. **2.** stranger, outsider.

acquiesce *vb.* yield, accede, consent, defer, give in. *It is often wise to acquiesce to people who are smarter than you.* **Ant.** fight, defy, resist.

acquire *vb.* obtain, attain, get, gain, procure, secure, achieve, receive, realize. *After spending several months in Japan, he acquired a taste for Oriental cooking.* **Ant.** lose, forfeit, forgo, relinquish.

acquisition *n.* **1.** acquirement, attainment, obtainment, gain. *Acquisition of knowledge is a* *desirable goal.* **2.** possession, purchase, property, belongings. *The book collector's latest acquisition is a rare first edition.*

acquit *vb.* **1.** excuse, forgive, exonerate, absolve, clear, exempt. *The defendant was acquitted of all charges after new evidence proved his innocence.* **2.** behave, comport, conduct, deport. *The new police officer acquitted herself well on her first dangerous assignment.* **Ant. 1.** condemn, sentence, convict. **2.** misbehave, misconduct.

acre *n.* 43,560 square feet, 160 square rods, .405 hectare, parcel, plot, lot. *We bought a new house with an acre of land.*

acreage *n.* land, real estate, parcel, plot, property, holding. *The farmer had to sell some of his acreage in order to pay his taxes.*

acrid *adj.* sharp, bitter, pungent, stinking, harsh, caustic. *We began to cough as the air filled with the acrid fumes.* **Ant.** mild, sweet.

acrobat *n.* gymnast, performer, tumbler, tightrope walker, aerialist, stuntman, stuntwoman. *We gasped as we watched the acrobat nearly fall.*

act *n.* **1.** action, deed, accomplishment, achievement, feat, exploit. *The young woman received a medal for her act of heroism.* **2.** law, decree, statute, edict, bill, resolution. *War was declared by act of Congress.* **3.** pretense, pretension, show, fake, insincerity, deceit, affectation. *The young boy's tantrum was just an act to get attention.* *–vb.* **4.** perform, operate, function, behave, work, serve. *When the president was incapacitated, the vice president acted in his place.* **5.** portray, impersonate, pretend, simulate, play. *She acted so well that she got the lead in her next film.* **Ant. 1.** inaction, inactivity. **3.** sincerity, candor, forthrightness.

acting *n.* performance, pretending, impersonation, characterization, mimicry, portrayal, theatrics, dramatization, (slang) hamming it up. *His acting in the play was superb.*

action *n.* **1.** activity, work, effort, achievement, accomplishment, act, deed, feat, exploit. *The firefighter was praised for his actions.* **2.** combat, fighting, conflict, hostilities, warfare. *Did you see any action when you were in Vietnam?* **3.** activity, excitement, adventure, stimulation. *She likes movies with lots of action.* **Ant. 1.** inaction, inactivity. **2–3.** peace, quiet, serenity.

activate *vb.* turn on, start, mobilize, energize, animate, stimulate. *Dialing 911 activates your community's emergency-response program.* **Ant.** deactivate, turn off, halt, stop, arrest.

active *adj.* **1.** lively, energetic, dynamic, animated, spirited, vibrant, industrious. *Despite his stroke, he's still a very active person.* **2.** functioning, working, operating. *Our club has more than 100 active members.* **Ant. 1.** inactive, idle, lethargic. **2.** inactive, nonfunctioning.

activism *n.* involvement, advocacy, action, militancy, striking, boycotting. *Activism can help prevent and stop wars.* **Ant.** apathy, inaction, passivity.

activist *n.* doer, advocate, champion, mover and shaker, logroller, catalyst for change. *She was an activist in the human rights movement.*

activity *n.* **1.** action, work, effort, function, movement, commotion, tumult. *The laundromat is full of activity on Monday mornings.* **2.** project, pursuit, endeavor, undertaking, avocation, occupation. *She is busy with numerous after-school activities.* **Ant. 1.** inactivity, quiet, calm.

actor *n.* performer, entertainer, player, thespian, actress, artist, impersonator. *This movie features one of my favorite actors.*

actress *n.* thespian, leading lady, actor, starlet, prima donna. *She moved to Hollywood to become an actress.*

WORD SEARCH
group of: *cast, company, ensemble, repertory, troupe*
improvisation: *ad lib*
main role: *lead, leading man, leading lady*
minor role: *bit player, cameo, extra, (slang) spear carrier*
overacts, one who: *ham*
silent performer: *mime*
substitute: *stand-in, understudy*

actual *adj.* true, real, genuine, certain, verifiable, concrete, tangible. *Though he claimed illness, the actual reason he didn't go is that he can't stand parties.* **Ant.** false, fake, imaginary.

actuality *n.* reality, essence, fact, truth, substance. *Despite what she told her editor, in actuality she hadn't even started the book.*

actually *adv.* genuinely, really, truly, literally, indeed. *It did not actually happen like she said.*

acumen *n.* intelligence, smarts, shrewdness, sharpness, judgment, keenness. *Terry has the acumen necessary to succeed in business.* **Ant.** ignorance, stupidity, dullness.

acute *adj.* **1.** severe, intense, piercing, strong, sharp, keen. *He's in acute pain.* **2.** perceptive, discerning, discriminating, sensitive, intuitive, precise. *She has an acute understanding of what's going on.* **3.** critical, crucial, grave, serious, perilous, urgent. *This county has an acute shortage of low-income housing.* **Ant. 1.** mild, moderate, weak, dull. **2.** imperceptive, imprecise, inaccurate. **3.** noncritical, unimportant.

adage *n.* proverb, saying, maxim, epigram, cliche. *"An apple a day keeps the doctor away" is an example of an old adage.*

adamant *adj.* firm, resolute, unyielding, rigid, stubborn. *The teacher was adamant about turning in neat papers.* **Ant.** wishy-washy, flexible, soft.

adapt *vb.* modify, alter, adjust, accommodate, conform, reconcile, fit, change. *The small company is having trouble adapting to the latest changes in technology.*

adaptable *adj.* versatile, flexible, adjustable, accommodating, tractable. *This electric drill is adaptable for use as a screwdriver.* **Ant.** rigid, fixed, inflexible.

adaptation *n.* version, alteration, modification, revision, conversion. *His new novel is merely an adaptation of the same plot he's used before.*

adapter *n.* connector, fitting, coupling, plug. *We needed a special adapter to plug the machine into the outlet.*

add *vb.* **1.** join, affix, include, attach, append. *Before you ring up my purchases, please add this item.* **2.** total, sum up, calculate, compute. *He asked the waitress to add up his bill.* **3.** increase, augment, supplement, swell, enlarge. *The new project added significantly to her workload.* **Ant. 1.** remove, withdraw, eliminate. **2.** subtract, deduct. **3.** reduce, diminish, lessen.

addict *n.* **1.** substance abuser, user, (slang) junkie, fiend, (slang) dopehead. *The drug addict was required to get medical help.* **2.** fan, devotee, adherent, fanatic, enthusiast, lover. *She's a movie addict.*

addicted *adj.* hooked, dependent, obsessed, devoted, habituated. *Many people are addicted to chocolate.*

addiction *n.* obsession, fixation, preoccupation, mania. *He's been struggling to overcome his addiction to cigarettes.*

addition *n.* increase, raise, supplement, extension, expansion. *The new baby was a welcome addition to their family.* **Ant.** deduction, reduction, lessening.

additional *adj.* supplemental, extra, added, more, increased, further. *She will need additional income to afford the house she'd like.*

address *n.* **1.** location, place, residence, abode, dwelling, street number. *Please include your phone number and address.* **2.** speech, lecture, talk, presentation, oration. *The president's address will be carried on all major networks. –vb.* **3.** focus on, concentrate on, apply, direct, devote. *You're wasting your time by not addressing the real issue.* **4.** speak, talk, lecture, orate. *The principal will address the entire student body at tomorrow's assembly.*

adept *adj.* skilled, expert, capable, proficient, competent, deft. *He was quite adept at carpentry.* **Ant.** unskilled, bumbling, incompetent.

adequate *adj.* sufficient, enough, suitable, satisfactory, fitting, acceptable. *The student's work was not outstanding, but it was adequate for a passing grade.* **Ant.** inadequate, insufficient, unsuitable.

adhere *vb.* **1.** cling, stick, hold, attach, fasten. *This sticker won't adhere to my chrome bumper.* **2.** follow, keep, be faithful, be loyal, be devoted. *Despite the injustices she's suffered, she still adheres to her principles.* **Ant. 1.** disjoin, loosen, separate. **2.** be disloyal, be untrue.

adherent *n.* follower, disciple, observer, devotee, (slang) card-carrying member, believer, supporter. *She is an adherent of the Republican philosophy.* **Ant.** opponent, enemy, detractor.

adhesive *n.* binder, cement, glue, tape, (slang) stickum. *The adhesive was so old it had lost its stickiness.*

adjacent *adj.* next to, adjoining, touching, near, bordering, neighboring. *My property is adjacent to hers.* **Ant.** remote, distant, separate, removed.

adjourn *vb.* defer, delay, postpone, suspend, interrupt, discontinue. *The chairman adjourned the committee meeting till next week.* **Ant.** convene, assemble, gather.

adjudicate *vb.* judge, determine, try, settle, hear, process, arbitrate, mediate. *Only the most fair-minded people should adjudicate any dispute.*

adjust *vb.* **1.** set, regulate, change, order, repair, fix. *He had to adjust his VCRs tracking control to play the new movie.* **2.** adapt, reconcile, accommodate, attune, conform. *She's having difficulty adjusting to the demands of her new job.*

adjustment *n.* **1.** alignment, modification, ordering, fixing, regulating. *Your television's color control is out of adjustment.* **2.** accommodation, settlement, compromise, adapting. *The returning astronauts had trouble making the adjustment to Earth's gravity.*

ad-lib *vb.* improvise, invent, play it by ear, (slang) wing it, make up. *He got up on stage and ad-libbed for twenty minutes.*

administer *vb.* **1.** manage, direct, supervise, run, govern, control. *Who will administer the new research project?* **2.** provide, dispense, apply, give, distribute. *Paramedics administered first aid at the accident site.*

administration *n.* **1.** management, supervision, governing, commanding, regulation, superintendence. *The administration of their department was held in high regard.* **2.** government, command, management, leadership, bureaucracy, ministry, headquarters. *He was at the head of the administration for thirteen years.*

administrator *n.* manager, leader, bureaucrat, head, governor, minister, supervisor, superintendent. *As administrator, she was instrumental in improving the organization's efficiency.*

admirable *adj.* excellent, praiseworthy, commendable, superb, wonderful. *Her kindness is* *admirable.* **Ant.** bad, contemptible, despicable, worthless.

admiration *n.* esteem, high regard, reverence, approval, respect, awe. *She has great admiration for Hemingway's writing ability.* **Ant.** contempt, disdain, scorn, disapproval.

admire *vb.* respect, esteem, value, revere, venerate, honor. *I admire anyone who acts unselfishly for the benefit of others.* **Ant.** dislike, detest, scorn, hate.

admirer *n.* fan, supporter, disciple, devotee, follower. *He has a secret admirer.* **Ant.** detractor, opponent.

admissible *adj.* acceptable, allowed, proper, legal, legitimate, permissible. *There was an argument over whether the evidence was admissible in court.* **Ant.** inadmissible, illegal, unacceptable.

admit *vb.* **1.** confess, acknowledge, concede, confide, reveal. *George Washington admitted to chopping down a cherry tree.* **2.** let in, let enter, induct, initiate, install. *Three new members were admitted to the exclusive club.* **Ant. 1.** deny, conceal, withhold. **2.** obstruct, reject.

admonish *vb.* **1.** warn, caution, advise, forewarn. *He admonished her to be more careful behind the wheel.* **2.** scold, chastise, berate, tell off, rebuke, reprove. *My mother would always admonish me for going outside without a coat.* **Ant. 2.** praise, commend, compliment.

adolescence *n.* puberty, teen years, youth, pubescence. *She remembered feeling awkward during her adolescence.*

adolescent *n.* teenager, teen, youth, youngster, (slang) teenybopper, minor. *His sense of humor was that of an adolescent.*

adopt *vb.* **1.** embrace, assume, appropriate, take, use, employ. *The city council voted to adopt new methods for raising revenues.* **2.** take in, raise, take under one's wing, foster, parent. *They decided they would adopt an orphan.* **Ant. 1.** reject, spurn, discard, repudiate. **2.** disown, reject.

adorable *adj.* lovable, attractive, enchanting, captivating, lovely. *She got an adorable little bunny for her birthday.* **Ant.** unlovable, unlikable, offensive.

adoration *n.* worship, veneration, reverence, devotion, love, honor. *It's rare to find a slave who has much adoration for his master.* **Ant.** antipathy, dislike, aversion, detestation.

adore *vb.* love, cherish, revere, venerate, worship, idolize. *She adores her grandfather.* **Ant.** abhor, hate, despise, dislike.

adorn *vb.* decorate, embellish, ornament, beautify, furbish, trim. *She wore a blouse adorned with lace.* **Ant.** divest, strip, mar, deface.

adrift *adj.* aimless, rudderless, directionless, wandering, astray. *The tiny boat was adrift on an endless ocean.* **Ant.** anchored, on course.

adroit *adj.* skillful, dexterous, deft, proficient, sharp, nimble. *Linda proved to be just as adroit in the garden as she was on the tennis court.* **Ant.** unskilled, maladroit, bumbling.

adulation *n.* exaltation, praise, worshipping, flattery, adoration. *The adulation of the crowd convinced him that he was great enough to be King.* **Ant.** scorn, disdain, contempt.

adult *n.* **1.** grown-up, mature person, man, woman. *This movie is rated for adults only. –adj.* **2.** mature, grown-up, grown, aged, developed, experienced. *He was attacked by an adult bear.* **Ant. 1.** infant, child, adolescent. **2.** immature, inexperienced.

adulterate *vb.* contaminate, spoil, pollute, taint, corrupt, denature. *We would never adulterate our* *wild strawberries by topping them with whipped cream.* **Ant.** purify, clean, concentrate.

adulterer *n.* adulteress, philanderer, cheater, womanizer. *An adulterer risks destroying his marriage.*

adultery *n.* infidelity, unfaithfulness, cheating, sleeping around, affair. *Many marriages have been ruined by adultery.* **Ant.** faithfulness, fidelity, loyalty.

advance *vb.* **1.** move forward, go forward, proceed, progress, march. *The army advanced toward the enemy's castle.* **2.** improve, further, promote, upgrade, strengthen, assist, benefit. *The scientist's discovery advanced our knowledge of medicine.* **3.** propose, suggest, submit, offer, propound. *He advanced a controversial new theory on the origin of disease.* **4.** prepay, lend, loan. *His parents advanced him his next week's allowance.* –*n.* **5.** progress, progression, headway, advancement, improvement. *The computer industry has benefited from advances in technology.* **6.** promotion, upgrade, rise, elevation. *Her advance to personnel manager was the result of many years of hard work.* **7.** prepayment, down payment. *The writer received a large advance for her latest book.* **Ant.** **1.** recede, retreat, withdraw. **2.** hinder, impede, decrease. **3.** withhold, suppress. **5.** setback, reversal. **6.** demotion, reduction.

advantage *n.* asset, edge, favor, help, benefit, aid, service. *The boxer favored to win has the advantage of a longer reach.* **Ant.** disadvantage, drawback, hindrance.

advantageous *adj.* helpful, favorable, beneficial, valuable, fortunate. *He was in an advantageous position for a promotion.* **Ant.** disadvantageous, unfavorable, unhelpful.

advent *n.* coming, arrival, forthcoming, appearance, entry. *The advent of the space age began with a satellite called "Sputnik."* **Ant.** end, close, departure.

adventure *n.* escapade, venture, exploit, feat, hazard, peril, risk. *She dreams of leading a life full of adventure.*

adventurer *n.* thrill-seeker, daredevil, risk-taker, trailblazer, explorer. *The adventurer planned to travel around the world in a hot air balloon.*

adventurous *adj.* **1.** bold, daring, rash, intrepid, brave. *The adventurous boys snuck into a cemetery at midnight.* **2.** challenging, perilous, hazardous, risky, dangerous. *Their climb of Mt. Everest promised to be adventurous.* **Ant.** **1.** cautious, timid, cowardly. **2.** safe, boring, routine.

adversary *n.* opponent, foe, rival, competitor, enemy. *Her former instructor was her main adversary in the golf tournament.* **Ant.** ally, partner, colleague, friend.

adverse *adj.* unfavorable, bad, detrimental, hostile, destructive. *Adverse weather forced us to postpone our camping trip.* **Ant.** beneficial, good, favorable.

adversity *n.* misfortune, suffering, difficulty, trouble, calamity, hardship. *Try to show courage when faced with adversity.* **Ant.** success, fortune, good luck.

advertise *vb.* publicize, promote, proclaim, announce, feature, display. *The company advertised its latest product on television.*

advertisement *n.* commercial, plug, notice, spot, placard. *They ran all of their advertisements in the newspaper.*

advice *n.* counsel, guidance, recommendation, suggestion, opinion, warning, information. *She doesn't seem to want my advice.*

advise *vb.* **1.** counsel, recommend, suggest, urge, warn, caution. *His doctor advised him to lower his intake of cholesterol.* **2.** inform, notify, apprise, acquaint, tell. *We have been advised that there will be a big storm tomorrow.*

advisory *n.* report, caution, alert, warning, note, notification. *A severe weather advisory made us change our minds about going sailing.*

advocate *vb.* **1.** recommend, support, promote, endorse, encourage, defend, uphold. *He advocates stricter laws against drunk drivers.* –*n.* **2.** supporter, upholder, backer, champion, proponent, promoter. *She is an advocate of tougher environmental laws.* **Ant. 1.** oppose, discourage. **2.** opponent, adversary, critic.

aerobics *n.* exercise, workout, conditioning, cardiovascular workout, training, calisthenics. *She stays slim by practicing aerobics for 45 minutes every day.*

affair *n.* **1.** business, matter, concern, undertaking, activity, occasion, episode. *Starting your own company can be a complex affair.* **2.** celebration, festival, party, event, ceremony, function. *The senior prom will be quite an affair this year.* **3.** liaison, romance, relationship. *The actress is having an affair with her director.*

affect *vb.* **1.** influence, alter, change, transform, modify. *Our vacation plans were affected by the airline strike.* **2.** touch, move, stir, impress, upset, trouble. *He was deeply affected by reports of famine in Africa.*

affectation *n.* put-on, pretense, airs, performance, pose, show. *His English accent was a phony affectation.*

affection *n.* love, warmth, tenderness, fondness, liking, concern. *He has deep affection for his wife and children.* **Ant.** hate, loathing, dislike.

affectionate *adj.* loving, tender, warm, fond, devoted, caring. *She adores her kitten because it's so affectionate.* **Ant.** cold, distant, unfeeling, uncaring.

affidavit *n.* statement, testimony, deposition, declaration. *He was required to write what he witnessed in a formal affidavit.*

affiliate *vb.* **1.** associate, unite, incorporate, befriend. *She decided to affiliate only with people who agreed with her philosophy.* –*n.* **2.** associate, member, ally, brother, sister, branch. *The network oversaw dozens of affiliates.* **Ant. 1.** spurn, reject.

affiliation *n.* association, membership, relationship, alliance, union. *Her affiliation with the organization was strong.*

affinity *n.* attraction, liking, fondness, sympathy, affection. *My family has a natural affinity for car racing.* **Ant.** aversion, repulsion, dislike.

affirm *vb.* **1.** swear, declare, assert, claim, insist, maintain. *She affirmed that he was the one who stole her purse.* **2.** ratify, confirm, approve, endorse, uphold. *Congress failed to affirm the president's nominee for the Supreme Court.* **Ant. 1.** deny, refute, renounce. **2.** reject, veto, nullify.

affix *vb.* attach, stick, connect, fasten. *Affix the stamp to the envelope.*

afflict *vb.* plague, trouble, distress, burden, torment, beset. *She was afflicted with a bad cold.*

affliction *n.* misfortune, trouble, distress, hardship, adversity, pain, misery. *Chronic headaches are but one of his afflictions.* **Ant.** benefit, blessing, comfort.

affluent *adj.* wealthy, rich, prosperous, privileged. *She lives in an affluent neighborhood.* **Ant.** poor, impoverished, underprivileged.

afford *vb.* **1.** pay for, bear, manage, support. *I can't afford to take a vacation this summer.* **2.** provide, supply, furnish, offer, give. *This vista affords a panoramic view of the Grand Canyon.*

aficionado *n.* connoisseur, enthusiast, (slang) nut, fanatic, devotee. *Tina has always been a jazz aficionado.*

afraid *adj.* **1.** fearful, frightened, terrified, scared, anxious, nervous, alarmed. *He's afraid of heights.* **2.** sorry, remorseful, unhappy, hesitant, reluctant. *I'm afraid I won't be able to lend you the money for a new car.* **Ant. 1.** bold, courageous, fearless. **2.** happy, pleased.

afterlife *n.* hereafter, heaven, eternity, life after death, afterworld. *The medium said she could communicate with people in the afterlife.*

aftermath *n.* outcome, result, fallout, repercussions, wake, consequence. *In the aftermath of the earthquake, the government passed stronger building codes.* **Ant.** prelude, lead-up, preface.

age *n.* **1.** era, epoch, period, time, generation, season. *We live in the computer age.* **2.** years, eon, millennium, eternity. *I haven't been to a movie in ages.* *–vb.* **3.** mature, ripen, season, develop, grow old. *This cheese has aged nine months.*

aged *adj.* **1.** old, elderly, mature, advanced, ancient. *She takes care of her aged parents.* **2.** mellow, mature, ripe, ripened, developed. *He's a connoisseur of aged wines.* **Ant. 1.** young, youthful, juvenile. **2.** immature, green.

ageless *adj.* timeless, infinite, eternal, neverending. *A mountain appears ageless but in fact it will one day erode to mere sand and grit.* **Ant.** finite, limited.

agency *n.* organization, bureau, bureaucracy, office, department. *He got a job working for a government agency.*

agenda *n.* schedule, calendar, to-do list, plan, lineup, program, docket. *What's on your agenda this morning?*

agent *n.* **1.** delegate, representative, advocate, negotiator. *The writer had her agent negotiate the book contract.* **2.** power, force, means, medium, mechanism, instrument. *Scouring powder is an effective cleansing agent.*

aggravate *vb.* **1.** intensify, worsen, exacerbate, increase, exaggerate. *Scratching only aggravated his case of poison ivy.* **2.** irritate, annoy, exasperate, provoke, irk, bother. *She was aggravated by her neighbor's barking dogs.* **Ant. 1.** lessen, diminish, relieve. **2.** calm, soothe.

aggravation *n.* annoyance, bother, exasperation, vexation, irritation. *His noisy neighbors were a constant source of aggravation.*

aggression *n.* hostility, belligerence, combativeness, assault, attack. *A naval blockade is considered an act of aggression.* **Ant.** friendliness, peacefulness, peace.

aggressive *adj.* **1.** hostile, belligerent, combative, warlike, militant, offensive. *The nation's aggressive actions led to a war.* **2.** bold, forceful, assertive, competitive, vigorous, energetic. *We need an aggressive mayor to solve our city's problems.* **Ant. 1.** peaceful, friendly, defensive. **2.** timid, shy, retiring.

aggressor *n.* attacker, initiator, assailant, instigator, offender, antagonizer. *The aggressor was charged with assault and battery.* **Ant.** victim, defender, prey.

agile *adj.* **1.** athletic, nimble, spry, supple, lithe, limber. *The cat made an agile leap to the bookshelf.* **2.** quick, sharp, clever, keen, bright, perceptive. *Algebra isn't hard if you have an agile mind.* **Ant. 1.** clumsy, awkward, inept. **2.** slow, dull, sluggish.

agility *n.* nimbleness, dexterity, adroitness, flexibility, quickness, lightness. *A great deal of agility is required of pole vaulters.* **Ant.** clumsiness, slowness, awkwardness.

agitate *vb.* **1.** stir, mix, shake, churn, beat, toss. *A washing machine agitates clothes to clean them.* **2.** upset, excite, incite, arouse, provoke. *The revolutionary's speech agitated the mob.* **Ant. 2.** calm, soothe, pacify.

agitated *adj.* upset, disturbed, excited, worried, nervous, jittery. *Everyone was agitated when a major earthquake was predicted.* **Ant.** serene, tranquil, calm.

agnostic *adj.* freethinker, disbeliever, skeptic, doubter, thinker, philosopher. *An agnostic believes that God cannot be known.* **Ant.** believer, theist, zealot.

agonize *vb.* suffer, fret, worry, lose sleep over, grapple with. *I always agonize over what to wear to a job interview.*

agony *n.* pain, suffering, torment, anguish, distress, torture. *He was in agony with two broken legs.* **Ant.** comfort, pleasure, bliss, joy.

agree *vb.* **1.** consent, assent, concede, accept, allow. *She agreed to lend me ten dollars.* **2.** concur, coincide, correspond, harmonize, fit, match. *His account of the accident does not agree with mine.* **Ant. 1.** deny, oppose, dissent. **2.** disagree, differ, contradict.

agreement *n.* **1.** understanding, harmony, accord, conformity. *It looks as if the two sides will never be in agreement with each other.* **2.** deal, pact, compact, treaty, arrangement, settlement. *Management and union officials reached an agreement that ended the strike.* **Ant. 1.** disagreement, discord, dissension.

agriculture *n.* farming, agronomy, horticulture, agribusiness, husbandry, cultivation, crop-raising. *Two centuries ago, most people worked in one form of agriculture or another.*

aid *vb.* **1.** help, assist, support, serve, back. *Unless you aid me, I won't be able to finish the project in time.* –*n.* **2.** assistance, help, support, service, backing. *I wouldn't have been able to fix my car without your aid.* **Ant. 1.** obstruct, hinder, oppose. **2.** hindrance, obstacle.

AIDS *n.* acquired immune deficiency syndrome, sexually transmitted disease, immune failure. *It is possible to contract AIDS from a blood transfusion.*

ail *vb.* trouble, disturb, bother, distress, afflict. *She looks as if something ails her.*

ailment *n.* disorder, discomfort, sickness, illness, affliction, disease. *He constantly complains about his minor ailments.*

aim *vb.* **1.** point, direct, level, sight, focus. *He aimed his arrow at a makeshift target.* **2.** try, strive, plan, endeavor, seek, intend, attempt. *She aims for perfection in her writing.* –*n.* **3.** goal, target, intention, intent, objective, ambition. *His aim is to make the honor roll.*

aimless *adj.* directionless, unorganized, purposeless, pointless, erratic, unguided. *Some people lead aimless lives.* **Ant.** purposeful, intentional, systematic.

air *n.* **1.** atmosphere, sky, wind, breeze. *The kite floated through the air.* **2.** aura, quality, flavor, mood, appearance, character. *He's secretive because he likes to maintain an air of mystery.* –*vb.* **3.** ventilate, aerate. *This room needs to be aired out.* **4.** voice, express, declare, reveal, disclose, expose, communicate. *The personnel manager made herself available for employees who wanted to air their complaints.* **Ant. 4.** conceal, hide, suppress.

airborne *adj.* aloft, in flight, in the clouds. *The helicopter was airborne within seconds.*

aircraft *n.* craft, airplane, airliner, jet, helicopter, airship, flying machine. *We watched aircraft take off and land at the airport.*

WORD SEARCH

altitude measuring device: *altimeter*
automatic flying system: *autopilot*
body of: *fuselage*
boom as aircraft exceeds speed of sound: *sonic boom*
cockpit: *cabin*
course: *flight path*
crash-land in water: *ditch*
distress call: *Mayday*
drive on ground: *taxi*
exhaust trail left by jet: *contrail*
fall out of air due to low air speed: *stall*
faster than speed of sound: *supersonic; hypersonic*
flaps: *aileron, airfoil, spoiler*
flaps, tail: *elevator, rudder*
flight data recorder: *black box*
"hole" in the air, causing abrupt drop: *air pocket*
landing approach: *approach, glidepath*
landing, perfect: *three-point landing*
late-night flight: *red-eye*
lights on wingtips, flashing: *strobes*
motorless: *glider*
physics of flight: *aerodynamics*
rollover stunt: *barrel roll*
"rough" air: *turbulence*
shelter: *hangar*
traffic jam over airport: *stack*
unidentified: *UFO, bogey*
wind condition, crash-causing: *wind shear*
wind, opposing: *head wind*

air force *n.* air defense, air power, strategic air command, strike force. *The United States Air Force may be the most powerful in the world.*

WORD SEARCH

attack: *air strike, bombing run, dog fight, strafing*
emergency takeoff: *scramble*
fire upon enemy aircraft: *engage*
group of aircraft: *echelon, escadrille, squadron, wing*
information gathering mission: *reconnaissance*
single flight: *sortie*

airhead (slang) *n.* idiot, (slang) bubblehead, imbecile, moron, dope. *I'm such an airhead that this morning I went out with only one sock on.*

airport *n.* airfield, jetport, airstrip, air base, runway, landing strip, installation. *Let's go to the airport and watch the jets take off.*

WORD SEARCH

control center: *control tower*
control tower personnel: *air traffic controllers*
driveway leading to runway: *taxiway*
exhaust shield: *blast fence*
ground traffic directors: *marshalers*
lights that guide aircraft to runway: *approach lights, sequence flashers, barrette*
loading and refueling area: *apron*
luggage carrier: *skycap*
maintenance crew: *ground crew*
radio-guided landing system: *microwave landing system*
runway turnoff lane: *rollout*
shelter or maintenance building: *hangar*
takeoff strip: *runway*

airy *adj.* **1.** breezy, ventilated, open, fresh. *Having all the windows open gave the house an airy feeling.* **2.** light, ethereal, gossamer, diaphanous, sheer. *We could see through the airy curtains, which puffed open with the slightest breeze.* **Ant. 1.** closed, stuffy, suffocating. **Ant. 2.** heavy, thick, opaque.

aisle *n.* corridor, passage, passageway, walkway, path, lane. *Fire regulations prohibit sitting in the aisles of a movie theater.*

alarm *n.* **1.** warning, alert, signal, bell, buzzer, siren. *Many people have burglar alarms in their* *homes.* **2.** fear, fright, apprehension, dismay, distress, dread. *The smell of smoke filled her with alarm.* –*vb.* **3.** scare, frighten, startle, shock, disturb, dismay. *The sound of screeching brakes alarmed him.* **Ant. 2.** serenity, tranquillity. **3.** calm, reassure, relieve, comfort.

alarming *adj.* frightening, startling, disturbing, shocking, appalling. *She has an alarming lack of responsibility.* **Ant.** reassuring, soothing, comforting.

alarmist *n.* prophet of doom, Cassandra, scaremonger, Chicken Little. *People who panic easily tend to be alarmists.*

album *n.* collection, anthology, book, miscellany. *I like looking through old photo albums.*

alchemy *n.* transmutation, magic, sorcery, pseudo-science, pseudo-chemistry. *Through alchemy, lead was thought to be convertible into gold.*

alcohol *n.* liquor, spirits, intoxicant, (slang) booze, (slang) hard stuff. *One should never drive after drinking alcohol.*

alcoholic *n.* drunk, substance abuser, problem drinker, (slang) lush, (slang) bar fly. *An alcoholic suffers from a form of addiction.*

alcoholism *n.* addiction, substance abuse, drinking problem, illness, dependence. *Alcoholism can be a deadly disease.*

alcove *n.* recess, nook, niche, bay. *You can leave your shoes in the alcove.*

alert *adj.* **1.** attentive, awake, aware, watchful, vigilant, observant. *An alert employee spotted the shoplifter.* **2.** quick, nimble, lively, sharp, brisk, agile. *The alert child learned to read at an early age.* –*n.* **3.** warning, alarm, signal, siren. *There will be a practice air-raid alert at noon today.* –*vb.* **4.** warn, caution, advise, signal, notify. *Police alerted the bank's employees to expect a robbery.* **Ant. 1.** inattentive, unaware, unconcerned. **2.** slow, dull, listless.

alibi *n.* excuse, story, explanation, plea, defense. *The defendant could find no one to confirm his alibi.*

alien *adj.* **1.** strange, foreign, different, unfamiliar, exotic. *She's fascinated by the alien customs of primitive tribes.* **2.** opposed, incompatible, contradictory, inconsistent, unlike. *Lying is alien to her character.* –*n.* **3.** foreigner, stranger, outsider, immigrant. *Because he is a citizen of a different country, he is classified as an alien here.* **4.** extraterrestrial, space being, (slang) little green man, otherworldly creature. *A two-headed alien emerged from the spaceship.* **Ant. 1.** familiar, common, commonplace. **2.** compatible, consistent, like. **3.** native, citizen

alienate *vb.* estrange, distance, shut out, separate, divide. *Their hostile actions only served to alienate their neighbors.* **Ant.** unite, unify.

alignment *n.* positioning, calibration, straightening, fine-tuning, coordination. *All four wheels must be in perfect alignment.* **Ant.** misalignment, maladjustment.

alike *adj.* **1.** like, identical, similar, equal, even, matched. *No two snowflakes are exactly alike.* –*adv.* **2.** similarly, identically, equally, evenly, likewise. *The twins are hard to tell apart since they dress alike.* **Ant. 1.** different, unlike, opposite. **2.** differently, distinctly.

alive *adj.* **1.** live, living, existing, animate. *You need to water your lawn if you want to keep the grass alive.* **2.** lively, animated, active, alert, vivacious, vital, vigorous. *She seems to be more alive with the coming of spring.* **Ant. 1.** lifeless, dead, deceased. **2.** slow, lethargic, inactive.

allegation *n.* accusation, charge, claim, profession, assertion, insinuation. *Sally made the allegation that Paul stole the last cookie.*

allege *vb.* accuse, charge, claim, assert, insinuate, state, purport, attest. *I allege that Paul stole the last cookie.*

allegiance *n.* loyalty, faithfulness, devotion, fidelity, obedience. *He pledged allegiance to the fraternity and its members.* **Ant.** disloyalty, treachery, treason.

allergic *adj.* reactive, immune sensitive, hypersensitive, susceptible, averse to. *She was severely allergic to peanuts.*

allergy *n.* sensitivity, hypersensitivity, susceptibility, aversion, immune defense. *She has a peanut allergy.*

WORD SEARCH

doctor: *allergist*
pollen allergy: *hay fever*
red blotches, symptom: *hives*
severe, potentially fatal reaction: *anaphylaxis*
substance that causes allergic reaction: *allergen*

alleviate *vb.* relieve, ease, diminish, lessen, reduce, soften. *To alleviate symptoms, drink plenty of fluids and stay in bed.* **Ant.** worsen, aggravate, intensify.

alliance *n.* agreement, pact, bargain, understanding, treaty, union. *The two countries formed an alliance against their mutual enemy.*

allied *adj.* joined, combined, united, joint, connected, affiliated. *The peasants were allied with the middle class in the civil war.* **Ant.** disunited, unconnected, uncombined.

alligator *n.* reptile, creature, animal, predator, carnivore, gator. *I hope there aren't any alligators in the sewer.*

allocate *vb.* distribute, ration, mete, allot, appropriate. *It was my job to allocate funds from the treasury.* **Ant.** collect, hoard, save.

allot *vb.* assign, allocate, distribute, allow, share, divide. *The president allotted each person fifteen minutes for an interview.* **Ant.** withhold, deny, refuse.

allow *vb.* **1.** permit, let, authorize, grant, approve, sanction. *Smoking is not allowed at school.* **2.** allot, allocate, give, assign, provide. *Allow yourself enough time to get your homework done.* **Ant.** **1.** forbid, prohibit, refuse. **2.** withhold, deny.

allowance *n.* stipend, payment, salary, allocation, compensation, cut, recompense, percentage. *She was given an allowance of five dollars per week.*

alloy *n.* compound, mixture, composite, blend, amalgam, amalgamation. *Steel is an alloy of carbon and iron.*

allude *vb.* mention, suggest, hint, refer, imply, speak of. *He's sensitive about his size, so let's not allude to it.*

allure *vb.* **1.** fascinate, attract, captivate, enchant, draw, charm. *She was allured by his intelligence.* –*n.* **2.** attraction, lure, fascination, temptation, enticement, charm. *Dragons can't resist the allure of gold.* **Ant.** **1.** repel, alienate, estrange.

allusion *n.* reference, implication, hint, inference, suggestion. *When she said I was as emotionless as a Vulcan, she was making an allusion to* Star Trek.

ally *n.* **1.** colleague, friend, helper, partner, associate, assistant. *The criminal needed to find an ally to help with the robbery.* –*vb.* **2.** combine, join, unite, unify, connect. *The citizens allied together in their fight against crime.* **Ant.** **1.** enemy, foe, opponent. **2.** separate, divide.

almanac *n.* forecaster, annual, calendar, yearbook, publication. *We consulted the almanac to see when the next full moon would occur.*

almost *adv.* nearly, practically, about, mostly, largely, somewhat. *She's almost finished the book she's reading.* **Ant.** definitely.

alone *adv.* **1.** solitarily, singly, individually, separately. *He went to the movie alone.* –*adj.* **2.** secluded, isolated, unaccompanied, unattended, unescorted. *She was alone in the woods.* **Ant. 1–2.** accompanied, escorted, attended.

aloof *adj.* cold, cool, detached, distant, withdrawn, uninterested. *An aloof person has difficulty finding friends.* **Ant.** warm, friendly, involved.

aloud *adv.* audibly, out loud, openly, loudly, distinctly, clearly. *He enjoys reading aloud to himself.* **Ant.** silently, inaudibly.

alter *vb.* change, modify, vary, transform, revise, remake. *His new beard completely alters his appearance.* **Ant.** maintain, continue, keep.

alter ego *n.* **1.** other ego, dark side, id, counterpart. *My alter ego controls my most primitive instincts.* **2.** sidekick, buddy, friend, companion, soul mate. *My wife is my alter ego, and she makes most of the decisions.*

alternate *vb.* **1.** switch, interchange, rotate, intersperse, change. *Blue stripes alternate with yellow stripes on his shirt.* –*adj.* **2.** alternating, reciprocal, successive. *The American flag has alternate red and white stripes.* **3.** substitute, another, different, additional. *Since she missed her plane, she had to take an alternate flight.* –*n.* **4.** substitute, replacement, second, backup. *Since our elected delegate could not go to the meeting, we had to send an alternate.*

alternative *n.* choice, selection, possibility, option, preference. *She had difficulty choosing an ice cream flavor because there were so many alternatives.*

altogether *adv.* completely, entirely, wholly, totally, thoroughly, absolutely. *He missed the target altogether.* **Ant.** partially, partly, incompletely.

altruism *n.* selflessness, charity, kindheartedness, consideration, humanitarianism, philanthropy. *The selfless desire to help others is what altruism is all about.* **Ant.** selfishness, self-centeredness, cruelty.

altruistic *adj.* selfless, charitable, kindhearted, considerate, humanitarian, philanthropic. *Giving a gift anonymously is as close to an altruistic act as you can perform.* **Ant.** selfish, self-centered, cruel.

always *adv.* eternally, perpetually, forever, ever, unceasingly, continually. *I'll love you always.* **Ant.** never, rarely.

amass *vb.* accumulate, gather, pile, collect, stockpile, heap. *I hope to amass a large fortune someday.* **Ant.** dispose of, distribute, dump.

amateur *n.* **1.** nonprofessional, novice, beginner, apprentice, hobbyist. *The pro tennis player didn't want to compete against amateurs.* –*adj.* **2.** amateurish, nonprofessional, inexperienced, unskilled. *She joined an amateur theater group.* **Ant. 1.** professional, expert. **2.** professional, experienced.

amateurish *adj.* unprofessional, unskilled, untalented, inexperienced, incompetent, bumbling. *The band gave an amateurish performance and was rewarded with lukewarm applause.* **Ant.** professional, skilled, accomplished.

amaze *vb.* astonish, surprise, astound, bewilder, stun, impress. *Her command of the English language never ceases to amaze me.* **Ant.** bore, tire, anticipate, expect.

amazement *n.* astonishment, wonder, surprise, bewilderment, awe. *I was filled with amazement as I watched the magician perform.* **Ant.** boredom, apathy, indifference.

ambassador *n.* diplomat, delegate, agent, minister, representative, consul, emissary. *The ambassador will arrive in Russia today to smooth over the controversy.*

ambience *n.* atmosphere, aura, air, environment, mood. *A crackling fire in the woodstove gave the room a warm ambience.*

ambiguous *adj.* unclear, vague, equivocal, uncertain, questionable, duplicitous. *His ambiguous statements could have been understood in more than one way.* **Ant.** clear, unequivocal, concrete.

ambition *n.* **1.** desire, will, determination, drive, energy, resolve. *To succeed as a writer, you must have lots of ambition.* **2.** goal, end, aspiration, objective, purpose, dream. *Her ambition is to become a doctor.* **Ant. 1.** indifference, apathy, laziness.

ambitious *adj.* **1.** determined, dynamic, energetic, eager, intent. *He will probably succeed because he's so ambitious.* **2.** audacious, bold, daring, grandiose, difficult, challenging. *Humanity's desire to conquer space is an ambitious dream.* **Ant. 1.** purposeless, apathetic, lazy. **2.** modest, simply, easy.

ambivalent *adj.* mixed, contradictory, wavering, indecisive, of two minds, on the fence. *I often have ambivalent feelings during elections and don't know who to vote for.* **Ant.** decisive, single-minded, certain.

amble *vb.* walk, stroll, ramble, saunter, wander, drift. *The old man ambled through the park.* **Ant.** rush, run, sprint, dash.

ambrosia *n.* food fit for the gods, food fit for a king, delicacy, epicurean delight. *Grandmother's cooking often approached ambrosia, especially at Thanksgiving.* **Ant.** garbage, slop, refuse.

ambulance *n.* rescue vehicle, emergency vehicle, medical transport. *She was rushed to the hospital in an ambulance.*

ambush *vb.* attack, assault, jump, take by surprise, bushwhack. *We were ambushed by the enemy and taken completely by surprise.*

amenable *adj.* agreeable, willing, open, cooperative, responsive. *The team was amenable to most of the changes the coach outlined.* **Ant.** resistant, rejecting, closed.

amend *vb.* improve, better, correct, perfect, reform, revise, change, alter, modify. *To make that proposal legal, the constitution will have to be amended.* **Ant.** worsen, weaken, keep.

amendment *n.* improvement, upgrade, correction, change, addition, revision, attachment. *The amendment was passed by a three-to-one vote.*

amenity *n.* nicety, extra, luxury, frill, comfort. *The hotel's amenities included cable TV and a heated pool.*

amiable *adj.* friendly, agreeable, pleasant, congenial, gracious, sociable, cordial. *Small towns typically have an amiable atmosphere.* **Ant.** unfriendly, disagreeable, unpleasant.

amicable *adj.* peaceful, peaceable, friendly, cooperative, harmonious, civil. *The mediator hoped to find an amicable settlement to the international dispute.* **Ant.** hostile, belligerent, unfriendly.

ammunition *n.* (slang) ammo, ordnance, arms, munitions, explosives, shells. *They loaded up with ammunition and headed out to the enemy camp.*

WORD SEARCH

bullet storage compartment, gun's: *clip, magazine*
fragments, injury-causing: *shrapnel*
over-the-shoulder bullet belt: *bandolier*
projectile-less cartridge: *blank*
shot, one: *round*
stockpile of: *munitions dump*
wagon used to carry: *caisson*

amnesty *n.* forgiveness, pardon, excusing, dispensation, absolution, clemency. *The prisoners were finally granted amnesty and released.* **Ant.** condemnation, sentencing.

among *prep.* amid, amidst, amongst, between, in with. *The pirates divided the treasure among themselves.*

amorous *adj.* loving, romantic, affectionate, erotic, in the mood, demonstrative. *Indulging an amorous impulse, the couple kissed for more than an hour.* **Ant.** rejecting, hateful, repulsed.

amorphous *adj.* shapeless, vague, indistinct, formless, nondescript. *An amorphous cloud passed overhead and darkened the sky.* **Ant.** distinct, well-defined, distinctive.

amount *vb.* **1.** total, comprise, add up, come to. *His debts amount to several thousand dollars.* **2.** equal, approach, correspond, imply, suggest. *Her remark amounts to a rebuke.* –*n.* **3.** sum, total, extent, measure, quantity. *We have only a small amount of money left.*

ample *adj.* plentiful, abundant, sufficient, adequate, enough. *We have ample time for a leisurely dinner before the movie starts.* **Ant.** meager, scarce, insufficient, inadequate.

amplify *vb.* expand, enlarge, increase, extend, intensify, strengthen. *The cheerleaders used hand-held megaphones to amplify their voices.* **Ant.** reduce, decrease, diminish, lower.

amputate *vb.* sever, dismember, excise, lop off, cut off, remove. *After gangrene set in, the infected foot had to be amputated.*

amuse *vb.* entertain, please, occupy, interest, divert, charm. *The kitten's antics amused us all.* **Ant.** bore, weary, tire.

amusement *n.* **1.** pleasure, relaxation, entertainment, pastime, diversion. *What are your favorite amusements?* **2.** laughter, mirth, enjoyment, merriment, pleasure. *Watching the children play filled him with amusement.* **Ant.** **2.** sadness, displeasure.

amusing *adj.* entertaining, pleasurable, pleasing, pleasant, delightful, charming. *Her stories are always amusing.* **Ant.** boring, dull, uninteresting.

analogy *n.* comparison, correlation, similarity, relationship, semblance. *He made an analogy between busy beavers and industrial productivity.*

analysis *n.* examination, investigation, study, evaluation, dissection, review. *The laboratory made a chemical analysis.*

analytical *adj.* evaluative, critical, inquisitive, deep-thinking, interpretive. *The professor was far too analytical to be fooled by a simple prank.* **Ant.** unthinking, brainless, thoughtless.

analyze *vb.* examine, investigate, study, evaluate, scrutinize. *If you analyze your motives, you'll know the right thing to do.* **Ant.** ignore, disregard, neglect.

anarchist *n.* rebel, insurrectionist, agitator, terrorist, revolutionary, radical. *Anarchists are trying to topple the government.*

anarchy *n.* chaos, disorder, rebellion, revolution, mayhem, civil unrest, lawlessness. *Anarchy would result if we chose to abolish our legal system.* **Ant.** order, law and order, peace.

ancestor *n.* **1.** forebear, forefather, foremother. *His ancestors came to America in the 19th century.* **2.** predecessor, forerunner, precursor, antecedent, prototype. *The ancestor of the automobile was the horse-drawn carriage.* **Ant.** **1.** descendant, offspring, heir. **2.** successor, follower.

ancestry *n.* lineage, pedigree, heritage, family tree, progenitors, roots, bloodline. *She traced her ancestry all the way back to Ireland.*

anchor *vb.* **1.** fasten, attach, fix, affix, secure. *She anchored her bookshelves to the wall.* *–n.* **2.** mainstay, support, foundation, bulwark. *His religion is the anchor of his life.* *–n.* **3.** mooring, hold, hook, kedge, killick. *Let's set the anchor so we won't drift off with the current.* **Ant.** detach, disconnect, loosen.

WORD SEARCH

hoisting device: *capstan, windlass*

hoist, to: *weigh*

prongs: *flukes*

ancient *adj.* old, antique, aged, archaic, old-fashioned, primitive. *Grandfather still drives his ancient Model-T Ford.* **Ant.** recent, new, modern.

ancillary *adj.* subordinate, supplementary, auxiliary, secondary, adjunct. *We were careful to read the ancillary clauses that appeared in the contract's small print.* **Ant.** main, principle, head.

android *n.* robot, automaton, cyborg. *An android may look human, but its emotions are likely to be quite artificial.*

anecdote *n.* story, narrative, tale, yarn, account, reminiscence. *I love Grandmother's amusing anecdotes about her childhood.*

anemic *adj.* weak, listless, fatigued, run-down, feeble, pale. *She couldn't get out of bed and appeared anemic.* **Ant.** energetic, robust, strong.

anesthetic *n.* painkiller, anesthesia, analgesic, opiate, soporific. *They gave me an anesthetic to kill the pain.*

angel *n.* spirit, guardian spirit, cherub, heavenly being, seraph, divine messenger, immortal. *Gabriel and Raphael are well-known angels.* **Ant.** devil, demon.

angelic *adj.* heavenly, divine, otherworldly, sweet, saintly, ethereal. *An angelic stranger showed us the way out of the woods.* **Ant.** demonic, devilish, Satanic.

anger *n.* **1.** rage, wrath, ire, fury, vexation, annoyance, irritation, displeasure. *She insulted him in a fit of anger.* *–vb.* **2.** enrage, outrage, infuriate, incense, irritate, annoy, upset. *His cruel remark angered me.* **Ant. 1.** calm, peacefulness, forbearance. **2.** soothe, pacify, mollify, calm.

angry *adj.* mad, furious, irate, wrathful, enraged, infuriated, irritated, annoyed, upset. *Please don't be angry with me.* **Ant.** happy, content, pleased.

angst *n.* anxiety, apprehension, misgiving, uneasiness, dread, nervousness. *She had a classic case of teenage angst, perpetually worried about fitting in and being cool.* **Ant.** calmness, contentment, serenity.

anguish *n.* distress, agony, torment, misery, anxiety, despair, pain, suffering. *He was in anguish after breaking up with his girlfriend.* **Ant.** comfort, solace, pleasure.

animal *n.* **1.** fauna, creature, beast, game. *She doesn't like to see wild animals imprisoned in zoos.* **2.** beast, brute, barbarian, savage. *The football player was flattered when he was called an animal.*

animated *adj.* lively, spirited, energetic, vigorous, dynamic, exciting. *She was the most animated person at the party.* **Ant.** boring, dull, lifeless.

animosity *n.* antagonism, hate, enmity, hostility, antipathy, malice, dislike, bitterness. *He felt unjust animosity toward the person who got the job he had wanted.* **Ant.** friendship, kindness, love, sympathy.

annals *n.* archives, history, records, chronicles, registers. *In the annals of history, nobody has ever changed base metal into gold.*

annex *vb.* **1.** add, attach, append, acquire, appropriate, connect, join. *The imperialist coun-*

try annexed some of its neighbor's territory. –*n.* **2.** addition, extension, supplement, wing, branch. *A new annex for the library is under construction.* **Ant. 1.** detach, separate, disconnect.

annihilate *vb.* demolish, destroy, exterminate, kill, eradicate, obliterate. *The army's offensive annihilated all opposition.*

annotate *vb.* notate, commentate, footnote, expand on. *The editor wished to annotate Mark Twain's books, in order to explain to readers some of the slang and culture of the late 1800s.*

announce *vb.* proclaim, declare, report, disclose, reveal, publish. *She announced her candidacy for the U.S. Senate.* **Ant.** hide, conceal, withhold.

announcer *n.* emcee, broadcaster, reporter, herald, crier, voice-over. *The announcer exclaimed in a shrill voice how wonderful the product was.*

annoy *vb.* irk, irritate, bother, vex, pester, disturb, harass, distract. *Don't annoy your brother while he's using the computer.* **Ant.** comfort, soothe, please.

annual *adj.* yearly, perennial. *The annual* Farmer's Almanac *is scheduled to hit the market next week.*

annuity *n.* payment, investment, fund, allowance, retirement fund, security. *Grandpa's annuity pays him more than $20,000 a year.*

annul *vb.* invalidate, nullify, withdraw, cancel, void, rescind. *The endlessly fighting couple decided to annul their marriage.* **Ant.** validate, certify, sanction.

annulment *n.* nullification, cancellation, invalidation, repeal. *The annulment dissolved their marriage vows.*

anonymous *adj.* unknown, nameless, unidentified, incognito, secret, uncredited. *An anonymous phone call tipped off the police.* **Ant.** named, known, identified.

anorexia *n.* anorexia nervosa, eating disorder, dieting disorder, sickness, neurosis. *When she was suffering from anorexia, she lost 70 pounds.* **Ant.** obesity, gluttony, overeating.

anorexic *adj.* emaciated, wasting, starving, malnourished, skinny. *She lost 40 pounds and appeared anorexic.* **Ant.** fat, overweight, obese.

answer *n.* **1.** reply, response, acknowledgment, reaction, return. *She eagerly awaited an answer to her letter.* **2.** result, solution, resolution. *It is often difficult to find the right answers for a crossword puzzle.* –*vb.* **3.** respond, reply, acknowledge, rejoin, return. *He answered her letter.* **4.** be accountable, be responsible, pay, atone. *The law says that we must answer for our crimes.* **Ant. 3.** ask, question, inquire.

antagonist *n.* opponent, adversary, rival, competitor, foe, enemy. *He bravely faced his antagonist in the boxing ring.* **Ant.** friend, ally, partner.

antagonize *vb.* irritate, alienate, insult, offend, annoy. *The child's rude behavior antagonized everyone.* **Ant.** please, charm, appease.

antecedent *n.* forerunner, predecessor, precursor, ancestor. *The telegraph was the antecedent of the telephone.* **Ant.** follower, descendant, successor.

antediluvian *adj.* pre-Flood, ancient, prehistoric, B.C., archaic, outmoded. *Their office clerks were still writing letters by hand, an antediluvian practice in the age of word processors.* **Ant.** futuristic, progressive, 21st century.

antenna *n.* aerial, signal receiver, (slang) rabbit ears. *You could get a better radio signal by extending the antenna.*

anthem *n.* song, composition, hymn. *Do you know all the words to the National Anthem?*

anthology *n.* collection, compilation, compendium, omnibus, treasury. *I love to read anthologies of science fiction stories.*

antibiotic *n.* medicine, drug, treatment, cure, pill, penicillin. *The doctor prescribed an antibiotic for my strep throat.*

anticipate *vb.* expect, foresee, foretell, predict, forecast. *She anticipates a good turnout for her lecture.*

anticlimax *n.* disappointment, let down, (slang) bomb, much ado about nothing, disillusionment. *Watching the Red Sox lose the championship yet again was an anticlimax to their brilliant season.* **Ant.** climax, grand finale.

antics *n.* tomfoolery, horseplay, foolishness, pranks, shenanigans. *The antics of the Three Stooges are still making people laugh.*

antidepressant *n.* psychotropic drug, mood elevator, medication, pharmaceutical, Prozac, Zoloft. *Jane was struggling with blue moods so her doctor prescribed an antidepressant.*

antidote *n.* antitoxin, antivenin, remedy, cure, treatment. *A poisonous bite from a coral snake requires an immediate antidote.*

antipathy *n.* aversion, hatred, dislike, loathing, repugnance. *I feel antipathy toward criminals.* **Ant.** liking, appeal, affection.

antiquated *adj.* outdated, old, old-fashioned, archaic, outmoded, obsolete, dated. *The crank telephone is now thoroughly antiquated.* **Ant.** modern, updated, new.

antique *adj.* **1.** old, aged, ancient, antiquated, old-fashioned. *He collects antique cars.* –*n.* **2.** relic, curio, rarity, memorabilia, souvenir. *This store has an impressive assortment of antiques.* **Ant. 1.** new, recent, modern.

anti-Semitism *n.* fascism, Jew-hating, prejudice, Nazism, chauvinism. *Adolf Hitler practiced the most horrific form of anti-Semitism.*

antiseptic *adj.* germ-free, clean, sterile, disinfected, sanitary. *Surgeons must make sure their hands are antiseptic before operating.* **Ant.** septic, infected, dirty.

antisocial *adj.* **1.** unfriendly, aloof, cold, introverted, hermit-like, reclusive. *Sarah wasn't really antisocial at the party, she was just shy.* **2.** hostile, sociopathic, depraved, unfeeling, angry. **Ant. 1.** friendly, extroverted, social. **2.** friendly, warm, considerate.

antithesis *n.* opposite, reverse, contrary, contradiction, inverse. *The antithesis of fun is boredom.*

anxiety *n.* apprehension, uneasiness, distress, worry, concern, foreboding, suspense. *She was filled with anxiety when she heard about her friend's accident.* **Ant.** relief, peacefulness, calmness.

anxious *adj.* **1.** worried, uneasy, concerned, apprehensive, restless, fearful. *He felt anxious the night before he was to undergo surgery.* **2.** eager, desirous, keen, impatient, intent. *She was anxious to get tickets for the hit musical.* **Ant. 1.** confident, collected, relieved. **2.** reluctant, hesitant.

apart *adv.* **1.** distant, removed, away, aside. *I don't see how both bookstores can succeed, since they're less than a block apart.* **2.** alone, separately, individually, aside, isolated. *Our house sits apart from the others on the block.* **3.** asunder, into parts, into pieces. *He took the engine apart, but he couldn't get it back together.* **Ant. 1.** near, together.

apartment *n.* rental unit, flat, tenement, suite, room, duplex, walk-up, condominium. *It was a tiny apartment with only one bedroom.*

apathetic *adj.* indifferent, unconcerned, unfeeling, uninterested, unmoved, uncommitted, cold. *Too many people are apathetic about environmental issues.* **Ant.** concerned, interested, committed.

apathy *n.* indifference, unconcern, disinterest, passiveness, lethargy, coldness. *If people had less apathy, we'd be able to solve more of our problems.* **Ant.** enthusiasm, fervor, interest, concern.

ape *n.* primate, simian, mammal, gorilla, chimpanzee, animal. *Some zoologists like to refer to the human as the "naked ape."*

aperture *n.* opening, orifice, hole, slot, gap. *We reduced the camera's aperture in order to cope with the blinding sunlight.*

apex *n.* highest point, peak, zenith, top, pinnacle, summit, climax. *Winning an Oscar was the apex of her acting career.* **Ant.** lowest point, bottom, nadir.

aplomb *n.* poise, composure, confidence, self-assurance, equanimity. *He had to speak in front of 3,000 people, but he handled it with great aplomb.* **Ant.** awkwardness, insecurity, inexperience.

apocalypse *n.* end of the world, mass destruction, Armageddon, catastrophe, holocaust, devastation. *The prophets warned of a horrible apocalypse.*

apocryphal *n.* questionable, unsubstantiated, suspect, unproven, dubious. *The reports of aliens over Roswell appear largely apocryphal.* **Ant.** true, proven, authentic.

apologetic *adj.* sorry, contrite, repentant, regretful, remorseful. *I couldn't be mad at her because she was so apologetic.* **Ant.** unrepentant, unremorseful.

apologize *vb.* atone, take back, beg one's pardon/forgiveness, offer regrets, (slang) eat crow. *I apologize for being late.*

apology *n.* explanation, excuse, acknowledgment, confession, regret. *He offered an apology for his lateness.*

apostle *n.* missionary, champion, follower, advocate, disciple, evangelist. *She has long been regarded as an apostle of love.* **Ant.** detractor, critic, enemy.

appall *vb.* horrify, shock, alarm, dismay, outrage, stun, offend, revolt. *Investors were appalled by news of the stock-market crash.* **Ant.** reassure, please, comfort.

appalling *adj.* fearful, frightening, alarming, dreadful, horrible, awful. *There was an appalling loss of life during World War II.* **Ant.** reassuring, comforting, pleasing.

apparatus *n.* machinery, equipment, implements, tools, gear. *The local gym has installed a new set of weightlifting apparatus.*

apparel *n.* clothing, clothes, garments, attire, wear, outfit. *I'm looking for a store that sells men's apparel.*

apparent *adj.* plain, obvious, evident, clear, manifest, unmistakable. *Her love of teaching is apparent to her students.* **Ant.** doubtful, uncertain, obscure.

apparently *adv.* evidently, seemingly, plainly, clearly, obviously. *He apparently won't be coming to the party.*

appeal *n.* **1.** request, plea, entreaty, application, petition. *The court turned down her appeal for a new trial.* **2.** attraction, allure, charm, draw, fascination. *Diamonds have an appeal that's hard for some people to resist.* *–vb.* **3.** beg, beseech, plead, pray, implore. *Farmers victimized by the drought appealed for federal assistance.* **4.** attract, excite, interest, fascinate, tempt. *Chinese food does not appeal to me.* **Ant.** **1.** refusal, rejection, objection. **2.** repulsiveness, unpleasantness. **3.** reject, refuse, deny. **4.** repulse, revolt.

appealing *adj.* attractive, inviting, alluring, tempting, desirable. *That pizza certainly looks appealing.* **Ant.** unappealing, repugnant, disagreeable.

appear *vb.* **1.** seem, look, act, sound. *Though he appears to like school, he really can't stand it.* **2.** arise, rise, arrive, emerge, show up, turn up. *The sun appeared from behind a mountain.* **Ant. 2.** disappear, vanish.

appearance *n.* **1.** arrival, emergence, coming, advent, appearing. *Though it was a cloudy day, the sun made a brief appearance.* **2.** look, image, demeanor, visage, aspect. *Appearances can be deceiving.* **Ant. 1.** disappearance, withdrawal, vanishing.

appease *vb.* placate, pacify, calm, soothe, ease, allay, quench. *The sandwich appeased her hunger.* **Ant.** irritate, aggravate, provoke.

appendix *n.* supplement, addition, postscript, attachment. *This dictionary has an appendix which lists computer terms.*

appetite *n.* hunger, craving, desire, taste, want, need. *He hasn't been able to control his appetite for sweets.* **Ant.** aversion, revulsion, repugnance.

appetizer *n.* snack, tidbit, starter, hors d'oeuvre, finger food. *He ate a pile of appetizers before dinner and got sick.*

WORD SEARCH

Asian dough casing stuffed with minced vegetables or meat: *dim sum*
assortment of appetizers and other foods: *smorgasbord*
casing filled with vegetables or meat: *dumpling*
chicken wings served with celery sticks and blue cheese dressing: *buffalo wings*
cracker or bread with a spread: *canapé*
dough pillow filled with potato, meat or cheese: *knish*
drink, alcoholic: *aperitif*
goose liver spread: *paté de foie gras (paté)*
herring rollup: *rollmop*
Italian marinated vegetables: *antipasto*
mashed eggplant and garlic spread: *baba ghanouj*
salted sturgeon spread: *caviar*
tortilla chips with guacamole, salsa, melted cheese: *nachos*
vegetables served raw with a dip: *crudités*

appetizing *adj.* appealing, inviting, tempting, tantalizing, attractive. *Boiled fish and cabbage soup is not very appetizing.* **Ant.** unappetizing, unattractive, repugnant.

applaud *vb.* praise, acclaim, compliment, commend, approve. *We all applauded her decision to look for a better job.* **Ant.** criticize, condemn, ridicule.

applause *n.* clapping, ovation, praise, acclaim, accolades. *After the opera was over, the audience's applause lasted for quite some time.* **Ant.** booing, hissing, denunciation.

apple *n.* pome, fruit, pippin.

WORD SEARCH

varieties: *Baldwin, Cortland, Empire, Fuji, Gala, Golden Delicious, Granny Smith, Gravenstein, Jonathan, Liberty, Matsu (Crispin), Macoun, McIntosh, Northern Spy, Paulared, Red Delicious, Rome, russet, Winesap.*

appliance *n.* apparatus, implement, equipment, device, fixture. *Stoves and refrigerators are examples of kitchen appliances.*

applicable *adj.* relevant, pertinent, suitable, appropriate, fitting. *Though her idea has merit, it isn't really applicable to our problem.* **Ant.** inapplicable, inappropriate.

application *n.* **1.** use, purpose, function, relevance, pertinence. *Her new invention doesn't* *have any practical applications.* **2.** request, requisition, petition, form. *He has submitted his application for a driver's license.*

apply *vb.* **1.** use, utilize, employ, exercise, administer. *The accident was her first chance to apply her knowledge of first aid.* **2.** put, lay, spread, rub, deposit, smear. *He applied two coats of varnish to his snowshoes.* **3.** refer, pertain, relate, involve, concern. *This law applies to everyone.* **4.** devote, dedicate, give, assign, commit. *She applied herself wholeheartedly to her new job.*

appoint *vb.* designate, select, assign, place, name, nominate. *He has been appointed to temporarily fill the vacant congressional seat.* **Ant.** dismiss, discharge.

appointment *n.* **1.** assignment, designation, placement, selection, nomination. *She received an appointment to the Supreme Court.* **2.** engagement, meeting, booking, date. *He has a doctor's appointment this afternoon.*

appraisal *n.* evaluation, assessment, valuation, estimation, rating, estimate of worth. *We had to get our house appraised before we could get a new loan.*

appraise *vb.* evaluate, assess, value, estimate, measure, judge, price, rate. *The value of the land was appraised at $100,000.*

appreciate *vb.* **1.** realize, understand, comprehend, recognize, perceive. *He doesn't appreciate how much trouble he's caused.* **2.** value, esteem, prize, admire, honor, cherish. *It's difficult to work for someone who doesn't appreciate your efforts.* **Ant.** **1.** misunderstand, misjudge. **2.** dislike, disdain, scorn.

appreciation *n.* **1.** gratitude, thankfulness, thanks, gratefulness. *She expressed her appreciation for all the help she'd received.* **2.** awareness, understanding, comprehension, realization, sensitivity. *That uneducated man has no appreciation of the finer things in life.* **Ant.** **1.** ingratitude, ungratefulness. **2.** disregard, ignorance.

apprehend *vb.* catch, capture, arrest, seize, take into custody, (slang) collar. *The police announced that they had apprehended a suspect in the robbery.* **Ant.** release, free.

apprehension *n.* **1.** capture, arrest, seizure, (slang) collar, (slang) nabbing, jailing. *The community was relieved with the news of the criminal's apprehension.* **2.** anxiety, nervousness, uneasiness, foreboding, dread, bad feeling. *There is a certain amount of apprehension felt before a thunderstorm.* **Ant.** **1.** release, liberation. **2.** relief, calm, reassurance.

apprehensive *adj.* nervous, anxious, dreading, uneasy, fearful, frightened, on edge. *We were apprehensive about the approaching storm.* **Ant.** calm, relaxed, reassured.

apprentice *n.* trainee, beginner, student, learner, pupil, neophyte, (slang) rookie. *The carpenter took the boy under his wing as an apprentice.* **Ant.** teacher, mentor, master.

approach *vb.* **1.** approximate, equal, resemble, parallel, border. *His writing talent approaches that of Hemingway.* **2.** near, reach, gain, achieve, make. *The car slowed down as it approached town.* **3.** begin, start, commence, undertake, enter. *She approached her new job with a strong desire to succeed.* *n.* **4.** method, procedure, system, manner, style. *He pioneered a new approach for the treatment of disease.* **5.** access, entry, route, entrance, passage. *Heavy snowfall blocked all approaches to the remote village.* **Ant.** **1.** differ, diverge. **2.** recede, retreat, withdraw. **3.** finish, conclude, end. **5.** exit, outlet.

appropriate *adj.* **1.** suitable, proper, fitting, applicable, correct. *The invitation stated that appropriate attire was required.* *–vb.* **2.** confiscate, seize, commander, steal, take. *The ruthless dictator appropriated the private holdings of his enemies.* **3.** allocate, assign, allot, disburse, authorize. *The town council appropriated funds for construction of a new library.* **Ant. 1.** inappropriate, unfitting, unsuitable. **2.** return, relinquish, surrender. **3.** withhold, misappropriated.

approval *n.* **1.** admiration, acceptance, respect, favor, praise. *She worked hard to win her employer's approval.* **2.** permission, consent, authorization, sanctión, validation. *She needs her parents' approval before she can use the family car.* **Ant. 1.** disapproval, dissatisfaction. **2.** disapproval, prohibition.

approve *vb.* **1.** appreciate, like, respect, praise, commend, value. *I approve your choice of music.* **2.** permit, allow, condone, support, uphold, sanction. *His parents don't approve of his working during the school year.* **Ant. 1.** disapprove, dislike, criticize. **2.** disapprove, disallow.

approximate *adj.* **1.** estimated, rough, comparable, near, inexact. *The approximate time is two o'clock.* *–vb.* **2.** estimate, judge, gauge, reckon, compute. *She asked the mechanic to approximate the cost of repairs.* **Ant. 1.** exact, precise, accurate.

approximately *adv.* about, roughly, almost, nearly, around. *This test will take approximately one hour to complete.* **Ant.** exactly, precisely.

apron *n.* smock, pinafore, coverall, bib, garment. *It's a good idea to wear an apron when cooking with messy ingredients.*

apropos *adv.* fitting, appropriate, befitting, apt, suitable, timely. *It would be apropos to have the best man give a toast.* **Ant.** inappropriate, unbefitting, tacky.

aptitude *n.* gift, talent, ability, capability, flair, capacity. *This test will measure your scholastic aptitude.*

arbitrary *adj.* subjective, whimsical, capricious, unreasonable, irrational, inconsistent. *His business failed because he was prone to making arbitrary decisions.* **Ant.** objective, prudent, consistent.

arcade *n.* **1.** gallery, cloister, walkway, piazza. *The couple strolled through the arcade.* **2.** amusement facility, game room, entertainment center. *He went to the arcade to play video games.*

arcane *adj.* esoteric, secret, mysterious, incomprehensible, abstruse, enigmatic. *At the party, he shared some arcane knowledge of the universe, but nobody understood him.* **Ant.** comprehensible, knowable, simple.

archaic *adj.* old-fashioned, obsolete, outdated, ancient, antiquated. *Now that we're in the computer age, typewriters seem almost archaic.* **Ant.** new, modern, current.

archetype *n.* model, example, prototype, original, exemplar. *The computer giant's business plan is being used as an archetype throughout the industry.*

architect *n.* designer, draftsman or -woman, builder, planner, engineer, creator. *The architect designed a magnificent skyscraper.*

architecture *n.* building design, drafting, construction. *Examples of Gothic architecture surrounded us as we walked along the medieval streets.*

WORD SEARCH

British 16th-century style characterized by exposed beams: *Tudor*

classical orders: *Corinthian, Doric, Ionic, Tuscan, Composite*

drawing and plan: *blueprint*

18th-century style borrowing from classical, Renaissance and baroque: *Georgian*

European, elaborately decorated style from 1550–1700s: *baroque*

French, richly ornamental: *rococo*
futuristic style of the 1930s featuring chevrons, zigzags: *art deco*
Greek, early: *Byzantine*
Italian classical: *Renaissance*
Mediterranean style characterized by domes and horseshoe arches: *Islamic*
Middle Ages style characterized by pointed arches, flying buttresses: *Gothic*
19th-century ornamental house style: *Victorian*
revived style from an earlier period: *revival*
stucco and Arabesque designs, early Spanish: *Moorish*

archives *n.* records, files, annals, repository, chronicles, library, collection. *We had to search the archives to find the old newspaper story.*

ardent *adj.* passionate, zealous, fervent, intense, strong, impassioned, vehement. *He was an ardent supporter of equal rights.* **Ant.** indifferent, dispassionate, apathetic.

arduous *adj.* difficult, trying, exhausting, fatiguing, rigorous. *Her proposed climb of Mt. Everest will be an arduous undertaking.* **Ant.** easy, effortless, simple.

area *n.* **1.** expanse, extent, stretch, space, scope. *Our town covers an area of five square miles.* **2.** region, territory, terrain, district, zone. *Bears live in wilderness areas.* **3.** field, sphere, realm, domain. *That does not fall within my area of expertise.*

arena *n.* theater, stadium, amphitheater, coliseum, stage, ring. *The rock band completely sold out the arena.*

argue *vb.* **1.** quarrel, dispute, feud, disagree, haggle, bicker. *The children argued over whose turn it was to do the dishes.* **2.** assert, maintain, plead, discuss, debate. *She argued that the city should build a shelter for homeless people.* **Ant. 1.** agree, concur, concede.

argument *n.* **1.** quarrel, altercation, feud, dispute, disagreement. *When the referee called a foul, one of the players got into an argument with him.* **2.** case, grounds, reason, evidence, justification. *He doesn't have a valid argument to support his claim that the city should adopt a mass-transit system.* **Ant. 1.** agreement, harmony, unanimity.

argumentative *adj.* disagreeable, combative, quarrelsome, contentious, belligerent. *Sheila and Jake are too argumentative to make their marriage last.* **Ant.** agreeable, conciliatory, easygoing.

arid *adj.* dry, parched, waterless, withered, barren, sterile. *Without irrigation, you can't grow crops on arid land.* **Ant.** moist, wet, damp, fertile.

arise *vb.* rise, emerge, appear, originate, begin, start. *Misunderstandings can arise when people don't communicate properly.* **Ant.** sink, cease, end, disappear.

aristocracy *n.* nobility, gentility, upper class, elite, gentry, high society. *She was born of the aristocracy and therefore enjoyed great privileges.* **Ant.** peasantry, bourgeoisie.

aristocrat *n.* nobleman, noblewoman, blue blood, lord, high-born, snob, peer. *He was an aristocrat descended from royalty, or so he said.* **Ant.** peasant, low-born, loser.

arithmetic *n.* math, mathematics, figures, calculations, adding and subtracting. *You have to know basic arithmetic to be able function effectively in modern society.*

arm *n.* **1.** limb, branch, projection, extension, appendage. *Please don't sit on that chair's arm.* **2.** weapon, armament, ordnance, firearm, gun, ammunition. *Some people would like to see military arms turned into plowshares.* –*vb.*

3. prepare, protect, strengthen, fortify, equip, outfit. *She armed herself with an umbrella before venturing out into the storm.*

Armageddon *n.* end of the world, apocalypse, war, holocaust, final battle. *Some people believed that Armageddon would occur at the dawning of the new millennium.*

armed *adj.* equipped, outfitted, (slang) packing heat, loaded. *The bank robber was armed and dangerous.* **Ant.** unarmed, disarmed, unloaded.

arms *n.* weapons, ammunition, armament, ordnance, guns, bombs, munitions. *Lay down your arms and give peace a chance.*

army *n.* military unit, corps, troop, legion, host, horde, swarm, throng, force, defensive unit. *The army closed in on the enemy position.*

WORD SEARCH

ammunition storage: *munitions dump*
backup unit: *reserves*
eating facility: *mess*
infantry fighter: (slang) *grunt*
lodging: *billet, barracks*
medal for wounds: *Purple Heart*
ranks (in ascending order): *private, corporal, sergeant, sergeant major, chief warrant officer, lieutenant, captain, major, colonel, brigadier general, general*
recruit training ground: *boot camp*
uniform, camp: *fatigues*
unit (from smallest to largest): *squad, platoon, company, battalion, brigade, division, corps, field army*
vehicle, small transport: *humvee*

aroma *n.* fragrance, scent, smell, odor. *The aroma of a pie baking in the oven made my mouth water.* **Ant.** stink, stench, reek.

around *prep.* about, approximately, roughly, near. *I will be there around nine o'clock.*

arouse *vb.* awaken, waken, rouse, stir, excite, stimulate. *Her strange story aroused my curiosity.* **Ant.** settle, stifle, repress.

arraign *vb.* accuse, charge, indict, blame, incriminate, (slang) point the finger at. *The suspect was arraigned in court today.* **Ant.** acquit, exonerate, excuse.

arrange *vb.* **1.** place, order, group, position, organize. *He arranges his books according to subject matter.* **2.** plan, prepare, schedule, design, devise. *She arranged a picnic for all her employees.* **Ant.** **1.** disorder, disorganize, disarrange.

arrangement *n.* **1.** order, array, pattern, layout, setup, system. *She devised an unusual arrangement for her coin collection.* **2.** plan, preparation, provision, reservation. *Father made all the arrangements for our vacation.*

array *n.* collection, assortment, bunch, congregation, multitude, batch, lineup, arrangement. *The clothier displayed an array of new fashions.*

arrest *vb.* **1.** apprehend, capture, catch, seize, detain. *Police arrested two suspects in the recent robbery.* **2.** stop, stay, check, halt, obstruct, delay. *Radiation therapy should arrest the growth of your tumor.* –*n.* **3.** capture, apprehension, detention, seizure, restraint. *Police announced the arrest of a major drug dealer.* **Ant.** **1.** release, free, liberate. **2.** encourage, continue.

arrival *n.* coming, appearance, entrance, advent, approach. *We eagerly awaited the arrival of my sister's plane.* **Ant.** departure, leaving, withdrawal.

arrive *vb.* reach, attain, enter, come, approach, near. *She arrived at work ten minutes late.*

arrogance *n.* haughtiness, presumptuousness, conceit, pride, ego, braggadocio, imperiousness. *The swaggering fighter displayed an annoying arrogance.* **Ant.** modesty, humbleness, humility.

arrogant *adj.* haughty, presumptuous, pretentious, conceited, proud, egotistical. *His arrogant attitude made him quite unpopular.* **Ant.** modest, humble, unassuming.

arrow *n.* shaft, dart, bolt, projectile, missile. *William Tell's arrow pierced the apple and split it.*

WORD SEARCH
barb: *fluke*
feather: *vane*
holder: *quiver*
launcher: *bow, crossbow*
notch at one end: *nock*
shooter: *archer, bowman*

arsenal *n.* armory, munitions, dump, magazine, stockpile, depot. *The enemy had accumulated a formidable arsenal over the years.*

arson *n.* fire-setting, torching, pyromania.

WORD SEARCH
crime: *insurance fraud*
evidence of accelerant use: *hydrocarbon residue*
starter fluid: *accelerant*

art *n.* **1.** artwork, painting, drawing, engraving, etching. *He invited us over to view his collection of wilderness art.* **2.** skill, talent, craft, technique, knowledge. *She has mastered the art of making people feel welcome.*

WORD SEARCH
bigger-than-life depictions of everyday objects: *pop art*
broken color style of Monet and Renoir: *Impressionism*
cube style: *cubism*
cursive, swirling lines, 19th-century style characterized by: *art nouveau*
dots or points creating a whole: *pointillism*
dreamlike or nightmarish: *surrealism*
experimental: *avant-garde*
nonrepresentational: *abstract art*
optical effects that fool the eye: *op art*
ornamental style of the 16th to 18th centuries, rich: *baroque*
realistic or photograph-like depictions: *photorealism, hyperealism, tromp l'oeil, magic realism; representational*
shades of same color, form utilizing several: *chiaroscuro*
unschooled: *folk art*

artery *n.* blood vessel, vein, channel, conduit. *Major arteries can be found in the neck.*

article *n.* **1.** object, item, piece, thing, element. *This store carries a variety of religious articles.* **2.** composition, essay, story, feature, theme. *He makes his living writing magazine articles.*

articulate *adj.* eloquent, well-spoken, expressive, smooth-talking, facile, fluent. *Politicians give endless speeches and therefore must be articulate.* **Ant.** tongue-tied, inarticulate, ineloquent.

artificial *adj.* fake, phony, false, unreal, unnatural. *This ring is made with artificial diamonds.* **Ant.** real, genuine, authentic.

artillery *n.* gunnery, cannons, weaponry. *The squadron suddenly came under heavy artillery fire.*

artisan *n.* craftsman, technician, handicraftsman, artificer, artist. *The local crafts fair displayed the works of numerous artisans.*

artist *n.* **1.** painter, sculptor, photographer, writer, singer, composer. *Our museum will be displaying the work of a local artist.* **2.** master, professional, pro, expert, genius. *He's a real artist when it comes to making up excuses.* **Ant.** **2.** amateur, novice, beginner.

artistic *adj.* creative, artful, inventive, ornamental, decorative, masterful. *The little girl's snowwoman had two heads, but it was artistic.*

artistry *n.* creativity, skill, flair, virtuosity, style, inventiveness. *The artistry of the stained glass was breathtaking.*

ascend *vb.* climb, mount, scale, rise, advance. *A priest ascended the steps to the altar.* **Ant.** descend, fall, drop.

ascent *n.* climb, climbing, scaling, mounting, surmounting. *Their ascent of Mt. McKinley took three weeks.* **Ant.** descent.

ashamed *adj.* embarrassed, humiliated, chagrined, mortified, uneasy. *You should be ashamed to wear such sloppy attire to work.* **Ant.** unashamed, proud, honored.

ashes *n.* cinders, embers, soot. *Make sure the ashes have cooled before throwing them in the trash.*

ask *vb.* **1.** question, query, quiz, inquire, interrogate. *The new student had to ask for directions to her classroom.* **2.** request, seek, beg, plead, implore. *She asked him to stop smoking in her presence.* **3.** invite, summon, bid, beckon. *He asked her to dinner.* **Ant.** **1.** answer, respond, reply.

askew *adj.* crooked, awry, aslant, off. *The painting was slightly askew, so I adjusted it.* **Ant.** straight, level.

asleep *adj.* sleeping, dozing, napping, slumbering, dormant. *The house was quiet because everyone was asleep.* **Ant.** awake, up, active.

aspect *n.* **1.** look, appearance, manner, bearing, demeanor. *She does not like to hike in that forest because of its gloomy aspect.* **2.** facet, side, angle, phase, feature, point. *Have you analyzed all aspects of the problem?*

asphyxiate *vb.* suffocate, choke, smother, strangle. *A plastic bag placed over one's head can asphyxiate.*

aspiration *n.* goal, ambition, objective, desire, wish, dream, aim. *Her aspiration was to become the first female baseball player in the Major League.*

aspire *vb.* desire, want, wish, crave, yearn, seek. *He aspires to be a famous actor.*

assail *vb.* attack, criticize, accost, (slang) rip into, (slang) jump on, blast, malign, blister. *The boss assailed me for being chronically late.* **Ant.** compliment, praise, pat on the back.

assailant *n.* attacker, assaulter, aggressor, molester, mugger. *The assailant struck the victim and proceeded to steal her purse.*

assassin *n.* killer, murderer, slayer, executioner, triggerman. *An assassin was responsible for the death of Martin Luther King, Jr.*

assassinate *vb.* kill, murder, slay, execute, liquidate. *Terrorists assassinated our ambassador.*

assault *n.* **1.** attack, onslaught, offensive, rush, storming. *The goblin army was routed when the elves made their assault.* –*vb.* **2.** attack, rush, storm, raid, strike, charge. *An army of dwarves assaulted the goblins' last stronghold.* **Ant.** **1.** retreat, withdrawal. **2.** retreat, retire, withdraw.

assemble *vb.* **1.** gather, collect, accumulate, congregate, meet. *A crowd began to assemble at the accident site.* **2.** put together, fabricate, make, construct, manufacture. *It took him all day to assemble the model airplane.* **Ant.** **1.** scatter, disperse, disband. **2.** disassemble, dismantle.

assembly *n.* gathering, meeting, grouping, rally, convention. *Our principal will speak at tomorrow's assembly.* **Ant.** separation, dispersion.

assert *vb.* affirm, declare, announce, proclaim, swear. *Despite his team's recent loss, he still asserts that they're the best.* **Ant.** deny, refute, disavow.

assertion *n.* claim, avowal, declaration, statement, proclamation. *It's foolish to make assertions that you can't support.* **Ant.** denial, contradiction.

assertive *adj.* forceful, aggressive, insistent, forward, overbearing. *She's so assertive she won't* *take "no" for an answer.* **Ant.** timid, hesitant, shy.

assess *vb.* evaluate, appraise, weigh, measure, judge, check, determine, value. *After the storm, a survey crew was brought in to assess the damage.*

assessment *n.* evaluation, appraisal, weigh, measurement, judgment, check, determination, valuation. *They made a grim assessment of the damage.*

asset *n.* **1.** advantage, benefit, strength, blessing, resource. *Her strong arm is a great asset when it comes to playing tennis.* **2.** property, holdings, possessions, belongings, wealth, riches. *His savings account is just one of his numerous assets.* **Ant. 1.** disadvantage, liability, drawback.

assign *vb.* **1.** distribute, dispense, give, allocate, allot. *Her students think she assigns too much homework.* **2.** appoint, designate, name, nominate, delegate. *He was assigned to serve on the personnel committee.*

assignment *n.* responsibility, duty, task, chore, job. *I can't go out because I have homework assignments from three different classes.*

assimilate *vb.* adapt, adjust, acclimatize, fit in, integrate, blend in. *It took me more than a year to assimilate in Italy.*

assist *vb.* help, aid, support, further, advance. *She assisted him with his homework.* **Ant.** hinder, impede, hamper.

assistance *n.* help, aid, support, cooperation, backing. *He wouldn't have been able to finish the book without her assistance.* **Ant.** hindrance, opposition, resistance.

assistant *n.* **1.** aide, helper, attendant, subordinate, associate. *The manager hired an assistant because his store was getting very busy.* *–adj.* **2.** helping, aiding, assisting, accessory, attendant. *She was excited to get a job as an assistant editor.*

associate *vb.* **1.** relate, connect, identify, attach, combine. *Most people associate Thanksgiving with turkey dinners.* **2.** socialize, mingle, mix, accompany. *I don't like the people you associate with.* *–n.* **3.** partner, colleague, confederate, peer, coworker. *She took her business associates out to lunch yesterday.* **Ant. 1.** separate, divide, divorce.

association *n.* **1.** organization, alliance, syndicate, society, party. *He's a member of an association for screenwriters.* **2.** companionship, friendship, acquaintance, fellowship, intimacy. *My parents don't approve of my association with you.*

assorted *adj.* various, varied, mixed, miscellaneous, diverse. *This sofa is available in assorted color combinations.* **Ant.** identical, uniform, similar.

assortment *n.* variety, mixture, collection, selection, array. *This hardware store carries a large assortment of tools.*

assume *vb.* **1.** presume, suppose, postulate, suspect, infer. *His boss assumed he'd be at work on time.* **2.** adopt, embrace, acquire, take, undertake. *She assumed his responsibilities after he was fired.* **Ant. 1.** know, prove. **2.** renounce, abandon, relinquish.

assuming *adj.* presumptuous, arrogant, egotistical, overconfident. *She was an assuming prima donna, certain in the knowledge that everyone adored her.* **Ant.** unassuming, modest, humble.

assumption *n.* presumption, belief, supposition, conjecture, surmise. *He bought the used television on the assumption that it worked.*

assurance *n.* pledge, vow, oath, promise, guarantee. *She gave me her assurance that she would repay the loan.*

assure *vb.* reassure, promise, pledge, affirm, guarantee. *The mechanic assured us that our car would be ready by noon.* **Ant.** deny, refute, question.

assured *adj.* confident, self-assured, secure, bold, certain, cocky. *When Babe Ruth went to the plate, he was assured.* **Ant.** shaky, insecure, timid.

asteroid *n.* meteoroid, planetoid, rock, celestial object. *The extinction of the dinosaurs may have been caused by an asteroid striking the Earth 65 million years ago.*

asthma *n.* respiratory disease, obstructive pulmonary disease, chronic cough, breathing disorder, wheezing, allergy. *Inhaling pet dander always triggered her asthma.*

astonish *vb.* amaze, surprise, astound, startle, stun, dazzle. *She was astonished to learn she had just won the lottery.*

astonishing *adj.* amazing, surprising, astounding, startling, impressive. *He has the astonishing ability to recall everything he reads.* **Ant.** ordinary, routine, expected.

astonishment *n.* amazement, surprise, wonder, shock, bewilderment. *We were filled with astonishment as we watched the daredevil perform.* **Ant.** apathy, indifference, boredom.

astound *vb.* astonish, amaze, surprise, startle, stun. *The Wright brothers astounded the whole world with their first airplane flight.*

astray *adj.* lost, adrift, off the mark, far afield, off course. *Fifty miles from home, the dog had run seriously astray.* **Ant.** on course, correct, in the right direction.

astrology *n.* horoscopy, reading of the stars, divination, pseudoscience. *Astrology is widely considered to be nothing more than pseudoscience.*

astronaut *n.* spaceman, spacewoman, space explorer, cosmic explorer, cosmonaut, pilot. *The word astronaut means "sailor of the stars."*

astronomer *n.* stargazer, cosmologist, astrophysicist, scientist. *Astronomers believe that billions of planets exist in the universe.*

astronomy *n.* stargazing, cosmology, astrophysics, space study. *He took a class in amateur astronomy to learn more about locating comets.*

WORD SEARCH

building that houses telescope: *observatory*
device used to create spectrum to determine a celestial object's chemical makeup: *spectroscope*
distance measurement unit: *light-year, parsec, astronomical unit*
eclipse of one celestial body in front of another: *occultation*
great imaginary circle from north to south in the sky: *meridian*
locating measurements: *azimuth, declination, right ascension*
measured with respects to the stars, as: *sidereal*
optical device: *telescope*
orbit of satellite that appears opposite that of Earth's rotation: *retrograde*
orbital position of planet on opposite side of earth from the sun: *opposition*
overhead, point in sky directly: *zenith*
path of Sun, Moon and planets: *ecliptic*
planet discovery technique of watching for starlight to dim temporarily: *transit method*
radio signals from space, receives and magnifies: *radio telescope*
table of future positions of planets and stars: *ephemeris*
telescopes, combination of two or more: *interferometer*

See also MOON; PLANET; SPACE; SUN; UNIVERSE.

astute *adj.* sharp, shrewd, keen, clever, canny. *She got her wealth by making some very astute investments.* **Ant.** dumb, naive, stupid, unintelligent.

asylum *n.* refuge, sanctuary, haven, shelter, protection, retreat. *They gave the fugitive asylum in their underground security facility.*

asymmetrical *adj.* uneven, lopsided, mismatched, disproportionate, unbalanced, contrasting. *The building was asymmetrical, with one of its sides much larger than the others.* **Ant.** symmetrical, balanced, matching.

atheism *n.* nontheism, disbelief, impiety, skepticism, godlessness, doubt, denial. *Atheism is neither good nor bad, but the simple lack of belief in a god.* **Ant.** theism, belief, faith, piety.

atheist *n.* nonbeliever, skeptic, freethinker, doubter, agnostic. *Atheists believe that humans merely invented the concept of God.* **Ant.** theist, believer, follower.

athlete *n.* competitor, sportsman, Olympian, (slang) jock. *Michael Jordan was a great athlete.*

athletic *adj.* robust, vigorous, strong, muscular, sturdy. *His athletic body is the result of daily exercise.* **Ant.** frail, feeble, weak.

atmosphere *n.* **1.** air, sky, heavens. *Scientists hope to establish a space station well beyond Earth's atmosphere.* **2.** feeling, mood, tone, character, spirit. *This restaurant has a cozy atmosphere.*

WORD SEARCH

heat buildup due to trapping of solar radiation by carbon dioxide: *greenhouse effect*
layer: *stratum*
layer from 0–10 miles up: *troposphere*
layer from 10–30 miles: *stratosphere*
layer from 30–50 miles: *mesosphere*
layer from 50–300 miles: *thermosphere*
layer from 300 miles to space: *exosphere*
layer rich in ions: *ionosphere*
oxygen layer that protects living things from damaging rays of Sun: *ozone layer*
rising column of air: *thermal*

atom *n.* particle, jot, bit, scintilla. *Particles smaller than atoms are commonly known as subatomic particles.*

WORD SEARCH

center: *nucleus*
components of: *protons, neutrons, electrons*
fusing of two atoms to create energy: *fusion*
hypothetical fusion of atoms in a test tube: *cold fusion*
number of protons in nucleus: *atomic number*
number of neutrons and protons in nucleus: *mass number*
particle smaller than: *subatomic particle*
smasher: *accelerator, collider*
splitting of and resulting energy release: *fission*
study of: *nuclear physics*
two or more bound together: *molecule*
weight of: *atomic mass*

atomic *See* NUCLEAR.

atomic bomb *See* A-BOMB; NUCLEAR BOMB.

atone *vb.* amend, repent, redeem, do penance, make up for. *To clear your conscience, you should atone for your sins.*

atrocious *adj.* horrible, terrible, dreadful, evil, cruel, brutal. *The Nazis were guilty of committing atrocious crimes.* **Ant.** good, kind, benevolent.

atrocity *n.* outrage, horror, brutality, cruelty, crime. *The world was stunned by the news of the terrorist's atrocity.*

atrophy *vb.* waste, wither, weaken, degenerate, emaciate. *An astronaut's muscles in zero gravity will atrophy very quickly without vigorous exercise.* **Ant.** strengthen, grow, increase.

attach *vb.* **1.** join, connect, secure, fasten, add. *Please attach this donor's certificate to your driver's license.* **2.** bind, tie, attract, captivate, enamor. *The boy is very attached to his puppy.* **Ant. 1.** detach, unfasten, disconnect.

attachment *n.* **1.** accessory, addition, supplement, extension, extra. *Her new computer has space for a hard disk and other attachments.* **2.** bond, tie, devotion, love, fondness, affection. *He has a strong attachment to his grandfather.* **Ant. 2.** hatred, dislike, indifference.

attack *vb.* **1.** assault, charge, storm, rush, raid. *A band of Indians attacked the wagon train.* **2.** criticize, denounce, censure, revile, berate. *Congress attacked the president's stand on foreign policy.* *–n.* **3.** assault, offensive, onslaught, charge, invasion. *The soldiers were nervous because they were expecting an enemy attack.* **4.** spasm, fit, seizure, stroke, disease. *Exercise and proper diet are the best ways to prevent heart attacks.* **Ant. 1.** retreat, retire, withdraw. **2.** defend, uphold, support. **3.** retreat, withdrawal, defense.

attacker *n.* assailant, assaulter, batterer, mugger, thug, aggressor. *Her attacker was sentenced to five years in prison.*

attain *vb.* achieve, reach, acquire, gain, win, accomplish. *Van Gogh did not attain great fame as an artist until after his death.* **Ant.** lose, forfeit, miss.

attainment *n.* achievement, accomplishment, acquirement, realization, success, skill, talent. *Proficiency in foreign languages is just one of her numerous attainments.*

attempt *vb.* **1.** strive, endeavor, try, seek, venture, struggle. *She will attempt to swim the English Channel next week.* *–n.* **2.** try, effort, trial, attack, endeavor, undertaking. *His attempt to climb Mt. Everest was unsuccessful.*

attend *vb.* **1.** go to, be present at, visit, frequent. *She can't go on vacation because she has to attend summer school.* **2.** serve, tend, care for, wait on, minister to. *The paramedics attended to the most critical patients first.* **Ant. 1.** miss, be absent. **2.** ignore, neglect, disregard.

attendant *n.* servant, aide, assistant, helper. *He has a part-time job as a gas-station attendant.*

attention *n.* heed, notice, observance, regard, concentration. *This lecture will require everyone's full attention.* **Ant.** inattention, disregard, neglect.

attentive *adj.* observant, heedful, mindful, alert, watchful. *Please try to be more attentive when I speak to you.* **Ant.** inattentive, unobservant, heedless.

attest *vb.* verify, support, bear witness, affirm, confirm, substantiate. *I can attest to the allegation that Tim stole the last cookie.* **Ant.** deny, contradict, discredit.

attic *n.* garret, upper floor, storage space, clerestory, dormer, loft. *We store all our old clothes in the attic.*

attire *vb.* **1.** dress, clothe, array, bedeck, outfit. *The queen was attired in a luxurious gown.* *–n.* **2.** clothing, garments, apparel, outfit, costume. *The soldiers wore standard military attire.*

attitude *n.* mood, disposition, temperament, outlook, perspective. *His failing grades can be attributed to his poor attitude.*

attorney *n.* lawyer, counselor, legal representative, advocate, solicitor, barrister, DA. *Get an attorney to go over the contract before you sign it.*

attract *vb.* draw, pull, lure, catch, invite, entice. *Her odd behavior attracted everyone's attention.* **Ant.** repel, repulse, rebuff.

attraction *n.* appeal, allure, lure, bait, draw, fascination, charm. *The Grand Canyon is Ari-*

zona's biggest tourist attraction. **Ant.** repulsion, revulsion.

attractive *adj.* appealing, alluring, enticing, inviting, pleasing, pretty, handsome. *He certainly looks attractive in his new suit.* **Ant.** unattractive, unappealing, plain, ugly.

attribute *n.* feature, characteristic, quality, distinction, quirk. *She has many fine attributes, including a wry sense of humor.* –*vb.* credit, assign, blame, impute. *I would attribute our poor hitting skills with a lack of batting practice.*

attrition *n.* dwindling, reduction, decline, decimation, loss. *We will reduce the work force by natural attrition, not by layoffs.* **Ant.** gain, increase, growth.

atypical *adj.* abnormal, unusual, eccentric, irregular, uncommon. *Getting snow in July is atypical for our area.* **Ant.** normal, usual, common.

auction *n.* sale, sell-off, vendue, sale, bidding war. *We bid on several antiques at last night's auction.*

audacious *adj.* **1.** brave, courageous, gutsy, daring, intrepid, fearless, bold. *They made an audacious attempt to climb the mountain during a blizzard.* **2.** arrogant, cheeky, rude, brazen, shameless, presumptuous. *Her attempt to take the last of the cookies without asking was rather audacious.* **Ant. 1.** cowardly, fearful, cautious. **2.** courteous, polite.

audacity *n.* **1.** courage, bravery, guts, fearlessness, nerve, daring. *Climbing the icy cliff took a stunning amount of audacity.* **2.** arrogance, cheekiness, rudeness, nerve, shamelessness, gall, brass. *How they had the audacity to cut in line ahead of us, I'll never know.* **Ant. 1.** cowardice, fear, timidity. **2.** courtesy, politeness, deference.

audible *adj.* hearable, perceptible, clear, detectable, discernible, within earshot. *Unfortunately, their rude remarks were quite audible to everyone there.* **Ant.** inaudible, imperceptible, unclear.

audience *n.* **1.** spectators, onlookers, listeners, gallery, house. *The audience was restless before the concert began.* **2.** interview, reception, consultation, meeting, hearing. *Sir Lancelot could meet with King Arthur without having to formally request an audience.*

audit *vb.* examination, inspection, check, accounting, review, investigation. *The IRS agent performed an audit on their income tax return.*

audition *n.* tryout, test, trial, hearing, screen test. *Auditions for the starring role are being held today.*

auditorium *n.* theater, hall, concert hall, lecture hall, amphitheater, playhouse. *We gathered in the auditorium to hear the president's speech.*

augment *vb.* increase, enlarge, extend, raise, expand, swell. *She augmented her income by taking on an additional job.* **Ant.** decrease, lessen, diminish.

aura *n.* air, ambiance, emanation, (slang) vibe, atmosphere, mood. *We sensed the woman had an aura of great inner peace.*

aurora *n.* aurora borealis, northern lights, aurora australis, southern lights. *The aurora looked like colored ribbons curling across the sky.*

auspices *n.* sponsorship, patronage, support, approval, aegis. *We were given the okay to collect donations under the auspices of the local women's club.*

auspicious *adj.* favorable, propitious, timely, positive, felicitous, fortunate, opportune. *Spring is an auspicious time to plant a garden.* **Ant.** unfavorable, negative, bad.

austere *adj.* severe, rigid, strict, stern, harsh, stiff, formal. *Her austere look means we're in trouble.* **Ant.** cheerful, friendly, lenient.

authentic *adj.* genuine, real, true, actual, legitimate, pure. *An authentic first edition of any Dickens novel is incredibly valuable.* **Ant.** fake, imitation, unreal, false.

authenticate *vb.* verify, certify, validate, corroborate, substantiate, vouch. *We needed an expert to authenticate the archeological find.* **Ant.** discredit, falsify, unmask.

author *n.* writer, novelist, poet, creator, originator. *His dream is to become a best-selling author.*

WORD SEARCH

fake name: *pen name, pseudonym, nom de plume*
many books, author of: *polygraph*
publicizes books: *publicist*
sells books and handles book contracts: *literary agent*
writes a book secretly for someone else: *ghostwriter*

authoritative *adj.* scholarly, expert, documented, erudite, sound, reliable. *A dictionary must be highly authoritative.* **Ant.** ignorant, unschooled, amateurish.

authority *n.* **1.** command, power, influence, rule, domination. *I have to bow to my father's authority.* **2.** expert, master, genius, wizard, specialist. *She's an authority when it comes to discussing politics.* **3.** right, privilege, permission, approval, authorization. *Who gave you authority to use my computer?* **4.** police, sheriff, lawmakers. *She notified the authorities when she discovered her car was missing.* **Ant. 3.** refusal, denial, prohibition.

authorization *n.* authority, approval, permission, privilege, right. *The lawyer requested authorization to study certain police files.* **Ant.** refusal, denial, ban, prohibition. *n.* permission, go-ahead, empowerment, license, sanction. *We did not have the proper authorization to enter the sacred tomb.* **Ant.** denial, restriction, veto.

authorize *vb.* approve, permit, allow, entitle, enable. *The bank's manager is the only one authorized to grant loans.* **Ant.** prevent, disallow, disapprove.

autograph *n.* **1.** signature, inscription, endorsement. *He collects the autographs of famous ballplayers.* –*vb.* **2.** sign, inscribe, endorse, dedicate. *Would you mind autographing your book for me?*

automated *adj.* automatic, mechanized, robotic, computerized, self-operating. *The entire assembly line was automated.* **Ant.** manual, hand-made.

automatic *adj.* **1.** self-operating, self acting, self-moving. *Her new camera is completely automatic.* **2.** involuntary, unplanned, instinctive, spontaneous, uncontrolled. *His reaction was automatic when the dog ran in front of his car.* **Ant. 1.** manual. **2.** deliberate, planned, intentional.

automobile *n.* car, vehicle, transport, (slang) wheels, (slang) bucket of bolts, sedan, station wagon, hatchback, coupe. *My automobile ran out of gas.*

WORD SEARCH

alcohol, driving under the influence of: *DUI, OUI*
brakes, non-skid: *anti-lock brakes*
chauffeur-driven: *limousine*
explosion of fuel in exhaust system: *backfire*
frame: *chassis*
funeral: *hearse*
gauge, engine speed: *tachometer*
gauge, mileage: *odometer*
gauge, vehicle speed: *speedometer*

gear system: *transmission*
global satellite positioning system: *GPS*
hemispherical combustion chamber: *hemi*
license plate, personalized: *vanity plate*
pedal for manual transmission: *clutch*
police: *squad car, cruiser, prowl car*
pollution control apparatus: *catalytic converter*
powered by gasoline and electric: *hybrid*
shock absorber and mounting plate: *strut*
skid without traction over sheet of water: *hydroplane*
speed control, automatic: *cruise control*
starting without a key: (slang) *hotwiring*
turning force of engine crankshaft: *torque*
vibration of front end due to fault in tires or suspension system: *shimmy*
warning lights on dashboard: *hazard lights*

autonomy *n.* independence, self-reliance, sovereignty, self-rule, freedom, self-determination. *The island government was granted complete autonomy and could decide issues on their own.* **Ant.** dependence, subjugation, subjection.

autumn *n.* fall, harvest time. *Autumn is my favorite time of year.*

auxiliary *adj.* secondary, subsidiary, subordinate, supplemental, accessory. *The hospital has an auxiliary generator in case it loses power.*

available *adj.* obtainable, accessible, reachable, attainable, handy. *Since the restaurant had no available tables, we had to wait.* **Ant.** unavailable, unobtainable, inaccessible.

avalanche *n.* snowslide, snow collapse, inundation, cataclysm, deluge. *The west side of the mountain was closed due to a heightened risk of an avalanche.*

avant-garde *n.* **1.** vanguard, new school, innovators, cutting edge, pioneers. *They were the avant-garde of digital artists, employing techniques never seen before.* *–adj.* **2.** cutting edge, innovative, pioneering. **Ant. 1.** old school, dinosaurs. **2.** old school, antiquated.

avarice *n.* greed, gluttony, acquisitiveness, money-hunger, cupidity. *King Midas's avarice for gold is legendary.* **Ant.** generosity, benevolence.

avenge *vb.* revenge, vindicate, retaliate, repay, punish. *Rather than seeking to avenge injustices, try a little forgiveness.* **Ant.** forgive, pardon, excuse.

avenue *n.* **1.** street, road, boulevard, thoroughfare. *The village's avenues are paved with brick.* **2.** route, means, path, course, road. *Hard work is the best avenue to success.*

average *adj.* **1.** standard, normal, typical, ordinary, usual. *The average temperature of the human body is 98.6 degrees.* **2.** mean, middle, median, medium. *She ran the marathon at an average speed of six miles per hour.* *–n.* **3.** mean, median, par, norm, standard. *His score on the test was close to the national average.* **Ant. 1.** exceptional, extraordinary, unusual.

aversion *n.* repugnance, antipathy, hatred, revulsion, dislike. *She has an aversion to horror movies.* **Ant.** liking, attraction, fondness.

avert *vb.* prevent, thwart, stop, turn away, halt, shunt, deter. *They hoped to avert a disaster by draining some of the flood waters.* **Ant.** cause, invite, bring about.

aviator *n.* flyer, pilot, airman, aviatrix. *The famed aviator was the first to cross the ocean alone.*

avid *adj.* eager, passionate, enthusiastic, fervent, zealous, ardent, fanatical. *He was an avid postage stamp collector.* **Ant.** unenthusiastic, apathetic, indifferent.

avocation *n.* hobby, pastime, interest, sideline, pursuit. *There is nothing more satisfying than making your avocation your vocation.*

avoid *vb.* evade, elude, dodge, escape, duck, shun. *Let's go to an afternoon matinee in order to avoid the evening crowds.* **Ant.** face, confront, meet.

awaken *vb.* wake, awake, rouse, arouse, stir. *We were awakened by someone pounding on the front door.*

award *vb.* **1.** bestow, give, grant, accord, render. *The court awarded the woman custody of her children.* –*n.* **2.** reward, prize, trophy, decoration, citation. *The firefighter received an award for bravery.* **Ant. 1.** withhold, deny, refuse.

aware *adj.* mindful, conscious, informed, apprised, knowing. *Are you aware of the dangers of drug addiction?* **Ant.** unaware, unfamiliar, uninformed.

awesome *adj.* impressive, astonishing, awe-inspiring, breathtaking, magnificent, eye-popping, intimidating. *The sight of the shuttle taking off into space was awesome.* **Ant.** ho-hum, unimpressive, trivial.

awful *adj.* dreadful, terrible, horrible, appalling, bad, poor. *That was an awful thing to say to your friend.* **Ant.** delightful, wonderful, pleasant.

awfully *adv.* very, exceedingly, extremely, greatly, terribly. *I'm awfully glad to see you.*

awkward *adj.* **1.** clumsy, inept, ungraceful, uncoordinated, bungling, ungainly. *He made an awkward attempt to catch the ball.* **2.** embarrassing, disconcerting, difficult, ticklish, delicate. *We both felt uncomfortable during the awkward pause in our conversation.* **3.** unwieldy, unmanageable, cumbersome, unhandy. *The heavy hammer felt awkward to the small boy.* **Ant. 1.** graceful, coordinated. **2.–3.** pleasant, comfortable, easy.

awning *n.* canopy, shade, canvas, marquee. *We stood under the awning to escape the Sun's broiling rays.*

awry *adj.* **1.** crooked, askew, off, aslant. *The beam appeared awry, so we leveled it.* **2.** wrong, amiss, out of order, (slang) out of whack. *The play went awry after several actors forgot their lines.* **Ant. 1.** straight, level. **2.** right, correct.

ax *n.* chopper, broadax, hatchet, maul. *Grab the ax and cut some firewood.*

B

babble *n.* **1.** jabber, drivel, prattle, babel, gibberish, blabbing. *The politicians were debating vociferously, but it sounded like babble to me.* *–vb.* **2.** prattle, jabber, blab, stammer, blat, prate. *I couldn't listen to their nonsensical babble anymore.*

baby *n.* **1.** infant, newborn, toddler, tot, babe. *The baby slept soundly in its crib.* *–vb.* **2.** pamper, spoil, coddle, overprotect, indulge. *Everyone babied the youngest member of our family.* **Ant.** **1.** adult, grown-up. **2.** deny, neglect.

WORD SEARCH

bathtub: *bathinette*
bed: *cradle, bassinet*
bounce on one knee: *dandle*
loud cry: *squall*
diaper irritation: *diaper rash*
mouth soother: *pacifier, teething ring*
multiple: *twins, triplets, quadruplets, quintuplets, sextuplets*
prematurely born: (slang) *preemie*
seal-like cough: *croup*
song: *lullaby*
talk: *babble, coo, gurgle*
teeth, growth and appearance of: *teething*
walking: *toddling*

babysit *vb.* tend, watch, guard, mind, care for. *I have to babysit the twins on Saturday.*

babysitter *n.* sitter, nanny, nursemaid, governess, guardian, au pair. *We need to hire a babysitter to watch little Joey.*

back *n.* **1.** backside, reverse, rear, posterior, tail, spine. *What's on the back of your T-shirt?* *–adj.* **2.** behind, rearmost, hind, end, posterior. *You may exit through the back door.* *–vb.* **3.** reverse, withdraw, recede, retreat. *She backed the car out of the driveway.* **4.** support, favor, promote, encourage, endorse. *Who will you back in next month's election?* **Ant.** **1.** front, anterior. **2.** front, near, fore. **3.** forward, advance, progress. **4.** oppose, fight, undermine.

backer *n.* supporter, financier, sponsor, benefactor, underwriter. *We need a backer to help us pay for a new play production.*

backfire *vb.* blow up, explode, go awry, flop, bomb. *The plan could backfire if we aren't careful.* **Ant.** succeed, work, go smoothly.

background *n.* **1.** setting, environment, landscape, backdrop. *He helped build the background for the school play.* **2.** experience, preparation, upbringing, rearing. *The personnel manager questioned applicants about their educational background.* **Ant.** **1.** foreground, forefront. **2.** prospects, future.

backhoe *n.* excavator, digger, earth mover, heavy machinery. *Nowadays they use a backhoe instead of a shovel to dig graves.*

backing *n.* support, sponsorship, financing, underwriting, aid. *We got the backing of three major corporations to help us finance the operations.*

backlash *n.* reaction, repercussion, fallout, backfire, response, consequence. *The senator's much-publicized scandal is causing voter backlash.*

backlog *n.* accumulation, excess, back orders, critical mass, pile. *The backlog of orders requires us to hire additional workers.*

backstab *n.* backbite, betray, slander, double-cross, attack. *I refuse to backstab, no matter how difficult a person may be to work with.*

bacteria *n.* microorganisms, germs, pathogens, (slang) bugs, microbes, bacilli. *Disease-causing bacteria are all around us.*

bad *adj.* **1.** wicked, immoral, naughty, sinful, corrupt, evil. *The bad guys in movies often wear black clothes.* **2.** defective, faulty, incorrect, poor. *The mechanic fixed the car's bad brakes.* **3.** foul, decayed, rotten, spoiled, polluted. *I bit into a bad apple.* **4.** harmful, destructive, hurtful, deadly. *Large cities are often criticized for their bad air.* **5.** severe, dangerous, serious, critical, extreme. *The plane was delayed by a bad storm.* **6.** sorry, regretful, upset, apologetic. *She felt bad about having lied to him.* **7.** sick, unwell, weak, ill, indisposed, poor, miserable. *He stayed home because he was feeling bad.* **Ant. 1.** good, moral, virtuous. **2.** good, perfect. **3.** good, fresh, edible. **4.** helpful, healthy. **5.** trivial, minor, insignificant. **6.** pleased, unashamed. **7.** well, healthy.

bad breath *n.* halitosis, sour breath, (slang) dragon breath. *Eating onions or garlic will give you bad breath.*

badge *n.* shield, emblem, medal, symbol, insignia. *He claimed to be a police officer, but he wasn't wearing a badge.*

badger *vb.* harass, pester, bother, torment, tease, annoy, irritate. *He badgered me to return his book.* **Ant.** comfort, calm, soothe.

baffle *vb.* confuse, puzzle, perplex, befuddle, bewilder, mix up. *This math problem will baffle all but the brightest students.*

bag *n.* sack, tote, duffel, pouch, pack, haversack. *I bought a bag of potatoes.*

baggage *n.* luggage, bags, suitcases, carry-ons, valises, trunks, gear. *Load your baggage onto the train.*

baggy *adj.* loose, ill-fitting, sagging, droopy, billowing, slack. *Are baggy pants still in style?* **Ant.** tight, skintight, constricting.

bail *n.* bond, surety, security, money, deposit, warranty. *Bail was set at $10,000.*

bait *n.* **1.** lure, inducement, enticement, attraction, temptation. *Cheese makes a good bait for catching mice.* –*vb.* **2.** provoke, tease, goad, annoy, harass, tempt, lure. *Reporters baited the actor with personal questions.* **Ant. 2.** soothe, calm, humor, flatter.

bake *vb.* roast, cook, heat, broil. *Let's bake some cookies.*

bakery *n.* pattiserie, pastry shop, bread shop, cake shop, bagel shop. *I stopped at the bakery to buy a cake.*

balance *vb.* **1.** stabilize, equalize, steady, match. *The president tried to balance the nation's budget.* –*n.* **2.** equilibrium, poise, stability. *The gymnast lost her balance and fell to the ground.* **3.** remainder, residue, excess, difference, remains. *She will pay five dollars today and the balance tomorrow.* **Ant. 1.** topple, upset. **2.** imbalance, shakiness.

bald *adj.* bare, hairless, barren, smooth, exposed. *The Buddhist monk kept his head bald by shaving off his hair.* **Ant.** covered, hairy, unshorn, bristly.

balk *vb.* hesitate, falter, flinch, recoil, stop. *I would balk at any plans to expand the business right now.*

ball *n.* sphere, globe, orb, spheroid, toy. *Bounce the ball my way.*

ballet *n.* dance, toe dancing, choreography. *Dancing on the tips of one's toes is ballet's most difficult challenge.*

WORD SEARCH
dancer: *ballerina* (female), *danseur* (male)
director: *impresario*
knee bend: *plié*
leap from one foot to the other: *jeté*
midair split: *pas ciseaux, grand écart*
outfit: *leotard, tights, tutu*
posturing on one leg: *arabesque*
shoes: *toe shoes*
tiptoeing steps: *pas de bourrée, temps de point, en pointe*
whirl around: *pirouette*

balloon *n.* aerostat, lighter-than-air craft, vessel. *We visited the clouds in Uncle Jim's hot air balloon.*

WORD SEARCH
altitude gauge: *altimeter*
anchor line: *mooring line, tether*
basket: *gondola*
director: *balloonmeister*
gas heater: *burner*
ground crew: *chase crew*
pilot and passengers: *aeronauts*
sandbags or other weights used to control altitude: *ballast*

ballot *n.* **1.** vote, election, poll, polling, referendum. *The class president was elected by secret ballot.* **2.** ticket, slate, candidate list. *Three people had their names on the ballot for treasurer.*

ban *n.* **1.** prohibition, restriction, injunction, embargo, taboo. *Most countries have a ban on hunting whales.* *–vb.* **2.** forbid, disallow, prohibit, outlaw, censor. *Many dangerous chemicals are banned from being used on food crops.* **Ant. 1.** permission, sanction, approval. **2.** allow, endorse.

banal *adj.* trite, insipid, lackluster, dull, stale, inane. *The music was catchy, but the lyrics were painfully banal.* **Ant.** original, inventive, brilliant.

band *n.* **1.** group, gang, bunch, club, society, pack, company. *The police were searching for a band of car thieves.* **2.** ensemble, duo, combo, trio, quartet, pentad, sextet, septet, orchestra.

WORD SEARCH
administrator and adviser: *manager*
fan of: (slang) *groupie*
improvisational session: (slang) *jam*
main act: *headliner*
play date or location: *gig*
playing exceptionally well: (slang) *cooking*
set-up crew member: (slang) *roadie*
show booker: *agent*
show circuit: *tour*

bandage *n.* Band-Aid, gauze, dressing, swath, covering, strip. *I cut my hand and needed a bandage.*

bandit *n.* robber, outlaw, brigand, thief, hoodlum, gangster, pirate. *Bandits robbed the stage-coach.*

bang *n.* **1.** boom, noise, detonation, explosion, pop, crack, thud. *Lightning struck the tree and made a terrible bang.* *–vb.* **2.** strike, hit, beat, slam, smack, rap.

banish *vb.* exile, outlaw, deport, eject, expel. *The queen banished the evil sorcerer from her realm.* **Ant.** welcome, embrace, receive.

bank *n.* savings and loan, financial institution, lending institution, thrift, credit union, investment firm. *I save most of my money in the bank.*

WORD SEARCH
ATM: *automated teller machine*
check, guaranteed by bank: *certified check*

check, returned due to insufficient funds: *bounced check*
FDIC: *Federal Deposit Insurance Corporation*
loan, failure to pay off: *default*
loan payment, larger than usual: *balloon payment*
loan payment, late in making: *delinquent*
loan security: *collateral*
payment for use of bank's funds: *interest*
storage space for valuables: *safe deposit box*
teller's window: *wicket*

bankrupt *adj.* insolvent, broke, wiped out, ruined, (slang) belly-up, destitute. *The company went bankrupt after a series of bad business decisions.* **Ant.** rich, wealthy, solvent.

banner *n.* sign, streamer, pennant, flag, ensign. *We hoisted the championship banner and hung it from the gym ceiling.*

banquet *n.* feast, dinner, meal, regale, spread. *The king held a banquet for his knights.* **Ant.** snack, fasting.

banter *n.* jesting, joking, ribbing, teasing, repartee. *Their wise-guy banter sounded mean, but it was actually in fun.*

baptism *n.* rite, christening, initiation, sacrament, immersion, ritual. *All of the family members attended the baby's baptism.*

baptize *vb.* initiate, immerse, christen, consecrate, anoint. *The preacher will baptize the baby tomorrow.*

bar *n.* **1.** rod, rail, spar, grating, pole. *The prison had bars on its windows.* **2.** tavern, pub, saloon, alehouse. *The bar sold whiskey and beer.* **3.** ingot, slab, block. *Bars of gold were stored in the bank's vault.* **4.** barrier, hindrance, obstacle, obstruction, barricade. *The ship hit a sand bar.* *–vb.* **5.** block, stop, curb, restrict, lock. *The school barred its students from leaving campus.* **Ant.** **4.** aid, assistance, opening. **5.** admit, allow, unlock.

barbarian *n.* outlander, savage, vandal, brute, primitive. *Rome claimed to have civilized the barbarians of faraway lands.*

barbaric *adj.* uncivilized, uncultured, coarse, brutish, savage, cruel. *The pirates acted in the most barbaric manner.* **Ant.** civilized, cultured, refined, enlightened.

barbecue *vb.* **1.** roast, flamebroil, grill, rotisserie, cook. *Who doesn't love to barbecue chicken?* *–n.* **2.** roast, cookout, grilling, party.

barber *n.* haircutter, hairdresser, beautician, coiffeur, stylist. *The barber gave me a terrible shave.*

bare *adj.* **1.** naked, stripped, nude, uncovered, undressed. *The nurse gave him a shot in his bare behind.* **2.** empty, blank, barren, vacant, void. *She found nothing to eat in the bare cupboard.* **3.** simple, plain, undisguised, pure, basic. *Sherlock Holmes was interested in only the bare facts of a case.* *–vb.* **4.** uncover, expose, show, reveal. *Taking off his cap, he bared his head to the rain.* **Ant.** **1.** clothed, covered. **2.** filled, stocked. **3.** disguised, embellished. **4.** cover, conceal.

barely *adv.* just, scarcely, hardly, only. *She was barely tall enough to reach the cookie jar.* **Ant.** amply, profusely, sufficiently.

bargain *n.* **1.** agreement, understanding, pact, contract, treaty. *The suspect made a bargain in which he pleaded guilty to a lesser crime.* **2.** discount, reduction, deal, buy, steal. *There were many good bargains at the swap meet.* *–vb.* **3.** barter, negotiate, haggle, deal, dicker. *The president bargained for release of the hostages.*

barge *n.* flatboat, scow, freight carrier. *They loaded the barge with construction equipment and floated out into the bay.*

barn *n.* cow barn, stables, byre, stalls, shed, outbuilding, shelter. *Put the cows in the barn before it starts snowing.*

WORD SEARCH
construction of: *barnraising*
hay storage, top floor: *hayloft*
storage facility standing next to: *silo, granary*

barrel *n.* cask, drum, hogshead, keg, vessel, cylinder, firkin. *The barrel of rainwater was too heavy to move.*

WORD SEARCH
maker: *cooper*
stopper: *bung*

barren *adj.* bare, dead, empty, depleted, desolate, sterile, unfruitful. *The farmer was unable to grow crops on the barren land.* **Ant.** lush, fertile, fruitful.

barricade *n.* barrier, roadblock, blockade, impediment, obstruction. *To stop the bank robber, the police put up a barricade.*

barrier *n.* blockade, obstruction, obstacle, barricade, impediment, stop, bar. *The Great Wall of China was built as a barrier against nomadic barbarians.* **Ant.** passage, opening, entrance.

barter *vb.* trade, swap, bargain, exchange, negotiate. *I bartered my sandwich for her apple.*

base *n.* **1.** foundation, foot, stand, bottom, substructure. *I had my picture taken at the base of the Statue of Liberty.* **2.** station, post, headquarters, garrison, camp. *Scientists hope to establish a base on the Moon.* –*vb.* **3.** establish, ground, root, form, rest. *The writer based her tale of King Arthur on historical facts.* –*adj.* **4.** coarse, vile, low, immoral, vulgar, obscene. *People were offended by his base jokes.* **Ant. 1.** top, pinnacle, summit. **3.** invalidate, uproot. **4.** noble, honorable, exalted.

baseball *n.* sport, ball, game, national pastime. *Let's go play a game of baseball.*

WORD SEARCH
bat, illegal: *corked bat*
bat's warm-up weight: *donut*
bench, player's: *dugout*
bumbled play or catch: *error*
dirt track around outfield: *warning track*
fantasy league: *Rotisserie League*
fastball: (slang) *smoke, hummer, fireball*
fly balls: *blooper, pop up*
hits: *single, double, triple, home run*
hit often used as a sacrifice to move other player, tiny infield: *bunt*
hit, weak: *nubber, squibber*
hitter, reliable in critical situation: *clutch hitter*
hitter for pitcher: *designated hitter*
home run, four-run: *grand slam*
minor leagues: *AAA, AA, A, farm system, bush leagues*
out-of-play ball: *foul*
panic and perform badly: *choke*
pitch, curving or strangely breaking: *breaking ball, curveball, forkball, knuckleball, screwball, sinker, slider, spitball, split-fingered fastball*
pitch, slow and easy to hit: (slang) *lollipop*
pitch thrown deceptively slow: *change-up, off-speed pitch*
pitcher, closing: *closer, reliever, stopper*
pitcher, team's best: *ace*
pitcher's warm-up area: *bullpen*
player draw from schools and minor leagues: *draft*
player, first-year: *rookie*
player not currently under contract: *free agent*
runner, substitute: *pinch runner*
stands, hit fair ball that bounces into: *ground rule double*
strike out: (slang) *whiff, fan*

baseless *adj.* unsupported, groundless, unjustified, unfounded, unreasonable. *The judge refused to accept the baseless accusations against the defendant.* **Ant.** supported, justified, reasonable.

bashful *adj.* reserved, shy, sheepish, timid, demure. *The bashful child peeked at us from behind a couch.* **Ant.** forward, outgoing, brazen.

basic *adj.* fundamental, rudimentary, elementary, essential. *We will cover basic vocabulary in our first-year Spanish class.* **Ant.** advanced, additional supplementary.

basin *n.* sink, tub, vessel, font, washbowl. *You can wash your socks out in the basin.*

basket *n.* container, hamper, wickerwork, holder, pannier. *Toss your dirty clothes in the basket.*

basketball *n.* (slang) hoops, (slang) B-ball, ball, sport. *A good way to get in shape fast is to play full-court basketball.*

WORD SEARCH

backboard shot, close: *layup*
block opponents to get rebound: *box out*
midair catch ending in a slam dunk: *alley-oop*
positions: *guard, forward, center*
running break to basket: *fast break*
screen or legally getting in the way of an opponent: *pick*
screen play: *pick and roll*
shot granted for foul: *foul shot, free throw*
shot, long range: *three pointer, outside shot,* (slang) *Hail Mary,* (slang) *prayer*
shot missing everything, including the rim: (slang) *brick,* (slang) *air ball*
shot, nothing but net: *swish*
shot, one-handed arc: *hook*
slamming ball through hoop: *dunk, slam dunk*
violation: *foul*
violation, blocked shot over hoop: *goaltending*
violation, dribbing: *double dribble, traveling,* (slang) *walking, palming*

bastion *n.* stronghold, fortress, fortification, citadel, bulwark. *Harvard is a great bastion of learning.*

bat *n.* club, cudgel, baton, bludgeon, staff. *Hold the bat firmly and swing evenly.*

batch *n.* bunch, group, assortment, collection, lot. *We baked a batch of cookies.*

bath *n.* wash, wash-up, soak, cleansing, rinse, scrub. *A hot bath will make you feel great after a long, tiring day.*

bathe *vb.* wash, soak, clean, rinse, scrub, freshen up. *The Victorians tended to bathe only once or twice a week.*

bathing suit *n.* swimsuit, trunks, shorts, bikini, Speedo, maillot, cutoffs, one-piece. *Get your bathing suit and let's go for a swim.*

bathroom *n.* rest room, lavatory, toilet, washroom, men's room, ladies' room, powder room, (slang) john. *I went to the bathroom to freshen up.*

WORD SEARCH

British slang: *loo*
military: *latrine*
outdoor: *outhouse*

baton *n.* stick, staff, bat, club, wand. *She lead the band with a makeshift baton.*

battalion *n.* battle group, subdivision, group, unit, body. *The embattled army dispatched a battalion into the troubled area.*

battery *n.* **1.** electric cell, storage cell. *Did you buy batteries for the toy?* **2.** series, cluster, set, group, batch. *The applicant had to take a battery of tests.* **3.** beating, attack, maiming, onslaught, mayhem. *He was arrested for assault and battery.* **Ant. 2.** scattering, individual. **3.** kindness, gentleness.

battle *n.* **1.** fight, conflict, war, skirmish, confrontation. *The Germans fought the Americans in a battle for control of the Rhine River.* –*vb.* **2.** fight, clash, skirmish, feud, argue. *Two students battled for the lead in the school play.* **Ant. 1.** peace, armistice, truce. **2.** agree, concur.

battleship *n.* warship, naval vessel, cruiser, destroyer, fighting vessel. *The battleship cruised into the outer harbor and dropped anchor.*

bawdy *adj.* lascivious, ribald, raunchy, dirty, lewd. *The R-rated movie was a little too bawdy for my taste.* **Ant.** proper, wholesome, clean.

bawl *vb.* cry, whine, wail, blubber, sob, whimper. *The baby will bawl if you wake it too early.*

bay *n.* cove, harbor, inlet, bight, gulf. *We anchored in the bay and fished for mackerel.*

bayou *n.* creek, branch, waterway, marsh, outlet, inlet. *The bayou was a great place to watch for egrets.*

beach *n.* seacoast, coast, shore, bank, seashore, sand. *Waves washed driftwood up onto the beach.*

WORD SEARCH

bathhouse: *cabana*
channel, tiny: *rill*
coral or rock ridge just off shore: *barrier reef*
dangerous cross-current: *riptide*
debris, lost ship cargo and: *flotsam and jetsam*
pull of receding waves: *undertow*
sand ripples left by waves: *swash marks*
sand shelf or hummock: *berm*
sea spray: *spindrift*
seaweed and other vegetation washed ashore: *wrack*
strip connecting two landmasses: *isthmus, tombolo*
sweep of waves up beach: *swash*
tide, receding: *ebb tide*
wave, giant: *tsunami, eagre, tidal bore*
waves: *plunger, spiller, comber, train, graybeard*

beacon *n.* signal, light, beam, guide, lighthouse, radar. *The beacon warned ships to avoid the shallow reef.*

beam *n.* **1.** rafter, timber, brace, girder, support. *The ceiling of our cabin is constructed with open beams.* **2.** ray, shaft, streak, flash, stream. *A beam of sunlight broke through the clouds.* –*vb.* **3.** radiate, broadcast, transmit, gleam, shine. *The television program was beamed to us via satellite.* **Ant. 3.** retain, withhold, absorb.

bear *n.* bruin, mammal, omnivore, carnivore, grizzly. *A bear wandered into camp last night and scared us half to death.*

bear *vb.* **1.** tolerate, endure, suffer, stand, withstand. *He couldn't bear hearing such terrible sounds.* **2.** carry, haul, transport, bring, convey. *The hotel porter bore the luggage to our room.* **3.** produce, deliver, generate, make, form. *The apple trees bore fruit.* **4.** display, exhibit, show, possess. *My school diploma bears the principal's signature.* **5.** push, thrust, strain, drive, press. *You'll have to bear down on the saw to cut through that thick board.*

beard *n.* whiskers, bristles, stubble, five o'clock shadow, tuft. *He wore a beard similar to Abe Lincoln's.*

WORD SEARCH

forked: *swallowtail beard*
pointy and short: *Van Dyke*
rounded: *aureole*
slim and pointed: *stiletto*
spade-shaped: *Shenandoah*
square and long: *tile*
tuft: *goatee*
tuft under bottom lip: *barbiche*
twined: *screw beard*

bearing *n.* **1.** carriage, posture, conduct, demeanor, poise. *The princess had a regal bearing.* **2.** relevance, significance, reference, connection. *The judge claimed that the defendant's wealth had no bearing on the outcome of the trial.* **Ant. 2.** insignificance, irrelevance.

beast *n.* **1.** animal, mammal, creature. *The donkey is sometimes called a beast of burden.* **2.** monster, brute, savage, ogre. *"Beauty and the Beast" is a famous fairy tale.*

beastly *adj.* brutish, loathsome, cruel, repulsive, horrid, nasty. *We've had some beastly weather.* **Ant.** appealing, humane, cultured.

beat *vb.* **1.** hit, pound, batter, thrash, pummel. *He was robbed and beaten by a mugger.* **2.** whip, whisk, stir, mix. *Please beat the cookie dough.* **3.** defeat, win, overcome, conquer, vanquish. *Our team beat the opposing team by three points.* **4.** vibrate, pulse, pulsate, throb, tremble. *I could hear her heart beat.* –*n.* **5.** rhythm, cadence, meter, pulse, measure. *The audience clapped their hands to the beat of the music.* **Ant. 1.** fail, succumb, lose.

beautiful *adj.* gorgeous, enchanting, attractive, lovely, pretty, appealing. *These roses are beautiful.* **Ant.** ugly, hideous, unsightly, repulsive.

beautify *vb.* enhance, decorate, dress, glamorize, primp. *Adding, a fresh coat of paint is the simplest way to beautify a home.* **Ant.** deface, ruin, spoil.

beauty *n.* appeal, attractiveness, prettiness, loveliness, allure, charm, good looks, fairness. *The beauty of Miss America is unrivaled.* **Ant.** repulsiveness, ugliness, homeliness.

beckon *vb.* motion, summon, signal, hail, call, gesture. *The teacher beckoned me to come to her desk.*

become *vb.* turn into, emerge as, develop into, convert. *He became a werewolf when the Moon was full.*

becoming *adj.* seemly, befitting, proper, appropriate, right. *That hairstyle is very becoming on you.* **Ant.** unbecoming, unsuitable, unflattering.

bed *n.* bunk, mattress, futon, (slang) sack. *I was tired so I went to bed early.*

bed and breakfast *n.* inn, B&B, lodging, guest house, accommodations. *We plan on lodging at a bed and breakfast instead of a hotel.*

bedlam *n.* uproar, pandemonium, clamor, riot, turmoil, upheaval. *Bedlam erupted in the stadium when the home team lost.* **Ant.** peacefulness, order.

bedridden *adj.* disabled, infirm, handicapped, crippled, prostrate, incapacitated. *Mary is bedridden with a broken leg.* **Ant.** ambulatory, able-bodied.

beehive *n.* beegum, apiary, colony. *Don't mess around with that beehive unless you want to get stung.*

beer *n.* ale, lager, alcohol, (slang) brew, malt, bitter, (slang) suds. *They each had a beer at the bar.*

WORD SEARCH

cask: *keg, puncheon, tun.*
drinking vessel: *mug, stein, schooner*
manufacturer: *brewery*

before *prep.* **1.** in advance of, prior to, previous to, ahead of. *Please take out the trash before dark.* –*adv.* **2.** previously, earlier, formerly, already. *He didn't want to go to the movie because he had seen it before.* **Ant. 1.** after, later than. **2.** after, behind.

beg *vb.* plead, implore, ask, entreat, beseech. *She begged her parents for a larger allowance.* **Ant.** insist, demand, order.

beggar *n.* panhandler, pauper, derelict, mendicant, tramp, (slang) bum. *The beggar asked for a job instead of money.*

begin *vb.* start, commence, initiate, found, introduce, establish, launch. *She plans to begin a rock band.* **Ant.** stop, finish, end, terminate, abandon.

beginner *n.* neophyte, amateur, rookie, novice, tyro. *I can't beat anyone at chess because I'm just a beginner.* **Ant.** veteran, professional, expert.

behavior *n.* conduct, attitude, actions, performance, manners. *She received a demerit for bad classroom behavior.*

behead *vb.* decapitate, guillotine, lop off, decollate, execute. *We no longer behead criminals for their crimes, although some might think we should.*

behemoth *n.* giant, leviathan, monster, Goliath, titan, colossus. *The behemoth washed up on shore this morning, and the city hired a truck to haul it off.*

behind *prep.* **1.** in back of, beyond, after, following. *The parking lot is behind the store.* *–adv.* **2.** after, following, in back of, in the rear of. *The students walked behind the museum guide.* **3.** late, show, tardily, behindhand. *My watch is behind by one hour.* **Ant. 1–2.** before, in front of. **3.** early, ahead.

behold *vb.* see, observe, witness, view, notice. *Behold, the rabbit has disappeared.*

belated *adj.* late, tardy, overdue, delayed. *I sent Aunt Mary a belated birthday card.* **Ant.** timely, on time, prompt.

believe *vb.* accept, trust, affirm, hold, maintain. *She believes that life exists on other planets.* **Ant.** disbelieve, reject, doubt, question.

belittle *vb.* deride, degrade, disparage, insult, put down, diminish. *I'm breaking up with Angela because all she does is belittle me.* **Ant.** praise, build up, compliment.

bell *n.* ringer, dinger, campana, carillon, chimes. *Please don't ring the bell when my head is inside of it.*

WORD SEARCH

clapper: *tongue*
person who rings church bells: *sexton*
sound: *chime, clang, ding, dong, knell, peal, toll, tinkle, tintinnabulation*
tower: *belfry*

belligerent *adj.* unfriendly, hostile, argumentative, quarrelsome, warlike. *The United States considered Germany a belligerent nation during World War II.* **Ant.** friendly, peaceful, easy-going.

bellow *vb.* holler, roar, shout, thunder, boom, bark. *The drill seargent can bellow better than anyone.* **Ant.** whisper, murmur, mutter.

belly *n.* stomach, midsection, abdomen, gut, tummy, paunch. *The belly tends to put on fat more easily after middle age.*

belongings *n.* property, possessions, effects, goods. *Students keep their belongings in lockers.*

beloved *adj.* loved, cherished, adored, treasured, revered. *Grandfather was one of the most beloved figures in our family.* **Ant.** hated, despised, detested.

below *adv.* beneath, underneath, under, lower, down. *We drove below the freeway overpass.* **Ant.** above, over, atop.

belt *n.* cinch, band, sash, cord, cummerbund. *I ate so much I had to loosen my belt.*

bench *n.* seat, settee, pew, bleacher. *Let's sit on the park bench.*

benchmark *n.* standard, exemplar, touchstone, yardstick, bellwether. *A world record time is the benchmark against which all runners measure themselves.*

bend *vb.* curve, arc, bow, flex, crook, warp. **Ant.** straighten.

beneath *adv.* **1.** below, under, underneath, lower. *Our Christmas tree has a star above and lots of presents beneath.* *–prep.* **2.** below, under, underneath, unbefitting. *The school's seniors felt cleaning the auditorium was beneath them.* **Ant. 1–2.** above, over.

benediction *n.* blessing, prayer, invocation, grace, consecration. *Father Mike gave the benediction at the end of the service.*

benefactor *n.* supporter, financier, patron, underwriter, donor. *The school's benefactor donated a million dollars to the budget this year.*

beneficial *adj.* good, helpful, advantageous, useful, healthy. *Exercise is a beneficial activity.* **Ant.** harmful, bad, detrimental.

benefit *n.* gain, profit, perk, reward, help. **Ant.** loss, liability.

benevolence *n.* goodwill, kindness, humanitarianism, charity, compassion, goodness, generosity. *Thanks to the benevolence of a stranger, the lost bell was replaced.* **Ant.** cruelty, meanness, selfishness.

benign *adj.* **1.** harmless, innocuous, curable, mild, favorable, healthful. *The patient's tumor was benign and was safely removed.* **2.** kind, gentle, mild, merciful, compassionate, benevolent. *The phony witch was far more benign than she appeared.* **Ant. 1.** harmful, dangerous, malignant. **2.** mean, cruel, vicious.

bent *adj.* crooked, bowed, warped, twisted, contorted. *I had an accident on my bike and now the frame is bent.* **Ant.** straight.

bequeath *vb.* leave, bestow, give, will, endow. *When I die, I will bequeath all my cherished possessions to my nephew.* **Ant.** take, withdraw.

bereft *adj.* bereaved, destitute, lonely, desolate, wanting. *After her dog died, she was absolutely bereft.* **Ant.** fulfilled, enriched, contented.

berserk *adj.* crazy, crazed, insane, out-of-control, mad, maniacal. *The berserk juvenile was arrested for inciting a riot.* **Ant.** sane, calm, rational.

beset *vb.* plague, victimize, torment, bother, trouble. *The wicked witch beset the children with all kinds of troubles.*

best *adj.* **1.** greatest, finest, unrivaled, top, superior. *My friend and I have the best treehouse in the neighborhood.* *–n.* **2.** finest, first, foremost, champion. *She is among the best in that field of medical research.* *–vb.* **3.** beat, defeat, conquer, surpass. *He thinks he can best me at a game of table tennis.* **Ant. 1–2.** worst, poorest.

best-seller *n.* hot seller, hit, hot item, winner, success, chart buster. *It is every author's dream to write a best-seller.* **Ant.** dud, (slang) dog, loser.

bet *n.* **1.** wager, gamble, chance, stake, venture. *They made a bet on tomorrow's game.* *–vb.* **2.** gamble, wager, dare, challenge, risk. *She bet ten dollars that the spotted horse would win.*

betray *vb.* **1.** deceive, trick, forsake, desert, abandon. *The traitor betrayed her country by selling secret documents.* **2.** disclose, reveal, expose, divulge, show. *My father accidentally betrayed where he hid the candy.* **Ant. 1.** support, protect, guard. **2.** safeguard, guard.

betrayal *n.* treachery, double-crossing, treason, disloyalty, perfidy. *Stabbing me behind my back is a terrible betrayal.* **Ant.** loyalty, faithfulness, fidelity.

better *adj.* **1.** preferable, improved, superior, finer. *She hopes to get a better grade on the next test.* **2.** greater, larger, bigger, longer. *He spent the better part of his vacation painting the house.* **3.** improving, recovering, healthier, stronger. *She's feeling better today.* *–vb.* **4.** enrich, advance, improve, strengthen, enhance. *He went to school to better himself.* **Ant. 1.** poorer, inferior, second-rate. **2.** lesser, smaller. **3.** weaker, sicker. **4.** downgrade, lessen.

between *prep.* among, within, amidst, amongst, betwixt. *The number five is between four and six.*

beverage *adj.* drink, refreshment, pop, soda, liquid, cooler. *On a hot day, my beverage of choice is always lemonade.*

beware *vb.* mind, avoid, shun, heed, notice, watch. *Please beware of the vicious dog next door.* **Ant.** disregard, ignore, overlook.

bewilder *vb.* daze, confuse, obscure, disorient, puzzle. *The foreign city bewildered him.* **Ant.** explain, inform, enlighten.

bewitching *adj.* charming, enchanting, spellbinding, beguiling, mesmerizing, alluring. *Her performance in the play was absolutely bewitching.* **Ant.** repulsive, boring, ho-hum.

beyond *prep.* past, after, above, behind, farther on, yonder. *The store is just beyond the next intersection.*

bias *n.* **1.** preference, favoritism, prejudice, partiality, bent. *I have a bias for small pets like cats.* *–vb.* **2.** prejudice, predispose, influence, sway. *His fancy clothes biased the judges in his favor.* **Ant. 1.** fairness, impartiality.

Bible *n.* Holy Scriptures, the good book, Word of God, Gospel, Old Testament, New Testament. *The Sunday school class learned lessons from the Bible.*

bicker *vb.* argue, fight, quarrel, debate, haggle, squabble. *If they continue to bicker like this, I'm going to ask them to leave.* **Ant.** agree, concur, get along.

bicycle *n.* bike, two-wheeler, (slang) wheels, mountain bike, ten-speed.

WORD SEARCH
four-wheeler: *quadricycle*
historical: *ordinary, velocipede*
one-wheeler: *unicycle*
three-wheeler: *tri-wheeler, pedicab, trishaw*
two, built for: *tandem*

bid *vb.* **1.** propose, offer, submit, venture. *She bid one million dollars for the famous painting.* **2.** instruct, charge, command, order, direct. *The teacher bid us to do our homework.* *–n.* **3.** proposal, proposition, offer, submittal. *That company made a bid on the new construction project.* **Ant. 2.** prohibit, withhold, forbid. **3.** retraction, withdrawal.

big *adj.* **1.** large, huge, immense, enormous, giant, massive, gigantic. *Alaska is a big state.* **2.** significant, important, serious, vital, momentous. *Tomorrow's game is a big one for our team.* **Ant. 1.** small, tiny, little. **2.** small, insignificant, unimportant.

bigot *n.* chauvinist, racist, sexist, homophobe, anti-Semite. *He was a bigot who mistrusted anyone who didn't attend the same church he did.*

bigotry *n.* chauvinism, narrow-mindedness, prejudice, intolerance, discrimination, racism, sexism. *Her bigotry made her an enemy to nearly everyone.* **Ant.** acceptance, tolerance, fairness.

bike *n.* *See* BICYCLE.

bikini *See* BATHING SUIT.

bill *n.* **1.** charge, debt, tab, invoice, check. *I was a little shocked how high the restaurant bill was.* *–vb.* **2.** charge, invoice, tally. *If they forgot their wallet, we'll just bill them.* *–n.* **3.** legislation, proposition, act, proposal, draft, measure. *Congress passed a new anti-pollution bill today.*

billiards *n.* pool, (slang) stick.

WORD SEARCH
shot in which ball first hits cushion: *bricole*
shot in which cue ball hits cushion first or strikes two balls in succession: *carom*
cushion recoil shot: *bricole*
miss: *scratch*
stick: *cue*

billow *vb.* swell, puff, undulate, inflate, surge, balloon. *We watched as the storm clouds began to billow.* **Ant.** deflate, collapse.

bind *vb.* **1.** fasten, lash, constrict, tie, tether, secure. *He bound her sprained ankle with a bandage.* *–n.* **2.** dilemma, quandary, predicament, impasse, difficulty. *He found himself in a bind when his car broke down.* **Ant. 1.** loosen, untie, unfasten, free.

binge *n.* indulgence, overindulgence, gorging, immoderation, excess, bender. *I had an uncontrollable binge and ate twelve cookies.*

biodegrade *vb.* break down, degrade, decompose, disintegrate, dilute. *We only buy trash bags that biodegrade when disposed.*

biography *n.* life story, autobiography, memoirs. *The biography of Elvis Presley was a best-seller.*

biologist *n.* life scientist, ecologist. *Jean is studying to become a biologist.*

biology *n.* life science. *Biology is a fascinating subject.*

biopsy *n.* tissue sampling, excision, tissue removal, analysis. *Sharon had a biopsy performed on that strange spot on her arm.*

bird *n.* fowl, feathered friend. *Birds of a feather flock together.*

WORD SEARCH

beak, curving or hooked: *aquiline*
claw: *talon*
collar or fluff: *ruff*
crest on fowl: *comb*
eggs, group of: *clutch*
enclosure: *aviary*
expert: *ornithologist*
groom: *preen*
grooming: *preening*
grouping of: *flock, colony, rookery*
migratory route: *flyway*
mythical: *phoenix, roc*
nest: *aerie*
prey, of: *raptor*
sit on eggs: *brood*
wingless: *apterous*

birth *n.* **1.** childbirth, delivery, breeding, reproduction. *The zoo announced the birth of a baby panda bear.* **2.** ancestry, heritage, descent, lineage, background. *The man claimed to be of aristocratic birth.* **3.** beginning, debut, start, genesis, origin. *The year 1776 marked the birth of the United States of America.* **Ant. 1.** death. **3.** end, finish, termination.

birth defect *n.* deformity, congenital defect, abnormality, malformation, mutation. *The surgeons were able to correct the baby's birth defect with a simple procedure.*

birthmark *n.* mole, blemish, spot, beauty mark, port wine stain. *I have a birthmark on my arm that some people mistake for a tattoo.*

bishop *n.* high priest, cleric, clergyman, deacon. *The bishop lead the priests in prayer.*

bison *n.* buffalo, mammal, quadruped, herbivore, mammal. *We gasped when we saw a huge bison grazing along the side of the road.*

bistro *n.* bar, lounge, saloon, tavern, wine shop, club. *My mother opened a little bistro down on Fifth Street.*

bite *vb.* **1.** chew, crunch, gnaw, snap, nibble. *Vampires are reputed to bite people's necks.* *–n.* **2.** sting, edge, punch, prickle, nip. *He commented on the weather's cold bite.* **3.** puncture, prick, injury, wound. *I bandaged the dog bite on her leg.* **4.** snack, mouthful, morsel, nibble. *I haven't had a bite to eat all day.*

bitter *adj.* **1.** stinging, harsh, tart, acid, biting. *He finds black coffee too bitter to drink.* **2.** resentful, hostile, angry, spiteful, sore. *The team members were bitter over their loss.* **Ant. 1.** mild, bland, sugary, sweet. **2.** forgiving, pleasant, joyful.

bizarre *adj.* strange, weird, odd, outlandish, queer, otherworldly, peculiar. *The alien's appearance was bizarre.* **Ant.** ordinary, normal.

blabbermouth *n.* bigmouth, tattletale, informer, (slang) rat, whistleblower. *If you hadn't been such a blabbermouth, we wouldn't have been caught.* **Ant.** mute.

black *adj.* soot, ink, jet, coat, pitch, gunmetal, carbon, brunet, onyx, ebony. *A night as black as gunmetal.* **Ant.** white.

blackball *See* BLACKLIST.

blacklist *vb.* blackball, exclude, ostracize, ban, banish, reject. *Senator McCarthy was famous for wanting to blacklist anyone suspected of being a communist.* **Ant.** include, welcome.

black magic *n.* sorcery, necromancy, witchcraft, Satanism, evil forces.

blackmail *vb.* extort, (slang) milk, (slang) bleed, coerce, threaten. *The crime boss often used his privileged information to blackmail people.*

black market *n.* underground economy, bootleg market, underworld market. *It's illegal to buy DVDs on the black market.*

blade *n.* knife, razor, edged tool, cutter, point. *Early humans used stone blades for cutting.*

blah *adj.* bland, boring, dull, plain, humdrum. *The pizza was blah because it didn't have any toppings.* **Ant.** exciting, stimulating, extraordinary.

blame *n.* **1.** accusation, implication, reproach, fault, guilt. *She always receives the blame when things go wrong.* –*vb.* **2.** accuse, charge, fault, reprimand, reproach. *My brother blamed me for breaking the stereo.* **Ant. 1.** acquittal, exoneration, vindication. **2.** acquit, absolve.

blameless *adj.* guiltless, faultless, innocent, clean, clear, irreproachable. *The jury found the defendant blameless on all counts.* **Ant.** guilty, faulty.

bland *adj.* tasteless, dull, boring, uninteresting, flavorless, flat. *Many people think oatmeal is bland.* **Ant.** stimulating, exciting, zestful.

blank *adj.* **1.** bare, unfilled, clear, unmarked, barren. *Please get out a blank piece of paper for your essay.* **2.** empty, dull, vacant, expressionless. *She gave me a blank look when I asked for directions.* –*n.* **3.** void, emptiness, space, gap, hollowness. *We had to fill in the blanks with the correct answers.* **Ant. 1.** marked. **2.** sharp, attentive.

blanket *n.* cover, spread, quilt, comforter, afghan, coverlet. *Give me another blanket or I'll freeze.*

blasé *adj.* nonchalant, uncaring, cool, bored, apathetic, uninterested, indifferent. *He accepted the prize in a surprisingly blasé manner.* **Ant.** excited, enthusiastic, eager.

blasphemy *adj.* irreverence, disrespect, sacrilege, impiety, denouncing. *The atheist's comments were considered blasphemy by the church.* **Ant.** reverence, respect, worship.

blast *vb.* **1.** explode, detonate, burst, erupt, demolish. *The bomb blasted a hole in the building.* –*n.* **2.** surge, gust, flurry, gale, blow. *A blast of cold air entered through the open window.* **3.** burst, explosion, eruption, detonation, discharge. *The bomb's blast could be heard for miles.*

blastoff *n.* liftoff, launch, ignition, firing. *NASA reported that blastoff of the new rocket is scheduled for this afternoon at three o'clock.*

blatant *adj.* glaring, conspicuous, loud, flagrant, obnoxious. *The opponent was thrown out of the game for committing a blatant foul.* **Ant.** subtle, quiet, invisible.

blaze *vb.* **1.** flare up, flame, burn. *Rebellion blazed throughout the poverty-stricken country.*

–*n.* **2.** shimmer, shine, glow, glare, flash. *A blaze of light drew our attention to the flying saucer.* **3.** burning, flames, fire, conflagration. *When the forest burned, the blaze could be seen miles away.*

bleach *vb.* whiten, lighten, fade, blanch. *I have to bleach my socks in order to keep them white.*

bleak *adj.* grim, dismal, disheartening, barren, desolate. *My chances for doing well on tomorrow's test seem bleak.* **Ant.** promising, bright.

bleed *vb.* hemorrhage, spurt, flow, ooze, trickle. *I cut myself on the saw and began to bleed.*

blemish *n.* **1.** flaw, imperfection, defect, blotch, discoloration, impurity. *Pimples left blemishes on my face.* –*vb.* **2.** mar, flaw, spoil, mark, spot. *The painting was blemished with water stains.* **Ant. 1.** purity, perfection, flawlessness. **2.** improve, perfect.

blend *vb.* **1.** combine, mingle, merge, mix, unite. *Blue and yellow blended together produce green.* –*n.* **2.** combination, mixture, compound, merger, mingling. *The punch was a blend of orange and pineapple juices.* **Ant. 1.** split, separate, divide. **2.** division, separation.

blender *n.* food processor, mixer, chopper, liquefier, juicer. *Toss some carrots and tomatoes in the blender and make some vegetable juice.*

bless *vb.* anoint, sanctify, consecrate, dedicate, honor. *The priest blessed the temple after its construction.* **Ant.** curse, damn, blaspheme.

blessed *adj.* **1.** holy, sacred, sacrosanct, sainted, hallowed. *We pray under an icon of the blessed mother.* **2.** gifted, fortunate, favored, lucky. *She was blessed with a natural ability to sing.* **Ant. 1.** cursed, damned, punished. **2.** unfortunate, lacking, ill-favored.

blessing *n.* godsend, good fortune, luck, benefit, boon, gift. *The rain was a blessing to all the worried farmers in the valley.* **Ant.** punishment, torment.

blight *n.* **1.** disease, affliction, decay, withering, scourge. *Blight ruined the farmer's crops.* –*vb.* **2.** ruin, spoil, contaminate, shrivel, wither. *The one mistake blighted the politician's career.* **Ant. 1.** bounty, blessing. **2.** foster, favor, benefit.

blimp *n.* dirigible, airship, zeppelin. *Some companies like to advertise on the sides of blimps.*

WORD SEARCH

balloon: *gas bag*
gas: *helium*
ground crew: *riggers*
mooring post: *mast*
passenger compartment: *gondola, car*
weights for controlling ascent and descent: *ballast bags*

blind *adj.* **1.** unseeing, sightless, visionless, unsighted. *The blind man used a cane to cross the street.* **2.** unaware, ignorant, dense, naive, unknowing. *He was blind to her faults.* –*n.* **3.** cover, shade, screen, shield, concealment. *The deer hunter built a blind to conceal himself.* –*vb.* **4.** make sightless, daze, dazzle, stun. *She was blinded by his good looks and didn't notice his shortcomings.* **Ant. 1.** seeing, sighted. **2.** observant, aware.

blinding *adj.* dazzling, glaring, bright, brilliant, electric. *The sun was so blinding, I nearly drove off the road.* **Ant.** dim, dark, shadowy.

blindness *n.* sightlessness, glaucoma, cataracts, myopia, retinitis pigmentosa. *My grandfather's blindness rarely slows him down.* **Ant.** sight, vision.

bliss *n.* delight, ecstasy, happiness, joy, rapture, enchantment. *Our vacation in Hawaii was pure bliss.* **Ant.** grief, anguish, misery, depression.

blissful *adj.* pleasurable, enraptured, joyous, exhilarated, delighted, happy. *She spent a blissful* *day at the beach.* **Ant.** miserable, unhappy, distressful.

blister *n.* swelling, bleb, canker, ulcer, sore, boil. *My new sneakers are giving me blisters.*

blitz *n.* blitzkrieg, onslaught, offensive, strike, attack. *The army launched a terrifying blitz against the enemy.* **Ant.** retreat, backpedaling, surrender.

blizzard *n.* snowstorm, tempest, gale, storm, squall. *A blizzard trapped the Donner Party in the High Sierra.*

bloat *vb.* swell, enlarge, expand, stretch, inflate, distend. *Eating those three pizzas caused my stomach to bloat.* **Ant.** contract, wither, shrink, deflate.

blob *n.* glob, mass, clump, ball, daub. *Who left this blob of toothpaste on the sink?*

bloc *n.* alliance, coalition, partnership, ring, group, cartel. *The environmentalists formed a bloc that gave them great power in Washington.*

block *vb.* **1.** interfere, impede, obstruct, prevent, stop. *A tall man sitting in the front blocked our view.* –*n.* **2.** square, bar, slab, chunk, brick. *They built the wall with cement blocks.* **3.** obstacle, barrier, barricade, hindrance, constraint. *Hair and dirt formed a block in our drainpipe.* **Ant. 1.** advance, unblock, open. **3.** passageway, entrance, opening.

blockade *n.* barrier, obstacle, obstruction, hurdle, stoppage. *A naval blockade kept enemy ships from leaving the harbor.* **Ant.** access, opening, entry.

blond *adj.* golden-haired, sandy-haired, platinum-haired, flaxen-haired, (slang) towheaded, strawberry blond. *My hair turns increasingly blond the longer it is exposed to the sun.* **Ant.** brunet, black.

blood *n.* life fluid, hemoglobin, gore. *Vampires have a taste for blood.*

bloodbath *n.* slaughter, carnage, murder, gore, holocaust. *Many Civil War battles were little more than bloodbaths.*

bloodthirsty *adj.* homicidal, predatory, vampiric, murderous, violent. *The bloodthirsty dictator ruled with an iron fist.* **Ant.** peaceful, pacifistic, Christian.

bloom *vb.* **1.** blossom, flourish, flower, sprout, prosper. *Their friendship bloomed into love.* –*n.* **2.** flower, blossom, bud. *The gardener tended her blooms with care.* **Ant. 1.** shrivel, fade, wither.

blossom *vb.* **1.** bloom, thrive, grow, flower, flourish. *The beginning violinist eventually blossomed into a virtuoso.* –*n.* **2.** flower, bud, bloom. *She stuck a lily blossom in her hair.* **Ant. 1.** wither, wilt, fade.

blouse *n.* shirt, pullover, slipover, garment. *I wear my favorite blouse to job interviews.*

blow *n.* **1.** smack, hit, punch, cuff, whack. *I received a strong blow to my leg when the bike ran into me.* **2.** shock, surprise, jolt, jar. *It came as quite a blow to learn I failed the test.* –*vb.* **3.** puff, exhale, expel, huff, breathe. *She blew air into the balloons.* **4.** sail, drift, flutter, fly, waft. *We watched tumbleweeds blow past us in the desert.* **5.** erupt, explode, detonate, burst. *People hurriedly left when they learned the volcano was about to blow.* **Ant. 2.** comfort, relief, pleasure. **3.** inhale.

blue *adj.* sky-blue, aquamarine, indigo, turquoise, azure, teal, beryl. *Her eyes were robin's-egg blue.*

blue collar *adj.* working class, labor force, proletariat, unskilled, middle class, lower class. *My father has always been a blue collar guy, working mostly in warehouses and construction sites.* **Ant.** upper class, professional, executive.

blueprint *n.* draft, rendering, plan, design, layout, scheme. *The blueprint for the new skyscraper was immensely complex.*

blues *n.* depression, sadness, dejection, heavyheartedness, doldrums, unhappiness. *I get the blues whenever it rains for more than three days.* **Ant.** joy, happiness, euphoria.

bluff *n.* **1.** fake, deception, lie, bragging, boast. *We discovered his threats were just a bluff.* **2.** crag, cliff, precipice, scarp. *The eagle built its nest high up on the bluff.* *–vb.* **3.** fool, deceive, trick, delude, mislead. *The robber bluffed the police into thinking she had a bomb.* **Ant. 1.** fact, truth, candor.

blunder *n.* **1.** error, mistake, indiscretion, lapse, slip. *Buying the wrong kind of milk was a blunder on his part.* *–vb.* **2.** bungle, slip, stumble, stagger, flounder. *She blundered into a beehive.* **Ant. 1.** accomplishment, success, achievement.

blunt *adj.* **1.** unsharpened, dull, edgeless, unpointed. *Her knife was too blunt to cut the rope.* **2.** frank, candid, tactless, abrupt, short, direct. *He was quite blunt in telling me he disliked my shirt.* *–vb.* **3.** dull, deaden, numb, stifle, impair, lessen. *Lack of sleep blunted our senses.* **Ant. 1.** sharp, pointed, edged. **2.** subtle, indirect, tactful. **3.** sharpen, excite, stimulate.

blur *n.* **1.** smear, haze, blot, cloud, smudge. *The hummingbird flew by in a blur of color.* *–vb.* **2.** obscure, shroud, confuse, smear, cloud. *Wearing someone else's glasses can blur your vision.* **Ant. 1.** clarity. **2.** clarify, focus, define.

blurt *vb.* blab, gush, spout, tattle, let slip. *A good way to lose friends is to blurt out all of their secrets at a party.* **Ant.** hush, shutup.

bluster *n.* boasting, bluff, crowing, bravado, bragadoccio. *The boxer displayed plenty of bluster, but it vanished as soon as his opponent knocked him down.* **Ant.** cowardice, fear, anxiety.

board *n.* **1.** timber, plank, beam, wood, two-by-four, slat. *We need to replace that rotten board with a new one.* **2.** committee, cabinet, directors, trustees, advisers. *We were told we would have to ask the town zoning board about our plans.* **3.** meals, food, dinners, suppers, breakfasts. *Hotel prices in Europe usually include room and board.* *–vb.* **4.** enter, mount, embark. *Passengers were instructed to board the airplane.* **5.** quarter, house, lodge, accommodate, feed. *Host families boarded the foreign-exchange students for a month.* **Ant. 4.** depart, disembark, leave, vacate.

boast *vb.* **1.** brag, gloat, swagger, flaunt, crow. *She boasted that she could run the mile in less than four minutes.* *–n.* **2.** brag, bragging, bravado, bluster. *We disbelieved his boast that he knew the famous rock star.* **Ant. 1.** disavow. **2.** disavowal.

boastful *adj.* vain, conceited, pretentious, arrogant, cocky. *The boastful student said he was very rich.* **Ant.** humble, modest.

boat *n.* vessel, craft, motorboat, yacht, sailboat, ship, tub, hulk. *I have a small boat I use to shuttle back and forth between islands.*

WORD SEARCH

air-propelled: *airboat*
carrier with flat bottom: *barge, scow*
emergency: *lifeboat*
fishing: *dragger, dogger, longliner, trawler, whaler*
Italian, poled: *gondola*
living quarters, permanent: *houseboat*
Oriental, flat-bottomed: *junk, sampan*
passenger shuttle: *ferry*
race or exhibition: *regatta*
rowers: *canoe, kayak, dinghy, dory, gig, skiff*
rowing racer: *shell, scull*
sailboat, multiple-hulled: *catamaran, trimaran*
waves caused by: *wake*

body *n.* 1. figure, frame, form, physique, build. *The model spent long hours trying to get his body in top condition.* 2. corpse, carcass, cadaver, remains. *The body of the dead king was carried through the city.* 3. group, assembly, society, council, organization. *The town council is our local governing body.* **Ant.** 1. spirit, soul, psyche, intellect.

body building *n.* weight lifting, resistance training, (slang) pumping iron, (slang) getting ripped, body sculpting, training. *Because of body building, skinny Joel can now lift more than 20 pounds.*

bodyguard *n.* escort, guard, security, protector, shield. *The president's daughter couldn't travel anywhere without a bodyguard.*

bog *n.* marsh, wetland, fen, quagmire, slough, swamp. *The bog is a good place to look for frogs.*

bogus *adj.* fake, imitation, counterfeit, phony, artificial. *The lost treasure turned out to be completely bogus.* **Ant.** real, legitimate, authentic.

bohemian *n.* nonconformist, gypsy, dropout, free spirit, artist, nonconformist. *The bohemian enjoyed hitchhiking across the country whenever he felt like it.* **Ant.** conformist.

boil *n.* pustule, pimple, carbuncle, sore, fester. *He developed an ugly and painful boil on his neck.* *–vb.* bubble, steam, roil, seethe, simmer, cook. *It's a good idea to boil water taken from a river before drinking it.*

boisterous *adj.* noisy, rowdy, uproarious, loud, tumultuous, unrestrained, unruly. *It was a very boisterous party.* **Ant.** calm, quiet, restrained, tranquil.

bold *adj.* 1. fearless, brave, adventuresome, reckless, courageous. *The two bold girls spent the night in a haunted house.* 2. vivid, bright, striking, strong, powerful. *One should never wash bold colors in bleach.* **Ant.** 1. fearful, cowardly, timid. 2. dull, pale, colorless.

bolster *v.* brace, fortify, strengthen, prop up, reinforce, support. *We nailed in additional beams to bolster the frame.* **Ant.** weaken, undermine.

bolt *n.* 1. fastening, spike, rivet, pin, peg. *The shelf fell down when its restraining bolt broke.* 2. flash, brand, missile, arrow, dart. *A bolt of lightning hit the tree.* *–vb.* 3. run, rush, dash, sprint, flee. *Students bolted from class when the bell rang.* 4. fasten, lock, latch, bar, secure. *She bolts the front door before going to sleep.* **Ant.** 3. stroll, ramble, saunter. 4. unlock, unlatch, open.

bomb *n.* 1. explosive, charge, missile, shell, weapon of mass destruction, mine, torpedo, atom bomb, (slang) physics package. *A special police squad was called to search for the bomb.* *–vb.* 2. blow up, bombard, blast, shell, destroy, level, (slang) blow to smithereens. *They will bomb the enemy position at midnight.* 3. fail, lose, flop, (slang) blow it, (slang) choke, (slang) lay an egg. *They barely rehearsed, so I knew their show would bomb.* **Ant.** 3. succeed, excel, triumph.

WORD SEARCH

earth-penetrating: *bunker buster*
exploding part: *warhead*
explosive materials used in: *TNT, trinitrotoluene, nitroglycerin*
fire-starting: *incendiary bomb*
gasoline-filled bottle: *Molotov cocktail*
guided: *smart bomb*
jelled gas incendiary: *napalm*
lead pipe, contained in: *pipe bomb*
low tech atomic bomb used to spread radiation: *dirty bomb*
puttylike explosive: *plastic explosive*
sub-marine: *mine, torpedo*
timed charge, having a: *time bomb*
underground: *mine*

unguided: *dumb bomb*
See also MISSILE; NUCLEAR BOMB.

bombastic *adj.* pompous, grandiloquent, pretentious, inflated, turgid. *His writing was bombastic and silly.* **Ant.** unpretentious, plain-speaking, spare.

bomber *n.* terrorist, demolition experts, radical, arsonist, revolutionary. *The bomber didn't care how many innocent people he killed.*

bona fide *adj.* authentic, genuine, real, legitimate. *According to the professor, we had uncovered a bona fide T-Rex bone.* **Ant.** fake, phony, questionable.

bonanza *n.* rich vein, gold mine, windfall, treasure trove. *The squirrel discovered a bonanza of acorns under the old oak tree.*

bond *n.* **1.** connection, relationship, tie, allegiance, attachment. *People who face extreme danger together tend to form a strong bond. –vb.* **2.** bind, connect, tie, attach, join. *Mary is very friendly and bonds with others quickly.* **Ant. 1.** disconnection, detachment. **Ant. 2.**

bondage *n.* slavery, enslavement, subjugation, servitude, bonds, shackles. *They were released from their bondage soon after the Civil War ended.* **Ant.** freedom, liberty, free will.

bonus *n.* addition, reward, extra, benefit, gratuity. *The employees received bonuses for their excellent work.*

booby trap *n.* ambush, pitfall, deadfall, blind, tripwire. *We set up a booby trap in the woods to catch the thief.*

book *n.* volume, publication, tome, hardcover, paperback, work, novel, opus, text, manuscript. *On a rainy day, I love to curl up with a good book.*

WORD SEARCH

category of fiction: *genre*
compilation of notable articles, essays or short stories: *anthology*
condensed from a longer work: *abridged*
glowing testimonial on cover: *blurb*
hater of: *bibliophobe*
introduction: *foreword*
last word: *epilogue*
logo of publisher: *colophon*
lover of: *bibliophile, bookworm*
pages attached at center, creating fold in cover: *spine*
passion for collecting: *bibliomania*

bookkeeping *n.* accounting, record keeping, auditing, crediting and debiting. *The IRS agent wanted to make sure my bookkeeping was accurate.*

booklet *n.* pamphlet, brochure, circular, literature, folder. *Turn to the first page of your booklet for instructions.*

bookworm *n.* reader, book lover, bibliophile, bibliomaniac. *It's no big deal to a bookworm to read two books per week.*

boom *n.* **1.** blast, bang, explosion, roar, report. *We heard the space shuttle's sonic boom.* **2.** improvement, upswing, growth, expansion, rise. *California experienced an economic boom during the Gold Rush. –vb.* **3.** resound, thunder, rumble, roar, reverberate. *A cannon shot boomed over the valley.* **4.** prosper, thrive, flourish, swell, advance. *Business boomed during the tourist season.* **Ant. 2.** slump, decline, recession. **4.** dwindle, fail, collapse.

booming *adj.* flourishing, thriving, prospering, profiting, exploding, succeeding. *The personal computer business is booming.* **Ant.** failing, slumping, declining.

boondoggle *n.* waste, extravagance, pork, frivolity, white elephant. *The government invested all of our tax money in yet another boondoggle.*

boor *n.* clod, clodhopper, lout, (slang) yahoo, bumpkin, oaf. *The boor burped loudly again and again and never excused himself.* **Ant.** gentleman, gentlewoman.

boost *vb.* **1.** lift, raise, elevate, hoist, heft. *He boosted himself over the wall.* **2.** expand, increase, build up, develop, promote. *Hosting the Olympics helped to boost the local economy.* *–n.* **3.** raise, lift, hoist, heave, shove. *Will you give me a boost up?* **Ant.** **1.** drop, lower. **2.** decrease, diminish, curtail, reduce.

boot *n.* footwear, shoe, overshoe, clodhopper, wader. *I wear my boots to slog through puddles.*

WORD SEARCH

Eskimo: *mukluk*
hiking boot, heavily treaded: (slang) *wafflestomper*
horseback-riding, for: *jodhpur*
leather knee-high: *Wellington*
leather, western tooled: *cowboy*
military: *combat boot, jackboot*
rubber: *galosh*
work shoe, heavy: *brogan*

booth *n.* stall, cubicle, stand, compartment, hut, shed, kiosk. *Get your ticket at the booth around the corner.*

bootleg *adj.* illegal, pirated, black market, underground, smuggled. *Ironically, bootleg whiskey could be bought nearly everywhere during Prohibition.* **Ant.** legal, legitimate.

bootlegger *n.* smuggler, black marketer, scofflaw, runner, pirate, distiller. *The bootlegger was arrested for mass-marketing copied DVDs.*

booty *n.* pillage, spoils, loot, takings, plunder. *The raiders hid their booty on a desert island.*

bordello *n.* *See* BROTHEL.

border *n.* verge, margin, edge, perimeter, rim. *Thankfully the pit bull stopped at the border of its yard.*

borderline *adj.* marginal, ambiguous, iffy, indefinite, unclear. *My ability to sing is borderline at best.*

bore *vb.* **1.** exhaust, tire, weary, fatigue. *The lecture bored me.* **2.** burrow, tunnel, gouge, mine, drill. *The termite bored its way into the tree trunk.* *–n.* **3.** nuisance, pest, bother, annoyance, irritation. *She found the self-centered actor to be a real bore.* **Ant.** **1.** interest, intrigue, excite. **2.** fill, cap, plug.

boring *adj.* unexciting, tedious, wearisome, dull, monotonous, tiring. *He fell asleep during the boring movie.* **Ant.** exciting, amusing, arousing, delightful, thrilling.

borough *n.* neighborhood, section, quarter, berg, community, town. *Of all the boroughs of New York, I like Brooklyn the best.*

borrow *vb.* obtain, get, appropriate, adopt, assume. *May I borrow your book?* **Ant.** lend, return.

boss *n.* **1.** manager, supervisor, director, executive, employer, administrator. *My boss scheduled me to work on Christmas Eve.* *–vb.* **2.** command, direct, order, control. *My older brother bosses me around when my parents leave.* **Ant.** **1.** worker, employee, subordinate, helper. **2.** follow, obey.

bossy *adj.* tyrannical, dictatorial, domineering, pushy, controlling. *My sister is too bossy for most people.* **Ant.** passive, deferential, easygoing.

botch *vb.* flub, goof, bungle, fumble, fail, ruin. *Don't botch your tax returns or you may be audited.* **Ant.** succeed, accomplish, achieve.

bother *vb.* **1.** pester, aggravate, irritate, annoy, harass, disturb. *Noisy crickets bothered me all* *night.* –*n.* **2.** irritation, annoyance, problem, worry, vexation, nuisance. *It's too much of a bother to clean my room.* **Ant. 1.** please, placate, comfort. **2.** enjoyment, pleasure, ease.

bottle *n.* vessel, container, glass, decanter, flagon, flask, vial, carafe. *The table was set with a bottle of fine wine.*

bottom *n.* **1.** foot, underside, ground, base, foundation, underpart, lowest part. *Her friend waited for her at the bottom of the water slide.* **2.** rump, buttocks, posterior, behind. *He tripped and fell on his bottom.* –*adj.* **3.** ground, lowest, deepest, undermost. *The gift shop is on the bottom floor.* **Ant. 1.** summit, top, peak, pinnacle. **3.** upper, highest.

bouillon *n.* broth, stock, flavoring, soup base, consommé. *I like to add lots of bouillon to my Mulligan stew.*

boulevard *n.* avenue, parkway, concourse, street, thoroughfare. *The boulevard was wide enough to allow cars to drive around the downed power line.*

bouncer *n.* security personnel, guard, enforcer, ejector, protector. *The bouncer wouldn't allow anyone underage into the bar.*

bound *adj.* **1.** secured, wrapped, tied, roped, shackled. *The captive was found bound and gagged.* **2.** sure, fated, destined, certain. *Your lie is bound to create more problems.* **3.** committed, obligated, beholden, compelled, obliged. *The renegade felt bound to no laws.* –*vb.* **4.** spring, jump, bounce, leap, skip. *She bounded over the mud puddle.* **5.** enclose, restrict, encircle, limit, delimit. *A fence bounds the baseball field.* –*n.* **6.** boundary, perimeter, border, extremity. *The river marks the bounds of our property.* **7.** leap, hop, spring, jump, bounce. *Superman can leap over tall buildings in a single bound.* **Ant. 1.** unfastened, loose, untied. **3.** free, released. **4.** hobble, shuffle, crawl.

boundary *n.* rim, border, edge, frontier, perimeter, fringe, frame, extent. *The fence marks the boundary of our property.*

boundless *adj.* infinite, limitless, endless, immense, perpetual, immeasurable. *Some astronomers believe the universe is boundless.* **Ant.** limited, bounded, restricted, narrow.

bountiful *adj.* abundant, plentiful, teeming, copious, ample, fat. *The garden supplied a bountiful crop of beans this year.* **Ant.** sparse, lean, scarce.

bouquet *n.* arrangement, bunch, posy, corsage, nosegay, spray. *The living room was decorated with fragrant bouquets of lilacs and roses.*

bourgeois *adj.* middle-class, common, traditional, conventional. *Watching TV every night has long been a bourgeois pastime.* **Ant.** upper class, elite, unconventional.

bout *n.* match, contest, round, competition, course, term. *Rocky lost his last bout to a younger boxer.*

boutique *n.* shop, gift store, booth, concession, franchise. *I bought a funky coffee mug at the new boutique.*

bow *n.* **1.** curtsy, greeting, salaam, obeisance. *The magician gave a bow at the end of his act.* **2.** prow, fore, head, front. *A lookout was posted at the ship's bow.* –*vb.* **3.** bend, concede, yield, submit, capitulate. *The private refused to bow to the sergeant's foolish orders.* **4.** curtsy, kneel, salaam, stoop. *All the citizens bowed as their queen passed by.* **Ant. 2.** stern, rear. **3.** contest, oppose, resist.

bowels *n.* intestines, innards, guts, viscera, insides, entrails. *Diarrhea is hard on the bowels.*

bowling *n.* tenpins, candlepins, duckpins, kegling. *Bowling is great fun but it makes an awful racket.*

WORD SEARCH

central pin: *kingpin*
curving shot: *hook*
machine that sets pins: *pinsetter*
one game: *string*
shot leaving an opening between pins: *split*
ten pins knocked down with one ball: *strike*
ten pins knocked down with two balls: *spare*

box *n.* **1.** crate, container, trunk, carton, receptacle. *She packed her things in several boxes.* *–vb.* **2.** spar, cuff, fight, belt, hit, strike. *The two men boxed for the championship title.* **3.** enclose, package, confine, cage. *Traffic boxed us in on all sides.* **Ant. 3.** release, liberate.

boxing *n.* pugilism, fighting, sparring, prizefighting, fisticuffs. *Boxing continues to be one of the most controversial sports.*

WORD SEARCH

hold or embrace opponent: *clinch*
practice equipment: *punching bag, speedbag*
practice with partner: *spar*
punches: *cross, jab, uppercut, one-two punch, roundhouse, haymaker*
weight division (lightest to heaviest): *flyweight, bantamweight, featherweight, lightweight, welterweight, middleweight, light heavyweight, heavyweight, cruiserweight*
win by disabling opponent: *knockout, technical knockout (TKO)*
win by points: *decision*

boy *n.* lad, youth, male, young man, guy, child, junior, (slang) sprout. *The boy prefers to jump in the mud rather than walk around it.*

boycott *n.* **1.** rejection, ban, exclusion, spurning, repudiation. *Students organized a boycott of the school cafeteria because its food was so bad.* *–vb.* **2.** refuse, reject, ostracize, ban, bar. *Upset consumers boycotted the company's products.* **Ant. 1.** support, patronage, usage. **2.** accept, use, purchase.

boyfriend *n.* beau, sweetheart, flame, (slang) honey, steady, (slang) boy toy. *Moira broke up with her boyfriend again last week.*

brace *n.* **1.** prop, reinforcement, backing, support, band, crutch, splint. *The runner wore a brace around his knee.* *–vb.* **2.** bolster, strengthen, hold, reinforce, fortify, prepare. *The astronauts braced themselves for the takeoff.* **Ant. 2.** weaken, cripple, undermine.

bracelet *n.* jewelry, armlet, chain, band, ornament, bangle. *She always wore her favorite charm bracelet.*

brag *vb.* **1.** boast, exaggerate, exult, gloat. *The warrior bragged that she could kill the dragon with one sword blow.* *–n.* **2.** boast, bragging, exaggeration, pretension, self-praise. *Unfortunately, no one believed her brags that she could slay the dragon so easily.* **Ant. 1.** disavow, disclaim. **2.** disavowal.

braggart *n.* boaster, egotist, blusterer, blowhard, peacock. *Everybody cheered when the braggart struck out with just three pitches.*

braid *n.* plait, twine, knot, interlacing, weave. *Sarah likes to weave her hair in braids.*

brain *n.* mind, encephalon, head, intellect, organ, seat of reason, center of consciousness. *Albert Einstein had an exceptionally powerful brain.*

WORD SEARCH

connector of hemispheres: *corpus callosum*
muscle coordinator: *cerebellum*
nerve cell: *neuron*
perception, memory and reasoning, center of: *cerebrum*
regulator of blood pressure and body temperature: *hypothalamus*
regulator of breathing: *medulla oblongata*
regulator of hunger, thirst, aggression: *limbic system*

scan of brain waves: *electroencephalogram (EEG)*
sections in each hemisphere, one of four: *lobe*
sense heat, cold, pressure: *thalamus*
side, right or left: *hemisphere*
speech muscles, controls: *Broca's area*

brainstorm *vb.* think, problem-solve, create, invent, ponder, analyze. *Thomas Edison, one of the greatest inventors of all time, knew how to brainstorm.*

brainwash *vb.* indoctrinate, condition, program, train, convince, persuade. *They brainwashed him into believing that cookies tasted rotten.*

brake *n.* **1.** restraint, curb, reign, check, constraint. *The president put the brakes on the economy in an attempt to avoid inflation.* –*vb.* **2.** slow, decelerate, slacken, halt, stop. *The trolley braked to avoid hitting the pedestrian.* **Ant. 1.** accelerator, starter. **2.** accelerate, quicken, speed.

branch *n.* **1.** stem, limb, bough, fork, arm, extension. *Our treehouse is supported by four thick branches.* **2.** division, bureau, department, member, section. *He works at the West Valley library branch.* –*vb.* **3.** fork, separate, divide, spread, diverge. *The river branches into two smaller streams.* **Ant. 1.** trunk, main part. **2.** headquarters, main office.

brand *n.* **1.** label, trademark, seal, stamp, mark. *The ranchers placed a brand on all their livestock.* **2.** kind, make, type, variety, nature. *What cereal brand do you normally eat?* –*vb.* **3.** mark, stamp, label, stain, stigmatize. *His past behavior has branded him an unreliable person.*

brash *adj.* bold, nervy, brazen, reckless, rude, headlong, impulsive. *The obnoxious loudmouth made a brash attempt to cut in line.* **Ant.** thoughtful, wary, cautious.

brassy *adj.* bold, cocky, brash, nervy, impudent, insolent. *Cutting in line requires an exceedingly brassy personality.* **Ant.** timid, passive, meek.

brat *n.* spoiled child, imp, enfant terrible, holy terror, devil, rascal. *The brat screamed and whined until he got his way.* **Ant.** model child, angel.

bravado *n.* bluster, swaggering, boastfulness, cockiness, muscle-flexing, braggadocio. *The challenger strutted about with false bravado.* **Ant.** cowardice, timidity, reservation.

brave *adj.* **1.** fearless, courageous, gallant, heroic, daring, bold. *The brave woman rescued a drowning child from icy waters.* –*vb.* **2.** dare, face, challenge, confront, defy. *He left his cabin and braved the blizzard outside.* **Ant. 1.** cowardly, timid, fainthearted. **2.** retreat, withdraw.

bravery *n.* courage, boldness, daring, intrepidity, fearlessness, guts. *The firemen received medals for their bravery.* **Ant.** cowardice, fearfulness, timidity.

brawl *n.* **1.** scuffle, ruckus, fight, riot, uproar, dispute. *Police broke up the barroom brawl.* –*vb.* **2.** fight, quarrel, battle, scuffle. *Players brawled on the football field.*

brawny *adj.* muscular, powerful, strapping, beefy, Herculean, husky, burly. *The brawny wrestlers swaggered into the ring.* **Ant.** skinny, frail, slight.

brazen *adj.* insolent, forward, outspoken, defiant, rash. *The brazen student told the principal he was doing a lousy job.* **Ant.** shy, timid, reserved.

break *vb.* **1.** wreck, smash, fragment, shatter, snap, crack, splinter. *The plate broke when I dropped it.* **2.** beat, exceed, surpass, pass, top. *The swimmer broke the world record in the 100-meter freestyle.* **3.** disclose, inform, reveal, communicate. *He broke the news of the girl's death to her parents.* **4.** burst, erupt, initiate, begin. *The crowd* *broke into singing.* –*n.* 5. rupture, fault, crack, opening, gap, rift, split. *The earthquake left a break in the concrete of our patio.* 6. rest, interlude, intermission, pause, lull. *Employees get a 45-minute lunch break.* 7. chance, stroke of luck, opportunity. *Being chosen to costar in the film was the actor's big break.* **Ant.** 1. fix, heal, repair. 2. fail, miss. 3. conceal, withhold, hide. 4. cease, halt. 5. mending, repair. 6. continuation.

breakable *adj.* fragile, brittle, delicate, flimsy. *Most of the items in the glass shop are breakable.* **Ant.** unbreakable, sturdy, solid.

breakdown *n.* failure, malfunction, collapse, short circuit, bust, rupture, crash. *The computer system suffered a major breakdown.*

breakthrough *n.* advance, innovation, discovery, progress, invention. *There are amazing breakthroughs in medicine every day.*

breakup *n.* parting, split, separation, rift, dissolution, disbanding. *Ted and Alice had a painful breakup, but now they're back together again.* **Ant.** banding, bonding, pair-up.

breast *n.* mammary, bust, bosom, chest, teat, udder. *Liz was relieved that her daughter was too young to get breast implants.*

breathe *vb.* respire, draw breath, exhale, inhale, gasp. *I like to breathe deeply of the fresh spring air.*

breathless *adj.* shortwinded, winded, gasping, panting, asthmatic, wheezing. *All the runners were breathless by the time they reached the finish line.*

breathtaking *adj.* exciting, awesome, electrifying, thrilling, overwhelming, stunning. *The Grand Canyon is known for its breathtaking scenery.* **Ant.** ordinary, ho-hum, soporific.

breed *vb.* 1. reproduce, procreate, create, generate, produce, cultivate. *Many animals breed during the spring months.* –*n.* 2. type, kind, species, variety, stock, race. *What breed of dog do you have?*

breeze *n.* wind, draft, zephyr, whiff, sough. *After the hot spell, it was a relief to feel the cool breeze come off the ocean.*

brevity *n.* shortness, quickness, briefness, conciseness, terseness. *The students appreciated the brevity of their principal's speech.* **Ant.** lengthiness, longwindedness, verbosity.

brew *vb.* cook, boil, simmer, ferment, steep, stew. *It's a real art to brew the perfect cup of coffee.*

bribe *n.* 1. payoff, inducement, incentive, hush money, graft. *The mob member tried to offer the shopkeeper a bribe to keep quiet.* –*vb.* 2. pay off, induce, corrupt, entice, (slang) grease one's palm. *The mob members tried to bribe Joe into not calling the police about their illegal activity.*

brick *n.* block, stone, soldier, clinker. *The chimney was constructed from sturdy bricks.*

bridge *n.* 1. span, connector, viaduct, connection, overpass, link, structure. *We crossed the old bridge carefully.* –*vb.* 2. connect, link, cross, unite, join. *Their shared interest in music bridged the gap in ages.*

WORD SEARCH

cable and girder: *suspension bridge*
fear of crossing: *gephyrophobia*
opens and closes for marine traffic: *drawbridge, bascule, swing bridge*
railroad bridge framework: *trestle*

brief *adj.* 1. momentary, abrupt, swift, temporary, quick, fleeting. *A butterfly's life span seems brief compared to that of a human.* –*vb.* 2. instruct, advise, inform, explain. *The president's advisers briefed him on the overnight development.* **Ant.** 1. prolonged, extended, lengthy, long. 2. conceal.

bright *adj.* **1.** dazzling, illuminated, shining, radiant, glowing. *The road sign was painted bright yellow.* **2.** smart, clever, intelligent, alert, quick. *The bright child was moved a grade ahead.* **3.** promising, favorable, hopeful, cheerful, joyful. *The outlook on the patient's condition is bright.* **Ant. 1.** dim, dark, faded. **2.** stupid, dumb, slow. **3.** grim, hopeless.

brilliance *n.* **1.** glow, radiance, splendor, shine, brightness. *The moonlight's brilliance made it possible to take a midnight walk.* **2.** intelligence, genius, cleverness, wisdom. *The brilliance of his poetry impressed all of us.* **Ant. 1.** darkness, dimness, gloom. **2.** stupidity, mediocrity.

brilliant *adj.* **1.** gleaming, afire, shining, sparkling, intense. *Sunlight reflected off her brilliant diamond.* **2.** profound, ingenious, clever, intelligent, splendid, glorious. *The lawyer's defense of her client was simply brilliant.* **Ant. 1.** dull, drab, dark. **2.** unimpressive, awful, stupid, dumb.

bring *vb.* **1.** bear, fetch, tote, get, convey. *Will you bring me a glass of water?* **2.** invoke, produce, cause, create, start. *Sad movies bring tears to my eyes.* **3.** make, motivate, persuade, induce, force. *I couldn't bring myself to eat the green beans.* **Ant. 1.** send, leave, take away. **2.** prevent, stop, quench, suppress.

brink *n.* edge, verge, border, threshold, line, brim. *Crawling out to the hole in the ice, they were poised over the brink of disaster.*

brisk *adj.* **1.** lively, swift, quick, busy, energetic. *You should brush your teeth in a brisk manner.* **2.** sharp, exhilarating, nipping, crisp, keen, bracing. *We stood shivering in the brisk wind.* **Ant. 1.** slow, sluggish. **2.** dead, stagnant, mellow.

brittle *adj.* weak, breakable, fragile, crumbly, delicate. *The dead leaves were quite brittle.* **Ant.** strong, unbreakable, sturdy, solid, durable.

broad *adj.* **1.** spacious, extensive, outstretched, wide, sweeping, large. *Books about gorillas will be listed under the broad category of African animals.* **2.** bare, plain, visible, direct, glaring. *The crime was committed in broad daylight.* **Ant. 1.** confining, meager, limited. **2.** obscured, unclear, hidden.

broadcast *n.* **1.** program, show, telecast, transmission, newscast. *The station's news broadcast comes on at six o'clock.* *–vb.* **2.** announce, televise, transmit, send, air, beam. *The Olympics were broadcast to almost all countries around the world.*

broad-minded *adj.* liberal-minded, open-minded, unbiased, tolerant, free-thinking, unprejudiced. *She was a broad-minded politician who was open to varied viewpoints.* **Ant.** narrow-minded, prejudiced, closed-minded.

brochure *n.* advertisement, circular, pamphlet, leaflet, sales presentation, flier. *The brochure included a price list for cottage rentals.*

broken *adj.* **1.** fractured, damaged, shattered, destroyed, mangled, smashed, crushed, injured. *The doctor put a cast on my broken arm.* **2.** discontinued, interrupted, unconnected, intermittent. *Earth received a broken and garbled message from the distant space probe.* **Ant. 1.** mended, repaired, fixed. **2.** continuous, unbroken, connected.

broken-hearted *adj.* sad, depressed, dejected, blue, devastated, forlorn, grief-stricken. *She was broken-hearted over the loss of her pet.* **Ant.** happy, euphoric, ecstatic.

broker *n.* agent, go-between, mediator, intermediate, middleman, businessperson. *We hired a broker to locate a parcel of land for us.*

brooch *n.* breastpin, pin, clasp, ornament, clip, jewelry. *Grandmother always wore a beautiful brooch on her lapel.*

brook *n.* stream, branch, tributary, creek, rill. *The boys fished for trout down at the brook.*

brothel *n.* bordello, house of ill repute, house of prostitution, bawdy house, whorehouse, (slang) cathouse. *When I asked my Dad what a brothel was, he told me it was none of my business.*

brown *adj.* auburn, tan, cocoa, chocolate, chestnut, coffee, brunet, fawn, henna. *Her eyes were as brown as the Mississippi River.*

browse *vb.* **1.** look over, scan, peruse, flip, skim, survey, windowshop. *He browsed through the store's sports equipment.* **2.** graze, feed, nibble, pasture. *Sheep browsed on the clover.*

bruise *n.* **1.** blemish, discoloration, abrasion, mark. *The apple had a bruise where it hit the ground.* *–vb.* **2.** injure, hurt, scrape, bump, wound. *Your unkind words bruised his feelings.*

brush *n.* **1.** shrubs, undergrowth, wood, bushes, thicket. *The jackrabbit hid from the coyote in the desert brush.* **2.** meeting, encounter, clash, engagement. *He had a brush with death when his car turned over.* *–vb.* **3.** sweep, whisk, groom, clean, polish. *She brushed the snarls out of her sister's hair.* **4.** graze, skim, touch, scrape. *The waiter brushed our table as he passed by.*

brusque *adj.* blunt, curt, rough, gruff, discourteous, abrupt. *We were offended by the brusque treatment from the clerk.* **Ant.** polite, gracious, friendly.

brutal *adj.* barbaric, unmerciful, savage, cruel, mean, vicious, harsh, ruthless. *The critics wrote brutal reviews of that movie.* **Ant.** kind, gentle, merciful, humane, tender.

brutality *n.* savagery, viciousness, violence, cruelty, barbarism, harshness. *The brutality displayed by both fighters was shocking.* **Ant.** compassion, humanity, affection.

brute *n.* ogre, savage, beast, monster, animal, barbarian, Neanderthal. *Bigfoot has been described as quite a brute.*

buckle *n.* **1.** catch, fastener, clasp, hook. *After losing weight, I could tighten my belt buckle one more notch.* *–vb.* **2.** hook, attach, clasp, fasten, join, strap. *The motorcyclist buckled on her helmet.* **3.** crumple, collapse, warp, bend, distort. *The submarine's prow buckled when it hit a reef.* **Ant.** **2.** unbuckle, loosen, undo, release. **3.** straighten, unbend.

buddy *n.* friend, pal, chum, companion, sidekick, comrade. *I'm going to play golf this Saturday with my best buddy.* **Ant.** enemy, stranger, rival.

budge *vb.* move, stir, go, slide, shift, yield. *Though we pushed and pulled, the mule refused to budge.* **Ant.** stay, remain.

budget *n.* **1.** financial plan, expenses, costs, allowance, program. *The governor set aside a portion of the state budget for health care.* *–vb.* **2.** plan, program, forecast, allocate, ration. *You must budget your time for both fun and work.*

buff *n.* enthusiast, expert, devotee, fanatic, connoisseur, (slang) nut. *Uncle Joe has been a train buff for most of his life.*

buffalo *n.* bison, animal, mammal, quadruped, herbivore. *We watched the buffalo graze next to the stream.*

buffet *n.* counter, shelf, sideboard, credenza, salad bar, smorgasbord. *The buffet was nearly overflowing with food.*

buffoon *n.* clown, fool, bozo, joker, idiot, oaf. *The buffoon thought that burping loudly at the table was hilarious, but it actually spoiled our dinner.*

bug *n.* **1.** insect, pest, vermin, (slang) creepy-crawler. *I couldn't identify the bug crawling up my arm.* **2.** flaw, defect, imperfection, mistake. *The* *computer was frustrating to use because it had several bugs.* –*vb.* **3.** bother, pester, annoy, irritate, irk, vex, plague. *It really bugs me when people are late.*

build *vb.* **1.** create, make, manufacture, construct, fashion, assemble, erect, forge, develop. *Let's build a snowman.* –*n.* **2.** figure, shape, physique, body, frame. *That athlete has a great build.* **Ant. 1.** wreck, demolish, destroy, dismantle.

building *n.* construction, structure, edifice, high rise, skyscraper, unit, erection. *The sky-high building all but eclipsed those around it.*

WORD SEARCH

arch series: *arcade*
brickwork patterns: *checkerwork, basketweave, English bond, Flemish bond*
concrete embedded with steel bars, mesh: *reinforced concrete*
face of: *facade*
inscribed stone: *cornerstone*
inscription on cornerstone: *epigraph*
gallery between two main floors: *mezzanine*
monster-like ornament: *gargoyle*
rooftop wall: *parapet*
supports: *beams, buttresses, flying buttresses, girders, joists, piers*
windows, nonopening: *deadlights*
wing: *annex, ell*

bulge *n.* **1.** swelling, bump, prominence, lump, hump, protuberance. *The tree branch was diseased and had an ugly bulge on it.* –*vb.* **2.** swell, protrude, inflate, balloon, distend, grow. *My forehead began to bulge where I hit it against the door.*

bulky *adj.* hulking, cumbersome, unwieldy, lumpish, ponderous, portly, ungainly, big. *My ski jacket is too bulky to pack in a suitcase.* **Ant.** compact, manageable, small.

bull *n.* **1.** steer, bullock, animal, mammal, quadruped, herbivore. *Farmer Frank's bull is the size of a tank.* **2.** lies, fabrication, bunk, falsehood, exaggeration, (slang) baloney. *He claimed to have psychic powers but we knew it was a bunch of bull.*

bulldozer *n.* earthmover, plow, heavy machinery. *The bulldozer cleared the field of shrubs and boulders in less than a day.*

bullet *n.* shot, shell, slug, ball, cartridge, projectile, trajectile, pellet. *The bullet bounced off the rock with a sharp twang.*

WORD SEARCH

cartridge without projectile: *blank*
container: *cartridge*
diameter: *caliber*
glowing military: *tracer*
nonlethal riot control: *baton rounds*
receptacle: *clip, magazine*

bulletin *n.* announcement, news flash, report, communication, dispatch. *The weather bulletin came over the radio an hour before the storm arrived.*

bullfight *n.* corrida, sport, spectacle. *I like Spain a lot but I don't care for its bullfights.*

WORD SEARCH

cheer: *olé*
fighter: *matador, torero*
horseman who lances bull's neck: *picador*
lance used by picador: *pic*
matador's shelter: *burladero*
red cape: *capa*
team of assistants: *cuadrilla*

bully *n.* **1.** tormentor, oppressor, ruffian, persecutor. *No one liked the school bully.* –*vb.* **2.** terrorize, scare, harass, threaten, abuse. *She bullied her younger brother into washing the dishes.* **Ant. 2.** charm, persuade, entice.

bumbling *adj.* fumbling, uncoordinated, incompetent, oafish, bungling, blundering. *I could not perform ballet without looking like a bumbling idiot.* **Ant.** competent, coordinated, smooth.

bump *n.* **1.** bulge, lump, protuberance, swelling, nodule. *It's best to slow down when driving over speed bumps.* **2.** whack, knock, jolt, thump, crash. *We felt a bump as our boat touched the dock.* *–vb.* **3.** whack, slam, collide, jar, knock, bounce. *I bumped my knee against the table.* **Ant. 1.** hole, depression.

bumpy *adj.* lumpy, corrugated, potholed, jarring, washboard, rough. *The road was so bumpy, we broke a shock absorber.* **Ant.** smooth, flat, glassy.

bunch *n.* **1.** group, clump, cluster, crowd, assemblage, heap, stack, pile. *A bunch of us went up to the park yesterday.* *–vb.* **2.** amass, collect, cluster, huddle. *People bunched around the snack bar.* **Ant. 2.** scatter, disband, disperse.

bundle *n.* **1.** stack, package, sack, pack, collection, bunch. *He bought a bundle of logs for his fireplace.* *–vb.* **2.** wrap, swaddle, package, group, bunch. *We bundled the newspapers for recycling.* **Ant. 2.** disperse, scatter.

bungle *vb.* botch, blunder, fumble, mishandle, miscalculate, flub. *We need someone who won't bungle the job.* **Ant.** succeed, perform, ace.

bungling *adj.* bumbling, oafish, blundering, incompetent, stumbling, uncoordinated. *The bungling player dropped the ball at the one-yard line.* **Ant.** successful, competent, coordinated.

buoy *n.* float, marker, beacon, light, bell, navigational aid. *We were told never to touch the lobster buoys.*

burden *n.* **1.** weight, cargo, load, baggage, payload. *The camel collapsed under its heavy burden.* **2.** trouble, hardship, grief, misfortune, duty, responsibility. *Managing two stores was a burden she could have done without.* *–vb.* **3.** weight, load, overload, encumber, tax. *Please don't burden me with more responsibilities.*

bureau *n.* **1.** dresser, chest, commode, highboy, chiffonier. *Fold your clothes neatly and put them in your bureau.* **2.** department, division, office, branch, wing, institution. *I have to get my license renewed at the bureau of motor vehicles.*

bureaucrat *n.* administrator, official, civil servant, public servant, politician. *The bureaucrat delayed the investigation with the usual red tape.*

burgeon *vb.* grow, proliferate, mushroom, expand, spread, multiply. *The sandwich franchise really began to burgeon about 30 years ago.* **Ant.** shrink, diminish, dwindle.

burglar *n.* robber, thief, ransacker, prowler, criminal. *The burglar crept from the house with his bag of loot.*

burial *n.* interment, entombment, inhumation, funeral. *Many relatives attended the burial at the cemetery.*

burlesque *n.* satire, parody, caricature, lampoon, spoof, comedy. *The college put on an old-time burlesque, which poked fun at national politics.*

burly *adj.* big, heavy, muscular, strong, brawny, hulking. *The burly wrestler stepped into the ring and taunted his challenger.* **Ant.** scrawny, skinny, anorexic.

burn *vb.* **1.** blaze, scorch, ignite, singe, sear, overcook. *Her father burned the hamburgers on the barbecue.* **2.** hurt, sting, smart, throb, ache. *My eyes burned from the chlorinated water.* **Ant. 1.** extinguish, douse, quench. **2.** relieve, soothe.

burning *adj.* 1. blazing, fiery, scorching, flaming, smoldering. *Firefighters sprayed water on the burning house.* 2. biting, stinging, smarting, sharp, cutting. *Hot peppers can leave as burning sensation in your mouth.* 3. excited, raging, passionate, urgent, impatient. *I have a burning desire to be with you.* **Ant.** 2. soothing, dulling, numbing. 3. indifferent, uncaring.

burnout *n.* exhaustion, weariness, fatigue, disillusionment, disenchantment, breakdown. *If you work too many hours, you'll suffer from burnout.* **Ant.** invigoration, enlivening, restoration.

burrow *n.* 1. hole, den, shelter, excavation, tunnel, warren. *The animal rushed back into its burrow.* –*vb.* 2. excavate, dig, tunnel, hollow out.

burst *vb.* 1. explode, break, rupture, erupt, gush. *The water balloon burst when it hit the wall.* –*n.* 2. outpouring, flow, rush, eruption. *The musician's popular song was received with a burst of applause.*

bury *vb.* 1. entomb, enclose, inter, enshrine. *The dead man was buried in our local cemetery.* 2. cover, hide, conceal, screen, cloak, veil. *He buried the sensitive information in a secret file.* **Ant.** 1. unearth, exhume. 2. expose, disclose, reveal.

bus *n.* public transport, motor coach, motor vehicle, mass transport, jitney. *I rode the bus into town.*

bush *n.* shrub, vegetation, hedge, briar, scrub, plant. *We saw the cat hiding behind the holly bush.*

business *n.* 1. enterprise, company, store, corporation, firm. *My uncle owns a business which rents videos.* 2. work, occupation, job, trade, pursuit, career. *My mother is in the hotel business.* 3. selling, commerce, marketing, dealings. *The store opens for business at nine o'clock.* 4. concern, interest, affair, problem. *It's none of your business.*

businessman/woman *n.* entrepreneur, merchant, trader, capitalist, tycoon, mogul. *You've got to out-hustle your competitors in order to be a good businesswoman.*

bustle *n.* activity, hubbub, commotion, hurly-burly, flurry, comings and goings. *Many people love the bustle of Wall Street.* **Ant.** inactivity, stillness, calm.

busy *adj.* 1. industrious, engaged, occupied, active, working. *She was too busy to speak with me.* 2. moving, crowded, bustling, hectic. *Stores are often very busy during the holidays.* **Ant.** 1. idle, unoccupied, inactive. 2. motionless, empty, relaxed.

busybody *n.* meddler, snoop, gossip, blabbermouth, interloper, (slang) buttinski. *My mother-in-law is a busybody and doesn't know when to mind her own business.*

butt/buttocks *n.* bottom, rump, seat, derriere, (slang) fanny, gluteus maximus. *One's buttocks tend to go numb from sitting during a long airline flight.*

button *n.* 1. knob, disk, dial, switch, control. *Please push the elevator button for the fifth floor.* 2. fastener, link, buckle, stud. *We used pieces of coal for the snowman's buttons.* –*vb.* 3. fasten, clasp, buckle, close. *He doesn't like shirts that button up the front.*

buttress *n.* 1. support, reinforcement, brace, abutment, prop, beam, arch. *The arched ceiling was supported by a large buttress.* –*vb.* 2. support, reinforce, prop, brace, hold, fortify, strengthen. *When fighting a court case, always be sure to buttress your arguments with evidence and facts.*

buxom *adj.* full-figured, voluptuous, shapely, busty. *She was by no means fat, but was in fact curvaceous and buxom.* **Ant.** skinny, bony, anorexic.

buy *vb.* purchase, acquire, obtain, get, procure, order. *Where did you buy your jacket?* **Ant.** steal, rent, sell, lease.

buzz *n.* drone, whizz, whir, hiss, hum. *The buzz from the lumber yard's saws echoed throughout the neighborhood.*

by *prep.* **1.** next to, close to, beside, alongside, near. *Our school is by the courthouse.* –*adv.* **2.** near, close to, through. *We watched the parade pass by.*

bystander *n.* witness, observer, onlooker, passerby, spectator. *A bystander claimed to have witnessed the accident first-hand.*

C

cab *n.* taxi, cabriolet, hack, ride, transport. *Let's take a cab uptown.*

cabaret *n.* nightclub, dinner theater, boîte, supper club, disco. *They put on a great show at the cabaret last night.*

cabin *n.* **1.** cottage, lodge, chalet, bungalow, shack. *She went to her mountain cabin for the weekend.* **2.** room, quarters, chamber, compartment, stateroom. *The ship's captain asked all passengers to return to their cabins.*

cabinet *n.* cupboard, chest, repository, closet, box, console. *We put the dishes back in the cabinet.*

cabinetmaker *n.* carpenter, craftsman, artisan, woodworker, furniture maker. *The cabinetmaker took over a week to finish each piece.*

cable *n.* **1.** cord, rope, line, strand, wire. *The aerial tramway runs on a thick cable.* **2.** telegram, cablegram, wire, message. *She received a cable informing her of the package's arrival.* *–vb.* **3.** wire, telegraph. *The student cabled his parents for more money.*

cache *n.* hoard, store, stockpile, supply, savings. *Pioneers often kept caches of meat for the hard winter months.*

cactus *n.* plant, succulent, saguaro, cholla, cereus, prickly pear. *Arizona is home to many different types of cactus.*

cadaver *n.* corpse, body, carcass, remains, (slang) stiff, mummy, the deceased. *The medical examiner prepared the cadaver for an autopsy.*

cadence *n.* beat, tempo, rhythm, meter, measure. *The cadence of the music was so slow, it was impossible to detect any kind of rhythm.*

cafeteria *n.* lunchroom, coffee shop, restaurant, cafe, snack bar, diner. *Many students dislike our cafeteria's food.*

cage *n.* **1.** pen, enclosure, dungeon, prison, coop, pound, box. *She keeps her canary in a bird cage.* *–vb.* **2.** confine, jail, imprison, impound, enclose, restrain. *The evil sorceress caged the prince in her dungeon.* **Ant. 2.** release, free.

cagey *adj.* cunning, tricky, crafty, sly, wily, shrewd. *The fox is a cagey animal and one that is difficult to trap.* **Ant.** stupid, incautious, dense.

cajole *vb.* persuade, coax, talk into, (slang) sweet-talk, flatter, wheedle. *Try all you want, but you'll never cajole me into going to the wrestling matches.*

cake *n.* confection, dessert, sweet, treat, baked good, pastry.

WORD SEARCH

cake baked in a ring mold and soaked in rum syrup: *savarin*
carrots and spices, made from: *carrot cake*
chocolate or cocoa, made from: *devil's food cake*
Christmas favorite with candied fruits: *fruitcake*
liquid mixture: *batter*

open tart with pastry cream and fruit: *flan*
overturned when served, fruit on bottom when baked: *upside-down cake*
pound of each of main ingredients, made from: *pound cake*
rich, frosted layer cake flavored with ground nuts: *torte*
spiral sponge cake filled with jelly: *jellyroll*
sponge cake topped with ice cream and meringue: *baked Alaska*
tube-shaped: *Bundt cake*

calamity *n.* disaster, catastrophe, mishap, tribulation, blow, misfortune. *Losing our airline tickets turned into a real calamity.* **Ant.** blessing, boon, godsend.

calculate *vb.* **1.** compute, determine, figure, estimate, work out. *This problem asks us to calculate the square root of 256.* **2.** plan, expect, intend, mean. *I didn't calculate on the delay and thus missed my bus.*

calculating *adj.* scheming, designing, plotting, crafty, shrewd, wily. *She was an aloof but calculating woman who often got her way.* **Ant.** naive, artless, unthinking.

caliber *n.* diameter, gauge, bore. *The detective tried to determine the caliber of the gun barrel.*

calibrate *vb.* adjust, align, balance, tune, correct, fix. *The butcher was required to calibrate his scales once a year.*

call *vb.* **1.** shout, yell, exclaim, cry, hail, say. *Did you hear someone call my name?* **2.** telephone, phone, dial, ring. *I called the hotel for reservations.* **3.** command, order, summon, ask, invite. *The judge called the witness to the stand.* **4.** label, name, title, designate. *Our softball team is called the Matadors.* –*n.* **5.** scream, shout, cry, yell, holler. *Give a call if you need anything.* **6.** summons, appeal, bidding, invitation, declaration, order, command. *The president issued a call to arms.*

callous *adj.* hard, tough, unsympathetic, uncaring, indifferent, insensitive, cold. *Some people criticized the mayor for being callous toward the poor.* **Ant.** tender, sympathetic, caring, soft.

callow *adj.* immature, inexperienced, juvenile, sophomoric, childish, unsophisticated. *Fred was a callow student who made the teacher's job doubly difficult.* **Ant.** mature, adult, experienced.

calm *adj.* **1.** relaxed, tranquil, untroubled, still, peaceful, composed. *Few public speakers feel truly calm when giving a speech.* –*vb.* **2.** quiet, soothe, pacify, assuage, lull. *The teacher attempted to calm his rowdy students.* **Ant.** **1.** excited, agitated, upset. **2.** disturb, excite, agitate.

camaraderie *n.* friendship, rapport, fellowship, sociability, comradeship, fraternization. *One of the best things about being on a team is the camaraderie among players.* **Ant.** hostility, unfriendliness, coldness.

camel *n.* mammal, animal, quadruped, herbivore, dromedary. *A camel can travel for long distances without water.*

camera *n.* 35-millimeter, Polaroid (trademark), Kodak (trademark), Nikon (trademark), camcorder. *He earned his living taking pictures with his camera.*

WORD SEARCH

converts light images into electronic signals to create digital photos: *CCD, charged coupled device*
focuser: *range finger, viewfinder*
illuminator: *flash*
image storage memory chip: *card*
lens for shooting distant objects: *telephoto lens, zoom lens*
lens for shooting tiny objects: *macro lens*
lens for special effects: *filter*
lens for wide angle shots: *wide-angle lens, fish-eye, bugeye*

opens and closes during shot: *shutter*
reduced image of stored photo in a digital camera: *thumbnail*

camouflage *n.* **1.** cloak, disguise, mask, screen, concealment. *The hunters used some small branches for camouflage. –vb.* **2.** conceal, disguise, cover, mask, cloak. *Butterflies have colors that camouflage them from predators.* **Ant. 2.** expose, reveal, show.

camp *n.* **1.** encampment, bivouac, shelter, cover, base, cantonment. *We decided to make camp at the river's edge. –vb.* **2.** encamp, bivouac, pitch a tent, rough it, station. *I don't like to camp where there are bears.*

campaign *n.* **1.** plan, operation, drive, effort, offensive, maneuvers. *Napoleon's military campaign bogged down in Russia. –vb.* **2.** run, canvass, crusade, stump, push. *She is campaigning for the office of class treasurer.*

campus *n.* grounds, quad, yard, alma mater, dorm. *We all decided to live on campus instead of at home during our senior year at college.*

can *n.* tin, container, vessel, receptacle. *I hope you plan to recycle that empty can of soda.*

canal *n.* channel, waterway, aqueduct, conduit, passage, duct. *We had to sail through at canal to get to the other side of the city.*

cancel *vb.* stop, drop, delete, repeal, revoke, nullify, void. *The network canceled the low-rated television series.* **Ant.** maintain, keep, confirm, uphold.

cancellation *n.* deletion, discontinuance, recall, withdrawal, annulment. *Fans were upset by the show's cancellation.* **Ant.** continuation, reintroduction.

cancer *n.* disease, carcinoma, malignancy, tumor, neoplasm, growth. *Chemotherapy is an effective treatment for patients with cancer.*

WORD SEARCH
blood and marrow, of: *leukemia*
breast removal: *mastectomy*
cancer causing: *carcinogenic*
cause: *carcinogen*
deadly: *malignant*
harmless form: *benign*
mass: *tumor, neoplasm, growth*
medical field: *oncology*
skin, of: *melanoma*
spread of: *metastasis*
tissue removal and testing for: *biopsy*
treatment: *chemotherapy, radiation*

candid *adj.* **1.** truthful, direct, frank, honest, forthright, open, sincere. *Please be candid about your feelings.* **2.** informal spontaneous, unrehearsed, unplanned. *He likes taking candid photographs of people.* **Ant. 1.** fake, untruthful, insincere. **2.** formal, rehearsed, planned.

candidate *n.* office seeker, nominee, runner, contender, hopeful, applicant. *She was running as a candidate for governor.*

candle *n.* taper, light, torch, rush, glim, tea light. *Be sure to blow out the candle before you go to bed.*

candor *n.* honesty, truthfulness, frankness directness, straightforwardness, [illegible]. *The film critic's candor was appreciated by some actors and resented by others.* **Ant.** dishonesty, indirectness, elusiveness.

candy *n.* sweets, confection, bonbon, sweet treat, candy bar, drop, wafer, kiss. *Halloween offers kids a motherload of candy.*

cane *n.* staff, stick, walking stick, alpenstock, crook, rod. *After I broke my ankle, I had to walk with a cane.*

canker *n.* lesion, ulcer, ulceration, sore, blister, cold sore, herpes. *The worst thing you can do is pour salt on a canker.*

cannibal *n.* man-eater, headhunter, barbarian, carnivore, savage, murderer. *Legend has it that the forest is still inhabited by cannibals.*

cannon *n.* gun, howitzer, mortar, heavy artillery, weapon, pom-pom. *They fired their cannons at the old building and toppled it.*

canoe *n.* outrigger, kayak, dugout, longboat, boat. *Indians traveled in canoes.*

WORD SEARCH
carry between bodies of water: *portage*
equipment and apparel: *duffel*
side edges: *gunwales*
underside: *keel*

canon *n.* law, doctrine, statute, decree, dogma. *According to institutional canon, board members should be at least 45 years of age.*

canopy *n.* shade, awning, cover, baldachin, tilt. *We hunkered down under the canopy to escape the sun's heat.*

cantankerous *adj.* grouchy, ornery, nasty, crabby, testy, ill-tempered. **Ant.** cheerful, jolly, easygoing.

canteen *n.* flask, receptacle, bottle, jug. *When traveling through the desert, it's a good idea to carry a full canteen.*

canvas *n.* duck, fabric, cloth, tent cloth, sail cloth, hemp, cotton. *The sail was made from a strong canvas which the wind could not tear.*

canyon *n.* gorge, valley, chasm, pass, gulch, box canyon. *There is no greater spectacle in the world than the Grand Canyon.*

cap *n.* hat, (slang) lid, beret, beanie, tam o' shanter. *You look like a geek when you wear your cap sideways.* See HAT.

WORD SEARCH
kerchief worn around and tied in the back, popularized by pirates and contestants on the game show, *Survivor: buff* (also known as a do-rag)

capable *adj.* able, skillful, competent, efficient, talented, experienced, qualified. *Our company is looking for a capable programmer.* **Ant.** incapable, unskilled, incompetent.

capacity *n.* **1.** size, dimensions, content, volume, range, measure, space. *This bottle has a capacity of two liters.* **2.** ability, competence, potential, aptitude, intelligence. *The child is unschooled but has a large capacity for learning.* **3.** position, role, job, function. *In his capacity as student-body president, he spoke to the reporter.* **Ant. 2.** inability, incapacity, incompetence.

cape *n.* mantle, wrap, cloak, capote, pelisse, poncho. *A dashing man in a cape appeared in the shadows.*

capital *n.* money, assets, funds, principal, savings. *My capital is all tied up in stocks and bonds.* **Ant.** deficit, debts.

capitalism *n.* free enterprise, open market, free market, commercialism, private enterprise, mercantilism. *The strongest economic system has proven to be capitalism.* **Ant.** socialism, communism.

capitalist *n.* investor, financier, business man/woman, entrepreneur, tycoon, millionaire. *He was a dyed-in-the-wool capitalist who loved to invest in new schemes.*

capitulate *vb.* yield, submit, give in, acquiesce, surrender, (slang) cave in. *My boss told me it was okay to capitulate on the first and third clauses in the contract.* **Ant.** fight, defy, hold firm.

caprice *n.* whim, whimsy, impulse, notion, fancy. *I don't want a leader who makes major decisions by mere caprice alone.*

capricious *adj.* impulsive, whimsical, fickle, unpredictable, frivolous. *I made a lot of capricious decisions when I was young.* **Ant.** thoughtful, predictable, stable.

capsize *vb.* overturn, tip, keel over, upset, roll over. *If you don't sit down, the canoe will capsize.*

capsule *n.* pill, tablet, pellet, ampule. *The doctor told me to get plenty of rest and take one antibiotic capsule at night.*

captain *n.* **1.** commander, skipper, master, chief, leader, head. *The team captains chose five players each.* *–vb.* **2.** lead, skipper, pilot, head, command, direct. *She has captained the starship for the last ten years.*

caption *n.* heading, subtitle, title, legend, inscription. *The caption under the comic was hilarious.*

captivate *vb.* enchant, charm, dazzle, fascinate, tantalize, delight. *The sight of Saturn's rings captivated the spaceship's passengers.* **Ant.** repel, disgust, offend.

capture *vb.* **1.** catch, hold, trap, seize apprehend. *In chess, you lose when the other player captures your king.* *–n.* **2.** seizure, arrest, ensnaring, trapping, taking. *The prince was held for ransom following his capture by pirates.* **Ant. 1.** liberate, release. **2.** release, freeing, liberation.

car *n.* automobile, sedan, (slang) wheels, vehicle, coupe, station wagon, SUV, transport. *We like to take a long ride in the car on Sundays.*
See also AUTOMOBILE.

caravan *n.* convoy, file, column, train, procession, company, troop. *A caravan of nomads straggled over the sand dunes.*

carcass *n.* corpse, cadaver, body, (slang) road kill, carrion, remains. *The carcass had been in the road for three days.*

carcinogenic *adj.* mutagenic, cancer-causing, tumor-forming, toxic, hazardous. *Cigarettes are very carcinogenic.*

care *vb.* **1.** protect, attend, watch, mind, tend. *A baby-sitter cared for the young children until their parents returned.* **2.** like, wish, crave, want, desire. *Would you care for another slice of pizza?* *–n.* **3.** worry, concern, burden, sorrow, responsibility. *Our lazy cat doesn't have a care in the world.* **4.** caution, wariness, attention, concentration, thought. *One should take care when using a power saw.* **5.** safekeeping, custody, protection, guardianship, keep, charge. *I left my dog in my neighbor's care.* **Ant. 1.** neglect, ignore. **2.** hate, dislike reject. **3.** relaxation, enjoyment, pleasure. **4.** disregard, recklessness. **5.** neglect.

careen *vb.* tilt, lurch, tip, swerve, lean, pitch. *We hung on for our lives as the car began to careen out of control.*

career *n.* job, occupation, business, employment, work, living trade, vocation. *Teaching is my career.*

carefree *adj.* untroubled, unworried, cheerful, happy, easygoing, joyful, merry. *The princess had a carefree life as a child.* **Ant.** troubled, burdened, worried, difficult.

careful *adj.* thoughtful, cautious, concerned, wary, guarded, mindful, accurate. *Be careful that you don't miss any problems on the test.* **Ant.** careless, unthinking, mindless, negligent.

caregiver *See* CARETAKER.

careless *adj.* forgetful, thoughtless, unthinking, uncaring, unwary, negligent. *It was careless* *of him to leave the door unlocked.* **Ant.** careful, exact, cautious.

caress *n.* **1.** stroke, touch, cuddle, embrace, hug, kiss. *The child gave her puppy a caress.* –*vb.* **2.** touch, brush, graze, stroke, massage. *A gentle breeze caressed his face.*

caretaker *n.* caregiver, attendant, conservator, custodian, sitter, guardian, maintenance man. *We asked the caretaker of the inn to please turn on the air conditioner.*

cargo *n.* freight, load, payload, shipment, lading, consignment. *It took more than eight hours to load all of the cargo on to the ship.*

caricature *n.* cartoon, portrait, sketch, depiction, take-off, spoof, mockery. *Editorial cartoonists love to draw caricatures of politicians.*

carnage *n.* slaughter, bloodshed, bloodbath, massacre, gore, butchery. *The carnage of many Civil War battles is difficult to imagine.*

carnival *n.* fair, festival, jubilee, amusement park, jamboree, exposition. *Mardi Gras may be the world's biggest carnival.*

carnivore *n.* meat-eater, flesh-eater, predator, hunter. *The lion is a formidable carnivore.* **Ant.** vegetarian, vegan.

carom *n.* rebound, ricochet, glance, bounce. *We watched the ball carom off the wall and into the outfielder's outstretched glove.*

carouse *vb.* party, drink, revel, cut loose, wassail. *Some young guys like to carouse on weekends.*

carpenter *n.* woodworker, woodwright, craftsman, craftswoman, builder, artisan. *The carpenter built a beautiful spiral staircase.*

WORD SEARCH

aligned: *level, plumb, true*
grooves, cut: *dado, rabbet*
joint: *miter, mortise*
sawing support: *sawhorse, sawbuck*
tools: *saw, plane, miter box, chisel, bevel, level, adze, sander*

carpet *n.* rug, throw, floor covering, mat, runner, area rug. *She purchased an expensive Persian carpet for her living room.*

carriage *n.* coach, buggy, cart, trap, gig, stagecoach. *The queen and king were brought to the palace in a carriage.*

carry *vb.* **1.** bear, move, lug, bring, cart, transport, convey. *He carries his schoolbooks in a backpack.* **2.** support, shoulder, bear, maintain, undertake. *Do you think this bridge can carry the weight of a two-ton truck?* **3.** offer, supply, provide, furnish. *The local market carries three types of onions.* **Ant.** **1.** drop, let fall. **3.** remove, omit, withhold.

cartel *n.* partnership, bloc, coalition, monopoly, syndicate, consortium. *The oil cartel controls crude oil prices around the world.*

cartography *n.* map-making, chart-making, mapping. *As part of her geography course, Jill is learning cartography.*

carton *n.* box, container, case, package, crate. *I dropped a carton full of books on my toe.*

cartoon *n.* caricature, drawing, funny, comic, animated feature. *As a kid, I consumed a steady diet of Saturday morning cartoons.*

carve *vb.* **1.** sculpt, whittle, fashion, shape, form, chisel. *She likes to carve animals out of pieces of wood.* **2.** partition, slice, divide, quarter, split, chop. *Politicians carved the large district into three smaller ones.*

Casanova *n.* womanizer, Don Juan, (slang) player, heartbreaker, (slang) stud, Lothario. *He fancied himself a Casanova, but most women were immune to his charms.*

cascade *n.* **1.** waterfall, fall, rapids, cataract. *She hiked up to the stream's cascade.* *–vb.* **2.** plunge, fall, rush, surge, avalanche. *His marbles cascaded to the ground when their bag broke.* **Ant. 2.** trickle, drip, leak.

case *n.* **1.** example, sample, situation, event, happening, occasion. *In this case, I think you are correct.* **2.** lawsuit, argument, plea presentation, explanation. *The lawyer presented his case to the jury.* **3.** holder, container, canister, box, carton, package. *She keeps her glasses in a leather case.* **4.** patient, invalid, subject. *The doctor has several difficult cases.*

cash *n.* money, currency, dollars, legal tender, (slang) dough, (slang) Benjamins. *I ran out of cash, so I had to use my credit card.*

cashier *n.* teller, clerk, counter person, bursar. *The cashier gave me the incorrect amount of change.*

casino *n.* gambling hall, gaming house. *A great way to lose your money fast is to gamble it away in a casino.*

cask *n.* barrel, keg, firkin, hogshead, vessel, tun. *The castaways had only one cask of water.*

casket *n.* coffin, sarcophagus, box, pall. *Six of John's closest friends and relatives carried the casket to the grave.*

casserole *n.* dish, concoction, mishmash, terrine, melange, potpourri. *Aunt Mary served a delicious casserole.*

cast *n.* **1.** casing, support, splint, brace. *Doctors put a cast on his broken arm.* **2.** mold, copy, replica, pattern, impression. *This museum makes casts of famous actors, then fills them with wax.* **3.** look, appearance, demeanor, suggestion, shade, trace. *In "Dr. Jekyll and Mr. Hyde," Mr. Hyde has an evil cast to his face.* **4.** launch, throw, fling, toss, heave. *In a game of horseshoes, each player is allowed three casts.* *–vb.* **5.** toss, hurl, send, throw, emit, project. *A fisherman cast his line into the lake.* **6.** award, allot, bestow, give, select. *Who did you cast your ballot for?* **7.** set, sculpt, shape, mold, arrange. *The artist cast her sculpture in bronze.*

castaway *n.* outcast, pariah, exile, reject, stray, waif. *Robinson Crusoe is probably the world's most famous castaway.*

caste *n.* social order, class, rank, place, station, status. *The rigid hierarchical divisions of some societies result from a caste system.*

castle *n.* fortress, citadel, hold, keep, palace, manor, mansion, tower. *Ireland is famous for its impressive castles.*

WORD SEARCH

bridge to: *drawbridge*
domestic staff: *chamberlain, steward*
door, giant, grated: *portcullis*
knights' jousting practice area: *tiltyard*
owner: *lord*
prison, underground: *dungeon*
privy: *garderobe*
tower, main inner: *donjon*
tower, small: *turret*
trench around, water-filled: *moat*
yard area: *bailey, courtyard, ward*
wall ringing outer grounds: *curtain wall*
wall, roof: *parapet*

castrate *vb.* geld, neuter, sterilize, (slang) fix, emasculate, eunuchize. *The farmer said he would castrate his bull in order to curtail its bad behavior.*

casual *adj.* informal, relaxed, offhand, loose, nonchalant, carefree. *There's no need to dress up for a casual dinner party.* **Ant.** formal, stiff, reserved.

casualty *n.* injury, fatality, victim, loss, sufferer. *It is sad when civilians become casualties of war.*

cat *n.* feline, pet, pussy, kitty, tabby, grimalkin, carnivore, mouser. *The cat is particularly fond of snoozing.*

WORD SEARCH

black and white: *piebald*
bred of its own kind only: *purebred*
frill around neck: *ruff*
foot coloration: *gloves, mittens*
gray or blue gray: *blue*
intoxicant: *catnip*
kitten group: *litter*
mating cry or howl: *caterwaul*
mixed breed: *mongrel*
soles of feet: *pads*
striped: *tabby, tiger*
throat patch of white: *locket*
tortoiseshell and white: *calico*
traces of color: *ghost markings*

cataclysm *n.* upheaval, disaster, eruption, catastrophe, calamity, devastation. *The volcano produced a terrible cataclysm when it erupted.*

catalog *n.* **1.** directory, list, inventory, index, schedule, program. *We looked through the store's clothes catalog.* *–vb.* **2.** classify, record, list, arrange, categorize, rank. *Library personnel have cataloged all the books on their shelves.*

catalyst *n.* stimulus, activator, activist, agitator, reactant, impetus. *John Muir's writings were a catalyst for the preservation of huge tracts of wild lands.*

catapult *n.* launcher, sling, slingshot, siege engine, trebuchet.

catastrophe *n.* tragedy, misfortune, disaster, devastation, calamity, ruin. *The catastrophe would have been avoided if the stoplight had been working.* **Ant.** good fortune, blessing.

catch *vb.* **1.** seize, snatch, grasp, grab, capture, trap. *He caught several fish.* **2.** discover, detect, surprise, find, startle. *My mother caught me taking the cookies she was saving.* **3.** overtake, reach, attain, intercept. *She caught and passed the two leading runners on the final lap.* **4.** understand, comprehend, perceive, discern, hear. *I didn't catch what you were saying.* *–n.* **5.** grab, snatch, capture, seizure, snare. *The baseball player made a spectacular catch.* **6.** hook, fastener, clasp, lock, latch. *The catch on the door is stuck.* **7.** snag, trick, trap, snare. *The catch in this contract is that you must pay by tomorrow.* **Ant.** **1.** miss, free, release. **5.** miss, drop, fumble. **7.** boon, advantage, blessing.

catch-22 *n.* no-win situation, lose-lose situation, Gordian knot, dilemma, horns of a dilemma.

category *n.* type, brand, class, classification, grouping. *How many categories of music can you name?*

catharsis *n.* purification, cleansing, renewal, rebirth, expurgation, replenishment. *The vacation we took in the Bahamas was a wonderful catharsis to the stress of our daily lives.* **Ant.** burnout, stress, exhaustion.

cattle *n.* livestock, cows, steers, herd, ruminants, herbivores. *The ranchers took three days to round up their herd.*

catty *adj.* back-biting, back-stabbing, malicious, vicious, nasty, mean. *I hate when catty people insult others behind their back.* **Ant.** kind, considerate, easygoing.

caucus *n.* meeting, assembly, gathering, convention, conclave, session. *The committee met as a caucus before the meeting scheduled for Tuesday evening.*

cauldron *n.* kettle, vat, pot, boiler. *The witch tossed a few eyes of newt into the bubbling cauldron.*

cause *vb.* **1.** create, provoke, generate, kindle, incite, motivate. *What caused the fire?* *–n.* **2.** origin, source, creator, reason, motive, root. *The cause of the plane crash was a faulty engine.* **3.** belief, goal, ideal, object, principle. *The activist fought for environmental causes.* **Ant. 1.** prevent, block, halt. **2.** outcome, result.

caustic *adj.* corrosive, acid, burning, astringent, cutting, biting. *Battery acid is a caustic substance.* **Ant.** benign, soothing.

caution *n.* **1.** care, discretion, wariness, alertness, vigilance. *We proceeded with caution on the icy road.* *–vb.* **2.** warn, alert, advise, counsel, admonish. *A sign cautioned us to slow down because there was a curve ahead.* **Ant. 1.** carelessness, rashness.

cautious *adj.* careful, watchful, attentive, alert, wary, vigilant, aware, guarded. *One should be cautious when crossing a busy street.* **Ant.** rash, daring, careless, foolhardy.

cavalier *adj.* indifferent, casual, uncaring, rough, arrogant, devil-may-care. *The boss was completely cavalier in his attitude about doubling our workload without increasing our pay.* **Ant.** conscientious, caring, thoughtful.

cave *n.* cavern, grotto, chamber, tunnel, hole, passage, cavity. *It's always a good idea to bring plenty of flashlights when exploring a cave.*

WORD SEARCH

chamber, large: *gallery*
explorer/exploring: *spelunker/spelunking*
geological formation characterized by caves and sinkholes: *karst*
icicle hanging from roof: *stalactite*
icicle sprouting from floor: *stalagmite*
inhabitant: *troglodyte*
study of: *speleology*
underwater passage: *sump, syphon*
vertical shaft: *chimney*

caveat *n.* warning, caution, advisory, admonition, advisement, forewarning. *The harbor master issued a stern caveat about going out sailing without checking the weather first.*

cave-in *n.* collapse, rupture, toppling, breakdown, burst, landslide. *Everyone who worked in the mine worried about a cave-in.*

caveman *n.* prehistoric human, hominid, Stone Age human, primitive human, Neanderthal, Cro-Magnon, hominoid, troglodyte. *Contrary to a number of inaccurate movies, a caveman never came face to face with a dinosaur.*

cavernous *adj.* gaping, commodious, abysmal, hollow, sunken, yawning. *We entered the cavernous warehouse with trepidation.*

cavity *n.* hole, pit, crevasse, gap, hollow, cavern, crater, opening. *The explosion made a large cavity in the ground.*

cease *vb.* stop, discontinue, suspend, quit, terminate, halt, desist, conclude. *Will this rain never cease?* **Ant.** continue, start, begin.

cede *vb.* surrender, yield, relinquish, give, release, grant. *The team was forced to cede the title to their challengers.* **Ant.** keep, retain, hold.

celebrate *vb.* observe, honor, commemorate, keep, glorify. *Some friends and I celebrated my birthday at an amusement park.* **Ant.** ignore, forget, dishonor, desecrate.

celebrity *n.* **1.** star, notable, heroine, hero, dignitary, personage. *Many celebrities showed up for the Academy Awards ceremony.* **2.** popularity, fame, renown, note, stardom. *The triumphant space explorers welcomed their newfound celebrity.* **Ant. 2.** nonrecognition, obscurity, oblivion.

celestial *adj.* astronomical, heavenly, astral, stellar, universal, galactic, of the sky. *It was an evening of breathtaking celestial beauty.*

celibate *adj.* chaste, virtuous, abstinent, virginal, continent. *Priests must remain celibate at* *all times.* **Ant.** promiscuous, loose, sexually active.

cell *n.* enclosure, cubicle, lockup, stall, cage, pen. *The bank robber was put in the prison's holding cell.*

cement *n.* **1.** plaster, concrete, mortar, glue, stucco, asphalt. *She wrote her name in the wet cement of the new sidewalk.* –*vb.* **2.** bind, glue, seal, fix, stick, join, connect. *He cemented the broken wing on his model airplane.*

cemetery *n.* graveyard, burial ground, resting place, mortuary. *My uncle is buried in that cemetery.*

WORD SEARCH

burial space: *plot*
burial vault: *crypt, sepulcher, tomb*
crucifixion depiction: *calvary*
grave robber: *ghoul*
massive: *necropolis*
memorial: *shrine*
mourning statues: *weepers*
poor person's: *potter's field*
RIP: *rest in peace (resquiescat in pace)*
stone memorial: *gravestone, headstone, monument*
tomb house: *mausoleum*
underground vault: *catacombs, crypt*
urn vault: *cinerarium*
vault: *sepulcher*

censor *vb.* **1.** ban, forbid, edit, suppress, purge, delete. *Many countries censor political books and magazines.* –*n.* **2.** examiner, inspector, abridger, reviewer, editor. *The station's censor deleted bad language with loud "bleeps."* **Ant.** **1.** allow, accept, approve.

censorship *n.* expurgation, sanitizing, removal, editing, deletion, cutting, (slang) cleaning up. *Censorship often raises public interest in the censored work.* **Ant.** freedom of speech, freedom of expression.

censure *n.* **1.** condemnation, rebuke, criticism, scolding, disapproval. *He received his parent's censure for staying out all night.* –*vb.* **2.** blame, criticize, reprimand, scold, reproach, judge. *The school board censured the teacher for her nontraditional teaching style.* **Ant.** **1.** praise, approval, endorsement. **2.** praise, encourage.

census *n.* count, head count, population, tally, demographics, statistics. *According to an international census, the world is populated with more than 6 billion people.*

center *n.* **1.** middle, midway, focus, heart, core, hub, pivot, crux. *The center of the Earth is thought to be made up of nickel and iron.* –*vb.* **2.** converge, focus, concentrate, centralize, consolidate. *Their conversation often centers around sports.* **Ant.** **1.** side, surface, exterior. **2.** spread, scatter, disperse.

central *adj.* **1.** middle, midmost, midway, inmost, inside. *Colorado is a central state.* **2.** prime, principal, dominant, pivotal, key, essential, main. *Tom Sawyer is the central character in Mark Twain's famous book.* **Ant.** **1.** outside, exterior, rim. **2.** minor, secondary.

ceremonial *adj.* ceremonious, formal, ritual, stately, solemn, courtly. **Ant.** casual, informal, relaxed.

ceremony *n.* **1.** celebration, rite, ritual, observance, services. *The graduation ceremony will take place on the football field.* **2.** etiquette, formality, protocol, solemnity, politeness. *The royal wedding was performed with a great deal of ceremony.* **Ant.** **2.** informality, casualness.

certain *adj.* **1.** convinced, definite, sure, positive, undoubting. *Are you certain you want to buy this car?* **2.** undeniable, evident, conclusive, guaranteed, reliable, foolproof. *I will only bet on a certain winner.* **3.** specific, particular, precise, express. *There are certain rules that I must discuss* *with you.* **Ant.** 1. uncertain, unsure. 2. uncertain, unreliable, questionable. 3. uncertain, vague, indefinite.

certainly *adv.* surely, unquestionably, positively, definitely, clearly, undoubtedly. *It's certainly cold out today.*

certificate *n.* document, certification, documentation, instrument, license, credential, diploma. *After I successfully completed the course, the school awarded me a certificate.*

certify *vb.* guarantee, verify, establish, validate, promise. *You'll need a witness to certify your signature on this document.* **Ant.** invalidate, question.

cesspool *n.* cesspit, sewer, septic tank, sump, cloaca. *I really don't care to discuss cesspools when I'm eating my dinner.*

chafe *vb.* rub, scrape, abrade, wear, rasp, scour. *My shoes were so tight they began to chafe.*

chagrin *n.* embarrassment, shame, humiliation, disgrace, mortification, discomfort. *To my chagrin, my pants fell down clear to my ankles.*

chain *n.* 1. metal links, cable, irons, shackles, manacles. *The dog had a chain around its neck.* 2. train, line, series, string, procession. *His request went up the chain of command to the commanding general.* –*vb.* 3. connect, secure, fasten, manacle, handcuff, restrain. *She chained her bike to the metal rack.* **Ant.** 3. unchain, release, free.

chair *n.* 1. seat, stool, bench, rocker, couch. *Pull up a chair and join us.* 2. chairwoman, chairman, leader, director, moderator, facilitator. *She was voted in as chair of the math department.* –*vb.* 3. oversee, facilitate, direct, moderate, lead. *He chaired the committee meeting.*

WORD SEARCH

canvas chair that folds up: *director's chair*
canvas sling: *sling chair, butterfly chair*
cruise ship chair, folding: *deck chair*
low, armless chair or lounge used in bedroom: *slipper chair*
pivoting, revolving chair for office: *swivel chair*
rocker that is usually painted or stenciled, spindle-backed: *Boston rocker*
royal's chair carried on poles: *sedan chair*
spindle-backed, wooden: *Windsor chair*
stuffed bag, usually used only by children or teens: *beanbag chair*
tilting, upholstered chair with unfolding footrest: *recliner*
wicker, round-backed: *basket chair*
wide chair for two people: *loveseat*
winged easy chair: *wing chair*
wooden bench, unupholstered: *settle*
wooden bench, usually upholstered: *settee*

chairman *n.* chair, director, presiding officer, speaker, president, chief. *The chairman was the most intelligent and articulate member of the board.*

challenge *n.* 1. dare, threat, provocation, summons, ultimatum. *Sir Lancelot received a challenge at the jousting tournament.* 2. trial, venture, test, puzzle, difficulty. *The obstacle course proved to be a difficult challenge.* –*vb.* 3. dare, summon, bid, defy, confront. *She challenged him to a game of chess.* 4. test, strain, try, tax, stimulate. *The computer malfunction challenged her problem-solving abilities.* 5. contradict, question, dispute, contest, object. *The lawyer challenged the defendant's statement.* **Ant.** 5. accept, believe, support.

champion *n.* 1. winner, victor, hero, conqueror, leader, title holder. *After winning the final game, he was crowned the champion.* 2. defender, supporter, backer, protector, guardian. *The humane society considers itself the champion of abused animals.* –*vb.* 3. promote, defend, support, protect, uphold, back, guard. *He championed the group's* *right to march.* **Ant.** 1. loser, fallen. 2. enemy, antagonist. 3. oppose, obstruct.

championship *n.* playoffs, showdown, elimination, competition, title match, tournament of champions. *Whoever wins the championship is the best team in the world.*

chance *n.* 1. opportunity, prospect, opening, occasion. *Don't blow it; this may be your big chance.* 2. fate, accident, happenstance, luck, coincidence. *It was only by chance that we found the hotel.* 3. possibility, probability, likelihood, odds, tendency. *There is a good chance that the game will be canceled.* 4. danger, gamble, risk, peril, venture. *When you cheat, there is always the chance that you will be caught.* *–adj.* 5. accidental, unforeseen, random, unexpected, uncertain. *My meeting him last Sunday was a chance occurrence.* *–vb.* 6. occur, happen, befall, transpire, result. *It chanced that my birthday fell on a holiday this year.* 7. risk, attempt, hazard, gamble, try. *The two hikers decided not to chance crossing the raging river.* **Ant.** 2. plan, proposal, intent. 3. impossibility, improbability. 5. expected, foreseen, planned.

change *vb.* 1. alter, vary, modify, transform, fluctuate, turn, shift. *The ship's captain changed course when she saw the iceberg.* 2. replace, exchange, swap, trade, substitute. *I went inside to change my dirty shirt.* *–n.* 3. transformation, difference, switch, variation, reversal. *A remarkable change came over her when she began exercising and eating right.* **Ant.** 1. maintain, remain, hold. 2. keep, maintain. 3. stability, sameness, permanence.

channel *n.* 1. canal, watercourse, passage, duct, strait, artery, route. *The tugboat guided the large ship into the main channel.* *–vb.* 2. route, direct, convey, conduct, guide, steer. *The teacher said we should channel our energy into our homework.*

chant *n.* plainsong, song, recitation, vocalization, canticle, psalm. *We found the Gregorian chants to be particularly haunting.*

chaos *n.* disorder, confusion, disarray, mess, disorganization, jumble. *His Hawaiian-print shirt is a chaos of colors.* **Ant.** organization, harmony, order, calm.

chaotic *adj.* out-of-control, wild, confused, disordered, turbulent, riotous. *The chaotic streets were a result of the riot.* **Ant.** ordered, peaceful, in control.

chaperone *n.* escort, guardian, protector, babysitter, watchful eye. *In Victorian times, a chaperone sometimes accompanied teenagers on dates.*

chaplain *n.* minister, clergyman, priest, reverend, parson, rabbi. *The chaplain led the group in prayer.*

chapter *n.* 1. section, episode, part, subdivision, portion. *He is writing the book's final chapter.* 2. group, branch, gathering, unit, assembly. *She joined the local chapter of the Sierra Club.*

character *n.* 1. individual, person, role, part, portrayal. *Frodo is the main character in J.R.R. Tolkien's "The Hobbit."* 2. honesty, morality, courage, integrity, respectability, sincerity. *Eleanor Roosevelt was a woman of renowned character.* 3. attitude, personality, temperament, quality, nature. *The dark and gloomy castle had a rather forbidding character.* 4. letter, figure, symbol, insignia, sign. *You can choose different characters for a computer printout.* 5. eccentric, oddball, nonconformist, maverick. *The old hermit was quite a character.* **Ant.** 2. dishonesty, corruption, immorality.

characteristic *adj.* 1. typical, distinctive, marked, representative, particular, specific. *I heard my friend's characteristic laugh.* *–n.* 2. feature, mannerism, trait, attribute, distinction, peculiarity, quirk. *His most noticeable characteristic is his kindness.* **Ant.** 1. uncharacteristic, atypical.

charge *vb.* 1. rush, surge, storm, attack, thrust, push. *The soldiers charged up the hill.* 2. bill, assess, ask, tax, fine. *The store charged forty dollars for this shirt.* 3. blame, accuse, indict, arraign, incriminate. *The city attorney's office charged her with one count of fraud.* 4. load, pack, instill, infuse, stack. *The singer's entrance charged the auditorium with excitement.* 5. order, urge, direct, bid, demand. *My father charged me to take out the trash.* –*n.* 6. price, bill, cost, expense, fare, fee. *The charge for a one-night stay in our hotel is sixty dollars.* 7. custody, care, guardianship, protection, keeping. *The young boy was left in his grandparent's charge.* 8. attack, offensive, drive, onslaught, thrust, push. *The cavalry charge overran the defenders' position.* 9. accusation, implication, complaint, allegation, citation. *The charge you are accused of is burglary.* 10. dependent, ward, responsibility, minor. *She became a charge of the state when her parents died.* **Ant.** 1. retreat, withdraw. 3. absolve, acquit. 4. empty, discharge. 8. withdrawal, retreat. 9. absolution, acquittal.

charisma *n.* magnetism, magnetic personality, dominance, charm, appeal, presence, power, authority. *John F. Kennedy had great charisma.*

charismatic *adj.* powerful, charming, magnetic, hypnotic, dominant, authoritative. *A charismatic personality often rises to prominence.* **Ant.** unappealing, dull, weak.

charitable *adj.* 1. giving, unselfish, generous, unsparing, humanitarian, nonprofit. *The charitable organization gave food and housing to the needy.* 2. lenient, tolerant, forgiving, kind, sympathetic. *This time I will be charitable and not punish you.* **Ant.** 1. selfish, ungenerous, stingy. 2. rigid, unforgiving.

charity *n.* 1. aid, contribution, endowment, alms, benefaction, assistance. *His extra money was earmarked for charity.* 2. generosity, benevolence, philanthropy, altruism, humanity. *The organization was famous for its charity.* **Ant.** 2. stinginess, selfishness, cold-heartedness.

charm *n.* 1. allure, appeal, captivation, pull, enchantment, attractiveness, magnetism. *The charm of the quaint old house convinced the couple to buy it.* 2. amulet, spell, chant, lucky piece. *The sorceress gave him a charm that scares away evil goblins.* –*vb.* 3. delight, captivate, enthrall, mesmerize, attract, bewitch, hypnotize. *A fakir charmed the king cobra with a flute.* **Ant.** 1. aversion, repulsion, revulsion. 3. disgust, revolt, repel.

charming *adj.* enchanting, captivating, delightful, pleasing, enjoyable, fascinating. *He has a charming smile.* **Ant.** repulsive, disagreeable, nauseating, unpleasing.

chart *n.* 1. layout, graph, plot, map, diagram, table, outline, scheme. *We could see by the chart that sales were down.* –*vb.* 2. map, lay out, outline, plot, draft. *The cartographer charted the explorer's route.*

charter *n.* 1. license, contract, permit, lease, agreement, compact, franchise. *The national board for our fraternity said it would revoke our charter if we didn't pay our dues.* –*vb.* 2. license, grant, sanction, allot, authorize. *The state chartered the bank to do business.* 3. rent, lease, hire, engage, employ. *We chartered a boat for the afternoon.*

chase *vb.* 1. pursue, follow, trail, tail, track. *The dog chased a car down the street.* 2. drive out, evict, repulse, dispel, disperse. *We chased the dog off our lawn.* –*n.* 3. hunt, pursuit, tracking, race, quest. *The rider was thrown off his horse during the chase.*

chaste *adj.* wholesome, virginal, innocent, celibate, righteous, uncorrupted. *The monks led a chaste life.* **Ant.** unchaste, wanton, corrupt.

chastise *vb.* punish, discipline, scold, berate, upbraid, (slang) give a tongue lashing, ream. *I didn't think you would chastise me just for eating the last slice of the pizza.* **Ant.** commend, compliment, reward.

chastity *n.* celibacy, abstinence, virtue, virginity, purity, innocence. *She planned on protecting her chastity until she was married.* **Ant.** promiscuity, sluttiness, wildness.

chat *vb.* **1.** talk, chatter, converse, gossip, discuss. *My hairdresser often chats with me about her friends and family.* –*n.* **2.** talk, discussion, conversation, visit. *He dropped by for a chat.*

chatter *vb.* **1.** babble, talk, jabber, gossip, prattle. *My younger brother chattered on about his soccer game.* –*n.* **2.** babble, talking, blather, gossip, jabbering, chatting. *The teacher quieted the students' chatter.*

chatterbox *n.* talker, blabbermouth, (slang) motormouth, (slang) windbag. *I don't mind a chatterbox as long as he listens as well as he talks.* **Ant.** wallflower, mute.

chauvinism *n.* bigotry, bias, sexism, racism, nationalism, prejudice, intolerance. *His chauvinism blinded him to the positive attributes of those who were different.* **Ant.** broad-mindedness, acceptance, tolerance.

chauvinist *n.* supremacist, racist, sexist, jingoist, bigot, nationalist. *He was a chauvinist who mistrusted anyone unlike himself.*

cheap *adj.* **1.** inexpensive, low-priced, thrifty, reduced, lowered, reasonable. *An imitation diamond is relatively cheap compared to a real one.* **2.** shoddy, trashy, poor, mean, low. *We stayed at a cheap motel.* **3.** miserly, stingy, ungenerous, grudging, tight. *He was too cheap to buy his mother a gift.* **Ant. 1.** expensive, unreasonable, high-priced. **2.** excellent, superior. **3.** generous, unselfish, unsparing.

cheapskate *n.* miser, (slang) penny-pincher, tightwad, skinflint, Scrooge. *I'm too much of a cheapskate to buy anything new, which is why I always shop at second-hand stores.* **Ant.** giver, philanthropist, benefactor.

cheat *vb.* **1.** defraud, swindle, deceive, bilk, trick, mislead. *He cheated me by charging $120 for a $15 watch.* –*n.* **2.** swindler, trickster, crook, con artist, fraud. *I refuse to play cards with that cheat.*

check *vb.* **1.** explore, review, inspect, examine, investigate. *Security guards checked for a prowler after they heard the alarm.* **2.** stop, prevent, brake, halt, inhibit, curb, slow, restrain. *A severe storm checked the ship's progress.* **3.** agree, correspond, concur, tally, harmonize. *The detective said the suspect's story checks with the facts.* **4.** mark, tally, note, register, score. *The teacher checked wrong answers with a red pen.* –*n.* **5.** inspection, examination, study, investigation. *All new cars are subject to a factory check before being shipped.* **6.** obstacle, barrier, restriction, block, rejection, stoppage. *His habitual tardiness is a check against his chances for promotion.* **7.** slash, mark, notation, impression. *When completing this form, please put a check next to those items you wish to order.* **8.** bill, tab, ticket, receipt. *We were shocked at the price of dinner when we received the check.* **Ant. 1.** overlook, neglect. **2.** encourage, start, release. **3.** contradict, disagree. **6.** start, promotion, advance.

cheer *vb.* **1.** shout, applaud, yell, encourage, acclaim. *We cheered for our team.* **2.** console, comfort, reassure, brighten, enliven. *He cheered his sad friend with funny stories.* –*n.* **3.** shout, yell, hooray, roar, cry. *She gave a cheer when she won the award.* **4.** sparkle, animation, merriment, joy, happiness. *The sunny wallpaper added a note of cheer to the hospital rooms.* **Ant. 1.** boo, hiss. **2.** discourage, demoralize. **3.** boo, hiss. **4.** discouragement, gloom, dejection.

cheerful *adj.* merry, joyous, happy, bright, carefree, jolly, playful, delighted. *The students were cheerful when they learned they had the day off from school.* **Ant.** depressed, sad, cheerless.

cheerless *adj.* bleak, gloomy, dismal, miserable, joyless. *The overcast winter day was totally cheerless.* **Ant.** cheerful, bright, joyous.

chef *n.* cook, culinary expert, cuisinier. *When the restaurant hired a better chef, business improved.*

cherish *vb.* love, honor, revere, respect, nurture, adore, value. *I cherish the time I've had with my daughter.* **Ant.** hate, detest, dislike.

chest *n.* **1.** box, container, trunk, dresser, case, locker. *My parents keep their family mementos in a wooden chest.* **2.** breast, bosom, pectorals, front. *Bodybuilders lift weights to expand their chests.* **Ant. 2.** back.

chew *vb.* crunch, munch, grind, gnaw, bite, eat, nibble. *I often chew gum when I watch movies.*

chic *adj.* stylish, fashionable, sophisticated, (slang) in, smart, chichi. *The actress always wore chic clothing.* **Ant.** unfashionable, unstylish, outmoded.

chicanery *n.* trickery, deception, deceit, cheating, subterfuge, dishonesty. *There is a lot of chicanery involved in con games.* **Ant.** honesty, integrity, truthfulness.

chicken *n.* fowl, hen, bird, biddy, rooster. *The chickens do a good job of eating all the bugs on the ground.*

chief *n.* **1.** leader, captain, head, ruler, director, boss, manager. *The police chief had a hundred officers under his command.* –*adj.* **2.** main, principal, first, primary, major, greatest. *Beef is the chief export of Argentina.* **Ant. 1.** follower, subject. **2.** minor, least, secondary.

chiefly *adv.* first, primarily, mainly, particularly, especially. *Expensive running shoes are bought chiefly by serious athletes.*

child *n.* young adult, youth, teenager, boy, girl, kid, adolescent, juvenile. *If you are a child, you can get in free with an adult.* **Ant.** adult, senior citizen, grown-up.

childhood *n.* youth, boyhood, girlhood, puberty, adolescence, teens. *The happiest time in my life was childhood.* **Ant.** adulthood, senescence, senior years.

childish *adj.* juvenile, sophomoric, adolescent, babyish, immature, callow, naive. *A childish prank ended in a broken window.* **Ant.** adult, mature, grown-up.

chill *n.* **1.** coolness, bite, frostiness, nip, crispness, coldness, briskness. *The chill of the mountain air surprised us.* –*vb.* **2.** cool, refrigerate, freeze, frost. *Please chill the soda before serving it.* –*adj.* **3.** cold, frosty, cool, icy, frigid, harsh. *He wore a hat in the chill wind.* **Ant. 1.** heat, warmth. **2.** warm, heat. **3.** warm, balmy, hot.

chilly *adj.* cold, frigid, cool, icy, frozen, harsh. *No one wanted to swim in the chilly water.* **Ant.** warm, hot, balmy.

chimney *n.* smokestack, flue. *We watched the smoke curl out of the chimney and join the clouds.*

chisel *vb.* **1.** sculpt, carve, shape, engrave, form. *The artist chiseled a totem from the large tree.* –*n.* **2.** blade, gouge, knife, edge. *The sculptor used a chisel and mallet.*

chivalrous *adj.* polite, courtly, mannerly, noble, virtuous. *Giving up your bus seat to an elderly rider is a chivalrous thing to do.* **Ant.** obnoxious, loutish, discourteous.

chivalry *n.* honor, gallantry, valor, courtesy, courtliness, heroism. **Ant.** cowardice, rudeness, dishonor.

choice *n.* **1.** selection, option, alternative, possibility, pick. *The theater gave us a choice between five different movies.* **2.** decision, wish, preference, judgment. *It's your choice whether or not you study for the test.* *–adj.* **3.** fine, superior, supreme, prime, first-rate. *He only buys the choice cuts of meat.* **Ant. 2.** force, coercion. **3.** inferior, poor.

choke *vb.* **1.** strangle, smother, suffocate, gasp, drown. *The man died after choking on a piece of meat.* **2.** block, stop, plug, obstruct, impede, clog. *Thick jungle choked the trail.* **Ant. 2.** unclog, unplug.

choose *vb.* decide, determine, select, prefer, like, pick, elect. *The players will choose a team captain on Saturday.* **Ant.** discard, reject, refuse.

choosy *adj.* selective, picky, fussy, exacting, discriminating, finicky. *The choosy feline would eat nothing but sushi.* **Ant.** undiscriminating, easy-to-please.

chore *n.* **1.** job, duty, task, errand, assignment. *Taking the trash out is one of my chores.* **2.** burden, trouble, nuisance, bother, annoyance, problem. *It's such a chore to walk to school every day.* **Ant. 2.** pleasure, enjoyment, delight.

chorus *n.* choir, chorale group, glee club, ensemble, singing group. *The chorus belted out a heavenly song in three-part harmony.*

christen *vb.* baptize, name, title, dub, designate. *The boatyard was scheduled to christen the new boat next Saturday.*

chronic *adj.* continual, endless, persistent, habitual, recurrent, established. *He suffers from chronic asthma.* **Ant.** infrequent, occasional, unusual.

chronicle *n.* **1.** record, history, story, biography, account, diary, narrative. *The medicine man recited a chronicle of the tribe.* *–vb.* **2.** report, record, document, log, register. *The reporter chronicled the events that led up to the catastrophe.*

chronological *adj.* sequential, ordered, in order, consecutive, serial, successive, dated. *The teacher asked us to put every student's birthday in chronological order.* **Ant.** random, casual, haphazard.

chubby *adj.* fat, chunky, tubby, overweight, lumpy, plump, pudgy. *We all tend to get a little chubby after holiday meals.* **Ant.** thin, skinny, slight.

church *n.* cathedral, chapel, sanctuary, temple, tabernacle. *They went to church on Easter Sunday.*

WORD SEARCH

baptism, area reserved for: *baptistery*
basin for baptism: *font*
bench: *pew*
bishop, of: *cathedral*
Buddhist: *pagoda*
confession booth in Catholic church: *confessional*
congregation's area: *nave*
crucifixion scenes, statuary: *calvary*
district: *parish*
house of clergy: *parsonage, rectory*
Jewish: *synagogue*
Muslim: *mosque*
platform or table: *altar*
preaching platform: *pulpit*
storage room for clergy apparel: *vestry*
tower: *belfry, steeple*
window, arched: *lancet*

churn *vb.* stir, swirl, agitate, whisk, beat, whip. *In the old days, we had to churn our own butter.*

chutzpah *n.* nerve, courage, guts, brassiness, boldness, audacity. *You need a lot of chutzpah to give a speech in front of ten thousand people.* **Ant.** timidity, cowardice, fear.

cigar *n.* stogie, corona, panatella, (slang) smoke, cheroot, Havana. *Many people don't care for the smell of a cigar.*

cigarette *n.* butt, (slang) smoke, (slang) coffin nail. *Cigarette smoking reduces lifespans significantly.*

cinch *vb.* belt, bind, girdle, clasp, fasten, latch. *She cinched her belt tighter.*

cinders *n.* ashes, coals, embers, clinkers, slag. *Unfortunately, the old barn was burned to cinders and we had to rebuild.*

circle *n.* **1.** hoop, ring, disk, wheel, orbit, circuit. *Covered wagons used to form circles for protection against attack.* –*vb.* **2.** loop, ring, enclose, surround, revolve. *Please circle those answers which you got wrong.* **Ant. 1.** square, rectangle, triangle.

circuitous *adj.* roundabout, circular, meandering, indirect, rambling. **Ant.** direct, straight.

circular *adj.* **1.** round, spherical, globular, disklike. *Pie dishes are always circular.* –*n.* **2.** advertisement, ad, flier, insert, handbill, brochure. *The newspaper was stuffed with advertising circulars.*

circulate *vb.* **1.** distribute, spread, disperse, pass, flow. *Turn on a fan to circulate the air.* **2.** visit, wander, travel, tour, journey. *The hostess circulated among her guests.* **Ant. 1.** keep, hold, retain. **2.** stop, stay.

circumspect *adj.* cautious, leery, wary, careful, guarded, apprehensive. *When he spied the pit bull, the mailman became noticeably circumspect.* **Ant.** bold, fearless, incautious.

circumstance *n.* happening, event, episode, fact, incident, occurrence, case. *The man died under suspicious circumstances.*

circumstantial *adj.* incidental, inconsequential, inconclusive, indirect, insignificant, speculative. *A criminal usually cannot be convicted through circumstantial evidence alone.* **Ant.** central, significant, important.

circus *n.* tent show, big top, exhibition, performance, extravaganza, hippodrome. *You never know what kind of spectacle you'll see at the circus.*

WORD SEARCH

arena: *ring*
laborer: *rouster, roustabout*
peripheral attraction: *sideshow*
procession: *caravan*

citadel *n.* fortress, fort, stronghold, bastion, safehold. *The walls of the ancient citadel were three feet thick.*

citation *n.* **1.** charge, penalty, ticket, writ, warrant. *The police gave her a citation for jaywalking.* **2.** honor, award, decoration, medal, recognition. *He received a citation for his outstanding work.* **3.** quotation, quote, reference, documentation, passage, mention. *Be sure to list the sources for all citations in your paper.*

citizen *n.* native, national, resident, member, subject. *Only citizens are allowed to vote.* **Ant.** alien, foreigner, nonresident.

city *n.* metropolis, urban center, municipality, megalopolis, downtown, community, urban sprawl. *You can see the lights of the city from outer space.*

WORD SEARCH

districts: *borough, business district, ghetto, residential district, ward*
official: *alderman, councilor, mayor*

city hall *n.* municipal building, town hall, city center, courthouse. *We had to get our fishing license at city hall.*

civic *adj.* community, municipal, metropolitan, civil, urban. *It is your civic duty to vote.*

civil *adj.* **1.** nonmilitary, civilian, public, secular, citizen. *The soldier was tried before a civil rather than military judge.* **2.** kind, mannerly, courteous, polite, pleasant, nice. *He told the two students to stop fighting and be civil to one another.* **Ant. 1.** military, religious. **3.** uncivil, insulting, impolite.

civilian *n.* **1.** nonmilitary person, private citizen, noncombatant. *After leaving the army, he had to get used to being a civilian again. –adj.* **2.** nonmilitary, civil, secular, public, lay. *The soldier put on his civilian clothes when he went into town.* **Ant. 1.** soldier, military person. **2.** military.

civility *n.* politeness, courtesy, respect, consideration, tact, respectfulness. *Despite disliking your cousin you should treat him with civility.* **Ant.** disrespect, impoliteness, rudeness.

civilization *n.* sophistication, progress, development, socialization, refinement, cultivation. *The Babylonians were an ancient culture with a high degree of civilization.* **Ant.** barbarism, savagery.

civilized *adj.* refined, cultured, urbane, educated, advanced, tamed, humanized. *We cannot have a civilized world without laws, ethics and morals.* **Ant.** uncivilized, wild, untamed.

claim *vb.* **1.** state, declare, insist, maintain, profess. *She claims to be descended from royalty.* **2.** take demand, seize, appropriate, request. *Colonists often claimed land belonging to the Indians. –n.* **3.** ownership, grant, deed, title, rights. *My claim to the money I found was denied.* **4.** declaration, assertion, statement, pronouncement, proclamation, avowal. *I don't believe his claim that he climbed Mt. Everest.* **Ant. 1.** deny, repudiate, disavow. **2.** relinquish, renounce, reject. **4.** disavowal, denial, repudiation.

clairvoyant *adj.* **1.** psychic, extrasensory, prescient, perceptive, having a sixth sense, telepathic. *The mystic used her clairvoyant powers to discern the location of the hidden key. –n.* **2.** psychic, mind reader, seer, prophet, sensitive. *The clairvoyant told the detectives where the body could be found.*

clam *n.* mollusk, quahog, cherrystone, littleneck, steamer, seafood. *The new restaurant specializes in fried clams.*

clammy *adj.* wet, moist, dank, damp, slimy, sweaty. *The clammy, overcast weather continued for three more days.* **Ant.** dry, arid, parched.

clamor *n.* **1.** commotion, shouting, noise, uproar, disturbance, loudness. *She went outside to see what the clamor was all about. –vb.* **2.** shout, yell, howl, argue, quarrel. *The small children clamored for attention.* **Ant. 1.** quiet, silence, peacefulness.

clamp *n.* vise, hold, grip, clasp, clip. *I placed the two wooden parts in a clamp and waited for the glue to set.*

clan *n.* band, family, group, gang, association, tribe, fraternity. *Their clan was made up of more than 77 family members.*

clang *vb.* ring, gong, reverberate, bong, toll, peal. *You can hear the church bells clang from a mile away.*

clarify *vb.* explain, define, show, interpret, described, illustrate. *We asked the teacher to clarify the example in our textbook.* **Ant.** confuse, obscure.

clarity *n.* clearness, lucidity, comprehensibility, intelligibility, legibility. *Hemingway's writing was admired for its simplicity and clarity.* **Ant.** fuzziness, distortion, cloudiness.

class *n.* **1.** section, session, lecture, seminar, subject. *Her calculus class starts at noon.* **2.** rank, category, species, group, classification, division, set. *Monkeys belong to a class of animals known as primates.* **3.** position, rank, status, caste, clique, standing, grade. *Most Americans consider themselves part of the middle economic class.* –*vb.* 4. classify, group, rank, label, categorize. *The company classes its new car as a luxury model.*

classic *adj.* 1. model, exemplary, quintessential, vintage, standard, archetypal, best. *The classic car was noted for its many innovations.* 2. representative, conventional, traditional, standard, prototypical. *The new car featured the classic lines of the past.* –*n.* 3. model, masterpiece, masterwork, exemplar, standard, ideal, paragon. *The Chevy Corvette has long been considered a classic.* **Ant.** 1. second-rate, poor, inferior. 2. unconventional, radical. 3. joke, also-ran, lemon.

classification *n.* categorization, grouping, assignment, arrangement, labeling. *Everything must be separated and labeled during classification.*

classified *adj.* secret, top secret, confidential, restricted, private. *The spy was especially nervous whenever she carried classified information.* **Ant.** public, open, unrestricted.

classify *vb.* arrange, rank, class, group, categorize, index, type, organize. *They classified their students by scholastic ability.*

classy *adj.* stylish, elegant, refined, superior, first-class, smart, chic. *She always looked sharp in her classy clothes.* **Ant.** low-class, cheap, unrefined.

clause *n.* provision, article, condition, passage, paragraph, specification. *Before you sign a contract, be sure to read every clause carefully first.*

claw *n.* 1. nail, talon, pincer, hook, spur. *A bear's claws can easily rip open the toughest flesh.* –*vb.* 2. scratch, slash, gouge, gash, rip, tear. *Cats claw each other viciously when fighting.*

clean *vb.* 1. wash, bathe, wipe, scrub, disinfect, neaten. *Will you please clean your hands before dinner?* –*adj.* 2. washed, wiped, spotless, stainless, bathed, sanitized. *I set the table with four clean plates.* 3. unpolluted, healthy, pure, uncontaminated, unspoiled. *One should drink only clean water.* 4. honorable, wholesome, virtuous, moral, upright. *She runs a clean business.* **Ant.** 1. soil, dirty. 2. messy, dirty, soiled. 3. polluted, contaminated, unhealthy. 4. dirty, immoral, unwholesome.

clean-cut *adj.* groomed, neat, clean-shaven, scrubbed, immaculate. *The military requires a clean-cut look.* **Ant.** unkempt, ungroomed, wild.

clear *adj.* 1. transparent, colorless, unclouded, translucent. *The ceramic pots were covered with a clear glaze.* 2. apparent, plain, distinct, evident, conclusive. *It's quite clear he did not know the answer.* 3. open empty, free, unblocked, unhindered. *He made sure the area was clear before firing the rifle.* –*vb.* 4. clarify, explain, enlighten, simplify, unravel. *Has my explanation cleared up the problem?* 5. empty, remove, free, unblock, open, unclog. *The plumber cleared the pipes.* 6. skip, pass, leap, fly over, make. *The high jumper cleared the pole at eight feet.* 7. free, acquit, absolve, exonerate, excuse. *The jury cleared him of all charges.* –*adv.* 8. fully, completely, totally, wholly, altogether. *She threw the ball clear across the field.* **Ant.** 1. muddy, clouded, murky. 2. unclear, perplexing, unapparent. 3. blocked, closed, clogged. 4. confuse, muddle. 5. block, clog, close. 7. accuse, blame.

clearance *n.* authorization, go-ahead, permission, okay, green light, sanction. *The pilot had to wait for clearance to take off.*

clemency *n.* forgiveness, pardon, mercy, kindness, charity. *Roy Bean did not earn the nickname "the hanging judge" by showing clemency.*

clergy *n.* ecclesiastics, ministry, churchmen, men of the cloth, clerics, priesthood. *Members of the clergy gathered before the congregation to lead them in prayer.*

clergyman *n.* ecclesiastic, preacher, priest, minister, cleric, rabbi, pastor, bishop, deacon, prelate. *Your clergyman may offer counseling on spiritual matters.*

WORD SEARCH

abbey's head, female: *abbess*
abbey's head, male: *abbot*
bishop, highest: *archbishop*
black, full-length garment: *cassock*
cape worn by pope, cardinal, bishop: *mozzetta*
Catholic head: *pope*
cloak, bishop's long: *cope*
garments: *vestments*
hat, bishop's: *miter*
home of: *rectory, parsonage, manse*
Islamic leader: *ayatollah*
Jewish leader: *rabbi*
monk's robe: *frock*
mosque's prayer leader: *imam*
pope's assistant: *cardinal*
pope's office and residence: *papacy, the Vatican*
priest's assistants: *acolyte, altar boy*
priest's collar: *clerical collar*
priest's long white robe: *alb*
priest's sleeveless mantle: *chasuble*
school: *seminary*
synagogue prayer leader: *cantor*

clerk *n.* salesman/woman, associate, cashier, teller, employee, bookkeeper. *The clerk helped me find the shoe department.*

clever *adj.* intelligent, sharp, witty, bright, shrewd, skillful. *She is clever enough to think her way out of difficult situations.* **Ant.** unintelligent, dumb, slow.

cliché *n.* trite line, banality, tired line, overused expression, platitude. *A cliché is a word, phrase or description used so often that it has lost its impact.* **Ant.** original, fresh line.

client *n.* customer, buyer, patron, shopper, protégé. *The stockbroker has several clients whose accounts he oversees.* **Ant.** seller, dealer, vender.

clientele *n.* clients, customers, regulars, patrons, business, followers. *My clientele consists of adventure-seeking millionaires.*

cliff *n.* ledge, overhang, overlook, precipice, drop-off, bluff, palisade. *It's not a good idea to camp out at the edge of a cliff.*

climate *n.* **1.** weather, clime, temperature, atmosphere. *Southern California has a sunny climate.* **2.** tone, attitude, feel, spirit, character. *The climate of the meeting was friendly.*

climax *n.* **1.** crisis, culmination, peak, summit, top. *The story's climax came when the giant trapped Jack.* –*vb.* **2.** culminate, top, intensify, peak, complete, terminate. *The argument climaxed in a fistfight.* **Ant. 1.** anticlimax, bottom. **2.** diminish, lessen, continue.

climb *vb.* **1.** scale, rise, ascend, lift, top, march, plod. *My friend and I climbed to the top of the hill.* –*n.* **2.** ascent, scaling, incline, elevation, march, plod. *The climb to the top was difficult.* **Ant. 1.** descent, sink. **2.** descent, dip.

clinch *vb.* **1.** establish, settle, complete, fix, secure. *Our volleyball team clinched the championship with its final win.* **2.** fasten, attach, bind, secure, grip, seize. *He clinched the buckle on his backpack.*

clincher *n.* closer, deathblow, finishing touch, capper, culmination. *The clincher was the seller's agreement to guarantee the house for a year.*

cling *vb.* stick, adhere, clasp, grip, hold fast, endure. *Lint tends to cling to my black sweater.*

clinic *n.* dispensary, infirmary, treatment facility, sick bay, medical center. *We got our flu shots at the local clinic.*

clique *n.* gang, club, circle, sorority, fraternity, set, crowd, faction. *He wanted to be part of the popular clique.*

cloak *n.* 1. cape, overcoat, shawl, jacket, coat. *The Phantom of the Opera wore a thick black cloak.* 2. screen, veil, mask, cover, disguise, shroud. *She used the bushes as a cloak behind which she changed her clothes.* –*vb.* 3. cover, hide, conceal, veil, screen, disguise. *The spy cloaked her identity.* **Ant.** 3. reveal, uncover, expose.

clock *n.* timepiece, chronometer, timer, watch, hourglass. *The clock is ten minutes fast.*

clod *n.* clodhopper, oaf, dolt, ignoramus, idiot, moron, halfwit. *Some social clod broke into the room and threw water balloons at everyone.* **Ant.** intellectual, scholar, socialite.

clog *n.* 1. blockage, jam, occlusion, clot, stoppage, congestion. *We need a plunger to get this clog out of the toilet.* –*vb.* 2. block, jam, occlude, clot, stop, congest. *Too much toilet paper will clog the toilet.*

clone *n.* double, copy, duplicate, match, remake, offshoot. *My clone will grow up to look exactly like me.*

close *vb.* 1. shut, secure, lock, block, bar, seal. *They close the store at nine o'clock.* 2. complete, finish, end, conclude, cease. *The festival closes with a big parade.* 3. join, attach, merge, connect, unite. *The doctor closed the wound with stitches.* 4. approach, near, surround, envelop, box. *The police closed in on the thief.* –*adj.* 5. near, nearby, imminent, impending, forthcoming. *When the snow begins to melt, spring is close.* 6. friendly, familiar, special, loyal, faithful. *I have two really close friends.* 7. similar, alike, resembling, comparable, parallel. *His hair color is close to the color of mine.* 8. tight, firm, secure, solid, careful. *The mother kept a close watch on her children.* –*n.* 9. end, ending, conclusion, termination, finish. *The environmentalist looked forward to the close of hunting season.* –*adv.* 10. near, nearby, closely, nigh, nearly. *Stand close to me.* **Ant.** 1. open, unlock, unbar. 2. open, begin, start. 3. open, separate. 5. far, distant. 6. cold, unfriendly, distant. 7. dissimilar, uneven, unequal. 8. loose, weak, careless. 9. start, beginning, opening. 10. far.

close call *n.* narrow escape, near miss, cliffhanger, (slang) close shave, photo finish. *The broken candle didn't cause a fire, but it was definitely a close call.*

close-minded *adj.* narrow-minded, unreceptive, blind, dogmatic, intolerant. *It's great to have your own opinions, but don't be close-minded.* **Ant.** open-minded, flexible, receptive.

closet *n.* storage, storeroom, walk-in closet, compartment, wardrobe, locker, cupboard. *Hang your jacket up in the closet, please.*

closure *n.* completion, culmination, conclusion, ending, fulfillment, tying up loose ends. *The couple had fought bitterly in the past but were now seeking closure.*

clot *vb.* coagulate, congeal, thicken, coalesce, set. *Blood tends to clot less efficiently when you're taking aspirin.*

clothing *n.* clothes, apparel, attire, dress, (slang) garb, (slang) duds. *Styles of clothing change decade by decade.*

cloud *n.* vapor, fog, haze, billow, overcast, moisture, nebula. *Storm clouds approached from the west.*

WORD SEARCH

bands and ripples: *cirrocumulus, mackerel sky*
fair weather: *cumulus, stratocumulus*
feathery: *cirrus*
gray, shapeless and full of rain: *nimbostratus*
layer, low and continuous: *stratus*
piece broken off by wind: *rack*
referring to: *nubilous*
sky-covering veils: *cirrostratus*

study of: *nephology*
swiftly moving patch of a storm cloud: *scud*
thunder and lightning producer: *thunderhead*

cloudy *adj.* 1. overcast, gloomy, dark, foggy, gray. *The sky is so cloudy that it looks like it may rain.* 2. vague, unclear, confused, uncertain, foggy. *My understanding of the problem is rather cloudy.* **Ant.** 1. clear, light. 2. clear, understandable, certain.

clout *n.* power, influence, (slang) pull, weigh, say, friends in high places. *The mayor has a lot of clout in his home town.*

clown *vb.* 1. joke, jest, play, fool, ridicule. *When she gets bored she often clowns in class.* –*n.* 2. buffoon, joker, jester, fool, comic. *He's such a clown in front of groups of people.*

club *n.* 1. group, gang, organization, league, team, society. *She likes skiing, so she joined the ski club.* 2. lodge, center, facility, haunt, hall, joint. *My friend and I play tennis at the sports club.* 3. bat, stick, hammer, cudgel, baton, mallet. *She used a club to drive off the vicious dog.* –*vb.* 4. whack, batter, bash, bat, hit, beat. *Chimpanzees tried to club the cheetah with sticks.*

clue *n.* 1. evidence, trace, hint, sign, suggestion, idea. *I haven't a clue as to where they went.* –*vb.* 2. suggest, intimate, hint, reveal, advise. *Clue me in as to what you want for your birthday.*

clump *n.* mass, bunch, cluster, lump, clod, thicket. *The police found the thief hiding behind a clump of bushes.*

clumsy *adj.* bungling, awkward, ungainly, bumbling, uncoordinated. *Colts are clumsy because of their long legs.* **Ant.** graceful, agile.

cluster *n.* 1. group, clump, collection, band, gathering, pack, mass. *Our galaxy is part of a large cluster that includes many other galaxies.* –*vb.* 2. gather, mass, group, collect, assemble. *We seem to have a lot of exams clustered around our vacation week.* **Ant.** 2. scatter, disperse.

clutter *n.* jumble, mess, litter, disorder, hodgepodge, disarray. *Clutter covered the apartment from one room to the next.* **Ant.** order, tidiness.

coach *n.* 1. manager, leader, director, trainer, teacher, instructor. *The basketball coach made his players run ten laps.* –*vbs.* 2. train, instruct, tutor, teach, guide, drill. *She coached him on what to say in court.* **Ant.** 1. student, player. 2. learn, study.

coagulate *vb.* clot, congeal, thicken, curdle, gel, cake. *The blood began to coagulate and the wound was quickly sealed.* **Ant.** liquefy, thin.

coalesce *vb.* fuse, merge, integrate, blend, combine, consolidate. *The party made everyone happy and the two warring factions gradually began to coalesce.* **Ant.** separate, divide, break apart.

coalition *n.* alliance, confederacy, union, partnership, faction, league. *We formed a coalition to fight city hall.*

coarse *adj.* 1. rough, bristly, uneven, scraggly, gnarled, rugged. *My grandfather has a coarse beard.* 2. rude, uncivilized, impolite, crude, ill-mannered. *The arrogant prince considered the peasants a coarse lot.* **Ant.** 1. soft, smooth, even. 2. polite, mannered, refined.

coast *n.* 1. seashore, shore, beach, shoreline, seaside. *A pirate ship was sighted off the coast.* –*vb.* 2. glide, skim, drift, slide, flow. *The bicyclist stopped pedaling and simply coasted along.*

coat *n.* overcoat, jacket, topcoat, windbreaker, outerwear, slicker. *Is it cold enough to wear a coat?*

WORD SEARCH

collar of black velvet, characterized by: *Chesterfield*

formal: *tuxedo*
plaid, short woolen: *mackinaw*
sport coat: *blazer*
spy: *trench coat*
toggle-buttoned: *toggle coat, duffel coat*

coax *vb.* persuade, urge, influence, charm, steer. *Do you think you can coax your mother into letting me stay the night?* **Ant.** force, intimidate, pressure.

cocaine *n.* drug, narcotic, controlled substance, crack, (slang) snow, (slang) blow, (slang) coke. *Cocaine is an addictive and dangerous drug.*

cockpit *n.* cabin, flight deck. *The airplane's cockpit was confined but cozy.*

cocktail *n.* mixed drink, cocktail, aperitif, (slang) hard stuff. *A bartender must know how to make dozens of different cocktails.*

coddle *vb.* mollycoddle, baby, spoil, indulge, pamper. *Grandparents love to coddle their grandchildren.* **Ant.** abuse, hurt, neglect.

code *n.* system, law, regulation, statute, principle, ethic. *She lives her life by a strong code of honor.*

coerce *vb.* pressure, force, intimidate, compel, frighten, harass. *The soldier coerced the prisoner into revealing the enemy's location.* **Ant.** ask, request, coax.

coffee *n.* beverage, drink, brew, dark, roast, French roast, decaf, (slang) Joe, (slang) java. *Many people have a difficult time getting moving in the morning without coffee.*

WORD SEARCH
boiled milk, with: *café au lait*
brew and filter: *percolate*
caffe latte with almond syrup: *café amaretto*
caffe latte with chocolate: *café mocha*
espresso capped with foamed milk: *cappuccino*
espresso with steamed milk, capped with foamed milk: *caffe latte*
half-size cup of espresso: *demitasse*
steam-pressed coffee served in a small cup: *espresso*
stimulant: *caffeine*

coffin *n.* casket, box, catafalque, sarcophagus, pall. *The vampire rose from his coffin and made a pot of coffee for the long night ahead.*

coherent *adj.* clear, intelligible, lucid, understandable, comprehensible, rational. *The drunk was staggering and barely coherent.* **Ant.** incoherent, unintelligible, irrational.

cohort *n.* colleague, associate, sidekick, collaborator, ally, buddy. *My cohort, Joseph, is helping me with the paperwork.*

coil *n.* **1.** ring, spiral, loop, roll, reel, circle. *He carries a coil of wire in his tool kit.* –*vb.* **2.** wind, twist, loop, roll, reel. *Please coil the rope when you're through using it.*

coin *vb.* create, originate, devise, invent, mint, issue. *She coined a new word to describe her computer's unusual malfunction.*

coincide *vb.* agree, concur, correspond, fit, accord, match. *My version of the accident doesn't coincide with the other driver's story.* **Ant.** disagree, differ, conflict.

coincidence *n.* accident, chance, fate, happening, fluke. *It was pure coincidence that we named our sons the same thing.* **Ant.** plan, intent.

cold *n.* **1.** chill, chilliness, frost, iciness, coolness, frigidity. *The cold of the night air made our breath fog up.* **2.** illness, sickness, virus, fever, bronchitis. *He went to the doctor about his bad cold.* –*adj.* **3.** chilly, chilled, cool, cooled, shivering, wintry, icy. *Put on a sweatshirt if you're cold.* **4.** unresponsive, indifferent, uncaring, unfriendly, chilly. *He gave me a cold greeting.* –*adv.* **5.** absolutely, completely, thoroughly, perfectly, precisely. *She had the material down cold.* **Ant. 1.** warmth, heat. **3.** hot, scorching, sweltering. **4.** warm, feeling, friendly. **5.** incompletely, imperfectly.

cold sore *n.* blister, herpes, canker sore, ulceration. *I don't want to eat anything salty because of the cold sore on my lip.*

coliseum *n.* stadium, arena, amphitheater, bowl, theater. *The concert was scheduled to be held in the coliseum.*

collaborate *vb.* team up, work together, cowrite, coauthor, cocreate, collude. *They decided to collaborate on a book.*

collapse *vb.* **1.** sink, deflate, crumble, disintegrate, fall, fail. *The hot-air balloon collapsed when a tree gashed a hole in it.* –*n.* **2.** breakdown, downfall, failure, exhaustion, disintegration. *The building was so old that no one was surprised by its collapse.*

collateral *n.* security, insurance, warranty, guarantee, bond, surety. *The bank requires some form of collateral for any loan it provides.*

colleague *n.* peer, associate, coworker, teammate, ally, companion, partner. *Her colleagues threw her a going-away party at work.* **Ant.** enemy, rival, competitor.

collect *vb.* **1.** gather, assemble, amass, accumulate, compile. *She collects postage stamps.* **2.** raise, acquire, obtain, receive, solicit. *You may collect $200 when you pass "Go."* **3.** compose, calm, control, recover, prepare. *I was so upset that I had to collect myself before I could speak.* **Ant. 1–2.** scatter, disperse, distribute.

collection *n.* assemblage, assembly, gathering, group, hoard. *Have you seen my coin collection?*

collective *adj.* joint, shared, common, united, unified, mutual. *It will take everyone's collective efforts to end pollution.* **Ant.** individual, separate, divided.

college *n.* school, university, academy, institution, campus, alma mater, seminary. *The college runs on a two-semester schedule from September to May.*

WORD SEARCH

advanced degree: *postgraduate degree, master's, doctorate*
brotherhood: *fraternity*
charge: *tuition*
course: *minor, major, elective*
graduates: *alumni*
graduate with honors (from lowest to highest): *cum laude, magna cum laude, summa cum laude*
grounds: *campus, quad, quadrangle*
housing: *dormitory*
male/female mixed: *coed*
official: *dean, regent, provost, registrar*
sisterhood: *sorority*
teacher: *professor*

collide *vb.* crash, hit, smash, strike, bump. *The two skiers were not injured when they collided on the slopes.*

collision *n.* crash, impact, accident, contact, encounter, meeting. *The large asteroid broke apart in its collision with the Moon.*

cologne *n.* perfume, fragrance, scent, toilet water. *The man in the elevator was wearing so much cologne, we could hardly breathe.*

colony *n.* settlement, outpost, dependency, satellite, community, province, possession. *They left the motherland and formed a new colony.*

color *n.* **1.** tint, shade, hue, tone, coloration, tinge. *What color do you plan to paint your bike?* –*vb.* **2.** tint, tinge, dye, stain, paint. *He colored his hair so the gray wouldn't show.*

colorful *adj.* **1.** brilliant, multicolored, gaudy, vivid, bright. *The circus performers wore colorful costumes.* **2.** eccentric, odd, unique, quaint, lively. *The old woman who sleeps on the park bench is a rather colorful character.* **Ant. 1.** pale, faded, dull. **2.** boring, uninteresting, colorless.

colossal *adj.* huge, large, gigantic, massive, mammoth, immense, enormous, mighty. *King Kong was a colossal ape.* **Ant.** small, tiny, little.

column *n.* pillar, support, post, pier, caryatid, shaft, monument. *The roof was held up by classical columns.*

coma *n.* unconsciousness, stupor, oblivion, catalepsy, vegetative state. *After being knocked unconscious, the accident victim lapsed into a long-term coma.*

comatose *adj.* unconscious, insensate, stuporous, cataleptic, unresponsive, in a vegetative state. *He remained in the hospital in a comatose state for three months.* **Ant.** conscious, awake, aware.

comb *vb.* groom, brush, dress, untangle, style, fix. *Comb your hair before you go to school.*

combat *n.* **1.** battle, fight, war, confrontation, conflict, dispute. *He was wounded in combat.* *–vb.* **2.** fight, battle, confront, attack, oppose, resist. *Some members of the community tried to combat drug use in their neighborhood.* **Ant. 1.** peace, truce, harmony.

combine *vb.* mix, scramble, join, blend, fuse, merge, unite, mingle. *To make chocolate milk, one must combine milk with cocoa.* **Ant.** scatter, separate, divide.

combustible *adj.* flammable, inflammable, ignitable, explosive, burnable, incendiary. *Gasoline and dry kindling are a combustible combination.* **Ant.** fireproof, fire retardant.

combustion *n.* burning, blazing, ignition, incineration, fire, oxidation. *The gas fumes were so thick that even the slightest spark would cause sudden combustion.*

come *vb.* **1.** move, approach, go toward, near, advance. *Come over here so I can show you how it's done.* **2.** show up, arrive, appear, turn up, materialize. *Do you think the package will come today?* **3.** occur, happen, chance, befall, transpire. *Halloween comes on October 31.* **4.** issue, arise, spring, emanate, originate. *She comes from France.* **5.** cover, reach, attain, go, extend. *These socks come all the way up to my knees.* **Ant. 1.** go, leave, depart.

comeback *n.* **1.** resurgence, rebirth, return, revival, rally. *The star basketball player had a remarkable comeback after his surgery.* **2.** retort, reply, rejoinder, riposte, repartee, answer.

comedian *n.* comedienne, comic, joker, humorist, cutup, stand-up, entertainer, clown. *The comedian had the audience in stitches.*

comedy *n.* humor, farce, hilarity, (slang) shtick, slapstick, lampoon, parody, satire. *The Three Stooges offered their own weird brand of slapstick comedy.*

comet *n.* celestial body, iceball, orbital debris, cosmic wanderer. *Many comets orbit the Sun but may take decades to return to view.*

comfort *vb.* **1.** cheer, ease, relieve, console, reassure. *She comforted the crying child.* *–n.* **2.** relief, reassurance, cheer, sympathy, satisfaction, consolation. *It was a comfort to know I could depend on my friends.* **3.** luxury, plenty, contentment, happiness, pleasure, enjoyment. *The queen and king lived in great comfort.* **Ant. 1.** irritate, annoy, upset. **2.** displeasure, trouble, worry. **3.** poverty, sorrow, discomfort.

comfortable *adj.* **1.** relaxed, restful, contented, untroubled, calm. *I felt comfortable talking to him, although I had only known him for a short time.* **2.** luxurious, pleasant, cozy, soft, pleasing, snug. *The chairs at school are not very comfortable.* **Ant. 1.** uncomfortable, anxious. **2.** uncomfortable, unpleasant.

comforter *n.* quilt, blanket, cover, bedspread. *I was nice and warm underneath the comforter.*

comical *adj.* humorous, funny, amusing, witty, entertaining. *It was a comical moment when the cat fell into the trash can.* **Ant.** sad, tragic, somber.

command *vb.* **1.** order, tell, demand, instruct, direct, charge. *She commanded her dog to sit.* **2.** control, head, direct, supervise, manage, rule. *She commands the city's police department.* –*n.* **3.** order, instruction, request, rule, directive, charge. *The knights obeyed the queen's commands.* **4.** control, authority, leadership, domination, power, regulation. *The general has one thousand soldiers under his command.* **Ant. 1.** beg, ask, plead.

commander *n.* leader, boss, captain, chief, head, director, (slang) head honcho. *The commander ordered us to put down our arms.*

commanding *adj.* powerful, dominating, imposing, imperious, formidable, authoritative. *The general had a commanding demeanor, even when he was tired.* **Ant.** passive, weak, deferential.

commemorate *vb.* memorialize, observe, honor, celebrate, remember. *Where it is legal, many people commemorate Independence Day by setting off firecrackers.* **Ant.** forget, dishonor, neglect.

commence *vb.* begin, start, initiate, launch, embark, undertake. *The meeting will commence at noon.* **Ant.** end, finish, terminate, conclude.

commencement *n.* beginning, opening, start, inauguration, genesis, onset. *The 1990s marked the commencement of the Internet age.* **Ant.** ending, closing, termination.

commend *vb.* praise, applaud, honor, compliment, celebrate, approve. *I must commend you on your beautiful speech.* **Ant.** criticize, condemn, disapprove.

commendable *adj.* praiseworthy, laudable, exemplary, excellent, admirable, meritorious. *Her work with the local charity office was commendable.* **Ant.** despicable, horrible, bad.

commendation *n.* praise, pat on the back, tribute, acclaim, approval, credit, (slang) brownie points. *He received a commendation for his heroics.* **Ant.** disapproval, demotion, criticism.

commensurate *adj.* equal, proportionate, corresponding, to scale, fitting. *The manager said that the pay scale was commensurate with one's experience.* **Ant.** disproportionate, inconsistent, divergent.

comment *vb.* **1.** remark, state, discuss, mention, express. *My grandfather always comments on how tall I have grown.* –*n.* **2.** remark, statement, mention, observation, explanation. *I was offended by her comment about the weight I have gained.*

commentator *n.* reporter, observer, pundit, analyst, reviewer, critic, news anchor. *The commentator reported that NASA would again delay the launch.*

commerce *n.* business, trade, traffic, industry, exchange. *That truck line is engaged in interstate commerce.*

commercial *adj.* **1.** business, mercantile, monetary, for profit, trade, industrial. *The commercial section of town is always bustling with activity.* –*n.* **2.** advertisement, ad, spot, plug, pitch. *There are too many commercials on television today.*

commission *n.* **1.** board, task force, council, committee, delegation. *The commission will require 30 days to investigate the charges.* **2.** fee, percentage, payment, compensation, share, cut.

commit *vb.* **1.** perform, do, execute, produce, enact, effect, pursue. *He was accused of having committed a serious crime.* **2.** promise, pledge, obligate, swear, bind. *Everyone must commit to bringing something for the party.*

committee *n.* board, commission, council, delegation, panel, task force. *A committee was formed to assess the city's long-term land management plan.*

common *adj.* **1.** typical, normal, usual, frequent, customary, habitual. *It's quite common for football players to get hurt.* **2.** mutual, communal, public, collective, joint. *A common wall separates the two properties.* **3.** plain, simple, average, unknown, ordinary, obscure. *No one listened to him because he was just a common foot soldier.* **4.** cheap, mean, low, vulgar, coarse, rude. *Her language was filled with common expressions she had heard on the streets.* –*n.* **5.** square, green, park, quad, mall. *Students gathered on the university common to hear the speeches.* **Ant. 1.** unusual, unique, uncommon. **2.** individual, personal. **3.** uncommon, special, extraordinary. **4.** cultured, refined.

commonly *adv.* usually, ordinarily, generally, normally, regularly. *She commonly goes to the beach on sunny weekends.* **Ant.** rarely, infrequently, never.

common sense *n.* sound judgment, savvy, intelligence, smarts, horse sense, wisdom, experience. *You don't need a college degree to drive a car, you just need common sense.* **Ant.** ignorance, stupidity, idiocy.

commotion *n.* uproar, frenzy, turmoil, disturbance, upheaval. *There was a commotion in the chicken coop when the fox got in.* **Ant.** calm, peacefulness, quiet.

communal *adj.* shared, mutual, cooperative, collective, common, community. *The neighborhood had a communal arrangement and shared everything.* **Ant.** private, sole, individual.

commune *n.* cooperative, kibbutz, collective, community. *Some people live in a commune and share everything equally.*

communicate *vb.* **1.** speak, talk, converse, confer, correspond. *My pen pal and I communicate through letters.* **2.** impart, share, inform, show, announce, teach. *The old sage communicated her wisdom to the young novice.*

communication *n.* **1.** conversation, speaking, talking, writing, rapport. *The problem stemmed from a lack of communication within the office.* **2.** message, dispatch, communique, notification, bulletin. *There has been no communication from the city since the earthquake.*

communism *n.* collectivism, Bolshevism, marxism, socialism. *Communism is a social system in which property is owned by the state.*

community *n.* society, city, neighborhood, town, state, population, group. *The farmer lived in a rural community.*

commute *vb.* **1.** travel, journey, drive, bus, shuttle. *Most of our students commute to school.* **2.** reverse, reduce, change, diminish, decrease. *A governor has the power to commute a criminal's sentence.*

compact *adj.* **1.** small, compressed, packed, dense, crowded. *She drives a compact car.* –*vb.* **2.** pack, condense, press, stuff, cram, compress. *A machine in our kitchen compacts the trash.* –*n.* **3.** agreement, contract, deal, treaty, pledge. *Management and labor signed a compact giving the workers a raise.* **Ant. 1.** large, loose. **2.** loosen, unpack, scatter.

companion *n.* **1.** friend, comrade, protector, attendant, partner, mate. *A dog makes a good companion.* **2.** accessory, complement, accompaniment, supplement, appendage. *This thin volume is the companion to the required text.* **Ant.** 1. enemy, stranger.

company *n.* 1. corporation, business, firm, partnership, establishment. *My sister works for a large engineering company.* 2. group, assembly, gathering, party, team, unit, circle. *These actors are from a local theater company.* 3. visitors, friends, guests, relatives, callers. *He's having company over for dinner tonight.* 4. companionship, fellowship, friendship, association, intimacy. *I don't feel comfortable in the company of strangers.* **Ant.** 3. host, hostess. 4. loneliness, solitude, isolation.

comparable *adj.* alike, similar, equal, corresponding, uniform, akin. *Their work output was comparable, yet he was paid a higher salary.* **Ant.** incomparable dissimilar, unlike.

compare *vb.* 1. relate, contrast, balance, review, consider. *It's best to compare prices before buying a car.* 2. match, equal, rival, resemble, equate. *A frozen pizza cannot compare to a homemade one.*

comparison *n.* analogy, match, parallel, resemblance, similarity. *There's no comparison between reading about spaceflight and actually voyaging through outer space.* **Ant.** difference, dissimilarity, discrepancy.

compassion *n.* sympathy, tenderness, kindliness, mercy, feeling, love, concern, caring, warmth. *Mother Teresa was a woman of great compassion who devoted her life to helping the poor and sick.* **Ant.** indifference, coldness, unconcern.

compassionate *adj.* sympathetic, tender, kind, merciful, loving. *A compassionate person never turns away anyone truly in need.* **Ant.** uncompassionate, unfeeling, heartless.

compatible *adj.* agreeable, agreeing, cooperative, harmonious, compliant. *Fortunately, my roommate and I are quite compatible.* **Ant.** incompatible, clashing, disagreeing.

compel *vb.* force, oblige, pressure, coerce, drive, urge, impel. *Losing my job compelled me to make some changes in my lifestyle.* **Ant.** stop, deter, prevent, block.

compensation *n.* 1. payment, settlement, damages, coverage, satisfaction. *He was awarded $1,000 in compensation for his work-related injury.* 2. pay, salary, wages, earnings, remuneration. *She doesn't receive adequate compensation for the work she performs.*

compete *vb.* contest, contend, strive, fight, vie, challenge, combat. *Two actors are competing for the starring role.* **Ant.** quit, surrender, yield.

competent *adj.* able, trained, skillful, dependable, capable, experienced, qualified. *Make sure you go to a competent dentist.* **Ant.** incompetent, unskilled, unqualified.

competition *n.* 1. contest, tournament, meet, game, match, bout. *The Olympics are a competition for athletes from all over the world.* 2. competitor, rival, challenger, opponent, adversary. *My competition in the wrestling tournament is said to be quite good.* 3. rivalry, opposition, struggle, contention, conflict. *There is a fierce competition between the top two students in our class.* **Ant.** 2. ally, comrade, teammate. 3. teamwork, cooperation.

competitive *adj.* rivaling, (slang) dog-eat-dog, aggressive, ambitious, combative, (slang) cutthroat. *A competitive nature is required to win at sports.*

competitor *n.* rival, opponent, challenger, adversary, contestant, contender. *Our competitor cut his prices, so we must follow suit.* **Ant.** partner, ally, teammate.

compile *vb.* assemble, gather, collect, accumulate, amass. *The coach compiled a list of his players' phone numbers.*

complacent *adj.* smug, self-satisfied, contented, confident, self-assured, secure. *As soon as you adopt a complacent attitude, your competitors will rise up and beat you.* **Ant.** insecure, uneasy, dissatisfied.

complain *vb.* criticize, protest, object, gripe, lament, whine. *The diner complained that his meat was undercooked.* **Ant.** approve, compliment, praise.

complaint *n.* 1. criticism, objection, condemnation, reprimand, rebuke. *She lodged a complaint with the hotel manager about the lack of towels.* 2. illness, sickness, disorder, infirmity, ailment. *The man suffered from several serious complaints.* **Ant.** 1. praise, approval, compliment. 2. remedy, cure.

complement *n.* 1. addition, companion, counterpart, accessory, supplement. *Your choice of wine was a fine complement to the dinner.* 2. quota, limit, totality, entirety, maximum. *The ship left, although its full complement of crew members was not on board.* –*vb.* 3. supplement, complete, perfect, fulfill, satisfy. *The illustrations really complement this book.* **Ant.** 3. ruin, lessen, diminish.

complete *vb.* 1. finish, conclude, end, perform, accomplish, fulfill. *She completed her homework five minutes before class started.* –*adj.* 2. entire, total, whole, full, absolute, uncut. *We bought the complete set of thirty volumes.* 3. thorough, in-depth, perfect, extensive, exhaustive, widespread. *The mechanic gave my car a complete tune-up.* **Ant.** 1. start, begin, initiate. 2. incomplete, partial, deficient. 3. spotty, partial, superficial.

complex *adj.* 1. complicated, difficult, involved, perplexing, intricate. *Mathematicians often use complex equations.* –*n.* 2. maze, network, system, labyrinth, structure. *We wandered around the mall complex.*

complexion *n.* color, tone, pigmentation, hue, cast, tinge. *She was a beautiful girl with a lovely complexion.*

complicate *vb.* confuse, muddle, involve, entangle, mix up. *Getting a second job will complicate your life.* **Ant.** simplify, clarify, disentangle.

complicated *adj.* complex, involved, difficult, intricate, hard, elaborate. *The musician played a very complicated piece of music.* **Ant.** easy, simple, uninvolved.

compliment *n.* 1. praise, acclaim, approval, commendation, congratulation, flattery. *She received several compliments on her excellent performance in the play.* –*vb.* 2. praise, acclaim, commend, congratulate, applaud. *He complimented her on her win in the track meet.* **Ant.** 1. disapproval, insult, complaint. 2. insult, condemn.

complimentary *adj.* 1. praising, approving, flattering, admiring, favorable. *His new book received complimentary reviews.* 2. free, gratis, gratuitous, donated. *I have two complimentary tickets for tonight's movie.* **Ant.** 1. uncomplimentary, unflattering, disapproving.

comply *vb.* follow, conform, observe, obey, satisfy, fulfill, consent. *My brother did not comply with my parents' rules.* **Ant.** disobey, evade, disregard, oppose.

compose *vb.* 1. create, conceive, produce, write, devise. *She composed a new play for her theater group.* 2. comprise, constitute, embody, form, fashion. *Copper and tin are the elements that compose bronze.* 3. settle, calm, quiet, soothe, arrange. *Try to compose yourself before you tell him the tragic news.* **Ant.** 1. destroy, demolish, take apart. 3. excite, upset, agitate.

composite *adj.* 1. combined, joined, mixed, blended, consolidated, melded. *The composite materials in sugar cookies are butter, flour and sugar.* –*n.* 2. combination, blend, mixture, consolidation, compound, amalgam. *Brass is a composite of copper and zinc.*

composition *n.* 1. arrangement, layout, content, formulation, makeup, organization. *The design was a highly formal composition of diverse elements.* 2. writing, creation, work, opus, draft, piece, thesis, dissertation. *He revised and polished his composition until it was flawless.*

composure *n.* self-control, calm, quiet, assurance, poise, dignity. *The angry man regained his composure and quietly sat down.* **Ant.** passion, agitation, excitement.

compound *vb.* 1. increase, augment, intensify, worsen, complicate. *You'll only compound the problem if you put it off any longer.* 2. mix, blend, mingle, combine, devise, make. *A pharmacist is a person who compounds medicinal drugs.* –*adj.* 3. multiple, complex, composite, complicated, mixed. *She has sustained a compound fracture of the left arm.* –*n.* 4. combination, composite, blend, mixture, fusion. *Brass is a compound made of copper and zinc.* **Ant.** 1. lessen, decrease, reduce. 2. separate, divide, isolate. 3. simple, elemental, unmixed.

comprehend *vb.* understand, grasp, perceive, appreciate, discern, follow. *I cannot comprehend why you like green beans.* **Ant.** misunderstand.

comprehensive *adj.* complete, thorough, sweeping, broad, extensive, inclusive. *The final exam will be a comprehensive test covering the entire year's work.* **Ant.** partial, incomplete, specialized.

compress *vb.* shrink, tighten, contract, compact, condense, shorten. *Compress your speech until only the relevant points remain.* **Ant.** expand, lengthen, draw out.

comprise *vb.* include, embrace, contain, cover, involve, enclose. *Eggs, toast and orange juice comprise my typical breakfast.*

compromise *n.* 1. bargain, arrangement, agreement, understanding, accommodation, settlement. *We made a compromise wherein each of us would pay for half.* –*vb.* 2. agree, accommodate, settle, negotiate, exchange, yield. *Why don't we compromise by staying at your house the first night and mine the second?* 3. risk, endanger, jeopardize, embarrass, discredit, expose. *By blurting out my identity, you have compromised my safety.* **Ant.** 1. argument, quarrel, disagreement. 2. argue, dispute, disagree. 3. support, strengthen, guard.

compulsion *n.* drive, impulse, obsession, force, desire, need. *He had a compulsion to check the stove burners three times before leaving his house.*

compulsive *adj.* obsessive, crazed, driven, uncontrollable, irresistible. *Her need to wash her hands ten times a day was rather compulsive.*

compulsory *adj.* enforced, required, necessary, mandatory, unavoidable, binding. *School is compulsory until the age of sixteen.* **Ant.** optional, elective, voluntary.

compute *vb.* calculate, determine, figure, add, ascertain. *Astronomers have computed the distance from the Earth to the Sun to be 93 million miles.*

computer *n.* calculator, data processor, (slang) number cruncher, microprocessor, PC, laptop, mainframe. *My computer added the figures in a fraction of the time my brain could have.*

WORD SEARCH

auxiliary device: *peripheral*

calculating and accounting program, rows and columns: *spreadsheet*

CDs to MP3 format, digitize: *rip*
CDs, write data or music onto: *burn*
chip: *microprocessor, integrated circuit*
choice list: *menu*
clean up hard drive: *defrag*
cursor manipulator: *mouse*
data storage: *memory*
data storage medium, portable: *disk, diskette, floppy disk, cartridge, CD-ROM*
eight bits of memory space: *byte*
enthusiast, expert: *hacker*
fail or freeze up: *crash, hang up*
fear or hatred of: *cyberphobia*
icon of a real person: *avatar*
infiltrating outside program that disrupts functioning: *virus, worm*
insidious software secretly loaded to spy on user's computing habits: *spyware; parasite; scumware*
linking computers, international network: *Internet, World Wide Web*
linking of several computers: *network*
messages sent over Internet between computers: *E-mail*
moving imagery to protect against permanently burning images on screen: *screen saver*
network of computers, in-house: *internet*
paper printout of data: *hard copy*
partial truths, computer intelligence that recognizes: *fuzzy logic*
physical components: *hardware*
pointer: *cursor*
portable version: *laptop; PDA (personal digital assistant)*
programs: *software*
receive data from other computers: *download*
sent data to other computers: *upload*
start up: *boot up*
storage area, temporary: *clipboard*
superimposed screen within screen: *window*
teaching aid: *tutorial*
telephone hookup device: *modem*
tray for CD: *caddy*
TV-like screen: *monitor*

comrade *n.* friend, partner, associate, teammate, companion, colleague. *The lost explorer's comrades searched the jungle for him.* **Ant.** enemy, stranger, outsider.

con *vb.* rip off, swindle, trick, cheat, defraud, deceive. *The thug tried to con the old lady out of her fortune.*

conceal *vb.* hide, camouflage, cover, mask, disguise, bury, cloak, veil. *He concealed the Easter eggs in different parts of the room.* **Ant.** reveal, expose, show.

concealment *n.* covering, masking, disguising, hiding, concealing. *The newspaper exposed the official's concealment of his dealings with terrorists.* **Ant.** showing, disclosure, presentation.

concede *vb.* **1.** accept, agree, grant acknowledge, recognize, allow. *Because of the article you showed me, I must concede that you were correct.* **2.** surrender, relinquish, resign, yield, transfer, deliver. *The champion conceded her title to this year's winner.* **Ant. 1.** reject, disagree, deny. **2.** win, defeat.

conceited *adj.* arrogant, vain, snobbish, smug, egotistical. *The conceited athlete thought he was the best in the state.* **Ant.** humble, modest, unassuming.

conceive *vb.* **1.** create, form, generate, initiate, produce, originate. *She conceived a plan to expand her company's business.* **2.** imagine, think, suppose, dream, consider, comprehend. *I can't conceive of a place I would rather be than in the mountains.*

concentrate *vb.* **1.** study, ponder, think, contemplate, analyze. *I must concentrate hard to memorize all these dates.* **2.** center, converge, focus, gather, collect, localize. *They concentrated* *their search in the local neighborhood.* **3.** condense, compress, reduce, consolidate, thicken. *Please concentrate the soup by adding less water than the directions call for.* **Ant.** **1.** ignore, neglect. **2.** scatter, spread. **3.** dilute, weaken.

concentration *n.* **1.** thought, attention, regard, study, application. *This problem requires my total concentration.* **2.** collection, mass, gathering, centralization, convergence. *There's a concentration of motels on the edge of town.* **Ant.** **1.** inattention, disregard. **2.** scattering, dispersion.

concept *n.* idea, theory, thought, notion, belief, conjecture. *My concept of your house is different now that I've seen it.*

conception *n.* birth, beginning, origination, genesis, inception, start. *Life begins at conception.* **Ant.** death, end, finish.

concern *n.* **1.** matter, affair, interest, business, consideration. *My brother's whereabouts is not my concern.* **2.** care, attention, regard, worry, anxiety. *Local citizens listened with concern to news of the approaching tornado.* –*vb.* **3.** disturb, distress, worry, perturb, bother, pain. *His continual sickness concerned his father.* **4.** affect, interest, involve, influence. *This talk does not concern you.* **Ant.** **2.** coldness, indifference, disregard.

concert *n.* **1.** performance, show, symphony, festival, recital. *Fans jumped onto the stage at the rock concert.* **2.** agreement, harmony, closeness, unity, accord. *The troop of soldiers marched in concert.* **Ant.** **2.** discord, disagreement, separation.

concession *n.* compromise, yielding, conceding, granting, capitulation, compromise. *We had to make several concessions before the other party would sign the contract.*

concise *adj.* short, brief, condensed, compact, abridged, consolidated. *The newscaster gave a concise review of the day's news.* **Ant.** lengthy, long, wordy, rambling.

conclude *vb.* **1.** finish, complete, end, terminate, halt, stop. *The performer concluded her show with her most popular song.* **2.** reason, decide, determine, deduce, assume, suppose. *When he didn't show up, we concluded that he didn't want to come.* **Ant.** **1.** begin, start, continue.

conclusion *n.* **1.** finish, close, completion, termination, end. *At the movie's conclusion, the audience applauded.* **2.** decision, judgment, determination, understanding, observation. *Have you reached a conclusion about what college you're going to attend?* **Ant.** **1.** beginning, start, opening. **2.** uncertainty, indecision.

conclusive *n.* convincing, irrefutable, definitive, clinching, incontestable, undisputable. *The detective had gathered conclusive evidence against the alleged murderer.*

concoct *vb.* devise, formulate, create, whip up, invent, fabricate. *The witch began to concoct a strange-smelling brew.*

concoction *n.* formulation, creation, invention, fabrication, recipe, compound, brew. *The concoction in the pot bubbled and steamed.*

concourse *n.* walkway, mall, passage, boulevard, promenade. *We were impressed by how large the airport's concourse was.*

concrete *n.* **1.** cement, pavement, asphalt, mortar. *Outside Mann's Chinese Theater, the concrete contains the handprints of movie stars.* –*adj.* **2.** direct, actual, real, physical, solid, conclusive. *She said she needed concrete proof before she would believe that ghosts exist.* **Ant.** **2.** vague, theoretical, obscure.

concur *vb.* agree, assent, consent, approve, ratify. *I must concur with your mother's decision not* *to let you attend the party.* **Ant.** disagree, disapprove, reject.

concussion *n.* shock, agitation, blow, jolt, shaking, pounding, impact. *The concussion from the earthquake shook the whole building.*

condemn *vb.* **1.** denounce, reproach, criticize, rebuke, accuse. *The media condemned the police officer for his cruel treatment of the suspect.* **2.** sentence, convict, doom, judge, ban. *The tribal council condemned the thief to twelve years as an outcast.* **Ant. 1.** applaud, admire, praise. **2.** acquit, free, excuse.

condemnation *n.* denunciation, reproach, criticism, rebuke, disapproval. *The Soviet Union received worldwide condemnation for its shooting down of an airliner.* **Ant.** praise, approval, acclaim.

condensation *n.* **1.** abridgement, summary, shortening, reduction, compression. *I only had time to read a condensation of* War and Peace. **2.** moisture, dew, liquefaction, sweating. *Condensation obscured our view through the window.*

condense *vb.* compress, reduce, shorten, compact, consolidate, trim. *He condensed his ten-page report down to five pages.* **Ant.** expand, increase, enlarge.

condescending *adj.* arrogant, supercilious, imperious, snobbish, patronizing, haughty. *He looked down his nose at us in condescending manner.* **Ant.** respectful, unpretentious, down-to-earth.

condiment *n.* flavoring, sauce, seasoning, sauce, spice, relish. *The restaurant had ketchup and mustard and eleven other condiments.*

condition *n.* **1.** state, shape, form, situation, status. *Our school's dirt racetrack was in poor condition after the heavy rains.* **2.** problem, illness, ailment, complaint, sickness. *The elderly woman suffers from an arthritic condition of the bones.* **3.** term, provision, restriction, demand, requirement, limitation. *I told her a secret, on the condition she tell it to no one else.* –*vb.* **4.** train, shape, practice, prepare, coach, equip. *The athletes conditioned themselves for the upcoming competition.*

condolence *n.* sympathy, support, compassion, comfort, pity, understanding. *We sent our condolences to the bereaved family.* **Ant.** congratulations, rejoicing.

condom *n.* contraceptive, prophylactic, protection, (slang) rubber, sheath. *Condoms help prevent pregnancies as well as sexually transmitted diseases.*

condone *vb.* pardon, forgive, excuse, disregard, justify, approve. *Her parents refused to condone her late-night partying.* **Ant.** criticize, condemn, disapprove.

conducive *adj.* promoting, instrumental, leading to, ancillary. *Chewing your food carefully is conducive to easy digestion.* **Ant.** adverse, counter.

conduct *n.* **1.** behavior, manner, actions, habits, performance. *His wild conduct at the formal dinner annoyed the host.* **2.** operation, management, administration, direction, supervision. *The manager's job is to oversee the conduct of all operations.* –*vb.* **3.** behave, carry, direct, handle, manage, supervise. *We were pleased that you conducted yourself in a mature manner.* **4.** lead, guide, convoy, escort, usher. *An usher conducted us to our seats.*

conductor *n.* maestro, band leader, director; leader, guide. *The conductor lead the orchestra with his body language as well as his baton.*

confederate *n.* ally, partner, associate, accomplice, colleague. *The criminal's confederates were also arrested.* **Ant.** opponent, enemy, rival.

confer *vb.* **1.** discuss, converse, consult, deliberate, talk. *I conferred with my dentist about getting braces for my teeth.* **2.** award, present, give, grant, bestow. *The queen conferred the highest honor of her realm on the brave warrior.* **Ant. 2.** revoke, withhold, deny.

conference *n.* meeting, discussion, talk, session, deliberation, interchange. *Our teachers have conferences with their students' parents each semester.*

confess *vb.* admit, concede, acknowledge, own, disclose, reveal. *He confessed to his roommate that he broke the stereo.* **Ant.** hide, deny, withhold.

confession *n.* admission, acknowledgment, telling, disclosure, assertion, revelation. *The prisoner made a written confession.* **Ant.** denial, disclaimer, repudiation.

confidant *n.* friend, intimate, buddy, pal, alter ego, sidekick. *I tell my confidant things that I would never tell anyone else.*

confide *vb.* tell, disclose, reveal, divulge, entrust, trust, impart. *I confide my secrets to my best friend.*

confidence *n.* **1.** self-reliance, sureness, certainty, assurance, conviction. *It takes confidence to run for political office.* **2.** faith, reliance, trust, belief, dependence, conviction. *I have confidence in your ability to pass the test.* **Ant. 1.** uncertainty, self-doubt. **2.** distrust, doubt, suspicion.

confident *adj.* **1.** certain, assured, convinced, sure, optimistic, positive. *I'm confident I can do the job.* **2.** self-assured, bold, daring, fearless, assertive. *My confident friend has no trouble asking people out on a date.* **Ant. 1.** doubtful, uncertain. **2.** hesitant, anxious, insecure.

confidential *adj.* private, secret, classified, restricted, undisclosed. *Only highly trusted employees could look at the confidential report.* **Ant.** open, circulated, public.

configuration *n.* arrangement, structure, shape, figure, conformation, contour. *The constellation of Sagittarius is in the configuration of a giant teapot.*

confine *vb.* **1.** restrict, limit, hold, imprison, cage, constrain, enclose. *The sheep were confined in a pen.* –*n.* **2.** limit, margin, boundary, edge, border. *Inmates were not allowed beyond the confines of the prison yard.* **Ant. 1:** free, loose, liberate.

confirm *vb.* uphold, verify, prove, affirm, establish. *The letter confirmed my worst suspicions.* **Ant.** oppose, contradict, refute.

confiscate *vb.* take, seize, impound, claim, secure, possess. *A teacher confiscated the student's squirt gun.* **Ant.** return, release, deliver.

conflagration *n.* fire, blaze, firestorm, wildfire, inferno, hellfire. *The small fire quickly grew out of control and within minutes became a full-blown conflagration.*

conflict *n.* **1.** fight, battle, struggle, clash, warfare, hostilities, combat. *The conflicts in the Middle East have been going on for years.* –*vb.* **2.** clash, disagree, struggle, contradict, differ. *My views on the environment conflict with his.* **Ant. 1.** peace, settlement, agreement. **2.** agree, concur.

conflicting *adj.* contrary, contrasting, opposing, contradictory, incompatible. *The news bureau refused to run the story because it received conflicting reports from eyewitnesses.* **Ant.** matching, harmonious, compatible.

conform *vb.* obey, follow, comply, observe, adapt, accommodate. *In the corporate world, one must conform to a formal dress code.* **Ant.** differ, disobey, oppose.

conformist *n.* follower, slave to fashion, emulator, copycat, (slang) sheep, (slang) one of the herd. *She was always a conformist, trying hard to please those in the majority.* **Ant.** nonconformist, freethinker, rebel.

confound *vb.* bewilder, confuse, perplex, puzzle, mystify, muddle. *The opponents were on the spot to confound the quarterback with every move.*

confront *vb.* meet, encounter, face, challenge, oppose, tackle, resist. *She confronted her fears by entering the haunted house.* **Ant.** avoid, flee, evade.

confrontation *n.* clash, showdown, challenge, defiance, conflict. *She had a confrontation with her boss involving her request for a raise.*

confuse *vb.* bewilder, puzzle, baffle, perplex, mystify. *The problems in my physics class often just confuse me.* **Ant.** clarify, enlighten, explain.

confusing *adj.* puzzling, obscure, baffling, perplexing, disturbing, disconcerting. *Finding an address in a big city can be confusing.* **Ant.** orderly, clear, simple.

confusion *n.* **1.** bewilderment, puzzlement, mystification, perplexity, disorientation. *His look of confusion told me he didn't understand my explanation.* **2.** turmoil, agitation, disorder, upheaval, disarray, disorganization. *There was a great deal of confusion at the airport due to the construction going on.* **Ant. 1.** clarification, enlightenment, explanation. **2.** orderliness, order, organization.

congeal *vb.* thicken, solidify, set, coagulate, jell, clot. *The sticky fluid quickly began to congeal in the cold air.* **Ant.** thin, become fluid.

congenial *adj.* friendly, pleasant, cordial, sociable, agreeable, affable, convivial. *At the party, everybody was warm and congenial.* **Ant.** unfriendly, standoffish, cold.

congenital *adj.* natal, inborn, innate, genetic, connate, inherent. *Unfortunately, the baby was born with a congenital defect.* **Ant.** acquired, caught.

congested *adj.* plugged, filled, jammed, choked, blocked, crowded, stuffed. *The freeways were congested with traffic.* **Ant.** empty, clear, uncrowded.

conglomerate *n.* company, firm, multinational, chain, partnership. *The conglomerate presided over several subsidiaries overseas.*

congratulate *vb.* compliment, praise, salute, applaud, cheer. *I congratulated him on his recent marriage.* **Ant.** criticize, rebuke, condemn.

congratulation *n.* best wishes, compliments, blessings, praise. *I sent her my congratulations when she graduated from college.* **Ant.** criticism, condemnation, reproach.

congregate *vb.* gather, assemble, mass, meet, collect, group, swarm, cluster. *Several dogs congregated about the fire hydrant.* **Ant.** separate, scatter, disband.

congregation *n.* parishioners, flock, gathering, group, assembly, mass. *The preacher was troubled by his diminishing congregation.*

congress *n.* assembly, senate, legislature, delegation, (in U.S.) House of Representatives, (in U.S.) Capitol Hill. *Congress met to debate the bill.*

WORD SEARCH

influence and persuasion from outside interest groups: *lobbying*
kill or remove bill from consideration: *table*
leader, assistant party: *whip*
leads House of Representatives: *Speaker of the House*
legislation, proposed: *bill*
legislative body, upper: *Senate*
legislative house: *chamber*

meeting of House and Senate: *joint session*
member of: *congressman, congresswoman, senator, representative, legislator, statesman*
persuade member of Congress to vote a certain way, one who tries to: *lobbyist*
speaking area: *floor*
speech, extremely long: *filibuster*

congressman *n.* congresswoman, member of Congress, senator, representative, legislator, statesman, politician. *We wrote to our congressman for help in the matter.*

conjecture *n.* guesswork, guess, speculation, theorizing, supposition, hypothesis, surmise. *They were predicting that it would snow, but it was nothing more than conjecture.*

conjure *vb.* beckon, summon, call forth, raise, invoke, cast a spell, bewitch. *The medium said she could conduct a seance and conjure the dead.*

connect *vb.* **1.** join, unite, attach, bind, couple, link, tie. *A small road connects the two towns.* **2.** equate, relate, identify, associate, correlate. *It took me a while to connect the voice I was hearing to my old friend from elementary school.* **Ant. 1.** disconnect, separate, split. **2.** dissociate, separate.

connection *n.* **1.** junction, union, conjunction, bond, coupling. *The television repairman said the problem was a faulty connection.* **2.** association, relationship, attachment, alliance, relation. *I no longer have any connections with that company.* **Ant. 2.** alienation, separation, detachment.

connive *vb.* scheme, plot, devise, finagle, conspire, wangle. *The thieves began to connive a way to break into the bank.*

connoisseur *n.* aficionado, expert, authority, devotee, epicure, buff, specialist. *He was a connoisseur of fine wines.*

conquer *vb.* overcome, defeat, subdue, master, crush, vanquish, overpower. *Attila the Hun tried to conquer Europe in the fifth century.* **Ant.** lose, fall, surrender.

conqueror *n.* victor, winner, champion, vanquisher, defeater. *Citizens of the defeated city-state were forced to pay tribute to their conquerors.* **Ant.** vanquished, defeated, loser.

conquest *n.* triumph, win, coup, victory, defeat, overthrow. *The dictator would not be satisfied until he had achieved yet another conquest against his opponents.* **Ant.** loss, defeat, destruction.

consecrate *vb.* sanctify, exalt, honor, anoint, hallow, bless. *The clerics said they would consecrate the unearthed tablets.* **Ant.** damn, vilify, curse.

conscience *n.* principles, standards, morals, ethics, scruples. *Doesn't it bother your conscience to lie?*

conscientious *adj.* responsible, reliable, trustworthy, sincere, dependable, dedicated. *She was a conscientious employee who never left before her work was done.* **Ant.** unreliable, irresponsible, undependable.

conscious *adj.* **1.** awake, aware, sensible, thinking, alert. *The doctors said we could visit him when he becomes conscious.* **2.** aware, knowledgeable, knowing, informed, mindful. *Are you conscious of the amount of pollution in our environment?* **3.** deliberate, willful, intentional, planned, purposeful. *We made a conscious effort to notice the shy girl.* **Ant. 1.** unaware, unconscious, asleep. **2.** unaware, unknowing, uninformed. **3.** unintentional, unconscious, accidental.

consecutive *adj.* successive, uninterrupted, continuous, unbroken, sequential. *He hit three consecutive home runs.* **Ant.** interrupted, broken, discontinuous.

consensus *n.* agreement, consent, accord, unanimity, concord. *The council reached a consensus on the date of the election.* **Ant.** disagreement, discord, dissension.

consent *vb.* **1.** agree, allow, accept, grant, approve, permit, sanction. *The actor consented to having his picture taken with me.* –*n.* **2.** agreement, permission, approval, endorsement, assent, leave, sanction. *You need the principal's consent to leave campus.* **Ant.** **1.** disagree, disapprove, refuse. **2.** disagreement, disapproval.

consequence *n.* **1.** aftermath, outcome, result, upshot, development. *All those cavities are the consequence of not brushing properly.* **2.** importance, significance, moment, note, seriousness. *What you do with your life is of no consequence to me.* **Ant.** **1.** source, cause, origin. **2.** unimportance, insignificance.

conservation *n.* preservation, protection, safekeeping, saving, environmentalism, management. *Conservation has saved thousands of acres of wilderness for future generations.* **Ant.** squandering, waste, development.

conservationist *n.* preservationist, environmentalist, environmental activist. *Conservationists long ago saw the need to protect open lands from development.*

conservative *adj.* **1.** right-wing, traditional, nonliberal, conventional, reactionary. *The Republicans are known for their conservative policies.* **2.** cautious, safe, prudent, careful, sparing, wary. *I try to be conservative with my spending.* –*n.* **3.** right-winger, rightist, traditionalist, conventionalist, reactionary. *The city's conservatives did not like the new dance club.* **Ant.** **1.** liberal, progressive, radical. **2.** risky, careless, daring. **3.** radical, liberal, progressive.

conserve *vb.* save, preserve, guard, maintain, protect, safeguard. *The marathon runner conserved her energy for the final mile.* **Ant.** waste, exhaust, consume.

consider *vb.* **1.** study, review, deliberate, contemplate, examine, evaluate. *Why don't you consider my offer and tell me your decision tomorrow?* **2.** judge, view, think, believe, regard, feel. *I consider smoking cigarettes an unhealthy habit.* **Ant.** **1.** disregard, ignore, overlook.

considerable *adj.* **1.** significant, important, noteworthy, great, major, impressive. *Winning the Nobel Peace Prize is a considerable honor.* **2.** large, substantial, abundant, sizable, extensive, massive. *It looked like he had gained a considerable amount of weight.* **Ant.** **1.** unimportant, trivial, minor. **2.** small, scant, meager.

considerate *adj.* thoughtful, kind, sensitive, concerned, tactful. *A considerate woman held the door open for me.* **Ant.** inconsiderate, thoughtless, unkind.

consideration *n.* **1.** thought, attention, study, reflection, regard, examination, deliberation. *I have agreed to your proposal after giving it much consideration.* **2.** thoughtfulness, concern, kindliness, respect, courtesy, regard. *Out of consideration for your neighbors, don't play your music too loud.* **3.** factor, concern, point, aspect, detail, item. *The distance one must drive is an important consideration in deciding which job to take.* **Ant.** **1.** inattention, oversight, omission. **2.** discourtesy, rudeness.

consist *vb.* contain, comprise, involve, include, embody. *My family consists of my mother, my two brothers and myself.*

consistency *n.* **1.** firmness, thickness, texture, composition, density, nature. *The soup had a thin consistency.* **2.** agreement, conformity, harmony, accord, compatibility, unity. *Her taste in movies has no consistency.* **Ant.** **2.** inconsistency, disagreement, incompatibility.

consolation *n.* comfort, solace, sympathy, pity, relief, condolence. *Karen lost the contest, but she was given a prize as consolation.*

console *vb.* comfort, aid, help, support, hearten, cheer. *We took him out for pizza to console him after he didn't get the job he wanted.* **Ant.** hurt, upset, bother, disturb.

consolidate *vb.* join, combine, unite, merge, pool, concentrate. *If we consolidate our efforts, we'll get the job done much faster.* **Ant.** separate, divide, part.

conspicuous *adj.* obvious, plain, visible, apparent, evident, noticeable, prominent. *I was upset because my pimple was so conspicuous.* **Ant.** invisible, concealed, unnoticeable.

conspiracy *n.* plot, scheme, intrigue, treason, deception, trick. *The two generals were involved in a conspiracy to topple the government.*

conspirator *n.* schemer, plotter, engineer, colluder, accomplice, partner in crime. *The three conspirators planned to rob the local bank.*

conspire *vb.* plot, scheme, collude, collaborate, machinate, wangle. *The two evil-doers conspired to take over the world.*

constant *adj.* **1.** unchanging, fixed, even, regular, uniform, steady. *The rower maintained a constant pace.* **2.** continual, nonstop, unbroken, uninterrupted, endless, persistent. *There has been a constant downpour all day.* **3.** devoted, faithful, loyal, dedicated, trustworthy. *The dog has been her constant companion for years.* **Ant.** **1.** changing, irregular, uneven. **2.** infrequent, occasional, erratic. **3.** unfaithful, disloyal, undependable.

constantly *adv.* regularly, continually, frequently, habitually, continuously. *He's constantly losing his car keys.* **Ant.** occasionally, seldom, rarely.

constellation *n.* configuration, formation, cluster, assemblage, array, asterism. *Most people recognize the constellation called the Big Dipper.*

WORD SEARCH

bear, great: *Ursa Major, the Big Dipper*
bear, little: *Ursa Minor, the Little Dipper*
dragon: *Draco*
hunter: *Orion*
lion: *Leo*
southern cross: *Crux*
swan: *Cygnus*
W, big: *Cassiopeia*

constipation *n.* irregularity, straining at stool. *If you have constipation, you should increase your fiber intake and drink more water.*

constituency *n.* electorate, voters, citizens, district, party members, residents. *The governor was exceptionally responsive to his constituency.*

constitution *n.* charter, laws, code, legislation, bill of rights, canon. *A modern society must form some sort of constitution to live by.*

constitutional *adj.* legal, lawful, statutory, chartered, approved. *Their ownership of guns was deemed constitutional.* **Ant.** unconstitutional, illegal, unlawful.

constrain *vb.* restrain, restrict, confine, bind, detain, contain. *We constrained the dog to the pole with a chain.* **Ant.** free, release, loose.

constrict *vb.* **1.** pinch, cramp, bind, squeeze, strangle. *The tight shirt collar constricted my throat.* **2.** obstruct, block, clog, close, congest, choke. *Dead trees constricted the stream.* **Ant.** **1.** loosen, unbind, swell. **2.** unclog, clear, open.

construct *vb.* build, make, create, erect, assemble, form, produce. *She spent all day constructing a treehouse in her backyard.* **Ant.** destroy, demolish, dismantle.

constructive *adj.* useful, helpful, valuable, beneficial, practical, usable. *I hate it when someone tells me they're giving me constructive criticism.* **Ant.** destructive, harmful, worthless.

consult *vb.* talk, confer, discuss, deliberate, counsel. *She and I consulted on the best time for a party.*

consultant *n.* adviser, specialist, professional, mentor, expert, authority. *A consultant was called in to figure out the mess.*

consultation *n.* council, conference, meeting, discussion, deliberation, analysis. *I was having computer troubles, so I called in an expert for a consultation.*

consume *vb.* **1.** absorb, eat, devour, drink, drain, use. *I was so thirsty that I consumed three cans of soda.* **2.** destroy, devastate, demolish, waste, ravage. *Fire consumed the old building.* **Ant. 1.** produce, supply, save. **2.** save, restore.

consummate *adj.* complete, perfect, accomplished, highest, supreme, masterful. *After practicing for 20 years, she became the consummate piano player.* **Ant.** imperfect, incomplete, amateurish.

consumption *n.* use, expenditure, depletion, usage, draining. *Americans drive so much that our national gasoline consumption is huge.* **Ant.** conservation, production, saving.

contact *n.* **1.** touch, connection, meeting, encounter, joining, impact. *The whole world burst into applause when the Apollo landing craft made contact with the Moon's surface.* *–vb.* **2.** communicate with, approach, reach, meet, touch, seek. *Scientists are trying to contact extraterrestrial life.*

contagious *adj.* catching, transmittable, infectious, spreadable, transmissible. *You should not be around someone with the measles, because it is a very contagious disease.* **Ant.** noncontagious, noninfectious.

contain *vb.* **1.** include, hold, carry, bear, retain, embrace. *This bottle contains apple juice.* **2.** restrain, control, check, limit, bind, suppress. *A large cage was used to contain the gorilla.* **Ant. 2.** free, release, loosen.

contaminate *vb.* pollute, poison, foul, soil, taint, defile, corrupt. *Toxic waste from the factory contaminated our drinking water.* **Ant.** clean, cleanse, purify.

contamination *n.* adulteration, fouling, pollution, taint, infection, defilement. *The contamination of our drinking water had been caused by bacteria.*

contemplate *vb.* ponder, consider, meditate, study, deliberate. *Please contemplate my request before answering.*

contemplation *n.* thought, thinking, reflection, deliberation, study. *She reached her decision after much contemplation of the problem.*

contemporary *adj.* modern, late, recent, up-to-the-minute, cutting-edge, new. *Contemporary fashion often borrows from the past.* **Ant.** old, old-fashioned, outdated.

contempt *n.* scorn, hatred, disrespect, revulsion, disgust, distaste, detestation. *I have great contempt for people who hurt others.* **Ant.** respect, admiration, affection.

contemptible *adj.* shameful, low, mean, revolting, dishonorable, offensive. *The way in which he treats his children is contemptible.* **Ant.** admirable, honorable, respectable, praiseworthy.

contend *vb.* **1.** battle, fight, struggle, compete, wrestle, contest. *Two chimpanzees contended for one banana.* **2.** claim, hold, maintain, assert, state, declare. *I still contend there's no way you* *can hike up there in a single day.* **Ant. 1.** surrender, quit, yield. **2.** reject, deny, disclaim.

contended *adj.* pleased, happy, satisfied, content, comfortable. *My teacher was not contented with my paper and asked me to rewrite it.* **Ant.** unhappy, discontented, concerned, irritated.

content *n.* **1.** insides, ingredients, substance, matter, subject. *The contents of the sealed box remain a mystery.* **2.** size, capacity, volume, area, scope, extent. *The container has a three-gallon content.* **3.** satisfaction, happiness, comfort, gladness, pleasure, delight. *She got some content out of knowing her rival had failed.* *–adj.* **4.** satisfied, pleased, delighted, happy, unworried, untroubled. *Are you content with your new apartment?* *–vb.* **5.** please, satisfy, delight, comfort, gladden, pacify. *I tried to content the baby with a lollipop.* **Ant. 3.** discontent, annoyance, displeasure. **4.** dissatisfied, displeased, troubled. **5.** upset, irritate, annoy.

contentious *n.* quarrelsome, antagonistic, argumentative, combative, belligerent. *The contentious couple couldn't stop arguing over who would wash the dishes.* **Ant.** agreeable, harmonious, peaceful.

contest *n.* **1.** competition, meet, tournament, trial, match, game. *I entered a drawing contest.* **2.** fight, battle, encounter, struggle, conflict, clash. *The couple is often engaged in a contest of wills.* *–vb.* **3.** fight, battle, struggle, contend, strive, compete. *Two top executives contested over control of the company.* **4.** challenge, oppose, dispute, argue, counter. *The millionaire's disinherited daughter contested his will.* **Ant. 2.** truce, peace, agreement. **3.** surrender, yield, quite. **4.** acknowledge, accept, adopt.

contestant *n.* competitor, entrant, participant, contender, rival. *There were more than fifty contestants in the chess tournament.*

context *n.* framework, setting, situation, circumstance, surroundings. *The problem arose from her hearing my statement out of context.*

contingency *n.* possibility, chance occurrence, act of God, eventuality, emergency, accident. *When hiking in the wilderness, it pays to be prepared for any contingency.*

contingent *adj.* depending, provisory, subject to, conditional. *Whether we go to Bermuda or not is contingent upon getting adequate vacation time from work.*

continual *adj.* **1.** unending, unbroken, nonstop, uninterrupted, ceaseless. *A continual stream of toxic waste entered the ocean from the factory.* **2.** constant, frequent, habitual, regular, repeated. *Their fighting is a continual thing.* **Ant. 1.** broken, erratic, fitful. **2.** infrequent, occasional.

continue *vb.* **1.** extend, proceed, progress, project, resume. *This road continues for fifty more miles before reaching the ocean.* **2.** remain, endure, stay, last, abide. *How long will you continue at your current job?* **Ant. 1.** discontinue, stop, pause. **2.** resign, quit, leave.

continuous *adj.* unbroken, unending, uninterrupted, constant, endless. *This spring provides us with a continuous water supply.* **Ant.** broken, disconnected, infrequent.

contort *vb.* twist, bend, distort, knot, deform. *The basketball player had to contort himself to get into the compact car.* **Ant.** straighten, smooth, unbend.

contour *n.* shape, outline, figure, profile, lines, silhouette. *My car has a distinctly box-like contour.*

contraband *adj.* illegal, illicit, unlawful, prohibited, black market, bootleg. *The detective uncovered a number of contraband items from Cuba.*

contraceptive *n.* birth control device, prophylactic, protection, condom, diaphragm, (slang) the pill.

contract *n.* **1.** agreement, arrangement, deal, understanding, compact, bargain. *The baseball player signed a contract to play for two years.* –*vb.* **2.** engage, agree, pledge, promise, undertake, vow. *A carpenter contracted to rebuild our kitchen cabinets for $500.* **3.** assume, acquire, develop, incur, catch. *She contracted malaria in the jungle.* **4.** compress, shorten, reduce, tighten, decrease, constrict. *I could feel my heart contract in fear.* **Ant. 2.** refuse, withdraw. **3.** evade, dodge, avoid. **4.** lengthen, expand, increase.

contraction *n.* tightening, condensing, compression, reduction, recession. *The pregnant woman in the waiting room was having contractions.*

contradict *vb.* refute, deny, differ, counter, challenge, oppose, dispute. *I must contradict you when you say the world is flat.* **Ant.** confirm, verify, support.

contradictory *adj.* contrary, opposing, disagreeing, conflicting, different. *We have contradictory views on the topic of disarmament.* **Ant.** similar, comparable, equivalent.

contraption *n.* apparatus, machine, device, (slang) gizmo, rig, appliance, gadget. *He invented a contraption that produced ice on demand.*

contrary *adj.* **1.** against, opposed, opposite, different, other. *Contrary to the advertisement, this cleanser does not remove tough stains.* **2.** disagreeable, stubborn, obstinate, unpredictable, unaccommodating, unfriendly. *Mules are known to be contrary animals.* **Ant. 1.** consistent, similar. **2.** agreeable, friendly, accommodating.

contrast *vb.* **1.** differentiate, deviate, differ, diverge, depart, vary. *Make the lettering light so it will contrast with the dark background.* –*n.* **2.** difference, variation, distinction, divergence, unlikeness. *There was quite a contrast between the owner's mansion and the worker's shack.* **Ant. 1.** compare, relate, resemble. **2.** similarity, resemblance.

contribute *vb.* **1.** give, donate, volunteer, bestow, grant, supply. *Will you contribute money to help save the whales?* **2.** influence, advance, promote, aid, supplement. *The prime minister's death contributed to the nation's downfall.* **Ant. 1.** take, keep, receive. **2.** avert, detract, curb.

contribution *n.* donation, gift, grant, offering, endowment, bestowal. *Would you like to make a contribution to local charity organizations?*

contrite *adj.* sorry, remorseful, repentant, ashamed, regretful, apologetic. *The man who hit my car had a contrite look.* **Ant.** unapologetic, unremorseful, unashamed.

contrition *n.* regret, sorrow, remorse, guilt, shame, repentance. *The toddler's contrition for stealing the last waffle was written all over his tearful face.* **Ant.** self-righteousness, pride, indifference.

contrivance *n.* gadget, device, apparatus, contraption, implement, machine. *The professor claimed that his complicated-looking contrivance was a time machine.*

WORD SEARCH

unnecessarily complex: *Rube Goldberg device*

contrive *vb.* invent, imagine, design, create, plan, improvise. *He contrived an illness to miss a day of school.*

control *vb.* **1.** rule, direct, manage, run, supervise, administer, govern, oversee. *Who really controls the government?* **2.** check, curb, restrain, contain, suppress, leash. *Try to control your anger.* –*n.* **3.** direction, management, supervision, command, regulation, rule. *It's out of my control.* **4.** check, curb, restraint, constraint, damper, block. *Congress must put stronger controls on the spending of government money.* **Ant. 2.** express, release, lose.

controversial *adj.* sensitive, delicate, questionable, debatable, arguable, doubtful. *The new law requiring dogs to wear diapers is highly controversial.* **Ant.** safe, certain, noncontroversial.

controversy *n.* debate, disagreement, dispute, argument, quarrel, strife, contention. *There's controversy surrounding the question of life on other planets.* **Ant.** agreement, harmony, accord.

convalescence *n.* recovery, recuperation, rehabilitation, strengthening, healing. *Expect a long convalescence after breaking a leg.*

convene *vb.* assemble, gather, collect, meet, congregate, rally. *Our Boy Scout troop will convene on Saturday for an awards ceremony.* **Ant.** disperse, disband, scatter.

convenience *n.* handiness, usefulness, advantage, comfort, benefit. *His cabin lacks the convenience of indoor plumbing.* **Ant.** inconvenience, disadvantage, hardship.

convenient *adj.* **1.** fitted, suitable, advantageous, useful, beneficial. *Let's make the appointment at a time that is convenient for you.* **2.** handy, near, nearby, accessible, available. *The neighborhood park is a convenient place for walking my dog.* **Ant. 1.** inconvenient, inappropriate. **2.** remote, inaccessible.

convent *n.* nunnery, abbey, cloister, religious institution. *She joined the convent seeking a spiritual retreat.*

convention *n.* **1.** tradition, custom, habit, rule, orthodoxy, code. *By convention, each speaker would be given twenty minutes to present his or her case.* **2.** conference, meeting, assembly, rally, congress, caucus.

conventional *adj.* normal, usual, traditional, customary, common, proper. *He would like a conventional wedding.* **Ant.** unusual, unconventional, uncommon.

converge *vb.* join, meet, unite, merge, approach, link. *Any two sides of a triangle converge at a single point.* **Ant.** diverge, separate, disperse, part.

conversation *n.* discussion, talk, chat, dialogue, conference. *I had a long conversation with my parents about my failing grades.*

converse *vb.* talk, discuss, chat, speak, communicate, confer. *I wish to converse with you in private.*

conversion *n.* change, metamorphosis, turnaround, transformation, switch, remodeling. *The conversion from garage to two-bedroom apartment was expensive.*

convert *vb.* **1.** turn, change, alter, transform, modify, reshape. *We had to convert our dollars to British pounds when we visited England.* –*n.* **2.** disciple, follower, recruit, believer, proselyte. *The converts were instructed in the teachings of their new religion.*

convey *vb.* **1.** carry, move, transport, transfer, bear, haul, deliver. *Trucks were used to convey the soldiers to their new base.* **2.** communicate, impart, send, tell, reveal, relate. *I spent a lot of time choosing a card that would convey just the right message.*

convict *vb.* **1.** condemn, sentence, blame, judge, doom. *The jury convicted the defendant on one count of murder.* –*n.* **2.** felon, criminal, violator, offender, lawbreaker, prisoner. *The convicts spent their work time making license plates.* **Ant. 1.** acquit.

conviction *n.* **1.** belief, faith, dogma, doctrine, opinion, view. *His conviction was that all people would go to heaven, not just a chosen few.* **2.** assurance, confidence, certainty, fervor. *He stated his opinion with such conviction that it was difficult to doubt him.* **Ant. 2.** doubt, uncertainty, indecision.

convince *vb.* persuade, influence, impress, sway, satisfy, assure. *I tried to convince her that I was telling the truth.*

convoy *vb.* **1.** escort, accompany, lead, conduct, usher, pilot, guide. *Two tugboats convoyed the damaged ship to safety.* –*n.* **2.** escort, guard, cover, protection, group, fleet. *During World War II, ships traveled with convoys to protect themselves from enemy submarines.*

convulsion *n.* spasm, seizure, contraction, throe, attack, tremor. *She had an allergic reaction and went into violent convulsions.*

cook *vb.* prepare, make, concoct, bake, roast, grill, fry. *Whose turn is it to cook dinner tonight?*

cookie *n.* confection, dessert, sweet, baked good, wafer, snap, macaroon. *Many people have an addiction to cookies.*

WORD SEARCH

buttery and crumbly and hailing from Scotland: *shortbread*
chocolate chip, famous: *tollhouse cookie*
coconut-flavored and chewy: *macaroon*
crispy, cinnamon-flavored, textured with oatmeal: *snickerdoodle*
dropped from spoon on to cookie sheet: *drop cookie*
dry, hard cookie flavored with almonds, chocolate, or anise seed: *biscotti*
ginger and molasses, flavored with: *ginger snap, gingerbread man*
hollow shell containing slip of paper with fortune or bit of wisdom: *fortune cookie*
molasses, dark and chewy and flavored with: *molasses cookie*
palm leaf, in the shape of a: *palmier*
sugar, made from brown or confectioner's sugar and sprinkled with granulated: *sugar cookie*

cool *adj.* **1.** chilly, cold, icy, freezing, nippy. *I love cool summer evenings.* **2.** composed, calm, controlled, collected, serene. *It's a rare person who can remain cool during an earthquake.* **3.** unfriendly, distant, indifferent, detached, apathetic. *He's rather cool toward his little sister.* –*vb.* **4.** lose heat, chill, refrigerate, ice, freeze. *My coffee needs to cool before I can drink it.* **5.** calm, moderate, control, dampen, quiet. *It would be best to let your temper cool before you speak to him.* **Ant. 1.** warm, hot, sweltering. **2.** excited, agitated, disturbed. **3.** friendly, attached, warm. **4.** heat, warm. **5.** aggravate, intensify.

cooperate *vb.* collaborate, coordinate, unite, combine, join. *The groups that cooperated the most were the first to finish.* **Ant.** fight, oppose, disagree.

cooperation *n.* participation, collaboration, teamwork, association, help. *I need your cooperation to finish this project on time.* **Ant.** opposition, hindrance, dissension.

coordinate *vb.* harmonize, match, balance, organize, adjust, order, arrange. *I try to buy clothes that coordinate well.* **Ant.** disorganize, jumble, disrupt.

cop *n.* (slang) police officer, peace officer, officer of the law, patrolman, sheriff, deputy. *The cop warned us to slow down or he would give us a ticket.*

See also POLICE.

cope *vb.* manage, control, survive, endure, handle. *She coped really well with the tragedy.*

copious *adj.* heavy, abundant, rich, overflowing, plentiful, lavish. *An editor's job is to cut an amateur writer's copious use of words.* **Ant.** scant, light, sparse.

copulate *vb.* have sexual intercourse, mate, make love, (slang) fool around, breed, sleep with someone. *Some chimpanzees in the wild copulate to relieve stress.*

copy *n.* **1.** reproduction, duplicate, imitation, replica, likeness, representation. *That painting is just a copy of the original.* –*vb.* **2.** imitate, mirror, repeat, mimic, echo, follow. *My little brother copies every movement I make.* **3.** duplicate, reproduce, replicate. *Please copy this report for me.* **Ant. 1.** original, prototype. **2.** invent, originate, develop.

copycat *n.* copier, imitator, impersonator, mimic, emulator, parrot. *When it came to Michael Jordan slam-dunking a basketball, everybody was a copycat.*

cord *n.* string, rope, thread, twine, line. *I need a piece of cord to tie this package.*

cordial *adj.* friendly, warm, gracious, sociable, kindly, pleasant, cheerful. *He was not very cordial to his girlfriend's former boyfriend.* **Ant.** unfriendly, cold, reserved.

core *n.* center, middle, heart, nucleus, kernel. *How many seeds does the average apple have in its core?*

cork *n.* stopper, plug. *We couldn't pull the cork from the wine bottle without a corkscrew.*

cornerstone *n.* keystone, mainstay, anchor, foundation, base, linchpin. *The right to vote is the cornerstone of democracy.*

corny *adj.* unsophisticated, (slang) hokey, stupid, trite, banal, hackneyed. *The movie was poorly written and too corny for my taste.* **Ant.** sophisticated, intelligent, profound.

coroner *n.* medical examiner, investigator, public officer, doctor, physician. *The coroner was called to examine the corpse.*

corporation *n.* company, enterprise, business, association, firm, partnership. *They both work for the same corporation.*

corpse *n.* cadaver, body, carcass, (slang) stiff, remains, the deceased. *The police located the corpse deep in the woods.*

corral *n.* pen, enclosure, confine. *We rounded up the horses and led them into the corral.*

correct *vb.* **1.** fix, repair, remedy, amend, rectify, right. *Can you correct the malfunction in my computer?* **2.** reprimand, reprove, rebuke, discipline, punish. *He corrected the small child for biting the dog.* –*adj.* **3.** right, exact, accurate, precise, proper, suitable. *You must have the correct change for this vending machine.* **Ant. 1.** ruin, spoil, damage. **2.** praise, compliment, excuse. **3.** wrong, bad, incorrect.

correction *n.* remedy, improvement, alteration, repair, modification, revision. *He typed my name wrong and had to make a correction.*

correspond *vb.* **1.** communicate, write, report, signal. *Although I'm moving away, we can still correspond.* **2.** agree, coincide, match, parallel, equate. *The red dots correspond to our team, the blue dots to the opposing team.* **Ant. 2.** disagree, differ, contrast.

corridor *n.* passageway, hall, hallway, walkway, avenue, lane, route. *The elevators are at the end of this corridor.*

corroborate *vb.* verify, validate, substantiate, confirm, document. *My new employer telephoned my old employer to corroborate the information on my job application.* **Ant.** invalidate, disprove, contradict.

corrode *vb.* erode, consume, deteriorate, disintegrate, rust. *Acid will corrode certain types of metal.*

corrosion *n.* erosion, rust, decomposition, deterioration, breakdown, decay. *Corrosion had worn a large hole in the frame of the old car.*

corrosive *adj.* erosive, caustic, cutting, mordant, acidic, scathing. *Acid is a highly corrosive substance.*

corrugated *adj.* pleated, ridged, wrinkled, creased, furrowed. *Cardboard is often corrugated to increase its strength.* **Ant.** smooth, flat.

corrupt *adj.* **1.** dishonest, immoral, crooked, dishonorable, wicked. *The corrupt police officer took bribes.* –*vb.* **2.** degrade, debase, taint, pollute, poison, blight. *The conservative minister believed rock music corrupts teenagers.* **Ant. 1.** honest, moral, honorable. **2.** improve, redeem, save.

corruption *n.* immorality, dishonesty, fraud, graft, vice, wickedness. *There's too much corruption in our local government.* **Ant.** morality, goodness, honesty, integrity.

cosmetic *adj.* beautifying, enhancing, corrective, decorative, superficial. *Martha wanted to have cosmetic surgery to smooth some of the lines on her face.*

cosmetics *n.* makeup, beauty products, beautifiers, beauty enhancers, preparations. *She applied her cosmetics so thickly that she ended up looking like a clown.*

cosmopolitan *adj.* worldly, urbane, sophisticated, cultured, cultivated, international. *She had traveled around the world and had a distinctly cosmopolitan aura about her.* **Ant.** provincial, small-town, unsophisticated.

cosmos *n.* space, universe, outer space, the great beyond, creation, macrocosm. *Crossing the cosmos at the speed of light would take billions of years.*

cost *n.* **1.** price, charge, expense, value, worth, bill. *The cost of the skis is $1,000.* –*vb.* **2.** damage, harm, injure, hurt, burden. *Dropping out of college has really cost me.*

costly *adj.* expensive, pricey, exorbitant, steep, stiff, high-priced. *Most sports cars are too costly for my budget.* **Ant.** inexpensive, cheap, economical.

costume *n.* outfit, ensemble, attire, uniform, habit, clothing. *She wore a pirate costume to the Halloween party.*

cottage *n.* cabin, bungalow, lodge, hut, shack, hovel. *His parents own a cottage in the country.* **Ant.** mansion, palace, manor.

couch *n.* sofa, divan, davenport, lounge, seating, futon. *All I want to do is stretch out on the couch and take a nap.*

couch potato *n.* Slang. slacker, slug, (slang) lazy-bones, do-nothing, sloth, shirker. *You can be a couch potato but only after your work is finished.*

cougar *n.* mountain lion, puma, panther. *Cougars are stealthy predators.*

cough *vb.* hack, hem, rasp, wheeze, hawk, clear throat. *I left the theater because I had to cough.*

council *n.* committee, board, assembly, panel, directorate, cabinet. *The city council voted to extend the library's hours.*

counsel *n.* **1.** advice, opinion, guidance, recommendation, instruction. *She sought her best friend's counsel on dating.* **2.** attorney, lawyer, adviser, counselor. *Counsel for the defense presented the first witness.* –*vb.* **3.** advise, guide, instruct, recommend, suggest. *I counseled my brother to take easy classes his first year of college.*

counselor *n.* **1.** legal representative, attorney, lawyer, advocate, solicitor, adviser. *He hired a* *counselor to represent him in court.* **2.** guide, adviser, mentor, mental health practitioner, psychologist, psychiatrist, confidant. *She went to a professional counselor for help with her addiction.*

count *vb.* **1.** number, tally, score, total, enumerate. *I counted fifteen people at the dinner party.* **2.** rely, depend, trust, reckon, bank. *You can count on my being there.* **3.** matter, regard, consider, weigh, tell. *Your opinion doesn't count, since you didn't see what happened.* *–n.* **4.** sum, tally, total, numbering, calculation. Do you have a count of the number of cassettes you own?

counter *adv.* **1.** opposite, contrary, contrarily, against. *One normally walks counter to the direction of traffic.* *–adj.* **2.** opposing, rival, different, opposite, conflicting. *The disillusioned soldier went to fight with the counter side.* *–vb.* **3.** return, retaliate, answer, combat, offset. *The boxer countered the punch with a right hook.* *–n.* **4.** tabletop, table, bar, stand, booth. *Please take your purchases to the check-out counter.*

counterfeit *adj.* **1.** fake, forged, imitation, false, bogus. *The bank refused to take the counterfeit money.* *–vb.* **2.** forge, copy, falsify, imitate, duplicate. *He makes his living counterfeiting passports and other legal documents.* *–n.* **3.** copy, reproduction, imitation, forgery, fake. *The dealer refused to buy the painting because she believed it to be a counterfeit.* **Ant.** **1.** genuine, original, authentic.

country *n.* **1.** nation, state, realm, domain, commonwealth. *He visited seven countries when he toured Europe.* **2.** countryside, terrain, territory, land, district. *They hiked for days through forested country.* *–adj.* **3.** rural, rustic, provincial, pastoral, secluded. *My friend just bought a country house.* **Ant.** **3.** city, urban, cosmopolitan.

coup *n.* masterstroke, coup d'état, victory, achievement, exploit, accomplishment. *Frank scored quite a coup by winning three chess matches in a row.*

coup/coup d'état *n.* overthrow, takeover, uprising, power grab, revolution. *The rebels mounted a coup d'état against the government and are now in power.*

couple *n.* pair, duo, twosome, brace. *I'd rather go to the movies as a couple than by myself.*

courage *n.* bravery, valor, daring, spirit, fearlessness, heroism. *It takes courage to say no to drugs.* **Ant.** cowardice, timidity, fear.

courageous *adj.* daring, brave, bold, gallant, fearless, heroic, unafraid. *The courageous woman was the only one willing to enter the cave to look for the lost dog.* **Ant.** cowardly, timid, fearful.

courier *n.* messenger, runner, carrier, emissary, (slang) gofer. *A courier left a package at our door.*

course *n.* **1.** route, path, passage, track, direction, way, approach. *He took the easiest course to success.* **2.** class, lecture, program, seminar, subject. *I signed up for a women's studies course.* **3.** development, progress, advance, flow, progression. *The course of history was changed by the discovery of electricity.* *–vb.* **4.** flow, rush, run, surge, race. *Sweat coursed down her face.*

court *n.* **1.** court of law, halls of justice, judiciary, bench, bar, tribunal. *We decided to settle the matter in small claims court.*

court *vb.* woo, pursue, date, take out, curry favor with, cajole. *Sandy had wanted to court Sam for more than a year before working up the courage to ask him out.* **Ant.** reject, shun, ignore.

WORD SEARCH

action against another party: *suit*
arrest order: *warrant*
break temporarily from proceedings: *adjourn, recess*

cases to be heard, schedule of: *docket*
decision: *verdict*
disrespect in court: *contempt of court*
formal document charging one with a crime: *indictment*
general jurisdiction court: *superior court*
guard: *bailiff*
hearing of charges and entry of plea: *arraignment*
highest U.S. court: *Supreme Court*
informal appearance before judge: *hearing*
inquiry by: *inquest*
judge's private room: *chambers*
judge's seat: *bench*
jury member: *juror*
jury that evaluates accusations before trial: *grand jury*
jury unable to decide: *hung jury*
negotiate plea, to: *plea bargain*
order by: *injunction*
party defending against claim for damages: *defendant, litigant*
party filing claim for damages: *plaintiff, litigant*
punishment for damages above and beyond actual loss: *punitive damages*
recorder of proceedings: *court stenographer, court reporter*
statement given by witness before trial: *deposition*
trial voided due to legal oversight or abuse: *mistrial*
witness seat during testimony: *witness stand*

courteous *adj.* polite, gracious, kindly, mannerly, thoughtful, considerate. *The courteous host introduced me to all his guests.* **Ant.** discourteous, impolite, inconsiderate, rude.

courtship *n.* dating, wooing, pair bonding, wining and dining, romance, engagement. *Their courtship lasted only a month before they decided to get married.*

cove *n.* bay, inlet, anchorage, bight, estuary, lagoon. *We brought the boat into the cove to escape the storm.*

covenant *n.* agreement, promise, contract, compact, pledge, pact. *The covenant forbid anyone from erecting a fence over six feet high.*

cover *vb.* **1.** coat, mantle, envelop, spread, overlay. *During cold winter nights, we cover ourselves with thick quilts.* **2.** shield, shelter, protect, house, defend, guard. *The canopy covered us from the sun.* **3.** disguise, conceal, hide, screen, cloak. *He tried to cover his embarrassment.* **4.** describe, investigate, study, report, recount. *My freshman geology class covers just the basics.* **5.** replace, substitute, double, alternate, relieve. *The backup pitcher covered for her until she got over the flu.* **6.** journey, travel, traverse, cross, pass. *I can normally cover five hundred miles in a single day's driving.* –*n.* **7.** top, lid, wrapper, roof, blanket, layer, jacket. *The trash can was so full I couldn't get the cover on.* **8.** disguise, camouflage, pretense, screen, cloak. *Superman used his Clark Kent identity as a cover.* **9.** shelter, concealment, protection, refuge, hiding. *The tree gave us cover from the sun.* **Ant.** **1.** expose, uncover, remove. **2.** expose, reveal. **3.** expose, reveal, unmask. **4.** omit, delete, pass over.

covert *adj.* hidden, masked, disguised, secret, stealthy. *She made covert glances at the boy sitting beside her.* **Ant.** overt, apparent, obvious.

cover-up *n.* concealment, evasion, closeting, burial, cooking the books, masking. *The company attempted a cover-up after their pollution record was revealed.* **Ant.** revelation, exposure, show.

covet *vb.* desire, wish, long for, hunger for, crave, envy. *He coveted a fast sports car.* **Ant.** reject, decline, spurn.

cow *n.* bovine, ruminant, heifer, calf, Holstein, guernsey, bull, animal. *The cow contentedly chewed its cud.*

WORD SEARCH
barn: *stable, byre*
chew cud: *ruminate*
milk gland: *udder*
regurgitated and rechewed food: *cud*
straw, hay, winter feed: *fodder*

cowardice *n.* fearfulness, faintheartedness, spinelessness, fear, fright. *Cowardice is a bad trait for a soldier to have.* **Ant.** bravery, courage, fearlessness.

cowardly *adj.* timid, uncourageous, fearful, fainthearted, scared. *In "The Wizard of Oz," the cowardly Lion searches for courage.* **Ant.** brave, fearless, courageous, bold.

cowboy *n.* rancher, cowpoke, cowpuncher, drover, cattle herder, bronco buster. *Cowboys must be well versed in stopping stampedes.*

WORD SEARCH
breeches, leather: *chaps, leggings*
burn mark that identifies ownership of cattle: *brand*
competition: *rodeo*
gathering of wandering cattle: *roundup*
hat: *Stetson*
rope: *lasso, lariat*
steal someone else's cattle: *rustle*
unbranded cow: *maverick*

cower *vb.* tremble, cringe, quail, quake, shrink, grovel. *The young boy cowered behind a rock when he saw the bear approaching.*

coy *adj.* modest, bashful, shy, shrinking, demure, blushing. *She was always coy with boys until she got to know them.* **Ant.** boisterous, loud, assertive.

coyote *n.* coy dog, canine, scavenger, carnivore, omnivore, mammal. *The coyote is sneaky and smart and will eat almost anything.*

cozy *adj.* snug, warm, comfortable, relaxing, sheltered, pleasant, homey. *We stayed at a cozy little inn on the beach.* **Ant.** cold, uncomfortable, unpleasant.

crabby *adj.* grouchy, touchy, testy, irritable, moody, nasty. *I woke up in a very crabby mood this morning.* **Ant.** sweet, happy, good-natured.

crack *vb.* **1.** break, split, burst, snap, fracture, splinter. *My glasses cracked when I stepped on them.* **2.** snap, clap, pop, crackle, beat, slap. *The cowboy cracked his whip at the wild mustang.* –*n.* **3.** burst, snap, bang, shot, pop, explosion. *We heard the crack of a hunter's rifle.* **4.** fissure, crevice, split, break, fracture. *We noticed there was a crack in the building's foundation.* **5.** joke, jest, wisecrack, quip, insult. *He made a crack about my new haircut.*

crackpot *n.* **1.** crank, (slang) nut, crackbrain, (slang) screwball, eccentric, made scientist. *Every person with a new idea is a crackpot until proven otherwise.* –*adj.* **2.** crazy, crackbrain, eccentric, (slang) nutty.

craft *n.* **1.** ability, proficiency, skill, artistry, talent. *His model airplane was built with great craft.* **2.** trade, occupation, work, job, profession. *Cabinetmaking is a difficult craft to learn.* **3.** deception, cunning, trickery, deceit, guile. *She used craft in trying to get the elderly man to sell his house.* **4.** vessel, boat, ship, plane, spaceship. *His yacht is a beautiful craft.* **Ant.** **1.** inability, unskillfulness, incompetency. **2.** frankness, openness, honesty.

craftsman *n.* artisan, artist, smith, wright, master, technician. *The craftsman perfected a new method of wood carving.*

crafty *adj.* shifty, sly, deceitful, scheming, tricky, cunning, crooked. *The Joker in "Batman" is a crafty villain.* **Ant.** honest, straightforward, direct.

cram *vb.* stuff, pack; jam, crowd, ram, squeeze. *She crammed all her clothes into one suitcase.* **Ant.** unpack, empty, remove.

cramp *n.* **1.** spasm, contraction, convulsion, twitch, seizure. *He experienced abdominal cramps after eating the garlic and anchovy pizza.* **2.** restraint, obstruction, hindrance, damper, control. *Lack of money has put a cramp in her formerly extravagant lifestyle.*

crane *n.* hoist, lift, derrick, davit, boom, heavy machinery. *The crane was capable of lifting a truck.*

cranky *adj.* *See* CRABBY.

crap *n.* Slang. **1.** (vulgar) excrement, feces, dropping, dung, poop, stool, guano. *Unfortunately, the dog left a crap in front of the mailbox again.* **2.** junk, trash, garbage, refuse, schlock. *Your room is a mess because it is loaded down with useless crap.* **3.** nonsense, (slang) bull, (slang) baloney, bunk, untruth, lie. *The shoplifter said he intended to pay for his items but the merchant knew that was crap.*

crappy *adj.* Slang. lousy, junky, sub-par, inferior, worthless, trashy. *A broken tree branch makes for a really crappy baseball bat.* **Ant.** superior, excellent, great.

crash *vb.* **1.** smash, bump, collide, hit, plow. *The skier crashed into a tree.* **2.** wreck, demolish, batter, destroy, break, shatter. *I crashed my car.* –*n.* **3.** bang, blast, crack, clatter, explosion. *We heard a distant crash of thunder.* **4.** collision, accident, pileup, wreck, smash. *He got hurt in the car crash.*

crass *adj.* insensitive, rude, crude, tacky, uncouth, unrefined, vulgar. *Burping at the table is considered crass.* **Ant.** sensitive, polite, courteous.

crater *n.* pit, craterlet, hole, depression, caldera, impact center. *Scientists know that the Moon is very old because of the craters on its surface.*

crave *vb.* desire, want, long for, hunger for, covet, need. *When I've been by myself for awhile, I often crave companionship.* **Ant.** dislike, reject, detest.

craving *n.* desire, need, longing, hunger, thirst, yearning. *Right now I have a craving for some junk food.* **Ant.** dislike, abhorrence, hate.

crawl *vb.* **1.** creep, drag, squirm, wiggle, wriggle. *The caterpillar slowly crawled across a leaf.* **2.** teem, swarm, abound, flow, bristle. *In the summertime, our kitchen crawls with ants.* –*n.* **3.** creep, walk, plod, trudge, shuffle. *Heavy rain slowed traffic to a crawl.* **Ant.** **1.** walk, run, dash. **3.** run, sprint, dash.

craze *n.* fad, mania, rage, trend, latest thing. *The snowboard craze is still going strong.*

crazy *adj.* **1.** stupid, foolish, insane, mad, insensible, reckless, irrational. *Walking alone in a big city is a crazy thing to do.* **2.** wild, infatuated, raving, excited, passionate, mad. *I'm crazy about chocolate-chip ice cream.* 3. strange, peculiar, bizarre, unusual, outrageous. *We've had some crazy weather lately.* **Ant.** **1.** sane, sensible, smart. **2.** indifferent, uninterested, unexcited. **3.** usual, normal, average.

creak *vb.* squeak, groan, squawk, rasp, grate, moan. I get scared when I hear the stairs creak in the middle of the night.

crease *n.* **1.** fold, ridge, crinkle, wrinkle, furrow, pleat. *There are creases in my new pants.* –*vb.* **2.** pleat, wrinkle, fold, crinkle, furrow. *Years of exposure to the weather has creased the old fisherman's face.*

create *vb.* make, produce, invent, devise, design, generate, build. *She can create fantastic graphics with her new computer software.* **Ant.** destroy, demolish, eliminate.

creation *n.* **1.** masterpiece, masterwork, artwork, production, invention. *The artist stood back and let people admire his creation.* **2.** formation, development, making, birth, nativity. *Scientists are exploring the mysteries behind the creation of the universe.* **Ant. 2.** extinction, destruction, death.

creative *adj.* inventive, imaginative, ingenious, artistic, visionary, productive. *I admire his creative nature.* **Ant.** unimaginative, unoriginal, uninspired.

creativity *n.* inventiveness, imagination, ingenuity, cleverness, resourcefulness, genius. *He experienced a burst of creativity and redecorated the entire first floor.*

creator *n.* originator, inventor, maker, designer, mastermind, architect, author. *She took credit as the new design's creator.*

creature *n.* being, animal, beast, mortal, soul. *She loves all the Earth's creatures.*

credentials *n.* qualifications, certification, degrees, accreditation, title, license. *Be sure your contractor has the proper credentials or you may be sorry.*

credibility *n.* reliability, integrity, character, trustworthiness, believability, track record. *He lied so much he lost all credibility.* **Ant.** dishonesty, lack of character.

credit *n.* **1.** recognition, commendation, acknowledgment, approval, acclaim. *Don't take all the credit for yourself.* **2.** deferred payment, charge, installment, time. *He bought a new car on credit.* **3.** asset, honor, boon, benefit, plus. *You're a credit to your profession* –*vb.* **4.** recognize, acknowledge, attribute, assign, honor. *Who is credited with the discovery of electricity?* **5.** accept, trust, believe, hold, deem. *I credit what she says as the truth.* **Ant. 1.** discredit, disapproval, blame. **2.** cash, check. **3.** liability, handicap, hindrance. **4.** question, distrust, disbelieve.

creed *n.* belief, doctrine, dogma, tenet, faith. *Though he considers himself religious, he doesn't hold to a specific creed.*

creek *n.* stream, brook, rivulet, branch, run. *You won't catch any fish in that little creek.*

creep *n.* **1.** jerk, (slang) sleazebag, pervert, (slang) slimeball, worm, snake. *We noticed some creep lurking in the shadows and called the police.*– *vb.* **2.** crawl, drag, squirm, wiggle, wriggle, sneak, steal. *The spider crept across its web.* **Ant. 2.** walk, run, dash.

creepy *adj.* scary, weird, macabre, gruesome, eerie, hair-raising, horrible. *A graveyard at midnight is rather creepy.*

cremate *vb.* burn, incinerate, consume, reduce to ashes. *Some people choose to cremate their loved ones after they die.*

crescendo *n.* surge, increase, rise, climax, culmination, crest, boiling point. *The orchestra reached a rousing crescendo and then went stone silent.* **Ant.** decrescendo, dissipation, reduction.

crest *n.* top, peak, summit, ridge, tip, crown. *I'll race you to the crest of that hill.* **Ant.** bottom, base, foot.

crevasse *n.* *See* CREVICE.

crevice *n.* fissure, crack, chasm, cleft, cranny, opening. *The rock climbers pulled their way up through a narrow crevice and continued on.*

crew *n.* hands, team, squad, band, company, group. *The crew of the starship were eager for shore leave.*

crime *n.* misdeed, violation, offense, transgression, wrongdoing, felony, misdemeanor. *It is a crime to steal.* **Ant.** virtue, legality.

criminal *adj.* **1.** illegal, unlawful, immoral, wrong, dishonest. *The selling of drugs is a criminal act.* *–n.* **2.** offender, culprit, crook, felon, outlaw. *The police are looking for the criminals who robbed our local bank.* **Ant.** **1.** legal, lawful, honest.

cringe *vb.* shrink, flinch, wince, cower, recoil, quail. *As the leper advanced toward me, I couldn't help but cringe.*

cripple *vb.* disable, weaken, damage, paralyze, stop, incapacitate. *The loss of our two star players crippled our team.* **Ant.** assist, encourage, strengthen.

crisis *n.* emergency, disaster, predicament, plight, climax, crux. *The big crisis last weekend was our house catching on fire.*

crisp *adj.* brittle, crunchy, friable, firm, fresh. *The crackers were fresh and crisp.* **Ant.** soggy, soft, gooey.

criterion *n.* standard, measure, yardstick, guideline, scale, gauge. *The criterion we use to qualify new employees is their ability to speak French.*

critic *n.* **1.** reviewer, analyst, judge, evaluator, pundit, expositor. *The critic gave the movie a rotten review.* **2.** fault-finder, detractor, belittler, complainer, nitpicker, mudslinger. *The critic in the back seat constantly found fault with my driving.*

critical *adj.* **1.** urgent, important, crucial, grave, decisive, momentous. *It is critical that a snakebite victim get help as soon as possible.* **2.** disapproving, discriminating, condemning, derogatory, severe. *My boss is too critical about the job I do.* **Ant.** **1.** irrelevant, insignificant. **2.** uncritical, indiscriminating.

critical mass *n.* flashpoint, crisis point, boiling point, moment of truth, climax. *The rebellious behavior of the crowd rapidly reached a critical mass, and the police were quickly called in.*

criticize *vb.* censure, denounce, fault, ridicule, condemn, judge. *My parents criticize almost everything I do.* **Ant.** praise, commend, acclaim.

critique *n.* review, examination, commentary, analysis, assessment. *Our class project is to attend an opera and write a critique on it.*

crook *n.* thief, burglar, robber, pickpocket, shoplifter, felon. *The police put the crook in handcuffs and hauled him off.*

crooked *adj.* bent, curved, twisted, warped, serpentine, lopsided. *The bicycle seat was uncomfortable because it was crooked.* **Ant.** straight, aligned, level.

crop *n.* **1.** harvest, yield, reaping, product, production. *The farmer hurried to harvest his crop before it rained.* *–vb.* **2.** trim, clip, cut, mow, shear. My task is to crop our overgrown hedges.

cross *n.* **1.** crucifix, crux, rood. *Many Christians wear a cross as a symbol of their devotion.* **2.** blend, hybrid, combination, crossbreed, mixture. *–vb.* **3.** traverse, ply, transit, span, pass. *It'll take us all day to cross the lake in this old rowboat.* **4.** mingle, mix, interbreed, combine, crossbreed. *If you cross a goat and a sheep, you end up with a geep.* **5.** crisscross, intertwine, interlock, twist, weave. *When she crosses her arms like that, it means she's angry.* *–adj.* **6.** opposed, opposing, contrary, opposite, counter. *We've been working to cross purposes.* **7.** angry, mad, sullen, moody, touchy. *Why are you so cross today?* **Ant.** **7.** agreeable, pleasant, amiable.

WORD SEARCH

bind to a cross and torture: *crucify*
cross-bearer: *crucifer*
cross-shaped: *cruciform*

cross with circle: *Celtic cross*
Egyptian cross with top loop: *ankh, ansate cross*
horizontal beam: *transom*

crouch *vb.* squat, stoop, bend, kneel, dip, bow. *The catcher crouched behind home plate.*

crow *n.* raven, rook, jackdaw, bird. *The old crow loved nothing more than to poke through our garbage.*

crowbar *n.* pry bar, wrecking bar, lever, pinch bar, tire iron. *We had to pry off the wood with a crowbar.*

crowd *n.* **1.** horde, throng, mob, mass, assemblage, group. *I don't go to the beach on weekends because I can't stand crowds.* **2.** clique, gang, circle, set, party. *Parents often warn their children not to hang around with the wrong crowd.* **3.** spectators, viewers, audience, listeners. *The crowd clapped at the end of the performance.* –*vb.* **4.** assemble, congregate, cluster, collect, huddle. *Everyone crowded around the snack table.* **5.** jam, shove, push, squeeze, compress, cram. *People crowded into the elevator.* **Ant. 4.** disperse, disband, scatter.

crowded *adj.* mobbed, packed, jammed, congested, wall-to-wall, overflowing. *The mall is extremely crowded during the Christmas rush.* **Ant.** deserted, empty, vacant.

crown *n.* coronet, tiara, diadem, circlet. *The queen doesn't look fully dressed without her crown.*

crucial *adj.* critical, essential, important, urgent, grave, vital. *It is crucial that you don't become dehydrated in the desert.* **Ant.** unessential, trivial, unimportant.

crucify *vb.* hang, nail to cross, bind to cross, rack, torture, torment. *The Romans used to crucify condemned criminals.*

crud *n.* matter, rot, filth, dirt, goo, muck, (slang) crap. *We had a lot of crud on our shoes so we took them off on the porch.*

crude *adj.* **1.** coarse, primitive, unfinished, unrefined, unpolished. *She made a crude telescope out of a tube and magnifying glass.* **2.** rude, vulgar, uncivilized, tasteless, offensive, revolting, gross. *He made a crude remark at the party.* **Ant. 1.** refined, processes, finished. **2.** courteous, polite, elegant.

cruel *adj.* savage, vicious, ruthless, barbaric, merciless, heartless. *It was very cruel of you to tease him about his lost puppy.* **Ant.** kind, considerate, compassionate.

cruelty *n.* viciousness, meanness, brutality, cold-heartedness, barbarity, cold-bloodedness. *In the old days, prisoners of war were often treated with terrible cruelty.* **Ant.** kindness, humanity, compassion.

cruise *vb.* **1.** navigate, sail, coast, float, travel, journey. *Her dream is to cruise the seven seas.* –*n.* **2.** voyage, sail, journey, trip, tour. *Let's go on a cruise next summer.*

crumble *vb.* collapse, fragment, disintegrate, powder, decay. *The cake crumbled in my hand.*

crumbly *adj.* brittle, friable, fragile, insubstantial, delicate. *These shortbread cookies are too crumbly.* **Ant.** solid, gooey.

crumple *vb.* crinkle, squash, rumple, crush, smash. *I crumpled up the newspaper to fit it in the trash can.*

crunch *vb.* grind, break, crumble, shatter, chomp, munch. *I like to stuff 20 potato chips in my mouth simultaneously and crunch them.*

crunchy *adj.* brittle, crisp, crackling, chewy. *The prefer vegetables where they are raw and crunchy.* **Ant.** gooey, liquid, soft.

crusade *n.* **1.** campaign, drive, movement, action, struggle. *He's waging a personal crusade to save our neighborhood.* –*vb.* **2.** march, drive, fight, battle, struggle. *A group called M.A.D.D. crusades for tougher laws against drunk drivers.*

crusader *n.* campaigner, activist, champion, visionary, reformer. *He was an aggressive crusader for more stringent pollution controls.*

crush *vb.* **1.** smash, squash, pulverize, stomp, grind, squeeze, mash. *We crushed the aluminum cans for recycling.* **2.** destroy, overcome, quash, overwhelm, topple, demolish. *His rejection crushed her.*

crutch *n.* prop, support, staff, aid. *I need a crutch until my broken leg heals.*

crux *n.* heart, core, meat, nitty gritty, gist, root. *We got to the crux of the matter by ignoring meaningless details.*

cry *vb.* **1.** weep, sob, bawl, wail, lament. *She cried at her friend's wedding.* **2.** shout, yell, call, scream, clamor. *The stranded climber cried for help.* –*n.* **3.** shout, yell, call, scream, bellow. *He gave a cry of warning when he saw the forest fire.*

crypt *n.* tomb, vault, mausoleum, chamber, burial place. *My grandfather is buried in a crypt below the old church.*

cryptic *adj.* secret, mysterious, hidden, perplexing, obscure. *There was a cryptic message in the bottle I found on the beach.* **Ant.** obvious, clear, apparent.

cubicle *n.* compartment, room, booth, cell, office, stall, chamber. *I have a spacious office now, but I used to work in a small cubicle.*

cuddle *vb.* snuggle, embrace, hug, nuzzle, caress. *She likes to cuddle soft furry animals.*

cue *n.* signal, sign, hint, indication, tip, prompt. *The actor entered the stage right on cue.*

cuisine *n.* food, fare, (slang) eats, (slang) grub, dishes, menu. *The French are famous for their delicious cuisine.*

culminate *vb.* climax, end, conclude, finish, terminate, complete. *The wedding culminated with a big dance.* **Ant.** begin, start, commence.

culprit *n.* criminal, offender, lawbreaker, wrongdoer, transgressor. *Who is the culprit who ran off with my backpack?*

cult *n.* sect, band, devotees, following, believers, disciples. *He ran away and joined a religious cult.*

cultivate *vb.* **1.** farm, till, plow, garden, plant. *Farmers cultivate many kinds of crops.* **2.** promote, encourage, support, foster, develop, improve. *It is important to cultivate a sense of self-worth in children.* **Ant. 2.** hinder, obstruct, discourage.

cultivation *n.* **1.** planting, farming, agriculture, gardening. *The farmer explained the steps necessary for successful rice cultivation.* **2.** promotion, advancement, encouragement, fosterage, development. *I really work on the cultivation of my friendships.* **Ant. 2.** hindrance, obstruction, discouragement.

culture *n.* civilization, society, attainments, accomplishments, refinement. *We are studying the culture of medieval Europe in our history class.*

cultured *adj.* civilized, sophisticated, enlightened, educated, knowledgeable. *She felt quite cultured after spending four years at a European university.* **Ant.** uncultured, crude, uneducated.

cumbersome *adj.* awkward, unwieldy, burdensome, weighty, clumsy, bulky. *A long run-on sentence can be quite cumbersome to read.* **Ant.** manageable, easy, compact.

cunning *adj.* **1.** crafty, sly, calculating, deceptive, scheming, shrewd. *The cunning businesswoman sold the house for two times what it was worth.* –*n.* **2.** craftiness, trickery, slyness, guile, deception. *Watch out for the cunning behind his charm.* **3.** skill, genius, talent, mastery, cleverness. *The shipwrecked man had to use his cunning to survive in the wilderness.* **Ant. 1.** clumsy, artless, naive. **2.** sincerity, openness, frankness. **3.** clumsiness, awkwardness.

cup *n.* glass, mug, tumbler, goblet, drinking vessel, chalice, stein. *I began drinking from a cup when I was two.*

curator *n.* caretaker, custodian, conservator, keeper, steward, guardian. *The museum's curator gave us a fascinating tour of the dinosaur floor.*

curdle *vb.* congeal, coagulate, clot, thicken, solidify, ferment. *The milk was so old it had actually begun to curdle like cottage cheese.* **Ant.** thin, liquefy.

cure *n.* **1.** remedy, treatment, medicine, antidote, corrective. *Do you think any cure exists for the problem of poverty?* *–vb.* **2.** heal, remedy, correct, alleviate, relieve, lessen. *The doctor prescribed medicine to cure my illness.* **Ant. 1.** sickness, illness, ailment. **2.** sicken, worsen, weaken.

curiosity *n.* **1.** inquisitiveness, questioning, interestedness, interest. *Please relieve my curiosity by telling me how this works.* **2.** eccentricity, novelty, wonder, peculiarity, oddity. *The exotic stranger was a curiosity to the local residents.* **Ant. 1.** indifference, disregard, unconcern.

curious *adj.* **1.** inquisitive, questioning, searching, investigative, nosy, snooping. *I am curious about the meaning of your name.* **2.** peculiar, unusual, weird, strange, odd, exotic, rare. *That's a curious object you found on the beach.* **Ant. 1.** indifferent, uninterested. **2.** normal, usual, conventional.

curl *vb.* curve, coil, bend, turn, warp, twist, corkscrew. *The cat loves to curl up by the fire.*

currency *n.* money, coin, cash, bills, legal tender. *When traveling abroad, you need to exchange your dollars for the local currency.*

current *adj.* **1.** present, latest, prevailing, popular, voguish. *She wore only current fashions.* *–n.* **2.** flow, course, stream, tide, flood. *The swimmer got caught in a current and was pulled away from shore.* **Ant. 1.** past, antique, outmoded, unpopular.

curriculum *n.* studies, courses, classes, subjects, lessons. *The curriculum appeared to be heavy with math courses.*

curse *n.* **1.** oath, profanity, swearing, blasphemy, obscenity. *I would rather he didn't voice so many curses.* **2.** spell, invocation, charm, hex, jinx. *The wizard's curse changed her into a tree.* **3.** torment, burden, misfortune, plague, affliction. *Buying cars that break down seems to be my curse in life.* *–vb.* **4.** swear, blaspheme, cuss, fulminate. *People sometimes curse when they're angry.* **5.** burden, plague, afflict, torment, harass, trouble. *She says she is cursed by bad luck.* **Ant. 3.** blessing, joy, relief. **4.** bless, commend, praise. **5.** assist, relieve, help.

cursed *adj.* jinxed, star-crossed, bedeviled, doomed, ill-fated, damned. *The troubled expedition was cursed from the very beginning.* **Ant.** blessed, fortunate.

curt *adj.* brusque, brief, short, abrupt, impolite, to the point. *His directions were curt and somewhat rude.* **Ant.** courteous, long-winded, polite.

curtail *vb.* shorten, reduce, trim, cut, lessen, decrease, restrict. *To lose weight, one must curtail one's eating.* **Ant.** increase, extend, expand.

curtain *n.* drapes, shade, veil, portiere, valance. *I closed the curtain to block out the sunlight.*

curvaceous *adj.* shapely, voluptuous, buxom, full-figured, hourglass-figured, statuesque. *Mae West was famous for her curvaceous figure.*

curve *n.* **1.** arc, bend, bow, turn, crook, crescent. *This roller coaster has lots of dips and curves.* *–vb.* **2.** bend, bow, hook, arch, curl, swerve. *The road curves to the left just ahead.*

cushion *n.* **1.** pillow, pad, padding, buffer, mat. *His sofa is comfortable because of its thick cushions.* *–vb.* **2.** pillow, soften, lessen, dampen, cradle. *The helmet cushioned the blow to his head.*

custodian *n.* caretaker, keeper, curator, steward, manager, cleaner. *We called the custodian to repair the broken window.*

custody *n.* **1.** guardianship, supervision, trusteeship, charge, protection. *If my parents should ever die, my grandparents will get custody of me.* **2.** holding, detention, possession, confinement, imprisonment. *That criminal is now in police custody.*

custom *n.* tradition, convention, practice, fashion, procedure. *It is the custom in Japan to take off your shoes before entering a house.* **Ant.** oddity, abnormality, rarity.

customary *adj.* usual, habitual, common, regular, normal. *She greeted me with her customary smile.* **Ant.** unusual, uncommon, rare.

customer *n.* shopper, purchaser, buyer, patron, client. *The store was full of customers buying gifts for the holidays.* **Ant.** seller, vendor.

cut *vb.* **1.** slash, slice, carve, chop, clip, nip. *I cut the tags off my new clothes.* **2.** cross, traverse, move, pass, ply. *He cut across the lawn to reach the building.* **3.** shorten, reduce, edit, abridge, condense, delete. *The playwright decided to cut her play by several scenes.* **4.** halt, stop, interrupt, thwart, obstruct. *The mechanic yelled for me to cut the engine.* –*adj.* **5.** severed, separated, sliced, pared, sectioned, divided. *I put a cut banana in my oatmeal.* **6.** shortened, reduced, abridged, condensed. *We saw the cut version of the movie.* –*n.* **7.** wound, incision, nick, gash, slash. *I put a bandage on my cut.* **8.** reduction, decrease, lessening, decline, fall. *The city will be faced with a major budget cut next year.* **Ant.** **3.** expand, add, increase. **4.** begin, start, activate. **6.** expanded, extended, lengthened. **8.** increase, raise, boost.

cutback *n.* downsizing, belt-tightening, decrease, reduction, lowering, reversal. *The company announced a cutback in research and development.*

cute *adj.* adorable, attractive, cherubic, angelic, sweet-faced, darling, charming. *Babies, puppies, and kittens are almost always cute.* **Ant.** repulsive, ugly, disgusting.

cutthroat *adj.* ruthless, merciless, dog-eat-dog, pitiless, cold-blooded, sociopathic. *Competition became cutthroat when too many stores opened near the mall.* **Ant.** collaborative, helpful, charitable.

cutting edge *adj.* forefront, leading edge, trailblazing, vanguard, avant-garde, fore. *The computer company had long been at the cutting edge of new technology.* **Ant.** following, tail end, last.

cyberspace *n.* electronic medium, databank, computer memory, Internet, World Wide Web, communication network. *She met her new boyfriend in a chat room in cyberspace.*

cycle *n.* revolution, rotation, period, series, succession, sequence. *The rinse cycle on this washing machine lasts ten minutes.*

cyclone *n.* windstorm, whirlwind, tornado, twister, hurricane, waterspout. *The cyclone had winds in excess of 100 miles per hour.*

cylinder *n.* chamber, barrel, tube, drum, pipe. *The engine was powered by eight cylinders.*

cynic *n.* skeptic, doubting Thomas, scoffer, realist, nonbeliever, pessimist. *Cynics believe everyone has a hidden motive.* **Ant.** optimist, believer, Pollyanna.

cynical *adj.* doubting, unbelieving, disbelieving, skeptical, suspicious. *I'm too cynical to believe in psychic phenomena.* **Ant.** believing, accepting, unsuspicious.

cyst *n.* vesicle, sac, bleb, blister. *Sarah had to go to her doctor to have a cyst removed.*

D

dab *n.* **1.** pat, touch, morsel, bit, speck. *She put another dab of butter on her pancakes.* –*vb.* **2.** swab, daub, smear, touch, wipe. *He dabbed a little cologne on his neck.*

dabble *vb.* fool, tinker, fiddle, putter, dally. *I'm not an artist, but I do dabble around with paints.*

dagger *n.* knife, dirk, stiletto, blade, pocketknife. *Brutus killed Caesar with a dagger.*

dainty *adj.* **1.** delicate, fine, petite, exquisite, graceful, refined. *She prepared dainty sandwiches for her tea party.* **2.** finicky, fussy, discriminating, particular, scrupulous. *His cat is a dainty eater.* **Ant.** **1.** unappealing, gross, vulgar. **2.** hearty, robust.

dam *n.* **1.** bank, dike, levee, wall, barrier, barrage. *The dam was harnessed to generate electricity for the local towns.* –*vb.* **2.** block, check, impede, stop, hold back. *We were afraid the beavers would dam the river again.*

damage *vb.* **1.** hurt, injure, harm, wound, break, cripple, wreck. *High winds damaged our barn.* –*n.* **2.** hurt, injury, harm, destruction, devastation, blow. *Her car received minor damage in the accident.* **Ant.** **1.** repair, fix, heal.

damages *n.* compensation, reimbursement, amends, expenses, losses, costs. *The accident victim sued the negligent company for damages.*

damp *adj.* **1.** moist, wet, soggy, dank, clammy, sodden. *The grass is still damp from yesterday's rain.* **2.** indifferent, uncaring, lukewarm, spiritless, unenthusiastic. *I received a damp response to my proposal.* –*n.* **3.** moisture, wetness, dankness, sogginess, clamminess. *The damp seemed to penetrate to his bones.* **Ant.** **1.** dry, arid. **2.** enthusiastic, warm. **3.** heat, dryness.

dance *vb.* **1.** prance, frolic, cavort, leap, skip. *We danced with joy when our team won the championship.* –*n.* **2.** ball, prom, party, hop, social. *There's a big dance at school this weekend.*

WORD SEARCH

bend over backwards under pole: *limbo*
ballroom, classical: *waltz*
Bohemian, high-energy: *polka*
Brazilian: *samba, bossa nova, lambada*
clickety-clacking: *tap*
country and western or rural: *line dance, square dance, Texas two-step*
Cuban: *rhumba, conga, mambo*
designs dance steps and sequences: *choreographer*
design of steps and sequences: *choreography*
French, high-kicking: *can-can*
Hawaiian: *hula*
Latin American: *cha cha, salsa*
1920s: *Charleston*
1930s: *shag, Lindy hop*
1940s: *jitterbug*
1960s, Chubby Checker: *twist*
1970s hip tapping: *bump*
1980s prostrate movements: *breakdance*

1990s, running in position: *running man*
robot-like movements: *locking*
Russian squat: *cossack*
slamdance, area where dancers: *mosh pit*
slam into each other as a dance: *slamdance, mosh*
secret, all-night dance party: *rave*
Spanish: *flamenco, fandango, bolero, tango*
step design: *choreography*
tip-toeing: *ballet*
two-step, ballroom: *foxtrot*
wooden shoes: *clog*

dancer *n.* danseuse, danseur, ballerina, (slang) hoofer, terpsichorean. *The dancers whirled and stomped their way across the floor.*

danger *n.* risk, threat, hazard, peril, jeopardy, menace. *Smokey the Bear warns about the dangers of unwatched campfires.* **Ant.** safety, security, safeness.

dangerous *adj.* unsafe, threatening, risky, hazardous, menacing, perilous. *Rattlesnakes are dangerous if provoked.* **Ant.** safe, harmless, innocuous.

dangle *vb.* hang, drag, trail, droop, swing, sag. *She dangled a fishing line in the lake.*

dank *n.* moist, damp, clammy, wet, muggy, humid. *We entered the dank cave.* **Ant.** dry, arid, parched.

dare *vb.* **1.** defy, challenge, taunt, goad, provoke. *I admit I broke the window, but my brother dared me to do it.* **2.** venture, risk, challenge, face, brave, confront. *She dared to run the rapids in a fragile kayak.* *–n.* **3.** bet, provocation, challenge, taunt. *He swallowed the goldfish on a dare.*

daredevil *n.* thrill-seeker, stunt person, show-off, adventurer, (slang) hot dog. *Daredevils often wind up in a hospital bed.* **Ant.** coward, armchair adventurer.

daring *adj.* adventurous, bold, courageous, brave, fearless, gallant. *She made a daring leap across the chasm.* **Ant.** timid, cowardly, fearful.

dark *n.* **1.** night, nightfall, nighttime, darkness, blackness. *He wants to get back before dark.* *–adj.* **2.** lightless, unlit, black, sunless. *It gets dark here about nine o'clock.* **3.** deep, dim, dusky, swarthy, murky. *His hair is a dark brown.* **4.** glum, brooding, gloomy, sullen, dreary, cheerless. *She's in a dark mood.* **Ant.** **1.** dawn, daytime. **2.** light, bright, lit. **3.** pale, pastel, fair. **4.** happy, joyful, cheerful.

dark horse *n.* underdog, longshot, sleeper, outside shot, unknown, giant slayer. *Of the seven candidates, two were considered dark horses.* **Ant.** favorite, frontrunner, sure bet.

darling *n.* **1.** love, beloved, sweetheart, jewel, favorite. *Her youngest grandson is her darling.* *–adj.* **2.** loved, treasured, valued, dear, favorite. *This is my darling nephew.*

dart *vb.* **1.** leap, sprint, rush, spring, bolt, fly, dash. *I thought I was going to be first in line until he darted in front of me.* *–n.* **2.** dash, rush, spring, leap, bolt, sprint, bound. *The runner made a dart for the finish line on the final lap.* **3.** bolt, shaft, arrow, quarrel, projectile. *Can you throw the dart into the bull's-eye?*

dash *vb.* **1.** hurry, rush, sprint, race, hasten. *She had to dash to the station to catch her bus.* **2.** ruin, spoil, thwart, frustrate, foil. *Our dream of victory was dashed in the semifinals.* **3.** hurl, fling, slam, thrust, smash. *Heavy surf dashed against the pier.* *–n.* **4.** race, rush, run, sprint, dart. *We all made a dash for the exit when class was over.* **5.** touch, bit, hint, suggestion, trace. *This soup needs a dash more salt.*

dashing *adj.* audacious, bold, jaunty, gallant, debonair, rakish, flamboyant. *The dashing young man caught everyone's attention as he entered.* **Ant.** shy, retiring, awkward.

data *n.* information, facts, statistics, figures, details. *My driver's license contains data on my height, weight and address.*

date *n.* **1.** time, day, month, year, season, period. *I've forgotten the date of your birthday.* **2.** appointment, engagement, rendezvous, meeting. *Let's make a date to meet here tomorrow at five o'clock.* **3.** escort, companion, boyfriend, girlfriend, friend. *Do you have a date for the prom?*

daunt *vb.* thwart, deter, dishearten, intimidate, frighten. *The great importance of her assignment did not daunt her.* **Ant.** encourage, rouse, stir.

daunting *adj.* intimidating, discouraging, frightening, dispiriting, disheartening, scary. *Filing a tax return can be a daunting task.* **Ant.** encouraging, heartening.

dawdle *vb.* idle, dally, fiddle, poke, daydream, loaf. *She dawdled all day and had no time left to finish her homework.* **Ant.** hurry, rush, hustle.

dawn *n.* **1.** sunrise, daybreak, sunup, morning, daylight. *He gets up at dawn to go jogging.* **2.** birth, emergence, beginning, awakening, start, appearance. *It was the dawn of a new age.* *–vb.* **3.** begin, start, arise, originate, emerge. *A new day dawned for the settlers.* **4.** register, strike, appear, occur, hit. *It finally dawned on me what he was trying to say.* **Ant.** **1.** sunset, evening, dusk. **2.** ending, finish, termination. **3.** end, finish, terminate.

day *n.* **1.** daytime, daylight, sunlight, sunshine. *He works during the day and parties at night.* **2.** age, epoch, period, time, generation. *The old woman liked to talk about how things were during her day.*

day care *n.* childcare, babysitter, nursery school, preschool, kindergarten. *I have to drop the children off at day care before going to work.*

daydream *n.* fantasy, reverie, fancy, musing, visualization, castle in the air. *Without a winning ticket, winning the lottery is only a daydream.*

daze *vb.* **1.** stun, confuse, bewilder, muddle, dazzle, blind. *The strong sunlight momentarily dazed me when I stepped outside.* *–n.* **2.** muddle, confusion, bewilderment, trance, stupor. *The man was in a daze after he ran into a tree.*

dazzling *adj.* brilliant, stunning, blinding, vivid, overpowering, exciting. *The skaters gave a dazzling performance.* **Ant.** dull, ordinary, routine.

deacon *n.* cleric, clergyman, deaconess. *The deacon lead the congregation in prayer.*

dead *adj.* **1.** lifeless, deceased, perished, extinguished, expired. *She buried the dead sparrow in her backyard.* **2.** uninterested, bored, unresponsive, emotionless, cool. *The audience seems rather dead tonight.* **3.** obsolete, extinct, discontinued, defunct, passé. *At one time, Hebrew was considered a dead language.* **4.** spiritless, dull, listless, boring, uneventful. *Dance clubs are usually dead on week nights.* **5.** motionless, stationary, still, standing, quiet. *After losing power, the boat was dead in the water for two hours.* **6.** absolute, complete, total, outright, utter. *The train came to a dead stop to avoid the moose.* *–n.* **7.** silence, hush, stillness, quiet, calm. *The dead of the night was broken by a loud crash.* *–adj.* **8.** directly, exactly, straight, right. *The beach is dead ahead.* **9.** totally, entirely, completely, thoroughly, absolutely, utterly. *You're dead wrong about this.* **Ant.** **1.** alive, living, live. **2.** alive, wild, responsive. **3.** existing, modern, current. **4.** lively, active, spirited. **5.** alive, moving, operative. **6.** partial, incomplete.

deadbeat *n.* debtor, freeloader, (slang) bum, burden to society, loafer, layabout. *The deadbeat refused to work or pay his bills.*

deaden *vb.* numb, extinguish, quench, diminish, dampen, blunt, lessen. *Novocaine will* *deaden the pain of a toothache.* **Ant.** stimulate, rouse, excite.

deadline *n.* time limit, due date, zero hour, cutoff. *If I didn't turn in the story by the deadline, I would be fired.*

deadlock *n.* gridlock, stalemate, impasse, standstill, hung jury, logjam. *In debates between Democrats and Republicans, expect frequent deadlocks.*

deadly *adj.* poisonous, fatal, lethal, toxic, harmful, dangerous, hazardous. *Arsenic is a deadly substance.* **Ant.** safe, harmless, innocuous.

deadpan *adj.* expressionless, blank, stony-faced, poker-faced, wooden. *It's wise to maintain a deadpan expression when playing poker.*

deal *vb.* **1.** distribute, bestow, dispense, assign, give. *Deal each person five cards.* **2.** trade, bargain, transact, sale, retail. *The store says it only deals in one type of computer.* **3.** consider, concern, treat, handle, manage. *This article deals with pollution issues.* *–n.* **4.** contract, agreement, arrangement, pact, negotiation. *I made a deal with my sister in which she agreed to do my chores for ten dollars.* **5.** amount, quantity, allotment, extent, degree. *I don't have a great deal of time for recreation.* **Ant.** **1.** receive, take, collect. **3.** ignore, overlook.

dealer *n.* salesman, broker, retailer, wholesaler, buyer, seller, merchant, trader. *The local car dealer had something of a shady reputation.*

dealership *n.* sales outlet, store, franchise, shop, market, concession. *The car dealership was open seven days a week.*

death *n.* passing, dying, demise, departure, termination, extinction. *He missed school because of a death in his family.* **Ant.** life, existence, birth.

WORD SEARCH

after death: *posthumous*
fear of: *necrophobia*
herald of, mythical: *banshee*
march: *dirge*
mercy killing: *euthanasia*
omen: *knell*
study: *thanatology*
watch: *vigil*

debacle *n.* disaster, catastrophe, ruin, breakdown, devastation, fiasco. *The riot turned the trial into a debacle.*

debatable *adj.* disputable, contestable, unsettled, controversial, undecided, moot. *Whether humans will ever set foot on Mars is debatable.* **Ant.** settled, decided, proven.

debate *vb.* **1.** ponder, deliberate, contemplate, consider, think. *He debated which college to attend.* **2.** discuss, argue, dispute, question, contest. *The existence of a supreme being has been debated throughout much of human history.* *–n.* **3.** discussion, argument, dispute, disagreement, wrangle. *We got into a debate over whether or not it was a good movie.*

debility *n.* infirmity, handicap, weakness, frailty, disease, sickness. *The loss of her pinky fingernail was only a temporary debility.*

debonair *adj.* suave, carefree, charming, cool, jaunty, cheerful, urbane. *Being well-schooled in the social graces, he was unusually debonair.* **Ant.** crude, unrefined, tacky.

debrief *vb.* **1.** question, interrogate, probe, quiz, inquire, gather intelligence. *The commanding officer wanted to debrief the prisoners of war before they spoke to the media.* **2.** censor, silence, quiet, hush up, mute, muzzle. *The farmer claimed to have seen an alien, so we'll have to debrief him.*

debris *n.* trash, wreckage, junk, waste, rubble, flotsam, garbage. *Space debris orbits the Earth.*

debt *n.* indebtedness, obligation, bill, arrears, liability. *She is in debt to her parents for $100.*

debunk *vb.* disprove, expose, refute, hold up to ridicule, puncture, deflate. *The scientist loved to debunk psychics and dowsers.* **Ant.** prove, confirm, substantiate.

debut *n.* premiere, opening, first appearance, entry, introduction, inauguration. *She made her singing debut on a church stage.* **Ant.** finale, exit, farewell.

decadent *adj.* in decay, degenerating, declining, on the wane, self-indulgent, gone bad. *She couldn't abide by his decadent lifestyle.* **Ant.** progressing, healthy.

decapitate *vb.* behead, guillotine, decollate. *The female praying mantis is known to decapitate the male during mating.*

decay *vb.* **1.** deteriorate, rot, decompose, disintegrate, decline. *Vegetables were starting to decay in the untended garden.* *–n.* **2.** deterioration, decomposition, disintegration, rot, rotting. *That old abandoned house is in a bad state of decay.* **Ant. 1.** flourish, thrive, grow. **2.** health, vigor, development.

deceit *n.* deception, dishonesty, trickery, cheating, cunning, fraud. *He used deceit to cheat us out of our rightful inheritance.* **Ant.** honesty, truthfulness, sincerity.

deceive *vb.* fool, mislead, trick, delude, dupe, misinform. *She deceived me into believing she had completed all her work.*

decelerate *vb.* brake, check, slow down, halt, stop, cease. *The space shuttle decelerated as it entered the atmosphere.* **Ant.** accelerate, speed up, start.

decency *n.* modesty, dignity, propriety, suitability, seemliness. *Pornography offends my sense of decency.*

decent *adj.* **1.** modest, proper, respectable, dignified, tasteful. *My pants are so torn they are no longer decent to wear.* **2.** sufficient, reasonable, adequate, passable. *That was the first decent meal he's had all week.* **3.** mannerly, kind, generous, thoughtful, courteous, considerate. *It was decent of you to offer to pay for dinner.* **Ant. 1.** indecent, immodest, improper. **2.** insufficient, inadequate. **3.** unmannerly, unthoughtful, inconsiderate.

deception *n.* dishonesty, trickery, sleight of hand, lie, fraud, subterfuge. *The con artist had perfected the art of deception.* **Ant.** honesty, truthfulness, credibility.

deceptive *adj.* deceitful, misleading, tricky, dishonest, shifty, treacherous. *The con man was deceptive and shrewd.*

decide *vb.* choose, select, elect, pick, resolve, judge. *He couldn't decide which jacket to wear.*

decipher *vb.* solve, puzzle out, figure out, decode, understand, crack. *The spy failed to decipher the secret code.*

decision *n.* verdict, conclusion, determination, resolution, judgment, opinion. *Have you reached a decision about where you want to go?*

decisive *adj.* determined, firm, resolute, fixed, conclusive, deciding, final. *She made a decisive move that won the game.* **Ant.** indecisive, undetermined, inconclusive.

declare *vb.* announce, proclaim, express, pronounce, claim, assert. *The United States declared its independence from Britain in 1776.*

decline *vb.* **1.** reject, refuse, shun, veto, deny, rebuff. *She declined her friend's offer to stay the night.* **2.** decrease, wane, ebb, subside, lessen, lower. *Deaths due to pneumonia have declined since the introduction of penicillin.* *–n.* **3.** wane, ebb, downswing, decrease, lessening, lowering. *Smoking is on the decline.* **4.** slope, descent, dip, slant, angle. *The astronauts drove their moon buggy down the decline.* **Ant. 1.** accept, consent, adopt. 2. rise, increase. 3. rise, upswing, upturn. 4. ascent, incline.

decode decrypt, decipher, solve, figure out, puzzle out, translate. *The enemy was not able to decode the secret telegraph signals it picked up.*

decompose *vb.* rot, decay, putrefy, break down, biodegrade, compost. *If garbage and leaves are left to decompose, they will turn into rich fertilizer.*

decontaminate *vb.* clean, sterilize, disinfect, sanitize, wash, distill. *You must decontaminate yourself after exposure to bacteria.* **Ant.** contaminate, infect, pollute.

decor *vb.* decorations, style, theme, ornamentation, scheme, layout. *The decor of the apartment was shabby chic.*

decorate *vb.* adorn, ornament, garnish, festoon, bedeck, trim, embellish. *He decorated his room with posters.*

decorum *n.* manners, propriety, etiquette, civility, protocol, demeanor, properness. *A somber decorum is expected at funerals.* **Ant.** bad manners, rudeness, impropriety.

decoy *n.* ruse, lure, fake, plant, facade, enticement. *Ducks are often attracted by wooden decoys that resemble them.*

decrease *vb.* 1. reduce, lower, lessen, diminish, cut, shrink. *The state decreased the speed limit to 55 mph.* –*n.* 2. reduction, lowering, lessening, cutback, diminishing, slackening. *I asked my boss for a decrease in my workload.* **Ant.** 1. increase, lift, raise. 2. increase, lift, extension.

decree *n.* 1. edict, ruling, proclamation, law, command, ordinance, regulation. *The king's decree says no one may hunt in the royal forest.* –*vb.* 2. rule, command, proclaim, instruct, order, dictate, demand. *Our leader has decreed that all members of the commune must shave their heads.*

decrepit *adj.* old, dilapidated, ancient, deteriorated, rickety, run-down. *We were terrified to go flying in that decrepit plane.*

dedicate *vb.* devote, inscribe, address, offer, give, consecrate. *The book was dedicated to the author's husband.*

dedicated *adj.* committed, devoted, goal-oriented, focused, single-minded, determined. *You have to be a dedicated athlete in order to make it into the big leagues.* **Ant.** halfhearted, lazy, uncommitted.

deduce *vb.* infer, conclude, reason, interpret, assume, analyze. *Even though there were very few clues, Sherlock Holmes deduced the identity of the criminal.*

deduct *vb.* subtract, remove, withdraw, take, eliminate. *Please deduct the price of the broken lamp from my allowance.* **Ant.** add, increase, extend.

deed *n.* act, action, work, feat, performance, task, enterprise, turn. *Robin Hood is known for the good deeds he did for the poor.*

deep *adj.* 1. extensive, vast, immeasurable, cavernous, fathomless. *I was unable to see to the bottom of the deep hole.* 2. profound, critical, important, vital, intense. *Her words almost always have an underlying deep meaning.* 3. absorbed, immersed, engrossed, preoccupied, engaged. *I was deep in thought.* 4. powerful, sincere, earnest, impassioned, intense. *He has a deep love for his country.* **Ant.** 1. shallow. 2. shallow, trivial, superficial. 4. shallow, light, weak.

deer *n.* whitetail, buck, doe, stag, hart, fawn, roe, quadruped, herbivore.

WORD SEARCH

antlers: *rack*
antler covering: *velvet*
bellowing cry: *bell*

feeding area: *yard*
meat: *venison*
smelly secretion: *musk*
tail: *flag*

deface *vb.* blemish, mark, disfigure, ruin, spoil, vandalize, scratch. *The graffiti artists tried to deface the entire front of the store.*

defamatory *adj.* slanderous, libelous, smearing, injurious, damaging, denigrating. *Making a defamatory statement may result in a lawsuit.* **Ant.** flattering, complimentary, reverential.

defame *vb.* slander, libel, smear, denigrate, malign, insult. *The paper tried to defame the politician by printing half-truths.* **Ant.** compliment, praise, flatter.

defeat *vb.* **1.** conquer, vanquish, master, overcome, overthrow. *The Allies defeated the Axis powers in World War II.* –*n.* **2.** loss, downfall, failure, ruin, setback. *She took her team's defeat very hard.* **Ant. 1.** lose, surrender, yield. **2.** victory, triumph, success.

defect *n.* **1.** fault, flaw, error, mistake, failing, snag. *The cars were recalled due to a defect in their brakes.* –*vb.* **2.** desert, bolt, mutiny, secede, leave. *The foreign diplomat defected to the United States.*

defection *n.* desertion, changeover, switchover, conversion, withdrawal. *News of the diplomat's defection was on the front page.*

defective *adj.* flawed, faulty, broken, marred, warped, imperfect. *He returned the defective merchandise to the manufacturer.* **Ant.** perfect, faultless, unmarred.

defend *vb.* protect, safeguard, guard, shield, shelter, save. *She hired a lawyer to defend her in court.* **Ant.** attack, assail, endanger.

defendant *n.* accused, litigant, suspect, party, prisoner. *The defendant was ill-prepared to plead his case.* **Ant.** plaintiff, accuser, victim.

defense *n.* protection, preservation, guard, security, support. *A moat was the castle's first line of defense.*

defenseless *adj.* powerless, vulnerable, weak, helpless, unprotected, unguarded. *The poor, defenseless mouse didn't have a chance against the old tomcat.* **Ant.** powerful, fortified, guarded.

defer *vb.* **1.** delay, postpone, suspend, table, shelve. *She asked her apartment manager if she could defer payment to the end of the month.* **2.** yield, submit, accede, listen, assent, obey. *He defers to her because she's his boss.*

deferential *adj.* submissive, acquiescent, reverential, compliant, respectful, obeisant. *Most students are deferential toward their teachers, but every classroom has its rebels.* **Ant.** domineering, overbearing, rebellious.

defiant *adj.* disobedient, rebellious, recalcitrant, insubordinate, unruly, stubborn. *The defiant student refused to do his homework.* **Ant.** obedient, submissive, agreeable.

deficient *adj.* lacking, incomplete, wanting, insufficient, short. *The accident was attributed to the driver's deficient judgment.* **Ant.** complete, sufficient, adequate.

deficit *n.* shortage, shortfall, insufficiency, deficiency. *It looks like we're going to have another budget deficit this year.*

define *vb.* describe, explain, specify, depict, characterize, label. *If you can't define that word, consult a dictionary.*

definite *adj.* **1.** specific, fixed, determined, particular, clear. *Let's establish a definite time and place for the game.* **2.** certain, positive, sure, settled, conclusive, decided. *It's not definite that I'll be able to attend.* **Ant. 1.** indefinite, unspecific, vague. **2.** uncertain, unsure.

definitely *adv.* certainly, obviously, decidedly, conclusively, positively. *It was definitely a raccoon I saw.* **Ant.** possibly, perhaps, maybe.

definition *n.* **1.** description, explanation, specification, depiction. *Instead of giving the definition of a word, a thesaurus lists synonyms.* **2.** sharpness, distinctness, clarity, clearness, visibility. *This television is known for its high definition.*

definitive *adj.* defining, conclusive, precise, consummate, complete, perfect. *Stevie Ray Vaughn was the definitive modern blues artist.*

deflate *vb.* contract, collapse, empty, shrink, deplete, exhaust. *We watched the hot air balloon come down in the field and slowly deflate.* **Ant.** inflate, fill, expand.

deflect *vb.* divert, veer, ricochet, bounce off, turn aside, diverge. *The pitcher had just enough time to deflect the sizzling line drive with the back of his glove.*

deform *vb.* mar, disfigure, mutilate, distort, maim. *The Phantom of the Opera wore a mask because a fire had deformed his face.*

deformity *n.* malformation, disfigurement, abnormality, contortion, imperfection, flaw. *The Hunchback of Notre Dame was severely judged by his deformity.*

deft *adj.* skillful, adept, adroit, clever, proficient, crack, handy. *The carpenter was known for his deft hands.* **Ant.** unskilled, bumbling, inexpert.

defunct *adj.* dead, extinct, out of business, deceased, (slang) kaput, (slang) gone belly up, gone. *Unfortunately, the phone line was disconnected because the company is now defunct.* **Ant.** thriving, alive and well, booming.

defy *vb.* disobey, disregard, resist, spurn, withstand, challenge, dare. *The child defied his babysitter by refusing to go to bed.* **Ant.** obey, follow, observe, respect.

degrade *vb.* humiliate, shame, dishonor, debase, reduce, demean, lower. *She refused to degrade herself by supporting his lie.*

degree *n.* **1.** grade, level, tier, rank, step, height. *To an above-average degree, writers tend to be introverts.* **2.** certificate, diploma, credentials, sheepskin, shingle, testimonial. *After four hard years at college, I am finally getting my bachelor's degree.*

WORD SEARCH

B.A.: *bachelor of arts*
baccalaureate: *bachelor's degree*
below master's and doctorate: *undergraduate; associate's, bachelor's*
B.S.: *bachelor of science*
ceremonies, award: *commencement*
C.E.: *civil engineer*
D.D.S.: *doctor of dental science*
D.Th.: *doctor of theology*
graduating with great honor: *magna cum laude*
graduating with highest honor: *summa cum laude*
highest: *doctorate, Ph.D.*
M.A.: *master of arts*
M.B.A.: *master of business administration*
M.D.: *doctor of medicine*
Ph.D.: *doctor of philosophy*
recognition of life achievement, not formal schooling: *honorary degree*

dehydrate *vb.* dry, desiccate. *We plan to dehydrate our food to make it last longer on the trail.* **Ant.** hydrate, saturate, drench.

deify *vb.* exalt, worship, revere, idolize, venerate, put on a pedestal. *She was a superstar, deified by her fans.* **Ant.** denigrate, abuse, criticize.

deity *n.* god, goddess, supreme being, creator, divinity, spirit, idol. *As an atheist, Deanna refuses to believe in any kind of deity.*

dejected *adj.* depressed, unhappy, sorrowful, disheartened, downcast, despondent. *He was dejected because he couldn't find his lost dog.* **Ant.** happy, joyous, cheerful.

delay *vb.* **1.** interrupt, postpone, detain, suspend, prolong, hinder, impede. *Rain delayed the game.* –*n.* **2.** wait, lag, postponement, stay, suspension, interruption, break. *The pilot said there would be a ten-minute delay before takeoff.*

delegate *vb.* **1.** assign, relegate, name, designate, charge. *My manager delegated to me the job of sweeping out the store.* –*n.* **2.** representative, spokesperson, diplomat, envoy, ambassador. *Most countries send delegates to the United Nations.*

delete *vb.* erase, eradicate, cancel, remove, cut, omit. *She accidentally deleted an important computer file.* **Ant.** insert, add, include.

deleterious *adj.* damaging, harmful, destructive, hurtful, injurious, pernicious. *Acid has a deleterious effect on most substances.* **Ant.** helpful, benign, beneficial.

deliberate *vb.* **1.** examine, consider, weigh, ponder, study. *The jury deliberated for two weeks before reaching a verdict.* –*adj.* **2.** intentional, planned, thoughtful, calculated, prearranged. *His remark was a deliberate attempt to insult me.* **Ant.** **2.** spontaneous, hasty, rash.

deliberately *adv.* intentionally, purposefully, willfully, thoughtfully, wittingly. *Did you deliberately slam the door in my face?* **Ant.** unintentionally, unwittingly.

delicacy *n.* **1.** fineness, fragility, flimsiness, slightness, frailness. *The delicacy of the spider web delighted us.* **2.** tact, finesse, sensitivity, consideration, gentleness. *Use delicacy when telling someone they have bad breath.* **3.** tidbit, morsel, treat, luxury. *Frogs' legs are considered a delicacy in France.* **Ant.** **1.** coarseness, roughness. **2.** bluntness, insensitivity.

delicate *adj.* **1.** fragile, frail, flimsy, fine, slight, small. *Be careful—this is very delicate china.* **2.** difficult, touchy, ticklish, dangerous, critical. *The surgeon performed a delicate operation.* **3.** tactful, sensitive, considerate, careful, diplomatic. *She tried to be delicate when she told him she no longer loved him.* **Ant.** **1.** rough, coarse, sturdy. **2.** easy, safe. **3.** inconsiderate, insensitive, careless.

delicious *adj.* appetizing, rich, luscious, tasty, savory, pleasing, delightful. *That cream pastry was delicious.* **Ant.** sickening, unpleasant, terrible.

delight *vb.* **1.** thrill, excite, please, cheer, amuse, gladden. *Winning the award delighted him.* –*n.* **2.** excitement, pleasure, joy, happiness, rapture, exhilaration. *It was such a delight to see you after all these years.* **Ant.** **1.** displease, sadden, depress. **2.** displeasure, unhappiness.

delightful *adj.* pleasurable, pleasant, enjoyable, agreeable, happy. *We had a delightful time on our vacation.* **Ant.** unpleasant, depressing, unhappy.

delinquent *n.* **1.** criminal, lawbreaker, hoodlum, miscreant, felon, (slang) punk, offender. *The juvenile delinquent would end up in jail if he continued to break the law.* –*adj.* **2.** lax, slack, irresponsible, remiss, negligent, derelict. *He was delinquent with all of his bills.* **Ant.** **1.** law abider. **2.** responsible, conscientious.

delirious *adj.* confused, muddled, incoherent, bewildered, hallucinating, (slang) out of it. *His high fever made him somewhat delirious.* **Ant.** lucid, rational, clear-thinking.

deliver *vb.* **1.** transfer, transmit, send, convey, bear, present. *Mail is delivered every day except holidays and Sundays.* **2.** speak, voice, utter, give, impart, communicate. *The woman delivered a moving speech.* **3.** rescue, save, free, release, protect, liberate. *The aliens said they came to deliver Earth from its impending doom.* **Ant. 1.** keep, hold, retain.

deliverance *n.* emancipation, rescue, saving, liberation, freeing, release. *The prisoners of war hoped that their deliverance from captivity would be soon.*

delivery *n.* transfer, conveyance, transmittal, transmission, distribution. *The messenger had several deliveries to make.*

delude *vb.* deceive, mislead, fool, dupe, trick, misguide. *I deluded myself into believing she liked me.*

deluge *n.* **1.** avalanche, flood, downpour, overflow, inundation, barrage. *The newspaper received a deluge of letters protesting the article.* –*vb.* **2.** flood, swamp, drown, engulf, inundate, overrun, submerge. *The school was deluged by calls from angry parents.*

delusion *n.* illusion, misbelief, misconception, fantasy, hallucination. *He has delusions of grandeur.* **Ant.** fact, reality, actuality.

deluxe *adj.* choice, select, prime, splendid, luxurious. *Let's order a deluxe pizza.* **Ant.** common, ordinary, average.

demand *vb.* **1.** require, claim, ask, need, want, invoke. *I demand my rights.* –*n.* **2.** order, bidding, command, ultimatum, direction, requirement. *Will our government meet the terrorist's demands?*

demanding *adj.* difficult, hard, burdensome, tough, painstaking, arduous. *Writing a book is a demanding task.* **Ant.** easy, simple, trouble-free.

demean *vb.* degrade, demote, disgrace, debase, humble, shame. *I don't think it's a good idea to demean anyone.* **Ant.** idolize, elevate, flatter.

demented *adj.* crazy, mentally unstable, insane, psychotic, deranged, irrational. *People once believed that a full moon could cause one to become demented.* **Ant.** sane, rational, stable.

dementia *n.* senility, mental deterioration, mental disturbance, mental deficiency, Alzheimer's disease, psychosis. *She was suffering from a form of dementia and didn't always make sense.* **Ant.** clear-thinking, sharpness, alertness.

democracy *n.* government by and for the people, constitutional government, republic, commonwealth, equality. *We live in a democracy where everyone has a say in how we shall be governed.* **Ant.** autocracy, tyranny, dictatorship.

democratic *adj.* representative, equal, constitutional, common, of and for the people, egalitarian, libertarian. *The democratic process gives everyone a chance to be heard.* **Ant.** dictatorial, tyrannical, autocratic.

demolish *vb.* wreck, ruin, destroy, break, devastate, pulverize, annihilate. *The meteorite demolished the house on which it fell.* **Ant.** build, restore, create.

demon *n.* devil, fiend, ghoul, ogre, hobgoblin, spook, evil spirit. *The sorcerer called a demon from the pool of darkness.*

demonic *adj.* fiendish, diabolical, Satanic, devilish, hellish, bedeviled. *Stephen King has a flair for bringing demonic themes to life.* **Ant.** angelic, heavenly, divine.

demonstrate *vb.* **1.** protest, march, rally, picket, strike. *Protestors demonstrated outside the White House.* **2.** show, display, exhibit, illustrate, describe. *This model demonstrates how a nuclear-power plant works.*

demonstration *n.* **1.** march, protest, rally, parade, picketing. *She plans to attend tomorrow's antiwar demonstration.* **2.** show, exhibit, exhibition, display, presentation. *The inventor plans to conduct a public demonstration of his antigravity device.*

demonstrator *n.* protester, marcher, striker, boycotter, conscientious, objector, rioter. *The demonstrator marched in front of his company and complained loudly about poor working conditions.*

demoralize *vb.* dishearten, deflate, depress, discourage, dispirit, crush. *The opponent's fourth touchdown served to thoroughly demoralize the hometown team.* **Ant.** encourage, hearten, charge.

demote *vb.* lower, downgrade, reduce, degrade, displace. *The lieutenant was demoted to private for his refusal to follow orders.* **Ant.** elevate, raise.

demure *adj.* reserved, shy, quiet, modest, coy, blushing. *Her demure behavior concealed a burning passion.*

den *n.* lair, shelter, retreat, sanctuary, hideaway, nest. *The coyote pups were not yet old enough to leave their den.*

denial *n.* refusal, veto, disapproval, disavowal, disclaimer. *Her denial of the charges against her caused an uproar in the courtroom.* **Ant.** acceptance, affirmation, approval.

denigrate *vb.* criticize, put down, defame, belittle, vilify, malign. *Our local movie critic tends to denigrate science fiction films.* **Ant.** praise, compliment, flatter.

denomination *n.* sect, faith, order, group, body, school. *What church denomination did she say she belongs to?*

denote *vb.* indicate, symbolize, designate, signify, represent, mark. *Red circles denote danger zones on this map.*

denounce *vb.* condemn, attack, assail, criticize, rebuke, upbraid. *Students gathered in the administration building to denounce the school's discriminatory practices.*

dense *adj.* compact, compressed, thick, congested, massed. *The fog was so dense I couldn't see anything.* **Ant.** sparse, thin, scattered.

dent *n.* indentation, hollow, (slang) ding, dimple, depression, concavity. *A collision with a shopping cart resulted in a dent in my car.*

dentures *n.* false teeth, implants, (slang) choppers, partials. *Now that my teeth have all fallen out, I find it hard to eat without my dentures.*

deny *vb.* **1.** contradict, disaffirm, dispute, protest, disavow. *She denied any knowledge of the theft.* **2.** withhold, refuse, veto, forbid, prohibit. *My parents denied my request to use the car.* **Ant. 1.** affirm, concede, admit. **2.** grant, allow, permit.

depart *vb.* leave, exit, withdraw, go, embark. *What time will the train depart?* **Ant.** arrive, enter, appear.

department *n.* division, section, bureau, branch, unit. *She heads the personnel department.*

departure *n.* **1.** leaving, exit, withdrawal, embarking, takeoff, parting. *The time of our departure is nine o'clock.* **2.** shift, change, deviation, divergence, swerving. *Allowing employees to wear blue jeans was a departure from the usual rules.* **Ant. 1.** arrival, coming, entrance. **2.** conformity, adherence.

depend *vb.* **1.** rely, bank, count, trust, believe. *You can depend on her to have the work done in time.* **2.** hinge, rest, turn, hang, stand. *Whether or not we go depends on the weather.*

dependable *adj.* trustworthy, trusty, reliable, responsible, faithful, conscientious. *She needs a dependable person to take care of her house while she's away.* **Ant.** undependable, unreliable, untrustworthy.

depict *vb.* describe, portray, picture, characterize, represent. *Antarctica is often depicted as a cold and forbidding place.*

deplete *vb.* drain, exhaust, empty, consume, weaken, reduce, diminish. *Running your radio* *all night will deplete the batteries.* **Ant.** restore, replenish, increase.

deplorable *adj.* wretched, miserable, pathetic, regrettable, contemptible, shameful. *She left her room in a deplorable condition.* **Ant.** acceptable, good, agreeable.

deploy *vb.* spread out, station, disperse, position, distribute, arrange. *The soldiers were told that they should be prepared to deploy in three hours.* **Ant.** gather, amass, muster.

deport *vb.* expel, eject, evict, remove, banish, dislodge. *Foreign citizens crossing U.S. borders without proper papers are deported.*

depose *vb.* oust, remove, dethrone, overthrow, impeach, unseat. *The citizens enacted a plan that would quickly depose the king.* **Ant.** install, empower, seat.

deposit *vb.* **1.** place, set, put, insert, lay, bank. *I just deposited $100 in my checking account.* –*n.* **2.** precipitation, sediment, silt, dregs, alluvium. *The chemist boiled the solution until only a blue deposit remained.* **3.** money, assets, savings, payment, installment. *His deposits total over $10,000.* **Ant. 1.** withdraw, remove.

depraved *adj.* evil, wicked, immoral, corrupt, vile, base, foul. *The depraved count murdered several hundred villagers.* **Ant.** good, moral, virtuous.

depreciate *vb.* lower, reduce, devalue, deflate, cut, decrease, diminish. *Inflation depreciates the value of money.* **Ant.** increase, raise, boost.

depress *vb.* **1.** sadden, dishearten, discourage, deject, dispirit. *Losing his job depressed him.* **2.** lower, reduce, flatten, level, sink. *The dollar's loss of value depressed the stock market.* **Ant. 1.** gladden, encourage, cheer. **2.** raise, lift, boost.

depressed *adj.* unhappy, miserable, downcast, sorrowful dejected. *The astronaut was very depressed when her mission was unsuccessful.* **Ant.** happy, joyous, delighted.

depression *n.* **1.** melancholy, sadness, despair, despondency, hopelessness. *He went through a period of depression after breaking up with his girlfriend.* **2.** crater, cavity, hole, hollow, pit. *There was a big depression in the ground where the meteorite hit.* **3.** recession, decline, slump, stagnation, crash. *The economy is headed toward a depression.* **Ant. 1.** cheerfulness, optimism, happiness. **3.** boom, progress.

deprive *vb.* strip, divest, rob, deny, withhold, remove, seize. *Loud music next door deprived him of a good night's sleep.*

deputy *n.* assistant, aide, sidekick, second-in-command, agent, subordinate. *The deputy filled in when the sheriff was busy.*

deranged *adj.* crazy, psychotic, mentally unstable, psychopathic, insane, irrational. *The deranged criminal was considered armed and dangerous.* **Ant.** sane, rational, stable.

derelict *adj.* **1.** abandoned, deserted, discarded, forsaken, forlorn. *The derelict ship rusted away.* **2.** negligent, slack, lax, delinquent, loose, lazy. *He's been derelict in doing his chores.*

deride *vb.* belittle, scorn, knock, ridicule, mock, tease, taunt. *Please don't deride my belief in UFOs.*

derision *n.* ridicule, disrespect, contempt, disdain, disparagement, scorn. *At the meeting, her suggestion was met with derision.* **Ant.** respect, honor, acceptance.

derive *vb.* obtain, reap, extract, come, arise, gather, get. *This potion is derived from bat wings.*

derogatory *adj.* disparaging, disrespectful, contemptuous, belittling, unflattering, sarcastic. *The teacher had the student removed from class for* *his derogatory remarks.* **Ant.** complimentary, flattering, respectful.

descend *vb.* **1.** drop, fall, plunge, sink, dive, subside, submerge. *The submarine descended to the bottom of the sea.* **2.** come, spring, issue, derive. *He is descended from native American Indians.* **3.** pounce, swoop, attack, assault, invade. *Barbarian hordes descended on the unprotected village.* **Ant.** **1.** ascend, rise, climb.

descendant *n.* offspring, issue, family, progeny, brood, daughter, son. *She is a descendant of 18th-century immigrants.* **Ant.** ancestor, parent.

descent *n.* **1.** fall, plunge, drop, dip, droop, settling, decline. *The gull made a quick descent and plucked a fish from the water.* **2.** ancestry, heritage, lineage, parentage, origin, roots, stock. *He is of Arabic descent.* **Ant.** **1.** ascent, climb, rise.

describe *vb.* depict, define, portray, illustrate, picture, relate, recount. *The police asked her to describe what she saw last night.*

description *n.* account, report, depiction, portrayal, sketch. *Can you give a description of the thief?*

desecrate *vb.* violate, spoil, profane, dishonor, disrespect, debase. *The vandals broke into the shrine and desecrated it.* **Ant.** honor, respect, worship.

desegregate *vb.* integrate, unite, join, associate, bring together, commingle. *They decided to desegregate schools to encourage diversity.* **Ant.** segregate, separate, divide.

desert *vb.* abandon, forsake, leave, quit, renounce. *My friends deserted me when things got bad.*

desert *n.* wasteland, barrens, badlands, flats, dunes, arid plain. *You have to be tough to survive in the desert.*

WORD SEARCH

cactus: *saguaro*
eroded area comprised of mesas, gullies, channels: *badlands*
dune, crescent-shaped: *barchan*
dune, elongated: *seif dune, sword dune*
dune, pyramidlike: *pyramid*
dune, starlike: *star*
dune, whalelike: *whaleback*
dusty whirlwind, compact: *dustdevil*
illusion: *mirage*
rain that evaporates before it reaches the ground: *phantom rain*
riverbed, dried-up: *arroyo*
mosaiclike ground comprised of colored pebbles: *desert pavement, gibber plain, reg*
mountain, flat-top and eroded: *mesa, butte*
nomad, Arab: *Bedouin*
temporary lake after rain: *playa*
salty plain that was once a lake: *salt flat*
vegetation fed by spring, isolated area of: *oasis*

deserted *adj.* empty, vacant, abandoned, uninhabited, desolate, lonely. *The ghost town was deserted.* **Ant.** crowded, mobbed, teeming.

deserter *n.* runaway, defector, truant, fugitive, refugee, traitor. *Deserters will face long prison terms.* **Ant.** joiner.

deserve *vb.* merit, earn, warrant, qualify, rate. *After working so many extra hours, he deserves the promotion.*

design *vb.* **1.** plan, fashion, arrange, draft, develop, imagine, visualize. *Engineers have designed the car so that it is both comfortable and fast.* –*n.* **2.** plan, pattern, scheme, arrangement, outline, diagram. *She oversaw the design and building of her new house.* **3.** intent, objective, intention, purpose, aim, goal, desire. *It was not my design to get your position on the team.*

designate *vb.* name, nominate, appoint, select, assign, choose. *The teacher has designated me as group leader.*

desirable *adj.* attractive, inviting, agreeable, valuable, worthy, excellent. *This is a desirable job because of the high salary and pleasant environment.* **Ant.** undesirable, unattractive, repulsive.

desire *vb.* **1.** want, wish for, fancy, covet, crave. *She's desired a new car for some time.* –*n.* **2.** wanting, wishing, yearning, longing, attraction, craving. *He felt a strong desire to see his family again after so many years.* **Ant. 2.** aversion, distaste, dislike.

desk *n.* table, work station, rolltop, ambo, escritoire, secretary. *We were not surprised to see that our math teacher had fallen asleep at her desk again.*

desolate *adj.* barren, deserted, empty, bleak, godforsaken, abandoned. *The Arizona desert was one of the most desolate places I had ever seen.* **Ant.** crowded, mobbed.

despair *n.* hopelessness, dismay, distress, depression, dejection. *They felt despair when they realized there was no way to save him.* **Ant.** hopefulness, hope, optimism.

desperado *n.* outlaw, criminal, gunman, criminal, thug, bandit, bandito. *The desperado held up the town bank and fled on horseback.*

desperate *adj.* **1.** frantic, hasty, wild, risky, reckless. *He made a desperate grab for his hat as it flew out the window.* **2.** hopeless, despairing, wretched, despondent, depressed. *She felt desperate because she had no date and the dance was only one day away.* **Ant. 1.** cautious, careful. **2.** happy, hopeful, optimistic.

desperation *n.* **1.** desperation, despondency, gloom, hopelessness, futility, discouragement. *His desperation over being lost in the woods grew by the hour.* **2.** recklessness, frenzy, rashness, foolhardiness, carelessness. *Stealing food for his family was an act of desperation borne of poverty.*

despicable *adj.* detestable, disgraceful, shameful, contemptible, loathsome, unforgivable. *Knocking over gravestones is a despicable act of vandalism.* **Ant.** commendable, admirable, laudable.

despise *vb.* detest, hate, loathe, scorn, dislike, abhor, disdain. *I've always despised a person who says nasty things about others.* **Ant.** like, admire, respect.

despondent *adj.* depressed, downhearted, melancholic, heartbroken, suicidal, forlorn. *He was despondent over the loss of his beloved pet.* **Ant.** euphoric, ecstatic, joyful.

despot *n.* dictator, tyrant, autocrat, authoritarian, master, oppressor. *The evil despot outlawed the right to vote.*

destination *n.* goal, objective, stop, end, target, aim. *The plane's destination is Beijing.*

destiny *n.* fortune, luck, lot, fate, providence. *She felt that it was her destiny to become president.*

destitute *adj.* impoverished, poor, penniless, broke, needy. *The massive earthquake left thousands of people homeless and destitute.* **Ant.** rich, affluent, wealthy.

destroy *vb.* wreck, ruin, demolish, level, raze, devastate, crush. *A mudslide destroyed several houses in our neighborhood.* **Ant.** restore, save, preserve.

destruction *n.* ruination, devastation, wrecking, razing, demolition, leveling. *Rabbits are responsible for the destruction of our garden.* **Ant.** preservation, conservation.

detach *vb.* disconnect, unfasten, separate, free, loosen. *She had trouble detaching the gum from her shoe.* **Ant.** attach, fix, secure.

detail *n.* **1.** part, item, particular, specific, feature, aspect. *His paintings are known for their fine attention to detail.* –*vb.* **2.** itemize, specify, depict, recount, relate. *He detailed all his expenses.*

detain *vb.* **1.** delay, slow, hinder, retard, check, impede. *She was detained by an important phone call.* **2.** arrest, hold, stop, restrain, imprison, confine. *Security personnel detained the woman after finding a gun in her baggage.*

detect *vb.* see, discover, uncover, notice, spot, observe, find. *The doctor could detect no signs of infection.*

detective *n.* investigator, sleuth, undercover agent, (slang) private eye, (slang) gumshoe, (slang) snoop. *Sherlock Holmes is the best known of all fictional detectives.*

WORD SEARCH

canine trained to detect drugs, bombs, arson: *sniffer dog*
chemical used to detect presence of blood: *Luminol*
clue: *lead*
crime lab specialist: *criminalist*
death, determines cause of: *coroner, medical examiner*
drugs and other substances, machine used to identify: *gas-chromatography mass spectrometer*
explosives, machine used to detect: *X-ray diffraction machine*
identification through analysis of DNA in blood, semen, hair, etc: *DNA fingerprinting*
interrogation technique, intense and outmoded: *third degree*
fingerprints, study of: *dactylography*
fingerprints, technique that reveals hidden: *super glue fuming*
footprint casts: *moulages*
fibers, chemicals, particles, field specializing in identification of: forensic chemistry lie detector: *polygraph*
London detective organization, famous: *Scotland Yard*
medical evidence surrounding case, field specializing in: *forensic medicine*
observation of suspect, long-term: *surveillance, stakeout*
recording device, carrying a secret: *wired*
scientific detection facility: *crime lab*
solve a case: *crack*
strangulation, hemorrhage under eyelid that indicates: *petechial hemorrhage*
unaffiliated with police department, detective: *private investigator; private eye*

detente *n.* peace, harmony, truce, amnesty, suspension of hostilities, relaxation. *The two nations entered a new era of detente after long, difficult negotiations.* **Ant.** hostility, animosity, war.

detention *n.* restraint, internment, delaying, arrest, retention. *He was held in detention for running in the halls.* **Ant.** freedom, liberation, release.

deter *vb.* discourage, prevent, stop, thwart, block, hinder. *Hopefully, our new alarm system will deter burglars.* **Ant.** encourage, reassure, stimulate.

detergent *n.* cleanser, soap, cleaner, solvent, degreaser, scouring powder. *Even strong detergent won't wash out the smell of a skunk.*

deteriorate *vb.* degrade, fall apart, decay, crumble, rot, degenerate, corrode. *Anything left out in the elements will eventually deteriorate.* **Ant.** strengthen, grow, harden.

determination *n.* resolve, resoluteness, tenacity, drive, persistence, perseverance. *Through hard work and determination, the team finally won the state championship.* **Ant.** lack of resolve, indifference, apathy.

determine *vb.* settle, decide, ascertain, resolve, discover. *Have you determined which movie you're going to see?*

determined *adj.* decided, fixed, settled, purposeful, firm, resolute. *His determined look made me realize I couldn't talk him out of going.* **Ant.** undetermined, indecisive, undecided.

deterrent *n.* check, roadblock, impediment, stumbling block, hurdle, obstacle, curb. *A police radar gun serves as a good deterrent to speeders.*

detest *vb.* hate, dislike, despise, loathe, abhor, disdain. *I really detest worms.* **Ant.** love, like, adore.

dethrone *vb.* depose, expel, kick out, remove, impeach, oust. *The silly king was dethroned, and he spent the rest of his days working as a court jester.* **Ant.** install, empower, seat.

detonate *vb.* explode, set off, blow, discharge, fire, touch off. *The police roped off the area in fear that the bomb might detonate before it was defused.*

detonation *n.* explosion, discharge, firing, blow-up, boom, roar. *We heard a distant detonation, which was the road crew blowing up some ledge.*

detour *vb.* **1.** route, direct, skirt, bypass. *Due to construction work, we were detoured onto a side street.* –*n.* **2.** bypath, byroad, byway, diversion, digression. *I know we're late, but I need to make a quick detour to the rest room.*

detrimental *adj.* damaging, harmful, destructive, injurious, deleterious, pernicious. *Smoking is detrimental to your health.* **Ant.** helpful, healthy, beneficial.

devalue *vb.* degrade, cheapen, reduce, lower, lessen, drop. *Failure to apply a fresh coat of paint might devalue your home and reduce its asking price.* **Ant.** enrich, increase, upgrade.

devastate *vb.* ravage, waste, ruin, destroy, despoil, raze, level. *Locusts devastated the farmer's crops.*

devastation *n.* destruction, ruin, annihilation, wreckage, demolition, fallout. *The hurricane brought widespread devastation.*

develop *vb.* **1.** enlarge, expand, improve, broaden, increase. *Lifting weights developed my biceps.* **2.** generate, invent, form, fashion, establish, organize. *Scientists spent years developing a spacecraft that could surpass the speed of light.* **3.** acquire, get, contract, obtain, gain. *He developed a serious case of pneumonia.*

developer *n.* investor, builder, real estate mogul, land baron, speculator, businessman, businesswoman. *The developer planned to clear the last area of forest to put in a mall.*

development *n.* **1.** evolution, growth, rise, progress, history. *The development of the laser promises to benefit medical science.* **2.** event, incident, happening, occurrence, episode. *Stay tuned to this station for the latest developments.*

deviant *adj.* abnormal, anomalous, unusual, weird, unorthodox, irregular. *His distaste for pizza was somewhat deviant.* **Ant.** normal, usual, regular.

deviate *vb.* stray, diverge, wander, turn, depart. *His account of the accident seems to deviate from the facts.*

device *n.* **1.** gadget, instrument, equipment, apparatus, implement, tool. *The aliens had devices that allowed them to read our minds.* **2.** scheme, strategy, plot, design, intrigue. *My parents used several devices to try to get me to choose the college they preferred.*

devil *n.* demon, imp, fiend, ogre, evil-doer, Satan, Lucifer. *The little devil stole the last piece of pie.* **Ant.** angel, do-gooder, saint.

devilish *adj.* evil, nasty, fiendish, villainous, impish, diabolical. *He was a devilish prankster* *who irritated everyone.* **Ant.** angelic, saintly, good.

devious *adj.* underhand, sneaky, tricky, scheming, calculating, deceitful. *That was a devious way of getting your needs met.* **Ant.** honest, straightforward.

devise *vb.* invent, conceive, formulate, forge, construct, arrange. *She devised a way to turn lead into gold.*

devote *vb.* give, commit, surrender, pledge, dedicate, offer, apply. *She devoted many hours to the project.*

devoted *adj.* loyal, faithful, dedicated, committed, true. *Her dog is her devoted companion.* **Ant.** unfaithful, disloyal, untrue.

devotee *n.* fan, fanatic, buff, enthusiast, aficionado, adherent. *Joe has broken his legs four times during crash-landings, but he is still a devotee of hang gliding.*

devotion *n.* dedication, attachment, loyalty, faithfulness, love, regard. *She appreciates her husband's devotion.* **Ant.** indifference, disinterest, disregard.

devour *vb.* gobble, swallow, gulp, consume, eat, finish. *He devoured two hamburgers in less than three minutes.*

devout *adj.* faithful, pious, earnest, sincere, heartfelt, reverent. *He is a devout Catholic.*

dexterity *n.* skill, agility, facility, proficiency, adroitness. *The basketball player was known for her dexterity on the court.* **Ant.** clumsiness, awkwardness, ineptitude.

diabetes *n.* metabolic disorder, insulin insufficiency, disease, illness. *To help prevent diabetes, get plenty of exercise and watch your diet.*

diabolic *adj.* satanic, demonic, fiendish, evil, wicked, infernal. *The schemes of mass murderers are often diabolic.* **Ant.** angelic, heavenly, divine.

diagnosis *n.* identification, educated guess, conclusion, determination, opinion, analysis. *My entire body was covered in red spots, so it was easy to make a diagnosis.*

diagram *n.* sketch, drawing, outline, blueprint, picture, illustration. *Please draw a diagram of the building.*

dialect *n.* speech, vernacular, idiolect, accent, language, local tongue, idiom. *The foreigner spoke with a dialect that I couldn't identify.*

dialogue *n.* conversation, talk, exchange, chat, discourse. *I couldn't follow the play's dialogue.*

diameter *n.* caliber, width, breadth, size, measurement. *I don't know how many miles in diameter the Sun is, but I do know it's gargantuan.*

diarrhea *n.* loose stool, (slang) Montezuma's revenge, flux, trots, (slang) Aztec two-step, gastrointestinal distress. *Sheila drank the water in Mexico and got a bad case of diarrhea.* **Ant.** constipation.

diary *n.* journal, log, logbook, chronicle, record. *The ship's captain kept a diary of his journeys.*

dichotomy *n.* division, split, break, separation, rift, subdivision. *There is quite a dichotomy between what the Republicans and the Democrats believe.* **Ant.** convergence, connection, meeting.

dicker *vb.* haggle, higgle, negotiate, bargain, talk down. *Prices in the bazaar are not carved in stone, so customers must dicker with merchants.*

dictate *vb.* **1.** communicate, speak, say, utter, transmit. *The lawyer dictated a letter to her secretary.* **2.** direct, ordain, command, order, decree, determine. *I won't let you dictate where I go.* **Ant. 2.** follow, obey.

dictator *n.* despot, tyrant, autocrat, oppressor, totalitarian, strongman. *Once the dictator took control of the country, the quality of life quickly deteriorated.*

diction *n.* expression, enunciation, articulation, vocabulary, usage, language. *His perfect diction makes it possible for listeners to understand every word he utters.*

dictionary *n.* lexicon, glossary, reference, vocabulary, book, tome. *If you don't know the definition to this word, look it up in the dictionary.*

die *vb.* **1.** perish, expire, decease, end, succumb, fail. *When the plane began shaking, he thought he was going to die.* **2.** thirst, hunger, desire, want, crave, yearn, long. *She's dying for a tall glass of lemonade.* **Ant. 1.** live, survive, exist.

diet *n.* regimen, regime, abstinence, deprivation, fasting, calorie counting. *I've tried dozens of diets and none of them has worked.*

differ *vb.* **1.** vary, deviate, contrast, disagree, conflict. *Estimates to fix his car differed by as much as $500.* **2.** disagree, dispute, squabble, quarrel, argue, wrangle. *We differed on where to go for our vacation.* **Ant. 1.** match, correspond, coincide. **2.** agree, concur.

difference *n.* **1.** dissimilarity, contrast, divergence, variation, deviation. *Do you think there is a big difference between people in New York and those in Los Angeles?* **2.** argument, dispute, squabble, quarrel, feud, clash. *I quit after my boss and I had some major differences.* **Ant. 1.** similarity, likeness. **2.** agreement, harmony, accord.

different *adj.* **1.** separate, distinct, assorted, varied, unrelated. *She painted her car several different colors.* **2.** unusual, strange, odd, unique, extraordinary. *He has a different way of doing things.* **3.** dissimilar, unlike, contrasting, opposed, divergent. *My taste in movies is quite different from hers.* **Ant. 2.** ordinary, common, usual. **3.** identical, alike, same.

difficult *adj.* hard, troublesome, tough, laborious, strenuous, exhausting, tedious. *It's difficult writing a twenty-page paper the night before it's due.* **Ant.** easy, simple, pleasant.

difficulty *n.* strain, trouble, labor, problem, bother, ordeal, trial. *After gaining twenty pounds, he had difficulty getting into his jeans.*

diffuse *adj.* spread out, strewn, scattered, dispersed. *In some parts of the universe, stars are highly diffuse.* **Ant.** concentrated, thick, dense.

dig *vb.* **1.** scoop, burrow, excavate, tunnel, shovel, mine. *She dug for clams.* *–n.* **2.** jab, poke, prod, thrust, push. *Give the mule a light dig in the ribs to get it going.*

digest *vb.* **1.** absorb, assimilate, grasp, understand, comprehend. *Give me a minute to digest what you said.* *–n.* **2.** summary, abstract, condensation, abridgment, brief. *I just finished reading a digest of his latest book.*

dignified *adj.* poised, classy, distinguished, regal, aristocratic, self-respecting. *Leaders must maintain a dignified air or risk losing respect.* **Ant.** undignified, silly, goofy.

dignitary *n.* VIP, personage, official, (slang) bigwig, (slang) bigshot, celebrity. *The dignitary from Egypt was expected to visit the governor today.*

dignity *n.* formality, respectability, reserve, solemnity, loftiness. *His sense of dignity would not allow him to act so foolishly.*

digress *vb.* deviate, wander, stray, drift, depart, veer, straggle. *Sorry, but I seem to have digressed from my topic.*

dilapidated *adj.* broken-down, decaying, crumbling, deteriorated, falling apart. *The dilapidated house threatened to collapse with the next strong breeze.* **Ant.** sound, solid, new.

dilate *vb.* expand, enlarge, widen, swell, broaden, inflate. *The optometrist's solution dilated the pupils of my eyes.* **Ant.** shrink, contract, constrict.

dilemma *n.* quandary, bind, predicament, question, stalemate, perplexity. *Two parties are going on tonight, and it's a dilemma trying to decide which one to attend.*

dilettante *n.* dabbler, amateur, hobbyist, tyro, layman, nonprofessional. *I'm trying to master painting, but I'm just a dilettante.* **Ant.** master, professional, expert.

diligence *n.* persistence, perseverance, earnestness, exertion, application. *It takes diligence to successfully pan for gold.* **Ant.** laziness, sloth, lethargy.

diligent *adj.* industrious, persevering, hardworking, painstaking, persistent, zealous. *She gets good grades because she's diligent in her studying.* **Ant.** lazy, indifferent, careless.

dilute *vb.* **1.** thin, mix, weaken, cut, adulterate. *She dilutes her orange juice with water.* *–adj.* **2.** diluted, thin, watery, weak, adulterated. *The cook's vegetable soup is usually very dilute.* **Ant.** **1.** thicken, concentrate. **2.** thick, concentrated, strong.

dim *adj.* **1.** low, soft, weak, dark, murky, indistinct. *This light is too dim for reading.* **2.** discouraging, somber, unpromising, depressing, ominous. *The surrounded troops thought their prospects were pretty dim.* **Ant.** **1.** bright, brilliant, strong. **2.** hopeful, promising.

dimension *n.* measure, size, magnitude, extent, expanse, spread, range, volume. *Do you understand the full dimensions of the problem?*

diminish *vb.* lessen, reduce, decrease, recede, shrink, lower, dwindle, subside. *The sound diminished as we got farther away.* **Ant.** increase, magnify, enlarge.

din *n.* noise, clamor, uproar, racket, commotion. *The din of my neighbor's stereo is getting on my nerves.* **Ant.** silence, stillness, quiet.

dine *vb.* eat, feed, feast, sup, banquet. *Let's dine out tonight.*

diner *n.* café, lunch counter, eatery, restaurant, (slang) greasy spoon. *We stopped at a diner and ordered a big breakfast.*

dingy *adj.* shabby, dirty, seedy, run-down, grimy, drab, gloomy. *The cheap motel had small and dingy rooms.* **Ant.** luxurious, shiny, clean.

dinner *n.* supper, meal, repast, feast, banquet, feed. *Kids, time for dinner!*

dinosaur *n.* saurian, sauropod, terrible lizard, prehistoric beast, theropod. *Kids are universally fascinated by dinosaurs.*

dip *vb.* **1.** immerse, submerge, soak, plunge, dunk. *She dipped her feet in the pool's cool water.* **2.** sink, set, settle, descend, drop. *The sun dipped below the horizon.* **Ant.** **2.** rise, climb, ascend.

diploma *n.* certificate, parchment, document, degree, (slang) sheepskin, award. *Companies hiring today require a high school diploma as a bare minimum.*

diplomacy *n.* statesmanship, tact, people skills, sensitivity, charm, politics. *Solving international problems requires great diplomacy.* **Ant.** insensitivity, rudeness, brusqueness.

diplomat *n.* envoy, ambassador, emissary, mediator, negotiator, consul. *Diplomats from two nations met to sign the treaty.*

diplomatic *adj.* tactful, sensitive, charming, politic, prudent, discreet, strategic. *When settling* *a dispute, it pays to be diplomatic.* **Ant.** rude, insensitive, brusque.

dire *adj.* 1. grievous, awful, alarming, terrible, horrible, fearsome. *She was suffering from a dire illness.* 2. critical, urgent, vital, desperate, crucial. *The accident victims were in dire need of care.*

direct *vb.* 1. run, manage, lead, supervise, administer, control. *She is responsible for directing the play.* 2. point, guide, aim, steer, lead, send. *Will you direct me to the post office?* 3. command, instruct, tell, charge, bid, order. *My instructions directed me to meet him at the train station.* –*adj.* 4. straight, short, true, unwinding, unswerving. *Is this path the most direct route to the top?* 5. frank, honest, candid, blunt, truthful, sincere. *Please be direct with me.* **Ant.** 4. indirect, roundabout, winding. 5. indirect, subtle, devious.

direction *n.* 1. path, course, heading, way, route, bearing. *In which direction did they go?* 2. administration, management, control, supervision, handling, leadership. *The business has profited under his direction.* 3. instruction, command, order, guidelines, teaching. *My boss told me to follow his directions carefully.*

directly *adv.* straight, right, immediately, quickly, promptly, instantly. *If you land on this space, you go directly to jail.* **Ant.** later, eventually, indirectly.

director *n.* leader, supervisor, head, orchestrator, foreman, general. *The director has the last word in how things will be handled.*

dirigible *n.* balloon, zeppelin, blimp, airship, lighter-than-air vehicle. *It's rare to see a dirigible in the sky today.*

dirty *adj.* 1. soiled, filthy, unwashed, grimy, unclean, stained. *I took my dirty clothes to the laundry.* 2. indecent, obscene, smutty, vulgar, pornographic. *He has a dirty mind.* 3. illegal, crooked, dishonorable, deceitful, villainous, corrupt. *The politician made some dirty deals.* 4. angry, annoyed, offended, resentful, bitter. *She gave me a dirty look.* –*vb.* 5. soil, smear, tarnish, smudge, stain, blacken. *The scandal has dirtied her name.* **Ant.** 1. clean, spotless, washed. 2. clean, decent, virtuous. 3. clean, legal. 5. clean, sanitize, wash.

disability *n.* debility, handicap, infirmity, impairment, weakness, injury. *Although she was blind from birth, she never let her disability stop her from doing what she wanted.* **Ant.** ability, strength, advantage.

disable *vb.* cripple, handicap, incapacitate, impair, weaken, debilitate. *It's easy to disable a computer; just unplug it.* **Ant.** enable, facilitate, strengthen.

disadvantage *n.* handicap, detriment, drawback, minus, liability, burden. *Your lack of education is a real disadvantage.* **Ant.** advantage, strength, plus.

disagree *vb.* differ, conflict, clash, argue, quarrel, debate. *They disagreed over which team had the better quarterback.* **Ant.** agree, concur, reconcile.

disagreeable *adj.* 1. unpleasant, disgusting, repulsive, distasteful, repellent. *She finds the thought of eating cooked snails rather disagreeable.* 2. unfriendly, surly, irritable, grouchy, sullen. *He doesn't get along with anyone because of his disagreeable nature.* **Ant.** 1. agreeable, pleasant, appealing. 2. agreeable, friendly.

disagreement *n.* quarrel, dispute, fight, clash, rift, split. *We had a disagreement over who could use the car.* **Ant.** agreement, concurrence, accord.

disappear *vb.* vanish, dematerialize, dissolve, vaporize, depart, fade. *The ship disappeared in the Bermuda Triangle.* **Ant.** appear, emerge, materialize.

disappoint *vb.* disillusion, dissatisfy, sadden, dishearten, discourage, frustrate. *The producers disappointed me by making a bad movie.* **Ant.** please, satisfy, delight.

disappointment *n.* dissatisfaction, frustration, regret, letdown, disillusionment. *The children made their disappointment obvious when their trip to the circus was postponed.* **Ant.** satisfaction, contentment, happiness.

disapprove *vb.* criticize, dislike, condemn, reject, deplore, denounce. *His parents disapprove of the way he dresses.* **Ant.** approve, praise, commend.

disarm *vb.* neutralize, defang, disable, take the teeth out of, mollify, charm. *The beauty contestant could disarm any man with her smile.*

disarming *adj.* charming, winning, irresistible, likable, appealing. *Lisa has a disarming way of getting what she wants.*

disaster *n.* catastrophe, tragedy, misfortune, calamity, accident, mishap. *At least 1,500 people died in the* Titanic *disaster.*

disastrous *adj.* calamitous, ruinous, catastrophic, devastating, tragic, fatal. *The company suffered a disastrous loss of revenues.* **Ant.** fortunate, beneficial, helpful.

disband *vb.* separate, split, break up, divide, dissolve, fold. *The group had been together for twenty years but finally decided to disband.* **Ant.** join, unite, form.

disbelief *n.* doubt, distrust, skepticism, scorn, rejection, incredulity. *His story of the purple aliens was met with disbelief.* **Ant.** belief, acceptance, trust.

discard *vb.* **1.** eliminate, dispose, dump, drop, shed, scrap, abandon. *Please discard your litter in the trash can. –n.* **2.** reject, castaway, scraps, throwaway, garbage. *Put your discards in this pile.* **Ant. 1.** retain, keep, save.

discern *vb.* ascertain, decipher, discover, distinguish, see, notice. *I think I've discerned the purpose of her visit.*

discerning *adj.* discriminating, judicious, astute, intelligent, perceptive, sharp. *It takes a discerning eye to notice the difference between a star and a planet.* **Ant.** undiscerning, stupid, blind.

discharge *vb.* **1.** explode, detonate, shoot, burst, activate. *Pulling this pin will discharge the bomb.* **2.** gush, ooze, emit, eject, leak, empty. *Sewer pipes discharged polluted wastes into the ocean.* **3.** release, free, dismiss, fire, relieve. *The soldier was honorably discharged after serving four years. –n.* **4.** blast, explosion, shooting, firing, detonation. *The rifle's discharge shattered the peacefulness of the forest.* **5.** emission, ejection, flow, seepage, issue, secretion. *Automobile discharge is a major source of pollution.* **6.** release, dismissal, expulsion, removal. *She was informed of her discharge from the company.* **Ant. 3.** hold, keep, hire.

disciple *n.* follower, supporter, apostle, devotee, adherent, believer. *A disciple of* Star Trek *is often a fan of science fiction.* **Ant.** master, leader, teacher.

disciplinarian *n.* tyrant, authoritarian, slavedriver, punisher, dictator, controller. *A disciplinarian does not always have to rule with an iron fist.*

discipline *n.* **1.** practice, drilling, preparation, instruction, training. *It takes years of discipline to learn how to rock-climb.* **2.** regulation, restriction, direction, control, punishment, correction. *My parents are strict when it comes to discipline.* **3.** subject, specialty, major, curriculum. *The instructor is very knowledgeable in his* *discipline.* –*vb.* **4.** train, drill, school, prepare, instruct, toughen. *She disciplined herself to feel no pain.* **5.** punish, correct, chastise, reprimand, criticize. *I disciplined my dog for tearing up the neighbor's flower garden.*

disclaimer *n.* disavowal, denial, caveat, caution, notice. *Many manufacturers place disclaimers on their products that absolve them of legal responsibility.*

disclose *vb.* reveal, tell, divulge, expose, unmask, show, release. *I can't disclose the source of my information.* **Ant.** hide, conceal, mask.

disclosure *n.* admission, confession, revelation, declaration, exposé, acknowledgment. *The public disclosure proved embarrassing.* **Ant.** cover-up, censoring, secret.

disco *n.* discotheque, dance hall, nightclub, club. *They danced at the disco all night.*

discomfort *n.* uneasiness, distress, suffering, misery, ache, pain. *Is your sprained knee giving you much discomfort?* **Ant.** comfort, ease, pleasure.

disconcerted *adj.* perturbed, disturbed, rattled, uneasy, ruffled, troubled. *My mother always becomes disconcerted during a storm.* **Ant.** calm, untroubled, serene.

discontented *adj.* dissatisfied, displeased, unhappy, impatient, frustrated. *She is discontented with her job.* **Ant.** satisfied, pleased, happy.

discontinue *vb.* stop, cease, end, terminate, suspend, interrupt. *My parents threatened to discontinue my allowance if I didn't behave.* **Ant.** continue, maintain, start.

discord *n.* conflict, hostility, friction, strife, disharmony. *The mounting discord between the two nations was cause for concern.* **Ant.** harmony, peace, accord.

discount *n.* **1.** reduction, deduction, decrease, lessening, rebate. *You can get a discount if you buy two of the same items.* –*vb.* **2.** reduce, lessen, decrease, subtract, deduct. *This store discounts everything by 25 percent.* **3.** disregard, ignore, overlook, omit, slight. *The jury discounted my testimony, since I hadn't seen the crime.* **Ant. 2.** hike, raise, boost.

discourage *vb.* **1.** deject, dismay, unnerve, dishearten, depress, disenchant. *I was discouraged by the fact that no publisher seemed interested in my book.* **2.** dissuade, warn, caution, deter, restrain. *The ranger strongly discouraged those who lacked training from attempting the climb.* **Ant. 1.** encourage, hearten, excite. **2.** encourage.

discouragement *n.* despair, setback, frustration, worry, dismay. *Her failure to win the lead part was a major discouragement to her.* **Ant.** encouragement, uplift, boost.

discourteous *adj.* rude, impolite, inconsiderate, ill-mannered, boorish, uncivil. *The store fired their cashier because he was discourteous to customers.* **Ant.** courteous, polite, civil.

discover *vb.* find, unearth, uncover, locate, detect, recognize, spot, see. *The California Gold Rush occurred in 1848, after gold was discovered at Sutter's Mill.* **Ant.** miss, overlook.

discovery *n.* detection, unearthing, uncovering, finding, find, locating. *William Herschel is credited with the discovery of the planet Uranus in 1781.*

discredit *vb.* reject, dispute, debunk, disprove, challenge, puncture, explode. *The goal of many scientists is to discredit psychics and other practitioners of the occult.* **Ant.** prove, support, credit, back up.

discreet *adj.* guarded, cautious, diplomatic, tactful, careful. *Please be discreet when telling them the nature of my problem.* **Ant.** indiscreet, incautious, careless.

discrepancy *n.* inconsistency, conflict, disparity, error, incongruity, disagreement. *The accountant found a discrepancy between the receipts and what was recorded in the ledger.* **Ant.** match, consistency, agreement.

discretion *n.* judgment, preference, inclination, thoughtfulness, wisdom. *Television viewers should use their own discretion in deciding what to watch.*

discrimination *vb.* **1.** bigotry, prejudice, bias, intolerance, racism, sexism. *It is unlawful for employers to practice discrimination based on sex, creed or color.* **2.** judgment, insight, discernment, discretion, forethought. *Use some discrimination in choosing a car.*

discuss *vb.* talk about, debate, review, examine, consider, study. *Let's discuss this before we go ahead and do it.*

discussion *n.* debate, conversation, talk, discourse, conference, meeting. *He fell asleep during the class discussion.*

disdain *vb.* loathe, despise, hate, abhor, spurn, hold in contempt. *I disdain racial intolerance.* **Ant.** like, admire, respect.

disease *n.* illness, sickness, ailment, malady, affliction. *Leprosy is one of the least contagious diseases.*

WORD SEARCH

blood: *anemia, hemophilia, leukemia*
bone: *osteoarthritis, osteoporosis, rickets*
brain and nervous system: *Alzheimer's disease, aphasia, encephalitis, epilepsy, Huntington's chorea, meningitis, multiple sclerosis, Parkinson's disease, stroke*
circulatory: *aneurysm, arteriosclerosis, hypertension, ischemia, phlebitis, thrombosis*
contagious: *chicken pox, diphtheria, measles, plague, tuberculosis, whooping cough*
deficiency: *beriberi, pellagra, rickets, scurvy*
digestive: *appendicitis, cirrhosis of the liver, colitis, Crohn's disease, diabetes, gallstones, hepatitis, pancreatitis, peptic ulcer, typhoid fever*
ear: *tinnitus, vertigo*
eye: *cataract, conjunctivitis, glaucoma, pinkeye, retinitis pigmentosa*
food poisoning: *botulism, salmonella, trichinosis*
germ killer: *antibiotic, antibody*
heart: *arrhythmia, congestive heart failure, coronary artery disease, ischemic heart disease, tachycardia*
identification of: *diagnosis*
imagined: *hypochondriasis*
immune breakdown: *AIDS (acquired immunodeficiency syndrome)*
joints: *arthritis, gout, rheumatism*
kissing disease: *mononucleosis*
lockjaw: *tetanus*
lungs: *asthma, black lung disease, bronchitis, cystic fibrosis, emphysema, pneumonia, tuberculosis*
muscles: *muscular dystrophy, myasthenia gravis, tendonitis*
outcome, physician's predicted: *prognosis*
recurring or perpetual: *chronic*
sexually transmitted: *AIDS, chlamydia, gonorrhea, herpes, syphilis*
skin: *dermatitis, eczema, impetigo, lupus, psoriasis, scabies, vitiligo*
spreading throughout a region: *epidemic*
spreading from nation to nation: *pandemic*
tick, transmitted by: *Lyme disease*
tropical: *dengue fever, leprosy, malaria, yellow fever*
tumorous: *cancer*

disenchanted *adj.* disillusioned, disenfranchised, disappointed, disabused, worldly-wise. *Kara thought she wanted to work on a trash truck for the rest of her life but became disenchanted after her first day on the job.* **Ant.** enchanted, spellbound, enraptured.

disfigure *vb.* deface, deform, damage, scar, blemish, flaw. *The fire disfigured a valuable painting.*

disgrace *n.* **1.** dishonor, shame, embarrassment, humiliation, stain, taint. *We viewed our loss to the worst team in the league as a major disgrace.* –*vb.* **2.** dishonor, shame, discredit, tarnish, embarrass, humiliate. *The warrior's dishonorable actions disgraced his tribe.* **Ant. 1.** honor, glory. **2.** honor, credit, distinguish.

disgraceful *adj.* shameful, embarrassing, degrading, shocking, scandalous, humiliating. *It's disgraceful that many hardworking people earn so little.* **Ant.** worthy, becoming, honorable.

disguise *vb.* **1.** camouflage, mask, conceal, veil, cloak, cover. *Batman disguises himself by wearing a mask.* –*n.* **2.** camouflage, mask, costume, veil, guise, covering. *Everyone must wear a disguise to the costume party.* **Ant. 1.** uncover, reveal, disclose.

disgust *vb.* **1.** sicken, revolt, shock, nauseate, repel, appall. *The movie's gore and blood disgusted me.* –*n.* **2.** revulsion, repulsion, distaste, repugnance, loathing. *I could not hide the disgust I felt at the slovenly way in which he ate.* **Ant. 1.** please, delight. **2.** pleasure, satisfaction, liking.

dish *n.* plate, platter, saucer, bowl, vessel. *Please wash out the cat's dish and refill it with food.*

disheveled *adj.* messy, sloppy, ruffled, unkempt, tousled, disorderly. *She looked rather disheveled after her twelve-hour flight.* **Ant.** neat, tidy, trim.

dishonest *adj.* crooked, deceitful, untrustworthy, dishonorable, false, corrupt. *Never buy a car from a dishonest dealer.* **Ant.** honest, honorable, trustworthy.

dishonor *n.* shame, disrespect, humiliation, embarrassment, scandal, degradation. *The vandal brought dishonor to himself and his family.* **Ant.** honor, respect, praise.

disillusioned *adj.* *See* DISENCHANTED.

disinfect *vb.* sterilize, sanitize, decontaminate, purify, cleanse, kill germs. *You must thoroughly disinfect your hands before performing surgery.* **Ant.** infect, contaminate.

disintegrate *vb.* shatter, crumble, decompose, fragment, decay. *The ancient bones disintegrated as soon as the tomb was opened.*

disjointed *adj.* disconnected, loose, separated, broken, displaced, choppy. *It was hard to follow the movie's plot because it was so disjointed.* **Ant.** connected, cohesive, joined.

dislike *vb.* **1.** hate, detest, despise, loathe, abhor. *She dislikes tests.* –*n.* **2.** hatred, loathing, revulsion, disgust, abhorrence, aversion. *He has a strong dislike of war.* **Ant. 1.** like, love, admire. **2.** like, love, admiration.

disloyal *adj.* unfaithful, traitorous, treasonable, false, untrue, treacherous. *I think it's rather disloyal of him to root for the other school's team.* **Ant.** loyal, faithful, true.

dismal *adj.* bleak, gloomy, cheerless, dreary, somber, depressing, drab. *This has been a rather dismal winter.* **Ant.** cheerful, sunny, bright.

dismantle *vb.* disassemble, tear down, remove, raze, strip, fell. *Stagehands dismantled the backdrop when the play was over.* **Ant.** build, assemble, construct.

dismay *vb.* **1.** dishearten, distress, alarm, discourage, frighten, appall. *She was dismayed by all the homework she had to do.* –*n.* **2.** distress, discouragement, dread, alarm, agitation, concern. *I felt enormous dismay upon realizing how much farther I had to walk.* **Ant. 1.** encourage, hearten, relieve. **2.** encouragement, assurance.

dismember *vb.* amputate, cut up, lop off, mutilate, disarticulate. *The serial killer would always dismember his victims.*

dismiss *vb.* **1.** excuse, release, free, discharge, expel, fire. *The teacher dismissed him from class after he became ill.* **2.** disregard, reject, rebuff, scorn, discredit. *Don't dismiss what she has to say.* **Ant. 1.** accept, admit, hire. **2.** accept, receive, consider.

dismissal *n.* release, discharge, removal, suspension, expulsion. *His poor attitude at the office was the reason for his dismissal.*

disobedient *adj.* rebellious, defiant, unruly, insubordinate, ungovernable. *She took her disobedient dog to training school.* **Ant.** obedient, submissive.

disobey *vb.* defy, disregard, ignore, flout, resist, oppose. *The soldier was court-martialed for disobeying orders.* **Ant.** obey, heed, follow.

disorderly *adj.* **1.** messy, untidy, disorganized, chaotic, confused. *His room is always disorderly.* **2.** unruly, disruptive, unlawful, lawless, improper. *She was arrested for disorderly conduct.* **Ant. 1.** tidy, neat, clean. **2.** civil, lawful, proper.

disoriented *adj.* confused, lost, muddled, bewildered, directionless, blind. *It is easy to become disoriented in the forest.*

disown *vb.* reject, spurn, throw out, disclaim, repudiate, forsake. *She threatened to disown her own daughter.* **Ant.** adopt, claim, own.

disparage *vb.* criticize, put down, belittle, malign, ridicule, defame. *He would often disparage others for minor imperfections.* **Ant.** compliment, praise, commend.

disparity *n.* inequality, difference, imbalance, disproportion, gap. *There continues to be a disparity in the wages received by male and female workers.* **Ant.** equality, consistency, balance.

dispassionate *adj.* detached, unemotional, disinterested, unfeeling, impartial, objective. *We need a dispassionate umpire to call balls and strikes and not favor one side or another.* **Ant.** impassioned, biased, passionate.

disperse *vb.* scatter, disband, dissolve, separate, spread. *Police dispersed the unruly crowd.* **Ant.** assemble, gather, collect.

display *vb.* **1.** exhibit, show, expose, reveal, demonstrate, array. *Where are they displaying your artwork?* –*n.* **2.** show, exhibition, exhibit, presentation, demonstration. *That was a fine display of skateboarding.*

dispose *vb.* **1.** incline, motivate, induce, move, tempt. *I'm disposed toward being charitable today.* **2.** discard, unload, dump, throw out, distribute. *Where should he dispose of his trash?*

disprove *vb.* debunk, dispel, invalidate, refute, expose, discredit. *The scientist took every opportunity to disprove the existence of psychic powers.* **Ant.** prove, verify, validate.

disputable *adj.* debatable, questionable, moot, unsettled, contestable, unresolved. *Whether life ever existed on Mars or not is disputable.* **Ant.** undisputable, settled, resolved.

dispute *vb.* **1.** question, challenge, oppose, doubt, argue, contradict. *She disputed his claim to royalty.* –*n.* **2.** argument, disagreement, quarrel, feud, conflict, debate. *The two countries are in a dispute over which owns the land.* **Ant. 1.** support, affirm, confirm. **2.** agreement, accord.

disregard *vb.* **1.** ignore, forget, overlook, skip, reject, neglect. *Disregard the last note I sent, since I've changed my mind.* –*n.* **2.** indifference, neglect, inattention, oversight, disdain. *I'm angry with my friend because of her disregard for my feelings.* **Ant. 1.** heed, regard, notice. **2.** regard, attention, interest.

disrepair *n.* decay, ruin, deterioration, dilapidation, wreckage. *The house had fallen into disrepair and needed extensive renovation.*

disreputable *adj.* dishonorable, unsavory, shady, infamous, notorious, dishonest. *The loan shark had a disreputable track record.* **Ant.** honorable, respectable, noble.

disrespect *n.* **1.** disregard, insolence, irreverence, rudeness, discourtesy, flippancy. *His disrespect of the teacher landed him in the principal's office.* –*vb.* **2.** disregard, insult, offend, slight, take lightly. *Disrespect the law and you'll find yourself in jail.* **Ant. 1.** respect, regard, honor. **2.** respect, regard, revere.

disrespectful *adj.* rude, impolite, discourteous, irreverent, brash. *He was cautioned against being disrespectful in court.* **Ant.** respectful, polite, courteous.

disrupt *vb.* interrupt, upset, halt, disturb, disorganize, agitate. *A dog entered the church and disrupted the wedding ceremony.*

dissatisfied *adj.* disappointed, discontented, displeased, unhappy. *My parents seem dissatisfied with everything I do.* **Ant.** pleased, happy, satisfied.

dissect *vb.* analyze, examine, study, scrutinize, inspect, explore. *If we were to closely dissect the current controversy, we would find both parties to blame.*

disseminate *vb.* distribute, disperse, broadcast, scatter, spread, circulate. *The publicity office disseminates all university news.* **Ant.** gather, collect.

dissent *vb.* **1.** disagree, oppose, object, differ, protest. *Several people dissented with the coach's decision to forfeit the game.* –*n.* **2.** opposition, protest, objection, discord, disagreement. *There was dissent among the students when told school tours would be extended.* **Ant. 1.** agree, consent, concur. **2.** agreement, consent, accord.

dissension *n.* disagreement, conflict, contention, friction, discord, dissent. *The dissension between parties caused widespread gridlock.* **Ant.** agreement, accord, harmony.

dissertation *n.* report, treatise, thesis, paper, study, composition. *I found a good topic on which to write my dissertation.*

dissident *n.* dissenter, protestor, objector, rebel, separatist, nonconformist. *The dictator's first political act was to remove all dissidents from the government.*

dissimilar *adj.* different, unlike, contrasting, opposite, distinct, disparate. *A circle, a square, and a triangle are dissimilar shapes.* **Ant.** similar, alike, matching.

dissipate *vb.* disappear, run out, thin, scatter, exhaust, deplete. *The rain finally began to dissipate.* **Ant.** grow, concentrate, mushroom.

dissolve *vb.* **1.** melt, liquefy, disappear, vanish, fade, disintegrate. *This powder dissolves when added to water.* **2.** end, terminate, conclude, cancel, dismiss, disband. *Since no one attended the meetings, we decided to dissolve our club.* **Ant. 1.** solidify, thicken, congeal. **2.** continue, begin, start.

dissuade *vb.* discourage, deter, talk out of, advise against, (slang) throw cold water on, curb. *I would strongly try to dissuade anyone from swimming off the Maine coast in January.* **Ant.** persuade, convince, talk into.

distance *n.* length, span, stretch, expanse, space, gap, interval. *The distance between school and the arcade is about five blocks.*

distasteful *adj.* unsavory, disgusting, repugnant, gross, repulsive, unpalatable. *Spreading manure on the garden is a distasteful job, but* *someone must do it.* **Ant.** pleasant, savory, appealing.

distend *vb.* bloat, expand, swell, enlarge, spread, inflate, fatten, balloon. *The dog's stomach distended from eating too much food.* **Ant.** shrink, contract, constrict.

distill *vb.* extract, purify, refine, concentrate, decoct, boil down. *We will have to distill the water in order to drink it.*

distinct *adj.* **1.** individual, separate, different, discrete, dissimilar. *Scottish clans each have a distinct plaid from which their kilts are made.* **2.** clear, obvious, plain, apparent, evident, certain, unmistakable. *Skunks give off a distinct odor.* **Ant. 1.** similar, identical, like. **2.** indistinct, vague, unclear.

distinction *n.* **1.** separation, differentiation, division, discernment, discrimination. *Only an expert can discern the distinction between these two bird species.* **2.** importance, prominence, rank, consequence, significance. *The vineyard advertised its product as a wine bought by people of distinction.*

distinctive *adj.* particular, special, unique, unusual, different. *That artist has a very distinctive painting style.* **Ant.** typical, average, usual.

distinguish *vb.* **1.** differentiate, determine, decide, identify, detect, recognize. *How can I distinguish between the twins?* **2.** honor, memorialize, dignify, glorify, ennoble. *The knight's distinguished himself by his bravery.*

distinguished *adj.* famous, renowned, celebrated, prominent, illustrious, eminent. *The distinguished scientist is known for her brilliant research.* **Ant.** undistinguished, unknown.

distort *vb.* warp, deform, twist, contort, knot, misshape. *Anger distorted his features.*

distortion *n.* misinterpretation, misrepresentation, lie, inaccuracy, exaggeration, falsification. *Politicians may use distortion to smear a rival's voting record.* **Ant.** truth, accuracy, reality.

distract *vb.* divert, interrupt, sidetrack, disturb, annoy, trouble. *I was distracted by my neighbor's barking dog.*

distraught *adj.* upset, beside oneself, anxious, frantic, troubled, agitated. *She was distraught over her two flat tires.* **Ant.** calm, cool, tranquil.

distress *vb.* **1.** upset, disturb, worry, trouble, sadden, depress. *The queen was distressed when her knights failed to return.* –*n.* **2.** agony, sorrow, anguish, misery, sadness, depression. *I felt great distress over not being accepted at the university.* **Ant. 1.** comfort, console, relieve. **2.** relief, solace, comfort.

distribute *vb.* give, dispense, deliver, allocate, spread, scatter. *A group on the corner distributed religious pamphlets.* **Ant.** take, collect, gather.

distributor *n.* wholesaler, dealer, outlet, merchandiser, jobber, trader. *The distributor said he could provide 1,000 units at half price.*

distribution *n.* **1.** dispersion, dispensation, spreading, scattering, circulation. *His job is to oversee distribution of the company's products.* **2.** placement, location, arrangement, order, disposition. *This map shows the distribution of our defense forces.*

district *n.* area, territory, region, section, zone, community. *She lives in the Richmond district.*

distrust *n.* **1.** mistrust, suspicion, disbelief, misgiving, skepticism, wariness. *It's always wise to have a certain amount of distrust around wild animals.* –*vb.* **2.** mistrust, doubt, question, disbelieve, suspect, be leery of. *Always distrust a skunk.* **Ant. 1.** trust, faith, belief. **2.** trust, believe, have faith in.

disturb *vb.* **1.** bother, annoy, interrupt, pester, harass. *Loud construction work outside disturbed him as he studied.* **2.** trouble, upset, confuse, distress, worry. *I am disturbed by my friend's odd behavior.*

disturbance *n.* **1.** commotion, tumult, turmoil, uproar, racket. *The principal investigated the disturbance in the school cafeteria.* **2.** interruption, distraction, annoyance, vexation, bother. *Where can I work without disturbance?* **Ant. 1–2.** peace, quiet, calm.

ditch *n.* gully, trench, channel, drain, conduit, excavation. *Rainwater flows through the ditch and into the culvert.*

diva *n.* lead singer, prima donna, vocalist, goddess. *The diva walked on stage and received a standing ovation before she sang a single note.*

dive *vb.* **1.** plunge, plummet, jump, leap, fall, pitch. *I dove for cover when I heard the explosion.* *–n.* **2.** lunge, plunge, descent, drop, jump, leap. *The swimmer executed a graceful dive.*

diverge *vb.* separate, divide, split, fork, swerve, part. *This corridor diverges into two passageways.* **Ant.** merge, join, unite.

diverse *adj.* varied, assorted, diversified, unlike, mixed. *Her favorite restaurant has a diverse selection of international foods.* **Ant.** identical, similar, same.

diversify *vb.* mix, spread out, branch out, expand, vary, broaden. *The company diversified in an attempt to increase profits.* **Ant.** limit, reduce, concentrate.

diversity *n.* difference, variance, variety, distinctiveness, dissimilarity. *The diversity of our population is one of this country's strengths.* **Ant.** similarity, uniformity, likeness.

divert *vb.* deflect, shift, sidetrack, swerve, shunt. *Engineers diverted the runaway train onto a secondary track.*

divide *vb.* **1.** separate, part, split, cut, partition. *The teacher divided the class into two groups.* **2.** distribute, dispense, share, allot, dole. *The pirates divided the booty amongst themselves.* **Ant. 1.** join, unite, combine.

divine *adj.* **1.** holy, sainted, sacred, heavenly, blessed, godly. *It was once thought in Japan that the emperor ruled by divine right.* *–vb.* **2.** prophesy, predict, foresee, foretell, anticipate, portend. *The fortune-teller claimed she could divine the future.*

division *n.* branch, part, section, portion, component. *My favorite team won the championship in the western division.*

divisive *adj.* discordant, polarizing, alienating, at odds, fault-finding, hostile. *The speaker's harsh opinions proved divisive.* **Ant.** uniting, harmonious, agreeable.

divorce *n.* **1.** disunion, separation, split, dissolution, severance. *My parents are going to get a divorce.* *–vb.* **2.** separate, disunite, split, detach, part, divide. *I divorced myself from their argument.* **Ant. 1.** union, unity, harmony. **2.** join, unite, merge.

divulge *vb.* tell, reveal, confide, bare, expose, disclose, release. *She refused to divulge her secret to us.* **Ant.** hide, conceal, cloak.

dizzy *adj.* light-headed, reeling, off balance, unsteady, vertiginous, wobbly. *Spin around fast ten times and see how dizzy you get.* **Ant.** steady, balanced, clear-headed.

DNA *n.* genetic code, double helix, nucleic acid, deoxyribonucleic acid, nucleotide chains, code of life. *Every person on the planet can be identified by their DNA.*

do *vb.* **1.** perform, execute, administer, undertake, fulfill. *Please do what I tell you.* **2.** finish, conclude, end, complete, accomplish. *Have you done your homework?* **3.** suffice, serve, satisfy, answer, work. *Will this room do, or would you like to see another?* 4. render, give, pay, afford, bear. *Do me a favor and quit talking so much.* 5. cover, traverse, manage, fare, proceed. *She can do a mile in under five minutes.*

docile *adj.* gentle, passive, subdued, agreeable, tame, obedient, manageable. *Tranquilizers made the tiger docile.* **Ant.** unruly, rebellious, wild.

dock *n.* pier, wharf, landing, berth, marina, slip. *Tie your boat at the dock.*

docket *n.* agenda, schedule, ticket, program, calendar. *The judge had a lot of cases on the docket today.*

doctor *n.* physician, M.D., medical practitioner, osteopath, healer, medic, (slang) doc. *See a doctor about that cough.*

WORD SEARCH

anesthesia specialist: *anesthetist, anesthesiologist*
animal: *veterinarian*
bones, joint and muscle specialist: *orthopedist*
children's: *pediatrician*
digestive: *gastroenterologist*
disease specialist: *pathologist*
drug specialist: *pharmacologist*
ear, nose and throat: *otolaryngologist*
elderly patients, treats: *gerontologist*
epidemics: *epidemiologist*
eye: *ophthalmologist*
foot: *podiatrist*
heart: *cardiologist*
incompetent: *quack*
listening device: *stethoscope*
mental: *psychiatrist*
national medical chief: *surgeon general*
nervous system: *neurologist*
oath taken by: *Hippocratic oath*
prayers, attempts to cure by: *faith healer*
pregnancy and birth: *obstetrician*
skin: *dermatologist*
spine and back straightener: *chiropractor*
training, in: *intern*
urinary tract and kidney specialist: *urologist*
women's reproductive system: *gynecologist*

doctrine *n.* creed, principle, dogma, belief, teaching, theory, maxim. *The cult members obeyed their leader's doctrines.*

document *n.* 1. paper, record, certificate, credential, voucher, deed. *You need the right documents to get into certain countries.* –*vb.* 2. record, verify, certify, authenticate, chronicle. *Scholars have documented the existence of the ancient civilization.*

documentary *n.* film, narrative, docudrama, investigative report, travelogue, chronicle. *He was flying to Africa to film an animal documentary.*

doddering *adj.* faltering, senile, feebleminded, shaky, shuffling, infirm. *The doddering old man forgot what his appointment was for.* **Ant.** sharp, robust, strong.

dodge *vb.* 1. duck, sidestep, dart, swerve, shift, bolt. *The matador dodged out of the way of the charging bull.* –*n.* 2. dark, duck, sidestep, swerve, shift. *The rabbit escaped the hawk by making a dodge into the brush.*

dog *n.* canine, hound, mongrel, (slang) mutt, (slang) pooch, (slang) flea bag. *Please leash your dog.*

WORD SEARCH

bark: *bay, howl, yelp*
cheeks, lower: *chops*
chest hair, white or colored: *apron*
chin hairs: *beard*
black or dark brown: *sable*
disease: *distemper, heartworm, mange, rabies*
ears, dangly: *lop ears*
father: *sire*
fear of: *cynophobia*
female: *bitch*

foot cushions: *pads*
gray or black on white: *badger-marked*
gray or gray-streaked: *grizzled*
hairstyling, poodle's fancy: *pompon*
hairs that bristle on the neck and back when frightened or angry: *hackles*
lineage: *pedigree*
long-legged and light: *racy*
lover of: *philocynic*
low to the ground and thick-bodied: *cloddy*
mixed breed: *mongrel*
mother: *dam*
multicolored: *parti-colored*
muzzled, sharply: *snipy*
nose, multicolored: *butterfly nose*
patchy-colored: *pied*
reddish brown or purple brown: *liver*
sniffing out game in field: *quartering*
streaked or spotted: *brindle*
streak on head: *blaze*
tail: *brush, bobtail, ringtail, plum, whip, screwtail*
throat frill: *ruff*
white with black spots: *harlequin*
yellowish brown: *fawn*

dogged *adj.* tenacious, persistent, persevering, determined, stubborn, relentless. *The detective's dogged pursuit of the truth was admirable.* **Ant.** irresolute, half-hearted.

dogma *n.* belief, doctrine, views, convictions, gospel, canon. *Atheism and theism are two opposite dogmas.*

dogmatic *adj.* opinionated, overpositive, closed-minded, narrow-minded, biased, prejudiced. *The preacher was so dogmatic in his views that no amount of persuasion would change his mind.* **Ant.** open-minded, liberal-minded, unbiased.

doldrums *n.* depression, lassitude, malaise, listlessness, blues, (slang) blahs. *I fall into the doldrums whenever it rains for more than three days straight.*

dollar *n.* bill, legal tender, (slang) buck, note, greenback, currency. *A dollar no longer buys as much as it used to.*

dollop *n.* blob, mass, lump, modicum, quantity, spoonful. *Give me a big dollop of whipped cream on my pie.*

dolly *n.* handtruck, cart, car, carrier, transport. *A dolly is useful to transport a heavy load.*

dolphin *n.* cetacean, mammal, sea creature, denizen of the deep. *Dolphins are among the most intelligent animals in the sea.*

dolt *n.* idiot, moron, imbecile, simpleton, dunce, ignoramus. *He knew that if he quit high school he would be considered a dolt.* **Ant.** genius, Einstein, Rhodes scholar.

domain *n.* territory, area, region, zone, realm, empire. *This valley is the domain of our people.*

dome *n.* roof, vault, bubble, arch, hemisphere, rotunda. *The new baseball stadium is covered by a dome.*

domestic *adj.* **1.** family, home, household, residential. *They prefer the domestic life.* **2.** tame, tamed, domesticated, trained, broken. *Sheep, cows and goats are all domestic animals.* **3.** native, internal, homemade, endemic, indigenous. *Are these computers of domestic make?* **Ant.** **2.** wild, feral, untamed. **3.** foreign, non-native, exotic.

domesticate *vb.* tame, break, train, civilize, master, gentle. *It's not easy to domesticate a wild animal.*

dominant *adj.* strongest, prominent, prime, controlling, principal. *Usually, the dominant wolf in the pack becomes the leader.* **Ant.** weakest, subordinate, inferior.

dominate *vb.* **1.** control, rule, command, overpower, direct. *The talkative man dominated the conversation.* **2.** pervade, overspread, overrun, characterize, permeate. *Rose bushes dominate our garden.*

domineering *adj.* overbearing, bossy, controlling, tyrannical, imperious, bullying. *A domineering boss has trouble retaining employees.* **Ant.** easygoing, passive, shy.

donate *vb.* give, present, bestow, offer, impart, confer, grant. *My parents donated some old furniture for the school rummage sale.*

donation *n.* contribution, gift, handout, offering, present, aid, alms. *We gave a $50 donation to the church.*

done *adj.* finished, completed, concluded, ended, through. *Is the turkey done yet?* **Ant.** incomplete, undone, unfinished.

Don Juan *n.* playboy, ladies man, (slang) player, Casanova, Lothario, smooth operator. *They called him a Don Juan because he had romanced more than 50 women.*

donkey *n.* ass, mule, burro, jenny, jack, beast of burden. *The donkey refused to be ridden, no matter how many treats it was given.*

donor *n.* contributor, donator, giver, benefactor, supporter. *We need more donors for the blood drive.*

donut *n.* doughnut, sinker, cruller, olicook, dessert. *A donut is a favorite breakfast pastry.*

doom *n.* **1.** destiny, lot, fate, death, extinction, ruin. *The soldiers faced their impending doom with bravery.* –*vb.* **2.** fate, destine, predetermine, ordain, condemn. *His efforts are doomed to fail.*

door *n.* entrance, portal, gate, hatch, entranceway, exit. *Please close the door.*

doorbell *n.* chime, ringer, buzzer, bell, dinger. *Please ring the doorbell before entering.*

doozy *n.* Slang. (Slang) humdinger, (slang) lulu, (slang) something, (slang) the bomb, (slang) dilly, exception. *That grammatical error was a doozy.*

dope *n.* idiot, moron, imbecile, (slang) dummy, dunce, (slang) nitwit. *I was really a dope for forgetting my books again.* **Ant.** intellectual, genius, (slang) Einstein.

dormant *adj.* inactive, sleeping, lethargic, sluggish, passive. quiet. *Bears remain dormant during the winter months.* **Ant.** active, wakeful, alert.

dormer *n.* window, gable, projection, lucarne. *Adding a dormer to the second floor will allow more light into the bedroom.*

dormitory *n.* dorm, dorm room, hall, quarters, living quarters, house, student housing. *We lived in a dormitory until we graduated.*

dose *n.* measure, portion, quantity, quota, allowance. *Make sure you take the correct dose of medicine.*

dossier *n.* file, record, profile, history, report. *The CIA compiled an extensive dossier on the infamous terrorist.*

dot *n.* point, spot, speck, mark, period, iota. *She arrived on the dot.*

double *adj.* twin, binary, pair, dual, two-fold, duplex. *The theater was presenting a double feature.*

double-cross *vb.* betray, deceive, (slang) two-time, (slang) stab in the back, cheat. *Criminals sometimes double-cross one another.*

doubt *vb.* **1.** suspect, distrust, mistrust, question, disbelieve. *Do you doubt my word?* –*n.* **2.** misgiving, disbelief, uncertainty, suspicion, skepticism. *I have doubts about whether she'll really show up.* **Ant. 1.** trust, believe, accept. **2.** trust, belief, certainty.

doubtful *adj.* unlikely, questionable, uncertain, debatable, dubious. *It's doubtful that she'll* *get off work in time to join us.* **Ant.** probable, likely, certain.

dour *adj.* morose, grim, gloomy, glum, harsh, sullen, surly. *Many students on Monday morning have a dour look on their faces.* **Ant.** cheerful, smiling, happy.

douse *vb.* drench, soak, wet, saturate, dunk, slosh. *Always douse a campfire thoroughly before leaving it.*

down *adj.* **1.** dejected, discouraged, depressed, despondent, melancholy. *He's been feeling down ever since he lost his job.* –*adv.* **2.** downward, downhill, below, beneath, underneath. *She fell down.* –*vb.* **3.** swallow, gulp, take, drop, fell. *He downed a soda.* **Ant. 1.** up, elated, happy. **2.** up, upward.

downfall *n.* **1.** fall, crash, ruin, collapse, overthrow, breakdown, destruction. *Who can say when the downfall of civilization will occur?* **2.** rainstorm, shower, cloudburst, thunderstorm, deluge. *There's a heavy downfall outside.*

downgrade *vb.* degrade, reduce, diminish, devalue, minimize, demote. *The teacher said she would downgrade our papers if we failed to use proper punctuation.*

downhearted *adj.* sad, depressed, unhappy, low, miserable, blue. *Joe was downhearted after losing the race.* **Ant.** happy, elated, euphoric.

downplay *vb.* minimize, make light of, devalue, lessen, downgrade. *Frank always downplays his weaknesses and highlights his strengths.* **Ant.** highlight, maximize, hype.

downpour *n.* deluge, torrent, rainstorm, cloudburst, gullywasher, precipitation. *We ran as fast as could to get out from under the sudden downpour.*

downsize *vb.* cut, reduce, pare, decrease, shrink, lay off. *The company announced that it would downsize by laying off 100 workers.* **Ant.** expand, grow, mushroom.

downtrodden *adj.* afflicted, persecuted, unfortunate, abused, oppressed, subjugated. *The people had been downtrodden long enough and rose up in protest against their government.* **Ant.** uplifted, empowered.

doze *vb.* **1.** nap, sleep, slumber, snooze, drowse. *He dozed off in class today.* –*n.* **2.** nap, slumber, snooze, siesta. *She fell into a doze beside the stream.*

drab *adj.* dull, dreary, lusterless, dingy, dismal, somber, gloomy. *We need some new furniture to liven up this drab room.* **Ant.** vivid, colorful, bright.

Draconian *adj.* severe, strict, harsh, cruel, extreme, brutal. *The dictator took Draconian measures to punish his enemies.* **Ant.** civil, compassionate, kind.

draft *n.* **1.** outline, sketch, overview, synopsis, plan. *Have you finished the first draft of your novel?* **2.** breeze, flow, stream, current, wind. *There's a cold draft coming through the window.* **3.** induction, conscription, impressment, call, summons. *During the Vietnam War, some men avoided the draft by going to Canada.* –*vb.* **4.** draw, sketch, diagram, outline, design, plan. *Engineers drafted plans for the new spaceship.* **5.** induct, conscript, impress, summon, call. *The United States drafts men into the armed forces during times of war.*

drag *vb.* **1.** tug, haul, draw, lug, tow, pull, trail. *The lion dragged its kill to its den.* **2.** plod, creep, crawl, straggle, limp. *The boring lecture seemed to drag on for hours.* **Ant. 1.** push, shove, thrust. **2.** rush, race, speed.

dragon *n.* firedrake, serpent, monster, mythical beast, creature. *The fire-breathing dragon came in handy whenever we needed to have our coffee warmed up.*

drain *vb.* **1.** sap, empty, extract, tax, deplete, withdraw. *The hot sun drained me of my energy.* **2.** leak, drip, ooze, seep, flow, discharge. *The infected wound was lanced so the pus would drain.*

drama *n.* story, production, play, melodrama, tragedy, tear-jerker. The Elephant Man *is a drama about a deformed man and his ill treatment by society.*

dramatic *adj.* intense, striking, sensational, emotional, theatrical. *Shaving off his beard created a dramatic change in his appearance.*

dramatize *vb.* play up, exaggerate, amplify, perform, act, embellish, intensify. *Hollywood likes to dramatize real events and make them appear bigger than life.* **Ant.** play down, diminish, understate.

drape *n.* curtain, shade, window dressing, blind, valence. *Let's close the drape so the sun won't wake the baby.*

drastic *adj.* extreme, radical, forceful, severe, intensive, harsh. *Don't you think starving yourself is a drastic way to lose weight?*

draw *vb.* **1.** sketch, diagram, picture, outline, trace, depict. *The pirates drew a map of where they had buried the treasure.* **2.** charm, attract, lure, tempt, invite, allure. *Tales of wondrous beauty drew people to the islands.* **3.** extract, pull, remove, take, acquire, obtain. *The doctor drew a blood sample.* **4.** lengthen, extend, prolong, continue, elongate. *He drew out his story until everyone was quite bored.* **5.** drag, tug, tow, haul, lead, pull. *We'll need two horses to draw this wagon.* *–n.* **6.** tie, stalemate, checkmate, deadlock, truce. *The judge finally declared the game a draw.* **Ant. 2.** repulse, repel. **4.** shorten, reduce. **5.** push, shove.

drawback *n.* problem, flaw, defect, weakness, handicap, block, hurdle. *Your plan has several serious drawbacks.*

dread *vb.* **1.** fear, cower, cringe, worry, tremble, quail. *I dread giving my speech in front of the entire class.* *–n.* **2.** fear, terror, dismay, alarm, fright, anxiety. *They beheld the werewolf with dread.* **Ant. 2.** bravery, courage, confidence.

dreadful *adj.* fearful, frightful, ghastly, horrible, awful, offensive. *The roach-infested hotel we stayed in was simply dreadful.*

dream *n.* **1.** reverie, fantasy, vision, desire, wish, hope. *Her dream is to write a best-seller.* *–vb.* **2.** conceive, daydream, think, wish, desire. *I dream about making a million dollars.*

dreamer *n.* visionary, thinker, deep thinker, castlebuilder, scatterbrain. *A dreamer may often have his head in the clouds.*

dreary *adj.* uninteresting, tedious, wearisome, dismal, cheerless, bleak. *Washing a sink full of dishes can be a dreary task.* **Ant.** interesting, exciting, cheerful.

drench *vb.* soak, drown, saturate, douse, flood, splash, immerse. *We were drenched by a sudden thunderstorm.*

dress *n.* **1.** clothing, apparel, attire, garb, wardrobe, covering. *We found the dress of the alien visitors rather odd.* *–vb.* **2.** clothe, outfit, garb, attire, adorn, deck. *Dress yourself for cold weather.* **3.** treat, bandage, splint, bind, remedy. *The doctor dressed her patient's wound.*

WORD SEARCH

African chemise with bell sleeves: *dashiki*
ankle-length: *maxi*
calf-length: *midi*
full and puffy: *bouffant*
Hawaiian: *muumuu*
Hindi wrap: *sari*
Japanese sashed wraparound: *kimono*
knitted: *sweater dress*
loose gown: *peignoir*

Roman, bare-shouldered: *toga*
shapeless, long: *Mother Hubbard*
tight with back slit: *sheath*

dresser *n.* bureau, chest, chest of drawers, chiffonier. *Fold your clothes neatly and put them in the dresser.*

dressy *adj.* classy, elegant, smart, chic, formal, flashy, stylish. *I don't have any dressy clothes to wear to a formal wedding.* **Ant.** casual, sloppy, grungy.

dribble *vb.* drip, drizzle, seep, weep, slobber, drool. *Be careful to slowly dribble water onto the plants so as not to drown them.*

drift *vb.* **1.** wander, tramp, ramble, amble, meander. *She drifted from job to job.* –*n.* **2.** course, flow, trend, tendency, bearing. *The country is experiencing a drift toward conservatism.* **3.** meaning, direction, sense, object, implication. *He didn't quite get the drift of the conversation.* **4.** heap, pile, bank, mass, mound. *A deer was caught in the snowdrift.*

drifter *n.* transient, hobo, vagabond, tramp, wanderer, nomad. *The drifter stopped people on the sidewalk to ask for spare change.*

drill *n.* **1.** training, workout, exercise, instruction, routine. *Her soccer coach makes the players perform numerous drills.* –*vb.* **2.** bore, pierce, ream, penetrate. *A carpenter drilled several holes in the board.* **3.** train, instruct, coach, teach, school, tutor. *Paramedics are drilled in proper lifesaving techniques.*

drink *vb.* **1.** imbibe, quaff, swallow, sip, gulp. *She drinks two cups of coffee every morning.* –*n.* **2.** beverage, liquid, water, alcohol. *Would you like a drink?*

drinkable *adj.* potable, palatable, purified, sterilized, clean, sanitized. *The water was drinkable only after we boiled it.* **Ant.** toxic, poisonous, contaminated.

drip *vb.* drop, sprinkle, dribble, trickle, leak, weep, seep. *Watch the raindrops drip from the tree limbs.*

drive *vb.* **1.** steer, guide, operate, ride, control. *He just learned how to drive a car.* **2.** push, propel, thrust, move, shove, hurl. *This spray will drive the insects away.* **3.** press, overwork, tax, spur, motivate, urge. *The coach drove his players hard.* –*n.* **4.** ride, trip, journey, excursion, run. *It was a long drive up the ski lodge.* **5.** push, thrust, movement, advance, surge. *The team's final drive resulted in a touchdown.* **6.** ambition, initiative, energy, hustle, aggressiveness. *I admire her drive to better herself.* **7.** road, driveway, path, route. *There is a winding drive up to the mansion.*

drivel *n.* nonsense, foolishness, blather, twaddle, (slang) hogwash, (slang) rot. *She liked to hear herself talk, but much of what she said was drivel.*

driver *n.* motorist, commuter, operator, chauffeur, racer. *The police clocked the driver at 100 miles per hour.*

drizzle *n.* mist, rain, fog, spray, sprinkle, moisture. *The forecast is calling for drizzle in the morning.*

drone *vb.* buzz, hum, thrum, whir, hizz, murmur. *I love to hear the bees drone around the new blooms.*

drool *n.* **1.** slobber, slaver, spittle, drivel, saliva, spit. *Drool dripped down the dog's chin as he sniffed the plate of hamburgers.* –*vb.* **2.** slobber, salivate, dribble. *Let the dog have a bite of your pizza or he'll drool all over us.*

droop *vb.* drop, sag, slump, sink, wilt, dip, bend, bow. *His long mustache droops at the ends.* **Ant.** rise, stand, stiffen.

drop *n.* **1.** bead, tear, speck, dab, particle, splotch. *The leaves sparkled with drops of dew.* **2.** fall, descent, plunge, abyss, chasm, precipice. *It's* *a long drop from where we stand on this ledge.* **3.** decline, decrease, reduction, downslide, lessening. *Her drop in weight concerns us.* –*vb.* **4.** fall, plunge, descend, sink, plummet, dive. *Strong winds caused pine cones to drop from the trees.* **5.** abandon, leave, dismiss, omit, discontinue, forgo. *The band dropped the last song from its act.* **6.** reduce, cut, decrease, diminish, lessen, lower. *The store has recently dropped its prices.* **Ant. 2.** rise, climb, ascent. **3.** increase, rise, gain. **4.** rise, soar, ascend. **6.** increase, augment.

droppings *n.* excrement, manure, dung, guano, cow chips, (slang) meadow muffins. *The golf course is having trouble with goose droppings on the fairway.*

drought *n.* dry spell, aridity, shortage, insufficiency, scarcity. *We've had such a long drought that the pond has completely dried up.*

drown *vb.* submerge, immense, flood, deluge, inundate. *She drowned her pancakes in syrup.*

drowsy *adj.* sleepy, tired, listless, dozy, groggy. *If you feel drowsy, go to bed.* **Ant.** alert, wakeful, rested.

drudgery *n.* menial labor, toil, taskwork, chores, work, (slang) grunt work. *I hate the drudgery involved in keeping a house clean.*

drug *n.* pharmaceutical, medicine, treatment, remedy, cure, pill, prescription. *The physician prescribed a new drug for his patient's ailment.*

drunk *adj.* **1.** intoxicated, inebriated, tipsy, sodden, stupefied. *Drunk drivers are the cause of many fatal accidents.* –*n.* **2.** drunkard, inebriate, sot, lush, alcoholic. *The drunk stumbled from the bar and fell into a gutter.* **Ant. 1.** sober, abstinent.

drunkard *n.* alcoholic, drunk, substance abuser, (slang) wino, (slang) lush, problem drinker. *The drunkard staggered down the sidewalk.*

dry *adj.* **1.** arid, rainless, parched, waterless, dehydrated. *We followed the dry riverbed for several miles.* **2.** deadpan, droll, subdued, subtle, sarcastic. *She has a dry sense of humor.* –*vb.* **3.** dehydrate, parch, wither, shrivel, wilt. *The sun dried my skin.* **Ant. 1.** wet, damp, soggy. **3.** wet, soak, dampen.

dual *adj.* double, twin, binary, duplex, matched, twofold. *The shop was so busy it had to have dual cash registers.*

dubious *adj.* questionable, debatable, doubtful, uncertain, unclear. *Receiving the award for most talkative student is a dubious honor.* **Ant.** certain, sure, definite.

duck *vb.* squat, bend, drop, dodge, swerve, veer. *She ducked to avoid the ball heading straight for her.*

duct *n.* conduit, pipe, shaft, airway, passage, chimney. *The air duct filtered out moist air from the shower.*

due *adj.* **1.** expected, awaited, scheduled, payable, anticipated. *When is the term paper due?* **2.** justified, fitting, adequate, sufficient, appropriate, proper. *Her behavior has given me due cause for alarm.* **Ant. 2.** inappropriate, insufficient, inadequate.

dull *adj.* **1.** boring, uninteresting, dreary, wearisome, tedious, monotonous. *It's hard not to fall asleep reading this dull textbook.* **2.** blunt, pointless, unsharpened, edgeless. *This knife is too dull to carve the turkey.* **3.** colorless, pale, faded, lusterless, softened, muted. *I think a dull color would look better than this bright yellow.* –*vb.* **4.** lessen, fade, dim, reduce, soften, deaden. *Age has dulled her vision.* **Ant. 1.** interesting, lively, exciting. **2.** sharp, pointed. **3.** sharp, vivid, bright. **4.** sharpen, increase, improve.

dullard *n.* dolt, imbecile, moron, idiot, dunce, nitwit. *Only a dullard can't recite the alphabet in order.*

dumb *adj.* stupid, moronic, imbecilic, unintelligent, slow, ignorant, uneducated. *His comments about not needing a diploma were really dumb.* **Ant.** smart, intelligent, brilliant.

dumbfound *v.* astonish, floor, stun, flabbergast, stupefy, render speechless. *The sight of a flying saucer would dumbfound most people.*

dummy *n.* **1.** mannequin, doll, figure, puppet, muppet, scarecrow, jackstraw. *The ventriloquist made his dummy speak like someone from Brooklyn.* **2.** idiot, moron, imbecile, dunce, ignoramus, (slang) nitwit. *Sorry to be such a dummy, but could you tell me who is buried in Grant's tomb?*

dump *n.* **1.** landfill, dumpsite, refuse yard, junkyard, hazardous waste site, recycling facility. *The local dump was once the favorite haunt of bears and seagulls.* –*vb.* **2.** empty, discard, unload, junk, scrap, throw out.

dunce *n.* idiot, fool, moron, imbecile, ignoramus, (slang) nitwit, simpleton. *He forgot to comb his unruly hair and felt like a dunce.* **Ant.** scholar, genius.

dune *n.* hill, ridge, sand pile, sand drift, barrow, hummock. *We were astonished to see that the wind had carved a giant dune into the shape of a whale.*

WORD SEARCH

crescent-shaped: *barchan*

elongated dune that can stretch for miles: *whaleback*

long and up to 300 feet high: *sief dune*

star-shaped: *star dune*

dung *n.* excrement, feces, droppings, manure, guano, (slang) crap. *The horse stall smelled distinctly of fresh dung.*

dungarees *n.* pants, trousers, jeans, overalls, denims, Levis. *My old dungarees have holes in both knees.*

dungeon *n.* keep, prison, hold, donjon, confine, stronghold. *The thief was locked away in the king's dungeon for many years.*

dunk *vb.* submerge, immerse, dip, plunge, drop. *Her friends tried to dunk her into the swimming pool.*

duplicate *vb.* **1.** reproduce, repeat, copy, replicate, clone. *Several labs have tried to duplicate the scientist's findings.* –*n.* **2.** copy, reproduction, likeness, double, facsimile. *Make a duplicate of your term paper in case the teacher loses the original.*

duplicity *n.* double-dealing, deception, backstabbing, dishonesty, disloyalty, artifice. *He frequently spoke out of both sides of his mouth, having long ago mastered the art of duplicity.* **Ant.** loyalty, honesty, faithfulness.

durable *adj.* strong, sound, enduring, reliable, dependable, stout. *That company makes durable clothing.* **Ant.** weak, flimsy, fragile.

duration *n.* space, span, stretch, course, extent, term, sentence. *Please do not smoke for the duration of the flight.*

dusk *n.* twilight, sunset, evening, darkness, night. *The park closes at dusk.*

dust *n.* particles, lint, grit, soot, particulate, fibers, scales. *People are horrified to learn that house dust is composed mostly of dead skin cells.*

duty *n.* **1.** chore, job, assignment, task, responsibility, function. *My duty at summer camp was to wash the dishes.* **2.** tax, tariff, fee, toll, dues, levy. *The foreign ship had to pay a duty to enter port.*

dwarf *n.* midget, little person, runt, gnome, pygmy, (slang) shrimp. *The dwarf we met yesterday was small in statute but big of heart.*

dwell *vb.* live, reside, stay, abide, inhabit, populate. *No one dwells in this bleak and forbidding land.*

dwindle *vb.* fade, wither, ebb, shrink, diminish, disappear. *The stream dwindles into nothing about five miles from here.* **Ant.** increase, grow, thrive.

dye *vb.* **1.** color, stain, tint, shade, paint. *She dyed her hair green.* –*n.* **2.** color, stain, tint, paint, pigment. *Do you think the dye will wash out?*

dynamic *adj.* vigorous, active, energetic, electrifying, spirited, lively. *Berkeley was a dynamic place in which to live during the sixties.* **Ant.** inactive, dull, listless.

dynamite *n.* explosive, blasting material, demolition material, TNT, nitroglycerin. *They used dynamite to blow up the old bridge.*

dynasty *n.* family rule, succession of power, ascendancy, crown, regency, rule. *The same family dynasty had ruled the land for more than 120 years.*

dysfunctional *adj.* maladjusted, troubled, abnormal, impaired, sick, unhealthy. *Both parents were alcoholics and were considered dysfunctional.* **Ant.** functional, normal, healthy.

dyslexia *n.* learning disorder, reading disorder, handicap, learning impairment. *Having dyslexia can make it more difficult to learn how to read.*

E

eager *adj.* avid, keen, enthusiastic, excited, intent, willing. *We were eager to start the canoe trip.* **Ant.** adverse, reluctant, unconcerned.

eagle *n.* raptor, bird of prey, predator, Falconiforme. *Losing more and more of their habitat, some eagles are taking up residence on bridges near large cities.*

WORD SEARCH

claws: *talons*
group of: *convocation*
hooked beak, describing: *aquiline*
nest: *aerie*

earn *vb.* **1.** make, collect, receive, gain, acquire, draw, realize. *She earns enough money to live comfortably.* **2.** deserve, merit, warrant, reap, achieve. *I feel that I've earned my vacation.* **Ant. 1.** spend, forfeit, lose.

earnest *adj.* serious, sincere, eager, intent, determined, heartfelt. *They made an earnest attempt to clear up the misunderstanding.* **Ant.** insincere, halfhearted, frivolous.

earnings *n.* income, wage, net, pay, profit, salary, proceeds. *My earnings for the job weren't as high as I expected.* **Ant.** expenses, expenditures, outlay.

earring *n.* earbob, bauble, ornament, jewelry, girandole. *Freda screamed when she dropped her earring down the sink.*

earth *n.* **1.** planet, world, globe, sphere, orb. *Ozone depletion is an environmental problem that threatens the entire Earth.* **2.** soil, ground, dirt, sod, land, turf. *The farmer surveyed the parched earth of his fields.*

WORD SEARCH

green color of: *terre verte*
inhabitant of: *earthling, tellurian*
outermost layer: *crust, lithosphere*
personification of: *Gaia*
pertaining to: *terrene*
shape: *oblate, spheroid*
study of its structure: *geology, tectonics*
subsurface: *astheosphere, core, mantle*

earthling *n.* tellurian, inhabitant of the Earth, human, man, woman, terra. *The shadowy figures next door were indeed earthlings, and not extraterrestrial aliens.* **Ant.** alien, extraterrestrial, (slang) little green man.

earthly *adj.* terrestrial, terrene, worldly, mundane, physical, temporal. *Making lots of money is an earthly desire that fades with age.* **Ant.** extraterrestrial, ethereal, otherworldly.

earthquake *n.* tremor, temblor, convulsion, shock, upheaval, seismic event. *The earthquake shook the building.*

WORD SEARCH

center of: *epicenter*
continental motion responsible for: *plate tectonics*
following tremor: *aftershock*

fracture in the Earth where quake originates: *fault*
ground undulations: *primary waves, compressional waves, Love waves*
magnitude scale: *Richter scale, Mercalli intensity scale*
pertaining to: *seismic*
preceding warning tremor: *foreshock*
recorder of Earth's vibrations: *seismograph*
sea wave caused by, massive: *tsunami*
study of: *seismology*

earthy *adj.* folksy, unrefined, down-to-earth, unsophisticated, unpretentious, rough. *The original pioneers were tough, earthy people who didn't have the need to refine themselves.* **Ant.** sophisticated, refined, dainty.

ease *n.* **1.** comfort, naturalness, readiness, leisure, easiness, facility. *He swims with ease.* –*vb.* **2.** relieve, comfort, soothe, lessen, diminish, decrease. *Her kind words eased his grief.* **Ant. 1.** difficulty, discomfort, effort. **2.** worsen, aggravate.

easy *adj.* **1.** simple, effortless, painless, light, undemanding. *The first part of the obstacle course is easy.* **2.** comfortable, relaxed, carefree, untroubled, satisfying. *Her summer on the French Riviera was full of easy living.* **3.** lenient, permissive, pleasant, easygoing, friendly. *He's an easy person to work for.* **Ant. 1.** hard, difficult, strenuous. **2.** awkward, uncomfortable, miserable. **3.** unfriendly, harsh, strict.

easygoing *adj.* relaxed, tolerant, untroubled, happy-go-lucky, laid-back, gentle, placid. *His easygoing manner made him a pleasure to work with.* **Ant.** difficult, temperamental, mean.

eat *vb.* **1.** devour, consume, ingest, swallow, chew. *I feel like I could eat a horse.* **2.** rust, wear, corrode, erode, dissolve. *Rust has slowly eaten away at the iron gate.*

eavesdrop *vb.* listen in, spy, pry, snoop, wiretap, bug. *Don't eavesdrop or you might hear something unpleasant about yourself.*

ebb *vb.* **1.** recede, decrease, decline, reduce, lessen, diminish. *The storm began to ebb in the evening.* –*n.* **2.** withdrawal, retreat, lowering, decrease, decline. *Some beautiful shells were uncovered when the tide was at low ebb.* **Ant. 1.** increase, heighten, intensify. **2.** rising, advancement.

eccentric *adj.* **1.** odd, peculiar, weird, queer, strange, bizarre. *Her eccentric habits made her friends feel uncomfortable.* –*n.* **2.** crank, misfit, character, nonconformist, screwball, crackpot. *Eccentrics may be a little strange, but they can make life interesting.* **Ant. 1.** normal, ordinary, regular. **2.** conformist, conventionalist.

eccentricity *n.* peculiarity, oddness, quirk, idiosyncrasy, abnormality, weirdness. *His most notable eccentricity was his refusal to drive a car.*

echo *vb.* **1.** reverberate, resound, ring, reply, resonate. *A shotgun blast echoed throughout the canyon.* **2.** imitate, mimic, impersonate, copy, parrot, repeat. *The macaw echoed everything I said.* –*n.* **3.** answer, reflection, response, repetition, reaction. *He shouted a greeting in the large hall and listened for an echo.*

eclectic *adj.* selective, diverse, multi-faceted, assorted, wide-ranging, broad. *Jasmine has eclectic tastes in music and enjoys the best of jazz one day and the best of country, rock, or classical the next.* **Ant.** limited, narrow.

eclipse *n.* **1.** masking, shadowing, veiling, covering, darkening. *There will be a lunar eclipse tonight.* –*vb.* **2.** obscure, darken, shadow, dim, conceal, hide. *Our view was partially eclipsed by the trees.* **3.** overshadow, surpass, outdo, exceed, outshine, transcend. *His effort at the high jump eclipsed all other attempts.* **Ant. 2.** uncover, expose, clear.

economical *adj.* frugal, thrifty, economic, prudent, saving, sparing. *It is more economical to buy the large box of cereal.* **Ant.** generous, wasteful, extravagant.

economize *vb.* save, conserve, skimp, scrimp, pinch. *Inflation has forced us to economize.* **Ant.** spend, waste, squander.

economy *n.* **1.** income, earnings, production, enterprise. *The national economy is threatened by a recession.* **2.** frugality, thrift, thriftiness, prudence, restraint. *We need to practice economy now that Father has retired.* **Ant. 2.** extravagance, squandering, waste.

ecosystem *n.* environment, habitat, ecological community, environs, living system. *An oil spill is a disaster to any ecosystem.*

ecstasy *n.* pleasure, delight, rapture, joy, bliss, elation. *The double fudge cake was pure ecstasy.* **Ant.** misery, suffering, torment.

ecstatic *adj.* delighted, overjoyed, happy, elated, joyful. *She was ecstatic when she got the part in the movie.* **Ant.** gloomy, despondent, unhappy.

eddy *n.* vortex, current, countercurrent, swirl, whirlpool. *We watched the floating leaf swirl as it was pulled into an eddy.*

Eden *n.* garden, paradise, utopia, heaven on earth, garden of Adam and Eve. *The desert was a parched but beautiful Eden.*

edge *n.* **1.** rim, border, margin, boundary, brim, verge. *The old man lived in a little shack on the edge of town.* **2.** advantage, lead, superiority, jump, start. *Her quickness gave her an edge over the competition.* –*vb.* **3.** border, outline, trim, rim, hem. *We edged the herb garden with chives.* **4.** inch, slide, creep, stalk, sneak. *The cat slowly edged closer to the unsuspecting mouse.* **Ant. 1.** center, middle, interior. **2.** disadvantage, hindrance. **4.** rush, run, race.

edgy *adj.* tense, uptight, anxious, nervous, jumpy, (slang) wired. *The guy was biting his nails and pacing and was obviously edgy.* **Ant.** calm, serene, relaxed.

edible *adj.* palatable, consumable, comestible, digestible, fit to eat. *It's very difficult to tell which mushrooms in the wild are edible and which are poisonous.* **Ant.** inedible, unpalatable, toxic.

edict *n.* order, command, decree, law, rule, statute, proclamation. *A herald announced the king's edict in the town square.*

edit *vb.* correct, revise, amend, check, alter, arrange. *The book will be finished as soon as it has been edited.*

edition *n.* issue, copy, number, volume, printing. *Book collectors prefer the first printing of a first edition.*

editorial *n.* commentary, opinion, (slang) think piece, observation, essay, article, viewpoint. *She wrote an editorial on homelessness.*

educate *vb.* teach, tutor, train, instruct, school, inform, coach. *The job of a teacher is to educate.*

education *n.* schooling, learning, instruction, training, study. *He attended a prestigious school in order to get a good education.*

educational *adj.* instructional, informative, enlightening, edifying, scholastic, academic, illustrative, eye-opening. *The computer offers many new educational opportunities.*

educator *n.* teacher, instructor, professor, tutor, mentor, trainer. *Being an educator requires great patience.*

eerie *adj.* spooky, ghostly, weird, creepy, strange, unearthly. *I have an eerie feeling that someone is watching us.*

effect *n.* **1.** result, outcome, upshot, consequence, aftermath. *The full effect of today's elec-*

tion will not be known for years. **2.** impact, influence, impression, bearing, effectiveness. *The rain came too late to have an effect on this year's harvest.* **3.** operation, action, execution, force, power. *The new law will go into effect on the first of next year.* –*vb.* **4.** make, produce, accomplish, cause, create, realize. *The airline strike has effected a change in our vacation plans.* **Ant. 1.** origin, source, beginning. **4.** prevent, stop, block.

effective *adj.* **1.** useful, helpful, efficient, practical, competent. *I need to find a more effective studying method.* **2.** active, current, operational, operative. *Do you know when the new store hours become effective?* **3.** powerful, forceful, impressive, striking, successful. *The ending of the horror movie was so effective that I couldn't sleep all night.* **Ant. 1.** useless, worthless, ineffective. **2.** inoperative, inactive, inert. **3.** weak, pointless, unimpressive.

effeminate *adj.* unmanly, feminine, sissyish, emasculate, soft, delicate. *Most men have an effeminate side but wouldn't dare show it in public.* **Ant.** masculine, tough, macho.

efficacy *n.* effectiveness, proficiency, productiveness, power, potency. *The physician prescribed a medication known for its efficacy.*

efficient *adj.* effective, competent, productive, capable, practical. *Alphabetical filing is an efficient method of organization.* **Ant.** ineffective, inefficient, unworkable.

effigy *n.* likeness, figure, representation, dummy, mock-up. *The protesters set fire to an effigy of the hated dictator.*

effort *n.* **1.** attempt, endeavor, venture, try, struggle. *Try to make an effort to be on time.* **2.** energy, force, exertion, work, labor, toil. *The effort needed to build Hoover Dam was immense.*

effortless *adj.* easy, painless, simple, smooth, light, natural. *The gazelle made an effortless leap over the fence.* **Ant.** hard, difficult, strenuous.

egalitarian *adj.* equal, fair-minded, liberal, democratic, unbiased, just. *The club was egalitarian in nature and only elected leaders by vote.* **Ant.** unfair, biased, prejudiced.

ego *n.* self, psyche, self-image, self-esteem, self-respect. *My ego was somewhat deflated after failing to score a single basket.*

egocentric *adj.* egotistical, conceited, self-centered, self-absorbed, selfish, narcissistic. *He had an egocentric personality and assumed he was superior to everyone.*

egotism *n.* conceit, egomania, self-centeredness, selfishness, self-absorption, narcissism. *His arrogance and egotism were sickening to behold.*

eject *vb.* **1.** project, emit, expel, erupt, spew, discharge. *Foul fumes ejected from the exhaust pipe.* **2.** banish, dismiss, exclude, remove, evict. *He was ejected from the club for unruly behavior.* **Ant. 1.** retain, keep, hold. **2.** admit, receive, introduce.

elaborate *adj.* **1.** ornate, detailed, fancy, complex, complicated. *We were impressed by his elaborate needlepoint designs.* –*vb.* **2.** explain, clarify, specify, expand, embellish, expound. *Would you elaborate on your plans to run for office?* **Ant. 1.** simple, plain, basic. **2.** condense, summarize, simplify.

elastic *adj.* flexible, pliable, stretchable, adaptable, bendable. *This elastic belt is suitable for all waist sizes.* **Ant.** stiff, inflexible, rigid.

elated *adj.* delighted, excited, happy, overjoyed, joyful, cheerful. *She was elated to find a gold coin on the sidewalk.* **Ant.** sad, unhappy, gloomy, morose.

elder *adj.* **1.** older, senior, ranking, superior, earlier. *He is the elder brother of a family of five.*

–*n.* **2.** senior, veteran, ancestor, patriarch, matriarch. *All important decisions were made by the tribal elders.* **Ant. 1.** younger, newer, later. **2.** junior, youth, novice.

elderly *adj.* old, ancient, aged, olden, mature. *The elderly woman lives with her grandson.* **Ant.** young, youthful, juvenile.

elect *vb.* select, pick, vote, choose, decide, opt, determine. *We elected to have our annual picnic at the beach.*

election *n.* vote, voting, balloting, referendum, selection. *Who do you plan to vote for in next week's election?*

WORD SEARCH

attacks on opponents, verbal: *mudslinging, smear campaign*
assembly of party members to choose candidate: *caucus*
candidate's beliefs, goals for office: *platform*
candidate list: *ballot, ticket*
district or group of voters: *constituency*
district, voting: *precinct*
enthusiasm-generating assembly: *rally*
grin and shake hands with everyone: *glad-hand*
mail-in vote: *absentee ballot*
nominating election: *primary*
speak from city to city: *barnstorm, stump*
victory by large majority of votes: *landslide*
vote for an issue rather than a candidate: *referendum, proposition*
voting statistics: *poll*
will and dictates of the people clearly understood through votes: *mandate*

elective *adj.* optional, chosen, voluntary, electoral, discretionary. *We were told that we would have four mandatory courses and two elective ones.* **Ant.** mandatory, required, forced.

electricity *n.* voltage, power, wattage, current, charge, (slang) juice. *Save electricity by turning out lights.*

WORD SEARCH

atom: *electron*
drop of voltage through power line: *brownout*
generator: *dynamo*
loss of power: *blackout, power outage*
medium that restricts current: *insulator*
medium that will carry electricity with little resistance: *conductor*
medium that will carry electricity with zero resistance: *superconductor*
regulator of current: *rheostat*
unit of power: *amp, ampere, ohm, volt, watt, joule*

electrify *vb.* thrill, excite, dazzle, stun, stagger, shock. *Michael Jordan could electrify a crowd just by slam-dunking a basketball.* **Ant.** anesthetize, put to sleep, bore.

elegance *n.* richness, grandeur, opulence, grace, dignity, refinement. *The coronation ceremony was conducted with great elegance.* **Ant.** tastelessness, plainness, crudeness.

elegant *adj.* grand, majestic, stylish, refined, dignified, tasteful, opulent. *She looked elegant in her new evening gown.* **Ant.** plain, common, tasteless.

element *n.* part, piece, component, ingredient, substance, factor. *Vegetables and fruits are important elements of a proper diet.* **Ant.** mass, sum, whole.

elementary *adj.* **1.** basic, fundamental, principal, primary, elemental. *Food, water and shelter are elementary human needs.* **2.** simple, plain, clear, easy, uncomplicated. *Surely you can do an elementary thing like combing your own hair.* **Ant. 1.** secondary, unimportant, lesser. **2.** complex, complicated.

elephant *n.* pachyderm, herbivore, mammal, quadruped, beast, animal. *Elephants are among nature's most intelligent animals.*

WORD SEARCH
call: *bellow, trumpet*
driver: *mahout*
extinct: *mammoth, mastadon*
female: *cow*
male: *bull*
nose: *snout, trunk*
outcast, vicious: *rogue*
run at to intimidate: *charge*
sexual frenzy of male: *musth, rut*
tooth: *tusk*
tusk: *ivory*
young: *calf*

elevate *vb.* lift, raise, hoist, boost, uplift, erect. *The stage was elevated to allow a clear view for the spectators.* **Ant.** lower, drop, depress.

elevation *n.* height, altitude, lift, rise, prominence, loftiness. *My mountain cabin is at an elevation of five thousand feet.*

elf *n.* dwarf, gnome, pixie, brownie, leprachaum, fairy. *An elf would probably make a good jockey because of its size and stature.*

elicit *vb.* bring out, draw, extract, call forth. *His rude remarks only served to elicit boos from the crowd.*

eligible *adj.* qualified, suitable, suited, fitting, acceptable. *You are eligible for our grand prize of one million dollars.* **Ant.** ineligible, unqualified, unsuitable.

eliminate *vb.* remove, omit, exclude, expel, erase, drop, cancel. *She eliminated sugar from her diet.* **Ant.** include, admit, obtain.

elite *adj.* the best, the highest, the select, aristocracy, crème de la crème, upper class. *At the country club, he hobnobbed with an elite class of people.* **Ant.** lower class, dregs of society.

elixir *n.* potion, formula, concoction, nostrum, mixture, compound, curative. *The witch concocted a magic elixir.*

eloquent *adj.* persuasive, expressive, articulate, fluent, poetic, impassioned. *The writer's eloquent prose made me cry.* **Ant.** dull, ordinary, weak.

elucidate *vb.* clarify, explain, illuminate, illustrate, simplify. *We asked the teacher to elucidate further on the subject.* **Ant.** obfuscate, muddy.

elude *vb.* avoid, dodge, escape, evade, shun, duck. *The rabbit eluded the hunter by running into a brush thicket.* **Ant.** encounter, face, chase.

elusive *adj.* **1.** evasive, illusory, fleeting, slippery, tricky. *We are searching for the elusive unicorn.* **2.** baffling, puzzling, mysterious, confusing, deceptive. *She gave us an elusive theory when we wanted hard facts.*

emaciated *adj.* wasted, lean, scrawny, anorexic, malnourished, gaunt, raw-boned. *The prisoners had become noticeably emaciated from lack of nourishment.* **Ant.** fat, obese, plump.

E-mail *n.* electronic mail, online mail, message, flash, correspondence, missive. *He sent me an E-mail from halfway across the world.*

emanate *vb.* issue, exude, discharge, flow, arise, emit, spring. *A small cloud of gas appeared to emanate from the swamp.*

emancipate *vb.* liberate, free, release, deliver, redeem, unchain. *The rebels wished to emancipate their country from foreign invaders.* **Ant.** enslave, subjugate, dominate.

emasculate *vb.* castrate, weaken, take the teeth out of, effeminate, enervate, debilitate. *Ranchers may physically emasculate an ornery bull in order to make it more manageable.* **Ant.** strengthen, fortify, toughen.

embargo *n.* ban, prohibition, proscription, blockage, stoppage, restriction. *They placed an embargo on all imported pesticide.*

embark *vb.* **1.** start, begin, undertake, commence, enter. *The movie actor embarked on a stage career.* **2.** board, go aboard, sail, leave, depart. *All passengers must embark in ten minutes.* **Ant. 1.** finish, end, terminate. **2.** disembark, land.

embarrass *vb.* shame, humiliate, upset, discomfort, humble. *Why did you embarrass me in front of our friends?*

embarrassment *n.* chagrin, shame, uneasiness, discomfort, bewilderment. *His racist remark was an embarrassment to us all.*

embassy *n.* consulate, foreign office, ministry, diplomatic office, chancellery. *While traveling abroad we had to go to the U.S. embassy to resolve the problem.*

embellish *vb.* adorn, decorate, garnish, enhance, enrich, elaborate. *The country singer embellished his suit with rhinestones.*

embezzle *vb.* steal, defraud, swindle, cheat, pilfer, rob, misuse. *How much money did she embezzle from her employer?*

emblem *n.* sign, symbol, badge, insignia, trademark, label. *The lumber company has a drawing of a tree on their emblem.*

embody *vb.* represent, personify, incarnate, manifest, symbolize. *The bald eagle embodies the image we like to have about the United States.*

embrace *vb.* **1.** hug, hold, clasp, caress, enfold, grasp. *They embraced their long-lost son.* **2.** include, cover, enclose, contain, involve, encompass. *A successful treaty must embrace the concerns of all involved parties.* **Ant. 2.** exclude, omit, ignore, neglect.

embroider *vb.* exaggerate, embellish, aggrandize, fabricate, invent, stretch the truth. *Michael liked to embroider descriptions of things that happened to him at work.* **Ant.** understate, play down.

emerge *vb.* appear, rise, arise, surface, issue, show, spring. *A sea serpent emerged from the depths of the ocean.* **Ant.** sink, disappear, recede, retreat.

emergency *n.* crisis, extremity, predicament, difficulty, accident. *Call an ambulance and tell them it's an emergency.*

emergency room *n.* ER, trauma center, critical care facility, medical crisis unit, intensive care unit (ICU). *Macky broke his leg and had to be rushed to the hospital.*

emigrate *vb.* move, migrate, resettle, relocate, depart, leave. *My father's job will force us to emigrate from Canada.*

eminent *adj.* important, famous, renowned, celebrated, prominent, notable. *Arthur C. Clarke is an eminent science-fiction writer.* **Ant.** unimportant, unknown, unremarkable.

emissary *n.* representative, envoy, messenger, agent, attaché, ambassador. *The United States sent an emissary to relay a message to the emir.*

emission *n.* discharge, issuance, emanation, leakage, outpouring, seepage. *Emissions from the coal-fired power plant exceeded federal pollution standards.*

emit *vb.* discharge, expel, release, issue, shed, eject. *My car is emitting some rather noxious fumes.* **Ant.** retain, keep, hold.

emotion *n.* feeling, passion, sentiment, reaction, excitement. *You can hear the deep emotion in her voice.*

emotional *adj.* **1.** sensitive, feeling, moving, stirring, touching, heartwarming. *The family reunion was an emotional moment.* **2.** excited, excitable, hysterical, passionate, temperamental. *An emotional person makes a terrible poker player.* **Ant. 1.** cold, unfeeling, unemotional. **2.** calm, placid, reserved.

emotionless *adj.* dead, stony, cold, apathetic, indifferent, unfeeling. *The crook was completely emotionless, even when told he might spend ten years in jail.* **Ant.** emotional, passionate, enraged.

empathize *vb.* understand, comprehend, identify with, stand in another's shoes, relate to, appreciate, sympathize. *As a light sleeper, I can empathize with insomniacs.*

empathy *n.* understanding, appreciation, affinity, communion, sympathy, rapport. *Unable to find clothes that fit me properly, I have empathy for other oddly-sized people.*

emperor *n.* sovereign, monarch, czar, ruler, empress, czarina. *Charlemagne was crowned emperor by Pope Leo III.*

emphasis *n.* stress, weight, accent, force, importance, attention. *I enjoy games that put more emphasis on fun than on winning.*

emphasize *vb.* stress, accent, highlight, spotlight, press. *She emphasized the need for donations to keep the day-care center open.* **Ant.** minimize, underplay, understate.

emphatic *adj.* strong, definite, powerful, forceful, decisive, assertive. *She made an emphatic denial of any knowledge of the theft.* **Ant.** weak, hesitant, indecisive.

empire *n.* kingdom, dominion, rule, territory, realm, holdings. *His empire stretched for 150 miles in every direction, yet the king was dissatisfied.*

employ *vb.* **1.** hire, retain, engage, enlist, contract. *Businesses should employ more handicapped people.* **2.** use, apply, utilize, operate, handle. *He employed a crowbar to open the crate.* **Ant. 1.** fire, discharge, dismiss.

employee *n.* worker, laborer, hand, servant, helper, assistant. *The employees are demanding a higher wage.* **Ant.** employer, boss, manager.

employer *n.* boss, manager, proprietor, hirer, contractor. *My new employer is an easy person to work for.* **Ant.** employee, servant, worker.

employment *n.* **1.** job, placement, work, position, profession, occupation. *I hope you enjoy your employment with our firm.* **2.** use, usage, using, operation, service, application. *The employment of smoke alarms is an excellent safety measure.*

empower *vb.* enable, entitle, authorize, vest, commission, entrust. *Her goal was to empower the homeless people so they could help themselves.*

emptiness *n.* nothingness, vacancy, void, desolation, vacuum, vacuity. *The emptiness of space is mindboggling.* **Ant.** fullness, richness.

empty *vb.* **1.** clear, drain, void, deplete, exhaust. *She emptied the glass of its contents.* –*adj.* **2.** vacant, void, unfilled, unoccupied, blank. *He opened the barrel and discovered that it was empty.* **3.** meaningless, worthless, senseless, purposeless, futile. *All we received was a bunch of empty promises.* **Ant. 1.** fill, pack, stock. **2.** full, complete, packed. **3.** meaningful, worthwhile, valuable.

emulate *vb.* copy, take after, imitate, mimic, use as a role model, ape. *When you don't know how to act in a certain situation, emulate someone who does.*

enable *vb.* allow, permit, empower, qualify, authorize, license. *A college degree will enable you to get a better job.* **Ant.** disallow, disqualify, stop, prevent.

enact *vb.* legislate, establish, pass, institute, order, authorize, decree, transact. *They might try to enact a new provision in the law.*

enchant *vb.* **1.** bewitch, charm, hex, conjure. *The evil witch enchanted the prince by turning him into a frog.* **2.** delight, please, fascinate, enthrall, captivate. *The children were enchanted by the puppet show.* **Ant. 1.** release, exorcise, free. **2.** bore, tire, repel.

enchanting *adj.* charming, fascinating, captivating, intriguing, alluring. *It was an enchanting evening.*

enclose *vb.* **1.** encircle, surround, confine, envelop, contain. *The lions in the zoo were enclosed by a deep moat.* **2.** include, insert, place, append, add. *He enclosed his receipt when he mailed the letter of complaint.*

encompass *vb.* **1.** surround, encircle, envelop, ring, circumscribe. *We erected a fence to encompass the entire yard.* **2.** include, embody, comprehend, take in. *The new tax rules would encompass all waterfront properties.*

encore *n.* curtain call, recall, standing ovation, command performance, reprise. *The diva ran off the stage, but the crowd demanded an encore.*

encounter *vb.* **1.** meet, face, confront, engage, experience. *The king's soldiers encountered heavy resistance from the Cyclops.* –*n.* **2.** meeting, confrontation, collision, conflict, clash, brush. *He had an encounter with a grizzly bear on the narrow mountain trail.* **Ant. 1.** avoid, escape, elude. **2.** avoidance, evasion.

encourage *vb.* **1.** persuade, inspire, support, spur, hearten, urge. *She was encouraged to run for class president.* **2.** foster, promote, boost, heighten, increase, advance. *Brushing after meals encourages the development of healthy teeth and gums.* **Ant. 1.** dissuade, discourage, deter. **2.** retard, prevent, hinder.

encouragement *n.* reassurance, support, encouraging, help, aid, assistance. *He needed little encouragement to complete the marathon.* **Ant.** discouragement, hindrance, constraint.

encroach *vb.* intrude, trespass, infringe, invade, interlope, infiltrate. *Urban sprawl will soon encroach upon our most unspoiled open lands.* **Ant.** retreat, recede.

encumber *vb.* burden, saddle, weigh down, hamper, oppress, load down. *His boss tended to encumber him with too many responsibilities.* **Ant.** unencumber, lighten, free.

encyclopedia *n.* reference book, fact book, volume, tome, information resource, glossary. *Consult an encyclopedia for general information on your topic.*

end *n.* **1.** limit, border, boundary, extremity, edge, tip. *There's a good restaurant on the west end of town.* **2.** conclusion, close, finish, finale, completion, termination. *The cowboy rode off into the sunset at the end of the movie.* **3.** aim, goal, objective, intent, intention, purpose. *She's going to need plenty of time and money to achieve her end.* –*vb.* **4.** finish, stop, halt, close, terminate, conclude, cease. *Let's end this meeting at a reasonable time.* **Ant. 1.** center, middle, heart. **2.** start, beginning, opening. **4.** start, initiate, open, begin.

endanger *vb.* threaten, risk, imperil, jeopardize, expose. *Mountain climbing sounds like just another way to endanger your life.* **Ant.** protect, safeguard, preserve.

endangered *adj.* threatened, jeopardized, at risk, imperiled, facing extinction, vulnerable. *The rhinoceros is an endangered species.* **Ant.** safe, secure, protected.

endearing *adj.* lovable, adorable, dear, sweet, charming, winning. *The child had an endearing smile.* **Ant.** repulsive, disgusting, sickening.

endeavor *vb.* **1.** attempt, try, undertake, strive, aim, venture, seek. *We endeavored to save the old theater from being demolished.* –*n.* **2.** effort, attempt, try, undertaking, struggle, exertion. *Scott's endeavor to be the first man to reach the South Pole ended in failure.*

endless *adj.* eternal, infinite, limitless, everlasting, unending, ceaseless. *The line for concert tickets seemed to be endless.* **Ant.** finite, limited, definite.

endorse *vb.* support, back, approve, confirm, recommend, certify. *The actress was asked to endorse a new line of cosmetics.* **Ant.** condemn, criticize, disapprove.

endowment *n.* gift, funding, contribution, donation, grant, bequest. *The philanthropist gave a large endowment to the school.*

endurance *n.* stamina, durability, persistence, fortitude, hardiness, tolerance. *Triathlon athletes must have incredible endurance.* **Ant.** weakness, weariness, frailty.

endure *vb.* **1.** last, continue, remain, persist, hold, stay, prevail. *I need a house paint that will endure for many years.* **2.** suffer, experience, bear, tolerate, withstand, sustain. *The lost desert patrol endured thirst and heat exhaustion before they were rescued.* **Ant. 1.** fail, decay, perish. **2.** escape, avoid, succumb.

enemy *n.* foe, opponent, adversary, rival, antagonist, nemesis. *I wouldn't want to make a dragon my enemy.* **Ant.** friend, ally, partner.

energetic *adj.* active, vigorous, lively, tireless, animated, dynamic. *The energetic puppy tired us out.* **Ant.** tired, weary, lazy.

energize *vb.* invigorate, stimulate, electrify, enliven, spark, refresh. *Vigorous exercise can tire you out, but it can also energize you.* **Ant.** sap, drain, tire.

energy *n.* **1.** power, strength, force, might, muscle, effort. *You are wasting energy trying to push that boulder off the road.* **2.** vigor, vitality, drive, zip, zest, punch, pep. *The school wants cheerleaders who have lots of energy.* **Ant. 2.** sluggishness, laziness, lethargy.

enforce *vb.* compel, force, require, impose, execute, invoke. *The speed limit is strongly enforced in this state.*

engage *vb.* **1.** occupy, involve, engross, concern, absorb, preoccupy. *I was so engaged in the conversation that I lost track of time.* **2.** hire, retain, employ, contract, commission. *The club engaged a caterer for their annual banquet.* **3.** pledge, commit, promise, betroth. *They are engaged to be married in June.*

engaging *adj.* charming, captivating, enchanting, pleasing, likable, delightful. *The comedian had a very engaging personality.* **Ant.** unlikable, unpleasant, dull.

engine *n.* motor, power plant, powerhouse, dynamo, turbine, (slang) workhorse. *Listen to that engine roar.*

engineer *n.* technologist, builder, inventor, tinkerer, mechanic, troubleshooter. *The computer engineers created yet another innovation this year.*

engrave *vb.* carve, etch, cut, inscribe, chisel, scratch. *Her initials were engraved on the bracelet.*

engross *vb.* involve, immerse, absorb, occupy, preoccupy, engage. *She was engrossed in trying to complete the jigsaw puzzle.* **Ant.** bore, tire, weary.

enhance *vb.* enrich, improve, better, magnify, heighten, intensify. *A good polishing will enhance the appearance of your shoes.* **Ant.** lessen, reduce, diminish, decrease

enigma *n.* puzzle, riddle, mystery, secret, problem, question. *The Loch Ness monster will remain an enigma until there is documented proof of its existence.*

enjoy *vb.* like, appreciate, delight, love, relish, fancy, savor. *She enjoyed her day at the beach.* **Ant.** dislike, hate, despise.

enjoyment *n.* pleasure, delight, satisfaction, happiness, amusement, joy, fun. *He experienced many hours of enjoyment at the zoo.* **Ant.** misery, suffering, displeasure.

enlarge *vb.* increase, extend, expand, augment, lengthen, broaden, widen. *The playground will be enlarged to include a tennis court.* **Ant.** decrease, reduce, shrink.

enlighten *vb.* educate, inform, instruct, explain, clarify, teach. *Would you please enlighten me on your country's customs?* **Ant.** confuse, mislead, perplex.

enlist *vb.* **1.** enroll, register, enter, volunteer, sign up. *He enlisted in the army for two years.* **2.** recruit, engage, secure, procure, obtain. *Will you help us enlist donors for the blood drive?*

enliven *vb.* brighten, cheer, vitalize, excite, animate, stimulate, rouse. *A good rock band would enliven this party.* **Ant.** dampen, deaden, subdue

enmity *n.* hatred, malevolence, animosity, venom, hostility, malice. *The enmity between the two combatants was obvious, especially when they spit at each other.* **Ant.** love, affection, friendliness.

enormous *adj.* huge, giant, immense, gigantic, colossal, tremendous, mammoth. *Some dinosaurs were enormous creatures.* **Ant.** tiny, small, slight.

enough *adj.* **1.** adequate, ample, sufficient, plenty, abundant. *Do you have enough chairs for your classroom? –adv.* **2.** adequately, sufficiently, satisfactorily, passably, amply. *I'm tired enough to sleep through an earthquake.* **Ant. 1.** scant, meager, inadequate.

enrage *vb.* anger, madden, infuriate, inflame, provoke, incense. *His rude manners enraged her.* **Ant.** please, delight, calm.

enrich *vb.* improve, better, enhance, upgrade, develcp, embellish. *The farmer enriched his field with fertilizers.* **Ant.** downgrade, degenerate, impoverish.

enroll *vb.* register, enlist, join, engage, enter, serve. *We must enroll in school by Friday.* **Ant.** withdraw, drop, leave, quit.

enrollment *n.* roster, register, record, roll, registration. *My history class has an enrollment of thirty students.*

enslave *vb.* indenture, subjugate, subdue, dominate, master, control. *The captured Athenians were enslaved by the Spartans.* **Ant.** free, liberate, release.

ensure *vb.* insure, assure, confirm, guarantee, secure, certify, warrant. *Your term paper is good enough to ensure a passing grade.*

entangle *vb.* snare, catch, trap, involve, ravel, ensnarl. *The fly found itself entangled in a spider's web.* **Ant.** disentangle, free, extricate.

enter *vb.* **1.** arrive, go in, come in, penetrate, intrude. *She entered the room with a flourish.* **2.** begin, start, join, commence, enroll. *He is going to enter a ballet class in the fall.* **3.** register, list, catalog, record, write. *Please enter your answers in the appropriate space.* **Ant. 1.** leave, exit, escape. **2.** end, finish, conclude.

enterprise *n.* **1.** project, undertaking, operation, program, venture, business. *Her lemonade stand proved to be a profitable enterprise.* **2.** drive, energy, ambition, zeal, courage, boldness. *The boxer lacked the enterprise to become a champion.*

enterprising *adj.* entrepreneurial, go-getting, venturesome, ambitious, hustling, inventive. *She was an enterprising young woman with a head for business.* **Ant.** lazy, unambitious, slothful.

entertain *vb.* **1.** amuse, divert, delight, please, engross, interest. *We hired a comedian to enter-*

tain our guests. 2. heed, consider, imagine, harbor, foster, contemplate. *The workers would not entertain the thought of a salary decrease.* **Ant.** 1. bore, weary, tire. 2. reject, neglect, ignore.

entertainment *n.* amusement, diversion, pastime, performance, play. *We were all looking forward to the evening's entertainments.*

enthusiasm *n.* zeal, eagerness, fervor, passion, ardor, excitement. *We cheered our team with enthusiasm.* **Ant.** apathy, coldness, unconcern.

enthusiastic *adj.* eager, passionate, zealous, avid, fervent, ardent. *The school band has many enthusiastic musicians.* **Ant.** indifferent, half-hearted, reluctant.

entice *vb.* coax, tempt, lure, induce, attract, persuade. *A neighbor enticed her into buying a ticket for the church raffle.* **Ant.** discourage, dissuade, frighten.

entire *adj.* complete, whole, intact, total, full, undivided, unbroken. *He sold his entire collection of science-fiction books.* **Ant.** partial, incomplete, divided.

entirely *adv.* wholly, altogether, fully, completely, perfectly. *Your solution to the puzzle is entirely right.* **Ant.** partially, partly, somewhat.

entitle *vb.* 1. allow, authorize, permit, enable, sanction, license. *This coupon entitles you to one free snow cone.* 2. name, title, dub, call, designate. *Benny Goodman was entitled the King of Swing.*

entourage *adj.* retinue, attendants, staff, escort, bodyguards, cortege. *He was followed everywhere by his entourage.*

entrance *n.* 1. entry, portal, doorway, door, gate, access. *The entrance to the museum is located on the other side.* 2. admission, entry, admittance, approach, arrival, coming. *The queen's entrance was accompanied by much fanfare.* –*vb.* 3. fascinate, enchant, wonder, delight, charm, enrapture. *I was entranced by the dancing fairies.* **Ant.** 1. exit, outlet, egress. 2. exit, departure, leaving. 3. bore, disinterest, disappoint.

entrepreneur *n.* businessperson, enterpriser, industrialist, risk-taker, speculator, go-getter, developer. *The intrepid entrepreneur transformed the rundown section of town into a thriving shopping area.*

entropy *n.* deterioration, decay, disintegration, degeneration, degradation. *In the end, entropy destroys everything, even the universe itself.* **Ant.** rebirth, invigoration, reconstruction.

entrust *vb.* commit, assign, trust, delegate, consign, charge. *The dying pirate entrusted his treasure map to the cabin boy.*

entry *n.* 1. entrance, door, doorway, gate, threshold. *There's a stalled car blocking the parking lot's entry.* 2. admission, admittance, entrance, access, initiation. *Minors are not allowed entry into taverns.* 3. item, account, statement, note, record. *She has just finished making an entry in her diary.* **Ant.** 1. exit, outlet, egress. 2. exit, departure, leaving.

enunciate *vb.* pronounce, articulate, speak clearly, mouth, voice clearly, say, frame each word carefully. *He tended to enunciate words with a lisp.*

envelop *vb.* enfold, wrap, surround, cover, encircle, enclose. *The forest fire enveloped five thousand acres.*

envelope *n.* cover, wrapper, wrapping, jacket, case, sheath. *The Earth's envelope of air protects us from harmful solar radiation.*

envious *adj.* jealous, covetous, desirous, yearning, resentful. *She was envious of her friend's new sports car.*

environment *n.* surroundings, habitat, setting, element, conditions, neighborhood. *Eskimos live in a cold environment.*

environmentalist *n.* conservationist, ecologist, environmental activist, environmental advocate, green party member. *The environmentalists pooled their resources to purchase the last piece of undeveloped land.*

envoy *n.* representative, messenger, agent, emissary, courier, ambassador, delegate. *An envoy was sent to the embassy to deliver the president's message directly.*

envy *vb.* **1.** covet, desire, want, crave, resent, begrudge. *The farmer envied his neighbor's new team of horses.* –*n.* **2.** jealousy, resentment, spite, grudging, malice. *Envy of her classmates affected her attitude toward them.*

ephemeral *adj.* transient, fleeting, evanescent, short-lived, transitory, brief. *Comets and meteors are highly ephemeral.* **Ant.** permanent, long-lasting, eternal.

epic *adj.* grand, huge, heroic, mythical, legendary, grand. *It was a downpour of epic proportions.* **Ant.** trivial, insignificant, small.

epidemic *n.* **1.** plague, outbreak, pestilence, scourge, contamination. *An epidemic of measles broke out in our summer camp.* –*adj.* **2.** widespread, prevailing, rampant, extensive, prevalent. *Incidents of crime have reached epidemic proportions.*

epilepsy *n.* seizure disorder, neurological disorder, convulsions, catalepsy. *My friend Eddy had epilepsy, but surgery has stopped his seizures.*

WORD SEARCH

dream-like symptoms signaling impending seizure: *aura*

major seizure with unconsciousness: *grand mal*

minor or brief unconsciousness without convulsions: *petit mal*

epiphany *n.* revelation, insight, enlightenment, illumination, understanding, grasp. *It's not unusual for an astronaut to experience an epiphany the first time he or she sees the Earth from space.*

episode *n.* **1.** incident, event, occurrence, scene, experience, affair. *He frequently has episodes in which he feels like he is another person.* **2.** installment, chapter, scene, act, section, part. *In the last episode, our hero was about to be eaten by giant termites.*

epitaph *n.* inscription, memorial, legend, commemoration, wording, engraving. *The epitaph on my great grandfather's headstone has nearly worn away.*

epitome *n.* perfect example, perfect representation, embodiment, archetype, ultimate, model. *Some drivers consider the Rolls Royce the epitome of what a luxury car should be.*

epoch *n.* era, time, period, age, interval, span. *The development of the Internet marks a new epoch in world communication.*

equal *adj.* **1.** even, uniform, identical, similar, same, like. *She divided the pie into four equal slices.* –*vb.* **2.** match, correspond to, amount to, reach, tally. *One plus two equals three.* –*n.* **3.** match, rival, peer, equivalent, parallel. *He has not met his equal on the basketball court.* **Ant. 1.** uneven, unbalanced, different.

equality *n.* parity, evenness, balance, uniformity, par, sameness. *It is difficult to attain equality with others without a good education.* **Ant.** inequality, disparity.

equate *vb.* identify, compare, liken, equalize, associate, treat. *It is wrong to equate money with happiness.*

equilibrium *n.* stability, balance, steadiness, poise, evenness, symmetry. *She lost her equilibrium and fell off the log.*

equip *vb.* supply, provide, furnish, outfit, prepare, fit. *Travelers to Alaska should equip themselves with plenty of warm clothes.*

equipment *n.* gear, material, instruments, supplies, outfit, kit. *Let's check our camping equipment before we leave.*

equitable *adj.* fair, even, just, impartial, objective, unbiased, reasonable. *I'm sure that we can reach an equitable settlement for your damaged property.* **Ant.** uneven, unfair, unjust.

equivalent *adj.* equal, alike, similar, comparable, identical. *One gallon is equivalent to four quarts.* **Ant.** unequal, dissimilar, different.

equivocate *vb.* evade, sidestep, mince words, beat around the bush, hedge, waffle. *Politicians often equivocate when it comes to controversial issues.*

ER *See* EMERGENCY ROOM.

era *n.* age, epoch, period, generation, time. *The industrial era started in the late 18th century.*

eradicate *vb.* erase, eliminate, remove, destroy, exterminate, demolish. *I wish we could eradicate suffering from our lives.* **Ant.** create, establish, generate.

erase *vb.* remove, cancel, delete, scratch, eliminate, clear. *Would you please erase the writing on the blackboard?* **Ant.** add, restore, insert.

erect *adj.* **1.** upright, raised, vertical, straight, stiff, rigid. *The prairie dogs were standing erect outside their burrows.* –*vb.* **2.** build, construct, raise, establish, create. *A monument to the pioneers will be erected in the town square.* **Ant. 1.** stooped, limp, prone. **2.** demolish, destroy, raze.

erode *vb.* waste, wear, deteriorate, decay, eat. *Each spring the hills are slowly eroded by rain.*

erogenous *adj.* erotogenic, sexual, sensitive, sensuous, sensual, erotic. *Some parts of the body, such as the earlobes, are highly erogenous.*

erosion *n.* wear, deterioration, wasting, corrosion, disintegration, weathering. *Erosion reduced the once mighty boulder to a tiny nubbin.*

erotic *adj.* sexy, sexual, sensual, amatory, carnal, titillating. *It is illegal to admit children under eighteen to theaters showing erotic movies.*

erotica *n.* pornography, X-rated materials, adult materials, sexual imagery, smut. *The magazine contained mild erotica, and nobody under age 18 could buy it.*

errand *n.* chore, task, job, duty, assignment, undertaking, mission. *He will return after he completes his errand.*

erratic *adj.* irregular, unpredictable, unsteady, uneven, odd, eccentric. *My computer has been acting very erratic lately.* **Ant.** regular, normal, constant.

erroneous *adj.* wrong, incorrect, false, mistaken, inaccurate, faulty, untrue. *The reports of pink elephants on Main Street were erroneous.* **Ant.** right, correct, true, accurate.

error *n.* mistake, blunder, slip, oversight, fallacy, inaccuracy. *There are too many errors in your report.* **Ant.** accuracy, correctness.

erudite *adj.* educated, scholarly, learned, pedantic, literate, brainy. *The professor was the most erudite woman I had ever met.* **Ant.** ignorant, stupid, uneducated.

erupt *vb.* burst, explode, expel, eject, spew, gush, discharge. *Steam erupted from the broken pipe.*

eruption *n.* upheaval, cataclysm, blast, ejection, explosion, surge. *The eruption blew the top of the mountain off.*

escalate *vb.* rise, increase, grow, intensify, heighten, deepen. *Tensions invariably escalate when we fail to listen to another's point of view.* **Ant.** decline, fall, diminish.

escapade *n.* caper, adventure, high jinks, stunt, antics, tomfoolery. *We took off on another wild escapade and later regretted it.*

escape *vb.* **1.** flee, fly, run, break out. *The prisoners planned to escape from the evil prince's dungeon.* **2.** avoid, elude, dodge, evade, bypass. *There is no way to escape the final exam.* **3.** leak, erupt, issue, flow, seep. *Gas is escaping from the fuel line.* –*n.* **4.** breakout, getaway, flight, departure, release. *Their only escape from the dragon was through a haunted forest.* **Ant. 1.** capture, apprehend, imprison. **2.** meet, face, confront. **4.** capture, imprisonment, retention.

escort *vb.* **1.** conduct, guide, lead, usher, accompany, attend, chaperon. *I would be pleased to escort you to the dance.* –*n.* **2.** guard, retinue, attendant, companion, guide, chaperon. *The queen's escort walked with her to the carriage.*

escrow *n.* collateral, security, insurance, surety, bond, guarantee. *We had to put money in escrow to pay for future property taxes.*

esoteric *adj.* arcane, incomprehensible, abstruse, obscure, mysterious, deep. *Einstein is famous for his esoteric theories of time and space.* **Ant.** obvious, comprehensible, simple.

ESP *n.* extrasensory perception, psychic powers, telepathy, mindreading skills, clairvoyance, (slang) third eye. *Few scientists believe that ESP exists.*

especially *adv.* specially, particularly, notably, chiefly, principally. *I bought this gift especially for you.*

espionage *n.* spying, undercover work, (slang) cloak and dagger, intelligence, surveillance. *Espionage is among the world's most hazardous work.*

espouse *vb.* support, advocate, take up, champion, adopt, advance. *I espouse the conservation of land worldwide.* **Ant.** reject, spurn, fight.

essay *n.* article, paper, piece, composition, discourse, theme, study. *Your essay on the Boston Tea Party is due tomorrow.*

essence *n.* **1.** nature, character, basis, substance, meaning, spirit. *The essence of the rock singer's appeal is his boyish looks.* **2.** odor, perfume, scent, fragrance, smell. *An essence of roses lingered in the room.*

essential *adj.* vital, necessary, important, required, fundamental, critical. *It is essential that you show up in class tomorrow.* **Ant.** unimportant, unnecessary, inessential.

establish *vb.* **1.** found, form, create, settle, organize, build. *England established colonies all over the world.* **2.** prove, verify, confirm, substantiate, demonstrate. *New research has established the dangers of consuming too much cholesterol.* **Ant. 1.** abolish, eliminate, discontinue. **2.** disprove, refute, deny.

establishment *n.* **1.** institution, foundation, organization, business, company. *What is the name of the establishment you work for?* **2.** founding, formation, construction, start, installation. *The city council voted funds for the establishment of a new library.* **Ant. 2.** closing, removal, ending.

estate *n.* **1.** assets, holdings, wealth, possessions, property. *My grandfather's estate was valued at over a million dollars.* **2.** manor, residence, acreage, plantation. *I often dream of living on a sprawling estate in the country.*

esteem *n.* **1.** respect, admiration, honor, reverence, regard. *The mayor of this town is held in high esteem.* –*vb.* **2.** value, regard, respect, admire, revere, treasure. *Abraham Lincoln is esteemed as one of America's greatest presidents.* **Ant. 1.** contempt, disdain, ridicule. **2.** belittle, disregard.

estimate *vb.* **1.** guess, reckon, judge, evaluate, calculate, figure. *I estimate that it will be another hour before the plane arrives.* –*n.* **2.** evaluation, assessment, guess, judgment, opinion, appraisal. *The dealer gave him an estimate of the value of his coin collection.*

estranged *adj.* alienated, distant, remote, hostile, separated, divorced. *The couple had too many arguments and grew increasingly estranged.* **Ant.** close, intimate, friendly.

estuary *n.* mouth, outlet, waterway, tidewater, drain. *You catch some big fish down at the estuary when the tide is right.*

eternal *adj.* everlasting, endless, unending, ceaseless, perpetual, continual. *Romeo and Juliet pledged eternal love to each other.* **Ant.** temporary, limited, passing.

eternity *n.* infinity, forever, timelessness, immortality, perpetuity. *We seemed to wait an eternity for the bus, but really it was only twenty minutes.*

ethereal *adj.* otherworldly, heavenly, celestial, divine, supernal, unearthly. *The moonlight cascading over her face gave the model a distinctly ethereal appearance.* **Ant.** mundane, earthly.

ethical *adj.* moral, proper, virtuous, upright, honorable. *She lost the election but was admired, for running an ethical campaign.* **Ant.** unethical, improper, corrupt.

ethics *n.* morals, principles, moral code, standards, values, mores. *The mayor reconsidered his ethics and apologized for his actions.*

ethnic *adj.* cultural, racial, tribal, folk, native. *New York is home to more ethnic groups than any other city in the world.*

etiquette *n.* manners, conduct, behavior, customs, decorum, protocol, courtesy. *Please show me the proper etiquette for meeting the queen.*

eulogy *n.* tribute, praise, honor, homage, encomium, acclamation. *My brother delivered a beautiful eulogy at my grandfather's funeral.*

euphemism *n.* polite word, substitute, replacement, delicacy, pretense. *"Heck" has long been a euphemism for* hell, *but soldiers in battle are unlikely to ever say that war is "heck."*

euphoria *n.* joy, happiness, ecstasy, elation, rapture, bliss. *The slugger's grand slam home run caused great euphoria throughout the stadium.* **Ant.** misery, depression, despondency.

euthanasia *n.* mercy killing, assisted suicide, putting out of misery, putting to sleep. *The animal shelter must sometimes practice euthanasia to put sick animals out of their misery.*

evacuate *vb.* leave, vacate, withdraw, abandon, depart, clear. *We must evacuate the building before it collapses.* **Ant.** enter, occupy, return.

evade *vb.* avoid, elude, shun, escape, dodge, neglect. *She's been evading me all evening.* **Ant.** encounter, confront, face, meet.

evaluate *vb.* assess, rate, appraise, value, judge, estimate. *Would you evaluate the worth of my stamp collection?*

evangelism *n.* preaching, proselytizing, testifying, hearing witness, (slang) bible thumping. *The church used evangelism to spread the word about its faith.*

evangelist *n.* preacher, minister, revivalist, missionary, crusader for God. *He was an old-time evangelist who preached fire and brimstone.*

evaporate *vb.* vaporize, dissipate, vanish, disappear, fade, dissolve. *The sorcerer waved his arms, and the pile of gold evaporated.* **Ant.** solidify, appear, materialize.

evasion *n.* avoidance, escape, dodge, elusion, shirking, equivocation. *Her evasion of the truth ruined her reputation.* **Ant.** facing, confrontation, meeting.

evasive *adj.* elusive, slippery, deceitful, shifty, dodging, misleading. *The detective found the suspect's answers highly evasive.* **Ant.** direct, straightforward, honest.

even *adj.* **1.** level, flat, smooth, plane, uniform. *This table's top doesn't appear to be even.* **2.** steady, constant, regular, stable, uniform, unchanging. *Her heart was beating at an even rate.* **3.** equal, balanced, parallel, similar, fair, just. *The two soccer teams seemed to be an even match.* –*vb.* **4.** equalize, balance, adjust, level, square. *The successful field goal evened the score.* **Ant. 1.** rough, uneven, coarse. **2.** unsteady, irregular, changing. **3.** unfair, unequal, different.

evening *n.* sunset, sundown, dusk, twilight, nightfall. *The weather tends to be cooler in the evenings.* **Ant.** morning, sunrise, dawn.

event *n.* **1.** occurrence, episode, happening, occasion, incident, experience. *College graduation was an important event in my life.* **2.** competition, match, game, contest, tournament. *The Olympics feature a wide variety of sporting events.*

eventful *adj.* momentous, notable, memorable, fateful, exciting, unforgettable. *It was an eventful day at the carnival.* **Ant.** ordinary, usual, dull, unexciting.

eventually *adv.* ultimately, finally, sometime, someday, hereafter. *Eventually the Sun will burn out but I would not stock up on extra flashlights at this time.* **Ant.** now, immediately, never.

ever *adv.* always, constantly, continuously, eternally, forever. *In many fairy tales, the people live happily ever after.* **Ant.** never.

every *adj.* all, each, any, whole, total. *Please pick up every item you dropped.* **Ant.** one, some.

evict *vb.* eject, remove, expel, dismiss, oust. *She was evicted because she did not pay her rent.*

evidence *n.* proof, facts, documentation, confirmation, verification. *Do you have any evidence that you were kidnapped by little green men from outer space?*

evident *adj.* clear, plain, obvious, apparent, certain, unmistakable, distinct. *It is evident that you are not enjoying the concert.* **Ant.** unclear, uncertain, doubtful.

evil *adj.* **1.** wicked, sinful, bad, wrong, immoral. *The sorcerer wanted to rule the kingdom for his own evil purpose.* –*n.* **2.** sin, sinfulness, wickedness, vice, corruption. *The warrior thought his king's command to remove evil from the world was a pretty tall order.* **Ant. 1.** good, moral, virtuous. **2.** good, virtue, righteousness.

evildoer *n.* criminal, devil, felon, demon, sociopath, psychopath. *A person's upbringing often dictates whether he or she will grow up to be an evildoer or not.* **Ant.** good Samaritan, philanthropist, angel.

evoke *vb.* summon, awaken, invoke, provoke, arouse, induce. *Sunny days at the beach always evoke memories of my Hawaiian vacation.* **Ant.** suppress, prevent, repress.

evolution *n.* survival of the fittest, natural selection, law of the jungle, phylogeny, adaptation, succession. *Darwin's theory of evolution changed how we looked at our creation.*

evolve *vb.* develop, grow, progress, emerge, result, unfold. *Her profitable chain of restaurants evolved from a single hot dog stand.*

exacerbate *vb.* aggravate, worsen, intensify, inflame, provoke, rub salt into a wound. *Verbal insults only exacerbate an argument.* **Ant.** diminish, soften, mitigate.

exact *adj.* **1.** right, correct, accurate, true, precise, specific. *You need the exact combination to* *open the lock.* –*vb.* 2. demand, take, force, extract, levy, impose. *The law exacts a heavy penalty for reckless driving.* **Ant.** 1. wrong, imprecise, inexact.

exacting *adj.* demanding, meticulous, particular, painstaking, strict, precise. *Some delicate plants require exacting care.* **Ant.** undemanding, imprecise, sloppy.

exaggerate *vb.* overstate, amplify, embellish, magnify, inflate, stretch. *He exaggerated when he said he could hold his breath for five minutes.* **Ant.** understate, underrate, minimize.

exalted *adj.* revered, glorified, honorable, noble, dignified, lordly. *It is customary to bow when the tribe's exalted chief enters.* **Ant.** lowly, common, humble.

examination *n.* 1. inspection, observation, study, survey, probe. *My doctor gave me a thorough examination.* 2. test, quiz, exam, interrogation, midterm, final. *She has to study for tomorrow's history examination.*

examine *vb.* 1. inspect, study, probe, explore, investigate, search. *The art expert examined the painting carefully.* 2. question, quiz, test, ask, query, interrogate. *It was the district attorney's turn to examine the witness.*

example *n.* model, sample, specimen, type, instance, illustration. *This museum has many examples of Indian pottery.*

exasperate *vb.* annoy, irritate, aggravate, bother, irk, provoke, anger. *His constant humming exasperates me.* **Ant.** calm, tranquilize, soothe.

excavate *vb.* uncover, unearth, dig, quarry, exhume. *The archaeologists are excavating an Aztec temple.* **Ant.** fill, cover, bury.

exceed *vb.* surpass, excel, outdo, better, beat, pass, transcend. *Her score on the exam exceeded the instructor's expectations.*

excel *vb.* prevail, predominate, surpass, outdo, best, better, exceed. *A man with his height and speed should excel in basketball.*

excellence *n.* quality, perfection, eminence, supremacy, superiority. *Her music is famous for its excellence.* **Ant.** mediocrity, inferiority, shortcoming.

excellent *adj.* superior, fine, choice, outstanding, great, splendid, wonderful. *This is an excellent day to go sailing.* **Ant.** terrible, awful, inferior.

except *prep.* but, excepting, excluding, barring, besides, save. *The room was silent except for the ticking of a clock.* **Ant.** including, counting, adding.

exception *n.* 1. deviation, anomaly, exclusion, exemption, limitation. *There is an exception to every rule.* 2. objection, complaint, disagreement, criticism, offense. *The senator took exception to his colleague's speech.* **Ant.** 1. consistency, conformity. 2. agreement, acceptance, support.

exceptional *adj.* rare, unusual, uncommon, extraordinary, unique, remarkable. *He has exceptional strength for such a small boy.* **Ant.** ordinary, common, average.

excerpt *n.* extract, passage, selection, fragment, piece, section. *Our teacher read us an excerpt from* David Copperfield.

excess *n.* 1. surplus, abundance, oversupply, glut, profusion. *I wish I had an excess of money.* –*adj.* 2. abundant, surplus, excessive, extra, spare. *Save your excess energy for the uphill hike.* **Ant.** 1. shortage, lack, need. 2. sparse, meager, scanty.

excessive *adj.* extreme, unreasonable, overdone, undue, excess. *His excessive shouting made him hoarse.* **Ant.** deficient, conservative, insufficient.

exchange *vb.* 1. trade, swap, barter, switch, change, replace. *The boys exchanged baseball trading cards.* –*n.* 2. interchange, trade, swap, dealing, transfer. *There will be a cultural exchange between the two countries.*

excite *vb.* arouse, stimulate, incite, stir, provoke, awaken. *If you excite the horses, they might stampede.* **Ant.** quiet, calm, soothe.

excitement *n.* stimulation, adventure, thrill, arousal, frenzy, commotion. *I had too much excitement for one day.* **Ant.** boredom, serenity, quiet.

exclaim *vb.* proclaim, declare, yell, shout, blurt. *"You're out!" the umpire exclaimed.* **Ant.** whisper, mumble, murmur.

exclamation *n.* shout, outcry, yell, bellow, scream. *He made an exclamation of dismay when he saw the rattlesnakes.* **Ant.** whisper, mumble, murmur.

exclude *vb.* ban, bar, prohibit, preclude, remove, eliminate. *The Galactic Council excludes Martians from its meetings.* **Ant.** include, allow, permit.

exclusive *adj.* 1. selective, restrictive, closed, preferential, privileged. *The exclusive club would not let anyone join unless they made at least a million dollars a year.* 2. high-priced, luxurious, posh, expensive, swank, chic. *We're spending our vacation time at an exclusive resort.*

excommunicate *vb.* ostracize, exclude, banish, blackball, censure, ban. *The church threatened to excommunicate anyone who refused to abide by its tenets.* **Ant.** welcome, take in, include.

excrement *n.* dung, feces, waste, manure, droppings, guano. *Animal excrement is an excellent fertilizer for the garden.*

excruciating *adj.* agonizing, painful, unbearable, unendurable, torturous, insufferable. *His broken leg caused him excruciating pain.* **Ant.** delightful, soothing, anesthetizing.

excursion *n.* trip, outing, voyage, tour, journey, expedition. *We are going on an excursion to Israel.*

excusable *adj.* forgivable, pardonable, extenuating, condonable, allowable, understandable. *Being late for work due to a car accident is excusable.* **Ant.** inexcusable, unforgivable.

excuse *vb.* 1. pardon, forgive, tolerate, indulge, overlook. *Please excuse my carelessness.* 2. free, exempt, release, absolve, dismiss, spare. *The judge excused her from jury duty.* –*n.* 3. reason, alibi, plea, explanation, defense. *I will accept no excuses for being late.* **Ant.** 1. blame, punish, condemn. 2. obligate, compel, oblige.

execute *vb.* 1. kill, murder, assassinate, dispatch, eliminate. *They executed the spy at sunrise.* 2. perform, accomplish, complete, fulfill, implement. *The figure skater executed his routine with ease.*

execution *n.* killing, capital punishment, putting to death, lethal injection, electrocution, beheading, lynching. *The murderer's execution was carried out by lethal injection.*

executive *adj.* 1. managerial, supervisory, administrative, directing, official. *We need a person with executive skills to manage this department.* –*n.* 2. manager, official, officer, administrator, director. *She was the youngest executive in the office.*

exemplary *adj.* model, ideal, prototypical, classic, quintessential, superb. *His angelic behavior in school was exemplary.* **Ant.** terrible, substandard, awful.

exemplify *vb.* embody, depict, represent, typify, epitomize. *Her conduct exemplifies the high standards we should all maintain.*

exempt *adj.* immune, excused, free, released, spared, excepted. *Women are exempt from the draft.* **Ant.** responsible, liable, subject.

exercise *n.* **1.** workout, drill, exertion, activity, training. *He does twenty minutes of aerobic exercise every day.* *–vb.* **2.** train, drill, practice, work out, condition. *A good athlete must exercise daily.* **3.** use, apply, employ, implement, utilize. *Citizens should exercise their right to vote.*

exert *vb.* use, employ, apply, utilize, wield. *She exerted all her energy in planning the charity event.*

exertion *n.* effort, work, energy, strain, strength, action. *I don't like jogging because it requires too much exertion.* **Ant.** rest, leisure, inactivity.

exhale *vb.* breathe, respire, blow, pant, huff, wheeze. *Be sure to exhale fully when exercising.* **Ant.** inhale.

exhaust *vb.* **1.** tire, weaken, fatigue, enfeeble, weary. *The long swim exhausted him.* **2.** deplete, use, spend, expend, drain, finish, consume. *We must not exhaust Earth's natural resources.* **Ant.** **1.** refresh, revive, renew. **2.** restore, replenish, conserve.

exhaust *n.* discharge, fumes, outflow, gas, smoke, carbon monoxide. *Be careful not to breathe in the car's exhaust.*

exhaustion *n.* fatigue, weariness, tiredness, draining, depletion. *The soldiers collapsed in exhaustion after their long march.* **Ant.** strength, energy, replenishment.

exhaustive *adj.* thorough, complete, extensive, full, total, profound. *She made an exhaustive search of all files.* **Ant.** incomplete, partial, superficial.

exhibit *vb.* **1.** show, display, reveal, present, demonstrate, expose. *I wish to exhibit our new line of computer software.* *–n.* **2.** show, showing, display, demonstration, exhibition. *The art museum has a fine exhibit of bronze sculptures.* **Ant.** **1.** hide, conceal, suppress.

exhilarate *vb.* stimulate, excite, energize, invigorate, cheer, delight. *The skiers were exhilarated by the fresh snowfall.* **Ant.** sadden, depress, dishearten.

exhume *vb.* unearth, disinter, dig up, resurrect. *The police department sought permission to exhume the body after new evidence was uncovered.* **Ant.** bury, inter, entomb.

exile *vb.* **1.** banish, remove, eject, expel, deport, oust. *The defeated rebel was exiled for his crimes.* *–n.* **2.** expulsion, banishment, removal, deportation, dislocation. *All convicted criminals will face exile.* **3.** refugee, outcast, deportee, expatriate, alien. *The exiles were seeking a new country.* **Ant.** **1.** recall, return, restore.

exist *vb.* **1.** live, survive, endure, subsist, remain, last. *A camel can exist many days without water.* **2.** occur, happen, arise, emerge, prevail. *I don't believe a better opportunity will ever exist.* **Ant.** **1.** die, expire, perish. **2.** disappear, vanish, cease.

existence *n.* **1.** reality, presence, actuality, fact, occurrence. *The possibility of the existence of life on other planets is highly debatable.* **2.** being, survival, life, condition, endurance. *The polar research team's existence was threatened by the severe cold.* **Ant.** **1.** nonexistence, fantasy, fiction.

exit *n.* **1.** egress, outlet, opening, door, doorway. *All auditorium exits must be kept open.* **2.** departure, leaving, withdrawal, retreat, exodus. *The actress made a hasty exit when she saw the photographers approaching.* *–vb.* **3.** leave, go, depart, withdraw, retreat, retire. *He exited the room quietly.* **Ant.** **1.** entrance, entry, inlet. **2.** entrance, arrival, return. **3.** enter, come, arrive.

exodus *n.* flight, exit, departure, withdrawal, migration, emigration. *Moses led the Israelites' exodus from Egypt.* **Ant.** return, influx, immigration.

exonerate *vb.* acquit, free, clear, excuse, vindicate, discharge. *The new evidence was used to exonerate the suspect.* **Ant.** condemn, convict, charge.

exorbitant *adj.* unreasonable, excessive, overpriced, extreme, enormous. *The drought has raised the price of vegetables to an exorbitant level.* **Ant.** reasonable, modest, fair, just.

exorcism *n.* purging, expulsion, casting out, banishment, ceremony. *The priest performed an exorcism to rid the troubled woman of evil spirits.*

exotic *adj.* foreign, strange, unfamiliar, unusual, unique, different. *I often dream of traveling to exotic lands.* **Ant.** familiar, normal, ordinary.

expand *vb.* increase, enlarge, widen, grow, stretch, spread. *Her dance class expanded from a part-time hobby to a thriving business.* **Ant.** decrease, shrink, contract.

expect *vb.* **1.** hope, await, look, anticipate, foresee. *She expects to get off work early today.* **2.** demand, require, want, insist, wish. *The teacher expects all homework to be completed by tomorrow morning.* **3.** guess, predict, suppose, presume, believe, assume. *I expect it will rain this afternoon.*

expectation *n.* hope, promise, anticipation, confidence, prospect. *She had great expectations when she left for college.*

expecting *adj.* *See* PREGNANT.

expedient *adj.* useful, helpful, practical, profitable, beneficial, worthwhile. *Since her boss was in a bad mood, she felt it would not be expedient to ask for a raise.* **Ant.** futile, ineffective, useless.

expedite *vb.* speed up, hasten, (slang) grease the wheels, facilitate, accelerate, rush. *To expedite matters, we'll try to eliminate government red tape.* **Ant.** slow, bog down, stop.

expedition *n.* journey, trip, voyage, safari, mission, exploration. *In 1856, Sir Richard Burton led an expedition to discover the source of the Nile River.*

expel *vb.* discharge, eject, oust, banish, exile, remove. *The unruly student was expelled from school.* **Ant.** admit, accept, invite.

expend *vb.* spend, exhaust, consume, waste, dispense, disperse. *She expended too much energy for such a small profit.* **Ant.** save, receive, conserve.

expenditure *n.* expense, cost, outlay, payment, disbursement, investment. *The company was forced to reduce its expenditures and cut waste.* **Ant.** income, receivable, profit.

expense *n.* cost, price, amount, payment, charge, outlay. *The trip's expense was over their budget.*

expensive *adj.* costly, exorbitant, overpriced, steep, extravagant. *Diamond rings are expensive items.* **Ant.** cheap, reasonable, moderate.

experience *vb.* **1.** feel, know, encounter, undergo, meet, enjoy. *You can't know how much fun a roller coaster is until you experience one.* –*n.* **2.** incident, event, ordeal, encounter, adventure, episode. *The airplane crash was an experience I hope to never have again.* **3.** knowledge, practice, background, skill, training. *The orchestra needs a conductor with experience.* **Ant. 1.** miss, avoid, evade. **3.** inexperience.

experienced *adj.* trained, practiced, accomplished, skilled, qualified. *We are hiring only experienced workers.* **Ant.** unskilled, untrained, inexperienced.

experiment *n.* **1.** trial, test, research, analysis, examination, investigation. *We performed some experiments in my science class. vb.* **2.** test, try, study, analyze, examine, investigate. *The football team experimented with some new plays.*

experimental *adj.* exploratory, speculative, trial, pilot, hypothetical, theoretical. *Being a test pilot for experimental aircraft is dangerous.* **Ant.** proven, tested, confirmed.

expert *n.* **1.** authority, master, specialist, professional, genius. *The candle maker is an expert at her craft. –adj.* **2.** proficient, skilled, experienced, masterful, practiced. *This rug was made by expert weavers.* **Ant. 1.** amateur, novice, beginner. **2.** inept, unskilled, untrained.

expertise *n.* skill, training, experience, proficiency, knowledge. *It takes a lot of expertise to succeed as a stuntman.*

expire *vb.* **1.** end, terminate, discontinue, stop, lapse. *Your club membership has expired.* **2.** die, decease, succumb, perish, pass. *With one last breath the old man expired.* **Ant. 1.** begin, start, continue. **2.** live, thrive.

explain *vb.* **1.** clarify, define, interpret, teach, demonstrate, describe. *The astronomer explained the difference between a lunar eclipse and a solar eclipse.* **2.** account, justify, excuse, rationalize, answer. *Can you explain why you failed your math test?*

explanation *n.* reason, account, answer, cause, motive. *I hope you have a good explanation for your tardiness.*

explicit *adj.* clear, graphic, unambiguous, frank, express, specific, straightforward. *The motion picture featured explicit scenes of violence.* **Ant.** unclear, ambiguous, indirect.

explode *vb.* burst, erupt, blast, detonate, discharge. *The time bomb might explode at any moment.*

exploit *vb.* **1.** use, utilize, manipulate, apply, work. *She exploited every available opportunity to get a part in the school play. –n.* **2.** adventure, achievement, feat, act, deed, accomplishment. *The African explorer's exploits were well documented in his autobiography.*

exploration *n.* examination, inspection, scrutiny, trailblazing, survey, probe. *The complete exploration of space would take billions of years.*

explore *vb.* **1.** examine, probe, investigate, research, pry. *We must explore new ways to produce energy.* **2.** travel, search, traverse, survey, scout. *Coronado explored much of southwest America while searching for the Seven Cities of Cibola.*

explorer *n.* trailblazer, searcher, investigator, surveyor, researcher, adventurer. *Explorers in uncharted terrain must be prepared for any emergency.*

explosion *n.* blast, detonation, burst, outburst, eruption. *When the bomb went off, the explosion was heard for miles.*

explosive *adj.* **1.** volatile, inflammable, fulminant, charged, reaching critical mass, unstable. *The fuel tank was highly explosive. –n.* **2.** bomb, charge, munition, warhead, dynamite, nitroglycerin. *The bomb squad gingerly removed the explosive.*

export *vb.* ship overseas, trade internationally, transport, sell abroad. *The goal is to export as many goods as you import.* **Ant.** import.

expose *vb.* reveal, uncover, bare, disclose, open, show, exhibit. *An informer exposed the details of the government's secret plot.* **Ant.** cover, hide, conceal.

exposé *n.* uncovering, muckraking, disclosure, (slang) kiss-and-tell, revelation, investigative report. *The scandalous exposé proved embarrassing to the guilty parties.*

exposure *n.* disclosure, discovery, revealing, revelation, uncovering. *The politician feared public exposure of his secret trust fund.* **Ant.** hiding, concealment, covering.

expound *vb.* explain, express, detail, spell out, illustrate, describe. *Mary could expound for hours on her views of the environment.*

express *vb.* **1.** state, speak, say, declare, utter, tell. *You should express your opinions clearly.* **2.** show, reveal, exhibit, represent, symbolize, signify. *Art often expresses the philosophical viewpoints of the artist.* –*adj.* **3.** distinct, specific, exact, precise, particular, explicit. *The express purpose of her trip to Arizona was to see the Grand Canyon.* **4.** speedy, fast, quick, rapid, swift. *The letter will arrive tomorrow if you send it by express mail.* **Ant. 2.** conceal, hide, suppress. **3.** indirect, vague, general. **4.** slow, sluggish, creeping.

expression *n.* **1.** phrase, statement, declaration, saying, cliché. *Have you ever heard the expression "The early bird gets the worm"?* **2.** look, appearance, air, aspect, countenance. *She knew by his expression that he was surprised.* **3.** representation, depiction, show, communication, delivery. *Her stare was an expression of displeasure.*

expressionless *adj.* blank, stony, deadpan, wooden, vacant, vacuous. *The dead fish was remarkably expressionless.* **Ant.** animated, lively, expressive.

expressive *adj.* eloquent, articulate, graphic, vivid, descriptive, meaningful. *Sarah has the most expressive body language I've ever seen.* **Ant.** inexpressive, blank, stony.

expressway *n.* highway, freeway, causeway, beltway, interstate, turnpike. *We drove on the expressway and arrived fifteen minutes early.*

expulsion *n.* ejection, eviction, dismissal, exile, banishment. *Fighting will result in expulsion from the playground.* **Ant.** inclusion, acceptance.

expunge *vb.* delete, erase, take out, remove, cut, extirpate. *Her job as editor was to expunge superfluous words.*

exquisite *adj.* delicate, elegant, beautiful, precious, perfect, lovely. *My mother does exquisite needlepoint.* **Ant.** ugly, common, plain.

extend *vb.* **1.** expand, lengthen, stretch, broaden, spread, increase. *The contest deadline has been extended to the end of the month.* **2.** offer, grant, give, present, bestow. *The master of ceremonies extended his welcome to the audience.* **Ant. 1.** shorten, reduce, decrease. **2.** withdraw, remove.

extension *n.* addition, expansion, attachment, increase, augmentation. He has received a six-month extension on the deadline for his book.

extensive *adj.* vast, large, broad, wide, widespread, spacious, ample. *He owns an extensive ranch in Wyoming.* **Ant.** small, limited, restricted.

extent *n.* size, span, amount, degree, measure, range, reach. *There is no limit to the extent of her magical powers.*

extenuating *adj.* lessening, mitigating, moderating, justifiable, attenuating, diminishing, qualifying. *I was late due to extenuating circumstances.*

exterior *n.* **1.** outside, surface, shell, face, covering. *The building's exterior was covered with graffiti.* –*adj.* **2.** outer, outside, external, outward, outermost. *The patio is equipped with exterior lighting.* **Ant. 1.** inside, center, interior. **2.** inner, interior, internal.

exterminate *vb.* destroy, kill, murder, eliminate, slaughter. *The mad scientist's new weapon will exterminate every living thing on Earth.* **Ant.** save, conserve, create.

external *adj.* outside, outer, outermost, exterior, outward, surface. *He gave no external indi-*

cations of the anger he was feeling. **Ant.** inside, internal, inner.

extinct *adj.* vanished, dead, lost, deceased, departed. *Both the dodo and the passenger pigeon are extinct species of birds.* **Ant.** living, thriving, flourishing.

extinction *n.* elimination, annihilation, death, termination, disappearance, obsolescence. *The extinction of the dinosaurs occurred 65 million years ago.* **Ant.** birth, development, proliferation.

extinguish *vb.* **1.** put out, quench, smother, douse, suffocate. *Please extinguish the campfire before you leave.* **2.** destroy, demolish, eliminate, erase, crush. *The quarterback's injury extinguished our hopes for winning the championship.* **Ant. 1.** light, start, ignite. **2.** heighten, foster, increase.

extol *vb.* praise, acclaim, honor, laud, applaud, glorify, celebrate. *Let us extol the virtues of summer.* **Ant.** disparage, condemn, vilify.

extort *vb.* blackmail, exact, extract, force, coerce, cheat, fleece. *The bully extorted lunch money from the other students.*

extra *adj.* **1.** additional, more, spare, surplus, excess, further. *Extra guards were hired to protect the gold shipment.* –*n.* **2.** addition, supplement, bonus, plus, accessory. *The boss added a little extra to my check.* –*adv.* **3.** especially, unusually, uncommonly, extremely, particularly. *She prefers her chili extra hot.* **Ant. 1.** fewer, less, lesser. **3.** barely, scarcely, less.

extract *vb.* **1.** remove, withdraw, pry, extort, pluck. *The spy extracted the secret plans from a security guard.* –*n.* **2.** essence, concentrate, extraction, juice. *Vanilla extract is a common ingredient in candies.* **3.** excerpt, selection, quotation, passage, fragment. *The magazine printed an extract from the author's latest novel.* **Ant. 1.** install, insert, implant.

extradite *vb.* turn over, return, transfer. *The sheriff's office announced that they would extradite the prisoner to the city of New York this afternoon.*

extraneous *adj.* extra, unnecessary, inessential, superfluous, needless, irrelevant. *Let's not waste time arguing over extraneous matters.* **Ant.** essential, necessary, needed.

extraordinary *adj.* unusual, uncommon, rare, exceptional, unique, amazing. *My teacher has an extraordinary amount of patience.* **Ant.** usual, common, normal, average.

extrapolate *vb.* infer, deduce, postulate, assume, theorize, make an educated guess. *We cannot extrapolate from our knowledge of the existence of water on Mars that life was present on the planet also.*

extraterrestrial *n.* alien, E.T., otherworldly visitor, space being. *Have extraterrestrials visited Earth?* **Ant.** earthling, native.

extravagant *adj.* **1.** lavish, wasteful, excessive, exorbitant, spendthrift. *His extravagant buying sprees will have to stop.* **2.** wild, fanciful, fantastic, outrageous, foolish, outlandish. *The prospector told an extravagant tale of a lost gold mine.* **Ant. 1.** thrifty, frugal, economical. **2.** realistic, true, reasonable.

extrasensory perception *See* ESP.

extreme *adj.* **1.** farthest, furthest, outermost, utmost, ultimate. *There's an oasis at the extreme south end of the desert.* **2.** severe, excessive, intense, harsh, drastic, great. *The factory workers wore ear plugs as protection against the extreme noise.* –*n.* **3.** limit, end, boundary, ultimate, height, depth. *Marathon runners must often push their endurance to the extreme.* **Ant. 1.** near, nearest, closest. **2.** moderate, reasonable, average.

extremely *adv.* very, quite, exceedingly, unusually, especially. *She has been extremely kind to us.*

extremist *n.* radical, zealot, fanatic, immoderate, revolutionist, hard-liner. *Beware of extremists on either side of an issue.* **Ant.** moderate, centrist.

extricate *vb.* free, extract, liberate, disentangle, untie, relieve. *After an exhaustive effort, I finally managed to extricate myself from the foot-deep mud.*

extrovert *n.* socializer, people person, partyer, gregarious person, life of the party, backslapper. *The extrovert tends to be comfortable at parties and on dance floors.* **Ant.** introvert, loner, hermit.

extroverted *adj.* outgoing, friendly, personable, social, unreserved, talkative. *Her extroverted personality made her the perfect candidate for a position in sales.* **Ant.** introverted, introspective, aloof.

exuberance *n.* enthusiasm, vitality, exhilaration, eagerness, excitement. *He was full of exuberance on the day of his wedding.* **Ant.** despair, dejection, depression.

exuberant *adj.* spirited, exciting, lively, zestful, enthusiastic. *She enjoyed the exuberant style of the rock band.* **Ant.** lethargic, dispirited, solemn.

exude *vb.* discharge, excrete, emit, ooze, issue, secrete. *The corpse soon began to exude a foul odor.*

exultant *adj.* joyful, jubilant, ecstatic, euphoric, elated, gleeful. *The students were absolutely exultant when their basketball team won the state championship.* **Ant.** miserable, depressed, downhearted.

eye *n.* **1.** sight, eyesight, perception, vision, viewpoint. *She has a great eye for details.* –*vb.* **2.** watch, observe, scan, gaze, stare, view, ogle. *Our cat eyed the fish in the aquarium.*

WORD SEARCH

cavity: *orbit, socket*
close up vision: *nearsightedness, myopia*
clouding of lens: *cataract*
colored portion: *iris*
colors, inability to differentiate some: *color blindness*
cross-eyed, condition of being: *esotropia, strabismus, exotropia*
discharge: *rheum*
distance vision: *farsightedness, hyperopia*
distortion, peripheral: *astigmatism*
double, seeing: *diplopia*
fluid between cornea and lens: *aqueous humor*
focusing body: *lens*
focusing layer, innermost: *retina*
light-reactive center: *pupil*
pressure causing defects and blindness: *glaucoma*
specialist: *ophthalmologist, oculist*
specks appearing in front of: *floaters*
transparent outer membrane: *cornea*
white of: *sclera*

eyesight *n.* *See* VISION.

eyesore *n.* mess, dump, fright, pigsty, monstrosity, horror. *The local landfill has always been an eyesore.*

eyewitness *n.* witness, spectator, observer, viewer, onlooker. *Were there any eyewitnesses to the bank robbery?*

F

fable *n.* myth, legend, tale, story, parable, allegory. *My favorite fable is the one about the tortoise and the hare.*

fabric *n.* **1.** cloth, textile, material, weave, goods. *Denim is the fabric commonly used to make blue jeans.* **2.** structure, texture, organization, framework, construction. *The fabric of space is distorted by intense gravitational fields.*

WORD SEARCH

canvas: *duckcloth, sailcloth*
crinkled: *crepe, seersucker*
gingham, light: *chambray*
glazed cotton in upholstery and drapes: *chintz*
glossy: *satin, étoile*
goathair: *angora, mohair*
goat leather, soft: *chamois*
heavy, floral-patterned: *brocade*
hunting jacket: *mackinaw*
jeans material: *denim, dungaree*
leather, soft: *suede*
print designs, decorated with numerous small: *calico*
ribbed: *corduroy*
sample of: *swatch*
sheer: *gauze, chiffon, gossamer, organza, voile*
sheets, bed: *muslin, percale*
shiny and rustling: *tafetta*
silk, artificial or man-made: *rayon*
suit: *tweed, serge*
stretchy, man-made: *spandex*
tablecloth, heavy: *damask*
thick and soft as velvet: *velveteen, moleskin*
towels: *terry cloth*
wool: *fleece*
wool, brushed and softened: *flannel*
wool, combed: *worsted*
wrinkle-resistant, synthetic: *polyester*

fabricate *vb.* make, manufacture, assemble, construct, create, devise. *He fabricates computers from components made by other manufacturers.* **Ant.** disassemble, demolish, destroy.

fabrication *n.* lie, falsehood, prevarication, fib, invention, fiction. *That he had won the lottery turned out to be a complete fabrication.* **Ant.** truth, fact, reality.

fabulous *adj.* marvelous, amazing, incredible, remarkable, fantastic. *She had a fabulous time on her summer vacation.* **Ant.** ordinary, routine, common.

facade *n.* front, mask, face, veneer, guise, put-on, disguise. *Pretending to be happy when you're not is a facade.*

face *n.* **1.** features, countenance, visage, expression, look, aspect. *Clowns paint their faces to look funny.* **2.** front, facade, surface, exterior, outside. *He climbed straight up the cliff's main face.* **3.** reputation, honor, prestige, image, repute. *The politician hoped to save face by denying any knowledge of the scandal.* –*vb.* **4.** meet, encounter, confront, brave, challenge. *I can't face the day without my morning coffee.* **5.** front, overlook, look, border, meet. *My bedroom window faces west.* **Ant.** 2. back, reverse.

facelift *n.* cosmetic surgery, plastic surgery, (slang) nip and a tuck. *Margery wants to have a facelift to eliminate her wrinkles.*

facetious *adj.* humorous, funny, amusing, comic, witty, clever. *She wrote a facetious story about meeting a goldfish from outer space.* **Ant.** serious, grave, solemn.

facilitate *vb.* simplify, accelerate, expedite, ease, assist. *The payroll department uses a computer to facilitate the processing of checks.* **Ant.** hinder, obstruct, delay.

facility *n.* 1. complex, system, network, office, building. *The hospital has a modern research facility.* 2. ease, skill, dexterity, proficiency, ability, talent. *My two-year-old nephew reads with surprising facility.* **Ant.** 2. difficulty, clumsiness, inability.

facsimile *n.* copy, duplicate, reproduction, replica, twin, double. *We roughed out a pretty good facsimile of the original diagram.*

fact *n.* truth, reality, certainty, actuality, event, act. *It is a known fact that Mars is an arid planet.* **Ant.** fiction, falsehood, lie.

faction *n.* group, sect, coalition, bloc, partnership, clique, camp. *The leftist faction protested the ruling.*

factor *n.* consideration, element, part, component, influence. *There are many factors to consider when looking for a job.*

factory *n.* plant, shop, workshop, mill, works. *My father works at the local automobile factory.*

factual *adj.* true, real, actual, certain, accurate, correct. *The witness gave a factual account of the crime.* **Ant.** erroneous, untrue, fictional.

faculty *n.* teachers, academics, professors, instructors, fellows, staff. *Students and faculty will meet to discuss the dress code.*

fad *n.* whim, craze, rage, fancy, fashion, vogue. *She ignores the latest clothing fads by dressing as she pleases.*

fade *vb.* pale, dim, dull, blanch, weaken, lessen, diminish. *Too many washings have faded the colors of her dress.* **Ant.** brighten, increase, grow.

fail *vb.* 1. abort, miscarry, flounder, falter, collapse, miss. *The goblin attack failed when the dwarves rallied their forces.* 2. decline, weaken, dwindle, wane, ebb, sink. *His health is beginning to fail.* 3. neglect, avoid, evade, ignore, omit. *My friend failed to water my plants while I was on vacation.* **Ant.** 1. succeed, win, triumph. 2. thrive, prosper, flourish.

failing *n.* defect, flaw, imperfection, weakness, shortcoming, deficiency. *Greed is a serious human failing.* **Ant.** strength, talent, strong point.

failsafe *adj.* foolproof, safeguarded, covered, insured, guaranteed, secure. *A failsafe generator will provide electrical power at the hospital in an emergency.*

failure *n.* 1. failing, nonsuccess, disappointment, defeat, frustration. *Her last book was a commercial failure.* 2. bankruptcy, default, collapse, breakdown, crash. *There have been a lot of failures in the savings-and-loan industry.* 3. delinquency, negligence, neglecting, omission, dereliction. *Failure to make timely payments can result in the repossession of your car.* **Ant.** 1. success, victory, triumph. 2. prosperity, solvency.

faint *adj.* 1. weak, feeble, indistinct, dim, slight, low. *Mission Control received a faint signal from the distant space probe.* 2. dizzy, lightheaded, woozy, giddy, fatigued. *She felt faint from working in the hot sun all day.* –*vb.* 3. swoon, collapse, pass out, black out. *He fainted when he heard about the stock-market crash.* **Ant.** 1. strong, clear, distinct.

fainthearted *adj.* timid, frightened, scared, cowardly, mousy, spineless. *Fainthearted people should not bother to see the latest horror movie.* **Ant.** brave, courageous, strong.

fair *adj.* **1.** just, honest, impartial, unprejudiced, legitimate. *The defendant felt the jury had reached a fair verdict.* **2.** average, moderate, adequate, passing, tolerable. *She has a fair chance of winning the election.* **3.** clear, open, cloudless, sunny, bright. *Fair weather is predicted for the day of our picnic.* **4.** lovely, attractive, beautiful, pretty, comely. *In fairy tales, dragons have a tendency to abduct fair maidens.* **5.** light, pale, creamy, light-colored, blond. *He sunburns easily because of his fair complexion.* –*adv.* **6.** justly, fairly, legally, honestly, honorably, rightly. *She may have won, but she didn't play fair.* –*n.* **7.** show, exhibit, exposition, pageant, display. *The county fair opens this weekend.* **Ant. 1.** prejudiced, biased, dishonest. **2.** superior, poor. **3.** cloudy, stormy, inclement. **4.** unattractive, ugly, homely. **5.** dark, dusky, swarthy. **6.** unfairly, dishonestly.

fairy *n.* pixie, elf, mythical being, dwarf, gnome, sprite. *The tooth fairy prefers teeth without cavities.*

faith *n.* **1.** belief, confidence, dependence, reliance, trust. *I have a lot of faith in her reliability.* **2.** creed, doctrine, sect, teaching, orthodoxy. *There are many different religious faiths in the world.* **Ant. 1.** doubt, uncertainty, mistrust.

faithful *adj.* **1.** reliable, trustworthy, loyal, steadfast, devoted. *My dog is a faithful companion.* **2.** exact, precise, accurate, close, correct. *This painting is a faithful reproduction of the original.* **Ant. 1.** disloyal, faithless, unfaithful. **2.** inexact, imprecise.

fake *n.* **1.** fraud, forgery, imitation, counterfeit, fabrication. *He just paid $100,000 for a painting that turned out to be a fake.* –*adj.* **2.** false, imitation, phony, bogus, unreal, artificial. *Her ring is set with a fake diamond.* –*vb.* **3.** pretend, simulate, feign, assume, counterfeit. *She faked interest in her friend's boring story.* **Ant. 2.** real, genuine, authentic.

fall *vb.* **1.** collapse, drop, plunge, tumble, crash. *During the earthquake, my books fell off their shelves.* **2.** lessen, diminish, reduce, descend, lower, decline. *Their voices fell to a whisper when the teacher entered the room.* **3.** succumb, submit, yield, surrender, capitulate. *During World War II, France fell to the invading German army.* **4.** happen, occur, chance, arrive, come. *Easter always falls on a Sunday.* –*n.* **5.** plunge, drop, descent, tumble, crash. *She took a bad fall on her bike.* **6.** downfall, ruin, collapse, seizure, capture, overthrow. *Historians still debate the reasons for the fall of Rome.* **Ant. 1–2.** rise, climb, ascend. **3.** withstand, resist, repel. **5.** rise, ascent, climb.

fallacious *adj.* untrue, false, erroneous, incorrect, wrong, mistaken. *Her statements concerning the reality of fairies were fallacious.* **Ant.** true, correct, right.

fallacy *n.* error, falsehood, mistake, untruth, misconception, illusion. *Ghosts are based more on fallacy than reality.* **Ant.** truth, fact, reality.

fallible *adj.* imperfect, prone to error, faulty, defective, human, errant. *Teachers may know a lot, but they are fallible.* **Ant.** infallible, perfect, inerrant.

fallout *n.* consequences, repercussions, result, aftermath, wake, backlash. *The fallout from her unpopular decision would be severe.*

fallow *adj.* uncultivated, unseeded, inactive, barren, resting, dormant. *The farmer let half of his fields lie fallow.* **Ant.** seeded, cultivated, productive.

false *adj.* **1.** incorrect, untrue, mistaken, erroneous, inaccurate. *The witness perjured himself* by making a false statement in court. 2. artificial, fake, bogus, counterfeit, spurious. *She's living under a false name.* **Ant.** 1. true, correct, accurate. 2. real, genuine, authentic.

false teeth *See* DENTURES.

falsify *vb.* fake, misrepresent, forge, alter, distort, misstate. *It's a crime to falsify a legal document.*

falter *vb.* hesitate, waver, vacillate, fluctuate, stumble. *The knight's determination faltered when he saw the size of the dragon.*

fame *n.* reputation, repute, renown, celebrity, distinction, honor. *Marie Curie's fame spread when she won her second Nobel Prize.* **Ant.** obscurity, anonymity, dishonor.

familiar *adj.* 1. known, accustomed, well-known, common, everyday. *It's sure nice to see a familiar face.* 2. acquainted, versed, aware, apprised, informed, experienced. *She's not familiar with the facts of the case.* 3. friendly, close, intimate, cordial, informal. *Soldiers are not supposed to get too familiar with their officers.* **Ant.** 1. unfamiliar, unknown, rare. 2. unaware, ignorant, uninformed. 3. remote, distant, formal.

familiarize *vb.* acquaint, get to know, study, enlighten, school, acclimatize. *The plant's new employees have to familiarize themselves with how the machinery works.*

family *n.* 1. clan, brood, tribe, kin, relatives, relations. *His family includes his parents, a brother and two sisters.* 2. group, class, division, order, category, classification. *Donkeys and zebras are members of the horse family.*

famine *n.* starvation, hunger, privation, scarcity, want, need. *The recent African drought resulted in widespread famine.* **Ant.** abundance, bounty, glut.

famished *adj.* starving, hungry, ravenous, malnourished, emaciated, weak with hunger. *I haven't eaten all day and I'm absolutely famished.* **Ant.** satiated, full, gorged.

famous *adj.* well-known, celebrated, renowned, eminent, distinguished, popular. *Elvis Presley was a famous singer.* **Ant.** unknown, obscure, unpopular.

fan *n.* admirer, follower, devotee, enthusiast, addict. *Some science-fiction fans are so devoted they publish their own magazines.*

fanatic *n.* 1. zealot, extremist, partisan, fiend, freak. *The religious fanatic started a new cult.* –*adj.* 2. fanatical, extremist, zealous, fervent, enthusiastic. *She's a fanatic supporter of environmental causes.*

fanaticism *n.* zeal, overenthusiasm, devotion, dogma, single-mindedness, passion. *His fanaticism for sports made him neglect his schoolwork.*

fanciful *adj.* imaginary, fantastic, made-up, illusory, unreal, fictitious, mythical. *He had some fanciful notions about the Moon being made from green cheese.* **Ant.** real, factual, down-to-earth.

fancy *adj.* 1. ornate, elegant, elaborate, exceptional, special. *He showed up at the party wearing very fancy clothes.* –*n.* 2. liking, fondness, inclination, desire, want. *I wish she hadn't developed a fancy for expensive restaurants.* 3. imagination, fantasy, whim, notion, idea. *It's his fancy to become president someday.* –*vb.* 4. like, favor, relish, enjoy, crave. *He fancies women with superior intellects.* 5. imagine, suppose, believe, think, presume. *She fancies herself a better artist than Picasso.* **Ant.** 1. plain, simple, ordinary. 2. dislike, distaste, aversion.

fanfare *n.* trumpeting, hoopla, (slang) ballyhoo, display, fuss. *They always have a big fanfare before the Super Bowl.*

fang *n.* incisor, tooth, canine tooth, (slang) chopper. *The snake's fang measured more than an inch in length.*

fanny *n.* (slang) butt, posterior, rear, seat, rump, buttocks. *Sit your fanny down and get your homework done.*

fantasize *vb.* imagine, picture, envision, visualize, take a flight of fancy, dream up. *She liked to fantasize about one day becoming a famous ballerina.*

fantastic *adj.* **1.** great, exceptional, marvelous, terrific, superb. *You look fantastic today.* **2.** unbelievable, odd, weird, bizarre, absurd, crazy. *He told a fantastic story about being abducted by creatures from outer space.* **Ant. 1.** ordinary, average, common. **2.** believable, reasonable.

fantasy *n.* imagination, fancy, illusion, daydream, fiction. *Mermaids are creatures of fantasy.*

far *adv.* **1.** much, considerably, greatly, immeasurably, quite. *Dinner was far better than I expected.* *–adj.* **2.** distant, remote, removed, faraway, inaccessible. *She lives on the far side of town.* **Ant. 1.** less, little, barely. **2.** close, near, adjacent.

farce *n.* comedy, mockery, nonsense, travesty, burlesque, satire. *The poorly judicated trial turned into a farce.*

fare *vb.* **1.** manage, proceed, prosper, thrive, happen. *She's faring well at her new job.* *–n.* **2.** charge, cost, fee, price, amount. *Airline fares have gone down since deregulation.* **3.** food, provisions, board, menu, diet. *If you think you wouldn't like prison fare, don't commit a crime.*

farfetched *adj.* unbelievable, incredible, improbable, unlikely, implausible. *Her story of being kidnapped by elves was farfetched.* **Ant.** believable, credible, plausible.

farm *vb.* **1.** cultivate, grow, till, raise, sow, plant. *The land he farms belongs to his neighbor.* *–n.* **2.** farmstead, plantation, ranch, acreage, spread. *My sister's farm has more than three hundred acres of soybeans.*

WORD SEARCH

animal employed to pull: *draft animal*
changing fields and crops: *crop rotation*
chicken house: *coop*
corn storage facility: *corn crib*
crop planted to control erosion: *cover crop*
crops sold for money, not feed: *cash crops*
feed for animals: *fodder*
feed that has been stored: *silage*
field left unseeded for a season, the state of a: *fallow*
harvesting rig, grain: *combine*
hay cutter: *mower, sickle, scythe*
hay fork: *pitchfork*
hay into blocks, rig that compresses and ties: *baler*
hay pile: *windrow, haycock*
horse enclosure: *corral*
farming to feed family only: *subsistence farming*
pesticide spraying by air: *crop dusting*
plowed channel in soil: *furrow*
separator of seeds, grain and straw: *thresher*
soil-breaking implements: *cultivator, harrow, tiller*
storage building for fodder, usually cylindrical: *silo*
storage building, grain: *granary*
tenant farmer: *sharecropper*

farmer *n.* grower, planter, agriculturist, agrarian, sharecropper, agronomist. *The farmer has the longest workday of anyone.*

farming *n.* agriculture, agronomy, cultivation, husbandry, agribusiness, sharecropping. *Farming is a difficult occupation.*

farsighted *adj.* prescient, wise, perceptive, forward-thinking, foresighted, provident. *It was* *particularly farsighted to develop computers for home use.* **Ant.** nearsighted, myopic, unthinking.

fascinate *vb.* enrapture, charm, enchant, captivate, delight, absorb. *She fascinated the audience with tales of her adventures.* **Ant.** bore, weary, disenchant.

fascinating *adj.* enthralling, captivating, engrossing, absorbing, interesting. *He has a fascinating collection of antique bottles.* **Ant.** boring, uninteresting, dull.

fascism *n.* totalitarianism, nationalism, dictatorship, Naziism, militarism. *It is difficult to imagine any government more troubling to its citizen than fascism.* **Ant.**

fashion *vb.* **1.** form, make, shape, create, construct. *She fashioned a belt out of soda-can pull tabs.* *–n.* **2.** style, taste, custom, vogue, convention, practice. *Bell-bottom trousers were once in fashion.*

fashionable *adj.* stylish, chic, in vogue, trendsetting, (slang) hot, modern, smart. *Is it still fashionable to get one's nose pierced?* **Ant.** old-fashioned, outdated, outmoded.

fast *adj.* **1.** speedy, quick, rapid, swift, fleet. *He likes fast cars.* **2.** immovable, fixed, firm, secure, tight. *She kept a fast grip on her daughter's hand.* *–adv.* **3.** swiftly, rapidly, quickly, hastily, speedily. *Please don't drive so fast.* **4.** firmly, securely, soundly, tightly, solidly. *The climber held fast to his safety rope.* **Ant.** **1.** slow, sluggish. **2.** insecure, loose, uncertain. **3.** slowly, slow, leisurely. **4.** loosely, insecurely.

fasten *vb.* secure, fix, attach, bind, tie, connect. *She fastened the tent line to a tree.* **Ant.** free, release, loosen.

fastener *n.* holder, latch, buckle, lock, button, catch. *Make sure all of the fasteners are secured.*

fastidious *adj.* meticulous, exacting, detail-oriented, picky, fussy, discriminating. *She was fastidious in keeping every single hair in its place.* **Ant.** sloppy, unparticular, casual.

fat *adj.* **1.** obese, overweight, stout, corpulent, plump, heavy. *If you think you're fat, you should try eating less and exercising more.* **2.** thick, broad, wide, immense, extensive, large. *An unabridged dictionary is a fat book.* *–n.* **3.** grease, lard, tallow, oil, blubber. *He fried the meat in its own fat.* **Ant.** **1.** slender, thin, lean. **2.** narrow, thin, small.

fatal *adj.* **1.** lethal, mortal, deadly, terminal, killing. *We were all saddened to hear about the fatal plane crash.* **2.** disastrous, ruinous, catastrophic, critical, crucial. *Telling her boss to go jump in a lake was a fatal mistake.* **Ant.** **1–2.** harmless, beneficial, minor.

fate *n.* destiny, fortune, lot, luck, providence, chance. *It seems to be my fate to buy losing lottery tickets.*

fated *adj.* destined, preordained, predetermined, in the stars, in the cards. *Some people seem to be fated for greatness.*

father *n.* dad, parent, papa, protector, sire, (slang) pop. *My father was my greatest role model.*

fatigue *n.* **1.** weariness, tiredness, exhaustion, feebleness, weakness. *Her fatigue was caused by hiking all day with a heavy pack.* *–vb.* **2.** weary, tire, exhaust, weaken, drain. *Playing softball in the hot sun fatigued him.* **Ant.** **1.** strength, vigor, vitality. **2.** refresh, renew, restore.

fatty *adj.* adipose, blubbery, marbled, lardy, tallowy, greasy. *Cut off the fatty parts of the meat if you want to reduce your calorie intake.* **Ant.** lean.

faucet *n.* spigot, tap, valve, cock. *Get a drink from the faucet.*

fault *n.* **1.** responsibility, guilt, lapse, blame, crime, error. *It's not my fault you can't find your car keys.* **2.** defect, blemish, flaw, imperfection, shortcoming. *Her new car had so many faults she had to return it to the dealer.*

faultfinding *adj.* nit-picking, critical, overcritical, hairsplitting, quibbling, caviling. *She was a faultfinding, cranky woman who drove everyone crazy with her constant complaints.*

faulty *adj.* defective, imperfect, damaged, deficient, unsatisfactory, bad. *His car doesn't run well because it has a faulty valve.* **Ant.** perfect, satisfactory, good.

faux *adj.* fake, artificial, phony, simulated, imitation, synthetic. *The faux diamonds were so well made, they appeared genuine.* **Ant.** real, authentic, true.

favor *n.* **1.** service, courtesy, kindness, boon, good deed. *She did me a favor by lending me lunch money.* **2.** approval, admiration, esteem, regard, respect. *The candidate promised to cut taxes in an attempt to win our favor.* –*vb.* **3.** approve, support, prefer, like, advocate. *I favor spending public funds to help the homeless.* **Ant.** **2.** disfavor, disapproval, antipathy. **3.** disapprove, dislike.

favorable *adj.* good, promising, auspicious, beneficial, advantageous, satisfactory. *Her new play received favorable reviews.* **Ant.** bad, adverse, unsatisfactory.

favorite *adj.* **1.** preferred, liked, esteemed, special, choice. *What's your favorite movie?* –*n.* **2.** preference, choice, fancy, liking, beloved. *Vanilla ice cream is my favorite.*

favoritism *n.* partiality, bias, discrimination, prejudice, nepotism, preferential treatment. *It is better to hire people according to their qualifications, not out of favoritism.*

fawn *vb.* flatter, toady, (slang) kiss up to, grovel, kowtow, fall all over. *The underlings tend to fawn over the boss.* **Ant.** reject, lord over, dominate.

fax *n.* **1.** facsimile, copy, duplicate, transmission, reproduction, document. *We always send a fax when the information must arrive quickly.* –*vb.* **2.** transmit, send, forward, relay, convey, copy. *Fax the information to their office right away.*

faze *vb.* bother, disturb, discompose, perturb, upset, unnerve. *Deadlines don't faze veteran reporters.*

fear *n.* **1.** dread, terror, fright, horror, anxiety, phobia. *He has a fear of high places.* –*vb.* **2.** dread, be afraid, apprehend, mistrust. *She fears the dark.*

fearless *adj.* brave, courageous, valiant, valorous, gallant. *The fearless maiden told the dragon to leave her alone.* **Ant.** cowardly, fearful, afraid.

feasible *adj.* possible, practical, achievable, attainable, reasonable. *It's not yet feasible to send colonists to other planets.* **Ant.** impractical, impossible, unfeasible.

feast *n.* **1.** banquet, meal, dinner, occasion, celebration. *The queen held a feast in honor of her son's marriage.* –*vb.* **2.** dine, banquet, feed, gorge, glut, indulge. *On Thanksgiving Day, we usually feast on turkey.*

feat *n.* deed, act, achievement, accomplishment, maneuver, trick. *Balancing three pails of water on your head is quite a feat.*

feather *n.* plume, plumage, penna, quill, down, eider. *The recipe said to pluck every feather from the chicken before cooking it.*

feature *n.* **1.** highlight, attribute, quality, trait, characteristic. *She knew exactly what features she wanted in a new computer.* –*vb.* **2.** star, highlight, headline, emphasize, promote. *This movie features my favorite actress.*

feces *n.* excrement, dung, stool, (slang) crap, droppings, guano. *Rodent feces is a form of food contamination.*

federation *n.* alliance, union, partnership, association, league, confederacy. *The federation of authors helps mediate contract disputes with publishers.*

fee *n.* charge, payment, price, cost, compensation, stipend. *My agent's fee is 10 percent of everything I make.*

feeble *adj.* weak, frail, fragile, infirm, delicate, ineffective. *The old man's voice was so feeble we could barely understand him.* **Ant.** strong, vigorous, effective.

feed *vb.* **1.** sustain, nurture, nourish, maintain, support. *My parents have a large family to feed.* **2.** eat, consume, devour, ingest, take. *Birds feed on worms.* **3.** give, deliver, dispense, provide, supply. *I need to feed more paper into my computer's printer. –n.* **4.** food, edibles, provisions, fodder, nourishment. *What do cows use for feed?* **Ant. 1.** starve, famish. **3.** withhold, deny, deprive.

feedback *n.* response, criticism, evaluation, assessment, sentiment, fallout. *She asked the teacher for feedback on her poetry.*

feel *n.* **1.** touch, handle, finger, stroke, manipulate, grope. *I had no idea what the fabric was like until I felt it.* **2.** know, experience, understand, perceive, sense. *A kitten feels pleasure when you pet it.* **3.** think, believe, consider, hold, assume. *She feels we should pay more attention to her. –n.* **4.** touch, sensation, feeling, texture, finish. *I like the feel of satin.*

feeling *n.* **1.** sensation, perception, reaction, response, awareness. *He had a bad feeling in his stomach when he saw the vampire.* **2.** view, belief, thought, opinion, conviction. *She had a feeling I would be late again.* **3.** emotion, sentiment, attitude, mood, temper. *Winning the award gave him a feeling of happiness. –adj.* **4.** warm, emotional, sensitive, caring, sympathetic, compassionate. *She's a very feeling person.* **Ant. 4.** unfeeling, insensitive, cold.

feign *vb.* fake, make up, invent, pretend, simulate, put on. *Every once in a while she would feign illness to get out of school.*

feisty *adj.* spunky, tough, strong, fiery, spirited, lively. *I avoided arguing with her because she was too feisty.* **Ant.** meek, mild, weak-willed.

feline *adj.* catlike, predatory, stealthy, graceful, slinky, sly. *Christine slinks into a room with feline grace.*

fell *vb.* raze, level, hew, cut down, destroy. *Every hour of every day, 500,000 rain forest trees are felled.* **Ant.** raise, grow.

fellowship *n.* communion, fraternization, association, togetherness, friendship, comradeship, brotherhood. *The church group met for fellowship and prayer every Sunday night.*

felon *n.* criminal, convict, lawbreaker, culprit offender. *Three felons escaped from the state prison.*

felonious *adj.* criminal, evil, wicked, illegal, unlawful, larcenous. *He had a long record of felonious behavior.* **Ant.** moral, good, angelic.

felony *n.* crime, criminal act, offense, violation, sin, evil deed. *He was convicted of a felony and served five years in prison.*

female *n.* **1.** girl, woman, lady, femme, gal, matron. *In most animal groups, the female is slightly smaller than the male. –adj.* **2.** feminine, girlish, womanly, ladylike. *The female form tends to be more curvaceous than that of the male.*

feminine *adj.* female, womanly, ladylike, girlish, genteel, effeminate. *She was proud of her feminine virtues.* **Ant.** masculine, male, manly.

fence *n.* **1.** barrier, railing, wall, enclosure, barricade. *This fence is here to keep the cows in the right pasture.* *–vb.* **2.** enclose, encircle, surround, encase, wall. *She fenced her backyard.*

feng shui *n.* geomancy, furniture arranging, interior design, harmonizing, space design, orientation. *We employed feng shui to arrange our living room for optimum results.*

ferocious *adj.* fierce, savage, brutal, violent, cruel, wild. *That ferocious dog should be sent to the pound.* **Ant.** tame, docile, submissive.

ferry *n.* boat, vessel, transport, mass transit vehicle, raft, barge. *Let's take a ferry over to the island.*

fertile *adj.* productive, fruitful, rich, prolific, fecund. *The farmer felt himself lucky to have such fertile fields.* **Ant.** sterile, barren, unproductive.

fertilize *vb.* enrich, feed, dress, compost, manure, germinate. *It's a good idea to fertilize your garden every spring.*

fertilizer *n.* soil enhancement, enrichment, compost, dressing, plant food, humus, manure. *Every garden needs fertilizer to thrive.*

fervent *adj.* ardent, zealous, passionate, enthusiastic, intense, heated. *The charity worker made a fervent appeal for donations.* **Ant.** dispassionate, apathetic, cool.

fervor *n.* intensity, passion, enthusiasm, zeal, ardor, spirit, fever. *My neighbors' fervor for lawn ornaments is somewhat embarrassing.* **Ant.** apathy, indifference, coolness.

festival *n.* celebration, jubilee, gala, holiday, fete. *The town is having a festival to celebrate its 100th anniversary.*

festive *adj.* gay, joyful, happy, merry, jubilant, joyous. *Everyone at the wedding was in a festive mood.* **Ant.** unhappy, sad, somber.

festivity *n.* merrymaking, revelry, play, celebration, mirth, partying. *I'm looking forward to the festivity of the holidays.*

fetch *vb.* get, retrieve, bring, obtain, grab, convey, deliver. *I enjoy having my dog fetch the newspaper, but I don't care for the drool on the front page.*

fetid *adj.* stinky, smelly, malodorous, putrid, foul, reeking. *We all held our noses as a fetid odor arose from the meat-packing plant.* **Ant.** sweet-smelling, fragrant, fresh.

fetish *n.* erotic fixation, turn-on, mania, obsession, fascination, preoccupation. *My wife has a foot fetish and loves to tickle toes.* **2.** charm, magical object, talisman, amulet. *The witch doctor used a fetish to protect himself from evil spirits.*

feud *n.* **1.** fight, conflict, strife, quarrel, vendetta, dispute. *Romeo and Juliet's love affair was tragic because their families were engaged in a feud.* *–vb.* **2.** quarrel, fight, bicker, clash, squabble. *He's always feuding with his parents.*

fever *n.* **1.** temperature, inflammation, flush, illness, sickness. *She stayed home from school because she had a fever.* **2.** turmoil, heat, ferment, panic, fluster, agitation. *We felt the fever of excitement as the big game drew near.* **Ant. 2.** calm, serenity, tranquility.

few *adj.* limited, scarce, scanty, meager, infrequent, occasional. *There are still a few apples left on the tree.* **Ant.** many, numerous, plentiful.

fiancé *n.* betrothed, significant other, (slang) honey, (slang) sweetheart, wife-to-be, husband-to-be. *I asked my fiancée if she wouldn't mind being married in Las Vegas.*

fiasco *n.* mess, disaster, ruin, defeat, failure. *The football game between the elephants and the mice was a fiasco for the mice.* **Ant.** victory, success, triumph.

fib *n.* **1.** lie, falsehood, untruth, fabrication, deception. *I told a fib when I said I liked his new shirt.* *–vb.* **2.** lie, falsify, misrepresent, misstate, fabricate. *She fibbed when she said she had been studying all day.* **Ant. 1.** truth, fact.

fickle *adj.* changeable, capricious, erratic, whimsical, variable, unpredictable, (slang) blowing hot and cold. *Fickle people change their minds often.* **Ant.** stable, constant, reliable.

fiction *n.* story, tale, yarn, fantasy, falsehood, lie. *His account of seeing a UFO was pure fiction.* **Ant.** nonfiction, reality, fact.

fictitious *adj.* imaginary, made-up, untrue, created, fabricated, mythical. *He claimed the fish was ten feet long, but that estimate was probably fictitious.* **Ant.** true, factual, real.

fidelity *adj.* faithfulness, truthfulness, loyalty, integrity, reliability, dedication. *They maintained their fidelity through fifty years of marriage.* **Ant.** infidelity, disloyalty, unfaithfulness.

fidget *vb.* squirm, jiggle, wiggle, twitch, fret, jitter. *Most kids fidget if they have to sit in one place for too long.*

field *n.* **1.** ground, plot, meadow, pasture, area, region. *We need to find an open field for our softball game.* **2.** occupation, profession, vocation, line, business, activity. *What field do you plan to go into after you graduate?*

field trip *n.* outing, expedition, junket, day trip, jaunt, tour. *We're taking a field trip to the science museum.*

fiendish *adj.* evil, devilish, demonic, Satanic, diabolical, villainous. *The dictator hatched a fiendish plot to take over the world.* **Ant.** saintly, kind, angelic.

fierce *adj.* violent, savage, ferocious, furious, wild, powerful. *A fierce storm knocked down all the town's power lines.* **Ant.** gentle, moderate, tame.

fight *n.* **1.** struggle, conflict, battle, combat, quarrel, brawl. *The school bully picked a fight with a smaller boy.* *–vb.* **2.** battle, combat, struggle, contend, clash, quarrel. *The villagers fought bravely to defend their homes against Viking raiders.*

fighter *n.* combatant, battler, brawler, scrapper, boxer, pugilist. *The veteran fighter lost his bout with the young upstart.* **Ant.** pacifist, dove.

figurative *adj.* metaphorical, symbolic, emblematic, representative, illustrative. *His remarks were figurative and were not intended to be taken literally.* **Ant.** literal, exact.

figure *n.* **1.** diagram, drawing, picture, illustration, sketch. *She drew a figure of a dragon.* **2.** number, numeral, digit, cipher, integer. *The accountant was busy jotting down figures in his notebook.* **3.** form, shape, silhouette, outline, pattern. *We could barely make out the figure of someone walking in the distance.* **4.** personage, personality, person, character, notable. *The president is an important public figure.* *–vb.* **5.** calculate, reckon, compute, tally, assess. *She figured out the total of her purchases.*

figure of speech *n.* expression, metaphor, simile, imagery, trope. *"Building castles in the sky" is a figure of speech used to describe someone who likes to daydream.*

figurehead *n.* straw man, puppet, token, front, dupe. *The so-called president was merely a figurehead, as the nation's real power lay in the hands of his advisers.*

figurine *n.* statuette, sculpture, knicknack, figure, carving, objet d' art. *The old jade figurine represented a Chinese goddess.*

file *n.* **1.** record, archive, dossier, folder, portfolio. *The company's personnel files need reorganizing.* **2.** line, column, queue, row, rank. *The soldiers marched by in a long file. –vb.* **3.** organize, classify, arrange, sort, store. *Please file these documents.* **4.** apply, petition, seek, solicit, submit. *The couple filed for a divorce.* **5.** march, hike, walk, parade, troop. *The audience filed out of the theater when the movie was over.*

filibuster *n.* speech, monologue, tirade, exhortation, discourse, dissertation. *The Congressman delivered a filibuster that went on for over seven hours.*

filigree *n.* tracery, ornamentation, decoration, delicate lines. *The mirror was decorated with delicate filigree.*

fill *vb.* **1.** stuff, pack, load, stock, crowd, jam. *The mall was filled with shoppers.* **2.** occupy, pervade, suffuse, permeate, saturate. *Smoke filled the air.* **3.** replenish, refill, resupply, supply, provide, charge. *Please fill the gas tank.* **Ant. 3.** empty, drain, deplete.

film *n.* **1.** coating, layer, scum, covering, veil, sheet. *The oil spill left a greasy film all over the sand.* **2.** motion picture, (slang) flick. *I don't like films with subtitles.*

See also MOVIE.

filter *n.* **1.** strainer, sieve, screen, sifter, net. *Please use a fresh filter each time you make a pot of coffee. –vb.* **2.** strain, filtrate, purify, cleanse, drain. *The backpackers filtered the stream water before drinking it.* **3.** trickle, seep, ooze, leak, flow. *Sunlight filtered through the clouds.*

filth *n.* dirt, scum, grime, pollution, sewage, sludge. *The kids played in the muddy field and came home covered in filth.*

filthy *adj.* dirty, foul, grimy, soiled, muddy, unclean. *It's time to wash these filthy clothes.* **Ant.** clean, washed, cleansed.

finagle *vb.* manipulate, arrange, wangle, engineer, contrive, (slang) weasel. *He liked to finagle deals through dishonest means.*

final *adj.* last, concluding, ultimate, terminating, decisive, ending. *The prince and the princess were married in the movie's final scene.* **Ant.** first, beginning, opening.

finale *n.* conclusion, end, close, finish, cap, completion, climax. *We stuck around for the grand finale, which won a standing ovation.* **Ant.** opening, introduction, beginning.

finance *n.* **1.** money matters, budgeting, banking, investment, economics. *Money fascinates her, so she'll probably enter a career in finance. –vb.* **2.** pay for, underwrite, bankroll, capitalize, support, back, pick up the tab.

financial *adj.* fiscal, monetary, pecuniary, economic, money. *I agreed to baby-sit for a small financial consideration.*

financier *n.* underwriter, investor, venture capitalist, angel, banker, (slang) sugar daddy. *The inventor needed a financier to underwrite the development of his invention.*

finalize *vb.* conclude, close, complete, (slang) dot all the Is and cross all the Ts, cap, wind up. *The mortgage company announced that it would finalize the loan on Tuesday.* **Ant.** open, begin, break ground.

find *vb.* discover, detect, locate, perceive, gain, attain, recover. *Where did you find your missing car keys?* **Ant.** lose, misplace, mislay.

fine *adj.* **1.** excellent, superior, admirable, outstanding, exceptional. *You did a fine job on that report.* **2.** thin, small, little, minute, delicate, sheer. *Be sure to read the fine print at the bottom of a contract. –n.* **3.** penalty, charge, payment, assessment, settlement. *She had to pay a fine on the library books she returned late. –vb.* **4.** assess, charge, levy, tax penalize. *He was fined fifty dol-*

lars for speeding. **Ant.** 1. poor, inferior, mediocre. 2. coarse, thick, large.

finesse *n.* skill, adroitness, artfulness, savvy, knack, shrewdness, expertise. *The woodcarver worked with great finesse.* **Ant.** incompetence, clumsiness, inexperience.

fine-tune *vb.* adjust, tweak, balance, align, attune, calibrate. *We need to fine-tune the motor to make it run better.*

finicky *adj.* fussy, picky, discriminating, choosy, particular, fastidious. *The finicky cat would eat nothing but fresh tuna.* **Ant.** unparticular, easy-to-please, undiscriminating.

finish *vb.* 1. complete, conclude, end, cease, stop, terminate. *You can watch TV after you finish your chores.* 2. consume, devour, deplete, exhaust, empty, kill. *Finish your supper or you'll be sent straight to bed.* –*n.* 3. conclusion, end, close, completion, finale. *If you start something, you should see it through to the finish.* 4. surface, texture, coating, polish, exterior. *She sanded the table until it had a perfectly smooth finish.* **Ant.** 1. start, begin, commence. 3. beginning, opening, start.

finite *adj.* limited, fixed, terminable, confined, restricted, ending. *There appear to be a finite number of stars in the sky, but in fact no astronomer could ever count them all.* **Ant.** infinite, endless, interminable.

fire *n.* 1. blaze, combustion, burning, conflagration, inferno. *It took three engine companies to put out the fire.* 2. passion, ardor, heat, fever, spirit. *His voice was full of fire when he spoke about is adventures in Afghanistan.* 3. shooting, bombardment, shelling, firing. *The soldiers were pinned down by heavy fire.* –*vb.* 4. light, ignite, kindle, burn, inflame. *An arsonist fired two buildings last night.* 5. dismiss, discharge, release, depose, terminate. *The manager was forced to fire one of her employees.* 6. arouse, stir, excite, stimulate, inspire. *Her stories about spaceflight fired my imagination.* 7. shoot, discharge, detonate, shell, snipe. *The sheriff fired his revolver at the desperado.* **Ant.** 2. apathy, indifference, cool. 4. extinguish, douse, quench. 5. hire, employ, engage. 6. cool, calm, quiet.

WORD SEARCH

fear of: *pyrophobia*
fire hazard: *firetrap*
god: *Vulcan*
intense, widespread fire: *firestorm*
land cleared to stop a fire's progress: *firebreak*
predicting the future by peering into flames: *pyromancy*
sets fires for insurance or revenge: *arsonist*
sets fires for pleasure: *pyromaniac, firebug*
setting a fire intentionally for insurance or other: *arson*
setting fires for pleasure: *pyromania*
worshipper: *pyrolater*

fire alarm *n.* smoke alarm, alert, heat sensor, early warning system. *Luckily the fire alarm warned residents to evacuate the burning building.*

firearm *n.* gun, rifle, pistol, revolver, shotgun, (slang) shooting iron. *The thug was arrested for carrying a concealed firearm.*
See also GUN.

fireball *n.* meteor, meteorite, bolide, shooting star. *The fireball we saw was actually re-entry debris from an old satellite.*

firecracker *n.* squib, petard, cherry bomb, bottle rocket. *Firecrackers are illegal in our state.*
See also FIREWORKS.

fireplace *n.* hearth, chimney, blaze, fireside, inglenook, stove. *Get warm by the fireplace.*

fireproof *adj.* nonflammable, noncombustible, fire-resistant, flameproof, fire-retardant. *Asbestos is a fireproof material.* **Ant.** flammable. combustible, explosive.

fireworks *n.* pyrotechnics, incendiary devices, rockets. *Fireworks were displayed as the finale to the town's Fourth of July celebration.*

WORD SEARCH

child's: *bottle rocket, sparkler*
hisses and sputters: *fizgig, squib*
pinwheel-like: *catherine wheel*

firm *adj.* 1. stiff, hard, rigid, solid, compact. *After hiking through the bog, it was nice to be on firm ground again.* 2. steady, fixed, settled, definite, immovable, unwavering. *It's my firm opinion that animals should be treated humanely.* –*n.* 3. company, business, organization, corporation, establishment. *He works for a law firm.* –*vb.* 4. strengthen, harden, toughen, improve, tone. *She exercises regularly to firm her muscles.* **Ant.** 1. resilient, soft, limp. 2. unsteady, movable, wavering. 4. soften, weaken.

first *adj.* 1. initial, opening, beginning, original, earliest. *The first chapter is good, but the rest of the book is mediocre.* 2. highest, preeminent, chief, main, foremost. *The president's wife is known as the first lady.* **Ant.** 1. last, concluding, ending. 2. secondary, subordinate.

fiscal *adj.* monetary, financial, budgetary, revenue, money. *The city council met to discuss fiscal matters.*

fisherman *n.* angler, fisher, piscator, harvester of the sea, gill-netter, lobsterman. *A fisherman always pays close attention to the weather and the tides.*

fishing *n.* angling, casting, trolling, trawling, wetting a line. *He went fishing and caught a bass and an old boot.*

WORD SEARCH

ball, floating signal: *bobber*
basket, fisherman's: *creel*
chair, boat: *fighting chair*
corral, fish: *weir*
gear box: *tackle box*
illegal fishing: *poaching*
net hung from floats: *gill net, seine*
net drawn together by two boats: *purse seine*
spear: *harpoon, gaff*
taking of bait by fish: *strike*
weight: *sinker*

fission *n.* atom splitting, atom smashing, atomic reaction, dividing, scission. *Nuclear fission can be harnessed for good or evil.*

fit *adj.* 1. suitable, proper, right, appropriate, fitting. *This food isn't fit for a dog.* 2. healthy, sturdy, robust, well, hale, hardy. *She's looking fit as a result of all the exercise she's been getting.* –*vb.* 3. conform, suit, correspond, harmonize, agree. *The punishment should fit the crime.* 4. equip. outfit, prepare, ready, furnish. *The ship was fitted out for a long voyage.* –*n.* 5. seizure, spasm, spell, outburst, tantrum. *The spoiled child always had a fit when he couldn't get what he wanted.* **Ant.** 1. improper, unsuitable, inappropriate. 2. weak, unfit, sick.

fitness *n.* health, robustness, strength, vigor, endurance, vitality. *Your level of fitness increases when you exercise every day.* **Ant.** weakness, sickness, vigor.

fitting *adj.* suitable, proper, appropriate, seemly, becoming. *Boisterous chatter isn't fitting in church.* **Ant.** unbecoming, improper, wrong.

fix *vb.* 1. repair, mend, remedy, restore, patch. *We need to get someone to fix the washing machine.* 2. attach, secure, fasten, tie, connect, anchor. *The soldiers were ordered to fix bayonets.* 3. set, settle, decide, determine, establish. *They fixed a time for their next meeting.* –*n.* 4. predicament, quandary, mess, jam, dilemma. *That is quite a fix you've gotten yourself into.* **Ant.** 1. break, damage. 2. loosen, unfasten, remove.

fixation *n.* obsession, preoccupation, mania, compulsion, fascination, fetish. *His constant gambling was a fixation.*

fixture *n.* fitting, attachment, contrivance, part, component, appurtenance. *We need special wiring for this light fixture.*

flabby *adj.* fat, blubbery, pendulous, saggy, sloppy, out-of-shape. *I got flabby when I stopped exercising.* **Ant.** muscular, toned, thin.

flag *n.* pendant, emblem, banner, standard, colors. *The flag was positioned at half-mast in honor of the deceased president.*

flagrant *adj.* bold, obvious, brazen, glaring, conspicuous, shocking. *Knocking someone down on the basketball court is a flagrant foul.* **Ant.** inobvious, hidden, concealed.

flamboyant *adj.* showy, colorful, loud, flashy, garish, ostentatious, wild. *Her flamboyant personality lip up a room.* **Ant.** dull, reserved, understated.

flame *n.* **1.** fire, blaze, flare, light, glow, flash. *When the oil tank burned, the flames towered hundreds of feet high. –vb.* **2.** flare, burn, blaze, flash, fire. *She burned herself when the whole book of matches flamed up in her hand.*

flammable *adj.* inflammable, combustible, incendiary, explosive. *Use care around flammable liquids.* **Ant.** noncombustible, fireproof, fire-retardant.

flap *vb.* flutter, vibrate, wave, beat, flail, swish. *The caged bird flapped its wings in a vain attempt to fly away.*

flash *n.* **1.** flare, blaze, sparkle, glitter, streak, burst. *We could see lightning flashes in the distance.* **2.** second, instant, moment, minute, wink, jiffy. *I'll be back in a flash. –vb.* **3.** flare, flame, blaze, gleam, glare. *I lost my night vision when he flashed a light in my eyes.* **4.** streak, race, rush, dash, speed, dart. *The car flashed by so quickly we couldn't see the driver.*

flashback *n.* memory, remembrance, recollection, reliving, recall, recurrence. *My dreams are sometimes comprised of flashbacks from childhood.*

flashy *adj.* showy, ostentatious, glitzy, glittery, gaudy, flamboyant. *Liberace liked to wear flashy clothes covered in sequins.* **Ant.** dull, plain, colorless.

flat *adj.* **1.** level, horizontal, even, smooth, plane. *He prefers hiking across flat ground.* **2.** absolute, definite, unqualified, positive, unconditional. *She gave me a flat refusal when I asked her to do my homework.* **3.** dull, lifeless, tasteless, dead, weak, stale. *This root beer has gone flat. –adv.* **4.** exactly, precisely, evenly, specifically, just dead. *He ran the mile in four minutes flat.* **Ant. 1.** round, curved, rough. **Ant. 2.** qualified, conditional, vague. **3.** tasty, savory, interesting.

flatten *vb.* level, squish, squash, squeeze, crush, plane. *We need to flatten all of these boxes before we can fit them into the recycler.*

flatter *vb.* overpraise, praise, compliment, extol, exalt, please. *He flattered her by saying she looked like a movie star.* **Ant.** insult, belittle, displease.

flatterer *n.* complimenter, sycophant, apple polisher, (slang) kiss-up, toady. *Flatterers look like friends, the way wolves look like dogs.* **Ant.** critic, detractor, fault-finder.

flattery *n.* compliment, praise, sycophancy, fawning, smarm, bootlicking. *His false flattery was beginning to grate on my nerves.* **Ant.** criticism, faultfinding, disapproval.

flaunt *vb.* display, show off, vaunt, advertise, strut. *He flaunts his good looks.* **Ant.** conceal, hide, cloak.

flavor *n.* **1.** taste, flavoring, seasoning, relish, tang. *A little salt will enhance the flavor of this stew.* *–vb.* **2.** season, spice, tinge, color, lace. *She flavors her spaghetti sauce with oregano.*

flaw *n.* fault, defect, blemish, shortcoming, imperfection. *This shirt is inexpensive because it has a minor flaw.*

flee *vb.* escape, run, fly, bolt, evade, elude. *Bambi and his friends fled from a terrible forest fire.*

fleet *adj.* **1.** rapid, swift, quick, fast, speedy, hurried. *The robber made a fleet getaway.* *–n.* **2.** flotilla, squadron, armada, navy, convoy. *The fleet returned to harbor after a training exercise at sea.* **Ant. 1.** slow, sluggish, unhurried.

fleeting *adj.* brief, quick, short-lived, temporary, transient, ephemeral. *The appearance of the comet was fleeting.* **Ant.** permanent, lasting, enduring.

flesh *n.* meat, body tissue, beef, brawn, muscle, fat. *Vegetarians have many reasons for not eating animal flesh.*

flex *vb.* bend, curve, crook, stretch, contract, tense, expand. *We asked the wrestler if he would flex his biceps.*

flexible *adj.* bendable, pliable, elastic, versatile, adaptable. *She repaired the leaking pipe with a flexible piece of plastic.* **Ant.** stiff, rigid, hard.

flick *vb.* snap, flip, tap. *I have no flick all this lint off before I can put on this sweater.*

flicker *vb.* flutter, flash, blink, twinkle, waver. *We could see the light of a jack-o-lantern flickering on their porch.*

flier *n.* *See* FLYER.

flight *n.* **1.** soaring, flying, sailing, trip, crossing. *She's suffering from jet lag after her transatlantic flight.* **2.** swarm, wing, flock, formation, squadron. *A flight of geese passed overhead.* **3.** escape, getaway, retreat, exodus, withdrawal. *Moses led the Israelites during their flight from Egypt.*

flighty *adj.* scatterbrained, whimsical, capricious, (slang) ditzy, fickle, wild. *The young man was simply too flighty to be placed in a management position.*

flimsy *adj.* frail, fragile, delicate, feeble, weak, unsubstantial. *Not wanting to miss your favorite soap opera is a pretty flimsy excuse for being late to work.* **Ant.** solid, strong, substantial.

flinch *vb.* wince, shrink, start, cower, cringe, withdraw. *The boy flinched when the dentist began drilling.*

fling *vb.* **1.** toss, throw, cast, hurl, pitch, heave. *After missing the easy catch, the outfielder stomped away and flung his glove down.* *–n.* **2.** chance, try, attempt, venture, trial, go. *Anyone willing to give snipe hunting a fling?*

flip *vb.* **1.** toss, flick, throw, pitch, spin, snap. *Let's flip a coin to decide who goes first.* **2.** somersault, handspring, acrobatic move. *Part of his dance was an incredible back flip.*

flippant *adj.* disrespectful, irreverent, insolent, rude, fresh, sassy. *Her flippant remarks were insensitive.* **Ant.** respectful, reverent, polite.

flirt *vb.* tease, entice, lead on, make a pass at, tantalize, trifle. *She liked to flirt with all the boys.*

flirtatious *adj.* teasing, enticing, inviting, tantalizing, coquettish, provocative. *Flirtatious behavior was discouraged at the school dance.*

float *vb.* skim, drift, glide, ride, slip, swim. *As we watched the stream, a piece of wood floated past.* **Ant.** sink, submerge, drown.

flock *n.* **1.** herd, pack, company, group, swarm, band, crowd. *The shepherd tended his flock.* *–vb.* **2.** rush, run, go, converge, throng, swarm. *People flocked to the store that was giving away free pizza.*

flog *vb.* whip, lash, thrash, flagellate, strap, flail, flog. *The captain threatened to flog anyone who even whispered of a mutiny.*

flood *n.* **1.** deluge, inundation, torrent, overflow, surge. *Relief workers helped victims of the flood.* *–vb.* **2.** deluge, inundate, submerge, overflow, overwhelm. *During the Christmas season, the post office is flooded with mail.*

floor *n.* **1.** story, level, tier, stage, deck. *She lives on the third floor of her apartment building.* **2.** flooring, base, planking, linoleum, tile, parquet. *This floor needs to be waxed.*

flop *vb.* **1.** fail, (slang) blow it, (slang) bomb, fold, (slang) lay an egg, fall short. *He was so afraid he would flop, he practiced his lines all night.* *–n.* **2.** failure, (slang) bomb, disaster, loser, (slang) dud, (slang) turkey. *My experiment of concocting a beverage out of grape juice and milk was a flop.* **Ant. 1.** succeed, win, triumph. **2.** success, win triumph.

flotilla *n.* fleet, armada, argosy, squadrons, vessels. *The navy sent a flotilla of vessels to safeguard against smuggling.*

flounder *vb.* wallow, struggle, tumble, lurch, falter, waver. *A small boat floundered helplessly in the heavy waves.*

flourish *vb.* **1.** grow, succeed, prosper, thrive, develop, bloom. *Her bookstore flourished because she picked a good location.* **2.** brandish, wave, wield, swing, flaunt, display. *The knight flourished his broadsword in the dragon's face.* *–n.* **3.** show, exhibition, display, fanfare, embellishment. *The magician pulled a rabbit from her hat with a great deal of flourish.* **Ant. 1.** decline, fail, wither.

flow *vb.* **1.** stream, pour, gush, run, cascade, surge. *Water flowed from the broken fire hydrant.* *–n.* **2.** stream, course, sweep, current, progression. *An accident interrupted the flow of traffic.*

flower *n.* **1.** blossom, bloom, bud, bouquet, posy. *She sent him flowers as a token of her affection.* **2.** prime, zenith, acme, height, vigor. *Philosophy was in its flower during Greece's golden age.* **3.** best, choice, pick, select, elite. *These students are the flower of our class.* *–vb.* **4.** blossom, bloom, bud, flourish, prosper, thrive. *Her talent flowered when she began taking music lessons.* **Ant. 2.** nadir, low point. **3.** worst, least, poorest.

fluctuate *vb.* waver, vacillate, vary, sway, oscillate, wobble. *The price of wheat fluctuates from year to year.* **Ant.** stabilize, settle, persist.

fluent *adj.* expressive, articulate, eloquent, smooth-talking, fluid, loose-tongued. *He was fluent in three languages.* **Ant.** tongue-tied, halting, inarticulate.

fluffy *adj.* downy, soft, plush, feathery, fleecy. *The freshly laundered towels were as fluffy as snow.*

fluid *n.* **1.** liquid, solution, juice, drink, beverage. *The triathlete was dehydrated because he didn't consume enough fluids during the race.* *–adj.* **2.** liquid, watery, flowing, liquefied, most, wet. *This fluid mixture becomes a solid mass when frozen.* **Ant. 2.** solid, hard, firm.

fluke *n.* quirk, accident, break, fortuity, serendipity, stroke of luck. *That we all happened to meet at the same time and at the same place was a fluke.*

flunk *vb.* fail, (slang) bomb, (slang) strike out, flop, (slang) crash and burn, not make the grade. *I'm going to have to study harder or I'll flunk the math test.* **Ant.** pass, excel, surpass.

flush *vb.* **1.** redden, blush, color, burn, flame. *He flushed with anger when I insulted him.* **2.**

flood, wash, rinse, hose, douse. *She flushed food scraps down the garbage disposal.* –*n.* **3.** blush, redness, rosiness, ruddiness, glow. *Her face had a healthy flush after her vigorous hike.* –*adj.* **4.** even, level, flat, straight, true. *He wanted his new countertop to be flush with the stove.*

fly *vb.* **1.** soar, float, glide, wing, sail, coast. *Canadian geese fly south for the winter.* **2.** rush, hasten, hurry, dash, bolt, tear. *She flew out of the room to answer the phone.*

fly-by-night *adj.* unreliable, undependable, disreputable, untrustworthy, unprofessional, irresponsible. *The loan company looked suspiciously like a fly-by-night operation, so I took my business elsewhere.* **Ant.** reliable, dependable, professional.

flyer *n.* flier, pilot, aviator, aviatrix, navigator, airman. *Charles Lindbergh is the world's most famous flyer.*

flying saucer *n.* unidentified flying object, UFO, spaceship, bogey, extraterrestrial vessel, aircraft. *Bobby thought she saw a flying saucer but it was really only the planet Venus.*

foam *n.* froth, lather, bubbles, suds, spume, fizz. *I like to shake my soda to create a foam.*

focus *n.* **1.** center, heart, middle, hub, core, point. *The movie star enjoyed being the focus of attention.* –*vb.* **2.** focalize, concentrate, center, aim, direct. *This course will focus on 20th-century writers.* **Ant. 1.** edge, fringe, margin.

foe *n.* enemy, adversary, rival, opponent, antagonist, competitor. *They are friends at work but foes on the tennis court.* **Ant.** friend, ally, associate.

fog *n.* **1.** mist, haze, steam, vapor, cloud. *The airport was closed due to heavy fog.* –*vb.* **2.** mist, cloud, obscure, conceal, screen. *Our breath fogged the windshield.* **Ant. 2.** clear, reveal, brighten.

WORD SEARCH

dense mass: *fog bank*
forms below this temperature: *dew point*
freezing fog that creates frost: *rime*
trapped and blinded by, a ship: *fogbound*

foghorn *n.* diaphone fog signal, warning signal, siren, guide, navigational aid, auditory beacon. *We knew we were approaching shore when the foghorn sounded louder.*

foibles *n.* weaknesses, faults, imperfections, flaws, failings, frailties. *Everyone has foibles, but some have more than others.*

foil *vb.* thwart, frustrate, hinder, prevent, baffle. *An alert guard foiled the robbery attempt.* **Ant.** aid, abet, support.

fold *vb.* **1.** crease, pleat, double, bend, plait. *I always have trouble folding a map properly.* **2.** fail, close, collapse, crash, bomb. *The new play folded after only three performances.* **3.** clasp, embrace, wrap, enfold, envelop. *He folded his arms in anticipation of a long wait at the doctor's office.* –*n.* **4.** pleat, crease, wrinkle, crimp, bend. *A cat played with the curtain's folds* **Ant. 1.** straighten, smooth, flatten. **2.** succeed, thrive, prosper. **3.** unfold, unwrap, open.

folder *n.* file, binder, sheath, envelope, cover. *Put your important papers in a folder to protect them.*

foliage *n.* greenery, leaves, leafage, umbrage, canopy. *Many people like to view the fall foliage in New England.*

folklore *n.* myths, legends, old wives tales, urban myths, tradition, superstition. *According to folklore, a rabbit's foot is considered good luck.*

follow *vb.* **1.** result, ensue, succeed, arise, issue. *From her line of reasoning, it follows that she believes in extraterrestrial life.* **2.** trail, tail, track, shadow, accompany, attend. *Mary's little* *lamb followed her everywhere.* 3. comprehend, understand, fathom, grasp, perceive. *I wasn't able to follow the movie's intricate plot.* 4. heed, obey, mind, regard, observe. *Our cake was a disaster because we didn't follow the directions.* **Ant.** 1. precede, forerun. 2. elude, evade, avoid. 3. misunderstand, misinterpret. 4. ignore, disobey, forsake.

follower *n.* disciple, fan, adherent, minion, sidekick, pupil. *The cult leader's followers acted much like sheep.* **Ant.** leader, director, pacesetter.

folly *n.* foolishness, nonsense, idiocy, stupidity, absurdity, inanity. *Since Alaska was considered worthless, its purchase was thought to be folly.* **Ant.** wisdom, sanity, prudence.

fond *adj.* 1. liking, loving, affectionate, devoted, tender, warm. *The lovers exchanged fond glances.* 2. partial to, enamored of, stuck on, addicted to. *Many people are fond of TV.* **Ant.** 1. distant, hostile, cool. 2. averse, indifferent.

fondle *vb.* caress, pet, stroke, coddle, cuddle, embrace. *She loves to fondle her teddy bear.*

food *n.* provisions, rations, victuals, fare, nourishment. *We'd better go to the grocery because we're low on food.*

food poisoning *n.* sickness, illness, nausea, sour stomach, salmonella, ptomaine poisoning, botulism. *Eating spoiled seafood will cause a severe case of food poisoning.*

fool *n.* 1. idiot, moron, dunce, simpleton, dummy, buffoon, clown. *You're a fool if you think you can pass this test without studying.* –*vb.* 2. cheat, trick, dupe, deceive, hoax. *Abraham Lincoln said you can't fool all of the people all the time.* **Ant.** 1. sage, genius.

foolish *adj.* unwise, stupid, dumb, thoughtless, silly, senseless. *It is foolish to spend all your money on lottery tickets.* **Ant.** wise, bright, smart, sensible.

foolproof *adj.* failsafe, user-friendly, goof-proof, idiot-proof, simple. *Cutting an onion under running water is a foolproof way of preventing tears.* **Ant.** tricky, complex, complicated.

foot *n.* bottom, base, foundation, footing, support. *They camped at the foot of the mountain.* **Ant.** head, top, peak.

football *n.* sport, game, athletic competition. *Football is a rough and aggressive sport.*

WORD SEARCH

dropped ball after having possession: *fumble*
encroachment on opposing side before ball is snapped: *encroachment, offsides*
extra point kick after touchdown: *conversion*
faking a handoff then running with the ball hidden: *bootleg*
field: *gridiron*
foul: *clipping, face mask, unnecessary roughness*
kickoff: *punt*
long pass requiring small miracle to be caught: *Hail Mary*
pass stolen by opposing player: *interception*
position in which quarterback takes the snap from several feet away: *shotgun*
positions: *center, noseguard, nose tackle, defensive back, safety, cornerback, quarterback, halfback, fullback, running back, wide receiver*
quarterback run and evasion of defense: *scrambling, quarterback sneak*
score: *touchdown*
short lateral or surprise pass: *flea-flicker*
surprise rush by large number of defensemen: *blitz*
three-point kick through goalposts: *field goal*
two-point score: *safety*

footprint *n.* print, track, tread, impression. *The detective followed the muddy footprints that led to the thief's apartment.*

forage *vb.* root about, look, search, scavenge, sniff out, seek, rummage. *The pigs were let loose to forage for roots and nuts.*

forbid *vb.* prohibit, ban, disallow, prevent, bar, outlaw. *She thinks the city council should forbid smoking in all restaurants.* **Ant.** allow, permit, approve.

forbidden *adj.* prohibited, outlawed, illegal, taboo, proscribed, verboten. *It is usually forbidden to use foul language in school.* **Ant.** allowed, permitted.

forbidding *adj.* frightening, scary, menacing, threatening, sinister. *That deserted house looks forbidding on dark and stormy nights.* **Ant.** agreeable, pleasant, inviting.

force *n.* **1.** strength, power, might, vigor, energy. *The wind was blowing with great force.* **2.** army, troop, squadron, legion, corps, unit. *An enemy force besieged the castle.* *–vb.* **3.** oblige, compel, coerce, require, persuade. *Sickness forced him to postpone his vacation.* **4.** push, drive, pull, wrench, break, thrust. *Since the window was stuck, we had to force it open.* **Ant. 1.** weakness, feebleness, ineffectiveness.

forceful *adj.* powerful, strong, dynamic, energetic, vigorous, potent. *The lawyer made a forceful appeal on behalf of her client.* **Ant.** weak, powerless, feeble.

foreboding *n.* premonition, apprehension, dread, intuition, misgiving. *The knight had a foreboding that something bad would happen if he entered the dragon's lair.*

forecast *n.* **1.** prediction, prophecy, prognosis, foretelling. *The forecast is for continued rain.* *–vb.* **2.** predict, foretell, prophesy, conjecture, surmise. *She claims to be able to forecast the future.*

foreign *adj.* alien, exotic, strange, unknown, unfamiliar, distant. *He likes to travel to foreign lands.* **Ant.** known, familiar, native.

foreigner *n.* alien, immigrant, outsider, stranger, visitor. *The foreigners spoke with strange accents.* **Ant.** native, indigene, aborigine.

foreman *n.* manager, supervisor, overseer, superintendent, boss. *She was designated to be the jury's foreman.*

foremost *adj.* leading, principal, main, first, head, chief. *Getting home safely was the lost hiker's foremost thought.* **Ant.** secondary, last, least.

foreplay *n.* making out, fondling, warm-up, heavy petting, sexual activity, cuddling. *Spouses often complain of a lack of foreplay from their mates.*

forerunner *n.* predecessor, forebear, forefather, prototype, ancestor, precursor. *The forerunner of the home computer was the calculator.* **Ant.** follower, successor, descendant.

foresee *vb.* anticipate, expect, envision, predict, foretell. *He should have foreseen the threat posed by the storm.*

foresight *n.* farsightedness, forethought, vision, anticipation, prophecy. *It took great foresight to see how successful home computers would be.* **Ant.** hindsight.

forest *n.* woods, woodland, timber, grove, thicket, copse. *Most of North America was once covered with forests.*

WORD SEARCH

cut area littered with logging debris: *slash*
grassy clearing in: *glade*
logging, high-intensity: *clearcutting*
pertaining to: *arboreal*
top of trees, leafy: *canopy, crown*
tropical forest receiving heavy rainfall: *rain forest*
wind-toppled trees: *windthrow, windfall, deadfall*

foretell *vb.* forecast, predict, divine, foresee, presage. *The palm reader foretold that I would meet an attractive stranger.*

forever *adv.* always, eternally, endlessly, perpetually, everlastingly. *I will love you forever.*

foreword *n.* preface, introduction, prologue. *You can't judge a book by its foreword.* **Ant.** epilogue.

forefeit *vb.* lose, renounce, relinquish, sacrifice, yield. *She had to forfeit her title when it was discovered she had used steroids.* **Ant.** keep, retain.

forge *vb.* **1.** mold, cast, make, shape, create, construct. *They forged a lasting friendship.* **2.** falsify, counterfeit, fake, imitate, simulate. *He forged his mother's signature on a note to his teacher.* **3.** push, plod, struggle, strive, drive. *The dog sledder forged ahead despite the heavy snow.*

forgery *n.* fake, fraud, counterfeit, sham, imitation, copy. *The valuable signature of George Washington turned out to be a forgery.*

forget *vb.* misremember, misrecollect, overlook, miss, disregard. *She forgot my name.* **Ant.** remember, recall, recollect.

forgetful *adj.* absent-minded, inattentive, abstracted, (slang) out-to-lunch, amnesic, remiss, oblivious. *He was a forgetful he once neglected to put on socks in the morning.* **Ant.** sharp, alert, aware.

forgive *vb.* pardon, excuse, absolve, condone, reprieve. *I forgive you this time, but please don't let it happen again.* **Ant.** blame, accuse, condemn.

forgiveness *n.* pardon, absolution, dispensation, amnesty, mercy, clemency. *The best way to cure a grudge is through forgiveness.* **Ant.** grudge, condemnation, revenge.

forgo *vb.* relinquish, renounce, forfeit, surrender, abandon. *If you expect to lose weight, you'll have to forgo sweets.* **Ant.** keep, retain.

fork *vb.* **1.** divide, branch, split, part, diverge. *When the road forks, bear left to reach my house.* –*n.* **2.** branch, branching, split, division, angle. *There's a fork in the road just ahead.*

forlorn *adj.* desolate, hopeless, wretched, miserable, dejected, pitiful. *The lost puppy had a forlorn look.* **Ant.** cheerful, happy, hopeful.

form *n.* **1.** shape, figure, contour, outline, pattern, build. *The sorceress took on the form of a swan.* **2.** species, type, variety, kind, class, aspect. *What form of transportation do you prefer?* **3.** method, system, style, manner, procedure. *The gymnast trained hard to improve her form.* **4.** mold, cast, die, framework, pattern. *Work crews constructed a wooden form before pouring the cement.* **5.** document, paper, application, questionnaire. *You'll have to fill out these forms if you wish to apply for a driver's license.* –*vb.* **6.** shape, create, fashion, make, construct, devise. *The goad of our founding fathers was to form a more perfect union.*

formal *adj.* **1.** official, correct, conventional, orthodox, regular. *If you hope to be considered for this job, you'll have to submit a formal application.* **2.** ceremonial, ritualistic, elaborate, elegant, fancy. *The couple planned to have a formal wedding.* **3.** rigid, stiff, aloof, reserved, proper, cool. *She makes me feel uneasy because her manners are so formal.* **Ant.** **1.** unofficial, unconventional. **2.** informal, unceremonious. **3.** friendly, warm, casual.

format *n.* form, system, arrangement, configuration, plan, size, setup. *Eight-track tapes are an outmoded recording format.*

formation *n.* configuration, pattern, design, layout, arrangement. *That cloud formation looks like a person's head.*

former *adj.* previous, prior, earlier, past, preceding, erstwhile. *He's still on good terms with his former boss.* **Ant.** current, present, later.

formidable *adj.* awesome, impressive, intimidating, forbidding, difficult. *Goliath was a formidable opponent for David.* **Ant.** weak, insignificant, easy.

formula *n.* system, method, plan, prescription, recipe, procedure, guideline. *The alchemist claimed to have a secret formula for changing lead into gold.*

forsake *vb.* renounce, forswear, abandon, desert, leave, quit. *She forsook smoking once she became aware of its dangers.*

fort *n.* fortress, fortification, stronghold, stockade, base. *The soldiers hastily constructed a crude log fort.*

forte *n.* specialty, skill, area of expertise, strong point, strength, ability. *Making impromptu speeches was her forte.* **Ant.** weakness, weak area.

forth *adv.* onward, forward, out, outward, ahead. *The brave knight rode forth to confront his opponent.*

forthcoming *adj.* pending, upcoming, approaching, on the horizon, imminent, impending. *The theater showed previews of forthcoming movies.* **Ant.** past, prior.

forthright *adj.* honest, direct, frank, blunt, straightforward, candid. *If one is going to offer constructive criticism, one must be forthright.* **Ant.** indirect, dishonest, mealy-mouthed.

fortify *vb.* strengthen, reinforce, shore up, buttress, gird, build up. *We must fortify the old roof or a heavy load of snow will cave it in.* **Ant.** weaken, undermine, debilitate.

fortitude *n.* courage, bravery, valor, resolution, determination. *For some people, it takes a lot of fortitude to say they're sorry.* **Ant.** cowardice, weakness, timidity.

fortunate *adj.* lucky, blessed, favored, charmed, well-off, happy. *You're fortunate to have such a good friend as her.* **Ant.** unfortunate, unlucky, unhappy.

fortune *n.* **1.** money, wealth, riches, prosperity, affluence. *She made her fortune in real estate.* **2.** fate, chance, luck, destiny, providence, accident. *It was his good fortune to buy a winning lotto ticket.* **Ant.** **1.** poverty, destitution. **2.** misfortune, design, intent.

fortune-teller *n.* seer, psychic, soothsayer, diviner, prognosticator, prophet. *The fortune-teller told me I would soon meet someone tall, dark and handsome.*

forum *n.* meeting, gathering, assembly, discussion, seminar. *The city council held a public forum to discuss the need for new taxes.*

forward *adj.* **1.** bold, brazen, assertive, aggressive, arrogant. *Her forward behavior alienated her colleagues.* **2.** front, fore, foremost, headmost, anterior. *She found a seat in the forward part of the bus.* –*adv.* **3.** onward, ahead, along, outward, before. *I'm looking forward to Christmas vacation.* –*vb.* **4.** advance, encourage, foster, promote, further. *She's been working to forward the cause of world peace.* **Ant.** **1.** timid, retiring, modest. **2.** back, rear, posterior. **3.** backward, behind. **4.** hinder, impede, obstruct.

fossil *n.* remains, relic, remnant, impression, specimen, imprint. *We found a fossil of an ancient sea creature.*

foul *adj.* **1.** disgusting, offensive, repulsive, indecent, obscene, dirty. *Foul language is inappropriate in the classroom.* **2.** rainy, stormy, wet, blustery, bleak, bad. *We shouldn't take the yacht out in this foul weather.* **Ant.** **1.** proper, decent, inoffensive. **2.** good, fair, clear.

found *vb.* establish, create, institute, develop, originate. *Our family business was founded by my grandfather.*

foundation *n.* **1.** base, support, underpinning, foot, bed, bottom. *Our house is built on a concrete block foundation.* **2.** establishment, institution, organization, association, society. *He works for a nonprofit foundation.*

founder *vb.* sink, swamp, submerge, wallow, go down. *The ship began to founder in the high seas.*

fountain *n.* spray, spout, fount, font, jet, geyser. *Water flowed from the fountain in a steady stream.*

foyer *n.* hall, lobby, entrance, vestibule, reception area. *Please meet the guests in the foyer.*

fracas *n.* fight, brawl, scuffle, melee, donnybrook, rumble. *The police had to be called to break up the fracas.*

fraction *n.* part, portion, piece, fragment, section. *Only a small fraction of our graduating class went on to college.*

fracture *vb.* **1.** break, split, crack, fragment, shatter, splinter. *She fractured her leg playing basketball.* –*n.* **2.** break, split, crack, rupture, fissure. *Her fracture took six weeks to heal.*

fragile *adj.* brittle, breakable, delicate, frail, feeble, weak. *This crystal vase is very fragile.* **Ant.** strong, sturdy, unbreakable.

fragment *n.* **1.** portion, part, piece, section, segment. *There was nothing but fragments left when he dropped the vase.* –*vb.* **2.** splinter, shatter, burst, crumble, disintegrate. *The ancient bones fragmented in her hands when she picked them up.*

fragrance *n.* aroma, scent, smell, odor, perfume. *He likes the fragrance of roses.* **Ant.** stink, reek, stench.

fragrant *adj.* aromatic, sweet-smelling, ambrosial, perfumed, sweet, savory. *Lilacs are deliciously fragrant.*

frail *adj.* fragile, delicate, weak, feeble brittle, breakable. *This parchment is old and frail.* **Ant.** strong, sturdy, tough.

frailty *n.* weakness, vulnerability, debility, infirmity, Achilles heel. *The old man's frailty prevented him from climbing stairs.* **Ant.** strength, power, vigor.

frame *n.* **1.** mounting, framework, casing, housing, edging, border. *She bought a frame for her new painting.* **2.** physique, body, build, figure, shape. *He has such a small frame he'll never make much of a football player.* –*vb.* **3.** mount, border, enclose, surround, encase. *We should frame this picture before sending it to Grandmother.* **4.** formulate, fashion, construct, devise, design. *The lawyer framed her questions in an easily understandable manner.*

franchise *n.* chain, store, dealership, distributorship, enterprise, outfit, shop. *Mike wants to run his own fast-food franchise.*

frank *adj.* honest, straightforward, forthright, candid, explicit, blunt. *Use care when making frank comments.* **Ant.** dishonest, euphemistic, insincere.

frantic *adj.* frenzied, excited, agitated, frenetic, nervous, distraught. *The groom became frantic when the bride was late getting to the church.* **Ant.** composed, calm, serene.

fraternity *n.* brotherhood, fellowship, kinship, society, club, order, house. *When I go to college, I hope to get into my brother's fraternity.* **Ant.** sorority.

fraud *n.* **1.** deceit, deception, trickery, duplicity, dishonesty. *He was arrested for fraud when he sold a counterfeit painting.* **2.** cheat, swindler, faker, pretender, impostor. *She claims to be a wealthy princess, but she's actually just a fraud.* **Ant. 1.** honesty, integrity, fairness.

fraudulent *adj.* deceptive, dishonest, criminal, crooked, devious, treacherous. *The crook earned his money through fraudulent means.* **Ant.** honest, legitimate, legal.

fray *n.* **1.** fight, brawl, scuffle, tussle, row, battle. *The personnel manager and the company accountant got into a fray over employee benefits.* *–vb.* **2.** ravel, tatter, frazzle, shred, wear. *Too many washings have frayed her jeans.*

freak *adj.* **1.** odd, unusual, abnormal, strange, unexpected, weird. *A freak snowstorm hit our town last July.* *–n.* **2.** abnormality, oddity, curiosity, deviation, anomaly, monstrosity. *A snake with two heads is a freak of nature.* **Ant.** **1.** normal, ordinary, expected.

free *adj.* **1.** complimentary, gratis, gratuitous, chargeless, costless. *She has two free tickets for today's baseball game.* **2.** independent, liberated, emancipated, autonomous, self-governing. *India became a free nation in 1948.* **3.** available, open, idle, vacant, empty, unclaimed. *Now that Grandfather has left, our guest room is free.* **4.** loose, unconfined, unrestrained, unbridled, untied. *The prisoner was set free.* *–vb.* **5.** release, loose, liberate, emancipate, untie, unleash. *Activists broke into the science building and freed the lab animals.* **Ant.** **1.** expensive, costly, paid. **2.** dependent, enslaved, restricted. **3.** taken, occupied, unavailable. **4.** confined, restrained, tied. **5.** restrain, confine, imprison.

freedom *n.* independence, liberty, emancipation, liberation, release. *Abraham Lincoln gave America's slaves their freedom.* **Ant.** slavery, servitude, bondage.

freelance *adj.* independent, self-employed, at-large, autonomous, unaffiliated. *He sometimes covered local news as a freelance reporter.* **Ant.** staff, affiliated, salaried.

freeway *n.* highway, expressway, superhighway, beltway, autobahn. *Be sure to observe the speed limit as you drive on the freeway.*

freeze *vb.* **1.** ice, frost, refrigerate, chill, cool. *You should freeze this meat if you aren't going to use it till next week.* **2.** stop, halt, harden, stiffen, immobilize. *She froze in her tracks when she saw the bear.* *–n.* **3.** frost, chill, nip, bite, sting. *Last night's freeze killed my tomato plants.* **4.** halt, stop, restraint, moratorium, suspension. *The president put a freeze on new taxes.* **Ant.** **1.** thaw, warm, heat.

freezer *n.* ice box, ice chest, cooler, refrigeration unit. *Take the chicken out of the freezer so it'll be thawed by tomorrow.*

freezing *adj.* frigid, ice-cold, biting, raw, wintry, bone-chilling. *The weather in Maine is freezing, at least in the winter.* **Ant.** warm, hot, balmy.

frenzy *n.* furor, turmoil, rage, rush, agitation. *There was a frenzy of last-minute activity as the cast prepared for opening night.*

frequent *adj.* **1.** common, usual, habitual, regular, customary. *This airline offers discounts for frequent fliers.* *–vb.* **2.** patronize, haunt, visit, attend, go to. *He frequents that bar.* **Ant.** **1.** rare, unusual, uncommon. **2.** avoid, shun, spurn.

fresh *adj.* **1.** unspoiled, unfaded, wholesome, new, recent. *Are these eggs fresh?* **2.** refreshing, invigorating, healthy, clean, pure. *Let's step outside to get some fresh air.* **3.** wise, bold, impudent, forward, rude. *Don't get fresh with me.* **Ant.** **1.** stale, spoiled, old. **2.** stale, impure, polluted. **3.** polite, courteous, respectful.

fret *vb.* worry, agonize, anguish, fuss, lose sleep over, work oneself up, (slang) sweat bullets. *Don't fret over a little spilled milk.* **Ant.** relax, (slang) chill.

friction *n.* **1.** rubbing, abrasion, grinding, grating, chafing. *If you don't keep oil in the* *engine, friction will wear it out.* **2.** conflict, antagonism, discord, disagreement, dissension. *There was a lot of friction between the two stepbrothers.* **Ant. 2.** harmony, agreement, compatibility.

friend *n.* comrade, companion, intimate, pal, acquaintance, ally. *They have been friends since childhood.* **Ant.** stranger, adversary, foe.

friendly *adj.* sociable, personable, warm, outgoing, extroverted, companionable. *You have to be exceptionally friendly to deal with the public daily.* **Ant.** unfriendly, mean, aloof.

friendship *n.* fellowship, comradeship, companionship, intimacy, amity, closeness. *I truly value your friendship.* **Ant.** coolness, indifference, animosity.

fright *n.* terror, fear, dread, alarm, panic, scare. *The passengers were filled with fright when the pilot parachuted out of the plane.* **Ant.** bravery, courage, fortitude.

frighten *vb.* scare. terrify, shock, alarm, terrorize, daunt. *Her pit bull frightens me.* **Ant.** reassure, encourage, comfort.

frightening *adj.* terrifying, scary, fearful, alarming, intimidating. *Last night's thunderstorm was frightening.* **Ant.** calming, reassuring, encouraging.

frigid *adj.* icy, freezing, cold, chilly, piercing, biting. *How can she enjoy swimming in the frigid water of a mountain lake?* **Ant.** warm, hot, temperate.

fringe *n.* border, margin, edge, rim, periphery, limit. *He lives on the fringe of poverty.* **Ant.** center, core, heart.

frisky *adj.* playful, frolicsome, coltish, kittenish, lively, active. *The party-goers suddenly turned frisky and began throwing friends into the pool.* **Ant.** lifeless, dead, slothful.

fritter *vb.* squander, waste, lavish, (slang) blow, spend, throw away. *You'll be sorry if you fritter away all of your savings.* **Ant.** save, conserve, (slang) tighten one's belt.

frivolous *adj.* silly, foolish, senseless, trivial, petty, unimportant. *His parents thought his comic book collection was a frivolous waste of money.* **Ant.** serious, sensible, important.

frolic. *vb.* **1.** cavort, romp, frisk, play, prance, sport. *She enjoys watching the bear cubs frolic at the zoo.* *–n.* **2.** merriment, gaiety, fun, romp, revel, caper. *The millionaire's daughter enjoyed a life full of frolic.*

front *n.* **1.** head, top, fore, beginning, forefront, forepart. *He likes to sit at the front of the bus.* **2.** surface, face, facade, bearing, demeanor. *She tried to maintain a brave front despite her depression.* **3.** coalition, alliance, affiliation union, merger. *The workers formed a united front against management's demands.* *–adj.* **4.** first, initial, beginning, headmost, foremost. *The only seats we could find were in the front row.* **Ant. 1–4.** back, rear.

frontier *n.* **1.** boundary, border, edge, perimeter, rim. *The frontier between the United States and Canada is not fortified.* **2.** hinterland, outskirts, backwoods, bush, outback, boondocks. *Lewis and Clark led an expedition that explored America's frontier.*

frost *n.* condensation, rime, frozen dew, snow, ice crystals, hoarfrost. *I'm late because I had to scrape so much frost off of my windshield this morning.*

frosting *n.* icing, topping, glaze, spread. *Please don't lick the frosting off the cake.*

frothy *adj.* foamy, lathery, bubbly, soapy, fizzy, effervescent. *The shaving cream is ready to apply when it is worked into a frothy lather.*

frown *vb.* **1.** scowl, glower, pout, glare, mope, sulk. *She frowned at me when I told her I didn't like her new dress.* –*n.* **2.** scowl, glower, grimace, pout, glare. *His frown means he's unhappy with me.* **Ant. 1–2.** smile.

frozen *adj.* iced, iced-over, gelid, chilled, cooled, solidified, hardened. *The pond was frozen solid.* **Ant.** thawed, fluid, melted.

frugal *adj.* thrifty, stingy, pennypinching, economical, parsimonious, scrimping. *They had always been frugal and refused to use credit cards.* **Ant.** extravagant, lavish, profligate.

fruit *n.* yield, harvest, crop, return, reward, result. *He's living a life of ease enjoying the fruits of his labor.*

fruitful *adj.* fertile, plentiful, abundant, prolific, successful. *The Thanksgiving holiday was started by pilgrims celebrating their first fruitful harvest.* **Ant.** scarce, meager, scanty.

fruition *n.* fulfillment, completion, realization, consummation, achievement. *If you want your dreams to come to fruition, you should be persistent.*

fruitless *adj.* unproductive, useless, pointless, futile, unprofitable, ineffective. *My attempts at growing rich by raising earthworms has been largely fruitless.* **Ant.** fruitful, productive, rewarding.

frumpy *adj.* frumpish, dowdy, unfashionable, slovenly, plain. *She looked so frumpy I thought she was wearing a potato sack.* **Ant.** chic, stylish, sharp.

frustrate *vb.* foil, thwart, balk, defeat, discourage, hinder. *Efforts to help the flood victims are being frustrated by the impassable roads.* **Ant.** encourage, help, support.

frustration *n.* bafflement, thwarting, defeat, discouragement, obstruction, failure. *Figuring out one's taxes can be an exercise in frustration.*

fry *vb.* sear, brown, sauté, sizzle, singe. *I'll fry up a couple of eggs for breakfast.*

frying pan *n.* skillet, wok, spider, cooking utensil. *The burned frying pan is going to be hard to clean.*

fuel *n.* gas, propellant, combustible, oil, kindling, power, source. *My car runs better when I use high octane fuel.*

fugitive *n.* refugee, runaway, renegade, deserter, exile. *Police mounted a massive search for the two fugitives.*

fulfill *vb.* satisfy, meet, accomplish, complete, finish, achieve. *She has to take only one more course to fulfill her graduation requirements.*

full *adj.* **1.** filled, stuffed, replete, saturated, brimming, loaded. *We won't need to stop for gas since we already have a full tank.* **2.** complete, whole, entire, solid, thorough. *He's feeling tired after putting in a full day at the office.* **Ant. 1.** empty, vacant, void. **2.** incomplete, partial.

fumble *vb.* mishandle, mismanage, muff, bumble, botch. *He lost his job when he fumbled an important assignment.*

fume *n.* gas, smoke, exhaust, steam, vapor, smog, pollution. *The fumes from the bus exhaust made us cough.*

fun *n.* pleasure, amusement, enjoyment, merriment, gaiety, sport, recreation. *Are we having fun yet?*

function *n.* **1.** purpose, role, operation, job, use, capacity. *The function of this wire is to carry electricity to the starter.* **2.** ceremony, affair, gathering, party, celebration. *The local church held a fund-raising function.* –*vb.* **3.** work, act, perform, serve, operate. *Her watch also functions as a miniature calculator.*

functional *adj.* practical, suitable, useful, serviceable, efficient, workable. *A chair is a highly* *functional piece of furniture.* **Ant.** impractical, inefficient, unworkable.

fund *n.* **1.** savings, endowment, investment, account, portfolio. *She makes weekly contributions to her retirement fund.* **2.** wealth, riches, money, capital, assets, cash. *He invests his surplus funds in real estate.* –*vb.* **3.** finance, capitalize, endow, patronize, support. *She hasn't yet found anyone to fund her research project.*

fundamental *adj.* **1.** primary, basic, essential, major, indispensable, necessary. *A fundamental knowledged of English is essential for success.* –*n.* **2.** basic, rudiment, principle, essential, foundation. *She has mastered the fundamentals of computer programming.* **Ant. 1.** superficial, secondary, superfluous.

fund-raiser *n.* charity event, pledge drive, telethon, philanthropic enterprise. *We're planning to hold a fund-raiser to help pay for a new community center.*

funds *n.* money, capital, cash, resources, finances, currency. *It's wise to keep extra funds around for emergencies.*

funeral *n.* burial, services, obsequies, exequies, interment, last rites. *A funeral is a somber affair.*

WORD SEARCH

announcement of death: *obituary*
bulger's observance, military: *taps*
burial at sea: *deep six*
burial cloth: *shroud*
car that conveys coffin to cemetery: *hearse*
coffin carriers: *pallbearers*
praise for deceased, formal: *eulogy*
procession: *cortege*
song of lament: *dirge, requiem*
toll of bell signaling death: *knell*
undertaken: *mortician*

fungus *n.* growth, thallophyte, mold, mildew. *Watch out for the disgusting fungus growing in the cellar.*

funnel *vb.* channel, direct, conduct, siphon, filter. *Let's funnel the gasoline into the tank to prevent spillage.*

funny *adj.* humorous, amusing, comic, comical, odd, strange. *She told a funny story about the time she forgot her husband's name.* **Ant.** serious, grave, humorless.

furious *adj.* **1.** angry, irate, mad, incensed, infuriated, wrathful. *My parents were furious when I stayed out past midnight.* **2.** wild, turbulent, violent, raging, fierce, savage. *A furious windstorm knocked down all the local power lines.* **Ant. 1.** pleased, gratified, happy. **2.** mild, tame, calm.

furnace *n.* heater, burner, stove, incinerator, smelter, forge, kiln. *The home furnace should be cleaned annually for maximum efficiency.*

furnish *vb.* equip, supply, provide, outfit, appoint, distribute. *The instructor will furnish everything needed for the class.*

furniture *n.* furnishings, seating, cabinetry, chairs, tables, bureaus. *Victorian houses were crammed full of furniture.*

furor *n.* uproar, rage, outrage, outburst, ruckus, to-do. *A furor arose over the increased development in the neighborhood.*

furrow *n.* channel, trench, trough, groove, rut, cut. *The farmer spent all day plowing furrows into his field.*

furry *adj.* hairy, woolly, shaggy, bushy, downy, bristly, hirsute. *Animals who live in cold climates are often furry.* **Ant.** bald, bare, clean-cut.

further *adj.* **1.** additional, more, supplementary, extra, spare. *There will be further details on* *the eleven o'clock news.* **2.** farther, yonder, remoter, yon. *That further mountain is the one we're hoping to climb.* –*vb* **3.** aid, assist, promote, advance, forward, help. *She hoped that taking night classes would further her career.* **Ant. 2.** nearer, closer. **3.** hinder impede, obstruct.

furtive *adj.* secret, sly, covert, clandestine, hidden, concealed. *She stole a furtive glance at the boy sitting next to her.* **Ant.** open, direct, unconcealed.

fury *n.* **1.** rage, anger, wrath, ire, furor, frenzy. *She had to face her father's fury when she wrecked his car.* **2.** intensity, severity, might, power, force. *We were astonished by the fury of the storm.* **Ant. 1–2.** calmness, serenity, tranquility.

fuse *vb.* join, merge, weld, link, blend, combine. *The chemist fused two metals together to create a new alloy.* **Ant.** separate, divide, split.

fusion *n.* union, blend, merger, integration, melding, joining. *The band plays a fusion of jazz and rock.* **Ant.** fission, split, division.

fuss *n.* bother, trouble, stir, fretting, ado, disturbance. *I don't want anybody making a big fuss over my birthday.*

fussy *adj.* picky, choosy, discriminating, fastidious, finicky, particular. *She was fussy and would wear only name-brand jeans.* **Ant.** easy to please, unparticular, undiscriminating.

futile *adj.* useless, vain, unproductive, unavailing, ineffective. *He made a futile attempt to quit smoking.* **Ant.** effective, productive, successful.

futon *n.* mattress, sofa, couch, bed, fold-out, convertible. *I don't want to sleep on the futon because it's too short.*

future *adj.* coming, pending, imminent, prospective, later. *She agreed to meet him at some unspecified future date.* **Ant.** past, former, previous.

futuristic *adj.* innovative, cutting-edge, modern, ultramodern, visionary, groundbreaking. *He designed a futuristic city in which all of the commercial buildings were located in one gigantic mall.* **Ant.** old fashioned, antiquated, outmoded.

fuzzy *adj.* hairy, furry, napped, frizzy, hirsute, downy, bristly. *My jaw gets fuzzy quickly if I forget to shave.*

G

gab *vb.* talk, chatter, converse, babble, (slang) chit chat, (slang) shoot the breeze, jabber. *It didn't matter what the subject was, the girls just liked to gab.*

gabby *adj.* talkative, chatty, verbose, loquacious, (slang) motormouthed, windy. *Eddy is exceptionally gabby, but he can be a good listener too.*

gadget *n.* device, contraption, instrument, appliance, tool. *I can't get this gadget to work.*

gaffe *n.* mistake, error, blunder, faux pas, slip, lapse, goof. *He made a major gaffe by drinking from his finger bowl.*

gag *vb.* **1.** choke, retch, vomit, upchuck, heave. *Lemons tend to make me gag.* –*n.* **2.** joke, prank, practical joke, stunt, trick, jest. *We pulled a funny gag on the teacher.*

gain *vb.* **1.** get, earn, acquire, obtain, attain, win, achieve. *The runner managed to gain the lead after the tenth lap.* –*n.* **2.** increase, improvement, profit, advantage, addition, enrichment. *There was a gain in productivity amongst auto workers this year.* **Ant. 1.** lose, forfeit, worsen. **2.** decrease, decline, loss.

gait *n.* stride, step, tread, pace, walk, carriage. *Her thoroughbred runs with a graceful gait.*

gala *n.* celebration, jubilee, party, festival, ball, affair. *Are you going to the New Year's gala?*

galaxy *n.* star system, star cluster, island universe. *We live in a huge galaxy called the Milky Way.*

gale *n.* wind, storm, tempest, blow, squall, outburst. *We shouldn't go sailing in this gale.*

gall *n.* **1.** boldness, nerve, cheek, audacity, impudence. *He has a lot of gall to ask me for a loan.* –*vb.* **2.** annoy, anger, irritate, irk, provoke, bother, vex. *Her arrogant attitude galled him.* **Ant. 1.** humility, meekness, politeness. **2.** please, cheer, delight.

gallant *adj.* **1.** brave, courageous, heroic, valiant, fearless, bold. *Sir Lancelot was a gallant knight.* **2.** courteous, polite, noble, civil, thoughtful, kind. *The gallant young woman gave her bus seat to an old man.* **Ant. 1.** cowardly, timid, fearful. **2.** rude, impolite, discourteous.

gallery *n.* **1.** passage, passageway, hallway, corridor, aisle. *A long gallery led to the ballroom.* **2.** museum, salon, studio, showroom, arcade. *She exhibited her sculptures at a local gallery.*

gallop *vb.* **1.** run, race, dash, rush, hurry, scurry, scamper. *The wild horses galloped away from the cowboys.* –*n.* **2.** run, gait, speed, clip, ride, dash. *The pony express rider managed a steady gallop to the next station.* **Ant. 1.** walk, crawl, amble. **2.** walk, crawl.

galvanize *vb.* stimulate, spur, jolt, energize, inspire, electrify, arouse. *The loss of another old-*

growth forest to development served to galvanize the environmental group.

gambit *n.* play, maneuver, ploy, stratagem, tactic, action. *The enemy's gambit to blow up the bridge failed.*

gamble *vb.* **1.** bet, risk, chance, wager, venture. *Don't gamble what you can't afford to lose.* *–n.* **2.** risk, chance, hazard, wager, bet, venture. *Investing in the stock market can be a gamble.*

game *n.* **1.** contest, competition, match sport, tournament. *Tonight's basketball game will be for the city championship.* **2.** amusement, entertainment, pastime, recreation, fun. *The children went to the park to play games.* **3.** prey, quarry, victims, animals, fish, fowl. *I'll never understand why she likes to hunt big game.* **Ant.** **2.** work, toil, labor.

gamut *n.* extent, range, sweep, scope, area, spectrum. *My grandfather's talents ran the gamut from chess master to master chef.*

gang *n.* group, band, crew, team, troop, ring, club, company. *A gang of boys were hanging around the drinking fountain.*

gangling *adj.* tall, lanky, rangy, spindly, skinny, long-limbed. *The gangling youth was constantly asked if he played basketball.* **Ant.** short, stout, fat.

gangrene *n.* decay, putrefaction, rot, wasting, tissue death. *When gangrene set in, the explorer's frostbitten toes had to be amputated.*

gangster *n.* hood, hoodlum, criminal, crook, thug. *The bank was held up by gangsters.*

gap *n.* opening, break, space, rift, breach, split, hole. *The mouse escaped through a gap in the floor.*

gape *vb.* stare, gaze, glare, gawk, peer, ogle. *She gaped at the enormous amount of food on the table.*

garage *n.* shelter, carport, car barn, building, hangar. *Park your car in my garage.*

garb *n.* clothes, clothing, apparel, dress, attire, outfit. *Next Halloween, I plan to wear pirate garb.*

garbage *n.* trash, rubbish, waste, junk, debris, refuse. *Please pick up the garbage on the lawn.*

garbled *adj.* distorted, jumbled, confused, warped, twisted. *She could not understand the garbled loudspeaker announcement.* **Ant.** clear, straight, understandable.

garden *n.* **1.** plot, bed, patch, nursery, conservatory, garth. *She liked to tend to her beautiful rose garden.* *–vb.* **2.** cultivate, grow, raise. *I like to garden, but I don't like getting dirty.*

WORD SEARCH

beauty, plant grown strictly for its: *ornamental*
box that is used as a mini greenhouse: *cold frame*
enclosed garden: *garth*
glass container, in a: *terrarium, bottle garden*
medicinal ingredients or seasonings, garden that provides: *herb garden*
night-flowering garden: *moon garden*
pests: *aphid, cutworm, gypsy moth, slug, Japanese beetle*
plant that dies after first year: *annual*
plant that returns on its own year after year: *perennial*
section: *bed, plot*
soil enrichment material: *compost, manure*
soilless growing method: *hydroponics*
tiny niche garden: *pocket garden*
tool: *hoe, rake, trowel, sprinkler*
tree and shrub garden: *arboretum*
weed smothering substance: *mulch*
World War II, provided domestic food during: *victory gardens*

gargantuan *adj.* gigantic, massive, huge, towering, colossal, immense. *He drove up in a* *gargantuan truck that overshadowed everything around it.* **Ant.** tiny, miniature, microscopic.

garish *adj.* gaudy, ostentatious, flashy, loud, ornate, chintzy. *The wallpaper was ornate and garish.* **Ant.** tasteful, understated, classy.

garlic *n.* herb, clove, bulb, seasoning, flavoring. *Garlic tastes great but it gives you bad breath.*

garment *n.* clothing, clothes, attire, garb, apparel, outfit, dress. *She hung her garments in the closet.*

garnish *vb.* **1.** decorate, embellish, adorn, enhance, trim, deck. *She garnished her salad with sprigs of watercress.* –*n.* **2.** decoration, ornament, adornment, trimming, embellishment. *A little garnish on the plate will make the food look more attractive.*

gas *n.* **1.** vapor, effluvium, fume, emission, steam, smoke. *The methane gas in the landfill had to be vented.* **2.** gasoline, fuel, petrol, propellant, combustible. *Fill the car's tank with gas.*

gash *n.* **1.** slash, wound, cut, slit, slice. *The pirate had an ugly gash on his right cheek.* –*vb.* **2.** cut, slice, wound, slash, tear, slit, rip. *She gashed her hand on a piece of broken glass.*

gasp *vb.* **1.** pant, puff, huff, wheeze, gulp, choke. *The hiker gasped for air as she reached the high mountain pass.* –*n.* **2.** gulp, wheeze, huff, heave, pant, puff. *He made one last gasp before dying.*

gate *n.* entrance, entry, portal, door, doorway. *Please close the gate so the dog won't get out.*

gather *vb.* **1.** group, assemble, collect, accumulate, mass, convene. *A small crowd gathered around the street performers.* **2.** harvest, reap, collect, garner, take. *It is time to gather the fruit from the trees.* **3.** understand, assume, conclude, deduce, infer, reckon. *I gather that dinner will be late.* **Ant. 1.** separate, disperse, disassemble.

gathering *n.* assembly, crowd, company, group, grouping, throng. *We are expecting a large gathering for our school reunion.*

gauche *adj.* tactless, ill-mannered, boorish, crude, graceless, unsophisticated. *They stuffed their faces with appetizers in a very gauche manner.* **Ant.** tactful, refined, sophisticated.

gaudy *adj.* loud, flashy, garish, vulgar, tawdry, tasteless. *Our neighbor placed a gaudy pink flamingo in his garden.* **Ant.** tasteful, subtle, quiet.

gauge *n.* **1.** measure, test, standard, yardstick, model, pattern. *Test scores are used as a gauge to determine scholastic success.* **2.** tester, measurer, instrument, meter. *Tire pressure can be checked with a gauge.* –*vb.* **3.** estimate, measure, assess, judge, evaluate, appraise. *It is difficult to gauge distances by mere eyesight.*

gaunt *adj.* lean, thin, scrawny, skinny, lanky, bony. *The gaunt man looked like he hadn't eaten in a week.* **Ant.** plump, fat, obese.

gawk *vb.* gape, ogle, stare, gaze, look, eyeball. *The bystanders stood and gawked at the site of the accident.*

gay *adj.* **1.** happy, cheerful, jolly, merry, joyful, joyous, gleeful. *Everyone at the party was in a gay mood.* **2.** colorful, bright, brilliant, vivid, intense, showy. *The painter used gay colors to brighten up the reception area.* **Ant. 1.** gloomy, sad, solemn. **2.** dull, sedate, drab.

gay *adj.* homosexual, lesbian, bisexual, (slang) out of the closet, Sapphic. *Jonathan spends much of his time fighting for gay rights.* **Ant.** heterosexual.

gaze *vb.* **1.** stare, peer, look, gape, watch, scan. *I could gaze at the stars for hours.* –*n.* **2.** look, stare, gape, scrutiny, glare. *The child looked upon the magician with a gaze of wonderment.*

gazebo *n.* belvedere, summerhouse, platform, garden house, bandstand, structure, shelter. *The barbershop quartet will perform a concert from the park's gazebo.*

gear *n.* **1.** outfit, equipment, apparatus, effects, belongings. *Have you collected all your camping gear?* **2.** mechanism, cog, cogwheel, cam, wheel. *The machine worked perfectly after we oiled its gears.*

geek *n.* Slang. goon, mutant, weirdo, oddball, sideshow specimen. *I feel like a geek whenever I wear clothes that don't fit.*

gem *n.* mineral, jewel, precious stone, semi-precious stone, bauble, rock. *She wore a polished gem on the end of a gold chain.*

WORD SEARCH

blue: *aquamarine, sapphire, turquoise*
cutter, expert: *lapidary*
diamond, faux: *zircon*
iridescent: *moonstone, opal, pearl*
purple: *amethyst*
red: *ruby, garnet*
study of: *gemology*
weight: *carat, karat*
yellow: *topaz*

genealogy *n.* lineage, family tree, ancestry, descent, bloodline, pedigree. *Grandma traced her genealogy back to the Middle Ages.*

general *adj.* **1.** typical, regular, usual, conventional, customary. *Shaking hands is a general form of greeting.* **2.** basic, comprehensive, overall, vague, inexact, indefinite. *She has a general knowledge of Spanish.* **3.** widespread, prevalent, universal, common, popular. *There will be a general strike tomorrow.* **Ant. 1.** uncommon, unique, unusual. **2.** exact, specific, specialized. **3.** local, limited, individual.

generally *adv.* usually, commonly, ordinarily, chiefly, normally, frequently. *I generally go to bed at ten o'clock.* **Ant.** rarely, seldom, occasionally.

generate *vb.* create, produce, make, cause, devise, develop. *The old battery barely generated enough electricity to start the car.* **Ant.** destroy, eliminate, demolish.

generation *n.* **1.** creation, birth, origination, production, spawning, genesis. *The plant scientist was cited for his generation of new hybrids.* **2.** age group, offspring, spawn, contemporaries. *Members of the baby boom generation will soon enter their senior years.*

generator *n.* dynamo, alternator, energy converter. *We have an emergency generator in the cellar in case of a power failure.*

generic *adj.* general, universal, common, comprehensive. *Feeling blah on Monday is a generic complaint.* **Ant.** specific.

generous *adj.* **1.** charitable, unselfish, kindly, considerate, thoughtful. *Your generous offer of help is appreciated.* **2.** ample, large, liberal, abundant, big. *There is a generous amount of space in our backyard.* **Ant. 1.** mean, selfish, miserly. **2.** tiny, small, meager.

genesis *n.* birth, origin, inception, start, beginning, creation. *The genesis of the home computer age began in the late 1980s.* **Ant.** death, end, close.

genial *adj.* friendly, agreeable, cordial, pleasant, cheerful, comfortable. *We enjoyed the restaurant's genial atmosphere.* **Ant.** uncomfortable, unfriendly, unpleasant.

genie *n.* jinni, supernatural being, conjurer, wizard, spirit. *The genie granted the startled woman three wishes.*

genitals *n.* sexual organs, reproductive organs, genitalia, privates, pudendum. *It's a good idea to protect one's genitals from injury during sports.*

genius *n.* **1.** talent, ability, gift, flair, aptitude, brilliance. *Mozart's genius is still appreciated today.* **2.** mastermind, master, prodigy, brain, expert. *You don't have to be a genius to work a computer.* **Ant. 2.** idiot, moron, imbecile.

genocide *n.* extermination, annihilation, massacre, eradication, elimination. *Genocide is the widespread massacre of population.*

genre *n.* category, type, kind, class, style, sort. *He liked to write in the mystery genre.*

genteel *adj.* refined, cultured, polite, civil, gentlemanly, ladylike. *His genteel manner was most welcome in our house.* **Ant.** rough, unrefined, uncultured.

gentle *adj.* **1.** kind, tender, warmhearted, pleasant, harmless, docile. *He may act tough, but he's actually a very gentle person.* **2.** easy, mild, light, moderate, smooth, soft. *We hiked up a gentle grade to the waterfall.* **Ant. 1.** mean, cruel, tough. **2.** hard, difficult, rough.

genuine *adj.* real, true, actual, factual, authentic. *The merchant assured the magician that his magic ring was the genuine article.* **Ant.** false, phony, fake, counterfeit.

genus *n.* class, classification, order, category, type, sort. *What genus of mammal does the horse fall under?*

germ *n.* microbe, microorganisms, pathogen, (slang) bug, bacterium, virus. *Always wash your hands thoroughly to keep germs away.*

germane *adj.* pertinent, relevant, relating, connected, applicable, apropos. *Her comments about cats during our discussion of World War II were not germane.* **Ant.** irrelevant, unconnected.

germicide *n.* germ killer, antiseptic, disinfectant, bactericide, antibiotic. *All surfaces must be cleaned with a powerful germicide before surgery can be performed.*

germinate *vb.* grow, generate, sprout, develop flower. *An infinite number of seeds germinate in the spring.*

gestation *n.* pregnancy, incubation, development, maturation. *The gestation period for elephants is greater than that for humans.*

gesture *n.* **1.** sign, movement, signal, motion, indication. *At an art auction, buyers use hand gestures to make bids.* –*vb.* **2.** sign, wave, signal, motion, beckon. *The usher gestured for us to follow him.*

get *vb.* **1.** obtain, acquire, receive, attain, gain, secure. *She got an award for selling the most raffle tickets.* **2.** persuade, cause, induce, convince, influence. *How can I get you to change your mind?* **3.** become, turn, grow, begin go. *Public speaking gets easier as you practice it.* **4.** prepare, make, fix, do, ready. *He's getting dinner ready.* **5.** understand, realize, learn, comprehend, grasp, catch. *I didn't get the meaning of her story.* **6.** come, arrive, approach, reach, near. *When will we get there?* **Ant. 1.** lose, surrender, forfeit. **2.** dissuade, discourage, deter. **3.** remain, stay, continue. **5.** misunderstand, confuse, misinterpret. **6.** leave, go, depart.

geyser *n.* spout, gusher, fountain, jet, spring. *The geyser of super-heated water shot sixty feet in the air.*

ghastly *adj.* horrible, gruesome, hideous, terrible, dreadful, frightful. *She was frightened by the goblin's ghastly appearance.* **Ant.** beautiful, attractive, lovely.

ghetto *n.* slum, rundown quarter, inner city, blighted area. *The city tried to rejuvenate the ghetto with new investments.*

ghost *n.* **1.** phantom, specter, spirit, spook, shade, wraith. *That house is haunted by a ghost.* **2.** trace, suggestion, hint, shadow. *He doesn't have a ghost of a chance to win the race.*

ghostly *adj.* spectral, phantom, phantasmic, spooky, spiritual, supernatural. *I broke into a cold sweat when I saw a ghostly figure float across the room.*

ghoul *n.* grave robber, demon, fiend, devil, demon, evil spirit. *He decided to dress as a ghoul on Halloween.*

giant *adj.* **1.** huge, gigantic, enormous, monstrous, colossal, mammoth. *Tokyo is being attacked by a giant lizard.* –*n.* **2.** colossus, titan, behemoth, monster, ogre. *The sorcerer's treasure was guarded by a two-headed giant.* **Ant. 1.** tiny, small, miniature. **2.** dwarf, midget, pygmy.

gibberish *n.* blather, (slang) gobbledygook, drivel, nonsense, mumbo jumbo, gibber. *The hysterical woman was speaking gibberish, so we couldn't help her.*

giddy *adj.* lighthearted, lightheaded, dizzy, silly, flighty, (slang) ditzy, scatterbrained. *On Christmas Eve, the children are giddy with excitement.* **Ant.** sober, serious, somber.

gift *n.* **1.** present, offering, contribution, donation, grant. *She brought a gift to the birthday party.* **2.** talent, ability, aptitude, genius, flair, knack. *He has a gift for getting into trouble.*

gifted *adj.* talented, skilled, adept, capable, creative, inventive. *The talent contest featured many gifted performers.* **Ant.** untalented, unskilled, mediocre.

gig *n.* show, performance, date, engagement, appearance, concert. *The band has a gig tomorrow at nine o'clock.*

gigantic *adj.* giant, huge, enormous, monstrous, immense, colossal, titanic. *A gigantic spaceship hovered over the city.* **Ant.** small, tiny, little.

giggle *vb.* laugh, chuckle, titter, chortle, snicker, tee-hee. *During church services, she started to giggle uncontrollably.*

gimmick *n.* stunt, scheme, trick, angle, ruse, ploy. *Advertisers use various gimmicks to sell their products.*

gingerly *adv.* delicately, carefully, lightly, cautiously, guardedly. *The bomb technicians gingerly removed the timer mechanism.* **Ant.** roughly, heavily, awkwardly.

girl *n.* female, gal, lass, belle, mademoiselle, maiden, miss. *The girls like to play kickball, while the boys play football.*

gist *n.* essence, point, heart, sum, bottom line. *I don't want to hear trivia, just the gist of the story.*

give *vb.* **1.** provide, supply, present, bestow, grant, donate, furnish. *Her parents gave her a pony for her birthday.* **2.** yield, collapse, buckle, fail, loosen, slacken. *The bridge gave under the truck's weight.* **3.** allow, permit, grant, offer, allot, allocate. *Motor vehicles should always give the right-of-way to pedestrians.* **Ant. 1.** get, receive, take. **3.** deny, disallow, refuse.

gizmo *n.* gadget, apparatus, device, contraption, mechanism, widget. *He didn't know what the name of the tool was, so he called it a gizmo.*

glacier *n.* ice mass, snow mass, snow pack, ice pack, ice floe. *Glaciers sometimes carry natural cargoes of boulders for miles.*

WORD SEARCH

boulder pushed miles from its native area by: *erratic*
breaking away of large chunks: *calving*
deposit of rocks and gravel left by: *drift, till, drumlin, esker, kame, moraine*
floating in ocean, large chunk: *iceberg*
scratches in bedrock left by: *striations*
study of: *glaciology*

glad *adj.* happy, delighted, cheerful, pleased, joyful, elated. *I'm so glad you could come to my party.* **Ant.** sad, unhappy, upset, awful.

gladiator *n.* fighter, swordsman, combatant. *Gladiators often met with violent deaths.*

glamorous *adj.* attractive, exciting, alluring, enchanting, charming. *She thought becoming a fashion model would be glamorous.* **Ant.** dull, ordinary, tedious.

glamour *n.* appeal, charm, magnetism, star power, fascination, enchantment. *The fashion model always carried an aura of glamour.*

glance *vb.* **1.** look, scan, browse, peek, glimpse, peer. *He glanced at the calendar to check the time of his next appointment.* **2.** ricochet, reflect, bounce, rebound, skim. *The rock glanced off the wall and landed harmlessly on the ground.* *–n.* **3.** look, glimpse, squint, peek, peep. *She stole a quick glance at the boy sitting next to her.* **Ant. 1.** study, stare, examine. **3.** examination, scrutiny, inspection.

gland *n.* organ, body part, component, element. *The thymus, thyroid and pituitary are all glands.*

glare *vb.* **1.** stare, scowl, glower, frown, scrutinize. *Why is that rude man glaring at me?* **2.** shine, flare, blaze, flash, dazzle. *Bright sunlight glared off the snow.* *–n.* **3.** light, shine, brightness, glimmer, flash, brilliance. *Sunglasses will eliminate the glare.* **4.** stare, scowl, frown, glower, look. *The ogre's fierce glare told me that I was in trouble.*

glaring *adj.* **1.** flagrant, obvious, conspicuous, blatant, prominent. *The telephone company made a glaring error when they charged me $10,000 for a three-minute call to Idaho.* **2.** bright, brilliant, intense, blazing, strong. *She painted her car a glaring shade of red.* **Ant. 1.** inobvious, inconspicuous, hidden. **2.** soft, subdued.

glass *n.* tumbler, cup, cooler, highball, delmonico, cordial. *A delmonico is a tall glass holding about 10 ounces of fluid.*

glasses *n.* eyeglasses, spectacles, (slang) specs, corrective lenses, bifocals. *I can't see well without my glasses.*

glaze *n.* finish, coat, patina, luster, lacquer, varnish. *He polished the car until he could see his reflection in its glaze.*

gleam *n.* **1.** glimmer, shine, radiance, sparkle, reflection, glow. *His new car has a beautiful gleam.* *–vb.* **2.** shine, sparkle, glimmer, glow, glisten, beam, radiate. *A lantern gleamed from the far end of the corridor.*

glee *n.* joy, merriment, joyfulness, gladness, ecstasy. *The children shouted with glee when we told them we were going to the circus.* **Ant.** sadness, sorrow, dejection.

glib *adj.* facile, offhanded, shallow, superficial, quick, silver-tongued. *We knew by his glib comments that he had given little thought to the matter.* **Ant.** thoughtful, deep, profound.

glide *vb.* slide, flow, skim, coast, skate, float, slip, fly. *The sailboat glided gracefully over the water.* **Ant.** stagger, crawl, shuffle.

glimmer *n.* **1.** gleam, twinkling, glimmering, shimmer, flicker, flash. *All she could see of the retreating car was the glimmer of its rear lights.* **2.** hint, suggestion, trace, speck, inkling. *There was only a glimmer of hope that the crash victims survived.* *–vb.* **3.** twinkle, flicker, shine, sparkle, shimmer. *Stars glimmered in the night sky.*

glimpse *vb.* **1.** observe, witness, view, sight, spot, see. *We glimpsed a deer running through the forest.* *–n.* **2.** glance, peek, look, view, squint, peep. *She caught a glimpse of the burglar.* **Ant. 1.** stare, scrutinize.

glint *n.* sparkle, gleam, flash, glitter, scintillation. *Sarah has a beautiful glint in her eyes when she smiles.*

glisten *vb.* shine, glimmer, sparkle, gleam, glow, flash, twinkle. *Her wet hair glistened in the sunlight.*

glitch *n.* malfunction, error, mistake, (slang) bug, snag, snafu. *My computer had a major glitch so I had to reboot.*

glitter *vb.* **1.** sparkle, shine, glisten, glimmer, twinkle. *From the top of the hill we could see city lights glittering below.* *–n.* **2.** glamour, grandeur, splendor, excitement, thrill. *The farm boy left home to seek the glitter of Hollywood.*

glitz *n.* flash, showiness, gaudiness, garishness. *Its easy to be attracted by the glitz and glamour of Hollywood.*

gloat *vb.* bask, brag, revel, triumph, delight, wallow. *A good winner does not gloat over her victories* **Ant.** despair, regret, envy, grudge.

glob *n.* blob, mass, dollop, globule, gob, lump. *I dropped a glob of ice cream on my new shirt.*

global *adj.* worldwide, universal, international planetary, widespread. *The border dispute had global significance.* **Ant.** local, regional, limited.

globe *n.* **1.** ball, sphere, orb, spheroid, oval. *The Japanese use small glass globes as floats for their fishing nets.* **2.** Earth, planet, world, geosphere, land. *Ferdinand Magellan was the first person to sail around the globe.*

gloom *n.* **1.** sadness, unhappiness, misery, despair, dejection. *War has brought much gloom upon the Earth.* **2.** dimness, darkness, shade, shadow, murkiness. *The gloom of the cave was broken by the spelunker's lantern.* **Ant.** **1.** happiness, cheer, delight. **2.** light, brightness, brilliance.

gloomy *adj.* **1.** sad, unhappy, depressed, miserable, downcast, dismal, cheerless. *She has been in a gloomy mood since she lost the contest.* **2.** dreary, dark, murky, overcast, shadowy, dim, dull. *The poor lighting in the room created a gloomy atmosphere.* **Ant.** **1.** happy, cheerful, gay. **2.** bright, brilliant, sunny.

glorify *vb.* celebrate, exalt, honor, venerate, idolize, revere. *It's not a good idea to glorify money above all else.* **Ant.** disparage, disrespect, dishonor.

glorious *adj.* wonderful, splendid, marvelous, gorgeous, superb, beautiful. *It's a glorious day to go surfing.* **Ant.** awful, terrible, horrible.

glory *n.* **1.** honor, praise, fame, prestige, recognition. *The young police officer had dreams of glory.* **2.** grandeur, splendor, magnificence, elegance, majesty. *The full moon rose in a blaze of glory.* **Ant.** **1.** dishonor, disgrace, obscurity.

glossary *n.* lexicon, word list, vocabulary, dictionary, nomenclature. *When you need to know the meaning of a word, consult the book's glossary.*

glossy *adj.* shiny, shimmering, glowing, lustrous, glassy, gleaming. *Most magazines nowadays are printed on glossy paper.* **Ant.** dull, tarnished.

glow *vb.* **1.** shine, flicker, sparkle, glimmer, blaze, glare. *His secret decoder ring also glows in the dark.* *–n.* **2.** shine, light, brightness, gleam, shimmer, radiance. *The candle's glow was the only visible light.*

glower *vb.* scowl, frown, lower, glare, (slang) shoot a dirty look. *The boy was too angry to reason with, so we just let him glower at us from the corner.* **Ant.** grin, beam.

glowing *adj.* **1.** favorable, rave, passionate, enthusiastic, complimentary. *We received glowing reports on the work of our volunteers.* **2.** ruddy, vivid, bright, flushed. *I could tell the child was healthy by her glowing face.* **Ant.** **1.** critical, disapproving, condemning. **2.** pale, pallid, white.

glue *n.* **1.** adhesive, paste, cement, mucilage, mortar. *You need to add more glue if you want the picture to stick.* *–vb.* **2.** stick, paste, cement, affix, bind, fasten. *He glued the model airplane parts together.*

glum *adj.* dispirited, downhearted, gloomy, sad, sullen, morose. *Everyone sat around looking glum after the home team lost.* **Ant.** happy, cheerful, joyful.

glut *n.* **1.** surplus, excess, overload, oversupply, abundance. *A glut of fruit resulted in lower produce prices.* *–vb.* **2.** saturate, flood, fill, overload, stuff. *Holiday traffic glutted the freeways.* **Ant. 1.** scarcity, shortage, want.

glutton *n.* gourmand, (slang) pig, (slang) hog, overeater, epicure. *The glutton ate everything in sight but soon suffered an upset stomach.*

gnarled *adj.* knotty, knotted, twisted, contorted, distorted, crooked. *An old gnarled tree stood in the center of the cemetery.* **Ant.** straight, smooth, unblemished.

gnaw *vb.* chew, bite, nibble, champ, munch, eat. *The baby is teething so she loves to gnaw on things.*

gnome *n.* dwarf, fairy, pixie, elf. *The gnome of legend typically lives underground and guards a treasure.*

go *vb.* **1.** leave, depart, exit, withdraw, retire. *We need to be going very soon.* **2.** move, proceed, progress, advance, travel, approach. *Anyone want to go to a movie?* **3.** work, run, function, operate, perform, act. *How do you make this machine go?* **4.** reach, run, stretch, extend, expand. *This trail goes about ten miles to an abandoned mine.* **5.** fit, suit, agree, belong, conform, blend, harmonize. *Pickles and ice cream do not go together.* **Ant. 1.** stay, remain, arrive, return.

goad *vb.* urge, push, prod, incite, spur, provoke, exhort. *Don't let anyone goad you into doing something illegal.*

goal *n.* aim, purpose, object, objective, end, target, ambition. *It will be easier to succeed if you clearly define your goals.*

gobble *vb.* bolt, wolf, devour, cram, gorge, swallow whole. *Don't gobble your food or you might choke.*

goblin *n.* hobgoblin, bogeyman, spirit, imp, elf, ghost. *Watch out for ghosts and goblins on Halloween.*

god/God *n.* Supreme Being, the Almighty, the Creator, Lord, Holy Spirit, Jehovah, Allah. *There are many beliefs about the existence of God.*

WORD SEARCH

appearance by: *theophany*
cry of praise: *hosanna*
disbelief in: *atheism, nontheism*
God cannot be known, belief that: *agnosticism*
half god, half human: *demigod*
multiple gods, belief in: *polytheism*
one god, belief in only: *monotheism*
study of: *theology*
universe and its natural laws are God, belief that: *pantheism*

godforsaken *adj.* desolate, abandoned, forgotten, condemned, forlorn, wretched. *The godforsaken stretch of desert was as flat as a Euclidian plane.* **Ant.** blessed, cheerful.

godless *adj.* atheistic, nontheistic, impious, freethinking, agnostic, pagan, sacrilegious. *Godless people can be moral and ethical without necessarily believing in a higher power.* **Ant.** God-fearing, devout, pious.

godsend *n.* gift, blessing, windfall, manna, miracle, boon. *The farmer's bumper crop was a godsend.*

gold *adj.* yellow, gilt, honey, flaxen, auric, caramel, tawny. *Trees in New England turn red and gold every fall.*

gold digger *n.* parasite, user, leech, sponge, opportunist, exploiter. *The millionaire was worried about gold diggers befriending him only for his money.*

gold mine *n.* mother lode, bonanza, cash cow, goose that laid the golden egg. *During the 1990s, the personal computer market turned into a veritable gold mine.*

golf *n.* sport, pastime. *Let's go play eighteen holes of golf.*

WORD SEARCH

average number of shots for each hole, determined: *par*
clubs: *chipping iron, driver, mashie, niblick, putter, wood, wedge*
curving fairway: *dogleg*
curving shot: *hook, slice*
flag stick: *pin*
free shot granted in casual game: *Mulligan*
grounds: *course, fairway, green, links, putting green, rough*
helper: *caddy*
hole reached in one shot: *ace, hole in one*
long shot: *drive*
par, one stroke over: *bogey*
par, one stroke under: *birdie*
par, two strokes over: *double bogey*
par, two strokes under: *eagle*
pin, ball's launching: *tee*
sand hazard: *sand trap, bunker*
short shot, very: *putt*
turf hacked out by club: *divot*
warning, shouted: *fore!*

good *adj.* **1.** fine, excellent, pleasant, enjoyable, agreeable, nice. *Did you have a good time at the fair?* **2.** virtuous, kind, honorable, upright, honest, obedient, moral. *Santa Claus knows if you've been bad or good.* **3.** proper, suitable, fit, right, useful, adequate, capable. *A canoe is good for calm waters, but we'll need a raft for the rapids.* –*n.* **4.** benefit, welfare, advantage, interest, gain, success. *It is patriotic to work for the good of your country.* **5.** virtue, value, worth, merit, kindness. *There is a little good in everyone.* **Ant.** **1.** terrible, bad, unpleasant. **2.** bad, disobedient, naughty. **3.** improper, worthless, useless. **4.** loss, harm, disadvantage. **5.** evil, wickedness, corruption.

good-bye *n.* **1.** farewell, parting words. *We said our good-byes and left.* –*interj.* **2.** farewell, bye-bye, adios, adieu, aloha, ciao, hasta la vista, sayonara. *He shouted back, "Good-bye, Jim," and never returned.*

good-looking *adj.* attractive, beautiful, handsome, pretty, cute, becoming. *Kara is a really good-looking woman.* **Ant.** repulsive, ugly, gross.

good-natured *adj.* easygoing, amiable, nice, even-tempered, good-humored, pleasant. *The Labrador Retriever is a good-natured dog.* **Ant.** mean, cantankerous, prickly.

goodness *n.* virtue, wholesomeness, integrity, kindness, morality, good-heartedness. *You can count on the goodness of people to help out in an emergency.* **Ant.** immorality, evil, criminality.

goodwill *n.* kindness, humanitarianism, goodness, altruism, benevolence, amity. *The charity drive generated widespread goodwill.* **Ant.** cruelty, ill will, hostility.

goody-goody *adj.* prudish, prissy, uptight, Victorian, puritan, moral, correct. *It's hard to have fun when someone is acting goody-goody.* **Ant.** devilish, wild, immoral.

gooey *adj.* viscous, sticky, pasty, tacky, gelatinous, (slang) gloppy. *The sauce was too gooey, so we added more water.*

goofy *adj.* silly, foolish, childish, sophomoric, (slang) nerdy, dopey. *The goofy dance had the children giggling uncontrollably.* **Ant.** serious, uptight.

goon *n.* (slang) geek, lummox, freak, (slang) dork, weirdo. *Everyone called him a goon, but he was actually a nice guy.*

gore *n.* bloodshed, slaughter, carnage. *I don't care for movies with violence and gore.*

gorge *n.* **1.** canyon, ravine, crevice, abyss, chasm. *The wagon train could not find a way across the deep gorge. –vb.* **2.** stuff, glut, fill, cram, sate. *I have a stomachache because I gorged myself during dinner.*

gorgeous *adj.* beautiful, pretty, lovely, attractive, stunning, glorious, splendid. *The hills are gorgeous when the leaves turn gold in autumn.* **Ant.** ugly, drab, plain.

gorilla *n.* great ape, primate, simian, mammal, beast, creature. *Gorillas are social animals that are very similar to human beings.*

gory *adj.* bloody, sanguine, bloodstained, blood-drenched, violent, homicidal, murderous. *I don't allow my children to see gory movies.*

gospel *n.* truth, God's word, fact, reality, chapter and verse. *According to gospel, it is always better to forgive.*

gossamer *n.* Something diaphanous, airy, delicate, fine, or feathery. *She wore a dress as thin as gossamer.*

gossip *n.* **1.** rumor, hearsay, chatter, babble, talk. *Movie stars must get tired of all the gossip about them.* **2.** gossiper, tattler, snoop, meddler, chatterbox, busybody. *Don't believe anything a gossip tells you. –vb.* **3.** talk, tattle, prattle, blab, chatter, babble. *I have better things to do than to sit around and gossip.*

gouge *vb.* **1.** scratch, scrape, excavate, scoop out. *The toddler tried to gouge a hole in the cake frosting. –n.* **2.** hole, scratch, excavation, groove, gash, furrow. *We found a gouge the size of a toddler's thumb in the cake frosting.*

gourmet *n.* epicure, epicurean, connoisseur, gourmand, gastronome, bon vivant. *She was a gourmet with discriminating tastes.*

govern *vb.* manage, direct, lead, control, run, guide, supervise, regulate. *Our weekly meetings are governed by the club president.* **Ant.** follow, comply, obey.

government *n.* administration, management, control, regulation, rule, guidance. *In a democracy government is controlled by the people.*

WORD SEARCH

absence of, complete: *anarchy*
authoritarian: *totalitarianism*
betrayal of one's own: *treason*
citizens in charge of: *commonwealth, democracy, republic*
clergy, headed by: *hierocracy, theocracy*
dictated by one ruler or small group: *dictatorship, despotism, tyranny*
female: *matriarchy*
independence from others: *sovereignty*
king's: *monarchy*
male: *patriarchy*
military: *martial state*
privileged class, by: *aristocracy*
secret police, controlled by: *police state*
seizure of: *coup d'état*
self-governing: *autonomous*

governor *n.* director, administrator, head, chief, ruler, leader, commander. *The governor of Maine will give a speech today.*

gown *n.* dress, apparel, attire, frock, garment. *She bought a new gown for the formal dinner party.*

grab *vb.* **1.** grasp, seize, grip, clutch, clasp, hold, take. *He grabbed his child's arm and pulled her back to the curb. –n.* **2.** grasp, lunge, pass, clutch, seizure. *She made a grab for the frog, but it hopped away.* **Ant. 1.** release, free, loose.

grace *n.* **1.** charm, elegance, gracefulness, culture, refinement, manners. *The hostess handled the uninvited guest with grace.* **2.** mercy, charity, pardon, forgiveness, leniency. *The criminal was freed by the grace of the empress.* –*vb.* **3.** honor, dignify, glorify, exalt, favor. *The club's founder graced the banquet with his presence.* **4.** adorn, embellish, enrich, beautify, ornament, decorate. *We graced the funeral site with flowers.* **Ant.** **1.** clumsiness, crudeness, coarseness. **2.** cruelty, harshness, disfavor. **3.** dishonor, shame, insult.

graceful *adj.* elegant, limber, lovely, beautiful, delicate. *Ballet dancers are very graceful.* **Ant.** clumsy, awkward, graceless.

gracious *adj.* kind, courteous, polite, friendly, cordial, genial. *Her gracious manners were appreciated by the guests.* **Ant.** haughty, unkind, cool.

grade *n.* **1.** incline, slope, ramp, slant, tilt. *The cross-country skier found the steep grade to be tough going.* **2.** category, type, class, degree, level, step, group. *Crossword puzzles are often classified into grades of difficulty.* –*vb.* **3.** order, classify, rank, sort, class, evaluate, arrange. *The judges graded the contestants according to their talent and creativity.*

gradual *adj.* slow, moderate, steady, measured, continual, continuous. *The tide's gradual advancement eventually destroyed the sand castle.* **Ant.** sudden, instant, abrupt.

graduate *vb.* **1.** finish, complete, succeed, prevail, promote. *After four years of college, I finally graduate this semester.* **2.** calibrate, mark, score, measure, grade. *This thermometer is graduated in centigrade degrees.* –*n.* **3.** alumnus, alumna, bachelor, fellow. *She is a recent law-school graduate.* **Ant.** **1.** fail, flunk, drop out.

graffiti *n.* defacement, slogans, graphics, epigrams, scribbles. *The store owner had to clean the graffiti off his walls with a sandblaster.*

graft *n.* **1.** join, implant, transplant, set, inset, splice. *The botanist grafted two different plants together.* –*n.* **2.** transplant, implant, inset, insert. *His burned arm was treated with a skin graft.* **3.** corruption, bribery, fraud, theft, cheating, extortion. *The new governor's first priority is to eliminate political graft.*

grammar *n.* composition, language, structure, syntax, semantics, sentence construction. *When making a point, whether in a speech or in print, always use good grammar.*

grand *adj.* **1.** royal, majestic, stately, impressive, magnificent. *She lives in a grand mansion in Beverly Hills.* **2.** total, complete, full, comprehensive, final. *The grand total of his prize was twenty thousand dollars.* **3.** fine, good, wonderful, great, superb, marvelous. *They had a grand time at the picnic.* **Ant.** **1.** mediocre, inferior, unimpressive. **2.** partial, incomplete, fractional. **3.** bad, awful, terrible.

grandeur *n.* splendor, majesty, glory, magnificence, resplendence. *The backpackers delighted in the grandeur of the wilderness.* **Ant.** plainness, squalor, commonness.

grandiose *adj.* great, grand, magnificent, impressive, theatrical, pompous. *His grandiose manner of speaking was too affected for our tastes.* **Ant.** understated, subdued, modest.

grandstand *n.* stands, bleachers, seating, box seats, decking. *Every available space in the grandstand was taken up by fans.*

grant *vb.* **1.** allow, permit, give, sanction, award, bestow, present. *A genie granted three wishes to the poor fisherman.* **2.** concede, allow, accept, concur, admit, agree. *He finally granted that my conclusions were correct.* –*n.* **3.** allotment, award, allowance, bequest, endowment, gift. *The researcher needs a grant if she is to continue her studies.* **Ant.** **1.** disallow, deny, refuse. **2.** reject, dispute, deny.

graphic *adj.* vivid, lifelike, realistic, explicit, descriptive, striking, detailed. *They gave the movie an R rating for its graphic violence.* **Ant.** vague, understated.

grapple *vb.* contend, struggle, battle, cope, deal. *I don't feel like grappling with unhappy customers today.*

grasp *vb.* **1.** seize, grab, clutch, grip, catch, hold. *She grasped at her toy boat as it floated down the creek.* **2.** understand, perceive, comprehend, see, follow. *I can't seem to grasp the meaning of your story.* –*n.* **3.** hold, reach, possession, grip, clasp. *The football was almost in my grasp.* **4.** understanding, perception, knowledge, sense. *My grasp of Latin is very poor.* **Ant.** **1.** release, free, loose. **2.** misunderstand, confuse, misjudge.

grass *n.* turf, lawn, sward, meadow, pasture, green, fescue, timothy. *I mow the grass every Saturday.*

grateful *adj.* thankful, indebted, pleased, gratified, appreciative. *She was grateful for the cool weather.* **Ant.** ungrateful, thankless, unappreciative.

gratify *vb.* please, satisfy, delight, content, charm. *I was gratified with my test results.* **Ant.** disappoint, displease, dissatisfy.

grating *adj.* harsh, jarring, strident, grinding, rasping, scraping. *We all cringed when a loud, grating noise echoed up from the street.*

gratitude *n.* thanks, thankfulness, appreciation, gratefulness. *I wish to express my gratitude for your help.* **Ant.** ingratitude, ungratefulness.

gratuitous *adj.* unnecessary, for show, unjustified, needless, inessential, superfluous. *The movie was filled with gratuitous scenes of violence.* **Ant.** necessary, justified, needed.

gratuity *n.* tip, bonus, reward, gift, offering, extra. *It's customary to leave a modest gratuity for the waiter.*

grave *n.* **1.** tomb, crypt, plot, vault, mausoleum. *The vampire rose from his grave.* –*adj.* **2.** serious, thoughtful, solemn, somber, earnest. *The librarian gave me a grave look that meant "Be quiet and study."* **3.** urgent, important, critical, crucial, vital, severe. *Pollution of the Earth is of grave concern to all.* **Ant.** **2.** playful, merry, gay. **3.** unimportant, trivial, minor.

graveyard *n.* cemetery, necropolis, (slang) boneyard, burial ground, city of the dead, memorial grounds. *There is no spookier place than a graveyard at midnight.*

gravity *n.* **1.** force, pull, weight, gravitational pull, pressure, attraction. *In general, the larger the celestial body, the stronger its gravity.* **2.** seriousness, weight, importance, magnitude, significance, enormity. *We were all struck by the gravity of the riot.* **Ant.** insignificance, triviality.

gravy *n.* drippings, sauce, natural juices. *This potato is great with a little gravy poured over it.*

gray *adj.* ash, leaden, silvery, smoky, stone, slate, battleship gray. *I hate gray, overcast days.*

graze *vb.* **1.** feed, browse, eat, pasture. *Cows were grazing in the meadow.* **2.** brush, glance, rub, scrape, scratch, skim. *Branches grazed his arms as he ran through the forest.*

grease *n.* **1.** oil, fat, lard, lubricant, ointment, salve. *She doesn't like foods that have a lot of grease.* –*vb.* **2.** oil, lubricate, anoint, daub, smear. *You need to grease your bike chain.*

greasy *adj.* oily, slippery, fatty, oleaginous, unctuous, waxy. *Our local diner tends to serve only greasy food.*

great *adj.* **1.** big, large, huge, enormous, immense, vast, tremendous. *Buffalo used to* *travel in great herds across the plains.* **2.** important, remarkable, outstanding, famous, notable, prominent. *We should learn about the great leaders of our country.* **3.** chief, primary, leading, important, major, principal. *One of the great concerns of the people is the rising crime rate.* **Ant. 1.** small, tiny, meager. **2** unimportant, trivial, unremarkable. **3.** minor, lesser, secondary.

greatly *adv.* tremendously, immensely, enormously, vastly, largely. *I greatly appreciate your help.* **Ant.** little, somewhat.

greed *n.* hunger, craving, avarice, greediness, desire. *Greed for gold destroyed the two miners' friendship.* **Ant.** unselfishness, generosity, charity.

greedy *adj.* selfish, grasping, avaricious, miserly, desirous. *Don't be so greedy and give me some of your cake.* **Ant.** unselfish, generous, charitable.

green *adj.* emerald, kelly, aquamarine, leaf, pea, moss, sea green, beryl, grass. *In spring, the grass turns a lush green.*

greet *vb.* welcome, receive, meet, address, accept, hail. *Tourists in Hawaii are greeted by girls wearing leis.* **Ant.** ignore, neglect, shun.

greeting *n.* salutation, hello, acknowledgement, hail, nod, salute. *A friendly greeting always makes one feel welcome.*

gregarious *adj.* friendly, social, personable, outgoing, extroverted, affable. *People in sales are often gregarious.* **Ant.** Aloof, reserved, shy.

gridlock *n.* knot, entanglement, jam, impasse, logjam, block, obstruction. *So many people disagree on this issue, I expect to have a gridlock when we vote.*

grief *n.* sorrow, sadness, distress, misery, agony, anguish, despair. *The beggar's life was one of much grief.* **Ant.** happiness, joy, bliss.

grief-stricken *adj.* despairing, desolate, in mourning, heartsick, heartbroken, anguished. *Sandy was grief-stricken for months after her dog died.*

grievance *n.* complaint, gripe, bone to pick, ax to grind, wrong, objection, problem. *If you have a grievance with the food, tell the chef.*

grieve *vb.* **1.** mourn, weep, lament, bemoan, deplore. *He grieved the death of his friend.* **2.** distress, sorrow, sadden, depress, dishearten. *It grieves me that nations cannot live peacefully together.* **Ant. 1.** praise, celebrate, rejoice. **2.** delight, comfort, please.

grievous *adj.* dreadful, horrible, shameful, painful, unfortunate, tragic. *The assassination of President Kennedy was a grievous incident in American history.* **Ant.** pleasant, happy, joyous.

grill *vb.* **1.** interrogate, examine, question, quiz. *I wish my parents wouldn't grill me about where I've been.* **2.** barbecue, broil, cook, sear, fry. *She grilled the steak over a charcoal fire.*

grim *adj.* **1.** severe, harsh, stern, cold, hard, forbidding. *The grim-looking border guard asked to see my passport.* **2.** ghastly, sinister, horrible, terrible, grisly, gruesome. *The pile of bones in the werewolf's den left a grim impression on its discoverer.* **Ant. 1.** kind, merciful, gentle. **2.** pleasing, pleasant, cheerful.

grime *n.* dirt, filth, soil, mess, dust. *He hosed the grime off the sidewalk.*

grimy *adj.* Filthy, dirty, dingy, smudged, grubby, sooty, muddy. *Don't even think about eating dinner with those grimy hands.* **Ant.** clean, sparkling, immaculate.

grin *vb.* **1.** smile, beam, smirk, laugh. *She grinned at the chipmunk's antics.* –*n.* **2.** smile, smirk, beam, simper. *Wipe that silly grin off your face.* **Ant. 1.** frown, snarl, scowl. **2.** frown, sneer, grimace.

grind *vb.* **1.** sharpen, whet, smooth, polish, file. *The swashbuckler's sword was ground to a sharp edge.* **2.** crush, crumble, pulverize, crunch, pound. *The giant was grinding rocks into powder with his bare hands.* *–n.* **3.** toil, bore, tedium, drudgery, labor. *This job has become a real grind.* **Ant. 3.** joy, pleasure, amusement.

grip *vb.* **1.** hold, clasp, grasp, clutch, clench, grab. *The softball player gripped her bat tightly.* **2.** hold, attract, retain, enthrall, fascinate. *I'm impressed by a movie that grips the viewer's interest till the end.* *–n.* **3.** hold, grasp, clutch, clinch, clasp, control. *She had a pretty tight grip on the rope.* **Ant. 1.** release, free, loose. **2.** lose, repel, bore.

gripe *n.* **1.** complaint, peeve, grievance, protest, lament. *The chef was tired of the customers' gripes about her cooking.* *–vb.* **2.** complain, grumble, fuss, grouch, whine, protest, mutter. *He was always griping about his problems.* **Ant. 1.** praise, complaint, compliment, flattery. **2.** approve, flatter, praise.

grisly *adj.* gruesome, grim, shocking, hideous, horrid, horrible, frightful. *His grisly zombie costume won first prize at the Halloween party.* **Ant.** pleasant, handsome, pretty.

grit *vb.* **1.** clench, gnash, grind, grate, scrape. *She gritted her teeth and ignored the insults.* *–n.* **2.** dirt, sand, gravel, dust, soot. *The sandstorm left tons of grit all over the house.* **3.** guts, nerve, spunk, courage, pluck, spirit, fortitude. *The early American pioneers had a lot of grit.* **Ant. 3.** cowardice, meekness, timidity.

groan *vb.* **1.** moan, complain, sob, mumble, grumble, whimper. *She groaned when she saw the poor condition of her house.* *–n.* **2.** whine, wail, moan, whimper, cry. *We heard a mysterious groan come from behind the bushes.*

groggy *adj.* dazed, shaky, unsteady, muddled, confused, dizzy, sleepy. *She usually feels a little groggy in the mornings.* **Ant.** alert, awake, sharp.

groom *vb.* **1.** brush, clean, preen, comb, spruce. *He took his dog to the pet shop to be groomed.* **2.** train, prepare, coach, develop, educate. *The new worker is being groomed for a management position.*

groove *n.* **1.** rut, trench, channel, furrow, slot. *A phonograph needle follows the groove on a record.* **2.** habit, routine, rut, custom, pace. *I slowly got into the groove of working on an assembly line.*

grope *vb.* probe, fumble, feel, search, hunt, flounder. *He groped in the grass for his lost contact lens.*

gross *adj.* **1.** total, entire, whole, complete. *What is the gross profit of your business?* **2.** rude, coarse, improper, crude, obscene, vulgar, indecent. *No one is impressed by gross language.* **3.** outrageous, glaring, extreme, complete, flagrant. *Did you really expect to get away with such a gross violation of the rules?* **Ant. 1.** net, partial, limited. **2.** proper, clean, decent. **3.** vague, obscure, minor.

grotesque *adj.* bizarre, queer, weird, strange, freakish, fantastic, unnatural. *A grotesque gargoyle flew into the village.* **Ant.** normal, ordinary, routine.

grouch *n.* grump, (slang) sourpuss, complainer, grumbler, crab, (slang) bear. *I'm a grouch until I have my first cup of coffee.*

grouchy *adj.* grumpy, cross, testy, irritable, surly, sulky. *My coach gets grouchy when we lose.* **Ant.** cheerful, agreeable, pleasant.

ground *n.* **1.** land, earth, soil, turf, dirt, terrain. *She was relieved when the plane finally landed on the ground.* **2.** field, area, region, territory, property. *Traveling salesmen have to cover a lot of ground.* **3.** basis, reason, foundation, rationale, motive, cause. *Do you have grounds for your action?*

groundbreaking *adj.* pioneering, trailblazing, innovating, cutting edge, spearheading. *The doctor was noted for his groundbreaking work in cancer prevention.* **Ant.** old, used, antiquated.

groundless *adj.* baseless, unsupported, unfounded, conjectural, unjustified. *The detective's suspicions proved groundless when the suspect's alibi was verified.* **Ant.** supported, proven, factual.

grounds *n.* **1.** property, estate, land, acreage, area, lot. *The guard patrolled the perimeter of the grounds every hour.* **2.** basis, rationale, reason, cause, motive. *Physical abuse is grounds for divorce.*

groundswell *n.* uprising, surge, wave, tsunami, rush, force to be reckoned with. *The environmental movement has received a groundswell of support.*

group *n.* **1.** collection, gathering, assembly, bunch, crowd, batch, band. *A small group of people gathered around the campfire.* **2.** set, category, division, class, branch. *Swedish, Danish and German are all part of the Indo-European language group.* –*vb.* **3.** classify, collect, sort, arrange, organize, gather, assemble. *We grouped the test results according to their final scores.* **Ant.** **3.** separate, divide, disperse.

grove *n.* thicket, copse, stand, orchard, woods. *There's a grove of oak trees near our house.*

grovel *vb.* cringe, cower, fawn, stoop, kowtow. *The slave groveled in the presence of his master.*

grow *vb.* **1.** develop, expand, extend, enlarge, increase. *The dragon grew to an enormous size.* **2.** cultivate, breed, raise, tend, produce, nurture. *My mother grows tomatoes in our garden.* **3.** turn, become, wax, develop, get. *My sick friend is growing stronger every day.* **Ant.** **1.** shrink, decrease, lessen.

growl *vb.* snarl, rumble, grumble, give a guttural warning, gnarl. *The dog tended to growl at everyone who approached.*

growth *n.* development, increase, growing, progress, expansion, advancement. *The doctor kept a chart of the child's growth.* **Ant.** decline, decrease, regression.

grubby *adj.* dirty, grimy, filthy, soiled, mud-stained, (slang) grungy. *You can't prepare dinner with grubby hands.* **Ant.** clean, sparkling, immaculate.

grudge *n.* **1.** resentment, bitterness, spite, malice, ill will. *She's held a grudge against him ever since he beat her in checkers.* –*vb.* **2.** begrudge, resent, envy, refuse, deny. *You shouldn't grudge her small victory.* **Ant.** **1.** liking, goodwill, friendliness. **2.** allow, accept, celebrate.

grueling *adj.* difficult, hard, strenuous, tiring, exhausting, taxing, trying. *The last mile of the race was a grueling uphill run.* **Ant.** easy, light, effortless.

gruesome *adj.* ugly, hideous, horrible, horrid, frightening, scary, repulsive. *The Phantom of the Opera removed his mask to reveal a gruesome face.* **Ant.** beautiful, handsome, pleasing.

gruff *adj.* surly, grumpy, rude, crude, abrupt, blunt, coarse, rough. *The waiter's gruff manner ruined our dinner party.* **Ant.** polite, pleasant, civil, friendly.

grumble *vb.* complain, gripe, fuss, protest, growl, mutter, grouch. *He grumbled about the high price of our theater tickets.* **Ant.** praise, compliment, applaud.

grump *n.* grouch, griper, complainer, whiner, (slang) bear, (slang) crab, (slang) sourpuss. *I'm usually a grump in the morning, so leave me alone.*

grumpy *adj.* grouchy, crabby, cranky, irritable, surly, moody, testy. *Goldilocks met three grumpy bears.* **Ant.** pleasant, cheerful, sweet.

grungy *adj.* dirty, grimy, dingy, unclean, messy, (slang) scuzzy. *My clothes get grungy after working in the garden.* **Ant.** clean, sparkling, shining.

guarantee *n.* **1.** warranty, promise, pledge, assure, insurance, commitment. *Our flying carpets come with a six-month guarantee.* *–vb.* **2.** promise, pledge, assure, insure, certify, warrant, vouch. *I guarantee there will be no charge for repairs.*

guarantor *n.* insurer, backer, sponsor, underwriter, bondsman, warrantor. *As a co-signer on the loan, my wife is serving as a guarantor.*

guard *vb.* **1.** protect, defend, watch, shield, patrol, oversee. *The loyal dog guarded his master's property.* *–n.* **2.** sentry, watchman, sentinel, protector, defender, guardian. *A guard was appointed to watch the queen's jewelry.*

guarded *adj.* defensive, cautious, discreet, careful, restrained. *The old prospector was guarded about the location of his gold mine.* **Ant.** open, frank, careless.

guardian *n.* protector, trustee, custodian, caretaker, warden, keeper. *Cinderella's stepmother was a terrible guardian.* **Ant.** foe, enemy, opponent.

guerrilla *n.* bush fighter, resistance fighter, soldier, freedom fighter, warrior, mercenary. *An army of guerrillas are hiding out deep in the mountains.*

guess *vb.* **1.** assume, suppose, think, estimate, believe, imagine. *I guess the meeting will start late.* *–n.* **2.** estimate, opinion, assumption, notion, theory. *Your guess is as good as mine.* **Ant. 1.** know, prove, see. **2.** fact, truth, actuality.

guest *n.* visitor, caller, patron, customer, company. *We will be having some guests for dinner.* **Ant.** host, hostess.

guidance *n.* counseling, advice, mentoring, direction, counsel, instruction, help. *If you lose your way, ask a teacher for guidance.*

guide *vb.* **1.** lead, direct, conduct, escort, accompany, steer, pilot. *Sacagawea guided the Lewis and Clark expedition.* *–n.* **2.** escort, conductor, director, pilot, leader. *We hired a guide to take us through the caves.* **3.** example, model, pattern, sign, beacon, directory. *She used my dress as a guide for making hers.* **Ant. 1.** follow, misguide, mislead.

guidebook *n.* handbook, manual, field guide, how-to book, bible, tome. *The guidebook featured illustrations of the constellations.*

guideline *n.* direction, indication, instruction, rule, code, key. *Be sure to follow the guidelines carefully.*

guild *n.* association, club, group, union, federation, fraternity, sorority. *Writers belonging to a guild enjoy many benefits.*

guile *n.* trickery, trickiness, cunning, deception, deceit, slyness. *The thief used guile to steal the woman's jewels.* **Ant.** honesty, sincerity, truthfulness.

guilt *n.* **1.** fault, sin, offense, crime, misdeed, misbehavior, misconduct. *The criminal refused to admit her guilt.* **2.** shame, disgrace, dishonor, humiliation, blame, wrong. *He felt guilt over the way he treated his neighbor.* **Ant. 1.** innocence, sinlessness, honesty. **2.** honor, pride, esteem.

guilty *adj.* **1.** criminal, illegal, accountable, responsible, culpable. *The defendant was found guilty.* **2.** ashamed, regretful, sorry, shameful, sheepish. *If you didn't lie, then why do you look so guilty?* **Ant. 1.** innocent, guiltless, blameless. **2.** proud, noble, satisfied.

guinea pig *n.* test subject, testee, examinee, rodent, lab animal, cavvy. *It's best to avoid being a guinea pig and wait several years before trying an experimental drug.*

guise *n.* facade, cover, semblance, appearance, form, mode. *The spy was operating under the guise of an innocent librarian.*

guitar *n.* musical instrument, acoustic, six-string, twelve-string, (slang) axe, electric guitar. *I want to learn how to play bass guitar.*

WORD SEARCH

acoustic steel guitar: *Dobro*
Appalachian version played on lap: *dulcimer, zither*
country twanger: *banjo*
country whiner mounted on legs, electric: *steel guitar*
East Indian version with very long neck: *sitar*
four-string, low-sounding: *bass guitar*
Hawaiian with nasal tone: *Hawaiian guitar*
Japanese: *koto*
middle ages version: *lute*
small four-string: *mandolin*
tiny: *ukulele*

gulch *n.* valley, trench, wash, arroyo, channel, ravine, gully. *We lived on the banks of a gulch through which whitewater flowed.*

gulf *n.* **1.** bay, estuary, fjord, cove, lagoon. *Let's go sailing in the gulf.* **2.** gap, abyss, rift, space, distance. *There's a large gulf between developed and undeveloped nations.*

gullible *adj.* naive, innocent, trustful, trusting, unsuspecting, easy. *The little girl was so gullible, she believed that the Moon is really made out of cheese.* **Ant.** skeptical, suspicious, cynical.

gully *n.* ravine, defile, gorge, channel, furrow, trench. *Erosion formed small gullies on the hillside.*

gulp *vb.* **1.** swallow, swill, guzzle, bolt, wolf. *The dog gulped down its dinner.* –*n.* **2.** swallow, swig, mouthful, sip, dose. *She felt better after taking several large gulps of water.*

gummy *adj.* sticky, gooey, chewy, viscid, tacky. *My foot stuck to the floor because some kind of gummy substance was on my shoe.*

gun *n.* firearm, revolver, pistol, rifle, shotgun, weapon. *A gun should always be locked and kept away from children.*

WORD SEARCH

ammunition holder: *clip, cylinder, magazine*
back explosion: *backfire*
barrel end: *muzzle*
case: *holster*
locking mechanism: *safety*

gunfire *n.* gunshot, discharge, shot, detonation, volley, fusillade. *We called the police after we heard gunfire coming from the alley.*

gung ho *adj.* enthusiastic, eager, ardent, fanatical, (slang) psyched, fired up. *The boss likes his employees to exhibit gung go behavior, whether they're tired or not.* **Ant.** unenthused, apathetic, bored.

gurgle *vb.* burble, bubble, ripple, murmur, trickle, tinkle. *I like to listen to the rain gurgle down the gutters.*

guru *n.* mentor, teacher, guide, master, spiritual leader, maharishi. *The guru taught his students well and was much revered.*

gush *vb.* spurt, flood, spew, surge, jet, stream. *We watched the water gush out of the broken pipe.*

gust *n.* blast, outburst, burst, flurry, puff, rush, draft. *His hat was blown away by a gust of wind.*

gusto *n.* zest, relish, pleasure, enjoyment, exhilaration, enthusiasm. *Grandfather always approached hard work with gusto.* **Ant.** dread, apathy, boredom.

gutless *adj.* cowardly, timid, fainthearted, spineless, weak, fearful. *You can't be gutless and fight in a war.* **Ant.** brave, bold, intrepid.

guts *n.* courage, bravery, nerve, backbone, spunk, boldness. *You have to have guts to parachute out of an airplane.* **Ant.** fear, cowardice, timidity.

gutsy *adj.* brave, courageous, plucky, spunky, bold, intrepid. *Mary is gutsy for trying parasailing during a storm.* **Ant.** cowardly, timid, gutless.

gutter *n.* sewer, drain, ditch, trough, channel. *She swept the fallen leaves out of the gutter.*

guy *n.* man, male, boy, (slang) dude, gentleman, fellow, chap. *Einstein was a guy who liked to use his head.*

guzzle *vb.* swig, gulp, quaff, (slang) chug-a-lug, tipple, (slang) down. *Don't guzzle your soda or you might choke.*

gym *n.* gymnasium, fitness center, court, workout facility, arena, hall. *Let's go down to the gym and play basketball.*

gymnastics *n.* athletics, acrobatics, tumbling, vaulting, exercises, somersaults. *You must be exceptionally coordinated to excel in gymnastics.*

gyp *vb.* rip off, swindle, scam, bilk, rook, bamboozle. *The con artist tried to gyp me into buying a fake Rolex watch.*

gypsy *n.* wanderer, nomad, drifter, vagabond, rover, Bohemian. *The gypsy traveled from town to town, making money telling fortunes.*

gyrate *vb.* revolve, spin, whirl, rotate, spiral, go around, circle. *We watched the top gyrate for two full minutes.*

H

habit *n.* practice, custom, routine, tendency, trait, ritual. *She has a habit of always interrupting me.*

habitat *n.* home, environment, terrain, biosphere, realm, range, ecosystem. *The natural habitats of many wild animals are vanishing.*

habitation *n.* home, residence, dwelling, house, housing, lodging. *The traditional habitation of the Eskimo is called an igloo.*

habitual *adj.* customary, usual, routine, regular, normal. *He can't get started in the morning without his habitual cup of coffee.* **Ant.** occasional, rare, uncommon.

habituated *adj.* accustomed, familiar, acclimated, insured, adapted, hardened. *It takes a while to become habituated to the culture of another country.*

hacienda *n.* estate, mansion, house, plantation, ranch. *We stayed overnight at my uncle's hacienda.*

hack *vb.* chop, cut, axe, split, slash, gash, slice, mangle. *Soldiers hacked their way through the thick jungle.*

hacker *n.* computer programmer, (slang) computer wiz, (slang) cracker, (slang) cyber punk. *The company hired a hacker to de-bug its computer programs.*

hackneyed *adj.* trite, clichéd, unoriginal, pedestrian, banal, stock. *The teacher criticized the student's hackneyed writing.* **Ant.** original, fresh, imaginative.

hag *n.* witch, crone, virago, shrew, harridan, ogress. *On Halloween, we dressed up as old hags and scared everyone away.*

haggard *adj.* weary, worn, gaunt, drawn, pale, fatigued, tried. *She looked haggard after her long hike through the desert.* **Ant.** refreshed, energetic, robust.

haggle *vb.* argue, quarrel, bicker, dispute, disagree. *They're constantly, haggling over whose turn it is to use the computer.*

hail *vb.* **1.** call, summon, signal, flag, shout at. *She hailed a taxi.* **2.** greet, welcome, acclaim, cheer, applaud. *Everyone hailed the good news from the peace conference.* **Ant. 2.** ignore, disregard, condemn.

hair *n.* locks, mane, curls, tress, strands, (slang) do. *Comb your hair before going to school.*

WORD SEARCH

back comb: *tease*
braid: *plait, cue, pigtail, fishbone braid, French braid*
braided rows close to scalp: *cornrows*
curl: *corkscrew, ringlet*
curls, styled with: *perm, permed*
curly like a poodle: *poodle cut*
fake: *toupee, wig*
hairy, abnormally: *hirsute*

Jamaican braids: *dreadlocks*
knot: *bob, bun, chignon*
1980s and 90s cut, short on sides, very long in back: *mullet*
pile of the 1950s, high: *beehive*
point of hair tapering to forehead: *widow's peak*
puffy, African-American style of the '70s: *Afro*
punk: *mohawk, porcupine, spiked*
remover: *depilatory, electrolysis*
short cut, women's: *bob*
straight cut with bangs: *pageboy*
sweep of hair combed back from forehead: *pompadour*
very short, men's: *buzz, crew cut, flattop.*
unruly tuft: *cowlick*

hairdresser *n.* hair stylist, barber, hair cutter, beautician, coiffeur. *I have an appointment with the hairdresser at one o'clock.*

hair-raising *adj.* terrifying, frightening, horrifying, spine-tingling, shocking, petrifying. *Rollercoaster rides are becoming more and more hair-raising.* **Ant.** *soothing, calming, soporific.*

hairy *adj.* hirsute, shaggy, fuzzy, furry, woolly, bushy, downy. *Collies are hairy dogs that must be shaved in summer to help keep them cool.* **Ant.** bald, hairless, glabrous.

halcyon *adj.* tranquil, serene, peaceful, untroubled, calm, relaxed. *We spent the afternoon by the brook fishing in halcyon contentment.* **Ant.** troubled, agitated, anxious.

hale *adj.* healthy, robust, hearty, fit, sound, well. *It's a pleasure to see you looking so hale again.* **Ant.** unhealthy, sick, weak.

halfhearted *adj.* lukewarm, cool, indifferent, passive, apathetic, lackluster, unenthusiastic. *His halfhearted attempt at the long jump failed to qualify him for the finals.* **Ant.** wholehearted, enthusiastic, eager.

halitosis *n.* bad breath, (slang) dragon breath, foul breath, offensive breath, (slang) garbage breath. *An old-fashioned remedy for halitosis is to chew on mint leaves.*

hall *n.* hallway, corridor, foyer, passageway, walkway, gallery. *Please remove your coat and shoes in the hall.*

hallmark *n.* characteristic, sign, indicator, symbol, stamp, badge. *The hallmark of a talented basketball guard is ball-handling skill.*

hallowed *adj.* sacred, holy, consecrated, blessed, sanctified, dedicated. *The evil demon could not enter hallowed grounds.* **Ant.** profane, secular, unholy, unsanctified.

hallucination *n.* delusion, illusion, mirage, vision, fantasy, dream, apparition. *Her hallucinations were caused by illness.*

WORD SEARCH
alcoholic's: *delirium tremens*
amputee's false sensation of lost limb: *phantom limb pain*
causes, anything that: *hallucinogen*
crosses senses: *synesthesia*
odor: *phantosmia*

halo *n.* nimbus, aureole, glory, radiance, ring, circle. *The Moon sometimes has a halo around it, which is actually an optical illusion caused by ice crystals in the Earth's atmosphere.*

halt *vb.* **1.** stop, cease, wait, desist, pause, hold, quit. *Traffic halted to let the ducklings cross the road.* *–n.* **2.** stop, end, finish, discontinuance, close, standstill, termination. *Let's put a halt to senseless violence.* **Ant. 1.** continue, proceed, start. **2.** beginning, start, resumption.

halve *vb.* divide, cut in two, bisect. *We'll halve the last cookie and share equally.*

hammer *n.* **1.** mallet, gavel, sledge, maul, claw hammer. *Where are the hammer and nails?* *–vb.* **2.** pound, drive, beat, tap, pummel, bang, knock, batter. *The carpenter hammered the pieces of wood together.*

hamper *vb.* hinder, obstruct, impede, prevent, restrain, thwart, inhibit. *The muddy track hampered the horse's performance.* **Ant.** aid, assist, promote, help.

hamstring *n.* hobble, handicap, cripple, disable, incapacitate, prostrate. *The new law preventing sprawl may hamstring anyone planning to develop large tracts of land.* **Ant.** help, aid, assist.

hand *n.* **1.** assistance, aid, help, support, lift. *Do you need a hand with painting the house?* **2.** role, part, share, responsibility. *The principal had a hand in getting an orchestra to play at the school fair.* **3.** laborer, worker, employee, aide, assistant. *We need to hire more hands to work on the farm.* –*vb.* **4.** give, pass, deliver, present, transmit, transfer. *Please hand me the salt.*

handbook *n.* guidebook, how-to, bible, manual, reference, field guide. *Be sure to consult the company handbook whenever you have a question about procedure.*

handicap *n.* **1.** disadvantage, hindrance, drawback, impediment, burden, disability. *His stuttering was a handicap when meeting new people.* –*vb.* **2.** impede, hamper, hinder, disable, inhibit, frustrate, limit. *Severe heat handicapped their efforts to battle the fire.* **Ant. 1.** advantage, help, benefit. **2.** aid, assist, boost.

handle *vb.* **1.** touch, feel, grasp, finger, hold. *Please handle the glasses with care.* **2.** manage, operate, manipulate, control, direct, run, work. *The farmer handled his tractor expertly.* –*n.* **3.** knob, shaft, grip, hilt, handgrip. *Take hold of the handle and pull.*

handsome *adj.* **1.** attractive, fine, good-looking, comely, pleasing, fair. *She thought the waiter was very handsome.* **2.** generous, liberal, large, ample, big, abundant, plentiful. *He received a handsome reward for finding the lost dog.* **Ant. 1.** ugly, plain, unattractive. **2.** small, stingy, meager.

handwriting *n.* script, penmanship, hand, calligraphy, (slang) hen scratching, scribble. *His handwriting was shaky and completely illegible.*

WORD SEARCH

poor: *cacography*
slip of the pen, psychological: *lapsus calami*
study of: *graphology*
time-saving: *shorthand*

handy *adj.* **1.** near, close, available, accessible, ready, convenient. *The photographer always kept his camera handy.* **2.** useful, efficient, clever, skillful, proficient, adept, inventive. *Her chauffeur was handy at maneuvering through traffic.* **Ant. 1.** unavailable, far, remote. **2.** useless, clumsy, ineffective.

hang *vb.* **1.** suspend, dangle, droop, drape, sling, attach. *He hung his jacket in the closet.* **2.** depend, rest, stand, wait, hinge. *My promotion hangs on the decision of my boss.* **3.** lynch, execute, kill, string up. *Let's hang the horse thief at sunrise.*

hangout *n.* haunt, stomping ground, retreat, club, home away from home, gathering spot. *Let's go to the hangout and talk.*

haphazard *adj.* careless, aimless, disorganized, random, purposeless, casual, chaotic. *Her belongings were tossed around the room in a haphazard manner.* **Ant.** organized, careful, neat, orderly.

hapless *adj.* unlucky, unfortunate, star-crossed, jinxed, woeful, cursed. *The hapless baseball team lost their tenth game in a row.* **Ant.** lucky, fortunate, blessed.

happen *vb.* occur, take place, arise, befall, result, appear, transpire. *A nice thing happened yesterday.*

happiness *n.* pleasure, joy, delight, cheer, bliss, enjoyment, ecstasy. *Her years in Europe were a time of great happiness.* **Ant.** misery, unhappiness, sadness, sorrow.

happy *adj.* glad, joyful, cheerful, elated, pleased, joyous, delighted, merry. *I'm happy that everything turned out so well.* **Ant.** sad, unhappy, gloomy, depressed.

happy-go-lucky *adj.* untroubled, carefree, unconcerned, devil-may-care, lighthearted, casual. *She was too happy-go-lucky to be perturbed by a parking ticket.* **Ant.** troubled, anxious, angry.

harangue *n.* tirade, scolding, exhortation, diatribe, lecture, chewing out. *The police officer addressed a scathing harangue to the speeder and issued him a ticket.*

harass *vb.* bother, annoy, pester, trouble, torment, disturb, harry, plague. *She was always being harassed by salespeople.*

harbinger *n.* sign, herald, forerunner, signal, portent, omen. *A flock of birds flying south is a harbinger of winter.*

harbor *n.* **1.** port, dock, anchorage, bay, lagoon. *We went to the harbor to watch the boats.* **2.** haven, refuge, shelter, retreat, sanctuary. *The local church served as a temporary harbor for the homeless.* *–vb.* **3.** protect, shelter, house, shield, guard, hide. *The resistance movement harbored refugees from the government.*

hard *adj.* **1.** difficult, tough, exacting, laborious, exhausting, strenuous. *The test was not as hard as I expected.* **2.** severe, harsh, rough, cruel, brutal, vicious, unpleasant. *A drought brought hard times to the village.* **3.** stern, strict, demanding, firm, unrelenting, unfeeling. *The new professor was a hard teacher.* **4.** solid, firm, dense, hardened, rigid, stiff, strong. *The camper found it difficult to sleep on the hard ground.* **Ant.** **1.** easy, simple, effortless. **2.** comfortable, pleasant, nice. **3.** lenient, lax, relaxed. **4.** soft, flexible, elastic.

hardly *adv.* barely, rarely, scarcely, narrowly, just. *There was hardly enough time to eat between classes.* **Ant.** easily, usually, certainly.

hardship *n.* misfortune, adversity, burden, difficulty, trouble. *The drought victims endured one hardship after another.*

hardy *adj.* strong, robust, fit, healthy, sturdy, tough, vigorous. *Exercise and a good diet made him hardy.* **Ant.** weak, feeble, unhealthy.

harem *n.* seraglio, wives, concubines. *The sultan's palace included rooms that housed his harem.*

harlot *n.* prostitute, streetwalker, strumpet, hussy, whore, (slang) ho. *One must be careful not to appear like a harlot when wearing scanty outfits.*

harm *n.* **1.** hurt, injury, pain, damage, abuse. *The one bad movie has done a lot of harm to her acting career.* **2.** evil, mischief, wickedness, wrong, sin, malice. *Don't try to convince me that there's no harm in telling a lie.* *–vb.* **3.** hurt, damage, injure, mistreat, abuse. *My dog won't harm you.* **Ant.** **1.** good, assistance, help. **2.** kindness, goodness, benefit. **3.** help, heal, cure.

harmful *adj.* dangerous, injurious, hurtful, damaging, unhealthy, unsafe, bad. *Cigarettes are harmful to your health.* **Ant.** safe, harmless, healthy, beneficial.

harmless *adj.* safe, beneficial, innocent, gentle, inoffensive, benign, good. *Hamsters are harmless creatures.* **Ant.** harmful, dangerous, vicious, unsafe.

harmonious *adj.* **1.** friendly, agreeable, cordial, congenial, pleasing. *The friends settled their* *argument in a harmonious fashion.* **2.** tuneful, melodious, melodic, harmonic, musical. *The choir was known for its harmonious renditions of classic songs.* **Ant. 1.** disagreeable, unfriendly quarrelsome. **2.** discordant, harsh.

harmony *n.* agreement, conformity, accord, concord, unity. *Her views on the environment are in harmony with my own.* **Ant.** disagreement, discord, conflict.

harried *adj.* stressed, troubled, harassed, hassled, tormented, pestered. *A mother of five children is constantly harried.* **Ant.** untroubled, calm, relaxed.

harrowing *adj.* alarming, terrifying, scary, upsetting, traumatic. *Being trapped on the cliff ledge was a harrowing experience.*

harsh *adj.* **1.** rough, coarse, grating, jarring, discordant, unpleasant. *His harsh voice really gets on my nerves.* **2.** cruel, severe, mean, tough, unkind, merciless, brutal, heartless. *The prisoners complained of harsh treatment from the guards.* **Ant. 1.** pleasing, pleasant, smooth. **2.** kind, lenient, merciful.

harvest *n.* **1.** crop, yield, produce, outcome, fruit, reward. *The farmers had a good harvest.* *–vb.* **2.** reap, gather, pick, collect. *Our neighbors helped us harvest the corn.*

hash *n.* mixture, hodgepodge, miscellany, mishmash, medley, mess. *We used a variety of leftovers to make a big hash for dinner.*

hassle *n.* **1.** quarrel, dispute, fight, argument, squabble, struggle. *Two people got into a hassle over the one parking space.* *–vb.* **2.** harass, harry, bother, argue, fight, squabble. *My father is always hassling me about getting a haircut.*

haste *n.* hurry, speed, rush, dispatch, rapidity, quickness, swiftness. *She left with haste when my pet rattlesnake got loose.* **Ant.** delay, slowness, sluggishness.

hasten *vb.* race, hurry, rush, speed, quicken, run, dash. *She hastened to catch the bus.* **Ant.** slow, delay, drag, slacken.

hasty *adj.* quick, fast, speedy, swift, rapid, sudden. *It's foolish to make hasty decisions.* **Ant.** slow, deliberate, leisurely.

hat *n.* cap, chapeau, headgear, (slang) lid. *He liked to pull his hat down over his eyes.*

WORD SEARCH

bowl-like and narrow-brimmed: *bowler, derby*
cowboy: *Stetson, ten-gallon hat*
creased down middle of crown, men's: *fedora, homburg*
Crockett's, Davy: *coonskin cap*
domelike, women's soft: *cloche*
graduate's square with tassel: *mortarboard*
Jewish skullcap: *yarmulke*
kerchief worn around head and tied in the back, popularized by pirates: *buff, do-rag*
Mexican, broad-brimmed: *sombrero*
pancake-like: *beret, tam-o'shanter*
Sherlock Holmes' tweed; *deerstalker*
stovepipe-like of the 19th century: *top hat*
straw hat, men's: *Panama*
straw hat, women's: *boater, picture hat*
winter, long, knitted: *stocking cap*

hatch *vb.* **1.** concoct, devise, plan, create, produce, invent, generate. *He's always hatching schemes to make money.* **2.** breed, incubate, brood, produce. *We hatched the chicken eggs in an incubator.*

hate *n.* **1.** hatred, loathing, hostility, revulsion, malice, scorn. *I can't live in a place where there is so much hate.* *–vb.* **2.** loathe, dislike, detest, despise, abhor, scorn. *The cowboy hated city life.* **Ant. 1.** love, liking, affection. **2.** love, like, adore, cherish.

hateful *adj.* detestable, horrid, vile, despised, odious, offensive. *The travelers avoided the canyon where the hateful goblins lived.* **Ant.** lovable, adorable, likable, decent.

hatred *n.* hate, revulsion, aversion, animosity, hostility. *I have a lot of hatred for people who are cruel to animals.* **Ant.** friendliness, love, affection.

haughty *adj.* proud, arrogant, prideful, conceited, vain, pompous. *Everybody acts so haughty at those high-class charity balls.* **Ant.** humble, modest, simple.

haul *vb.* **1.** heave, pull, draw, drag, tow, tug, carry. *Help me haul the hay bales into the barn.* *–n.* **2.** load, burden, weight, cargo, freight. *There's a huge haul of fish coming into the market today.*

haunt *vb.* **1.** obsess, plague, torment, distress, frighten, terrorize. *Lately she's been haunted by nightmares.* *–n.* **2.** hideaway, hangout, rendezvous, spot, place. *The old haunts aren't what they used to be.*

haunting *adj.* unforgettable, upsetting, disturbing, distressing, hypnotic. *The wolves' haunting howls echoed through the night.*

have *vb.* **1.** own, possess, hold, carry, retain, keep. *Do you have the car keys?* **2.** get, acquire, obtain, take, gain. *I'll have another glass of lemonade.* **3.** experience, undergo, endure, know, enjoy. *Have a good time at the party.*

haven *n.* shelter, retreat, asylum, refuge, sanctuary. *My mountain cabin is my haven from city life.*

havoc *n.* ruin, disaster, destruction, chaos, disorder, devastation. *A motorcycle gang spread havoc through the small town.* **Ant.** peace, calm, order, serenity.

hawker *n.* vendor, pitchman, salesman, peddler, huckster, merchant. *It was common to see hawkers peddling patent medicines on the streets in the 1800s.*

hayseed *n.* (slang) hick, yokel, clodhopper, hillbilly, rustic, (slang) rube. *Being from a small town, I sometimes feel like a hayseed when I visit New York.*

haywire *n.* crazy, disordered, (slang) out of whack, (slang) out of kilter, confused, amok. *Last night our toaster went haywire and burst into flames.*

hazard *n.* **1.** danger, risk, peril, threat, chance. *Heat exhaustion is a common hazard of desert hiking.* *–vb.* **2.** venture, risk, guess, gamble, dare, offer, attempt. *I'll hazard a guess that we will be home by Sunday.* **Ant. 1.** protection, security, safeguard.

hazardous *adj.* dangerous, perilous, risky, unsafe, chancy. *It is hazardous to skate on thin ice.* **Ant.** safe, reliable, secure.

hazardous waste *n.* toxic waste, pollution, contaminated materials, pathogenic materials, nuclear waste. *The corporation promised to clean up its worst hazardous waste sites.*

haze *n.* vapor, mist, murk, fog, smog, smoke. *We could barely make out the lighthouse through the haze.*

hazy *adj.* **1.** foggy, cloudy, misty, murky, bleary, overcast, dim. *The sky is frequently hazy near the ocean.* **2.** unclear, obscure, faint, uncertain, muddled, vague, unsure. *Her thoughts have been a little hazy since she hurt her head.* **Ant. 1.** sunny, clear, bright. **2.** certain, clear, unconfused.

head *n.* **1.** brain, mind, intellect, mentality, aptitude. *Use your head to solve that problem.* **2.** director, supervisor, leader, chief, boss, commander. *They had a meeting with the head of the office.* **3.** start, beginning, front, top, source, peak. *The people at the head of the line have been here for* *hours.* –*vb.* **4.** lead, direct, command, supervise, manage, control, preside. *The police chief will personally head the investigation.* **5.** go, proceed, start, move, turn, steer. *He headed for the exit.* –*adj.* **6.** leading, chief, main, principal, presiding, commanding. *I will speak only to the head supervisor.* **Ant. 2.** employee, follower, subordinate. **3.** back, bottom, rear. **4.** follow, conclude. **5.** withdraw, retreat. **6.** inferior, lowest.

headline *n.* heading, caption, title, banner. *A newspaper headline is reserved for the day's most important event.*

headquarters *n.* HQ, command post, base, center of operations, nerve center. *Call headquarters and ask for directions.*

headstrong *adj.* stubborn, obstinate, willful, bullheaded, pigheaded. *The headstrong woman insisted she was right.* **Ant.** submissive, meek, docile.

headway *n.* progress, improvement, advance, movement, gain, progression. *He made some headway toward getting a job.*

heady *adj.* intoxicating, arousing, exhilarating, stimulating, exciting. *The kitchen was filled with a heady aroma of freshly baked bread.*

heal *vb.* cure, remedy, restore, repair, mend, treat, ease. *Broken bones take a long time to heal.* **Ant.** hurt, wound, damage, worsen.

healer *n.* doctor, physician, shaman, medicine man, practitioner, faith healer. *Some people believe that a faith healer might cure disease through the placebo response.*

health *n.* well-being, fitness, vitality, healthiness, soundness. *It is important to take care of your health.* **Ant.** sickness, illness, disease, weakness.

healthy *adj.* well, fit, strong, robust, hearty, wholesome, hale, sound. *She exercises in order to maintain a healthy body.* **Ant.** sick, ill, unfit, weak, feeble.

heap *vb.* **1.** pile, stack, lump, amass, collect, load, gather. *They heaped the garbage into one big pile.* –*n.* **2.** mass, pile, stack, collection, mound, load, clump, hill. *The dump truck deposited a large heap of dirt.*

hear *vb.* listen, heed, attend, hearken, detect, perceive. *Can you hear the birds singing?*

hearing *n.* inquiry, interview, inquisition, inquest, audience, review. *The evidence against the accused will be presented at the hearing.*

hearsay *n.* rumor, talk, gossip, secondhand information, scuttlebutt. *Evidence based on hearsay is not admissible in court.*

heart *n.* **1.** kindness, feeling, sympathy, love, mercy, tenderness, compassion. *Have a heart and give the child a cookie.* **2.** spirit, courage, bravery, spunk, desire, valor. *The boxer has no skill but lots of heart.* **3.** center, core, middle, interior, nucleus. *A minotaur lived in the heart of the labyrinth.* **4.** essence, root, source, basis, foundation, focus. *We need to sit down and discuss the heart of the problem.* **Ant. 1.** hatred indifference, coldness, **2.** cowardice, fear, shyness. **3.** outside, outskirts, exterior.

heartache *n.* heartbreak, broken heart, sadness, sorrow, grief, anguish. *Country music songs are often about heartache.* **Ant.** joy, euphoria, ecstasy.

heart attack *n.* coronary occlusion, coronary thrombosis, cardiac arrest, myocardial infarction, blockage. *To prevent a heart attack, watch your cholesterol and blood pressure and get plenty of exercise.*

heartbreaking *adj.* heart-wrenching, sad, painful, agonizing, tragic, pitiful. *The movie's heartbreaking ending had the audience in tears.* **Ant.** joyful, happy, cheering.

heartbroken *adj.* devastated, crushed, depressed, miserable, sad. *The child was heartbroken over the loss of his teddy bear.* **Ant.** euphoric, elated, joyful.

heartburn *n.* reflux, pyrosis, brash, indigestion. *If you have heartburn, try an antacid.*

heartfelt *adj.* insincere, genuine, real, deep, impassioned, ardent. *She gave us her heartfelt thanks for helping.* **Ant.** insincere, fake, forced.

heartily *adv.* sincerely, fervently, totally, warmly, earnestly, keenly. *I heartily recommend the duck in orange sauce.* **Ant.** coolly, indifferently.

heartless *adj.* cruel, mean, unfeeling, ruthless, merciless, pitiless, callous. *The heartless landlord threw the family out in the streets.* **Ant.** merciful, kind, humane, generous.

heat *n.* **1.** warmth, warmness, hotness, swelter, temperature. *It was difficult to work in the heat of the day.* **2.** excitement, fervor, passion, intensity, fever, frenzy. *The crowd lost control in the heat of the moment.* –*vb.* **3.** warm, cook, reheat, boil, simmer. *He heated water for a cup of tea.* **Ant. 1** cold, cool. **2.** calmness, peacefulness. **3.** cool, chill.

heathen *n.* pagan, nontheist, atheist, agnostic, infidel, nonbeliever. *The minister warned that heathens would have trouble getting into heaven.* **Ant.** believer, convert, Christian, Jew, Muslim.

heave *vb.* hoist, haul, raise, boost, lift, pull, push, fling. *Laborers heaved the crates onto the truck.*

heaven *n.* **1.** paradise, bliss, ecstasy, nirvana, rapture, joy. *It was heaven to float in the swimming pool on a hot day.* **2.** afterlife, paradise, nirvana, eternity, hereafter. *She believes that she will go to Heaven after she dies.* **Ant. 1.** torment, agony, suffering. **2.** hell, nothingness, oblivion.

heavenly *adj.* glorious, divine, ethereal, spiritual, extramundane, sublime. *Eating chocolate swirl ice cream is a heavenly experience.* **Ant.** hellish, horrible, devilish.

heavy *adj.* **1.** weighty, bulky, massive, hefty, dense. *The chair was too heavy to lift.* **2.** excessive, abundant, severe, intense, fierce, forceful. *Heavy winds blew down the telephone lines.* **3.** sad, gloomy, depressing, sorrowful, dismal, unendurable. *He's been in a heavy mood since the death of his cat.* **4.** boring, tiresome, tedious, difficult, dreary, dull. *I find my algebra class to be heavy going.* **Ant. 1.** light, weightless, lightweight. **2.** light, minimal, slight. **3.** happy, carefree, cheerful. **4.** light, easy, interesting.

heckle *vb.* harass, pester, jeer, taunt, hassle, annoy. *Comedians hate it when members of the audience heckle them.*

hectic *adj.* frantic, wild, mad, excited, chaotic, feverish. *Shopping is always hectic on Christmas Eve.* **Ant.** quiet, calm, slow, peaceful.

hedge *n.* **1.** boundary, fence, border, barrier. *We couldn't look into the garden due to the high hedges.* **2.** protection, guard, security, insurance. *Health insurance acts as a hedge against unexpected medical expenses.* –*vb.* **3.** evade, avoid, dodge, parry, sidestep. *When I asked about specifics, the senator hedged the question.*

hedonist *n.* pleasure-seeker, bon vivant, partyer, voluptuary, debauchee, glutton. *The hedonist tends to indulge in too much of a good thing.*

heed *vb.* **1.** follow, regard, obey, notice, mind, observe. *She would not have been arrested had she heeded the officer's warning.* –*n.* **2.** attention, mind, notice, care, regard, consideration. *Pay heed to the instructions.* **Ant. 1.** ignore, disregard, disobey. **2.** disregard, inattention.

hefty *adj.* heavy, weighty, massive, large, ample, powerful. *The truck tire proved to be surprisingly hefty.* **Ant.** light, small, insignificant.

heifer *n.* calf, yearling, ruminant, herbivore, mammal. *A mother cow is often protective of her heifer.*

height *n.* **1.** tallness, stature, highness, elevation, altitude. *What is the height of that building?* **2.** peak, maximum, crest, climax, pinnacle, apex, zenith. *This is the height of the fishing season.* **Ant.** **1.** depth, deepness, lowness. **2.** minimum, depth.

heinous *adj.* evil, abominable, wicked, despicable, monstrous, revolting. *The perpetrators of the heinous crime could expect life in prison.* **Ant.** angelic, saintly, moral.

heir *n.* beneficiary, inheritor, recipient, receiver. *I like to dream that I will be the heir to a fortune.*

heirloom *n.* inheritance, legacy, hand-me-down, cherished possession, bequest. *My favorite quilt is a family heirloom, handed down from my great grandmother.*

heist *n.* robbery, hold-up, (slang) stick-up, theft, larceny, thievery. *The robber was sentenced to 20 years in prison for an armored car heist.*

helicopter *n.* aircraft, (slang) chopper, (slang) whirlybird, (slang) eggbeater. *The helicopter hovered overhead for five minutes.*

hell *n.* Hades, Gehenna, underworld, netherworld, depths, eternal punishment, inferno. *The preacher warned about the fire and brimstone world of hell.* **Ant.** heaven, Shangri-la, paradise.

hellion *n.* devil, troublemaker, minion of the devil, demon, rogue, rascal. *Boys in groups can sometimes turn into little hellions.*

hellish *ant.* infernal, satanic, stygian, evil, wicked, cruel, diabolical. *Fighting fires is an often hellish job.* **Ant.** heavenly, wonderful.

helm *n.* wheel, control, driver's seat, tiller, seat of power, leadership. *In stormy seas, the most experienced sailor should take the helm.*

helmet *n.* headgear, head protector, hardhat. *Don't even think about riding your bike without a helmet.*

help *vb.* **1.** aid, assist, benefit, support, sustain, serve. *The boy scout helped a little old man cross the street.* **2.** control, relieve, ease, cure, mend, prevent. *A cup of mint tea should help your stomachache.* *–n.* **3.** assistance, aid, support, backing, service, cooperation. *Can I get some help moving these boxes?* **Ant.** **1.** hinder, impede, obstruct. **2.** worsen, aggravate, harm. **3.** opposition, noncooperation, obstruction.

helper *n.* aid, hand, assistant, (slang) gofer, handmaid, right-hand man, subordinate. *I need a helper to hold this piece of wood for me.*

helpful *adj.* useful, beneficial, valuable, supportive, productive, worthwhile. *A list of recommended readings would be helpful.* **Ant.** useless, worthless, harmful.

helpless *adj.* powerless, defenseless, weak, feeble, vulnerable. *The lamb was helpless against the pack of coyotes.* **Ant.** strong, powerful, protected.

helter-skelter *adj.* chaotic, haphazard, disorderly, confused, jumbled, random. *The house was a disaster area, with everything spread around helter-skelter.* **Ant.** ordered, arranged, neat.

henchman *n.* helper, underling, aid, flunky, subordinate, (slang) yes man. *The crime boss and his henchman met to discuss future scams.*

henpeck *vb.* nag, needle, badger, harass, pester, (slang) bug, (slang) ride. *Some women have to henpeck their husbands to get them to perform household chores.*

herald *n.* **1.** messenger, forerunner, crier, proclaimer, courier. *A herald announced the birth of the princess.* *–vb.* **2.** announce, proclaim, broadcast, declare, trumpet. *"New and improved!" heralded the commercial.*

herbicide *n.* defoliant, weed killer, poison. *Mr. Smith uses a herbicide to kill the dandelions in his yard.*

herd *n.* **1.** pack, crowd, flock, group, drove, swarm, gathering. *The campsite was invaded by a herd of boy scouts.* *–vb.* **2.** drive, guide, lead, group, collect, gather. *Let's herd the horses into the barn.*

hereditary *adj.* inborn, inherent, innate, genetic, congenital, inbred. *The ability to run fast is partially hereditary.* **Ant.** acquired, learned.

heresy *n.* dissension, unorthodoxy, apostasy, blasphemy, freethinking, nonconformity. *Although he turned out to be right, Galileo was imprisoned by the Catholic Church for heresy.* **Ant.** conformity, agreement, orthodoxy.

heretic *n.* disbeliever, dissenter, nonconformist, renegade, infidel. *Martin Luther was considered a heretic.* **Ant.** believer, loyalist, traditionalist.

heritage *n.* legacy, inheritance, tradition, birthright. *She is proud of the heritage handed down from her African ancestors.*

hermit *n.* recluse, misanthrope, loner, anchorite, lone wolf. *Although he had plenty of money, he chose to live as a hermit in a remote section of the forest.*

hero *n.* heroine, champion, idol, favorite, model, inspiration, ideal. *My childhood hero was the Lone Ranger.* **Ant.** villain, coward.

heroic *adj.* brave, valiant, daring, gallant, bold, courageous, fearless, intrepid. *The heroic princess saved the bungling knight from being eaten by a dragon.* **Ant.** cowardly, scared, timid, fearful.

heroin *n.* drug, narcotic, illicit substance. *Heroin is a powerfully addictive drug.*

hesitant *adj.* reluctant, doubtful, undecided, indecisive, uncertain. *She was hesitant to lend money to her irresponsible friend.* **Ant.** decided, decisive, certain.

hesitate *vb.* pause, delay, waver, wait, falter, balk. *The adventurer hesitated briefly before entering the dark and mysterious cavern.* **Ant.** continue, resolve, proceed.

hex *n.* curse, spell, jinx, whammy, evil eye. *The old witch threatened to place a hex on our family.*

hiatus *n.* break, rest, interim, gap, interruption, suspension, pause. *The actors were on a hiatus until the show resumed in the fall.*

hibernate *vb.* sleep, winter, hole up, lie low, lie dormant. *Bears put on a thick layer of fat in the fall so they can hibernate through the winter.*

hick *n.* yokel, ignoramus, (slang) hayseed, (slang) hillbilly, (slang) clodhopper. *He called himself a poorly educated hick, but in reality he had a lot of common sense.*

hide *vb.* **1.** conceal, cover, cloak, screen, mask, veil, disguise. *The pirates hid their treasure in a cave.* *–n.* **2.** fur, pelt, skin, leather. *A fox hide looks better on a fox than on a human.* **Ant. 1.** reveal, uncover, expose, display.

hideous *adj.* ugly, repulsive, ghastly, horrible, terrifying, gruesome. *I saw some pretty hideous creatures last Halloween.* **Ant.** beautiful, attractive, pleasing.

hierarchy *n.* order, ranking, chain of command, strata, corporate ladder, pecking order. *We located the responsible party high up in the organization's hierarchy.*

high *adj.* **1.** tall, towering, elevated, lofty, soaring. *Redwoods are very high trees.* **2.** extreme, severe, excessive, acute, unreasonable, serious. *With finals approaching, many students are suffering from high stress.* **3.** shrill, raised, sharp, piercing. *The whistle had a very high pitch.* **4.** prominent, important, powerful, superior, great, eminent. *She was promoted to a high position in the office.* **Ant. 1.** low, short, little. **2.** small, limited, reasonable. **3.** deep, lowered. **4.** inferior, secondary, insignificant.

highbrow *adj.* intellectual, cultivated, erudite, scholarly, cultured, learned. *Mrs. Morley only reads highbrow literature and wouldn't be caught dead looking at a tabloid.* **Ant.** lowbrow, uncultivated, ignorant.

high-class *adj.* upper-class, superior, first-rate, upper crust, deluxe. *In order to get into the high-class restaurant, I had to wear a suit and tie.* **Ant.** low-class, inferior, cheap.

highlight *n.* high point, best part, feature, focus, headline. *The highlight of the game occurred when a crazy fan streaked naked across the field.*

high-strung *adj.* tense, uptight, taut, temperamental, edgy, excitable. *The high-strung tennis player lost his temper easily.* **Ant.** easy-going, relaxed, calm.

highway *n.* expressway, freeway, parkway, beltway, turnpike, autobahn, road. *The highway is a faster route than a back road.*

hijack *vb.* skyjack, rob, (slang) carjack, kidnap, abduct. *The police uncovered the terrorist's plan to hijack the airplane.*

hike *vb.* **1.** walk, trek, tramp, march, ramble, rove, trudge. *The backpackers hiked to their next campsite.* **2.** raise, boost, lift, increase, upgrade. *The gas stations hiked their prices again.* –*n.* **3.** trek, walk, journey, tramp, jaunt, march. *She enjoys a morning hike in the hills.* **4.** raise, boost, increase, expansion. *The president opposes a tax hike.* **Ant. 2.** reduce, cut, lower. **4.** reduction, cut, decrease.

hilarious *adj.* funny, delirious, hysterical, riotous, laughable, uproarious. *The circus clowns were hilarious.* **Ant.** sad, solemn, depressing.

hill *n.* rise, knoll, mound, hilltop, elevation, prominence. *Her cabin sits on a hill overlooking a wooded valley.* **Ant.** hollow, valley, bottom.

WORD SEARCH

hilly: *rolling, tumulose*
low areas between hills: *intervale*

hinder *vb.* delay, obstruct, stop, prevent, stall, detain, interrupt, impede. *Darkness hindered our ability to complete the climb.* **Ant.** support, aid, assist, help.

hindrance *n.* obstacle, obstruction, delay, interference, restriction. *Lack of money need not be a hindrance to having a good time.* **Ant.** help, assistance, aid, support.

hindsight *n.* retrospect, wisdom of experience. *In hindsight, I would choose not to eat ten cookies in a row again.* **Ant.** foresight, prophecy.

hinge *vb.* **1.** revolve, depend, pivot, rely, rest. *The jury's decision hinges on the testimony of one witness.* –*n.* **2.** joint, pivot, bearing, axis. *Please oil the hinges on the gate.*

hint *vb.* **1.** suggest, imply, tip, mention, insinuate. *The teacher hinted that there would be a surprise test on Tuesday.* –*n.* **2.** clue, tip, suggestion, implication, allusion. *If you won't tell me the answer, then at least give me a hint.* **3.** taste, trace, tinge, pinch, dash. *Good spaghetti sauce should have just a hint of oregano.* **Ant. 1.** declare, state, announce. **3.** abundance, surplus, excess.

hip *adj.* (slang) with it, sophisticated, cool, enlightened, stylish, au courant. *To be hip, you* *have to wear the right clothes and know all the cool slang.*

hip hop *n.* rap, black urban music, gangsta rap. *My Dad loves rock and roll but hates hip hop.*

hippie *n.* nonconformist, free spirit, beatnik, (slang) flower child, deviant, (slang) freak. *Long-haired hippies wearing peace symbols were a common sight in the late 1960s.*

hire *vb.* employ, engage, appoint, retain, contract. *The store hired two more people.* **Ant.** fire, dismiss, release.

Hispanic *adj.* Spanish, Latino, Hispano. *Miami has a large Hispanic population.*

historic *adj.* important, consequential, weighty, momentous, notable, famous, celebrated. *I vividly remember the historic landing on the moon by* Apollo 11.

history *n.* chronicle, record, account, report, story, annals, saga, narrative. *The history of America is full of great deeds.*

histrionics *n.* theatrics, melodramatics, dramatics, show, display, performing. *The man complained about his parking ticket with absurd histrionics.*

hit *vb.* **1.** strike, knock, punch, beat, slam, slug, pound. *Try to hit the ball on the first pitch.* **2.** touch, affect, overwhelm, move, stir, impress. *The seriousness of the situation finally hit me.* –*n.* **3.** blow, knock, bump, impact, stroke, slam, punch. *The quarterback took a hard hit when he was tackled.* **4.** triumph, success, winner, sensation, smash. *Her first novel was a surprise hit.* **Ant.** **4.** loser, failure, flop.

hitch *vb.* **1.** tie, tether, fasten, harness, join, bind, attach. *The cowboy hitched his horse to a post.* **2.** hike, tug, pull, yank, raise. *She hitched up her pants and waded across the stream.* –*n.* **3.** snag, obstacle, problem, catch, drawback, difficulty. *His lateness threw a hitch in our plan to see the seven o'clock movie.* **Ant.** **1** untie, release, unfasten. **2.** lower, release, drop.

hit man *n.* trigger man, enforcer, assassin, hired gun, thug. *The Mafia boss hired a hit man to take out his rival.*

hoard *vb.* **1.** store, collect, accumulate, stockpile, amass, save. *Pack rats are famous for hoarding objects.* –*n.* **2.** collection, mass, stock, stockpile, cache, reserve, supply. *A hoard of diamonds was found by the police officer.* **Ant.** **1.** waste, spend, surrender.

hoarse *adj.* harsh, rough, raspy, grating, scratchy, cracked, coarse. *All this yelling is making me sound hoarse.* **Ant.** full, clear, smooth.

hoax *n.* **1.** trick, fraud, deception, deceit, sham, joke. *The cockroach festival was a hoax.* –*vb.* **2.** deceive, trick, fool, dupe, swindle. *I can't believe you were hoaxed into a snipe hunt.* **Ant.** **1.** truth, actuality, fact.

hobble *vb.* limp, falter, stagger, shuffle, totter. *Blisters covered my feet, so I couldn't do anything but hobble painfully.*

hobby *n.* pastime, recreation, diversion, amusement, avocation. *Her hobby is collecting stamps.*

hobo *n.* tramp, transient, drifter, rover, derelict, homeless person, vagrant. *A hobo passing through town asked us for spare change.*

hockey *n.* sport, game, contact sport, athletic competition. *Ice hockey is one of the roughest sports.*

WORD SEARCH

bumping opponent away from puck: *check, body check*
goal defense player: *goalie*
hard, driving shot: *slapshot*
illegal shot from behind center red line: *icing*

illegal striking of opponent: *roughing, slashing, spearing, high-sticking*
penalty advantage when opposing team is one player short: *power play*
positions: *center, forward, wing, backline, defenseman*
puck drop commencing play: *face-off*
three goals scored by one player in single game: *hat trick*

hodgepodge *n.* mixture, mélange, miscellany, jumble, potpourri, mess. *For dinner, we're having a hodgepodge of leftovers.*

hog *n.* pig, sow, boar, swine, shoat, piglet. *The hog at the fair tipped the scales at a whopping 800 pounds.*

hoist *vb.* pull, yank, raise, lift, heave, elevate. *She hoisted a bucket out of the well.*

hold *vb.* **1.** have, retain, keep, own, possess. *He holds two tickets to the concert.* **2.** grasp, grip, clutch, seize, clench. *Please hold my hand.* **3.** contain, enclose, include, accommodate. *This silo holds a large surplus of wheat.* **4.** remain, stick, adhere, stay, persist, last, endure. *My repairs will hold until you can get the car to a mechanic.* **5.** think, consider, believe, judge, conclude, maintain. *I hold that new research will lead to an improved product.* **6.** conduct, direct, manage, execute. *The tennis finals will be held this weekend.* –*n.* **7.** grip, grasp, clutch, clamp, embrace. *Get a firm hold on the bat.* **8.** control, possession, sway, power, rule, authority. *Take hold of yourself and don't panic.* **Ant.** **2.** release, relinquish, remove. **4.** loosen, yield. **5.** deny, reject, disavow. **6.** cancel, postpone.

hole *n.* **1.** opening, gap, break, leak, crack, slot. *There's a hole in your blue jeans.* **2.** fault, defect, flaw, discrepancy, inconsistency. *There are numerous holes in your line of reasoning.* **3.** depression, pit, concavity, crater, hollow. *You'll need to dig that hole deeper.*

holiday *n.* vacation, leave, break, celebration, festival. *Next Monday is a holiday for all government workers.*

holistic *adj.* whole, integrated, comprehensive, complete, systemic, integral. *Many physicians today take a holistic approach to treating sick patients.* **Ant.** partial, individual, divided.

holler *vb.* shout, roar, yell, bellow, thunder, bark. *It is far better to present the facts than to holler idle threats.*

hollow *adj.* **1.** vacant, empty, void, unfilled, depressed, sunken. *The bandits hid their loot in a hollow spot under the floor.* **2.** meaningless, false, vain, pointless, worthless. *A person who cheats will inherit a hollow victory.* –*n.* **3.** cavity, hole, depression, crater, pocket, basin. *The squirrel stored nuts in a hollow of the tree.* –*vb.* **4.** dig, scrape, scoop, excavate, shovel. *Tribesmen hollowed out the log in order to make a canoe.* **Ant.** **1.** full, filled, raised. **2.** meaningful, substantial, valuable.

holocaust *n.* annihilation, genocide, extermination, massacre, mass killing, devastation, destruction. *Millions of Jews were killed in the Holocaust of World War II.*

holy *adj.* sacred, saintly, sanctified, hallowed, revered, divine, religious. *Jerusalem is a holy city for three religions.* **Ant.** secular, unsanctified, unholy.

homage *vb.* tribute, praise, honor, respect, reverence, devotion. *Her documentary paid homage to the Apollo astronauts.* **Ant.** criticism, disrespect, dishonor.

home *n.* **1.** house, residence, residency, dwelling, abode, habitation. *He bought a home in the country.* **2.** habitat, haunt, refuge, retreat, homeland, site. *Argentina is the home of the gaucho.*

homebody *n.* introvert, (slang) couch potato, (slang) stick-in-the-mud. *I'm perfectly happy to remain a homebody and never leave the house.* **Ant.** extrovert, man about town, party animal.

homeless *adj.* vagrant, destitute, evicted, dispossessed, impoverished, penniless. *The shelter provided homeless men and women a place to stay until they could get back on their feet.*

homely *adj.* ugly, plain, unattractive, unappealing, repulsive. *He was such a great guy that nobody noticed how homely he was.* **Ant.** handsome, pretty, beautiful.

homesick *adj.* wistful, heartsick, lonely for home, nostalgic, longing, yearning. *Many kids get homesick during the first day at summer camp.*

homespun *adj.* plain, homemade, simple, unpretentious, down-home, folksy. *We love Karen's down-to-earth, homespun humor.* **Ant.** manufactured, mass-produced, sophisticated.

homicidal *adj.* murderous, bloodthirsty, maniacal, enraged, irrational, violent. *The police were on the lookout for a homicidal maniac.* **Ant.** pacific, peaceful, loving.

homicide *n.* murder, manslaughter, killing, assassination, slaughter. *Several gang members were arrested for homicide.*

homogenous *adj.* similar, like, identical, uniform, unmixed, the same. *Japan has a largely homogenous population.* **Ant.** dissimilar, unlike, mixed.

homosexual *adj.* **1.** gay, lesbian, same-sex, bisexual. *We have a friend who is very open about his homosexual orientation.* –*n.* **2.** gay person, gay, lesbian, bisexual. *Homosexuals gathered at the town square to petition for equal rights.*

honest *adj.* **1.** truthful, honorable, reliable, upright, trustworthy, ethical. *We need an honest person to handle the financial arrangements.* **2.** candid, frank, forthright, genuine, real, true. *I'm looking for honest facts, not what the politicians want me to hear.* **Ant. 1.** dishonest, deceitful, unethical. **2.** false, deceiving.

honk *vb.* beep, toot, blow, blast, blare, sound. *Honk your horn only when necessary.*

honor *n.* **1.** distinction, regard, respect, esteem, prestige, acclaim, renown. *The Olympic athlete returned to her country with honor.* **2.** honesty, virtue, decency, integrity, character. *The gentleman's honor was at stake.* –*vb.* **3.** respect, revere, regard, dignify, exalt. *We will honor the senator with a parade.* **4.** take, accept, acknowledge, recognize. *The bank refused to honor my check.* **Ant. 1.** shame, disgrace, humiliation. **2.** dishonesty, shame, dishonor. **3.** dishonor, disgrace, humiliate. **4.** reject, deny, refuse.

honorable *adj.* honest, ethical, virtuous, trustworthy, reliable. *Honorable people do not tell lies.* **Ant.** disreputable, corrupt, dishonest.

hoodlum *n.* hood, thug, ruffian, gangster, (slang) gangbanger, punk, troublemaker. *The hoodlums down on the corner were arrested for vandalism.*

hoodwink *vb.* trick, fool, mislead, deceive, cheat, bamboozle. *Don't let any con artists hoodwink you with their fast talk.*

hook *n.* **1.** clip, clasp, pin, hanger, fastener. *Hang your jacket on the hook.* –*vb.* **2.** fasten, attach, secure, latch, link, join. *Please hook the door on the bird cage.*

hoopla *n.* excitement, ballyhoo, fuss, to-do, bustle, furor. *There was a high level of hoopla at the party last night.*

hop *vb.* jump, leap, leapfrog, spring, bound, hurdle, vault. *Please hop over my flower bed, not in it.*

hope *vb.* **1.** wish, desire, trust, expect, anticipate, believe. *We can only hope the trapped min-*

ers are still alive. –n. **2.** trust, faith, assurance, reliance, confidence, belief. *Our football team placed all their hopes on the rookie quarter-back.* **3.** longing, yearning, expectation, desire, ambition, anticipation. *The college graduate has great hopes for the future.* **Ant. 1.** despair, doubt, fear. **2.** distrust, doubt, disbelief. **3.** hopelessness, despair, pessimism.

hopeful *adj.* optimistic, confident, assuring, expectant, promising, encouraging. *There are hopeful signs of a break in the storm.* **Ant.** hopeless, despairing, depressing.

hopeless *adj.* pessimistic, despairing, depressing, discouraging, helpless, useless, desperate. *Bailing water out of the rapidly sinking boat was a hopeless task.* **Ant.** hopeful, optimistic, favorable.

horde *n.* pack, multitude, swarm, herd, mob, crowd, legion, throng, troop. *Hordes of lemmings jumped into the sea.*

horizon *n.* skyline, vista, limit, range, azimuth, offing. *The captain watched the horizon for signs of an approaching storm.*

horizontal *adj.* level, even, flat, plane, straight, prone. *Your radio-controlled car will work best on a horizontal surface.* **Ant.** vertical, sloped, uneven, bumpy.

horn *n.* **1.** antler, spike, tusk, outgrowth. *An animal's horns can be a great defensive weapon against predators.* **2.** musical instrument, wind instrument, bugle, trumpet, coronet. *Little Bo Beep was advised to blow her horn to keep her flock under control.*

horrible *adj.* terrible, awful, gruesome, dreadful, horrid, frightful, hideous. *We have to report the horrible accident to the police.* **Ant.** delightful, wonderful, good, nice.

horrify *vb.* shock, dismay, scare, revolt, petrify, appall, send chills down one's spine. *Stephen King's books are guaranteed to horrify readers.*

horror *n.* **1.** terror, dread, fear, fright, panic, dismay, alarm, repulsion. *He shook with horror when the vampire entered his room.* **2.** cruelty, atrocity, outrage, torment, abomination. *We need to put a stop to the horrors committed by terrorists.* **Ant. 2.** good, kindness, happiness.

hors d'oeuvre *See* APPETIZER.

horse *n.* equine, steed, stallion, mare, mount, pony, nag. *The horse has served as a beast of burden for thousands of years.*

WORD SEARCH

beige with black mane: *buckskin*
beige with light mane: *dun*
black and white: *piebald*
bronze- or copper-colored: *chestnut, sorrel*
brownish red with black mane: *bay*
brownish with gray and white sprinkles: *roan*
bushy tail: *broomtail*
buttermilk or golden: *palomino*
castrated male: *gelding*
cry of: *neigh, whinny*
four, under the age of: *colt, filly*
gaits: *walk, trot, lope, canter, gallop, rack, volt, fox trot*
leap, playful: *gambado*
newborn: *foal*
nose and mouth area: *muzzle*
pen: *corral*
pertaining to: *equine, equestrian*
pulling, strong horse used for: *draft horse*
shelter: *stable, stall*
stand up on rear legs: *rear*
trot in place for show: *piaffe*
white splash between eyes: *star*
white streak on face: *blaze, race*
wild: *bronco, mustang*

horseman *n.* equestrian, rider, cowboy, jockey, bronco buster. *A cattle driver in the 1800s had to be an expert horseman.*

horseplay *n.* antics, hijinks, clowning, tomfoolery, fun, teasing. *The boys' horseplay resulted in a broken window.*

horticulture *n.* gardening, agriculture, cultivation, farming, floriculture. *His goal was to grow ornamental plants for sale, so he went to school to study horticulture.*

hospitable *adj.* friendly, gracious, warm, generous, cordial, sociable, open. *Texans are known for being hospitable people.* **Ant.** cold, unfriendly, unwelcome.

hospital *n.* medical center, infirmary, treatment facility, dispensary, ward, sick bay. *Mary broke a leg and had to be rushed to the hospital.*

hospitality *n.* accommodation, graciousness, entertainment, consideration, geniality, welcome. *They invited us in for tea and cakes, and we thanked them for their hospitality.*

host *n.* **1.** hostess, innkeeper, welcomer, entertainer, emcee. *I will be your host for the length of your stay.* **2.** horde, multitude, army, swarm, legion, crowd, mob. *A host of Vandals sacked Rome.*

hostile *adj.* unfriendly, opposing, aggressive, warlike, belligerent, unfavorable. *The hostile guard searched my suitcase thoroughly.* **Ant.** friendly, agreeable, allied, peaceful.

hostility *n.* ill will, unfriendliness, malevolence, meanness, enmity, antagonism. *The two nations worked together to eliminate their mutual hostility.* **Ant.** friendliness, warmth, goodwill.

hot *adj.* **1.** heated, scorching, scalding, burning, blazing, boiling. *I moved away from Phoenix because it's too hot there.* **2.** spicy, pungent, biting, sharp, peppery, zesty. *The chicken gumbo was too hot for my taste.* **3.** passionate, violent, intense, fierce, excited, emotional, frenzied. *Congress got into a hot debate today.* **4.** good, excellent, successful, marvelous, popular. *The rock concert was really hot.* **Ant.** **1.** cold, cool, freezing. **2.** bland, mild, flat. **3.** quiet, calm, unemotional. **4.** dull, boring, bad.

hotel *n.* inn, lodge, hostel, motel, tavern, lodging. *We stayed at the hotel on the beach.*

hound *vb.* chase, pester, nag, bug, dog, pursue, persecute. *Telemarketers will hound you all day long if they think you'll answer the phone.*

house *n.* dwelling, home, residence, shelter, habitation, abode. *My house is on the corner.*

WORD SEARCH

access to attic: *scuttle*
beam, supporting: *joist*
domelike structure atop roof: *cupola*
double-sloped roof reminiscent of barn: *gambrel*
framing members: *studs*
passage between house and garage: *breezeway*
protruding room and window on roof: *dormer*
siding boards: *clapboards*
styles: *bungalow, Cape Cod, cottage, colonial, Federal, Georgian, ranch, saltbox, townhouse, Tudor, Victorian.*

housekeeper *n.* maid, homemaker, housewife, domestic, cleaner. *The housekeeper has a full-time job.*

housewife *n.* homemaker, lady of the house, stay-at-home Mom, matron, domestic manager. *Alice is content to be a housewife and doesn't choose to pursue a career outside the home.*

hovel *n.* shack, hut, cabin, shanty, shed, hole. *His home was just a little hovel near the railroad tracks.* **Ant.** castle, mansion, palace.

hover *vb.* **1.** float, drift, hang, flutter, fly. *The helicopter hovered in the air.* **2.** hang, loiter, linger, wait, loom. *The boss hovered over her secretary until the letter was typed.* **3.** vacillate, waver, vary, falter, seesaw. *His final decision has hovered between yes and no for the last hour.*

howl *vb.* **1.** yell, yowl, cry, wail, screech, shriek, bellow, bay. *The coyotes howled at the moon.* –*n.* **2.** yelp, scream, cry, clamor, yowl, wail. *She let out a howl when the hammer hit her thumb.*

hub *n.* center, middle, core, focus, midpoint, heart, nucleus. *The bus station is the hub of the city's transportation system.*

hubbub *n.* commotion, fuss, hullabaloo, clamor, uproar, noise. *There was a great hubbub as Santa Claus entered the mall.* **Ant.** stillness, inactivity, silence.

hubris *n.* arrogance, insolence, pride, egotism, overconfidence, conceit. *It was pure hubris that made the bigshot think he was entitled to cut in line.* **Ant.** modesty, humility.

huckster *n.* peddler, hawker, salesman, merchant, tradesman, haggler. *The huckster tried to sell us three apples for five dollars but we didn't bite.*

huddle *vb.* **1.** bunch, crowd, mass, cram, cluster, snuggle, gather. *The football team huddled together to plan the next play.* –*n.* **2.** mass, heap, pile, jumble, mess, clump, bunch. *There was a huddle of unpaid bills on her desk.* **Ant.** **1.** separate, divide, scatter, disperse.

hue *n.* color, tint, shade, cast, tinge, tone, complexion. *Please paint the reception room in hues that are relaxing.*

hug *vb.* **1.** embrace, cuddle, hold, grasp, squeeze, enfold, caress. *The little girl hugged her teddy bear.* –*n.* **2.** embrace, squeeze, caress, press, clasp. *Give your dear old grandmother a big hug.*

huge *adj.* enormous, large, giant, massive, immense, gigantic, colossal. *Jack woke up to see a huge beanstalk growing in his yard.* **Ant.** small, tiny, little.

hulking *adj.* bulky, massive, lumbering, heavy, powerful, husky. *The hulking wrestler stepped into the ring.*

human *adj.* **1.** imperfect, fallible, mortal, flesh-and-blood, civil, civilized. *If you make mistakes, remember that you're only human.* –*n.* **2.** anthropoid, man, woman, person, *Homo sapiens*, being, individual, mammal. **Ant.** **1.** inhuman, perfect, immortal.

humane *adj.* kind, merciful, thoughtful, good, tender, compassionate. *Feeding the starving kittens was a humane act.* **Ant.** cruel, heartless, mean.

humanitarian *adj.* **1.** altruistic, charitable, philanthropic, giving, generous, kind, compassionate. *Among other humanitarian acts, she liked to give part of her pay to the homeless shelter.* –*n.* **2.** philanthropist, (slang) do-gooder, good Samaritan, benefactor, Robin Hood, giver. *The millionaire was a humanitarian who donated to charities throughout his life.* **Ant.** **1.** selfish, cruel, unfeeling. **2.** cheapskate, miser.

humanity *n.* **1.** humankind, human race, mankind, man, men and women, society, people. *The history of humanity is full of triumphs and tragedies.* **2.** compassion, sympathy, empathy, benevolence, kindness, goodness. *The philanthropist was cited for his humanity.*

humankind *n.* humanity, human race, mankind, Homo sapiens, family of man. *Humankind has existed on Earth for a relatively short time.*

humble *adj.* **1.** modest, unassuming, unpretentious, meek, respectful. *The college president was quite humble despite his many accomplishments.*

2. poor, lowly, low, simple, common, obscure. *She started in a humble job and worked her way to the top.* –*vb.* **3.** shame, lower, humiliate, chasten, demean, debase. *The defeated prince was humbled in front of his captors.* **Ant. 1.** vain, proud, arrogant, pompous. **2.** rich, important, prestigious. **3.** praised, exalted, promoted.

humdrum *adj.* dull, boring, blah, tedious, routine, monotonous. *She was getting tired of her humdrum job.*

humid *adj.* muggy, sticky, damp, steamy, moist, clammy, sultry. *The hot summer days in New York tend to be humid.* **Ant.** dry, arid, parched.

humiliate *vb.* shame, embarrass, disgrace, degrade, dishonor, humble, demean. *She was humiliated when she slipped on the banana peel.* **Ant.** honor, exalt, dignify, elevate.

humiliation *n.* shame, embarrassment, dishonor, degradation, lowering. *It was a great humiliation for him to have to ask for help.* **Ant.** honor, prestige, pride, exaltation.

humility *n.* modesty, humbleness, meekness, unpretentiousness, lowliness. *The priest taught that humility is a virtue.* **Ant.** conceit, pride, arrogance.

humor *n.* **1.** ridiculousness, funniness, comedy, amusement, fun, wit. *She didn't see the humor of the situation.* **2.** temperament, mood, disposition, attitude, sentiment, character. *The boss has been in bad humor ever since we lost the contract.* –*vb.* **3.** indulge, pamper, gratify, coddle, oblige, favor. *Let's humor him and maybe he will just go away.* **Ant. 1.** seriousness, gravity, solemnity. **3.** oppose, contradict.

humorist *n.* comedian, comedienne, joker, wit, clown, (slang) stand-up. *The famous humorist has written a newspaper column for twenty years.*

humorous *adj.* funny, hilarious, witty, comical, amusing, laughable. *It wasn't what she said but the way she said it that was so humorous.* **Ant.** sad, serious, grave, sober.

hump *n.* lump, bulge, mound, knob, swelling, ridge, rise. *Would you like your camel with one hump or two?*

hunch *n.* **1.** feeling, thought, intuition, impression, sensation, notion, suspicion. *I have a hunch that you will win first place.* –*vb.* **2.** arch, vault, curve, bend, stoop, tense. *Hunching your back is bad for your posture.*

hunchbacked *adj.* humpbacked, crookbacked, buffalo humped, deformed, gibbous. *Slouching can make you appear hunchbacked, so stand up straight.*

hunger *n.* **1.** starvation, famine, hungriness, appetite. *There is still hunger in many parts of the world.* **2.** desire, want, craving, longing, yearning, thirst, need. *The library is a good place to satisfy your hunger for knowledge.* –*vb.* **3.** desire, want, crave, yearn, itch, wish, long. *She hungered for the job of chairperson.*

hungry *adj.* **1.** starving, starved, famished, empty, ravenous. *Our church donated food to feed the hungry children.* **2.** eager, greedy, desirous, avid, needful, craving. *The dictator was hungry for power.* **Ant. 1.** full, sated, satiated. **2.** indifferent, satisfied.

hunk *n.* **1.** chunk, piece, lump, block, slab, glob. *Cut off a hunk of meat for me.* **2.** Adonis, (slang) stud, (slang) beefcake, (slang) looker, (slang) dreamboat. *The quarterback was a hunk.*

hunt *vb.* **1.** track, stalk, chase, pursue, shoot. *We will be hunting for quail during the weekend.* **2.** search, look, probe, seek, quest, scour. *I spent an hour hunting for my keys.* –*n.* **3.** chase, search, pursuit, quest, hunting. *He was offended by the idea of a fox hunt.*

hurdle *n.* **1.** barrier, obstacle, obstruction, barricade, hazard, block. *The oral exam is the last* *hurdle in completing this class.* –*vb.* **2.** jump, leap, vault, scale, bound, hop, spring. *The mail carrier hurdled over a hedge to escape from a dog.*

hurl *vb.* throw, heave, fling, cast, pitch, toss, sling, launch. *In a fit of rage, she hurled the broken typewriter into the trash.*

hurricane *n.* tropical storm, typhoon, storm, monsoon, tempest, cyclone. *A hurricane is expected to hit the Gulf Coast.*

hurried *adj.* hasty, rushed, pushed, speedy, frantic, abrupt. *His hurried letter had too many mistakes.*

hurry *vb.* **1.** hasten, rush, speed, race, run, scurry. *We hurried through our dinner in order to arrive at the theater on time.* –*n.* **2.** haste, rush, flurry, bustle, dispatch, quickness, speed. *The commuter was in a hurry to get to her train on time.* **Ant. 1.** linger, dawdle, delay. **2.** slowness, delay, sluggishness.

hurt *vb.* **1.** injure, harm, damage, cripple, wound, mar, pain. *You'll hurt your back if you try to lift that crate.* **2.** distress, grieve, upset, insult, offend, abuse. *I didn't mean to hurt his feelings.* **3.** limit, hinder, impede, impair, inhibit, lessen. *The pitcher's injury hurts our team's chances for the championship.* –*n.* **4.** injury, harm, damage, pain, ache, pang. *The hurt in her ankle did not affect her ability to run.* **5.** suffering, torment, discomfort, insult, embarrassment, humiliation. *He was experiencing the hurt of being betrayed by a friend.* –*adj.* **6.** injured, damaged, painful, wounded, impaired. *Androcles pulled a thorn out of the lion's hurt paw.* **Ant. 1.** repair, restore, heal. **2.** praise, compliment, please. **3.** aid, benefit, improve, help. **6.** healed, cured, improved.

hurtful *adj.* harmful, injurious, destructive, damaging, deleterious, mean. *I find your criticism more hurtful than constructive.* **Ant.** helpful, nice, beneficial.

hurtle *vb.* fly, plunge, rush, hurl, zip, tear. *We watched the racers hurtle past us at top speed.*

husband *n.* spouse, groom, mate, (slang) hubby, companion. *Her husband did most of the housework while she held an office job.*

hush *n.* silence, stillness, quiet, peace, calm, lull. *Nothing soothes jangled nerves better than the hush of the north Maine woods.*

husky *adj.* **1.** brawny, muscular, stout, burly, beefy, powerful. *The wrestler was husky and intimidating.* **2.** hoarse, rough, whiskey-voiced, throaty, rasping, guttural. *Her voice was so husky she sounded like a man.* **Ant. 1.** skinny, anorexic, wispy.

hustle *vb.* **1.** hurry, hasten, speed, rush, dash, scurry. *She was always hustling from one meeting to the next.* –*n.* **2.** hurry, fuss, turmoil, stir, flurry, movement, activity. *The play went smoothly, but you should have seen the hustle backstage.* **Ant. 1.** linger, dawdle, loiter. **2.** calmness, peacefulness, rest.

hut *n.* shack, cabin, camp, shelter, shanty, lean-to. *We built a hut to protect us from the elements.*

hutch *n.* chest, cabinet, locker, box, trunk. *My wife stores quilts in a cedar hutch.*

hybrid *n.* cross, mixed breed, composite, crossbreed, mix, mongrel. *The hybrid may take on some of the best or worst characteristics of its parents.*

hygienic *adj.* clean, sanitary, disinfected, aseptic, germ-free, pure. *A hospital must be hygienic.* **Ant.** dirt, unclean, infected.

hymn *n.* spiritual, psalm, choral, anthem, song, ode. *The choir sang a hymn of praise.*

hyperactive *adj.* overactive, unrestrained, wild, frenetic, unruly, unfocused. *The child was running back and forth and throwing things in a hyperactive frenzy.* **Ant.** inactive, unmoving, still.

hypnotic *adj.* spellbinding, mesmerizing, entrancing, stupefying, soporific, somnolent. *The changing patterns on my screensaver can be hypnotic.*

hypnotize *vb.* mesmerize, charm, entrance, enchant, transfix, fascinate. *He was hypnotized by her gorgeous green eyes.*

hyperbole *n.* exaggeration, (slang) hype, embellishment, embroidering, inflation. *Advertisements often use hyperbole to make the sales pitch more effective.* **Ant.** understatement, truth, modesty.

hypocrite *vb.* deceiver, imposter, pretender, fraud, fake. *A person who preaches simple living and then buys a Cadillac is a hypocrite.*

hypocritical *adj.* false, deceptive, insincere, deceitful, dishonest. *It is hypocritical to insult your friends behind their backs.* **Ant.** sincere, honest, honorable.

hypothesis *n.* theory, assumption, conjecture, speculation, proposition. *The detective's hypothesis was that the butler did it.*

hypothetical *adj.* theoretical, unproven, guessed, conjectural, supposed, imaginary. *The scientists' discussion of interstellar spaceflight was purely hypothetical.* **Ant.** factual, actual, true.

hysteria *n.* hysterics, frenzy, madness, agitation, outburst, panic, mania. *A false report of aliens landing on Earth caused mass hysteria.* **Ant.** calm, tranquility, serenity.

hysterical *adj.* **1.** uncontrollable, frenzied, panicky, emotional, wild, raving. *We could not control the hysterical man.* **2.** funny, hilarious, laughable, comical, absurd. *Her new comedy is hysterical.* **Ant.** **1.** controlled, calm, composed. **2.** serious, sad, solemn, somber.

I

icon *n.* symbol, idol, image, representation, likeness, picture. *Donald Trump has long been an icon of financial success.*

iconoclast *n.* cynic, skeptic, critic, detractor, nonbeliever, denouncer. *Henry Thoreau was an iconoclast who thumbed his nose at society's conventions.*

icy *adj.* frozen, freezing, gelid, frosty, frigid, glacial. *It's dangerous to drive after a freezing rain when the roads are icy.*

idea *n.* thought, opinion, concept, belief, notion, assumption, conviction. *Your idea is original but impractical.*

ideal *adj.* **1.** perfect, model, fitting, pure flawless. *This is an ideal place for a campsite.* –*n.* **2.** model, standard, inspiration, concept, objective. *The Declaration of Independence is based on the ideal that all people are created equal.*

idealist *n.* romantic, visionary, optimist, utopian, dreamer. *Many great people were idealists.* **Ant.** cynic, pessimist, fatalist.

idealistic *adj.* Utopian, romantic, unrealistic, Pollyannaish, naive, visionary. *Striving to achieve world peace is an idealistic but noble goal.* **Ant.** realistic, cynical, moderate.

identical *adj.* same, alike, twin, uniform, duplicate. *The two women were wearing identical dresses.* **Ant.** different, distinct, unlike.

identify *vb.* recognize, know, distinguish, place, verify, tell, name. *Can you identify the person who robbed the bank?*

idiom *n.* language, dialect, tongue, vernacular, parlance, jargon. *It is sometimes difficult to understand the idiom of another culture.*

idiosyncrasy *n.* quirk, peculiarity, characteristic, distinction, eccentricity, mannerism. *His most puzzling idiosyncrasy was his preference for a manual typewriter instead of a word processor.*

idiot *n.* fool, moron, simpleton, dummy, dunce, imbecile. *Anyone who would drive recklessly is an idiot.*

idiotic *adj.* stupid, imbecilic, moronic, childish, infantile, asinine. *Some people regard slapstick humor as idiotic.* **Ant.** brilliant, intelligent, genius.

idle *adj.* **1.** lazy, loafing, sluggish, shiftless, listless, lethargic. *The rich man didn't have to work and thus led an idle life.* **2.** unused, unproductive, futile, fruitless, useless. *Idle factories are a sign of a stagnant economy.* –*vb.* **3.** laze, loaf, lounge, bum, loiter. *A beach is a great place in which to idle away the day.* **Ant. 1–2.** busy, active, occupied. **3.** work, labor, toil.

idol *n.* **1.** image, statue, god, symbol, icon, effigy. *The explorer was accused of stealing the sacred idol of Chtulu.* **2.** hero, favorite, darling, inspiration, star, superstar. *Elvis Presley was my mother's idol.*

idolize *vb.* exalt, put on a pedestal, revere, worship, admire, look up to. *Most young basketball players idolize the stars of the game.* **Ant.** reject, disparage, disrespect.

idyllic *adj.* peaceful, pastoral, tranquil, carefree, unspoiled, heavenly, ideal. *The sheep ranging over the sunlit hills offered an idyllic picture.*

iffy *adj.* questionable, doubtful, tentative, unresolved, up in the air, dubious. *The weather in Austin, Texas, is always iffy; if you don't like it, just wait a few minutes.* **Ant.** certain, settled, guaranteed.

ignite *vb.* **1.** light, burn, fire, kindle. *She ignited the campfire with just one match.* **2.** excite, rile, inflame, rouse, agitate. *The army's actions served only to ignite the crowd's anger.* **Ant. 1.** extinguish, quench, douse. **2.** calm, ease, soothe, quiet.

ignoramus *n.* moron, idiot, imbecile, dolt, simpleton, (slang) pea-brain. *The last thing we need is an ignoramus running the country.* **Ant.** genius, Rhodes scholar, intellectual.

ignorance *n.* stupidity, inexperience, naivete, innocence, illiteracy, unenlightenment. *Little hurts a nation's economy more than the ignorance and illiteracy of its citizens.* **Ant.** knowledge, enlightenment, scholarship.

ignorant *adj.* **1.** unaware, uninformed, innocent, unknowing, unfamiliar. *The defendant was ignorant of the events leading to her arrest.* **2.** illiterate, unlearned, uneducated, unschooled, untaught. *How could he have graduated from high school and still be so ignorant?* **Ant. 1.** informed, knowledgeable, aware. **2.** literate, educated.

ignore *vb.* neglect, overlook, disregard, avoid, omit, snub, skip. *She ignored the shouting from the next apartment.* **Ant.** notice, heed, acknowledge.

ill *adj.* **1.** sick, ailing, sickly, unwell, diseased, unhealthy. *He was too ill to go to school today.* **2.** evil, bad, sinister, harmful, wicked, unfavorable, hostile. *An ill wind is blowing through town.* –*n.* **3.** harm, evil, abuse, wickedness, misfortune, injury. *They were afraid that the witch would do them ill.* **Ant. 1.** well, healthy, strong. **2.** good, beneficial, helpful.

ill-at-ease *adj.* uncomfortable, nervous, self-conscious, shy, bashful, anxious. *Many people are ill-at-ease when it comes to public speaking.* **Ant.** relaxed, calm, serene.

illegal *adj.* unlawful, illicit, criminal, banned, unauthorized, forbidden, prohibited. *I refuse to do anything that's illegal.* **Ant.** legal, permitted, lawful.

illegible *adj.* unreadable, obscure, unintelligible, unclear, indistinct. *The doctor's prescription is illegible.* **Ant.** readable, clear, legible.

illegitimate *adj.* illegal, unlawful, unauthorized, improper, wrongful. *Blackmail is an illegitimate way of raising money.* **Ant.** legal, lawful, proper.

illicit *adj.* illegal, prohibited, unlawful, improper, forbidden, criminal. *Mr. Jones was arrested for possession of illicit substances.*

illiterate *adj.* uneducated, untaught, unschooled, ignorant, untutored. *One who cannot read is considered illiterate.* **Ant.** educated, learned, schooled.

illness *n.* sickness, malady, disease, affliction, ailment, disorder. *He contracted a mysterious illness when he was in the jungle.*

illogical *adj.* irrational, unsound, absurd, unreasonable, inconsistent, preposterous. *It was illogical to try out for the swim team since you don't know how to swim.* **Ant.** logical, sensible, reasonable, sound.

illuminate *vb.* **1.** brighten, lighten, light, emblaze. *Fireworks illuminated the night.* **2.** clarify, clear, explain, enlighten, interpret, reveal. *These recommended readings will help illuminate our class lectures.* **Ant. 1.** darken, dim, cloud. **2.** confuse, complicate, obscure.

illusion *n.* **1.** vision, mirage, delusion, apparition, phantom. *We thought we saw a ghost on the staircase, but it was just an illusion.* **2.** fallacy, misbelief, fantasy, misconception, dream. *The musician knew that his dream of success was more than an illusion.* **Ant. 1.** reality, actuality, fact. **2.** truth, certainty, probability.

illustrate *vb.* **1.** show, demonstrate, explain, clarify, illuminate. *Could you illustrate your point with examples?* **2.** depict, picture, draw, decorate, embellish. *The artist was asked to illustrate a children's book.*

illustrious *adj.* distinguished, celebrated, famous, noted, prominent, renowned. *She had an illustrious career as an architect.* **Ant.** obscure, undistinguished, lowly.

image *n.* likeness, resemblance, picture, depiction, form, portrait. *The escaped convict's image was broadcast on the evening news.* **2.** idea, thought, notion, concept, impression, perception. *I have an image of what Heaven should be like.* **3.** idol, statue, effigy, fetish. *He would not bow down to a graven image.*

imaginary *adj.* unreal, nonexistent, fictional, imagined, fantastic, mythical. *Hobbits and elves are imaginary creatures.* **Ant.** real, factual, historical, actual.

imagination *n.* creativity, invention, inventiveness, inspiration, originality. *A science-fiction writer needs a lot of imagination.*

imagine *vb.* **1.** dream, fantasize, picture, envision, conceive, visualize. *She imagined what it would be like to live on Mars.* **2.** suppose, assume, think, believe, gather, suspect, guess. *I imagine it must be cold in Alaska.*

imbecile *n.* fool, moron, dolt, idiot, simpleton, blockhead. *I feel like an imbecile for forgetting your birthday.*

imbroglio *n.* predicament, mess, confusion, quandary, trouble, entanglement. *The police were called to settle an imbroglio involving several people outside the local tavern.*

imbue *vb.* infuse, suffuse, instill, impregnate, saturate, permeate. *We want to imbue in our children a strong sense of right and wrong.*

imitate *vb.* copy, duplicate, mimic, simulate, mirror, reproduce. *I hate it when she imitates my actions.*

imitation *n.* **1.** copy, simulation, reproduction, duplication, counterfeit, replica. *This painting is a cheap imitation of the original.* –*adj.* **2.** artificial, phony, simulated, fake, false, copied. *The imitation diamonds looked real to me.* **Ant. 1.** original. **2.** real, authentic, original.

immaculate *adj.* pure, spotless, clean, unstained, unblemished, perfect, flawless. *The restaurant's kitchen was immaculate.* **Ant.** dirty, filthy, imperfect, flawed.

immaterial *adj.* irrelevant, impertinent, inconsequential, inapplicable, unimportant, insignificant. *The judge rejected the attorney's information as immaterial.* **Ant.** relevant, pertinent, important.

immature *adj.* **1.** young, early, undeveloped, unformed, incomplete, unripe. *The immature fruit is not yet ready to pick.* **2.** juvenile, infantile, childish, irresponsible, inexperienced. *It was immature to lose your temper.* **Ant. 1.** mature, old, grown. **2.** mature, responsible.

immeasurable *adj.* boundless, infinite, vast, unfathomable, bottomless, limitless. *The universe* *appears to be immeasurable, but some astronomers like to try and measure it anyway.* **Ant.** measurable, finite, limited.

immediate *adj.* **1.** direct, adjacent, adjoining, closest, nearest, next. *The bank is on your immediate left.* **2.** instant, prompt, sudden, swift, timely, speedy, direct. *The immediate arrival of the paramedics saved her life.* **Ant. 1.** far, distant, remote. **2.** slow, delayed, pending.

immediately *adv.* directly, instantly, promptly, presently, now. *We will begin the class immediately.* **Ant.** later, shortly, eventually.

immense *adj.* large, enormous, great, vast, huge, gigantic, colossal. *The explorers were astounded by the immense size of the pyramid.* **Ant.** small, little, tiny.

immerse *vb.* **1.** submerge, dunk, dip, plunge, soak, drench. *The hippopotamus immersed itself in the cool river.* **2.** absorb, engross, involve, engage, occupy, preoccupy. *She was totally immersed in the book she was reading.*

immigrate *vb.* migrate, resettle, move, colonize. *My neighbors immigrated to Asia.*

imminent *adj.* near, approaching, immediate, impending, forthcoming, threatening. *The town was an imminent danger from the cyclone.* **Ant.** distant, remote, unlikely.

immoral *adj.* wrongful, unethical, sinful, evil, corrupt, wicked, bad. *Stealing is an immoral act.* **Ant.** moral, good, ethical.

immortal *adj.* eternal, everlasting, undying, deathless, endless. *The Greek gods and goddesses were considered to be immortal.* **Ant.** mortal, temporary, perishable.

immortality *n.* endurance, indestructibility, deathlessness, eternity. *Humans have been searching for the secrets of immortality for centuries.* **2.** fame, renown, celebrity. *It is the goal of some stars to become so famous that they achieve immortality.* **Ant. 1.** mortality, limit, death. **2.** anonymity, obscurity.

immovable *adj.* **1.** unmovable, immobile, set, stationary, fixed, stable. *The trail crew blasted a path through the immovable boulders.* **2.** firm, unchangeable, stubborn, inflexible, unbending, steadfast. *The teacher remained immovable about the date of the exam.* **Ant. 1.** mobile, moveable, portable. **2.** flexible, changeable.

immune *adj.* invulnerable, resistant, safe, unaffected, protected, spared. *She is immune to poison ivy.* **Ant.** susceptible, vulnerable.

immunity *n.* resistance, protection, defense, exemption, impunity, exception. *The diplomat was granted immunity from criminal prosecution.* **Ant.** susceptibility, vulnerability, liability.

immutable *adj.* unchangeable, fixed, unalterable, irreversible, permanent. *The laws of physics are immutable.* **Ant.** changeable, alterable, unfixed.

impact *n.* **1.** contact, force, crash, collision, strike, blow. *It doesn't take much of an impact to shatter a watermelon.* **2.** influence, effect, impression, force, power. *His experiences in the army have had quite an impact on him.*

impair *vb.* damage, harm, injure, weaken, mar, hurt, ruin. *Reading in dim light can impair your vision.* **Ant.** improve, better, enhance.

impartial *adj.* fair, neutral, objective, unbiased, evenhanded, unprejudiced. *Ideally, your judge will be impartial.* **Ant.** partial, biased, subjective, prejudiced.

impasse *n.* block, dead end, roadblock, deadlock, bottleneck, stalemate, standstill. *The parties reached an impasse and needed a tie-breaking vote.* **Ant.** passage, clearance, clearing.

impassioned *adj.* passionate, fervent, ardent, zealous, vehement, enthusiastic. *The president gave an impassioned speech calling for more land conservation.* **Ant.** apathetic, indifferent, bored.

impatient *adj.* restless, anxious, fidgety, jumpy, eager, hurried. *After waiting one hour, she started to get impatient.* **Ant.** patient, composed, unhurried.

impeach *vb.* charge, indict, incriminate, impugn, denounce, discredit. *In light of the scandal, both political parties agreed to impeach the president.*

impeccable *adj.* flawless, faultless, perfect, unblemished, spotless, immaculate. *The gymnast's routine was impeccable.* **Ant.** faulty, imperfect, flawed, defective.

impede *vb.* delay, slow, hinder, inhibit, block, thwart, obstruct. *The senator was indicted for impeding the investigation.* **Ant.** assist, further, support.

impediment *n.* obstacle, barrier, hindrance, deterrent, stumbling block, obstruction. *The lack of a college degree can be a great impediment in the work place.* **Ant.** aid, help, boost.

impending *adj.* approaching, oncoming, nearing, imminent, threatening, forthcoming, looming. *The wizard spoke of impending doom.*

impenetrable *adj.* impervious, impassable, dense, bullet-proof, bomb-hardened, reinforced. *The enemy erected a line of impenetrable fortresses.* **Ant.** penetrable, weak, vulnerable.

imperative *adj.* mandatory, compulsive, required, essential, urgent, necessary. *It is imperative that you pay your taxes on time.* **Ant.** unimportant, optional, unnecessary.

imperfect *adj.* flawed, faulty, defective, blemished, impaired. *The dishonest jeweler tried to sell an imperfect diamond.* **Ant.** perfect, flawless, ideal.

imperfection *n.* flaw, deficiency, shortcoming, failing, weakness, disfigurement. *My dog has far too many imperfections to win a best-in-show prize.* **Ant.** perfection, flawlessness.

imperial *adj.* royal, majestic, lordly, regal, grand. *Please refer to the queen as your "imperial majesty."*

imperil *vb.* endanger, risk, jeopardize, hazard, expose. *Careless handling of toxic chemicals imperiled the workers.* **Ant.** protect, preserve, safeguard.

imperious *adj.* overbearing, domineering, arrogant, haughty, lordly, commanding. *The professor was far too imperious to be liked by his students.* **Ant.** modest, easy going, submissive.

impermeable *adj.* airtight, water-tight, waterproof, impenetrable, impervious. *The plastic wrap formed an impermeable membrane that even air could not penetrate.* **Ant.** permeable, porous, open.

impersonal *adj.* objective, detached, disinterested, indifferent, neutral, impartial. *I was upset because my friend sent me a rather impersonal card.* **Ant.** personal, private, intimate.

impersonate *vb.* imitate, mimic, mock, parody, do an impression of, caricature. *The comedian gets lots of laughs when he impersonates the president.*

impertinent *adj.* **1.** irrelevant, immaterial, beside the point, unrelated, not germane. *Please hold off on any impertinent questions, as we have limited time in our meeting.* **2.** rude, impudent, insolent, disrespectful, fresh, (slang) mouthy. *One more impertinent comment from you, Mr. Rogers, and you'll be seeing the principal.* **Ant. 1.** relevant, related, germane. **2.** polite, considerate, respectful.

impetuous *adj.* impulsive, thoughtless, rash, headlong, reckless, careless. *Young children are* *given to impetuous acts.* **Ant.** careful, thoughtful, cautious.

impetus *n.* stimulus, spur, goad, spark, catalyst, incentive. *Lack of money was the impetus that made me get a job.*

implement *n.* **1.** tool, instrument, device, utensil, apparatus, appliance. *Do you have the right implement to do the job? –vb.* **2.** start, enact, execute, begin, achieve, accomplish. *We will implement our plan tomorrow.*

implicate *vb.* connect, associate, involve, include, entangle, embroil. *A famous actress was implicated in the scandal.* **Ant.** exclude, eliminate, acquit.

implication *n.* association, connection, link, involvement, suggestion, incrimination. *His long discussion about weight loss was an implication that we should exercise more.*

implicit *adj.* implied, suggested, understood, inferred, tacit, unexpressed. *My mother's surly facial expression was an implicit message to stay away from the cake.* **Ant.** explicit, spoken, direct.

implied *vb.* suggested, alluded to, inferred, indicated, implicated, implicit. *His accusatory tone implied that he believed that I took the last donut.*

implode *vb.* blow, collapse, cave in, fold. *We were worried that the igloo we made from wet snow might implode if people stood on its roof.*

implore *vb.* beg, plead, beseech, entreat, urge. *The peasants implored their king to lower taxes.*

imply *vb.* suggest, hint, indicate, signify, mean, denote. *Her absence implies that she is mad at you.*

impolite *adj.* rude, discourteous, disrespectful, uncivil, inconsiderate. *The children were impolite to their baby-sitter.* **Ant.** polite, mannerly, civil.

important *adj.* **1.** significant, essential, crucial, meaningful, valuable, worthwhile. *I have something important to tell you.* **2.** influential, prominent, distinguished, imposing, powerful. *You have to be an important person to get your name in "Who's Who."* **Ant. 1–2.** unimportant, inconsequential, insignificant.

impose *vb.* **1.** put, institute, levy, introduce, place, order. *The park rangers imposed a fee for campsite use.* **2.** intrude, interfere, inconvenience, bother, trouble. *I don't want to impose on you by staying overnight.*

imposing *adj.* grand, majestic, striking, stately, impressive. *The Empire State Building is one of the most imposing skyscrapers in New York.* **Ant.** ordinarily, unimpressive, unimposing.

impossible *adj.* inconceivable, unworkable, unbelievable, unthinkable, ridiculous, absurd. *It's impossible to be in two places at once.* **Ant.** possible, feasible, plausible.

impostor *n.* imitator, impersonator, fraud, deceiver, pretender, phony. *The man in the general's uniform was just an impostor.*

impotent *adj.* ineffectual, powerless, weak, inadequate, unproductive, incapable. *Their shouting to scare away the skunk was completely impotent.* **Ant.** potent, powerful, effective.

impound *vb.* hold, retain, confine, keep, imprison, seize, confiscate. *The police department may impound your car if you park it in front of a fire hydrant.*

impractical *adj.* unworkable, unrealistic, unfeasible, futile, absurd. *It is impractical to carry the piano up five flights of stairs.* **Ant.** practical, pragmatic, workable.

impregnable *vb.* invincible, unyielding, indestructible, indomitable, impenetrable. *The enemy experimented with ways of constructing an impregnable fortress.*

impregnate *vb.* inseminate, fertilize, procreate, make pregnant, fecundate. *The male may impregnate a female, but only if he has a high sperm count.*

impress *vb.* **1.** affect, influence, strike, move, touch. *The new teacher impressed me as being very strict.* **2.** imprint, mark, print, indent, stamp. *The postmark was impressed on the envelope.*

impression *n.* **1.** impact, effect, feeling, influence, sensation. *She wanted to make a good impression on the interviewer.* **2.** indentation, imprint, stamp, mark, depression. *The watchband was so tight that it left an impression on his wrist.* **3.** thought, idea, opinion, hunch, notion, sense. *Do you get the impression that he doesn't like me?*

impressionable *adj.* suggestible, susceptible, pliable, easily brainwashed, gullible, vulnerable. *Children are impressionable and can be easily misled.*

impressive *adj.* imposing, striking, awesome, majestic, stirring, inspiring. *The queen's coronation was an impressive ceremony.* **Ant.** ordinary, routine, unimpressive.

imprison *vb.* incarcerate, jail, lock up, confine, pen, detain. *They decided to imprison the soldiers until the war was over.* **Ant.** free, liberate.

improbable *adj.* unlikely, doubtful, questionable, implausible, dubious. *It is improbable that you will see any robins in the winter.* **Ant.** likely, certain, possible, plausible.

impromptu *adj.* impulsive, unrehearsed, unprepared, spontaneous, improvised. *The host's impromptu dance kept everybody in a light mood.* **Ant.** planned, rehearsed, prepared.

improper *adj.* **1.** incorrect, wrong, faulty, erroneous, unsuitable, inappropriate. *Did you know that's the improper way to hold a tennis racket?* **2.** indecent, naughty, immoral, unbecoming, lewd, offensive. *His obscene remarks were crude and improper.* **Ant.** **1.** fitting, proper, correct. **2.** decent, moral, proper.

impropriety *n.* mistake, error, goof, faux pas, gaffe, blunder. *By eating the pie with her hands, she was guilty of a social impropriety.*

improve *vb.* better, perfect, enhance, upgrade, amend, refine, correct. *The pianist sought to improve her technique.* **Ant.** impair, worsen, damage.

improvement *n.* betterment, enhancement, correction, progress, development. *The teacher noticed an improvement in his students' grades.* **Ant.** worsening, decline, weakening.

improvise *vb.* invent, make up, devise, create, ad-lib. *I forgot the recipe, so I'm going to improvise.*

imprudent *adj.* unwise, unadvisable, incautious, thoughtless, careless, rash, foolish. *It was imprudent to go camping in the desert without water.* **Ant.** cautious, thoughtful, careful.

impudent *adj.* insolent, offensive, rude, disrespectful, impertinent, fresh, (slang) smart-alecky. *The wise-cracking student was so impudent that he had to be removed from class.* **Ant.** respectful, polite, reverent.

impugn *vb.* attack, assail, challenge, criticize, question, refute. *We listened to the lawyer impugn the reputation of the defendant.*

impulse *n.* urge, whim, desire, fancy, itch, need. *She had the impulse to jump into the pool with her clothes on.*

impulsive *adj.* impromptu, rash, abrupt, spontaneous, sudden, unplanned. *He went on an impulsive buying spree.* **Ant.** planned, cautious, deliberate.

impunity *n.* immunity, freedom, exemption, exception, license, privilege. *The graffiti artists mistakenly thought they could vandalize private* *property with impunity.* **Ant.** liability, punishment, consequence.

impure *adj.* contaminated, tainted, sullied, unclear, polluted, adulterated. *The water here is impure and undrinkable.*

inaccessible *adj.* unreachable, remote, unattainable, distant, out of reach. *The log cabin was inaccessible by road.* **Ant.** accessible, reachable, close.

inaccurate *adj.* wrong, incorrect, false, mistaken, erroneous, imprecise. *The gas-station attendant gave me inaccurate directions.* **Ant.** accurate, correct, right.

inactive *adj.* idle, inert, still, sedentary, inoperable, dormant. *The volcano has been inactive for decades.* **Ant.** active, busy, productive.

inadequate *adj.* insufficient, deficient, meager, short, scanty, incomplete. *The stock clerk ordered an inadequate supply of pencils.* **Ant.** sufficient, adequate, ample.

inadmissible *adj.* unacceptable, restricted, unfitting, inappropriate, unsuitable, unqualified. *The evidence, unfortunately, was inadmissible in court.* **Ant.** admissible, allowed, legal.

inadvertent *adj.* accidental, unintentional, unplanned, unwitting, involuntary, undeliberate. *She spilled the milk all over the floor, but it was inadvertent.* **Ant.** intentional, designed, deliberate.

inane *adj.* silly, senseless, foolish, ridiculous, empty, stupid, absurd. *Not being able to find your sock is an inane reason for waking me up.* **Ant.** sensible, reasonable, intelligent.

inanimate *adj.* lifeless, dead, inert, inorganic. *Someone must have shifted the table, because inanimate objects do not move themselves.* **Ant.** alive, living, animate.

inappropriate *adj.* improper, unfit, unsuitable, wrong, unseemly. *It is inappropriate to talk during the minister's sermon.* **Ant.** appropriate, proper, suitable.

inattentive *adj.* absentminded, heedless, distracted, preoccupied, negligent, oblivious, remiss. *Driving on the highway in no time to be inattentive.* **Ant.** attentive, alert, observant.

inaugurate *vb.* **1.** begin, start, introduce, commence, open, launch. *The health club inaugurated a morning exercise session.* **2.** induct, install, instate, invest, initiate. *The new president was inaugurated with much ceremony.* **Ant. 1.** end, conclude, finish. **2.** remove, impeach, oust.

inborn *adj.* innate, genetic, congenital, natural, inherited, in the genes. *She had an inborn talent for artistic endeavors.* **Ant.** acquired, attained, learned.

incantation *n.* magic spell, magic charm, invocation, chant, hex, hocus-pocus. *The wizard uttered an incantation that made the rabbit suddenly vanish.*

incapable *adj.* incompetent, ineffective, inefficient, inept, unqualified, powerless, weak. *The business went bankrupt because of its incapable administrators.* **Ant.** competent, effective, strong.

incapacitated *adj.* disabled, paralyzed, crippled, immobilized, handicapped, put out of action. *The fishermen were incapacitated by the foot-thick mud.* **Ant.** able, healthy.

incarcerate *vb.* imprison, jail, confine, hold, restrain, lock up. *The police officer decided to incarcerate the staggering drunk.* **Ant.** free, release, liberate.

incense *vb.* anger, irritate, enrage, infuriate, inflame, provoke. *The waitress was incensed when* *her customer refused to tip her.* **Ant.** cheer, calm, soothe.

incense *n.* aromatic, scent, fragrance, pastille, spice, essence. *Sarah likes to burn incense while she meditates.*

incentive *n.* motivation, encouragement, motive, spur, inducement, cause, reason. *The theater offered two tickets for the price of one as an incentive to draw customers.* **Ant.** discouragement, deterrent, curb.

inception *n.* start, beginning, birth, origin, outset, initiation. *The inception of baseball occurred more than a century ago.* **Ant.** end, close, death.

incessant *adj.* constant, continual, ceaseless, endless, relentless, unending. *I wish that dog would stop its incessant howling.* **Ant.** occasional, sporadic, irregular.

incest *n.* sexual abuse, molestation, statutory crime, rape. *Incest can have serious psychological consequences.*

incident *n.* event, occurrence, experience, happening, episode. *Were you involved in that bizarre incident in the library?*

incidental *adj.* secondary, subordinate, minor, unimportant, trivial, casual. *Any financial reward in the lawsuit is incidental to the principles involved.* **Ant.** major, primary, dominant.

incinerator *n.* furnace, burner, crematory, gas chamber. *What can't be recycled is consumed in the town incinerator.*

incisive *adj.* sharp, penetrating, piercing, cutting, to the point, trenchant. *Her revelatory report was incisive and authoritative.* **Ant.** dull, superficial, shallow.

incite *vb.* rouse, arouse, induce, urge, provoke, instigate, encourage. *The speaker was accused of inciting the crowd into rioting.* **Ant.** dissuade, restrain, discourage.

inclement *adj.* stormy, foul, rough, nasty, harsh, raw. *We had a spell of inclement weather last week.* **Ant.** clement, nice, pleasant.

inclination *n.* leaning, preference, disposition, bias, bent, predilection. *My inclination is to go fishing earlier rather than later.*

incline *vb.* lean, bend, slope, slant, tilt. *The tree inclines to the left.* *–n.* **2.** hill, slope, grade, bank, rise. *Ivy was planted on the incline to keep it from eroding.*

inclined *adj.* likely, apt, prone, willing, disposed, liable. *I'm inclined to agree with you.* **Ant.** unlikely, unwilling, disinclined.

include *vb.* involve, contain, encompass, embody, comprise, encircle, cover. *The price of dinner includes a free drink.* **Ant.** exclude, omit, preclude.

incognito *adj.* in disguise, masked, concealed, anonymous, clandestine. *Nobody recognized me because I was traveling incognito.*

incoherent *adj.* unintelligible, incomprehensible, indistinct, confused, muddled, disjointed. *The football player was incoherent after his concussion.* **Ant.** coherent, clear, intelligible.

income *n.* revenue, salary, wage, earning, pay, profit. *She makes a good income from her realty business.*

incomparable *adj.* unequaled, matchless, unrivaled, unique, unparalleled, supreme. *The incomparable beauty of Beethoven's Ninth Symphony has to be heard to be understood.* **Ant.** ordinary, mediocre, fair, average.

incompatible *adj.* mismatched, opposite, contradictory, clashing, antagonistic, contrary. *Dogs and cats are often incompatible.* **Ant.** compatible, suited, matching.

incompetent *adj.* incapable, unfit, ineffective, inefficient, inept, unqualified. *The incompetent dishwasher broke most of the dishes.* **Ant.** competent, able, fit, effective.

incomplete *adj.* unfinished, undone, partial, fragmentary, wanting, lacking, deficient. *The jigsaw puzzle was still incomplete at the end of the day.* **Ant.** complete, whole, done, finished.

incomprehensible *adj.* unintelligible, unknowable, inscrutable, baffling, mysterious, unexplainable. *What may lie beyond the edge of the universe is incomprehensible.* **Ant.** comprehensible, understandable, knowable.

inconceivable *adj.* unbelievable, unthinkable, incredible, unlikely, unimaginable. *It was inconceivable that the butler would steal the diamonds.* **Ant.** believable, plausible, likely.

inconclusive *adj.* unclear, unresolved, indefinite, unresolved, unproven, open, debatable. *The scientist's study proved inconclusive.* **Ant.** conclusive, clear, definite.

incongruous *adj.* clashing, contrasting, incompatible, conflicting, odd, unsuited. *Love and war make an incongruous pair.* **Ant.** compatible, harmonious.

inconsequential *adj.* insignificant, trivial, neglible, ineffective, unimportant, trifling. *The company's minor losses were largely inconsequential.* **Ant.** consequential, momentous, critical.

inconsiderate *adj.* selfish, thoughtless, unthinking, tactless, negligent. *The inconsiderate neighbor refused to turn down his radio.* **Ant.** considerate, thoughtful, kind.

inconsistent *adj.* **1.** contradictory, illogical, contrary, incompatible, conflicting. *The professor's theory is inconsistent with the scientific facts.* **2.** erratic, fickle, changeable, uncertain, unstable. *The boxer's inconsistent style confused his opponent.* **Ant. 1.** consistent, logical, uniform. **2.** stable, unchanging, steady.

inconspicuous *adj.* indistinct, obscure, unapparent, unnoticeable, muted, dim. *We barely noticed the inconspicuous sparrow in the tree.* **Ant.** obvious, conspicuous, clear.

inconvenient *adj.* annoying, awkward, untimely, bothersome, unhandy, troublesome. *You arrived at an inconvenient time.* **Ant.** convenient, timely, handy.

incorporate *vb.* include, involve, integrate, merge, mix, blend. *The technicians want to incorporate a faster modem into the computer.*

incorrect *adj.* wrong, false, mistaken, inexact, inaccurate, untrue. *You will fail the test if you have more than ten incorrect answers.* **Ant.** right, true, correct, accurate.

incorrigible *adj.* irreformable, irredeemable, intractable, incurable, beyond help, a lost cause. *Disciplinary action did little to counter the tryant's incorrigible behavior.* **Ant.** redeemable, reformable, curable.

increase *vb.* **1.** enlarge, expand, grow, magnify, inflate, extend, multiply. *Her book collection has increased so much she needs more shelves.* *–n.* **2.** growth, expansion, enlargement, gain, advance, rise, addition. *The increase in his wages was well deserved.* **Ant. 1.** decrease, lessen, diminish. **2.** decrease, drop, reduction.

incredible *adj.* unbelievable, extraordinary, unimaginable, amazing, fantastic. *The explorer told an incredible story about being captured by Amazon warriors.* **Ant.** credible, ordinary, believable.

incredulous *adj.* disbelieving, skeptical, distrusting, dubious, unconvinced, doubting, questioning. *Telling children that pigs can fly is guaranteed to bring an incredulous response.* **Ant.** credulous, believing, trusting.

increment *n.* step, rise, gain, addition, increase, notch. *We will increase speed by increments of five miles per hour.*

incriminate *vb.* accuse, charge, blame, implicate, point the finger at, involve. *He refused to testify on the grounds that he might incriminate himself.*

incurable *adj.* malignant, deadly, terminal, hopeless, fatal, lethal. *I worry that my chronic hiccups may be incurable.* **Ant.** curable, benign, treatable.

incursion *n.* infiltration, advance, inroad, invasion, foray, encroachment. *They set up roadblocks to help stall an incursion by terrorists.*

indebted *adj.* obligated, owing, beholden, bound, grateful, appreciative. *I'm indebted to the store clerk who found my lost wallet.*

indecent *adj.* immodest, improper, immoral, offensive, obscene, shameful, tasteless. *The rock singer has been criticized for his indecent behavior on stage.* **Ant.** decent, tasteful, proper.

indecisive *adj.* **1.** unsettled, doubtful, unclear, dubious, arguable, debatable. *She argued that the opinion-poll results were indecisive.* **2.** faltering, hesitant, wavering, uncertain, tentative. *The indecisive shopper couldn't decide what color socks he wanted.* **Ant. 1.** conclusive, certain, decided. **2.** definite, sure, decisive.

indeed *adv.* surely, definitely, certainly, really, honestly, truly. *She is indeed the daughter of the king.*

indefensible *adj.* insupportable, inexcusable, unforgivable, weak, untenable. *His excuse was indefensible, so the judge threw the book at him.* **Ant.** supportable, defensible.

indefinite *adj.* uncertain, unknown, unsettled, unsure, vague, doubtful, confusing. *The governor will be out of the state for an indefinite period of time.* **Ant.** definite, exact, certain, specific.

indelible *adj.* lasting, permanent, fixed, indestructible, unforgettable, ingrained. *The first moon landing left an indelible memory.* **Ant.** temporary, erasable, forgettable.

indelicate *adj.* tacky, rude, rough, coarse, crude, gross. *The diner seated next to us was so indelicate as to burp throughout his dinner.* **Ant.** delicate, tactful, refined.

indent *vb.* dent, impress, dimple, depress, hollow, mark. *Indent the start of all new paragraphs.*

independence *n.* freedom, liberty, autonomy, self-government, emancipation. *The rebels fought to win independence for their country.* **Ant.** dependence, subjection, slavery.

independent *adj.* free, uncontrolled, self-reliant, self-governing, separate, unattached. *The millionaire's donation made the art museum financially independent.* **Ant.** dependent, reliant, subject, controlled.

indescribable *adj.* nondescript, amorphous, indistinct, inexpressible, beyond words. *The emperor lived in a palace of indescribable luxury.*

indestructible *adj.* impregnable, unbreakable, immortal, deathless, durable, permanent. *Made of heavy metal, the toy truck was practically indestructible.* **Ant.** destructible, vulnerable, fragile.

index *n.* catalog, file, register, glossary, directory. *This subject should be mentioned in the book's index.*

indicate *vb.* **1.** suggest, imply, mean, signify, reveal, represent. *The dark clouds indicate a storm is coming.* **2.** point, show, designate, specify, state. *Please indicate where you want me to place the chair.*

indication *n.* sign, evidence, telltale, portent, signal, hint. *The sudden drop in temperature was an indication of an impending cold spell.*

indicator *n.* sign, guide, pointer, dial, gauge, barometer. *The inflation rate is a good indicator of the economy's growth.*

indict *vb.* accuse, charge, arraign, incriminate, cite, impute. *The grand jury moved to indict all parties suspected of the offenses.*

indictment *n.* charge, accusation, arraignment, incrimination, citation, legal statement. *The grand jury handed down a formal indictment.*

indifferent *adj.* **1.** unconcerned, uncaring, unmoved, insensitive, apathetic, neutral. *The doctor seemed indifferent to his patient's medical complaint.* **2.** ordinary, mediocre, average, passable, uninspired. *She was disappointed in the indifferent performance by the string quartet.* **Ant. 1.** concerned, caring, interested. **2.** special, exceptional.

indigenous *adj.* native, aboriginal, original, natural, endemic, homegrown. *Native Americans are indigenous to our country.* **Ant.** foreign, alien

indigent *adj.* impoverished, poor, destitute, needy, poverty-stricken, (slang) broke, penniless. *The indigent vagrant panhandled for spare change.* **Ant.** wealthy, rich, affluent.

indignant *adj.* angry, irate, incensed, mad, offended, wrathful. *He was indignant when his date didn't show up.* **Ant.** serene, pleased, calm.

indignity *n.* insult, humiliation, embarrassment, abuse, affront. *Yesterday I suffered the indignity of running out of toilet paper at the worst possible moment.*

indirect *adj.* roundabout, oblique, circuitous, divergent, deviating, vague, sidelong. *She indicated in an indirect manner her intention to raise her bid.*

indiscreet *adj.* careless, incautious, rash, reckless, foolish, thoughtless. *I would not have told him my secret if I had known he was so indiscreet.* **Ant.** discreet, careful, prudent.

indiscretion *n.* impropriety, injudiciousness, mistake, slip, lapse, transgression, faux pas. *The president's many indiscretions got him into trouble.*

indiscriminate *adj.* careless, undiscriminating, unparticular, casual, uncritical, haphazard. *An indiscriminate word may cause a great deal of anguish.* **Ant.** discriminating, choosy, selective.

indispensable *adj.* essential, necessary, required, needed, vital, basic. *A paint brush is an indispensable item for an artist.* **Ant.** dispensable, disposable, unnecessary.

indistinct *adj.* vague, unclear, obscure, faint, blurred, hazy, uncertain. *The approaching figures were indistinct in the fog.* **Ant.** clear, distinct, defined.

individual *adj.* **1.** personal, private, separate, special, particular, single, exclusive. *Everyone has their individual likes and dislikes.* –*n.* **2.** person, being, entity, character, somebody, human. *That individual just won a million dollars.* **Ant. 1.** public, general, common, universal.

individuality *n.* personality, character, distinction, self, uniqueness, originality. *Individuality is what sets you apart from the rest of the herd.*

indoctrinate *vb.* instruct, imbue, teach, enlighten, train, brainwash, program. *The cult indoctrinates its new members with an intense educational program.* **Ant.** deprogram.

indolent *adj.* lazy, slothful, shiftless, inactive, idle, listless. *If you are indolent, you won't succeed at anything but being a couch potato.* **Ant.** industrious, hard-working, productive.

indomitable *adj.* invincible, unconquerable, unbeatable, dominant, staunch, omnipotent. *The dictator's stronghold over the citizenry appeared indomitable.* **Ant.** beatable, weak, defeatable.

induce *vb.* cause, prompt, influence, persuade, impel, inspire, urge, convince. *She was induced to move out of the city because of the increase in crime.* **Ant.** dissuade, discourage, hinder, prevent.

indulge *vb.* satisfy, gratify, humor, favor, pamper, spoil, placate. *They indulged their child in her every whim.* **Ant.** deny, forbid, thwart, abstain.

indulgence *n.* **1.** luxury, excess, privilege, allowance, satisfaction. *The trip to Hawaii was a well-deserved indulgence.* **2.** understanding, tolerance, patience, forgiveness, leniency. *I ask for your indulgence if I talk too long.* **Ant. 1.** denial, repression. **2.** intolerance, impatience.

industrious *adj.* hardworking, persistent, diligent, productive, active, tireless. *You must be industrious in order to succeed in your own business.* **Ant.** lazy, sluggish, slothful.

industry *n.* **1.** commerce, business, trade, manufacture, enterprise. *There's been an increase in industry since the trade agreement was signed.* **2.** persistence, diligence, zeal, energy, productiveness. *Good workers are prized for their industry.*

ineffective *adj.* inefficient, useless, worthless, vain, futile, unproductive, fruitless. *Our air conditioner was ineffective during last week's heat wave.* **Ant.** effective, useful, beneficial.

ineffectual *adj.* weak, incompetent, inept, useless, powerless, ineffective. *The townspeople voted against their ineffectual councilman.* **Ant.** competent, powerful, capable.

inefficient *adj.* ineffective, inadequate, incapable, unsuccessful, incompetent, unable. *The new pollution controls were inefficient in reducing smog.* **Ant.** efficient, successful, able.

inept *adj.* incompetent, unskilled, bumbling, untrained, maladroit, (slang) all thumbs. *The collapse of the new stairs proved that the contractor was inept.* **Ant.** competent, skilled, expert.

inert *adj.* unmoving, fixed, motionless, static, inactive, immobile, passive. *You have to lie inert while the X ray is being taken.* **Ant.** active, moving, mobile.

inertia *n.* inactivity, stasis, lifelessness, immobility, passivity, paralysis. *The congressman was criticized for his inertia on environmental issues.* **Ant.** motion, activity, movement.

inevitable *adj.* certain, sure, destined, unavoidable, inescapable, fate. *It is inevitable that Central High will win the football championship this year.* **Ant.** unsure, uncertain, doubtful.

inexpensive *adj.* cheap, reasonable, modest, low-priced, economical. *I'm shopping for an inexpensive watch.* **Ant.** expensive, costly, high-priced.

inexperienced *adj.* untrained, unskilled, new, novice, beginning. *This mountain road is too dangerous for an inexperienced driver.* **Ant.** experienced, expert, trained, skilled.

inexplicable *adj.* mysterious, unknown, unexplainable, incomprehensible, baffling, inscrutable. *Unidentified flying objects may be inexplicable, but it doesn't necessarily mean that they're spaceships from other worlds.* **Ant.** explicable.

infallible *adj.* perfect, faultless, flawless, unfailing, unerring, reliable. *She has an infallible ear for music.* **Ant.** faulty, imperfect, unreliable.

infamous *adj.* notorious, scandalous, shameful, villainous, ill-famed. *Al Capone was an infamous gangster.* **Ant.** honorable, respectful, esteemed.

infamy *n.* reputation, fame, disrepute, notoriety, ignominy, villainy. *Hitler's infamy quickly spread around the world.* **Ant.** repute, honor.

infant *n.* baby, tot, child, newborn, babe. *The infant slept peacefully through the night.*

infantile *adj.* babyish, childish, spoiled, selfish, juvenile, unsophisticated. *Crying over spilled milk is infantile behavior.* **Ant.** mature, adult, sophisticated.

infatuated *adj.* smitten, enamored, bewitched, enchanted, beguiled, enraptured. *She was infatuated with the new boy, but she did not love him.* **Ant.** repulsed, repelled, disgusted.

infect *vb.* **1.** contaminate, taint, poison, sicken, afflict. *Many children at the summer camp were infected with a cold virus.* **2.** influence, affect, touch, stir, move. *His humorous personality infected the entire group.*

infectious *adj.* contagious, catching, infective, transferable, communicable. *Flu is an infectious disease.* **Ant.** noninfectious, incommunicable.

infer *vb.* conclude, reason, guess, reckon, deduce, suppose, presume. *I infer from your statement that you admit your part in the crime.*

inferior *adj.* poor, substandard, secondary, lesser, lower, mediocre. *She regretted using an inferior brand of paint for the house.* **Ant.** superior, better, higher.

infernal *adj.* hellish, diabolic, Stygian, satanic, demonic, evil. *The volcano spewed forth all matter of infernal materials.*

infertile *adj.* sterile, barren, infecund, impotent, unproductive. *Mary had so much trouble conceiving a child that she feared she might be infertile.* **Ant.** fertile, fecund, prolific.

infest *vb.* overrun, plague, swarm, beset, invade, ravage, fill. *The old wooden house was infested with termites.*

infidel *n.* nonbeliever, atheist, heretic, non-Christian, non-Muslim, heathen. *Whether you're considered an infidel or not, you have the right to believe or not believe what you wish.* **Ant.** believer, Christian, Muslim.

infidelity *n.* unfaithfulness, disloyalty, betrayal, adultery, cheating, treachery. *She filed for divorce because of her husband's repeated infidelity.* **Ant.** fidelity, faithfulness, loyalty.

infiltrate *vb.* penetrate, impregnate, invade, intrude, permeate, pass through. *Pollution from pesticides can sometimes infiltrate into groundwater.*

infinite *adj.* endless, limitless, unlimited, boundless, immense, enormous. *The number of stars in the universe is almost infinite.* **Ant.** limited, finite, restricted.

infinitesimal *adj.* microscopic, minute, negligible, slight, subatomic, atomic. *The odds of winning the state lottery are sometimes infinitesimal.* **Ant.** massive, stupendous, immense.

infinity *n.* endlessness, limitlessness, eternity, forever, infinitude, perpetuity. *Peering through a telescope at the universe is peering through infinity.*

infirm *adj.* weak, fragile, feeble, sick, frail, faltering. *My grandmother is too infirm to do her own grocery shopping.* **Ant.** strong, robust, powerful.

infirmary *n.* hospital, dispensary, sick bay, clinic, treatment facility, pharmacy. *If you've got a migraine, maybe you should go to the infirmary and get treatment.*

inflammation *n.* redness, swelling, tenderness, irritation, immune response. *The doctor gave me some medication to reduce the inflammation.*

inflame *vb.* rouse, incite, enrage, provoke, aggravate, ignite. *She was inflamed with anger when her sister tore the dress.*

inflammatory *adj.* arousing, inciting, explosive, incendiary, rabble-rousing, provocative. *Her inflammatory remarks caused an uproar.* **Ant.** soothing, pacifying, mollifying.

inflate *vb.* expand, distend, blow up, swell, enlarge. *He inflated the balloon with one huge breath.* **Ant.** deflate, collapse.

inflexible *adj.* **1.** rigid, stiff, unbending, firm, hard. *This inflexible bar will break if you try to bend it.* **2.** stubborn, steadfast, unbending, unyielding, immovable, headstrong. *She is inflexible regarding her decision to move to California.* **Ant. 1–2.** elastic, flexible, yielding.

inflict *vb.* impose, wreak, perpetrate, apply, subject, give. *The bombing inflicted heavy casualties.*

influence *n.* **1.** effect, sway, power, control, important, weight. *She has a great deal of influence with the school board.* –*vb.* **2.** sway, persuade, move, direct, control, affect, impress. *The contestant was disqualified for trying to influence the judges.* **Ant. 1.** ineffectiveness, unimportance.

influential *adj.* effective, powerful, persuasive, potent, forceful, inspiring. *Charisma can be a highly influential force.* **Ant.** ineffective, impotent, powerless.

influenza *n.* flu, viral infection, virus, (slang) bug, respiratory virus, chills and fever. *It's wise for the elderly to get an annual vaccine to protect against influenza.*

influx *n.* inflow, arrival, inpouring, tide, flood. *An influx of tourists has clogged the highways.* **Ant.** exit, outflow, recession.

inform *vb.* tell, advise, enlighten, notify, acquaint, teach, educate. *Please inform the doctor that I will be late for my appointment.*

informal *adj.* casual, natural, easy, relaxed, simple, unofficial. *The speaker had an informal style that kept everybody at ease.* **Ant.** formal, official, stiff, rigid.

information *n.* facts, news, data, knowledge, intelligence, material. *We need more information in order to make a decision.*

informer *n.* informant, whistle-blower, (slang) tattletale, (slang) weasel, (slang) rat, snitch. *The informer approached the police with damaging evidence against the gang.*

infraction *n.* violation, lawbreaking, breach, offense, transgression, malfeasance. *A parking ticket is a relatively minor infraction, but it can be an expensive one.*

infrastructure *n.* framework, underpinning, foundation, support, base. *Without a solid infrastructure of good employees, a company cannot survive.*

infrequent *adj.* uncommon, occasional, irregular, unusual, sporadic. *Earthquakes are infrequent but frightening events.* **Ant.** common, frequent, usual.

infringe *vb.* intrude, encroach, trespass, violate, contravene, step on one's toes. *I don't want to infringe on my neighbor's sleep by blasting my stereo after midnight.*

infuriate *vb.* enrage, outrage, inflame, madden, anger, incense, rile. *His arrogant attitude infuriated his supervisor.* **Ant.** please, delight, satisfy.

infuse *vb.* instill, imbue fill, suffuse, ingrain, permeate. *She used an atomizer to infuse the room with the fragrance of lavender.*

ingenious *adj.* clever, imaginative, inventive, skillful, resourceful, creative. *The inventor created an ingenious device that irons your clothes while you sleep.* **Ant.** unoriginal, ordinary, unimaginative.

ingenue *n.* young woman, innocent, naif, babe in the woods, debutante, juvenile. *The* *young ingenue showed promise of becoming a big star.*

ingenuity *n.* inventiveness, creativity, imagination, cleverness, resourcefulness, intelligence. *The inventor used his ingenuity to solve the engineering problem.*

ingrained *adj.* intrinsic, innate, dyed-in-the-wool, deep-rooted, fixed. *Honesty should be ingrained in every child.* **Ant.** superficial, surface.

ingratiate *vb.* court, (slang) kiss up to, charm, flatter, cajole, curry favor. *You might try to ingratiate yourself with the supervisor if you want a job.* **Ant.** disrespect, insult, offend.

ingredient *n.* element, particle, part, factor, item, piece, aspect, feature. *Blueberries are a primary ingredient in blueberry muffins.*

inhabit *vb.* live, reside, dwell, occupy, abide, lodge. *The hollow tree was inhabited by two squirrels.*

inhabitant *n.* resident, denizen, citizen, native, occupant, lodger. *The inhabitants of the old Victorian mansion were composed largely of ghosts.*

inhale *vb.* breathe, draw a breath, inspire, sniff, gasp. *It's unhealthy to inhale automobile fumes.* **Ant.** exhale.

inherent *adj.* essential, natural, inborn, inbred, ingrained, innate, elemental. *The ability to fly is an inherent trait of a bat.* **Ant.** alien, superficial, artificial.

inheritance *n.* legacy, bestowal, endowment, heritage, estate, bequest. *Her late uncle left her a large inheritance.*

inherited *adj.* innate, hereditary, inborn, inbred, genetic, in the genes. *Sarah inherited her green eyes from her mother.*

inhibited *adj.* shy, reserved, reticent, self-conscious, guarded, uptight. *He was too inhibited to dance.* **Ant.** uninhibited, spontaneous, unguarded.

inhibition *n.* shyness, reserve, reticence, self-consciousness, withdrawal, bashfulness. *Inhibitions prevented some of the students from braving the dance floor.* **Ant.** spontaneity, freedom, abandon.

inimitable *adj.* incomparable, peerless, unrivaled, unequaled, unmatched, unparalleled. *The inimitable Jimmy Hendrix was one of the all-time great electric guitar players.*

initial *adj.* first, beginning, starting, primary, basic, original, opening. *We passed the initial phase of the test.* **Ant.** ending, last, concluding, final.

initiate *vb.* **1.** start, begin, commence, open, introduce, launch. *Our club initiates a membership drive every six months.* **2.** induct, inaugurate, receive, install, enter. *The pledges were initiated into the fraternity.* **Ant. 1.** accomplish, finish, complete. **2.** remove, oust, ban.

injection *n.* shot, vaccine, infusion, inoculation, dose. *One painless injection can prevent the flu all year long.*

injure *vb.* harm, damage, mar, hurt, wound, impair. *He injured his arm while playing baseball.* **Ant.** heal, aid, benefit.

injurious *adj.* harmful, hurtful, damaging, deleterious, destructive, pernicious. *Smoking is injurious to your health.* **Ant.** helpful, healthy, healing.

injury *n.* wound, hurt, trauma, (slang) boo boo, break, contusion. *It's important to wear a helmet when riding a bike to prevent head injury.*

injustice *n.* unfairness, wrong, unjustness, disservice, inequity. *The lawyer felt that her client had suffered an injustice.* **Ant.** justness, fairness, right.

inkling *adj.* indication, idea, notion, hint, glimmer, clue. *I had an inkling that a telemarketer would call at the dinner hour.*

inn *n.* lodging, bed and breakfast, accommodation, roadhouse, resort, motel. *An old inn often has more charm than a new hotel.*

innate *adj.* natural, instinctive, inborn, inbred, inherent. *The figure skater had an innate talent for the sport.* **Ant.** learned, acquired, cultivated.

inner *adj.* interior, inside, inward, internal, central. *The inner core of the sphere was metallic.* **Ant.** outer, outside, exterior, outward.

innocent *adj.* **1.** guiltless, blameless, sinless, faultless, not guilty. *The jury found the defendant innocent.* **2.** harmless, innocuous, inoffensive, simple, safe, unknowing. *How could such an innocent encounter be so tragic?* **Ant. 1.** guilty, sinful, responsible. **2.** offensive, harmful.

innocuous *adj.* harmless, benign, painless, innocent, inoffensive, bland. *Even an innocuous pastime is better than none.* **Ant.** harmful, deleterious, damaging.

innovation *n.* invention, novelty, change, alteration, introduction. *The inventor felt that his self-polishing shoes would be an important innovation in the fashion industry.*

innovator *n.* inventor, creative thinker, pioneer, trailblazer, experimenter, discoverer. *Computer firms count on their team of innovators for new improvements.*

innuendo *n.* allusion, suggestion, hint, implication, insinuation. *The story was nothing but rumor and innuendo.*

innumerable *adj.* countless, many, limitless, unlimited, infinite, numerous. *The mosquitoes at this campsite are innumerable.* **Ant.** limited, few, countable.

inoculation *n.* immunization, vaccination, shot, injection, booster. *It's wise to get an inoculation against chicken pox.*

inoffensive *adj.* innocent, harmless, innocuous, unoffending. *She tried to make her criticism as inoffensive as possible.* **Ant.** offensive, insulting, harmful.

inordinate *adj.* excessive, unreasonable, disproportionate, exorbitant, immoderate, extravagant. *The shoe store was charging an inordinate amount for a pair of running shoes, so we went elsewhere.*

inquest *n.* inquiry, investigation, probe, hearing, inquisition, examination. *The coroner held an inquest to determine the victim's cause of death.*

inquire *vb.* **1.** ask, seek, question, query, quiz. *I'm here to inquire about the room for rent.* **2.** examine, investigate, search, explore, study, research. *This research project will inquire into the mysteries of the atom.*

inquiry *n.* questioning, interrogation, query, inquisition, grilling, cross examination. *Congress will schedule a formal inquiry into the scandal next week.*

inquisitive *adj.* inquiring, prying, curious, snooping, nosy, searching. *An inquisitive raccoon investigated every corner of the garage.* **Ant.** indifferent, uninterested, unconcerned.

insane *adj.* **1.** crazy, mad, lunatic, demented, unbalanced, deranged, psychotic. *After spending twenty years alone in the mountains, the hermit was slightly insane.* **2.** senseless, foolish, silly, stupid, dumb, idiotic, moronic, absurd. *It was insane to dive head first into that shallow pond.* **Ant. 1.** sane, sound, rational. **2.** wise, reasonable, sensible.

insanity *n.* mental illness, craziness, psychosis, derangement, dementia, lunacy. *Continuing to* *arm the world with more and more nuclear weapons is insanity on a grand scale.* **Ant.** sanity, mental health, stability.

WORD SEARCH

alcoholic's form of: *delirium tremens, hallucinosis, Korsakoff's psychosis*
conscience, utterly lacking in: *sociopathic, psychopathic*
delusion that one is larger than life: *delusions of grandeur*
disordered thought processes and moods: *schizophrenia*
multiple personality: *multiple personality, split personality*
odor hallucination: *phantosmia*
persecution, delusion of: *paranoia*
removal of brain lobe in attempt to treat: *prefrontal lobotomy*
seeing things: *hallucinating*
shock therapy: *electroconvulsive therapy*
stupor, extreme: *catatonia*
talking, nonstop: *logomania*
See also MENTAL ILLNESS; PHOBIA.

insatiable *adj.* limitless, unsatisfiable, unquenchable, uncontrolled, demanding. *He has an insatiable appetite for ice cream.* **Ant.** limited, satisfied, controlled.

insect *n.* bug, pest, vermin, (slang) creepy crawler, arthropod. *Even well-kept homes are infested with at least a few insects.*

insecure *adj.* **1.** unstable, unsafe, dangerous, unsteady, hazardous, shaky. *The stack of barrels looked insecure, so we tied them down.* **2.** unsure, uncertain, nervous, anxious, hesitant, uneasy. *I feel insecure about speaking in front of so many people.* **Ant. 1.** stable, safe, secure. **2.** confident, assured, certain.

insensitive *adj.* unconcerned, unfeeling, callous, hard, tough, cold. *You didn't have to be so insensitive about her feelings.* **Ant.** sensitive, warm, caring, feeling.

inseparable *adj.* indivisible, unseparable, undividable, impartible. *The two friends are inseparable.* **Ant.** separable, dividable, partible.

insert *vb.* inject, place, put, implant, enter. *She inserted a dime into the parking meter.* **Ant.** remove, eject, withdraw.

inside *adj.* **1.** inner, interior, inward, internal, indoor. *The inside dining area will be warmer at night.* **2.** private, personal, intimate, confidential, secret. *The director told an inside joke about the film industry.* –*n.* **3.** interior, inner part, inner space. *Please paint the inside of the house too.* **Ant. 1.** outer, outward, external. **2.** public, popular. **3.** exterior.

insidious *adj.* stealthy, sneaky, treacherous, covert, surreptitious, dangerous, perilous. *Cancer is often an insidious disease.* **Ant.** overt, open.

insight *n.* understanding, perception, knowledge, wisdom, judgment, vision. *New insights can be gained through the exploration of space.*

insightful *adj.* perceptive, observant, sharp, intelligent, aware, wise. *A psychiatrist must be compassionate and insightful.* **Ant.** stupid, dense, ignorant.

insignia *n.* badge, emblem, patch, decoration. *The air force cadet wore his insignia proudly.*

insignificant *adj.* trivial, unimportant, trifling, meaningless, inessential, paltry. *An insignificant amount of rain fell on the crops.* **Ant.** significant, important, meaningful.

insincere *adj.* dishonest, false, deceitful, deceptive, untrue, untruthful. *Her feelings for her friend proved to be insincere.* **Ant.** sincere, honest, truthful.

insinuate *vb.* suggest, imply, hint, convey, indicate, state. *Are you insinuating that I didn't study for the test?*

insipid *adj.* dull, tasteless, bland, shallow, flavorless, vapid. *Many television programs are insipid and uninspiring.* **Ant.** flavorful, rich, interesting.

insist *vb.* demand, require, command, request, urge, stress. *The security guard insisted on seeing the intruder's identification.*

insistent *adj.* demanding, pushy, persistent, tenacious, determined, firm. *My mother was always insistent about wearing a scarf, even when it wasn't cold out.*

insolent *adj.* insulting, disrespectful, rude, surly, arrogant, defiant. *The insolent student had to stay after school as punishment.* **Ant.** polite, courteous, respectful.

insolvent *adj.* indebted, ruined, bankrupt, in arrears, (slang) broke, in the red. *The company became insolvent as a result of financial mismanagement.* **Ant.** solvent, in the black, profitable.

insomnia *n.* sleeplessness, insomnolence, tossing and turning, sleep disorder, restlessness, wakefulness. *He suffered from chronic insomnia and rarely slept more than five hours per night.* **Ant.** somnolence, sleep, slumber.

inspect *vb.* examine, investigate, observe, study, search, scan, scrutinize. *She inspected the motorcycle before buying it.* **Ant.** overlook, ignore, neglect.

inspection *n.* examination, scrutiny, survey, scan, probe, check. *The mortgage company scheduled a house inspection for next week.*

inspector *n.* examiner, investigator, auditor, checker, reviewer, assessor. *The inspector examines the kitchens for cleanliness once a week.*

inspiration *n.* **1.** stimulus, incentive, encouragement, motivation, influence. *Her story should be an inspiration to all.* **2.** idea, thought, revelation, enlightenment. *Where did you get the inspiration to create a TV that turns itself off during commercials?*

inspire *vb.* encourage, stimulate, arouse, motivate, stir, prompt, excite. *Reading that novel inspired me to write a book.* **Ant.** discourage, deter, dishearten.

install *vb.* set, place, seat, hook up, put in, situate. *Let's install the microwave over the stove.*

installment *n.* **1.** installation, positioning, seating, fixing, emplacement, setting up. *The appliance store scheduled the installment of our dishwasher for two o'clock.* **2.** part, section, segment, chapter, serial, episode. *I can't wait for the next installment of my favorite comedy show.*

instance *n.* moment, example, case, occasion, occurrence. *The traveler could think of many instances of being lost in a foreign country.*

instant *n.* **1.** moment, minute, second, flash, wink, jiffy. *The meteor could only be seen for an instant. –adj.* **2.** immediate, quick, prompt, swift, rapid, hasty. *I hope you don't expect an instant reply to your proposal of marriage.* **Ant. 2.** delayed, slow, lengthy.

instantly *adv.* immediately, instantaneously, suddenly, directly, rapidly, quickly. *A lifeguard instantly jumped into the pool to save the drowning child.* **Ant.** later, eventually, slowly.

instead *adv.* alternatively, rather, alternately, in lieu of. *The baseball game is canceled, so we're going to a movie instead.*

instigate *vb.* start, goad, foment, incite, prompt, spark, spur. *A reliable way to instigate a debate is to share your political views with the opposition.* **Ant.** end, discourage, quell.

instigator *n.* initiator, troublemaker, spark, spur, rabble-rouser, fomenter. *The police promptly arrested the instigator of the riot.*

instill *vb.* implant, imbue, infuse, impart, inject, indoctrinate. *Parents try hard to instill values in their children.* **Ant.** remove, take out, expunge.

instinct *n.* tendency, aptitude, feeling, intuition, impulse, capacity. *She has a natural instinct for painting.*

instinctive *adj.* innate, natural, involuntary, (slang) gut, intuitive, inherent. *Dogs have an instinctive desire to mark their territories.* **Ant.** acquired, learned, artificial.

institute *vb.* **1.** establish, start, begin, originate, found, initiate. *The library instituted a summer reading program.* –*n.* **2.** school, academy, institution, college, university, organization, establishment. *He is studying painting at the art institute.* **Ant. 1.** finish, conclude, discontinue.

institution *n.* **1.** custom, practice, tradition, convention. *Thanksgiving dinners are a national institution.* **2.** institute, school, university, college, organization, establishment. *There is an institution for almost every field of study.*

instruct *vb.* **1.** teach, educate, inform, train, tutor, enlighten, coach. *Today you will be instructed by a substitute teacher.* **2.** direct, command, order, dictate, told, charge. *He was instructed to leave the application on the desk.*

instruction *n.* direction, education, training, enlightenment, schooling, lesson. *The staff needs proper instruction to use the computers correctly.*

instructor *n.* teacher, trainer, guide, educator, guide, mentor. *The instructor showed us what to do if we met a bear on the trail.*

instrument *n.* tool, device, implement, machine, apparatus, utensil. *The television repairman had many strange instruments in his toolbox.*

instrumental *adj.* useful, helpful, beneficial, handy, effective, valuable. *Radio and television are instrumental in providing information to the public.* **Ant.** useless, worthless, ineffective.

insubordinate *adj.* disobedient, defiant, dissentious, rebellious, contrary, troublesome. *The boss strongly dislikes insubordinate employees.* **Ant.** deferential, agreeable, compliant.

insufferable *adj.* intolerable, unbearable, agonizing, excruciating, unendurable. *He experienced insufferable torture at the hands of the enemy.*

insufficient *adj.* inadequate, incomplete, deficient, skimpy, slim. *There was insufficient evidence to convict the defendant.* **Ant.** adequate, enough, sufficient.

insular *adj.* isolated, insulated, sequestered, lonely, separated, secluded. *She lived an insular life on an uninhabited island.*

insult *vb.* **1.** offend, humiliate, affront, outrage, ridicule, mock, belittle, scorn. *The waiter was insulted by the small tip.* –*n.* **2.** offense, outrage, slander, scorn, indignity, abuse. *I've had enough of your insults.* **Ant. 1.** flatter, praise, compliment. **2.** respect, flattery, praise.

insulting *adj.* offensive, hurtful, denigrating, derogatory, cutting, disparaging. *The comic's put-downs were too insulting for my tastes.* **Ant.** flattering, complimentary, sweet.

insurance *n.* protection, security, coverage, assurance, indemnity, safeguard. *We purchased insurance to cover our bills in case of an accident.*

insure *vb.* protect, safeguard, guarantee, warrant, assure. *The stereo system was insured against any damage for one year.*

insurgent *n.* **1.** rebel, revolutionary, dissident, mutineer, anarchist. *Insurgents stormed the palace.* –*adj.* **2.** rebellious, mutinous, revolutionary, disobedient, lawless. *The dictator jailed everyone found engaging in insurgent activities.* **Ant.** **1.** loyalist, patriot. **2.** loyal, obedient, patriotic.

insurmountable *adj.* impossible, insuperable, invincible, unbeatable, hopeless, out of reach.

insurrection *n.* revolution, mutiny, rebellion, coup, revolt, uprising. *Peasants planned an insurrection against their king.* **Ant.** submission, obedience.

intact *adj.* whole, complete, unbroken, undamaged, perfect, entire, unharmed. *There was not one dish intact after the earthquake.* **Ant.** broken, incomplete, damaged.

intangible *adj.* imperceptible, impalpable, invisible, untouchable, immaterial, elusive. *We don't really know if there is an afterlife; heaven is intangible.* **Ant.** tangible, physical, palpable.

integrate *vb.* blend, mix, combine, unify, fuse, harmonize. *All the suggestions were integrated into one long list.* **Ant.** segregate, separate, part, divide.

integrity *n.* virtue, honesty, honor, goodness, uprightness, morality. *The mayor's integrity was the issue in question.* **Ant.** corruption, dishonesty, immorality.

intellect *n.* intelligence, (slang) smarts, (slang) brains, reason, wits, understanding. *Albert Einstein had a superior intellect.*

intellectual *adj.* **1.** learned, academic, thoughtful, intelligent, scholarly, studious. *She is fascinated by philosophy, psychology, and related intellectual subjects.* –*n.* **2.** scholar, academician, thinker, intellect, sage. *It is incorrect to think that only intellectuals like to read.* **Ant.** **1.** ignorant, unlearned, thoughtless. **2.** idiot, dummy, moron.

intelligence *n.* **1.** intellect, aptitude, brightness, brains, wisdom. *Stop acting like you have the intelligence of a hamster.* **2.** information, knowledge, news, reports, data, facts. *The president requested to see all the intelligence on the oil crisis.* **Ant.** **1.** stupidity, ignorance.

intelligent *adj.* smart, wise, clever, bright, astute, brilliant. *She's too intelligent to wait on tables the rest of her life.* **Ant.** stupid, dumb, ignorant.

intelligible *adj.* clear, comprehensible, plain, understandable, unambiguous, unmistakable. *We found a hastily scrawled note that was barely intelligible.* **Ant.** unintelligible, unclear, ambiguous.

intend *vb.* mean, aim, plan, expect, propose, resolve. *Do you intend to mow the lawn today?*

intense *adj.* extreme, severe, great, powerful, strong, acute. *The chess champion played with intense concentration.* **Ant.** weak, mild, moderate.

intensify *vb.* increase, strengthen, magnify, reinforce, concentrate. *We'll have to intensify our efforts if we want to finish on time.* **Ant.** reduce, diminish, lessen.

intensity *n.* strength, power, force, magnitude, concentration, volume. *It rained with great intensity.*

intensive *adj.* thorough, full, total, exhaustive, concentrated, hard. *An intensive study of the problem will be undertaken.* **Ant.** careless, partial, superficial.

intent *n.* **1.** purpose, intention, aim, goal, plan, object, design. *His intent was to organize a softball team.* –*adj.* **2.** resolute, firm, determined, insistent, intense, fixed. *The pitcher was intent on striking out the batter.* **Ant.** **2.** purposeless, uncaring, indifferent.

intention *n.* intent, purpose, aim, plan, goal, design. *A good intention is preferable to an evil action.*

intentional *adj.* intended, deliberate, purposeful, planned, willful. *The intentional misspelling of my name was supposed to be a joke.* **Ant.** accidental, unplanned, unintended.

intercede *vb.* mediate, moderate, arbitrate, referee, intervene. *The attempt to intercede in the gang war was met with suspicion.*

intercept *vb.* stop, block, obstruct, seize, arrest, grab, interrupt. *A posse intercepted the outlaws at the pass.*

interchangeable *adj.* switchable, convertible, same, reciprocal, mutual, identical. *Luckily, the toy's numerous components were interchangeable.*

intercourse *n.* copulation, coitus, mating, sex, lovemaking, (slang) the wild thing. *Mammals cannot procreate without sexual intercourse.*

interest *n.* **1.** attention, regard, care, absorption, notice. *It was with great interest that the archaeologist studied the relics.* **2.** benefit, good, advantage, concern, welfare. *Do you ever look out for anybody's interests other than your own?* **3.** percentage, dividend, profit, yield, gain. *He received a good interest on his savings account.* **4.** share, ownership, portion, part, stake, investment. *Her interest in the toy company was inherited from her father.* –*vb.* **5.** intrigue, fascinate, concern, attract, engage, absorb. *He was interested in starting a rock band.* **Ant.** **1.** neglect, unconcern, apathy. **2.** loss, disadvantage.

interesting *adj.* fascinating, engaging, entertaining, absorbing, inviting, appealing. *Work is easy when it's interesting.* **Ant.** dull, boring, tedious, monotonous.

interfere *vb.* intrude, intervene, interrupt, meddle, conflict, intercede. *Don't interfere with the decision of the referee.* **Ant.** support, aid, assist.

interim *n.* interval, break, interlude, meantime, pause, intermission. *In the interim between games, we strolled about the stadium.*

interior *n.* **1.** inside, middle, center, nucleus, core. *The interior of the cabin needed painting.* –*adj.* **2.** inner, internal, indoor, inside, enclosed. *The interior lighting was inadequate for reading.* **Ant.** **1.** exterior, outside. **2.** outer, outdoor, external.

interloper *n.* intruder, trespasser, meddler, outsider, busybody. *My mother-in-law is nice, but during her extended visits she sometimes acts like an interloper.*

interlude *n.* interval, break, pause, intermission, gap, lull. *There was an interlude between the storms.*

intermediate *adj.* middle, moderate, halfway, intervening, midway. *If you pass this class, you can advance to the intermediate level.*

intermission *n.* break, interlude, rest, stop, pause, recess. *There will be a brief intermission between Acts 1 and 2.*

intermittent *adj.* recurrent, spasmodic, occasional, periodic, irregular, alternating. *The wind was intermittent throughout the day.* **Ant.** steady, continuous.

internal *adj.* inner, inside, inward, interior. *The accident victim had internal injuries.* **Ant.** outer, external, exterior.

international *adj.* global, worldwide, universal, multinational, intercontinental, cosmopolitan. *The environmental movement is now international in scope.* **Ant.** local, regional, domestic.

Internet *n.* World Wide Web, computer network, medium, (slang) information superhighway, cyberspace, interconnection. *I can contact someone halfway around the world on the Internet.*

WORD SEARCH

abandoned Web site: *ghost site, Orphan Annie*
actively connected: *on-line*
ad at top of webpage: *banner ad*
address: *URL (uniform research locator)*
ads, annoying and unwanted: *spam*
ads sent via instant messaging: *spim*
ads that pop up, annoying: *pop-up ads*
antagonism and insults exchanged with another party on-line: *flaming*
audio file, compressed: *MP3*
bank of stored files: *archive*
blog contributor: *blogger*
browsing aid, electronic: *browser, search engine*
browsing sites: *surfing*
camera that sends video or pics over Internet: *webcam*
chatting medium: *chat room, instant messaging*
coding used for security purposes: *cryptography, encryption*
connect to: *log on*
connector, network: *router*
converse in real time: *chat, instant message*
correspondence, private: *e-mail*
data holding to compensate for differing processing rates, temporary: *buffering*
device connecting computer to phone lines: *modem*
device that photographs and transmits hard copy and photos: *scanner*
discussion forum: *newsgroup*
failure of online network resulting in a frozen keyboard: *crash*
favorite site instant link: *bookmark*
file sent with e-mail, large: *attachment*
glowing link leading to another site: *hyperlink, hotlink*
host computer of network: *server*
inoperable or inaccessible: *down*
medium: *cyberspace*
message medium: *bulletin board*
message, put up a: *post*
motion picture file: *MPEG (Motion Picture Experts Group)*
option list: *menu*
photograph or image, compressed: *JPG (Joint Photographic Experts Group)*
photograph or graphic that when clicked on reveals larger version of itself, miniature: *thumbnail*
picture or representation of real person, small: *avatar*
picture or representation, small: *icon*
record on-line information for private use: *download*
reload a web page for updated data: *refresh*
search engines, popular: *Google, Yahoo*
searcher of new Internet resources: *crawler*
simulated: *virtual*
site or page of individual or organization: *home page, web site, web page*
software that may be shared online: *shareware*
sorting system to block unwanted e-mail: *filter*
spy program: *spyware, adware, keylogger*
stealing of copyrighted material from: *pirating*
terrorism online: *cyberterrorism*
transmission medium, high speed: *broadband, DSL*
transmission, phone line: *dial-up*
video transmission, live: *streaming*
virus, self-replicating: *worm*
visits to web site, tallied: *hits*
web log: *blog*
web site builder: *web designer*
web site manager: *webmaster*
undeliverable e-mail, return: *bounce*
wireless signals over, transmitter of: *wi-fi, Wi Max*

interpret *vb.* **1.** explain, define, construe, clarify, illustrate. *I don't know how to interpret her actions.* **2.** translate, paraphrase, decipher, reword, restate. *Since the traveler could not understand Japanese, he needed someone to interpret for him.*

interpretation *n.* understanding, view, reading, perception, definition, slant, take. *My interpretation of the play differed from the critics'.*

interrogate *vb.* question, quiz, query, probe, examine, ask. *The suspect was interrogated by the police for hours.*

interrupt *vb.* disturb, interfere, intercept, break, stop, intrude. *His nap was interrupted by a blasting car horn.* **Ant.** resume, continue.

intersect *vb.* cross, crisscross, meet, cut, bisect, traverse, crosscut. *Make a left turn where the highway intersects Main Street.*

interval *n.* period, pause, gap, interlude, interim, break, rest, interruption. *We need a longer interval between classes.*

intervene *vb.* interfere, mediate, intrude, interrupt, intercede. *The police intervened before any serious harm occurred.*

intervention *n.* interference, interruption, intrusion, incursion, intercession. *The president called for military intervention in the Middle East.*

interview *n.* **1.** conference, dialogue, meeting, discussion, conversation, evaluation. *I'm scheduled for an interview with the personnel manager.* –*vb.* **2.** question, converse, query, ask, examine, evaluate. *A reporter interviewed the politician regarding her stand on civil rights.*

interviewer *n.* questioner, interrogator, inquisitor, inquirer, prober. *It made me nervous when the interviewer asked what my main weaknesses were.*

intestines *n.* bowels, guts, viscera, innards, entrails, colon. *One's intestines may bloat uncomfortably after eating beans.*

intimacy *n.* closeness, caring, fondness, familiarity, friendship. *The family retained their intimacy despite their separation.* **Ant.** indifference, aloofness.

intimate *adj.* **1.** close, familiar, personal, dear, near, loving. *The two friends have an intimate relationship.* **2.** secret, private, personal, confidential, innermost. *The actress revealed her most intimate thoughts in her book.* **3.** thorough, solid, exhaustive, deep, profound, complete. *He has an intimate knowledge of the workings of Congress.* –*vb.* **4.** hint, imply, suggest, allude, insinuate, indicate. *She intimated that he was guilty of the crime.* **Ant.** **1.** impersonal, unfamiliar, remote. **2.** open, public, known. **3.** shallow, superficial, limited. **4.** declare, state, claim.

intimation *n.* suggestion, tip, hint, allusion, insinuation, innuendo. *The boss gave an intimation that she was going to resign soon by removing the files from her office.*

intimidate *vb.* scare, frighten, threaten, menace, dismay, alarm, terrify, terrorize. *Don't let that bully intimidate you.*

intimidating *adj.* threatening, frightening, scary, inhibiting, emasculating, unnerving. *My opponent is an intimidating chess player.*

intolerable *adj.* unbearable, unendurable, insufferable, excessive, unreasonable. *This summer's heat is intolerable.* **Ant.** tolerable, bearable, comfortable, endurable.

intolerant *adj.* biased, prejudiced, bigoted, disdainful, hostile, resentful. *The old man was intolerant of people from foreign lands.* **Ant.** tolerant, fair, accepting.

intoxicated *adj.* **1.** drunk, drunken, tipsy, high, inebriated. *She was arrested for driving while intoxicated.* **2.** enthralled, enchanted, excited, elated, moved. *The dancers were intoxicated by the loud and rhythmic music.* **Ant.** **1.** sober, dry, straight. **2.** bored, unmoved.

intrepid *adj.* fearless, bold, brave, heroic, valiant, courageous, daring. *An intrepid knight* *rode out to slay the dragon.* **Ant.** cowardly, frightened, meek, timid.

intricate *adj.* complex, complicated, elaborate, involved, detailed. *His latest novel has a confusingly intricate plot.* **Ant.** simple, uncomplicated, plain.

intrigue *vb.* **1.** fascinate, interest, captivate, excite, enthrall, charm. *The story of your adventures intrigues me.* –*n.* **2.** scheme, plot, conspiracy, espionage, ruse. *The rebellious army officers hoped their intrigues would be successful.* **Ant. 1.** bore, tire, weary.

intriguing *adj.* interesting, fascinating, captivating, arousing curiosity, provocative, enthralling. *The thriller's plot was highly intriguing.* **Ant.** boring, unengaging, dull.

intrinsic *adj.* inherent, innate, inner, natural, internal, basic. *The aggression of the male moose in the fall is of an intrinsic nature.* **Ant.** extrinsic, external, unnatural.

introduce *vb.* **1.** present, announce, acquaint, familiarize. *I would like to introduce you to my husband.* **2.** propose, submit, present, offer, advance, originate. *The congressman introduced a bill to outlaw slingshots.* **Ant. 2.** withdraw, remove. eliminate.

introduction *n.* **1.** opening, start, beginning, commencement, launching, initiation. *The 20th century ushered in the introduction of numerous innovations.* **2.** preface, foreword, prologue, preamble, prelude. *I often skip a book's introduction and jump directly to the first chapter.* **Ant. 1.** end, finale, closing. **2.** afterword, epilogue.

introspective *adj.* introverted, contemplative, self-analyzing, pensive, self-aware, soul-searching. *Mary is introspective and likes to analyze her own thought processes.* **Ant.** oblivious, unaware, unthinking.

introvert *adj.* bookworm, homebody, loner, (slang) lone wolf, wallflower, quiet, person. *Joe is a dyed-in-the-wool introvert who loves nothing more than curling up with a good book.* **Ant.** extrovert, party animal, people person.

introverted *adj.* introspective, reserved, solitary, quiet taciturn, thoughtful. *Introverted people often prefer quiet, one-on-one relationships.* **Ant.** extroverted, outgoing, unreserved.

intrude *vb.* trespass, encroach, infringe, intervene, impose, invade, interfere. *It's impolite to intrude on someone's privacy.*

intruder *n.* interloper, trespasser, infiltrator, invader, (slang) gate crasher, prowler. *The security system sensed an intruder and sounded an alarm.*

intrusive *adj.* obtrusive, invasive, unwelcome, unwanted, meddlesome, interfering. *I find your nosy questions to be highly intrusive.*

intuition *n.* instinct, insight, perception, intuitiveness, hunch. *Her intuition told her it was dangerous to drive across the bridge.*

intuitive *adj.* instinctive, (slang) gut, perceptive, psychic, innate. *Animals are often intuitive enough to know when it is going to rain.*

inundate *vb.* flood, overflow, overwhelm, swamp, saturate, engulf. *The graduate was inundated with job offers.*

invade *vb.* attack, assault, raid, penetrate, overrun, swarm. *Wild dogs invaded the chicken coop.*

invalid *adj.* void, null, worthless, useless, unusable, ineffective. *All passes for the movie are invalid on weekends.* **Ant.** useful, valid, effective.

invalidate *vb.* void, nullify, negate, annul, repeal, revoke. *The new rules will invalidate the existing ones starting next week.* **Ant.** validate, sanction.

invaluable *adj.* valuable, priceless, precious, expensive, costly, rare. *Rembrandt's paintings are invaluable.* **Ant.** cheap, worthless, common.

invasion *n.* attack, strike, assault, incursion, onslaught, offensive. *The army planned on launching a new invasion soon.* **Ant.** retreat, exit.

invective *n.* verbal attack, insults, verbal abuse, tongue-lashing, tirade, condemnation. *I couldn't listen to his invective anymore and left the party early.*

invent *vb.* **1.** create, produce, originate, develop, conceive. *The person who invented the alarm clock should be shot.* **2.** imagine, pretend, fabricate, fake, falsify. *She invented a story to explain her absence from school.* **Ant. 1.** copy, imitate, duplicate.

invention *n.* **1.** creation, device, gadget, contraption, innovation. *I hope the professor's newest invention doesn't explode like the last one.* **2.** inventing, creating, creation, development, origination. *The invention of the airplane changed our world.* **3.** inventiveness, creativity, originality, newness, freshness, novelty. *The artistic invention of Picasso is unequaled in the 20th century.* **4.** lie, falsehood, fabrication, fib, fiction, story. *His account of his journey to Atlantis is pure invention.* **Ant. 2.** imitation, copying, reproduction. **3.** conformity, staleness, dullness. **4.** truth, fact, reality.

inventor *n.* creator, innovator, father, mother, originator, pioneer, discoverer. *To protect his creation, the inventor applied for a patent.*

inventory *n.* **1.** supply, reserve, surplus, goods, stock, merchandise. *The store owner must sell his inventory by April.* **2.** list, catalog, tally, count, index, roster. *She made an inventory of the things she needed for her classroom.*

invest *vb.* **1.** empower, endow, authorize, license, delegate, charge, entrust.. *The police are invested with the duty to enforce the law.* **2.** spend, allot, venture, supply, give. *He invested a lot of money in his stamp collection.*

investigate *vb.* probe, examine, explore, study, research, inspect. *A committee was appointed to investigate UFO sightings.*

investigation *n.* inquiry, probe, inquest, examination, review, audit. *The detective began a covert investigation.*

investigator *n.* detective, inspector, examiner, auditor, fact finder, inquisitor. *The investigator dusted for fingerprints.*

investment *n.* money-maker, speculation, financial instrument, financial venture, security, nest egg. *It's wise to diversify your investments.*

investor *n.* capitalist, venture capitalist, speculator, shareholder, stockholder, financier. *The investor put up half of his savings to develop the property.*

invigorating *adj.* refreshing, stimulating, bracing, vitalizing, energizing. *A cold shower is invigorating.* **Ant.** weakening, enervating, tiring.

invincible *adj.* invulnerable, unbeatable, unconquerable, untouchable, secure. *The sorceress thought she was invincible.* **Ant.** beatable, vulnerable, weak.

invisible *adj.* imperceptible, impalpable, imperceivable, transparent, indiscernible, concealed. *Ghosts are invisible except on Halloween; then they wear sheets.*

invitation *n.* summons, request, call, bidding, solicitation. *I got your wedding invitation yesterday.*

invite *vb.* request, ask, welcome, summon, bid, beckon. *She invited her friends to have dinner at her house.*

inviting *adj.* appealing, alluring, enticing, tempting, seductive, magnetic. *The smells com-*

ing from the kitchen were deliciously inviting. **Ant.** repellent, repulsive, disgusting.

invoice *n.* bill, account, statement, bill of lading, manifest, itemization. *There appears to be an overcharge on this invoice.*

invoke *vb.* summon, address, entreat, beseech, call, beg. *The sorcerer invoked the spirits to grant his wish.*

involuntary *adj.* **1.** mandatory, unwilling, forced, coerced, compulsory. *The soldier was on an involuntary assignment.* **2.** automatic, spontaneous, instinctive, unintentional, uncontrolled. *When the doctor hit her knee with a hammer, her leg responded with an involuntary jerk.* **Ant. 1.** voluntary, willing, optional. **2.** intentional, controlled.

involve *vb.* **1.** include, embrace, contain, entail, imply. *A full checkup on your car will involve an oil change.* **2.** absorb, engage, occupy, concern, preoccupy, entangle. *I do not wish to become involved in your problems.* **Ant. 1.** exclude, omit, disregard. **2.** disentangle, disengage.

irate *adj.* angry, enraged, mad, angered, wrathful, infuriated, incensed. *She was irate with the man who stole her idea.* **Ant.** pleased, happy, glad.

ire *n.* anger, wrath, fury, displeasure, rage, indignation. *Don't risk the wizard's ire or he'll turn you into a toadstool.* **Ant.** serenity, contentment, peace.

irk *vb.* irritate, annoy, vex, bother, trouble, peeve, provoke. *It really irks me when people are late.* **Ant.** cheer, delight, satisfy.

ironic *adj.* **1.** sarcastic, biting, cutting, cynical, caustic, satiric. *Her ironic humor is not always appreciated.* **2.** strange, inconsistent, weird, contradictory, curious, odd. *Isn't ironic how I always manage to lose something after I organize my room?* **Ant. 1.** tactful, inoffensive. **2.** consistent, understandable.

irrational *adj.* illogical, unreasonable, absurd, ridiculous, crazy. *It's irrational to think you can catch fish in a bathtub.* **Ant.** rational, logical, sane, sensible.

irrefutable *adj.* indisputable, incontrovertible, proven, certain, undeniable, unquestionable. *We have irrefutable evidence that donuts are fattening, namely my stomach.* **Ant.** refutable, debatable, questionable.

irregular *adj.* **1.** uneven, unequal, unbalanced, rough, rugged. *The irregular surface of this table makes it hard to work on.* **2.** unusual, odd, erratic, abnormal, unconventional, peculiar, strange. *Your request to paint the office purple is highly irregular.* **Ant. 1.** even, level, smooth. **2.** normal, conventional, common.

irrelevant *adj.* unconnected, unrelated, unfitting, immaterial, unimportant. *His comments were irrelevant to the issues.* **Ant.** relevant, related, applicable.

irrepressible *adj.* uncontrollable, uninhibited, lively, vivacious, unrestrainable, unbridled. *The comic's irrepressible antics had the audience in stitches.* **Ant.** quiet, passive, low-key.

irresponsible *adj.* undependable, unreliable, careless, unaccountable, devil-may-care, thoughtless. *Failing to show up for work is irresponsible.* **Ant.** responsible, reliable, conscientious.

irreverent *adj.* disrespectful, profane, impious, irreligious, uncivil. *The irreverent person was asked to leave the temple.* **Ant.** reverent, respectful, pious.

irrigate *vb.* water, wash, soak, drench, flood, sprinkle. *We have to irrigate the garden in times of drought.*

irritable *adj.* testy, touchy, sensitive, peevish, impatient, cross. *I'm a very irritable person when I get up too early in the morning.* **Ant.** mellow, calm, agreeable.

irritate *vb.* **1.** anger, annoy, bother, provoke, pester, irk. *She was irritated by her roommate's sloppiness.* **2.** pain, chafe, redden, inflame, aggravate. *That brand of soap irritates my skin.* **Ant. 1.** placate, comfort, appease. **2.** relieve, ease, soothe.

Islamic *adj.* Muslim, Moslem, Muhammadan, Mohammedan, Shiite, Sunni. *Our Muslim neighbors follow the Islamic code stringently.*

island *n.* **1.** isle, islet, atoll, archipelago. *My friend lives on a Caribbean island.* **2.** haven, shelter, refuge, retreat, sanctuary. *The campfire was a little island of warmth surrounded by the cold of the night.*

WORD SEARCH

coral ring: *atoll*
group of: *archipelago*
river, in: *holm*

isolate *vb.* separate, segregate, detach, seclude, disconnect, remove. *Our first step should be to isolate the problem.*

isolation *n.* seclusion, solitude, confinement, loneliness, abandonment, cloister. *You can experience total isolation in Antarctica.*

issue *n.* **1.** matter, question, problem, topic, subject, concern. *Housing development is an important issue in our community.* **2.** copy, edition, number, volume, publication. *He collects old issues of science-fiction magazines.* –*vb.* **3.** distribute, circulate, release, dispatch, dispense. *The ice-cream parlor issued coupons for a free sundae.* **4.** flow, emerge, arise, discharge, spring, emit. *Oil issued from the leak in the pipe.* **Ant. 3.** revoke, withdraw, cancel.

item *n.* **1.** thing, article, element, object, unit, particular. *I need one more item from the store.* **2.** story, feature, account, article, report. *Did you read the item in the paper about the labor strike?*

itemize *vb.* detail, specify, register, list, record, document, count, number. *Every school expense must be itemized.*

itinerant *adj.* traveling, transient, roaming, wandering, rambling, migratory. *The farmer hired some itinerant workers to pick his apples.*

itinerary *n.* route, course, plan, program, tour, way, schedule. *The Grand Canyon is one of many stops on our itinerary.*

J

jab *vb.* **1.** poke, prod, push, thrust, nudge, elbow, punch. *She jabbed a knife into the watermelon.* –*n.* **2.** poke, prod, blow, punch, hit, dig. *A jab to the stomach knocked the wind out of him.*

jacket *n.* cover, wrapping, wrapper, coat. *Please put the record back in its jacket.*

WORD SEARCH

khaki: *bush jacket, safari jacket*
leather flight jacket: *bomber jacket*
lightweight: *golf jacket, windbreaker*
parka wit hood: *snorkel*
plaid wool: *lumber jacket, mackinaw*
seaman's: *pea jacket, pea coat*
winter, insulated: *parka*

jaded *adj.* dulled, wearied, bored, blasé, indifferent, cloyed. *By the time he walked into the seventh museum in one day, he was thoroughly jaded.* **Ant.** interested, fascinated, enthused.

jagged *adj.* notched, pointed, serrated, toothed, barbed, rough, irregular. *Saws have jagged edges* **Ant.** smooth, even, straight.

jail *n.* **1.** prison, penitentiary, jailhouse, stockade, brig. *He has spent the past ten years in jail.* –*vb.* **2.** imprison, incarcerate, detain, confine, lock up. *She was jailed for drunk driving.* **Ant.** **2.** free, release, liberate.

jalopy *n.* car, automobile, (slang) bucket of bolts, (slang) clunker, (slang) rattletrap, (slang) junker. *I've been driving the same old jalopy for 25 years.*

jam *vb.* **1.** press, pack, crowd, force, squeeze, cram, stuff. *He jammed so many clothes in the drawer that he couldn't close it.* **2.** block, obstruct, clog, stop, cease. *Her gun jammed when she attempted to fire it.* –*n.* **3.** crowd, crush, press, horde, throng, mob. *We were stuck for hours in a traffic jam.*

janitor *n.* custodian, maintenance man, caretaker, cleaner, superintendent. *The school janitor spends a great deal of time mopping floors.*

jar *n.* **1.** bottle, container, vessel, receptacle, jug. *Please pass me that jar of peanut butter.* –*vb.* **2.** annoy, irritate, upset, disturb, perturb. *The sound of squeaking chalk jarred my nerves.* **3.** shake, vibrate, rattle, rock, quake. *A sonic boom jarred our house.* **Ant.** **2.** soothe, comfort, calm.

jargon *n.* lingo, vernacular, language, talk, argot, shop talk, slang. *Musicians have their own jargon and like to use words like "jam" and "cooking."*

jaunt *n.* excursion, outing, day trip, short trip, stroll, cruise. *We took a jaunt down to the coast for the day.*

jazz *n.* music, bop, bebop, fusion jazz, improvisational music, smooth jazz. *Jazz is performed by some of the world's best musicians.*

jealous *adj.* **1.** envious, envying, covetous, desirous, resentful. *She was jealous when she saw my new computer.* **2.** suspicious, mistrustful, insecure, anxious, possessive. *He was so jealous of his wife that he didn't like her to go out alone.*

jealousy *n.* envy, suspicion, resentment, mistrust, anxiety, doubt. *Jealousy can destroy friendships.*

jeans *n.* pants, dungarees, Levis, Lees, trousers, slacks. *I would rather wear jeans than a three-piece suit.*

jeopardize *vb.* risk, imperil, endanger, menace, threaten. *Smoking jeopardizes your health.* **Ant.** save, protect, defend.

jeopardy *n.* risk, danger, peril, threat, vulnerability. *Her life was in jeopardy when she entered the burning building to save her friend.* **Ant.** safety, security.

jerk *n.* **1.** jolt, shake, twitch, pull, tug, yank. *The car started with a jerk because he had it in the wrong gear.* –*vb.* **2.** pull, tug, yank, snap, pluck. *She jerked on the leash in an effort to control her disobedient dog.*

jest *n.* **1.** joke, quip, witticism, wisecrack. *She must have a strange sense of humor because no one appreciates her jests.* –*vb.* **2.** joke, fool, tease, kid, wisecrack. *We thought he was jesting when he said he didn't want supper.*

Jesus Christ *n.* Son of God, Savior, teacher, Messiah, Lord, spiritual leader. *Many people believe that it's impossible to go wrong when using Jesus Christ as a moral compass.*

jet *vb.* **1.** spurt, spray, squirt, stream, gush, rush. *Water jetted from the broken fire hydrant.* –*n.* **2.** spurt, spray, squirt, geyser, stream. *The drinking fountain sent a jet of water into my eyes.*

jetty *n.* breakwater, seawall, barrier, riprap, groin. *We like to fish off the end of the pier.*

Jew *n.* Semite, Israelite, Hebrew, Judaist, Hasid. *Abraham is proud of being a Jew.*

jewel *n.* gem, gemstone, ornament, bauble, semi-precious stone. *India was the jewel in the crown of the former British Empire.*

jewelry *n.* jewels, gems, stones, ornaments, gold, silver. *She wore lots of expensive jewelry.*

Jewish *adj.* Semitic, Hebrew, Israelite, Hasidic. *The Jewish people have a long history.*

jilt *vb.* reject, dump, drop, spurn, ditch, break off. *Mary didn't want to jilt her boyfriend while he was away at war.*

jingle *vb.* **1.** tinkle, clink, clang, ring, chime. *Loose change jingled in her purse.* –*n.* **2.** tinkle, tinkling, ringing, chime, chiming. *We could hear the jingle of the sleigh's bells.* **3.** tune, melody, carol, chorus, chant. *Where did you hear that cute jingle?*

jinx *n.* curse, hex, spell, enchantment, charm. *He had so much bad luck he thought someone had placed a jinx on him.*

jitterbug *n.* swing dance, Lindy Hop. *The jitterbug was a popular style of dance during the 1930s and 1940s.*

jittery *adj.* shaky, nervous, quivering, nervous, anxious, tense. *Caffeine makes me feel jittery.* **Ant.** calm, serene, steady.

job *n.* **1.** employment, work, occupation, position, situation. *He's looking for a summer job.* **2.** task, duty, chore, role, function. *She has some jobs to do around the house before she can go out.*

jockey *n.* rider, equestrian. *Jockeys must be small and lightweight to compete.*

jog *vb.* run, trot, dash, speedwalk, race. *Eddy Buttfield likes to jog, but he is so slow that even old snails pass him.*

join *vb.* **1.** connect, combine, couple, assemble, fasten, unite, link. *Please join hands.* **2.** enroll, enlist, enter, sign up. *She joined a chess club.* **Ant.** **1.** divide, separate, detach. **2.** leave, quit, resign.

joint *n.* **1.** juncture, junction, coupling, connection, link. *He repaired the pipe's leaking joint.*

–adj. **2.** mutual, combined, shared, common, collective, concerted. *It took our joint efforts to put out the fire.* **Ant. 2.** individual, independent, separate.

joke *n.* **1.** jest, witticism, gag, prank, trick. *Putting a rubber snake in his friend's bed was a foolish joke.* *–vb.* **2.** jest, fool, kid, tease, taunt, ridicule. *She was only joking when she said you should dye your hair pink.*

jolly *adj.* merry, jovial, mirthful, jocular, exuberant, high spirited. *Santa Claus is not quite as jolly when he has a migraine.* **Ant.** gloomy, miserable, depressed.

jolt *n.* **1.** jerk, jump, shake, lurch, surprise, shock. *He got quite a jolt when he touched the frayed electrical wire.* *–vb.* **2.** jar, jerk, shake, shock, disturb, startle. *We were all jolted by the news of our friend's death.*

jostle *vb.* push, bump, shove, joggle, elbow. *Greedy shoppers jostled each other to get at the sale items.*

jot *vb.* scribble, write, record, register, mark. *She jotted down her friend's address and phone number.*

journal *n.* **1.** diary, notebook, log, register, record book. *He kept a daily journal while he was in the army.* **2.** newspaper, magazine, periodical, review, publication. *Her article on ecology was published in a scientific journal.*

journalism *n.* reporting, investigative reporting, news gathering, print media, fourth estate. *She learned how to write an exposé in her journalism class.*

journalist *n.* reporter, correspondent, newscaster, newswoman, newsman. *The president granted an interview to several journalists.*

journey *n.* **1.** trip, excursion, tour, expedition, voyage, cruise. *I can't wait to hear about his journey to the North Pole.* *–vb.* **2.** travel, tour, trek, voyage, wander. *She plans to journey through Asia next year.*

jovial *adj.* cheerful, jolly, merry, gay, joyful, joyous. *The circus clown was always jovial.* **Ant. 1.** sad, depressed, melancholy, gloomy.

joy *n.* happiness, delight, ecstasy, glee, rapture, elation. *He was filled with joy when she accepted his marriage proposal.* **Ant.** misery, sadness, sorrow.

joyous *adj.* joyful, happy, glad, jubilant, cheerful, merry. *The family's reunion after years of separation was a joyous occasion.* **Ant.** joyless, sad, unhappy.

jubilant *adj.* ecstatic, elated, exhilarated, thrilled, excited. *She was jubilant when she got the unexpected promotion.* **Ant.** disappointed, dejected, despondent.

judge *n.* **1.** justice, magistrate, jurist. *Our municipal judge has just been appointed to the state supreme court.* **2.** referee, umpire, moderator, evaluator, assessor, critic. *The judges gave the gymnast a perfect 10.* *–vb.* **3.** determine, decree, decide, rule, try. *The suspect's guilt or innocence will be judged in a court of law.* **4.** evaluate, appraise, rate, rank, analyze. *She was asked to judge our local beauty contest.*

judgment *n.* **1.** verdict, decision, ruling, finding, determination. *The jury will deliver its judgment tomorrow.* **2.** discretion, sense, intelligence, wisdom, discernment. *She showed good judgment when she picked me as her friend.*

judgmental *adj.* critical, faultfinding, self-righteous, holier-than-thou, censorious. *We are sometimes judgmental toward the very things we ourselves are guilty of.* **Ant.** nonjudgmental, accepting.

judicious *adj.* prudent, wise, thoughtful, sensible, mindful, careful. *The teacher's selection of* *one boy and one girl to represent the class was judicious.* **Ant.** injudicious, careless, senseless.

jug *n.* pitcher, flask, jar, bottle, carafe. *The peasant girl used a jug to carry water from the well.*

juggernaut *n.* god, monster, colossus, titan, institution, force to be reckoned with. *The new computer company is quickly becoming a juggernaut.*

juggle *vb.* maneuver, manipulate, fake, alter, tamper, modify. *He juggled his tax receipts to make it look like he had more deductions.*

juice *n.* extract, fluid, squeezings, essence, nectar, distillation. *Squeeze the juice from an orange carefully.*

juicy *adj.* succulent, moist, dripping, liquid, watery. *These nectarines are incredibly juicy.* **Ant.** dry, desiccated.

jumble *vb.* **1.** disorder, disorganize, disarrange, unsettle, mix. *Somehow she managed to jumble her computer files.* –*n.* **2.** muddle, mess, tangle, confusion, mixture. *Your report is just a jumble of unrelated facts.* **Ant.** **1.** order, organize, arrange. **2.** arrangement, order.

jumbo *adj.* oversized, huge, immense, colossal, giant, large. *He prefers jumbo shrimp.* **Ant.** small, tiny, average.

jump *vb.* **1.** leap, bound, vault, skip, spring, hop. *Fortunately, she had her parachute on when she jumped out of the plane.* –*n.* **2.** bound, leap, vault, spring, hurdle, rise. *His specialty is the high jump.*

junction *n.* joint, link, connection, intersection, interchange. *This road ends at its junction with Highway 5.*

juncture *n.* **1.** moment, time, period, point, stage. *At this juncture, nobody really knows what the weather will be on Mother's Day.* **2.** joint connection, coupling, link, union, convergence. *We found a leak at the juncture of the two pipes.*

jungle *n.* rain forest, bush, wilds, woods, wilderness. *Tigers in jungles.*

junior *adj.* lower, lesser, subordinate, secondary, younger. *She's junior partner in that law firm.* **Ant.** senior, higher, older.

junk *n.* debris, litter, trash, rubbish, garbage, refuse. *Please clean all that old junk out of your closet.*

junkyard *n.* scrapyard, refuse yard, recycling facility, dump, auto graveyard. *I went to the junkyard to find some spare parts for my car.*

jurisdiction *n.* **1.** authority, dominion, rule, command. *The police officer's jurisdiction ended at the city line.* **2.** bailiwick, province, bounds, district, territory. *The judge's jurisdiction encompassed the entire county.*

jury *n.* peers, panel, judges, grand jury, petit jury, inquest. *The jury found the defendant guilty on all counts.*

just *adj.* **1.** fair, impartial, unbiased, reasonable, equitable. *Considering what he had done, his punishment was just.* –*adv.* **2.** exactly, precisely, perfectly, completely, fully. *This present is just what I wanted.* **3.** barely, scarcely, narrowly, hardly, merely. *We had just made it to the theater when the movie started.* **4.** recently, lately, formerly, previously. *I just saw her at the store.* **Ant.** **1.** unfair, unreasonable, biased.

justice *n.* fairness, impartiality, justness, equity, rightness. *Slavery is a practice that denies justice to its victims.* **Ant.** injustice, unfairness, inequity.

justice of the peace *n.* official, magistrate, notary public, witness. *My wife and I got married by a justice of the peace at City Hall.*

justify *vb.* **1.** confirm, verify, substantiate, corroborate, vindicate. *She justified my faith in her when she repaid the loan.* **2.** excuse, explain, rationalize, support, defend. *He justified his crime by claiming he needed the money to feed his family.*

jut *vb.* **1.** protrude, extend, project, bulge, stick out. *A huge boulder jutted out over the cliff's edge.* –*n.* **2.** protrusion, extension, projection, outthrust. *We beached our boat on a jut of land.*

juvenile *adj.* **1.** young, youthful, immature, childish, adolescent. *Juvenile delinquents vandalized the local park.* –*n.* **2.** child, youngster, youth, minor, kid. *Juveniles are not entitled to vote.* **Ant. 1.** adult, mature, grown-up. **2.** adult, elder.

juvenile delinquent *n.* hoodlum, (slang) gangbanger, troublemaker, rowdy, punk, hooligan. *It is important to prevent a juvenile delinquent from becoming a full-fledged criminal.*

K

keen *adj.* **1.** sharp, fine, thin, honed. *Be careful; that knife has a keen edge.* **2.** clever, bright, brilliant, shrewd, quick. *She has a keen mind.* **3.** eager, enthusiastic, avid, ardent, zealous. *He was keen on going to the circus.* **Ant. 1.** dull, blunt. **2.** dense, stupid. **3.** apathetic, indifferent.

keep *vb.* **1.** hold, retain, have, possess. *You may keep the record you borrowed.* **2.** restrain, retard, impede, hinder, confine. *The rain kept us from going on a picnic.* **3.** support, sustain, maintain, provision, provide for. *She kept my dog while I was on vacation.* **4.** continue, persist, persevere, endure. *You keep saying you'll try harder, but you don't.* **5.** fulfill, observe, obey, honor. *He kept his promise to be home in time for dinner.* *–n.* **6.** upkeep, sustenance, subsistence, living, livelihood. *It's about time you got a job and paid for your own keep.* **7.** dungeon, cell, stronghold, tower. *The kidnapped prince was locked in the castle's inner keep.* **Ant. 1.** discard, release, abandon. **2.** free, liberate. **4.** stop, halt, cease. **5.** neglect, ignore, disregard.

keepsake *n.* memento, souvenir, remembrance, token, reminder. *I like to take home a keepsake from every foreign city I visit.*

keg *n.* barrel, cask, drum, tank, container. *They bought a keg of beer for their party.*

kettle *n.* cauldron, pot, vessel, vat, boiler. *The old witch tossed a dried bat wing into the kettle.*

key *n.* **1.** solution, explanation, answer, resolution, clue. *The missing piece of evidence was the key to solving the crime.* *–adj.* **2.** main, leading, primary, decisive, crucial. *She's the key member of our band, and we can't perform without her.* *–vb.* **3.** adjust, adapt, suit, fit, harmonize. *He keyed his comments to the audience's level of understanding.* **Ant. 2.** minor, insignificant, inconsequential.

keyboard *n.* organ, synthesizer, electric piano. *Modern keyboards are capable of mimicking virtually any other instrument.*

kick *vb.* **1.** boot, hit, strike, push, shove. *Only a cruel person would ever kick a dog.* *–n.* **2.** boot, punt, blow, stroke, hit. *He gave the football a hard kick.*

kickback *n.* payoff, (slang) payola, bribe, payment, cut, percentage. *The CEO of the company is under investigation for taking kickbacks.*

kid *vb.* **1.** tease, taunt, joke, jest, ridicule. *She was only kidding when she said she saw some Martians in your backyard.* *–n.* **2.** child, youngster, youth, daughter, son. *He took his kids to a movie.* **Ant. 2.** adult, grown-up, elder.

kidnap *vb.* abduct, capture, seize, steal, carry off. *The princess was kidnapped by an evil wizard.* **Ant.** return, release, free.

kill *vb.* **1.** slay, murder, slaughter, assassinate, execute. *The hunter killed a deer.* **2.** ruin, destroy, end, halt, terminate, extinguish. *His mismanagement of the important project killed his chances for a promotion.* **Ant. 2.** revitalize, begin, sustain.

killer *n.* murderer, assassin, (slang) hit man, gunman, homicidal, maniac, predator. *Many murders can be attributed to a serial killer.*

killing *n.* **1.** murder, slaughter, slaying, homicide, bloodshed. *Many people get upset over the killing of laboratory animals.* –*adj.* **2.** lethal, deadly, fatal, deathly, murderous. *The shuttle disaster was almost a killing blow to our space program.*

killjoy *n.* (slang) stick-in-the-mud, spoilsport, (slang) wet blanket, (slang) gloomy Gus, (slang) party pooper, naysayer.

kin *n.* family, relatives, relations, kinsfolk. *Police would not release the victim's name until his next of kin could be notified.*

kind *adj.* **1.** amiable, friendly, considerate, gentle, benign, loving, caring. *A kind woman held the door open for me.* –*n.* **2.** manner, variety, type, sort, class, make. *What kind of car do you drive?* **Ant.** **1.** unkind, unfriendly, inconsiderate.

kindle *vb.* **1.** ignite, light, fire, torch, burn. *She kindled the campfire with only one match.* **2.** arouse, excite, stir, provoke, stimulate. *His warm smile kindled her interest.* **Ant 1–2.** extinguish, quench, smother.

kindness *n.* charity, humanity, generosity, favor, graciousness. *Acts of kindness are their own reward.*

kindred *n.* like, related, similar, corresponding, matching, close. *My sister and I are not twins, but we are kindred spirits.* **Ant.** unlike, unrelated, contrasting.

king *n.* monarch, sovereign, emperor, ruler, lord. *Everyone was required to bow before the king.*

kingdom *n.* realm, domain, dominion, country, nation. *Before the 19th century, Germany was divided into numerous small kingdoms.*

kink *n.* **1.** twist, crimp, crinkle, gnarl, knot. *After swimming all day, her hair was full of kinks.* **2.** pang, spasm, cramp, crick. *He got a kink in his back from trying to lift the heavy weight.*

kinky *adj.* unconventional, outlandish, peculiar, perverted, strange, twisted. *Sarah has some rather kinky tastes when it comes to romance.* **Ant.** normal, ordinary, standard.

kiosk *n.* booth, stall, stand. *I bought a new watch from the kiosk in the mall.*

kismet *n.* fate, destiny, predestination, lot, Providence, God's will. *My wife and I believe it was pure kismet that brought us together.*

kiss *n.* peck, (slang) smooch, (slang) lip lock, (slang) French, slobber. *I gave my daughter a glass of water and a kiss goodnight.*

kit *n.* outfit, set, gear, instruments, equipment, tackle. *I love playing drums, but I hate hauling my drum kit to shows.*

klutz *n.* oaf, lummox, bungler, (slang) bull in a china shop, (slang) butterfingers. *Don't entrust glassware to a klutz.*

knack *n.* skill, talent, aptitude, gift, ability. *She has a knack for knowing just the right thing to say.*

kneel *vb.* bow, curtsy, kowtow, salaam. *You must kneel in the presence of the queen.*

knickknack *n.* bric-a-brac, gewgaw, doodad, gimcrack, objet d'art, conversation piece. *The baseball smashed the living room window and knocked over Mother's favorite knickknack.*

knife *n.* **1.** blade, cutlery, dagger, pocketknife, jackknife. *Knives are useful tools, but they should be handled with caution.* –*vb.* **2.** stab, cut, pierce, slash, lacerate. *The goblin crept forward with the intention of knifing the unsuspecting dwarf in the back.*

knit *vb.* **1.** weave, stitch, braid, crochet, hook. *He likes to knit sweaters in his spare time.* **2.** heal, mend, attach, fasten, join, unite. *The doctor said* *my broken arm will knit in two months.* **Ant. 2.** separate, split, divide.

knob *n.* **1.** handle, hold, handhold, grip, stud. *She put new knobs on her closet doors.* **2.** lump, bump, knot, knurl, protuberance. *We can't use this piece of wood because it has too many knobs.*

knock *vb.* **1.** rap, tap, beat, strike, pound, hammer. *Let's knock on the door and see if anyone's home.* –*n.* **2.** blow, thump, rap, tap, pounding. *Did you hear a knock at the door?*

knoll *n.* hill, hummock, mound, hillock, hump, swell. *We could hear a dog barking just over the knoll.*

knot *n.* **1.** tie, bow, loop, hitch, braid, plait. *The climber secured himself to the rope with a strong knot.* **2.** burl, knurl, knob, bulge. *This is inferior lumber because it has so many knots.* **3.** tangle, snarl, kink, twist, gnarl. *He should brush the knots out of his hair.* **4.** group, cluster, bunch, clump, collection. *A knot of people gathered at the scene of the accident.* –*vb.* **5.** tie, fasten, secure, hitch, fix. *She knotted her hair into a bun.* **Ant. 5.** untie, undo, loosen.

know *vb.* understand, comprehend, perceive, recognize, realize. *Do you know how to drive?*

know-how *n.* expertise, savvy, proficiency, mastery, command, experience. *My nephew has to know-how to fix just about any computer problem.* **Ant.** ignorance, stupidity, lack.

know-it-all *n.* (slang) walking encyclopedia, intellectual, professor, (slang) brain, (slang) blowhard, (slang) windbag. *I hate to be a know-it-all, sir, but touchdowns are not scored in hockey.* **Ant.** ignoramus, idiot, know-nothing.

knowledge *n.* **1.** understanding, experience, familiarity, consciousness, awareness. *His knowledge of computers is very limited.* **2.** scholarship, learning, information, facts, data. *She has assembled a vast body of knowledge about the environment.* **Ant. 1.** ignorance, unfamiliarity.

knowledgeable *adj.* learned, educated, enlightened, informed, smart, scholarly, well-read. *When it comes to weather, the farmer is almost as knowledgeable as the meteorologist.* **Ant.** ignorant, uneducated, stupid.

kook *n.* eccentric, character, weirdo, neurotic, (slang) nut case, (slang) looney tune. *Some kook is going around the neighborhood and warning that the end of the world is near.*

kosher *adj.* proper, approved, acceptable, okay, all right, permitted. *Abe asked if the meal was kosher, and we told him it was.* **Ant.** unacceptable, improper, unapproved.

knowtow *vb.* bow, bow and scrape, kiss feet, stoop, kneel, cringe, grovel. *My grandmother refuses to kowtow to anyone.* **Ant.** dominate, intimidate, browbeat.

kudos *n.* praise, acclaim, credit, esteem, applause, glory, pat on the back. *Kudos to the sophomore class for raising the most money for charity.* **Ant.** criticism, dishonor, boos.

L

label *n.* **1.** tag, sticker, mark, stamp, ticket, slip. *The label on a can will tell you what's in it.* –*vb.* **2.** tag, mark, name, stamp, ticket, classify, designate. *Please label all the items on sale.*

labor *n.* **1.** work, toil, effort, drudgery, task, exertion. *Much labor goes into building a house.* **2.** employees, workers, laborers, manpower. *There is a dispute between labor and management about the pay increase.* –*vb.* **3.** work, toil, drudge, slave, strain, strive. *The workers labored from dawn to dusk.* **Ant. 1.** rest, leisure, relaxation. **3.** rest, idle, loaf.

laboratory *n.* lab, testing, facility, analysis center, workshop. *The patient's blood was analyzed in the laboratory.*

laborer *n.* worker, blue-collar worker, drudge, hand, (slang) grunt, employee. *A laborer for most of his life, my father preferred to work with his hands.*

laborious *adj.* strenuous, difficult, burdensome, hard, arduous, tiresome, demanding. *Moving a piano can be a laborious task.* **Ant.** light, easy, simple, effortless.

labyrinth *n.* maze, network, complex, entanglement, tangle, web. *The city was a labyrinth of streets and boulevards.*

laceration *n.* cut, rip, tear, slash, gash, slice. *My old and dull razor gave me a nasty laceration this morning.*

lack *n.* **1.** want, shortage, scarcity, need, dearth, absence, deficiency. *She got the job in spite of her lack of experience.* –*vb.* **2.** need, want, require, miss. *He lacks the motivation to succeed in his work.* **Ant. 1.** abundance, plenty, surplus. **2.** have, own, possess, hold.

lackadaisical *adj.* disinterested, indifferent, listless, languid, unmotivated, spiritless, half-hearted. *His homework was only partially finished due to his lackadaisical attitude.* **Ant.** enthusiastic, interested, spirited.

lackey *n.* toady, stooge, (slang) yes man, flunky, underling, servant. *The Mafia boss was accompanied by his favorite lackey.*

lackluster *adj.* dull, bland, blah, drab, colorless, unexciting. *The team put in a lackluster performance and lost by a large margin.* **Ant.** brilliant, colorful, exciting.

lady *n.* woman, female, matron, mademoiselle, senorita, maiden. *My daughter is trying to behave like a lady, but she still burps at the dinner table.*

ladylike *adj.* feminine, genteel, refined, cultured, proper, courtly. *It's hardly ladylike to chew with your mouth open.*

lag *vb.* **1.** tarry, linger, dawdle, loiter, straggle, falter, delay. *Try not to lag too far behind us.* –*n.* **2.** slowdown, lateness, tardiness, slack, delay, drag. *What is causing the lag in the game?* **Ant. 1.** lead, hurry, go ahead. **2.** advance, acceleration.

lagoon *n.* pool, shallow, tidal pond, body of water, backwater. *We took a quick swim in the blue waters of the lagoon.*

lair *n.* **1.** burrow, den, cave, hole, nest. *The coyotes rested peacefully in their lair.* **2.** retreat, hideout, hideaway, sanctuary. *The bandits hid the gold in their lair.*

laissez-faire *n.* freedom, nonintervention, free enterprise, deregulation, latitude, hands-off policy. *Our laissez-faire trading policy with Mexico has proven beneficial in some ways and harmful in others.* **Ant.** restraint, regulation, restriction.

lake *n.* loch, pond, tarn, basin, reservoir. *Let's go swimming in the lake.*

WORD SEARCH

crater lake: *caldera*
desert lake, fleeting: *playa*
glacial: *ice scour, kettle, moraine lake*
glacial series of: *paternoster lakes*
mountain lake: *tarn*
mountainside basin: *cirque*
outlet: *bayou*
pertaining to: *lacustrine*

lame *adj.* **1.** crippled, disabled, limping, deformed, handicapped. *She could not run in the race because of her lame leg.* **2.** poor, weak, unconvincing, feeble, inadequate, sorry, flimsy. *I'm getting tired of your lame excuses.* **Ant. 1.** healthy, agile, functioning. **2.** convincing, plausible.

lament *n.* **1.** cry, moaning, lamentation, wailing, mourning, weeping, sorrow. *The warriors' laments for their fallen leader could be heard throughout the countryside.* –*vb.* **2.** moan, weep, wail, mourn, cry, grieve, deplore. *The children lamented the death of their cat.* **Ant. 1.** celebrating, delight. **2.** celebrate, cheer, enjoy.

lamp *n.* light, beacon, illuminant, lantern.

lampoon *vb.* make fun of, ridicule, satirize, parody, mock, (slang) send up. *Comedians love to lampoon political life.*

lance *vb.* **1.** cut, pierce, puncture, slash, perforate. *A doctor lanced the wound.* –*n.* **2.** spear, javelin, pike, harpoon, weapon. *The knights attacked with their lances.*

land *n.* **1.** ground, soil, turf, field, terra firma. *The sailors have not seen land for six months.* **2.** country, nation, homeland, region, province, realm, territory. *This is the land of his ancestors.* –*vb.* **3.** arrive, disembark, settle, light, debark. *Someday astronauts will land on Mars.* **4.** get, gain, secure, win, obtain, hook. *The sales representative landed three more commissions this week.*

landfill *n.* dump, waste site, disposal area. *The landfill is full of old toxic materials and should be cleaned up.*

landlord *n.* landholder, property owner, mortgage holder, lessor, proprietor, slumlord. *Landlords like to collect their rents on time.*

landslide *n.* mudslide, rockslide, collapse, avalanche. *The landslide flowed over the main highway and cut off traffic.*

lane *n.* passage, road, way, path, route, alley, byway, track. *The lane was wide enough for only one car.*

language *n.* **1.** speech, tongue, dialect, idiom, vernacular. *The official language of Spain is Spanish.* **2.** jargon, vocabulary, phrasing, expression, lingo. *Programmers use technical language that can't be understood if you aren't familiar with computers.*

languid *adj.* weak, listless, lethargic, sluggish, enervated, faint. *Most of us had become languid in the broiling heat.* **Ant.** strong, energetic, lively.

languish *vb.* sicken, weaken, fade, wither, decline, deteriorate. *She languished while dieting because she didn't get enough protein.* **Ant.** flourish, revive, recover, thrive.

lanky *adj.* lean, slender, thin, skinny, gaunt, bony, scrawny. *The basketball player was tall and lanky.* **Ant.** plump, chubby, stocky, muscular.

lapse *n.* **1.** error, mistake, slip, blunder, neglect, disregard. *The accident was caused by the driver's lapse of attention.* **2.** descent, decline, drop, regression, deterioration, slump. *Her lapse into a coma was distressing to her doctors.* **3.** interval, intermission, period, interlude, interruption. *There was a lapse of three months in which the Venusians received no contact from Mars.* –*vb.* **4.** decline, slip, fall, worsen, sink, fade, degenerate. *His memory has lapsed as he's grown older.* **5.** stop, expire, terminate, cease, end. *They will look for a new apartment as soon as their lease has lapsed.* **Ant.** **2.** advance, improvement, development. **4.** improve, progress, increase. **5.** continue, proceed, start.

larceny *n.* theft, robbery, burglary, stealing, fraud, embezzlement. *Larceny is a serious crime.*

larder *n.* storage, pantry, store, supply, provisions, stock. *We have a large stockpile of food in our larder.*

large *adj.* big, huge, massive, immense, enormous, vast, great, extensive, sizable. *The large turnout at the concert was unexpected.* **Ant.** small, little, tiny.

lark *n.* prank, frolic, fling, caper, escapade, romp, spree, whim. *His taking the day off work was just one of his occasional larks.*

lascivious *adj.* indecent, improper, immoral, obscene, vulgar. *He was ejected from the party for rude and lascivious behavior.* **Ant.** moral, decent, proper.

lash *n.* **1.** whip, cane, flail, strap, thong, scourge. *In times now past, students were punished with a lash.* **2.** stroke, blow, whip, hit. *You deserve twenty lashes with a wet noodle.* –*vb.* **3.** whip, beat, flog, thrash, flail. *It is cruel to lash horses.* **4.** scold, berate, criticize, attack, castigate, upbraid. *The teacher lashed out at the students for their unruly behavior.* **5.** tie, rope, bind, fasten, secure, tether. *The sailor lashed the sail to the mast.* **Ant.** **4.** praise, commend, compliment. **5.** untie, unbind, release.

lasso *n.* lariat, rope, thong, noose. *Let's try to rope that calf with the lasso.*

last *adj.* **1.** final, ending, conclusive, closing, ultimate, terminal. *This is the last time I'll eat at this restaurant.* –*vb.* **2.** endure, persist, continue, remain, survive, abide. *How long is this rain going to last?* **Ant.** **1.** beginning, first, starting. **2.** end, stop, cease, expire.

lasting *adj.* enduring, continuing, permanent, perennial, persistent, lingering. *Doctors have a lasting commitment to save lives.* **Ant.** temporary, brief, passing, momentary.

latch *vb.* **1.** lock, bolt, fasten, secure, catch, close. *The dog escaped because you didn't latch the gate.* –*n.* **2.** bolt, hook, lock, fastening, clamp. *The latch on this suitcase is difficult to open.* **Ant.** **1.** open, unlock, unlatch.

late *adj.* **1.** tardy, overdue, behind, slow, delayed, detained. *He was late for his appointment.* **2.** deceased, dead, departed, gone. *The late senator was known for her achievements in civil rights.* **3.** recent, new, fresh, advanced, modern. *This car is the manufacturer's latest model.* **Ant.** **1.** early, prompt, punctual. **2.** alive, existing, surviving. **3.** early, old, first.

lately *adv.* recently, currently, presently, of late. *Lately he's been acting a little strange.* **Ant.** formerly, originally, once.

latent *adj.* dormant, hidden, inactive, inert, sleeping, unrealized. *Some people believe that telepathy is a latent power of the mind.* **Ant.** realized, developed, active.

later *adv.* **1.** afterwards, subsequently, next, successively. *We will eat dinner later.* –*adj.* **2.** following, ensuing, subsequent, successive, succeeding. *I will get back to you at a later date.* **Ant. 2.** earlier, prior, first.

latitude *n.* scope, freedom, liberty, range, extent, choice, leeway. *The teacher gave her students a lot of latitude in choosing their science projects.*

latter *adj.* later, final, ending, ensuing, successive, last. *The latter part of the movie was more entertaining.* **Ant.** former, earlier, beginning.

lattice *n.* framework, openwork, screen, grating, trellis. *Grandfather erected a lattice for the roses to climb.*

laud *vb.* praise, acclaim, extol, compliment, commend, cheer. *The boss makes it a point to laud exceptional performances.* **Ant.** criticize, disparage, denigrate.

laugh *vb.* **1.** giggle, chuckle, roar, guffaw, snicker, chortle, titter. *The children laughed at the clown.* –*n.* **2.** giggle, chuckle, snicker, roar. *Everybody needs a good laugh now and then.* **Ant. 1.** cry, weep, mourn, frown. **2.** crying, weeping.

laughable *adj.* funny, hilarious, comical, humorous, amusing, ridiculous. *If the incident weren't so embarrassing it would be laughable.* **Ant.** serious, solemn, somber, sad.

laughter *n.* giggling, chuckling, tittering, cackling, guffawing, merriment. *Our house is always full of laughter.*

launch *vb.* **1.** begin, initiate, start, originate, introduce, establish, inaugurate. *A new sports program will be launched in June.* **2.** propel, fire, thrust, shoot, eject. *Cape Kennedy launched a space shuttle today.* **Ant. 1.** stop, terminate, end.

launder *vb.* wash, clean, scrub, cleanse, scour. *He laundered his clothes.*

lavish *vb.* **1.** squander, waste, shower, bestow, overindulge. *The millionaire lavished her money on her friends.* –*adj.* **2.** liberal, extravagant, abundant, bountiful, generous, plentiful. *I didn't expect such a lavish banquet.* **Ant. 1.** save, retain, withhold. **2.** scanty, economical, stingy.

law *n.* rule, regulation, statute, decree, edict, mandate, code, principle. *Every society has laws that must be observed.*

WORD SEARCH

incriminate oneself, legal refusal to: *pleading the Fifth*
jargon of: *legalese*
jawbreaker, habitual: *scofflaw, recidivist*
lured illegally into crime by police: *entrapment*
lawlessness: *anarchy*
philosophy or science of: *jurisprudence*
punishment laws: *penal code*
reading of rights during arrest: *Miranda rule*
second prosecution, law against: *double jeopardy*
time limit for prosecution: *statute of limitations*

lawbreaker *n.* criminal, felon, scofflaw, outlaw, violator, transgressor. *Lawbreakers will be prosecuted.*

lawful *adj.* legal, legitimate, authorized, permitted, sanctioned, permissible. *The demonstration was conducted in a lawful manner.* **Ant.** unlawful, illegal, illicit, prohibited.

lawless *adj.* anarchic, ungoverned, uncivilized, unregulated, felonious, barbarous. *In the 1800s, the unorganized territories were largely lawless.* **Ant.** lawful, regulated, governed.

lawn *n.* yard, grass, turf, grounds, green, sward. *If you roll around on the lawn your clothes will be covered with grass strains.*

lawsuit *n.* case, action, litigation, claim, suit, prosecution. *The company filed a lawsuit for patent infringement.*

lawyer *n.* attorney, counsel, counselor, advocate, barrister. *The defendant knew he would need a good lawyer.*

lax *adj.* slack, neglectful, loose, careless, lenient, casual, negligent. *The students were often lax about getting their homework done on time.* **Ant.** precise, careful, strict, rigid.

laxative *n.* cathartic, purging agent, physic. *Eddy was advised to take a laxative for his constipation.*

lay *vb.* **1.** place, deposit, put, set, settle, establish, fix. *Please lay the suitcases on the bed.* **2.** assign, charge, attribute, place, credit, put. *Let's lay the responsibility on someone else.* *–n.* **3.** position, arrangement, alignment, orientation, contour. *She surveyed the lay of the land.*

layer *n.* thickness, stratum, tier, level, fold, coating. *It was so cold that he slept under four layers of blankets.*

layoff *n.* dismissal, discharge, cutback, downsizing, loss of employment. *Fifty workers lost their jobs in the layoff.*

lazy *adj.* sluggish, idle, inactive, listless, slow, slothful, lethargic. *She was too lazy to get out of bed.* **Ant.** active, energetic, industrious, busy.

lead *vb.* **1.** guide, direct, show, conduct, escort, steer, pilot. *Would you lead me to the nearest hospital?* **2.** command, head, direct, supervise, manage, govern. *The senior staff member always leads the meetings.* **3.** exceed, surpass, outperform, head, best, better. *Our team was leading by seven points at halftime.* *–n.* **4.** start, advantage, edge, precedence, advance, jump. *The marathon runner took an early lead.* **5.** hint, clue, cue, suggestion, indication. *The detectives needed more leads to solve the murder.* **Ant. 1.** follow, tail, trail. **2.** follow, obey, heed. **3.** trail, lag, succeed. **4.** disadvantage, handicap. **5.** misdirection, diversion.

leader *n.* director, chief, head, commander, manager, supervisor, superior, boss. *Take me to your leader.* **Ant.** follower, disciple, subordinate.

leadership *n.* supervision, government, command, control, direction, guidance. *You must have great leadership skills to run a company successfully.*

leading *adj.* greatest, ranking, foremost, outstanding, number one, preeminent. *The leading experts say that smoking takes ten years off from your life.* **Ant.** following, trailing.

league *n.* alliance, union, organization, coalition, federation, fellowship, order. *She belongs to the League of Women Voters.*

leak *vb.* **1.** drip, ooze, seep, flow, dribble, trickle, escape. *Water slowly leaked out of the pipe.* **2.** disclose, reveal, divulge, relate, tell. *The president's adviser leaked secrets to a journalist.* *–n.* **3.** hole, opening, break, fissure, puncture, crack. *We need to fix the leak in the pipes.* **Ant. 2.** conceal, hide, suppress.

lean *vb.* **1.** recline, tilt, slant, bend, slope, tip. *This pole leans slightly to the right.* **2.** depend, rely, trust, count. *Sometimes you need someone to lean on.* **3.** tend, incline, aim, favor, verge, trend. *She can't decide which college to attend, but she's leaning toward Harvard.* *–adj.* **4.** skinny, slender, thin, willowy, lithe, lanky. *Movie cowboys are frequently tall and lean.* **5.** meager, scant, spare, barren, inadequate, poor. *We've had lean times ever since Mother lost her job.* **Ant. 4.** fat, plump, portly. **5.** full, ample, substantial.

leaning *n.* tendency, inclination, preference, penchant, proclivity, bias. *My leaning is to always vote for the Democrat.*

leap *vb.* **1.** jump, spring, vault, bound, hop, hurtle, skip. *Look before you leap. –n.* **2.** jump, vault, hop, bound, skip, hurtle, spring. *It's a long leap to the other side of the stream.*

learn *vb.* **1.** master, acquire, absorb, assimilate, memorize. *Have you learned the history lesson for today?* **2.** discover, determine, ascertain, detect, comprehend, unearth. *Astronomers want to learn how the universe began.*

learned *adj.* educated, scholarly, literate, knowledgeable, informed. *My teacher is a learned individual.* **Ant.** illiterate, ignorant, uneducated.

learning *n.* education, schooling, edification, scholarship, erudition, enlightenment. *Mark Twain's learning came informally, outside of school.*

lease *vb.* **1.** rent, let, engage, secure, sublease, charter. *They leased the house for one year. –n.* **2.** agreement, contract, arrangement, pledge, guarantee. *I signed a six-month lease on the apartment.*

leash *vb.* **1.** restrain, control, fasten, rein, check, hold, tie. *All dogs must be leashed while in the park. –n.* **2.** harness, strap, thong, tether, line, rope, restraint. *Hold the leash tight or the dog will get away from you.*

least *adj.* smallest, littlest, slightest, minimal, trivial. *The traffic ticket is the least of your problems.* **Ant.** largest, biggest, major.

leave *vb.* **1.** go, depart, exit, flee, abandon, desert. *The gunfighter was told to leave town by sunset.* **2.** will, bequeath, bequest, commit, entrust, release. *The millionaire left his entire fortune to his cat.* **3.** maintain, retain, keep, sustain. *Leave the books where they are. –n.* **4.** allowance, permission, consent, freedom, approval, authorization. *The ambassador has leave to address the assembly.* **5.** vacation, absence, furlough, sabbatical, liberty. *She took a one-month leave to go to Europe.* **Ant. 1.** stay, return, arrive. **4.** denial, refusal, rejection.

lecherous *adj.* lewd, lustful, unrestrained, lascivious, salacious, licentious. *Kate was disgusted by the lecherous look the dirty old man gave her.* **Ant.** prudish, wholesome.

lectern *n.* stand, support, desk, ambo. *I had to give a speech in front of the school and nearly fainted at the lectern.*

lecture *vb.* **1.** speak, address, talk, instruct, expound, preach, sermonize. *The doctor lectured us about physical fitness. –n.* **2.** speech, address, talk, discourse, oration, sermon, lesson. *We heard a lecture on Tasmanian devils.*

ledge *n.* shelf, ridge, edge, projection, shoulder. *The only way to cross the cliff was by a two-foot-wide ledge.*

ledger *n.* account book, journal, record book. *You can't run a profitable business without keeping track of your expenses in a ledger.*

leech *n.* parasite, bloodsucker, sponge, (slang) bum, extortionist. *Don't let that leech take advantage of you.*

leery *adj.* wary, cautious, guarded, uncertain, suspicious, chary. *I tend to be leery of anyone who offers get-rich-quick schemes.* **Ant.** trusting, confident, gullible.

leeway *n.* flexibility, latitude, margin, scope, room, range, slack. *She left little leeway in her busy schedule.*

leftovers *n.* remnants, remains, remainders, surplus, leavings. *Leftovers for dinner again?*

left-wing *adj.* leftist, liberal, progressive, radical, left, communistic. *Her left-wing politics don't* *mix well with my conservative views.* **Ant.** conservative, right-wing, rightist.

legacy *n.* inheritance, bequest, hand-me-down, birthright, heritage, heirloom. *The legacy of lax environmental laws is global warming.*

legal *adj.* lawful, legitimate, permissible, sanctioned, permitted. *Is it legal to park here?* **Ant.** illegal, unlawful, illicit.

legalize *vb.* legitimize, sanction, decriminalize, permit, legislate, allow. *Many people would like to see the legislature legalize firecrackers in our state.* **Ant.** criminalize, ban, prohibit.

legend *n.* myth, fable, story, tale, saga, tradition, fiction. *The legend of Paul Bunyan originated in the northern United States.*

legendary *adj.* **1.** mythical, fabled, imaginary, fictitious, fanciful. *Two examples of legendary figures are Robin Hood and Hercules.* **2.** famous, famed, known, celebrated, renown. *The adventures of Annie Oakley are legendary.* **Ant. 1.** historical, factual, authenticated. **2.** unknown, ordinary.

legible *adj.* readable, clear, distinct, understandable, plain, decipherable. *She has very legible handwriting.* **Ant.** illegible, unclear, unreadable.

legion *n.* **1.** army, division, regiment, brigade, corps, troops, battalion. *He left to join the Foreign Legion.* **2.** multitude, mass, crowd, horde, throng, host, mob, army. *A legion of goblins surrounded the unwary travelers.*

legislation *n.* bill, act, law, ordinance, regulation, charter. *Enacting legislation for stricter pollution controls is a priority of environmental groups.*

legislator *n.* lawmaker, lawgiver, representative, politician, assemblyperson, councilman, councilwoman. *We are asking our legislator to toughen the local noise ordinances.*

legislature *n.* congress, senate, (in U.S.) House of Representatives, parliament, assembly, council. *The legislature will pass a number of new laws this year.*

legitimate *adj.* legal, lawful, rightful, proper, true, valid, genuine, just. *We feel that our complaints are legitimate.* **Ant.** illegal, unjustified, improper.

leisure *n.* relaxation, ease, comfort, rest, recreation, freedom, liberty, vacation. *After a busy day, she looked forward to a few hours of leisure.*

leisurely *adj.* casual, relaxed, unhurried, restful, comfortable, easy. *We spent a leisurely day at the beach.* **Ant.** hectic, hurried, rushed.

lend *vb.* give, donate, furnish, contribute, grant, loan, bestow, supply. *Can you lend me a hand with my homework?* **Ant.** keep, withdraw, borrow.

length *n.* distance, measure, reach, extent, span, range, stretch. *The carpenter measured the board's length.*

lengthen *vb.* extend, prolong, stretch, expand, elongate, increase. *He lengthened his stay at the hotel to one week.* **Ant.** shorten, decrease, curtail, cut.

lenient *adj.* merciful, kind, tolerant, gentle, lax, forgiving, sparing. *The judge is very lenient with first-time offenders.* **Ant.** strict, harsh, stern, severe.

lesbian *n.* homosexual, sapphist, gay woman. *I couldn't care less whether my neighbor is a lesbian or a heterosexual.*

lesion *n.* injury, wound, trauma, cut, laceration, contusion. *I was still covered in lesions two weeks after contracting chicken pox.*

less *adj.* **1.** fewer, smaller, slighter, lesser, reduced, shorter. *There are less calories in frozen* *yogurt than in ice cream.* –*adv.* **2.** under, little, barely, meagerly, slightly, lesser. *She likes to eat at the less-known restaurants.* **Ant. 1.** more, greater, increased, added.

lessen *vb.* reduce, diminish, dwindle, decline, decrease, shrink, ease. *His kind words lessened her sorrow.* **Ant.** increase, raise, enlarge.

lesson *n.* **1.** instruction, teaching, lecture, exercise, assignment, study. *She has been taking tennis lessons.* **2.** example, message, moral, warning, caution. *Let that be a lesson to you.*

let *vb.* **1.** allow, permit, grant, consent, authorize, sanction. *Please let the person talk.* **2.** rent, lease, hire, sublease, sublet, charter. *The cabin was let for the summer.* **Ant. 1.** forbid, prohibit, refuse. **2.** buy, sell.

letdown *n.* disappointment, comedown, anticlimax, washout, disenchantment. *It was a letdown that the Red Sox game was rained out.*

lethal *adj.* fatal, deadly, dangerous, destructive, mortal, killing. *My cat had a close encounter of the lethal kind with the neighborhood pit bull.* **Ant.** safe, harmless, beneficial.

lethargic *adj.* listless, tired, slothful, languid, sluggish, fatigued. *He was too lethargic to get up off the couch.* **Ant.** energetic, lively, active.

letter *n.* **1.** character, symbol, sign, figure, type. *This printer runs at the rate of 120 letters per second.* **2.** note, message, memorandum, document, communication, memo. *She sent a letter to her lawyer.* **3.** exactness, strictness, preciseness, substance, specifics. *The officer observed the letter of the law.*

levee *n.* embankment, bank, mound, dam, breakwater. *The floodwaters broke through the levee, submerging the town.*

level *adj.* **1.** even, smooth, flat, horizontal, plane. *Place the bowl on a level surface.* **2.** equal, aligned, flush, proportionate, even. *The top of the porch is level with my bedroom window* –*n.* **3.** degree, stage, position, layer, plane, station. *The level of workmanship in her sculptures is of the highest quality.* –*vb.* **4.** grade, even, flatten, smooth, plane, equalize. *Let's level the table so our drinks won't slide.* **5.** destroy, raze, demolish, flatten, wreck, devastate. *The Alaskan earthquake leveled the town of Valdez.* **Ant. 1.** uneven, rough, slanted. **2.** unequal, unbalanced, mismatched. **4.** roughen, coarsen. **5.** build, construct, establish.

leviathan *n.* giant, colossus, titan, behemoth, monster, hulk. *The blue whale is the leviathan of the sea.* **Ant.** (slang) shrimp, dwarf, mouse.

levity *n.* lightness, lightheartedness, frivolity, humor, foolishness, silliness. *We injected some levity into the proceedings by wearing lampshades on our heads.* **Ant.** seriousness, somberness, gravity.

levy *n.* tax, tariff, toll, duty, revenue, dues. *The government has decided to charge a levy for passing over the new bridge.*

lewd *adj.* lecherous, lascivious, libidinous, licentious, salacious. *The movie's humor was too lewd for my wife's taste.* **Ant.** prudish, G-rated, wholesome.

lexicon *n.* dictionary, glossary, thesaurus, reference. *The professor is compiling a lexicon of Appalachian slang.*

liability *n.* **1.** responsibility, culpability, accountability, obligation, burden. *Liability rests with the shopkeeper should someone get hurt in his store.* **2.** burden, drawback, hindrance, handicap, impediment, millstone. *We thought about picking Edith for our team, but we knew she'd be a liability.*

liable *adj.* **1.** prone, inclined, subject, likely, apt, susceptible. *This hot weather is liable to con-*

tinue throughout the summer. **2.** responsible, accountable, answerable, obligated, chargeable. *The truck driver is liable for the damages to your car.* **Ant. 1.** unlikely, improbable, disinclined. **2.** exempt, unaccountable.

liaison *n.* **1.** alliance, union, association, connection, affiliation. *I formed a liaison with a Japanese company to help me sell more widgets overseas.* **2.** love affair, romance, tryst, fling. *We suspected the boss might be engaged in a liaison with his receptionist.*

liar *n.* fibber, falsifier, fabricator, perjurer, storyteller. *The witness for the prosecution proved to be a liar.*

libel *n.* **1.** lies, falsehood, slander, defamation, smear, innuendo, malicious gossip. *News reporters must use great care in checking facts or they can be sued for libel.* –*vb.* **2.** lie, slander, defame, smear, malign, discredit. *When you publicize a story, use great care not to libel someone.*

liberal *adj.* **1.** generous, abundant, lavish, ample, bountiful, unsparing. *Most gardens will flourish with liberal amounts of fertilizer.* **2.** openminded, broad, tolerant, flexible, unprejudiced, unbiased. *Her liberal attitude allows her to see all sides of an issue.* **3.** progressive, left-wing, leftist. *The senator is considered a liberal Democrat.* **Ant. 1.** stingy, sparse, miserly. **2.** narrow-minded, biased, prejudiced. **3.** conservative, reactionary, right-wing.

liberate *vb.* free, emancipate, release, extricate, manumit, rescue. *The infantry unit was deployed to liberate the hostages.* **Ant.** enslave, incarcerate, shackle.

liberation *n.* freedom, liberty, emancipation, release, extrication, manumission, rescue. *They won their liberation after being held captive for nearly a year.* **Ant.** enslavement, incarceration, subjugation.

liberty *n.* **1.** freedom, independence, liberation, right, privilege. *We often take our liberties for granted.* **2.** permission, allowance, leave, license, sanction, right. *The hospital volunteers have the liberty to use the employee's lounge.* **Ant. 1.** bondage, enslavement, suppression.

libido *n.* sex drive, desire, lust, urge, sexuality, Eros, passion. *Stay our of the pasture when the bull's libido goes into overdrive.*

library *n.* book depository, book collection, reference center, research, facility, institution, athenaeum. *The library is a good place to find obscure facts.*

license *n.* **1.** permission, liberty, allowance, right, freedom, sanction. *I have my parents' license to use the car.* **2.** permit, certificate, authorization, pass. *May I please see your driver's license?* –*vb.* **3.** allow, permit, sanction, authorize, warrant, approve, commission. *She is licensed to practice physical therapy.* **Ant. 1.** denial, forbiddance, ban. **3.** forbid, prohibit, oppose.

lid *n.* cover, top, cap, seal. *Be sure to screw the lid on tightly.*

lie *vb.* **1.** recline, rest, sprawl, stretch, lounge. *Lie on the bed until you feel better.* **2.** sit, be situated, be located, be found, belongs, extends. *The Emerald City lies north of the poppy field.* **3.** falsify, fabricate, perjure, fib, misstate, misinform. *The thief lied about where he found the wallet.* –*n.* **4.** falsehood, untruth, fib, perjury, falsification, deceit. *Is it true that George Washington never told a lie?* **Ant. 1.** stand, sit, get up. **4.** truth, fact, veracity.

lifelike *adj.* realistic, natural, faithful, true, virtual. *Special effects in the movies today are very lifelike.* **Ant.** fake, phony, artificial.

lifestyle *n.* way of life, behavior, inclinations, habits, orientation, conduct. *Frank's lifestyle consists largely of being a couch potato.*

lift *vb.* 1. elevate, raise, hoist, boost, heave. *The movers lifted crates onto the truck.* 2. rescind, cancel, revoke, recall, repeal, reverse. *The government lifted martial law as soon as the riots ceased.* –*n.* 3. elation, boost, inspiration, encouragement, uplift. *Your get-well card gave me a lift.*

liftoff *n.* launch, blastoff, ignition, takeoff, firing. *Liftoff of the new rocket is scheduled for seven o'clock.*

light *n.* 1. brightness, illumination, brilliance, radiance, shine, glow. *An eerie light glowed throughout the cavern.* 2. lamp, lantern, torch, candle, match. *Did anyone bring a light?* 3. understanding, approach, aspect, viewpoint, insight, attitude. *Some writers are important because they shed new light on old matters.* –*adj.* 4. bright, brilliant, radiant, sunny, shining, gleaming, illuminated. *She prefers a light and airy dining room to a dark and stuffy one.* 5. whitish, pale, bleached, blond, fair. *People with light complexions get sunburned easily.* 6. lightweight, airy, buoyant, flimsy, slight. *Why does he always get to carry the light pack?* 7. mild, weak, slight, faint, gentle, little, minor, trivial. *The rain was too light to be beneficial to the crops.* 8. cheerful, gleeful, jolly, happy, carefree, gay. *The children are in a light mood because they are going to the circus.* –*vb.* 9. ignite, fire, kindle, burn, spark. *Whose turn is it to light the campfire?* 10. brighten, illuminate, shine, lighten, glow. *One candle will light a dark room.* 11. land, alight, perch, descend, settle, roost. *A sparrow lighted on the branch.* **Ant.** 1. dark, darkness, gloom. 4. dark, gloomy, shadowy. 5. dark, shaded. 6. heavy, hefty, weighty. 7. strong, substantial, serious. 9. somber, sad. 10. douse, extinguish, quench. 11. ascend.

lighten *adj.* reduce, decrease, lessen, alleviate, ease, empty. *Let's lighten the load so the wheelbarrow won't so hard to push.* **Ant.** increase, burden, weigh down.

lighthearted *adj.* merry, jovial, happy, joyful, carefree, cheerful, playful. *Everybody at the party was lighthearted.* **Ant.** miserable, depressed, downhearted.

lightly *adv.* softly, gently, slightly, delicately, gingerly, easily. *Tread lightly on the antique needlepoint carpet so as not to tear it.* **Ant.** heavily, intensely, violently.

lightning *n.* bolt, flash, stroke, electrical discharge. *To avoid being struck by lightning, never stand under a tree during a storm.*

WORD SEARCH

cloud borne from: *cumulonimbus, thunderhead*
ghostly version seen around ship masts and trees: *St. Elmo's fire*
globular: *ball lightning*

like *vb.* 1. favor, admire, love, fancy, enjoy, appreciate. *She likes surfing and beach volleyball.* –*adj.* 2. similar, same, identical, equal, comparable, corresponding. *Grandmother gave me five dollars, and she gave my brothers a like amount.* **Ant.** 1. dislike, loathe, hate. 2. unlike, dissimilar, different.

likely *adj.* 1. reasonable, possible, plausible, credible, probable. *This is a likely spot for our tent.* 2. probably, presumably, doubtlessly. *It's likely to rain tonight.* **Ant.** 1. unlikely, improbable, doubtful, unreasonable.

likeness *n.* 1. resemblance, semblance, similarity, comparison. *The likeness between the two sisters is uncanny.* 2. portrait, picture, image, representation, depiction. *The likeness of Abraham Lincoln appears on a penny.* **Ant.** 1. difference, disparity, dissimilarity.

limb *n.* appendage, extremity, part, member, arm, leg. *It would be difficult to live life fully without limbs.*

limber *adj.* 1. flexible, pliable, agile, elastic, bending, nimble. *Monkeys are very limber ani-*

mals. –*vb.* **2.** loosen, relax, stretch, unwind, slacken. *The quarterback limbered his muscles before the game.* **Ant. 1.** inflexible, stiff, rigid. **2.** stiffen, tighten.

limbo *n.* nowhere, oblivion, edge, border. *Kate would be in limbo professionally until she obtained her diploma.*

limit *n.* **1.** end, edge, extent, boundary, border, rim, fringe. *The planet Pluto marks the limits of the Venusian empire.* –*vb.* **2.** confine, restrict, restrain, curb, check, narrow. *Let's limit the number of applicants to ten.*

limited *adj.* restricted, defined, confined, restrained, fixed, finite. *There is a limited supply of pens available.* **Ant.** infinite, unlimited, endless.

limitless *adj.* unlimited, infinite, eternal, neverending, boundless, immeasurable. *The universe appears limitless, even through powerful telescopes.* **Ant.** limited, measurable.

limp *vb.* **1.** hobble, stagger, falter, halt, stumble, wobble. *The pirate with the wooden leg limped onto the ship.* –*n.* **2.** lameness, hobble, falter, shuffle. *The woman was described as having a pronounced limp.* –*adj.* **3.** flabby, soft, loose, slack, weak, floppy. *He took up weightlifting because he was tired of his limp muscles.* **Ant. 3.** firm, tough, strong, rigid.

line *n.* **1.** row, file, sequence, column, rank, procession. *Please form a line in front of the auditorium.* **2.** stroke, mark, stripe, dash, streak. *Draw a line connecting point A to point B.* **3.** cord, string, rope, thread, strand, cable. *The campers strung up a line to hang their food.* **4.** series, progression, succession, lineage, strain, ancestry. *Our poodle comes from a long line of champions.* **5.** pattern, system, principle, course, procedure, method. *Her solution didn't follow the conventional line of thought.* **6.** business, occupation, work, vocation, calling, trade. *His line is computer maintenance.* **7.** make, brand, kind, type, variety. *She sells several lines of perfume.* **8.** phrase, expression, story, tale. *Don't give me that old line about your dog eating your homework.* –*vb.* **9.** align, file, arrange, array, rank, range, order. *The recruits were lined up according to height.* **10.** inlay, panel, back, border, rim. *His jacket was lined with silk.* **11.** crease, furrow, wrinkle, score, groove, streak. *Worry has lined his face.* **Ant. 9.** disarray, disorder.

lineage *n.* ancestry, pedigree, family tree, descent, genealogy, bloodline. *She traced her lineage back to the early Europeans.*

linger *vb.* stay, remain, idle, tarry, persist, loiter, delay, dawdle. *The foul odor lingered long after the room was cleaned.* **Ant.** depart, disappear, hasten.

lingerie *n.* undergarments, underwear, underclothes, (slang) undies, underthings. *Most men are embarrassed to be seen in a women's lingerie store.*

lingo *n.* language, vocabulary, vernacular, jargon, argot, slang. *It's sometimes difficult to understand what surfers are talking about unless you know their lingo.*

linguist *n.* polyglot, bilinguist, interpreter, translator. *The hospital is hiring a new linguist to interpret for its foreign patients.*

liniment *n.* ointment, lotion, balm, unguent, embrocation. *That liniment you put on my aching back has an unpleasant odor.*

link *n.* **1.** bond, connection, tie, attachment, association, relationship. *Scientists are investigating the links between pollution and the rise in cancer.* –*vb.* **2.** connect, tie, associate, bond, attach, join. *The detective tried to link the crimes to her prime suspect.* **Ant. 2.** disconnect, separate, disassociate.

lion *n.* lioness, king of beasts, carnivore, predator, meat-eater, big cat. *Lions work as a team to bring down prey.*

WORD SEARCH
group: *pride*
hair: *mane*

lip *n.* **1.** brim, rim, edge, verge. *The lip of the tea cup is cracked.* **2.** insolence, impudence, mouth, back talk, disrespect, sass. *When I ask you to do your chores, I don't want to hear any lip.*

lip service *n.* insincerity, show, hollow words, empty talk, tokenism. *Politicians often pay only lip service to the needs of their constituents.*

liquefy *vb.* dissolve, melt, thaw. *We need to liquefy the fruit in order to make smoothies.*

liquid *adj.* **1.** fluid, flowing, molten, liquefied, smooth. *Water is the liquid form of ice.* *–n.* **2.** fluid, water, drink. *Adding liquid to flour will make a paste.* **Ant. 1–2.** solid.

liquidate *vb.* convert to cash, cash out, close out, sell out, sell stock. *The furniture store is going to liquidate its stock to get some much needed cash.*

liquor *n.* alcohol, intoxicant, spirits, drink, booze. *Liquor and driving do not mix.*

list *vb.* **1.** itemize, index, catalog, record, register, file, tabulate. *Please list your qualifications on the application form.* *–n.* **2.** register, slate, record, roll, inventory, roster. *Santa is making a list and checking it twice.*

listen *vb.* hear, attend, heed, hark, harken. *The soldiers listened carefully to their colonel's order.* **Ant.** ignore, disregard, neglect.

listless *adj.* sluggish, spiritless, lifeless, dull, inactive, lethargic. *This hot weather makes me feel listless.* **Ant.** lively, energetic, alert, active.

litany *n.* list, listing, rundown, account, compilation, repetition. *We heard a litany of complaints about our math teacher.*

literal *adj.* actual, true, real, exact, precise, faithful, accurate. *Not every passage in the Bible is intended to be taken in a literal sense.* **Ant.** figurative, metaphorical.

literally *adv.* actually, truthfully, exactly, really, verbatim, truly. *When I said I was hungry enough to eat a horse, I didn't mean it literally.* **Ant.** figuratively, metaphorically.

literary *adj.* literate, bookish, scholarly, cerebral, formal, erudite. *Joe is writing a literary novel, but he expects it to sell poorly.*

literate *adj.* educated, schooled, learned, informed, cultured, intelligent. *Anyone with a library that large must be quite literate.* **Ant.** illiterate, unschooled, unlearned, ignorant.

lithe *adj.* supple, flexible, limber, pliant, pliable, elastic, bending. *Dancers usually have lithe bodies.*

litigate *vb.* sue, prosecute, file suit, contest, bring legal action, press charges. *The dog-bite victim decided to litigate.*

litigation *n.* lawsuit, prosecution, suit, legal action, trial, court case. *Because mediation failed, litigation was the only way to resolve the matter.*

litter *vb.* **1.** clutter, scatter, strew, disorder. *Thoughtless drivers have littered the roadside with trash.* *–n.* **2.** trash, clutter, waste, refuse, rubbish, mess, debris, junk. *Remember to pick up your litter before you leave.* **Ant. 1.** clean up, tidy, police.

little *adj.* **1.** small, tiny, wee, petite, miniature, minute. *A little dog snapped at the mailman.* **2.** brief, short, limited, momentary, meager, scant, slight. *The track star had little time to rest between events.* *–adv.* **3.** slightly, hardly, somewhat, rather, scarcely. *She was a little tired from* *the long drive to New York.* **Ant. 1.** big, large, huge. **2.** ample, plentiful. **3.** very, certainly.

liturgy *n.* ritual, service, rite, ceremony. *We plan to attend the liturgy this afternoon.*

live *vb.* **1.** exist, endure, continue, survive, thrive, last. *Some species of tortoises live to be hundreds of years old.* **2.** reside, abide, dwell, stay, settle, inhabit. *She lived in France for two years.* –*adj.* **3.** living, alive, existing, surviving, vital, active. *I'd rather see live animals in a zoo than stuffed ones in a museum.* **Ant. 1.** die, decease, expire. **3.** dead, lifeless, deceased.

livelihood *See* LIVING.

lively *adj.* spirited, active, vigorous, brisk, energetic, bouncy. *The folk dancers did a lively rendition of the Mexican hat dance.* **Ant.** dull, boring, sluggish.

livid *adj.* **1.** enraged, furious, angry, mad, inflamed, irate. *He was livid over the rude behavior of the salesperson.* **2.** purple, lurid, discolored, bluish. *Whenever she was enraged, her face turned livid.* **Ant. 1.** calm, happy, pleased. **2.** rosy, bright.

living *n.* **1.** livelihood, income, earning, subsistence, career, vocation. *She makes a decent living as a writer.* –*adj.* **2.** alive, existing, live, organic, vital. *The guru advised us to have respect for all living things.* **Ant. 2.** nonexistent, dead, inert.

load *n.* **1.** weight, burden, cargo, freight, haul. *Take the next load to the shipping docks.* **2.** trouble, duty, pressure, worry, charge, responsibility. *Raising a child can be too heavy a load for some people.* –*vb.* **3.** fill, stack, pack, weight, burden, pile, stuff. *The farmers loaded the wagon with hay.* **Ant. 3.** empty, unload, unpack.

loaf *vb.* idle, lounge, loiter, rest, laze, loll. *It feels nice to just loaf in the sun.* **Ant.** work, toil, labor.

loan *vb.* **1.** lend, advance, allow, credit, finance. *Can you loan me twenty dollars till Monday?* –*n.* **2.** advance, credit, lending, allowance, mortgage. *The loan must be paid off in three years.*

loathe *vb.* hate, detest, despise, abhor, scorn, abominate. *I may dislike beets, but I really loathe lima beans.* **Ant.** love, like, adore, relish.

loathsome *adj.* atrocious, abominable, repulsive, repellent, foul, disgusting. *Ogres are truly loathsome creatures.* **Ant.** lovable, adorable, delightful, charming.

lob *vb.* toss, loft, throw, pitch, fling, flip. *Lob the ball gently so the little girl can catch it.*

lobby *n.* entrance, hall, foyer, anteroom, entry, waiting room. *I'll meet you in the lobby.*

lobby *vb.* influence, influence peddle, pressure, sway, push, (slang) pull strings. *We want to lobby for stronger environmental laws.*

lobbyist *n.* influence peddler, persuader, special-interest representative, (slang) mover and shaker, campaigner, (slang) string-puller. *The lobbyists in Washington are paid to influence politicians.*

local *adj.* nearby, close, neighboring, adjoining, surrounding. *Why go into the city when you can get that item in the local store?* **Ant.** faraway, distant.

locate *vb.* **1.** find, discover, detect, uncover, discern, unearth. *The explorer hoped to locate the lost city of Atlantis.* **2.** situate, place, fix, establish, station, put. *He plans to locate the gas station at the town's busiest intersection.*

location *n.* place, site, area, situation, locale, position, spot, point. *This is a great location for a hamburger stand.*

lock *vb.* **1.** latch, bolt, fasten, padlock, secure. *Did you lock the door?* **2.** join, link, grasp, hold, clasp, unite. *He locked his hands around the bar* *and pulled himself up. –n.* **3.** bolt, padlock, latch, clamp, hook. *The lock on the gate is rusty.* **Ant. 1.** unlock, open, unlatch. **2.** release, free, loosen.

locker *n.* compartment, cabinet, closet, storage unit, footlocker, trunk. *Hang your clothes up in your locker.*

lodge *vb.* **1.** stay, room, shelter, reside, board, quarter, accommodate. *The travelers were lodged at the local inn.* **2.** catch, position, settle, fix, place, put. *Her kite was lodged in a tree. –n.* **3.** inn, hotel, chalet, cabin, cottage, hut, hostel. *The lodge at the national park has no vacancies.*

lodger *n.* guest, boarder, tenant, renter. *We will be getting a new lodger this afternoon.*

lodging *n.* accommodation, hotel, motel, inn, bed and breakfast, hostel, rooming house. *We need to find lodging for the night.*

loft *n.* attic, garret, clerestory, upper level, studio. *The children liked to play hide and seek in the loft.*

lofty *adj.* **1.** haughty, proud, exalted, lordly, arrogant, snobbish. *The count's lofty treatment of his servants was embarrassing to watch.* **2.** towering, high, tall, elevated, soaring. *The climber's goal was to reach the lofty pinnacle.* **Ant. 1.** modest, humble, unassuming. **2.** short, low, stunted.

log *vb.* **1.** enter, write in, record, note, register, report. *I'll log the new information into the computer. –n.* **2.** record book, journal, account, ledger, diary, chronicle. *Enter the new information in the log.*

WORD SEARCH

logger: *lumberjack*
logging chute: *flume, sluice*
mass transported down river: *drive*
pile: *rollway*
sport of knocking opponent off from: *birling*

logic *n.* reasoning, deduction, sense, rationale, good judgment, inference. *Insisting that the earth is flat defies logic.*

logical *adj.* rational, reasonable, sound, sensible, valid, clear. *She devised a logical plan to accomplish her project.* **Ant.** irrational, illogical, unsound.

logistics *n.* management, administration, organization, coordination, handling, governance. *The logistics of maintaining an army in a foreign country is daunting.*

logo *n.* symbol, trademark, logogram, emblem, name, colophon. *Companies like to use logos to build name recognition.*

loiter *vb.* linger, dawdle, tarry, delay, idle, loaf, lag. *The shop owner did not like people to loiter in front of his store.* **Ant.** hurry, pass, speed, hasten.

lone *adj.* single, sole, alone, solitary, individual. *A lone coyote howled on the mesa.*

loneliness *n.* isolation, emptiness, seclusion, alienation, remoteness, detachment. *A vacation on a deserted island might be fun until loneliness sets in.* **Ant.** companionship, friendship, intimacy.

lonely *adj.* **1.** lonesome, alone, friendless, forsaken, companionless, forlorn. *I've been feeling lonely since you moved away.* **2.** isolated, secluded, remote, deserted, unpopulated. *Their house was in a lonely canyon off the main road.* **Ant. 1.** popular, sociable. **2.** populous, crowded, congested.

loner *n.* hermit, recluse, lone wolf, introvert, outcast, misanthrope. *The loner prefers his own company.*

long *adj.* **1.** extensive, lengthy, extended, prolonged, protracted. *It's going to be a long wait at the dentist's office. –vb.* **2.** crave, wish, yearn, desire, covet, hunger, thirst. *She longed for a chocolate shake.* **Ant. 1.** short, brief, small, contracted.

longevity *n.* long life, endurance, durability, staying power. *The longevity of the tortoise is impressive.*

longing *n.* want, yearning, desire, hunger, thirst, yen. *I have a longing for a vanilla ice cream cone.*

long-winded *adj.* wordy, verbose, rambling, prolix, endless, interminable. *I can't bear to hear another politician's long-winded speech.* **Ant.** brief, condensed, to-the-point.

look *vb.* **1.** see, watch, glance, gaze, observe, behold, view. *Look at that cute puppy.* **2.** appear, seem, sound, show, exhibit. *The penguins looked like they were wearing tuxedos.* *–n.* **3.** glance, gaze, peek, glimpse, peep. *Let's take a look at the house on the corner.* **4.** appearance, expression, manner, demeanor, bearing. *Her joyful look tells me that she received good news.*

lookout *n.* **1.** sentinel, guard, sentry, watchman, patrol. *We posted a lookout at the top of the hill.* **2.** watchtower, observatory, perch, crow's nest. *We had two men posted atop the lookout.*

loom *vb.* tower, rise, reach, appear, threaten, menace. *A hurricane loomed over the Florida coast.*

loony *adj.* crazy, insane, irrational, maniacal, (slang) nutty, demented. *We tend to see more loony behavior during a full moon.* **Ant.** rational, sane, level-headed.

loop *n.* **1.** circle, coil, noose, ring, spiral, knot. *The cowboy formed a loop at the end of his rope.* *–vb.* **2.** coil, twist, circle, knot, bend, turn. *The sailor looped the line to form a knot.*

loose *adj.* **1.** free, untied, unfastened, unfettered, liberated, unrestricted. *The escaped tiger roamed loose in the city.* **2.** slack, baggy, sagging, drooping. *The loose clothing made him look ten pounds heavier.* **3.** vague, inexact, indefinite, undefined, careless, general. *Her loose work habits caused her to make many mistakes.* **4.** wanton, immoral, sinful, wild, fast, reckless. *His loose lifestyle is responsible for his poverty.* *–vb.* **5.** untie, free, release, liberate, unbind, unfasten. *Every morning they loosed the horses into the meadow.* **Ant.** **1.** tied, bound, secured. **2.** tight, confining. **3.** exact, precise, clear. **4.** moral, virtuous, disciplined. **5.** tie, bind, secure.

loot *vb.* **1.** rob, steal, burglarize, plunder, ransack, pilfer. *Outlaws looted the stagecoach.* *–n.* **2.** booty, plunder, spoils, take, prize, haul. *I know where the pirates hid their loot.*

looter *n.* thief, plunderer, raider, burglar, shoplifter, pilferer. *During a riot, shop owners must protect their property from looters.*

lopsided *adj.* uneven, unbalanced, slanted, distorted, unequal, disproportionate. *The basketball game between the dwarves and the giants was a little lopsided.* **Ant.** even, balanced, equal.

loquacious *adj.* talkative, gabby, chatty, garrulous, verbose, (slang) motor-mouthed. *The loquacious student was recommended for a job in talk radio.* **Ant.** taciturn, reserved, quiet.

lord *n.* master, governor, baron, head, nobleman, royalty, aristocrat. *In his castle, he considered himself lord and master.*

lose *vb.* **1.** misplace, mislay, miss, forget, overlook. *The shopper lost her car in the vast parking lot.* **2.** forfeit, surrender, drop, succumb, yield. *The soccer team lost their third game in a row.* **Ant.** **1.** find, retrieve, locate. **2.** win, succeed, triumph.

loser *n.* failure, also-ran, (slang) Charlie Brown, (slang) flop, (slang) dud, the defeated, (slang) zero. *Even though she came in second, she felt like a loser.* **Ant.** winner, champion, number one.

loss *n.* **1.** deprivation, depletion, decrease, removal, want, need. *When the new roommate moved in, we had trouble adjusting to the loss of privacy.* **2.** ruin, destruction, wrecking, demolition, waste. *The high-speed chase resulted in the loss of three police cars.* **3.** defeat, failure, losing, undoing. *The recent loss ruined our football team's chances for championship.* **Ant. 1.** return, increase, gain. **2.** saving, preservation. **3.** win, triumph, victory.

lost *adj.* **1.** missing, mislaid, misplaced, stray, absent. *The search-and-rescue team was called out to look for a lost hiker.* **2.** destroyed, demolished, wrecked, ruined, obliterated. *All my possessions were lost in the fire.* **Ant. 1.** found, recovered, returned. **2.** saved, preserved.

lot *n.* **1.** plenty, abundance, quantity, much. *She brought lots of fried chicken to the picnic.* **2.** tract, land, parcel, plot, property, acreage. *We played, baseball in a vacant lot across the street.* **3.** portion, share, allotment, part, piece, measure. *The items for auction were divided into lots.* **4.** fate, destiny, fortune, plight, circumstance, chance. *Snow White's lot in life was to bite a poisoned apple.* **Ant. 1.** little, few, scant.

lothario *n.* womanizer, (slang) player, rake, Don Juan, Cassanova, philanderer. *Eddy fancies himself as a lothario, but most women think differently.*

lotion *n.* cream, ointment, balm, salve, embrocation, conditioner. *Be sure to put on plenty of suntan lotion before you go out.*

lottery *n.* drawing, game of chance, raffle, sweepstakes, gamble. *Someday I'll win the lottery and retire to Jamaica.*

loud *adj.* **1.** noisy, deafening, shrill, blaring, boisterous, booming. *Please don't play your music so loud.* **2.** gaudy, garish, flashy, showy, vulgar. *He dresses so loud that he stands out in a crowd.* **Ant. 1.** quiet, soft, silent. **2.** sedate, tasteful, conservative.

loudmouthed bigmouthed, obnoxious, boisterous, blustering, strident, bellowing. *The coach is a loudmouthed jerk, and I don't want to play for him.* **Ant.** quiet, reserved, shy.

lounge *vb.* **1.** relax, idle, laze, loaf, rest, recline. *The hotel guests lounged by the swimming pool.* *–n.* **2.** waiting room, lobby, anteroom, parlor, salon. *The lounge is a good place to meet people.*

lousy *adj.* poor, inferior, bad, shoddy, shabby, inadequate. *Judging from my wilted vegetables, I'm a lousy gardener.* **Ant.** excellent, good, great.

lovable *adj.* adorable, endearing, sweet, dear, winning, charming, cuddly. *Children are lovable even when they're being little devils.* **Ant.** despicable, repulsive, repellent.

love *n.* **1.** adoration, affection, warmth, devotion, tenderness, attachment. *There is much love between our family members.* *–vb.* **2.** adore, cherish, treasure, like, value. *She loved the sincerity and caring of all her friends.* **Ant. 1.** hatred, loathing, malice. **2.** hate, loathe, detest, abhor.

love handle *n.* Slang. fat, flab, blubber, (slang) spare tire, middle age spread. *As I age, I seem to grow bigger love handles.*

lovelorn *adj.* loveless, forsaken, bereft, spurned, rejected, lovesick. *The lovelorn bachelor searched for a mate.*

lovely *adj.* beautiful, attractive, enchanting, adorable, captivating. *The lovely sunset inspired me to write a poem.* **Ant.** ugly, unattractive, plain.

lovemaking *n.* sex, intercourse, copulation, mating, foreplay, making out. *Lovemaking is the subject of the* Kama Sutra.

lovesick *adj.* longing (slang) head over heals, lovelorn, (slang) having it bad, pining, infatuated, (slang) ga ga.

lover *n.* sweetheart, mate, suitor, paramour, flame, steady, heartthrob. *We saw lovers holding hands in the park.*

loving *adj.* affectionate, tender, caring, adoring, warm. *His kitten has a very loving nature.* **Ant.** unloving, uncaring, aloof.

low *adj.* **1.** little, small, paltry, slight, trivial, reduced. *The socks were so low in price that she bought a dozen pairs.* **2.** sad, downcast, depressed, unhappy, gloomy, morose. *I'm feeling a little low today.* **3.** degrading, terrible, rude, vulgar, mean, vile, awful. *I have seen some pretty low tricks, but that was the worst.* **4.** humble, modest, lowly, inferior, common. *The peasant boy endured his low status in the village.* **Ant. 1.** high, elevated, substantial. **2.** happy, delighted, elated. **3.** fine, admirable, decent. **4.** high, exalted, important.

lower *vb.* **1.** drop, submerge, dip, sink, let down, depress. *I refused to watch the cook lower the live lobster into the boiling water.* **2.** reduce, decrease, lessen, cut, depreciate, shorten. *We need to lower the price on widgets.* **Ant.** raise, lift, elevate.

low-key *adj.* mellow, quiet, subdued, underrated, restrained, muted. *The party was so low-key that I nearly fell asleep.* **Ant.** loud, blaring, unrestrained.

loyal *adj.* faithful, true, steadfast, devoted, trustworthy, dependable. *She has been a loyal employee for the last ten years.* **Ant.** unfaithful, disloyal, false, traitorous.

loyalty *n.* fidelity, faithfulness, allegiance, honor, reliability, steadfastness, devotion. *Military leaders demand complete loyalty from their troops.* **Ant.** disloyalty, infidelity, dishonor.

lubricate *vb.* grease, oil, slicken. *We must lubricate all moving parts to increase their lifespan.*

lucid *adj.* **1.** clear, understandable, accurate, sensible, rational, intelligible. *I wish someone could give a lucid explanation for what happened.* **2.** transparent, translucent, clear, light, bright. *The windows were so dirty they were no longer lucid.* **Ant. 1.** vague, confused, unclear. **2.** dim, dark, murky, gloomy.

Lucifer *n.* *See* SATAN.

luck *n.* fortune, chance, fate, fluke, accident. *Winning the lottery is purely a matter of luck.* **Ant.** design, skill, determination.

lucky *adj.* fortunate, fortuitous, favored, successful, blessed. *You were lucky to miss the traffic jam on the freeway.* **Ant.** unfortunate, unlucky, luckless.

lucrative *adj.* money-making, profitable, prosperous, rewarding, wealth-producing, remunerative. *My chocolate-covered ant business didn't turn out to be as lucrative as I'd hoped.* **Ant.** unprofitable, money-losing, expensive.

ludicrous *adj.* silly, ridiculous, absurd, crazy, laughable, preposterous, bizarre. *The sight of the grown man wearing a hat with moose antlers was ludicrous.* **Ant.** serious, sensible, solemn.

lug *vb.* carry, drag, heave, tug, haul, pull, bear, tote. *Do you really want to lug that sofa up the stairs?*

luggage *n.* baggage, bags, suitcases, trunks, effects, gear. *Please check your luggage at the counter.*

lukewarm *adj.* **1.** warm, tepid, mild, temperate. *She likes her bath water to be lukewarm.* **2.** indifferent, halfhearted, unenthusiastic, cool, aloof. *Congress was lukewarm over the senator's proposal.* **Ant. 1.** cold, hot, freezing, burning. **2.** excited, concerned.

lull *n.* **1.** calmness, pause, stillness, hush, quiet, break, interval. *The sudden lull meant they were in the eye of the hurricane.* *–vb.* **2.**

calm, quiet, hush, soothe, pacify, still. *The mother lulled her crying baby with a song.* **Ant. 1.** continuation, turbulence. **2.** excite, rouse, agitate.

lumber *n.* timber, planks, wood, boards, studs, posts, two-by-fours. *Our neighbors bought enough lumber to build a garage.*

luminous *adj.* glowing, radiant, shining, lighted, bright, illuminated. *The sorcerer had a luminous blue glow surrounding him.* **Ant.** dark, dim, dull.

lummox *n.* oaf, clod, (slang) klutz, (slang) clodhopper, (slang) big ape, moron. *The lummox bumped into all the other dancers and knocked them to the floor.*

lump *n.* **1.** piece, chunk, clump, clod, block, mass. *She tossed several lumps of coal into the stove.* **2.** bump, swelling, bulge, mass, knot. *He didn't know where the lump on his elbow came from.* –*vb.* **3.** combine, assemble, collect, amass, pool, merge. *They lumped all the camping equipment together for everyone to use.* **Ant. 3.** separate, divide, split.

lunacy *n.* craziness, insanity, madness, foolishness, psychosis, idiocy. *Many people believed that the Wright Brothers' pursuit of human flight was lunacy.* **Ant.** sanity, rationality, sense.

lunatic *n.* psychopath, sociopath, maniac, madman. *The lunatic was seen howling at the Moon at midnight.*

lunch *n.* meal, dinner, luncheon, bite to eat, dejeuner, repast. *I know it's time for lunch when my stomach starts growling.*

lunge *vb.* **1.** charge, plunge, thrust, lurch, attack, rush, dive. *The dog lunged at the intruder.* –*n.* **2.** charge, attack, plunge, pounce, jab, stab. *The cat made a lunge at the fleeing mouse.* **Ant. 1.** recoil, parry.

lungs *n.* respiratory organs. *You can damage your lungs by smoking.*

lurch *vb.* pitch, tumble, sway, teeter, toss, swing, reel, roll. *The small boat lurched to the side every time a wave hit.*

lure *vb.* **1.** attract, entice, draw, tempt, allure, coax, bait. *Don't be lured into accepting an easy but ineffective solution.* –*n.* **2.** bait, trap, decoy, enticement, draw, attraction, temptation. *The spy used his charm as a lure to get top-secret information.* **Ant. 1.** repel, repulse, rebuff.

lurid *adj.* shocking, startling, sensational, gruesome, grisly, grim, horrid. *The lurid headline read: "Man Eats His Own Heart."* **Ant.** mild, lighthearted, tame, cheerful.

lurk *vb.* prowl, creep, slink, sneak, skulk. *We knew a tiger was lurking near our campsite.*

luscious *adj.* delicious, succulent, delightful, tasty, delectable, savory. *The apple pie was luscious.* **Ant.** flavorless, nauseating, tasteless.

lush *n.* luxuriant, rich, abundant, profuse, prolific, verdant. *The garden always appears unusually lush after it has been fertilized.* **Ant.** barren, sparse, thin.

lust *n.* **1.** craving, passion, desire, longing, thirst, appetite, urge. *King Midas had a lust for riches.* –*vb.* **2.** desire, crave, long, hunger, yearn, covet, want. *The violinist lusted for a chance to lead the orchestra.*

luster *n.* brightness, gloss, shine, sheen, gleam, glow, radiance. *The luster of the antique car greatly increased its value.* **Ant.** dullness, tarnish, drabness.

luxurious *adj.* lavish, opulent, rich, elegant, splendid, magnificent, lush. *The duke lived in a luxurious palace.* **Ant.** poor, spare, shabby, simple.

luxury *n.* extravagance, extra, indulgence, treat, lavishness, immoderation. *He liked to surround himself with luxury and thus owned* *the best of everything.* **Ant.** bare necessity, poverty, lack.

lying *n.* dishonesty, prevarication, fabrication, deceit, fibbing, misrepresentation. *The voters were tired of the politician's lying.* **Ant.** honesty, truth, straightforwardness.

lynching *n.* hanging, execution, mob justice, vigilante justice, (slang) stringing up. *Lynching by vigilantes was a common travesty of justice in the 1800s.*

lyrical *adj.* musical, melodic, songful, tuneful, singing. *Her voice has a lyrical ring.*

M

macabre *adj.* gruesome, deathly, horrifying, morbid, ghastly, grisly. *The horror movie was filled with macabre scenes.*

machine *n.* **1.** appliance, mechanism, engine, device, apparatus, gadget. *The mechanic said my car was a fine machine.* **2.** structure, organization, party, association, agency, body. *New York City's bureaucracy is a large and complex machine.*

machismo *n.* maleness, masculinity, strength, virility, dominance, fierceness, potency. *Some people are turned off by swaggering machismo.* **Ant.** femininity, weakness, impotence.

macho *adj.* masculine, virile, male, tough, strong, dominant, fierce. *He believed he was macho enough to fight everyone in the room and win.* **Ant.** feminine, effeminate, weak.

mad *adj.* **1.** angry, furious, infuriated, enraged, irate, irritated. *I was mad at him for breaking my glasses.* **2.** crazy, deranged, insane, demented, unbalanced, lunatic. *The mad dog was put to sleep.* **3.** hysterical, excited, infatuated, passionate, wild. *The fans reacted with mad cheering when their team scored a touchdown.* **Ant. 1.** pleased, glad. **2.** sane. **3.** disinterested, indifferent.

madcap *n.* wild, reckless, crazy, foolish, rash, impulsive. *I enjoy madcap, physical comedy as well as the more cerebral stuff.* **Ant.** stuffy, prim, proper.

maddening *adj.* infuriating, frustrating, vexing, aggravating, irritating. *Getting tied up in traffic can be maddening.* **Ant.** mollifying, soothing, relaxing.

madhouse *n.* insane asylum, mental institution, psychiatric hospital (slang) nut house, (slang) laughing academy. *A house full of screaming kids can resemble a madhouse.*

madly *adv.* fiercely, passionately, insanely, wildly, fervently, intensely, deliriously. *I feel madly about you.* **Ant.** calmly, indifferently.

madman *n.* maniac, lunatic, psychopath, sociopath, psychotic. *The police were on the lookout for a madman.*

madness *n.* **1.** insanity, insaneness, craziness, lunacy, wackiness, daftness, derangement. *Some people consider war true madness.* **2.** recklessness, folly, silliness, foolishness, absurdity, idiocy. *It is madness for you to attempt to sail around the world by yourself.* **Ant. 1.** sense, sanity. **2.** wisdom, prudence.

maelstrom *n.* whirlpool, vortex, eddy, swirl, Charybdis, turmoil. *The storm water circled the sewer in a turbulent maelstrom.*

maestro *n.* master, conductor, composer, instructor. *The maestro gesticulated madly as he conducted the orchestra.*

Mafia *n.* Cosa Nostra, the mob, organized crime, the Syndicate, the underworld, Black

Hand. *The police have a plan to crack down on the Mafia and their illegal activities.*

WORD SEARCH

chief: *boss, capo, don, godfather*
code of silence: *omertà*
loans money at exorbitant rates: *loanshark*
low-ranking member: *soldier*
member of: *goodfella, Mafioso, mobster, wiseguy*
stolen goods: *swag*
stolen goods, receiver of: *fence*

magazine *n.* periodical, journal, publication, monthly, digest, weekly. *She likes to read all the magazines in her dentist's waiting room.*

magic *n.* **1.** sorcery, voodoo, witchcraft, wizardry, bewitchment, enchantment. *Do you believe in magic? –adj.* **2.** alluring, enchanting, charming, bewitching, spellbinding. *It was a magic night.* **Ant. 2.** ordinary, plain.

magical *adj.* supernatural, mystical, spellbinding, enchanting, mesmerizing, entrancing. *The performers put on an absolutely magical show.*

magician *n.* enchanter, sorcerer, sorceress, conjurer, medium, illusionist, mage. *We had a magician do tricks at the party.*

magnanimous *adj.* noble, forgiving, tolerant, high-minded, benevolent, chivalrous. *Our magnanimous neighbor always lets us play baseball in his backyard.* **Ant.** mean, unforgiving, intolerant.

magnate *n.* tycoon, mogul, capitalist, industrialist, (slang) bigwig, (slang) bigshot. *Macky wants to become the next popcorn magnate.*

magnetic *adj.* captivating, appealing, charismatic, alluring, enchanting. *She has a magnetic personality that draws people to her.* **Ant.** repulsive, offensive, disgusting.

magnificent *adj.* fantastic, impressive, superb, extraordinary, wonderful. *On the Fourth of July, we watched a magnificent fireworks display.* **Ant.** poor, ordinary, terrible.

magnify *vb.* enlarge, increase, exaggerate, dramatize, inflate. *Dwelling on the problem will only magnify it.* **Ant.** reduce, diminish, minimize.

magnitude *n.* degree, importance, intensity, significance, consequence, weight. *The magnitude of the earthquake was greater than we had originally thought.*

maharishi *n.* spiritual guide, mystic, guru, teacher. *For life's difficult problems, consult your maharishi.*

mail *n.* **1.** letters, postcards, messages, packages. *Did I receive any mail today? –vb.* **2.** send, dispatch, post, express, forward. *Make sure you mail the bills by Monday.*

maim *vb.* mutilate, maul, mangle, cripple, disfigure, disable, injure. *An artillery shell maimed the soldier.*

main *adj.* primary, principal, central, chief, foremost, major, crucial. *Most of the science books are in the main library.* **Ant.** secondary, minor, trivial.

mainly *adv.* primarily, principally, mostly, predominantly, chiefly, especially. *This movie theater is mainly a hangout for teenagers.* **Ant.** slightly, partly, partially.

mainstay *n.* backbone, support, pillar, buttress, foundation, anchor. *Potatoes, blueberries, and lobsters are mainstays of the Maine economy.*

mainstream *adj.* general, average, typical, standard, middle-of-the-road, universal, widespread. *Citizens in mainstream America tend to reject war.* **Ant.** radical, extreme, fringe.

maintain *vb.* **1.** continue, keep, support, sustain, uphold, preserve. *He maintains his yard quite well.* **2.** assert, claim, insist, contend, swear, declare. *I still maintain that traveling to Asia would be more enjoyable than traveling to Australia.* **Ant. 1.** discontinue, abandon, end. **2.** recant, disclaim.

majestic *adj.* awesome, impressive, grand, elegant, stately, magnificent, imposing. *The eagle is considered a majestic bird.* **Ant.** puny, undistinguished, humble.

major *adj.* **1.** main, primary, principal, greatest, largest. *He's finally playing in the major leagues this year.* **2.** important, great, foremost, leading, significant. *The museum considered the discovery a major find.* **Ant. 1.** minor, lesser, smaller. **2.** insignificant, unimportant.

majority *n.* preponderance, bulk, the most, greatest portion, lion's share. *The majority of people believe in equal rights for everyone.* **Ant.** minority, fraction, trifling.

make *vb.* **1.** create, produce, construct, fashion, build, prepare, develop. *Do you know how to make an ice-cream float?* **2.** force, compel, pressure, coerce, drive. *You can't make me go if I don't want to.* **3.** reach, get, attain, gain, acquire. *I hope to make senior salesclerk by this summer.* **4.** deliver, accomplish, cause, start, begin. *The president will make a speech this Sunday.* **5.** total, come to, amount to, equal. *With the jacket, it makes fifty dollars.* **Ant. 1.** destroy, demolish, wreck.

make-believe *adj.* fantasy, imagination, pretend, fancy, dream, fiction. *Children love to play make-believe.* **Ant.** reality, truth.

makeshift *adj.* slapdash, stopgap, thrown together, improvised, emergency, jury-rigged. *The castaway built a makeshift raft and drifted away.*

make-up *n.* cosmetics, foundation, face paint, beauty aid, rouge, blush. *Mary hates to be seen without her make-up.*

maladjusted *adj.* maladapted, disturbed, neurotic, inadequate, unfit, dysfunctional. *A maladjusted person may have trouble conforming to society's norms.* **Ant.** adjusted, normal, adapted.

malady *n.* disease, illness, sickness, ailment, affliction, infirmity. *He was afflicted with a strange malady that appeared to be caused by a virus.*

malaise *n.* unease, depression, discomfort, the blahs, lassitude, sickness, angst. *After interest rules were raised, the entire country suffered from an economic malaise.* **Ant.** health, vigor, vitality.

malcontent *n.* whiner, grouch, complainer, faultfinder, grumbler, (slang) bellyacher. *The classic malcontent is never happy unless he is miserable.*

male *adj.* **1.** masculine, manly, macho, virile, tough, boyish. *Male behavior is sometimes rough and tumble.* –*n.* **2.** man, guy, gentleman, fellow, chap, boy. *The man of the house can cook, clean and mow the lawn.* **Ant. 1.** female, feminine, effeminate. **2.** woman, female, lady.

malevolent *adj.* malicious, cruel, mean, hateful, vicious, vindictive, hostile. *Hitler was a malevolent dictator.* **Ant.** kind, compassionate, nice.

malformation *n.* deformity, abnormality, anomaly, irregularity, monstrosity, freak. *Unfortunately, the baby was born with a slight malformation, which had to be corrected.*

malformed *adj.* deformed, abnormal, misshapen, irregular, distorted, misproportioned. *The pumpkin was hideously malformed.*

malfunction *n.* failure, snag, breakdown, defect, (slang) bug, (slang) snafu. *A malfunction caused the computer to freeze up.*

malice *n.* spite, maliciousness, vengefulness, venom, malevolence. *Holding malice in your* *heart may actually shorten your lifespan.* **Ant.** forgiveness, kindness, compassion.

malicious *adj.* vicious, slanderous, hateful, spiteful, nasty, mean. *He told the other kids some really malicious things about me.* **Ant.** nice, kind, friendly.

malign *vb.* defame, slander, smear, denigrate, slur, insult. *Sally tried to malign her friend in public, but her plan backfired when she was maligned herself.* **Ant.** compliment, flatter, revere.

malignant *adj.* fatal, lethal, deadly, cancerous, harmful. *The doctors must operate, since it is a malignant tumor.* **Ant.** good, healthy, benign.

malingerer *n.* shirker, slacker, idler, loafer, clockwatcher. *Malingerers soon find themselves looking for new employment.*

mall *n.* shopping center, shopping complex, shopping mecca, marketplace. *We go to the mall for back-to-school shopping.*

malleable *adj.* pliable, flexible, moldable, plastic, yielding, movable. **Ant.** inflexible, rigid.

malnutrition *n.* malnourishment, nutrient deficiency, wasting, anorexia nervosa. *She appeared to be suffering from malnutrition because she was so thin.*

malodorous *adj.* stinking, smelly, noxious, reeking, foul, rotten. *The barn is particular malodorous when it gets humid.* **Ant.** sweet-smelling, ambrosial, fragrant.

malpractice *n.* carelessness, incompetence, negligence, ineptitude, mistake, oversight. *Doctors must take out insurance to protect themselves from malpractice suits.*

mammoth *adj.* huge, enormous, gigantic, colossal, monstrous, oversized, immense. *The meteorite left a mammoth hole in the ground.* **Ant.** tiny, little, small, undersized.

man *n.* **1.** male, guy, fellow, gentleman, chap. *Look for a tall man with a beard.* **2.** mankind, womankind, humankind, human, *Homo sapiens. Man is the only animal that blushes.*

manacle *n.* handcuff, shackle, iron, bond, chain. *Release the prisoners from their manacles.*

manage *vb.* **1.** oversee, supervise, run, direct, administer, guide. *Our boss manages the store quite well.* **2.** cope, function, survive, operate. *Thanks for offering your help, but I think I can manage.* **3.** arrange, manipulate, maneuver, contrive. *How did you manage to get the day off work?*

manageable *adj.* controllable, compliant, docile, governable, obedient, tame. *Wild animals are rarely manageable in captivity.* **Ant.** unmanageable, wild, disobedient.

management *n.* **1.** bosses, executives, managers, supervisors. *The unhappy customer complained to the store's management.* **2.** supervision, running, overseeing, administration, guidance, handling. *The management of this apartment building takes a lot of time and effort.*

manager *n.* boss, supervisor, administrator, chief, superintendent. *My manager scheduled me to work the entire weekend.* **Ant.** employee, underling.

mandate *n.* will of the people, directive, order, command, authority, decree, go-ahead. *The governor received a mandate from the voters to curb spending.*

mandatory *adj.* required, necessary, essential, imperative, requisite, compulsory. *A mandatory background check is required for all gun purchases.* **Ant.** elective, optional, unnecessary.

maneuver *n.* **1.** move, movement, tactic, ploy, gambit. *His pawn captured my queen in a maneuver I hadn't anticipated.* –*vb.* **2.** jockey, contrive, plot, scheme, conspire. *She maneuvered to get a better position in the company.* 3. move, direct, deploy, manipulate, steer. *He maneuvered the television so everyone in the room could see it.*

mangle *vb.* damage, mutilate, twist, ruin, maul, tear. *A vicious gust of wind mangled our kite.*

mangy *adj.* shabby, filthy, dingy, dirty, ragged, scruffy. *Please groom your mangy dog.*

manhandle *vb.* strongarm, rough up, dominate, arm-twist, bully, abuse. *The police try not to manhandle a suspect unless it becomes absolutely necessary.* **Ant.** coddle, baby, mother.

mania *n.* passion, obsession, craze, fascination, craving, enthusiasm, compulsion. *He has a mania for word games.* **Ant.** dislike, indifference.

maniac *n.* psychopath, psychotic, sociopath, lunatic, (slang) nut, madman. *Police reported that a maniac was on the loose.*

maniacal *adj.* crazy, insane, psychotic, sociopathic, psychopathic, (slang) nuts. *Hitler had a maniacal desire to conquer the world.* **Ant.** sane, stable, rational.

manic *adj.* agitated, overexcited, worked-up, crazed, unbalanced, hyperactive, driven. *She had a manic drive to build a new house in less than a week.*

manifest *adj.* 1. evident, obvious, plain, apparent, clear, unmistakable. *Many early pioneers believed it was their manifest destiny to colonize the American West.* –*vb.* 2. show, display, express, indicate, demonstrate. *Her anger manifests itself as sarcasm.* **Ant.** 1. concealed, masked, hidden. 2. conceal, veil, hide.

manifestation *n.* form, exhibition, display, example, demonstration, evidence. *Increased shoplifting can be a manifestation of high unemployment.*

manifesto *n.* proclamation, declaration, notice, notification, doctrine. *The government delivered its new manifesto to the people.*

manifold *adj.* multifold, multiple, varied, various, multifaceted. *Reasons for pulling the troops out were manifold.*

manipulate *vb.* mold, shape, work, steer, maneuver, guide. *He manipulates people into doing things they don't want to do.*

mankind *n.* womankind, humankind, humanity, human beings, *Homo sapiens*, man. *How many more centuries will mankind survive?*

manly *adj.* masculine, macho, virile, tough, strong, red-blooded, potent. *The marine projected a particularly manly image.* **Ant.** female, feminine, effeminate.

man-made *adj.* manufactured, artificial, human-made, built, fabricated, synthetic. *Man-made flowers pale in comparison to the real thing.* **Ant.** natural, real, organic.

manner *n.* 1. fashion, way, style, method, pattern. *I was reassured by the friendly manner in which she spoke* 2. type, kind, sort, class, category, variety. *What manner of beast is this?*

mannered *adj.* affected, pretentious, phony, fake, put-on, artificial. **Ant.** natural, genuine, real.

mannerism *n.* habit, peculiarity, eccentricity, characteristic, quirk. *He likes to crack his knuckles in public, and that's just one of his annoying mannerisms.*

mannerly *adj.* polite, courteous, considerate, gracious, refined, nice. *Children should be raised to behave in a mannerly fashion.* **Ant.** rude, discourteous, boorish.

manners *n.* etiquette, niceties, social graces, civilities, courtesy, politeness. *Use your best manners when you're in church.*

mansion *n.* estate, manor, palace, villa, residence. *The duke and duchess often vacation at their country mansion.*

manual *n.* 1. handbook, instruction book, guidebook, workbook. *The computer came with an operator's manual.* –*adj.* 2. physical, arduous, strenuous, heavy. *He spent the summer doing manual labor.*

manufacture *vb.* produce, make, build, create, assemble, fabricate. *The company, manufactures airplane parts.*

manufacturer *n.* maker, assembler, builder, producer, mill, company. *The widget manufacturer doubled its production this year.*

manure *n.* excrement, dung, fertilizer, guano, droppings, waste matter. *Farmers often spread their fields with cow manure.*

manuscript *n.* draft, original, typescript, document, script. *She has just completed the manuscript for her latest novel.*

many *adj.* 1. numerous, countless, innumerable, considerable, abundant. *There were many people at Disneyland.* –*n.* 2. multitude, masses, majority, scores, crowd. *Do you think the needs of the many should outweigh the needs of the few?* **Ant.** 1. few, limited, scant. 2. few.

map *n.* 1. chart, guide, graph, sketch, atlas. *The map so you don't get lost.* –*vb.* 2. plan, outline, arrange, chart, graph, diagram. *She mapped out her strategy for getting a promotion.*

mapmaker *n.* cartographer, surveyer, mapper, topographer. *Mapmakers sometimes rely on satellite photographs to verify their work.*

mar *vb.* blemish, deface, disfigure, spoil, deform, damage. *Please be careful not to mar the beautiful finish of the wood.*

marathon *n.* footrace, cross-country race, endurance race, run, 26-miler, course, contest. *Completing a marathon requires months of training beforehand.*

marauder *n.* raider, attacker, pillager, looter, invader, pirate. *We must protect the castle from marauders.*

march *vb.* 1. parade, walk, step, tramp, pace. *Our school band marched in the New Year's Day parade.* –*n.* 2. walk, hike, trek, tramp, parade. *She took her girl-scout troop on a march to the lake.* 3. advance, progress, advancement, progression, passage. *No one can stop the march of time.*

WORD SEARCH
formation, in: *close order drill*
manner: *lockstep*
straight-leg: *goosestepping*

margin *n.* 1. border, boundary, edge, fringe, rim. *When you type your paper, leave a one-inch margin on all sides.* 2. room, safeguard, allowance, latitude, range, leeway. *Leave some margin in your itinerary for possible delays.*

marginal *adj.* borderline, trivial, insignificant, minimal, slight, limited. *Unfortunately, profits were marginal last month.*

marijuana *n.* cannabis, hemp, (slang) pot, drug, (slang) weed, (slang) ganja. *Marijuana use is illegal in all 50 states.*

marina *n.* dockage, docking, harbor, moorings, berth, boatyard, landing. *I tie up my dinghy down at the marina.*

marinate *vb.* soak, steep, pickle, infuse, flavor. *The steak is even more delicious when you marinate it before cooking.*

marine *adj.* maritime, oceanic, sea, aquatic, pelagic, nautical. *The marine weather report issued a small-craft warning.*

mariner *n.* sailor, seaman, seafarer, naval officer, (slang) salt, skipper, mate. *A smart mariner always keeps his eye on the weather.*

marionette *n.* puppet, dummy, doll, figure. *Soldiers sometimes feel as if they're being controlled like helpless marionettes.*

marital *adj.* matrimonial, wedded, married, conjugal, connubial, nuptial. *Marital relations are often troubled.*

maritime *adj.* oceanic, marine, sea, aquatic, nautical, seagoing. *The city reserved the seafront for maritime businesses only.*

mark *n.* **1.** streak, spot, blemish, blotch, smudge, stain. *She tried to bleach out the ink mark on her blouse.* **2.** sign, indication, measure, stamp, label, symbol. *The mark of a talented writer is the ability to involve the reader.* **3.** target, goal, objective, standard, norm. *Your work has not been up to the mark.* *–vb.* **4.** spot, streak, stain, mar, blemish, disfigure. *The oil stain permanently marked his jeans.* **5.** identify, tag, indicate, signify, name, specify. *She marked her place in the book by bending a page corner.* **6.** heed, notice, obey, mind, note, respect. *Mark my words: He won't be coming back.* **Ant. 6.** ignore, disregard.

market *n.* **1.** marketplace, supermarket, mart, grocery. *Will you please pick up some milk while you're at the market?* **2.** desire, demand, need, want, call. *Is there a market for your new product?* *–vb.* **3.** sell, retail, vend, merchandise, dispense. *The company tried marketing its cereal in a new package.*

marksman *n.* sharpshooter, crack shot, dead shot. *Only a trained marksman could hit the distant target.*

maroon *vb.* strand, abandon, leave behind, desert, put ashore, forsake. *Robinson Crusoe was marooned on an island.*

marriage *n.* wedding, nuptials, union, alliance, affiliation. *She was very nervous on the day of her marriage.*

WORD SEARCH

contract protecting assets of spouse from the other: *prenuptial agreement*

multiple spouses, having: *bigamy, polygamy*

single spouse, having a: *monogamy*

marry *vb.* wed, (slang) tie the knot, exchange wedding vows, walk down the aisle. *I planned to marry Eddy, but I'm glad I didn't.* **Ant.** divorce, annul, split up.

marsh *n.* wetland, estuary, fen, moor, bog, swamp. *A marsh is a critical component of wildlife habitat.*

WORD SEARCH

hollow: *swale*

marshal *n.* **1.** sheriff, law officer, police officer. *A marshal broke up the fight in the saloon.* *–vb.* **2.** gather, array, deploy, collect, muster, mobilize, assemble. *We must marshal our forces for an all-out attack.* **Ant. 2.** scatter, disperse.

marshy *adj.* boggy, fenny, swampy, wet, mucky, soggy. *We had a hard time hiking through the marshy area.*

martial *adj.* military, militant, hostile, aggressive, warlike, combative. *The nomadic tribe was known for its martial tendencies.* **Ant.** peaceful, gentle, friendly.

martyr *n.* sufferer, hero, saint, idol. *He was called a martyr after dying for his beliefs.*

martyrdom *n.* suffering, torture, self-sacrifice, crown of thorns, persecution, torment. *A mother of triplets lives a life of intense love and martyrdom.*

marvel *n.* wonder, spectacle, sight, sensation, phenomenon. *The Pyramids are Egypt's most famous marvels.*

marvelous *adj.* terrific, fabulous, great, fantastic, wondrous, exceptional, superb. *We had a* *marvelous day at the park.* **Ant.** terrible, bad, horrible, awful.

masculine *adj.* manly, virile, macho, tough, two-fisted, red-blooded, potent. *He thought he was quite masculine when he managed to open the pickle jar.* **Ant.** feminine, effeminate, female.

mash *vb.* smash, crush, squash, pound, beat. *She mashed her crackers and added them to her soup.*

mask *n.* 1. disguise, cover, veil, camouflage. *Everyone must wear a mask to the costume party.* *–vb.* 2. disguise, cover, veil, hide, shroud, camouflage. *Bruce Wayne masked himself so no one would know he was Batman.* **Ant.** 2. expose, reveal, uncover.

masquerade *n.* costume party, ball, disguise, pose, facade, getup. *At the masquerade, I had trouble identifying everyone.*

mass *n.* 1. pile, heap, mount, stack, collection, clump. *He has a huge mass of snow to shovel off the walks.* 2. gathering, horde, crowd, mob, throng, host, assembly. *There was a mass of people waiting for the store to open.* 3. matter, material, massiveness. *Your weight will be different on the Moon, but your mass remains the same.* *–vb.* 4. gather, crowd, clump, cluster, assemble. *Cattle massed around the feed troughs.*

massacre *n.* 1. slaughter, killing, annihilation, execution, extermination, genocide. *The terrorist attack resulted in the massacre of many innocent people.* *–vb.* 2. slaughter, kill, annihilate, execute, exterminate. *Renegade soldiers massacred everyone in the village.*

massage *n.* 1. rub, rubdown, kneading, back rub. *She enjoys a good massage after her workouts.* *–vb.* 2. rub, knead, stroke, press, caress. *He massaged my forehead to ease my tension.*

massive *adj.* large, huge, enormous, mammoth, gigantic, big, immense. *There was a massive demonstration outside the White House.* **Ant.** tiny, little, small, slight.

master *n.* 1. controller, manager, administrator, head, ruler. *She is the master of her own fate.* *–adj.* 2. main, principal, primary, chief, controlling. *The hotel manager has a master key to all the rooms.* 3. expert, practiced, experienced, proficient, skilled. *She is a master swordswoman.* *–vb.* 4. learn, grasp, conquer, overcome, vanquish. *It took him five years to master the Russian language.* **Ant.** 1. servant, subject. 2. lesser, minor, secondary. 3. unskilled, amateurish, incompetent.

masterful *adj.* expert, virtuoso, proficient, accomplished, skilled, crack. *Jimmy Hendrix was masterful at playing the guitar.* **Ant.** unskilled, amateurish, inexperienced.

mastermind *n.* engineer, architect, creator, ringleader, designer, orchestrator. *The mastermind behind the theory of relativity was Albert Einstein.*

masterpiece *n.* masterwork, magnum opus, tour de force, showpiece, classic, model. *The novelist's lifelong dream was to write a masterpiece.*

mastery *n.* 1. rule, upper hand, control, domination, command, sway. *The dictator had achieved absolute mastery over the citizens he governed.* 2. expertise, skill, proficiency. *Stevie Ray Vaughn's mastery of the blues was astonishing.*

masturbation *n.* autoeroticism, self-gratification, onanism. *People once mistakenly believed that masturbation would cause blindness.*

match *n.* 1. mate, partner, consort, prospect, wife, husband. *She's a perfect match for you.* 2. correspondence, parallel, equivalence, replication, complement. *The match between the old and new paint was perfect.* 3. competitor, contestant, rival, equal, par. *He's no match for you in sports.* 4. competition, meet, contest, tournament, game. *She won the wrestling match.* 5. marriage, union, coupling, alliance, affiliation. *It was a match made in heaven.* –*vb.* **6.** correspond, fit, harmonize, tally, agree, couple. *His socks don't match.* **7.** rival, equal, meet, challenge. *There's no way I can match him in strength.*

matching *adj.* corresponding, coordinating, like, twin, identical, duplicate. *It always makes good fashion sense to wear matching socks.* **Ant.** clashing, opposite, unlike.

mate *n.* **1.** companion, partner, spouse, lover, counterpart, equal. *Ted is still looking for someone who could be his lifelong mate.* –*vb.* **2.** procreate, breed, copulate, pair up. *In spring, many animals mate.*

material *n.* **1.** cloth, fabric, textile, weave. *He chose a flowered material for the new curtains.* **2.** matter, substance, elements, stuff, components. *A truck brought the building materials to the construction site.*

materialize *vb.* appear form, emerge, manifest, rise, take shape. *The ghosts who were predicted to appear at midnight failed to materialize.* **Ant.** vanish, disappear, dissolve.

maternal *adj.* motherly, parental, nurturing, protecting, doting, loving. *A woman's maternal instincts are her children's best protection.* **Ant.** paternal, fatherly.

math *n.* mathematics, arithmetic, computation, calculation, equations, figures. *Don't count on your calculator to do your math for you.*

matriarch *n.* mother, grandmother, head of the household, empress, queen, matron. *Grandma enjoyed her role as family matriarch.* **Ant.** patriarch.

matronly *adj.* mature, motherly, dignified, serious, mellow. *A kind matronly woman offered to take us in for the night.*

matted *adj.* tangled, snarled, knotted, snagged, uncombed. *The terrier's hair was matted and desperately needed combing.*

matter *n.* **1.** material, substance, elements, components, stuff. *The planet Jupiter is made up of a gaseous matter.* **2.** problem, trouble, distress, ailment, sickness, difficulty. *What's the matter with him?* **3.** issue, point, question, topic, subject, concern. *It's a matter of right and wrong.* **4.** importance, significance, consequence, import. *It was of no matter that she came a few minutes late.* **Ant. 4.** insignificance, meaninglessness.

matter-of-fact *adj.* impassive, cool, businesslike, dry, unemotional, phlegmatic. *The murderer's matter-of-fact confession of his crime shocked the detective.*

mature *adj.* **1.** grown, adult, developed, wise, sensible. *Apologizing was the mature thing to do.* –*vb.* **2.** develop, evolve, broaden, ripen, season. *Spending four years away at college has matured her.* **Ant. 1.** immature, childlike, juvenile.

maturity *n.* adulthood, development, responsibleness, wiseness, experience. *His maturity showed in the calm way in which he dealt with the problem.* **Ant.** immaturity, youthfulness, childishness.

maudlin *adj.* sentimental, overemotional, (slang) sappy, mushy, teary, (slang) drippy. *The movie was so maudlin I almost threw up.*

maul *vb.* mangle, brutalize, batter, rend, injure, strike. *The angry tiger mauled its trainer.*

mausoleum *n.* tomb, sepulchre, grave. *My grandfather's remains rest in a mausoleum.*

maverick *n.* nonconformist, independent, rebel, individual, dissenter, vanguard. *John was a maverick who always did things his own way.* **Ant.** conformist, sheep.

maxim *n.* saying, truth, adage, truism, proverb, saw. *I've learned the hard way that the old maxim, "haste makes waste" is painfully true.*

maximum *adj.* **1.** greatest, largest, extreme, utmost, top, peak. *The maximum speed you can* *drive on this freeway is 55 mph.* –*n.* **2.** utmost, top, most, extreme, limit, bound. *One hundred dollars is the maximum I am willing to spend.* **Ant. 1.** minimal, lowest, smallest. **2.** minimum, least.

maybe *adv.* perhaps, possibly, perchance. *Maybe we'll have pizza for dinner.*

mayhem *n.* chaos, confusion, havoc, pandemonium, disorder, violence. *The riot caused widespread mayhem.* **Ant.** peace, tranquility, inactivity.

maze *n.* labyrinth, network, tangle, confusion, puzzle, jungle. *We got lost in a maze of narrow streets.*

meadow *adj.* field, grassland, pasture, range, veldt, prairie. *The children picked buttercups and dandelions in the meadow.*

meager *adj.* skimpy, sparse, inadequate, scarce, slender, insufficient, slight. *We dislike the restaurant because of the meager portions they serve.* **Ant.** large, plentiful, abundant.

meal *n.* repast, feast, feed, fare, banquet, dinner. *Let's stop into the nearest hamburger joint for a meal.*

mealymouthed *adj.* indirect, euphemistic, insincere, overnice, mincing, prim. *We need a critic who is blunt and never mealymouthed.* **Ant.** direct, blunt, frank.

mean *vb.* **1.** intend, plan, expect, want, wish. *Did you mean to throw that away, or was it a mistake?* **2.** signify, denote, imply, indicate, symbolize, represent. *The Spanish word "hola" means "hello" in English.* –*adj.* **3.** nasty, rude, unpleasant, disagreeable, grouchy, vicious, cruel. *The mean man screamed at us to get away from his driveway.* **4.** cheap, shoddy, squalid, miserable, shabby, wretched. *The old shack was a mean-looking place.* **5.** average, normal, standard, medium. *The mean temperature of the human body is 98.6 degrees Fahrenheit.* –*n.* **6.** median, norm, average, par, center. *The mean for yesterday's test was 75 points.* **Ant. 3.** nice, kind, considerate. **4.** fancy, expensive, superior. **5.** extreme, maximum, minimum.

meander *vb.* twist, wind, snake, wander, switchback, ramble. *The river meanders through the valley for miles.*

meaning *n.* sense, significance, idea, implication, intent, purpose. *Philosophers study the meaning of life.*

meaningful *adj.* significant, important, profound, worthwhile, useful. *She's looking for a more meaningful job.* **Ant.** meaningless, senseless, useless.

meaningless *adj.* senseless, purposeless, worthless, valueless, useless. *Watching TV all day is a meaningless waste of time.* **Ant.** meaningful, significant, worthwhile.

means *n.* resources, power, wealth, assets, money, capital. *Humans do not have the natural means for flight, but they do have the know-how and technology.*

measly *adj.* paltry, meager, trifling, meager, puny, scanty. *They wanted to pay me a measly five dollars to mow their lawn, so I refused.* **Ant.** huge, significant, massive.

measurable *adj.* quantifiable, quantitative, calculable, assessable. *Astronomers are unsure whether the universe is measurable.*

measure *vb.* **1.** parcel, ration, portion, gauge, allot. *Please measure out one cup of sugar.* –*n.* **2.** measurement, size, amount, quantity, volume, weight. *I don't think you put in the correct measure.* **3.** sample, example, model, test, pattern, standard, precedent. *His response will give you a measure of his commitment to the relationship.* **4.** procedure, action, course, step. *I put an alarm in my car as a measure against theft.*

measurement *n.* gauging, assessment, dimension, estimation, computation. *The measurement showed that Fran won the long-jump competition.*

meat *n.* flesh, beef, chop, roast, cutlet, steak. *I was a vegetarian once, but I missed the taste of meat too much.*

meat-eating *adj.* carnivorous, flesh-eating, predacious, bloodthirsty. *The meat-eating dinosaurs had teeth like saw blades.* **Ant.** vegetarian, vegan, herbivorous.

mechanical *adj.* technological, machine-driven, motorized, automated, robotic. *None of us could figure how the mad scientist's mechanical device functioned.*

mechanism *n.* device, component, instrument, gear, machine, contrivance. *The mechanism required electricity to run.*

medal *n.* award, honor, medallion, trophy, prize. *The swimmer received two bronze medals at the Olympics.*

meddle *vb.* interfere, intrude, pry, snoop, intervene. *Don't meddle in my affairs.*

meddlesome *adj.* interfering, officious, meddling, obtrusive, nosy, intrusive. *She was annoyed with her mother's meddlesome nature.*

media *n.* press, communications industry, news industry, radio, television, reporters. *The media will pay dearly for a scandalous story.*

mediate *vb.* intercede, moderate, negotiate, umpire, referee, intervene. *I tried to mediate between my two arguing friends.*

mediation *n.* arbitration, negotiation, intercession, compromise, settlement, moderating. *Mediation is far less stressful than enduring a formal court trial.*

medicinal *adj.* curative, therapeutic, remedial, helpful, soothing. *Some people believe herbs have a medicinal effect.* **Ant.** poisonous, harmful, destructive.

medicine *n.* medication, drug, prescription, antibiotic, potion. *Have you taken any medicine for your headache?*

WORD SEARCH

allergy reliever: *antihistamine*
aging, field of: *geriatrics, gerontology*
bloodclotting, prevents: *anticoagulant*
body's natural immunity component: *antibody*
breathing passages, opens: *bronchodilator*
cure-all: *panacea*
diabetes blood sugar regulator: *insulin*
fake medicine used in medical studies: *placebo*
fungal-derived medicine for bacterial infection: *antibiotic*
heart stimulant: *digitalis*
pain reliever: *analgesic, anesthetic*
poison, counteracts: *antidote, antivenin*
quack medicine: *patent medicine, nostrum*
reduced effectiveness of medicine over time: *tolerance*
relieves symptoms but does not cure: *palliative*
sleep, induces: *hypnotic, soporific*
vomiting, induces: *emetic*

medieval *adj.* of the Middle Ages, of the Dark Ages, Gothic, archaic, antiquated. *Castles were a common sight in medieval times.*

mediocre *adj.* inferior, unimpressive, undistinguished, average, ordinary. *We felt the carpenter did a mediocre job on our proof.* **Ant.** fantastic, exceptional, great, superior.

meditate *vb.* think, ponder, reflect, study, consider, contemplate. *I must meditate on my choices before I decide.*

meditation *n.* reverie, rumination, contemplation, reflection, musing, focus. *He used meditation to help calm himself down before bed.*

medium *n.* 1. means, agency, instrument, device, way, tool. *She writes poetry as a medium for expressing her feelings.* 2. environment, atmosphere, surroundings, setting, element. *The high-school student felt out of his medium in the university class.* 3. psychic, seer, clairvoyant, diviner, fortune teller, soothsayer. *The medium said she could communicate with spirits beyond the grave.* –*adj.* 4. middle, intermediate, average, normal, common, ordinary. *She chose a medium shade of brown.* **Ant.** 4. extreme, distinctive, uncommon.

medley *n.* mixture, assortment, variety, miscellany, melange, mix. *The singer performed a medley of his favorite songs.*

meek *adj.* unassertive, mild, gentle, docile, submissive, passive, shy, unassuming. *Clark Kent was a meek and mild-mannered reporter.* **Ant.** bold, assertive, aggressive, forward.

meet *vb.* 1. contact, greet, encounter. *He would like to meet the president.* 2. assemble, group, rally, collect, convene. *Let's all meet at the mall.* 3. reach, equal, satisfy, match, fulfill. *Your work does not meet my expectations.* 4. reach, adjoin, border, cross, front. *The river meets the sea about twenty miles from here.* –*n.* 5. competition, contest, match, tournament, game, race. *The track meet was held last Saturday.* **Ant.** 1. avoid, miss, elude.

melancholy *adj.* 1. sad, depressed, downcast, dejected, gloomy, unhappy, forlorn. *I was feeling very melancholy after my best friend moved away.* –*n.* 2. sadness, depression, despair, despondency, sorrow. *He expressed his melancholy in his poetry.* **Ant.** 1. happy, glad, cheerful. 2. happiness, joy, exhilaration.

meld *vb.* blend, mix, mingle, merge, amalgamate, fuse. *Talented musicians in the 1970s tried to meld rock with jazz and came up with jazz fusion.* **Ant.** separate, split, divide.

melee *n.* riot, fight, brawl, free-for-all, fracas, donnybrook. *The police had to be called to break up the melee.*

mellow *adj.* 1. gentle, mild, light, delicate, moderate. *She likes food that has a mellow rather than spicy flavor.* –*vb.* 2. soften, improve, mature, season, develop. *His temper has mellowed over the years.* **Ant.** 1. harsh, sharp. 2. harden.

melodious *adj.* melodic, musical, tuneful, euphonic, symphonic, songlike. *The songbird whistled a melodious tune.* **Ant.** discordant, cacophonous.

melodramatic *adj.* dramatic, exaggerated, theatrical, overemotional, sensational, maudlin. *She said she'd die without an ice cream cone, but I think she was being a tad melodramatic.* **Ant.** understated, subtle, undramatic.

melody *n.* song, tune, theme, strain, ballad. *I recognize that melody from somewhere.*

melt *vb.* dissolve, liquefy, thaw, defrost, soften, *Her frozen yogurt melted in the sun.* **Ant.** freeze, harden, solidify.

member *n.* initiate, participant, constituent, component, element. *He's a member of the sailing club.*

membership *n.* enrollment, rolls, body, constituency, roster, associates. *Their membership consisted of one hundred men and eighty-nine women.*

memento *n.* souvenir, token, keepsake, memorial, remembrance, memorabilia. *I always take home a memento from every major city I visit.*

memo *n.* memorandum, note, reminder, message, notice, communication. *The memo informed all of the employees that the company president would be visiting today.*

memoir *n.* journal, diary, autobiography, recollections, reflections. *The memoirs of the late actress have just been published.*

memorabilia *n.* mementos, keepsakes, collectibles, tokens, souvenirs, reminders. *George likes to collect baseball memorabilia.*

memorable *adj.* unforgettable, important, significant, momentous, eventful, remarkable. *My college graduation was a memorable day.* **Ant.** forgettable, unimportant, insignificant.

memorial *n.* **1.** monument, shrine, testimonial, statue, monolith, commemoration. *The Vietnam Memorial honors those who died fighting in that war. –adj.* **2.** commemorative, testimonial, eulogizing, honoring. *A memorial service was held for the police officer who was killed in the line of duty.*

memory *n.* **1.** remembrance, recollection, recall, retention. *I have a good memory for people and places.* **2.** fame, renown, repute, glory, reputation, distinction. *The late Mohandas Gandhi's memory lives on as an inspiration to people everywhere.* **Ant. 1.** forgetfulness.

menace *n.* **1.** danger, threat, risk, hazard, peril. *Criminals are a menace to society. –vb.* **2.** threaten, endanger, terrorize, frighten, intimidate. *The school bully menaced many of the students.* **Ant. 1** blessing, friend, boon. **2.** guard, help, aid.

mend *vb.* fix, repair, patch, heal, restore, stitch. *He spent the afternoon mending the holes in his socks.*

menial *adj.* **1.** lowly, humble, degrading, servile, base. *New employees are given the most menial tasks. –n.* **2.** servant, domestic, underling, helper, subordinate, slave. *Don't treat me like a menial.* **Ant. 1.** elevated, dignified, stately. **2.** lord, master, superior.

menopause *n.* change of life, climacteric, hormonal change, transition. *Many women approach menopause with dread because it marks the passage through middle age.*

mental *adj.* **1.** cerebral, abstract, intellectual, thinking, cognitive, reasoning. *I like mental games that test my intelligence.* **2.** disturbed, neurotic, psychotic, lunatic, insane. *This hospital treats mental patients.*

mental hospital *n.* psychiatric hospital, mental health facility, insane asylum, mental institution, psychiatric ward, rehab facility. *Uncle Joe suffered from a severe case of posttraumatic stress syndrome and had to be treated at a mental hospital.*

mental illness *n.* emotional illness, brain disorder, mental disorder, psychosis, neurosis, personality disorder, insanity. *The stigma of mental illness can sometimes be as bad as the malady itself.*

WORD SEARCH

compulsion or preoccupation, unhealthy: *mania, obsessive compulsive disorder*
erroneous beliefs: *delusions*
fear, an irrational: *phobia*
fear that everyone is out to get you, irrational: *paranoia*
mood swings disorder: *manic depression*
nervousness: *anxiety*
personalities, exhibiting multiple: *multiple personality*
sadness, severe and prolonged: *depression*
seeing things that aren't there: *hallucinations*
shock therapy: *electroconvulsive therapy*
stress term, outmoded: *nervous breakdown*
stupor: *catatonia*
trauma, psychological difficulty following: *posttraumatic stress syndrome*

See also INSANITY; PHOBIA.

mentality *n.* intelligence, intellect, judgment, understanding, temperament. *He acts like he has the mentality of a two-year-old.*

mention *vb.* **1.** remark, state, say, hint, indicate, announce, declare. *Did I mention that I spoke with your sister?* –*n.* **2.** reference, allusion, hint, suggestion, indication, comment, remark. *There was no mention of my accident on the evening news.* **Ant. 1.** neglect, forget, omit. **2.** silence, omission.

mentor *n.* teacher, guide, instructor, guru, instructor, adviser. *The best-selling author liked to act as a mentor to new writers.* **Ant.** student, learner, neophyte.

menu *n.* bill of fare, selection. *Do they have any low-carb selections on the menu?*

mercenary *n.* **1.** hired soldier, hireling campaigner, legionnaire. *The rebel leader used mercenaries to overthrow the government.* –*adj.* **2.** predatory, greedy, selfish, ravenous, grasping. *We were appalled by the corporation's mercenary tactics.* **Ant. 2.** sharing, unselfish, generous.

merchandise *n.* **1.** stock, wares, goods, commodities, staples. *There was a sale on all merchandise in the store.* –*vb.* **2.** sell, retail, distribute, promote, market. *The company merchandises its products through local distributors.*

merchant *n.* storekeeper, retailer, saleswoman, salesman, vendor. *The city's commercial district has many kinds of merchants.*

merciful *adj.* kind, compassionate, softhearted, humane, sympathetic, feeling. *The child decided to be merciful and let the fly go instead of killing it.* **Ant.** merciless, cruel, vicious.

merciless *adj.* cruel, vicious, inhumane, brutal, heartless. *The dictator is often a merciless leader.* **Ant.** merciful, kind, compassionate.

mercy *n.* compassion, kindness, pity, tenderness, softness, generosity, charity. *The harsh judge showed no mercy when it came time for sentencing.* **Ant.** cruelty, ruthlessness, harshness.

mere *adj.* simple, plain, sheer, bare, only. *The mere thought of getting in a boat makes me seasick.*

merge *vb.* converge, combine, fuse, join, unite. *A side road merges onto the highway up ahead.* **Ant.** diverge, split, separate.

merger *n.* alliance, union, consolidation, incorporation, fusion. *The two small airlines agreed on a merger into a single larger airline.*

meridian *n.* zenith, apex, peak, pinnacle, crowning point. *At the meridian of his career, Michael Jordan was unstoppable.*

merit *n.* **1.** credit, value, worthiness, worth, justification. *Your idea for saving money has a lot of merit* –*vb.* **2.** deserve, warrant, justify, rate, earn. *His acting performance merits an award.* **Ant. 1.** discredit, worthlessness.

merry-go-round *n.* carousel, ride. *A merry-go-round is a feature of many carnivals.*

mesa *n.* plateau, tableland. *The mesa is a creation of erosion over millions of years.*

mesh *n.* netting, webbing, screen, strainer, grid, openwork. *I wore a mesh shirt to keep cool.*

mesmerize *vb.* enchant, entrance, hypnotize, spellbind, bewitch, cast a spell on. *The hypnotist mesmerized his subject and made him cluck like a chicken.*

mess *n.* **1.** clutter, disarray, dump, eyesore, pigpen, disorder. *The kids need to clean up their mess when they've finished playing.* **2.** predicament, entanglement, quagmire, trouble, difficulty, quandary. *Unless you want to get in a real mess with the law, I suggest you pay your parking tickets.*

message *n.* **1.** note, communication, notice, notification. *Are there any telephone messages for me?* **2.** idea, content, meaning, point, theme, moral. *The movie's message was that everyone needs friends.*

messenger *n.* courier, carrier, runner, bearer, deliverer. *In big cities, bicycle messengers deliver packages between office buildings.*

messy *adj.* untidy, disorderly, disorganized, unkempt, jumbled, dirty. *She could never find anything in her messy room.* **Ant.** orderly, tidy, clean, organized.

metamorphosis *n.* transformation, change, transmogrification, rebirth, transmutation, conversion. *The metamorphosis of caterpillar to butterfly is a miracle of nature.*

metaphor *n.* figure of speech, analogy, likening, simile, trope. *The "lion's share" is a metaphor signifying the "most."*

metaphysical *adj.* supernatural, immaterial, spiritual, impalpable, unearthly, mystical. *My guru was more concerned with metaphysical matters than with physical ones.* **Ant.** physical, earthly, mundane.

meteor *n.* meteorite, fireball, bolide, meteoroid. *Let's stay up and watch the meteor shower tonight.*

WORD SEARCH

erroneous term: *shooting star*
fireball: *bolide*

method *n.* manner, design, technique, program, system, fashion, mode. *What method of transportation did you use?*

methodical *adj.* systematic, ordered, orderly, step-by-step, robotic, machine-like. *Joe has a methodical way of painting that helps him finish his work quickly* **Ant.** sloppy, random, disordered.

methodology *n.* methods, procedures, way, mode, practices, system. *My methodology for getting rid of mosquitoes is to slap them firmly with my hand.*

meticulous *adj.* careful, painstaking, stickling, exact, fastidious, particular. *Her clothes were always perfectly ironed, as she was meticulous about her appearance.* **Ant.** careless, sloppy, slack.

metropolis *n.* city, capital, downtown, municipality, megalopolis. *Los Angeles is America's largest metropolis.*

mettle *n.* heart, courage, character, spirit, mental toughness, guts, resolve. *You've got to have a lot of mettle to climb Mt. Everest.* **Ant.** cowardice, fear, anxiety.

microbe *See* MICROORGANISM.

microcosm *n.* miniature world, miniature reality. *Toxic fish in our river are merely a microcosm of a worldwide problem.*

microorganism *n.* microbe, germ, (slang) bug, bacillus, bacterium, virus. *You never know what kind of microorganisms may take up residence in your body.*

microscopic *adj.* infinitesimal, tiny, minute, indiscernible, imperceptible. *The water was unhealthy because it contained microscopic parasites.* **Ant.** huge, immense, gigantic, large.

microwave *vb.* heat, cook, warm, (slang) zap, (slang) nuke. *I like to microwave popcorn because it only takes two minutes.*

middle *adj.* **1.** central, midmost, midway, halfway, intermediate. *I'm the middle child in the family.* –*n.* **2.** center, midpoint, heart, midst, focus, core. *Can I sit in the middle?* **Ant. 1.** final, end, initial, beginning. **2.** outskirts, fringe, edge.

middle class *n.* bourgeoisie, hoi polloi, working class, Middle America, working people, the masses. *The middle class is shrinking due to economic stagnation.*

middleman *n.* intermediary, mediator, go-between, broker, agent, wholesaler. *In order to make more profit, our company must eliminate the middleman.*

midget *n.* dwarf, little person, homunculus, pygmy, gnome, Lilliputian. *A midget's true stature is determined by his heart.* **Ant.** giant, behemoth.

mighty *adj.* powerful, forceful, vigorous, gigantic, huge, massive. *She gave a mighty heave and pushed the rock out of the way.* **Ant.** weak, feeble, small.

migrant *adj.* traveling, itinerant, moving, transient, wandering, drifting. *The farmer hired migrant workers to harvest his apples.*

migrate *vb.* move, journey, travel, relocate, resettle, immigrate. *When did your family migrate to California?*

mild *adj.* **1.** gentle, easygoing, calm, soft, tender, tranquil, serene. *His mild nature made him easy to work with.* **2.** moderate, light, trivial, average, weak. *She received a mild burn after spending the day on the beach.* **Ant. 1.** harsh, angry, rough. **2.** severe, serious, strong.

mildew *n.* fungi, growth, mold. *Everything in the damp cellar smells like mildew.*

militant *adj.* warlike, aggressive, combative, fierce, activist, belligerent. *The militant environmental group bombed a whaling boat.* **Ant.** peaceful, passive, nonaggressive.

military *n.* **1.** service, armed forces, militia, troops, army, navy, air force, marines. *During the Vietnam War, men were drafted into the military.* *–adj.* **2.** soldierly, militaristic, martial, combative, warlike. *He liked the military lifestyle.*

mill *n.* factory, manufactory, production line, plant, works, foundry. *The old wood mill turned out an astonishing number of boards each day.*

mimic *vb.* **1.** impersonate, copy, echo, reproduce, imitate, mirror. *The hunter mimicked the call of the bird.* *–n.* **2.** mime, pantomimist, impersonator, imitator, copyist. *The street mimic repeated everything I did.*

mince *vb.* chop, dice, cube, hash, fragment, slice. *The recipe says to finely mince the onions.*

mind *n.* **1.** intellect, brain, reasoning, intelligence, rationality. *You can solve the problem if you just use you mind.* **2.** memory, remembrance, recall, awareness. *The smell brings apricots and honey to mind.* *–vb.* **3.** care, resent, dislike, object to, deplore. *Do you mind if I borrow your jacket?* **4.** watch, tend, attend, heed, notice. *Will you mind the children until I return?* **Ant. 4.** ignore, neglect.

mind-boggling *adj.* astonishing, stunning, overwhelming, staggering, mind-blowing, unbelievable. *The number of stars in the universe is mind-boggling.*

mindful *adj.* attentive, thoughtful, observant, considerate, heedful, aware. *Smokers need to be mindful of the rights of nonsmokers.* **Ant.** thoughtless, inconsiderate.

mindless *adj.* thoughtless, stupid, brainless, idiotic, imbecilic, bovine. *Golf is a mindless game only to those who don't play.* **Ant.** intelligent, brilliant, cerebral.

mind reader *n.* psychic, mentalist, telepathist, clairvoyant. *The self-professed mind reader was good only at guessing people's thoughts, not reading them.*

mindset *n.* attitude, view, perspective, thinking, position, opinion. *My mindset had always been to favor more land conservation.*

mine *n.* quarry, deposit, vein, lode, excavation, shaft, pit. *Working in a coal mine is hazardous.*

mingle *vb.* mix, socialize, circulate, merge, blend. *To meet people at parties, one must mingle.* **Ant.** separate, scatter, disperse.

miniature *adj.* midget, mini, pygmy, tiny, small, diminutive. *The miniature horse was so small I thought it was a dog.* **Ant.** giant, oversized, large.

minimize *vb.* reduce, lessen, diminish, limit, curtail. *The businesswoman tried to minimize her losses when the stock market collapsed.* **Ant.** maximize, increase, expand.

minimum *adj.* least, smallest, tiniest, lowest, slightest. *Two hundred is the minimum crew needed to run this starship.* **Ant.** maximum, greatest, largest.

minion *n.* follower, subordinate, flunkey, lackey, dependent. *The terrorist leader claimed to have many devoted minions.* **Ant.** leader, dictator, boss.

minister *n.* **1.** preacher, pastor, reverend, priest, evangelist. *The minister gave an interesting sermon.* *–vb.* **2.** care, attend, serve, tend, assist. *Nurses minister to the sick.*

minor *adj.* **1.** slight, light, small, insignificant, unimportant. *There's nothing to worry about; it's only a minor cut.* *–n.* **2.** child, juvenile, teen, adolescent, youth, youngster. *In many states, you are a minor until you reach the age of twenty-one.* **Ant. 1.** major, serious, severe. **2.** adult, grown-up.

minuscule *adj.* tiny, microscopic, mini, minute, small, infinitesimal. *Even a minuscule amount of a glazed donut is fattening.* **Ant.** gigantic, gargantuan, huge.

minute *adj.* microscopic, small, tiny, little, infinitesimal, slight. *The bug was so minute I had trouble seeing it.* **Ant.** large, huge, gigantic, enormous.

minutiae *n.* details, trivia, trifles, inessentials, nonessentials. *The media gives us more minutiae about movie stars than we really need to know.*

miracle *n.* wonder, marvel, blessing, phenomenon, rarity. *It was a miracle that anyone survived the horrible plane crash.*

miraculous *adj.* wondrous, magical, extraordinary, unbelievable, amazing. *The deathly ill man made a miraculous recovery.* **Ant.** ordinary, natural, common.

mirage *n.* illusion, refraction of light, apparition, hallucination, vision, phantom. *The sight of water in a bone-dry desert is often nothing more than a mirage.*

mire *n.* bog, slush, ooze, mud, soggy ground, marsh, quagmire. *You'll need some waterproof boots if you plan to slog through the mire.*

mirth *n.* happiness, cheerfulness, joyfulness, amusement, merriment, gaiety. *Her funny jokes and kind humor filled me with mirth.* **Ant.** sadness, melancholy, depression.

misanthrope *n.* people-hater, hermit, recluse, loner, man-hater, woman-hater, cynic. *The town misanthrope liked to keep to himself, mainly because people irritated him.* **Ant.** people person, extrovert.

misbehave *vb.* act out, disobey, transgress, break rules, offend, make trouble. *Bored children can be expected to misbehave.* **Ant.** behave, follow rules, conform.

miscarriage *n.* **1.** abortion, stillbirth, spontaneous abortion, premature delivery. *Unfortunately, Aunt Rita had a miscarriage and lost the baby.* **2.** malfunction, failure, misfire, miss. *Acquitting the alleged murderer was a miscarriage of justice.*

miscellaneous *adj.* varied, various, mixed, assorted, diverse. *His garage is full of miscellaneous junk.* **Ant.** uniform, identical, similar.

miscellany *n.* assortment, variety, mixture, collection, medley, potpourri. *Women often carry a miscellany of items in their pocketbooks.*

mischief *n.* deviltry, devilment, trouble, naughtiness, pranks, horseplay. *Boys have a penchant for getting into mischief.*

mischievous *adj.* playful, prankish, impish, teasing, exasperating. *The mischievous child hid in the closet when we tried to find him.*

misconception *n.* misunderstanding, distortion, urban myth, old wives tale, misinterpretation, erroneous notion. *It was once a popular misconception that the Sun orbited the Earth.* **Ant.** fact, truth.

misconduct *n.* misbehavior, wrongdoing, impropriety, bad behavior, transgression. *Any misconduct will result in a penalty.*

misconstrue *vb.* misunderstand, misinterpret, mistake, misjudge, distort. *If you don't listen carefully, you may misconstrue what I'm trying to say.* **Ant.** understand, comprehend.

misdemeanor *n.* offense, misdeed, violation, indiscretion, misconduct, wrongdoing. *He was a small-time criminal with a record consisting of misdemeanors and parking tickets.*

miser *n.* scrooge, penny pincher, tightwad, skinflint, hoarder. *The miser died a rich but unhappy man.*

miserable *adj.* **1.** unhappy, depressed, sad, heartsick, dejected, despondent, forlorn. *I am miserable when all my friends leave town.* **2.** unpleasant, joyless, troublesome, wretched, pitiful. *He said it was miserable camping in the rain.* **Ant. 1.** happy, joyous, cheerful. **2.** comfortable, untroubled.

miserly *adj.* penny-pinching, tight, stingy, parsimonious, frugal, cheap. *My miserly neighbor offered me a dime to shovel the snow off of his driveway.* **Ant.** generous, giving, charitable.

misery *n.* pain, torment, suffering, sorrow, distress, agony, anguish. *I was in great misery when I broke my leg.* **Ant.** relief, pleasure, comfort.

misfire *vb.* fail, miss, backfire, (slang) shoot blanks, fizzle. *We will surely misfire if we fail to plan carefully.*

misfit *n.* oddball, freak, outcast, square peg, individual, (slang) fish out of water. *A four-foot basketball player may be somewhat of a misfit in the NBA.*

misfortune *n.* tragedy, calamity, disaster, trouble, catastrophe. *It was a misfortune that you lost your money so early in the trip.* **Ant.** blessing, advantage.

misgiving *n.* doubt, fear, reservation, worry, uncertainty, anxiety. *She had misgivings about scuba diving in the shark-infested waters.* **Ant.** confidence, assurance, reliance.

misguided *adj.* misinformed, misled, mistaken, wrong, astray, off the beaten path. *The misguided player ran the wrong way.* **Ant.** informed, right, correct.

mishap *n.* accident, misfortune, snag, difficulty, disaster, calamity. *We arrived late due to a mishap on the way.*

mislead *vb.* deceive, delude, dupe, misguide, misdirect, misinform. *The salesman tried to mislead me into believing his car was the better buy.*

misplace *vb.* mislay, lose, forget, displace. *He seems to have misplaced his car keys again.*

misrepresentation *n.* distortion, lie, exaggeration, misstatement, fabrication, misquote.

Unfortunately, the report was a gross misrepresentation of the facts.

miss *vb.* 1. overlook, neglect, bypass, skip, disregard. *I missed the freeway off-ramp.* 2. long for, yearn for, desire, want. *We missed him the entire time he was away.* 3. avoid, escape, avert, dodge, elude. *The dog just missed being hit by the car.* –*n.* 4. failure, error, mistake, blunder, fumble. *Three misses and you're out.*

missile *n.* projectile, rocket, shell, shot, weapon. *The jet was brought down by a surface-to-air missile.*

mission *n.* 1. assignment, appointment, task, commission, quest, enterprise. *The scientist is being sent on a mission to Antarctica.* 2. purpose, objective, calling, job, vocation. *I often wonder about my mission in life.*

missionary *n.* minister, apostle, evangelist, outreach worker, preacher, messenger. *The church sent a missionary to teach religion to people in the remote village.*

mist *n.* 1. fog, cloud, haze, vapor, drizzle. *We were barely able to see the castle through the mist.* –*vb.* 2. fog, cloud, blur, film. *My glasses misted over in the sauna.*

mistake *n.* 1. error, fault, blunder, miscalculation, flaw, oversight. *It's my mistake that we got lost.* –*vb.* 2. confuse, mix up, misjudge, misidentify, miscalculate, misunderstand. *I mistook the stranger for my brother.*

mistaken *adj.* incorrect, flawed, erroneous, false, faulty, inexact, misunderstood. *It was a case of mistaken identity.* **Ant.** correct, accurate, true

mistreat *vb.* abuse, maltreat, torment, harass, brutalize, batter, strike. *We got angry at her for mistreating her dog.*

mistreatment *n.* abuse, maltreatment, manhandling, arm-twisting, (slang) stepping on, (slang) roughing up. *Mistreatment of prisoners goes against the Geneva Convention.* **Ant.** coddling, babying, spoiling.

mistress *n.* lover, paramour, girlfriend, sweetheart, courtesan, concubine, (slang) other woman. *Beth suspects that her husband might be keeping a mistress.*

mistrust *vb.* 1. distrust, disbelieve, doubt, suspect, question. *I mistrusted you after you told me that lie.* –*n.* 2. distrust, doubt, suspicion, question, skepticism, wariness. *I hold all salespersons in some mistrust.* **Ant.** 1. trust, believe, accept. 2. trust, belief, confidence.

misunderstand *vb.* misconstrue, misinterpret, misjudge, mistake, confuse. *Because he misunderstood your directions, he put two cups of salt in the cake batter.*

misunderstanding *n.* 1. disagreement, difference, dispute, discord, squabble, quarrel. *Even small misunderstandings can turn into major arguments.* 2. misreading, misinterpretation, misconception, mistake, error. *She took the wrong road due to her misunderstanding of the directions.* **Ant.** 1. harmony, accord, agreement. 2. understanding, comprehension.

mitigate *vb.* lessen, soften, diminish, lighten, alleviate, moderate. *Icing a burn can help mitigate pain.* **Ant.** increase, worsen, deepen.

mix *vb.* 1. blend, mingle, merge, scramble, stir, fuse. *The recipe called for all ingredients to be mixed thoroughly.* –*n.* 2. mixture, combination, compound, mingling, jumble, scramble. *Our dog is a retriever and collie mix.* **Ant.** 1. separate, isolate, divide.

mixed-up *adj.* confused, perplexed, puzzled, muddled, lost, befuddled. *This is the most mixed-up group of travelers I've ever seen.*

moan *n.* 1. groan, wail, sob, keen, whimper. *I could hear the moans of the patient in the next* *room.* –*vb.* 2. groan, wail, sob, keen, whimper, cry. *They moaned about all the homework they were assigned.*

moat *n.* trench, foss, gully, ditch, defensive barrier. *Many castles are surrounded by protective moats full of water.*

mob *n.* 1. crowd, gathering, horde, throng, swarm, group, pack, host. *An angry mob surrounded the bank, demanding their money back.* –*vb.* 2. surround, crowd, swarm, deluge, inundate, attack. *The famous actress was mobbed by fans seeking her autograph.*

mobile *adj.* movable, moving, portable, flowing, migratory, roving, nomadic. *The retired couple went camping in their mobile home.* **Ant.** immobile, stationary, fixed, immovable.

mobility *n.* movement, advancement, promotion, betterment, progress. *She's looking for a job that has potential for upward mobility.* **Ant.** immobility, rigidness, fixity.

mobilize *vb.* assemble, organize, summon, muster, marshal. *The senator mobilized all her supporters for her reelection campaign.* **Ant.** disband, demobilize, release.

mobster *n.* gangster, (slang) gangbanger, (slang) goodfella, mafioso, (slang) wiseguy, criminal. *Mobsters believe crime pays, but they often end up in jail for it.*

mock *vb.* 1. ridicule, insult, abuse, jeer, taunt, tease, deride. *Don't mock my taste in music, even if it is old-fashioned.* –*adj.* 2. fake, false, imitation, artificial, sham, pretend. *The stage crew built a mock spaceship.* **Ant.** 1. praise, compliment, admire. 2. real, authentic, genuine.

mockery *n.* 1. ridicule, insulting, jeering, taunting, teasing, scorn. *The winning team's mockery of the losing team was in bad taste.* 2. sham, joke, laughingstock, absurdity, farce. *Through your cruel jokes and laughter, you have made a mockery of me.* **Ant.** 1. praise, respect, approval.

mode *n.* 1. manner, way, technique, method, system. *Horse-drawn carriages are an old-fashioned mode of transportation.* 2. fad, vogue, fashion, trend, style. *Skinny ties have been out of mode for years.*

model *n.* 1. prototype, representation, replica, example, duplicate. *Engineers designed a model of the space shuttle before it was actually built.* 2. subject, source, pattern, mold, archetype. *Her life story served as a model for the television show.* –*vb.* 3. show, display, wear, demonstrate, parade. *He modeled the designer's clothes in Paris.*

modem *n.* modulator/demodulator, device, peripheral, data converter, translator. *It takes a long time for me to download data because my modem is outdated.*

moderate *adj.* 1. reasonable, average, medium, fair, mild, passable. *Our business had had moderate success.* –*vb.* 2. check, curb, tame, subdue, reduce, lessen, diminish. *He must moderate his spending.* 3. lead, manage, direct, chair, oversee, facilitate. *The club president moderated the meeting.* **Ant.** 1. immoderate, extreme, excessive. 2. increase, intensify.

moderately *adv.* reasonably, fairly, mildly, passably, somewhat. *The Japanese rock band is moderately popular in the United States.* **Ant.** unreasonably, extremely, excessively.

moderation *n.* restraint, self-control, temperance, discipline, frugality. *In all things, one should practice moderation.* **Ant.** immoderation, excess.

moderator *n.* master of ceremonies, emcee, speaker, mediator, presiding officer, chairperson. *The moderator was responsible for keeping order at the meeting.*

modern *adj.* current, contemporary, up-to-date, present, recent, latest, new. *We want our dining room furnished in a modern decor.* **Ant.** old, old-fashioned, outdated.

modernize *vb.* update, renovate, rejuvenate, refurbish, reform. *The new computer allowed us to modernize our bookkeeping procedures.*

modest *adj.* **1.** shy, humble, unassuming, bashful, blushing, unpretentious. *He has a lot to be proud about but is quite modest when people praise him.* **2.** limited, moderate, adequate, small, passable. *The couple retired on a modest income.* **Ant. 1.** immodest, proud, arrogant. **2.** grand, generous, impressive.

modesty *n.* **1.** humbleness, humility, diffidence, bashfulness, shyness. *The famous singer's modesty was surprising.* **2.** decency, reserve, propriety, decorum, discretion. *His sense modesty is so strong that he refuses to take off his shirt in the pool.* **Ant. 1.** boastfulness, arrogance, vanity. **2.** immodesty, showiness.

modify *vb.* change, adjust, remodel, revise, transform, reshape, alter. *The shop modified the racing bike to fit my needs.*

mogul *n.* magnate, tycoon, baron, (slang) mover and a shaker, (slang) bigwig, (slang) big shot. *A media mogul typically owns newspapers, magazines, and television stations.*

moist *adj.* damp, wet, clammy, dank, dewy, muggy, watery. *Please use a moist rag to wipe the table.* **Ant.** dry, arid, parched.

moisten *vb.* moisturize, dampen, wet, water, spray. *Since he doesn't like to lick stamps, he moistens them with a sponge.* **Ant.** dehydrate, dry, parch.

moisture *n.* dew, moistness, dampness, wetness, vapor, water, damp. *The lost and dehydrated hiker tried to lick moisture from leaves.* **Ant.** dryness.

moisturizer *n.* lotion, cream, emollient, salve, oil. *I need to buy some moisturizer for my dry skin.* **Ant.** desiccant, drying agent.

mold *n.* **1.** fungus, mildew, blight, rot, lichen. *I threw out the bread because of the mold spotting its surface.* **2.** cast, die, frame, model, pattern, shape, form. *She makes candles by pouring wax into copper molds.* *–vb.* **3.** form, shape, fashion, sculpt, knead, pattern. *The potter molded the clay into a beautiful vase.*

moldy *adj.* moldering, rotting, musty, mildewing, decayed, stale. *Don't put away your wet clothes or they'll get moldy.*

mole *n.* nevus, blemish, spot, beauty mark, freckle. *The old witch's nose had a giant mole.*

molest *vb.* abuse, harass, assault, torment, annoy, plague. *Please stop molesting that poor dog.*

mollify *vb.* soothe, appease, soften, calm, mellow, pacify. *Her soft words were meant to mollify the angry toddler.* **Ant.** intensify, inflame, aggravate.

mollycoddle *vb.* baby, coddle, pamper, spoil, indulge, wait on. *Don't mollycoddle the kids or they'll turn into brats.*

molt *vb.* shed, exfoliate, peel, slough off, cast off. *The snake began to molt and eventually lost all of its old skin.*

molten *adj.* melted, liquefied, volcanic, red-hot, smelted, igneous. *A molten river of lava poured out of the volcano.* **Ant.** frozen, solidified, icy.

moment *n.* minute, second, instant, jiffy, twinkling. *Can you wait here a moment while I run back and get my sunglasses?*

momentary *adj.* brief, transitory, fleeting, passing, ephemeral, short-lived. *After a momentary lapse, the game resumed.* **Ant.** infinite, never-ending.

momentous *adj.* important, major, significant, memorable, eventful. *The baby's birth was a momentous occasion for the new parents.* **Ant.** insignificant, unimportant, trivial.

momentum *n.* drive, energy, impulse, speed, thrust, velocity. *The car gained so much momentum that it crashed through the brick wall.*

monarch *n.* king, queen, ruler, sovereign, emperor, empress, czar, shah, pharaoh, majesty. *Queen Victoria was Great Britain's monarch from 1837 to 1901.*

monastery *n.* religious community, abbey, friary, cloister, convent, retreat. *The monastery was a strikingly peaceful place.*

monetary *adj.* pecuniary, financial, fiscal, capital. *I own a bookstore for reasons other than monetary gain.*

money *n.* cash, currency, funds, revenue, capital, wealth. *How much money did you spend for your car?*

mongrel *n.* mixed breed, crossbreed, mutt, hybrid, half-breed, cur. *The mongrel may have characteristics of several breeds.* **Ant.** purebred, thoroughbred.

monitor *n.* **1.** overseer, director, supervisor, mentor, examiner. *Everyone in class gets to be lunchroom monitor for a week.* –*vb.* **2.** oversee, supervise, observe, check, examine. *Nurses monitored the patient's condition twenty-four hours a day.*

monk *n.* brother, monastic, friar. *The monk had taken a vow of silence and could not speak.*

monkey *n.* simian, primate, ape, omnivore, mammal, chimpanzee. *Monkeys are highly social animals.*

monolith *n.* slab, monument, block, obelisk. *A monolith had been erected to honor the war dead.*

monolithic *adj.* massive, immovable, gigantic, permanent, immovable, like a rock. *The city bristles with block after block of monolithic skyscrapers.* **Ant.** tiny, flimsy, fleeting.

monologue *n.* soliloquy, talk, speech, discourse, lecture, oration. *The comic delivered an absolutely hilarious monologue.*

monopolize *vb.* corner, dominate, control, own, appropriate, absorb. *By federal law, companies cannot monopolize any business.* **Ant.** share, divide.

monopoly *n.* control, domination, corner, cartel, bloc. *Little Timmy gained a monopoly on lemonade sales by selling glasses for a penny each.*

monotonous *adj.* unchanging, unvarying, dull, boring, tedious, dreary, routine. *The dairy's newest employee got the monotonous job of counting the holes in the Swiss cheese.* **Ant.** exciting, invigorating, changing.

monster *n.* ogre, brute, fiend, beast, demon, ghoul. *Mary Shelley is the creator of the monster known as Frankenstein.*

monstrous *adj.* **1.** horrible, terrifying, frightful, gruesome, evil, foul, vile, diabolical. *The museum displayed the monstrous devices from a medieval torture chamber.* **2.** huge, enormous, gigantic, colossal, immense, mammoth. *He has a monstrous appetite.* **Ant.** **1.** pleasing, kindly, gentle. **2.** small, tiny, minute.

montage *n.* composition, arrangement, scheme, patchwork, mosaic, miscellany. *The art students assembled a montage of school photographs on the wall.*

monument *n.* remembrance, memorial, shrine, reminder, commemorative. *We went to the Washington Monument while visiting the capital.*

monumental *adj.* **1.** huge, enormous, mammoth, gigantic, massive, immense. *The building* *of the pyramids was a monumental effort.* **2.** historic, immortal, impressive, striking, memorable, enduring. *The monumental Apollo XI lunar landing took place in 1969.* **Ant. 1.** tiny, small, insignificant. **2.** forgettable, unimportant.

mooch *vb.* cadge, beg, (slang) sponge, panhandle, (slang) bum off. *Don't mooch any more french fries, please.* **Ant.** give, donate.

mood *n.* temperament, temper, spirit, humor, attitude, disposition. *Our argument left me in a bad mood.*

moody *adj.* changeable, variable, temperamental, melancholy. *My friend's so moody he can go from happy to sad in a moment's time.*

moon *n.* satellite, orb, sphere, planetoid, celestial body. *Many planets in our solar system are orbited by a moon.*

WORD SEARCH

decrease during second half of phase: *wane*
hole from meteorite impact: *crater*
increase during first half of phase: *wax*
line or crack from meteorite impact: *ray*
mound: *dome*
orbital point closest to Earth: *perigee*
orbital point farthest from Earth: *apogee*
phases: *new, crescent, quarter, gibbous, full*
plains once thought to be seas: *mares*
seasonal: *harvest, hunter's*
shadow: *umbra*
study of: *selenology*

moonlight *n.* moonshine, moonbeam, luminescence, radiance, effulgence, albedo. *We could just make out the glowing eyes of two deer in the moonlight.*

moor *n.* **1.** heath, marsh, swamp, bog, quagmire, wasteland, grassland. *She crossed the moors to get to the old Celtic ruins. –vb.* **2.** anchor, fasten, bind, rope, secure, hitch. *The sailors moored their ship to the dock.* **Ant. 2.** untie, unfasten, release.

moot *adj.* debatable, unsettled, open for discussion, unresolved, arguable, controversial. *Whether there is a superior sex is a moot question.* **Ant.** resolved, determined, indisputable.

mop *n.* **1.** swab, swabber scrubber, sponge. *The mop was quite dirty after being used to clean the floor. –vb.* **2.** swab, wash, wipe, sponge, scrub. *She mopped the sweat from her forehead.*

mope *vb.* droop, sulk, grouch, pout, brood, pine, languish. *She moped about the house all summer because she had nothing to do.*

moral *n.* **1.** lesson, teaching, proverb, meaning, significance, dictum. *The story's moral was that one should never trust a stranger. –adj.* **2.** good, upright, ethical, decent, honorable, honest, righteous. *They wanted a moral man as their rabbi.* **Ant. 2.** immoral, unethical, dishonest.

morale *n.* mood, spirit, heart, resolve, attitude, temper, will. *The survivors' morale dipped after the rescue plane failed to see them.*

morality *n.* righteousness, goodness, justice, fairness, correctness, fitness, integrity. *She questioned the morality of taking the kittens to the pound.* **Ant.** immorality, badness, injustice.

moralize *vb.* preach, sermonize, pontificate, lecture, pass judgment. *If you try to moralize too often with your children, they'll stop listening.*

morals *n.* principles, standards, moral code, moral compass, scruples, ideals, ethics. *Parents should instill morals in their children.*

morass *n.* swamp, marsh, bog, wallow, quagmire ooze. *Our car got stuck in a morass of mud.*

moratorium *n.* suspension, postponement, deferment, delay, discontinuance, stop. *The city council voted for a temporary moratorium on all new development.*

morbid *adj.* unwholesome, sickly, unsound, unhealthy, grim, gruesome, macabre. *The writer* *has a morbid interest in death.* **Ant.** wholesome, sound, healthy.

more *adj.* **1.** additional, supplemental, supplementary, added, extra. *May I have some more soda?* –*adv.* **2.** further, longer, above, beyond. *The movie runs more than two hours.* **Ant. 1–2.** less.

morgue *n.* mortuary, funeral parlor, charnel house, crematorium. *The detective brought in family members to identify the body in the morgue.*

moribund *adj.* dying, failing, terminal, expiring, sinking fast, growing extinct. *The typewriter business became increasingly moribund as word processors were introduced.* **Ant.** thriving, robust, growing.

morning *n.* dawn, sunrise, sunup, daybreak, A.M., forenoon. *I don't function well in the morning until I've had coffee.*

moron *n.* idiot, imbecile, ignoramus, dope, nitwit, dullard. *I felt like a moron when I left my car lights on all night.* **Ant.** genius, savant, scholar.

moronic *adj.* imbecilic, idiotic, stupid, bovine, infantile, dumb. *Wearing a turkey on your head for Halloween may strike some as moronic.* **Ant.** intelligent, brilliant, smart.

morphine *n.* narcotic, drug, pain reliever, pain killer, anesthetic, opiate. *Medics use large quantities of morphine on the battlefields.*

morose *adj.* sullen, sulky, grim, gloomy, somber, depressed. *She seemed rather morose at the family reunion.* **Ant.** cheerful, joyful, happy.

morsel *n.* bite, mouthful, scrap, crumb, shred, pinch, bit. *I haven't had a morsel to eat all day.*

mortal *adj.* **1.** transitory, passing, temporary, impermanent, short-lived. *Humans are mortal beings with short life spans.* **2.** fatal, lethal, deadly, killing, critical. *The soldier received a moral wound in battle.* **Ant. 1.** immortal, permanent, eternal.

mortality *n.* vulnerability, impermanence, humanity, humanness, weakness. *Her brush with death made her aware of her own mortality.* **Ant.** immortality, invulnerability.

mortgage *n.* contract, pledge, title, loan agreement. *It's a great time to get a mortgage when interest rates are low.*

mortician *n.* undertaker, funeral director, embalmer. *The mortician told me that business lately was unusually dead.*

mortify *vb.* humiliate, shame, disgrace, embarrass, deflate, dismay. *Losing my swimming trunks in the pool after a dive tends to mortify me.*

mortuary *n.* funeral home, funeral parlor. *The deceased was being prepared in the mortuary for eventual burial.*

mosaic *n.* collage, miscellany, inlay, jumble, hodgepodge. *The mosaic was constructed of more than a thousand individual tiles.*

mosque *n.* house of worship, temple, church, house of God. *A mosque is where Muslims go to pray.*

WORD SEARCH
prayer tower: *minaret*

moss *n.* lichen, liverwort, Spanish moss, club moss, peat moss, growth, vegetation. *Moss grows thick and lush in the forest near our house.*

most *adj.* **1.** greatest, maximum, utmost, foremost, largest, extreme. *This is the most fun I've had in weeks.* *n.* **2.** utmost, peak, maximum, optimum. *I want the most you can give.* –*adv.* **3.** extremely, very, quite, unusually, exceptionally. *He was most charming.* **Ant. 1–2.** least, minimum.

mostly *adv.* mainly, primarily, chiefly, principally, largely. *The soup was mostly water.*

motel *n.* motor inn, hotel, motor court, road house, accommodations. *We have reservations to stay at a motel tonight.*

mother *n.* mom, matriarch, caregiver, parent, nurturer. *The platypus has a face only a mother could love.*

motion *n.* **1.** movement, action, change, mobility, activity. *Her hyperactive child is constantly in motion.* **2.** gesture, sign, signal, nod, wave. *My father made a motion for me to join him.* **3.** suggestion, recommendation, proposal, submission. *Someone at the meeting made a motion that fees be reduced.* *–vb.* **4.** gesture, wave, signal, sign, indicate. *The teacher motioned for us to be quiet.*

motivate *vb.* encourage, move, spur, prompt, influence, persuade. *Watching the Olympics motivated the athlete to continue his training.* **Ant.** discourage, deter, hinder.

motive *n.* cause, incentive, reason, purpose, goal, objective, intention, basis. *Have the police determined the motive for the murder?*

motley *adj.* diverse, heterogenous, varied, miscellaneous, multifarious. *The population of New York is a motley group.* **Ant.** homogenous, the same, unvarying.

motor *n.* engine, power plant, dynamo, (slang) workhorse, generator, transformer. *The motor roared to life.*

WORD SEARCH

close air to carburetor: *choke*
cooling system: *fan, radiator, water pump*
cylindrical plugs that pump up and down and compress air-fuel mix: *pistons*
drive train: *clutch, transmission, driveshaft, differential*
energy unit: *horsepower, rpm (revolutions per minute)*
exhaust burner: *catalytic converter, afterburner, turbocharger*
filters dirt and dust: *air filter, fuel filter, oil filter*
fuel vaporizer: *carburetor*
main framework: *engine block*
overtaxing of: *redlining*
piston housing: *cylinder*
system that converts fuel into fine spray and injects it into cylinders: *fuel injection system*
valve operator: *camshaft*

motorboat *n.* speedboat, powerboat, outboard, cruiser, bass boat, yacht. *In a motorboat, we can cross the pond in 60 seconds.*

motorcade *n.* parade, procession, caravan, cavalcade. *The governor's car was only one in a long motorcade.*

motorcycle *n.* motorbike, (slang) wheels, dirt bike, (slang) chopper, (slang) iron horse, (slang) sled, scooter. *Highway patrol personnel must be able to ride a motorcycle.*

WORD SEARCH

accelerator: *throttle*
engine shutoff: *kill switch*
miniature: *moped, mini bike, pocket bike*
safety bar for passenger: *sissy bar* (slang)

motor home *n.* mobile home, trailer, R.V., camper, (slang) tin can. *We like to vacation in our motor home, but we never call it "camping."*

motto *n.* slogan, saying, canon, maxim, precept, proverb, dictum. *Alaska's state motto is "North to the future."*

mound *n.* hill, hump, rise, pile, heap, knoll, dome. *Termites build large nesting mounds out of saliva and soil.* **Ant.** hole, depression, hollow.

mount *n.* **1.** mountain, peak, summit, promontory, pinnacle. *Mount McKinley is the highest point in North America.* **2.** horse, steed, mare, stallion, bronco, mustang. *Cavalrymen were concerned with the welfare of their mounts.* *–vb.* **3.** rise, climb, surge, increase, grow, soar, ascend.

Tension mounted in the arena. **4.** install, position, locate, fix, set, put, place. *He mounted his trophy on the wall.* **Ant. 3.** descend, lower, lessen.

mountain *n.* mount, hill, peak, summit, pinnacle, point, promontory. *It was faster going down the mountain than climbing up it.* **Ant.** bottomland, dale, valley.

WORD SEARCH

air at high altitude: *rarefied*
altitude above 4,800 feet: *alpine*
chain: *cordillera, range, sierra*
cloud over: *banner*
flat-topped: *butte, mesa, plateau*
glow at sunrise or sunset: *alpenglow*
gully: *couloir*
lake: *tarn*
low between peaks: *saddle*
needle-like peak: *matterhorn*
pass: *col, defile*
peak: *horn, summit*
ridge: *hogback, sawback, spur*
rise: *shoulder*
rock, steep and weathered: *crag*
rubble: *scree, talus*
side: *flank*
snowslide: *avalanche*
study: *orography*

mourn *vb.* grieve, lament, sorrow, suffer, regret, weep, despair. *We mourned the loss of our loved one.*

mournful *adj.* sorrowful, joyless, sad, cheerless, painful, unhappy, distressing, grim. *The funeral was a mournful occasion.* **Ant.** happy, joyous, merry, cheerful.

mouse *n.* **1.** rodent, vermin, mammal, vole. *We have a mouse in our house, but it doesn't make much noise, se we let it stay.* **2.** controller, (slang) clicker, device. *Click on the icon with your mouse.*

mouth-watering *adj.* salivary, savory, appetizing, succulent. *That mouth-watering apple pie looks delicious.*

move *vb.* **1.** carry, bear, cart, lug, convey, shift, budge. *It will take two people to move this dresser.* **2.** go, proceed, advance, transfer, depart. *Our family recently moved to Illinois.* **3.** touch, disturb, affect, impress, shock, disquiet. *The sorrowful movie moved me.* **4.** persuade, force, oblige, impel, require. *Complaints from the community finally moved the government to take action.* **5.** suggest, submit, recommend, propose. *I move that we quit for the day.* –*n.* **6.** shift, step, measure, undertaking, deed, feat. *Changing careers was a big move in her life.* **7.** maneuver, tactic, ploy, device, stratagem. *His last chess move was quite clever.* **Ant. 2.** stay, remain.

movement *n.* **1.** motion, action, activity, stir, displacement. *He noticed the deer when he saw movement in the bushes.* **2.** drive, trend, inclination, tendency, drift. *There's been a recent movement in the city council to increase parking fines.*

mover and shaker *n.* doer, go-getter, producer, enterpriser, catalyst, (slang) sparkplug. *Kevin is such a mover and a shaker, he'll probably be a millionaire soon.* **Ant.** do-nothing, (slang) lightweight, nonentity.

movie *n.* motion picture, film, cinema, picture, feature. *My favorite movie is* Star Wars.

WORD SEARCH

actor, small role: *bit player, cameo appearance, extra*
advertising clips of new movie: *trailer*
animal handler: *wrangler*
assistant, set: *grip*
award: *Academy Award, Oscar*
black and white to color, process of converting: *colorization*
body motion capture via bodysuit sensors, natural: *motion capture, mocap*
clapper: *slate*
daytime, movie run in the: *matinee*
directs action: *director*
electrician, lights: *gaffer*

electrician's assistant: *best boy*
financing and hiring head: *producer*
illegally copied and distributed movie: *pirated*
joining of two pieces of film: *splicing*
lip synchronizing: *looping*
music of: *score*
object used in: *prop*
past, scene from character's: *flashback*
photographer, motion picture: *cinematographer*
real person's life story: *biopic*
record dialogue and sound effects: *Foley, dub*
rolling credits at end of movie: *crawl*
set on which scene is currently being shot: *hot set*
setting up a scene: *blocking*
shot, moving: *dolly shot, tracking shot*
shot, wide, side-to-side: *pan*
shot, zooming in: *zoom*
special effect, double scene: *split screen*
special effect, fade out: *dissolve*
special effect, gunshot wound: *squib*
special effects, metamorphosing: *morphing*
special effects, superimposition: *blue screen, matte shot*
trailer used as a dressing room while on location: *honeywagon*
writer: *screenwriter*

mow *vb.* cut, shear, trim, shave, clip, crop. *I mowed the lawn.*

much *adj.* 1. considerable, abundant, ample, substantial, plentiful. *He never seems to have much money.* –*adv.* 2. greatly, abundantly, highly, largely, considerably, overly. *I love you very much.* 3. frequently, often, repeatedly, regularly, habitually. *She goes to the movies too much.* **Ant.** 1. inadequate, insufficient, little.

muckraker *n.* investigator, investigative reporter, journalist, whistle-blower, exposer, (slang) scandal-monger. *The newspaper's best muckraker was assigned to dig up scandalous information.*

muckraking *n.* investigating, probing, uncovering, exposing, whistle-blowing. *Muckraking is a reporter's main pursuit.*

mud *n.* ooze, muck, mire, slime, slop, swamp, quagmire, morass. *We trudged through the rain and mud.*

muddled *adj.* confused, bewildered, befuddled, mixed-up, lost, disoriented. *The drunken man was so muddled, he couldn't even recall his own name.* **Ant.** clear, lucid, sharp.

muddy *adj.* mucky, silty, miry, sedimentary, dirty, oozing. *The baseball field is becoming too muddy to play on safely.*

mudslinging *n.* defamation, slander, name-calling, smear campaign, insulting, offending. *Politicians sometimes practice mudslinging to discourage votes for the opposition.*

muffle *vb.* dampen, mute, quiet, hush, silence, cloak, shroud. *Thick walls muffled the sound of the neighbor's shouting.* **Ant.** heighten, intensify, increase, amplify.

muffler *n.* mute, silencer, baffle. *The muffler is needed to reduce engine noise.*

mug *vb.* hold up, rob, purse-snatch, (slang) stick up, (slang) jump, assault. *She was afraid the shady characters across the street were looking for someone to mug.*

mugging *n.* hold-up, robbery, purse-snatching, (slang) stick-up, assault. *To avoid a mugging, stay away from dangerous areas of town after dark.*

muggy *adj.* humid, sticky, damp, clammy, moist, steaming. *The weather was hot and muggy.* **Ant.** dry, arid.

mule *n.* hinny, jackass, donkey, burro, jenny. *My son can be as stubborn as a mule.*

mull *vb.* ponder, consider, think, weigh, contemplate, reflect, muse. *I'll have to mull over whether I want to build a deck or not.*

multiply *vb.* increase, double, mushroom, reproduce, breed, generate. *The roaches seemed to multiply at an incredible speed.*

multitude *n.* crowd, gathering, swarm, mass, pack, assembly, throng, horde. *A multitude of people showed up to hear the president speak.*

mumble *vb.* mutter, murmur, whisper, stammer. *Sometimes it's difficult to understand him because he mumbles.*

mummify *vb.* dry, preserve, desiccate, embalm, swaddle. *The ancient Egyptian practice was to mummify their dead.*

mummy *n.* cadaver, corpse, the embalmed, the entombed, (slang) stiff. *There were gasps of shock when the mummy was revealed under its sarcophagus.*

munch *vb.* chew, crunch, nosh, bite, snack, nibble. *I like to munch on popcorn.*

municipal *adj.* city, civic, civil, metropolitan, urban, community, town. *Determining fair pay for police and fire department is a prickly municipal problem.*

municipality *n.* city, town, metropolis, village, community, borough. *Do I get my fishing license through my municipality or through my state?*

munitions *n.* weapons, ammunition, bombs, ordnance, arsenal. *Great care must be taken when working around a munitions dump.*

murder *n.* **1.** killing, slaying, slaughter, assassination, homicide, extermination. *Lee Harvey Oswald was the man responsible for the murder of President John F. Kennedy.* –*vb.* **2.** kill, slay, slaughter, assassinate, massacre, exterminate. *Terrorists murdered several passengers on the airplane.*

WORD SEARCH

accidental, unintentional: *involuntary manslaughter*
brother, of: *fratricide*
ethnic, racial, religious or political group, of: *genocide*
father, of: *patricide*
heat of passion shooting without malice aforethought: *manslaughter*
hired: *contract killing*
mass: *massacre*
mother, of: *matricide*
planned: *premeditated, first-degree murder*
politically motivated ambush: *assassination*
random act: (slang) *wilding*
self: *suicide*
serial: *serial killing*
sister, of: *sororicide*
suspected: *foul play*
unplanned with malice aforethought: *second-degree murder*

murky *adj.* gloomy, dark, dusky, dim, hazy, nebulous, obscure. *A nighttime fog made the harbor particularly murky.* **Ant.** clear, light, bright.

murmur *vb.* mutter, mumble, whisper, sigh, coo, sough. *When the show was delayed, the audience began to murmur with impatience.*

muscle *n.* abductor, adductor, flexor, constrictor, extensor, tendon. *Some men like to show off their muscles.*

muscular *adj.* brawny, strapping, Herculean, sinewy, husky, rippling. *Everyone got out of the muscular man's way.* **Ant.** skinny, flaccid, undeveloped.

muse *n.* spirit, inspiration, creativity, talent, genius. *I turn to my muse for new ideas for songs.*

museum *n.* gallery, treasury, collection, exhibit, repository, archives. *Let's go to the science museum and look at the dinosaur skeletons.*

mushy *adj.* maudlin, sentimental, sappy, gushy, lovey-dovey, saccharine. *That romantic comedy was too mushy for my taste.* **Ant.** cold, hard, unfeeling.

music *n.* songs, singing, instrumentation, rhythm, melody, tune. *Does he like rock music?*

WORD SEARCH

arrangement: *composition*
closing passage: *coda*
connection between two musical passages: *bridge*
expert musician: *virtuoso*
horizontal lines on which notes are written: *staff*
melody, dual: *counterpoint*
movie, written for: *score*
multiple rhythms played at same time: *polyrhythmic*
pause or silence: *rest*
performing without notes: *playing by ear*
pitch, above correct: *sharp*
pitch, below correct: *flat*
play informally with other musicians: *jam*
repeated section: *refrain*
return to original theme: *reprise*
school of: *conservatory*
tune, displeasing and out of: *dissonant*
tune, pleasing and in: *consonant*

musical *adj.* lyrical, instrumental, orchestral, operatic, symphonic, tuneful, melodic. *Mozart was a musical genius.* **Ant.** unmusical, discordant.

musician *n.* performer, artist, instrumentalist, singer, song stylist, virtuoso, vocalist. *Being on the road is a difficult part of every musician's life.*

must *vb.* should, ought to, have to, need to. *I must get to the post office today.*

mustache *n.* moustache, moustachio, whiskers, (slang) peach fuzz, (slang) soupstrainer. *My father once sported a handlebar mustache.*

WORD SEARCH

drooping over chin: *Fu Manchu, horseshoe*
M-shaped: *regent*
rectangular: *boxcar, toothbrush, Hitler*
T-form with chin tuft: *Roman T*
thick and overgrown: *walrus*
turned-up ends, having: *handlebar, Hindenburg*

musty *adj.* mouldy, fusty, stale, decaying, dusty. *The cellar smells terribly musty today.* **Ant.** fresh, clean, sweet.

mutant *n.* miscreation, deviation, mutation, alteration, freak of nature, monster. *Many of the frogs we found were mutants with three legs.*

mutation *n.* miscreation, deviation, alteration, anomaly, variation, accident. *The fruit flies exposed to radiation all exhibited signs of having undergone a mutation.*

mute *adj.* silent, speechless, voiceless, still, aphonic, mum. *The man used sign language because he was deaf and mute.*

mutinous *adj.* rebellious, insurrectionary, riotous, insubordinate, traitorous, subversive. *Much of the crew of the pirate ship had grown mutinous.* **Ant.** loyal, obedient, subordinate.

mutter *vb.* murmur, mumble, maunder, talk under one's breath, whisper. *I can't hear what you're saying when you mutter.*

mutual fund *n.* stock fund, bond fund, investment, growth fund, (slang) nest egg. *I invested most of money in a mutual fund made up of many stocks.*

muzzle *vb.* restrain, restrict, silence, shut up, hush up, quit. *In the United States, not even the president can muzzle the media.*

N

nab *vb.* grab, catch, seize, capture, trap, snare, arrest. *The shoplifter was nabbed as he left the store.* **Ant.** free, release, liberate.

nag *vb.* **1.** pester, harass, annoy, bother, irritate, torment, badger. *My parents are always nagging me about getting a job.* –*n.* **2.** nuisance, pest, complainer, whiner, grouch. *I wish my brother would stop being a nag.* **Ant. 1.** appease, soothe.

nail *vb.* hammer, strike, pound, tap, drive, hit. *A carpenter nailed the bookshelves to the wall.*

naive *adj.* innocent, simple, unworldly, unsophisticated, unaffected. *How can a person with her experience be so naive?* **Ant.** sophisticated, experienced, worldly.

naiveté *n.* inexperience, ignorance, innocence, unsophistication, credulity, gullibility. *The slick operator hoped to take advantage of the child's obvious naiveté.* **Ant.** experience, wisdom, worldliness.

naked *adj.* **1.** nude, bare, unclothed, undressed, stripped, uncovered, exposed. *It's against the law to go naked on a public beach.* **2.** plain, simple, unconcealed, open, evident, obvious. *He was afraid that the witness would tell the naked truth.* **Ant. 1.** clothed, dressed, covered. **2.** guarded, shielded, concealed.

name *n.* **1.** title, label, term, designation, appellation. *What is the name of that red flower?* **2.** reputation, repute, character, fame, distinction. *The attorney hopes to make a name for herself by winning this case.* –*vb.* **3.** title, call, label, term, designate, dub. *He named the puppy Patches.* **4.** appoint, designate, elect, assign, choose, nominate. *Last week the club named a new president.*

nanny *n.* babysitter, nursemaid, au pair, governess, nurse, mammy. *We need to hire a nanny to take care of the kids next month.*

nap *n.* **1.** sleep, snooze, slumber, doze, siesta, rest. *I think I'll take a little nap before dinner.* –*vb.* **2.** drowse, sleep, doze, rest, snooze. *The director was caught napping during the board meeting.*

narcissistic *adj.* vain, egotistical, conceited, self-infatuated, egocentric, self-absorbed. *When it comes to preening in front of a mirror, we are all a little narcissistic.*

narcotic *n.* drug, opiate, hypnotic, pain reliever, anesthetic, tranquilizer. *Narcotics can be dangerous and highly addictive.*

narrate *vb.* tell, recite, relate, recount, describe, report. *The speaker presented slides and narrated the story behind them.*

narration *n.* telling, recounting, description, account, detailing, chronicling. *The opening narration described an imaginary time long, long ago in a place far, far away.*

narrator *n.* storyteller, reporter, relater, recounter, author. *The narrator described the action in vivid detail.*

narrow *adj.* **1.** slender, thin, tight, slim, close, restricted. *The bridge was too narrow for the truck to cross.* **2.** bigoted, biased, intolerant, shallow, limited. *People with narrow minds shut themselves off from much of life's pleasure.* **Ant. 1.** wide, broad, spacious. **2.** receptive, unbiased, tolerant.

narrow-minded *adj.* closed-minded, small-minded, prejudiced, bigoted, intolerant, tunnel-visioned. *A racist is narrow-minded.* **Ant.** broad-minded, liberal, tolerant.

nasty *adj.* **1.** unpleasant, disagreeable, disgusting, distasteful, terrible, awful. *Washing dishes is a nasty job.* **2.** mean, cruel, vicious, hateful, vile, beastly. *Scrooge was a nasty person.* **Ant. 1.** enjoyable, pleasant, nice. **2.** sweet, kind.

nation *n.* country, kingdom, commonwealth, republic, domain, dominion, realm. *Monaco is an extremely small nation.*

national *adj.* nationwide, federal, interstate, coast-to-coast. *The national chess championship will be held next week.*

nationality *n.* nativity, extraction, race, citizenship, lineage, ethnic group. *What nationality are you?*

native *n.* **1.** citizen, resident, inhabitant, dweller. *She is a native of California.* –*adj.* **2.** local, original, natural, domestic, native-born. *The platypus is native to Australia.* **Ant. 1.** alien, foreigner, immigrant. **2.** foreign, imported.

natty *adj.* dapper, chic, smart, sharp, (slang) snazzy, (slang) dressed to the nines. *Eddy is looking natty with his new haircut.*

natural *adj.* **1.** instinctive, basic, fundamental, inborn, inbred, inherent. *Raccoons have a natural tendency to wash their food before eating it.* **2.** normal, regular, customary, typical, spontaneous. *If you just act natural, you will do well in your interview.* **Ant. 1.** learned, unnatural, alien. **2.** contrived, artificial.

naturalist *n.* ecologist, environmentalist, zoologist, botanist, field observer, (slang) tree hugger. *If it weren't for outspoken naturalists, the world would be more polluted than it is.*

naturally *adv.* **1.** certainly, surely, plainly, normally, usually. *Naturally, the queen will lead the procession.* **2.** freely, simply, normally, sincerely, honestly, candidly. *The children were behaving naturally until they spotted the photographer.* **2.** artificially, strangely, pretentiously.

nature *n.* **1.** world, universe, cosmos, creation. *Not even scientists understand all the laws of nature.* **2.** characteristic, disposition, trait, attribute, instinct, personality. *It is her nature to examine every aspect of a question.* **3.** essence, type, sort, character, kind, style, brand. *What is the nature of your visit?*

naughty *adj.* bad, disobedient, mischievous, misbehaving, troublesome. *Putting the goldfish in our soup was a naughty thing to do.* **Ant.** nice, behaved, obedient, good.

nausea *n.* sickness, queasiness, squeamishness, vomiting. *My nausea was caused by eating spoiled meat.*

nauseated *adj.* **1.** disgusted, revolted, offended, repulsed, upset. *She was nauseated by the violent movie.* **2.** ill, sick, queasy, squeamish, unwell. *Mountain driving tends to make me nauseated.*

nautical *adj.* marine, naval, maritime, oceanic, boating. *The sailor was an expert in the nautical arts.*

navigate *vb.* pilot, steer, guide, direct, sail. *It is unsafe to navigate this channel by night.*

navigator *n.* plotter, chartsman, pilot, helmsman, aviator, sailor. *The navigator plotted the quickest route home.*

navy *n.* marine defense, sea force, armada, fleet, argosy, flotilla. *The navy sent a convoy to defend the port from the enemy.*

WORD SEARCH

aircraft transport: *aircraft carrier, flattop*
armed, heavily: *battleship*
group of ships: *convoy, squadron*
mine destroyer: *minesweeper*
officers (in ascending order): *chief warrant officer, ensign, lieutenant, lieutenant commander, commander, captain, rear admiral, vice admiral, admiral, fleet admiral*
patrol torpedo boat: *PT boat*
simultaneous gunfire on target: *salvo*
sonic locator: *sonar*
speedy warship: *destroyer*
underwater vessel: *submarine, U-boat*

naysayer *n.* pessimist, opponent, critic, dissenter, defeatist, prophet of doom. *In the eyes of a naysayer, any man with a new idea is a crank.* **Ant.** supporter, champion, advocate.

Nazi *n.* fascist, nationalist. *Nazis were the worst kind of extremists.*

near *adj.* **1.** close, nearby, adjacent, neighboring, adjoining, bordering. *The nearest country to the south of the United States is Mexico.* –*vb.* **2.** approach, advance, draw near, move toward. *The train neared the station.*

nearly *adv.* about, almost, near, practically, approximately, roughly. *It's nearly six o'clock.*

nearsighted *adj.* myopic, shortsighted, (slang) blind as a mole, (slang) blind as a post. *I'm too nearsighted to drive without my glasses.* **Ant.** farsighted, hyperopic.

neat *adj.* **1.** clean, tidy, orderly, straight, immaculate. *His task is to keep the kitchen neat.* **2.** clever, skillful, effective, competent, great, wonderful. *That was a neat slam dunk.* **Ant.** **1.** dirty, sloppy, messy. **2.** incompetent, inept, awful.

neatly *adv.* orderly, tidily, cleanly, uniformly, in good order. *Fold your clothes neatly before you put them away.* **Ant.** sloppily, messily, haphazardly.

necessary *adj.* needed, essential, required, indispensable, important. *Pack only what is necessary for the trip.* **Ant.** unnecessary, nonessential, optional.

necklace *n.* strand, chain, locket, jewelry, choker, pendant. *The queen wore a necklace of emeralds the size of golf balls.*

necktie *n.* tie, cravat, ascot, bow tie, jabot, Windsor. *Every boy should learn how to tie his own necktie.*

need *vb.* **1.** require, want, lack, miss, yearn, cover, crave. *What the coach needs is a quarterback who can throw the ball.* –*n.* **2.** requirement, want, lack, necessity, demand. *The hospital is in need of more nurses.* **3.** poverty, distress, want, neediness, destitution. *This homeless shelter helps those who are in need.* **Ant.** **1.** have, possess. **2.** abundance, excess. **3.** wealth, affluence.

needless *adj.* unnecessary, nonessential, useless, pointless, purposeless. *It is needless for you to accompany me to the market.* **Ant.** essential, useful, necessary, required.

needlework *n.* needlepoint, knitting, crochet, embroidery, sewing, stitching. *In the 1800s, most girls were required to be proficient in needlework.*

needy *adj.* poor, penniless, destitute, broke, impoverished, bankrupt. *Will you donate food for a needy family?* **Ant.** rich, wealthy, affluent.

nefarious *adj.* villainous, evil, wicked, sinister, abominable, bad. *The captain and his nefarious crew of pirates pillaged the village.* **Ant.** good, angelic, saintly.

negate *vb.* nullify, cancel, void, counteract, nullify, neutralize. *Neglecting to pull weeds from* *your garden negates any effort to fertilize your crop.* **Ant.** augment, boost, enhance.

negative *adj.* opposed, denying, contrary, pessimistic, skeptical, rejecting. *The negative attitude of the jury worried his attorney.* **Ant.** positive, approving, optimistic.

neglect *n.* **1.** disregard, negligence, inattention, neglectfulness, omission. *The poor condition of his car is due to neglect.* –*vb.* **2.** disregard, ignore, overlook, forget, slight. *She neglected her garden and now it's nothing but weeds.* **Ant. 1.** attention, concern, care. **2.** regard, notice.

neglectful *adj.* negligent, delinquent, derelict, remiss, irresponsible, inattentive, careless. *The neglectful homeowner chose to put off repairing his steps until they collapsed.* **Ant.** attentive, conscientious, caring.

negligee *n.* nightie, nightgown, chemise, peignoir, deshabille. *A flimsy negligee won't keep you warm in winter.*

negligent *adj.* forgetful, careless, indifferent, neglectful, heedless. *The cracks in the wall are evidence of negligent workmanship.* **Ant.** careful, vigilant, attentive.

negotiate *vb.* **1.** arrange, settle, bargain, discuss, arbitrate, transact. *The leaders met secretly to negotiate peace terms.* **2.** handle, manage, clear, make, surmount. *The driver was going too fast to negotiate the turn.*

negotiator *n.* arbitrator, mediator, haggler, go-between, intermediary, middleman. *The warring nations needed a skilled negotiator to bring the hostilities to an end.*

Negro *n.* black, person of color, negroid, African, African American. *The skin tone of the equatorial Negro is often darker than that of people in more northern or southern latitudes.*

neighborhood *n.* **1.** community, environs, locality, surroundings, area. *This is a real friendly neighborhood.* **2.** range, order, area, vicinity, extent. *That car's value is in the neighborhood of $20,000.*

nemesis *n.* retribution, vengeance, vindication, just deserts, punishment, comeuppance. *The buck turned nemesis as it turned and attacked the prostrate hunter.*

neophyte *n.* beginner, amateur, novice, tyro, intern, debutant, (slang) rookie. *She was such a neophyte, she didn't even know how to turn on the computer.* **Ant.** expert, veteran, master.

nerd *n.* (slang) dork, (slang) geek, (slang) dweeb, (slang) goober, (slang) nebbish, (slang) goofball. *I like* Star Trek *and wear thick glasses, but I'm only a nerd on the outside.*

nerve *n.* **1.** courage, bravery, fearlessness, boldness, fortitude. *Do you have the nerve to dive off that cliff?* **2.** gall, arrogance, rudeness, cheek, insolence, brashness. *He had the nerve to go to the party uninvited.* **Ant. 1.** cowardice, fearfulness. **2.** reserve, shyness, politeness.

nerve-racking *adj.* stressful, frazzling, distressing, disquieting, disturbing. *Processing tax returns at tax time is nerve-racking.* **Ant.** relaxing, pacifying, soothing.

nervous *adj.* edgy, excitable, shaky, agitated, jumpy, uneasy, anxious. *Public speaking makes me nervous.* **Ant.** steady, calm, confident, relaxed.

nervous breakdown *n.* emotional collapse, (slang) burnout, nervous exhaustion, clinical depression, stress, posttraumatic stress disorder. **Ant.** serenity, calm, peace.

nervousness *adj.* anxiety, tension, stress, angst, apprehension, jitters. *Too much nervousness can affect your speech-making performance.* **Ant.** calm, relaxation, serenity.

nervy *adj.* **1.** impudent, insolent, fresh, rude, flip, brash. *She was pretty nervy to cut in line like that.* **2.** brave, intrepid, bold, gutsy, plucky, daring. *You have to be plenty nervy to climb Mt. Everest.* **Ant. 1.** polite, courteous, deferential. **2.** cowardly, spineless, mousy.

nest *n.* aerie, roost. *We found the falcon perching at its nest.*

nest egg *n.* savings, security, investment, (slang) stash. *It's wise to have a nest egg saved for a rainy day.*

nestle *vb.* snuggle, settle, cuddle, nuzzle, burrow. *The piglets nestled close to their mother.*

net *n.* **1.** netting, mesh, web, trap, snare. *The fishing boats pulled in their nets. –vb.* **2.** catch, snare, trap, capture, snag, bag. *The rangers plan to net the bear and release him in a less populated area.* **3.** make, earn, gain, clear, realize, collect. *We netted a $300 profit.*

network *n.* interconnection, affiliations, organization, chain, relationship, system. *The Internet is an international network of computers.*

neurosis *n.* emotional disorder, nervous disorder, personality disorder, maladjustment, anxiety disorder, phobia, mania. *My worst neurosis is a fear of spiders.*

WORD SEARCH

combat neurosis: *posttraumatic stress syndrome*
death, excessive fear of: *necrophobia*
dieting to the point of emaciation: *anorexia nervosa*
dieting and bingeing with forced vomiting: *bulimia*
fear, irrational: *phobia*
fire-setting, fascination with: *pyromania*
health, excessive worry over one's: *hypochondria*
obsession or crazed desire: *mania*
panic, uncontrollable bouts of: *panic disorder*
repeated thoughts, rituals: *obsessive-compulsive disorder*
steal, compulsion to: *kleptomania*

neurotic *adj.* irrational, maladjusted, emotionally disturbed, dysfunctional, anxious, phobic. *I am quite neurotic when it comes to spiders.* **Ant.** rational, well-adjusted, normal.

neuter *vb.* castrate, emasculate, geld, spay, (slang) fix, (slang) cut. *To control the pet population, always spay and neuter your cats and dogs.*

neutral *adj.* **1.** uninvolved, indifferent, impartial, unaligned, uncommitted. *The governor preferred to remain neutral on controversial issues.* **2.** ordinary, average, intermediate, indefinite. *A dress in a neutral color would be your safest choice.* **Ant. 1.** biased, partial, partisan.

neutralize *vb.* counteract, offset, nullify, negate, cancel, deactivate. *It's critical to neutralize a snakebite's poison as quickly as possible.*

neverending *adj.* perpetual, infinite, everlasting, eternal, forever, endless. *The solution to a neverending cycle of violence is not more violence.* **Ant.** finite, terminal, limited.

nevertheless *adv.* nonetheless, yet, however, regardless, anyway. *She's sick; nevertheless, she is going on a date.*

new *adj.* **1.** recent, latest, current, modern. *His new CD player has excellent sound quality.* **2.** unknown, unfamiliar, unexplored, uncharted, remote. *The explorer realized that she was in new territory.* **3.** original, fresh, creative, novel, unique, unusual. *We seem to have run out of new ideas.* **Ant. 1.** old, used, ancient. **2.** familiar, explored, traveled. **3.** unoriginal, stale, common.

newborn *n.* neonate, infant, babe, baby, weanling, suckling. *Even ugly newborns quickly become adorable to their parents.*

WORD SEARCH
prematurely, born: (slang) *preemie*

newly *adv.* recently, lately, freshly, anew, of late. *This newly revised almanac has lots of updated material.*

news *n.* information, data, report, knowledge, word, account. *We are expecting news about the hurricane.*

newscast *n.* broadcast, telecast, bulletin, dispatch, report. *I always watch the six o'clock newscast.*

newscaster *n.* broadcaster, newsman, newswoman, anchor, reporter, announcer. *The newscaster must use care to report the news in an unbiased manner.*

newsletter *n.* report, bulletin, paper, journal, publication, monthly. *I get a monthly newsletter that keeps me informed of changes in the stock market.*

newspaper *n.* publication, daily, weekly, tabloid, chronicle, gazette. *The newspaper tends to focus only on bad news.*

WORD SEARCH
assigns stories to reporters: *editor*
beating all competitors to a story: *scoop*
correction of a printed inaccuracy: *retraction*
error checker: *copy editor*
hawking on street corners: *bootjacking*
large story: *feature*
light publicity piece: *puff piece*
personal opinion piece: *editorial*
reporter's name line: *byline*
stories presented by pictures: *photojournalism*

next *adj.* 1. following, coming, ensuing, subsequent. *Would you call the next applicant?* 2. adjacent, nearest, closest, bordering, adjoining. *The Johnsons live in the next house.* –*adv.* 3. after, thereafter, successively, later. *Whose turn is it next?* **Ant.** 1. preceding, previous. first. 2. farthest, distant, remote.

nibble *vb.* 1. nip. chew, munch, bite, peck, gnaw. *The mice nibbled at the cheese.* –*n.* 2. taste, bite, crumb, morsel, tidbit, snack, bit. *I'll have just a nibble of that cake.*

nice *adj.* pleasant, agreeable, pleasurable, delightful, enjoyable, good. *They had a nice day at the zoo.* **Ant.** terrible, unpleasant, awful, miserable.

niche *n.* 1. corner, nook, alcove, recess, hollow, cavity, hole. *The hiker set her pack in a niche behind the tree.* 2. calling, position, place, trade, purpose. *He has not yet found his niche in life.*

nickname *n.* pet name, moniker, (slang) handle, cognomen, diminutive. *My good friend's nickname is Eddy Munster, but his real name is Carey.*

night *n.* evening, dark, nighttime, nightfall, darkness. *Vampires and werewolves come out at night.* **Ant.** day, daytime, daylight.

nightclub *n.* club, night spot, lounge, disco, bar, cabaret, supper club. *We went to the nightclub and saw a great band.*

nightmare *n.* bad dream, incubus, succubus, phantasmagoria, night terrors, hypnogogic imagery, *I had a nightmare and awoke in a cold sweat.*

nightmarish *adj.* surreal, otherworldly, horrific, hallucinatory, weird, creepy, strange. *Whales stranding themselves on shore and struggling to survive present a nightmarish scene.*

nimble *adj.* agile, spry, speedy, active, lively, quick, swift. *Jack was so nimble he could jump over the candlestick.* **Ant.** slow, awkward, clumsy, plodding.

nirvana *n.* enlightenment, bliss, awakening, blessedness, perfection, tranquillity. *He meditated with the goal of achieving nirvana.*

nit-pick *vb.* quibble, split hairs, pettifog, make a federal case out of nothing. *If you are given a gift you don't like, it's bad manners to whine, complain or nit-pick about it.*

nobility *n.* aristocracy, status, rank, eminence, elite, upper class. *She belonged to nobility and believed she was better than most.*

noble *adj.* **1.** exalted, lordly, aristocratic, titled, high-ranking. *The prince could only marry a woman of noble birth.* **2.** honorable, generous, virtuous, moral, superior, heroic. *The rescue failed, but it was a noble attempt.* **3.** stately, grand, majestic, splendid, glorious, awesome. *Colorado is blessed with noble mountains.* *–n.* **4.** lord, lady, aristocrat, noblewoman, nobleman. *The nobles were stunned by the peasant's rebellion.* **Ant. 1.** common, lowborn. **2.** cowardly, despicable. **3.** unimpressive, modest, forgettable. **4.** serf, peasant, commoner.

nobody *n.* nothing, nonentity, zero, flunky, (slang) nebbish, lightweight. *It's easy to feel like a nobody when you're the last one picked for a team.* **Ant.** somebody, bigshot, VIP.

noise *n.* sound, clamor, clatter, racket, uproar, din, disturbance, commotion. *Do you have to make all that noise in the morning?* **Ant.** quiet, silence, peace, hush.

noisy *adj.* loud, deafening, blaring, clamorous, resounding, boisterous, thunderous. *The fireworks show was a noisy event.* **Ant.** quiet, peaceful, still, noiseless.

nomad *n.* wanderer, migrant, rover, pilgrim, vagabond, drifter, gypsy. *She was a nomad roaming from town to town.*

nomadic *adj.* roving, drifting, wandering, rambling, migratory. *Tony lived a nomadic lifestyle, hitchhiking from town to town.* **Ant.** settled, rooted, stationary.

nominal *adj.* **1.** pretended, theoretical, supposed, surface, token. *Her leadership of the group is purely nominal.* **2.** trivial, trifling, small, slight, minimum, insignificant. *The nominal effects of the boycott will not hurt our business.* **Ant. 1.** real, true, genuine. **2.** considerable, large, substantial.

nominate *vb.* propose, choose, appoint, designate, select, name. *Who did you nominate for secretary?*

nonchalant *adj.* casual, indifferent, unconcerned, cool, easygoing, composed. *He had a nonchalant attitude about the final exam.* **Ant.** anxious, concerned, disturbed.

noncommittal *adj.* equivocal, undecided, indecisive, (slang) on the fence, guarded, cautious. *I'm still noncommittal about the election in November.* **Ant.** committed, certain, decisive.

nonconformist *n.* individualist, eccentric, freethinker, dissenter, rebel, original. *She was considered a nonconformist because she liked to do things her own way.* **Ant.** conformist, follower.

nondescript *adj.* indescribable, undistinctive, plain, vague, undistinguished, amorphous. *He had a perfectly forgettable, nondescript face.* **Ant.** distinctive, distinguished, eye-catching.

nonexistent *adj.* inexistent, made up, imaginary, fictitious, mythical, hypothetical. *Human rights are nonexistent as far as most tyrants are concerned.*

nonpartisan *adj.* independent, centrist, neutral, unbiased, objective, individualistic. *We need more nonpartisan politics and less infighting.* **Ant.** partisan, leftist, rightist.

nonprofit *n.* underwritten, funded, charitable, sponsored, subsidized, supported. *Most philanthropic organizations are nonprofit businesses.* **Ant.** for-profit.

nonsense *n.* silliness, stupidity, folly, foolishness, senselessness. *How much more of this nonsense do we have to take?* **Ant.** sense, reason.

nonsensical *adj.* senseless, silly, absurd, foolish, preposterous, incomprehensible. *Many people believed that Robert Goddard's ideas for spaceflight were nonsensical.* **Ant.** serious, astute, sensible.

nonviolence *n.* peace, peacefulness, pacifism, nonaggression, passive resistance, peacefulness. *We believe we can bring about change through nonviolence.*

nook *n.* niche, recess, cranny, corner, inglenook, alcove. *It's cozier to eat in the breakfast nook than in the dining room.*

norm *n.* standard, average, the usual, mean, rule, accepted practice. *Having one hundred inches of snow or more a year is the norm for northern Maine.* **Ant.** anomaly, oddity, abnormality.

normal *adj.* usual, standard, average, typical, routine, ordinary. *It was a pretty normal day until the flying saucer arrived.* **Ant.** unusual, abnormal, odd.

nose *n.* snout, olfactory organ, proboscis, (slang) sniffer, (slang) snoot, (slang) beak. *I have a cold and my nose is running like a faucet.*

nostalgia *n.* longing, wistfulness, pining, remembrance. *Sixties music gives my mother a sense of nostalgia.*

nosy *adj.* curious, prying, snooping, meddlesome, inquisitive. *The nosy guest peered in our closets.*

notable *adj.* noteworthy, distinguished, important, prominent. *She has made notable contributions to the field of biology.* **Ant.** unimportant, inconsequential.

notarize *vb.* authenticate, certify, witness, endorse, validate, register. *You will have to notarize your signature to validate your contract.*

notch *n.* nick, groove, cleft, gouge, slice, scratch. *I put a notch in the door to measure how tall my son had grown in a year.*

note *vb.* **1.** notice, regard, observe, watch, perceive. *Please note the differences between the two species of moths.* –*n.* **2.** message, record, memo, memorandum, letter. *Leave a note on the bulletin board.* **3.** notice, heed, regard, attention, mark. *Did you take note of the deadline for term papers?* **4.** bills, currency, banknote, legal tender. *The ransom was to be paid in ten- and twenty-dollar notes.* **Ant.** **1.** ignore, disregard, neglect. **3.** unconcern, indifference.

notebook *n.* tablet, binder, scratch pad, journal, log, chronicle. *I left my homework assignment in my notebook.*

nothingness *n.* zero, void, naught, nil, (slang) zilch, (slang) zip, (slang) nada. *The universe is made up largely of nothingness.*

notice *vb.* **1.** see, observe, heed, note, recognize. *Did you notice the size of that wrestler?* –*n.* **2.** attention, regard, interest, concern, note. *She took notice of the unsafe conditions at the factory.* **3.** announcement, bulletin, sign, statement, notification. *He received a notice regarding his overdue bills.* **Ant.** **1.** miss, overlook, disregard. **2.** unawareness, inattention.

notify *vb.* inform, advise, tell, mention, reveal, apprise. *Please notify me when the king arrives.*

notion *n.* idea, belief, thought, view, opinion, concept. *Where did you get such a weird notion?*

notoriety *n.* infamy, scandal, disrepute, disgrace, dishonor, shame. *Billy the Kid achieved much notoriety.* **Ant.** honor, esteem, standing.

notorious *adj.* infamous, renowned, celebrated, scandalous. *Los Angeles is notorious for its smog.*

nourish *vb.* nurture, feed, support, supply, sustain, strengthen. *You need some fertilizer to nourish your plants.* **Ant.** starve, deprive.

nourishing *adj.* nutritious, fortifying, sustaining, filling, replenishing. *That was a very nourishing meal.*

nourishment *n.* food, sustenance, support, nutrition. *The starving kitten was in need of nourishment.*

novel *adj.* original, new, unusual, unique, different, imaginative, odd, strange. *The movie had a novel conclusion.* **Ant.** unoriginal, usual, common, typical.

novel *n.* book, story, fiction, narrative, best-seller, saga, tale. *A novel is more complex than a short story.*

novelist *n.* author, writer, wordsmith, storyteller, (slang) hack. *Stephen King is my favorite novelist.*

novelty *n.* **1.** change, innovation, originality, variation, surprise. *Ethiopian food was a novelty to her.* **2.** knickknack, curio, trinket, bauble. *The Indian trading post offered many novelties.*

novice *n.* beginner, starter, learner, apprentice, trainee, newcomer, rookie. *All experts start out as novices.* **Ant.** master, expert, veteran.

now *adv.* presently, immediately, at once, instantly, directly. *Take out the trash now.* **Ant.** later, eventually, sometime.

noxious *adj.* toxic, harmful, poisonous, injurious, damaging, foul, lethal. *It is dangerous to work with noxious chemicals.* **Ant.** safe, harmless, healthful.

nozzle *n.* spout, valve, head, snout, conduit, sprayer. *Water is ejected from the nozzle at high velocity.*

nuance *n.* gradation, variation, shade, subtlety, distinction, refinement. *You'll notice a very slight nuance of flavor difference between cooking methods.*

nubile *adj.* sexually attractive, sexy, seductive, ripe, shapely, curvaceous, tempting. *Teenage boys are rarely indifferent to the nubile females around them.*

nuclear *adj.* atomic, subatomic, thermonuclear. *Nuclear power can be a negative or a positive force.*

nuclear bomb *n.* atomic bomb, hydrogen bomb, A-bomb, H-bomb, thermonuclear bomb, megaton weapon, kiloton weapon. *Few weapons are as destructive as a nuclear bomb.*

WORD SEARCH

atoms, splitting of: *fission*
billowing cloud following explosion: *mushroom cloud*
bomb that kills people but leaves buildings intact: *neutron bomb*
crude form that produces more radiation than blast effects: *dirty bomb*
detonation location: *ground zero*
electrical surges, blast effect causing damaging: *electromagnetic pulse*
fiery portion of blast: *firestorm*
illness from fallout: *radiation sickness*
minimum atomic material needed for chain reaction: *critical mass*
missile's bomb portion: *warhead*
precipitation of radioactive material: *fallout*

nucleus *n.* center, core, heart, focus, crux, basis. *We have three veteran players to form the nucleus of this year's team.*

nude *adj.* naked, unclothed, bare, au naturel, (slang) in the raw, (slang) in one's birthday suit, stripped. *Many people are uncomfortable on nude beaches.* **Ant.** clothed, attired, dressed.

nudge *vb.* **1.** push, shove, poke, jostle, touch, elbow. *He nudged her to get her attention.* –*n.* **2.** push, prod, poke, elbowing, punch, touch. *It will take more than a nudge to get the elephant to move.*

nuisance *n.* bother, annoyance, pest, pain, irritation, trouble, inconvenience. *Younger siblings can be a nuisance.* **Ant.** delight, blessing, pleasure, joy.

nuke *vb.* (slang) bomb, obliterate, destroy, incinerate, (slang) fry, (slang) blow back to the Stone Age, level. *The last thing any nation needs is a dictator who believes it's okay to nuke a rival nation.*

null *adj.* invalid, void, nonexistent, useless, ineffective, inoperative. *The election was declared null because of cheating.* **Ant.** valid, binding, useful.

nullify *vb.* cancel, negate, invalidate, kill, neutralize, revoke. *Congress may vote to nullify the current law and enact a new one.*

numb *adj.* unfeeling, deadened, insensitive, paralyzed, frozen. *I've been sitting cross-legged so long my legs are numb.* **Ant.** alive, responsive, sensitive.

number *n.* **1.** digit, figure, numeral, unit, integer. *What is the number of your hotel room?* **2.** amount, quantity, sum, total, volume, mass. *A large number of people are expected at the fair.* *–vb.* **3.** count, figure, total, calculate, add, estimate, reckon, tally. *She numbered the deer population at about five hundred.*

numerous *adj.* many, abundant, numberless, countless, plentiful. *It was only one of numerous ways he could have played that chess move.* **Ant.** few, scarce, limited.

nun *n.* sister, prioress, abbess, ecclesiast, mother superior. *Ask the nun to pray for you.*

nurse *n.* **1.** attendant, orderly, aide. *The nurse made sure his patient took her pills.* *–vb.* **2.** nurture, doctor attend, care for, nourish. *His family nursed him until he was well enough to take care of himself.*

nursery *n.* child care facility, day care center, nursery school, preschool. *We'll have to drop the children off at the nursery at nine o'clock.*

nursing home *n.* assisted living center, convalescent home, home for the elderly. *I'll move into a nursing home when I can no longer care for myself.*

nurture *vb.* **1.** nourish, feed, nurse, strengthen, sustain. *She nurtured the baby squirrel back to health.* **2.** raise, rear, develop, foster, support. *Imagination is a trait that must be nurtured.*

nut *n.* mental case, (slang) kook, (slang) weirdo, (slang) loon, (slang).

nutrient *n.* nutriment, mineral, vitamin, food, protein, carbohydrate. *You need dozens of different nutrients to keep you healthy.*

nutrition *n.* nourishment, food, sustenance, foodstuffs, nutrients. *The right nutrition is important to your health.*

nutritious *adj.* healthful, nourishing, wholesome, beneficial. *She starts each day with a nutritious breakfast.* **Ant.** unhealthful, unwholesome.

nuts *n.* crazy, insane, demented, deranged, cracked, (slang) potty, (slang) psycho screwball, (slang) nutter.

nylons *n.* stockings, hosiery, hose. *Is that a run I see in your nylons?*

O

oaf *n.* lummox, clod, clodhopper, dunce, ignoramus, (slang) klutz. *Nobody suspected he was an oaf until he got on the dance floor.*

oak *n.* acorn tree, shade tree, hardwood. *I'm going to take a nap under the oak tree.*

oar *n.* paddle, scull, pole, blade. *Paddle with your oar toward shore.*

oasis *n.* **1.** spring, watering hole, wadi. *We would have died of thirst if it hadn't been for the oasis.* **2.** sanctuary, refuge, haven, asylum. *The restaurant was an oasis in a desert of greasy spoons.*

oath *n.* **1.** vow, avowal, pledge, bond, promise. *Every elected official must take an oath of office.* **2.** swearword, swearing, curse, profanity, blasphemy. *He yelled an oath at the reckless driver.* **Ant. 2.** blessing, benediction.

obedience *n.* compliance, submission, deference, subservience. *The dictator demanded complete obedience from his underlings.* **Ant.** rebellion, opposition, defiance.

obedient *adj.* dutiful, obliging, respectful, obeying, submissive, compliant. *The soldiers were obedient to their commanding officer.* **Ant.** disloyal, disobedient, rebellious.

obelisk *n.* monolith, monument, shaft, column, tower, pylon. *The obelisk was tall enough to see for miles around.*

obese *adj.* fat, overweight, heavy, plump, portly, fleshy, stout. *The obese woman had trouble climbing the stairs.* **Ant.** underweight, skinny, thin, lean.

obesity *n.* fatness, plumpness, overweight, corpulence, rotundness, chubbiness. *A diet rich in fat and sugar may result in obesity.* **Ant.** thinness, skinniness, emaciation.

obey *vb.* follow, comply, submit, observe, respect, heed, conform. *Always obey the law.* **Ant.** disobey, defy, resist, refuse.

obituary *n.* obit, death notice, necrology. *I read my old school chum's obituary with great sadness.*

object *n.* **1.** thing, article, form, device, entity. *What is that object over there?* **2.** goal, aim, purpose, objective, target, end, point. *The object of this game is to put the ball in the basket.* –*vb.* **3.** oppose, protest, disapprove, complain, refuse, challenge. *He objected to the unfairness of the test.* **Ant. 3.** approve, agree, praise, assent.

objection *n.* disapproval, opposition, disagreement, protest, complaint. *Do you have any objections to the change in plans?* **Ant.** agreement, approval, acceptance.

objectionable *adj.* disagreeable, undesirable, unbefitting, unacceptable, offensive, unpleasant. *Objectionable odors rose from the garbage bin.* **Ant.** acceptable, pleasant, welcome.

objective *adj.* **1.** impartial, impersonal, unprejudiced, unbiased, detached, fair. *We want a judge who will be objective about our case.* –*n.*

2. goal, purpose, aim, object, intention, mission, target. *The secret agent's objective was to destroy the missile site.* **Ant.** 1. biased, prejudiced, subjective.

objectivity *n.* neutrality, detachment, dispassion, disinterest, fairness. *The only fair way to referee a game is with complete objectivity.* **Ant.** subjectivity, bias, prejudice.

obligation *n.* 1. agreement, contract, stipulation, commitment, pledge, promise. *We met our legal obligations by giving part of our profits to the building fund.* 2. duty, responsibility, requirement, liability, debt. *Doctors have an obligation to cure the sick.* **Ant.** 2. choice, freedom, decision.

obligatory *adj.* required, necessary, essential, binding, compulsory, peremptory. *The president tossed out the obligatory first pitch.* **Ant.** optional, unnecessary.

oblige *vb.* 1. require, obligate, compel, force, coerce, make, constrain, bind. *Since you broke the glass, you are obliged to buy it.* 2. favor, please, serve, accommodate, help, assist. *The waiter obliged her with a complimentary dessert.* **Ant.** 1. free, release, option. 2. displease, disfavor.

oblique *adj.* slanting, inclined, angled, askew, sloping, canted, leaning. *That painting is hung at a slightly oblique angle.* **Ant.** level, straight, balanced.

obliterate *vb.* 1. destroy, annihilate, raze, level, ruin, crush. *The bombers obliterated an entire town.* 2. erase, remove, delete, blot, cancel. *A coffee spill obliterated several names and numbers in her address book.* **Ant.** 1. build, restore, create. 2. add, keep, preserve.

oblivious *adj.* unaware, unobservant, unmindful, heedless, neglectful. *The driver was oblivious to the honking cars.* **Ant.** aware, mindful, conscious, heedful.

obnoxious *adj.* annoying, offensive, objectionable, unpleasant, disagreeable. *He's been obnoxious ever since he won the argument.* **Ant.** pleasant, agreeable, congenial.

obscene *adj.* vulgar, indecent, offensive, pornographic, foul, dirty. *There was too much obscene language in the play.* **Ant.** clean, decent, proper, acceptable.

obscenity *n.* 1. swear word, cuss word, curse, four-letter word, expletive oath. *Uttering an obscenity may be acceptable if you've just dropped an anvil on your toe.* 2. indecency, offensiveness, filth, lewdness, vulgarity, dirtiness, pornography. *Your town's obscenity laws may prohibit the selling of pornography.*

obscure *adj.* 1. unclear, vague, indistinct, uncertain, puzzling. *The meaning of his writings remains obscure.* 2. unknown, unnoticed, undiscovered, nameless, insignificant, minor. *The painting was by an obscure French artist.* –*vb.* 3. confuse, confound, muddle, cloud, mask, bewilder. *Don't obscure the issue.* 4. cover, hide, screen, shade, veil, block, conceal. *Dense forest obscured our view.* **Ant.** 1. clear, distinct, obvious. 2. famous, renown, celebrated. 3. clarify, clear, simplify. 4. reveal, expose, uncover.

obsequious *adj.* servile, fawning, compliant, submissive, toadying, ingratiating. *You don't need to be obsequious with your teacher, just respectful.* **Ant.** defiant, rebellious, domineering.

observant *adj.* watchful, vigilant, alert, attentive, perceptive. *An observant person will be able to spot the owl in the tree.* **Ant.** inattentive, careless, unobservant.

observation *n.* 1. watching, viewing, seeing, examination, observance, notice. *The police continued their observation of the suspect's house.* 2. comment, opinion, remark, view, assertion, declaration. *Your observation that the professor was* *angry is unnecessary.* **Ant. 1.** inattention, neglect, ignoring.

observe *vb.* **1.** watch, see, notice, witness, view, behold. *Please observe how the tennis player swings her racket.* **2.** celebrate, keep, honor, commemorate, remember. *My family observes the religious holidays.* **3.** obey, follow, heed, respect, comply, conform. *A tourist must observe the laws of the country that he or she is visiting.* **Ant. 1.** ignore, disregard, overlook. **2.** dishonor, violate, profane. **3.** disobey, break, infringe.

observer *n.* watcher, eyewitness, examiner, inspector, onlooker, lookout. *The fish and game department sent out an observer to watch for illegal poaching.*

obsessed *adj.* fixated, driven, preoccupied, crazed, possessed, consumed, gripped. *Obsessed with football, he watched three games in a row.*

obsession *n.* passion, compulsion, mania, fixation, preoccupation. *He has an obsession for antique cars.*

obsolete *adj.* old-fashioned, outdated, outmoded, dated, extinct, antiquated. *Calculators have made the slide rule obsolete.* **Ant.** current, fashionable, new, modern.

obstacle *n.* barrier, obstruction, hurdle, hindrance, impediment. *Heat and exhaustion were the marathon runner's primary obstacles.* **Ant.** aid, help, advantage.

obstetrics *n.* tocology, labor and delivery, midwifery, childbirth. *Obstetrics is an important branch of medicine.*

obstinate *adj.* stubborn, headstrong, inflexible, unyielding, determined. *The obstinate salesperson would not lower her price.* **Ant.** flexible, pliable, yielding.

obstruction *n.* obstacle, barrier, block, impediment, interference, barricade, bar. *The fallen tree was an obstruction to traffic.* **Ant.** freeing, clearing, aid, opening.

obtain *vb.* get, gain, acquire, achieve, secure, procure, attain. *The warrior's task was to obtain the ring of power.* **Ant.** lose, relinquish, surrender, give.

obtrusive *adj.* **1.** interfering, intruding, pushy, meddlesome, bold, forward. *I would be finished with my work if my boss were not so obtrusive.* **2.** prominent, outstanding, protruding, glaring, conspicuous, obvious. *A giraffe would be obtrusive in a herd of horses.* **Ant. 1.** reserved, patient, unassuming. **2.** concealed, inconspicuous.

obvious *adj.* plain, clear, unmistakable, evident, visible, apparent, distinct. *There was an obvious tone of distress in her voice.* **Ant.** indistinct, obscure, subtle, hidden.

occasion *n.* **1.** time, event, occurrence, incident, juncture, moment. *The wedding was a special occasion for all.* **2.** opportunity, chance, excuse, break, opening. *You might not get another occasion to speak.*

occasional *adj.* irregular, random, infrequent, sporadic, rare. *Except for an occasional hiker, this wilderness is unpopulated.* **Ant.** regular, frequent, constant.

occasionally *adv.* sometimes, irregularly, sporadically, periodically. *I occasionally get an overwhelming desire for a banana split.* **Ant.** continuously, regularly, usually, often.

occult *adj.* supernatural, mystical, magical, esoteric, arcane, secret, otherworldly. *She liked reading about psychic predictions and other occult practices.*

occupant *n.* resident, tenant, inhabitant, lodger, dweller, occupier. *The last occupants left the apartment in a mess.*

occupation *n.* **1.** profession, trade, calling, business, vocation, work, employment, job, pursuit. *Electronics has been his occupation for ten years.* **2.** conquest, control, ownership, rule, possession. *The British occupation of India ended in 1947.*

occupied *adj.* busy, preoccupied, engaged, employed, engrossed. *The bathroom is occupied.*

occupy *vb.* **1.** dwell, live, reside, inhabit, use, hold, utilize. *She occupied this apartment till last summer.* **2.** employ, engage, use, fill, busy, engross, entertain. *During the slow hours, the security guard occupied himself by reading.* **3.** seize, capture, conquer, obtain, control. *The soldiers were ordered to occupy the seaport.* **Ant. 1.** vacate, depart, leave. **3.** surrender, evacuate, liberate.

occur *vb.* happen, arise, befall, transpire, take place, develop, appear. *When will the next eclipse occur?*

occurrence *n.* event, incident, occasion, happening, episode, affair, experience. *The lunar landing was an unforgettable occurrence.*

ocean *n.* sea, body of water, expanse, (slang) bounding main, the deep, the abyss. *In 1492, Columbus sailed the ocean blue.*

WORD SEARCH

bottom, any one region of: *province*
bottom depression: *cauldron*
current, Atlantic's famous: *Gulf Stream*
current of Pacific that alters weather patterns worldwide: *El Niño*
currents, circular: *gyres*
depth measurement, six-foot: *fathom*
windless, flat calm region: *doldrums*
foam: *spume*
mountain under: *seamount*
shallow area presenting danger to boats: *shoals*
spray: *spindrift*
study of: *oceanography*
tides, maximum: *spring tide*
tides, minimum: *neap tide*
wave, giant: *tsunami*
waves: *plunger, spiller, swell, graybeard*
waves that oppose and crash into one another: *cross seas*

odd *adj.* **1.** unusual, strange, weird, extraordinary, peculiar, bizarre, curious. *There are some pretty odd characters in* Alice in Wonderland. **2.** rare, irregular, chance, infrequent, sporadic. *On odd occasions Grandfather would pick up his guitar and sing folk songs.* **3.** single, uneven, unmatched, leftover, surplus, remaining. *Why do I always end up with an odd sock when I do laundry?* **Ant. 1.** normal, usual, ordinary, typical. **2.** regular, frequent, common. **3.** matched, even, mated.

oddity *n.* abnormality, irregularity, peculiarity, anomaly, strangeness, quirk. *Snowfall in July is quite an oddity here.*

odds *n.* chances, probability, likelihood, prospects, expectation. *The odds of my being struck by lightning are slightly better than my winning the lottery.*

odds and ends bits and pieces, hodgepodge, melange, assortment, oddments, miscellany. *We hope to dispose of a lot of odds and ends at the yard sale.*

ode *n.* poem, lyric, song, hymn. *I'm penning an ode to my sweetheart.*

odious *adj.* offensive, revolting, repugnant, disgusting, detestable, abhorrent. *I had the odious task of shoveling out the horse stalls.*

odor *n.* scent, smell, aroma, essence, stench, stink. *She could not remove the unpleasant odor from her kitchen.*

odyssey *n.* journey, voyage, quest, journey, trek, sojourn. *We are going on an odyssey to Arizona.*

off-balance *adj.* unsteady, unbalanced, unstable, leaning, toppling, tipping. *The washing machine tends to jump around when it is off-balance.* **Ant.** balanced, steady, stable.

off-beat *adj.* unusual, abnormal, weird, strange, quirky, unconventional. *He liked attention, so he wore a lot of offbeat clothes.* **Ant.** conventional, usual, traditional.

off-center *adj.* off kilter, misaligned, off-balance, askew, eccentric. *That painting is slightly off-center.*

off-color *adj.* suggestive, dirty, raunchy, indelicate, risque, tasteless. *Please, no off-color jokes during class.*

offend *vb.* displease, annoy, irritate, anger, provoke, upset, disturb. *His bad manners offended everyone.* **Ant.** please, delight, charm.

offender *n.* violator, perpetrator, culprit, malefactor, law-breaker, sinner. *The offender was given a short prison sentence.*

offense *n.* **1.** violation, crime, felony, misdemeanor, infraction, transgression. *The defendant was charged with several offenses.* **2.** insult, disrespect, affront, outrage. *He meant no offense by his comment about her appearance.*

offensive *adj.* insulting, obnoxious, rude, repugnant, revolting, sickening, nasty. *The comedian made offensive use of obscenities.* **Ant.** pleasing, respectful.

offer *vb.* **1.** propose, submit, suggest, advance, volunteer. *She offered a suggestion on how to cut expenses.* **2.** give, present, bestow, provide, show. *If you offer the dog a bone, he won't bite you.* –*n.* **3.** proposal, proposition, bid, suggestion, invitation. *He made me an offer that I could not refuse.*

offering *n.* donation, contribution, tithe, gift, sacrifice, alms, charity. *In church, we gave an offering of ten dollars.*

off-guard *adj.* **1.** unready, unprepared, unwary, careless, asleep, napping. *The boxer was off-guard and got slugged in the face.* –*vb.* **2.** unready, unprepared, unwary *We were caught off-guard and got completely soaked by the down-pour.* **Ant.** ready, prepared, alert.

offhand *adj.* **1.** unprepared, spur of the moment, impromptu, extemporaneous, unrehearsed, ad-lib. *His offhand speech was given without notes or preparation.* **2.** careless, brusque, abrupt, curt, terse, blunt. *She made an offhand comment that hurt my feelings.* **Ant. 1.** prepared, rehearsed, planned. **2.** thoughtful, tactful.

office *n.* **1.** position, post, role, capacity, function, duty, task, job. *The office of treasurer is open for nominations.* **2.** working space, room, suite, headquarters. *Come into my office, and we'll discuss the matter.*

officer *n.* policeman, policewoman, patrolman, constable, magistrate, lawman, (slang) cop, detective. *The officer kindly gave us a warning instead of a ticket.*

official *adj.* **1.** authorized, approved, formal, authentic, real, sanctioned. *The order is not official until the judge signs it.* –*n.* **2.** officer, executive, administrator, commissioner, agent. *An official from the government investigated the accident.* **Ant. 1.** unofficial, informal, unauthorized.

officiate *vb.* referee, umpire, oversee, supervise, manage, direct, chair. *We need an emcee to officiate at the conference.*

officious *adj.* meddlesome, prying, obtrusive, intrusive, interfering. *My mother-in-law can be bossy and officious at times.*

off-key *adj.* out of tune, flat, sharp, off-pitch, dissonant, discordant. *I tend to be tone-deaf, so I sing off-key a lot.* **Ant.** in tune

off-limits *adj.* restricted, prohibited, forbidden, banned, illegal, unlawful. *The oil refinery is off-limits to children.* **Ant.** unrestricted, open, free.

offspring *n.* progeny, children, young, spawn, descendants, heirs. *The mother bear will viciously protect its offspring from harm.*

often *adv.* frequently, regularly, repeatedly, constantly, usually, generally. *The stores are often crowded on weekends.* **Ant.** never, rarely, seldom.

ogle *vb.* eyeball, gaze, gawk, stare, leer, gape. *He went to the dance to ogle the girls.*

ogre *n.* giant, brute, monster, beast, caveman, bogeyman. *The hunchbacked ogre lurking in the forest was really just a play of shadows.*

oil *n.* petroleum, crude, lubricant, (slang) black gold, flammable liquid, grease. *We need plenty of heating oil for winter.*

ointment *n.* emollient, unguent, salve, balm, medicament. *I need some of that ointment to soothe my poison ivy.*

old *adj.* **1.** aged, elderly, aging, mature, ancient. *You're only as old as you feel.* **2.** worn-out, shabby, used, decaying, ragged, faded. *This old sweater is ready to fall apart.* **3.** past, bygone, olden, former. *My parents are always talking about the "good old days."* **Ant. 1.** young, immature, youthful. **2.** unused, new, fresh. **3.** recent, ongoing, current.

old-fashioned *adj.* outdated, antiquated, outmoded, obsolete, dated, conservative. *My neighbor uses an old-fashioned push mower.* **Ant.** new, modern, cutting-edge.

Olympics *n.* world championships, tournament, athletic competition, contest, Olympiad, games. *My favorite event in the winter Olympics is the luge.*

omen *n.* sign, warning, portent, indication, foreboding. *The Navajos believe that owls are an omen of death.*

ominous *adj.* sinister, threatening, menacing, disquieting, fateful, dire. *That ominous-looking castle is owned by the local vampire.* **Ant.** promising, favorable, encouraging

omission *n.* oversight, exclusion, exception, deletion. *We must take care to avoid omissions when compiling a dictionary.*

omit *vb.* **1.** delete, remove, exclude, skip, drop. *We omitted the offensive part of the story.* **2.** neglect, ignore, overlook, fail, avoid, forget. *The guide omitted telling the hikers about the swamp.* **Ant. 1.** add, return, include. **2.** remember, recall, recollect.

omitted *adj.* excluded, left out, overlooked, forgotten, expunged, passed over. *I'm afraid your name was accidently omitted from the honor roll.* **Ant.** included, put in, covered.

omnipotent *adj.* all-powerful, almighty, god-like, supreme. *Omnipotent rulers are unquestionably dangerous.* **Ant.** impotent, weak, ineffectual.

omniscient *adj.* all-knowing, all-seeing, god-like. *Even the most omniscient observer can overlook a detail.*

once *adv.* previously, formerly, earlier, before. *Once upon a time there was a beautiful princess.*

onerous *adj.* burdensome, troublesome, laborious, oppressive, arduous, demanding. *I have the onerous responsibility of painting the entire house.* **Ant.** easy, effortless, simple.

one-sided *adj.* biased, partial, unbalanced, partisan, slanted. *The argument was largely one-sided, but only because opponents weren't in attendance.* **Ant.** balanced, fair, unbiased.

on-line *adj.* connected, linked, plugged in, wired. *Go online and I'll send you an instant message.*

only *adj.* **1.** sole, single, solitary, alone, exclusive, unique. *This is the only gas station within a hundred miles.* –*adv.* **2.** just, merely, simply, solely, singly. *I only wanted to talk to you.* **Ant. 1.** many, several, numerous. **2.** also, furthermore, additionally.

ooze *vb.* seep, drip, trickle, leak, flow, drain, dribble. *Sap oozed from the tree.*

opaque *adj.* impenetrable, impervious, nontransparent, murky, unclear, abstruse. *The window grew increasingly opaque with condensation.* **Ant.** clear, transparent, lucid.

open *adj.* **1.** unclosed, uncovered, ajar, unshut, gaping. *He walked through the open door.* **2.** accessible, available, reachable, unrestricted, public. *The library is open on weekdays.* **3.** wide, expansive, exposed, clear. *Wild horses grazed on the open plains.* **4.** candid, free, honest, frank, fair, sincere, plain. *It is best to be open about your feelings.* **5.** unbiased, unprejudiced, impartial, objective, fair. *The professor has an open mind to any opposing theories.* –*vb.* **6.** unclose, unlock, unfasten, clear, unblock. *Please open the door.* **7.** begin, start, initiate, commence, launch, embark. *We will open our business in July.* **8.** expand, spread, extend, unfold, unfurl. *The bud opened to unveil a beautiful flower.* **Ant. 1–2.** closed, shut. **3.** narrow, cramped. **4.** closed, quiet, reserved. **5.** biased, prejudiced, intolerant. **6.** close, lock, seal. **7.** end, stop, terminate. **8.** shut, fold, close.

open-minded *adj.* receptive, broad-minded, liberal, accepting, impartial, tolerant. *A good politician must be open-minded at all times.* **Ant.** closed-minded, narrow-minded, intolerant.

opera *n.* musical, melodrama, libretto, drame lyrique, musical performance. *Opera is a show in which a performer gets his toes stepped on and then he sings about it.*

WORD SEARCH

comic opera: *buffa*
composition with several arias, duets, choruses: *cantata*
director: *impresario*
high pitch, false: *falsetto*
lead female: *prima donna, diva*
lead male: *primo uomo*
vocal solo, long: *aria*
voice, booming bass: *basso profundo*
voice, lowest female: *contralto*
voice, lowest male: *bass*

operate *vb.* work, run, use, perform, handle, manage. *I'm learning how to operate a sewing machine.*

operation *n.* **1.** performance, functioning, working, action, operating, running. *The mechanics checked the operation of the racing car.* **2.** force, effect, action, use, application, play. *Plan B will go into operation at midnight.*

WORD SEARCH

anesthetic agent: *ether*
anesthetic through unconsciousness: *general anesthesia*
anesthetic used to deaden sensation in a specific area: *local anesthetic*
appendix removal: *appendectomy*
birth delivery through abdomen: *cesarean section, C-section*
blood vessel flow, restores: *angioplasty, bypass*
brain, removal of small front portion: *lobotomy*
brain, spinal cord or nerve: *neurosurgery*
breast removal: *mastectomy*
cutting into flesh: *incising*
cyst removal: *cystectomy*
kidney removal: *nephrectomy*
nose-enhancing surgery: *rhinoplasty*

organ replacement: *transplant*
stitching up of wound: *suturing*
tissue removal: *excision*
tissue sampling: *biopsy*
tonsil removal: *tonsillectomy*
transplant of body tissue from one place to another: *graft*
tumor removal: *lumpectomy*
uterus removal: *hysterectomy*

opinion *n.* viewpoint, belief, conviction, view, idea, judgment, feeling. *Everyone is entitled to his or her own opinion.*

opium *n.* opiate, narcotic, soporific, laudanum, drug. *Opium is an illicit drug.*

opponent *n.* competitor, enemy, foe, adversary, rival, contestant, challenger. *The tennis player was well matched with his opponent.* **Ant.** colleague, ally, partner, teammate.

opportunity *n.* chance, occasion, time, turn, moment, advantage, opening. *The actress had an opportunity to star in a major film.*

oppose *vb.* defy, resist, protest, battle, contest, withstand, confront. *Pacifists oppose the use of violence.* **Ant.** support, endorse, advocate, defend.

opposite *adj.* **1.** conflicting, opposing, different, diverse, contrary, unlike. *Their friendship ended because of their opposite views on music.* **2.** facing, other, reverse, converse. *The football teams lined up on opposite sides of the field.* **Ant.** **1.** parallel, similar, consistent. **2.** same, identical, exact.

opposition *n.* **1.** resistance, rejection, disagreement, hostility, defiance, disapproval. *The opposition to her new tax proposal was overwhelming.* **2.** opponent, competitor, contender, rival, adversary, foe. *The score is tied, but the opposition has the ball.* **Ant.** **1.** approval, support, backing. **2.** ally, colleague, supporter.

oppress *vb.* subdue, tyrannize, keep down, crush, subjugate, depress, stifle, dominate. *The dictator tends to oppress his people.* **Ant.** liberate, emancipate, free.

oppressed *adj.* downtrodden, subdued, tyrannized, dominated, misused, burdened. *Nelson Mandela worked tirelessly to give hope to the oppressed people of his country.* **Ant.** free, liberated, empowered.

oppression *n.* tyranny, subjugation, domination, control, abuse, subjection, force. *The despot rules by oppression.* **Ant.** freedom, liberation, emancipation.

oppressive *adj.* **1.** tyrannical, cruel, brutal, harsh, repressive. *The people rebelled against their oppressive dictator.* **2.** burdensome, trying, depressing, overpowering, discouraging, difficult, exacting. *It can be oppressive to accept too many duties at one time.* **Ant.** **1.** liberating, humane, just. **2.** heartening, encouraging.

optimal *adj.* optimum, best, greatest, favorable, top, superlative. *The optimal time to see a rainbow is after a rain shower.* **Ant.** worst, unfavorable, terrible.

optimism *n.* positive thinking, hopefulness, enthusiasm, belief, confidence, buoyancy, bullishness. *Many underprivileged people have succeeded through sheer hard work and optimism.* **Ant.** pessimism, doubt, negative thinking.

optimistic *adj.* **1.** hopeful, hoping, confident, expectant, upbeat, assured. *The writer was optimistic about selling his book.* **2.** promising, encouraging, favorable, hopeful. *The optimistic weather forecast convinced them to go ahead with their picnic.* **Ant.** **1.** pessimistic, despairing. **2.** unpromising, unfavorable.

optimum *adj.* ideal, best, top, optimal, greatest, utmost. *The optimum time to go fishing may be early in the morning.* **Ant.** lowest, worst, poorest.

option *n.* choice, selection, election, alternative, preference, possibility. *They had the option of traveling in the storm or stopping at a hotel.* **Ant.** requirement, compulsion, necessity.

optional *adj.* voluntary, elective, unforced, discretional. *We are conducting an optional course in self-defense.* **Ant.** mandatory, required, compulsory.

opulent *adj.* rich, wealthy, lavish, affluent, well-off, plush, swank. *She lives in an opulent neighborhood.* **Ant.** poor, modest, indigent.

opus *n.* composition, work, volume, production, piece, score. *My latest opus, a novel, is 856 pages long.*

oracle *n.* prophet, seer, augur, prognosticator, fortune-teller, diviner, sage. *She unwisely consulted an oracle for predictions of her future.*

oral *adj.* verbal, spoken, said, uttered, vocal, voiced, vocalized, verbalized. *Had I known this was an oral exam, I would not have brought pen and paper.*

orange *adj.* reddish-yellow, salmon, peach, fox, flaming, mandarin, marigold. *The sunset painted the sky a brilliant orange.*

oration *n.* speech, talk, address, lecture, sermon, pontification. *Politicians must practice their skills in oration every day.*

orator *n.* speaker, lecturer, talker, speech-giver, preacher, pontificator. *The orator held the audience in rapt attention.*

orb *n.* sphere, spheroid, ball, globe, celestial body, moon. *The psychic gazed into her crystal orb and predicted that I would soon lose my money to a scam artist.*

orbit *n.* **1.** course, revolution, path, cycle, route, circuit. *Pluto's orbit around the Sun takes 247.7 years.* –*vb.* **2.** circle, revolve, rotate, encircle, compass. *Scientists tried to contact the alien ship as it orbited Earth.*

orchard *n.* grove, plantation, stand, tree farm, vineyard, garden. *Let's go to the orchard and pick some apples.*

orchestra *n.* symphony, ensemble, band, philharmonic, combo, quintet. *The orchestra played beautifully last night.*

orchestrate *vb.* arrange, direct, coordinate, conduct, lead, manage. *We need a leader who can orchestrate the actions of dozens of employees at the same time.*

ordain *vb.* appoint, install, instate, induct, pronounce, consecrate. *The church will ordain a new priest tomorrow.*

ordeal *n.* trial, test, hardship, torment, suffering, affliction, misery, pain. *The old prospector told us about his ordeal of being trapped in a mine.* **Ant.** delight, joy, relief.

order *n.* **1.** command, instruction, demand, direction, rule, mandate, decree. *Who gave the order to move the tables?* **2.** arrangement, system, method, sequence, organization, pattern. *The clerk files all certificates in numerical order.* **3.** peace, harmony, calm, control, discipline. *Let's have some order around here.* **4.** shipment, placement, merchandise, consignment. *My order arrived early.* **5.** condition, shape, commission, state, form. *The repairman checked the appliances to see if they were in working order.* –*vb.* **6.** command, instruct, dictate, direct, decree, require, compel. *A police officer order him to drop his gun.* **7.** arrange, classify, organize, file, align, array. *She ordered the agenda by placing the most important item on top.* **8.** purchase, request, obtain, reserve, buy. *He likes to order merchandise by mail.* **Ant. 1.** request, plea, suggestion. **2.** mess, disarray. **3.** anarchy, chaos, disorder. **6.** ask, request, plead. **7.** scramble, confuse.

orderly *adj.* 1. well-behaved, quiet, civil, controlled, disciplined, peaceful. *The crowd remained orderly throughout the day.* 2. methodical, systematic, neat, ordered, organized, regulated, uniform. *The books were aligned on the shelves in an orderly fashion.* **Ant.** 1. disorderly, undisciplined. 2. disorganized, unsystematic.

ordinance *n.* law, rule, regulation, fiat, command, edict. *The town has an ordinance prohibiting dogs on the beach during summer.*

ordinarily *adv.* normally, usually, generally, regularly, primarily. *Ordinarily I wouldn't do this sort of work.* **Ant.** rarely, occasionally, sporadically.

ordinary *adj.* 1. common, usual, normal, customary, conventional, regular, standard. *The instructor taught the class in her ordinary manner.* 2. plain, simple, unimpressive, unexceptional, commonplace. *I was surprised to see the millionaire dressed in ordinary clothes.* **Ant.** 1. unique, rare unusual. 2. exceptional, extraordinary.

organic *adj.* 1. living, alive, animate, biological. *Scientists are looking for signs of organic material on Mars.* 2. natural, unadulterated, nonchemical. *I like my vegetables to be organically grown, without pesticides or artificial fertilizers.* **Ant.** nonliving, inanimate, dead. 2. artificial, adulterated.

organism *n.* life, form, being, animal, creature, plant, cell. *We examined the pond's organisms under the microscope.*

organization *n.* 1. group, association, alliance, society, league, club. *Our organization was formed with the purpose of preserving our local landmarks.* 2. arrangement, structure, plan, form, formulation, order. *The lack of organization in the meeting was obvious.* **Ant.** 2. confusion, chaos, disorder.

organize *vb.* 1. arrange, order, classify, sort, group, catalog, categorize. *Please organize the applications in alphabetical order.* 2. found, start, form, establish, create, develop. *We organized a coin-collector's club.* **Ant.** 1. disorganize, disarrange, scramble. 2. dissolve, disband.

orgasm *n.* climax, ejaculation, shudder, throes, shiver, convulsion. *The male ejaculates sperm into the females at the point of orgasm.*

orient *vb.* orientate, situate, locate, position, fix, take bearings. *It is exceedingly difficult to orient yourself deep in the Maine woods.*

orifice *n.* opening, mouth, aperture, hole, cavity, slot. *The creature had a tiny orifice, which we assumed was its mouth.*

origin *n.* beginning, source, start, basis, foundation, root, birth, cause. *The origins of our nation should be taught to all citizens.* **Ant.** end, finish, termination.

original *adj.* 1. first, primary, initial, beginning, earliest. *The original owners of the house moved out years ago.* 2. creative, new, novel, unique, inventive, imaginative, fresh, different. *Her drama was one of the most original plays I've ever seen.* **Ant.** 1. next, secondary, final, last. 2. imitate, ordinary, old.

originality *n.* freshness, novelty, inventiveness, creativity, imagination, ingenuity. *His painting of pigs flying to the Moon won first prize for originality.*

originate *vb.* 1. begin, start, arise, commence, derive, spring. *The use of paper money originated in China.* 2. invent, create, devise, produce, discover, introduce, conceive. *He is known for originating the potion that makes people invisible.* **Ant.** 1. end, terminate, conclude. 2. imitate, copy, reproduce.

originator *n.* inventor, creator, father, mother, pioneer, architect, instigator. *The originator of the invention was granted a patent.*

ornament *n.* **1.** decoration, adornment, embellishment, trimming, ornamentation. *We hung party ornaments from the ceiling.* –*vb.* **2.** decorate, beautify, adorn, embellish, trim, garnish. *Her evening gown was ornamented with diamonds.*

ornamental *adj.* decorative, embellishing, enhancing, garnishing, beautifying. *Placing an angel on top of the Christmas tree is a nice ornamental touch.*

ornate *adj.* decorated, ornamental, elaborate, fancy, embellished, florid. *The necklace was very ornate.* **Ant.** plain, unadorned, undecorated.

orphan *n.* motherless child, fatherless child, waif, foundling, castaway, stray. *The orphan dreamed of having two parents.*

orphanage *n.* foster home, group home, institution, asylum, refuge. *The orphanage takes in parentless children of all ages.*

orthodox *adj.* traditional, accepted, conventional, established, standard. *His religious paintings are done in an orthodox style.* **Ant.** radical, unorthodox, unconventional.

oscillate *vb.* alternate, swing, vibrate, pulsate, flicker, waver, sway. *Caution lights set up along the highway were set to oscillate.*

osmosis *n.* diffusion, absorption, mingling, mixing, blending, commingling. *The plant takes in liquid through osmosis.*

ostensible *adj.* seeming, outward, apparent, evident, pretended, external. *The shopkeeper's ostensible reason for patronizing his rival's boutique was to find a bargain, but his real reason was to spy.* **Ant.** real, root, true.

ostentatious *adj.* vain, flaunting, pretentious, pompous, boastful, flashy, showy, conspicuous. *The country singer looked ostentatious in his rhinestone suit.* **Ant.** modest, simple, reserved.

ostracism *n.* banishment, exile, expulsion, rejection, shunning, excommunication. *The cult punished those who failed to follow the rules with ostracism.* **Ant.** inclusion, acceptance, welcoming.

ostracize *vb.* banish, exile, exclude, reject, shun, excommunicate. *The group will ostracize all those who break the laws.* **Ant.** include, welcome, accept.

other *adj.* **1.** additional, added, more, extra, further. *I have one other photograph to show you.* **2.** different, contrasting, alternate, separate, opposite. *The other version of the story has a bad ending.* **Ant.** **1.** less, fewer. **2.** alike, similar, identical.

otherworldly *adj.* alien, extraterrestrial, unearthly, ethereal, mystical, metaphysical. *His face appeared otherworldly, but in fact it was simply covered in mud.* **Ant.** terrestrial, earthly, mundane.

ottoman *n.* footstool, hassock, divan. *Rest your feet on the ottoman set before the sofa.*

oust *vb.* eject, expel, remove, dismiss, evict, banish. *An unruly spectator was ousted from the audience.* **Ant.** install, admit, invite, receive.

outback *n.* back country, wilderness, hinterland, wasteland, desert, barrens. *The outback is a wasteland largely inhabitable by humans.*

outbreak *n.* outburst, eruption, explosion, epidemic, upheaval. *Doctors are warning us about a possible outbreak of the flu.* **Ant.** decrease, waning, reduction.

outburst *n.* outbreak, explosion, eruption, outpouring, flood, rush, torrent. *His outburst of anger was sudden and unexpected.* **Ant.** control, restraint, repression.

outcast *n.* exile, outsider, derelict, outlaw, vagabond, castaway. *The scholar felt like an outcast among the athletes.*

outclass *vb.* exceed, surpass, outdo, outdistance, overshadow, transcend. *The boxer totally outclassed his opponent.*

outcome *n.* result, end, conclusion, consequence, effect, aftermath. *We are awaiting the outcome of the election.*

outcry *n.* cry, uproar, scream, clamor, tumult, shout, outburst. *There was an outcry of disagreement to the court's decision.* **Ant.** murmur, whispering, calm.

outdated *adj.* obsolete, old fashioned, outmoded, antiquated, passé, prehistoric. *Record players have become seriously outdated.* **Ant.** modern, innovative, cutting edge.

outdo *vb.* surpass, exceed, beat, excel, best, better, overcome, outshine, outclass. *She was determined to outdo her competition.* **Ant.** equal, match.

outdoorsman *n.* sportsman, woodsman, naturalist, camper, hiker, adventurer, hunter. *Old Joe hikes, fishes and hunts, and is a dyed-in-the-wool outdoorsman.* **Ant.** (slang) couch potato.

outer *adj.* outside, outward, external, exterior, remote, outlying. *The spaceship was headed for the outer edge of the galaxy.* **Ant.** inner, interior, inside, nearer.

outfit *n.* **1.** costume, clothing, ensemble, dress, garb. *The model was wearing a cute outfit.* **2.** group, company, troop, band, gang, team, crew. *His outfit from the army got together for a reunion.* *–vb.* **3.** equip, rig, furnish, supply, provide, provision. *Scuba divers must be outfitted with special equipment.*

outflow *n.* effluence, outpouring, gush, emanation, stream, effusion. *The outflow from the dam is carefully controlled, according to drought conditions.* **Ant.** influx, inflow, entrance.

outgoing *adj.* **1.** leaving, departing, outbound, exiting. *The outgoing traffic is especially heavy on Fridays.* **2.** sociable, friendly, warm, extroverted, unreserved. *He was chosen as the game show's host because he was so outgoing.* **Ant. 1.** entering, returning, approaching. **2.** reserved, shy, timid.

outgrowth *n.* result, consequence, effect, outcome, product, development. *Lower food prices were the outgrowth of a bountiful harvest.*

outhouse *n.* privy, toilet, backhouse, latrine, outbuilding. *The log cabin had no indoor plumbing, so we had to use an outhouse.*

outing *n.* trip, excursion, expedition, jaunt, junket. *We went on an outing to the zoo.*

outlandish *adj.* wild, weird, unusual, odd, offbeat, alien. *You see many outlandish costumes on Halloween.*

outlast *vb.* outlive, endure, prevail, outdistance, stand the test of time. *A stone building will likely outlast one made of wood.*

outlaw *n.* **1.** criminal, bandit, fugitive, lawbreaker, desperado, outcast, rebel. *Jesse James was a famous outlaw of the old West.* *–vb.* **2.** abolish, forbid, prohibit, exclude, ban, bar, banish. *Someone should outlaw singing in the shower.* **Ant. 2.** legalize, allow, permit.

outlet *n.* passage, channel, route, opening, vent, exit. *This lake's outlet is a stream that flows into the ocean.*

outline *n.* **1.** silhouette, shape, contour, frame, tracing, border, edge. *All they could see was the outline of the mountains in the early dawn.* **2.** sketch, summary, draft, plan, brief, scenario. *He provided the publisher with an outline of his novel.* *–vb.* **3.** summarize, brief, sketch, draft, trace. *Would you outline your planned activities for the week ahead?* **Ant. 2.** specifics, particulars.

outlook *n.* **1.** viewpoint, attitude, perspective, stance, angle, standpoint. *We would all benefit if* *we adopted a more positive outlook.* **2.** prospect, future, opportunity, chance, forecast, expectation, promise. *The outlook for her investment seems excellent.* **3.** view, overlook, vista, panorama, scene, lookout. *The outlook from the rock was worth the climb.*

outlying *adj.* distant, remote, backcountry, frontier, rural, isolated. *Outlying areas tend to be safest from burglaries.* **Ant.** close, immediate, near.

outmoded *adj.* old-fashioned, outdated, antiquated, obsolete, passé, (slang) horse-and-buggy. *The crank telephone was outmoded long ago.* **Ant.** new, modern, cutting-edge.

output *n.* production, yield, product, run, turnout. *The toy factory increased its output during the holiday season.*

outrage *n.* **1.** insult, affront, offense, slander, contempt. *Your remarks about the president are an outrage.* **2.** atrocity, evil, barbarism, brutality, cruelty. *The terrorist attack was an outrage.* –*vb.* **3.** insult, anger, enrage, offend, shock, infuriate, affront. *The minister was outraged by the attacks on his character.* **Ant.** **1.** compliment, praise, flattery. **2.** help, good, blessing. **3.** please, soothe, calm.

outrageous *adj.* **1.** atrocious, brutal, vicious, evil, fiendish, monstrous, inhumane. *Outrageous crimes were committed by the Nazis in World War II.* **2.** shocking, disgraceful, shameful, offensive, horrible, awful. *Such outrageous behavior will not be permitted at this school.* **3.** excessive, unreasonable, enormous, extreme, immense. *The cost of housing is getting outrageous.* **Ant.** **1.** humane, beneficial, kind. **2.** decent, acceptable, proper. **3.** reasonable, fair.

outright *adj.* out-and-out, complete, total, entire, unqualified, downright. *I'd rather buy a car outright than have to make monthly payments on it.*

outside *adj.* **1.** outer, exterior, outward, external, outdoor. *Please open the outside door.* **2.** foreign, alien, outlying, unfamiliar, strange. *The astronauts discovered that an outside force was controlling their ship.* **3.** small, limited, improbable, slight, marginal. *There's an outside chance that my horse will win the race.* –*n.* **4.** exterior, surface, face, front. *The outside of the barn needs painting.* **Ant.** **1.** inside, interior, indoor. **2.** known, familiar. **3.** excellent, likely, probable. **4.** inside, interior, center.

outsider *n.* stranger, newcomer, foreigner, alien, intruder, interloper. *Moving into a new neighborhood always makes me feel like an outsider.*

outspoken *adj.* candid, plain, blunt, frank, direct, honest. *It's refreshing to listen to such an outspoken individual.* **Ant.** reserved, tactful, guarded, timid.

outstanding *adj.* **1.** remarkable, exceptional, excellent, prominent, foremost. *His school record is outstanding.* **2.** unpaid, overdue, unsettled, due, owed, uncollected. *She took out a loan in order to pay her outstanding bills.* **Ant.** **1.** ordinary, common, average. **2.** paid, settled, collected.

outward *adj.* outer, external, exterior, surface, apparent. *Judging by his outward appearance, the dog is malnourished.*

outweigh *vb.* override, exceed, surpass, eclipse, take precedence, transcend. *My need to go to the bathroom outweighs your need to comb your hair.*

outwit *vb.* outsmart, outthink, outfox, beat, outshine, get the better of. *It's possible to outwit chess opponents only with great concentration and practice.*

oval *adj.* ovoid, elliptical, oviform, egg-shaped. *The racetrack is oval in shape.*

ovation *n.* applause, cheers, clapping, acclamation, tribute, (slang) a hand. *The violinist received a standing ovation.*

over *adj.* ended, finished, concluded, done, completed, terminated. *Sorry folks, the show is over.* **Ant.** beginning, starting, opening.

overall *adj.* total, complete, general, sweeping, entire, extensive, expansive. *The mechanic made an overall inspection of the car.* **Ant.** partial, incomplete, fragmentary.

overbearing *adj.* domineering, oppressive, overpowering, overwhelming. *The coach's overbearing attitude took the fun out of our game.* **Ant.** casual, subdued, timid.

overblown *adj.* exaggerated, inflated, overdone, excessive, overworked, blown out of proportion. *The rumors concerning my shutting down the company are overblown.* **Ant.** understated, underworked, flaccid.

overcast *adj.* cloudy, hazy, dark, murky, foggy, misty, gloomy. *How am I going to get a tan on an overcast day?* **Ant.** sunny, bright, clear.

overcome *vb.* conquer, defeat, beat, surmount, prevail, overwhelm. *The poor farmboy overcame great odds to become a millionaire.* **Ant.** surrender, submit, yield.

overdue *adj.* late, tardy, belated, delayed, behind. *The stagecoach was ten hours overdue.* **Ant.** punctual, early, premature.

overflow *vb.* **1.** spill, flood, swamp, gush, overrun. *Excess water overflowed into the street.* –*n.* **2.** spillage, flooding, deluge, excess, surplus. *A dam was built to catch the overflow from the water-treatment plant.*

overhaul *vb.* renovate, revise, fix, repair, restore, service, rebuild. *The mechanic planned to overhaul the old motor.*

overhead *n.* expenses, costs, outlay, disbursement, upkeep, payroll. *The overhead in my bookstore is roughly $3,000 per month.*

overjoyed *adj.* ecstatic, elated, euphoric, thrilled, jubilant, rapturous. *Sally's overjoyed reaction was the result of having received a raise.*

overlook *vb.* neglect, ignore, omit, forget, skip, miss. *I will overlook your past mistakes.* **Ant.** notice, remember.

overpower *vb.* subdue, dominate, beat, crush, master, conquer. *Don't let the big men on their team overpower you.* **Ant.** surrender, yield, submit.

overrate *vb.* exaggerate, overpraise, overvalue, overestimate. *She overrated the quality of that movie.* **Ant.** underrate, minimize, undervalue.

overrule *vb.* repeal, cancel, reject, veto, revoke, rescind, disallow, overturn. *The Supreme Court overruled the original decision.* **Ant.** sustain, allow, accept, permit.

oversee *vb.* supervise, administer, manage, handle, direct, regulate, run. *The captain will oversee the loading of his ship.*

overshadow *vb.* eclipse, dwarf, outclass, outshine, outdo, tower over. *No matter where he played, our star tennis player tended to overshadow all competitors.*

oversight *n.* **1.** error, omission, slip, blunder, mistake, neglect. *Her name was left off the list due to an oversight.* **2.** control, management, direction, supervision, directorship. *The city council was given oversight of the summer festival.*

overstate *vb.* exaggerate, embellish, overdo, magnify, inflate. *You overstated the extent of damage done to your car.* **Ant.** understate, minimize, underplay.

overt *adj.* open, unconcealed, obvious, explicit, plain, naked. *The rioters were overt in* *their destruction of public property.* **Ant.** covert, undercover, secret.

overtake *vb.* pass, outdistance, (slang) blow by, (slang) leave in the dust, (slang) leave in one's wake. *The champion usually waits until the end of the race to overtake his competitors.* **Ant.** fall behind, lapse, recede.

overthrow *vb.* **1.** conquer, overpower, destroy, vanquish, defeat, overturn, upset. *Rebels conspired to overthrow the government.* *–n.* **2.** toppling, takeover, coup, revolution, rebellion, collapse, fall. *The overthrow of the dictator was supported by the army.* **Ant. 1.** restore, support, uphold. **2.** preservation, protection.

overture *n.* offer, opening, bid, tender, suggestion, proposal. *The millionaires made an overture to buy our property, but we weren't interested.*

overweight *adj.* obese, heavy, fat, corpulent, roly-poly, blubbery. *The number of overweight Americans increases every year.* **Ant.** underweight, anorexic, malnourished.

overwhelm *vb.* overpower, overcome, devastate, shatter, defeat, beat, crush. *The baseball team was overwhelmed by their opponents.*

own *adj.* **1.** private, individual, personal, particular. *Bring your own pen for the test.* *–vb.* **2.** possess, have, hold, keep, retain, maintain. *Do you own the house on the corner?* **3.** admit, confess, declare, acknowledge, profess, grant, allow. *The child owned up to breaking the vase.* **Ant. 3.** deny, disclaim, refute, disavow.

owner *n.* possessor, holder, keeper, bearer, custodian. *Can you prove that you are the owner of his bicycle?*

P

pace *n.* **1.** step, stride, gait. *The goalposts were 30 paces apart.* **2.** rate, speed, velocity, tempo, quickness. *He reads at a slower pace than his classmates. –vb.* **3.** walk, tread, amble, stroll, stride, traipse. *The caged lion restlessly paced back and forth.*

pacifist *n.* peacemaker, peace lover, dove, conciliator, appeaser, antiwar demonstrator, passive resister. *Pacifists believe all conflicts can be resolved nonviolently.* **Ant.** warmonger, hawk, fighter.

pacify *vb.* quiet, calm, appease, soothe, allay, placate, tranquilize, lull, soothe. *The officer attempted to pacify the angry crowd.* **Ant.** anger, enrage, agitate, excite, aggravate.

pack *n.* **1.** package, parcel, knapsack, bundle, load, packet. *The traveler picked up his pack of belongings.* **2.** group, bunch, crowd, gang, band, mob, herd. *The pack of wild dogs searched for food in the hills. –vb.* **3.** load, fill, cram, store, compress, stuff. *She told the movers to pack the books into two boxes.* **Ant. 3.** unload, empty, unpack.

package *n.* parcel, box, carton, pack, container, bundle. *Jane received a package from her aunt today.*

packed *adj.* full, crammed, jammed, stuffed, filled, overflowing. *The ballroom was packed with eager dancers.* **Ant.** empty, vacant, hollow.

pact *n.* contract, agreement, treaty, alliance, compact, arrangement, settlement. *The opposing leaders agreed to a pact on peace terms.*

pad *n.* **1.** cushion, padding, mattress, stuffing. *You will sit more comfortably if you place a pad on the wooden bench.* **2.** tablet, notebook, notepad, writing pad. *He wrote the message on a pad by the telephone. –vb.* **3.** stuff, fill, cushion, expand. *The bed should be padded for extra comfort.*

paddle *n.* **1.** oar, scull, pole. *Anyone who wants to row must have her own paddle. –vb.* **2.** row, oar. *She paddled the boat across the lake.*

pagan *n.* heathen, non-Christian, non-believer, atheist, infidel, idolater. *Christians were preceded in history by pagans.*

page *n.* **1.** paper, sheet, leaf. *I have to read 30 pages in my textbook before tomorrow's class.* **2.** messenger, attendant, servant. *The senator asked his page to deliver a message. –vb.* **3.** call, summon. *Would you page the bellboy?*

pageant *n.* spectacle, show, display, extravaganza, parade. *Every year the villagers held a pageant honoring their founding fathers.*

pageantry *n.* show, exhibition, spectacle, grandeur, glitter, extravaganza. *We like to attend Mardi Gras to watch the pageantry.*

pager *n.* (slang) beeper, communication device, receiver. *You can contact Kate through her pager if you can't reach her by other means.*

pail *n.* bucket, canister, container, vessel. *The pail was filled with water.*

pain *n.* 1. ache, hurt, discomfort, pang, agony, soreness. *My father has a pain in his back whenever he bends over.* 2. suffering, misery, grief, sorrow, torment, anguish, torment, distress. *The children's insults caused the boy much pain.* –*vb.* 3. hurt, ache, torment, agonize. *Does your shoulder pain you when I touch it?* **Ant.** 1. comfort, relief. 2. delight, joy, pleasure. 3. relieve, comfort, ease.

painful *adj.* 1. aching, sore, agonizing, hurting, hurtful, racking, throbbing, inflamed. *She woke up with a painful headache.* 2. distressing, difficult, unpleasant, disagreeable, grievous. *Visiting her sick friend in the hospital was a very painful experience.* **Ant.** 1. painless, soothing. 2. pleasurable, enjoyable, easy.

painkiller *n.* analgesic, anesthetic, palliative, anodyne, opiate, drug. *After Mack broke his leg, he had to take painkillers for several days.*

painstaking *adj.* exacting, careful, meticulous, thorough, diligent. *The vaccine for polio was discovered through painstaking research.* **Ant.** careless, haphazard, slipshod.

paint *vb.* 1. color, draw, sketch, coat. *The artist painted the canvas with a dark shade of blue.* –*n.* 2. color, pigment, enamel, stain. *The house will need two coats of paint.*

painting *n.* picture, portrait, sketch, canvas. *The painting on the wall is by Picasso.*

pair *n.* 1. couple, two, duo, doubles, twosome. *A pair of lovebirds were perched on the highest branch of the tree.* –*vb.* 2. match, join, mate, couple, unite, combine. *The fighters were paired off and assigned times for the boxing competition.*

palace *n.* mansion, castle, chateau, royal residence. *Her house was as beautiful as a king's palace.* **Ant.** hovel, shack.

palatable *adj.* tasteful, delicious, enjoyable, agreeable, savory, pleasant, appetizing. *Horses find sugar cubes to be very palatable.* **Ant.** distasteful, repugnant, disagreeable.

palatial *adj.* grand, stately, luxurious, majestic, ornate, opulent. *The millionaire lived in a palatial mansion in Beverly Hills.*

pale *adj.* colorless, ashen, pallid, sickly, anemic. *The beautiful green pasture turned a pale gray under the moonlight.* **Ant.** bright, vivid.

pall *n.* 1. cover, shroud, darkness, veil, shadow. *The dark clouds cast a pall over the school picnic.* –*vb.* 2. bore, fade, weary, weaken, displease, depress. *The routine of driving the same road every day has started to pall.* **Ant.** 1. lightness, brightness. 2. excite, interest, delight, please.

pallid *adj.* pale, wan, sallow, white, sickly, anemic. *His bout with the flu gave him a pallid complexion.* **Ant.** rosy, glowing, flushed.

pallor *n.* paleness, whiteness, wanness, sallowness. *The pallor in her face appeared terribly unhealthy.* **Ant.** rosiness, color, pinkness.

palpable *adj.* perceptible, touchable, tangible, perceivable, physical, real. *A light fog is barely palpable in the dark.*

palpitate *vb.* pulsate, throb, flutter, tremble, pulse, beat. *His heart palpitates whenever he has to talk in front of an audience.*

paltry *adj.* small, insignificant, trivial, trifling, meager, petty, worthless. *She would not accept a job that paid such a paltry wage.* **Ant.** important, significant, major, worthy.

pamper *vb.* spoil, favor, indulge, coddle, cater to. *She pampers her cat like a child.* **Ant.** neglect, ignore, mistreat.

pamphlet *n.* booklet, leaflet, brochure, handbill, folder. *This pamphlet explains the purpose of our organization.*

pan *n.* 1. skillet, pot, utensil, saucepan. *The bacon is sizzling in the pan.* –*vb.* 2. criticize, condemn, attack, denounce. *The author's latest book was severely panned by the critics.* **Ant.** 2. praise, encourage, recommend.

panacea *n.* cure-all, catholicon, fix-all, remedy, elixir, (slang) magic bullet, nostrum. *Scientists gave up looking for panaceas years ago.*

panache *n.* dash, flair, élan, self-confidence, verve, style. *The actress made her appearance with great panache.*

pancake *n.* flapjack, hotcake, batter cake, crepe, fritter, blintz. *There is nothing tastier than pancakes smothered in maple syrup.*

pander *vb.* indulge, gratify, cater to, serve, attend, satisfy, humor. *The movie pandered to those who loved to see explosions and car crashes.*

panel *n.* 1. committee, jury, group, assembly, board. *The site for the new library will be decided by a panel of community members.* 2. partition, board, section, divider. *We will need six wall panels to finish the entire room.*

pang *n.* pain, hurt, twinge, throb, ache, stab. *A sudden pang occurred when he bumped the table with his elbow.*

panic *n.* 1. terror, fear, alarm, fright, hysteria, dread, frenzy. *The bad financial news caused a panic in the stock market.* –*vb.* 2. terrorize, alarm, scare, frighten, stampede, terrify. *The first rule in an earthquake is not to panic.* **Ant.** 1. calm, composure. 2. calm, soothe.

panorama *n.* view, overview, perspective, scenic view, vista, scope. *The south rim of the Grand Canyon offers many breathtaking panoramas.*

pant *vb.* gasp, puff, wheeze, huff, blow. *The pace of the hike was tough enough to make her pant.*

pantry *n.* larder, closet, cupboard, buttery, storeroom, stockroom. *The pantry is getting low on rice and beans.*

pants *n.* trousers, jeans, slacks, breeches, shorts, dungarees. *She bought two pairs of pants and a shirt.*

paper *n.* 1. notepaper, writing paper, stationery. *Bring plenty of paper for the essay test.* 2. essay, article, report, composition, dissertation, manuscript, study. *The doctor submitted her paper on childhood illnesses to the medical institute.* 3. newspaper, journal, publication, tabloid, periodical. *The Grumpville Gazette is our town paper.* 4. document, certificate, deed. *The paper proves that you are the owner of the car.*

par *n.* average, standard, norm, usual, mean, equal. *I would have to sink my next putt to make par for the course.*

parable *n.* fable, allegory, lesson, moral tale. *Aesop's fables are excellent examples of parables.*

parade *n.* 1. procession, display, pageant, show, march, review. *The circus began with a parade through town.* –*vb.* 2. march, strut, walk, step, file. *The soldiers paraded down the field.*

paradigm *n.* model, archetype, example, prototype, ideal, standard. *A man who cooks, cleans and cares for his children is the male paradigm for the 21st century.*

paradise *n.* heaven, utopia, Eden, bliss, nirvana, ecstasy, euphoria. *Many fishermen think paradise is a fishing pole and a rushing stream.* **Ant.** hell, purgatory, misery.

paradox *n.* inconsistency, contradiction, enigma, mystery. *How he can eat so much and remain thin is a paradox to me.*

paragon *n.* model, highest example, exemplar, ideal, paradigm, archetype. *Michael Jordan was a basketball paragon.*

parallel *adj.* 1. side by side, alongside, abreast, *Draw two lines parallel to each other.* 2. alike, similar, resembling, like, corresponding. *There are two parallel thoughts on that issues. –n.* 3. comparison, similarity, likeness, correspondence, resemblance. *The teacher discussed the parallels between the governments of Canada and Australia. –vb.* 4. follow, run aside, run along to, run abreast of. *The cars paralleled each other through most of the race.* 5. match, duplicate, resemble, equal, correspond. *The subject of her report parallels mine.* **Ant.** 1. nonparallel. 2. unlike, divergent, different. 3. difference, diversity. 5. diverge, differ.

paralysis *n.* incapacitation, immobility, palsy, insensitivity, prostration, disability, paraplegia, quadriplegia. *A spinal injury can result in paralysis.*

paralyze *vb.* stun, freeze, immobilize, cripple, deaden, disable. *The suddenness of the action left him paralyzed with indecision.*

paramedic *n.* emergency medical technician, EMT, medical assistant, ambulance attendant, rescue squad member. *The paramedic checked for pulse and respiration.*

paramount *adj.* supreme, superior, dominant, principal, foremost, preeminent. *Getting your homework done is of paramount importance.* **Ant.** least, secondary, minor.

paranoia *n.* delusions, psychosis, distrust, suspicion, mental illness. *Paranoia is characterized by the irrational thought that people are out to get you.*

paranoid *adj.* delusional, suspicious, distrustful, fearful, anxious, mentally ill. *He was so paranoid he was convinced the football team was gossiping about him in the huddle.*

paranormal *adj.* supernatural, metaphysical, occult, mysterious, otherworldly, inexplicable. *He investigated all things paranormal, including ghosts.*

paraphernalia *n.* stuff, things, effects, equipment, gear, tackle. *My father used to take along 20 pounds of paraphernalia to catch a single one-pound fish.*

paraphrase *vb.* rephrase, summarize, reword, restate, interpret, repeat roughly. *The professor's speech was too long to repeat, so I'll paraphrase what she said.*

parcel *n.* 1. package, bundle, packet. *The parcel is to be delivered by Friday. –vb.* 2. divide, allocate, assign, allot, distribute. *All assignments have been parceled out to the workers.* **Ant.** 2. collect, combine.

parched *adj.* dry, thirsty, dehydrated, scorched. *He was parched from hiking through the desert without water.* **Ant.** wet, moist, watered.

pardon *vb.* 1. forgive, excuse, absolve, overlook, release. *The president has the power to pardon criminals. –n.* 2. forgiveness, release, amnesty, excuse. *The convict received a pardon.* **Ant.** 1. condemn, sentence. 2. condemnation, sentencing.

pare *vb.* 1. peel, skin, clip, trim, cut. *He pared the apple before eating it.* 2. reduce, cut, diminish, lessen, decrease, cut back. *She will have to get a higher-paying job or pare her living expenses.* 2. increase, boost, raise, inflate.

pariah *n.* outcast, castaway, reject, exile, refugee, undesirable. *In public places, smokers are becoming pariahs.*

parity *n.* equality, evenness, equivalence, symmetry, likeness, uniformity. *Wrestlers must have a certain parity of size or the match won't be fair.* **Ant.** inequality, unevenness, disparity.

park *vb.* 1. place, leave, deposit, put. *Park the car in the garage. –n.* 2. garden, grounds, green, sanctuary, reserve, parkland, preserve. *Some of the activities you can do in the park include strolling, birdwatching, and picnicking.*

parliament *n.* legislature, (in Britain) House of Lords, (in Britain and Canada) House of Commons, assembly, congress, government body. *Parliament will assemble today to discuss a new bill.*

parochial *adj.* provincial, local, regional, limited, narrow, small-town, insular. *She was wary of people who were different, as she had a parochial view of the world.* **Ant.** cosmopolitan, worldly, broad.

parody *n.* **1.** satire, take-off, imitation, burlesque, travesty. *That comedian does a very funny parody of the president.* –*vb.* **2.** satirize, spoof, lampoon, mock, ridicule, imitate, mimic. *The play parodied many aspects of our society.*

parson *n.* clergyman, minister, cleric, rector, preacher. *I asked the parson of our church to pray for my family's welfare.*

part *n.* **1.** piece, portion, section, segment, fraction, element, division, item. *Part of the jigsaw puzzle is missing.* **2.** share, role, participation, interest, function, task. *We should all take a part in protecting our natural resources.* –*vb.* **3.** divide, separate, open, split, detach. *He parted his hair down the middle.* **4.** leave, depart, exit, go. *The band parted company after the concert.* **Ant.** **1.** whole, entirety, all, totality. **3.** unite, combine, attach, join. **4.** stay, remain, linger.

partake *vb.* participate, engage, enjoy, share, take. *All are welcome to partake in the festival.* **Ant.** exclude, abstain, refrain.

partial *adj.* **1.** incomplete, part, limited, unfinished, fragmentary, fractional. *A partial schedule of activities will be available.* **2.** biased, prejudiced, one-sided, partisan, unfair, unjust, unbalanced. *We lost the game because the referee was partial to the opposing team.* **3.** fond, favoring. *She's quite partial to ice cream.* **Ant.** **1.** all, whole, complete. **2.** fair, impartial, balanced, just.

partiality *n.* bias, prejudice, preference, favoritism, leaning, liking. *My partiality for vanilla ice cream is well known.* **Ant.** objectivity, dispassion.

participate *vb.* take part, partake, join in, engage in, cooperate. *The game will be more enjoyable if everybody participates.* **Ant.** refrain, abstain.

particle *n.* piece, bit, trace, speck, shred, iota, fragment, scrap. *The dog left a particle of food in his dish.*

particular *adj.* **1.** special, distinctive, specific, notable, singular, exact. *She likes to wear a particular style of clothing.* **2.** detailed, fussy, demanding, precise, careful, finicky, picky, specific. *His roommate is very particular about cleaning the apartment.* –*n.* **3.** facts, detail, specific. *The officers, knew the particular about the accident on Main Street.* **Ant.** **1.** general, vague, unspecified. **2.** careless, uncritical, undemanding, indifferent.

partisan *adj.* partial, biased, one-sided, sectarian, prejudiced, close-minded. *The Democrat was strongly partisan in his viewpoint and completely rejected the Republican's argument.* **Ant.** unbiased, bipartisan, open-minded.

partition *n.* **1.** divider, wall, barrier, screen. *A partition was placed in the room in order to make two separate meeting areas.* **2.** division, separation, detachment, split-up, distribution. *The partition of the courts resulted in a civil and criminal branch.* –*vb.* **3.** divide, separate, break up, apportion, split, distribute. *The real-estate company partitioned the land into one-acre lots.* **Ant.** **2.** unification, joining.

partly *adv.* partially, somewhat, relatively, slightly. *The information was only partly correct.* **Ant.** completely, totally.

partner *n.* associate, mate, colleague, accomplice, collaborator, friend, ally. *They decided to be partners on the project.*

partnership *n.* association, alliance, corporation, connection. *The two businesses formed a partnership.*

party *n.* 1. celebration, festivity, get-together. *You are invited to my birthday party.* 2. group, alliance, assembly, organization, coalition, association. *The disagreement split the union into two separate parties.* 3. person, participant, individual, being, human. *She was the party responsible for the disturbance.*

pass *vb.* 1. move, go, travel, proceed, progress. *The train will pass by Santa Fe in an hour.* 2. cease, end, die, lapse, elapse, expire, depart, terminate. *All things must pass.* 3. give, hand over, deliver, convey. *Please pass the salt.* 4. approve, enact, authorize, ratify, establish, okay, confirm. *The law was passed by Congress.* 5. complete, satisfy, accomplish, qualify, achieve. *He must study if he wants to pass this course.* 6. exceed, surpass, excel, transcend, outshine. *She passed everyone's expectations.* 7. ignore, disregard, overlook, neglect. *Due to a lack of time, the committee passed over the housing problem.* 8. spend, expend, occupy, use, fill, while. *She passed the time reading.* –*n.* 9. passageway, gap, route, course, way, pathway, passage. *Is there a pass through these mountains?* 10. permit, permission, ticket, authorization. *You must have a pass to enter this building.* 11. throw, toss, cast, pitch. *The pass to the wide receiver was incomplete.* **Ant.** 1. stop, cease. 2. begin, start, continue. 3. keep, retain, hold. 4. disapprove, reject, deny, defeat. 5. fail, flunk. 6. falter, fall behind. 7. consider, notice. 8. waste, squander.

passable *adj.* 1. acceptable, allowable, adequate, tolerable, fair, satisfactory. *His work is not very good, but it is passable.* 2. clear, navigable, unobstructed. *The road will not be passable until a maintenance crew removes the fallen tree.* **Ant.** 1. unacceptable, inadequate, unsatisfactory. 2. impassable, obstructed, closed.

passage *n.* 1. movement, passing, progression, course, motion, transition, flow. *The situation improved with the passage of time.* 2. voyage, journey, travel, expedition, trip. *The passages of the early explorers were filled with dangers.* 3. passageway, course, route, corridor, path, channel. *There must be a passage out of this cave.* 4. paragraph, sentence, section, portion, selection. *Please read a passage from* Moby-Dick.

passageway *n.* passage, corridor, walkway, hall, path, alley. *We found a secret passageway through the cave.*

passé *adj.* old-fashioned, outdated, outmoded, antiquated, obsolete, stale. *She predicted that nose rings would soon be considered passé.* **Ant.** fashionable, chic, in vogue.

passenger *n.* rider, commuter, traveler, tourist. *This ferry can transport both cars and passengers.*

passion *n.* 1. love, desire, affection, fondness, liking, devotion. *The passion he felt for her was overwhelming.* 2. emotion, fervor, feeling, intensity, zeal, zest. *She wrote about her adventures with deep passion.* **Ant.** 2. indifference, apathy.

passionate *adj.* 1. emotional, ardent, impassioned, intense, excitable, fervid, excited. *When people talk about their hobbies, they tend to become quite passionate.* 2. erotic, amorous, desirous, loving. *She often has passionate thoughts about her boyfriend.* **Ant.** 1. apathetic, cold, cool, indifferent.

passive *adj.* inactive, quiet, submissive, apathetic, resigned, nonresistant, unresisting. *He* *is often too passive and submits to other people's desires too readily.* **Ant.** active, assertive, aggressive.

passport *n.* identification, ID, proof of citizenship, authorization, credentials, permit. *You need a passport to fly overseas.*

past *adj.* **1.** finished, done, gone, ended, over, expired, elapsed. *People worry too much about their past problems.* **2.** previous, preceding, former, prior, recent. *She has been looking for a job in the past week.* –*n.* **3.** yesteryear, yesterday, ancient times, olden times. *The days of the horse and carriage are in the past.* –*prep.* **4.** by, beyond. *The runners raced past the halfway point.* **Ant. 1.** ahead, coming. **2–3.** present, future.

paste *n.* **1.** glue, adhesive, binder, bond. *He attached the poster to the wall with a little paste.* –*vb.* **2.** stick, glue, fasten, attach, cement. *She pasted the photograph onto the page of her scrapbook.*

pastime *n.* entertainment, amusement, recreation, enjoyment, diversion, sport, hobby. *Bird-watching is a popular pastime.*

pastor *n.* minister, clergyman, priest, parson. *He is the pastor of our church.*

pastoral *adj.* idyllic, peaceful, simple, rustic, rural, ideal. *He longed for the pastoral life, raising sheep on a rolling farm far from the city.* **Ant.** urban, citified, metropolitan.

pastry *n.* baked good, dessert, sweet, treat. *A meal should not be made up entirely of pastry.*

pasture *n.* meadow, field, meadowland, grassland. *The cows grazed in a green pasture.*

pat *vb.* **1.** tap, hit, strike, rap. *She patted him on the shoulder to get his attention.* **2.** stroke, fondle, caress, pet. *Puppies like to be patted on the head.* –*n.* **3.** tap, hit, strike, rap. *A gentle pat on the head reminded the child to behave.*

patch *vb.* **1.** repair, mend, fix, sew up, restore. *A tailor patched my suit.* –*n.* **2.** spot, lot, space, area, tract, clearing. *This patch of ground will be used as a garden.*

patchwork *n.* miscellany, hodgepodge, melange, pastiche, jumble. *Our organization is a patchwork of experts on different subjects.*

patent *n.* title, grant, right, protection, registration, certification. *Thomas Edison was awarded an astonishing number of patents for his inventions.*

path *n.* walk, way, lane, route, pathway, road, trail, course, lane. *The path to the waterfall is very steep.*

pathetic *adj.* pitiful, sad, touching, pitiable. *The hungry cat meowed in a pathetic way.* **Ant.** laughable, amusing.

pathological *adj.* **1.** diseased, morbid, unhealthy, infected, contaminated. *The doctor observed his patient's pathological decline.* **2.** compulsive, habitual, obsessive, sick, unhealthy. *His desire to wash his hands fifty times a day was pathological.*

pathology *n.* infection, growth, spread, immune breakdown, malignancy, disease manifestation. *He went to medical school to study the pathology of cancer.*

pathos *n.* sympathy, pity, sorrow, sadness, poignancy, heartache. *The story was filled with pathos and made many readers cry.*

patience *n.* **1.** endurance, persistence, diligence, perseverance, tenacity. *It takes patience to learn to play a musical instrument.* **2.** calmness, tolerance, composure, serenity, self-control. *She has the patience of a saint.* **Ant. 1.** impatience, hastiness. **2.** impatience, intolerance.

patient *adj.* **1.** persistent, enduring, persevering, tenacious, determined. *It takes a patient* *person to wait in a long line.* **2.** calm, serene, uncomplaining, resigned. *Please be patient because he is a slow learner.* –*n.* **3.** invalid, shut-in, case, inmate. *The hospital currently has two hundred patients.* **Ant. 1.** impatient, restless. **2.** impatient, excitable.

patriarch *n.* father, grandfather, man, head of the household, leader, chief, master, elder. *The patriarch of the family was respected for his wisdom.* **Ant.** matriarch.

patriot *n.* flag-waver, nationalist, loyalist, statesman. *He was a dyed-in-the-wool patriot and believed his country could do no wrong.* **Ant.** traitor, turncoat, subversive.

patriotic *adj.* loyal, nationalistic, public-spirited, devoted. *It was her patriotic duty to serve her country.* **Ant.** treasonable, subversive, traitorous.

patrol *vb.* guard, watch, defend, protect. *Volunteers are needed to patrol the neighborhood.*

patronize *vb.* **1.** support, endorse, frequent, deal with. *You should patronize the local stores.* **2.** condescend, disrespect, disdain, humor. *That professor tends to patronize his students.* **Ant. 1.** boycott, spurn. **2.** flatter, respect.

patter *n.* pitch, spiel, line, chatter, talk, recitation. *The street vendor's amusing patter attracted potential customers from everywhere within earshot.*

pattern *n.* **1.** design, motif, decoration, figure. *He wore a shirt with a floral pattern.* **2.** model, example, prototype, guide, ideal. *The Beatle's musical style became the pattern for many bands.* –*vb.* **3.** fashion, imitate, model, follow, emulate, copy. *The architect patterned her house after a Spanish castle.*

paucity *adj.* dearth, lack, scarcity, shortage, deficiency, absence. *There was a paucity of candidates running for local office this year.* **Ant.** abundance, wealth, surplus.

paunch *n.* fat, bulge, potbelly, (slang) spare tire, stomach, (slang) middle age spread. *During the long winter, I tend to develop a paunch around my mid-section.*

pauper *n.* poor person, indigent, beggar, tramp, hobo, homeless person. *Without a job, you will quickly become a pauper.* **Ant.** millionaire, multimillionaire, (slang) moneybags.

pause *vb.* **1.** cease, stop, wait, break, hesitate, rest, delay. *She paused in the middle of her aerobics.* –*n.* **2.** halt, hesitation, stop, rest, wait, interlude, break, interruption. *His bitter remark caused a pause in the conversation.* **Ant. 1.** continue, proceed, perpetuate. **2.** continuation, progression.

pave *vb.* surface, cover, tar, asphalt. *A maintenance crew paved the street in front of our house.*

pavement *n.* blacktop, tar, asphalt, concrete, roadway, macadam, cobble. *In July, the pavement is too hot for bare feet.*

pawn *vb.* **1.** pledge, deposit, hock, secure. *The musician pawned his trumpet for twenty dollars.* –*n.* **2.** puppet, instrument, tool, stooge, toy, agent. *She wanted to make her own decisions and not be just another of her employer's pawns.*

peace *n.* **1.** harmony, accord, amity, friendship. *All nations, should work to achieve world peace.* **2.** quiet, tranquillity, calm, serenity, peacefulness. *He deserves a little peace after a hard day's work.* **Ant. 1.** war, discord, conflict. **2.** turmoil, chaos, disorder.

peaceful *adj.* **1.** nonviolent, peaceable, nonaggressive, pacifistic, agreeable. *The two countries entered into peaceful negotiations.* **2.** calm, serene, quiet, tranquil, restful, composed, peaceable. *The house seemed very peaceful after her guests departed.* **Ant. 1.** hostile, warlike, violent. **2.** noisy, disturbed, restless.

peacemaker *n.* diplomat, dove, makepeace, pacifist, mediator, conscientious objector. *We need a peacemaker, not a warmonger.* **Ant.** warmonger, hawk, incendiary.

peak *n.* **1.** top, summit, tip, pinnacle, crest, point, apex. *The climbers reached the highest peak.* **2.** climax, limit, maximum, top, zenith, apex. *The peak of her career was winning the Nobel Prize.* **Ant. 1.** bottom, base, foot. **2.** minimum, nadir, bottom.

peasant *n.* serf, farmer, peon, countryman, worker. *Peasants tended the king's fields.*

peccadillo *n.* fault, sin, offense, shortcoming, indiscretion, transgression. *The media loves to expose a peccadillo and the public loves to read about one.*

peculiar *adj.* odd, unusual, strange, distinctive, abnormal, queer, unique. *The platypus is a peculiar animal.* **Ant.** common, usual, ordinary, general.

peculiarity *n.* feature, particularity, trait, oddity, uniqueness, characteristic. *Singing in the shower is one of his peculiarities.*

pedantic *adj.* nit-picking, meticulous, scholarly, didactic, professorial, overprecise, (slang) hairsplitting. *Her criticism of my paper was needlessly pedantic.*

peddle *vb.* sell, vend, hawk, market, barter. *The salesman peddled his goods at the fair.*

peddler *n.* salesman, vendor, hawker. *The street peddler was given a citation for doing business without a license.*

pedestrian *n.* **1.** walker, hiker, stroller. *The pedestrian walked across the street.* –*adj.* **2.** dull, slow, uninteresting, commonplace, ordinary, unimaginative, mundane. *She did not like the author's pedestrian style.* **Ant. 2.** interesting, exciting, compelling.

pedigree *n.* lineage, bloodline, genealogy, family tree, descent, roots. *We traced our pedigree all the way back to an English noblewoman.*

peek *vb.* **1.** glimpse, glance, look, peep. *The boy peeked around the corner.* –*n.* **2.** glimpse, glance, look, peep. *Let's take a peek through the telescope.*

peel *vb.* pare, skin, husk, strip, shuck, shell. *Be careful with the knife when you peel that apple.*

peer *vb.* **1.** examine, stare, gaze, look, pry. *She peered at the sky, wondering if it were going to rain.* –*n.* **2.** equal, counterpart, match, colleague. *The young lawyer gained the respect of his peers.*

peerless *adj.* unrivaled, unmatched, superior, incomparable, unequaled, best, greatest. *When it came to hitting home runs, Mark McGwire was peerless.* **Ant.** second-rate, inferior.

peevish *adj.* irritable, ill-tempered, grouchy, moody, touchy, crabby. *Don't ask favors of your father when he is feeling peevish.* **Ant.** cheerful, contented, happy.

pejorative *adj.* disparaging, negative, deprecatory, belittling, degrading, uncomplimentary. *Any more pejorative remarks like that and you'll be removed from class.* **Ant.** complimentary, reverent, flattering.

pelt *n.* **1.** hide, skin, fur, coat. *The trapper brought his beaver pelts to the market.* –*vb.* **2.** hit, strike, beat, batter, pummel, bombard. *Stop pelting that person with snowballs.*

pen *n.* **1.** ballpoint, quill, fountain pen. *All applications must be completed with a pen.* **2.** corral, coop, cage, compound, enclosure, stockade. *Herd the cattle into the pen.* –*vb.* **3.** write, compose, draft, inscribe. *He penned a letter to the editor.* **4.** confine, cage, restrain, coop. *The horses have been penned up too long.*

penalize *vb.* punish, discipline, chastise, chasten, castigate. *They should not penalize her for stating her opinion.* **Ant.** award, reward, praise.

penalty *n.* punishment, discipline, fine, sentence, retribution, (slang) slap on the wrist. *The opposing team was given a stiff penalty for cheating.* **Ant.** reward, award, bonus.

penance *n.* reparation, atonement, repentance, remorse, penalty. *My penance for stealing the last cookie was to apologize and sweep the floor.*

penchant *n.* liking, fondness, affinity, inclination, weakness, attachment. *I have a penchant for old science fiction movies.*

pending *adj.* forthcoming, impending, upcoming, on the horizon, imminent, coming. *Her promotion at the bank is pending.*

penetrate *vb.* **1.** pierce, enter, puncture, bore, impale. *I can't get the nail to penetrate the wall.* **2.** permeate, infiltrate, saturate, invade, fill. *Outside sounds penetrated the conference room.*

penis *n.* sexual organ, genitalia, male organ, genitals. *In its normal state, the penis retracts like an accordion to protect itself from injury.*

penitentiary *n.* federal prison, jail (slang) pen, penal institution, (slang) slammer. *For an extended stay in your local penitentiary, try robbing a bank.*

pennant *n.* flag, streamer, banner, colors, pendant, standard. *She waved the team pennant every time they scored.*

pension *n.* allowance, grant, allotment, annuity, benefit. *He receives a pension from the government.*

pensive *adj.* reflective, meditative, absorbed, thoughtful, dreamy, melancholy. *Viewing the old photographs left her in a pensive mood.* **Ant.** happy, carefree, frivolous.

peon *n.* drudge, laborer, worker, farm worker, menial, slave, serf. *The forced labor made the children feel like peons.*

people *n.* humans, folks, men and women, children, populace, individuals, persons. *People from all walks of life come here to visit.*

pep *n.* energy, vitality, vim, vigor, get-up-and-go, zip. *Parents must have a lot of pep to care for young children.* **Ant.** lifelessness, exhaustion, slothfulness.

peppy *adj.* energetic, lively, vigorous, perky, spirited, (slang) zippy. *Cheerleaders must adopt a peppy attitude at game time.* **Ant.** tired, lethargic, run down.

perceive *vb.* **1.** understand, realize, comprehend, grasp, know, apprehend, recognize. *He was beginning to perceive the basis for their misunderstanding.* **2.** notice, see, observe, discover, discern, distinguish, note, recognize. *Look closely and you will perceive a light stain on the fabric.* **Ant. 1.** misunderstand, misconceive. **2.** overlook, miss, ignore.

percentage *n.* part, proportion, fraction, share, piece. *A small percentage of the profits will be given to charity.*

perceptible *adj.* perceivable, palpable, discernible, observable, apparent, conspicuous. *The comet was barely perceptible above the glare of the city lights.* **Ant.** imperceptible, invisible, impalpable.

perception *n.* comprehension, awareness, understanding, apprehension, sense, conception. *My perception of the proper golf swing is amateurish at best.*

perceptive *adj.* aware, knowing, sharp, alert, sensitive, insightful, conscious. *Few people are perceptive enough to figure out a magician's trickery.* **Ant.** obtuse, dense, dull.

perennial *adj.* returning, perpetual, recurrent, everlasting, enduring, continuous. *The gardener preferred to plant perennial flowers rather than annuals.* **Ant.** short-lived, temporary.

perch *vb.* light, roost, alight, rest, settle, sit. *We watched the robin perch at its nest.*

percolate *vb.* filter, filtrate, percolate, strain, drip, leach. *The last thing we want is for pollution to percolate down into the groundwater.*

perfect *adj.* **1.** exact, precise, complete, accurate, right. *The house was drawn in perfect detail.* **2.** flawless, faultless, ideal, unblemished, excellent. *The dancer's performance was perfect.* *–vb.* **3.** accomplish, complete, achieve, develop, attain. *Scientists are trying to perfect nuclear fusion.* **Ant. 1.** incorrect, incomplete, unfinished. **2.** flawed, faulty.

perfection *n.* flawlessness, excellence, faultlessness, supremacy, acme, ideal. *The gymnast aims for perfection.* **Ant.** faultiness, imperfection, inaccuracy.

perfectionist *n.* stickler, nitpicker, fussbudget, quibbler. *It can be very difficult to work for a perfectionist.*

perform *vb.* **1.** act, play, portray, enact, present. *He will perform the role of Hamlet.* **2.** do, achieve, accomplish, execute, effect, complete, fulfill. *Athletes are paid to perform.*

performance *n.* **1.** show, presentation, exhibition, production, entertainment. *The tenor gave an impressive performance.* **2.** execution, fulfillment, accomplishment, completion. *The athlete's performance at the Olympics was excellent.*

perfume *n.* fragrance, scent, cologne, essence, bouquet, emanation. *She wore an absolutely delicious-smelling perfume.*

perfunctory *adj.* routine, unenthusiastic, required, automatic, mechanical, blasé. *The clerk gave me a perfunctory thank-you and left.*

perhaps *adv.* maybe, possibly, conceivably, perchance. *Perhaps we shall meet again.*

peril *n.* danger, risk, hazard, jeopardy, threat, pitfall. *The explorers faced many perils in the jungle.* **Ant.** safety, security.

perilous *adj.* dangerous, hazardous, threatening, precarious, chancy, risky. *Mountain climbing is a perilous hobby.* **Ant.** safe, secure, harmless.

perimeter *n.* border, edge, limit, outline, periphery, skirt, edge. *A guard patrolled the perimeter of the property.*

period *n.* time, span, interval, term, duration. *She engages in a short period of meditation daily.*

periodic *adj.* recurrent, regular, cyclical, intermittent, at intervals, sporadic. *We get periodic rainstorms here.*

peripheral *adj.* outside, external, neighboring, sideline, surrounding. *The bomb produced some peripheral damage far from its target.*

periphery *n.* perimeter, outskirts, limit, edge, boundary, border. *We could see a faint set of footprints along the periphery of the room.*

perish *vb.* die, expire, cease, end, decease, vanish. *Many animals perished in the forest fire.* **Ant.** thrive, endure, appear.

perjury *n.* lying, dishonesty, deception, falsification, false testimony, prevarication. *Committing perjury is a criminal offense.*

perky *adj.* jaunty, buoyant, self-confident, lively, vivacious, spirited, animated. *Everyone in the restaurant liked the perky waitress with the perpetual grin.* **Ant.** sedate, depressed, somber.

permanent *adj.* lasting, stable, enduring, constant, perpetual. *She was relieved to find a more* *permanent place to live.* **Ant.** temporary, transient, fleeting, momentary.

permeate *vb.* pervade, fill, spread, penetrate, saturate, suffuse. *The smell of rotten eggs tends to permeate the kitchen.*

permissible *adj.* allowed, permitted, acceptable, approved, lawful, authorized. *Dancing is permissible only on the dance floor.* **Ant.** prohibited, forbidden, taboo.

permission *n.* okay, authorization, consent, go-ahead, permit, sanction. *We need to get permission to use the weight room after hours.*

permissive *adj.* lenient, soft, liberal, indulgent, lax, agreeable. *Her permissive parents let her stay out until two in the morning.* **Ant.** restrictive, strict, tyrannical.

permit *vb.* **1.** allow, authorize, let, tolerate, consent, approve, condone. *The teacher will not permit anyone to leave the classroom.* –*n.* **2.** license, permission, authorization, pass, sanction, warrant. *Do you have a permit to camp in this park?* **Ant. 1.** forbid, refuse, disallow, prohibit.

pernicious *adj.* destructive, deadly, harmful, deleterious, lethal, mortal, injurious. *Smoking has a pernicious effect upon the lungs.* **Ant.** healthy, harmless, benign.

perpetual *adj.* everlasting, permanent, eternal, continuing, endless, continual, constant, ceaseless. *He was lulled to sleep by the perpetual motion of the ocean waves.* **Ant.** temporary, inconstant, brief, transitory.

perplex *vb.* confuse, puzzle, bewilder, confound, baffle, mystify. *The new computer program totally perplexed her.* **Ant.** enlighten, assure.

perquisite *n.* (slang) perk, fringe benefit, extra, bonus, reward. *A nice perquisite of owning your own bookstore is being able to read all the books you want for free.*

persecute *vb.* harass, oppress, torment, abuse, maltreat, hound, victimize, badger, bully. *It is wrong to persecute someone because of his or her religious beliefs.* **Ant.** support, uphold, favor, accommodate.

perseverance *n.* persistence, diligence, steadfastness, doggedness, dedication, drive, tenacity. *If you're going to learn how to throw a curveball, you have to have perseverance.*

persevere *vb.* persist, continue, strive, endure, pursue. *The marathon runner persevered despite the pain in her leg.* **Ant.** stop, falter, discontinue.

persist *vb.* continue, persevere, insist, remain, endure. *The accused man persisted in claiming his innocence.* **Ant.** waver, cease, vacillate.

persistent *adj.* determined, constant, stubborn, relentless, tireless, unceasing. *His persistent complaining is starting to annoy me.* **Ant.** inconstant, wavering, changeable.

personable *adj.* friendly, warm, gregarious, outgoing, extroverted, amiable. *You must be personable to be in sales.* **Ant.** standoffish, cold, aloof.

personal *adj.* private, individual, own, particular, intimate. *Keep out of my personal belongings.* **Ant.** public, common, general.

personality *n.* character, disposition, individuality, nature, temperament. *The leader of the group must have a strong personality.*

personify *vb.* represent, embody, exemplify, symbolize, epitomize, typify. *Santa Claus is often used to personify the spirit of giving.*

personnel *n.* staff, employees, work force, crew, faculty, members. *We need to hire some temporary personnel to handle the pre-Christmas rush.*

perspective *n.* **1.** view, vista, aspect, angle, viewpoint, scene, overview. *She had a different perspective of the city from the airplane.* **2.** judgment, understanding, viewpoint, outlook, appreciation, comprehension. *Read this and you will have a new perspective on reality.*

perspire *vb.* sweat, swelter, drip, moisten. *The laborers perspired under the hot sun.*

persuade *vb.* convince, induce, urge, influence, coax, prompt, sway, entice. *They persuaded her to go to the party.* **Ant.** discourage, dissuade.

persuasive *adj.* convincing, compelling, alluring, logical, inducing, effective, forceful. *The salesperson was very persuasive.* **Ant.** unconvincing, dubious, inconclusive.

pertain *vb.* concern, apply, belong, relate, befit. *The following message pertains to you.*

pertinent *adj.* relevant, germane, applicable, related, connected, pertaining. *Keep your remarks pertinent and try to stick to the subject at hand.* **Ant.** impertinent, irrelevant, immaterial.

perturb *vb.* disturb, worry, trouble, upset, disquiet, fluster, unsettle. *She was perturbed by his bizarre behavior.* **Ant.** calm, quiet, soothe, compose.

peruse *vb.* examine, read, review, scrutinize, study, scan, observe. *The children perused the old magazines.*

pervade *vb.* permeate, saturate, penetrate, suffuse, imbue, spread. *A negative attitude seemed to pervade the entire classroom.*

pervasive *adj.* widespread, permeating, spreading, prevalent, extensive, rampant. *The sweet fragrance of lilac was pervasive throughout the garden.* **Ant.** confined, limited, microscopic.

perverse *adj.* contrary, stubborn, obstinate, unreasonable, headstrong. *He gets a perverse pleasure from being obnoxious.* **Ant.** agreeable, reasonable, proper.

perversion *n.* sexual deviation, twist, (slang) kink, fetish, depravity, sickness. *John wondered if his fascination for teensy-weensy polka dot bikinis was a perversion.*

pervert *n.* sexual deviant, sex fiend, fetishist, masochist, sadist, voyeur. *A pervert has lusts that are inappropriate.*

perverted *adj.* distorted, corrupt, warped, depraved, sick, immoral, deviant, impaired. *He has a perverted sense of humor.* **Ant.** normal, balanced, sound, healthy.

pesky *adj.* irritating, annoying, irksome, bothersome, disturbing. *A pesky mosquito buzzed by my ears all night.*

pessimist *n.* defeatist, cynic, skeptic, (slang) gloomy Gus, prophet of doom, naysayer. *Only a pessimist is happy when he is miserable.* **Ant.** optimist, Pollyanna.

pessimistic *adj.* gloomy, cynical, hopeless, doubtful, despairing. *The baseball team is pessimistic about winning the game.* **Ant.** optimistic, hopeful.

pest *n.* nuisance, annoyance, irritation, bother, irritant, pain. *Her little brother can be a big pest when he won't leave her alone.*

pester *vb.* bother, annoy, harass, irritate, torment, disturb, badger, trouble. *Don't pester me while I'm working.*

pestilence *n.* plague, pest, epidemic, scourge, disease, curse. *The virus was a pestilence in the confined spaces of the city.*

pet *vb.* **1.** stroke, fondle, caress, pat. *The child petted her kitten.* –*n.* **2.** favorite, darling, beloved, love. *He is considered the teacher's pet.* –*adj.* **3.** favorite, cherished, precious, loved, beloved. *Her pet charity is the Heart Association.* **Ant. 3.** disliked, unloved, despised.

petite *adj.* small, little, dainty, diminutive, trim, tiny, wee. *The petite poodle fitted perfectly in the child's lap.* **Ant.** big, large, ample.

petition *vb.* **1.** ask, appeal, request, entreat, plead, seek, solicit. *The lawyer petitioned the court to declare a mistrial.* –*n.* **2.** proposal, request, appeal, application, plea, entreaty, suit. *Please sign this petition to hire more teachers.*

petrify *vb.* **1.** stun, paralyze, daze, numb, transfix, immobilize, shock. *A charging elephant petrified the hunters.* **2.** fossilize, solidify, harden, mineralize, calcify. *Under the right conditions, wood will petrify into stone.* **Ant. 2.** soften, liquefy.

petroleum *n.* oil, gas, natural gas, fuel, hydrocarbon, fossil fuel. *The nation has enough petroleum reserves to last several more decades.*

petty *adj.* **1.** small, trivial, little, unimportant, insignificant, minor, trifling, paltry. *She pays too much attention to petty details.* **2.** mean, spiteful, ornery, miserly, stingy. *The store manager is petty when it comes to refunding money.* **Ant. 1.** major, important, vital. **2.** generous, tolerant, bighearted.

petulant *adj.* irritable, moody, grouchy, crabby, touchy, peevish, ill-tempered. *I knew enough to leave him alone when he was in one of his petulant moods.* **Ant.** cheerful, lighthearted, good-humored.

phantom *n.* **1.** ghost, spirit, specter, apparition. *A phantom floated over the staircase.* –*adj.* **2.** unreal, illusory, spectral, hallucinatory, imaginary. *It is only that phantom marathon runner they are claiming to see.*

pharmacist *n.* druggist, apothecary, (British) chemist. *I need to ask my pharmacist about the side effects of my medication.*

pharmacy *n.* druggist, drugstore, apothecary, dispensary, (British), chemist. *I need to get some vitamins at the pharmacy.*

phase *n.* stage, aspect, feature, state, condition, level. *We are ready for the final phase of the experiment.*

phenomenal *adj.* extraordinary, miraculous, remarkable, amazing, fantastic. *The outfielder made a phenomenal catch.* **Ant.** ordinary, routine, unexceptional.

phenomenon *n.* wonder, marvel, sensation, spectacle, anomaly, peculiarity. *She liked to watch the skies for comets and other celestial phenomenon.*

philanderer *n.* adulterer, (slang) cheater, (slang) cheat, (slang) player. *Kirsten is divorcing her husband because he is a philanderer.*

philanthropist *n.* humanitarian, contributor, sponsor, financier, benefactor, giver. *The philanthropist is always looking for new ways to contribute to society.* **Ant.** miser, misanthrope, tightwad.

philanthropy *n.* humanitarianism, charity, giving, munificence, generosity, benefaction, altruism. *Her philanthropy benefited the children's hospital.* **Ant.** cheapness, miserliness, selfishness.

philosopher *n.* deep thinker, sage, theorist, wise man, wise woman, logician. *Plato was a great philosopher.*

philosophical *adj.* thoughtful, meditative, rational, contemplative, profound, abstract. *It's best to adopt a philosophical attitude about the aging process.*

philosophy *n.* thinking, thought, principles, reason, theory, logic, knowledge, viewpoint. *My basic philosophy has always been live and let live.*

phobia *n.* fear, aversion, dread, terror, repulsion, dislike. *She has a phobia of cats.* **Ant.** attraction, like, fondness.

WORD SEARCH
animals: *zoophobia*
blood: *hemophobia*
bridges: *gephyrophobia*
cats: *ailurophobia*
closed or small spaces: *claustrophobia*
dark: *nyctophobia*
death: *necrophobia*
dogs: *cynophobia*
fire: *pyrophobia*
foreigners: *xenophobia*
germs: *microphobia*
ghosts: *phasmophobia*
heights: *acrophobia*
lightning: *astraphobia*
number 13: *triskaidekaphobia*
ocean: *thalassophobia*
open spaces: *agoraphobia*
snakes: *ophidiophobia*
spiders: *arachnophobia*
thunderstorms: *brontophobia*
water: *hydrophobia*
work: *ergophobia*

phobic *adj.* fearful, anxious, dysfunctional, frightened, apprehensive, neurotic, disturbed. *I am quite phobic when it comes to mice.* **Ant.** fearless, rational, cool.

phony *adj.* **1.** fake, unreal, counterfeit, false, bogus, forged, fraudulent. *The art dealer was burdened with a phony Picasso painting.* *–n.* **2.** fake, counterfeit, imitation, hoax, forgery. *The old phony claimed to be Abraham Lincoln's grandson.* **Ant. 1.** real, true, genuine, authentic.

photocopy *n.* **1.** copy, reproduction, duplicate, reprint. *I need a photocopy of the contract for my files.* *–vb.* **2.** copy, reproduce, run off, duplicate, reprint. *Photocopy that contract for your files.*

photograph *n.* **1.** picture, film, print, shot, snapshot. *Would you please take a photograph of our family?* *–vb.* **2.** shoot, take, film, snap. *He photographed couples at the senior prom.*

photographer *n.* picture-taker, photojournalist, (slang) shutterbug, paparazzo, portrait artist, cinematographer. *The photographer took a close-up with his flash and blinded me.*

photography *n.* picture-taking, portraiture, still photography, cinematography, filming, shooting. *You'll need a camera for class if you plan to study photography.*

WORD SEARCH
border, photo: *mat*
chemical solution used to develop film: *fixer, stop bath*
dressing up shots in the lab: *airbrushing, computer enhancement, retouching*
dual imagery photo: *double exposure*
enlargement, photo: *blowup*
enlarging apparatus: *enlarger*
focus range: *depth of field*
glaring, errant photo: *overexposure*
image distortions in digital pictures: *artifacts*
image storage medium in digital camera: *memory chip, card*
lab: *darkroom*
lenses, effects: *filter, fisheye, long-focus lens, portrait lens, telephoto lens, wide-angle lens, zoom lens*
light-measuring device: *light meter*
light to electronic signals to digital photos, device converting: *charged couple device, CCD*
photograph, looks good in a: *photogenic*
reduced image of a stored digital photo: *thumbnail*
room, shooting: *studio*
three-dimensional imagery: *holography*
three-dimensional photo: *hologram*

phrase *n.* **1.** expression, clause, catchword, idiom, saying, sentence. *Have you heard the phrase "A stitch in time saves nine"?* *–vb.* **2.** express, state, voice, put, describe. *Perhaps you can phrase it in a different way.*

physical *adj.* **1.** material, substantive, real, objective, actual, existing, substantial. *Geology and geography study the physical nature of Earth.* **2.** bodily, corporeal, fleshly, carnal, mortal. *The physical concerns, of the human body should not negate spiritual matters.* **Ant. 1.** nonmaterial, intangible, **2.** spiritual, mental.

physician *n.* doctor, healer, medic, practitioner, surgeon. *If your pain continues, we will have to call a physician.*

physique *n.* build, form, shade, body, frame, appearance, anatomy, structure. *Look at the physique on that bodybuilder.*

piano *n.* keyboard, (slang) 88s, (slang) ivories, instrument, concert piano, grand piano. *Elton John is a great pop piano player.*

pick *vb.* **1.** select, choose, elect. *Who do you pick as your team captain?* **2.** gather, pluck, collect, take, detach, get. *They picked grapes during harvest season.* –*n.* **3.** choice, best, prize, cream. *That flower arrangement is the pick of their selection.* **Ant. 1.** reject, refuse, ignore. **3.** worse, reject, least.

picket *vb.* **1.** demonstrate, protest, boycott, blockade. *The workers are picketing for better working conditions.* –*n.* **2.** fence, post, stake, peg. *The pickets were set in the ground to form a barrier.* **3.** guard, patrol, lookout, sentinel, sentry, watch. *The picket sounded his bugle when the reinforcements arrived.*

picky *adj.* fussy, selective, choosy, finicky, particular, discriminating. *Toddlers can be picky eaters.* **Ant.** undiscriminating.

picture *n.* **1.** painting, drawing, photograph, illustration, depiction. *This is a picture of the Statue of Liberty.* **2.** movie, film, motion picture, cinema. Citizen Kane *is my favorite picture.* **3.** image, likeness, description, representation. *The real-estate agent made the property sound like a picture of serenity.* –*vb.* **4.** imagine, conceive, envision, fancy. *Picture yourself on a beach in Tahiti.*

picturesque *adj.* scenic, photogenic, photographic, idyllic, eye-catching, breathtaking. *The Pennsylvania farm lands are picturesque.*

piece *n.* **1.** portion, part, amount, unit, section, segment. *Would you like a piece of pie?* –*vb.* **2.** fix, patch, repair, restore. *Let's try to piece this old jalopy back together.* **Ant. 1.** all, total, entirety. **2.** break, tear, crack.

pier *n.* dock, wharf, breakwater. *The boat was docked at the pier.*

pierce *vb.* **1.** puncture, enter, stab, penetrate, prick, impale, stick. *The needle pierced his skin.* **2.** wound, affect, sting, hurt, pain, move. *The sight of the starving children pierced her heart.* **Ant. 2.** calm, soothe, please.

piety *n.* godliness, devoutness, devotion, faith, holiness, zeal. *Her piety was genuine, as she attended church every Sunday.* **Ant.** atheism, irreverence.

pig *n.* hog, swine, piglet, shoat, boar, sow. *Pigs like to wallow in the mud.*

pigment *n.* coloring, dye, paint, stain, tint, shade. *They added various pigments together to get indigo blue.*

pigpen *n.* pigsty, mess, wallow, rathole, hovel, dump. *There is little difference between my brother's room and a pigpen.*

pile *n.* **1.** heap, mass, stack, accumulation, collection, mound. *Rake all the leaves into one pile.* –*vb.* **2.** stack, amass, mass, accumulate, collect, assemble. *The boxes were piled in an orderly fashion.* **Ant. 2.** scatter, disperse, strew.

pilfer *vb.* steal, rob, plunder, thieve, swipe, lift, take, snatch. *She pilfered a magazine as soon as the attendant turned his back.*

pilgrimage *n.* journey, trip, voyage, tour, excursion, mission, expedition. *He went on a pilgrimage to his native country.*

pill *n.* capsule, drop, dose, tablet, lozenge, pellet. *Take your pill with food or water.*

pillage *vb.* **1.** rob, sack, plunder, loot, ransack, ravage, waste. *Many villages were pillaged during the war.* –*n.* **2.** theft, plundering, destruction, devastation, robbery. *The pillage continued throughout the night.*

pillar *n.* post, prop, column, support. *A series of pillars held up the ceiling of the cathedral.*

pillow *n.* cushion, headrest, pad, support, bolster. *She rested her head on a pillow.*

pilot *n.* **1.** aviator, helmsman, steersman, navigator, guide. *The pilot directed his ship through the icebergs.* –*vb.* **2.** steer, direct, guide, conduct, lead. *She piloted the plane to its destination.*

pimp *n.* Slang, procurer, agent, whoremonger, street thug, Madam, (slang) hustler, (slang) flesh peddler. *The pimp was arrested several times for promoting prostitution.*

pimple *n.* papule, pustule, (slang) zit, acne, boil, blemish, eruption. *I hate getting a pimple before a big social event.*

pin *vb.* **1.** fasten, fix, secure, staple, rivet, stick. *Please pin this announcement to the bulletin board.* **2.** hold, restrain, immobilize, pinion. *The wrestler pinned his opponent to the mat.* –*n.* **3.** brooch, clasp, stickpin, clip, ornament, tiepin. *She wore an emerald pin on her evening gown.*

pinch *vb.* **1.** tweak, nip, squeeze, compress, cramp. *He pinched his friend to keep him from falling asleep.* –*n.* **2.** tweak, nip, squeeze. *That was a painful pinch you gave me.* **3.** emergency, crisis, hardship, difficulty, predicament. *The flimsy tent is unreliable, but it will do in a pinch.* **4.** bit, speck, trace, little, iota. *A pinch of paprika will add flavor to the soup.* **Ant. 4.** lot, bunch, bundle.

pinnacle *n.* **1.** top, summit, apex, peak, zenith, crest, climax. *The author's third book was the pinnacle of his creative period.* **2.** spire, minaret, steeple, tower. *The pinnacle on the church was the highest structure in the city.* **Ant. 1.** bottom, low, nadir, depth.

pinpoint *vb.* locate, home in on, identify, triangulate, get a fix on. *We need to pinpoint precisely where the leak is coming from.*

pioneer *n.* **1.** settler, explorer, pathfinder, colonist, frontiersman. *Early pioneers opened the American West for further development.* **2.** originator, innovator, founder, developer, forerunner. *D. W. Griffith was a pioneer in the movie industry.* –*vb.* **3.** lead, start, initiate, develop, establish, originate. *The first satellites pioneered a massive development in space technology.* **Ant. 1.** descendant, successor. **2.** follower, disciple. **3.** follow, continue, succeed.

pious *adj.* devout, religious, holy, reverent, righteous, saintly. *The priest was a pious man.* **Ant.** impious, unholy, profane.

pipe *n.* conduit, tube, passage, cylinder, main, duct. *The contractor ran a drainage pipe from the house to the nearby gully.*

pipe dream *n.* fantasy, flight of fancy, daydream, delusion, chimera, castle in Spain. *Before 1969, landing a person on the Moon was a pipe dream to some.*

pipeline *n.* conduit, passageway, tube, main, passage. *The oil company would like to build new pipeline to carry its flow of crude.*

piquant *n.* sharp, biting, pungent, zesty, spicy, flavorful. *The piquant flavor of salsa sometimes makes my cheeks burn.* **Ant.** dull, flavorless, flat.

pique *vb.* excite, arouse, whet, provoke, (slang) turn on, stimulate. *Any possibility of making extra money will pique my interest.* **Ant.** dull, dampen, shut down.

piracy *n.* robbery, hijacking, marauding, thievery, looting, swashbuckling. *Piracy on the high seas was once a serious and common crime.*

pirate *n.* **1.** buccaneer, privateer, plunderer, marauder. *Beware of pirates on the high seas.* –*vb.* **2.** steal, rob, appropriate, plagiarize. *Songs are sometimes pirated by corrupt people in the recording industry.*

pistol *n.* gun, revolver, firearm, handgun, automatic, weapon. *The gunfighter pulled out his pistol and fired.*

pit *n.* **1.** hole, cavity, crater, well, shaft. *The pit was so deep that they could not see the bottom.* **2.** seed, kernel, nut, stone. *An avocado pit is very large.* –*vb.* **3.** match, set, oppose. *The winners of the semifinals will be pitted against each other.*

pitch *vb.* **1.** toss, throw, hurl, cast, heave, fling. *She pitched a rock over the cliff.* **2.** erect, raise, set up, place, establish. *Let's pitch the tent by the lake.* **3.** rock, toss, lurch, plunge, drop, reel, roll. *The waves pitched the small boat back and forth.* –*n.* **4.** toss, throw, delivery, hurl. *The batter could not hit the pitch.* **5.** slant, slope, angle, incline, grade. *The pitch of the roof was too steep to walk on.* **6.** talk, spiel, speech. *He is vulnerable to a good sales pitch.* **7.** level, point, degree, peak, height. *When the audience had reached the right pitch of excitement, the band entered the auditorium.*

pitcher *n.* hurler, (slang) ace, (slang) fireballer, closer, reliever, finesse pitcher. *Matt and Macky are our team's two best pitchers.*

WORD SEARCH

curveball, alternative term for any type of: *breaking ball*
illegal motion: *balk*
illegal pitch: *spitball*
left-handed: *southpaw*
pitches: *change-up, curveball, fastball, forkball, knuckleball, off-speed pitch, screwball, sinker, slider*

piteous *adj.* sad, pitiful, sorrowful, touching, heartbreaking, distressing, pathetic, poignant. *A hungry kitten is a piteous sight.* **Ant.** heartwarming, cheerful, delightful.

pitfall *n.* trap, catch, peril, drawback, hazard, snare. *Going into business for oneself is exciting, but there are many pitfalls.*

pithy *adj.* succinct, concise, pointed, focused, to the point, meaningful. *A pithy review of the movie is more likely to hold readers' attention.*

pitiful *adj.* piteous, pitiable, pathetic, heartbreaking, heartrending, sad. *The movie's sad ending was pitiful.*

pitiless *adj.* cruel, heartless, ruthless, merciless, mean, unfeeling, hardhearted, uncaring. *The dictator was pitiless toward his enemies.* **Ant.** kind, merciful, gentle, compassionate.

pittance *n.* small change, (slang) chicken feed, insufficiency, (slang) peanuts, modicum, slave wages. **Ant.** overcompensation, riches, wealth.

pity *n.* **1.** sympathy, mercy, compassion, charity, kindness, condolence. *Have pity for the starving children.* –*vb.* **2.** sympathize, lament, commiserate. *I pity that old beggar on the street corner.* **Ant. 1.** cruelty, apathy, pitilessness.

pivot *vb.* turn, depend, hang, revolve, rely, hinge. *The entire drama pivoted on the opening scene.*

pixie *n.* imp. elf, fairy, sprite, mythological being. *She was often compared to a pixie because of her size and vivacity.*

placate *vb.* calm, soothe, appease, pacify, quiet, satisfy. *Sometimes it is better to placate people* than to argue with them. **Ant.** anger, displease, dissatisfy.

place *n.* **1.** spot, area, location, site, region, section, point, locality. *There's a great place for camping across the river.* **2.** residence, home, dwelling, house, abode. *Come over to my place after the show.* **3.** position, post, situation, rank, station, standing. *He has a minor place in the business.* *–vb.* **4.** put, set, lay, arrange, deposit, situate. *Place the flower pot on the table.* **5.** hire, employ, assign, appoint, engage. *She was placed on the board of directors.* **6.** identify, remember, connect, recognize. *She could not place the face with the name.* **Ant. 4.** remove, detach, take away.

placebo *n.* sugar pill, fake, test substance, preparation, blank. *Some test subjects received real medicine while others were given only placebos.*

placid *adj.* calm, serene, tranquil, peaceful, quiet, untroubled. *The lake is placid now that the storm is over.* **Ant.** agitated, temperamental, turbulent.

plagiarism *n.* copying, imitation, cribbing, stealing, infringement, counterfeiting. *Plagiarism is an author's greatest source of shame.*

plague *n.* **1.** epidemic, disease, illness, pestilence. *The entire population was wiped out by a deadly plague.* **2.** affliction, trouble, hardship, scourge, annoyance. *A plague of locusts destroyed the entire crop.* *–vb.* **3.** afflict, trouble, torment, worry, pester, annoy, burden. *This house is plagued by bad plumbing.* **Ant. 2.** boon, blessing, godsend. **3.** bless, comfort, placate.

plaid *adj.* tartan, checkered, crossbarred, check patterned. *She looks like a Scottish lass in her plaid skirt.*

plain *adj.* **1.** simple, ordinary, undecorated, common, unassuming, unadorned, modest. *This sofa comes in either a flowery design or plain white.* **2.** clear, simple, obvious, understandable, apparent, certain, unmistakable. *It was very plain that he did not enjoy their company.* **3.** honest, straightforward, frank, candid, sincere, open, blunt. *It was good to hear some plain facts instead of lies.* **4.** homely, unattractive, ugly. *He has a plain face but a great personality.* *–n.* **5.** prairie, plateau, grassland, savanna. *Large herds of buffalo once roamed the Plains.* **Ant. 1.** ornate, fancy, decorated. **2.** unclear, indistinct, vague. **3.** dishonest, indirect, deceptive. **4.** pretty, beautiful, attractive.

plaintive *n.* sad, mournful, pitiful, piteous, sorrowful, wistful. *Many country and western songs are filled with plaintive lyrics.* **Ant.** joyful, happy, euphoric.

plan *n.* **1.** scheme, program, system, design, method, scenario, strategy. *We need to make an evacuation plan for our office.* *–vb.* **2.** arrange, intend, propose, devise, design, contrive, aim. *The senior class plans to hold a graduation party.*

plane *n.* **1.** airplane, aircraft, airliner, jet. *The plane left the airport at noon.* **2.** level, grade, stage, degree, elevation. *He seems to think on a different plane than I do.* *–adj.* **3.** level, even, flat, smooth, horizontal. *He sanded the board to a plane surface.*

planet *n.* world, sphere, orb, globe, planetoid, celestial body. *Humans may one day soon land on the planet Mars.*

WORD SEARCH

gas, comprised largely of: *gas planet*

method of discovering new planets by watching for brief dimming of distant stars: *transit method*

originating mass: *planetesimal*

path around Sun: *orbit*

planet outside of our solar system: *extrasolar planet*

study of: *planetology*

plank *n.* board, stud, two-by-four, four-by-four, two-by-six, beam, post. *We need one more plank to complete the floor.*

plant *n.* **1.** vegetation, flora, greenery. *The plants in the garden are beginning to bloom* **2.** factory, shop, workshop, works, mill, facility. *His father works at the auto plant.* –*vb.* **3.** sow, seed, scatter, transplant. *The farmer was ready to plant the corn.* **4.** put, implant, establish, place, deposit, instill. *Her testimony planted a grain of doubt in the jury.*

plantation *n.* farm, orchard, nursery, vineyard, tree farm, grove, cropland. *Uncle Joe grows kiwi and grapes on his plantation.*

plastic *adj.* flexible, pliable, pliant, malleable, supple, resilient. *Until it cools, molten rock ejected from a volcano is remarkably plastic.*

plate *n.* dish, platter, china. *My grandmother's Sèvres dinner service is missing a plate.*

plateau *n.* mesa, tableland, highland. *The ancient mountain had long ago eroded down to a plateau.*

platform *n.* stage, rostrum, dais, podium, stand, soapbox. *He took the platform to deliver his speech.*

platitude *n.* cliché, (slang) old saw, banality, trite remark, chestnut, bromide. *The politician spewed forth the usual platitudes we had all heard before.*

platonic *adj.* nonphysical, emotional, ideal, spiritual, celibate, intellectual. *The relationship with my first girlfriend was strictly platonic.* **Ant.** physical, sexual, lustful.

platoon *n.* unit, two squads, detachment, group. *A platoon was detached to defend the area.*

plausible *adj.* believable, likely, credible, reasonable, feasible, possible, probable. *He had a plausible reason for being late.* **Ant.** unbelievable, unlikely, implausible.

play *vb.* **1.** frolic, revel, romp, sport, cavort. *The children played until sunset.* **2.** compete, participate, contend, game. *Would you like to play a nice game of chess?* **3.** perform, act, present, enact, impersonate. *The actress played her role well.* –*n.* **4.** drama, performance, show, theatrical. *The summer theater will present a play by Shakespeare.* **5.** recreation, amusement, entertainment, diversion, pleasure, fun. *There will be time for play in the afternoon.* **Ant. 1.** work, labor, toll. **5.** work, drudgery, labor.

playboy *n.* pleasure seeker, (slang) swinger, philanderer, womanizer, hedonist, Lothario. *He described himself as a playboy and had no interest in marriage.*

player *n.* contestant, competitor, team member, participant, opponent, athlete. *Each player participating in the game shall abide by the rules or be assessed the appropriate penalties.*

playful *adj.* lively, amusing, prankish, joking, frisky. *The puppy bounced around in a playful manner.* **Ant.** serious, somber, solemn, sedate.

playwright *n.* author, writer, dramatist, screenwriter, storyteller, (slang) hack. *The playwright has had three of her works produced on Broadway.*

plaza *n.* common, square, court, green, quadrangle, mall. *I'll meet you at noon in the middle of the plaza.*

plea *n.* **1.** appeal, request, petition, prayer. *Will anybody answer his plea for help?* **2.** defense, excuse, explanation, alibi, claim. *Her plea of not guilty surprised the judge.*

plead *vb.* **1.** ask, beg, appeal, request, beseech, implore. *The writer pleaded for an extension on her deadline.* **2.** declare, answer, argue, dispute, reason, express. *When asked why he had failed the test, he pleaded ignorance.*

pleasant *adj.* **1.** nice, agreeable, enjoyable, pleasurable, good, pleasing, delightful. *Did you have a pleasant trip?* **Ant.** unpleasant, disagreeable, bad, awful.

please *vb.* **1.** like, choose, want, wish, prefer, desire. *He does what he pleases.* **2.** satisfy, delight, gratify, pleasure, amuse. *The newspaper reviews pleased the playwright.* **Ant. 2.** displease, offend, annoy.

pleasing *adj.* pleasurable, delightful, agreeable, pleasant, enjoyable, gratifying. *Bee balm has a very pleasing aroma.* **Ant.** repulsive, disgusting, sickening.

pleasure *n.* happiness, enjoyment, delight, gladness, joy, cheer. *The walks in the park brought her much pleasure.* **Ant.** unhappiness, distress, sadness.

plebeian *adj.* common, lower-class, base, vulgar, working-class, pedestrian. *She had plebeian tastes and would rather eat sardines than caviar.* **Ant.** high-class, aristocratic, upper-crust.

pledge *vb.* **1.** promise, vow, agree, guarantee, swear, affirm. *She pledged her loyalty to the group.* *–n.* **2.** oath, vow, promise, agreement, word, commitment. *We expect you to honor your pledge.*

plentiful *adj.* abundant, overflowing, teeming, copious, replete, great. *Fish are plentiful.* **Ant.** scant, rare, lacking.

plenty *n.* abundance, enough, lots, much, fullness, sufficiency. *There will be plenty to eat at the banquet.* **Ant.** scarcity, shortage, need.

plethora *n.* overabundance, excess, profusion, overflow, surplus, deluge. *We found a plethora of pebbles on the beach.* **Ant.** scarcity, paucity, dearth.

pliable *adj.* flexible, pliant, elastic, supple, malleable, plastic. *Rubber is a pliable material.* **Ant.** hard, rigid, unyielding.

plight *n.* condition, state, circumstance, predicament, dilemma, difficulty, trouble. *The plight of starving children should be the concern of all.*

plod *vb.* **1.** tramp, drag, trudge, lumber, tread, walk. *The hikers plodded wearily up the hill.* **2** toil, drudge, grind, labor, sweat. *She slowly plodded through her homework.*

plot *vb.* **1.** plan, scheme, conspire, concoct, contrive. *They were accused of plotting to overthrow the government.* *–n.* **2.** plan, conspiracy, scheme, design, intrigue. *He was unaware of the plot to steal his money.* **3.** story, theme, outline, narrative, scenario. *I can't read a book if the plot is dull.* **4.** area, space, tract, lot, clearing, section. *She was planning to buy a small plot of land in the country.*

plow *vb.* plough, till, cultivate, furrow, break, turn, prepare. *Spring is a good time to plow the fields.*

ploy *n.* tactic, play, gambit, move, maneuver, action. *To win, the chess master used his favorite ploy.*

pluck *vb.* pick, pull out, gather, harvest. *Pluck the strings of the guitar gently, as it is quite fragile.*

plucky *adj.* brave, courageous, (slang) gutsy, spunky, bold, tough. *You've got to be exceedingly plucky to ask a miser for a donation.* **Ant.** cowardly, mousy, timid.

plug *n.* **1.** stopper, cork, bung. *The plug prevented leaking.* *–vb.* **2.** stop, stuff, block, obstruct, seal. *The little Dutch boy plugged the leaking dike with his finger.* **Ant. 2.** open, uncork, unplug.

plumb *vb.* fathom, probe, delve, sound, investigate, explore. *To plumb the depths of the ocean is to explore another world.*

plummet *vb.* plunge, fall, dive, descend, drop, swoop. *Stock prices are expected to plummet when interest rates rise.* **Ant.** rise, ascend, skyrocket.

plump *adj.* fat, chubby, round, portly, pudgy, stout, fleshy. *Overeating has made him quite plump.* **Ant.** thin, skinny, slender, slim.

plunder *vb.* **1.** rob, loot, pillage, ransack, raid, ravage, steal. *The pirates plundered several coastal villages.* –*n.* **2.** spoils, loot, booty, takings, prize. *All plunder from the raid was divided among the pirates.*

plunge *vb.* **1.** immerse, dip, submerge, dunk, sink, douse. *The thirsty hiker plunged his cup into the stream.* **2.** dive, jump, splash, fall, plummet, descend. *She took a deep breath and plunged into the icy water.* –*n.* **3.** fall, dive, jump, drop, leap, descent. *Let's take a plunge into the lake.*

plus *n.* bonus, extra, advantage, benefit. *If you're a fastball pitcher, being able to throw a curve and a slider is a big plus.* **Ant.** minus, negative, liability.

plush *adj.* luxurious, lush, elegant, fancy, lavish, opulent. *She lived in a plush apartment in Beverly Hills.* **Ant.** simple, bare, poor, stark.

pneumonia *n.* lung inflammation, sickness, viral infection, pulmonary disease, illness. *A bad case of pneumonia requires hospitalization.*

poacher *n.* trespasser, thief, intruder, scofflaw, hunter. *The game warden is trying to catch the poacher responsible for killing the elephants.*

pocket *n.* **1.** pouch, receptacle, compartment. *My wallet is in my left pocket.* –*vb.* **2.** steal, take, lift, pilfer, swipe. *The shoplifter tried to pocket a diamond bracelet.*

pocketbook *n.* purse, handbag, clutch, wallet, billfold. *If you're going to the mall, you'll need your pocketbook.*

podium *n.* dais, platform, rostrum, stage. *John was asked to come up to the podium to deliver his speech.*

poem *n.* verse, rhyme, composition, ode, sonnet, epigram, lyric. *I like to write poems, but I can't always think of words that rhyme.*

WORD SEARCH

four lines: *quatrain*
heroic narrative: *epic*
Japanese: *haiku*
love: *madrigal*
rhymeless and with meter: *blank verse*
rhymeless and without meter: *free verse*
rhythm: *meter*
study of: *prosody*
two lines: *couplet*

poet *n.* versifier, rhymer, author, wordsmith, lyricist, writer, bard, author. *Longfellow was a famous poet.*

poetic *adj.* lyric, imaginative, lyrical, romantic, creative. *The author's poetic style differs from today's realistic writing.* **Ant.** realistic, prosaic, literal.

poetry *n.* verse, rhyme, poems, composition, balladry, creative writing. *Writing good poetry is not as easy as it seems.*

poignant *n.* touching, soul-stirring, moving, heartrending, emotional, sad. *We found the final scenes of* Romeo and Juliet *to be especially poignant.*

point *n.* **1.** tip, end, spike, prong, apex. *The spear had a sharp point.* **2.** cape, headland, promontory. *The ship sailed around the point and into the harbor.* **3.** purpose, idea, aim, reason, objective, end, intent, meaning. *Is there a point* *to this discussion.* **4.** moment, period, instant, time, juncture. *At that point, the losing football team made a last attempt to score.* **5.** location, position, spot, place, locality, site. *There are many points of interest in this city.* **6.** detail, item, particular, part, section. *The lawyers went over every point in the contract.* –*vb.* **7.** show, indicate, designate, signify. *The gardener pointed out the best places to plant roses.* **8.** aim, direct, guide, turn, focus, train. *Don't point your finger at me.*

pointed *adj.* **1.** sharp, spiked, peaked, pointy. *Be careful of the pointed end of that knife.* **2.** pertinent, incisive, telling, piercing, penetrating. *He made a rather pointed remark about the condition of the apartment.* **Ant. 1.** dull, blunt, rounded. **2.** vague, aimless, pointless.

pointless *adj.* meaningless, inconsequential, senseless, worthless, vain, purposeless. *It is pointless to complain unless you also go to the polls to vote.* **Ant.** important, consequential, worthy.

poise *n.* **1.** confidence, assurance, presence, composure, self-control. *The young dancers showed a lot of poise for their age.* –*vb.* **2.** balance, hover, suspend, hang. *The acrobat poised her body on the high wire.* **Ant. 1.** awkwardness, clumsiness.

poison *n.* toxin, toxic substance, venom, carcinogen, germ, killer. *Some mushrooms contain a deadly poison.*

poisonous *adj.* toxic, venomous, deadly, lethal, fatal. *The bite of a cobra is extremely poisonous.* **Ant.** beneficial, harmless, healthful.

poke *vb.* **1.** prod, jab, push, hit, shove, nudge, stab. *She playfully poked her boyfriend in the ribs.* –*n.* **2.** punch, jab, thrust, hit. *Do you want a poke in the nose?*

poker *n.* card game, game of chance, draw poker, stud poker, strip poker. *Playing poker is a great way of losing money.*

WORD SEARCH

reveal hands: *call*
sequence, five cards in: *straight*
stake: *ante, chips, kitty, pot*
suit, five cards of same: *flush, royal flush*
three of a kind and a pair: *full house*
withdraw: *fold*

polarize *vb.* contradict, take sides, oppose, conflict, diverge, differ. *Democrats and Republicans frequently polarize on the issues.* **Ant.** agree, come together, ally.

pole *n.* shaft, rod, staff, standard, mast, pile. *We shinnied up the flag pole and untangled the flag.*

police *n.* **1.** authorities, law enforcement, cops, troopers, officers, guards. *The police arrived at the scene of the crime.* –*vb.* **2.** protect, guard, regulate, patrol, control. *We hired more guards to police the fair.* **3.** clean, tidy, straighten, spruce up, clean up. *The janitors policed up the playground.* **Ant. 3.** mess, dirty, neglect.

WORD SEARCH

arrest: *apprehend,* (slang) *collar,* (slang) *bust*
baton: *billy club, nightstick*
book of recorded arrests: *blotter*
chase technique of stopping fleeing criminal by turning cruiser into tail of getaway car and spinning it around: *pit maneuver*
crackdown of crime and gang activity, massive: *sweep*
criminal method of operation: *MO, modus operandi*
criminal alert: *APB (All Points Bulletin)*
criminal, massive hunt for: *dragnet, manhunt*
drugs and prostitution squad: *vice squad*
electric gun used to incapacitate suspect through shock: *stun gun, Taser*
interrogation of criminal: *third degree*
investigator of crime-related death: *coroner*
lie detector: *polygraph*
military: *MP*

photo of criminal: *mug shot*
record, criminal's: *rap sheet*
register criminal at jail: *book*
rights at arrest, required reading of: *Miranda rule*
Special Weapons and Tactics squad: *S.W.A.T.*
spray used to incapacitate suspects: *pepper spray, mace*
surveillance: *stakeout*
vehicle: *cruiser, squad car*

See also DETECTIVE.

policy *n.* practice, program, procedure, system, approach, rule, custom, course, method, habit. *It is their policy to refer all complaints to the store manager.*

polish *vb.* **1.** shine, brighten, buff, burnish, wax, varnish, rub. *Please polish the furniture by Friday.* **2.** perfect, improve, refine, enhance. *The comedian needs to polish his routine.* –*n.* **3.** luster, shine, brightness, gloss, sheen, glaze, varnish. *Your silver has a beautiful polish.* **4.** refinement, grace, elegance, culture, cultivation, class, finish. *The princess exhibited the charm and polish expected of royalty.* **Ant. 1.** dull, tarnish, dim. **2.** cheapen, worsen, coarsen. **3.** dullness, flatness. **4.** boorishness, crudeness, coarseness.

polite *adj.* courteous, civil, respectful, gracious, well-mannered, considerate, cordial. *He was very polite to the judge.* **Ant.** rude, discourteous, insolent, impolite.

politically correct *adj.* inoffensive, proper, PC, mincing, sensitive, acceptable, tactful, mealymouthed. *To speak as a politician, you must behave in a politically correct manner at all times.* **Ant.** offensive, insensitive, rude.

politician *n.* office holder, legislator, representative, bureaucrat, public servant, politico, statesman. *A politician must have great powers of persuasion.*

politics *n.* government, legislature, affairs of state, statesmanship, civics, campaigning. *Someone once said that politics is war without bloodshed.*

WORD SEARCH

ambiguous or sneaky language sometimes used in: *doublespeak, weasel words*
analyst and observer of: *pundit*
backscratching between politicians, reciprocal: *logrolling*
blaming or passing responsibility to someone else: *passing the buck*
cause, one who works for a: *activist*
command of the people by word or vote: *mandate*
corruption profit: *graft*
economic policy that is hands-off: *laissez-faire*
group working on a common cause: *bloc, political action committee, lobby*
group that splits off from larger group because of disagreement: *faction, splinter group*
hedging on an issue, politician's: *waffling*
hostilities between two nations, suspension of: *détente*
hostility but no actual war between nations: *cold war*
insults traded between politicians or political groups: *mudslinging, smear campaign*
investigation and finger-pointing, overzealous: *McCarthyism, witch-hunt*
issue put forth to distract populace from larger, more important issue: *red herring*
law breaking to make a political point: *civil disobedience*
parties, by both: *bipartisan*
practice politics: *politick*
sensitivity toward all cultural groups, practicing: *politically correct*
speech, long-winded: *filibuster*
support for an issue, widespread public: *groundswell, grassroots support*

threat-making nation that is actually powerless: *paper tiger*
wasteful projects pushed through by local politicians, treasury for: *pork barrel*
waste of taxpayers' money, project that is: *boondoggle*

poll *n.* 1. survey, census, sampling, canvass. *The latest poll shows that ninety percent of the population likes pizza.* –*vb.* 2. interview, survey, question, canvass, inquire, sample. *One hundred students were polled about their political views.*

pollutant *n.* contaminant, pollution, runoff, toxin, poison, filth, waste. *One of the biggest pollutants of our water is runoff from chemically treated lawns and farms.*

pollute *vb.* contaminate, foul, poison, infect, dirty, taint, befoul. *An oil spill severely polluted the harbor.* **Ant.** clean, purify, cleanse.

pollution *n.* contamination, runoff, toxins, poison, filth, hazardous waste, sewage, smog. *Automobiles cause a great deal of air pollution.*

Pollyanna *n.* optimist, blind optimist, idealist, one who wears rose-colored glasses, Dr. Pangloss. *You're a hopeless Pollyanna if you believe the world to be nothing but a bowl of cherries.* **Ant.** realist, cynic, skeptic.

poltergeist *n.* ghost, (slang) spook, thing that goes bump in the night, doppelganger. *Poltergeists are often thought to haunt old houses.*

pompous *adj.* boastful, pretentious, arrogant, self-important, grandiose, vain, overbearing. *The chairperson of the board acts too pompous to be effective.* **Ant.** humble, modest, unassuming.

pond *n.* marsh, bog, body of water, lagoon, pool, basin, millpond. *We like to swim and fish down at the pond.*

ponder *vb.* consider, study, think, examine, reflect, deliberate, contemplate. *Let's ponder the problem and not act hastily.*

ponderous *adj.* cumbersome, unwieldy, bulky, massive, heavy, awkward. *Pulling the junked car out of the lake proved a ponderous task.*

pontificate *vb.* preach, sermonize, lecture, moralize, admonish, harangue. *I don't like to pontificate, but I will if you refuse to buckle your seatbelt.*

pool *n.* puddle, pond, swimming hole, reservoir, lagoon, spring. *The pool was icy cold.*

poor *adj.* 1. needy, impoverished, destitute, penniless, indigent, poverty-stricken, broke. *The old woman was too poor to buy a decent meal.* 2. bad, inferior, inadequate, worthless, substandard, lacking, deficient. *It is difficult to grow corn in poor soil.* 3. unlucky, unfortunate, pitiable, wretched, miserable, pitiful. *The poor man has been ill for six weeks.* **Ant.** 1. rich, wealthy, affluent. 2. good, worthy, excellent. 3. fortunate, lucky, enviable.

pop *vb.* bust, crack, explode, blow, report, go off. *We knew somebody had gotten a pin when we heard several balloons pop.*

pope *n.* pontiff, bishop of Rome, vicar of Christ, patriarch, religious leader. *A new pope will change the spiritual leadership of the Catholic Church.*

WORD SEARCH

cape: *fanon, mozetta*
court: *Curia*
crown: *tiara*
electing group: *Sacred College of Cardinals*
envoy: *legate*
head piece: *miter*
meeting to elect new pope: *conclave*
office or jurisdiction of: *papacy*
residence: *Vatican*
succession of popes: *papacy*

popular *adj.* 1. favorite, accepted, approved, well-liked, celebrated, famous. *She is the most* *popular girl in school.* 2. general, conventional, prevailing, common, current, familiar, widespread. *The erroneous opinion that most athletes are stupid is a popular belief.* **Ant.** 1. unpopular, disliked, unaccepted. 2. unpopular, uncommon.

popularity *n.* favor, acceptance, acclaim, fame, celebrity, renown. *Popularity may fade, but talent will endure.* **Ant.** unpopularity, disregard, disfavor.

populated *adj.* inhabited, peopled, occupied, settled. *Southern California is one of the most heavily populated areas in America.*

population *n.* people, inhabitants, residents, populace, citizenry. *The population of the Earth is increasing at a dangerous rate.*

populous *adj.* crowded, teeming, dense, swarming, concentrated. *They moved from populous New York to uncrowded New Mexico.* **Ant.** sparse, scattered, underpopulated.

porch *n.* veranda, steps, stoop, portico, deck, gallery. *Let's go sit on the porch and watch the fireflies.*

pornographic *adj.* sexually explicit, X-rated, obscene, erotic, sexy, lewd. *The pictures of naked indigenous peoples in* National Geographic *are not considered pornographic.*

pornography *n.* erotica, X-rated materials, adult materials, smut, (slang) porn. *Some say pornography is in the mind of the beholder.*

port *n.* landing, anchorage, harbor, wharf, dock, pier. *With a storm on the horizon, we headed for the nearest port.*

portable *adj.* movable, transportable, compact, transferable, light, lightweight. *A portable radio is essential at a beach party.* **Ant.** immovable, fixed, stationary.

portend *vb.* bode, auger, presage, forewarn, herald, harbinger. *Those black clouds on the horizon portend a severe thunderstorm.*

portent *n.* sign, omen, forewarning, augury, herald, prediction. *Folklore holds that squirrels with extra thick fur in the fall are portents of a harsh winter.*

portion *n.* 1. part, piece, section, segment, share, fraction. *Each lottery winner received a portion of the prize money.* –*vb.* 2. distribute, divide, allocate, disperse. *The inheritance was portioned out to his relatives.* **Ant.** 1. whole, all, entirety.

portly *adj.* stout, rotund, fat, pudgy, heavy, large. *The portly man had trouble fitting into the narrow chair.* **Ant.** thin, skinny, anorexic.

portray *vb.* depict, represent, describe, picture, characterize. *He was portrayed as a wicked old man.*

pose *vb.* 1. sit, posture, model, stand. *I can't get the baby to pose for the camera.* 2. impersonate, pretend, feign, act. *The secret agent entered the military base by posing as a general.* 3. state, assert, submit, propose, present, suggest. *The current plan poses difficulties for some people.* –*n.* 4. posture, position, stance, attitude. *I cannot hold this pose for long.*

posh *adj.* sumptuous, luxurious, elegant, grand, fancy, opulent. *She lived in a posh penthouse on the ninety-ninth floor.* **Ant.** cheap, chintzy, cut-rate.

position *n.* 1. place, location, spot, point, site, station. *The position of the Sun left no shade for our picnic.* 2. view, attitude, belief, opinion, viewpoint, stand, conviction. *The president stated his position on the pending trade bill.* 3. state, situation, place, condition, predicament. *Your stubbornness has placed me in an awkward* *position.* **4.** job, employment, status, place, post, rank, duty. *The clerk was promoted to a supervisory position.* –*vb.* **5.** situate, place, put, arrange, set, pose. *She positioned the furniture in a more orderly fashion.*

positive *adj.* **1.** sure, confident, definite, undoubting, convinced, certain, emphatic. *He was positive that they had been here before.* **2.** practical, beneficial, pragmatic, real, effective, useful, good. *We need some positive suggestions on running our business.* **3.** optimistic, good, affirmative, hopeful. *She believes in the power of positive thinking.* **Ant.** **1.** unclear, uncertain, dubious. **2.** impractical, useless, destructive, bad. **3.** negative, pessimistic.

possess *vb.* have, own, hold, enjoy, control. *Superman possesses the ability to leap tall buildings in a single bound.*

possessed *adj.* **1.** serene, controlled, collected, composed, poised, tranquil. *After a good sleep she was calm and possessed.* **2.** bedeviled, bewitched, spellbound, entranced, demonized, crazed, haunted. *In the movie, the* Exorcist, *a little girl was possessed by the devil.*

possession *n.* **1.** ownership, custody, control, title. *Both parties claimed possession of the automobile.* **2.** property, belonging, resource, asset, effect. *He does not have very many possessions.*

possessive *adj.* greedy, controlling, proprietary, acquisitive, grasping. *The little boy was too possessive of his toys and refused to share.* **Ant.** generous, charitable, giving.

possibility *n.* **1.** chance, likelihood, probability, prospect, odds. *What are the possibilities of getting tickets for the show?* **2.** potentiality, promise, potential. *The possibilities for advancement in that career are endless.*

possible *adj.* likely, feasible, practical, conceivable, imaginable, workable. *There are many possible answers to the question.* **Ant.** impossible, unlikely, unreasonable.

post *vb.* **1.** place, attach, install, put, fix. *Please post this notice on the bulletin board.* **2.** station, assign, position, situate, place. *The pilots were posted at an Alaskan air base.* **3.** inform, notify, report, advise, brief, enlighten. *Keep me posted on the situation.* –*n.* **4.** pole, stake, pillar, column. *Do we have enough fence posts for the job?* **5.** position, job, duty, station, function, role, assignment. *The treasurer is considered an important post in this organization.*

poster *n.* print, picture, lithograph, placard, bill, reproduction, work of art. *His room was filled with posters of rock and roll artists.*

posterity *n.* descendants, heirs, successors, offspring, progeny. *I'm writing my memoirs for posterity.*

postpone *vb.* delay, defer, put off, suspend, shelve, hold. *The game will be postponed due to rain.* **Ant.** expedite, advance

postscript *n.* P.S., epilogue, addendum, conclusion, afterthought, appendix. *In the letter, I added a postscript to remind my mother to send cookies.*

postulate *vb.* suppose, guess, assume, theorize, surmise, hypothesize. *Scientists postulate that computers will one day think like the human brain.*

posture *n.* stance, shape, carriage, pose. *He has terrible posture.*

pot *n.* **1.** kettle, vessel, boiler, cauldron, saucepan. *We need another pot in which to steam the vegetables.* **2.** marijuana, (slang) dope, (slang) weed, cannabis. *Joey, unfortunately, was arrested for trying to sell pot.*

potato *n.* tuber, (slang) spud, russet, yam, vegetable. *I like my potato mashed or fried.*

potent *adj.* strong, powerful, effective, mighty, forceful. *Self-confidence is a potent ingredient for success.*

potential *adj.* **1.** possible, latent, likely conceivable. *The potential hazards of cave exploring are overshadowed by its rewards.* –*n.* **2.** possibility, ability, capability, potentiality, capacity. *Her potential as a concert pianist is excellent.* **Ant. 1.** inconceivable, actual.

pothole *n.* chuckhole, rut, pocket, crater, cavity, frost heave. *The city has promised to repair the giant pothole on Main Street.*

potion *n.* elixir, concoction, mixture, blend, brew, tonic, remedy. *The witch created a potion that turned frogs into princes.*

potpourri *n.* miscellany, mixture, assortment, mishmash, mélange, hodgepodge. *Aunt Mary's stew was comprised of a potpourri of garden vegetables and herbs.*

pouch *n.* pocket, bag, sack, poke. *The female kangaroo has a pouch to carry its young.*

pounce *vb.* jump, attack, leap, spring, strike. *The lion pounced on an unsuspecting gazelle.*

pound *vb.* hammer, hit, beat, strike, drum, pommel. *She pounded on the door till someone finally heard.*

pout *vb.* mope, sulk, put on a long face, sniffle. *To get her way, the toddler sometimes whines and pouts.*

poverty *n.* need, destitution, want, lack, neediness. *There is much poverty in India.*

power *n.* **1.** energy, strength, force, might, potency. *He's an incredible tennis player because there's so much power in his swing.* **2.** ability, capability, talent, skill, faculty. *This magic ring gives special powers to its wearer.* **3.** authority, control, rule, command, mastery, domination. *The royalty of ancient Egypt held great power over their subjects.* –*vb.* **4.** energize, operate, activate. *Nuclear energy powers most submarines.* **Ant. 1.** weakness, feebleness. **2.** inability, incapacity.

powerful *adj.* **1.** strong, muscular, mighty, robust, vigorous, brawny, massive. *Two powerful wrestlers jumped into the ring and flexed their muscles.* **2.** influential, effective, potent, dominant, commanding, controlling, authoritative. *She is a powerful leader who gets things done.* **Ant. 1.** weak, flaccid, limp. **2.** ineffective, powerless, impotent.

powerless *adj.* ineffective, impotent, submissive, weak, incapable, helpless. *Humans are often powerless in the face of a natural catastrophe.* **Ant.** powerful, potent, effective.

practical *adj.* efficient, workable, achievable, sound, sensible. *A practical method of filing is alphabetically.* **Ant.** impractical, unworkable, unsound.

practice *vb.* **1.** train, rehearse, drill, exercise, discipline, study. *A great musician must always practice his skill.* **2.** do, perform, observe, follow, pursue. *Good manners should be practiced daily.* –*n.* **3.** training, discipline, repetition, preparation, rehearsal. *All football players must show up for team practice.* **4.** custom, habit, tradition, rule, routine, way, fashion. *It is our practice to have coffee in the morning.* **5.** operation, application, execution, use, usage, action. *The new regulations go into practice next week.*

practitioner *n.* professional, specialist, expert, doctor, nurse, therapist. *See your health care practitioner about getting this year's flu shot.*

pragmatic *adj.* practical, real, actual, real-world, workable, utilitarian. *Her ideas were pragmatic and not at all far-fetched.* **Ant.** unrealistic, idealistic, theoretical.

prairie *n.* grassland, meadow, veldt, plain, tundra, pasture. *There is no prettier sight than wildflowers growing in profusion on the prairie.*

praise *n.* **1.** approval, compliment, commendation, acclaim, applause. *She received high praise from her peers.* –*vb.* **2.** approve, compliment, commend, admire, applaud, laud, honor, celebrate. *They praised the lifeguard for rescuing the drowning child.* **Ant. 1.** disapproval, criticism, ridicule. **2.** disapprove, belittle.

praiseworthy *adj.* commendable, admirable, meritorious, laudable, worthy, honorable. *Your honesty with returning my wallet is praiseworthy.* **Ant.** despicable, horrible, objectionable.

prank *n.* practical joke, gag, stunt, trick, caper, sport. *Give the kids plenty of candy on Halloween or they may pull a prank on you.*

pray *vb.* appeal, beg, invoke, beseech, ask, request, plead, implore. *The condemned man prayed for mercy.*

prayer *n.* supplication, pleading, appeal, petition, imploring, request, benediction, grace. *Prayer can be helpful in times of trouble.*

WORD SEARCH

affirmation, often at end of prayer: *amen*
beads: *rosary*
evening: *vesper*
knee, get down on one: *genuflect*
mealtime: *grace*
nine-day: *novena*
saint's prayer for others: *intercession*

preach *vb.* **1.** sermonize, lecture, evangelize, moralize, proclaim, teach. *The evangelist preached on the street corner.* **2.** urge, advocate, counsel, advise. *The wise guru preached humility and moderation to his disciples.*

preacher *n.* minister, pastor, clergyman, cleric, reverend, man of the cloth, priest. *The preacher delivered a stirring sermon.*

precarious *adj.* hazardous, risky, perilous, treacherous, uncertain, unstable, unreliable, insecure. *Walking on the icy slope was a precarious undertaking.* **Ant.** safe, steady, dependable, certain.

precaution *n.* care, wariness, prudence, caution, safeguard, foresight, forethought. *The auto racer took every precaution to prevent mechanical breakdowns.* **Ant.** carelessness, neglect.

precede *vb.* lead, preface, go before, predate, introduce. *An overture usually precedes the singing in an opera.* **Ant.** follow, succeed, ensue.

precedence *n.* priority, preeminence, supremacy, importance, superiority. *Care of the environment must take precedence over industrial development.* **Ant.** second place, inferiority.

precedent *n.* model, example, prior instance, exemplar, classic case, antecedent. *The court case set a precedent for all future litigation.*

precept *n.* law, rule, principle, guideline, commandment, maxim. *The organization governs itself by a strict code of precepts.*

precious *adj.* **1.** valuable, expensive, costly, priceless, invaluable, rare. *The museum displayed many precious works of art.* **2.** beloved, darling, cherished, dear, favorite. *He still considers his wife precious after thirty years of marriage.* **Ant. 1.** worthless, cheap, common. **2.** hated, disliked, despised.

precipice *n.* drop-off, cliff edge, ledge, brink, overlook, height. *We approached the precipice with utmost caution.*

precipitate *vb.* accelerate, quicken, hasten, expedite, advance, drive. *Verbal abuse often precipitates violence.* **Ant.** prevent, slow, deter.

precise *adj.* **1.** exact, specific, definite, explicit, correct, accurate. *The researchers insisted on precise measurements.* **2.** inflexible, rigid, strict, unbending. *The health department has precise regulations concerning the serving of food in restaurants.* **Ant.** 1. approximate, vague, ambiguous. 2. informal, casual.

precision *n.* accuracy, exactness, correctness, care, attention. *The draftsman drew his plans with great precision.* **Ant.** carelessness, inaccuracy, vagueness.

preclude *vb.* prevent, stop, hinder, forestall, thwart, foil. *A rain shower will preclude plans for a picnic.* **Ant.** help, enable, allow, permit.

precocious *adj.* advanced, premature, bright, mature, gifted, early-blooming. *The precocious child could speak four languages by the age of five.* **Ant.** late-blooming, immature, behind.

precursor *n.* forerunner, harbinger, predecessor, herald, antecedent, vanguard. *Putting a satellite in orbit was a precursor to manned space flight.*

predator *n.* hunter, carnivore, meat-eater, killer, stalker, prowler. *The predator prowled the tall grass in search of prey.*

predecessor *n.* forerunner, precursor, forebear, ancestor, antecedent. *The predecessor of the automobile was the horse and carriage.* **Ant.** follower, offspring, progeny.

predestination *n.* predetermination, God's will, destiny, fate, karma, kismet. *People who believe in predestination believe they can do nothing to change the future.*

predicament *n.* dilemma, fix, mess, crisis, difficulty, condition. *If I had kept my mouth shut, I wouldn't be in this predicament.*

predict *vb.* prophesy, forecast, foresee, foretell, anticipate. *Can you predict my future?*

prediction *n.* prophecy, guess, prognostication, educated guess, forecast, divination. *The psychic's prediction was really nothing more than a guess.*

predilection *n.* liking, fondness, preference, leaning, partiality, bias. *I have a predilection for pizza.*

predispose *vb.* prime, bias, influence, make susceptible, prejudice. *Chronic stress may predispose you to illness.*

predominant *adj.* dominant, important, prevailing, primary, supreme, major, main. *Food, clothing, and shelter are some of the predominate concerns of human existence.* **Ant.** secondary, minor, lesser, subordinate.

preeminent *adj.* superior, foremost, dominant, incomparable, peerless, unsurpassed. *Michael Jordan was the preeminent basketball player for the 1990s.* **Ant.** inferior, minor, unimportant.

preempt *vb.* appropriate, usurp, seize, assume, take over, bump. *The football game is scheduled to preempt regular programming.*

preface *n.* 1. foreword, prologue, introduction, preamble, prelude. *A book's preface will often give you helpful information.* –*vb.* 2. begin, introduce, start, precede, open, initiate. *Television shows are usually prefaced by commercials.* **Ant.** 1. epilogue, postscript, appendix. 2. end, conclude, finish.

prefer *vb.* favor, choose, fancy, elect, select, like. *She prefers to listen to classical music.* **Ant.** dislike, reject, hate.

preference *n.* 1. liking, partiality, leaning, bias, prejudice, fancy. *Do you have a preference for either movie?* 2. advantage, priority, precedence, supremacy. *Emergencies are to get preference over routine medical services.* **Ant.** 1. disliking, aversion. 2. impartiality, equal treatment.

pregnancy *n.* gestation, fertilization, incubation, (slang) the family way, parturiency. *You must take great care of your health during a pregnancy.*

WORD SEARCH
abortion, spontaneous: *miscarriage*
dark line sometimes seen on belly: *linea nigra*
embryo, earliest form of: *blastocyst*
false pregnancy: *pseudocyesis*
fetal movement, mother's first perception of: *quickening*
fluid: *amniotic fluid*
fluid secreted by breasts before birth: *colostrum*
implantation of fertilized eggs, artificial: *in vitro fertilization*
nausea: *morning sickness*
organ providing nutrients to fetus: *placenta*
sympathetic pregnancy symptoms of father: *couvade*
three month division: *trimester*

pregnant *adj.* **1.** expecting, expectant, gestational. *She took a leave of absence because she was pregnant.* **2.** meaningful, important, significant, expressive, weighty. *After a pregnant pause, he continued with his statement.* **3.** fertile, fruitful, rich, full, teeming, productive. *The jungle is pregnant with animal life.* **Ant. 2.** trivial, meaningless, empty **3.** barren, sterile, poor.

prehistoric *adj.* ancient, primitive, primeval, antediluvian, olden, past, early. *Many mammals from prehistoric days became extinct when the climate changed.* **Ant.** modern, late, future.

prejudice *n.* **1.** bias, intolerance, partiality, unfairness, preconception, prejudgment, bigotry. *The judge's prejudices interfered with her ability to try the case.* –*vb.* **2.** sway, bias, influence, predispose, warp. *His unruly behavior prejudiced the teacher against him.* **Ant. 1.** objectivity, open-mindedness.

preliminary *adj.* opening, introductory, beginning, preparatory, starting. *Each lawyer was allowed to make a preliminary statement.* **Ant.** final, concluding, ending.

prelude *n.* preface, prologue, warmup, introduction, preamble. *A comic opened as a prelude to the main act.*

premature *adj.* early, hasty, unexpected, untimely, ill-timed. *The marathon runner's departure from the pack was premature.* **Ant.** late, overdue, timely.

premeditated *adj.* planned, intended, prearranged, plotted, prepared. *The demonstration may look spontaneous, but it was premeditated.* **Ant.** spontaneous, unplanned, accidental.

premiere *n.* debut, opening, first showing. *The premiere was attended by numerous stars.*

premise *n.* foundation, basis, supposition, hypothesis, postulate, assertion, idea. *The premise of the novel was the decay of society caused by watching too much television.*

premium *n.* **1.** value, stock, appreciation, worth, price. *There's a high premium placed on honesty in these times.* **2.** reward, prize, compensation, bonus, gift. *When you buy three items, the store will give you an extra premium.*

premonition *n.* foreboding, intuition, gut feeling, (slang) bad vibes, hunch, apprehension, suspicion. *I had a premonition that the ship would sink, but it never did.*

preoccupied *adj.* engrossed, absorbed, engaged, involved, obsessed. *He seemed preoccupied with his job.*

preparation *n.* groundwork, priming, framework, development, provision. *Painting a house takes careful preparation.*

prepare *vb.* arrange, ready, anticipate, adapt, plan. *Prepare yourself for a shock.*

preponderance *n.* bulk, weight, (slang) lion's share, majority, dominance, supremacy. *The preponderance of the evidence proved that the defen-*

dant was guilty as charged. **Ant.** minority, insignificance, token amount.

preposterous *adj.* silly, ridiculous, unreasonable, outrageous, absurd, foolish, crazy. *Take that preposterous hat off your head.*

prerequisite *adj.* required, necessary, obligatory, imperative, mandatory, demanded. *Five of my courses are prerequisite, and two are elective.* **Ant.** unnecessary, elective, inessential.

prerogative *n.* right, due, choice, privilege, license, advantage. *When you turn eighteen, it becomes your prerogative to vote.*

preschool *n.* nursery school, kindergarten, day care center, child care center. *Are your children old enough for preschool?*

prescribe *vb.* order, recommend, select, direct, dictate, assign. *I'm hoping my doctor will prescribe a stronger pain medication for my leg.*

prescription *n.* order, directive, instruction, preparation, remedy, medicine, dosage. *The doctor gave me a prescription to take to the drug store.*

presence *n.* **1.** existence, appearance, attendance, occurrence, being. *The presence of smoke may indicate fire.* **2.** bearing, personality, appearance, feature, demeanor, air, manner, image. *His bulk and height gave him a towering presence.* **3.** company, vicinity, midst, neighborhood, proximity. *The murderer may be in our presence.*

present *vb.* **1.** give, grant, bestow, hand, provide, offer, confer. *The mayor presented her with the keys to the city.* **2.** introduce, acquaint. *May I present my mother?* **3.** show, exhibit, display, furnish, produce. *He presented his passport to the custom officer.* –*n.* **4.** gift, donation, offerings, gratuity. *Did you get any wedding presents?* **5.** now, today, moment. *Live for the present, not the past.* –*adj.* **6.** current, existing, existent, recent, immediate, latest. *The present situation appears to be out of control.* **7.** here, attending, near, nearby. *All clubs officers are present.* **Ant.** **1.** take, remove, reclaim. **5.** past, future. **6.** past, former, future, coming. **7.** absent, missing, away, gone.

presentable *adj.* groomed, respectable, decent, neat and clean, acceptable, passable. *Make sure you look presentable for your job interview.*

presentation *n.* **1.** demonstration, exhibition, show, pitch, performance, display. *The contractors made a strong presentation illustrating their building plans.* **2.** award, gift, bestowal. *A presentation was made for the top salesman of the year.*

preservation *n.* conservation, conservancy, saving, protection, safekeeping, perpetuation. *The organization was campaigning hard for the preservation of open land.* **Ant.** elimination, destruction, discarding.

preserve *vb.* **1.** save, protect, conserve, maintain, guard, keep, safeguard. *Help preserve our natural resources.* –*n.* **2.** jam, jelly, marmalade. *I like strawberry preserves on toast.* **3.** sanctuary, refuge, reserve, reservation, haven. *Endangered animals are often protected on wildlife preserves.*

preside *vb.* head, lead, officiate, administrate, govern, rule. *The judge presided over his court.*

president *n.* chief executive, head of state, commander-in-chief, CEO (chief executive officer), chairman, (slang) head honcho, (slang) big cheese. *Sally would make a great class president.*

press *vb.* **1.** push, depress, compress, squeeze, poke, crush. *She pressed down on the overstuffed suitcase.* **2.** hug, embrace, squeeze, clasp, snuggle. *He pressed the teddy bear closely to him.* **3.** iron, smooth, steam, flatten. *Please press these pants.* **4.** urge, insist, beg, entreat, demand, plead. *The child pressed her father for an answer to her question.* **5.** push, shove, crowd, surge, swarm, jam, cram. *The fans pressed against the* *rock star.* –*n.* 6. reporters, journalists, newspapers, media. *The Bill of Rights protects the freedom of the press.*

pressing *adj.* urgent, vital, critical, compelling, crucial, essential, necessary, important. *We have pressing business that must be taken care of immediately.* **Ant.** unnecessary, unimportant, trivial.

pressure *n.* 1. compression, density, force, power, gravity, weight. *The bridge collapsed under the pressure of the trucks.* 2. stress, strain, duress, tension, distress, anxiety. *The pressure of the job was too much for him.* –*vb.* 3. compel, coerce, push, force, persuade. *She was pressured into working on Sundays.*

prestige *n.* importance, distinction, influence, status, authority, reputation. *His father has much prestige in the community.* **Ant.** insignificance, obscurity.

prestigious *adj.* distinguished, esteemed, impressive, renowned, respected, important, eminent. *The Academy Award is a prestigious prize for a movie.*

presume *vb.* assume, suppose, believe, surmise, guess, imagine, think. *Don't presume the results till you have all the facts.*

presumptuous *adj.* overconfident, arrogant, forward, nervy, audacious, pompous. *It is presumptuous to assume you will be chosen homecoming queen.* **Ant.** unassuming, humble, modest.

pretend *vb.* 1. imagine, make believe, act, play, fantasize. *The children were pretending to be circus clowns.* 2. fake, feign, falsify, bluff, effect. *He pretended to be ill in order to miss school.*

pretense *n.* deceit, deception, fabrication, sham, fake, fraud, falsification, lie. *The uninvited guest got into the party by pretense.* **Ant.** truthfulness, honesty, candor.

pretentious *adj.* pompous, self-important, showy, gaudy, affected, smug. *The meal was good, but our waiter was very pretentious.* **Ant.** modest, unassuming, simple

pretext *n.* excuse, pretense, device, guise, reason, basis, alibi. *He needed a pretext to be in the gym during lunchtime.*

pretty *adj.* 1. beautiful, attractive, lovely, comely, fair, good-looking, cute. *Your girlfriend is very pretty.* –*adv.* 2. moderately, fairly, reasonably, somewhat, rather. *It's a pretty long drive to San Francisco.* **Ant.** 1. ugly, plain, homely, unattractive.

prevail *vb.* win, overcome, beat, dominate, conquer, succeed. *In the championship, the best team will almost always prevail.* **Ant.** lose, fail, flop.

prevailing *adj.* reigning, superior, dominating, dominant, predominant, preponderant. *According to prevailing wisdom, the Moon is not made out of green cheese.* **Ant.** failing, outmoded, inferior.

prevalent *adj.* common, prevailing, widespread, extensive, numerous, commonplace. *Trout are prevalent in mountain streams.* **Ant.** limited, rare, scarce.

prevent *vb.* stop, halt, obstruct, slow, thwart, defer, avoid, hinder, check. *Only you can prevent forest fires.* **Ant.** permit, allow, encourage.

prevention *n.* deterrence, preclusion, prohibition, thwarting, inhibition, stoppage, interception. *Disease prevention is almost always easier than disease treatment.*

previous *adj.* preceding, earlier, former, prior, foregoing, foregone. *The surfing was better in previous summers.* **Ant.** following, later, subsequent.

prey *n.* 1. victim, quarry, target, catch, chase, game. *The lion stalked her prey.* –*vb.* 2. victimize, seize, attack, hunt, exploit. *A gullible traveler may be preyed on by criminals.*

price *n.* **1.** cost, value, expense, worth, charge, amount, assessment. *What is the price of that diamond ring?* –*vb.* **2.** assess, value, rate, evaluate, appraise. *We priced the ring at $1,000.*

priceless *adj.* **1.** invaluable, irreplaceable, valuable, costly. *The Hope Diamond is a priceless gem.* **2.** fabulous, extraordinary, splendid, fantastic, unique, rare. *She has a priceless sense of humor.* **Ant. 1.** worthless, cheap. **2.** ordinary, common, dull, forgettable.

prick *vb.* pierce, stick, puncture, perforate, lance, stab. *Be careful around the roses or their thorns will prick you.*

pride *n.* **1.** satisfaction, delight, fulfillment, happiness, enjoyment. *That artist takes great pride in her sculptures.* **2.** self-esteem self-respect, dignity, self-worth, self-regard. *A person with pride does not beg.* **3.** arrogance, self-importance, conceit, vanity, egotism, snobbery disdain. *Pride goes before a fall.* **Ant. 1.** dissatisfaction, shame, embarrassment. **2.** self-hatred, guilt. **3.** *humility, modesty, humbleness.*

priest *n.* father, minister, man of the cloth, preacher, clergyman, cleric. *The priest crossed himself and said a silent prayer.*

prim *adj.* proper, prudish, upright, correct, straightlaced, stiff, Victorian. *She was a prim woman who rarely cut loose and had fun.* **Ant.** wild, casual, unrefined.

prima donna *n.* spoiled brat, crybaby, whiner, egotist, grouch, princess. *They don't allow prima donnas to ruin everyone's fun.*

primal *adj.* primeval, original, primitive, prehistoric, aboriginal. *As mammals, humans still have primal urges.*

primary *adj.* **1.** main, principal, dominant, chief, leading, fundamental, basic, key. *The defense of our nation is the primary duty of the military.* **2.** first, original, initial, prime, beginning, earliest. *Her little sister is still in primary school.* **Ant. 1.** lesser, minor, secondary. **2.** last, later, next, following.

primate *n.* simian, hominid, ape, monkey, mammal, chimpanzee, gorilla. *Primates are thought to be the most intelligent animals on Earth.*

prime *n.* peak, height, heyday, zenith, youth, springtime of life, best. *Teenagers are entering the prime of their lives.* **Ant.** worst, lowest, bottom.

prime minister *n.* premier, cabinet head, head, chief, executive, chief, minister, office holder. *The new prime minister took office last month.*

primer *n.* textbook, reference, how-to, introductory volume, reader. *I'm reading a primer on rose gardening.*

primeval *adj.* primordial, primitive, prehistoric, antediluvian, aboriginal, original. *Left uncut by man, trees in the primeval forest grew to tremendous size.* **Ant.** modern, late, recent.

primitive *adj.* **1.** crude, undeveloped, simple, unrefined, rough. *His woodcarvings are primitive but beautiful.* **2.** prehistoric, ancient, primeval, aboriginal, savage, uncivilized. *Primitive people survived primarily by hunting.* **Ant. 1.** refined, complex, sophisticated. **2.** modern, civilized.

primp *vb.* preen, groom, beautify, fix up, spruce up, neaten. *I usually primp in front of a mirror before I go out.*

principal *n.* **1.** head, headmaster, dean, director, superior, chief, leader. *The principal of our school is a likable person.* –*adj.* **2.** primary, main, leading, dominant, essential, foremost, first. *The principal ingredient in apple pie is apples.* **Ant. 2.** secondary, minor, incidental.

principle *n.* **1.** rule, standard, law, fact, precept, fundamental, tenet, assumption. *A major principle in physics is "for every action there is a reaction."* **2.** virtue, standards, ethics, morality, honor, integrity, honesty. *Martin Luther King was a man of principles.* **Ant. 2.** dishonor, immorality, dishonesty.

print *vb.* **1.** engrave, imprint, stamp, mark, indent. *The address of the chapel was neatly printed on the wedding invitation.* **2.** publish, issue, reissue, reprint. *The second edition of his novel has been printed.* *–n.* **3.** printing, letters, type, writing. *She would rather read books with large print.* **4.** etching, engraving, lithograph, reproduction. *Currier and Ives created prints showing early American scenes.* **5.** mark, stamp, imprint, impression. *Someone left a print in the wet cement.*

printer *n.* **1.** typesetter, compositor, publisher, photocopier. *I'll instruct the printer to set the pamphlets in big type.* **2.** electronic device, peripheral, component. *The printer is jammed with paper again.*

prior *adj.* earlier, former, preceding, previous, past. *We already studied that in a prior semester.* **Ant.** later, following, subsequent.

priority *n.* precedence, preeminence, rank, preference, leading concern. *World peace should take priority over everything else.*

prison *n.* jail, jailhouse, penitentiary, stockade, pen, dungeon, cell. *The convict spent twenty years in prison.*

WORD SEARCH

castle: *dungeon*
chained workers: *chain gang*
division: *ward*
drunks, cell for: *drunk tank*
early release for good behavior: *parole*
head: *warden*
isolation cell: *solitary confinement*
military: *stockade*
search of cell: *shakedown*
ship: *brig*
war camp: *concentration camp*

See also PRISONER.

prisoner *n.* convict, POW, criminal, (slang) jailbird, inmate, felon. *If he causes trouble, a prisoner may be placed in solitary confinement.*

WORD SEARCH

reform: *rehabilitation*
repeats criminal behavior after release: *recidivist*
serving life term: *lifer*
spousal relations visit: *conjugal visit*

prissy *adj.* proper, prim, prudish, straight-laced, (slang) goody-goody, puritanical. *Nobody expects you to act prissy in the great north woods.* **Ant.** informal, casual, wild.

pristine *adj.* untouched, clean, uncontaminated, unpolluted, unspoiled, pure. *There are few pristine bodies of water left in the world.* **Ant.** spoiled, contaminated, sullied.

privacy *n.* seclusion, solitude, separation, secrecy, sequestration, concealment. *We stayed in separate rooms because we both liked privacy.*

private *adj.* **1.** personal, own, individual, exclusive, peculiar, particular. *Do not trespass on that person's private property.* **2.** secret, hidden, confidential, covert, classified, concealed. *Several businessmen held a private meeting to discuss the merger.* **Ant. 1.** public, common, general. **2.** known, open, publicized.

privation *n.* deprivation, need, lack, want, hardship, security. *The victims of the tsunami suffered terrible privation.* **Ant.** satisfaction, fulfillment, riches.

privilege *n.* benefit, freedom, advantage, permission, liberty, entitlement, license. *The right to vote is a privilege.*

prize *n.* **1.** award, reward, premium, winnings, bounty, honor, purse. *The prize for first place was a week in Hawaii.* –*vb.* **2.** value, esteem, cherish, treasure, admire, appreciate. *The millionaire prized her art collection.* –*adj.* **3.** award-winning, valued, outstanding, champion, acclaimed. *His prize pig won a blue ribbon at the fair.* **Ant.** **2.** disregard, undervalue, dislike **3.** ordinary, mediocre.

probability *n.* odds, chances, likelihood, possibility, prospect, expectation. *There is little probability of being struck by lightning unless you stand outside in thunderstorms.*

probable *adj.* likely, believable, credible, presumable, feasible, reasonable, expected, promising, presumed. *It's probable that the mountains will have snow by Saturday.* **Ant.** unlikely, improbable, unreasonable.

probe *vb.* **1.** investigate, examine, scrutinize, explore, search, research, study, inspect. *Astronomers are probing the mysteries of the universe.* –*n.* **2.** examination, research, investigation, exploration. *A shipwreck was discovered during the probe of the ocean floor.*

problem *n.* **1.** dilemma, difficulty, predicament, issue, quandary. *Her tardiness is getting to be a problem.* **2.** puzzle, question, riddle, mystery. *Did you solve the geometry problem?* –*adj.* **3.** difficult, unruly, unmanageable, uncontrollable, stubborn. *This is a special class for problem students.* **Ant.** **2.** solution, answer. **3.** manageable, model, perfect.

procedure *n.* course, way, method, process, operation, action, policy, routine, strategy. *Each office follows a different procedure.*

proceed *vb.* continue, progress, advance, carry on, go. *Proceed to the next corner and turn right.* **Ant.** stop, retreat, halt, recede.

proceeds *n.* profits, take, winnings, earnings, income, net, gross. *The proceeds from the dance will go to charity.*

process *vb.* **1.** treat, prepare, handle, deal with, ready. *We will process your job application as soon as there is a vacancy.* –*n.* **2.** procedure, system, method, operation, way, conduct. *He is learning the process for baking bread.*

procession *n.* parade, march, file, caravan, line, cavalcade, train. *The funeral procession continued to the cemetery.*

proclaim *vb.* announce, declare, voice, state, herald, advertise. *The inventor proclaimed that he had developed an antigravity machine.*

proclamation *n.* announcement, declaration, statement, notice, pronouncement, edict. *The city distributed a proclamation concerning new leash laws.*

proclivity *n.* inclination, propensity, leaning, penchant, predilection, weakness. *She has a proclivity for saying the wrong thing.*

procrastinate *vb.* delay, stall, postpone, put off, hesitate, defer, dally. *She tends to procrastinate until the very last moment.* **Ant.** expedite, hasten, hurry.

procreate *vb.* reproduce, propagate, bear, spawn, beget, breed. *Many wild animals procreate in the spring.*

procure *vb.* get, obtain, acquire, secure, gain, win. *She is trying to procure tickets to the concert.*

prod *vb.* **1.** jab, poke, stab, nudge, push, goad. *He prodded the cattle into a pen.* **2.** excite, stir, prompt, encourage, push, spur, motivate. *The dance instructor prodded her students to practice daily.* **Ant.** **2.** discourage, dissuade, restrain.

prodigal *adj.* wasteful, extravagant, spendthrift, lavish, excessive, immoderate. *The prodigal lottery winner spent all of his money in less than a year.* **Ant.** thrifty, frugal, cheap.

prodigious *adj.* enormous, stupendous, extraordinary, monumental, Herculean, impressive, phenomenal. *His efforts in the local charity drive were prodigious.* **Ant.** tiny, insignificant, trivial.

prodigy *n.* genius, sensation, wonder, (slang) whiz kid, sensation, wunderkind, gifted student. *At the age of eight, she was playing the violin with exceptional skill; she was clearly a prodigy.*

produce *vb.* **1.** bear, yield, bring forth, supply, furnish, give. *This farmland produces many tons of corn yearly.* **2.** create, make, generate, originate, form, formulate. *The local factory produces microwave ovens.* **3.** show, present, exhibit, display, bring, demonstrate. *Why do you accuse her when you can't produce any proof?* *–n.* **4.** harvest, crop, resource, product. *Rice is China's major produce.* **Ant.** **3.** conceal, hide.

product *n.* **1.** result, outcome, output, effect, consequence, turnout, end. *Good health is a product of daily exercise and proper nutrition.* **2.** goods, merchandise, produce, stock, commodity. *Many products are imported from foreign countries.*

production *n.* manufacture, fabrication, creation, generation, assembly, construction. *We'll have to suspend production of widgets until we receive more raw material.*

productive *adj.* fruitful, profitable, rewarding, fecund, fertile, rich. *His fields were remarkably productive.* **Ant.** unproductive, infertile, worthless.

productivity *n.* output, production, capacity, turnout, yield. *Productivity has increased since we installed the new lighting.*

profane *adj.* **1.** wicked, sinful, obscene, blasphemous, worldly, secular. *He shocked the audience with his profane remarks.* *–vb.* **2.** debase, desecrate, abuse, offend, revile, violate, blaspheme. *Her behavior profaned the sanctity of the temple.* **Ant.** **1.** proper, reverent, pious. **2.** revere, respect, honor.

profanity *n.* swear word, obscenity, cuss word, four-letter word, expletive, oath. *Uttering any kind of profanity is prohibited on school grounds.*

profess *vb.* declare, claim, state, admit, avow, affirm, announce, proclaim, confirm. *The accused woman professed her innocence.*

profession *n.* **1.** career, occupation, vocation, employment, job, calling, field, business, work, discipline. *The profession of koala ranching is not in great demand.* **2.** declaration, avowal, announcement, statement, pledge, affirmation. *Their marriage ceremony was a profession of their love for each other.* **Ant.** **1.** hobby, pastime, avocation. **2.** denial, negation, withholding.

professional *adj.* expert, master, virtuoso, journeyman, specialist, authority. *If you're having work done on your house, be sure to hire a professional, not an amateur.* **Ant.** amateur, neophyte, incompetent.

professor *n.* teacher, instructor, scholar, educator, tutor. *She is a professor at Harvard University.*

proficient *adj.* skilled, competent, capable, qualified, talented. *It takes a proficient administrator to handle this department.* **Ant.** unskilled, incompetent, bad, inept.

profile *n.* **1.** outline, contour, side view, silhouette. *The artist wishes to draw your profile.* **2.** biography, character sketch, portrait. *There's a profile of the author on the back page of his book.* *–vb.* **3.** feature, highlight, write about, mention. *Our school yearbook profiled the homecoming queen.*

profit *n.* **1.** earnings, return, gain, income, pay, revenue, proceeds. *He made a respectable profit from the sale of his car.* **2.** benefit, improvement, advantage, advancement, good, value. *The time you spend studying will be of profit in the future.* *–vb.* **3.** gain, improve, advance, benefit, reap.

She learned to profit from her mistakes. **Ant. 1.** loss, debit, debt. **2.** harm, damage. **3.** lose, worsen.

profitable *adj.* **1.** lucrative, gainful, paying, moneymaking. *Computer programming can be a profitable profession.* **2.** rewarding, worthwhile, favorable, beneficial, productive, fruitful, valuable. *His volunteer work in the hospital was a profitable experience.* **Ant. 1.** unprofitable, losing. **2.** harmful, damaging, useless, vain.

profound *adj.* **1.** deep, penetrating, thoughtful, wise, intellectual, insightful, learned, serious. *The professor offered some profound advice.* **2.** thorough, severe, deep, total, exhaustive, intense. *Pollution may have a profound effect on the Earth's atmosphere.* **Ant. 1.** shallow, stupid, meaningless, silly. **2.** slight, superficial.

profuse *adj.* free-flowing, abundant, copious, plentiful, excessive, lavish. *Pressure must be applied to a wound to stop profuse bleeding.* **Ant.** sparse, meager, limited.

profusion *n.* outpouring, overflow, abundance, deluge, flood, plethora, excess. *We watched a profusion of salmon fight their way upstream.* **Ant.** dearth, scarcity, small amount.

progeny *n.* children, offspring, descendants, young, lineage, (slang) kids. *My grandparents are proud of their progeny and dote on them at every opportunity.*

prognosis *n.* outlook, forecast, prediction, turnout, yield. *The doctor's prognosis was that I would be fine.*

prognosticator *n.* seer, diviner, prophet, forecaster. *In Homeric legend, Cassandra was a prognosticator of the future.*

program *n.* **1.** agenda, schedule, plan, list, slate, docket. *The program for the festival includes both folk dancing and a juggling act.* –*vb.* **2.** schedule, arrange, slate, book, plan, engage, organize. *We programmed a wide range of activities for summer camp.*

progress *vb.* **1.** advance, improve, proceed, develop, grow, flourish. *The new research continued to progress at a steady pace.* –*n.* **2.** improvement, advancement, development, progression, growth. *The weight lifter measured her progress after each training session.* **Ant. 1.** regress, retreat, decay. **2.** regression, decline, loss.

progressive *adj.* modern, advanced, revolutionary, cutting-edge, pioneering, trailblazing. *The medical center is experimenting with progressive treatments for its patients.* **Ant.** regressive, antiquated, outmoded.

prohibit *vb.* stop, forbid, ban, disallow, hinder, deny, restrict, impede, prevent. *Camping is prohibited in most city parks.* **Ant.** allow, permit, let, legalize.

prohibition *n.* ban, outlawing, proscription, restriction, embargo, interdiction. *The legislature is considering a prohibition on fireworks.* **Ant.** acceptance, approval, legalization.

prohibitive *adj.* restrictive, forbidding, suppressive, repressive, restraining, obstructive. *The teacher's prohibitive demands made his students uneasy.* **Ant.** permissive, accepting, open, tolerant.

project *vb.* **1.** extend, bulge, protrude, jut, overhang. *The diving board projected out from the swimming pool.* **2.** plan, outline, design, calculate, estimate, determine. *The library is projected to be the most expensive aspect of the new university.* **3.** throw, cast, send, shoot, propel, discharge, launch. *A catapult projected the jet into the air.* –*n.* **4.** plan, design, proposal, scheme, undertaking, task, venture. *His latest project is to build a yacht.*

projection *n.* **1.** ledge, protrusion, overhang, bulge, extension, shelf. *A projection gave the mountain climbers a place to rest.* **2.** estimate, guess, prediction, forecast, evaluation. *We need a projection of the costs for building a new gymnasium.*

proliferate *vb.* grow, mushroom, expand, spread, multiply, increase. *Burger franchises tend to proliferate at a rapid pace.* **Ant.** decrease, die out, recede.

prolific *adj.* productive, fertile, fruitful, creative. *That prolific author has written more than a hundred books.* **Ant.** unproductive, unfruitful.

prologue *n.* preface, introduction, foreword, opening. *Be sure to read the prologue before starting the first chapter.*

prolong *vb.* extend, lengthen, stretch, continue, delay, draw out. *The snowstorm prolonged their stay for two more days.* **Ant.** abbreviate, shorten, limit, curtail.

promenade *n.* walk, walkway, footpath, avenue, mall, course. *Let's take a shortcut along the promenade.*

prominence *n.* **1.** notoriety, renown, fame, eminence, standing, importance, status. *Our math instructor achieved state prominence by winning the title of "teacher of the year."* **2.** projection, bump, bulge, eminence, protuberance, hump. *The mountain challenges hikers with numerous prominences.*

prominent *adj.* **1.** obvious, noticeable, conspicuous, evident, pronounced, visible. *The rock outcrop was quite prominent on the hillside.* **2.** important, famous, noted, notable, eminent, distinguished, celebrated, renowned. *That geologist is very prominent in her field.* **Ant. 1.** inconspicuous, hidden, indistinct. **2.** unimportant, unknown.

promiscuous *adj.* sexually active, (slang) easy, oversexed, fast, loose, wanton, indiscriminate. *Your odds of a contracting a sexually transmitted disease are extremely high if you engage in promiscuous behavior.* **Ant.** chaste, virginal, celibate.

promise *vb.* **1.** pledge, swear, assure, vow, guarantee, agree. *Do you promise to come back tomorrow?* *–n.* **2.** assurance, oath, vow, pledge, commitment, word. *He is expected to keep his promise.* **3.** ability, talent, capacity, prospect. *That pianist shows a lot of promise.*

promising *adj.* encouraging, favorable, optimistic, hopeful, reassuring. *His opening remarks got the lecture off to a promising start.* **Ant.** discouraging, unfavorable, bleak.

promontory *n.* headland, head, point, bluff, projection, height. *You can see for miles when standing atop a promontory.*

promote *vb.* **1.** help, aid, assist, support, encourage, advance. *Her nonviolent actions promoted a belief in her sincerity.* **2.** advertise, publicize, sell, boost, plug, push. *He promoted his book on local television shows.* **3.** elevate, raise, advance, exalt, upgrade. *The company promoted the clerk to a supervisory position.* **Ant. 1.** impede, hinder, discourage, obstruct. **3.** demote, downgrade.

promoter *n.* publicist, backer, booster, salesman, supporter, organizer. *The promoter ran ads on the radio for the upcoming concert.*

promotion *n.* **1.** publicity, selling, advertising, backing, supporting, plugging, touting. *You have to use a little hype to succeed in the art of promotion.* **2.** graduation, step up the ladder, upgrade, advance, raise. *The boss gave her a promotion and a raise.*

prompt *adj.* **1.** immediate, instant, quick, ready, punctual, quick, rapid, swift, efficient.

The firefighters took prompt action to extinguish the flames. –*vb.* **2.** suggest, hint, assist, remind, cue, help, nudge. *The actor needed to be prompted on his lines.* **3.** stimulate, arouse, impel, motivate, cause, inspire, convince. *The accusations prompted the senator to defend herself.* **Ant. 1.** lax, slow, late, overdue. **3.** discourage, deter, dissuade.

promptly *adv.* immediately, at once, instantly, now, quickly, pronto, (slang) PDQ. *I expect my paycheck to be mailed promptly.* **Ant.** slowly, eventually.

promulgate *vb.* proclaim, publicize, publish, state, announce, communicate, broadcast. *The company plans to promulgate its new policies to workers tomorrow.*

prone *adj.* **1.** inclined, likely, tending, apt, disposed, predisposed, subject. *He is prone to be upset over the outcome of football games.* **2.** flat, horizontal, face down, reclining, prostrate. *Lie in a prone position if you still feel dizzy.* **Ant. 1.** unlikely, averse, reluctant. **2** standing, upright, erect.

pronounce *vb.* **1.** proclaim, announce, state, declare, decree. *I now pronounce you husband and wife.* **2.** speak, say, voice, utter, articulate, enunciate, sound. *Her last name is hard to pronouncc.*

pronounced *adj.* distinct, clear, definite, unmistakable, obvious, evident. *The difference between a horse and a donkey is pronounced.* **Ant.** subtle, unnoticeable, minor.

proof *n.* evidence, verification, documentation, confirmation, certification, testimony. *Do you have proof that the watch is yours?*

proofread *vb.* check, fact-check, edit, correct, blue pencil, copy-edit, verify. *Let the editor proofread that manuscript for typos before sending it to the printer.*

prop *n.* support, brace, pillar, post, beam, upright. *We need at least one prop to hold up the temporary roof.*

propaganda *n.* disinformation, lies, distortion, deception, brainwashing, manipulation. *Propaganda is an effective psychological tool used to fool the public in times of war.*

propagate *vb.* reproduce, breed, multiply, beget, produce, bear, engender. *The nursery propagates thousands of plants and flowers.*

propel *vb.* move, push, drive, start, thrust, launch, shoot, eject, impel. *That toy boat is propelled by a rubber band.*

propeller *n.* prop, screw, blade, rotor. *For safety, stay well away from the airplane's propeller.*

propensity *n.* inclination, tendency, penchant, proclivity, bent, predilection. *The crook seemed to have a natural propensity for thievery.*

proper *adj.* right, correct, suitable, fitting, appropriate, conventional. *There is a proper technique for using chopsticks.* **Ant.** incorrect, wrong, unsuitable.

property *n.* **1.** belongings, possessions, assets, goods, effects, resources. *You can pick up your stolen property at the police station.* **2.** real estate, realty, land, acreage, acre, grounds, tract. *She bought a piece of property near the ski resort.*

prophecy *n.* prediction, forecast, divination, revelation, foretelling. *The gypsy's prophecy did not come true.*

prophesy *vb.* predict, forecast, foretell, divine, forewarn, soothsay. *The fortuneteller prophesied that he will meet a tall blond woman with a wart on her nose.*

prophet *n.* fortuneteller, predictor, soothsayer, oracle, seer, clairvoyant, diviner. *It is getting difficult to tell the true prophets from the false ones.*

propitious *adj.* favorable, auspicious, fortunate, opportune, timely, advantageous. *Spring is a propitious time to plant vegetables.* **Ant.** unfavorable, unfortunate, untimely.

proponent *n.* advocate, supporter, backer, champion, exponent, defender. *I am a proponent of sound environmental stewardship.* **Ant.** opponent, foe, detractor.

proportion *n.* **1.** part, share, section, percentage, piece, amount, division, fraction. *The board of directors distributed a proportion of the profits to each shareholder.* **2.** balance, relation, comparison, symmetry, perspective, correspondence. *Make sure that the deck is in correct proportion to the size of the house.* *–vb.* **3.** balance, adjust, arrange, adapt, shape, form, fit, conform. *The architect proportioned the rooms so they would complement each other.* **Ant. 1.** whole, all, entirety. **2.** imbalance, unevenness, disparity.

proposal *n.* **1.** offer, suggestion, intent, bid, motion, invitation, proposition. *She accepted his proposal of marriage.* **2.** plan, program, scheme, project, design, conception, draft, idea. *He submitted his proposal for a new civic center to the city council.*

proposition *n.* offer, suggestion, overture, proposal, presentation, proffer. *The developer made a proposition to install a ball field if the town council passed his building plans.*

propriety *n.* manners, properness, decorum, etiquette, politeness, appropriateness. *The highest form of propriety is expected while you're in church.* **Ant.** impropriety, rudeness, bad manners.

propulsion *n.* trust, force, power, energy, push, drive. *The jet boasted tremendous powers of propulsion.*

prosaic *adj.* dull, boring, blah, (slang) ho-hum, monotonous, humdrum, unimaginative. *The author's writing was prosaic, and I fell asleep reading it.* **Ant.** interesting, imaginative, exciting.

proscribe *vb.* ban, prohibit, outlaw, forbid, condemn, boycott. *The town council will vote today on whether to proscribe the use of motorized vehicles in the park.* **Ant.** allow, permit, accept.

prosecute *vb.* indict, charge, try, sue, accuse. *The district attorney plans to prosecute her for burglary.*

proselytize *vb.* espouse, persuade, convert, talk into, convince. *The new minister asked the congregation to help him proselytize throughout the neighborhood.* **Ant.** dissuade, talk out of, debunk.

prospect *n.* **1.** chance, expectation, hope, anticipation, likelihood, outlook, probability. *Her prospects for employment seemed excellent.* *–vb.* **2.** seek, search, explore, delve, dig, mine, sift. *He prospected for gold in Alaska.*

prospective *adj.* future, proposed, coming, expected, impending, eventual, anticipated, planned. *They are auditioning for the prospective soap opera.*

prospector *n.* miner, mineral hunter, rockhound, gold panner, wildcatter, speculator. *The old prospector panned the river for gold.*

prospectus *n.* financial statement, investment summary, plan. *Before I invest in a new mutual fund, I need to read the company's prospectus.*

prosper *vb.* thrive, succeed, flourish, advance, gain, boom, increase. *Her health has prospered since she started exercising.* **Ant.** decrease, fall, decline, fail.

prosperous *adj.* profitable, flourishing, successful, thriving, booming, lucrative. *She runs a prosperous candy shop in the mall.* **Ant.** unprofitable, failing, bankrupt.

prosperity *n.* success, wealth, fortune, affluence, riches, abundance. *The banker liked to brag about his prosperity.*

prostitute *n.* (slang) hooker, call girl, whore, street walker, (slang) ho, working girl, strumpet. *The vice squad arrested several prostitutes down on Seventh Street.*

prostrate *adj.* lying, prone, recumbent, supine, horizontal, flat. *The widow was prostrate with grief over the loss of her husband.*

protagonist *n.* principal, lead, hero, heroine, exponent, central figure. *Mark Twain's stories often employ children as protagonists.*

protect *vb.* guard, defend, shelter, safeguard, save, shield. *She tried to protect her children from the troubles of the world.* **Ant.** abandon, endanger, forsake, attack.

protection *n.* security, safety, safeguard, defense, shield, guard, assurance. *A burglar alarm offers some protection against robberies.* **Ant.** exposure, peril, danger.

protective *adj.* safeguarding, sheltering, maternal, paternal, shielding, defensive. *Mother bears are fiercely protective of their young.*

protégé *n.* student, understudy, star pupil, apprentice, charge, ward. *The artist was accompanied by his young protégé, who had artworks of his own to display.* **Ant.** mentor, teacher, guru.

protest *n.* **1.** objection, disagreement, complaint, opposition, disapproval. *She filed an official protest at city hall.* **2.** demonstration, picketing, boycott, strike. *The students held a protest in front of the administration building.* –*vb.* **3.** object, complain, dissent, oppose, disagree, resist. *The citizens protested the proposal for higher taxes.* **Ant.** **1.** agreement, endorsement, approval. **3.** approve, endorse.

protocol *n.* propriety, custom, code of conduct, decorum, manners, formalities. *We must follow strict protocol when visiting the president.*

prototype *n.* model, original, archetype, pattern, forerunner, antecedent. *NASA tested numerous prototypes of orbital spacecraft before the shuttle was built.*

protracted *adj.* prolonged, drawn out, lengthy, extended, elongated, stretched out. *We are hoping to avoid any protracted controversy.* **Ant.** shortened.

protrude *vb.* project, jut, extend, bulge, swell, stick out, overhang. *Pinocchio's nose protruded whenever he told a lie.*

proud *adj.* **1.** noble, dignified, honorable, grand, lofty, stately, revered. *Thanksgiving is a proud tradition in America.* **2.** self-important, arrogant, vain, haughty, boastful, disdainful, conceited, pompous, egotistical. *He is too proud to be seen with us.* **3.** honored, pleased, delighted, happy, glad, gratified. *I am proud of your actions.* **4.** splendid, glorious, magnificent, superb, enriching. *It was a proud moment when Armstrong walked on the Moon.* **Ant.** **1.** shameful, undignified, lowly. **2.** modest, humble, unassuming. **3.** ashamed, displeased, embarrassed, saddened. **4.** painful, humiliating, upsetting, regrettable.

prove *vb.* show, verify, confirm, establish, justify, affirm, certify, authenticate. *You must prove your citizenship in order to vote.* **Ant.** disprove, dispute, contradict, invalidate.

proverb *n.* saying, moral, platitude, maxim, truism. *There is a wise proverb that says "the early bird gets the worm."*

provide *vb.* give, produce, offer, present, supply, bestow, deliver. *The librarian will provide the books you need for your research.* **Ant.** deprive, withhold, refuse.

providing *conj.* if, supposing, provided, given, assuming. *I will pay for dinner, providing you pay for the movie tickets.*

province *n.* **1.** area, field, concern, limits, domain, extent. *The subject was not within the province of his knowledge.* **2.** territory, state, division, region, district. *Alberta is a province of Canada.*

provincial *adj.* narrow-minded, small-town, inexperienced, insular, parochial, unsophisticated. *She had been exposed to so few people outside her hometown that her attitudes were predictably provincial.* **Ant.** wordly, sophisticated, cosmopolitan.

provision *n.* **1.** arrangement, preparation, readiness, prearrangement, precaution, plan. *She made provisions in case she could not catch her plane.* **2.** condition, term, requirement, qualification, stipulation, restriction. *There was a provision in the will stating that she could not sell the house.*

proviso *n.* condition, stipulation, specification, requirement, provision, rider. *Our company agreed to provide a large discount, with the proviso that the buyer contract with nobody but us.*

provocation *n.* incitement, spark, instigation, inducement, stimulus, grounds. *Killer bees require little provocation to defend their hive.*

provocative *adj.* provoking, stimulating, aggravating, exciting, arousing, instigating. *The show was so provocative, half the audience stormed out before it was over.* **Ant.** inane, dull, uninteresting.

provoke *vb.* **1.** annoy, irritate, bother, irk, enrage, anger, aggravate, vex. *He provoked her with his endless complaining.* **2.** cause, prompt, incite, kindle, arouse, produce, awaken. *The decision of the court provoked anger in the community.* **Ant.** **1.** calm, soothe, relax, ease. **2.** appease, prevent, quell, stop.

prowess *n.* strength, skill, courage, bravery, heroism, valor, might, power. *Conan the Barbarian was a man of great prowess.* **Ant.** weakness, cowardice, fear, incompetence.

prowl *vb.* sneak, slink, lurk, stalk, creep, roam, steal. *Why are you prowling around in my yard?*

prowler *n.* lurker, hunter, stalker, predator, thief, burglar. *The police were called to investigate a report of a prowler.*

proximity *n.* nearness, closeness, vicinity, immediacy, propinquity. *Your proximity to the barbecue grill worries me.*

proxy *n.* agent, fill-in, surrogate, substitute, alternate. *I will send a proxy to witness the signing of the contract tomorrow.*

prude *n.* (slang) Goody Two-shoes, goody-goody, puritan, prig, (slang) Mrs. Grundy, Victorian. *She was too much of a prude to tell a naughty joke.*

prudent *adj.* **1.** cautious, discreet, careful, sensible, levelheaded, thoughtful, wise, cool. *A prudent person is less likely to leap to wrong conclusions.* **2.** frugal, thrifty, economical, sparing, saving. *With prudent spending, we should be able to stay within our budget.* **Ant.** **1.** reckless, rash, careless, foolish. **2.** wasteful, extravagant.

prudish *adj.* prim, prissy, formal, puritanical, repressed, stuffy. *He was a prudish man, insisting that all guests follow exact customs.* **Ant.** casual, tolerant, natural, free.

prune *vb.* trim, cut, clip, lop, crop, snip. *Prune the shrubs before they begin to look overgrown.*

pry *vb.* **1.** snoop, meddle, interfere, intrude, nose, peep, peer, poke. *Don't pry into my business.* **2.** lever, force, raise, lift, move, work, break. *The burglars attempted to pry open the safe.*

pseudonym *n.* pen name, alias, professional name, AKA, non de plume. *Some famous writ-*

ers prefer to use a pseudonym rather than their real name.

psyche *n.* mind, ego, soul, self, intellect, being, character. *Laughter is good for the psyche.*

psyched *adj.* (slang) excited, (slang) pumped, aroused, (slang) fired up, inspired, charged up. *We are so psyched about going to the amusement park tomorrow.* **Ant.** depressed, miserable, apathetic.

psychiatrist *n.* doctor, mental health practitioner, psychotherapist, psychoanalyst, therapist, (slang) shrink. *A psychiatrist is trained to diagnose a wide range of mental health problems.*

psychic *adj.* **1.** extrasensory, mindreading, telepathic, clairvoyant, intuitive, sensitive. *She claimed to have psychic powers, but I suspect she was really just a good guesser.* –*n.* **2.** mind-reader, telepathist, clairvoyant, prophet, mystic, predictor, medium. *A psychic can tell a lot about you, just as long as you give him or her a few hints first.*

psychological *adj.* mental, behavioral, conscious, emotional, psychic, intellectual. *Depression and anxiety are common psychological problems.*

psychopath *n.* sociopath, psychotic, lunatic, maniac, deranged person, (slang) psycho, (slang) nut case. *The police are on the lookout for a dangerous psychopath.*

psychotic *adj.* psychopathic, sociopathic, mentally ill, deranged, (slang) psycho, crazy, insane. *Psychotic behavior can often be controlled by drugs.* **Ant.** sane, stable, clear-headed.

pub *n.* bar, drinking establishment, tavern, public house, saloon, alehouse. *The men gathered at the pub for a beer.*

puberty *n.* adolescence, teen years, development, pubescence, awkward years. *Boys' voices can lower dramatically during puberty.*

WORD SEARCH

boys' change of voice: *ponticello*

public *n.* community, people, society, populace, masses, nation. *The public insists on absolute honesty from their politicians.*

publication *n.* book, magazine, newspaper, newsletter, dissemination. *I subscribe to a monthly publication about writing.*

publicity *n.* promotion, notice, hype, ballyhoo, plug, advertisement. *The best way to generate publicity is to appear on television.*

publicize *vb.* promote, advertise, hype, tout, (slang) plug, trumpet. *If you want to sell more products, you're going to have to publicize your company more.*

publish *vb.* release, issue, print, circulate, distribute. *A list of the crash victims will be published in the paper.*

puddle *n.* pool, wallow, drink, run-off. *Please don't walk through that puddle with your new shoes.*

pudgy *adj.* chubby, stout, fat, plump, chunky, overweight. *I've gotten a little pudgy from eating too much holiday candy.* **Ant.** thin, skinny, emaciated.

puffy *adj.* swollen, billowy, baggy, bloated, distended, inflated. *My face always looks puffy when I first get out of bed.* **Ant.** deflated, shriveled.

pugnacious *adj.* hostile, antagonistic, combative, contentious, belligerent, aggressive, bellicose. *The pugnacious student was suspended for fighting.* **Ant.** peaceful, pacifistic, passive.

puke *vb.* Slang vomit, throw up, (slang) hurl, (slang) ralph, regurgitate, upchuck, (slang) barf. *If you drink too much, be prepared to puke.*

pull *vb.* **1.** tow, tug, draw, drag, lug, haul. *The child pulled a toy wagon.* **2.** remove, extract, withdraw, yank, pluck, detach, take out. *She pulled the photograph out of the scrapbook.* **3.** divide, separate, rip, tear, shred, split. *The wrestler pulled the phone book apart with his bare hands.* **4.** move, go, drive, steer, maneuver. *A police officer signaled the driver to pull over.* **5.** wrench, strain, twist, dislocate, sprain. *She pulled a muscle in her neck.* –*n.* **6.** influence, power, leverage, weight, clout. *You must have a great deal of pull with the mayor.* **Ant. 1.** push, shove, thrust. **2.** insert, return, place, plant.

pulpit *n.* platform, lectern, dais, podium. *The preacher approached the pulpit and opened a Bible.*

pulse *n.* **1.** rhythm, throbbing, beat, cadence, vibration, drumming. *Electrical current has a steady pulse.* –*vb.* **2.** beat, throb, pulsate, palpitate, pound, drum, vibrate. *Her heart pulsed faster as she ran.*

pulverize *vb.* grind, demolish, atomize, shatter, crumble, crush. *The champion boxer pulverized his opponent.*

pummel *vb.* beat, pound, punch, sock, hit, strike, drub. *I have no desire to watch boxers pummel each other.*

pump *vb.* remove, draw, drain, suction, siphon. *We need to pump water into the fountain.*

pun *n.* wordplay, quip, malaprop, spoonerism, double entendre. *People who make puns should be "pun-ished."*

punch *vb.* **1.** hit, strike, box, knock, poke, whack, jab. *She punched him in the jaw.* –*n.* **2.** hit, thrust, blow, jab, poke, wallop, whack. *He deserves a punch in the face.*

punctual *adj.* timely, prompt, on time, exact, precise, dependable, reliable. *Please be punctual in arriving for the dinner party.* **Ant.** late, tardy, irregular.

puncture *n.* **1.** hole, rupture, opening, wound, cut, break, damage. *He has a puncture in his rear tire.* –*vb.* **2.** pierce, stick, prick, cut, punch, penetrate. *The balloon was punctured by the needle.*

pundit *n.* critic, authority, expert, scholar, know-it-all, observer. *Political pundits had much to write about Bill Clinton.*

pungent *adj.* **1.** sharp-tasting, spicy, strong, flavorful, peppery, seasoned, zesty. *Creole food has a very pungent taste.* **2.** biting, sharp, caustic, piercing, pointed, sarcastic, cutting. *Her sense of humor is too pungent for me.* **Ant. 1.** bland, mild, tasteless. **2.** dull, inane, banal, flat.

punish *vb.* penalize, chastise, discipline, chasten, admonish, sentence. *The thief was punished for his crime.* **Ant.** reward, excuse, praise, pardon.

punishment *n.* penalty, discipline, correction, payment, chastisement, sentence, penance, retribution. *The punishment should fit the crime.*

punitive *adj.* punishing, penalizing, penal, disciplinary, corrective, harsh. *The judge assessed punitive damages in addition to pain and suffering.*

punk *n.* hoodlum, juvenile delinquent, troublemaker, (slang) hood, rebel, nonconformist. *I was considered a punk simply because I wore a nose ring.*

puny *adj.* tiny, small, little, undersized, pint-sized. *The tiny fish was too puny not to throw back into the water.*

pupil *n.* student, learner, schoolmate, apprentice, trainee, scholar. *She is a pupil at Bullwinkle High School.*

puppet *n.* **1.** marionette, hand puppet, dummy. *The children were busy playing with puppets.* **2.** pawn, tool, slave, servant, instrument, stooge, dupe, flunky. *He is just a puppet of the government.*

purchase *vb.* **1.** buy, get, obtain, acquire, procure. *The farmer purchased a new tractor.* *–n.* **2.** buy, acquisition, investment, possession. *Your recent purchase was a bargain at any price.*

pure *adj.* **1.** clear, clean, unpolluted, untainted, uncontaminated, pristine, healthful. *She breathed the fresh, pure air of the wilderness.* **2.** genuine, unmixed, simple, real, undiluted, plain. *The necklace is made of pure gold.* **3.** innocent, virtuous, chaste, good, unworldly, unspoiled, uncorrupted. *The minister led a pure life.* **4.** total, absolute, complete, utter, thorough, sheer. *Pure skill and determination got the skier down the hill.* **Ant.** **1.** polluted, dirty, contaminated. **2.** imperfect, flawed. **3** corrupt, immoral, immodest, debauched. **4.** qualified, mixed.

purgatory *n.* limbo, punishment, atonement, penance, torment, hell. *The dentist's office can be a kind of purgatory when you eat too many sweets and fail to brush your teeth.*

purge *vb.* clear, expel, dump, remove, clean, cleanse, eliminate. *I need to purge my computer of viruses.*

purify *vb.* cleanse, clean, sanitize, decontaminate, clarify, filter, sterilize. *Stream water should always be purified before drinking.* **Ant.** pollute, dirty, infect, contaminate.

puritanical *adj.* prim, proper, straitlaced, severe, stuffy, prudish. *The school's ruling against dancing was puritanical.* **Ant.** wild, liberated, free-spirited.

purple *adj.* violet, lavender, amethyst, plum, heliotrope, lilac. *We looked out over a sea of purple flowers.*

purport *vb* profess, allege, maintain, mean, hold. *You don't purport to claim that psychics are from other planets, do you?*

purpose *n.* **1.** aim, intent, meaning, end, objective, intention, goal, ambition, mission. *My little brother's purpose in life is to drive my crazy.* **2.** use, application, function, reason, object, sense. *This item has no practical purpose.*

purposely *adj.* intentionally, deliberately, willingly, by design, on purpose. *I hope you didn't purposely ride your bike into the wet cement.* **Ant.** unintentionally, unwillingly, accidently.

purse *n.* pocketbook, clutch, handbag, wallet. *I think Mary left her purse on the beach.*

pursue *vb.* **1.** follow, hunt, chase, track, trail. *The police pursued the escaped convict.* **2.** continue, advance, cultivate, seek, undertake, follow. *The actress pursued her dream of stardom.*

push *vb.* **1.** shove, force, thrust, press, nudge, impel. *The boys pushed a wagon up the hill.* **2.** prod, encourage, inspire, prompt, coerce, pressure. *She had to be pushed into going to the party.* **3.** promote, advertise, sell, endorse, boost, tout, plug. *The store will be pushing their new toys till Christmas.* *–n.* **4.** nudge, shove, prod, thrust, jolt. *Give the door a push.* **5.** energy, ambition, drive, vitality, vigor, enterprise, initiative, pep. *A little push is needed to get this party going.* **Ant.** **1.** pull, drag, tow, draw. **2.** discourage, dissuade. **4.** pull, yank, jerk. **5.** apathy, laziness, inertia.

pushover *n.* weakling, (slang) wimp, (slang) wussy, mouse, coward, milquetoast. *Don't be a pushover, stand up for yourself.* **Ant.** fighter, pit bull, battler.

pushy *adj.* aggressive, bossy, domineering, overbearing, militant, presumptuous. *Avoid getting pushy or people will refuse to cooperate.* **Ant.** deferential, passive, submissive.

put *vb.* **1.** place, set, lay, settle, deposit, situate, position. *Put the sofa in the corner of the room.* **2.** express, say, state, word, phrase. *No matter how she put it, her friend couldn't understand.* **Ant.** **1.** take, remove, displace, dislodge.

putrefy *vb.* rot, spoil, decay, decompose, molder. *The food in the garbage can had begun to putrefy and stink.*

putrid *adj.* rotten, spoiled, decayed, decomposed, moldy, rancid, bad, foul, rank. *Meat that is left out too long will become putrid.* **Ant.** fresh, healthy, unspoiled.

putter *vb.* tinker, fiddle, trifle, toy, mess around, monkey around. *Grandfather likes to putter around his workshop.*

puzzle *n.* **1.** mystery, problem, dilemma, riddle, enigma, paradox. *It is a puzzle how he could pass that course without studying.* –*vb.* **2.** confuse, confound, bewilder, perplex, baffle, mystify, bemuse. *She was puzzled by his suspicious reaction to the question.*

puzzling *adj.* perplexing, bewildering, baffling, confounding, mysterious, mystifying. *North of the equator, a blizzard in July would be a rather puzzling sight.*

pyramid *n.* monument, memorial, mausoleum, shrine, architectural wonder, ziggurat. *It took thousands of workers to assemble Egypt's pyramids.*

Q

quack *n.* fraud, fake, charlatan, (slang) con artist, imposter, phony. *The healer turned out to be a quack with a fake medical degree.*

quagmire *n.* **1.** bog, morass, swamp, fen, slough, marsh. *It is almost impossible to pass through a quagmire on foot.* **2.** predicament, quandary, mess, plight, hole, entanglement. *The land developer fell into a quagmire of bureaucratic regulations.*

quail *vb.* cower, cringe, flinch, tremble, shudder, shake. *The rabbit quailed in fear when it was cornered by a dog.*

quaint *adj.* old-fashioned, charming, unusual, uncommon, curious, odd. *That mountain village is known for its quaint shops and boutiques.* **Ant.** modern, new, everyday.

quake *vb.* **1.** tremble, shudder, quiver, shake, shiver. *The children quaked with fear during the thunderstorm.* *–n.* **2.** earthquake, tremor, temblor. *The quake was felt thirty miles away.*

qualification *n.* **1.** prerequisite, requirement, capability, skill, talent. *You're wasting your time applying for that job, because you lack the proper qualifications.* **2.** limitation, restriction, reservation, condition. *I can say without qualification that she is the nicest person I've ever met.*

qualify *vb.* **1.** fit, suit, train, prepare, enable, entitle. *Her experience qualifies her for a promotion.* **2.** limit, restrict, modify, moderate, mitigate, change. *He qualified his statement by changing "always" to "usually."* **Ant.** **1.** disqualify, invalidate.

quality *n.* **1.** attribute, characteristic, trait, feature, property. *She has all the qualities necessary to make a good president.* **2.** value, worth, excellence, grade, status. *The inexpensive stereo turned out to be of poor quality.* *–adj.* **3.** excellent, fine, good, superior. *He got a quality education at Harvard.* **Ant.** **2.** mediocrity. **3.** poor, inferior.

qualm *n.* misgiving, uncertainty, regret, doubt, reservation. *She had no qualms about cheating on the test.*

quandary *n.* predicament, plight, jam, dilemma, fix, (slang) pickle. *Failure to file your taxes on time may land you in a quandary.*

quantity *n.* amount, number, measure, volume, mass. *She consumes soft drinks in large quantities.*

quarantine *n.* **1.** isolation, segregation, seclusion, detention. *The returning astronauts were placed in medical quarantine.* *–vb.* **2.** isolate, confine, segregate, seclude, detain. *Doctors quarantined the smallpox victims to stop the disease from spreading.*

quarrel *n.* **1.** argument, dispute, altercation, fight, disagreement. *The children got into a quarrel over whose turn it was to use the bike.* *–vb.* **2.** argue, dispute, fight, bicker, altercate. *They quarreled over who should pay the bills.* **Ant.** **1.**

agreement, peacefulness. **2.** agree, concur, cooperate.

quarry *n.* victim, prey, target, object, goal. *The con artist used the elderly as his quarry.*

quarter *n.* **1.** fourth, fourth part, one-fourth. *She ate a quarter of the pizza.* **2.** section, district, region, area, zone. *He grew up in the city's poorer quarter.* **3.** mercy, clemency, compassion, pity, leniency. *The gladiator gave no quarter to his opponent.* –*vb.* **4.** lodge, house, accommodate, station, post. *The troops were quartered in old-fashioned barracks.* **Ant. 3.** cruelty, brutality, harshness.

quarters *n.* residence, dwelling, lodgings, housing, accommodations. *She's looking for new living quarters.*

quaver *vb.* tremble, shake, quiver, shiver, shudder. *The singer's voice quavered when he got to the high notes.*

queasy *adj.* nauseous, nauseated, sick, squeamish, uneasy. *The sight of blood makes me queasy.*

queer *adj.* strange, uncommon, odd, unusual, peculiar, weird. *Her behavior was so queer everyone wondered what was wrong.* **Ant.** normal, conventional, usual.

quell *vb.* suppress, extinguish, silence, subdue, stifle. *She quelled his fears with her reassurances.* **Ant.** incite, arouse, encourage.

quench *vb.* slake, allay, sate, satisfy, extinguish, suppress. *It takes more than a soda to quench my thirst on hot days.*

query *n.* **1.** question, inquiry, request, interrogation. *Queries about repairs should be sent to the maintenance department.* –*vb.* **2.** ask, question, inquire, quiz, interrogate. *His parents queried him about his late night out.*

quest *n.* search, hunt, pursuit, pilgrimage, journey. *King Arthur sent his knights on a quest for the Holy Grail.*

question *n.* **1.** query, inquiry, interrogation, problem. *How many questions will there be on the test?* **2.** matter, issue, point, topic, subject. *The article dealt with the question of life on Mars.* **3.** doubt, uncertainty, confusion, controversy. *There is no question about her honesty.* –*vb.* **4.** ask, inquire, query, interrogate, quiz. *The teacher questioned me about my tardiness.* **5.** doubt, suspect, disbelieve, challenge, dispute. *She questioned his ability to take six classes and simultaneously hold a full-time job.* **Ant. 1.** answer, reply, respond. **5.** agree, confirm.

questionable *adj.* **1.** doubtful, debatable, suspect, unsure, uncertain. *It's still questionable as to whether or not I'll have the report done on time.* **2.** dubious, improper, unseemly, disreputable, suspicious. *Going to the movies every day is a questionable way to spend your entire life.* **Ant. 1.** certain, definite, proven. **2.** proper, legitimate.

quibble *vb.* haggle, cavil, split hairs, nitpick, bicker, argue. *Let's not quibble over trivial details.*

quick *adj.* **1.** fast, swift, hasty, rapid, speedy. *She had so much work to do she only had time for a quick lunch.* **2.** nimble, agile, alert, keen, sharp. *He has a quick mind.* **Ant. 1.** slow, unhurried, leisurely. **2.** dull, dense, sluggish.

quicken *vb.* accelerate, hasten, hurry, speed up. *You'd better quicken your pace, or we'll be late.* **Ant.** slacken, retard, hinder.

quickly *adv.* swiftly, speedily, rapidly, hastily, briskly, expeditiously. *Come in quickly, there's a storm coming.* **Ant.** slowly, slothfully.

quiet *adj.* **1.** silent, soundless, noiseless, hushed, still. *Please be quiet during the movie.* **2.** calm, peaceful, tranquil, restful, undisturbed. *She was looking forward to a quiet evening at home.* –*n.* **3.** silence, stillness, soundlessness, calm, tranquillity. *I can't think unless I have peace and quiet.* –*vb.* **4.** quieten, silence, hush, shut up, still. *The boisterous children were reluctant to* *quiet down.* **Ant. 1.** noisy, loud. **2.** restless, disturbed, fitful. **3.** disturbance, noise, tumult.

quip *n.* witticism, gibe, crack, wisecrack, bon mot, jest, repartee. *His quick wit always supplied him with a clever quip.*

quirk *n.* idiosyncrasy, peculiarity, mannerism, trait. *Putting peanut butter on ice cream is just one of his quirks.*

quit *vb.* **1.** stop, cease, discontinue, terminate, end. *Would you please quit making so much noise?* **2.** abandon, leave, resign, depart, renounce. *He quit his job to go back to school.* **Ant. 1.** start, begin, continue. **2.** stay, remain, maintain.

quite *adv.* **1.** completely, entirely, wholly, totally, thoroughly. *It was quite obvious that she was angry with me.* **2.** really, actually, truly, indeed, rather. *Getting a master's degree in one year is quite an accomplishment.* **Ant. 1.** barely, hardly, scarcely.

quiver *vb.* shake, tremble, shiver, quake, vibrate. *The dog quivered with fear when strangers came to the house.*

quixotic *adj.* idealistic, romantic, unrealistic, foolish, fanciful, starry-eyed. *It's a quixotic notion to think that all love affairs end happily ever after.* **Ant.** realistic, practical.

quiz *n.* **1.** test, examination, exam, puzzle. *She has an English quiz tomorrow.* *–vb.* **2.** ask, question, interrogate, query, inquire. *Stop quizzing me about how I spent my money.* **Ant. 2.** answer, reply, respond.

quota *n.* portion, share, allotment, ration, part. *The relief supplies were divided such that each person received a fair quota.*

quotation *n.* quote, excerpt, extract, passage, selection. *Her report included numerous quotations from Shakespeare.*

quote *n.* **1.** quotation, excerpt, extract, passage, selection. *You have too many quotes in your book report.* *–vb.* **2.** cite, mention, repeat, excerpt, extract. *The minister started his sermon by quoting from the Bible.*

R

rabbi *n.* master, teacher, clergy, clergyman. *If you have questions about the meaning of life, perhaps you should ask the rabbi.*

WORD SEARCH

school: *yeshiva*

rabbit *n.* bunny, hare, jackrabbit, doe, buck, mammal. *The rabbit's brown fur acts as camouflage among the summer foliage.*

rabble *n.* mob, crowd, masses, riffraff, horde. *The rabble of the city surrounded the king's carriage, demanding more food.* **Ant.** elite, nobility, aristocracy.

race *n.* **1.** contest, competition, campaign, run, sprint, relay, marathon. *Runners compete in races during the Olympics.* **2.** lineage, descent, breed, species, color. *The United States is a country made up of people from many races.* –*vb.* **3.** hurry, run, rush, dash, sprint, scramble. *She raced to class when the bell rang.* **Ant. 3.** crawl, creep.

WORD SEARCH

Auto Race

bumper-to-bumper tactic: *dogging*
curve: *ess-turn, hairpin, chicane*
custom-built or non-stock car: *formula car, Indy car*
drag racer: *dragster, rail, funny car*
driving directly behind competitor's car to create fuel-conserving vacuum: *drafting, slipstreaming*
flag directing hazardous car to exit track: *black flag*
flag, finish line: *checkered flag*
flag, hazard: *yellow flag*
flag signifying final lap: *white flag*
formula car race: *Grand Prix*
long distance race: *rally*
mechanical team: *pit crew*
mechanic, head: *crew chief*
NASCAR: *National Association for Stock Car Racing*
pass one track length ahead: *lap*
production car: *stock car*
service area: *pit*
starting position, front-inside: *pole position*
steel support inside car: *roll cage, roll bar*
straightaway, grandstand: *chute*
straightaway race: *drag race*
track that is 1-2 miles or longer: *superspeedway*

racism *n.* discrimination, prejudice, intolerance, bigotry. *Martin Luther King, Jr., fought against racism because he believed all people should live together in equality.*

racist *n.* bigot, chauvinist, white supremacist, black supremacist, xenophobe, klansman. *The racist often stereotypes others.*

rack *n.* **1.** frame, stand, holder, shelf. *He kept his wine bottles in a cellar rack.* –*vb.* **2.** convulse, agonize, toss, torment. *Her body was racked with fever.* **3.** comb, search, scour, scan, strain. *They racked their minds for an answer to the teacher's difficult question.*

racket *n.* **1.** noise, uproar, commotion, clatter, clamor, shouting, yelling. *The racket from the party could be heard three blocks away.* **2.** illicit business, swindle, fraud, extortion. *The police found out about the mobster's racket.* **Ant. 1.** quiet, silence, peacefulness.

racy *adj.* bawdy, dirty, suggestive, risqué, suggestive, off-color. *The comedian's racy remarks had to be censored for television.* **Ant.** wholesome, pure, G-rated.

radar Radio Detecting and Ranging System, tracking device, detection device, scanning system. *The flight controller watched the air traffic on his radar screen.*

radiant *adj.* **1.** bright, shining, brilliant, gleaming, glowing. *The campers woke up to a radiant morning perfect for hiking.* **2.** joyful, happy, merry, delighted, blissful, beaming. *A radiant smile lit the face of the young girl when she opened her present.* **Ant. 1.** dull, gloomy, dreary. **2.** unhappy, sad, heartbroken.

radiate *vb.* shine, glow, beam, illuminate, pour out, diffuse. *The Sun radiates light and heat.*

radiation *n.* emission, fallout, particle stream, nuclear decay. *Long exposure to radiation can be deadly.*

radical *adj.* **1.** extreme, drastic, severe, revolutionary, sweeping. *It was a radical decision for him to leave home and join the army.* –*n.* **2.** revolutionary, leftist, anarchist, extremist, communist, fascist, rightist. *A group of radicals held a march protesting against constitutional government.* **Ant. 1.** irrelevant, trivial. **2.** conservative, moderate.

radio *n.* receiver, transmitter, CB, crystal set, (slang) boom box, Marconi. *Turn up the radio.*

WORD SEARCH

AM: *amplitude modulation*
amateur two-way radio: *ham*
DAB: *digital audio broadcasting*
DJ: *disc jockey*
FM: *frequency modulation*
high definition radio: *digital radio*
hisses, pops, and phasing effects caused by signals reflected off tall buildings: *FM flutter*
identification letters: *call letters*
obnoxious radio show host: *shock jock*
pay radio covering entire nation or world: *satellite radio*
program type: *format*
unlicensed station: *pirate station*
range of radio frequencies: *band*

rag *n.* tatter, scrap, shred, remnant. *The homeless woman was dressed in rags.*

rage *n.* **1.** tantrum, fury, frenzy, rampage, uproar. *The tennis player flew into a rage when they called the ball out.* **2.** fashion, craze, style, fad. *Large weddings are all the rage.* –*vb.* **3.** rave, rant, rampage, yell, scream, seethe. *The manager raged when she found the mess.* **4.** flare, burn, blaze. *The fire raged for weeks.* **Ant. 1.** calm, peacefulness, quietness. **3.** remain calm, be satisfied, be delighted.

ragged *adj.* shabby, shaggy, seedy, patched, unkempt, tattered, shoddy. *The poor children were dressed in ragged clothes.* **Ant.** new, neat, clean, fine

raging *adj.* **1.** angry, enraged, furious, raving, irate, mad. *The raging bull charged the matador.* **2.** violent, stormy, howling, wild, windy, roaring. *Raging waters washed the sailor overboard.* **Ant. 1.** calm, peaceful, contented, composed. **2.** calm, still, quiet.

raid *n.* **1.** invasion, assault, onslaught, intrusion, sacking, foray. *The bandits made a raid on the village, looking for golf and loot.* –*vb.* **2.** attack, invade, assault, sack, ransack, pillage. *Vikings raided early English villages.*

raider *n.* attacker, invader, pillager, looter, bandit, pirate. *The raiders burned and destroyed the surrounding countryside.*

railing *n.* baluster, balustrade, banister, parapet, hand-hold. *Hang on to the railing when you go down the stairs.*

railroad *n.* rail line, railway, tracks, monorail, subway. *Slow down and look both ways at all railroad crossing.*

WORD SEARCH

brake operator: *brakeman*
bridge: *trestle*
driver: *engineer*
driving compartment, locomotive's: *cab*
engine: *locomotive*
fast train: *bullet train, express train*
freight cars: *boxcar, flatcar, gondola, hopper, platform car, refrigerator car, tank car*
hitching clamp: *coupler*
holding area, cars': *yard*
jump tracks: *derail*
magnetically levitated: *Maglev*
meal car: *dining car*
passenger cars: *coach, dining car, Pullman, sleeping car, sleeper, lounge car, observation car, smoking car*
rotating platform used to turn locomotives: *turntable*
shunting mechanism: *switch*
sidetrack dead-end: *spur*
signaling framework: *gantry*
single rail: *monorail*
sorting of cars in rail yard: *marshaling*
steam whistle's peep: *crow*
supervisor and fare collector: *conductor*
transport, hand-pumped: *handcar*
width of track: *gauge*
wooden plank on track: *tie, sleeper, crosstie*
yard supervisor: *yardmaster*

rain *n.* **1.** precipitation, rainfall, shower, downpour, torrent, drizzle, sprinkle, mist, cloudburst. *This is too much rain for the garden.* *–vb.* **2.** precipitate, downpour, drizzle, sprinkle, mist, come down in buckets. *Will it rain tomorrow?*

WORD SEARCH

cycle of rain and evaporation: *hydrologic cycle*
heavy rain, sudden: *spate*
study of: *hyetography*
temperature at which moisture condenses into rain: *dew point*
wind-driven: *scud*

rainbow *n.* spectrum, arc, band. *A pot of gold does not really appear at the end of a rainbow.*

raise *vb.* **1.** lift, uplift, elevate, lever, heave, boost. *The knights ordered them to raise the drawbridge.* **2.** erect, construct, build. *The construction crew raised the tallest skyscraper in the city.* **3.** nourish, grow, foster, cultivate, rear, nurture. *Many farmers raise chickens.* **4.** gather, collect, mass, accumulate. *The telethon for the earthquake victims raised more money than expected.* **5.** increase, better, advance, improve, upgrade. *The president hopes to raise the standard of living.* **6.** ask, propose. *He raised several important points during our talk.* **7.** excite, energize, arouse, kindle. *The television producers hoped to raise viewers' interest.* **Ant.** **1.** drop, lower. **2.** demolish, wreck, destroy. **5.** decrease, reduce, lower. **6.** suppress, check, squelch. **7.** extinguish, lessen.

rake *n.* **1.** hoe, spade, trowel. *The rusty old rake did a poor job of sweeping up the leaves.* **2.** playboy, rascal, womanizer, seducer, rogue. *That rake has chased after every attractive women he's met.* *–vb.* **3.** gather, clear, collect, catch. *They hope to rake together enough people to form a team.* **4.** scour, comb, search, ransack. *The police raked the neighborhood for the escaped prisoner.* **5.** machine-gun, shoot. *The gangsters raked the bank with bullets.*

rakish *adj.* dashing, jaunty, sporty, dapper, chic, debonair. *His new clothes made him appear rakish.*

rally *n.* **1.** assembly, meeting, conference, gathering, convention. *The students were called to a rally in the auditorium.* **2.** recovery, comeback, revival, improvement. *The team made a rally in the ninth inning to win the game.* *–vb.* **3.** gather, assemble, regroup. *The commander rallied his troops around him.* **4.** improve, recover, revive. *Her friends were relieved when she rallied from her illness.* **Ant.** **2.** failure, setback, deterioration. **3.** scatter, disband, separate. **4.** worsen, collapse, fail.

ram *vb.* drive, smash, butt, slam, hammer, hit. *Ram the tent stake into the ground.*

ramble *vb.* **1.** babble, blather, digress, chatter. *The instructor always rambles on about things unrelated to the class subject.* **2.** roam, wander, meander, drift. *They rambled around Europe last summer.* *–n.* **3.** stroll, walk, jaunt, saunter. *We went for a ramble in the forest.*

rambling *adj.* digressive, roundabout, wandering, discursive, circuitous, circumlocutory. *He delivered a rambling, unfocused speech.* **Ant.** to the point, concise.

rambunctious *adj.* raucous, wild, unruly, unrestrained, boisterous, noisy. *The children grew increasingly rambunctious.* **Ant.** quiet, restrained, subdued.

ramification *n.* result, consequence, fallout, complication, upshot, effect. *Lowering the age at which teenagers can drive would have negative ramifications.*

ramp *n.* incline, slope, rise, grade, jump, wedge. *The skateboarders climbed the ramp at blazing speed.*

rampage *n.* **1.** frenzy, spree. *The madman went on a rampage, destroying everything in his way.* *–vb.* **2.** rage, rant, rave, storm. *Rioters rampaged through the city.*

rampant *adj.* widespread, epidemic, uncontrolled, unrestrained, raging, unchecked. *Lawlessness was rampant in the Old West.* **Ant.** controlled, contained.

ramshackle *adj.* broken-down, rickety, decrepit, crumbling, dilapidated, tumble-down. *The migrant workers were housed in ramshackle shelters without running water.* **Ant.** sound, solid, luxurious.

ranch *n.* cattle farm, range land, grange, plantation, horse farm. *He owns a three hundred-acre horse ranch in Wyoming.*

rancid *adj.* rank, stinking, rotten, spoiled, repugnant, reeking, fetid, putrid. *The food became rancid in the heat.* **Ant.** fresh, sweet-smelling.

rancor *n.* ill will, hatred, animosity, malevolence, malice, enmity. *Rancor between the two parties kept them from reaching an agreement.* **Ant.** goodwill, friendship, love.

random *adj.* unplanned, undesigned, chance, haphazard, accidental. *Contest winners will be chosen in a random drawing.* **Ant.** planned, ordered, predetermined.

range *n.* **1.** reach, stretch, bounds, limit, span. *She felt the job was well within her range of talents.* **2.** line, variety, selection, series, scope. *The range of colors to choose from is overwhelming.* **3.** pasture, grasslands, plains. *The cattle grazed on the range.* **4.** ridge, chain, band, tier, series. *The Sierra Nevada is a large mountain range.*

rangy *adj.* long-limbed, gangling, leggy, lanky, lank. *Greyhounds are rangy, fast-running dogs.* **Ant.** short-limbed, stout.

rank *n.* **1.** position, status, class, grade, level, degree, seniority. *His rank of general impressed the public.* **2.** row, column, line, series, tier. *Ranks of bookshelves lined the library walls.* *–vb.* **3.** rate, count, stand, judge. *Getting my car fixed ranks high on my agenda.* **4.** arrange, array, align. *Please rank them according to height.* *–adj.* **5.**

lush, tropical, overgrown, dense. *The explorers walked through miles of rank plant life.* **6.** smelly, foul, stinky, rotten, putrid. *A rank odor rose up from his old sneakers.* **Ant. 5.** sparse, spotty, scanty. **6.** sweet, pleasant, fresh, fragrant.

rankle *vb.* irritate, annoy, anger, embitter, inflame, irk, gall. *Raising taxes will rankle most taxpayers.* **Ant.** delight, mollify, please.

ransack *vb.* **1.** rummage, scour, comb. *She ransacked her closet, looking for something to wear.* **2.** plunder, rob, pillage, loot, sack. *Their apartment was ransacked by burglars.* **Ant. 2.** return, repair, restore.

rant *vb.* rave, declaim, complain, fume, shout, vociferate. *Rant long enough and some people will give you your way.*

rap *n.* hip hop, music, urban black music, street music, inner city music. *My father hates rap music just like his father hated rock and roll.*

rapacious *adj.* plundering, predatory, marauding, thieving, savage, pillaging. *The rapacious crew of pirates would stop at nothing to gain riches.* **Ant.** charitable, giving, philanthropic.

rape *n.* **1.** sexual assault, molestation, sexual attack, ravishment, overpowering, violation. *Females of all ages must protect themselves from rape.* –*vb.* **2.** sexually assault, molest, attack, ravish, overpower, violate. *Most men who rape end up with long prison sentences.*

rapid *adj.* fast, swift, quick, speedy, brisk, hurried, accelerated, express. *The space shuttle's rapid climb into the sky was seen by millions of viewers.* **Ant.** slow, sluggish, gradual, crawling.

rapidly *adv.* quickly, swiftly, speedily, briskly, hurriedly, fast. *The snow rapidly turned to slush when the Sun rose.* **Ant.** gradually, slowly, sluggishly.

rapport *n.* affinity, compatibility, closeness, friendliness, harmony, understanding. *It's fun to discover you have a good rapport with someone.* **Ant.** alienation, hostility, difference.

rapture *n.* delight, ecstasy, joy, elation, enchantment, devotion. *The worshiper looked with rapture upon the religious artifact.* **Ant.** sorrow, distress, misery.

rare *adj.* unusual, scarce, uncommon, infrequent, limited, unique. *Finding the last rare stamp for our collection was difficult.* **Ant.** plentiful, frequent, ordinary, common.

rarely *adv.* seldom, infrequently, hardly, irregularly, occasionally. *Her car is covered with dust because she rarely washes it.* **Ant.** frequently, regularly, often.

rash *adj.* **1.** hasty, brash, thoughtless, sudden, careless, foolhardy. *In her anger, she made a rash decision and quit her job.* –*n.* **2.** outbreak, eruption, torrent, explosion, tumult. *The authorities were stumped by a rash of burglaries in the neighborhood.* **Ant. 1.** thoughtful, careful, calm, cautious.

rasp *vb.* grate, file, scrape, scratch, scour, abrade. *Rasp the side of the door slightly to keep it from sticking.*

raspy *adj.* rough, scratchy, gravelly, husky, whiskey-voiced, hoarse. *Old Joe's voice had grown raspy from too many cigarettes.*

rat *n.* rodent, vermin, pest, scavenger, mammal. *Rats are tough animals who can survive just about anywhere.*

rate *n.* **1.** speed, velocity, pace, gait. *At that rate you will never finish the puzzle.* **2.** fee, fare, rent, price, dues, cost. *The ski rental had daily and weekly rates posted inside the store.* –*vb.* **3.** grade, rank, evaluate, judge, consider. *I rate this food among the worst I've ever eaten.*

ratify *vb.* confirm, certify, verify, uphold, authorize, sanction, validate. *Both leaders must sign the treaty to ratify it.* **Ant.** invalidate, veto, oppose.

rating *n.* ranking, grade, score, classification, evaluation, mark. *The school achieved a high rating for computer literacy.*

ratio *n.* proportion, fraction, distribution. *The ratio of high-school teachers to students is about 1 to 30.*

ration *n.* **1.** quota, allotment, share, provision. *Their ration of gasoline was ten gallons.* **2.** stores, supplies, provisions, stocks. *The travelers bought rations in the nearest town.* –*vb.* **3.** distribute, assign, allocate, disperse. *Many countries had to ration scarce products during World War II.*

rational *adj.* logical, sensible, reasonable, wise, analytical, intelligent, well-grounded. *Vulcans act in a very rational manner.* **Ant.** irrational, crazy, unreasonable, rash.

rationale *n.* reasoning, argument, grounds, justification, explanation, thinking. *The rationale for fertilizing is to grow bigger, healthier crops.*

rationalize *vb.* justify, account for, intellectualize, convince, oneself, reason, explain away. *Criminals always like to rationalize their actions.*

rattle *vb.* **1.** shake, clatter, clank, jingle, clink, clang. *The small baby rattled its toy.* **2.** upset, confuse, shake, fluster, muddle. *The performer became rattled when someone yelled out.* **3.** chatter, babble, blather, blab, jabber. *My friend rattled on about her vacation.* –*n.* **4.** knocking, clatter, clank, clanging, clang. *We heard the rattle of the windows as the truck passed our house.*

raucous *adj.* loud, boisterous, riotous, uproarious, vociferous, blaring. *The city park can become quite raucous on the fourth of July.* **Ant.** still, silent, quiet.

raunchy *adj.* obscene, vulgar, lewd, dirty, explicit, X-rated, pornographic. *My daughter is not allowed to see raunchy movies.* **Ant.** wholesome, G-rated, clean.

ravage *vb.* **1.** destroy, ruin, devastate, waste, demolish, rape, violate. *The city was ravaged by the bombing.* –*n.* **2.** destruction, devastation, violation, rape, burning, razing. *The ravage caused by the bombs was still visible many years later.* **Ant.** **1.** build, repair, improve. **2.** repair, improvement.

rave *vb.* **1.** roar, rage, vociferate, rant, thunder, fume, explode. *He tended to rave at anyone who disagreed with him.* **2.** praise, enthuse, speak highly of, rhapsodize, gush. *Everyone raves about that movie.* **Ant.** **2.** criticize, disparage.

ravenous *adj.* **1.** starving, hungry, famished. *The travelers were ravenous after being lost in the desert with no food.* **2.** plundering, predatory, greedy, piratical, insatiable. *The company's ravenous methods gained it huge profits but bad publicity.* **Ant.** **1.** satiated. **2.** charitable.

ravine *n.* gully, gorge, valley, gulch, ditch, arroyo. *She fell into the ravine and came out covered in mud.*

ravishing *adj.* captivating, enchanting, bewitching, fascinating, beautiful, seductive. *The actress wore a ravishing gown.* **Ant.** repulsive, revolting, disgusting.

raw *adj.* **1.** unprepared, uncooked, unrefined, natural, unprocessed. *They feed the lions slabs of raw meat.* **2.** unschooled, untrained, immature, undisciplined, unsophisticated. *The raw power of the young man was impressive as he fought the trained boxer.* **3.** direct, candid, outspoken, blunt, frank. *His raw comments were received in silence by the offended audience.* **4.** harsh, wet, cold, numbing, biting, chilly. *The raw weather kept us inside.* **Ant.** **1.** prepared, cooked, refined. 2. trained, experienced, disciplined. 3. indirect, flowery. 4. warm, pleasant, mild.

raze *vb.* destroy, demolish, topple, crush, smash, ruin, wreck, annihilate. *The violent hurricane razed much of the coastal city.* **Ant.** build, repair, restore.

reach *vb.* 1. make, attain, achieve, arrive at. *Our horse will not reach the finish line in time.* 2. grasp, seize, stretch, clutch, grab. *She spilled her soda when she reached for the ketchup.* 3. span, extend, stretch, spread, approach. *The cost of the new stadium will reach into the millions.* 4. find, contact, get. *If he needs to reach me, have him telephone the hotel.* –*n.* 5. span, length, expanse, stretch. *The basketball player's reach was impressive.*

react *vb.* respond, answer, reply, act. *Paramedics react as quickly as possible to emergencies.*

reaction *n.* response, answer, reply, reflex, backlash. *The biologist recorded the dolphin's reaction to underwater sounds.*

readable *adj.* legible, clear, intelligible, decipherable, understandable, plain. *My handwriting is not as readable as it could be.* **Ant.** illegible, unintelligible, unclear.

ready *adj.* 1. prepared, set, equipped, willing, fit, eager. *Are you ready to leave?* 2. quick, swift, prompt, immediate, instant. *She had a ready answer to his question.* –*vb.* 3. prepare, equip, set, arrange. *The pilot was told to ready the engines for takeoff.* **Ant.** 1. unprepared, unready, unfit. 2. slow, delayed, late.

real *adj.* 1. genuine, actual, authentic. *That was a real diamond, not an imitation.* 2. factual, true, truthful, undeniable, valid, unquestionable. *She doesn't believe ghosts are real.* 3. sincere, heartfelt, honest, genuine. *Please give them a real round of applause.* **Ant.** 1. fake, imitation, unreal. 2. imaginary, mythological, unreal. 3. insincere, false.

realism *n.* 1. authenticity, naturalism, reality, naturalness. *The artist's use of lifelike colors added a strong sense of realism to his painting.* 2. reasonableness, straightforwardness. *She approached her problems with a realism that was admirable.* **Ant.** 1. unnaturalness, unreality, fantasy. 2. unreasonableness.

realistic *adj.* 1. pragmatic, practical, reasonable, sober, down-to-earth, achievable. *Set realistic goals and work hard to achieve them.* 2. representational, real, true-to-life, lifelike, photographic, graphic, faithful, true. *I like realistic paintings that depict nature exactly as it appears.* **Ant.** 1. unrealistic idealistic, impractical. 2. unrealistic, fake, abstract.

reality *n.* actuality, truth, existence, realness, fact. *The insane man had a warped sense of reality.* **Ant.** fantasy, unreality.

realize *vb.* 1. understand, comprehend, recognize, perceive, gather, appreciate. *My friend's kindness yesterday made me realize how much I really like him.* 2. complete, perfect, achieve, accomplish. *Their final goal was never fully realized.*

realm *n.* domain, kingdom, sphere, region, province. *The queen's realm extended to the sea.*

reap *vb.* harvest, cut, gather, obtain, acquire. *He hoped to reap the profits of his investments.* **Ant.** lose, miss.

rear *n.* 1. tail, back, end, posterior, rump. *The two tired runners fell to the rear.* –*adj.* 2. back, posterior, aft. *The rear window of our station wagon fogs up in cold weather.* –*vb.* 3. rise, tower, soar. *The bear reared up to defend its cubs.* 4. raise, develop, train, nurture, foster. *She rears thoroughbreds on her ranch.* **Ant.** 1. front, anterior, forepart. 2. front, leading. 3. drop, descend, sink.

reason *n.* 1. explanation, cause, justification, incentive, basis, excuse. *The reason he did not* *come was that his car broke down.* **2.** logic, sensibility, wisdom, rationality. *Will you listen to reason and take someone with you?* –*vb.* **3.** figure, understand, solve. *She was able to reason out the math problem.* **4.** argue, discuss, debate. *She won't listen to me, so will you reason with her?* **Ant. 2.** irrationality, stupidity.

reasonable *adj.* **1.** sensible, practical, logical, wise, intelligent, fair. *Your suggestion to split the cost between us seems reasonable.* **2.** fair, just, moderate, honest. *He bought the jacket at a reasonable price.* **Ant. 1.** unreasonable, impractical, unintelligent. **2.** unfair, unjust.

reasoning *n.* thinking, logic, rationale, analysis, cogitation, thought. *I know you believe that the Moon is made from green cheese, but what is your reasoning?*

reassure *vb.* assure, bolster, encourage, embolden, comfort, hearten. *Let me reassure you, there is life after high school.* **Ant.** discourage, frighten, unnerve.

rebate *n.* reimbursement, discount, bonus, incentive. *The dealership gave me a $500 rebate for buying a new car there.*

rebel *n.* **1.** agitator, malcontent, revolutionary, revolter, guerrilla. *The rebels launched an attack against government forces.* –*vb.* **2.** resist, defy, mutiny, revolt, strike, secede. *The students rebelled against the unreasonable school regulations.* **Ant. 2.** comply, obey, submit.

rebellion *n.* uprising, revolt, resistance, revolution, upheaval, insubordination. *The American Revolution was a rebellion against British control.*

rebellious *adj.* defiant, nonconforming, revolutionary, ungovernable, mutinous, resistant. *Her rebellious attitude sometimes got her into trouble.* **Ant.** conforming, obedient, passive.

rebound *vb.* bounce back, return, recoil, recover, ricochet, boomerang. *I try to rebound quickly after an illness.*

rebuff *n.* **1.** rejection, denial, refusal. *The manager's strong rebuff of my suggestion was upsetting.* –*vb.* **2.** reject, deny, refuse, decline, spurn. *If you always rebuff people's attempts to make friends, they will stop trying.* **Ant. 1.** acceptance, approval, agreement. **2.** accept, welcome.

rebuke *vb.* **1.** reprimand, scold, reproach, censure, chide. *He was strongly rebuked for arriving home late.* –*n.* **2.** reprimand, scolding, reproach, chiding. *What did I do to deserve your rebuke?* **Ant. 1.** praise, approve. **2.** praise, encouragement.

rebut *vb.* refute, retort, contradict, argue, oppose. *Every debater must be given a chance to rebut his opponent.* **Ant.** support, uphold, validate.

rebuttal *n.* refutation, retort, contradiction, argument, opposition, invalidation. *Always have a rebuttal prepared for your adversary's arguments.* **Ant.** support, agreement, validation.

recalcitrant *adj.* disobedient, defiant, rebellious, resistant, contrary, insubordinate. *He was fired for being consistently recalcitrant with his superiors.* **Ant.** obedient, agreeable, submissive.

recall *vb.* **1.** remember, recollect, recognize. *Do you recall the time we were in the amusement park and you got lost?* **2.** retract, revoke, withdraw, cancel. *They had to recall the automobiles because of faulty brakes.* –*n.* **3.** memory, recollection, remembrance. *His recall of the accident is hazy.* **Ant. 1.** forget. **3.** forgetfulness.

recant *vb.* take back, withdraw, retract, repeal, reverse, disavow, backpedal. *The newspaper decided to recant its inaccurate report.*

recapitulate *vb.* recap, recount, repeat, rehash, restate, review. *We will recapitulate the basic directions only once.*

recede *vb.* retreat, dwindle, diminish, regress, leave, subside. *We watched the harbor recede from view as our ship headed out to sea.* **Ant.** emerge, advance, increase.

receipt *n.* sales slip, proof of purchase, stub, voucher, record of sale. *You can't return your purchase without a receipt.*

receive *vb.* accept, assume, gather, get, hold, obtain, embrace, welcome. *The astronauts will receive awards at tonight's celebration.* **Ant.** refuse, reject, discard.

recent *adj.* latest, new, modern, novel, fresh. *The two freshmen were recent additions to our soccer team.* **Ant.** old, dated.

receptacle *n.* holder, repository, vessel, container, basket, box. *Insert the toothbrush into its receptacle.*

reception *n.* **1.** acceptance, welcome, admission. *What type of reception did the new songs receive?* **2.** party, tea, gathering, affair, hearing. *She went to the wedding reception.*

receptionist *n.* receiver, greeter, secretary, officer worker. *The receptionist, as always, greeted everyone with a smile.*

receptive *adj.* acceptant, open, sympathetic, open-minded, willing. *Do you think my parents will be receptive to my plan?* **Ant.** unreceptive, unsympathetic, close-minded.

recess *n.* **1.** intermission, break, pause, halt, rest. *We have our recess after English class.* **2.** hole, break, dent, nook, hollow, gap. *The injured sea gull hid itself in a recess of the cliff wall.* **Ant.** **1.** continuation.

recession *n.* **1.** decline, inflation, slump, slowdown, crisis. *Jobs are scarce during recessions.* **2.** indentation, hollow, nook. *The treasure was hidden in a recession in the cave floor.* **Ant.** **1.** improvement, recovery, upturn.

recharge *vb.* revive, renew, regenerate, rejuvenate, revitalize, energize. *Can we recharge those dead batteries?*

recipe *n.* formula, concoction, mix, blend, ingredients, specifications, prescription. *Ask Aunt Mary for her apple pie recipe.*

reciprocal *adj.* shared, give-and-take, mutual, coordinate, interdependent, corresponding. *They had reciprocal dishwashing duties; he washed and she dried.*

reciprocate *vb.* interchange, share, trade, swap, repay. *Do a good turn and sooner or later someone will reciprocate.*

recital *n.* narrative, story, account, reading, report, telling, performance. *I have to give a recital tomorrow night and I'm getting nervous.*

recite *vb.* repeat, quote, recount, narrate, speak. *The class recited the Pledge of Allegiance.*

reckless *adj.* wild, rash, thoughtless, careless, unthinking, irresponsible. *Her reckless behavior almost cost us our lives.* **Ant.** thoughtful, careful, responsible.

reckoning *n.* computation, counting, accounting, calculation, tally, totaling. *According to the waiter's reckoning, we spent nearly ninety dollars on dinner.*

recline *vb.* lounge, loll, repose, rest. *The sunbathers reclined on their lawn chairs.*

recluse *n.* hermit, monk, ascetic, loner. *The woman living up in the cave was a recluse.*

reclusive *adj.* solitary, retiring, isolated, hermitic, lone, cloistered, secluded. *Reclusive people prefer their own company.* **Ant.** outgoing, social, gregarious.

recognize *vb.* **1.** identify, place, detect, know, spot. *I'm sure I would recognize you in that disguise.* **2.** honor, reward, appreciate. *The scientist* *was recognized by the president for her outstanding achievements.* **3.** acknowledge, accept, sanction, endorse. *The United States decided to recognize the People's Republic of China in 1979.* **Ant. 2.** ignore, neglect. **3.** ignore, overlook.

recoil *vb.* react, bridle, jump, withdraw, cringe, flinch. *The horror movie's climactic scene made us recoil.*

recollect *vb.* recall, remember, place, reminisce. *I seem to recollect that you borrowed my skis last winter.* **Ant.** forget, overlook.

recommend *vb.* suggest, promote, endorse, commend, advocate. *He will recommend me for the job.* **Ant.** denounce, censure.

recommendation *n.* **1.** guidance, advice, suggestion, counsel. *I asked for the doctor's recommendation on my treatment.* **2.** endorsement, referral, approval, testimonial. *She needs a letter of recommendation to the program.* **Ant. 2.** criticism, condemnation.

reconcile *vb.* **1.** resign, adjust, adapt, submit. *He reconciled himself to doing his homework.* **2.** settle, heal, mend, resolve. *The two countries must reconcile their differences before a treaty can be signed.* **3.** reunite, conciliate, harmonize. *Someone should try to reconcile the two feuding coaches.*

reconnaissance *n.* survey, scouting, observation, look-see, mission, reconnoiter. *The spy plane was sent out on a mission of reconnaissance.*

reconsider *vb.* rethink, review, reexamine, reevaluate, reassess, take another look. *I hope you will reconsider my application for employment.*

recompense *n.* payment, repayment, compensation, remuneration, reparation, reward. *The neighbors are asking for recompense for the fence we damaged.*

record *n.* **1.** log, account, journal, report, chronicle, diary, transcript, history. *My parents keep a record of how much money I owe them.* **2.** unbeaten mark, ultimate time. *The athlete hoped to break the world record.* –*vb.* **3.** chronicle, register, document, note, log, tape. *The alien traveler wanted to record human behavior on Earth.* –*adj.* **4.** best, unbeaten, fastest, top. *The marathon runner crossed the finish line in record time.* **Ant. 3.** disregard, ignore, erase. **4.** slowest.

recording *n.* transcription, copy, reproduction, tape, CD, record, cassette, encoding. *Musical recordings have a much better sound quality now than thirty years ago.*

recount *vb.* tell, narrate, review, recapitulate, recap, relate, detail. *I wish you would recount how in the world you got three flat tires.*

recoup *vb.* recover, replace, regain, compensate, get back. *Whether you will recoup your investment in the stock market is questionable.*

recover *vb.* **1.** heal, improve, rally, revive, recuperate. *My brother needs time to recover from his cold.* **2.** retrieve, reclaim, regain, salvage. *I hope we can recover the things taken by the thieves.* **Ant. 1.** worsen, relapse, die. **2.** lose.

recovery *n.* **1.** recuperation, comeback, rehabilitation, regeneration. *His recovery after the climbing accident was miraculous.* **2.** retrieval, reclamation, repossession. *The sunken treasure's recovery was difficult.* **Ant. 1.** death, setback. **2.** loss.

recreation *n.* pastime, hobby, relaxation, sport, amusement. *Softball was their favorite form of recreation.* **Ant.** job, work.

recruit *vb.* **1.** enlist, enroll, induct, draft, obtain. *Please recruit people who can help us at the bake sale.* –*n.* **2.** enlistee, volunteer, selectee, draftee, soldier, private. *The new recruits were lined up outside the army barracks.*

rectify *vb.* correct, fix, mend, right, amend. *She hoped to rectify the problem by apologizing.*

recuperate *vb.* recover, get well, heal, mend, convalesce, rally, get better. *It takes a few days to fully recuperate from the flu.*

recur *vb.* reappear, return, repeat, continue. *We hope the computer malfunction does not recur.*

recurrent *adj.* repeating, repetitive, reappearing, regular, cyclical, periodic. *Vandalism is a recurrent problem around construction sites.*

red *adj.* crimson, rose, cherry, blood, vermilion, wine, coral, fuschsia. *I love the red and gold colors of autumn.*

redeem *vb.* **1.** retrieve, recover, regain, rescue, ransom. *The minister sought to redeem his followers' souls.* **2.** exchange, cash. *Can I redeem this coupon at the counter?* **3.** deliver, free liberate, absolve, acquit. *He hopes to redeem himself of his past failures.* **Ant. 1.** lose, abandon.

red herring *n.* diversion, distraction, distractor, attention-grabber, show-stealer, smokescreen. *Politicians sometimes used red herrings to distract the public from a more controversial issue.*

redneck *n.* (slang) good old boy, (slang) yahoo, conservative, farmer, bigot, ignoramus. *Please don't accuse me of being a redneck without knowing who I am.*

redolent *adj.* fragrant, odoriferous, aromatic, scented, smelling, evocative. *The Maine woods are redolent of balsam fir.*

redress *n.* amends, righting, recompense, reparation, compensation, restitution. *We will be seeking financial redress for our losses.*

red tape *n.* bureaucracy, delay, officialese, paper shuffling, regulatory process, impediment, channels. *Government red tape may slow things down considerably.*

reduce *vb.* **1.** lessen, cut, diminish, decrease, shorten, weaken, subtract, restrict. *Our football team must reduce the number of mistakes it makes.* **2.** humble, degrade, lower, demote. *The man was reduced to scavenging in the garbage when he lost his job.* **Ant. 1.** increase, strengthen, lengthen, extend. **2.** raise, boost.

redundant *adj.* repetitive, unnecessary, wordy. *Those two paragraphs are so much alike that it is redundant to include both of them.* **Ant.** necessary, vital.

reef *n.* shoal, bank, bar, sand bar, coral reef, atoll, shelf. *Boat captains should use care to avoid hitting a reef.*

reek *vb.* stink, smell, fume, give off a stench, emit odors, pollute. *The sardine factory tends to reek in July.*

reel *n.* **1.** spindle, bobbin, wheel. *The movie reel broke during the screening.* –*vb.* **2.** sway, stagger, roll, totter, rock, stumble. *The cowboy in the movie reeled from the punch.*

refer *vb.* **1.** direct, send, suggest, point. *May I refer you to another doctor?* **2.** mention, cite, quote, allude. *The author of the magazine article refers to several experts.* **3.** apply, pertain, touch, involve. *Her comments were meant to refer to only one person in class.* **4.** consult, address, turn, go. *Why don't you refer to your handbook for the answer?*

referee *n.* **1.** umpire, judge, moderator, arbitrator. *The referee was very fair in his calls during the game.* –*vb.* **2.** umpire, judge, moderate, arbitrate. *My mother refereed our soccer game.*

reference *n.* **1.** citation, mention, note, quotation, allusion, notice. *The book made reference to a secret government coverup.* **2.** testimonial, endorsement, plug, recommendation, backing. *Your references speak highly of you.*

refine *vb.* **1.** improve, perfect, polish, cultivate, better. *The sculptor will be more successful when* *she refines her technique.* **2.** purify, filter, strain, process, distill. *The metal was refined in the factory.* **Ant. 1.** worsen, coarsen. **2.** pollute, dirty, contaminate, defile.

refined *adj.* **1.** polished, cultured, finished, cultivated, well-bred, civilized. *She is a refined young woman with impeccable manners.* **2.** processed, distilled, purified, clarified, filtered, cleaned. *Cereals are made from refined grains.* **Ant. 1–2.** unrefined, course, rough.

refinement *n.* polish, cultivation, perfection, graciousness, gentility, taste. *Being a man of great refinement, he is always tactful and polite.* **Ant.** coarseness, roughness, crudeness.

reflect *vb.* **1.** mirror, flash, echo, reproduce. *Sunlight often reflects off our car window.* **2.** ponder, meditate, study, deliberate, contemplate. *I need some time alone to reflect on what just happened.* **3.** display, show, manifest, demonstrate, illustrate. *His positive outlook was reflected in the quality of his life.* **Ant. 1.** absorb. **3.** mask, obscure, veil.

reform *n.* **1.** improvement, correction, revision, change, betterment. *Social reforms led to the abolition of slavery.* –*vb.* **2.** improve, correct, change, rehabilitate, refashion. *The camp tried to reform criminals.*

reformatory *n.* penal institution, correctional facility, reform school, training facility, juvenile institution. *The reformatory is home for incorrigible juvenile delinquents.*

refrain *vb.* **1.** restrain, stop, resist, abstain, desist. *My brother could not refrain from yelling out during the movie.* –*n.* **2.** theme, melody. *The chorus sang the refrain in the production.* **Ant. 1.** persist, pursue.

refresh *vb.* freshen, revive, reinvigorate, renew, rejuvenate, stimulate. *She took a shower to refresh herself.* **Ant.** tire, drain, exhaust.

refreshing *adj.* reviving, regenerating, rousing, strengthening, invigorating, stimulating. *That cold soda was very refreshing.* **Ant.** tiring, weakening, depleting.

refreshment *n.* food, snacks, nourishment. *We bought refreshments after the game.*

refrigerate *vb.* cool, chill, freeze, ice, air condition. *You need to refrigerate that fish soon or it will spoil.* **Ant.** heat, boil, fry.

refuge *n.* shelter, sanctuary, asylum, haven, retreat, protection. *The wildlife refuge was protected from poachers.*

refugee *n.* exile, fugitive, evacuee, emigrant. *Thousands of refugees left their wartorn country.*

refund *vb.* **1.** repay, reimburse, return, restore. *The store will refund the money for the dress.* –*n.* **2.** rebate, repayment, reimbursement, return. *I returned the shirt and received a refund.* **Ant. 1.** keep, withhold.

refurbish *vb.* restore, fix up, renovate, rejuvenate, renew, recondition. *We need to refurbish the old barn before it falls down.*

refusal *n.* unwillingness, dissent, rejection, denial, opposition. *The dog's refusal to go farther forced his owner to carry him home.* **Ant.** acceptance, agreement, approval.

refuse *vb.* **1.** forbid, disallow, reject, veto, prohibit. *Did your mother refuse to let you go out Monday night?* –*n.* **2.** garbage, trash, rubbish, waste, litter. *Refuse piled up when the sanitation workers went on strike.* **Ant. 1.** allow, agree, accept, approve.

refute *vb.* disprove, counter, challenge, deny, rebut. *The executive tried to refute the statements written about him.* **Ant.** confirm, prove, establish.

regal *adj.* royal, majestic, stately, noble, splendid, imperial, grand. *The entire house was decorated in regal furnishings.* **Ant.** tawdry, cheap.

regale *vb.* amuse, entertain, enthrall, delight, captivate, enchant. *Grandfather liked to regale us with stories about his bear-hunting days.*

regalia *n.* finery, dress, attire, outfit, livery. *For the parade, the band members will be in their finest regalia.*

regard *vb.* **1.** consider, judge, view, think, rate. *I regard her as my best friend.* **2.** admire, value, honor, appreciate, respect. *I have always highly regarded this author's work.* **3.** watch, observe, scan, view. *The teacher silently regarded her class as they took the test.* *–n.* **4.** attention, notice, care, consideration. *Please give some regard to what I tell you.* **5.** respect, admiration, appreciation, honor. *We have enormous regard for the surgeons who saved his life.* **6.** matter, aspect, subject, respect. *In that regard, there can be no going back.* **Ant. 1.** reject, disregard. **2.** disregard, dislike, detest, dishonor. **3.** ignore, overlook. **4.** disregard, indifference. **5.** disregard, dislike, hatred, loathing. **6.** disregard.

regardless *adv.* despite, nonetheless, notwithstanding. *I will attend the concert regardless of what you say.*

regime *n.* government, administration, power, command, party, leadership. *The current regime is more open to peace than the one before it.*

region *n.* **1.** area, district, section, territory, zone. *The train finally reached the country's forested region.* **2.** scope, field, sphere. *Her region of expertise is business law.*

regional *adj.* geographical, territorial, provincial, sectional. *The two widely separated villages have regional differences.*

register *vb.* **1.** check in, sign up. *Did you register to vote yet?* **2.** display, express, portray, exhibit, record. *The surprise they felt was registered on their faces.* *–n.* **3.** log, logbook, journal, diary, record. *The museum has a register for visitors to sign.* **Ant. 2.** hide, conceal, mask.

regress *vb.* revert, reverse, go back, backslide, retreat, degenerate. *Without superior education, a society will regress.* **Ant.** progress, advance, go forward

regret *vb.* **1.** grieve, mourn, lament, repent. *We regret that we left before the banquet was over.* *–n.* **2.** remorse, concern, sorrow, disappointment, self-reproach, grief. *Try not to have too much regret over your lost necklace.* **Ant. 1.** celebrate, rejoice. **2.** satisfaction, comfort.

regretful *adj.* remorseful, sorrowful, sorry, repentant, apologetic. *I felt very regretful about the argument we had.* **Ant.** unremorseful, pleased, happy.

regular *adj.* **1.** normal, usual, common, standard, habitual, customary, frequent, established. *The bus will arrive at the regular time today.* **2.** uniform, flat, smooth, even. *The jeep moved across a regular and barren landscape.* *–n.* **3.** patron, client, starter. *Our store sends Christmas cards to customers who are regulars.* **Ant. 1.** unusual, uncommon, atypical, irregular, infrequent. **2.** irregular, uneven.

regulate *vb.* **1.** govern, supervise, control, direct. *Laws regulate the amount of money politicians receive.* **2.** arrange, adjust, set. *The new equipment in his fish tank will regulate the temperature.* **Ant. 1.** ignore, neglect. **2.** disrupt, jumble.

rehabilitate *vb.* restore, reform, save, redeem, improve, change. *At the reformatory, they try to rehabilitate young criminals.*

rehearse *vb.* prepare, review, practice, drill. *She will rehearse her speech before class.*

reign *n.* **1.** rule, sway, sovereignty, regency, regime, power. *The queen's reign lasted many* *years.* –*vb.* **2.** command, rule, govern, lead, manage. *The king reigned during the medieval ages.*

reimburse *vb.* pay back, recompense, repay, compensate, make good, settle. *We will reimburse you for your expenses.*

reinforce *vb.* strengthen, toughen, support, fortify, uphold, supplement. *The added logs will reinforce our dam.* **Ant.** weaken, lessen, cripple.

reiterate *vb.* recapitulate, recap, restate, retell, go over again, repeat. *I will reiterate the directions only once.*

reject *vb.* **1.** refuse, shun, decline, rebuff, discard, veto. *Don't reject his solution until you've tried it.* –*n.* **2.** discard, castoff, leftover, dregs. *The assembly-line rejects were thrown away.* **Ant. 1.** accept, choose, select, approve. **2.** chosen, selected.

rejection *n.* turndown, veto, refusal, dismissal, spurning, rebuff. *Their rejection of me for the school play was upsetting.* **Ant.** acceptance, selection, choice, approval.

rejoice *vb.* celebrate, exult, revel, glory. *The heroes in the comic book rejoiced over their defeat of the evil invaders.* **Ant.** mourn, grieve.

rejuvenate *vb.* renew, revive, revitalize, refurbish, restore, refresh, invigorate. *A cup of coffee can rejuvenate when you're tired.* **Ant.** exhaust, drain, sap.

relapse *vb.* **1.** backslide, reverse, lapse, revert, decline, deteriorate. *After being neat for a week, she relapsed into her messy habits.* –*n.* **2.** return, recurrence, reappearance. *The man had a relapse of his former illness.* **3.** backslide, decline, setback, reverse, deterioration. *The recovering patient suffered a relapse.* **Ant. 2.–3.** recovery, cure.

relate *vb.* **1.** repeat, describe, recount, tell, communicate, narrate. *Please relate the events of your year in Africa.* **2.** link, refer, pertain, apply. *His essay did not relate to the subject we've been studying.* **3.** identify, respond, empathize, understand. *I can really relate to the book's main character.* **Ant. 1.** conceal, hide. **2.** detach, disconnect, separate.

related *adj.* kindred, associated, connected, affiliated, linked, cognate. *I am related to my cousins.* **Ant.** unrelated, unconnected, independent.

relation *n.* **1.** association, connection, link, bond, relationship. *Relations were friendly between the two countries.* **2.** kin, relative. *She is a relation of mine.* **3.** relevance, connection, bearing, correlation. *His comments have no relation to our discussion.* **4.** narration, recitation, account, recital, report. *My sister's relation of the story was slightly exaggerated.* **Ant. 1.** disassociation, disconnection.

relationship *n.* kinship, association, friendship, alliance, marriage, tie, connection, link. *My relationship with my neighbor is a close one.*

relative *n.* kin, relation, blood tie, family member, sibling, cognate. *I have relatives all over New England.*

relax *vb.* **1.** rest, loaf, lounge, unbend, unwind. *They relax after school by playing video games.* **2.** calm, ease, quiet, soothe, loosen. *I think this music will relax you.* **Ant. 1.** work, labor, toil. **2.** tighten, tense, excite.

relaxation *n.* resting, unbending, unwinding, lounging, leisure. *Sitting in a sauna is a great method of relaxation.* **Ant.** tightening, laboring, working.

release *vb.* **1.** free, unfasten, unchain, unhook, detach, disconnect. *It took me a while to release the gate's latch.* **2.** free, loose, discharge, liberate. *The rangers will release the eagle after its wing heals.* **3.** unveil, distribute, exhibit, publish. *The company decided to release the movie during the* *summer.* –*n.* **4.** freedom, discharge, liberation. *The prisoner looked forward to his release.* **5.** distribution, circulation, publication. *The movie's release was awaited eagerly by fans.* **Ant. 1** fasten, chain, hook. **2.** cage, imprison, hold. **3.** conceal, withhold. **4.** imprisonment, detention. **5.** withdrawal.

relegate *vb.* assign, delegate, consign, entrust, commission. *The boss is planning to relegate me to dishwasher status.*

relent *vb.* bend, yield, soften, capitulate, relax. *My parents would not relent in their refusal to let me attend the party.*

relentless *adj.* harsh, ruthless, unyielding, unmerciful, hard. *Our leader set a relentless pace as we marched through the desert.* **Ant.** yielding, gentle, considerate, merciful.

relevant *adj.* connected, significant, related, associated, pertinent. *The detective discovered several relevant facts.* **Ant.** irrelevant, insignificant, unrelated.

reliable *adj.* trustworthy, dependable, honest, conscientious, responsible. *Reliable people can be trusted to do their jobs.* **Ant.** unreliable, untrustworthy, undependable.

reliance *n.* confidence, trust, conviction, belief, dependence. *He placed great reliance on the article's accuracy.* **Ant.** distrust, disbelief, independence.

relic *n.* artifact, remain, antique, remembrance, memento. *The old ship is a relic from World War II.*

relief *n.* **1.** release, respite, refreshment, comfort. *It was a relief to get out of the sun.* **2.** aid, help, comfort, rescue. *The Red Cross sent relief to the famine victims.* **3.** replacement, substitute, backup. *The team sent its reliefs into the game.* **Ant. 1.** suffering, discomfort, irritation, burden. **2.** neglect, harm.

relieve *vb.* **1.** lighten, reduce, release, remove. *The medicine helped to relieve the pain.* **2.** free, deliver, ease, release, discharge. *His forgiveness relieved me of my guilt.* **Ant. 1.** increase, maintain. **2.** burden, load.

religion *n.* belief, faith, spirituality, devotion, worship. *Freedom of religion is an important human right.* **Ant.** atheism, nihilism, unbelief.

WORD SEARCH

biblical texts rejected by some denominations: *apocrypha*
banishment from church: *excommunication*
cursing of God: *blasphemy*
dissenter: *heretic*
faith, abandonment of one's: *apostasy*
fellowship: *communion*
forgiveness of sins: *absolution*
God, seeing: *beatific vision*
healing illness through prayer: *faith healing*
kneel in worship: *genuflect*
laws, ecclesiastical: *canon*
literal interpretation of Bible, belief of: *fundamentalism*
nonbeliever in God: *atheist, nontheist*
offense to God: *abomination*
questioner of God's existence: *agnostic*
rite: *sacrament*
sect: *denomination*
spreading of word throughout world: *evangelism*
study of religion: *theology*
water sacrament, Christian: *baptism*

religious *adj.* **1.** spiritual, theological, devotional, devout, divine. *The religious painting hung in the church's entrance.* **2.** rigid, loyal, devoted, conscientious, unfailing. *He was religious about his daily exercising.* **Ant. 1.** irreligious, secular. **2.** unfaithful, unreliable.

relinquish *vb.* surrender, abandon, renounce, discard, release, forsake. *The small girl would* *not relinquish her doll.* **Ant.** keep, maintain, retain.

relish *vb.* enjoy, like, love, adore, savor, appreciate, (slang) dig. *I relish long walks on the beach.*

reluctant *adj.* unwilling, resistant, opposed, hesitant, slow. *He was very reluctant to show his parents his report card.* **Ant.** willing, enthusiastic, eager.

rely *vb.* depend, trust, count, lean. *If you're in trouble, you can rely on your friends.*

remain *vb.* stay, wait, linger, continue, persist, last. *Part of the group decided to remain behind.* **Ant.** leave, disappear, depart.

remainder *n.* excess, remains, leftovers, surplus, residual. *Put the remainder of the meal in the refrigerator.*

remark *vb.* **1.** comment, observe, state, express, mention. *The librarian remarked on how much I resemble my sister.* –n. **2.** comment, observation, statement, assertion, expression. *His cruel remark really angered me.*

remarkable *adj.* impressive, surprising, noteworthy, unbelievable, astonishing. *It was remarkable how quickly she rowed across the lake.* **Ant.** unremarkable, unimpressive, insignificant.

remedial *adj.* corrective, therapeutic, curative, healing, restorative. *I need to take some remedial golf lessons to improve my swing.*

remedy *n.* **1.** treatment, cure, antidote, corrective, therapy. *The medicine was a remedy for her fever.* –*vb.* **2.** cure, relieve, mend, heal, correct, rectify. *I think this should remedy the problem* **Ant. 1.** poison. **2.** worsen, intensify.

remember *vb.* recall, recollect, recognize, relive, reminisce. *There are many facts to remember for the test.* **Ant.** forget, neglect.

remembrance *n.* **1.** memory, recall, recollection. *Her remembrance of that day is rather hazy.* **2.** memorial, memento, keepsake, reminder. *They left flowers at the grave as a remembrance of their grandfather.* **Ant. 1.** forgetfulness.

remind *vb.* caution, warn, prompt, admonish, notify. *Remind him that he should clear away the dishes.*

reminder *n.* memo, notice, prompting, warning cue, suggestion. *My mother put a note on my door as a reminder that I have baseball practice today.*

reminisce *vb.* remember, recall, recollect, think back, review. *I like to reminisce about my childhood.*

remiss *adj.* forgetful, negligent, neglectful, slack, thoughtless, lazy. *She has been very remiss in doing her homework.* **Ant.** thorough, hardworking, earnest, careful.

remission *n.* arrestment, subsiding, reprieve, waning, lessening, abatement, alleviation. *Tests showed her cancer went into remission, and she was given a clean bill of health.*

remit *vb.* send, forward, transmit, mail, discharge. *Please remit payment within 30 days.*

remnant *n.* remainder, trace, remains, record, residue, leftover. *The explorers found the remnants of an ancient civilization.*

remodel *vb.* renovate, refurbish, overhaul, redo, redesign, rebuild. *We plan to remodel the children's room.*

remorse *n.* shame, guilt, self-reproach, regret, embarrassment, sorrow. *Doesn't the drunk driver have any remorse over the accident?* **Ant.** contentment, fulfillment, pride.

remote *adj.* **1.** faraway, distant, isolated, solitary, secluded. *The park ranger's cabin was in a* *remote forest area.* **2.** slim, faint, unlikely, improbable. *There is a remote chance we will get out early today.* **3.** withdrawn, detached, distant, disinterested. *He seemed very remote because he has a lot on his mind.* **Ant. 1.** close, nearby. **2.** likely, probable. **3.** interested, involved, animated.

removal *n.* **1.** erasure, transfer, extraction, evacuation, withdrawal. *The exterminators promised complete removal of the termites.* **2.** expulsion, discharge, ejection, dismissal. *They wanted his removal from office.* **Ant. 1.** replacement, introduction. **2.** confirmation, establishment.

remove *vb.* **1.** shed, unload, dislodge, move, shift, transplant, extract. *Please remove your books from the table.* **2.** erase, eliminate, delete, cancel. *See if you can remove the smudge on my cheek.* **3.** dismiss, discharge, unseat, discard. *The voters removed the judge from office.* **Ant. 1.** deposit, replace, keep. **2.** add, set, plant. **3.** install, instate, confirm.

remunerate *vb.* pay, compensate, repay, reimburse, recompense, reward. *I decided to remunerate the papergirl for her extra service with a tip.*

renaissance *n.* rebirth, resurgence, revival, renewal, regeneration, reawakening. *The electronics industry underwent a renaissance with the advent of the personal computer.*

render *vb.* present, deliver, give, furnish, provide, tender. *We'd be happy to render assistance, just give us a call.*

rendezvous *n.* **1.** date, meeting, encounter, appointment. *The couple arranged a midnight rendezvous by the fountain.* **2.** meeting place, haunt. *The fountain was their rendezvous.* *–vb.* **3.** meet, collect, assemble, gather. *They rendezvoused at the fountain.*

rendition *n.* interpretation, rendering, presentation, arrangement, performance, depiction. *The singer belted out her own rendition of the national anthem.*

renegade *n.* **1.** fugitive, outlaw, deserter, traitor, rebel. *The man committed a crime and is now a renegade from the law.* *–adj.* **2.** traitorous, disloyal, mutinous, treacherous, unfaithful. *Renegade soldiers kidnapped the queen.* **Ant. 1.** loyalist, follower. **2.** loyal, faithful.

renege *vb.* default, backpedal, reverse, break promise, go back on one's word, fail to fulfill. *He reneged on his promise to mow our lawn for free.* **Ant.** fulfill, satisfy, make good.

renew *vb.* refresh, regenerate, reestablish, revive, rejuvenate. *I need to renew my driver's license.* **Ant.** cancel, discontinue, abolish.

renewal *n.* continuation, resumption, restoration, recommencement, revival. *Did you get your library-card renewal yet?* **Ant.** cancellation, discontinuation.

renounce *vb.* relinquish, abandon, forgo, cease, discard. *The preacher said she must renounce her evil, ways.* **Ant.** maintain, keep, continue.

renovate *vb.* renew, remodel, repair, revive, regenerate. *A contractor has been hired to renovate the old house.* **Ant.** destroy, ruin.

renown *n.* fame, prominence, stardom, eminence, notoriety, celebrity. *She enjoyed great renown around the world.* **Ant.** obscurity, anonymity.

renowned *adj.* famous, prominent, eminent, notorious, celebrated, acclaimed. *He was renowned for his exceptional guitar-playing ability.* **Ant.** obscure, unknown, anonymous.

rent *vb.* **1.** lease, hire, charter, contract, sublet. *She will rent a sailboat for this afternoon.* *–n.* **2.** due, fee, payment, price, tariff. *My father pays the apartment rent.* **3.** tear, rip, gash, split, break.

The opposing quarterback dashed through a rent in our defensive line.

renunciation *n.* renouncement, rejection, forswearing, disavowal, abandonment, eschewal. *Her renunciation of the cult made front page news.* **Ant.** acceptance, adoption, approval.

repair *vb.* **1.** fix, mend, patch, restore, rebuild. *He repaired the hole yesterday.* –*n.* **2.** fixing, patching, reconstruction, mending, overhaul. *My car is in the shop for repairs.* **Ant. 1.** wreck, smash. **2.** destruction, damaging.

repartee *n.* witty comebacks, snappy comebacks, banter, quips, badinage, riposte, jesting. *The comedians' repartee had everyone in stitches.*

repast *n.* meal, feast, dinner, eats, food and drink, banquet. *I enjoyed a delicious repast and then settled down to take a nap.*

repay *vb.* reimburse, square, refund, compensate, pay back, settle. *Repay your debts promptly to avoid trouble.*

repeal *vb.* **1.** cancel, void, revoke, annul. *The unfair law was finally repealed by the voters.* –*n.* **2.** cancellation, annulment, withdrawal. *They voted for a repeal of the unpopular tax law.* **Ant. 1.** install, confirm. **2.** confirmation, validation.

repeat *vb.* **1.** restate, recount, recite. *Can you please repeat who you just told me?* **2.** redo, remake, replay, duplicate. *I hope she can repeat her excellent performance in tomorrow's game.* –*n.* **3.** rerun, replay, duplication, rebroadcast. *The television show was a repeat of a previously shown episode.*

repel *vb.* **1.** disgust, sicken, revolt, offend. *The sewer's smell really repels me.* **2.** repulse, resist, deflect, frustrate. *The army must repel the invaders.* **Ant. 1.** attract, delight, please. **2.** attract, invite.

repent *vb.* regret, lament, bewail, lament, deplore. *I hope the criminal repents her crime.* **Ant.** rejoice, celebrate.

repentance *n.* penitence, contrition, remorse, guilt, regret, compunction. *The toddler's repentance was genuine, so he escaped punishment for his cookie-thieving.*

repercussion *n.* consequence, result, fallout, backlash, reaction, impact. *If we a continue to pollute the air, the long-term repercussions will be serious.*

repetition *n.* repeat, duplication, recurrence, replay, rerun, reiteration. *The only way to play the piano fluidly is with repetition.*

repetitious *adj.* repetitive, repeating, duplicating, recurrent, redundant, tautological. *His speech was repetitious and thoroughly boring.*

replenish *vb.* refill, restock, restore, replace. *He went to the store to replenish our food supply.* **Ant.** empty, drain.

replete *n.* full, filled, abounding, overflowing, loaded, plentiful, crammed, packed. *The stream was replete with trout.* **Ant.** empty, bare, scant.

replica *n.* model, reproduction, imitation, duplicate. *The museum has a replica of a covered wagon.*

reply *vb.* **1.** answer, respond, retort, react. *You must reply to the invitation by the twelfth of December.* –*n.* **2.** answer, response, reaction, acknowledgment. *We are waiting for a reply to our letter.* **Ant. 1.** question, ask. **2.** question, inquiry.

report *n.* **1.** description, account, narrative, article, summary. *His book report was due today.* **2.** bang, crack, backfire, detonation. *The loud report of the rifle could be heard throughout the forest.* –*vb.* **3.** narrate, account, relate, describe, summarize state, disclose, reveal. *The scout* *reported that it was safe to continue.* **4.** arrive, appear. *You must report to the general in one hour.* **Ant. 1.** concealment, deletion. **2.** silence, quiet. **3.** conceal, hide.

reporter *n.* newsman, newswoman, journalist, muckraker, correspondent, member of the media, member of the press. *We sent our best reporter out to cover the story.*

repose *n.* rest, restfulness, sleep, slumber, peace of mind, tranquillity. *I achieve a great state of repose by meditating.* **Ant.** activity, bustle, stress.

repository *n.* depository, storehouse, warehouse, depot, archives, vault. *The Louvre is the repository of many famous artworks.*

repossess *vb.* reclaim, take back, regain, recover, retrieve. *If you fail to make payments, the dealership will repossess your car.*

reprehensible *adj.* reproachable, shameful, criminal, sinful, heinous, unforgivable, blameworthy. *The dictator's warlike actions were reprehensible.* **Ant.** virtuous, honorable, praiseworthy.

represent *vb.* **1.** stand for, act for, serve. *A lawyer will represent the defendant in court.* **2.** symbolize, characterize, illustrate, signify, exemplify. *This monument represents the millions who died during the war.*

representation *n.* **1.** description, depiction, portrayal, portrait, illustration. *The picture's abstract representation was confusing.* **2.** representatives, delegates. *Those two men are New York's representation in the Senate.*

representative *n.* **1.** delegate, emissary, spokesperson, envoy, ambassador. *Our school sent a representative to the competition.* **2.** legislator, congressman, congresswoman, assemblywoman, assemblyman. *The House of Representatives is formed from officials chosen in district elections.* *–adj.* **3.** typical, characteristic, descriptive, illustrative. *I hope his behavior is not representative of other students' behavior.* **4.** elected, democratic. *The United States has a representative government.*

repress *vb.* check, curb, restrain, suppress, quiet, crush. *You must repress your tendency to get into fights.* **Ant.** release, encourage, express.

reprieve *n.* postponement, cancellation, relief, stay, stay of execution, delay. *The criminal was granted a reprieve by the governor.*

reprimand *n.* rebuke, censure, admonishment, reproach, scolding, chastisement. *The children were given a reprimand for playing in the street.* **Ant.** approval, praise.

reprisal *n.* retaliation, revenge, retribution, vindication, vengeance, eye for an eye. *Terrorist attacks are often met with serious reprisals.*

reproach *vb.* **1.** reprimand, scold, criticize, condemn. *Don't reproach me for something I did not do.* *–n.* **2.** reprimand, scolding, criticism, condemnation. *She deserved your reproach for stealing money.* **Ant. 1.** praise, compliment. **2.** praise, compliment.

reproduce *vb.* **1.** copy, duplicate, photocopy, replicate, reprint. *Reproduce three copies of the contract for your records.* **2.** procreate, propagate, spawn, multiply, bear, sire, generate. *Rabbits reproduce quickly.*

reproduction *n.* **1.** copy, duplicate, photocopy, replication, reprint, imitation, fake, clone. *The art department needs a reproduction of the abstract.* **2.** procreation, propagation, spawn, generation, breeding, cloning. *Elephants require longer periods for reproduction than humans do.*

repudiate *vb.* reject, renounce, disavow, spurn, cast off, disapprove. *I repudiate all forms of government waste.* **Ant.** accept, approve, support.

repugnant *adj.* repulsive, disgusting, repellent, revolting, offensive, sickening. *Racism is repugnant to me.* **Ant.** honorable, praiseworthy, appealing.

repulsive *adj.* sickening, disgusting, revolting, offensive, disagreeable. *That monster costume is repulsive.* **Ant.** pleasing, attractive, agreeable.

reputable *adj.* trustworthy, respected, honored, dependable. *They went to a reputable doctor.* **Ant.** disreputable, untrustworthy.

reputation *n.* repute, standing, character, estimation, regard, stature. *She has a reputation as an honest person.*

request *vb.* **1.** ask for, call for, beg for, petition. *I requested a bicycle for my birthday.* –*n.* **2.** appeal, call, plea, summons, application. *Her request for more help was denied.* **Ant. 1.** refuse, reject. **2.** refusal, rejection.

requiem *n.* mass, service, memorial, eulogy, elegy. *The requiem for the lost soldier was moving.*

require *vb.* necessitate, direct, need, compel, command, demand. *The law requires you to be eighteen before you can vote.*

requirement *n.* necessity, essential, need, must, requisite, prerequisite. *A college degree is a requirement of many employers.*

requisite *n.* required, necessary, essential, obligatory, imperative, needed. *If you're going to build your own house, carpentry is a requisite skill.* **Ant.** unnecessary, optional, unneeded.

requisition *n.* **1.** request, call, summons, command, demand. *He sent in a requisition for more supplies.* –*vb.* **2.** request, demand, command. *The army requisitioned more equipment.* **Ant. 1.** refusal. **2.** refuse, reject.

rescind *vb.* repeal, revoke, recall, annul, reverse, cancel. *The city council is planning to rescind its harsh leash law.* **Ant.** implement, uphold, confirm.

rescue *vb.* **1.** save, deliver, recover, free, retrieve. *The lifeguard rescued the drowning man.* –*n.* **2.** saving, recovery, deliverance, retrieval. *We watched the rescue of the people caught in the fire.* **Ant. 1.** lose, abandon, relinquish, imprison. **2.** loss, abandonment.

research *n.* **1.** investigation, experimentation, exploration, analysis, study. *Much of the chemist's research was done in the laboratory.* –*vb.* **2.** investigate, study, explore, examine. *My friend and I will research our papers at the library.*

researcher *n.* investigator, detective, prober, analyst, fact-finder, scholar. *A historical researcher claims that the hoop skirt of the 1800s caused many accidents.*

resemblance *n.* likeness, similarity, sameness. *He bears a remarkable resemblance to his father.* **Ant.** difference, dissimilarity, distinction.

resemble *vb.* look like, take after, appear like, be similar to. *She resembles the famous television actress.* **Ant.** differ from, contrast with.

resent *vb.* be jealous of, be offended by, be annoyed by, dislike. *You should not resent your brother's success.* **Ant.** like, respect, admire, approve.

resentment *n.* bitterness, jealousy, displeasure, soreness, malice, anger, envy. *She felt resentment toward the winner.* **Ant.** pleasure, cheerfulness, friendliness.

reservation *n.* **1.** uncertainty, doubt, reluctance, hesitancy. *I have reservations about skiing down the steep slope.* **2.** booking, engagement. *I have a reservation at the restaurant.* **3.** preserve, territory, tract. *The United States took most of the Indians' land and resettled them on reservations.*

reserve *vb.* **1.** hold, retain, keep, preserve, save. *I reserve the right to change my mind.* **2.** book, schedule, retain, prearrange. *She reserved two tickets for next week's show.* –*n.* **3.** stock, supply, stockpile, store, savings. *She has an emergency food reserve.* **4.** coolness, restraint, remoteness, aloofness. *His reserve kept me from attempting to be friends.* –*adj.* **5.** unused, extra, backup, spare. *The reserve forces were called into battle.* **Ant.** **1.** give, relinquish, discard. **4.** friendliness, warmth.

reserved *adj.* reticent, retiring, inhibited, quiet, taciturn, shy, aloof. *He shunned small talk and tended to be reserved.* **Ant.** talkative, loquacious, loud.

reside *vb.* live, dwell, inhabit, abide, stay. *Our family resides in New York.*

residence *n.* home, household, habitation, dwelling, address. *The president's residence is the White House.*

resident *n.* citizen, dweller, inhabitant, householder, native. *My grandmother is a resident of a small town.*

residue *n.* remainder, remains, surplus, leavings, waste. *There is soap residue in the bathtub.*

resign *vb.* **1.** leave, quit, renounce. *Richard Nixon was forced to resign his position as president.* **2.** submit, surrender, abandon. *Resign yourself to several more hours of waiting.* **Ant.** **1.** keep, maintain.

resignation *n.* **1.** quitting, leaving, retirement, termination, withdrawal, notice. *We acknowledge your resignation with great sadness.* **2.** acceptance, submission, acquiescence, reconciliation, passivity, tolerance. *She accepted her position of second stringer with resignation.*

resigned *adj.* accepting, acquiescent, submissive, reconciled, stoical, passive. *I am resigned to my fate as a second-rate golfer.* **Ant.** rejecting, rebellious.

resilient *adj.* flexible, elastic, pliable, supple, tough, irrepressible. *You can't face life's many blows without being resilient.* **Ant.** inflexible, rigid, repressible.

resist *vb.* refuse, reject, oppose, withstand. *I was on a diet but could not resist eating the ice cream.* **Ant.** enjoy, accept.

resistance *n.* struggle, opposition, rebellion, defiance. *Our attempt at bathing the cat was met with resistance.*

resolute *adj.* determined, unbending, stubborn, unyielding, firm. *He was resolute in his decision to climb Mt. Everest.* **Ant.** irresolute, undecided, wavering.

resolution *n.* **1.** plan, goal, determination, objective, aim. *Her New Year's resolution is to stop smoking.* **2.** solution, answer, end. *The problem's resolution took a while.* **3.** proposal, recommendation, declaration. *The committee finally passed the resolution.*

resolve *vb.* **1.** settle, answer, fix. solve. *We must resolve the current crisis.* **2.** plan, propose, mean. *I resolve never to tell a lie again.* –*n.* **3.** determination, goal, intention. *Our resolve to build the fastest car has not weakened.*

resonant *adj.* resounding, reverberant, ringing, sonorous, echoing. *The bell's resonant clangs could be heard a mile away.*

resonate *vb.* resound, reverberate, echo, ring, vibrate, boom. *The pounding drum beat resonates through the nightclub walls.*

resort *vb.* **1.** turn, go, refer, employ, use. *Why did he resort to violence?* –*n.* **2.** retreat, hotel, hideaway. *The wealthy singer took a vacation at a Caribbean resort.* **3.** hope, choice, opportunity, option. *As a last resort, she will sell her house.*

resound *vb.* reverberate, echo, ring, resonate, vibrate. *We could hear our shouts resound off the canyon walls.*

resource *n.* **1.** asset, strength, wealth, capital, possession. *Oil is an important resource in the Middle East.* **2.** source, storehouse, reserve. *The library is a good resource for foreign-language tapes.*

resourceful *adj.* inventive, creative, clever, imaginative. *My friend is very resourceful in finding ways to skip her chores.* **Ant.** unresourceful, uninventive, unimaginative.

respect *n.* **1.** admiration, honor, praise, approval. *I have an enormous amount of respect for the famous astronomer.* –*vb.* **2.** honor, admire, praise, adore, revere, obey, follow, acknowledge. *The rabbi was respected by the community.* **3.** reference, matter, regard, aspect. *In that respect, I must disagree with you.* **Ant.** **1.** disrespect, scorn, contempt. **2.** disrespect, scorn, mock.

respectful *adj.* polite, considerate, courteous, mannerly, attentive. *We maintained a respectful silence at the funeral.* **Ant.** unrespectful, rude, impolite.

respite *n.* break, pause, recess, intermission, relaxation. *They took a respite from their work.* **Ant.** continuation.

respond *vb.* answer, reply, react, return, acknowledge. *I will respond to my pen pal's letter tomorrow.*

response *n.* reaction, feedback, reply, answer, acknowledgement. *The crowd's response was incredible.*

responsibility *n.* **1.** trust, charge, answerability, obligation. *It's my responsibility to take out the trash.* **2.** trustworthiness, reliability. *He is a person of responsibility.* **Ant.** **2.** untrustworthiness, unreliability.

responsible *adj.* **1.** answerable, accountable, obligated, chargeable. *You should not feel responsible for your friend's accident.* **2.** reliable, trustworthy, dependable, capable. *The leader must be a responsible person.* **Ant.** **1.** excusable, unaccountable. **2.** irresponsible, unreliable.

responsive *adj.* receptive, open, sensitive, awake, alive. *The politician was responsive to problems in her community.* **Ant.** unresponsive, indifferent, impassive.

rest *n.* **1.** sleep, relaxation, quiet, calm, peacefulness. *I need some rest after that exhausting race.* **2.** pause, break, recess, halt. *She took a rest from studying.* **3.** support, base, stand, platform. *The statue was set on a marble rest.* **4.** remainder, balance, residue. *The rest of you may go back to class.* –*vb.* **5.** sleep, relax, nap, pause, halt. *We will rest an hour before continuing our walk.* **6.** depend, hang, hinge, lie. *The game's outcome rests on this final toss.* **7.** lean, lay, set, prop. *Rest your umbrella against the wall.* **Ant.** **1.** unrest, work, excitement, disturbance. **5.** work, toil.

restaurant *n.* eatery, dining establishment, luncheonette, grill, steakhouse, diner, supper club. *Do we have to make reservations to eat at that restaurant?*

restful *adj.* **1.** peaceful, relaxing, calming, quieting. *The sound of the ocean waves was very restful.* **2.** peaceful, calm, quiet, untroubled. *The lake's surface was restful.* **Ant.** **1.** irritating, annoying, disturbing. **2.** agitated, troubled.

restitution *n.* reparation, amends, redress, recompense, remuneration, compensation. *The boys were forced to pay restitution for the windows they broke.*

restless *adj.* jumpy, fidgety, anxious, uneasy, sleepless. *The restless woman paced back and forth.* **Ant.** restful, calm, peaceful, relaxed.

restoration *n.* repair, reconstruction, revival, recovery. *The historic building is undergoing a restoration.*

restore *vb.* revive, renew, reclaim, refresh, reinstate, rebuild. *The artists will restore the old painting.*

restrain *vb.* check, stop, curb, hold, constrain, bind. *The cowboy restrained the bucking horse.* **Ant.** release, free.

restraint *n.* **1.** bonds, handcuffs, gag, ties. *The kidnapped man struggled against his restraints.* **2.** self-control, moderation, reserve, poise. *He acted with restraint, although he was very angry.*

restrict *vb.* limit, check, curb, constrain, constrict, restrain. *This movie's rating restricts it to people seventeen or older.*

restriction *n.* limitation, curb, regulation, constraint. *The contest restriction says you can only enter once.*

result *vb.* **1.** arise, issue, happen, flow, follow. *Arguments often result from misunderstandings.* **2.** conclude, end, terminate. *Her poor study habits will result in bad grades.* –*n.* **3.** outcome, product, consequence, aftermath. *The parrot's death was the result of poor care.* **Ant. 3.** source, cause.

resume *vb.* continue, restart, proceed, reestablish. *After a refueling stop, the plane will resume its flight.* **Ant.** discontinue, halt, stop.

résumé *n.* curriculum vitae, vita, employment history, work history, biography, bio, employment summary. *The ABC company needs to see my résumé.*

resurgence *n.* rebirth, renaissance, regeneration, revival, resurrection, renewal. *There has been a resurgence of interest in comets.* **Ant.** death, decline, decrease.

resurrection *n.* rebirth, regeneration, revival, renewal, restoration, rising from the dead. *There has been a resurrection of fashions from the 1960s.*

resuscitate *vb.* revive, revitalize, perform CPR, breathe life into, bring back from the dead. *Paramedics must learn how to resuscitate unconscious victims.*

retain *vb.* keep, hold, remember, grasp, preserve. *My friend retains facts much better than I do.* **Ant.** lose, dismiss.

retainer *vb.* charge, fee, stipend, allowance. *The private detective required a retainer before starting his investigation.*

retaliate *vb.* avenge, pay back, get even, reciprocate, take revenge, settle. *If you attack us, we will retaliate.*

retard *vb.* check, curb, block, slow, halt. *Hopefully this chemical will retard the fire's spread.* **Ant.** advance, encourage.

reticence *n.* quietness, shyness, reserve, restraint. *My friend's reticence was sometimes mistaken as conceit.* **Ant.** loudness, sociability.

reticent *adj.* quiet, silent, withdrawn, subdued, unsociable. *Some students are very reticent during final exams.* **Ant.** noisy, talkative, sociable.

retinue *n.* entourage, cortege, court, following, escort. *The king's retinue served his every whim.*

retire *vb.* withdraw, depart, retreat, leave, resign. *He will retire from his teaching position at the end of this semester.*

retiring *adj.* reserved, quiet, reticent, shy, inhibited, withdrawn, unsociable. *He was a retiring man who preferred his own company.* **Ant.** talkative, sociable, gregarious.

retort *n.* answer, reply, comeback, rebuttal, counter, riposte. *Attorneys like to have their retorts prepared ahead of time.*

retract *vb.* 1. withdraw, recant, recall. *Please retract your false accusation.* 2. withdraw, retreat, recoil. *We saw the turtle's head retract into its shell.* **Ant.** 1. confirm, endorse, uphold. 2. advance, protrude.

retreat *n.* 1. withdrawal, escape, about-face, pull-out, backpedaling, evacuation. *The general ordered a retreat from the front lines.* 2. sanctuary, getaway, haven, asylum, hideaway, cloister. *We have a cabin in the woods we use for a retreat.* –*vb.* 3. withdraw, escape, pull out, backpedal, backtrack, evacuate, flee. **Ant.** 1. advance, progression. 3. advance, progress, go forward.

retribution *n.* revenge, payback, retaliation, punishment, comeuppance, reprisal. *If an enemy attacks our shores, retribution will be severe.*

retrieve *vb.* recover, reclaim, regain, rescue, fetch. *Watch my dog retrieve the ball.*

retrospect *n.* reminiscence, reflection, review, hindsight, afterthought. *In retrospect, I wish I hadn't eaten so much pizza.*

return *vb.* 1. restore, replace, reinstall, repay, reestablish. *He will return the pen when he's finished.* 2. reappear, reoccur, recur, revisit. *We will return from our vacation in August.* –*n.* 3. restoration, replacement, reestablishment. *The quick return of our money was surprising.* 4. reappearance, recurrence, returning. *The ghost's return frightened him.* 5. profit, gain, earnings, yield. *She achieved huge returns on her investments.* **Ant.** 1. keep, hold. 2. depart, disappear. 3. removal, withdrawal. 4. departure, disappearance.

reunion *n.* reuniting, homecoming, gathering, get-together. *Are you coming to the family reunion?*

revamp *vb.* renovate, make over, revise, repair, rebuild, refurbish. *We need to completely revamp our operating procedures.*

reveal *vb.* display, uncover, expose, disclose, divulge. *Lifting up the leaf revealed a spider beneath it.* **Ant.** conceal, hide, mask.

revel *vb.* delight, enjoy, rejoice, luxuriate. *We will revel in the weekend's celebrations.*

revelry *n.* celebration, merry-making, partying, romping, festivity. *The police were called to tone down the New Year's revelry.*

revelation *n.* discovery, announcement, confession, disclosure. *The facts about his past were a shocking revelation.* **Ant.** coverup, concealment.

revenge *vb.* 1. avenge, punish, vindicate, reciprocate. *The team will try to revenge its loss in tomorrow's game.* –*n.* 2. vengeance, retaliation, retribution, repayment, satisfaction. *He wanted revenge against the person who had dishonored him.* **Ant.** 1. forgive, forget, ignore. 2. forgiveness, pardon.

revenue *n.* income, earnings, net, gross, profit, proceeds, gain. *Our yard sale generated a lot of extra revenue.*

reverberate *vb.* resonate, vibrate, echo resound, ring, rebound. *Thunder can reverberate for miles.*

revere *vb.* honor, adore, worship, admire, respect. *The pope is revered by virtually all Catholics.* **Ant.** dislike, scorn, hate, despise.

reverence *n.* respect, veneration, idolization, adoration, exaltation, awe. *While in church, you are expected to display a certain amount of reverence.* **Ant.** disrespect, irreverence, contempt.

reverent *adj.* honoring, respectful, awed, adoring, worshipping, deferential. *The members of the congregation were always reverent toward their minister.* **Ant.** irreverent, disrespectful, rude.

reverie *n.* daydreaming, fantasizing, flight of fancy, woolgathering, musing, deep thought, abstraction. *I was in a deep reverie when the oven timer suddenly brought me back to consciousness.*

reversal *n.* turnaround, about-face, overturning, switch, repeal, retraction. *His opinion underwent a complete reversal once he was exposed to the new information.*

reverse *adj.* **1.** opposite, contrasting, counter, inverse, back. *On the photograph's reverse side is a short message.* –*n.* **2.** opposite, converse, contrary. *She did the reverse of what she had originally planned.* –*vb.* **3.** invert, shift, upset, override, recall, repeal. *I will reverse my decision when I see evidence against it.* **Ant. 3.** keep, uphold, maintain.

revert *vb.* return, backslide, reverse, relapse. *We hope our dog does not revert to its old habits while we're gone.*

review *n.* **1.** evaluation, criticism, critique, commentary, editorial. *We read the movie review before we saw the movie.* **2.** reexamination, reevaluation, rundown, survey, study. *My review of the test material took less time than expected.* –*vb.* **3.** reexamine, reevaluate, restate, retrace, study. *Please review the steps with me once again.* **4.** criticize, critique, evaluate, examine. *A magazine writer reviewed the new novel.*

reviewer *n.* critic, analyst, judge, appraiser, evaluator, faultfinder, commentator. *Our local movie reviewer tends to nitpick.*

revile *vb.* verbally abuse, scold, vituperate, vilify, disparage, lambaste. *The local vandal was reviled by all.* **Ant.** praise, compliment, commend.

revise *vb.* change, alter, rewrite, redo, modify, rework. *The screenwriter must revise his script.*

revision *n.* rewrite, change, repair, editing, modification, second draft. *The editor ordered the writer to do a revision of the story.*

revival *n.* rebirth, renaissance, resurgence, return, reawakening restoration. *Swing music underwent a revival in the late 1990s.*

revive *vb.* reawaken, renew, freshen, resuscitate, recharge. *Doctors were able to revive the comatose woman.*

revoke *vb.* withdraw, cancel, void, repeal, nullify. *The judge will revoke the drunk driver's license.* **Ant.** restore, award, preserve.

revolt *vb.* **1.** rebel, mutiny, protest, riot. *The slaves revolted against their owners.* **2.** sicken, disgust, shock, offend, horrify. *Will the gory movie revolt us?* –*n.* **3.** rebellion, uprising, revolution. *A peasant led the revolt against wealthy landowners.* **Ant. 1.** obey, follow. **2.** please, attract, delight.

revolting *adj.* disgusting, repulsive, repellent, offensive, obnoxious, repugnant. *Rotting garbage is a revolting sight.* **Ant.** pleasant, delightful, appetizing.

revolution *n.* **1.** upheaval, uprising, overthrow, rebellion, revolt. *American patriots fought in a revolution against the British.* **2.** rotation, circle, cycle, spin. *The wheel made a complete revolution.* **Ant. 1.** counterrevolution, restoration.

revolutionary *adj.* **1.** new, pioneering, cutting edge, innovative, progressive, advanced. *Scientists have developed a revolutionary method for building computer chips.* **2.** rebellious, subversive, mutinous, insubordinate, insurrectionary, riotous. *The government is cracking down on revolutionary militia groups.* **Ant. 1.** outmoded, old, antique. **2.** conforming, sheepish.

revolve *vb.* rotate, circle, orbit, spin, reel. *The nine planets revolve around the Sun.*

revulsion *n.* disgust, nausea, distaste, repugnance, detestation, loathing. *Looking at maggots fills me with revulsion.* **Ant.** attraction, desire.

reward *n.* **1.** prize, payment, compensation. *We will give a reward to the person who finds our lost puppy.* –*vb.* **2.** repay, compensate, award, acknowledge. *The king will reward the brave knight with gold.* **Ant.** **1.** penalty, punishment. **2.** confiscate, punish.

rewarding *adj.* productive, fulfilling, beneficial, profitable, gratifying, compensating. *If you want a rewarding career, you must be educated.* **Ant.** unrewarding, unfulfilling, penalizing.

rhetoric *n.* eloquence, discourse, expressiveness, fluency, language, grandiloquence, oration, oratory. *Politicians use rhetoric to advance their ideas.*

rhetorical *adj.* grandiloquent, showy, insincere, bombastic, inflated, pretentious. *At election time, most Americans grow weary of the rhetorical sparring between candidates.*

rhyme *n.* alliteration, poem, verse, lyric, couplet, ode, limerick. *Children love to recite silly rhymes.*

rhythm *n.* pulsation, movement, throb, beat, meter. *They danced to the music's rhythm.*

ribald *adj.* vulgar, dirty, risqué, obscene, lewd, earthy, off-color. *Nobody under 18 is allowed in the nightclub because the show is particularly ribald.* **Ant.** wholesome, clean, G-rated.

rich *adj.* **1.** wealthy, prosperous, affluent. *England's royal family is very rich.* **2.** splendid, lavish, vivid, luxurious. *The painting's rich colors were breathtaking.* **3.** fertile, fruitful, bountiful. *The rich farmland produced an abundance of food.* **4.** fattening, sweet, creamy, flavorful. *This chocolate cake is too rich.* **Ant.** **1.** poor, poverty-stricken, impoverished. **2.** plain, cheap. **3.** unfertile, depleted, barren. **4.** bland, unappetizing

riches *n.* wealth, fortune, affluence, opulence, abundance, treasure, worth, money. *He controlled riches but rarely spent money on himself.* **Ant.** poverty, indigence, nothing.

rickety *adj.* unstable, wobbly, shaky, unsteady, fragile, teetering. *Don't sit in that rickety chair.* **Ant.** solid, strong, sturdy.

ricochet *vb.* rebound, bounce off, recoil, glance, deflect. *Be careful where you aim because bullets will ricochet off the rocks.*

rid *vb.* free, cleanse, clear, purge, purify. *The queen's soldiers will rid the forest of bandits.*

ride *n.* **1.** drive, conveyance, trip, cruise, spin, jaunt. *Do you need a ride to the library? –vb.* **2.** drive, travel, commute, tour, motor, journey. *Am I old enough to ride a horse?*

rider *n.* addition, supplement, clause, amendment, attachment, appendix. *We'll need to attach a rider to the contract to cover our additional requirements.*

riddle *n.* **1.** puzzle, mystery, problem, enigma. *He gave us a riddle to solve. –vb.* **2.** pierce, penetrate, honeycomb. *The old tree trunk was riddled with beetle holes.*

ridicule *n.* **1.** sarcasm, mockery, teasing, scorn, sneering. *I was very upset over the ridicule my idea received. –vb.* **2.** mock, insult, taunt, belittle. *He never ridicules his students.* **Ant.** **1.** praise, approval. **2.** praise, commend, applaud.

ridiculous *adj.* foolish, idiotic, silly, comical, laughable. *That clown looks ridiculous.*

rife *adj.* abundant, plentiful, copious, abounding, profuse, teeming. *I'm afraid my garden has become rife with insects.* **Ant.** lacking, deficient.

riffraff *n.* rabble, commoners, lower class, hoi polloi, (slang) scum, dregs. *He hung out with riffraff and got into trouble with the law.* **Ant.** upper class, elite, royalty.

rifle *n.* firearm, gun, carbine, shotgun, musket, Winchester, Remington. *Hunters clean their rifles with great care.*

rift *n.* **1.** crack, split, rent, opening, fissure, cleft. *Geologists have become wary of a growing rift running along the San Andreas fault in California.* **2.** disagreement, falling-out, gap, schism, estrangement, split. *The rift between the Democrats and Republicans will be difficult to mend.*

rig *n.* equipment, apparatus, gear, outfit, tackle, machine, vehicle. *We could just make out the oil drilling rig on the horizon.*

right *adj.* **1.** proper, good, honorable, fair, just. *That was the right thing to do.* **2.** correct, accurate, perfect, true, factual, faultless, proper. *His answer was right.* **3.** rational, sane, sensible. *She may act crazy, but she's in her right mind.* –*n.* **4.** permission, liberty, freedom, authorization. *Do I have the right to park here?* **5.** goodness, justice, honor, fairness, virtue. *The criminal's sense of right and wrong is distorted.* –*adj.* **6.** directly, quickly, instantly, promptly. *Don't worry; I'll be right over.* **7.** exactly, correctly, perfectly, properly. *The clothes do not fit right.* –*vb.* **8.** correct, fix, mend, repair. *We must right the injustice done to this woman.* **Ant. 1.** wrong, improper, dishonorable. **2.** wrong, incorrect, imperfect, faulted. **3.** irrational, insane. **5.** wrong, badness, injustice, sinfulness. **6.** indirectly, slowly. **7.** wrong, improperly, poorly.

righteous *adj.* virtuous, upright, moral, guiltless, angelic, saintly, good. *It's hard to fault a righteous person.* **Ant.** immoral, bad, sinful.

rigid *adj.* stiff, immovable, unbending, firm, set, inflexible. *The frozen fish were very rigid.* **Ant.** soft, bending, flexible, limp.

rigorous *adj.* tough, stern, demanding, challenging, severe. *She had a rigorous aerobic session.* **Ant.** easy, undemanding.

rile *vb.* anger, outrage, stir up, peeve, irk, aggravate. *I always find something in the news to rile me.* **Ant.** pacify, mollify, soothe.

rim *n.* edge, lip, border, brim, fringe, ledge. *The rim of my coffee cup is chipped.* **Ant.** inside, center.

rind *n.* peel, peeling, skin, hull, outer layer. *Are you supposed to eat the rind of a kiwi?*

ring *n.* **1.** hoop, loop, circle, coil. *The couple exchanged wedding rings.* **2.** gang, mob, band, club, clique. *The police broke up the gambling ring.* **3.** chime, dong, knell, peal, clang, sound. *The telephone's ring was very loud.* –*vb.* **4.** sound, chime, toll, jingle, knoll. *The church rings its bell on Christmas.* **5.** circle, encircle, surround, enclose, loop. *Please ring the fire pit with stones.*

ringleader *n.* boss, chief, head, leader, orchestrator, (slang) big cheese. *The police targeted the ringleader for arrest.*

rinse *vb.* wet, flush, clean, cleanse, splash. *Rinse off your feet before jumping in the pool.*

riot *n.* **1.** lawlessness, disorder, violence, uproar, protest, outbreak. *Many cars were burned during the riot.* –*vb.* **2.** rampage, protest, revolt, rage, rebel. *Angry workers rioted over the increase in food prices.*

riotous *adj.* anarchic, chaotic, rebellious, out-of-control, unruly, wild. *A riotous mob gathered to protest the controversial ruling.* **Ant.** peaceful, orderly, tranquil.

rip *vb.* **1.** tear, strip, split, shred. *Why did you rip apart the letter?* –*n.* **2.** tear, split, slit, rent, rupture. *I will sew the rip in my pants.*

ripe *adj.* mature, ready, developed, seasonable, timely. *That green banana is not ripe.* **Ant.** unripe, unready, unfit, raw.

ripen *vb.* age, mature, season, develop. *She left the green tomatoes on her counter to ripen.*

rip-off *n.* theft, thievery, (slang) gyp, robbery, fraud, cheat, swindle. *The students complained* *that charging three dollars for a cup of soda was a rip-off.*

riposte *n.* retort, comeback, response, rejoinder, repartee. *Almost instantly, the comedian came up with a clever riposte to the heckle she'd received.*

ripple *n.* wavelet, wave, riffle, lap, undulation, purl. *Gentle ripples lapped the shore.*

riptide *n.* undertow, undercurrent, current. *To escape a riptide, swim parallel to shore.*

rise *vb.* **1.** climb, ascend, soar, lift, rocket, surge, arise. *The Sun rises in the east.* **2.** increase, grow, swell, upswing, intensify, strengthen. *The temperature usually rises during the day.* *–n.* **3.** climb, soaring, ascent, mounting, uplift. *We watched the rise of the Sun from our porch.* **4.** increase, strengthening, upsurge, expansion. *There was a rise in crime during the holiday season.* **Ant. 1.** fall, descend, drop. **2.** fall, descend, decrease. **3.** fall, descent. **4.** fall, decrease, weakening.

risk *n.* **1.** gamble, uncertainty, hazard, danger. *Parachuting from that plane was a big risk.* *–vb.* **2.** gamble, dare, endanger, venture. *The gambler risked all his money on one last spin.* **Ant. 1.** certainty, safety, security.

risky *adj.* dangerous, perilous, hazardous, life-threatening, a gamble, chancy. *Starting a new business is always risky.* **Ant.** safe, secure, guaranteed.

risqué *adj.* suggestive, racy, daring, improper, indecent, ribald. *The comedian's act is too risqué for young audiences.* **Ant.** wholesome, clean, G-rated.

rite *n.* ritual, exercise, practice, custom, ceremony, formality. *A priest performs numerous rites for members of the church.*

ritual *n.* ceremony, rite, custom, habit, routine. *Brushing my teeth is part of my morning ritual.* **Ant.** departure, deviation.

ritzy *n.* luxurious, classy, elegant, posh, deluxe, (slang) snazzy. *You have to dress up to eat in a ritzy restaurant.* **Ant.** shabby, poor, cheap.

rival *n.* **1.** opponent, challenger, enemy, foe. *My rival in the competition was well-prepared.* *–adj.* **2.** opposing, competing, contending. *The rival team scored the first goal.* *–vb.* **3.** match, meet, approach, equal. *He rivals you in speed if not in strength.* **Ant. 1.** ally, friend, assistant, coworker. **2.** allied, cooperating.

rivalry *n.* contest, struggle, opposition, competition. *There was a friendly rivalry between our two schools.* **Ant.** cooperation, alliance, teamwork.

river *n.* waterway, tributary, branch, stream, brook, estuary. *Rafting on a river has become a popular pastime.*

WORD SEARCH

area of surrounding land that feeds river water: *watershed*
cross: *ford*
flood area alongside: *floodplain*
flood barrier/embankment: *levee*
loop of water separated from main river: *oxbow*
mill wheel, turns: *millrace*
referring to: *fluvial*
rotating current: *eddy*
sand ridge: *bar*
sediment mass deposited at mouth of river: *delta*
shallow surrounded by deep water: *shoal*
steep but narrow stretch of descending water: *chute*
tidal: *estuary*
underground: *aquifer, groundwater*
upwelling of current: *boil*
waterfall: *cataract*
winding portion: *meander, bend*

riveting *adj.* fascinating, engrossing, gripping, enthralling, spellbinding, mesmerizing. *The* *movie was absolutely riveting.* **Ant.** boring, dull, bland.

road *n.* street, path, lane, route, highway. *The winding road went up to the mountaintop.*

WORD SEARCH

circle: *rotary, cloverleaf, roundabout, circus*
cliff edge: *corniche*
curve: *ess, hairpin*
dead end: *cul-de-sac, impasse*
dividers, highway: *jersey barrier, median strip, island*
edge: *shoulder*
German expressway with no speed limit: *autobahn*
hole in: *chuckhole, pothole*
overhead crossover: *overpass*
paving material: *asphalt, blacktop, cobblestone, gravel, macadam*
ringing a city: *beltway*
slowdown device: *speed bump, speed table*
traffic jam: *bottleneck, gridlock*

roam *vb.* wander, drift, stray, ramble, rove, range. *The hobo roamed around America.*

roar *vb.* **1.** bellow, howl, thunder, yell, growl, thunder, blast, boom. *A bear will roar only when it needs to.* *–n.* **2.** bellow, howl, thunder, yell, growl, thunder, blast, boom. *Listen to the roar of crashing waves.*

roast *vb.* bake, cook, broil, brown, barbecue, sear, grill. *Roast the turkey for three hours.*

rob *vb.* burglarize, steal, thieve, pilfer, cheat. *The burglars robbed a bank.*

robber *n.* thief, mugger, crook, bandit, criminal, housebreaker. *The bank robber was quickly apprehended by the police.*

robbery *n.* stealing, (slang) stickup, mugging, holdup, thievery, theft, heist. *The suspects in the robbery were wearing ski masks.*

robe *n.* bathrobe, cassock, wrap, kimono, caftan, garment, gown. *I put on my robe to get the morning paper from the porch.*

robot *n.* automaton, android, cyborg, mechanical being, machine, golem. *A robot can sometimes be used in place of a human, especially for tedious jobs.*

robust *adj.* strong, healthy, sturdy, brawny, husky. *Santa Claus is a jolly and robust man.* **Ant.** scrawny, weak, sickly.

rock *n.* **1.** stone, boulder, pebble. *My sister enjoys skipping rocks in the lake.* **2.** sway, roll, pitch, bob, swing. *The rock of the boat made it difficult to stand.* *–vb.* **3.** shake, pitch, roll, sway, jar. *The earthquake rocked our house.*

WORD SEARCH

carving or drawing on a rock: *petroglyph*
conglomeration of rock types: *breccia, conglomerate*
deposited by glacier: *glacial erratics, till, drift*
formed or changed by heat and pressure: *metamorphic rock*
ground layer: *bedrock*
layers of: *strata*
lined with minerals: *geode*
molten: *lava, magma*
projecting: *ledge, outcrop*
rounded and small, naturally: *cobble*
sand, sediment or organic matter, comprised of: *sedimentary rock*
study of: *petrology*
weirdly shaped by windblown sand: *ventifact*

rock and roll *n.* music, pop music, rhythm and blues (R&B), heavy metal, metal, funk, hip-hop, rap, boogie. *Musicologists have catalogued more than a dozen subcategories of rock and roll.*

rocket *n.* missile, projectile, spacecraft, spaceship, space capsule, weapon. *NASA launched a rocket into space this morning.*

rocky *adj. 1.* stony, petrous, bouldered, cobbled, flinty, craggy, gravelly. *The riverbed is too rocky to walk across.* **2.** unstable, unsteady, shaky, wobbly, tottering, unbalanced. *Too many arguments make for a rocky relationship.* **Ant. 2.** stable, steady, balanced.

rococo *n.* ornate, ornamental, florid, elaborate, profuse, overdone. *The architecture of some rooms at Versailles is rococo, featuring shell motifs.*

rod *n.* staff, stick, pole, switch, shaft, cane, bar, dowel. *The sheepherder walks everywhere with a rod in his hand.*

rogue *n.* scoundrel, scamp, cad, rascal, deceiver, charlatan, swindler. *He had lied to everyone and had earned the reputation of a rogue.* **Ant.** saint, angel, choirboy.

roil *vb.* agitate, stir up, disturb, muddy, cloud, churn up. *We ran inside just as the storm clouds began to roil overhead.*

role *n.* part, character, portrayal, place. *She was given the role of Dorothy in* The Wizard of Oz.

role model *n.* hero, heroine, mentor, idol, good example, star. *Many children require a role model to learn how to behave correctly.*

roll *vb.* **1.** tumble, throw, toss, rotate, revolve, pitch. *Please roll the dice.* **2.** wrap, wind, whirl, twist, ball. *We must roll up our sleeping bags.* **3.** rumble, roar, thunder, boom. *The thunder rolled loudly.* –*n.* **4.** bun, biscuit, pastry, bread. *She ate cinnamon rolls for breakfast.* **5.** attendance, roster, register, list. *The teacher called the roll to see who was absent.* **6.** boom, thunder, clap, rumble. *The storm's loud roll startled me.*

romance *n.* love, love affair, courtship, flirtation. *He carried on a romance with the girl next door.*

romantic *adj.* **1.** passionate, emotional, sentimental, loving. *I have a romantic girlfriend who always sends me flowers.* –*n.* **2.** dreamer, idealist, visionary. *The poet was a romantic.* **Ant. 1.** unromantic, unemotional, unsentimental.

romp *vb.* play, frolic, cavort, revel, gambol, prance. *We watched the children romp around the playground.*

rookie *n.* beginner, neophyte, newcomer, freshman, (slang) tenderfoot, (slang) greenhorn. *Expect all rookies to make mistakes.* **Ant.** veteran, professional, expert.

room *n.* **1.** chamber, cubicle, compartment, lodgings, apartment. *My mother gets angry when my room is messy.* **2.** space, clearing, expanse. *Please give him more room to do his stunt.* –*vb.* **3.** live, dwell, stay, lodge. *The student rooms at the dormitory.*

roomy *adj.* spacious, capacious, voluminous, commodious, extensive, large. *The van was roomy enough to seat eight.* **Ant.** cramped, tight, confined.

root *n.* **1.** substructure, base, bottom, foundation. *The tree's roots were sticking up through the ground.* **2.** lineage, ancestry, heritage, bloodline. *I traced my family roots back to Africa.* –*vb.* **3.** cheer, applaud, clap, support. *We rooted for our soccer team.* **4.** fix, fasten, set, embed. *Fear rooted him to the ground.*

rope *n.* cord, cordage, cable, hawser, lanyard, line, strand. *The package was tied with rope.*

roster *n.* list, roll, register, inventory, index, muster. *I was happy to see my name added to the roster of starting players.*

rosy *adj.* pink, ruddy, blushing, blooming, roseate, rubicund. *Your cheeks are always rosy after you come in from the cold.*

rot *vb.* **1.** decay, spoil, mold, poison, corrupt. *These fruits will rot if you don't refrigerate them.* –*n.* **2.** decay, mold, corruption. *Dry rot weakened the cabin's timbers.*

rotary *n.* 1. roundabout, cloverleaf, circus. *Slow down when you enter the rotary. –adj.* 2. turning, spinning, twirling, rotating, revolving, gyrating. *I'm going to need a rotary sander to refinish the floor.*

rotate *vb.* revolve, spin, turn, whirl, circle. *Please rotate the observatory dome so we may view a different section of the sky.*

rotten *adj.* putrid, putrefying, rancid, decayed, spoiled, decomposed. *The meat was so rotten, even the dog spit it out.* **Ant.** fresh, good.

rotund *adj.* fat, plump, stout, obese, pudgy, full-figured. *She was becoming increasingly rotund from eating too much ice cream.* **Ant.** skinny, thin, emaciated.

rough *adj.* 1. coarse, scaly, rocky, jagged, uneven, scratchy. *The sandpaper felt very rough.* 2. difficult, hard, tough, harsh, brutal. *That was a rough test.* 3. unfinished, incomplete, crude. *This is a rough draft of my final paper. –vb.* 4. beat, thrash, pound, batter. *The thugs roughed up the frightened man.* **Ant.** 1. smooth, soft. 2. easy, mild. 3. final, finished, complete.

round *adj.* 1. circular, globular, oval, spherical, elliptical. *The Halloween pumpkin was round.* 2. arched, curved, bowed. *The paper was rounded at the corners. –n.* 3. series, circle, sequence, cycle. *A round of toasts was given before the meal.* 4. watch, tour, route, circuit. *The doctor completed her rounds. –vb.* 5. circle, orbit, skirt, go around. *The racing car rounded the turn.* 6. close, terminate, end, finish, conclude. *We will round off the celebration with a final song.* **Ant.** 1. square, rectangular. 2. straight. 6. start, open.

roundabout *adj.* indirect, circumlocutory, circuitous, meandering, winding, rambling. *He was trying to tell me in a roundabout way that my fly was unzipped.* **Ant.** direct, straightforward, blunt.

rouse *vb.* awaken, call, summon, animate, stir, arouse. *My father rouses me in the morning.* **Ant.** hush, soothe, quiet, still.

rousing *adj.* stirring, spirited, stimulating, vigorous, lively, brisk. *The audience gave the singer a rousing round of applause.* **Ant.** somnolent, sleepy, stupefying.

rout *n.* 1. defeat, conquest, beating, upset, licking. *The team's loss by a hundred points was a complete rout. –vb.* 2. overwhelm, defeat, conquer, vanquish, smash. *The attacking army routed the ill-prepared defenders.* **Ant.** 1. success, victory. 2. succeed, triumph.

route *n.* 1. path, course, way, track, road, lane. *The plane flies a direct route to London. –vb.* 2. direct, detour, send, dispatch. *The construction workers routed us onto a side road.*

routine *n.* 1. procedure, habit, pattern, custom, performance. *The gymnast practiced his routine before the competition. –adj.* 2. regular, usual, normal, customary. *Every six months I visit the dentist for a routine checkup.* **Ant.** 2. unusual, uncustomary, irregular.

rove *vb.* wander, drift, ramble, range, roam. *The photographer roved the country looking for great photo opportunities.*

row *n.* 1. line, column, string, chain, sequence. *Our car was parked at the row's end.* 2. quarrel, fight, argument, altercation, spat. *There was a row in the apartment below us. –vb.* 3. paddle, oar, scull, pull. *We rowed a boat across the lake.*

rowdy *adj.* wild, unruly, boisterous, rough, rambunctious, trouble-making. *A few soccer fans got too rowdy and were asked to leave the stadium.* **Ant.** behaved, polite, mild-mannered.

royal *adj.* 1. imperial, monarchical, noble, highborn. *Britain's royal family lives in a palace.* 2. magnificent, majestic, grand, splendid. *They* *gave us a royal welcome.* **Ant. 1.** common, plebeian. **2.** plain, modest, lowly.

royalty *n.* majesty, regality, nobility, sovereignty, kingship, queenship. *He claimed to be descended from royalty, but I suspect his ancestors were really just peasants.*

rub *vb.* **1.** massage, knead, scrub, stroke, scour. *Please rub my sore back.* *–n.* **2.** massage, rubdown, kneading, stroking. *A good back rub relaxes me.*

rubbish *n.* **1.** trash, garbage, waste, refuse. *The rubbish was unloaded into the dump.* **2.** nonsense, babble, gibberish. *That story you told is rubbish.*

ruckus *n.* uproar, commotion, rumpus, outburst, upheaval, disturbance. *A ruckus arose, and the police arrived to restore order.*

ruddy *adj.* red, pinkish, glowing, rosy, blooming, apple-cheeked, rubicund. *The old drunk's face was permanently ruddy from drinking too much.*

rude *adj.* **1.** impolite, insulting, discourteous, surly, inconsiderate, disrespectful. *The rude man ignored her when she spoke to him.* **2.** primitive, rough, crude, rustic, unpolished. *There was a rude shelter on the island.* **Ant. 1.** polite, courteous, considerate, courtly. **2.** finished, elegant, polished.

rudeness *n.* discourtesy, bad manners, tactlessness, crudeness, incivility, courseness. *Her rudeness annoyed everyone.* **Ant.** courtesy, politeness, manners.

rudimentary *adj.* **1.** basic, elementary, elemental, fundamental. *The alphabet is rudimentary knowledge for students.* **2.** incomplete, imperfect, simple, crude. *She had only a rudimentary understanding of what had happened.* **Ant. 1.** advanced. **2.** complete, finished, perfect.

rue *vb.* regret, repent, mourn, grieve. *You will rue the day you made that promise.*

ruffian *n.* tough, punk, gangster, criminal, thug, troublemaker, (slang) hood. *The police picked up the ruffian on the street corner for vandalizing the nearby shops.*

ruffle *vb.* **1.** disturb, upset, disorder, jumble, stir. *The wind ruffled the bird's feathers.* *–n.* **2.** frill, edging, flounce. *Ruffles covered the shirt's front.* **Ant. 1.** settle, smooth, calm.

rug *n.* carpet, mat, floor covering, runner, broadloom, throw rug. *The floor was covered by a rug to cut down on noise.*

rugged *adj.* harsh, stern, severe, rough, tough, solid, sturdy. *The mountains presented a rugged landscape to the hikers.* **Ant.** soft, frail, cultivated.

ruin *n.* **1.** destruction, downfall, collapse, decay, misfortune, disrepair. *Bad investments left him in financial ruin.* **2.** relics, remains, remnants, wreckage. *We visited the ruins of an ancient Roman coliseum.* *–vb.* **3.** destroy, spoil, wreck, shatter, smash. *The rain ruined my painting.* **Ant. 1.** creation, success, improvement. **3.** improve, create.

ruinous *adj.* disastrous, devastating, destructive, crushing, bankrupting, catastrophic. *I made a ruinous business decision and lost everything.* **Ant.** profitable, beneficial.

rule *n.* **1.** law, regulation, order, guideline, principle, maxim. *The school's rule says you need your parent's signature.* **2.** control, command, government, administration. *They suffered under the king's cruel rule.* *–vb.* **3.** control, command, lead, administer, govern. *The queen tried to rule her people with justice.* **4.** judge, decide, determine, resolve, settle. *The judge ruled that neither person should get the winnings.*

ruler *n.* leader, chief, head, dictator, president, king, administrator. *A dictator is a ruler who lays down the law without a popular vote.*

ruling *n.* judgment, decision, verdict, determination, finding, settlement. *The plaintiffs reacted with delight at the judge's ruling.*

rumble *vb.* 1. thunder, roar, boom, resound. *His voice rumbled from the next room.* –*n.* 2. thunder, roar, booming, roll, growl. *The avalanche's rumble was heard down in the valley.*

ruminate *vb.* think, contemplate, meditate, deliberate, consider, ponder, muse. *Don't ruminate in bed too long or you'll have insomnia.*

rummage *vb.* hunt, search, explore, ransack, probe. *He had to rummage through the attic to find the old painting.*

rumor *n.* 1. gossip, hearsay, report, story, whisper. *The rumor that I am leaving is incorrect.* –*vb.* 2. gossip, tattle, whisper, circulate. *It was rumored that the principal was being fired.*

rump *n.* rear, hindquarters, backside, posterior, buttocks, derriere. *Use care on the ice or you'll end up on your rump.*

rumple *vb.* wrinkle, crinkle, crumple, fold, ripple, bedraggle. *Don't lie around or you'll rumple your good clothes.*

run *vb.* 1. rush, hurry, race, dash, flee, gush, surge. *After hitting the ball, you must run to first base.* 2. operate, work, function. *The car runs on gasoline.* 3. campaign, compete. *The politician will run for office.* 4. vary, stretch, extend. *Their ages run from five to eighteen.* 5. unravel, separate, snag. *I hope the socks do not run.* 6. publish, print, show, display. *The article was run in today's paper.* –*n.* 7. race, dash, jog, sprint, marathon. *His crosscountry run took sixty days.* 8. stretch, series, streak. *She had a run of good test scores.* 9. freedom, control, liberty. *They have the run of the house while their parents are gone.* 10. snag, tear, pull. *She had a run in her stocking.* **Ant.** 1. walk, stroll, crawl. 2. stop, pause, quit, halt. 7. walk, stroll, crawl.

runaround *n.* evasion, (slang) buck-passing, delay, merry-go-round, headache, SNAFU. *I've tried to straighten out my telephone bill, but the company keeps giving me the runaround.*

runaway *n.* fugitive, refugee, escapee, truant, deserted, delinquent. *Many runaways end up living on the streets.*

rundown *n.* summary, outline, synopsis, sketch, briefing, abstract. *I need a rundown of the bills I owe.*

runt *n.* dwarf, midget, pygmy, pipsqueak, (slang) shrimp, lilliputian. *We picked out the runt of the litter and brought it home.*

runway *n.* airstrip, landing strip, airfield, taxiway, airport. *We have to get clearance before we can get on the runway.*

rupture *n.* 1. break, split, crack, fissure, rent. *The rupture in the tire was fixed.* –*vb.* 2. burst, split, crack, break, divide. *We must fix the dam before it ruptures.* **Ant.** 1. repair, mend. 2. repair, mend, heal, unite.

rural *adj.* country, agricultural, pastoral, rustic, farm. *They live in a rural area.* **Ant.** urban, cosmopolitan.

ruse *n.* trick, deception, dodge, hoax, ploy. *The thief's ruse misled the police.*

rush *vb.* 1. race, run, hurry, dash, hustle. *We must rush to the store before it closes.* –*n.* 2. sprint, dash, race, run. *There was a rush to the ticket booth when it opened.* **Ant.** 1–2. walk, crawl, stroll.

rust *vb.* oxidize, corrode, decay, crumble, weather, deteriorate. *If you leave your bike out in the rain, it will rust.*

rustic *adj.* **1.** country, rural, backwoods, farm, unsophisticated. *Our cabin was in a rustic setting.* –*n.* **2.** farmer, provincial, peasant. *The hillbilly was a rustic.* **Ant. 1.** urban, city, sophisticated. **2.** sophisticate.

rustle *vb.* crinkle, brush, crackle, whisper, flutter, swish. *Taffeta skirts tend to rustle as the wearer walks.*

rusty *adj.* oxidized, corroded, weathered, deteriorated, crumbling. *My bike is rusty from leaving it out in the rain so many times.*

rut *n.* **1.** furrow, groove, channel, trench, trough, ditch. *Avoid ruts in the mud unless you've got four-wheel drive.* **2.** routine, grind, treadmill, same old thing. *I need a change; my job has become such a rut.*

ruthless *adj.* unmerciful, heartless, cold, relentless, brutal, unfeeling. *She was ruthless toward her opponents.* **Ant.** merciful, compassionate, kind.

S

sabbatical *n.* leave, leave of absence, vacation, rest, break, hiatus. *I plan to go on a sabbatical until the fall.*

sabotage *n.* destruction, undermining, treachery, terrorist act, demolition, wrecking. *The terrorists secretly planned acts of sabotage.*

saboteur *n.* demolition expert, terrorist, agent provocateur, subversive, bomber, revolutionist. *The saboteur planted a bomb in enemy headquarters.*

sack *n.* **1.** bag, pouch, pack. *I take my lunch to school in a sack.* **2.** destruction, burning, plunder, devastation, pillage. *The sack of Rome by the Vandals occurred in 455.* *–vb.* **3.** bag, pack. *Clerks sack groceries at the market.* **4.** level, destroy, demolish, waste, pillage, plunder. *Vikings sacked a series of coastal villages.*

sacrament *n.* rite, ritual, ceremony, vow, oath, pledge. *Confirmation is a sacrament of the Christian church.*

sacred *adj.* holy, revered, hallowed, religious, blessed. *Mecca is a sacred Islamic city.* **Ant.** profane, secular.

sacred cow *n.* idol, juggernaut, hero, heroine, object of worship, taboo subject, protected institution. **Ant.** scapegoat, object of ridicule.

sacrifice *n.* **1.** offering, gift, homage. *The Aztecs of Mexico made sacrifices to their gods.* **2.** loss, surrender, relinquishment. *I sold my coin collection at a sacrifice.* *–vb.* **3.** offer, surrender, give, forfeit, cede, relinquish. *She sacrificed her free time to tutor her younger brother.* **Ant.** **2.** profit, return, gain.

sacrilege *n.* violation, desecration, profanation, disrespect, misuse, irreverence. *Vandalizing religious icons is sacrilege.*

sacrilegious *adj.* disrespectful, irreverent, blasphemous, impious, profane, unholy. *It is considered sacrilegious to take God's name in vain.* **Ant.** reverent, respectful, pious.

sacrosanct *adj.* sacred, holy, hallowed, consecrated, godly, divine, venerated. *The teachings of the church are sacrosanct.* **Ant.** unholy, impious, profane.

sad *adj.* unhappy, gloomy, depressed, mournful, melancholy, joyless. *The end of summer vacation was a sad event.* **Ant.** happy, joyful, glad, cheerful

sadden *vb.* depress, dispirit, distress, deject, grieve, upset. *Rainy Mondays always sadden me.* **Ant.** gladden, cheer, uplift.

saddle *n.* **1.** seat, pad, perch. *She kept slipping off the horse's saddle.* *–vb.* **2** equip, outfit, prepare. *The rider saddled his horse.* **3.** burden, weight, overwhelm, load, tax, strain. *We were saddled with extra paperwork.* **Ant.** **3.** relieve, unburden.

sadistic *adj.* cruel, perverse, severe, nasty, domineering, ruthless, brutal. *Hurting others for* *the pleasure of it is sadistic.* **Ant.** masochistic, kind, compassionate.

sadness *n.* depression, blue mood, downheartedness, melancholy, sorrow, unhappiness. *The prospect of moving away filled her with sadness.* **Ant.** glee, joy, happiness.

safari *n.* hunt, expedition, shoot, trek, caravan. *We're going on an African safari to shoot pictures of wild animals.*

safe *adj.* **1.** protected, secure, defended, guarded. *You must escape to a safe place.* **2.** harmless, sound, reliable. *Talking to strangers is not always safe.* **3.** unhurt, uninjured, undamaged, unbroken, intact. *Don't worry; your friend is safe.* –*n.* **4.** strongbox, vault, chest. *Robbers blew open the bank's safe.* **Ant. 1.** unsafe, unprotected. **2.** unsafe, harmful. **3.** hurt, injured.

safeguard *n.* **1.** protection, defense, armor, guard, shield. *Seatbelts are a safeguard against serious injuries.* –*vb.* **2.** armor, protect, guard, fortify, shield, screen. *High walls safeguard castles from attackers.* **Ant. 1.** threat, danger. **2.** risk, endanger.

safekeeping *n.* protection, security, care, guardianship, preservation. *It's wise to put your money into a bank for safekeeping.*

safety *n.* security, protection, immunity, invulnerability, defense, refuge. *For your safety, always wear a helmet when riding a bike.* **Ant.** peril, hazard, danger.

sag *vb.* **1.** droop, drop, sink, slump, flop. *His bag sagged with Halloween candy.* –*n.* **2.** droop, sinking, slump, dip, hollow. *We fixed the roof's sag.* **Ant. 1.** rise, soar. **2.** rise, upturn.

saga *n.* tale, history, narrative, chronicle, epic. *The Civil War saga will be a television miniseries.*

sagacious *adj.* clever, wise, shrewd, cunning, knowing, smart. *She asked the sagacious wizard for guidance.* **Ant.** stupid, dumb, ignorant.

sage *adj.* **1.** wise, expert, authoritative, intelligent, learned, astute. *If you and need sage advice, go to your guidance counselor.* –*n.* **2.** authority, guru, mentor, savant, wise man, wise woman, scholar. *The villagers consulted their eldest sage for guidance.* **Ant. 1.** moronic, imbecilic, stupid. **2.** moron, imbecile, idiot.

sail *n.* **1.** canvas, mainsail. *The boat's sail flapped in the wind.* **2.** cruise, outing, voyage, excursion. *They took an afternoon sail across the lake.* –*vb.* **3.** navigate, pilot, captain. *She sailed her boat in the harbor.* **4.** boat, cruise, yacht, skim, float. *He will sail down the river.* **5.** glide, slide, fly, flow, dart, shoot. *I sailed through the exam.* **Ant. 5.** plod, trudge.

WORD SEARCH

change course: *come about*
crew member: *hand*
dead calm area, sea's: *doldrums*
lean in wind, vessel's: *heel*
line fixture, pronged: *cleat*
line, sail-hoisting: *lanyard*
lines: *rigging*
mast, rear-most: *mizzenmast*
overhead: *aloft*
race: *regatta*
rope ladder or climbing lines: *ratlines*
sail, forward, triangular: *foresail, jib*
sail, largest: *mainsail*
sail, three-cornered: *spinnaker*
spar, bow: *bowsprit*
spar, large vertical: *mast*
spar on which bottom of sail is attached: *boom*
steerer: *helmsman*
wind-protected side of vessel: *lee, leeward*
wind side of vessel: *windward*
zigzagging course to counter opposing winds: *tacking*

sailboat *n.* boat, vessel, craft, yacht, wind-jammer, pleasure craft. *It is easy to overturn a sailboat if you don't know how to sail.*

WORD SEARCH
18th-century warship: *frigate*
fishing vessel: *smack*
fore- and aft-rigged vessel with two or three masts: *schooner*
hulled, double-: *catamaran*
hulled, triple-: *trimaran*
masted square rigger, multiple: *bark*
masted, single: *cutter, sloop*
masted, small, double-: *ketch*
19th-century transport, speedy: *clipper*
Oriental: *junk, sampan*
Spanish square rigger from 15th to 18th centuries: *galleon*
warship, speedy: *corvette*

sailor *n.* mariner, seafarer, seaman, sea dog, navy man, shellback. *The sailors had been at sea for a month and were anxious to walk on solid ground again.*

saint *n.* holy person, divine person, blessed person, martyr, Christian, angel. *Her endless good deeds made her a saint in the eyes of many.* **Ant.** demon, devil, sinner.

saintly *adj.* righteous, virtuous, good, holy, divine, blessed, angelic. *The philanthropist's generosity bordered on the saintly.* **Ant.** demonic, evil, devilish.

salacious *adj.* lustful, lecherous, lewd, libidinous, prurient, obscene. *The woman cast her husband a salacious glance in response to his advances.*

salad *n.* greens, tossed salad, vegetarian fare, vegan fare, coleslaw, cress salad, Caesar salad, fruit salad. *The salads she concocted were comprised of vegetables from around the world.*

salary *n.* wage, earnings, payment, fee, stipend. *The store's owner raised her employee's salary.*

sale *n.* **1.** closeout, markdown, discount, bargain, special. *We rushed to the holiday sale.* **2.** exchange, transfer, selling, buying, purchasing. *The house was up for sale.*

salesman *n.* peddler, vendor, solicitor, pitchman, merchandiser, sales representative, sales clerk. *Ask the salesman if he'll take 10 percent off.*

salient *adj.* prominent, projecting, outstanding, striking, primary, important, conspicuous. *The speaker's most salient point was that we should all live in peace.* **Ant.** insignificant, unnoticeable, inconspicuous.

saliva *n.* spit, spittle, slaver, slobber, sputum. *You need saliva in your mouth to help you swallow food.*

sallow *adj.* yellow, yellowish, sickly, jaundiced, pale, wan, pallid. *His illness gave his complexion a sallow cast.*

salon *n.* hairdresser's, beauty shop, barbershop, spa, beauty parlor. *I have an appointment at the hair salon at three o'clock.*

saloon *n.* bar, drinking establishment, pub, tavern, alehouse, (slang) honkytonk. *After work the men went to the local saloon to play darts and have a beer.*

salty *adj.* brackish, saline, briny. *The water in the ocean is very salty.*

salutation *n.* greeting, hail, hello, address. *Be sure to start your letter with a friendly salutation.*

salvage *n.* **1.** recovery, reclamation, rescue, saving, retrieval. *The shipwreck's salvage was carried out by professional divers. –vb.* **2.** save, reclaim, redeem, rescue, recover. *Do you think we can salvage this old coat?* **Ant. 1.** loss. **2.** discard, lose, waste.

salvation *n.* deliverance, saving, preservation, redemption, rescue, liberation. *The alcoholic's salvation depended on shunning his booze.* **Ant.** damnation, death, loss.

salve *n.* **1.** remedy, ointment, balm, lotion. *This cream is a salve for skin rashes. –vb.* **2.** ease, heal, relieve, pacify, reduce. *An apology would salve her wounded pride.* **Ant. 2.** annoy, irritate, inflame.

salvo *n.* discharge, broadside, firing, fusillade, cannonade, bombardment. *The navy ship commenced a deafening salvo to memorialize soldiers from previous wars.*

same *adj.* identical, exact, matching, duplicate, equal, similar. *My sister and I have the same last name.* **Ant.** different, unlike, unequal.

sample *n.* **1.** specimen, example, illustration, instance, taste. *He showed us samples of his poetry. –adj.* **2.** illustrative, representative, test, trial. *This is a sample sentence. –vb.* **3.** try, test, experience, taste, sip. *She asked if she could sample the different ice cream flavors.*

sanctify *n.* consecrate, purify, make sacred, bless, beatify, canonize, anoint. *The cleric said a special prayer to sanctify the shrine.* **Ant.** desecrate, profane, damn.

sanctimonious *adj.* self-righteous, holier-than-thou, preachy, hypocritical, overpious, unctuous. *His sanctimonious finger-pointing was a turn-off.*

sanction *n.* **1.** permission, consent, leave, approval, authorization. *Unless you have your parents' sanction, you cannot go.* **2.** penalty, pressure, punishment. *Sanctions were leveled against the terrorists' country. –vb.* **3.** authorize, confirm, certify, legalize, allow. *Their marriage was sanctioned by the priest.* **Ant. 1.** refusal, disapproval. **2.** reward. **3.** reject, ban, block.

sanctioned *adj.* authorized, certified, approved, confirmed, endorsed, warranted. *A day of free parking has been sanctioned by city hall.* **Ant.** disapproved, vetoed, rejected.

sanctity *n.* sacredness, holiness, purity, godliness, righteousness, inviolability. *Please respect the sanctity of the church by keeping your voices low.*

sanctuary *n.* hideout, refuge, shelter, protection, preserve. *The beautiful garden was her sanctuary from the world.*

sand *n.* **1.** grit, gravel, silt. *Sand got in her eye. –vb.* **2.** grind, file, scour, smooth. *Please sand the wood's rough edges.*

sandwich *n.* club, grinder, hero, submarine, hoagie. *I had a ham and cheese sandwich for lunch.*

sane *adj.* rational, sound, reasonable, sensible, balanced. *Why would a same man pretend he was crazy?* **Ant.** insane, irrational, mad, foolish.

sanguine *adj.* cheerful, optimistic, confident, buoyant, positive. *The soldier felt particularly sanguine despite the danger she was facing.* **Ant.** miserable, depressed, pessimistic.

sanitarium *n.* sanatorium, hospital, resort, health spa, institution, rehabilitation center, treatment facility. *My stay at the local sanitarium helped to relieve stress.*

sanitary *adj.* clean, healthy, sterile, disinfected, wholesome. *The park's rest room was not sanitary.* **Ant.** dirty, unhealthy, grimy, unclean.

sanitize *vb.* clean, disinfect, sterilize, make antiseptic. *You must sanitize every surface before performing any kind of surgery.* **Ant.** infect, dirty, soil.

sanity *n.* reason, rationality, saneness, sensibleness, normality. *People questioned Van Gogh's sanity after he cut off his ear.* **Ant.** insanity, madness, irrationality.

Santa Claus *n.* Saint Nicholas, Saint Nick, Kriss Kringle, Father Christmas. *Is Santa Claus coming to your house on Christmas Eve?*

sap *n.* **1.** juice, milk, fluid, lifeblood. *The tree's sap stuck to her hands. –vb.* **2.** drain, exhaust, reduce, weaken, deplete. *Fasting quickly sapped his strength.* **Ant. 2.** replace, restore.

sarcasm *n.* snideness, jeering, wisecracking, put-downs, mockery, ridicule. *Sarcasm is always insulting.*

sarcastic *adj.* insulting, mocking, sneering, scornful, bitter. *Why were you so sarcastic to your father?* **Ant.** pleasant, flattering, agreeable.

sardonic *adj.* sarcastic, nasty, snide, bitter, mocking, contemptuous, acid-tongued. *His sardonic remarks left few people unscathed.* **Ant.** sweet, complimentary, nice.

sash *n.* band, ribbon, belt, scarf, cummerbund. *A red sash was part of the band uniform.*

sass *vb.* talk back, (slang) wise off, (slang) give lip, (slang) mouth off, be impudent, be insolent. *Don't sass your mother.*

Satan *n.* the Devil, Lucifer, Prince of Darkness, Mephistopheles, Lord of the Flies, Beelzebub. *Many horror movies depict Satan in human form.*

satanic *adj.* demonic, evil, devilish, wicked, diabolical, fiendish. *Adolf Hitler's methods of world domination could only be described as satanic.* **Ant.** godly, angelic, saintly.

satellite *n.* moon, planetoid, orbiter, space station, spacecraft. *The Moon is a natural satellite of Earth; a space station is an artificial one.*

satire *n.* mockery, caricature, takeoff, send-up, spoof, lampoon. *The comedy trio frequently performs satires of television shows.*

satirical *adj.* mocking, ridiculing, lampooning, farcical, tongue-in-cheek, burlesque. *The play was a satirical depiction of Washington politics.*

satisfaction *n.* fulfillment, pleasure, gratification, comfort, delight, happiness. *Her high test scores gave her a great deal of satisfaction.* **Ant.** dissatisfaction, displeasure, unhappiness.

satisfactory *adj.* acceptable, adequate, sufficient, enough, passable. *The finished work was satisfactory.* **Ant.** unsatisfactory, unacceptable.

satisfy *vb.* **1.** gratify, please, comfort, pacify, content. *This drink will satisfy your thirst.* **2.** convince, persuade, assure, reassure. *Her explanation satisfied my doubts.* **Ant.** dissatisfy, displease.

satisfying *adj.* pleasing, gratifying, comforting, refreshing. *The meal was very satisfying.* **Ant.** dissatisfying, displeasing.

saturate *vb.* soak, drench, cover, waterlog, glut. *She saturates her vegetables with butter.*

sauce *n.* gravy, dressing, condiment, drippings, topping, seasoning, relish. *Would you like some chocolate sauce on your ice cream?*

saucy *adj.* disrespectful, rude, impertinent, flippant, insolent, bold, impudent. *Our local loudmouth was saucy enough to say anything to anybody.* **Ant.** polite, courteous, respectful.

saunter *vb.* **1.** stroll, promenade, amble, wander, straggle. *Even though she was quite late, she just sauntered into class.* –*n.* **2.** stroll, amble, ramble, jaunt. *He took a saunter in the park.* **Ant. 1–2.** run, race, dash.

savage *adj.* **1.** fierce, vicious, brutal, merciless, ruthless, cruel. *The hunter tried to fend off the tiger's savage attack.* –*n.* **2.** barbarian, brute, primitive, ruffian. *I get embarrassed when he acts like a savage.* **Ant. 1.** gentle, timid, tender.

savagery *n.* brutality, violence, barbarism, cruelty, viciousness, monstrosity. *The savagery of a lion's attack is frightening to behold.*

savant *n.* genius, intellectual, scholar, wise man, wise woman, sage, expert. *His IQ is high enough to put him into the category of a savant.* **Ant.** ignoramus, moron, idiot.

save *vb.* **1.** rescue, deliver, free, protect, help, safeguard. *Several people tried to save the beached whale.* **2.** keep, maintain, reserve, store. *You should save your work before you turn off the computer.* **Ant. 1.** risk, endanger. **2.** lose, spend, waste.

savings *n.* investment, nest egg, security, hoard, treasure, wealth. *It's wise to put away savings for a rainy day.*

savior *n.* lifesaver, messiah, deliverer, champion. *After killing the evil dragon, the knight was honored as the village's savior.*

savoir faire *n.* sophistication, worldliness, social grace, suavity, poise, urbanity. *Her savoir faire made her a natural party hostess.* **Ant.** clumsiness, awkwardness, backwardness.

savor *n.* **1.** taste, tang, flavor, nature, character. *The barbecued steaks had the savor of hickory smoke.* –*vb.* **2.** relish, enjoy, like, appreciate. *She savored the last bite of chocolate.*

savory *adj.* delicious, appetizing, ambrosial, delectable, mouth-watering. *The chef created a savory dish made out of chicken.* **Ant.** disgusting, unappetizing, unsavory.

savvy *adj.* **1.** aware, knowledgeable, educated, (slang) hip, (slang) with it, enlightened, sharp. *She was too savvy for swindlers to outsmart her.* –*n.* **2.** awareness, knowledge, experience, education, intelligence, (slang) smarts. *Do you have the savvy to succeed in business?* **Ant. 1.** uneducated, inexperienced. **2.** ignorance, stupidity, naiveté.

saw *n.* cutter, cutting tool, instrument, blade, handsaw, circular saw, jig saw. *Get a saw to cut that piece of wood.*

say *vb.* **1.** speak, state, utter, declare, recite, tell. *Can you say the names of the first three presidents?* –*n.* **2.** statement, expression, declaration. *I want a say in what we decide to do.*

saying *n.* proverb, expression, maxim, motto. *There is a saying that "two heads are better than one."*

scaffold *n.* framework, staging, platform, gallows, gantry. *The painters will need a scaffold to reach the third floor.*

scald *vb.* burn, char, sear, scorch, blister, heat. *The hot water scalded her hand.*

scale *n.* gauge, measure, gradation, calibration, degrees, ratio. *This test has a high scale of difficulty.*

scamp *n.* rascal, rogue, scoundrel, knave, imp, troublemaker. *Some scamp has stolen my last pencil.*

scamper *vb.* **1.** scurry, run, dash, race, scramble. *Mice scampered across the floor.* –*n.* **2.** scurry, dash, frolic, frisk, romp. *He heard the scamper of small children in the next room.*

scan *vb.* search, inspect, examine, explore, study, check. *The spaceship scanned the planet for signs of life.*

scandal *n.* disgrace, embarrassment, shame, dishonor. *The president had to resign because of the scandal.* **Ant.** honor, praise, flattery.

scandalous *adj.* disgraceful, shocking, odious, improper, sinful, outrageous. *Check the tabloid newspapers for the latest scandalous stories.*

scant *adj.* sparse, spare, wanting, insufficient, deficient, lacking. *We have scant space in our garage for any more junk.* **Ant.** plentiful, abundant, rich.

scanty *adj.* meager, skimpy, insufficient, sparse, inadequate. *The newspaper gave only scanty information on the plane crash.* **Ant.** abundant, sufficient.

scapegoat *n.* butt, whipping boy, fall guy, (slang) goat, (slang) patsy, victim. *The team needed a scapegoat to blame for their loss.*

scar *n.* **1.** blemish, mark, injury, disfigurement. *A childhood fall left a scar on her cheek.* *–vb.* **2.** mark, blemish, damage, disfigure, injure. *Fire scarred the inside of the building.*

scarce *adj.* rare, unusual, uncommon, infrequent. *Hunting has made grizzly bears scarce in the United States.* **Ant.** common, usual, frequent.

scarcely *adv.* barely, hardly, slightly, only, just. *She had scarcely enough time to finish the test.*

scarcity *n.* rarity, want, need, shortage, insufficiency. *There is a scarcity of water in the desert.*

scare *vb.* **1.** frighten, shock, alarm, startle, terrify. *Horror movies really scare me.* *–n.* **2.** fright, shock, alarm, start. *The accident gave him quite a scare.* **Ant. 1–2.** calm, comfort.

scarecrow *n.* strawman, malkin, jackstraw. *The birds have grown completely accustomed to the scarecrow and often perch on its head.*

scarf *n.* muffler, neckpiece, boa, tippet, bandanna, ascot. *Wear your scarf when it gets cold.*

scary *adj.* frightening, terrifying, unnerving, petrifying, shocking, intimidating. *Stephen King has written some very scary stories.* **Ant.** encouraging, reassuring, emboldening.

scathing *adj.* searing, acid, biting, sharp, vitriolic, bitter. *Our local critic gave the movie a scathing review.* **Ant.** mild, gentle, soft.

scatter *vb.* spread, disperse, sprinkle, strew, separate. *Wind scattered leaves over the sidewalk.* **Ant.** collect, group, unite.

scatterbrained *adj.* absent-minded, abstracted, daydreaming, flighty, giddy, brainless. *You can't be scatterbrained and expect to win a position as an airline pilot.* **Ant.** alert, sharp, focused.

scenario *n.* story, plot, concept, outline, synopsis, sketch. *The screenwriter roughed out a scenario for the new movie.*

scene *n.* **1.** landscape, location, locale, place, spot, region. *The artist painted an ocean scene.* **2.** episode, act, segment, event, part. *The movie's opening scene was violent.* **3.** disturbance, commotion, outburst, exhibition, display. *The angry man made a scene when they denied his request.*

scenic *adj.* beautiful, pretty, picturesque, unspoiled, spectacular. *He drove through a scenic part of the Rocky Mountains.* **Ant.** ugly, unattractive, ordinary.

scent *n.* **1.** smell, aroma, fragrance, odor. *Roses have a nice scent.* *–vb.* **2.** smell, sniff, detect, perceive, sense. *Our dog ran off when she scented the rabbit.* **3.** perfume, deodorize, aromatize. *We scented the room with incense.*

schedule *n.* **1.** program, timetable, calendar, agenda. *The college sent him its class schedule.* *–vb.* **2.** plan, arrange, slate, book, time. *The plane was scheduled to leave at one o'clock.*

scheme *n.* **1.** plan, design, idea, program, system, procedure. *The thief's scheme was foiled by the police.* *–vb.* **2.** plot, plan, intrigue, conspire. *Bandits schemed for a way to kidnap the prince.*

scheming *adj.* conniving, artful, crafty, sly, sneaky, calculating. *The dictator was always scheming for ways to wrestle away more power.* **Ant.** artless, innocent.

schism *n.* split, separation, division, rift, fragmentation, splintering. *The controversy caused a schism in the group.* **Ant.** union, alliance, unification.

scholar *n.* **1.** intellectual, academic, authority, specialist, sage. *An important scholar is speaking at our campus.* **2.** student, pupil, learner, disciple. *The professor is a scholar of Russian history.*

scholarly *n.* knowledgeable, educated, erudite, literate, intellectual, academic, pedantic. *Review-*

ers called the historian's new book well-researched and scholarly. **Ant.** ignorant, uneducated, stupid.

scholarship *n.* grant, funding, sponsorship, endowment, fellowship, gift. *She won a scholarship to attend the college of her dreams.*

school *n.* **1**, kindergarten, elementary school, high school, college, university. *My school has many students.* **2.** group, faction, set, doctrine, theory. *My father adheres to the school of thought that believes "children should be seen and not heard."* *–vb.* **3.** teach, instruct, educate, coach, train. *A judo instructor schooled her in the mysteries of the martial arts.*

science *n.* physical laws, hard facts, discipline, study. *Speleology is the science and study of caves.*

WORD SEARCH

agriculture: *agronomy*
air, dynamics of movement through: *aerodynamics*
animals: *zoology*
aviation: *aeronautics*
birds: *ornithology*
building design: *architecture*
cells: *cytology*
chemicals, applied: *chemical engineering*
chemistry of life: *biochemistry*
climate: *climatology*
crime: *criminology*
earth: *geology*
earthquakes: *seismology*
energy and heat: *thermodynamics*
energy and matter: *physics*
fluids: *hydraulics*
fossils, animal: *paleontology*
humans: *anthropology*
gene manipulation: *genetic engineering*
life processes: *biology*
machinery: *mechanics*
mapping: *cartography, topography*
metals: *metallurgy*
plants: *botany*
population studies: *demographics*
remains of earlier civilizations: *archaeology*
societies and social behavior: *sociology*
sound: *acoustics*
space: *astronomy, astrophysics*
substances, makeup, properties, and transformation of: *chemistry*
weather: *meteorology*

scientific *adj.* systematic, empirical, physical, observable, provable, precise, exact. *There is no scientific proof that astrology works.* **Ant.** unscientific, emotional.

scientist *n.* analyst, researcher, experimenter, lab technician, inquirer, investigator. *A scientist must be absolutely precise in her measurements.*

scintillating *adj.* sparkling, glittering, glinting, shimmering, shining, gleaming. *The crisp autumn sky was full of scintillating stars.* **Ant.** lackluster, dull.

scoff *vb.* jeer, mock, ridicule, knock, dismiss, discount. *People tend to scoff at anyone with a new idea.* **Ant.** support, uphold, respect.

scold *vb.* **1.** rebuke, reproach, reprimand, upbraid, criticize, berate. *Please don't scold him for being late.* *–n.* **2.** complainer, nag, faultfinder. *I try not to be a scold.* **Ant. 1.** praise, compliment.

scope *n.* range, spread, reach, sphere, extension. *The scope of the destruction was enormous.*

scorch *vb.* toast, singe, burn, char, bake, sear. *The hills were scorched by the fire.*

score *n.* **1.** count, tally, record, points. *The game's score is four to one.* **2.** groove, cut, scratch, nick, mark, notch. *The old table had scores along its surface.* *–vb.* **3.** earn, make, win, achieve. *We must score two goals to win the game.* **4.** nick, gash, scratch, mark, gouge. *Meteorites* *scored the starship's hull.* **5.** grade, judge, evaluate, rate, rank. *The judges will score our performances.*

scoundrel *n.* rogue, villain, knave, rascal, swindler. *That scoundrel drove off in my car.*

scour *vb.* **1.** scrub, rub, cleanse, wash, polish. *He scoured the pots after dinner.* **2.** comb, search, rake, scan. *They scoured the mountains for the lost hikers.*

scourge *n.* punishment, torment, misery, plague, curse, torture. *World War II may have been the greatest scourge of history.* **Ant.** blessing, godsend, boon.

scout *n.* **1.** guide, outrider, lookout, escort. *A scout was sent ahead to find the trail.* –*vb.* **2.** survey, inspect, examine, reconnoiter. *She scouted the area for a good camping place.*

scowl *vb.* **1.** frown, glower, glare, shoot a dirty look. *The father scowled at his misbehaving son.* –*n.* **2.** frown, glower, glare, dirty look, look of disapproval. *A scowl fell over his face.* **Ant. 1–2.** grin, smile.

scraggly *adj.* ragged, straggly, uneven, untrimmed, unpruned, ungroomed. *My hair is getting long and scraggly.* **Ant.** neat, even, trimmed.

scramble *vb.* **1.** race, rush, scurry, hurry, clamber, struggle. *She scrambled up the rocks.* **2.** mix, disorder, jumble, shuffle. *His father scrambled the eggs.* –*n.* **3.** rush, race, struggle, run, tumble. *There was a scramble for the exit when the fire broke out.* **Ant. 2.** order, arrange.

scrap *n.* **1.** bit, fragment, part, piece, portion, crumb. *I used a scrap of cloth for the patch.* –*vb.* **2.** junk, discard, abandon, throw away, reject. *He plans to scrap his old beat-up car.* **Ant. 2.** repair, fix, keep.

scrape *vb.* **1.** skin, peel, grind, graze, scour. *She scraped gum off the bottom of her shoe.* **2.** abrade, rub, scratch, skin, bruise. *He scraped his knees when he fell.* **3.** collect, gather, acquire, obtain, assemble. *He was barely able to scrape together enough money to buy a house.* –*n.* **4.** graze, abrasion, scuff, scratch, bruise, rub. *The fall left a scrape on his arm.* **5.** screech, grate, rasp. *The scrape of fingernails across a chalkboard is quite nerve-wracking.* **6.** dilemma, predicament, muddle, trouble, difficulty. *I hope she can get of this scrape.*

scrappy *adj.* game, plucky, gritty, aggressive, pugnacious. *On my team, I'd rather have someone who is scrappy than someone who is big.* **Ant.** passive, weak, lame.

scratch *vb.* **1.** scrape, rub, abrade, claw, graze. *Can you scratch my itchy back?* **2.** cancel, erase, eliminate, remove, delete, withdraw. *He was scratched from the team.* –*n.* **3.** scrape, gash, abrasion, mark, score. *The cat left a scratch on her hand.* **Ant. 2.** add, include.

scrawl *vb.* scribble, scratch, hen-scratch, doodle. *I watched the doctor scrawl out a prescription on his pad, but I couldn't decipher it.*

scrawny *adj.* skinny, bony, malnourished, spare, thin. *You don't find many scrawny players on a professional football team.* **Ant.** strapping, muscular, brawny.

scream *vb.* **1.** shriek, screech, howl, yell. *People often scream during scary movies.* –*n.* **2.** shriek, yell, cry, shout, screech. *We heard his screams for help.* **Ant. 1–2.** whisper, mumble, mutter.

screech *vb.* **1.** shriek, scream, squawk, squeal, cry. *The owl screeched all night long.* –*n.* **2.** shriek, scream, squeal, cry. *I was startled by the screech of the car's brakes.*

screen *n.* **1.** curtain, shade, mesh, netting, divider. *A screen in our doorway keeps out insects.* **2.** cover, veil, cloak, mask, disguise, shield. *The* *fog served as a screen for the attacking army.* –*vb.* **3.** filter, sift, sort, rate, grade, evaluate. *Television talk shows screen their phone callers.* **4.** shelter, veil, shield, protect, cloak. *Smoke screened our getaway.* **Ant.** **4.** reveal, disclose, show.

screw *n.* **1.** bolt, pin, fastener. *The desk was fastened to the floor with screws.* –*vb.* **2.** twist, twirl, whirl, turn, attach, fasten. *Please screw the lid back onto the jar.*

scribble *vb.* scrawl, scratch, doodle, dash. *Don't scribble over your test papers.*

scribe *n.* writer, scrivener, transcriber, calligrapher, clerk. *The scribe had a beautiful, practiced hand.*

scrimp *vb.* save, economize, (slang) pinch pennies, stint, be stingy, be frugal. *Scrimp long enough and you'll have enough for a down payment on a house.* **Ant.** spend, squander, (slang) blow.

script *n.* **1.** handwriting, cursive, calligraphy. *The invitation's letters were written in script.* **2.** screenplay, playbook, manuscript. *The actress read from the movie's script.*

scrooge *n.* misanthrope, cheapskate, skinflint, miser, hoarder, curmudgeon. *A scrooge is unpopular in most circles, especially around Christmas time.* **Ant.** giver, philanthropist, altruist.

scrounge *vb.* dig up, scrape for, bum, track down, beg, sponge. *I had to scrounge around for enough money to buy coffee this morning.*

scrub *vb.* **1.** scour, rub, brush, polish, wash, cleanse. *Please scrub the floor until it shines.* –*n.* **2.** rub, brush, polish, cleansing, washing. *That dirty shirt needs a good scrub.* **3.** brush, brushwood, bushes. *We walked through low scrub.*

scruffy *adj.* ungroomed, unkempt, untrimmed, mangy, bedraggled, ragged. *A scruffy dog wandered in.* **Ant.** groomed, trim, neat.

scruple *n.* qualm, hesitancy, misgiving, pang, second thought, apprehension. *A nagging scruple prevented the would-be thief from shoplifting.*

scrupulous *adj.* principled, upright, moral, ethical, proper, honest. *The scrupulous young student returned the lost wallet.* **Ant.** unscrupulous, unprincipled, immoral.

scrutinize *vb.* study, examine, observe, inspect, investigate. *He thoroughly scrutinized the car before buying it.*

scrutiny *n.* observation, inspection, watching, examination, investigation. *The teacher's scrutiny during the test prevented cheating.*

scuffle *n.* struggle, tussle, scrap, fight, fray, commotion. *A scuffle in the alley caught the police officer's attention.*

sculpture *n.* statue, figure, carving, bust. *Michelangelo is famous for his sculptures and paintings.*

scum *n.* filth, residue, dross, film, froth, refuse. *I'm going to skim the scum off the top of the pool water before going swimming.*

scurry *vb.* scamper, scuttle, scoot, dash, race, hurry. *Watch that squirrel scurry down the tree limb.*

scuttle *vb.* **1.** hurry, scamper, scurry, scramble, scoot. *The crab scuttled into the cave.* **2.** ditch, abandon, sink, wreck, destroy. The sailors were forced to scuttle their old leaky boat.

scuttlebutt *n.* news, gossip, scoop, rumor, word, talk. *We all gathered around the water cooler to hear the latest scuttlebutt.*

sea *n.* ocean, body of water, the deep, bounding main, surf, (slang) Davy Jones's locker. *The sea surged and swallowed up the ship.*

seal *n.* **1.** badge, stamp, emblem, sign, mark, insignia. *The state's seal must be on all official* *documents.* **2.** closure, fastening, seam, tape. *Don't use a jar if its seal is broken. –vb.* **3.** close, shut, bind, secure, fasten, plug. *Please seal the bottle so no water spills out.* **Ant. 3.** open, unseal, unbind.

seam *n.* closure, juncture, closing, fold, stitching, ridge, connection, suture. *For an even cut, be sure to tear the paper at the seam.*

seaman *n.* sailor, seafarer, mariner, merchant, marine, seadog, salt. *The seaman's skin was leathery from spending most of his life out on the ocean.*

seamy *adj.* sordid, unsavory, unwholesome, rough, dirty, objectionable. *For your safety at night, stay away from the seamy side of town.*

séance *n.* spiritual communion, spiritual contact, contact with the dead, conjuring, sitting, session. *At the séance, the spiritualist failed to contact any ghosts.*

sear *vb.* burn, scorch, singe, char, roast, blister. *The hot driveway seared his bare feet.*

search *vb.* **1.** seek, scour, explore, investigate, probe. *The librarian helped us search for the book. –n.* **2.** hunt, quest, pursuit, scouting, investigation. *Her search led her to the lost city.*

sea serpent *n.* monster, kraken, Loch Ness monster, oarfish, giant squid, zeuglodon. *Many tales of sea serpents probably arose from rare sightings of giant squid.*

seashore *n.* coast, strand, beach, seaside, seaboard, littoral. *Let's go down to the seashore and try to find some sand dollars.*

seasickness *n.* nausea, queasiness, motion sickness, illness, qualm. *I suffered from seasickness from the moment our boat left the dock.*

season *n.* **1.** era, time, term, span, period, quarter. *Christmas comes during the winter season. –vb.* **2.** spice, flavor, accent, enhance, embellish. *The cook seasons her food with herbs.*

seasoned *adj.* weathered, experienced, toughened, hardened, tempered, accustomed. *Seasoned hikers always know to bring plenty of extra socks.* **Ant.** unseasoned, inexperienced, green.

seasoning *n.* flavoring, spice, condiment, dressing, marinade, sauce, salt, pepper. *Garlic is a favorite seasoning of Italian chefs.*

seaweed *n.* kelp, sargasso, vegetation, plant, wrack, dulse. *Be careful that your feet don't get tangled in the seaweed*

secede *vb.* withdraw, disaffiliate, pull out, defect, renounce, quit. *The controversies leading up to the Civil War caused many southern states to secede from the Union.* **Ant.** join, confederate, merge.

secession *n.* withdrawal, defection, disaffiliation, expatriation, separation, breakup. *The government of the province discussed secession from the rest of the country.* **Ant.** merger, joining.

secluded *adj.* hidden, isolated, remote, unvisited, lonely. *The hermit's cave was in a secluded place.* **Ant.** public, open, visited.

seclusion *n.* isolation, solitude, privacy, retreat, sequestration, segregation. *A hermit likes to live in a seclusion.*

second *n.* moment, blink of an eye, heartbeat, tick of the clock, instant, flash, twinkling. *It takes only a second or two to fasten your seatbelt, so why not?*

secondhand *adj.* used, pre-owned, handed down, hand-me-down, old, broken-in. *You can save a lot of money buying secondhand cars.* **Ant.** new, firsthand.

second-rate *adj.* inferior, second class, low-grade, cheap, shabby, poor. *We stayed at a sec-*

ond-rate hotel without air-conditioning. **Ant.** first-rate, first class, superior.

secrecy *n.* concealment, covertness, silence, stealth, confidentiality, privacy, sneakiness. *The ice cream maker's recipes were kept in secrecy.* **Ant.** overtness, publicity, openness.

secret *adj.* 1. private, hidden, concealed, unrevealed, masked. *Our club has a secret password.* –*n.* 2. confidence, mystery, intrigue. *She wrote secrets in her diary.* 3. formula, recipe, cause, explanation, key, answer. *What's the secret of her success?* **Ant.** 1. open, unconcealed, disclosed. 2. disclosure, revelation.

secretary *n.* office worker, assistant, word processor, typist, organizer, filer, receptionist, bookkeeper, stenographer. *All appointments should be made through my secretary.*

secrete *vb.* hide, conceal, cache, stash, store, horde. *He secreted his money in a place where it could never be found by thieves.*

secretive *adj.* private, covert, cryptic, sneaky, stealthy, mysterious. *I already know you're going out with Steve, so stop being so secretive.* **Ant.** overt, open, public.

sect *n.* group, faction, party, camp, denomination, division, order. *A small sect broke off from the main group to practice their own beliefs.*

section *n.* 1. part, piece, portion, slice, segment. *She reads the business section of the newspaper.* –*vb.* 2. cut, divide, separate, split, slice. *Please section the cake into twelve pieces.* **Ant.** 1. whole, entirety. 2. join, unite.

sector *n.* section, segment, group, division, district, zone, class. *The working-class sector may vote differently from retirees.*

secular *n.* worldly, earthly, mundane, nonspiritual, nonreligious, lay, profane. *The secular population advocates a scientific teaching of evolution and creation.* **Ant.** religious, spiritual, ecclesiastical.

secure *adj.* 1. safe, protected, defended, unthreatened, sheltered. *Burglar alarms make him feel secure.* 2. certain, sure, guaranteed, assured, confident. *He has a secure position at the university.* –*vb.* 3. get, gain, win, obtain, acquire, procure. *She secured a place in line for us.* 4. tie, bind, attach, chain, fasten. *The sailors secured the boxes with rope.* 5. protect, shield, guard, safeguard, shelter. *The police secured the area where the robbery occurred.* **Ant.** 1. insecure, unprotected, unsafe. 2. insecure, uncertain. 3. lose, forfeit. 4. loose, unbind, untie. 5. expose, endanger.

security *n.* 1. safety, immunity, invulnerability, protection, safeguard, defense. *Installing smoke alarms provides an extra measure of security.* 2. confidence, fearlessness, certainty, soundness, peace of mind. *You must have great security in order to give a speech.* 3. pledge, guarantee, assurance, bond, escrow, surety, collateral. *We put up our home as security against the loan.* **Ant.** 1–2. insecurity, vulnerability, fear, anxiety.

sedate *adj.* calm, quiet, still, unexcited, composed, serious. *Being at the library requires sedate behavior.* **Ant.** agitated, excited, loud.

sedative *adj.* 1. calming, soothing, relaxing, numbing, narcotic. *Sleeping pills have a sedative effect.* –*n.* 2. drug, tranquilizer, narcotic. *The doctor prescribed a sedative for the pain.* **Ant.** 1. arousing, stimulating. 2. stimulant.

sedentary *adj.* inactive, stationary, idle, unmoving, motionless, vegetative, chair-bound. *A sedentary lifestyle is unhealthy.* **Ant.** active, busy, on-the-go.

sediment *n.* settlings, dregs, deposit, grounds, precipitate, lees. *Sediment had collected at the river bend until it formed a large bank.*

sedition *n.* insurrection, treason, incitement, rebellion, rabble-rousing, subversion. *Several government conspirators were convicted of sedition.*

seduce *vb.* tempt, snare, lure, trap, attract. *Don't be seduced by a criminal's fancy lifestyle.* **Ant.** repel, repulse, disgust.

seduction *n.* enticement, allure, temptation, persuasion, attraction, tease. *To lure bees, many flowers employ a kind of fragrant seduction.*

seductive *adj.* enticing, alluring, tempting, persuasive, tantalizing, beguiling, attractive, flirtatious. *The glamour of Hollywood can be seductive to those seeking the limelight.* **Ant.** repulsive, repellent, repugnant.

see *vb.* **1.** observe, view, notice, behold, detect. *Did he see the new movie yet?* **2.** discover, learn, determine, ascertain. *Please see if you can fix it.* **3.** understand, comprehend, perceive, grasp, realize. *Try to see my side of the argument.* **4.** imagine, visualize, envision, picture. *I can't see a way out of this crisis.* **5.** date, court, meet. *They started to see each other about a month ago.* **Ant. 1.** overlook, miss, ignore. **3.** misunderstand, disregard, ignore.

seedy *adj.* squalid, shabby, unkempt, rundown, neglected, disreputable. *We found a seedy little motel at the outskirts of town.* **Ant.** well-kept, luxurious sparkling.

seek *vb.* pursue, search for, look for, chase, solicit. *She will seek a job with her father's company.*

seem *vb.* appear, look, resemble, suggest. *It may not be a lot of money, but it seems like a fortune to me.*

seep *vb.* ooze, dribble, leak, drip, trickle. *Honey seeped out of the broken jar.* **Ant.** gush, surge, stream, rush.

seer *n.* clairvoyant, prophet, psychic, fortune-teller, prognosticator, oracle, medium. *She consulted with a seer to learn of her future.*

seesaw *n.* teeter-totter, ride. *I want you to counterbalance my weight on the seesaw, not catapult me into space.*

seethe *vb.* rage, fume, (slang) blow one's top, boil, (slang) foam at the mouth, (slang) see red, (slang) go ballistic. *The announcement of yet another tax hike made me seethe.*

segment *n.* **1.** part, portion, piece, section, slice. *The final segment of the show will be on tomorrow.* –*vb.* **2.** divide, split, section, separate, slice. *He segmented the candy bar into four pieces.* **Ant. 1.** whole, all, totality. **2.** join, combine.

segregate *vb.* separate, divide, isolate, dissociate, split up, insulate. *Some parents think schools should segregate the boys from the girls.* **Ant.** join, combine, desegregate.

segregation *n.* separation, apartheid, division, isolation, dissociation, split, insulation. *Some school districts have attempted to implement policies of racial segregation and failed.* **Ant.** integration, joining, desegregation.

seize *vb.* grab, grasp, capture, snatch, clutch. *Police seized the smuggler at the airport.* **Ant.** lose, drop.

seldom *adv.* rarely, infrequently, uncommonly, scarcely, hardly. *Busy students seldom have time to play.* **Ant.** frequently, commonly, always.

select *vb.* **1.** pick, choose, elect, draw, decide on. *Which movie video did you select?* –*adv.* **2.** first-rate, special, outstanding, elite, exclusive. *The soldier was part of a select army unit.* **Ant. 2.** ordinary, common.

selection *n.* **1.** choosing, picking, election, determination, nomination. *The judge waited for the selection of the jury.* **2.** variety, range, pick, choice, option. *The restaurant's dessert selection was rather limited.*

self *n.* ego, being, personality, mind, soul, character. *Interests of the self often take precedence over the interests of others.*

self-assured *adj.* confident, self-confident, secure, self-possessed, cocky, poised, fearless. *To win the public trust, politicians must be cool and self-assured.* **Ant.** insecure, unsure, uncertain.

self-centered *adj.* selfish, self-absorbed, narcissistic, egocentric, egotistical, conceited. *A self-centered minister cannot properly serve his congregation.* **Ant.** other-directed, altruistic, giving.

self-confidence *n.* self-assurance, security, poise, fearlessness, aplomb, positive, self-image, self-esteem. *You need great self-confidence to perform live on television.* **Ant.** insecurity, anxiety, uncertainty.

self-conscious *adj.* unsure, shy, modest, bashful, embarrassed. *She was self-conscious about her new haircut.* **Ant.** confident, bold, open, unreserved.

self-control *n.* self-restraint, self-discipline, willpower, strength, fortitude, stoicism. *A baker in a donut shop must practice great self-control or he'll eat up all his profits.* **Ant.** weakness, impulsiveness.

self-esteem *n.* self-respect, pride, confidence, self-assurance, ego, dignity, positive self-image, strength. *The greatest self-esteem is achieved through competence.* **Ant.** self-loathing, self-hatred.

selfish *adj.* self-centered, stingy, uncharitable, ungenerous, greedy. *The penny-pincher was a very selfish man.* **Ant.** unselfish, charitable, generous.

selfishness *n.* self-centeredness, self-absorption, egocentricity, narcissism, greed. *Scrooge's selfishness brought him great wealth but little happiness.*

self-reliant *adj.* independent, self-sufficient, autonomous, strong. *Children should be raised to be self-reliant as soon as possible.* **Ant.** dependent, needy, helpless.

self-respect *n.* self-esteem, pride, dignity, strength, self-worth, self-regard. *You win self-respect by doing what's right, not what's easy.* **Ant.** self-loathing, shame.

self-righteous *adj.* holier-than-thou, preachy, sanctimonious, pious, goody-goody, smug, hypocritical. *There is nothing more objectionable than someone getting up on their moral soapbox and delivering a self-righteous speech.* **Ant.** humble, self-effacing, self-critical.

sell *vb.* market, vend, peddle, trade, retail. *The store sells shoes at a cheap price.* **Ant.** buy, purchase.

seller *n.* dealer, vendor, trader, wholesaler, retailer, marketer, merchant. *The seller likes to haggle with his customers.* **Ant.** buyer, customer, patron.

semantics *n.* meaning, definitions, semiotics, interpretation, connotations, lexicology. *Let's not argue over semantics, let's argue the issue.*

semester *n.* term, session, period, interval, half-year. *She'll have to make up last semester due to her illness.*

seminal *adj.* influential, originating, basic, germinal, developmental, pioneering. *The invention of the modem was seminal in bringing about communication via the Internet.*

seminar *n.* meeting, conference, workshop, forum, symposium, group discussion. *I'm going to attend a seminar on investing in the stock market.*

senate *n.* assembly, governing body, high chamber, upper house, state council. *The bill was put before the senate for a vote.*

send *vb.* transmit, transfer, disseminate, launch, mail. *He sends Christmas cards to all his relatives.* **Ant.** get, receiver.

senile *adj.* demented, mentally deficient, disoriented, confused, feeble-minded, doddering. *My grandfather was afraid he was growing senile, but he really just had a bad memory.* **Ant.** sharp, lucid, clear-headed.

senior *adj.* **1.** older, elder, elderly. *My grandfather is a senior citizen.* **2.** ranking, superior, top, chief. *She's a senior officer at her bank.* –*n.* **3.** elder, superior, better, chief, head. *He is my senior at the office.* **Ant.** **1.** junior, younger. **2.** inferior, lower. **3.** junior, inferior.

sensation *n.* **1.** feeling, sense, perception, response, awareness, tingle, sight, sound. *Peering over the cliff gave me a dizzy sensation.* **2.** wonder, hit, phenomenon, fuss, uproar, excitement, furor. *The rock star's album was a worldwide sensation.*

sensational *adj.* spectacular, extraordinary, exciting, amazing, thrilling. *He performed a sensational dive.* **Ant.** ordinary, boring, dull.

sensationalism *n.* exaggeration, melodrama, tabloid journalism, yellow journalism, keyhole journalism, luridness. *The tabloid newspapers specialize in sensationalism.*

sense *n.* **1.** faculty, capacity, capability, function, sensation. *The dog's sense of smell was well-developed.* **2.** understanding, knowledge, awareness, perception. *I admired her strong sense of honor.* **3.** meaning, message, significance, content. *What he said had no sense to it.* –*vb.* **4.** perceive, feel, detect, recognize, discern. *He could sense someone hiding in his closet.* **Ant.** **3.** nonsense, gibberish. **4.** overlook, miss.

senseless *adj.* **1.** stupid, dumb, ridiculous, foolish, illogical. *Bringing snowshoes to the beach was rather senseless.* **2.** insensible, unconscious, unaware. *The boxer was knocked senseless.* **Ant.** **1.** sensible, smart, wise. **2.** conscious.

sensibility *n.* sensitivity, receptivity, responsiveness, sentience, perception. *A physician must have great sensibility to diagnose her patients.*

sensible *adj.* intelligent, thoughtful, wise, logical, reasonable. *Wearing heavy clothing is sensible in cold weather.* **Ant.** senseless, stupid, foolish.

sensitive *adj.* **1.** receptive, perceptive, sympathetic, responsive, understanding. *She is sensitive to her friends' problems.* **2.** tender, painful, sore, aching, delicate. *His bruise is still very sensitive.* **3.** accurate, precise, exact, subtle, responsive. *A seismograph is a sensitive measuring device.* **Ant.** **1.** insensitive, unfeeling, indifferent. **2.** insensitive, numb. **3.** inaccurate, approximate.

sensitivity *n.* feeling, perception, sense, sympathy, compassion, understanding, empathy. *The therapist discussed her client's problems with great sensitivity.* **Ant.** insensitivity.

sensual *adj.* sensory, physical, stimulating, arousing, exciting, lustful. *She found the massage to be a very sensual experience.* **Ant.** cerebral, spiritual, intellectual.

sensuous *adj.* sensory, stimulating, pleasing, sensual, physical. *A rollercoaster ride is a richly sensuous experience to some.*

sentient *adj.* feeling, conscious, sensitive, perceptive, responsive. *Humans are sentient beings.* **Ant.** unfeeling, unconscious, unresponsive.

sentimental *adj.* nostalgic, emotional, dreamy, romantic. *Her old boyfriend's letters made her feel sentimental.* **Ant.** unsentimental, unemotional.

sentinel *n.* guard, watchman, sentry, watch, lookout, picket. *The sentinel must be careful not to fall asleep at his post.*

separate *vb.* **1.** part, slip, divide, detach, sever. *Our teacher separates students who talk to each other.* *–adj.* **2.** different, individual, disconnected, distinct, isolated. *The zoo's lions and giraffes are kept in separate cages.* **Ant. 1.** join, unite. **2.** joined, connected.

separation *n.* **1.** division, partition, boundary, gap, space. *The Berlin Wall was a separation between East and West Berlin.* **2.** breakup, divorce, split, break, parting. *His parents' separation made him feel sad.* **Ant. 1.** union, junction. **2.** marriage, joining.

sepulcher *n.* vault, grave, mausoleum, crypt, resting place. *My late grandfather rests in a specially built sepulcher.*

sequel *n.* follow-up, continuation, spin-off, offshoot, epilogue. *A hit movie is almost always followed by several sequels.*

sequence *n.* series, string, chain, line, cycle, progression, arrangement. *The safe's combination is a sequence of numbers.*

sequester *vb.* isolate, quarantine, seclude, segregate, remove, withdraw, separate. *The ship's captain decided to sequester the flu-infected passengers.*

serendipity *n.* good fortune, happenstance, chance, fluke, fortuity, luck. *It was by sheer serendipity that I found my way out of the woods, in other words, it was a lucky accident.*

serene *adj.* calm, quiet, peaceful, restful, unexcited. *After the noisy city, the forest seemed very serene.* **Ant.** excited, agitated, stormy.

serenity *n.* peacefulness, calmness, restfulness, tranquillity. *The beautiful garden gave him a feeling of serenity.* **Ant.** excitement, anxiety, agitation.

serf *n.* villein, vassal, slave. *The serfs rebelled against their landlord's poor treatment.*

serial *adj.* in series, successive, consecutive, sequential, continuing, ongoing. *Police are on the lookout for a serial bank robber.* **Ant.** lone, single, isolated.

series *n.* sequence, run, succession, progression, cycle, row. *She endured a series of misfortunes.*

serious *adj.* **1.** grave, grim, reflective, solemn, sober, pensive. *My serious friend never laughs at jokes.* **2.** sincere, decided, earnest, definite, resolute. *Is she really serious about selling her car?* **3.** significant, important, crucial, consequential, momentous. *Deciding what college to attend is a serious decision.* **4.** dangerous, bad, alarming, grave, critical. *The patient's condition was serious.* **Ant. 1.** silly, jolly. **2.** insincere, undecided, joking. **3.** minor, unimportant, meaningless. **4.** mild, superficial.

seriously *adv.* gravely, solemnly, thoughtfully, earnestly. *He takes everything I say so seriously.* **Ant.** lightly, jokingly.

sermon *n.* lesson, lecture, speech, discourse, homily. *We heard the preacher's sermon.*

serpent *n.* snake, viper, reptile. *A monstrous serpent attacked the brave warrior.*

serpentine *adj.* snakelike, serpentlike, winding, twisting, coiled, tortuous. *We climbed a serpentine stairway to the top of the lighthouse.* **Ant.** straight, direct.

servant *n.* domestic, housekeeper, slave, menial, maid, butler. *My wealthy neighbors have servants who do all the cooking and cleaning.*

serve *vb.* **1.** give, pass, offer, deliver, supply. *The waiter served us our meal.* **2.** work, perform, labor, complete, spend. *He served two years in the Peace Corps.* **3.** help, aid, assist, attend, support. *I will serve you to my fullest ability.* **Ant. 3.** ignore, neglect.

service *n.* **1.** help, aid, assistance, support, attendance. *Please call room service.* **2.** army, navy, air force, marines, military. *His brother* *joined the service for four years.* 3. agency, department, bureau, facility, utility. *She joined the Forest Service.* 4. ceremony, ritual, rite, observance. *Church services were held on Sunday.* –*vb.* 5. repair, fix, restore, maintain, adjust. *Our car was serviced by trained mechanics.*

serviceable *adj.* operable, usable, workable, functional, ready. *The copy machine will be serviceable tomorrow.* **Ant.** inoperable, out of order, broken.

servile *adj.* slavish, submissive, subservient, deferential, groveling, fawning. *You'll be taken advantage of if you're too servile.* **Ant.** domineering, bossy, rebellious.

servitude *n.* slavery, bondage, serfdom, vassalage. *Peasants are usually in a landlord's servitude.*

set *vb.* 1. put, place, lay, rest, install. *Please set your things on the counter.* 2. arrange, order, adjust, fix, prepare. *She set the table for dinner.* 3. drop, sink, settle, descend, lower. *The Sun sets in the west.* 4. harden, solidify, stiffen, thicken. *The concrete must set before we can walk on it.* 5. start, begin, depart, embark. *They set off on their trip.* –*n.* 6. receiver, machine, apparatus. *Her television set is broken.* 7. packet, group, bunch, assortment, collection. *He bought a set of new dishes.* 8. stage, setting, scene. *We watched the actor on the movie set.* 9. bearing, posture, position, carriage. *Anger showed in the set of his shoulders.* 10. clique, crowd, clan, society, club. *Those of the jet set often drive fancy cars.* –*adj.* 11. fixed, regular, customary, habitual, definite. *She has a set way of doing things.* 12. decided, prepared, determined, arranged. *The time of our departure has already been set.* **Ant.** 1. remove, lift. 2. disarrange, disorder. 3. rise, ascend. 4. soften, liquefy. 5. finish, conclude. 11. flexible, impromptu.

setback *n.* defeat, loss, reversal, stumbling block, disappointment, regression, block. *Entrepreneurs face many setbacks but learn to overcome them.* **Ant.** progress, advance.

setting *n.* surroundings, backdrop, environment, locale, place, site, milieu. *The setting of the play is 19th-century New York.*

settle *vb.* 1. decide, agree, set, fix, choose. *She finally settled on the blue sweater.* 2. locate, live, dwell, reside, inhabit, colonize. *The emigrants decided to settle in Oregon.* 3. sink, drop, descend, subside, lower. *He settled into the soft chair.* 4. quiet, calm, soothe, pacify, tranquilize. *The medicine settled her upset stomach.* 5. heal, resolve, mend, close, terminate. *Please try to settle your argument.* **Ant.** 1. waver, hesitate. 3. ascend, rise. 4. upset, disturb.

settlement *n.* 1. community, colony, outpost, village. *The immigrants built a new settlement in the rural part of the state.* 2. resolution, agreement, arbitration, negotiation, disposition. *The litigants agreed on a settlement out of court.* 3. payment, payoff, discharge, reimbursement, deal. *The defendant paid a small settlement, and the case was closed.*

settler *n.* colonist, homesteader, pioneer, frontiersman, squatter. *The settlers had a tremendous amount of work to do to clear the land.*

sever *vb.* 1. separate, detach, dismember, part, amputate. *The dog's tail was severed in the accident.* 2. end, stop, discontinue, cease, dissolve. *The two warring nations severed all diplomatic ties.* **Ant.** 1. join, attach, unite. 2. continue, maintain.

several *adj.* some, a few, sundry, various, certain, divers. *He had several goldfish.* **Ant.** many, lots.

severe *adj.* 1. harsh, cruel, ruthless, fierce, violent. *School was canceled due to a severe snowstorm.* 2. serious, grim, stern, strict, grave. *The teacher gave the tardy student a severe look.* **Ant.**

1. mild, gentle, moderate. **2.** gentle, tender, cheerful.

severity *n.* harshness, seriousness, roughness, gravity. *The storm's severity kept people inside their homes.* **Ant.** mildness, gentleness, triviality.

sew *vb.* stitch, mend, tailor, hem, seam, embroider. *My mother wants to sew your loose buttons.*

sewage *n.* waste, runoff, sludge, discharge, pollution. *We were sickened by the raw sewage being discharged into the ocean.*

sex *n.* sexual intercourse, copulation, mating, fornication, reproduction, procreation, making love. *I first learned about sex in biology class.*

sex appeal *n.* sexiness, charm, animal magnetism, charisma, (slang) oomph, allure, virility. *In most cases, you need to have a certain amount of sex appeal to be a movie star.*

sexism *n.* discrimination, chauvinism, prejudice, bias, gender bias. *The manager was accused of sexism after he refused to pay the women on his staff the same salary as the men.*

sexual assault *n.* rape, molestation, violation, ravishment, date rape. *The police increased their patrols in light of the recent sexual assaults in the park.*

sexual harassment *n.* impropriety, sexual advances, flirtation, inappropriate behavior, misconduct exploitation, overtures. *Most major corporations have policies protecting against sexual harassment.*

sexy *adj.* attractive, appealing, alluring, beguiling, enticing, seductive. *Movie stars with looks and confidence are especially sexy.* **Ant.** unattractive, unappealing, repulsive.

shabby *adj.* **1.** worn, ragged, tattered, scruffy. *The homeless woman wore a shabby coat.* **2.** low, mean, dishonorable, unfair. *Calling people names is a shabby thing to do.* **Ant. 1.** fine, new, neat. **2.** honorable, nice, kind, considerate.

shack *n.* hut, shanty, hovel, shed. *The old miner lives in a shack.* **Ant.** mansion, palace.

shackle *n.* **1.** chain, manacle, bond, handcuff, cuff. *Slaves were often kept in shackles.* *–vb.* **2.** chain, bind, restrain, cramp. *Why did you shackle me with more work?* **Ant. 2.** free, unchain, aid.

shade *vb.* darken, dim, shroud, veil, hide, mask. *I had to shade my eyes from the Sun in order to see the ball.* **Ant.** light, illuminate.

shadow *n.* **1.** silhouette, outline, trace, image, shade. *The Sun made a shadow behind him.* **2.** hint, bit, touch, tinge, trace. *There's not a shadow of doubt concerning her honesty.* *–vb.* **3.** follow, trail, track, stalk, pursue. *The detective shadowed his suspect.*

shadowy *adj.* **1.** shaded, protected, sheltered, dark, murky. *The forest was cold and shadowy.* **2.** vague, unclear, obscure, indistinct, ghostly. *Shadowy figures were at the back of the alley.* **Ant. 1.** sunny, open, unshaded. **2.** clear, distinct.

shaggy *adj.* ungroomed, untrimmed, hairy, unkempt, woolly, uncombed. *The shaggy dog tends to shed more hair than others.* **Ant.** bald, neat, trim.

shake *vb.* **1.** vibrate, rattle, jiggle, tremble, jar. *An earthquake shook our house last night.* **2.** weaken, undermine, disturb, drain, diminish. *Nothing you say will shake my confidence in her.* *–n.* **3.** vibration, rattle, jiggling, trembling, quaking. *He gave the bottle a shake to mix its contents.* **Ant. 1.** settle, calm, quiet. **2.** increase, augment.

shallow *adj.* superficial, simple, empty, frivolous, trivial. *The movie star was very shallow.* **Ant.** deep, complex, complicated.

sham *n.* counterfeit, fake, imitation, forgery, fraud, phony, deception. *The diamond purported to be from a nearby mine turned out to be a sham.* **Ant.** genuine article, (slang) the real McCoy.

shaman *n.* priest, medicine man, healer, prognosticator, seer. *The shaman peered into the smoky fire to view the future.*

shambles *n.* ruin, devastation, wreck, disaster, mess, destruction. *After the New Year's Eve party, the house was a shambles.*

shame *n.* **1.** remorse, regret, dishonor, disgrace, humiliation, embarrassment. *She felt shame over her arrest.* **2.** disappointment, misfortune, disgrace. *It was a shame that you couldn't attend the party.* –*vb.* **3.** dishonor, disgrace, humiliate, embarrass. *He was shamed by the terrible way his friend acted.* **Ant. 1.** honor, pleasure, pride. **3.** honor, please.

shameful *adj.* dishonorable, disgraceful, humiliating, degrading. *Cheating on the test was a shameful thing to do.* **Ant.** honorable, admirable, noble.

shameless *adj.* unprincipled, disgraceful, conscienceless, unblushing, immodest, depraved. *When committing their crimes, many criminals are absolutely shameless.* **Ant.** ashamed, principled, contrite.

Shangri-la *n.* paradise, utopia, heaven on earth, Xanadu, Eden. *There is no Shangri-la, but there are some very pleasant places to visit on Earth.* **Ant.** hell, wasteland.

shanty *n.* shack, hut, hovel, cabin. *Old Joe lived in a shanty by the river's edge.*

shape *n.* **1.** figure, form, outline, contour, pattern. *The Earth has a circular shape.* **2.** condition, health, trim, state, order. *The overweight man was in bad shape.* –*vb.* **3.** form, mold, fashion, model, design. *The sculptor shaped the clay.*

shapeless *adj.* amorphous, formless, vague, irregular, indefinite, ill-defined. *The clouds formed shapeless masses.* **Ant.** well-defined, formed, distinct.

shapely *adj.* curvaceous, well-proportioned, fit, toned, statuesque, svelte. *Working out with weights and performing aerobics will make you more shapely.* **Ant.** shapeless, roly-poly, obese.

share *n.* **1.** part, piece, portion, segment, division. *They each got a share of the winnings.* –*vb.* **2.** divide, split, partition, apportion. *He shared his sandwich with his friend.*

shark *n.* **1.** fish, marine animal, predator, carnivore, marine hunter. *Don't trail bloody bait in the sea of you'll attract a shark.* **2.** swindler, (slang) rip-off artist, (slang) con artist, cheat, chiseler, crook. *The sharks running scams on the street will take your money if you're not careful.* **3.** expert, professional, pro, (slang) crackerjack, (slang) hotshot. *The pool shark was beating everyone that day.*

sharp *adj.* **1.** cutting, edged, keen, pointed, thorny. *A shark has very sharp teeth.* **2.** sudden, abrupt, rapid, steep. *There was a sharp drop to the valley below.* **3.** aware, intelligent, clever, shrewd, quick. *She is a sharp student.* **4.** harsh, cutting, bitter, stinging. *He had sharp words for the young thief.* –*adv.* **5.** suddenly, abruptly, rapidly, unexpectedly. *The driver stopped sharp when he saw the crack in the road.* **6.** exactly, promptly, precisely, punctually. *Please be there at one o'clock sharp.* **Ant. 1.** dull, blunt. **2.** gradual, gentle, slow. **3.** dull, unaware. **4.** gentle, soft, pleasant. **5.** slowly, gradually.

sharpen *vb.* point, hone, grind, edge, file. *Will you please sharpen the knife?* **Ant.** dull, blunt.

shatter *vb.* **1.** break, burst, smash, fragment, splinter. *The glass shattered when I dropped it.* **2.**

devastate, crush, dumbfound, overwhelm, destroy. *News of his death shattered her.* **Ant. 2.** uplift, reinforce.

shave *vb.* trim, shear, clip, crop, graze. *Some women prefer not to shave under their arms.*

shawl *n.* wrap, covering, manta. *It's a little cold outside, so take your shawl.*

shear *vb.* **1.** shave, cut, fleece, clip, trim. *The rancher sheared his sheep.* –*n.* **2.** scissors, pruners, clippers. *Please trim the bushes with these shears.*

sheath *n.* case, receptacle, holder, scabbard, covering, sleeve, wrapper. *For safety, keep that hunting knife in its sheath.*

shed *n.* **1.** shack, shanty, hut, barn, garage. *She keeps her tools in the shed.* –*vb.* **2.** discard, drop, remove, cast off. *Snakes shed their old skins.* **3.** cast, spread, shine, give, emit. *Her report should shed some light on the problem.* **Ant. 2.** keep, retain. **3.** withhold, repress.

sheen *n.* shine, gleam, luster, shimmer, gloss, sparkle. *After waxing, the kitchen floor always has a dazzling sheen.*

sheep *n.* ram, ewe, lamb, ruminant, ungulate, merino, cheviot. *The shepherd watches his flock of sheep.*

sheepish *adj.* shy, self-conscious, embarrassed, bashful, uncomfortable. *They were both rather sheepish on their first date.* **Ant.** confident, immodest, aggressive.

sheer *adj.* **1.** fine, thin, transparent, translucent, gauzy, clear. *She bought a pair of sheer panty hose.* **2.** absolute, total, complete, unrestrained, pure. *The movie was sheer entertainment.* **3.** abrupt, vertical, perpendicular, precipitous steep. *The rock climbers went up a sheer cliff.* **Ant. 1.** thick, coarse. **2.** partial, incomplete. **3.** sloping, gradual.

shelf *n.* counter, cupboard, board, mantle, bookcase, rack. *Put the book back on its shelf.*

shell *vb.* bomb, bombard, barrage, fire upon. *We knew the enemy would begin to shell us soon, so we dug trenches in preparation.*

shellac *n.* varnish, resin, finish. *Are you going to apply shellac to that table?*

shelter *n.* **1.** safety, protection, refuge, cover. *We ran for shelter when it began to rain.* **2.** accommodation, home, dwelling, habitation, quarters. *The city built a shelter for homeless people.* –*vb.* **3.** protect, guard, safeguard, defend, shield, cover. *The church sheltered the poor refugees.* **Ant. 1.** exposure, danger. **3.** uncover, expose.

shenanigans *n.* horseplay, (slang) monkey business, sport, mischief, nonsense. *If you kids don't stop your shenanigans right now, you're all going to your room.*

shepherd *n.* **1.** herder, tender, caretaker, guardian, sheep farmer. *The shepherd tends his flock and protects them from predators.* –*vb.* **2.** herd, tend, guard, protect, look after. *Learning how to shepherd a flock of sheep is not as easy as it looks.*

shield *n.* **1.** protection, guard, defense, screen, cover. *The spacecraft raised its shields against enemy fire.* –*vb.* **2.** protect, guard, shelter, cover, screen. *Her umbrella shielded her from the sun.* **Ant. 1.** danger, risk. **2.** endanger, uncover, expose.

shift *vb.* **1.** transport, transfer, relocate, move, carry. *The movers shifted the furniture to their truck.* **2.** change, switch, adjust, alter, vary. *The driver shifted into second gear.* –*n.* **3.** change, switch, move, alteration, turning. *We were surprised by the president's policy shift.* **4.** assignment, stint, period, duty. *She is working the late shift tonight.*

shiftless *adj.* lazy, indolent, good-for-nothing, slothful. *If you're shiftless and unmotivated, you'll end up without a job.* **Ant.** enterprising, hardworking, responsible.

shifty *adj.* deceitful, treacherous, devious, slippery, untrustworthy, dishonest. *A shifty character tried to talk the old lady out of her money.* **Ant.** honest, upright, trustworthy.

shimmer *vb.* **1.** twinkle, glimmer, sparkle, glisten, ripple. *The lake shimmered in the summer sun.* *–n.* **2.** sparkle, glimmer, twinkling, glittering, luster, glow. *The shimmer of his sequined costume caught our attention.*

shine *vb.* **1.** gleam, glow, beam, radiate, flash. *The doctor shined a light into my eyes.* **2.** polish, buff, burnish, wax. *Please shine the silverware for tonight.* **3.** excel, exceed, dominate, stand out. *Music is an area in which he shines.* *–n.* **4.** glow, gleam, brightness, sparkle, flash. *The new car has a nice shine.* **Ant. 2.** blacken, darken, dull. **3.** fail. **4.** darkness, dullness.

shiny *adj.* gleaming, bright, brilliant, scintillating, glinting, glossy. *The dime was new and shiny.*

ship *n.* **1.** boat, steamer, liner, freighter, yacht. *H crossed the ocean in a large ship.* *–vb.* **2.** embark, leave, depart, move. *The soldiers will ship out tomorrow.* **3.** send, transport, dispatch, transmit, forward. *She shipped the package to South America.*

WORD SEARCH

anchoring or securing of: *mooring*
anchor rope: *hawser*
barnacles and other marine life living on ship's bottom: *foul*
boarding platform: *gangplank*
body: *hull*
bottom fin: *keel*
bow's vibrations over waves: *panting*
bumpers comprised of tires or ropes: *fender, pudding*
captain: *skipper*
cargo and debris from wrecked ship: *flotsam, jetsam*
cargo hoist: *davit, derrick*
cargo list: *manifest*
cargo storage area: *hold*
crew member: *hand, mate*
crew quarters, structure that contains: *forecastle*
decks: *poop deck, weather deck*
depth below waterline, ship's: *draft*
depth numbers on bow: *draft marks*
drain: *scupper*
flag: *burgee, jack*
front: *bow, prow, fore*
hatch: *booby hatch, scuttle, companionway*
hospital: *sick bay*
kitchen: *galley*
lean: *heel, list*
living quarters: *cabin*
lookout's perch: *crow's nest*
meal room: *mess room*
merchant ship or fleet of same: *argosy*
navigational room: *chart room, pilot house*
observation platform: *bridge*
officers: *boatswain, purser, skipper, captain*
position finder: *loran*
pump, water: *bilge pump*
rising and falling fore and aft with waves: *pitching*
side looking from aft to bow, left: *port*
side looking from aft to bow, right: *starboard*
side-to-side rolling: *roll*
speed measurement, unit of: *knot*
stabilizing weight comprised of rocks, sand or iron: *ballast*
steer: *navigate, conn*
steering: *helm, rudder, tiller*
supplier: *chandler*
waiter: *cabin boy*
wall, compartment: *bulkhead*
whitewater trail: *wake*
window: *porthole*

shipshape *adj.* orderly, tidy, neat, trim. *Your room had better be shipshape when I come to inspect it, or else.* **Ant.** messy, disorganized, sloppy.

shirk *vb.* avoid, dodge, escape, evade, ignore. *He often tries to shirk his responsibilities.* **Ant.** fulfill, accomplish, do.

shirker *n.* slacker, malingerer, evader, dodger, (slang) deadbeat, (slang) bum. *Any shirkers found on this job will be terminated.* **Ant.** workaholic.

shirt *n.* blouse, pullover, jersey, T-shirt, turtleneck, shirtwaist. *He wore a button-down shirt.*

WORD SEARCH

African pullover: *dashiki*
floral: *Hawaiian, aloha shirt*
knotted shirt revealing a bare midriff: *calypso*
plaid wool: *Pendleton*
ruffed: *dandy*
short-sleeved pullover: *polo shirt*
sleeveless muscle shirt: *tank top*
sport pullover: *rugby shirt*
voluminous: *blouson*
western: *cowboy shirt*

shiver *vb.* **1.** tremble, shake, quiver, shudder, quake. *She shivered in the cold air.* –*n.* **2.** quiver, quake, shudder, tremble. *Scary movies send shivers down my spine.*

shock *n.* **1.** blow, jolt, jar, start, upset. *His bad report card gave him quite a shock.* **2.** paralysis, trauma, distress, collapse, stupor. *The accident victim was in a state of shock.* –*vb.* **3.** stagger, stun, upset, disturb, offend. *Her bad behavior really shocked us.*

shocking *adj.* startling, staggering, surprising, stupefying, astounding, breathtaking. *The violence of war is shocking.*

shoddy *adj.* poor, shabby, junky, inferior, second-rate, cheap. *The rickety chair was constructed with shoddy workmanship.* **Ant.** superior, first-rate, excellent.

shoe *n.* footwear, footgear, loafer, sneaker, running shoe, pump, boot, heels. *Make sure your shoe is tied.*

WORD SEARCH

aid to put on tight-fitting shoe: *shoehorn*
aid to remove tight-fitting shoe: *bootjack*
backless, woman's: *mule*
ballet: *toe shoe*
boat shoe, canvas: *deck shoe*
bottom: *sole*
brown and white oxford: *saddle shoe*
child's: *Mary Jane*
flap: *tongue*
infant's: *bootee*
laced over instep: *oxford*
lace hole: *eyelet*
loafer, slotted: *penny loafer*
low-heeled, woman's: *flat*
maker: *cordwainer*
mender: *cobbler*
Native American leather: *moccasin*
oxford with holes or perforations: *wing-tip*
raised: *platform shoe*
sandal-like with wood or cork sole: *clog*
sandals: *clogs, flip-flops, thongs*
sneakers, ankle-high: *hightops, basketball shoes*
sport field shoe providing added traction: *cleats*
strapless high-heel: *pump*
strapped high-heel: *slingback*
work shoe: *brogan, steel-toed shoe*

shoot *vb.* **1.** wound, hit, plug, nick, kill. *The soldier was shot in the leg.* **2.** fire, propel, discharge, project, eject. *He shoots arrows with an old Indian bow.* **3.** spring, leap, dash, rush, explode. *The runners shot out of the starting blocks.* –*n.* **4.** sprout, bud, sprig, twig. *The deer chewed on green shoots.*

shop *n.* **1.** store, market, boutique, outlet. *He bought her gift at a nearby shop. –vb.* **2.** buy, purchase, browse, look. *We went to shop at the mall.*

shopping *n.* buying, purchasing, browsing, sampling the merchandise, marketing, pricing. *Who does most of the shopping in your family?*

shopkeeper *n.* storekeeper, merchant, trader, retailer, dealer, monger, small businessman, small businesswoman. *Talk to the shopkeeper about getting a discount*

shoplift *vb.* steal, pilfer, filch, pocket, snatch, secrete. *The shopkeeper suspected the shifty-looking character might shoplift.*

shopper *n.* customer, bargain-hunter, patron, browser. *Shoppers get a little crazy around the holidays.*

shore *n.* **1.** beach, coast, seaside, waterfront, riverbank. *She found seashells on the shore. –vb.* **2.** hold, support, brace, buttress, reinforce, prop. *Workers tried to shore up the crumbling dam.* **Ant. 2.** weaken, destroy, overwhelm.

short *adj.* **1.** small, little, low, tiny, stunted, squat. *Horse jockeys are usually short.* **2.** brief, concise, momentary, fleeting. *He's only been waiting a short time.* **3.** abrupt, sharp, curt, rude, snappish. *The angry woman was very short with us. –adv.* **4.** suddenly, abruptly, quickly, forthwith. *The driver stopped short when she saw the injured animal. –n.* **5.** bermudas, cutoffs, trunks. *She wears shorts in the summer.* **Ant. 1.** tall, long, rangy. **2.** long, extended. **3.** patient, wordy. **4.** slowly, gradually. **5.** pants, trousers.

shortage *n.* scarcity, lack, shortfall, deficit, **drought**. *During gas shortages, people should drive as little as possible.* **Ant.** overabundance, surplus, excess.

shortchange *vb.* cheat, (slang) rip off, (slang) gyp. *I don't like to talk while I'm at the cash register because I'm afraid I'll shortchange someone.*

shortcoming *n.* failing, flaw, fault, drawback, defect. *I like her despite her shortcomings.* **Ant.** strength, virtue.

shorten *vb.* reduce, decrease, trim, cut, condense. *The sleeves were too long, so we shortened them.* **Ant.** lengthen, increase, extend.

shortfall *n.* shortage, deficit, deficiency, insufficiency, dearth, lack. *We suffered from a shortfall of orders last month and will have to scramble for new sales.* **Ant.** overstock, over-abundance.

short-lived *adj.* fleeting, brief, ephemeral, transient, quick, passing *The pet rock was a short-lived fad.* **Ant.** everlasting, infinite, neverending.

shortly *adv.* soon, presently, momentarily, directly, before you know it, any second now. *The train should be arriving shortly.*

short-sighted *adj.* myopic, nearsighted, unthinking, incautious, rash, blind, careless. *Failure to fill the car with gas before a long trip is short-sighted.* **Ant.** far-sighted, thoughtful, wise.

short-tempered *adj.* short-fused, hot-tempered, temperamental, crabby, touchy, cantankerous, irritable. *The badger is a short-tempered animal that should be avoided.*

shoulder *n.* **1.** rim, edge, ledge, bank, shelf. *His car hit the shoulder of the road. –vb.* **2.** push, shove, jostle, elbow, crowd. *She shouldered her way into the crowded room.* **3.** accept, carry, bear, assume, take. *I nced you to shoulder more of the work.*

shout *vb.* **1.** yell, scream, shriek, howl, roar. *The angry tennis players shouted at each other. –n.* **2.** yell, scream, cry, call, roar, howl. *We couldn't hear the announcer over the shouts of the crowd.* **Ant. 1–2.** whisper, mumble.

shove *vb.* **1.** push, move, thrust, jostle, shoulder. *He shoved the dog off the chair.* *–n.* **2.** push, nudge, boost, jostle, thrust, prod. *The toy began rolling when she gave it a shove.*

shovel *n.* spade, digger, digging implement, posthole digger, dredge, scoop. *I used a shovel to turn over the garden.*

show *vb.* **1.** display, exhibit, uncover, reveal, demonstrate. *Will you show your science project to the class?* **2.** lead, conduct, escort, steer. *Please show her to the door.* *–n.* **3.** performance, program, production, entertainment. *The theater's late show begins at midnight.* **4.** display, presentation, demonstration, exhibition. *Let's see a show of hands.* **Ant.** **1.** hide, conceal, cover. **4.** hiding, concealment.

showdown *n.* face-off, confrontation, clash, duel, moment of truth, turning point. *The championship teams will have a final showdown on Saturday.*

shower *n.* **1.** rainfall, downpour, sprinkle, drizzle, cloudburst, thunderstorm. The weatherman is predicting a shower. **2.** rinsing, cleansing, wash, wash-off, soak. *If you stink, you should really consider taking a shower.*

show-off *n.* exhibitionist, braggart, peacock, (slang) hot dog, (slang) showboat, blowhard. *Nobody likes a show-off, even when the person is truly talented.* **Ant.** shrinking violet

show off *vb.* exhibit, brag, peacock, (slang) showboat, strut, swagger, grandstand. *The star football player continued to show off, despite the crowd's boos.*

showpiece *n.* masterpiece, jewel in the crown, work of art, piece de resistance. *The chef's ice carving was a real showpiece.*

showy *adj.* flashy, ostentatious, garish, flamboyant, loud, gaudy. *That turquoise car is a little too showy for my tastes.* **Ant.** bland, plain, understated.

shred *n.* **1.** bit, scrap, piece, fragment, trace. *The criminal didn't leave a shred of evidence.* *–vb.* **2.** rip, tear, snip, slice, fragment. *The student shredded newspaper for his papier-mâché project.*

shrewd *adj.* clever, sharp, keen, intelligent, cunning, artful. *She made some shrewd business investments.* **Ant.** stupid, unwise, naive.

shriek *n.* **1.** scream, cry, squeal, screech, yell. *I let out a shriek when I saw the ghost.* *–vb.* **2.** scream, squeal, screech, yell, roar. *The people riding the roller coaster shrieked in delight.*

shrill *adj.* high-pitched, ear-piercing, intense, deafening, ear-splitting. *The shrill sound of the lunch whistle made us cover our ears.* **Ant.** low, quiet, imperceptible.

shrine *n.* memorial, tabernacle, monument, altar, reliquary, mausoleum. *The town constructed a shrine to remember the men killed in the war.*

shrink *vb.* **1.** retreat, retire, withdraw, cringe, cower. *He shrank from the horrible monster.* **2.** reduce, constrict, shrivel, shorten, decrease. *Jeans left too long in the dryer will shrink.* **Ant.** **1.** confront, face. **2.** increase, expand, lengthen.

shrivel *vb.* wither, wilt, shrink, fade, contract. *Plants shriveled during the drought.* **Ant.** grow, expand.

shrub *n.* bush, shrubbery, brush, hedge, thicket, scrub. *Shrubs should be pruned to keep them looking neat.*

shrunken *adj.* diminished, shriveled, contracted, compressed, withered, deflated. *The rotten pumpkin was shrunken beyond recognition.* **Ant.** enlarged, swollen, bloated.

shuck *vb.* shell, husk, remove, peel off. *I'll need at least an hour to shuck all that corn.*

shudder *vb.* **1.** shiver, tremble, shake, quake, convulse. *Just thinking about spinach makes him shudder.* –*n.* **2.** convulsion, shiver, tremble, quiver, twitch. *The dying porpoise gave one last shudder, then sank from view.*

shuffle *vb.* **1.** drag, hobble, scrape, limp, shamble. *A homeless man shuffled down the sidewalk.* **2.** mix, intermix, jumble, rearrange, disorder. *The gambler shuffled the card deck.* –*n.* **3.** limp, hobble, dragging, shambling. *She walks with an odd shuffle.* **Ant. 2.** order, arrange.

shun *vb.* avoid, reject, spurn, refuse, forgo. *Lepers were often shunned by other people.* **Ant.** welcome, accept, embrace.

shunt *vb.* divert, shift, sidetrack, switch, turn, lead. *The new rail line would shunt arriving trains on to an auxiliary track.*

shut *vb.* **1.** close, seal, secure, latch, block. *Shut the door behind you.* **2.** confine, cage, pen, enclose, lock. *The farmer shut the animals in the barn.* –*adj.* **3.** closed, sealed, blocked, unopened. *The road was shut for repairs.* **Ant. 1.** open, unseal. **2.** free, release. **3.** open, opened, unsealed.

shut out *vb.* (slang) blank, (slang) shut down, (slang) blow doors off from, (slang) skunk, rout. *The Red Sox shut out the Yankees last night.*

shutout *n.* rout, defeat, (slang) licking. *The game was a shutout, as only one team scored.*

shutter *n.* blind, shade, curtain, screen. *Shutters on our windows keep the sunshine out.*

shuttle *n.* orbiter, spacecraft, spaceship, vehicle, aircraft, rocket. *The shuttle is scheduled to blast off today.*

shy *adj.* **1.** bashful, modest, timid, sheepish, cautious. *The shy girl was afraid of speaking in front of her class.* **2.** short, under, deficient, lacking, scant. *The ball was several yards shy of a field goal.* –*vb.* **3.** flinch, jerk, quail, cringe, start. *The horse shied away from the crowd.* **Ant. 1.** immodest, bold, brash. **2.** over, above.

shyness *n.* bashfulness, reticence, inhibition, self-consciousness, diffidence, modesty. *His shyness kept him from asking anyone to dance.* **Ant.** overconfidence, cockiness, brazenness.

sick *adj.* **1.** ill, unwell, nauseated, queasy, troubled. *Roller coaster rides make him sick.* **2.** repulsive, offensive, disgusting, shocking. *That was a sick joke.* **3.** tired, weary, bored, fed up. *She was sick of doing homework.* **Ant. 1.** well, healthy. **2.** tasteful, pleasant. **3.** eager, fresh.

sicken *vb.* nauseate, turn one's stomach, disgust, revolt, repel, make ill. *The smell of rotting fish tends to sicken me.*

sickening *adj.* nauseating, stomach-turning, disgusting, revolting, repellent, distasteful. *His selfish attitude is sickening.*

sickle *n.* scythe, (slang) bushwhacker, grass-cutter, cutting implement, tool. *Grab a sickle and start cutting.*

sickly *adj.* ill, unwell, ailing, unhealthy, nauseated, weak. *She was too sickly to get out of bed* **Ant.** healthy, well, fit.

sickness *n.* illness, ailment, disease, affliction, disorder, infirmity, syndrome. *She suffered from a sickness the doctor couldn't identify.* **Ant.** wellness, health, fitness.

sideburns *n.* burnsides, (slang) muttonchops, whiskers. *My sideburns are getting too bushy.*

side effect *n.* reaction, byproduct, response, repercussion, symptom. *Does this drug have any side effects?*

sidestep *vb.* evade, dodge, elude, bypass, avoid, sidetrack. *Hopefully, the governor won't try and sidestep the tax issue.*

sideswipe *vb.* graze, glance off, scrape. *Don't get too close or you'll sideswipe that car.*

sidetrack *vb.* divert, digress, shunt, turn off. *Please stick to the topic and don't sidetrack.*

siesta *n.* nap, rest, (slang) snooze, (slang) catnap. *The hour following lunch is a great time to take a siesta.*

sieve *n.* strainer, sifter, filter, screen, mesh. *We need to strain the soil through a sieve.*

sift *vb.* rummage, filter, sort, search, probe. *The archaeologist sifted through the dirt for ancient pottery shards.*

sight *n.* **1.** vision, eyesight, seeing. *The old dog's sight was poor.* **2.** appearance, view, vision, glance, glimpse. *The sight of so much food made her mouth water.* **3.** wonder, marvel, scene, view, spectacle. *The Grand Canyon is quite a sight.* *–vb.* **4.** see, view, discern, glimpse, observe. *They sighted a plane flying overhead.* **Ant. 1.** blindness.

sign *n.* **1.** symbol, token, representation, indication, warning. *Geese flying south are a sign that winter has arrived.* **2.** gesture, signal, motion, wave, nod. *The coach gave a sign for the batter to bunt.* **3.** billboard, signpost, guidepost, bulletin. *The bus stopped at the stop sign.* *–vb.* **4.** endorse, initial, inscribe, autograph. *Your parents must sign your report card.* **5.** gesture, signal, flag, motion, wave. *The police officer gave a sign for our car to pass.*

signal *n.* **1.** indicator, sign, cue, alert, notice, go-ahead. *I waited for the traffic signal to turn green before stepping on the gas.* *–vb.* **2.** indicate, cue, alert, warn, communicate, semaphore. *Signal the waiter for service.*

signature *n.* autograph, inscription, endorsement, John Hancock, name, authorization. *You can't cash that check without a signature.*

significance *n.* importance, consequence, influence, weight, meaning. *The American Revolution has great significance in the history of the United States.*

significant *adj.* **1.** large, sizable, considerable, substantial, major. *I noticed a significant improvement in his dancing after he took lessons.* **2.** important, noteworthy, crucial, vital, valuable. *She felt that the last chapter was the only significant part of the entire book.* **Ant. 1.** insignificant, small, minor, trivial. **2.** insignificant, unimportant, meaningless, invaluable.

silence *n.* **1.** quiet, hush, stillness, noiselessness, speechlessness, muteness. *Mourners stood in silence beside the grave.* *–vb.* **2.** quiet, still, extinguish, subdue, calm, muffle. *The librarian silenced our loud talking* **Ant. 1.** loudness, noise, talkativeness. **2.** encourage, inflame.

silent *adj.* **1.** quiet, soundless, mute, speechless, noiseless. *We remained silent during the eulogy.* **2.** unspoken, unstated, undeclared, implicit, tacit. *We had a silent agreement.* **Ant. 1.** noisy, talkative, loud. **2.** spoken, declared.

silhouette *n.* outline, profile, contour. *We could see the couple's silhouette through the shade.*

silky *adj.* satiny, glossy, sleek, smooth, delicate. *Your skin is soft and silky.* **Ant.** rough, gritty, abrasive.

silly *adj.* foolish, ridiculous, comical, idiotic, stupid. *The circus clown was very silly.* **Ant.** serious, intelligent, sensible.

silt *n.* settlings, sediment, alluvium, wash. *The river is brown due to its high silt content.*

silverware *n.* silver, flatware, cutlery, eating utensils. *On Thanksgiving, Grandma always gets out the special silverware.*

similar *adj.* close, comparable, like, related, parallel. *My friend's taste in music is similar to mine.* **Ant.** dissimilar, different, contrary.

similarity *n.* resemblance, likeness, sameness, closeness, equivalence. *People commented on the similarity between the two brothers.* **Ant.** dissimilarity, difference, unlikeness.

simmer *vb.* stew, bubble, cook, boil, sizzle. *He let the soup simmer on the stove.*

simple *adj.* **1.** easy, uncomplicated, elementary, understandable, basic. *She answered the simple problems first.* **2.** uneducated, unsophisticated, unassuming, naive, unworldly. *The peasant was a simple man.* **3.** plain, unadorned, bare, natural, naked. *All we wanted was the simple truth.* **Ant.** **1** complicated, difficult, advanced. **2.** complicated, sophisticated, worldly. **3.** pretended, varnished.

simpleton *n.* ignoramus, dunce, moron, imbecile, fool, dolt. *The simpleton's problem is that he doesn't know what he doesn't know.* **Ant.** genius, intellectual, scholar.

simplicity *n.* easiness, directness, plainness, straightforwardness, openness. *She was surprised by the problem's simplicity.* **Ant.** complexity, difficulty, sophistication.

simplify *vb.* summarize, shorten, streamline, clarify, unravel. *He tried to simplify the long and complicated explanation.* **Ant.** elaborate, embellish

simulate *vb.* fake, imitate, copy, mimic, replicate, assume. *News programs sometimes simulate or re-enact crimes to increase viewer interest.*

simulation *n.* imitation, copy, fake, mimicry, replication, reproduction. *NASA showed a simulation of how the planetary probe landed.*

simultaneous *adj.* concurrent, synchronous, coexisting, parallel, coincident. *The network made a simultaneous broadcast to radio and television.*

sin *n.* **1.** wrong, violation, wickedness, offense, misdeed. *She confessed her sins to the priest.* –*vb.* **2.** err, stray, transgress, offend, trespass. *The minister said the thief had sinned.* **Ant.** **1.** sinlessness, goodness.

sincere *adj.* real, genuine, earnest, honest, heartfelt. *Do you think his apology was sincere?* **Ant.** insincere, fake, pretended.

sincerity *n.* genuineness, earnestness, frankness, honesty. *Hopefully, most donations to charities are given with sincerity.* **Ant.** insincerity, artificiality, emptiness.

sinewy *adj.* tough, strong, muscular, strapping, brawny, (slang) ripped. *The wrestler was in top shape and appeared unusually sinewy.* **Ant.** fat, lumpy, doughy.

sinful *adj.* immoral, evil, bad, wicked, criminal, wrong. *The lifelong criminal committed numerous sinful acts.* **Ant.** moral, virtuous, saintly.

sing *vb.* vocalize, intone, melodize, croon, chant. *He plans to sing several new songs at the concert.*

singe *vb.* char, sear, burn, brown, blacken, toast. *Be careful not to singe the meat.*

single-handed *adj.* alone, unassisted, unaided, independent. *Superman's single-handed efforts saved the world from destruction.*

singular *adj.* unique, one-of-a-kind, rare, exceptional, peculiar, unusual. *A blue moon is a singular occurrence.* **Ant.** common, ordinary, usual.

sinister *adj.* dangerous, wicked, threatening, evil, frightening. *In the movie, the two stars were stalked by a sinister figure.* **Ant.** harmless, safe.

sink *vb.* **1.** descend, fall, plunge, flounder, dip, slump, decline. *The ship began to sink after hitting the reef.* **2.** invest, risk, venture, drop. *Are you going to sink more money into the business?* **3.** bore, drill, dig, plant, lay. *Workers sank an oil well outside the city.* –*n.* **4.** basin, washbowl, washbasin. *Dirty dishes were piled in the sink.* **Ant. 1.** rise, lift, climb **2.** remove, withdraw.

sinuous *adj.* winding, serpentine, twisting, snaking, meandering, tortuous. *We made our way up the mountain on a sinuous, cliff-side road.* **Ant.** straight, unbending.

sip *vb.* sample, taste, slurp, siphon. *Can I have a sip of your soda?*

siren *n.* warning signal, alarm, Klaxon, whistle. *We could hear the warning siren from a mile away.*

sissy *n.* coward, weakling, (slang) wimp, (slang) wuss, effeminate man, (slang) scaredy cat. *He was called a sissy because he was afraid of his own shadow.* **Ant.** (slang) he-man, (slang) macho man, hero.

site *n.* place, location, position, spot, area. *The king found the perfect site for his new castle.*

sit-in *n.* protest, demonstration, rally, shutdown. *The organization planned to stage a sit-in to protest the toxic waste site.*

sitter *n.* babysitter, nanny, attendant, guardian, caretaker, wet nurse. *If we're going to see a movie tomorrow night, we'll need a sitter.*

situate *vb.* place, set, put, position, stand, station. *We must decide how to situate the new furniture in this room.* **Ant.** move, shift, remove.

situation *n.* predicament, circumstances, condition, state, case. *The situation at the accident was critical.*

sit-up *n.* crunch, exercise. *I hate doing sit-ups.*

sixth sense *n.* extrasensory perception, ESP, intuition, clairvoyance, psychic ability. *Dogs seem to have a sixth sense when it comes to detecting impending storms and earthquakes.*

size *n.* measurement, dimension, area, volume, expanse. *The salesman asked me for my shoe size.*

skate *vb.* ice-skate, figure skate, in-line skate, Rollerblade, blade, roller-skate, glissade. *Let's go skate on the pond.*

WORD SEARCH

arena: *rink*
flying spin: *Arabian*
forward to back turn: *choctaw*
ice resurfacing machine: *Zamboni*
jump, one revolution: *lutz*
jump, one-and-a-half revolution: *axel*
jump, two-and-a-half revolution; *double axel*
jump from one foot to another: *salchow*
jumping split with touching of toes: *Russian split*
jump with split legs: *split, stag*
pair stunt in which woman is held by feet and revolved with head near ice: *death spiral*
propelling oneself along the ice: *stroking*
spin in an arabesque position: *camel*
three-circle figure: *serpentine*
two-circle figure: *figure eight*

skateboard *n.* board, (slang) wheels. *Joe fell off of his skateboard and broke his arm.*

WORD SEARCH

axles, front and rear: *truck*
backwards, riding: *fakie*
cruises, board designed for long: *longboard*
curve, skate in a long curve: *carve*
flip board into air with foot: *kickflip*
front: *nose*
gathering, skateboarding: *jam*
platform of board: *deck*
ramp: *bank*

ride or scrape axles on top of railing or curb, intentionally: *grind*
rotation, half, mid-air: *180*
rotation, full, mid-air: *360*
rear: *tail*

skeleton *n.* bones, framework, scaffolding, inner structure. *Every bone of your skeleton is constantly regenerating itself.*

WORD SEARCH

breastbone, center: *sternum*
collarbone: *clavicle*
connective tissue: *cartilage*
ear bones: *incus, malleus, stapes*
fingers and toes: *phalanges*
foot bones: *metatarsal*
forearm: *radius, ulna*
"funny" bone between shoulder and elbow: *humerus*
hip: *pelvis, sacrum, coccyx*
jaw bones: *mandible, maxilla*
kneecap: *patella*
leg: *fibula, tibia, femur*
shoulder blade: *scapula*
skull: *cranium*
spinal column: *vertebrae*
tailbone: *coccyx*
upper-body framework: *ribs*

skeptic *n.* doubter, nonbeliever, questioner, cynic, doubting Thomas, scoffer. *Skeptics are rarely fooled by people claiming to be psychics.* **Ant.** believer, (slang) sucker, dupe.

skeptical *adj.* doubting, unbelieving, questioning, cynical, distrusting, unconvinced. *It's always wise to be skeptical when facing claims of the paranormal.* **Ant.** believing, naive, gullible.

skepticism *n.* doubt, disbelief, questioning, cynicism, distrust, mistrust. *Skepticism should be encouraged to counter pseudoscientific claims.* **Ant.** doubt, distrust, disbelief.

sketch *n.* **1.** drawing, diagram, chart, graph. *The artist drew a pencil sketch of my friend.* **2.** skit, scene, vignette. *The drama students acted out a sketch.* –*vb.* **3.** draw, pencil, outline, picture, graph. *The architect sketched her plans for the new building.*

sketchy *adj.* incomplete, vague, fuzzy, unfinished, crude. *She gave a sketchy explanation of where she had been.* **Ant.** complete, detailed, finished.

ski *vb.* schuss, slalom, snowplow, freestyle, snowboard. *They skied down the slope at top speed.*

WORD SEARCH

acrobatic form: *freestyle*
bump on hump, snow: *mogul*
cross country: *langlauf, Nordic skiing*
freestyle dance: *ballet*
jump, crouching: *gelendesprung*
lift, covered: *gondola*
parallel turn: *christie*
rifle shooting and skiing competition: *biathlon*
ski straight down the mountain: *schuss*
slowing or stopping position: *snowplow*
snow, deep and soft: *powder*
snow, old and granulated: *corn*
snow with hardened surface: *crust*
turns, series of quick: *wedelns*
uphill diagonal walking method: *herringbone*
zigzag course or race: *slalom*

skid *vb.* slide, slip, sideslip, fishtail, brake. *The car began to skid off the road.*

skill *n.* ability, talent, technique, trade, craft. *Painting is a skill that takes considerable practice to master.* **Ant.** inability, awkwardness, incompetency.

skillful *adj.* gifted, talented, capable, experienced, masterful. *We hired a skillful carpenter to build our new home.* **Ant.** unskillful, untalented, incapable, clumsy.

skimp *vb.* conserve, economize, pinch, scrimp, withhold. *The cook skimped on the sugar to save money.* **Ant.** waste, squander.

skimpy *adj.* scanty, small, puny, meager, inadequate. *Some people wore skimpy bathing suits at the beach.* **Ant.** large, enormous, extensive, lavish.

skin *n.* epidermis, dermis, derma, cuticle, hide, membrane, husk. *Sarah has beautiful skin.*

skinny *adj.* thin, slender, bony, anorexic, malnourished, lean. *If you want to be skinny, you'll have to exercise every day.* **Ant.** obese, fat, overweight.

skip *vb.* **1.** spring, bounce, jump, hop, leap. *She skipped from rock to rock.* **2.** miss, omit, neglect, dodge, avoid. *He got into trouble after he skipped class.* –*n.* **3.** spring, jump, hop, leap. *He took a skip over the crack in the sidewalk.* **Ant.** **1.** shuffle, drag. **2.** include, attend, cover.

skirmish *n.* **1.** battle, fight, clash, engagement, conflict. *A skirmish took place between two platoons.* –*vb.* **2.** battle, fight, struggle, clash, collide. *Soldiers skirmished for control of the hill.*

skirt *n.* **1.** dress, gown, frock, miniskirt, maxiskirt. *She wore her skirt just above the knees.* –*vb.* **2.** avoid, bypass, dodge, circle, sidestep. *The skirted the valley where the evil wizard lived.* **Ant.** **2.** confront, enter, meet.

WORD SEARCH

ballet: *tutu*
calico, ruffled hem: *prairie skirt*
giant skirt of 19th century: *crinoline, hoop skirt*
grass: *hula*
Malaysian wrap: *sarong*
tight-fitting with back slit: *sheath*
peasant-style: *dirndl*
puffy: *bouffant*
Scottish male's: *kilt*

skit *n.* sketch, playlet, act, parody, takeoff, vignette. *The comedy troupe put on a side-splitting skit.*

skittish *adj.* nervous, jumpy, edgy, jittery, restless, restive. *The horse becomes skittish when there is a storm brewing.* **Ant.** calm, relaxed, serene.

skulk *vb.* sneak, lurk, creep, slink, hide, steal. *The skunk likes to skulk behind the trash cans at night.*

skull *n.* cranium, head, sconce. *Hamlet holds a skull of his murdered father in Shakespeare's play.*

skunk *n.* polecat, animal, mammal, omnivore, quadruped, creature. *The skunk has a powerful spray from behind, so watch out.*

sky *n.* firmament, upper atmosphere, biosphere, cloudscape, vault, stratosphere, mesosphere, thermosphere. *The color of the sky is azure or cerulean.*

skydiving *n.* parachuting, freefalling, parasailing. *Skydiving is strictly a daredevil's sport.*

skyscraper *n.* high-rise, building, edifice, monolith, superstructure. *Tourists love to look up at the skyscrapers in New York City.*

slab *n.* hunk, block, piece, chunk, plank. *Cut me off a slab of that cake, will you?*

slack *adj.* **1.** loose, limp, relaxed, lax. *Keep the sail slack until the wind increases.* **2.** lazy, idle, negligent, sloppy. *The manager criticized them for being slack at their jobs.* –*adv.* **3.** loosely, limply, easily, relaxed. *The rope hung slack in her hands.* –*n.* **4.** decrease, decline, slowing, cutback. *Bad weather caused a slack in the store's business.* **Ant.** **1.** tight, rigid, tense. **2.** competent, careful, attentive. **3.** tightly, rigidly, stiffly. **4.** increase, upswing.

slacker *n.* shirker, malingerer, dodger, lagger, loafer, (slang) deadbeat. *Any slackers caught* *watching the clock will be reprimanded.* **Ant.** (slang) workhorse, (slang) workaholic.

slam *vb.* **1.** bang, smack, smash, dash, hurl. *The basketball player slammed the ball into the basket.* –*n.* **2.** banging, crashing, smack, smash. *We knew he was angry when we heard the slam of his door.*

slander *n.* **1.** falsehood, untruth, defamation, libel, distortion. *The actress sued the magazine for slander.* –*vb.* **2.** defame, smear, malign, slur, defile. *Her enemy slandered her good name.*

slang *n.* colloquialism, lingo, jargon, language, vernacular, street language. *In musical slang, a drummer who really knows how to play "has his chops down."*

slant *vb.* **1.** tilt, slope, pitch, cant, list. *The floor slanted where the ground had sunk.* **2.** bias, twist, distort, weight, prejudice. *He slants his speeches toward a liberal viewpoint.* –*n.* **3.** tilt, slope, pitch, leaning, list. *The tree grew with a slant because of strong northerly winds.* **4.** bias, distortion, viewpoint, prejudice, emphasis. *The newspaper is written with a conservative slant.*

slanting *adj.* inclined, leaning, tilting, diagonal, oblique, askew. *The picture on the wall is slanting and should be corrected.* **Ant.** straight, level, vertical.

slap *n.* **1.** smack, clap, blow, whack, bang. *The slap of waves hitting the beach lulled us to sleep.* –*vb.* **2.** smack, hit, whack, strike. *The loose sail slapped her in the face.* **3.** dash, fling, cast, toss, hurl. *Workers slapped paint on the house.*

slapdash *adj.* sloppy, careless, hasty, slipshod, haphazard, casual. *The tree house had been constructed in slapdash fashion and collapsed.*

slash *vb.* **1.** cut, slice, hack, gash, lacerate. *He accidentally slashed his hand on some broken glass.* **2.** cut, drop, trim, pare, reduce. *The editor slashed several pages from the manuscript.* –*n.* **3.** cut, gash, slit, slice, rent, tear. *Cereal fell through a slash in the box.* **4.** reduction, cut, drop, markdown. *The store advertised its price slash.* **Ant.** **2.** add, keep, maintain. **4.** increase, markup

slat *n.* lath, picket, stave, strip, paling. *Three of the slats in the fence are broken.*

slaughter *n.* **1.** massacre, killing, murder, bloodshed, butchering. *The slaughter on the battlefield sickened him.*–*vb.* **2.** massacre, annihilate, kill, butcher, exterminate. *Hunters slaughtered much of the deer herd.*

slaughterhouse *n.* abattoir, butchery, meat packing plant. *I found the slaughterhouse an unpleasant place to work at.*

slave *n.* servant, bondman, serf, menial, drudge, chattel. *A slave waited hand and foot on the plantation owner.*

slavery *n.* bondage, enslavement, servitude, serfdom, enthrallment *The captives were sold into slavery.* **Ant.** freedom, liberty, emancipation.

slavish *adj.* servile, subservient, obsequious, deferential, submissive. *Slavish behavior is disrespected, so please be assertive.* **Ant.** rebellious, defiant, stubborn.

slay *vb.* kill, murder, annihilate, assassinate, slaughter. *The knight rode out to slay the dragon.*

sleazebag *n.* (slang) scumbag, (slang) creep, (slang) slimeball, pervert, slob, pig. *I'm not a sleazebag, I just play one on TV.*

sleazy *adj.* creepy, (slang) scummy, dirty, greasy, oily, (slang) skanky, disreputable. *Those gangster clothes make you look sleazy.* **Ant.** wholesome, clean-cut, upright.

sled *n.* sleigh, toboggan, luge, cutter, sledge, bobsled. *Let's take our sleds to the top of the mountain.*

sleek *adj.* silky, shiny, glossy, smooth, glistening. *The tiger's fur was sleek from the rain.* **Ant.** dull, rough, coarse.

sleep *vb.* **1.** slumber, rest, repose, doze, nap. *My sister and I sleep in a bunk bed.* –*n.* **2.** slumber, rest, repose, snooze, nap. *The tired child needs a good night's sleep.* **Ant. 1.** arouse, awaken. **2.** wakefulness.

WORD SEARCH

between wakefulness and sleep: *hypnagogic*
body clock regulating: *circadian rhythm*
children's half-awake nightmare: *night terrors*
deep sleep: *sopor, stupor*
dream sleep: *REM sleep (rapid eye movement)*
excessive: *hypersomnia*
expert: *somnologist*
god of dreams: *Morpheus*
god of sleep: *Hypnos, Somnus*
grogginess from extreme oversleeping: *Rip Van Winkle Syndrome*
sleeping sickness: *narcolepsy*
sleeplessness: *insomnia*
twitch or spasm in arm or leg just before sleep onset: *myoclonic jerk*

sleepless *adj.* insomniac, restless, wakeful, (slang) wired, saucer-eyed, tossing and turning. *I don't want to spend another sleepless night counting sheep.* **Ant.** restful.

sleepy *adj.* drowsy, tired, weary, fatigued, exhausted, lethargic. *Never drive a car while you're sleepy.* **Ant.** alert, energetic, wide-awake.

sleet *n.* frozen rain, precipitation, hail. *The weatherman is predicting sleet today.*

sleigh *n.* sled, cutter, pung, conveyance, vehicle. *Here comes Santa in his sleigh.*

sleight-of-hand *adj.* trickery, legerdemain, deception, feint, prestidigitation, palming. *The magician's sleight-of-hand trick was far quicker than any of us could follow with our eyes.*

slender *adj.* slim, thin, lean, slight, narrow, reedy. *The slender trees bent with the wind.* **Ant.** thick, solid, fat.

sleuth *n.* detective, investigator, private eye, (slang) Sherlock, (slang) gumshoe. *One need not be a sleuth to determine who stole the last of the ice cream.*

slice *n.* **1.** piece, wedge, chunk, cut, portion. *Please give me a slice of pizza.* –*vb.* **2.** carve, segment, cut, divide, separate. *She sliced a tomato for her salad.*

slick *adj.* **1.** slippery, treacherous, sleek, glossy, shiny. *The road was slick from the gas spill.* **2.** smooth, suave, glib, sharp, cunning. *They distrusted the slick saleswoman.* –*n.* **3.** film, coating, scum, spill. *An oil slick washed up on the beach.* **Ant. 1.** rough, textured, coarse. **2.** amateurish, clumsy

slide *vb.* **1.** glide, slip, skim, skate, coast. *The softball player tried to slide into second base.* –*n.* **2.** chute, tube, trough, slope. *She went down the pool's slide.*

slight *adj.* **1.** small, slender, light, frail, delicate. *The boy seemed very slight on the large stage.* **2.** minor, unimportant, insignificant, modest. *There's a slight chance of snow today.* –*vb.* **3.** insult, snub, affront, rebuff, spurn. *He slighted her with his inattention.* –*n.* **4.** snub, insult, slur, affront. *Ignoring him was a slight.* **Ant. 1.** large, strong, solid. **2.** great, considerable.

slim *adj.* **1.** slender, thin, lean, slight, small. *The slim athlete was constantly exercising.* –*vb.* **2.** slenderize, reduce. *We joined a sports club to slim our waistlines.* **Ant. 1.** large, fat, thick.

slime *n.* **1.** scum, mucus, ooze, jelly, mire, muck. *The pool lining is covered with green slime.*

slimy *adj.* viscous, viscid, mucus-coated, scummy, mucky, vile, foul. *The bottom of the pond feels slimy.*

sling *n.* **1.** brace, support, band, strap, bandage. *Her broken arm is in a sling.* –*vb.* **2.** fling, cast, jerk, pitch, heave. *The cook slung raw hamburger onto the grill.*

slink *vb.* skulk, sneak, creep, lurk, prowl, tiptoe. *To our horror, we saw an intruder slink behind the shrubs.*

slip *vb.* **1.** glide, skim, slide, flow, slither. *She slipped between the bed covers.* **2.** skid, fall, trip, tumble. *He slipped on the ice.* **3.** decline, decrease, fall, lapse, sink. *The temperature slipped into the low twenties.* –*n.* **4.** blunder, error, mistake, oversight. *He made a slip in telling me about my gift.* **5.** fall, drop, downturn, decline. *A slip in the patient's condition worried the doctor.* **6.** stub, paper, note, certificate, coupon. *You should always save the sales slip.* **7.** undergarment, petticoat, chemise. *She wore a slip under her summer dress.* **Ant. 3.** increase, rise, improve. **4.** improvement, upturn, increase.

slippery *adj.* slick, greasy, sleek, smooth, satiny, waxy, glazed. *Black ice is extremely slippery.*

slipshod *adj.* sloppy, careless, slapdash, haphazard, shoddy, messy. *His hand-built chair was slipshod and quickly fell apart.* **Ant.** careful, meticulous, sharp.

slit *vb.* **1.** cut, split, rip, slash, slice. *She slit the envelope open.* –*n.* **2.** opening, groove, fissure, cut, slash. *He peered through a slit in the curtains.*

slither *vb.* snake, wriggle, slink, crawl, twist, turn. *Unfortunately, the snakes slither under the garage and take up residence there.*

sliver *n.* splinter, shard, fragment, bit. *Ow, I got a sliver of wood in my toe!*

slob *n.* pig, hog, animal, caveman, (slang) grub, (slang) grunge. *Only a slob would eat mashed potatoes with her hands.*

slobber *vb.* drool, dribble, drivel, slaver, salivate. *Please don't let the dog slobber all over the guests.*

slog *vb.* plod, labor, toil, trudge, wade, grind away. *They slogged up the mountain before finally collapsing in exhaustion.*

slogan *n.* motto, saying, catchphrase, jingle, expression, trademark. *The company used a catchy slogan to help potential customers remember its name.*

slope *vb.* **1.** slant, lean, bank, angle, incline. *The trail slopes uphill for the next mile.* –*n.* **2.** bank, ramp, angle, incline, descent. *Only experienced skiers should go down the steep slopes.* **Ant. 1.** flatten. **2.** horizontal, plane.

sloppy *adj.* messy, slovenly, disorderly, untidy, careless. *The sloppy diner spilled mustard on her shirt.* **Ant. 1.** neat, orderly, tidy.

slouch *vb.* **1.** droop, stoop, hunch, slump, bend. *Keep your shoulders back and don't slouch.* –*n.* **2.** incompetent, amateur, bumbler, laggard, clod, oaf. *He used to be a slouch at chess, but now he wins every match.*

slovenly *adj.* messy, sloppy, unclean, slack, careless. *I am disgusted by his slovenly habits.* **Ant.** neat, clean, careful.

slow *adj.* **1.** unhurried, plodding, sluggish, crawling, gradual, delayed. *The slow dripping of the water annoyed him.* **2.** dumb, dull, dense, obtuse, stupid. *The dog was too slow to learn new tricks.* –*vb.* **3.** delay, decelerate, moderate, slacken, break. *The car slowed in the heavy traffic.* **Ant. 1.** fast, hurried. **2.** smart, clever, bright. **3.** accelerate.

slowdown *n.* downturn, recession, slump, decline, depression, slackening. *Put away some* *extra savings to prepare for an economic slowdown.* **Ant.** boom, expansion, growth.

slowpoke *n.* sloth, slug, laggard, lagger, snail, foot-dragger. *Don't be a slowpoke or you'll be late for class.*

sludge *n.* ooze, muck, goo, waste, sewage, grease. *An engine runs better when it is free of sludge.*

sluggish *adj.* slow, crawling, listless, unhurried, plodding. *Cars are often sluggish in cold weather.* **Ant.** lively, quick, frisky.

slum *n.* ghetto, low-income district, inner city, skid row, shanty town. *She wanted to move out of the slum to a better part of town.*

slumber *vb.* **1.** sleep, doze, nap, snooze. *The baby looks peaceful when she slumbers.* –*n.* **2.** sleep, nap, rest, repose, siesta. *Our slumber was disturbed by a loud noise.*

slump *n.* downturn, decline, drop-off, rut, hard times, recession, depression. *Their best batter is in a slump and couldn't even hit a beachball.*

slur *vb.* slander, smear, insult, sully, cast aspersions, insult. *The newspaper can slur your reputation only if what they say is true.*

slurp *vb.* suck, sip, drink. *Please don't slurp your soup.*

sly *adj.* cunning, foxy, crafty, wily, crooked. *The sly politician gave out false information about his opponent.* **Ant.** open, honorable, straightforward.

smack *n.* **1.** hit, slap, whack, spank, blow. *She gave the dog a smack for biting the neighbor.* –*vb.* **2.** hit, whack, strike, slap, slam. *He smacked his head against the low doorway.* **3.** taste, smell, suggest, resemble. *That tale smacks of falsehood.*

small *adj.* **1.** little, tiny, petite, puny, miniature. *Only five people could fit in the small theater.* **2.** scant, meager, limited, piddling. *She has a small number of projects to finish.* **3.** minor, insignificant, unimportant, secondary, trivial. *We will deal with the small matters last.* **Ant.** **1.** big, large, gigantic. **2.** great, enormous. **3.** major.

smart *adj.* **1.** intelligent, bright, clever, brainy, sharp. *Marie Curie, winner of a Nobel Prize, was a very smart scientist.* –*vb.* **2.** sting, burn, hurt, throb, itch. *His scraped knee still smarts.* **Ant.** **1.** dumb, stupid, unintelligent.

smart-aleck *n.* (slang) wiseguy, (slang) wisenheimer, (slang) smart-ass, know-it-all, (slang) bigmouth. *The delinquent teen acted like a smart-aleck.*

smash *vb.* **1.** crush, shatter, pulverize, demolish, break. *The troll smashed the rocks blocking his path.* –*n.* **2.** blow, shattering, crash, bang. *Our car got quite a smash when it hit the tree.* **3.** hit, triumph, success, winner. *The new movie was a smash.* **Ant.** **3.** failure, flop.

smear *vb.* **1.** spread, coat, cover, layer, dab. *She smeared suntan lotion across her arms.* **2.** smudge, blur, streak, stain, soil. *The rain smeared the actor's makeup.* –*n.* **3.** smudge, blotch, streak, stain, spot. *The ink smear blotted out several words.*

smell *vb.* **1.** scent, sniff, detect, sense, perceive. *I could smell the cookies baking in the oven.* **2.** stink, reek. *The bus fumes really smelled.* –*n.* **3.** scent, odor, aroma, fragrance, stink. *The garbage gave off a horrible smell.*

smidgen *n.* bit, speck, trace, pinch, iota, crumb. *May I please have just a smidgen of that pie?*

smile *vb.* **1.** grin, beam, smirk. *We smiled for the photographer.* –*n.* **2.** grin, beam, smirk. *The happy boy gave us a big smile.* **Ant.** **1–2.** frown

smirk *n.* smile, grin, simper, sneer. *That smirk on your face is very disrespectful but cute.*

smite *vb.* hit, strike, smack, blast, demolish. *Lightning sometimes smites the tallest trees.*

smitten *adj.* infatuated, (slang) head over heels, enamored, in love, taken by, captivated, (slang) swept off one's feet. *Mary is absolutely smitten by Charlie.*

smock *n.* frock, camise, coverall

smog *n.* pollution, haze, pall, smoke, carbon monoxide, gas cloud. *When smog begins to obscure the Grand Canyon, it's time to take action.*

smoke *n.* fume, gas, soot cloud, hot air, exhaust, smog, pollution. *Smoke from the forest fire could be seen from miles away.*

smoke detector *n.* smoke alarm, fire alarm, heat sensor. *It's time to change the battery in the smoke detector.*

smokestack *n.* chimney, flue, funnel. *The company's smokestack was belching out a foul-smelling pollutant.*

smoky *adj.* fumy, thick, burning, choking, cloudy. *The kitchen is very smoky this morning, after you fried the bacon.*

smolder *vb.* fume, smoke, simmer, sizzle, fester. *His anger smoldered for days.*

smooth *adj.* **1.** even, polished, glassy, silky, unwrinkled. *A bowling ball is smooth to the touch.* **2.** easy, orderly, uneventful, untroubled. *The doctor hoped for a smooth operation.* **3.** suave, sophisticated, glib, slick, urbane. *The smooth politician expertly fended off questions of a personal nature.* –*vb.* **4.** flatten, even, sand, polish, press. *He smoothed out the crumpled letter.* **Ant.** **1.** rough, uneven, coarse, bumpy. **2.** uneven, difficult, troubled. **3.** unsophisticated. **4.** wrinkle, crumple, roughen.

smorgasbord *n.* spread, banquet, buffet, feast, spread, meal, appetizers. *My Swedish Grandma is preparing a smorgasbord for the family reunion.*

smother *vb.* suffocate, strangle, choke, extinguish, snuff. *The forest rangers smothered the fire with dirt.*

smudge *n.* **1.** smear, blotch, stain, blot. *She wiped the smudge off her windshield.* –*vb.* **2.** stain, smear, spot, soil, dirty. *The baby smudged his face with mud.* **Ant.** **2.** clean, cleanse.

smug *adj.* complacent, self-satisfied, cocky, pompous, self-righteous, holier-than-thou. *The champion was smug about his chances for winning but was shocked when he actually lost.* **Ant.** self-doubting, insecure, humble.

smuggle *vb.* traffic, sneak in, (slang) bootleg, secrete, run, import illegally. *Don't try to smuggle contraband into the country or you'll face a stiff jail sentence.*

smut *n.* pornography, (slang) porn, obscenity, X-rated material, adult material, erotica. *One person's erotic art may be another person's smut.*

snack *n.* tidbit, morsel, bite, nosh, refreshment. *I ate too many snacks and now I'm not hungry for supper.*

snafu *n.* mess, mistake, confusion, chaos, mix-up, (slang) screw-up. *We had quite a snafu down at the office today, but we eventually ironed it out.*

snag *n.* **1.** hitch, catch, obstacle, complication, difficulty. *Losing the plane tickets was a snag in our plans.* –*vb.* **1.** catch, pull, tear, rip. *He snagged his sweater on the fence.*

snake *n.* serpent, viper, rattlesnake, cobra, ophidian. *The zoo keeps its snakes in the reptile section.*

snap *vb.* **1.** click, crack, crackle, pop. *The audience snapped its fingers to the melody.* **2.** break, crack, fracture, separate. *She snapped the branch into two pieces.* **3.** clasp, join, catch, secure. *Please snap your jacket together in this cold weather.* **4.** nip, bite, chop. *The* *lizard snapped at the fly.* **5.** growl, grumble, snarl, bark. *She snapped at him when he asked a question. –n.* **6.** pop, crack, crackle, click. *I heard the snap of tree branches breaking.* **7.** catch, fastener, clasp. *The snap broke on his jeans.* **8.** nip, bite, chomp, snatch. *A crocodile's snap can be dangerous. –adj.* **9.** quick, sudden, hasty, abrupt. *Don't make a snap decision.* **Ant. 9.** thoughtful, careful, cautious.

snare *n.* **1.** trap, lure, decoy, net, noose. *A snare was set out to catch the injured raccoon. –vb.* **2.** trap, capture, hook, catch, seize. *The police snared the thief before he could get away.*

snatch *vb.* **1.** seize, grab, take, pluck, steal. *A mugger snatched the woman's purse. –n.* **2.** piece, part, fragment, portion, bit. *I overheard snatches of their conversation.*

sneak *vb.* **1.** slip, slink, creep, crawl, slither. *Let's sneak into the old haunted house tonight.* **2.** steal, smuggle, spirit, slip. *She tried to sneak a bowl of ice cream. –n.* **3.** scoundrel, rascal, knave, coward. *Only a sneak would leave without telling his friend. –adj.* **4.** covert, surprise, secret, underhand, unexpected. *The castle was captured in a sneak attack.*

sneaker *n.* sport shoe, running shoe, basketball shoe, walking shoe, boat shoe, deck shoe, footwear. *I play many different sports and require a cross-training sneaker*

sneaky *adj.* stealthy, devious, tricky, sly, underhanded, furtive (slang) weaselly. *Mice are sometimes sneaky enough to live underfoot without anyone noticing.*

sneering *adj.* mocking, ridiculing, sarcastic, scoffing, disdainful. *I don't like your sneering manner, sir.*

snicker *vb.* snigger, snort, sniggle, titter, chuckle, laugh. *If you children snicker one more time, I'm going to sent you to your rooms.*

snide *adj.* sarcastic, sardonic, nasty, malicious, hurtful, nasty. *I'm sick of your snide comments.* **Ant.** nice, complimentary, friendly.

snip *vb.* clip, cut, trim, shear, prune, chop. *Just snip off a little off the top, please.*

sniper *n.* assassin, shooter, gunman, ambusher, marksman, murderer. *The sniper turned out to be a first-rate sharpshooter.*

snippy *adj.* curt, short, smart-alecky, abrupt, brusque, snappish. *That clerk was more than rude, she was downright snippy!* **Ant.** courteous, kind, solicitous.

snob *n.* elitist, highbrow, (slang) stuffed shirt, parvenu, upstart, name-dropper. *The snob down the street acts as if he is embarrassed to be seen with us.*

snobbish *adj.* elitist, highbrow, snobby, (slang) stuck up, haughty, supercilious, (slang) snooty, pretentious. *Come down to earth and stop acting so snobbish.* **Ant.** humble, friendly, modest.

snoop *vb.* spy, pry, stick one's nose in, nose around. *Please don't snoop in my drawers.*

snooty *adj.* haughty, uppity, snobbish, snotty, supercilious, lofty. *Joe acts snooty because he believes he is better than everyone else.* **Ant.** down-to-earth, friendly.

snout *n.* nose, muzzle, nozzle, proboscis, beak. *The collie thrust his snout into the rabbit hole and snuffled excitedly.*

snow *n.* **1.** precipitation, snowflakes, flurries, hydrometeors, sleet, hail, blizzard, drift. *Maine receives well over six feet of snow every year. –vb.* **2.** precipitate, flurry, blizzard, blow, hail, sleet. *School was canceled this morning because it had snowed overnight.*

WORD SEARCH

bump or mound on ski trail: *mogul*
collapse, catastrophic: *avalanche*

compacted, old snow: *firn, crust*
granules, old, refrozen: *corn snow*
house of: *igloo*
pellets of: *graupel*
zero visibility due to whiteout: *blizzard*

snowboard *n.* board used to ride over snow. *Julie rented a snowboard during her winter holiday in Aspen.*

WORD SEARCH

airborne, getting: *catching air*
backwards stance, riding with a: *fakie*
crash or fall: *bail*
legs straightened, ride with one or both: *bone*
rotation, 180 degrees: *alley-oop*
rotation, 360 degrees: *caballerial*
run into rock or log: *bonk*
turn, make a turn: *carve*
vibrations, high speed: *chatter*
U-shaped ramp of snow: *half pipe*

snub *vb.* **1.** insult, slight, offend, spurn, shun. *The king snubbed his guest by refusing to shake his hand.* –*n.* **2.** insult, slight, rejection, discourtesy. *Not inviting him to your party was a snub.*

snug *adj.* **1.** cozy, safe, secure, comfortable, sheltered. *She felt snug in her warm bed.* **2.** tight, close-fitting, compact, close. *The shirt was a bit snug.* **Ant. 1.** unprotected, threatened. **2.** large, loose.

snuggle *vb.* cuddle, hug, nuzzle, embrace, nestle. *The girl snuggled with her puppy.*

soak *vb.* **1.** drench, flood, saturate, permeate, wet. *Rain soaked the dirt racing track.* **2.** mop, sop, dry, absorb. *She used a paper towel to soak up the spilled milk.*

soap *n.* detergent, cleanser, suds, wash powder, solvent. *Wash your hands with hot water and soap.*

soap opera *n.* melodrama, drama, program, play, show. *Soap operas have been playing on television for decades.*

soapy *adj.* sudsy, lathery, frothy, foamy, saponaceous. *I need to rinse out my soapy hair.*

soar *vb.* **1.** fly, glide, sail, float, wing, coast. *The falcon soared high in the sky.* **2.** rise, climb, mount, escalate, tower. *Temperatures soared during the summer.* **Ant. 2.** descend, fall.

sob *vb.* **1.** cry, weep, bawl, wail, snivel. *I sobbed when I heard the bad news.* –*n.* **2.** cry, wail, whimper, lamentation. *A sob escaped the unhappy man.* **Ant. 1–2.** laugh, giggle.

sober *adj.* **1.** serious, grim, grave, subdued, mellow. *The team's bad loss was a sober awakening.* **2.** dry, abstinent, temperate. *The sober man drove his drunken friend home.* **Ant. 1.** merry, joyful, silly. **2.** drunk, intoxicated.

sobriety *n.* soberness, abstinence, temperance, teetotalism, self-restraint. *The police are setting up roadblocks to check the sobriety of drivers.* **Ant.** drunkenness, intoxication, inebriation.

soccer *n.* football, sport. *Soccer is becoming one of our most popular sports.*

WORD SEARCH

goalie's long kick: *punt*
illegal position: *offside*
issue a card for a foul: *book, card, caution*
keeping the ball up in the air by bouncing off knee and other body parts: *juggling*
kick ball between defender's legs: *nutmeg*
officials: *linesmen, referee*
overhead kick: *bicycle kick, scissors kick*
penalty situation in which one team is a player short: *power play*
positions: *back, center back, center halfback, forward, fullback, goalkeeper, sweeper, winger*
running the ball downfield with feet: *dribbling*

soccer field: *pitch*
stop the ball's motion with body: *trap, kill*
three goals scored by one player in one game: *hat trick*

sociable *adj.* friendly, outgoing, hospitable, neighborly, cordial. *Ignoring your doorbell is not very sociable.* **Ant.** unsociable, unfriendly, withdrawn.

social *adj.* **1.** outgoing, sociable, friendly, amiable, extroverted. *Social people often like large parties.* **2.** community, communal, civic, common, public. *He's majoring in social studies.* **Ant. 1.** antisocial, introverted, solitary.

socialism *n.* Marxism, communism. *Some people believe we would have better health care under socialism.*

socialize *vb.* fraternize, mingle, befriend, associate, hobnob, entertain. *Some people like to socialize with friends after school.*

social security *n.* retirement income, disability insurance, unemployment insurance, old age insurance, government nest egg, entitlement program. *Most people will begin to collect social security at the age of sixty-five.*

society *n.* **1.** humanity, humankind, civilization, public, population. *Criminals are a danger to society.* **2.** group, association, organization, club, union. *She joined a bird-watching society.*

sociopath *n.* psychopath, antisocial personality, psychotic, maniac, lunatic, deranged person. *Police are on the lookout for a dangerous sociopath.*

sock *n.* **1.** stocking, hose, hosiery, anklet. *Her sock showed through the hole in her shoe.* **2.** punch, blow, smack, hit, strike. *The man was knocked out by a hard sock.* –*vb.* **3.** punch, hit, box, pound, smack. *The boxer socked his opponent.*

socket *n.* receptacle, receiving end, fitting, holder, chamber. *Plug the line into that socket over there.*

sod *n.* grass, turf, clod, sward, divot, clump. *To cover the bare spots in the yard, I'm going to put down some new sod.*

soda *n.* soft drink, pop, carbonated beverage, cola, ginger ale, root beer. *Grab a soda and quench your thirst.*

sofa *n.* couch, divan, lounge, davenport, chesterfield, convertible, futon. *We can seat four people on our sofa.*

soft *adj.* **1.** downy, silky, furry, smooth. *He fell asleep on the soft pillow.* **2.** mushy, squashy, spongy, doughy. *Please mash the potatoes until they become soft.* **3.** mellow, low, subdued, gentle, mild. *She likes listening to soft music.* **Ant. 1.** hard, stiff, rough. **2.** hard, solid, solidified. **3.** harsh, loud, strong, violent.

softhearted *adj.* compassionate, tender, sympathetic, merciful, lenient, easy. *Bill collectors can't afford to be softhearted.* **Ant.** hard, mean, cruel.

software *n.* program, instructions, disk, command. *You need a specific kind of software to run a word processing program.*

soggy *adj.* soaked, saturated, drenched, pasty, mushy. *The sandwich was soggy after she dropped it in the pond.* **Ant.** dry, hard.

soil *n.* **1.** earth, dirt, ground, humus, loam. *Farmers need fertile soil for their crops.* –*vb.* **2.** dirty, stain, muddy, smudge, foul. *The baby soiled her diapers.*

solace *n.* **1.** comfort, support, cheer, encouragement. *The priest's presence was a solace to the dying man.* –*vb.* **2.** comfort, cheer, console, hearten. *Her kind words solaced her heartbroken friend.* **Ant. 1.** upset, pain, agony. **2.** upset, distress, sadden.

solar system *n.* planetary system, celestial grouping. *There are nine planets and one Sun in our solar system.*

soldier *n.* warrior, service personnel, mercenary, fighter, GI, (slang) leatherneck. *A soldier is required to be exceptionally courageous.*

sole *adj.* only single, exclusive, lone, solitary. *He was the sole survivor of the terrible airplane crash.* **Ant.** multiple, shared.

solemn *adj.* grave, grim, unsmiling, somber, serious. *People were solemn during the funeral service.* **Ant.** frivolous, smiling, jolly.

solicit *vb.* request, seek, plead, beseech, beg. *That charity solicits money from people.*

solicitous *adj.* concerned, caring, attentive, worried, motherly, apprehensive. *We are quite solicitous with our children when they are sick.* **Ant.** uncaring, indifferent, apathetic.

solid *adj.* **1.** dense, hard, condensed, firm, compacted. *Ice is a solid form of water.* **2.** reliable, sound, steady, stable, worthy. *The actor gave a solid performance.* **3.** unbroken, continuous, uninterrupted. *She wore a solid yellow sweatshirt.* **Ant. 1.** liquid, gaseous. **2.** shaky, unsteady. **3.** discontinuous.

solidarity *n.* unity, unification, union, consensus, oneness, alliance, unanimity. *There was an impressive solidarity within our group on which way to vote.* **Ant.** division, dissension, individuality.

solidify *vb.* harden, thicken, set, fix, compress. *Molten lava eventually solidifies into rock.* **Ant.** dissolve, liquefy.

solitary *adj.* isolated, secluded, reclusive, individual, single. *The mountain man lived a solitary lifestyle.*

solitude *n.* aloneness, seclusion, loneliness, reclusion, isolation, remoteness. *With ever expanding urban sprawl, there are fewer and fewer places left in the world to experience true solitude.*

solo *adj.* **1.** lone, unaccompanied, single-handed, alone, unassisted. *We attended her first solo performance.* –*adv.* **2.** alone, unaccompanied, unassisted, single-handedly. *The piano player grew nervous whenever he had to perform solo.* **Ant. 1.** accompanied, group, assisted. **2.** accompanied, assisted.

solution *n.* **1.** answer, key, explanation, clarification, unraveling. *She figured out the solution to the math problem.* **2.** liquid, fluid, mixture, emulsion, solvent. *He heated the chemical solution.* **Ant. 1.** problem, question, dilemma.

solve *vb.* answer, resolve, untangle, unravel, explain. *It took several hours to solve the crossword puzzle.*

somber *adj.* grim, serious, gloomy, solemn, mournful. *We listened to her somber retelling of the story.* **Ant.** joyful, happy, gleeful.

somersault *n.* flip, roll, tumble, revolution. *The child was forbidden from performing backwards somersaults on his bed.*

song *n.* melody, tune, verse, hymn, refrain, ballad. *They danced to their favorite songs.*

WORD SEARCH

advertisement: *jingle*
award for best: *Grammy*
funeral: *dirge, requiem*
improvise: *vamp*
lyrics sung by multiple vocalists in timed succession: *canon, round*
multivoiced: *polyphonic*
passage: *refrain*
religious: *anthem, canticle, chorale, psalm, hymn*
sailor's: *shanty*
sung in counterpoint with another vocalist: *madrigal, call and response*
sung without instrumental accompaniment: *a cappella*
vocalizations impersonating jazz instruments: *scat*
words: *lyrics*

soon *adv.* quickly, rapidly, directly, shortly, promptly. *The starving child needs food as soon as possible.*

soot *n.* carbon, grit, particles, particulate, ash. *The firemen are taking samples of soot to determine if the fire was due to arson.*

soothe *vb.* relieve, ease, calm, relax, quiet. *A massage soothed his sore muscles.* **Ant.** irritate, upset, agitate.

soothing *adj.* calming, relaxing, tranquilizing, mollifying, comforting, softening. *Moisturizer is soothing on dry skin.* **Ant.** irritating, intensifying, aggravating.

sophisticated *adj.* **1.** worldly, urbane, experienced, refined, (slang) hip, cosmopolitan. *The sophisticated diners knew exactly what to do with their finger bowls.* **2.** complex, complicated, high-tech, intricate, involved, elaborate. *Computer technology is highly sophisticated.* **Ant. 1.** naive, unsophisticated, simple. **2.** simple, low-tech.

sophistry *n.* fallacious reasoning, deception, subterfuge, misrepresentation, chicanery. *The lawyer used sophistry more than evidence to make the defendant appear guilty.*

sophomoric *adj.* juvenile, adolescent, immature, inexperienced, callow, childish, foolish. *The teacher failed to find anything amusing in her student's sophomoric prank.* **Ant.** mature, adult, grown-up.

sorcerer *n.* wizard, warlock, conjurer, necromancer, witch, shaman. *The sorcerer turned the handsome prince into a flounder.*

sorcery *n.* wizardry, black arts, black magic, witchcraft, spellbinding, necromancy. *The witch used sorcery to influence others.*

sordid *adj.* vulgar, corrupt, unclean, dirty, foul. *The actor's sordid affair gained national attention.* **Ant.** clean, upstanding, moral.

sore *adj.* **1.** painful, tender, sensitive, bruised. *His cut is still very sore.* **2.** angry, annoyed, upset, irritated, resentful. *Are you still sore about yesterday's argument? –n.* **3.** injury, cut, gash, bruise, hurt, wound. *I bandaged the large sore on his leg.* **Ant. 2.** pleased, glad.

sorrow *n.* **1.** sadness, grief, anguish, unhappiness, distress. *We felt sorrow for the crash victims' families.* **2.** misfortune, disaster, loss, hardship, affliction. *His mother's death was a hard sorrow for him to bear. –vb.* **3.** mourn, grieve, despair, agonize, lament. *She sorrowed over the seal pup's death at the hands of hunters.* **Ant. 1.** gladness, happiness. **2.** joy, pleasure. **3.** celebrate.

sorrowful *adj.* sad, unhappy, gloomy, depressed, heartbroken. *The novel had a sorrowful ending.* **Ant.** happy, joyous, merry.

sorry *adj.* **1.** remorseful, apologetic, regretful, ashamed. *She said she was sorry for being rude.* **2.** sad, unhappy, downcast, depressed. *We are sorry you missed the party.* **3.** miserable, wretched, pitiful, sad. *My mother said my room was in a sorry state.* **Ant. 1.** happy, unremorseful. **2.** pleased, joyful. **3.** fine, decent.

sort *n.* **1.** kind, type, manner, variety, brand. *She's not the sort of person who tells lies. –vb.* **2.** sift, search, comb, rummage, probe. *She sorted through the trash for her lost letter.* **3.** arrange, organize, categorize, classify, index. *Please sort the papers by subject matter.*

sortie *n.* raid, attack, assault, mission, offensive. *The military is planning on launching a dozen sorties over enemy territory today.*

soul *n.* inner being, spirit, entity, psyche, ego, self. *Does a person's soul survive after death?*

sound *n.* **1.** noise, clamor, racket, blare, ring, creak. *He heard the sound of music coming from the auditorium. –vb.* **2.** ring, toll, reverberate, peal, rumble. *The alarm sounded throughout the* *city.* **3.** seem, appear, look. *Your trip sounds interesting.* **4.** pronounce, voice, express, articulate. *Please sound out the long words.* *–adj.* **5.** strong, sturdy, solid, undamaged, firm. *The inspector said the old house is still sound.* **Ant. 5.** unsound, unstable, shaky, damaged.

soup *n.* stew, broth, chowder, bouillon, stock, bisque. *My mother makes a great vegetable soup.*

WORD SEARCH

available ingredients, made from any: *Mulligan stew*
beef or veal with onions and paprika: *goulash*
beets, cabbage, potatoes, etc., often served cold with sour cream: *borscht*
broth from meat or vegetable stock, clear: *bouillon, consommé*
broth with beaten eggs: *egg drop soup*
Chinese specialty comprised of clear broth and dumplings: *won ton*
eggplant, zucchini, tomatoes, onions, etc.: *ratatouille*
hotly seasoned with tripe, meat, vegetables and dumplings: *pepper pot*
Indian specialty comprised of curried chicken with rice and coconut: *mulligatawny*
Japanese specialty comprised of fermented soy beans, onions and seaweed: *miso*
letter-shaped pasta, with: *alphabet soup*
liquid created when cooking meat or vegetables in seasoned water: *broth, stock*
meatless soup with pasta, barley, and beans or peas: *minestrone*
okra pods, seafood, ham and tomato soup: *gumbo*
onion soup topped with toast and cheese: *French onion soup*
seafood, any chunky: *chowder*
shellfish, creamy: *bisque*
Scottish specialty made from chicken, leeks and barley: *cock-a-leekie*
southwest or Mexican specialty with beans, ground beef, tomatoes and chilies: *chili*
Spanish specialty comprised of pureed tomatoes, cucumbers, peppers and onions, served cold: *gazpacho*
white wine broth with seafood and vegetables: *bouillabaisse*

sour *adj.* **1.** tart, vinegary, tangy, bitter, acidic. *Lemons have a sour taste.* **2.** spoiled, curdled, fermented, bad. *I think the old milk is sour.* *–vb.* **3.** spoil, curdle, ferment, turn. *The milk soured after several weeks.* **Ant. 1.** mild, pleasant, sweet. **2.** fresh, good.

source *n.* **1.** origin, head, beginning, start. *The river's source is high in the mountains.* **2.** informant, advisor, reference, authority. *He used several magazine sources for his term paper.* **Ant. 1.** end, termination, outcome.

souvenir *n.* keepsake, memento, reminder, remembrance. *Tourists often bring back souvenirs.*

sovereign *n.* **1.** monarch, emperor, ruler, lord, queen, king. *The peasants bowed before their sovereign.* *–adj.* **2.** monarchical, imperial, absolute, supreme. *The peasants resented the ruler's sovereign power.* **3.** independent, self-ruling, self-governing. *The United States is a sovereign nation.*

spa *n.* health facility, health club, resort, therapeutic facility, bath, tub. *I'm going to get a massage and a mudpack at the spa.*

space *n.* **1.** separation, gap, opening, break, span, interval. *Please leave a space between your first and last names.* **2.** area, expanse, room, distance, spread. *She needs her own personal space.* *–vb.* **3.** place, separate, order, arrange, distance. *He spaced his trophies a foot apart.*

WORD SEARCH

conglomeration of stars: *galaxy*
distance measurements: *astronomical unit, light-year, parsec*

galaxy, our: *Milky Way*
gas cloud, immense: *nebula*
object at the edge of the universe, bright: *quasar*

spacecraft *n.* spaceship, space vessel, rocket, capsule, orbiter, probe, shuttle. *Modern spacecraft are largely controlled by computers.*

WORD SEARCH

activity outside craft, astronaut's: *spacewalk, EVA (extravehicular activity)*
agency: *NASA, National Aeronautics and Space Agency*
cancel launch: *abort, scrub*
cargo: *payload*
chamber, pressure-equalizing: *airlock*
entry into Earth's atmosphere: *reentry*
firing of thrusters: *burn*
flight path: *trajectory*
gravity force exactly equal to that on Earth: *one g*
mission nerve centers: *mission control*
orbital altitude due to Earth's pull, loss of: *decay*
orbit matching that of Earth's rotation: *geosynchronous orbit*
sound, five times the speed of: *hypersonic*
rocket employed to slow vessel's speed: *retro rocket*
rocket providing additional lift: *booster*
wall: *bulkhead*

spacey *adj.* (slang) confused, unfocused, daydreaming, (slang) lost in a fog, (slang) out to lunch, weird. *Eddy is too spacey to be an airport flight controller.* **Ant.** sharp, focused.

spacious *adj.* roomy, sizable, large, uncrowded, vast. *The mansion was quite spacious.* **Ant.** crowded, small, tiny, narrow.

span *vb.* **1.** cover, cross, bridge, join, link. *A bridge spanned the river.* –*n.* **2.** length, range, stretch, duration, period. *A sequoia tree's life span can be several thousand years.*

spank *vb.* swat, hit, slap, wallop, smack, rap. *Many parents spank their toddlers who misbehave.*

spare *vb.* **1.** save, rescue, exempt, withhold, pardon. *The pig was spared from the slaughterhouse.* **2.** sacrifice, afford, lend, give, relinquish. *Can you spare a dollar?* –*adj.* **3.** extra, unused, substitute, reserve. *She used her spare tire to replace the one that had gone flat.* **4.** lanky, lean, skinny, thin, gaunt. *My aunt is strong despite her spare build.* **Ant.** **1.** condemn, doom, expose. **4.** large, stocky.

sparkle *vb.* **1.** glitter, twinkle, flash, shimmer, glimmer. *The gems sparkled in the treasure chest.* –*n.* **2.** spark, gleam, glitter, twinkle, dazzle. *There is a sparkle in his eyes when he laughs.*

sparse *adj.* scarce, scattered, scanty, thin, meager. *The Sahara Desert has sparse vegetation.* **Ant.** abundant, dense, lush, rank.

spartan *adj.* self-disciplined, demanding, strict, self-restrained, austere, rigid. *He put himself on a spartan diet to lose weight but was absolutely miserable.* **Ant.** undisciplined, lavish, undemanding.

spasm *n.* seizure, contraction, convulsion, fit, cramp. *She had a painful spasm in her lower back.*

spasmodic *adj.* convulsive, twitchy, spastic, fitful. *During sleep, dogs sometimes become spasmodic as they attempt to act out their dreams.*

spatter *n.* sprinkle, speckle, spot, shower, scatter. *Be careful or you'll spatter paint everywhere.*

speak *vb.* talk, communicate, vocalize, converse, discuss, lecture. *She can speak in both English and Japanese.*

speaker *n.* orator, speech-giver, lecturer, spokesman, spokeswoman, talker. *A speaker from the university will give a lecture on environmentalism today.*

spear *n.* **1.** lance, harpoon, javelin, spike. *Early American Indians used spears to hunt buffalo. –vb.* **2.** pierce, lance, impale, spit. *The warrior speared the buffalo.*

spearhead *vb.* originate, begin, initiate, start, launch, ignite, spark. *She is credited with spearheading the movement for equal rights.*

special *adj.* **1.** distinctive, unique, individual, particular, exceptional, extraordinary. *She gave her boyfriend a special gift. –n.* **2.** specialty, highlight, feature, selection. *The restaurant's Thursday special is roast beef.*

specialist *n.* expert, authority, ace, professional, master, devotee. *The city hired a tree specialist to save the dying elms.*

specialty *n.* focus, specialization, competence, strength, distinction. *The scientist's specialty is Greek archaeology.*

species *n.* classification, category, type, breed, kind. *Dogs belong to the canine species.*

specific *adj.* detailed, precise, exact, definite, particular. *Please give more specific directions to your house.* **Ant.** general, vague, inexact, ambiguous.

specify *vb.* state, indicate, define, stipulate, detail, clarify. *When placing an order, please specify your shirt size.*

specimen *n.* sample, example, representative, piece, cutting. *The geologist brought back several rock specimens.*

specious *adj.* sophistic, misleading, fallacious, hollow, deceptive, invalid, unsound. *The attorney employed a number of specious arguments that sounded good but were in fact erroneous.* **Ant.** valid, accurate, true.

speck *n.* fleck, particle, spot, drop, dot. *He wiped a speck of lint off his glasses.*

spectacle *n.* presentation, performance, pageant, extravaganza, sight. *We watched the fireworks spectacle.*

spectacular *adj.* sensational, impressive, remarkable, dramatic, magnificent. *The volcano erupted with a spectacular explosion.* **Ant.** unimpressive, ordinary, tame.

spectator *n.* watcher, observer, viewer, bystander, onlooker. *The spectators watched in horror as their team lost the championship.*

specter *n.* ghost, spirit, apparition, phantom, poltergeist, (slang) spook. *As a child I was always afraid a specter would fly out of my closet at night.*

speculate *vb.* **1.** guess, ponder, contemplate, conjecture, hypothesize. *We can only speculate about her chances of success.* **2.** trade, gamble, venture. *The investment firm speculates in real estate.*

speculation *n.* **1.** thought, thinking, reflection, contemplation, rumination. *It's only speculation right now, but I might open my own pizza parlor next year.* **2.** guess, guesswork, theory, conjecture, presumption. *That life exists on other planets is only speculation.*

speculative *adj.* conjectural, unproven, iffy, presumptive, theoretical, hypothetical. *Whether there is life on other planets is still speculative.* **Ant.** confirmed, factual, certain.

speech *n.* **1.** talk, oration, discussion, conversation, lecture. *The president's speech was televised nationally.* **2.** speaking, talking, dialect, language. *People's speech differs throughout the country.*

speechless *adj.* dumbstruck, mute, tongue-tied, dumbfounded, uncommunicative, silent, wordless. *He was struck speechless by the award.*

speed *n.* 1. quickness, swiftness, haste, velocity, rapidity, promptness. *He solved the problem with amazing speed.* –*vb.* 2. advance, further, promise, stimulate, assist. *Heat will speed the drying process.* 3. race, whiz, shoot, rush, fly, zoom. *We watched cars speed around the racetrack.* **Ant.** 1. slowness, sluggishness. 2. slow, halt. 3. walk, crawl.

speedy *adj.* rapid, swift, quick, fast, fleet. *The pizza parlor promises a speedy delivery.* **Ant.** slow, late, unhurried, leisurely.

spell *n.* 1. stretch, span, period, interval, bout. *We had a spell of bad weather.* 2. enchantment, charm, bewitchment, incantation. *The sorceress cast an invisibility spell to cloak our escape.*

spellbinding *adj.* enchanting, hypnotic, entrancing, mesmerizing, charming, magical. *I found the author's latest book to be absolutely spellbinding.*

spellbound *adj.* enchanted, hypnotized, entranced, mesmerized, charmed, bewitched. *I was spellbound by the actor's performance.*

spend *vb.* 1. pay, expend, invest, disburse, waste. *People often spend large sums of money on holiday gifts.* 2. pass, occupy, fill. *She is going to spend the weekend at the beach.* **Ant.** 1. conserve, keep, maintain, save.

spendthrift *n.* spender, squanderer, prodigal, wastrel, profligate. *Unfortunately, Mr. Johnston's son was a spendthrift and completely frittered away his inheritance.* **Ant.** miser, hoarder, pennypincher.

sphere *n.* 1. globe, ball, oval, orb, spheroid. *A bowling ball has the shape of a sphere.* 2. field, domain, realm, area, scope. *That subject is not within his sphere of knowledge.*

spice *n.* 1. seasoning, herb, flavoring, relish. *The chef added spices to the soup.* 2. relish, charm, appeal, zest. *Variety is the spice of life.* –*vb.* 3. season, flavor, accent, enliven. *She spiced her muffins with nutmeg and cinnamon.*

spike *n.* 1. peg, nail, stud, prong, point, barb. *Soccer shoes have spikes on their bottoms.* –*vb.* 2. pierce, prick, spear, stick, impale. *I spiked the marshmallows with a skewer.*

spill *vb.* 1. slosh, splash, empty, drop, pour. *Juice spilled out of the overturned glass.* –*n.* 2. seepage, leakage, leak, outflowing. *It took many months to clean up the oil spill.* 3. tumble, fall, plunge, roll, accident. *He took a bad spill on his bike.*

spin *vb.* 1. turn, whirl, twirl, revolve, rotate. *The contestants will spin a giant wheel.* 2. narrate, relate, tell, concoct, invent. *The old sailor liked to spin tall tales.* –*n.* 3. turn, twirl, rotation, revolution. *She gave the wheel a spin.* 4. ride, drive, jaunt, run. *We took a spin in the new car.*

spin-off *n.* outgrowth, offshoot, by-product, derivative. *The network executives are considering developing spin-offs from their latest hit show.*

spinster *n.* old maid, widow, divorcée. *The old spinster was perfectly happy never to have married.*

spirit *n.* 1. soul, essence, psyche, heart, life force. *Religious people believe their spirits will survive after death.* 2. ghost, phantom, shade, wraith, ghoul. *She was afraid of evil spirits in the haunted house.* 3. enthusiasm, energy, eagerness, zeal, bravery. *She lives life with a great deal of spirit.* 4. mood, emotions, morale, resolve, feelings. *Our spirits were low after the team's loss.* 5. alcohol, liquor, whiskey. *The liquor store sold several types of spirits.* –*vb.* 6. abduct, kidnap, seize, snatch. *A kidnapper spirited away the two children.* **Ant.** 1. body, flesh. 3. lifelessness, fearfulness, timidity.

spirited *adj.* lively, animated, energetic, enthusiastic, charged, dynamic. *We played a highly spirited game against the cross-town rivals.* **Ant.** lifeless, dispirited, dead.

spiritual *adj.* **1.** bodiless, nonmaterial, psychic, ghostly, supernatural. *The cemetery was haunted by spiritual creatures.* **2.** pious, devout, religious, holy, righteous. *The nuns led a spiritual life.* **Ant. 1.** physical, material. **2.** nonspiritual, secular, worldly.

spit *n.* saliva, expectorate, spittle, drool, sputum, (slang) loogie. *Do you really think I want a drink of soda with your spit in it?*

spite *n.* **1.** resentment, malice, hatred, revengefulness. *That cruel remark was said out of spite.* *–vb.* **2.** annoy, irritate, provoke, needle, nettle. *He missed the party just to spite you.* **Ant. 1.** love, kindness, forgiveness. **2.** please, delight, humor.

spiteful *adj.* malicious, vindictive, vengeful, mean, hateful, hurtful. *Some spiteful person put a tack in my chair.*

splash *vb.* splatter, spray, spurt, squirt, slosh, slop. *Don't splash that cold water on me.*

splendid *adj.* magnificent, brilliant, remarkable, excellent, beautiful. *We were pleased by her splendid musical performance.* **Ant.** poor, unremarkable, dreadful, awful.

splendor *n.* magnificence, brilliance, beauty, nobility, glory. *The splendor of the palace is awe-inspiring.* **Ant.** dullness, drabness, plainness.

splice *vb.* join, connect, bind, graft, link, unite. *The editor spliced two pieces of film together.* **Ant.** cut, break, disconnect.

split *vb.* **1.** divide, separate, break, allocate, allot. *The friends plan to split the prize money between them.* **2.** burst, break, splinter, snap, rip. *The man's bulging suitcase split open.* *–n.* **3.** break, rift, separation, tear, rent. *These pants have a split in the seam.* *–adj.* **4.** mixed, divided, separated, ruptured, broken. *The judges said it was a split decision.* **Ant. 1.** join, united, merge. **3.** merger, connection, closure. **4.** unbroken, unanimous.

spoil *vb.* **1.** ruin, wreck, destroy, damage, impair. *The rain spoiled our plans for a picnic.* **2.** rot, decay, mold, sour, curdle. *Meat left out of the refrigerator will spoil.* **3.** pamper, baby, indulge, overindulge, coddle. *His wealthy parents have spoiled him.* *–n.* **4.** loot, plunder, booty, takings. *The pirates gloated over the spoils.* **Ant. 1.** improve, better. **2.** keep, preserve. **3.** discipline, toughen.

spoiled *adj.* **1.** rotten, putrid, putrefied, decomposed, decayed, moldy. *That meat is spoiled.* **2.** overindulged, indulged, coddled, mollycoddled, pampered, babied. *The toy-throwing child was spoiled rotten.* **Ant. 1.** fresh, good, palatable. **2.** disciplined, deprived, hardened.

spokesman *n.* spokeswoman, speaker, PR person, representative, voice, prolocutor. *The spokesman for the company said the oil spill was an accident.*

sponsor *n.* **1.** supporter, endorser, promoter, adviser, patron. *Her sponsor in the drug recovery program is very supportive.* *–vb.* **2.** finance, support, endorse, back, promote. *A local business has agreed to sponsor our softball team.*

spontaneous *adj.* impulsive, unplanned, unhesitating, automatic, natural. *Small children's actions are often quite spontaneous.* **Ant.** planned, deliberate, calculated.

spoof *n.* parody, satire, take-off, lampoon, burlesque, comedy. *The comedy troupe loved to perform spoofs of Washington politics.*

spooky *adj.* creepy, scary, ghostly, haunted, macabre, eerie. *A cemetery is always spooky at night.*

sport *n.* 1. game, athletics, competition, contest, recreation. *Her favorite sport is volleyball.* –*vb.* 2. trifle, toy, play, frolic, romp. *The cat sported with an injured mouse.* 3. display, exhibit, bear, wear, show off. *The car sported a sunroof.* **Ant.** 1. work, job. 2. work, toil.

spot *n.* 1. place, location, site, position, point. *The campers found a good spot for their tent.* 2. dot, blot, mark, speck, dab. *The paint left a spot on her shirt.* –*vb.* 3. sprinkle, speck, mark, dot, stain. *Spilled ink spotted the table.* 4. detect, spy, see, observe, discover, perceive. *A detective spotted the suspicious man as he entered the airport.*

spotty *adj.* sporadic, irregular, intermittent, erratic, patchy, variable. *I'm afraid that your record for showing up on time is rather spotty.* **Ant.** regular, consistent, solid.

spouse *n.* husband, wife, mate, companion, partner, significant other. *I have been married to my current spouse for ten years.*

spout *vb.* 1. spurt, squirt, gush, spew, erupt, discharge. *Water spouted from the broken pipe.* –*n.* 2. vent, nozzle, nose, outlet. *Water shot out of the whale's spout.* 3. jet, spray, fountain, flow, spurt. *A spout of water and steam emerged from the geyser.* **Ant.** 1–3. drip, dribble, trickle.

sprain *vb.* wrench, twist, strain, tear ligaments. *Basketball players probably sprain their ankles more than any other athletes.*

sprawl *vb.* flop, loll, slump, slouch, lie. *The tired track runner sprawled on the field.*

spray *n.* 1. drizzle, droplets, shower, mist, foam, splatter. *Ocean spray soaked the front of the ship.* –*vb.* 2. shower, drizzle, splatter, spatter. *The gardener sprayed water on his flowers.*

spread *vb.* 1. stretch, extend, unfold, widen, increase. *The soldiers spread out to search the area.* 2. cover, coat, smear, smooth, blanket. *She spread jam on her toast.* 3. circulate, broadcast, distribute, radiate, scatter. *Please spread the word about the changes we've made.* –*n.* 4. expansion, growth, increase advance. *The fire's spread was aided by fierce winds.* 5. range, expanse, sweep, stretch. *The rancher's spread is enormous.* 6. cover, quilt, blanket, mantle. *The spread fell off my bed during the night.* **Ant.** 1. collect, compress. 3. confine, suppress. 4. shrinkage.

spreadsheet *n.* accounting program, accounting software, bookkeeping program. *Before you start in business, you should learn how to use a spreadsheet.*

spring *vb.* 1. jump, leap, bound, lunge, bounce. *A bobcat sprang from behind the bushes.* 2. release, trigger, discharge, free. *The mouse sprang the trap when it ate the cheese.* 3. emerge, arise, sprout, appear, spurt. *Flowers sprang up all over the hillside.* –*n.* 4. hop, bounce, jump, leap, buoyancy. *There was a spring in the joyful woman's walk.* 5. coil, spiral. *The mattress spring broke when I jumped on the bed.* 6. pool, water hole, well, fountain. *The moose drank from a mountain spring.* **Ant.** 1. crawl, slither, creep, drop.

springy *adj.* elastic, resilient, flexible, bouncy, rubbery. *This bed is too springy for my back.*

sprinkle *vb.* 1. spray, shower, powder, splatter, spread. *We sprinkled the cookies with tiny candies.* 2. drizzle, dribble, rain, shower, mist. *It may sprinkle during the night.* –*n.* 3. scattering, smattering, dash, touch, trace. *There was a sprinkle of gray in his hair.* 4. drizzle, shower, mist, dribble, rain. *Do we need an umbrella in this light sprinkle?*

sprint *vb.* run, dash, race, tear, rush, go all out. *Watch Mary sprint toward the finish line.*

sprout *vb.* 1. develop, grow, blossom, bud, bloom, flower. *New buds sprouted on the tree.*

–*n.* **2.** seedling, shoot, offshoot, stem. *She enjoys bean sprouts in her salad.*

spry *adj.* vigorous, lively, active, nimble, hearty, vital. *He was a spry eighty-year-old who still ran marathons.* **Ant.** lifeless, dead, bedridden.

spunk *n.* courage, guts, nerve, chutzpah, spirit, backbone, grit. *That cat's got a lot of spunk to go up against a pit bull.* **Ant.** cowardice, feebleness, spinelessness.

spunky *adj.* courageous, gutsy, plucky, gritty, tough, spirited. *You have to be pretty spunky to join the marines.* **Ant.** cowardly, feeble, spineless.

spur *n.* **1.** incentive, stimulus, goad, encouragement, motive. *The extra money was a spur to the artist's progress.* –*vb.* **2.** goad, prod, encourage, hasten, stimulate. *The will to succeed spurred her on to great accomplishments.* **Ant. 1.** discouragement, curb, obstacle. **2.** restrain, discourage.

spurious *adj.* false, fake, unauthentic, bogus, fraudulent, sham, apocryphal. *The signature on the document turned out to be spurious.* **Ant.** real, authentic, genuine.

spurn *vb.* reject, dismiss, rebuff, scorn, disregard. *He spurned her offer of help.* **Ant.** accept, welcome.

spy *n.* **1.** agent, secret agent, mole, operative, saboteur. *The spy was caught stealing secret information.* –*vb.* **2.** snoop, scout, peep, pry, eavesdrop. *He was accused of having spied for the enemy.* **3.** glimpse, see, detect, observe, notice. *She spied the famous singer entering through the back door.*

spying *n.* espionage, intelligence gathering, infiltration, eavesdropping, bugging. *If we're going to keep this new development secret, we need to safeguard against spying.*

WORD SEARCH

agency that collects intelligence worldwide, U.S. government: *CIA, Central Intelligence Agency*
CIA agent who secretly works for enemy: *mole*
coded communication science: *cryptology*
code form, put into: *encrypt, encipher*
code name: *cryptonym*
expose as a spy: *burn*
group of spies: *cell*
information that is gathered, secret: *intelligence*
narrow point, such as a bridge, where enemy travels are easily monitored: *chokepoint*
location where item is dropped off to be picked up by someone else later: *dead drop*
microphone, concealed: *bug, listening device*
misleading or phony information: *disinformation, counterintelligence*
penetration into enemy domain: *infiltration*
photo reduced to size of a pinhead: *microdot*
safe haven: *safe house*
secret code: *cipher*
secret, information that must be kept: *classified*
signaling technique in which telephone is rung a given number of times but nobody speaks: *dead telephone*
undercover or secret: *covert*
watching in secret: *surveillance*

squabble *vb.* **1.** argue, fight, wrangle, quarrel, disagree, scrap, quibble. *Every morning we heard the husband squabble with his wife over who would read the sports section first.* –*n.* **2.** argument, fight, quarrel, disagreement, scrap, wrangle, disagreement. *They had a minor squabble but quickly made up.* **Ant. 1.** agree, come to terms. **2.** agreement, accord.

squad *n.* unit, group, outfit, platoon, company, troop. *A special police squad was called in to dismantle the bomb.*

squalid *adj.* filthy, miserable, shabby, dingy, impoverished. *The poor family lived in squalid conditions.* **Ant.** royal, fine, attractive.

squall *n.* storm, gale, gust, flurry, tempest. *A sudden squall dropped ten inches of rain.*

squalor *n.* filth, shabbiness, seediness, dinginess, poverty, wretchedness. *They lived in squalor in a run-down tenement house.* **Ant.** luxury, splendor, affluence.

squander *vb.* waste, misspend, misuse, blow, lavish. *She squandered her money on fancy cars.* **Ant.** save, hoard.

square *n.* **1.** quadrangle, quad, rectangle, block, box. *My room is shaped like a square.* **2.** plaza, park, marketplace, commons. *A band was playing in the town square.* –*vb.* **3.** agree, match, fit, conform, correspond. *His story squares with all the news reports.* **Ant.** **1.** circle, triangle. **3.** disagree, differ.

squash *vb.* **1.** crush, smash, squeeze, mash, flatten. *The closing door squashed her hand.* **2.** suppress, strangle, smother, crush. *The dictator squashed all public demonstrations.* **Ant.** **2.** encourage, support, back.

squat *vb.* **1.** crouch, stoop, hunker, hunch, kneel. *The camper squatted down by the fire.* **2.** settle, encamp, inhabit, live, dwell. *A homeless family squatted in the abandoned building.* –*adj.* **3.** thickset, chunky, short, stocky, pudgy. *The squat man was unable to reach the top shelf.* **Ant.** **1.** stand. **3.** lean, lanky, slim.

squatter *n.* settler, claimant. *Squatters are laying claim to the unsettled land outside town.*

squawk *vb.* crow, hoot, screech, squeal, cry, protest. *The crows squawk whenever a hawk flies nearby.*

squeal *vb.* **1.** shriek, yelp, screech, wail. *The pigs squealed in delight when the farmer fed them.* **2.** inform, tell, betray, incriminate. *My brother squealed on me.* –*n.* **3.** shriek, yelp, screech, scream. *The small child let out a squeal when he saw the snake.*

squeamish *adj.* queasy, nauseous, sick, upset, shaky. *Do you become squeamish when you dissect frogs?*

squeeze *vb.* **1.** stuff, crowd, jam, pack, compress. *Ten people squeezed themselves into the tiny car.* **2.** wring, crush, twist, force, press. *She squeezed juice from the orange.* –*n.* **3.** embrace, hug, crushing, pinching, pressing. *Please give your beach towel a good squeeze to remove any excess water.*

squelch *vb.* hush, quiet, quell, crush, squash. *The harsh government squelched all forms of protest.* **Ant.** encourage, provoke, arouse.

squirm *vb.* wiggle, wriggle, twist, jerk, shift. *A worm squirmed in the bird's beak.*

squirt *vb.* **1.** splash, spray, spurt, splatter, jet. *Juice squirted from the ripe tomato.* –*n.* **2.** spurt, spray, fountain, jet, stream. *My brother hit me with a squirt from his water pistol.*

stabilize *vb.* steady, secure, brace, support, square, strengthen, fortify. *We placed a shim under the chair's broken leg to stabilize it.* **Ant.** destabilize, weaken, loosen.

stable *adj.* **1.** steady, fixed, firm, immovable, sound, enduring, lasting. *My parents have stable incomes that our family depends on.* –*vb.* **2.** pen, corral, house, quarter. *She stabled her horse in the nearest stall.* –*n.* **3.** barn, stall, corral, pen. *The donkeys were kept in a stable.* **Ant.** **1.** unstable, unsteady, shaky, momentary.

stack *n.* **1.** heap, pile, mound, batch, bundle. *He poured syrup on his pancake stack.* **2.** smokestack, chimney, funnel, flue. *Smoke billowed from the factory's stack.* –*vb.* **3.** heap, pile, lump, load, assemble. *The clerk stacked bottles on the shelf.* **Ant.** **3.** scatter, spread.

stadium *n.* arena, coliseum, athletic field, bowl, circus, amphitheater, sports complex. *We watched the game through binoculars from the last row of the stadium.*

staff *n.* 1. cane, stick, rod, pole, wand. *The sorceress used her staff to destroy the monster.* 2. crew, force, team, employees, personnel. *The famous restaurant has a talented staff.* –*vb.* 3. manage, tend, service, work. *Local residents staff the village inn.*

stage *n.* 1. phase, step, level, leg, period. *Our movie is in the first stage of production.* 2. platform, podium, dais, stand. *Curtains concealed the theater's stage.* 3. theater, arena, location, setting, place. *The South was the stage for many Civil War battles.* –*vb.* 4. perform, act, present, produce, dramatize. *The drama students staged a Shakespearean play.*

stagger *vb.* 1. stumble, reel, lurch, sway, totter. *The injured woman staggered into the hospital.* 2. stun, shock, startle, astound, jolt. *He was staggered by the news of his friend's death.* 3. alternate, fluctuate, zigzag, overlap. *The theater staggered its seats.*

stagnant *adj.* motionless, stationary, inactive, stale, polluted. *Frogs often live in stagnant ponds.* **Ant.** moving, running, fresh, unpolluted.

stagnate *vb.* stop, pause, idle, decline, fester, rot. *The rate of unemployment rose when the nation's economy stagnated.* **Ant.** grow, flow, flourish, expand.

staid *adj.* serious, restrained, sober, solemn, proper, formal. *Our math teacher was so staid and formal, he only rarely smiled.* **Ant.** silly, lighthearted, unrestrained.

stain *n.* 1. blot, blemish, mark, discoloration, smear. *She tried to remove the grass stains on her shoes.* –*vb.* 2. blemish, dirty, blotch, smear, discolor. *The vicious rumor stained his good name.*

stairs *n.* steps, staircase, flight, perron, companionway. *I'd rather take the stairs than the elevator, especially if it's only up two floors.*

stake *n.* 1. peg, spike, pin, picket, post. *A vampire can be killed by a stake through the heart.* 2. jackpot, spoils, winnings, wager, bet. *The stakes were high in the horse race.* –*vb.* 3. mark, outline, reserve, delimit. *The gold miner staked out a claim.* 4. peg, spike, fasten, secure, lash. *The campers staked their tent to the ground.* 5. bet, wager, gamble, invest, venture, risk. *I won't stake any money on his chances of winning.*

stale *adj.* hardened, moldy, dry, tasteless, bland. *These old doughnuts are rather stale.* **Ant.** fresh, tasty.

stalemate *n.* deadlock, draw, standstill, standoff, checkmate. *The driver and mechanic reached a stalemate concerning repair costs.* **Ant.** decision, resolution.

stalk *vb.* 1. hunt, pursue, shadow, track, trail. *Leopards often stalk antelope.* 2. stamp, march, stride, tramp, strut. *The angry woman stalked out of the room.* –*n.* 3. stem, shaft. *He enjoys eating raw celery stalks.*

stall *n.* 1. booth, stand, kiosk, store. *The farmer sold vegetables from a roadside stall.* 2. stable, shed, pen, corral. *He put hay in the horse's stall.* –*vb.* 3. stop, halt, interrupt, delay, linger. *The elevator stalled on the first floor.* **Ant.** 3. start, advance, continue.

stallion *n.* stud, steed, horse, mammal. *Nobody wanted to ride the white stallion because it was so aggressive.*

stalwart *adj.* strong, stout, powerful, firm, resolute, determined, staunch. *She is a stalwart supporter of equal rights.* **Ant.** weak, wishy-washy, spineless.

stamina *n.* endurance, energy, fitness, ruggedness, hardiness. *It takes stamina to be a triathlete.*

stammer *vb.* 1. stutter, falter, stumble, sputter. *People often stammer when giving speeches.* –*n.* 2.

stammering, stutter, stuttering. *Her stammer becomes noticeable when she is frightened.*

stamp *vb.* **1.** squash, mash, trample, crush, stomp. *Please make sure you stamp out your campfire.* **2.** label, mark, imprint, print, impress. *The postal clerk stamped "airmail" on the package.* *–n.* **3.** seal, mark, label, symbol, emblem. *Meat is required to have a USDA inspection stamp.*

stampede *n.* **1.** rush, flight, rout, scattering. *The rock band was overwhelmed by a stampede of fans.* **2.** flee, bolt, run, scatter, dash, panic. *The hunter's scent caused the elephants to stampede.*

stand *vb.* **1.** be upright, be vertical, be erect, rise. *Strong winds made it difficult to stand.* **2.** erect, place, set, put. *Please stand your skis in the corner.* **3.** last, remain, persist, exist, continue. *Egypt's pyramids have stood in the desert for thousands of years.* **4.** withstand, endure, bear, handle, undergo. *She didn't think she could stand the pain.* **5.** support, promote, argue, favor. *You should stand up for what you believe.* *–n.* **6.** resistance, defense, opposition, front. *The Indian tribe made a stand against the invading army.* **7.** viewpoint, opinion, position, policy. *What is your stand on this tissue?* **8.** rest, support, platform. *We set the figurine on a wooden stand.* **9.** booth, stall, counter, table. *She bought refreshments at a food stand.* **10.** grove, copse, woodland, thicket. *We walked through a stand of redwood trees.* **11.** bleachers, grandstand. *He watched the ballgame from the stands.* **Ant.** **1.** sit, lie, recline. **6.** withdrawal, retreat.

standard *n.* **1.** model, pattern, guidelines, principle, specification. *His family has strict standards of behavior.* **2.** flag, banner, pennant. *The castle's standard was placed on the highest tower.* *–adj.* **3.** usual, normal, regular, accepted, customary. *Driving on a road's left side is standard practice in Great Britain.* **Ant.** **3.** unusual, abnormal, atypical.

standby *n.* backup, stand-in, understudy, replacement, substitute, fill-in. *Sally has the credentials to serve as a standby if I get sick.*

standout *n.* star, superstar, winner, champion, talent, wunderkind, prodigy, savant. *With a closet full of trophies, she has proven herself a standout.* **Ant.** also-ran, second-stringer.

standpoint *n.* point of view, viewpoint, opinion, attitude, perspective. *From my standpoint, the Republicans are dead wrong.*

standstill *n.* stop, halt, gridlock, bottleneck, impasse, stalemate. *Traffic came to a standstill.* **Ant.** progression, advance, movement.

staple *n.* **1.** resource, necessity, feature, essential. *Corn was a staple of many American Indian diets.* *–adj.* **2.** primary, basic, essential, fundamental, chief. *The staple food of several Asian countries is rice.* **Ant.** **1.** extra, accessory. **2.** secondary, minor.

star *n.* **1.** sun, heavenly body, celestial body, red giant, white dwarf, quasar, pulsar. *Astronomers study distant stars.* **2.** celebrity, lead, principal, headliner, dignitary. *The talented actress was the star of the film.* *–vb.* **3.** feature, present, showcase, headline. *The movie will star my favorite actor.*

WORD SEARCH

brightens temporarily, star that: *nova, variable star*
brightness, measure of: *magnitude*
chart, position: *ephemeris*
collapsed star with immense gravity: *black hole, neutron star, pulsar*
concealment by another celestial body: *occultation*
exploding star: *supernova*
gassy birthplace of: *nebula*
group of stars in a major or minor configuration: *constellation, asterism*

mapping: *uranography*
massing of stars in which we live: *Milky Way*
massings containing billions or more stars: *galaxies*
pertaining to: *astral, stellar*
red sun, massive: *red giant*
shooting "star": *meteorite*
twinkling of: *scintillation*

stardom *n.* fame, notoriety, superstardom, renown, acclaim, prominence. *As a basketball player, Michael Jordan achieved great stardom.* **Ant.** obscurity, anonymity.

stare *vb.* **1.** gape, goggle, gaze, gawk, glare. *It's not polite to stare at people.* –*n.* **2.** gapping, goggling, ogling, scrutiny, regard. *I shut the door on the man's bold stare.*

stark *adj.* bare, austere, stripped, naked, barren, empty. *The Mexican desert was stark, unlike the lush forests of the north.* **Ant.** lush, rich, ornate.

start *vb.* **1.** begin, commence, activate, initiate. *My school starts on the eighth of September.* **2.** embark, leave, depart, set out. *They wish to start for the mountains later today.* **3.** establish, create, found, pioneer, launch. *My father started a new travel business.* **4.** jerk, twitch, flinch, jump, spring. *I started when the car honked its horn.* –*n.* **5.** beginning, onset, origin, inception, birth. *Runners lined up at the start of the race.* **6.** jerk, jar, jolt, twitch, spasm. *The loud noise gave him a start.* **Ant. 1.** finish, end, stop. **2.** delay, dawdle. **5.** finish, ending.

startle *vb.* surprise, scare, frighten, jolt, jar, shock. *The thunder's loud boom startled her.* **Ant.** calm, quiet, comfort, soothe.

starvation *n.* famine, hunger, deprivation, malnutrition. *Many villagers died of starvation after drought destroyed their crops.* **Ant.** plenty, abundance.

starve *vb.* hunger, famish, wither, perish, die. *Many deer starved during the long and harsh winter.*

state *n.* **1.** condition, stage, shape, form, situation. *Ice is a solid state of water.* **2.** republic, nation, country, dominion. *The state of Israel was founded in 1948.* –*adj.* **3.** governmental, federal, official, ceremonial. *The president attended the state dinner.* –*vb.* **4.** announce, declare, speak, proclaim, express. *Please clearly state your name and age.*

stately *adj.* dignified, important, lofty, distinguished, formal, impressive. *The government building was stately and imposing.* **Ant.** unimpressive, tacky, cheap.

statement *n.* announcement, proclamation, declaration, explanation, comment. *The spokeswoman read the president's prepared statement.*

state-of-the-art *adj.* cutting edge, modern, innovative, leading edge, advanced, trendsetting. *At the moment, my computer is considered state-of-the-art, but it will probably be obsolete within a year.* **Ant.** outmoded, old-fashioned, antediluvian.

statesman *n.* politician, diplomat, legislator, solon. *The elder statesman will be giving a speech this afternoon.*

static *adj.* **1.** changeless, stationary, unvarying, stagnant, fixed. *He was bored by his static life.* –*n.* **2.** interference, crackling, humming. *Static often makes phone conversation difficult.* **Ant. 1.** changing, moving, dynamic. **2.** silence, quiet.

station *n.* **1.** terminal, depot, stop. *We picked up my grandparents at the train station.* **2.** position, post, assignment, placement, place. *The security guard was criticized for leaving his station.* **3.** headquarters, station house, office, center. *Our class was given a tour of the fire station.* –*vb.* **4.** post, place, assign, position. *The soldiers will be stationed in Europe.*

stationary *adj.* motionless, fixed, unmoving, steady, changeless. *The clouds appeared stationary in the windless sky.* **Ant.** moving, running, changing, varying.

stationery *n.* notepaper, paper, letterhead. *The secretary wrote a memo on the company's stationery.*

statistics *n.* (slang) stats, numbers, percentages, data, facts, figures. *Her batting statistics were impressive.*

statue *n.* figure, likeness, image, sculpture, bust. *There is a huge statue of Abraham Lincoln in Washington, D.C.*

stature *n.* **1.** height, size, tallness. *That basketball player is a man of large stature.* **2.** status, rank, standing, importance, position. *The university's high stature was beyond question.* **Ant. 2.** inferiority, insignificance, lowliness.

status *n.* **1.** rank, standing, grade, position, significance. *Fancy cars are a symbol of high status to some people.* **2.** state, shape, condition, situation. *We questioned the park attendant on the status of the new ride.*

status quo *adj.* current state, present state of affairs, existing condition, present reality, norm. *I'd rather not change the rules but go with the status quo.*

statute *n.* law, ordinance, regulation, bill, act, legislation, rule. *The city has a statute prohibiting loud music played outside after nine o'clock.*

staunch *adj.* **1.** dedicated, loyal, devoted, firm, steadfast, solid. *The forest ranger was a staunch environmentalist.* *–vb.* **2.** stop, dam, check, halt, block. *She tried to staunch the flow of blood.* **Ant. 1.** unfaithful, shaky, hesitant, uncommitted. **2.** encourage, aid.

stay *vb.* **1.** remain, continue, dwell, persist, wait. *Let's stay at home since it's snowing.* **2.** check, curb, restrain, arrest, hinder. *The reinforced riverbank stayed the rising water.* *–n.* **3.** delay, suspension, postponement, deferment, break. *The lawyer requested a stay of sentencing.* **4.** vacation, visit, holiday, sojourn, stopover. *She enjoyed a one-week stay at camp.* **Ant. 1.** leave, go, depart. **2.** release, free. **3.** extension.

steadfast *adj.* constant, steady, unwavering, fixed, firm, stalwart, resolute. *The couple had been steadfast companions for over fifty years.* **Ant.** unsteady, disloyal, wavering.

steady *adj.* **1.** stable, constant, regular, fixed, continuous. *The unemployed woman hoped to find a steady job.* *–vb.* **2.** balance, stabilize, brace, secure, support. *The tightrope walker steadied himself with a long pole.* **Ant. 1.** unsteady, unstable, unreliable, shaky. **2.** unbalance, shake.

steak *n.* beef, meat, cut, sirloin, porterhouse, T-bone, filet mignon. *The diner ordered a steak large enough to feed a great white shark.*

steal *vb.* **1.** rob, filch, snatch, pilfer, thieve. *The thief stole a diamond necklace.* **2.** sneak, creep, slink, slip. *The prisoner stole past the sleeping guards.* **Ant. 1.** give, replace.

stealthy *adj.* sneaky, sly, devious, shady, shifty. *A stealthy robber crept into the house.* **Ant.** obvious, conspicuous.

steam *n.* **1.** vapor, condensation, mist, moisture. *Steam rose from the kettle's spout.* *–vb.* **2.** heat, boil, cook, simmer, stew. *The chef will steam our vegetables.* **3.** sail, cruise, ply, run. *The boat steamed into port.*

steep *adj.* **1.** sheer, sharp, abrupt, sudden, vertical. *The train chugged up the steep mountainside.* *–vb.* **2.** soak, immerse, submerge, saturate. *The anthropologist steeped herself in the local culture.* **Ant. 1.** gentle, gradual, horizontal.

steer *vb.* guide, drive, pilot, conduct, navigate. *The driver steered his car down the winding road.*

step *n.* **1.** footstep, footfall, tread, walk, stride, pace. *The cave echoed with the sound of our steps.* **2.** act, measure, move, action, deed, stage. *Writing an outline should be your first step.* **3.** rung, stair, foothold. *How many steps does your ladder have?* –*vb.* **4.** move, stride, walk, pace, tread. *I stepped closer to read the poster's small print.*

stereotype *n.* **1.** characterization, character type, classification, conception, type, image, misconception. *His perception that all Scottish people were stingy was based on a gross stereotype.* –*vb.* **2.** characterize, pigeonhole, typecast, categorize, type, label, generalize. *It is impossible to stereotype and be accurate; everyone is different and should be judged individually.*

sterile *adj.* **1.** unproductive, impotent, unfruitful, fallow, barren. *The farmer's fields had grown too sterile to produce viable crops.* **2.** clean, disinfected, antiseptic, sanitary, germ-free, pure. *Surgeons must perform operations in a sterile atmosphere.* **Ant. 1.** productive, fruitful, potent. **2.** infected, unclean.

sterilize *vb.* disinfect, clean, cleanse, purify. *A nurse sterilized my cut with alcohol.* **Ant.** infect, dirty.

stern *adj.* **1.** strict, sharp, severe, harsh, hard. *The police officer gave the motorist a stern warning.* –*n.* **2.** rear, back, end, tail. *The cargo was moved to the ship's stern.* **Ant. 1.** soft, gentle, kind. **2.** front, head.

stew *vb.* **1.** simmer, boil, cook, heat, seethe. *She let the meat and vegetables stew for several hours.* –*n.* **2.** mixture, mishmash, chowder. *His beef stew is quite good.*

stick *n.* **1.** branch, stem, switch, limb, twig. *We roasted the hot dogs on a stick.* –*vb.* **2.** puncture, pierce, prick, spear. *The nurse stuck a needle in my arm.* **3.** place, position, set, locate. *My boss stuck me in the back room.* **4.** fasten, glue, paste, tape, pin. *Please stick this to the bulletin board.* **5.** hold, cling, adhere, stay. *Stick to the job you were assigned.* **Ant. 3.** remove, dislodge. **4.** unfasten, detach. **5.** break, separate.

sticky *adj.* **1.** gummy, clinging, gluey, adhesive. *Honey is very sticky.* **2.** humid, moist, wet, clammy, muggy. *His shirt clung to his back in the sticky weather.* **Ant. 1.** slippery. **2.** dry, arid.

stiff *adj.* **1.** rigid, taut, inflexible, inelastic, hard. *The handkerchief was stiff with dried paint.* **2.** strong, forceful, powerful, keen, intense. *Our plane was flying into a stiff wind.* **3.** difficult, hard, tough, laborious. *There is a stiff climb to the top.* **4.** harsh, severe, stern, strict, unsparing. *The criminal was given a stiff sentence.* **Ant. 1.** bendable, flexible, supple. **2.** weak, faltering. **3.** gentle, easy. **4.** soft, gentle, mild.

stifle *vb.* smother, choke, strangle, suppress, restrain. *The writer felt stifled by the government's harsh rules.* **Ant.** encourage, free, release.

stigma *n.* disgrace, shame, dishonor, blemish, taint. *The exconvict spent the rest of his life with the stigma of being a murderer.* **Ant.** honor, glory, acclaim.

stigmatize *vb.* label, brand, characterize, disgrace, besmirch, dishonor. *To stigmatize is to label unfairly.*

still *adj.* **1.** motionless, calm, unmoving, peaceful, stationary. *A single ripple broke the pond's still waters.* **2.** silent, quiet, noiseless, hushed. *Late at night our house becomes very still.* –*n.* **3.** silence, quiet, hush, peacefulness, tranquillity. *The still of the night was broken by a loud crash.* –*adv.* **4.** yet, currently, nevertheless, nonetheless. *Are you still coming to the party?* –*vb.* **5.** silence, quiet, hush, calm, lull. *A lullaby* *stilled the crying baby.* **Ant.** 1. moving, turbulent, agitated. 2. noisy, loud, boisterous. 3. noise, commotion. 5. disturb, upset, agitate.

stimulant *n.* energizer, excitant, brace, (slang) upper, (slang) pick-me-up, (slang) shot-in-the-arm. *Caffeine is a powerful stimulant.* **Ant.** depressant, soporific, (slang) downer.

stimulate *vb.* arouse, excite, awaken, quicken, spur. *A tour of the hospital stimulated my desire to become a doctor.* **Ant.** deaden, kill, dull.

stimulating *adj.* arousing, exciting, enlivening, exhilarating. *It was an evening of stimulating conversation.* **Ant.** dreary, boring, dull.

sting *vb.* 1. prick, stab, bite. *The bee stung her face.* 2. burn, irritate, chafe, smart. *Salt water stung my eyes.* 3. pain, wound, insult, offend, anger. *I was stung by his cruel remark.* –*n.* 4. prick, bite, nip, puncture, stab. *A bee sting may hurt for some time.* 5. pain, hurt, distress, anguish. *The sting of her criticism stayed with him for days.* **Ant.** 2. soothe, caress. 3. soothe, please. 5. pleasure, caress.

stingy *adj.* 1. miserly, cheap, ungenerous, sparing, tight. *My stingy friend never pays for dinner.* 2. meager, slight, scanty, skimpy, lean. *The captives were given stingy amounts of food.* **Ant.** 1. generous, lavish. 2. abundant, profuse.

stink *vb.* 1. smell, reek. *This pile of unwashed clothes stinks.* –*n.* 2. stench, reek, odor, fume, smelliness. *The stink of the frightened skunk filled the cage.* **Ant.** 2. perfume, fragrance.

stipend *n.* payment, salary, fee, compensation, remuneration, allowance. *The substitute collected a small stipend for each time she sat in for the regular teacher.*

stipulate *vb.* specify, spell out, require, designate, arrange, state. *The contract stipulates clearly that the work must be completed by January.*

stipulation *n.* specification, requirement, designation, arrangement, statement, proviso, condition. *One stipulation of the contract is that the work must be checked by a qualified city inspector.*

stir *vb.* 1. whip, beat, churn, mix, agitate. *Please stir the soup before it burns.* 2. awaken, rouse, revive. *The bear stirred from its long hibernation.* 3. whip, incite, excite, encourage, enflame. *He stirred up trouble in the schoolyard.* –*n.* 4. movement, motion, rustle, flutter. *There was a stir in the audience when the popular singer entered.* 5. upheaval, commotion, excitement, uproar, disturbance. *The scandal caused quite a stir in the small town.* **Ant.** 3. calm, deaden. 4. stillness, silence. 5. dullness, boredom.

stitch *n.* 1. suture, loop, tack, tuck. *His deep wound required twelve stitches.* 2. garment, article, piece, scrap. *I don't have a stitch to wear.* 3. pain, ache, twinge, spasm, pang. *The runner got a stitch in her side.* –*vb.* 4. mend, repair, sew, suture, connect. *I stitched the tear in my shirt.*

stock *n.* 1. supply, store, inventory, hoard, reserve. *The store is running low on its stock of potato chips.* 2. shares, capital, investments. *I own stock in my mother's company.* 3. livestock, cattle, animals, herd. *The farmer rounded up his stock.* 4. parentage, lineage, ancestry, line, breed. *My dog comes from pedigree stock.* –*adj.* 5. regular, standard, basic, customary, staple. *Bread is a stock item at the supermarket.* –*vb.* 6. supply, furnish, equip, outfit. *She stocked her cabinets with canned goods.* **Ant.** 5. irregular, unusual, extra. 6. drain, empty.

stockade *n.* enclosure, pen, jail, prison, fort, palisade. *Lock the prisoners in the stockade until further notice.*

stockpile *n.* hoard, reserve, amassment, cache, larder, store. *The survivalist put away an impressive stockpile of beans and rice.*

stocky *adj.* thick, sturdy, burly, stout, solid. *The wrestler has a stocky build.* **Ant.** skinny, slender, delicate.

stodgy *adj.* staid, serious, proper, formal, uptight, stuffy, dull. *He was too stodgy to act silly with the rest of us.* **Ant.** wild, childish, silly.

stoic *adj.* impassive, indifferent, cool, detached, uncaring, resigned, stony. *He never complained about his chores and was, in fact, quite stoic about them.* **Ant.** reactive, hysterical, melodramatic.

stoke *vb.* stir, tend, turn coals, fill, refuel. *We need to stoke the fire before it goes out.*

stolid *adj.* impassive, stony, disinterested, indifferent, apathetic. *The stolid police officer was unmoved by my sob story.* **Ant.** passive, emotional, wild.

stomach *n.* **1.** belly, abdomen, gut, intestinal cavity. *His stomach hurt after eating so much candy.* **2.** liking, fondness, appetite, taste, desire. *She has no stomach for raw fish.* *–vb.* **3.** stand, endure, bear, abide, suffer. *She could not stomach the killing of animals for their furs.* **Ant.** **2.** dislike, distaste. **3.** condemn, reject.

stomp *vb.* stamp, tramp, trample, tread, squash, crush. *Stomp that bug!*

stone *n.* **1.** rock, pebble, cobble, boulder. *The old wall was built from stones.* **2.** gem, gemstone, jewel, diamond. *The jeweler polished the ring's stones.* *–vb.* **3.** pelt, bombard, batter. *In ancient times, criminals were sometimes stoned to death.*

WORD SEARCH

crystal-lined interior, globular stone with: *geode*
cuts and polishes, artist who: *lapidary*
cutter: *mason*
fire-starting: *flint*
massive: *boulder, megalith*
piles of: *rubble, scree, talus*
pit of: *quarry*
sharpening: *whetstone*
trailmarking pile of: *cairn*
turn into: *petrify*

Stone Age *n.* Paleolithic, Mesolithic, Neolithic, prehistoric era. *They didn't have toothbrushes or toilet paper in the Stone Age.*

stoned *adj.* (slang) high, under the influence, intoxicated, drugged, inebriated. *The man told the officer he was stoned, which was probably unwise.*

stonewall *vb.* obstruct, stall, impede. *The Congressman tried as hard as possible to stonewall the opposition.*

stoop *vb.* **1.** bend, crouch, duck, squat, bow. *The tall woman stooped to enter the low doorway.* **2.** sink, resort, fall, succumb. *Why did he stoop to such petty thievery?* *–n.* **3.** slump, slouch, bend, droop, dip. *The elderly man stands with a stoop.*

stop *vb.* **1.** halt, pause, discontinue, tarry, rest. *We stopped at a gas station.* **2.** block, check, restrain, bar, prevent, intercept. *He stopped the small child from running into the street.* **3.** quit, discontinue, cease, desist, suspend, terminate. *Please stop grinding your teeth.* *–n.* **4.** end, halt, delay, finish, discontinuation. *The rain forced the coaches to call a stop to the game.* **5.** layover, break, rest, stay. *The plane makes a stop in Chicago.* **6.** station, terminal, depot. *A bus stop is on the corner of Broadway and First.* **Ant.** **1.** continue, proceed. **2.** assist, encourage, speed. **3.** start, begin. **4.** start, continuation, resumption.

stopper *n.* plug, cork, bung, tap, tampion. *Quick, put the stopper in before all the water leaks out.*

storage *n.* cache, repository, stockpile, stowage, depot, bank. *Every spring we put our winter clothes into storage.*

store *n.* **1.** market, supermarket, mart, shop, outlet. *He went to the store to buy groceries.* **2.** supply, stock, reserve, accumulation, hoard, lot. *Our store of toilet paper is almost gone.* *–vb.* **3.** save, keep, hoard, stash, stockpile, collect. *She stores extra vegetables in her basement.*

storekeeper *n.* shopkeeper, merchant, proprietor, grocer, owner. *Ask the storekeeper if the lemons are on sale.*

storeroom *n.* storage, repository, stowage, depository, warehouse, depot, cache. *We put all of the extra apples in the storeroom for winter.*

storm *n.* **1.** tempest, blizzard, hurricane, gale, downpour. *The ship sank in a heavy storm.* **2.** outbreak, outburst, outcry, rush, blast. *The mayor's announcement provoked a storm of protest.* *–vb.* **3.** pour, howl, rain, snow. *It stormed for seven nights.* **4.** rage, rave, rush, thunder, stomp. *The angry woman stormed into the store, demanding a refund.* **5.** attack, assault, charge, assail, raid. *Peasants stormed their wicked landlord's castle.*

stormy *adj.* tempestuous, turbulent, wild, squally, blustery, violent. *Don't go out in your boat when it's stormy.* **Ant.** mild, calm, clear.

story *n.* **1.** tale, fable, legend, narrative, anecdote. *My favorite story is "Pinocchio."* **2.** report, account, tidings, description, version. *I don't know whether I believe his story.* **3.** floor, level, terrace, deck. *Her apartment is on the building's seventh story.*

storyteller *n.* raconteur, narrator, spinner of yarns, novelist, writer, author. *She was a talented storyteller who could hold anyone's attention for hours.*

stout *adj.* **1.** thickset, husky, brawny, stocky. *The humans and elves were accompanied by five stout dwarves.* **2.** bold, fearless, loyal, brave, determined. *The warrior was known to be of stout heart.* **Ant.** **1.** thin, lean, spare. **2.** fearful, weak, cowardly.

stove *n.* range, oven, heater, wood stove. *Be careful when you boil water on the stove.*

straggle *vb.* lag, stray, ramble, drift, tarry. *I was so tired that I straggled behind everyone else.*

straggler *n.* lagger, late arrival, stray, wanderer. *We watched with pity as the last stragglers in the race crossed the finish line.*

straight *adj.* **1.** unbent, unswerving, perpendicular, plumb, even. *Please stand in a straight line.* **2.** true, truthful, honest, reliable, accurate. *I want a straight answer this time.* **3.** orderly, tidy, arranged, neat. *Is your room straight?* **4.** continuous, unbroken, uninterrupted, consecutive. *There's been five straight days of bad weather.* *–adv.* **5.** directly, immediately, instantly, now. *Please go straight to bed.* **6.** straightly, upright, erectly, evenly. *The photographer asked us to stand up straight.* **Ant.** **1.** crooked, curved, bent. **2.** false, untruthful, unreliable. **3.** messy, disarranged. **4.** broken, interrupted. **5.** indirectly, eventually. **6.** crookedly, unevenly.

straightforward *adj.* direct, honest, plain, unambiguous, forthright, frank. *Her criticism of my paper was straightforward and painful.* **Ant.** indirect, ambiguous, dishonest.

strain *vb.* **1.** labor, struggle, strive, stretch, extend, fatigue, tax. *The runner strained to keep up with the group.* **2.** sprain, wrench, pull, twist. *He strained his back lifting the heavy box.* **3.** filter, sieve, drain, sift. *Please strain the peas.* *–n.* **4.** drain, drag, burden, stress, tension, pressure. *The unexpected medical expenses were a strain on our budget.* **5.** breed, family, variety, type, stock.

Where did you find this strain of wheat? **6.** melody, tune, theme. *I recognize that strain of music.* **7.** streak, trace, grain, trait. *There is a strong strain of rebellion in her.* **Ant. 1.** relax, loosen, yield.

strait *n.* narrow, channel, inlet, waterway. *Let's take the boat up into the strait and try to catch some bluefish.*

straitlaced *adj.* prim, proper, prudish, rigid, puritanical, upright. *Librarians aren't nearly as straitlaced as most would assume.* **Ant.** wild, untamed, uninhibited.

strand *vb.* **1.** ground, wreck, maroon, abandon. *The shipwreck stranded them on a desert island.* *–n.* **2.** shore, beach, coast, seashore. *He walked along a strand of white sand.* **3.** filament, fiber, thread, string. *There is a strand of hair in my soup.*

strange *adj.* weird, unusual, peculiar, odd, unfamiliar, exotic. *The science-fiction movie had some really strange creatures.* **Ant.** normal, usual, familiar.

stranger *n.* newcomer, outsider, foreigner, alien, immigrant. *She was a stranger to our town.* **Ant.** resident, friend, acquaintance.

strangle *vb.* choke, throttle, suffocate, smother, stifle. *The boa constrictor strangled the small animal.*

strap *n.* **1.** tie, fastening, thong, lash, belt. *His backpack strap broke.* *–vb.* **2.** lash, tie, fasten, bind, attach. *She strapped her boots into the snowshoe bindings.* **Ant. 2.** unfasten, untie, remove.

strapping *adj.* muscular, brawny, robust, strong, sturdy, husky, rugged. *The champion was a handsome man with a strapping physique.* **Ant.** skinny, flaccid, unsturdy.

strategic *adj.* essential, important, vital, crucial, critical, tactical. *The squadron knocked out all of the enemy's strategic military installations.* **Ant.** insignificant, inconsequential.

strategy *n.* tactic, plan, arrangement, method, blueprint. *The coach revealed a new strategy for tomorrow's game.*

stratum *n.* layer, level, bed, seam, stratification. *In which stratum did the paleontologist find the dinosaur bones?*

stray *vb.* **1.** wander, roam, rove, ramble, range, drift. *A little lamb strayed from the herd.* *–n.* **2.** lost animal, waif, vagabond. *Several strays showed up on her door-step.* *–adj.* **3.** lost, wandering, homeless, abandoned, unclaimed. *He fed the stray cat.*

streak *n.* **1.** band, stripe, line, bar, bolt. *There were streaks of gold in her sun-bleached hair.* **2.** period, interval, bout, spell, touch. *The gambler had a streak of bad luck.* *–vb.* **3.** mark, stripe, striate, band, stain. *His face was streaked with dirt and sweat.* **4.** flash, dash, race, sprint, fly, zoom. *Several bicyclists streaked across the finish line.* **Ant. 4.** crawl, limp.

stream *n.* **1.** river, creek, brook, rivulet, tributary. *She went fishing in the small mountain stream.* **2.** flow, jet, current, gush. *The kite soared on a stream of wind.* *–vb.* **3.** flow, rush, surge, cascade, spill. *A herd of caribou streamed past our cabin.*

street *n.* road, avenue, boulevard, highway, freeway, lane. *We crossed the street at a light.*

strength *n.* **1.** power, might, muscularity, brawn, vigor, force. *The elephant is an animal of great strength.* **2.** intensity, seriousness, firmness, resolution. *No one could question the strength of his convictions.* **3.** mainstay, forte, greatness, competence. *Debating is one of her strengths.* **Ant. 1–2.** weakness, feebleness. **3.** frailty, shortcoming.

strengthen *vb.* reinforce, renew, fortify, enhance, buttress. *The army was strengthened with two new battalions.* **Ant.** weaken, undermine.

strenuous *adj.* vigorous, energetic, laborious, active, tiring. *The doctor told the sick woman to avoid strenuous exercise.* **Ant.** relaxed, lazy, easy.

stress *n.* **1.** distress, strain, tension, anxiety, worry. *During exams, students often experience stress.* **2.** emphasis, weight, significance, importance, urgency. *There is a lot of stress placed on achieving good grades.* *–vb.* **3.** emphasize, underscore, accent, highlight. *Her parents stressed the importance of a good education.* **Ant. 1.** peacefulness, calm, serenity. **2.** unimportance, insignificance. **3.** deemphasize, ignore.

stretch *vb.* **1.** extend, expand, widen, lengthen, spread. *The desert stretched on for miles.* *–n.* **2.** spell, expanse, spread, distance, sweep. *The truck hit a stretch of rough road.* **3.** elasticity, give, spring, flexibility. *Rubber is a material with a lot of stretch.* **Ant. 1.** shrink, contract, retract, narrow.

strict *adj.* unyielding, stern, inflexible, rigid, exact. *His parents were strict about his curfew.* **Ant.** lax, flexible, permissive.

strident *adj.* loud, shrill, deafening, earsplitting, harsh, piercing. *The amplifier's strident feedback made everyone cover their ears in pain.*

strife *n.* conflict, fighting, hatred, unrest, discord. *Several Middle Eastern countries have experienced years of strife.* **Ant.** peace, quiet, calm.

strike *vb.* **1.** hit, smack, knock, punch, pound. *Her snowball struck me on the arm.* **2.** attack, charge, assault, raid. *A group of evil trolls struck the village just before midnight.* **3.** impress, affect, reach, please, seem. *Her idea struck me as a workable plan.* **4.** eliminate, cancel, remove, erase, delete. *A two-night stay in Paris was struck from the tour agenda.* **5.** ring, toll, sound. *The clock struck twelve.* **6.** picket, protest, walk out, boycott. *The workers will strike for better wages.* *–n.* **7.** blow, smack, knock, pounding. *We heard the strike of the blacksmith's hammer.* **8.** attack, assault, raid, charge. *The general launched a strike against the enemy.* **9.** walkout, protest, boycott. *The workers called a strike after negotiations broke down.* **Ant. 1.** caress, pat, stroke. **4.** add.

striking *adj.* arresting, staggering, stunning, eye-popping, conspicuous. *Sherry has striking green eyes.*

string *n.* twine, cord, thread, line, strand, fiber. *If you're going to fly a kite, you'll need a large ball of string.*

stringent *adj.* rigorous, strict, rigid, severe, tight, demanding, exacting. *The school's dress code was stringent: students were forbidden to wear sneakers.*

strip *vb.* **1.** peel, skin, scrape, remove, clear. *We plan to strip the old paint off our wall.* **2.** undress, disrobe, uncover. *He stripped before entering the bathtub.* *–n.* **3.** band, ribbon, belt, slat, stripe. *We pulled our boat up on a strip of beach.* **Ant. 1.** replace, add, restore. **2.** dress, cover.

stripe *n.* band, bar, streak, line, striation, score. *The tiger had stripes on her coat.*

stroke *n.* **1.** hit, blow, smack, clip, knock. *The ball entered the hole on the golfer's second stroke.* **2.** seizure, attack, collapse. *My grandmother suffered a stroke yesterday.* **3.** sounding, peal, knell, toll. *The New Year begins at the stroke of midnight.* **4.** flourish, movement, dash. *She marked the incorrect answers with a stroke of her pen.* **5.** happening, event, occurrence, accomplishment, achievement. *Finding you here was a stroke of good fortune.* *–vb.* **6.** caress, fondle, pet, rub, pat. *He stroked the kitten's head.*

stroll *vb.* **1.** walk, amble, meander, wander, ramble. *She strolled down the shaded avenue.*

–*n.* 2. walk, ramble, saunter, excursion. *We took a stroll along the beach.* **Ant.** 1. race, run, dash. 2. run, dash.

strong *adj.* 1. powerful, mighty, brawny, muscular, sturdy. *Weight lifters are quite strong.* 2. firm, unbending, deep, dedicated. *The monks had very strong religious beliefs.* 3. intense, potent, concentrated, sharp, bitter. *The cough medicine has a strong taste.* 4. distinct, notable, pronounced. *The sound of the waves was quite strong from where we stood.* 5. clear, sharp, quick, competent, keen. *He has a strong grasp of the essentials.* **Ant.** 1. weak, feeble, frail. 2. weak, shallow, shaky. 3. weak, bland, tasteless. 4. weak, inconclusive. 5. weak, slight, slim.

structure *n.* 1. building, construction, erection. *The parking structure has five levels.* 2. arrangement, form, pattern, construction, configuration. *The structure of the mineral was quite complex.* –*vb.* 3. build, form, construct, design, arrange. *This class will be structured around outside field trips.*

struggle *vb.* 1. fight, battle, wrestle, scuffle, labor. *The lion struggled to get out of its cage.* –*n.* 2. fight, battle, labor, striving, push. *Civil-rights activists wage a constant struggle against discrimination.* **Ant.** 1. surrender, yield.

strum *vb.* thrum, stroke, play, pluck, pick. *Strum the guitar softly.*

stubble *n.* whiskers, (slang) five o'clock shadow, bristles, beard, growth. *I need to shave this stubble before I begin to look like a caveman.*

stubborn *adj.* unmovable, unbending, headstrong, dogged, relentless. *The stubborn explorers refused to turn back.* **Ant.** wavering, hesitant, indecisive.

stucco *n.* plaster, cement. *Karen's beautiful villa is made of stucco.*

stuck-up *adj.* snobbish, snooty, supercilious, uppity, elitist, haughty. *We thought the new girl was acting stuck-up, but she was really just shy.* **Ant.** friendly, down-to-earth, folksy.

stud *n.* Casanova, Don Juan, playboy, (slang) skirtchaser, (slang) hunk. *The girls all think Eddy is a stud, but I think he's more of a dud.*

student *n.* pupil, scholar, learner, trainee. *There are five hundred students at my school.* **Ant.** teacher, professor.

studio *n.* workshop, workroom, atelier. *Would you like to go to my studio to view my drawings?*

studious *adj.* scholarly, academic, bookish, literary, hard-working, intellectual. *Her studious attitude won her a permanent place on the honor rolls.* **Ant.** lazy, illiterate, ignorant.

study *vb.* 1. read, learn, research, meditate, cram. *He usually studies at the library.* –*n.* 2. learning, examination, reading, research, exploration. *She finds the study of computer languages interesting.* 3. office, library, workroom, room. *My parents do their work in the study.*

stuff *n.* 1. goods, things, articles, material. *What sort of stuff did you buy at the store?* –*vb.* 2. pack, fill, cram, jam, load. *The pillow was stuffed with feathers.* **Ant.** 2. empty, drain, unpack.

stuffy *adj.* 1. suffocating, sweltering, airless, close, muggy. *He began to sweat in the stuffy room.* 2. congested, clogged, filled. *People with colds often suffer from stuffy noses.* 3. reserved, pompous, smug, dull, cold. *He is so stuffy at formal dinners.* **Ant.** 1. airy, ventilated. 2. open, unblocked. 3. friendly, natural.

stumble *vb.* trip, fall, stagger, blunder, tumble. *I stumbled over an exposed tree root.*

stump *vb.* perplex, puzzle, baffle, bewilder, mystify. *She was stumped by the difficult puzzle.*

stun *vb.* shock, surprise, astonish, jar, overwhelm. *News of his arrest stunned us.*

stunning *adj.* dazzling, electrifying, astonishing, striking, brilliant. *The football player made a stunning catch.* **Ant.** dull, unimpressive, unremarkable, mild.

stunt *vb.* **1.** dwarf, slow, curb, check, arrest. *Too much darkness will stunt a plant's growth.* –*n.* **2.** feat, exploit, trick, number, act, performance. *The motorcyclist's favorite stunt was riding through a burning hoop.* **Ant. 1.** speed, stimulate.

stunted *adj.* dwarfed, undersized, stubby, miniature, small, tiny. *All of the trees at the top of the mountain were stunted from the severe weather.* **Ant.** oversized, huge, overgrown.

stupefy *vb.* stun, daze, dumbfound, astonish, confuse. *We were stupefied by his decision to join the Foreign Legion.*

stupendous *adj.* huge, gigantic, gargantuan, astounding, great, prodigious, astronomical. *Hitting seventy home runs in a single baseball season is stupendous.* **Ant.** trivial, insignificant, inconsequential.

stupid *adj.* dumb, unintelligent, dense, mindless, foolish. *A stupid dog stood in the middle of the busy street.* **Ant.** intelligent, bright, clever.

stupidity *n.* ignorance, naiveté, dumbness, mindlessness, imbecility, idiocy. *Stupidity will get you nowhere very quickly.* **Ant.** intelligence, genius, brilliance.

stupor *n.* coma, daze, numbness, insensibility, lethargy. *The man was in a drunken stupor.*

sturdy *adj.* rugged, strong, tough, durable, solid. *She bought a sturdy backpack for her difficult journey.* **Ant.** fragile, frail.

stutter *vb.* **1.** stammer, sputter, falter, hesitate. *He often stutters when telling a lie.* –*n.* **2.** stammer, stammering, stuttering. *The speaker had a pronounced stutter.*

style *n.* **1.** fashion, design, form, pattern, shape, arrangement. *She wears a short hairstyle.* –*vb.* **2.** fashion, design, form, shape, arrange. *He styled his hair with a blow dryer.*

stylish *adj.* fashionable, elegant, chic, dapper, modish. *My stylish friend is always shopping for new clothes.* **Ant.** unstylish, unfashionable, outmoded.

stymie *vb.* thwart, obstruct, block, impede, stop, hinder. *Teachers would always stymie our attempts at food fights.* **Ant.** free, help, facilitate.

suave *adj.* smooth, gracious, diplomatic, courteous, refined, charming, tactful. *The diplomat was too suave to offend anyone.* **Ant.** rude, rough, unrefined.

subdue *vb.* pacify, check, overwhelm, restrain, silence. *Bystanders tried to subdue the violent woman.* **Ant.** inflame, arouse, excite.

subdued *adj.* unresponsive, unemotional, quiet, hushed, solemn. *The subdued audience did not react to his emotional speech.* **Ant.** excited, emotional, loud.

subject *n.* **1.** theme, topic, substance, matter, question. *The subject of my report is solar energy.* **2.** course, discipline, study, topic. *His favorite school subject is geography.* –*vb.* **3.** expose, bare, submit, give, treat. *She subjected me to hours of worry by not calling.*

subjective *adj.* personal, individual, biased, nonobjective. *Musical taste is subjective.* **Ant.** objective, impersonal, unbiased.

subjugate *vb.* enslave, dominate, control, conquer, subject, boss. *The goal of a dictator is to subjugate the masses.* **Ant.** empower, free, liberate.

sublime *adj.* majestic, lofty, elevated, transcendent, divine, holy. *He elevated his good deeds to the sublime when he sold all his possessions and gave away the proceeds to the poor.* **Ant.** low, pedestrian, ordinary.

submarine *n.* sub, U-boat, submersible, vessel. *German submarines sank many American ships in World War II.*

WORD SEARCH

air intake: *snorkel*
eyeglass, angled: *periscope*
locator: *sonar, sonobuoy*
missile: *torpedo*
observation tower: *conning tower, bridge*
tanks of water that control depth: *ballast tanks*
war hazard: *mine, depth charge*

submerge *vb.* 1. sink, plunge, dip, immerse. *The submarine submerged.* 2. drown, flood, engulf, deluge, immerse. *Floodwaters submerged the low field.* **Ant.** 1. surface, emerge. 2. uncover, bare.

submissive *adj.* subservient, nonresistant, docile, deferential, obeisant, servile. *It's never wise to be too submissive or you'll be walked on.* **Ant.** dominant, controlling, rebellious.

submit *vb.* 1. present, offer, proffer, propose. *The reporter submitted a story to his editor.* 2. yield, surrender, accept, endure, tolerate. *The patient refused to submit to any more testing.*

subordinate *n.* 1. assistant, aide, underling, junior, employee. *She gave the unpleasant jobs to her subordinates.* –*adj.* 2. inferior, lower, junior, auxiliary, secondary. *A vice president is subordinate to a president.* **Ant.** 1. superior, boss, chief. 2. superior, senior.

subpoena *n.* summons, writ, court order, notice, demand, instruction. *The witness received a subpoena to appear in court next Thursday at ten o'clock.*

subscribe *vb.* take, accept, support, buy, purchase. *The saleswoman wanted me to subscribe to several magazines.*

subsequent *adj.* next, following, ensuing, successive, succeeding. *Subsequent issues of the comic book will arrive each month.* **Ant.** previous, earlier.

subservient *adj.* submissive, servile, obeisant, subordinate, complaint, sycophantic. *The head of the company was always surrounded by subservient staff members.* **Ant.** dominant, rebellious, controlling.

subside *vb.* decrease, diminish, shrink, dwindle, lessen. *The waves subsided as the storm passed.* **Ant.** increase, rise, grow.

subsidiary *adj.* auxiliary, secondary, subordinate, secondary, supplementary, accessory. *Computers are often equipped with several subsidiary components.* **Ant.** main, primary, major.

subsidize *vb.* underwrite, finance, bankroll, sponsor, fund, pay for. *The school board voted to subsidize three new soccer teams.*

subsist *vb.* survive, live, last, remain, continue. *The lost explorers had to subsist on nuts and berries.* **Ant.** die, perish.

subsistence *n.* living, livelihood, sustenance, provisions, survival, means of support. *The farmer's subsistence was comprised only of what he could grow.*

substance *n.* 1. material, matter, ingredient, element. *The spaceship was made from a special substance.* 2. reality, solidity, actuality, essence, meaning. *There is no substance to your accusations.* 3. wealth, property, riches, means. *Only a person of substance could afford that expensive house.*

substantial *adj.* great, large, sizable, considerable, significant. *She won a substantial amount of money in the state lottery.* **Ant.** small, tiny, insignificant.

substantiate *vb.* corroborate, prove, authenticate, verify, certify, validate. *The detective's evidence helped to substantiate the defendant's story.* **Ant.** disprove, discredit, challenge.

substitute *n.* **1.** replacement, backup, alternative, relief, reserve. *Our class was taught by a substitute today.* *–vb.* **2.** replace, change, exchange, swap, switch. *I usually substitute margarine for butter.* *–adj.* **3.** alternative, temporary, secondary, replacement. *The substitute teacher was harassed by several students.* **Ant. 2.** keep, maintain. **3.** original, primary.

subterfuge *n.* deception, trick, ruse, machination, device, scheme. *The Trojan horse was the ultimate subterfuge.*

subterranean *adj.* underground, subsurface, sunken, buried, concealed. *Many animals prefer subterranean lairs.*

subtle *adj.* inobvious, delicate, elegant, understated, refined. *Your plea for money was not very subtle.* **Ant.** obvious, blunt.

subtract *vb.* remove, deduct, withdraw, diminish. *Five subtracted from twelve is seven.* **Ant.** add.

suburb *n.* suburbia, (slang) burbs, residential neighborhood, bedroom community, development, division. *We live in the suburbs in a neighborhood comprised of cookie-cutter houses.*

subversive *adj.* rebellious, insurrectionary, undermining, revolutionary, treasonous, destructive. *The terrorists' activities were highly subversive.* **Ant.** constructive, patriotic, loyal.

subway *n.* underground railway, (slang) tube, metro, rapid transit system, tunnel. *I rode the subway into town.*

succeed *vb.* prosper, flourish, thrive, triumph. *She wanted to succeed at her new job.* **Ant.** fail, falter, flounder.

success *n.* accomplishment, achievement, triumph, prosperity. *The wealthy man had great success with his investments.* **Ant.** failure, downfall, disaster.

successful *adj.* **1.** effective, victorious, fruitful, triumphant. *I was successful in convincing my friend to come with me.* **2.** rich, prosperous, wealthy, renowned. *She was a successful businesswoman.* **Ant. 1.** unsuccessful, ineffective. **2.** unsuccessful, unprosperous.

successive *adj.* consecutive, succeeding, following, adjacent, subsequent. *The earthquake was followed by two successive tremors.*

succinct *adj.* concise, to-the-point, pithy, condensed, short, brief. *His speech was not long-winded at all; in fact, it was quite succinct.* **Ant.** verbose, long-winded, wordy.

succulent *adj.* moist, juicy, fleshy, dripping, pulpy. *The interior of a cactus is often more succulent than one would think.* **Ant.** dry, parched, desiccated.

succumb *vb.* yield, surrender, submit, capitulate. *The tired woman succumbed to sleep.* **Ant.** resist, fight.

sucker *n.* dupe, victim, easy mark, (slang) patsy, (slang) pushover. *P. T. Barnum once observed that there was a sucker born every minute.*

sudden *adj.* unexpected, unannounced, unforeseen, abrupt, instant. *The driver was forced to make a sudden stop.* **Ant.** expected, gradual, foreseen.

sue *vb.* beg, plead, petition, appeal, ask, entreat. *The losing army sued for peace.*

suffer *vb.* **1.** hurt, ache, agonize. *The boy suffered from the pain in his leg.* **2.** sustain, experience, tolerate, endure, withstand, bear. *Do what I say, or suffer the consequences.*

sufficient *adj.* enough, adequate, abundant, satisfactory. *I think I have sufficient funds for only two more weeks.* **Ant.** insufficient, inadequate, unsatisfactory.

suffocate *vb.* smother, gag, choke, strangle. *The firefighter almost suffocated in the smoke-filled room.*

suggest *vb.* propose, offer, recommend, urge, advise. *I suggested that she take an aspirin for her headache.*

suggestible *adj.* impressionable, susceptible, malleable, naive, gullible. *Some people neglect to think critically and are therefore suggestible.* **Ant.** resistant, defiant, savvy.

suggestion *n.* advice, counsel, recommendation, proposal. *I followed his suggestion and bought the less expensive car.*

suggestive *adj.* **1.** remindful, reminiscent, expressive, indicative. *The color was suggestive of a red wine.* **2.** indecent, improper, shameless, tasteless. *He posed in a very suggestive manner.* **Ant. 2.** decent, tasteful, modest.

suit *n.* **1.** outfit, costume, attire, clothing, tuxedo. *He wears business suits to formal meetings.* **2.** appeal, petition, case, request, plea. *Her suit for leniency was denied.* –*vb.* **3.** satisfy, please, content, delight, fit. *My small car suits me just fine.* **4.** clothe, dress, equip, furnish. *The astronaut suited up for her space walk.* **Ant. 3.** dissatisfy, displease.

suitable *adj.* right, appropriate, proper, qualified, fit. *Do you think he is suitable for the job?* **Ant.** unsuitable, inappropriate, unfit.

suitcase *n.* valise, bag, carryall, overnight bag, grip, case. *The airlines mistakenly flew my suitcase to Los Angeles.*

sulk *vb.* **1.** pout, mope, grouch, grouse, brood. *She sulked when we said she couldn't come.* –*n.* **2.** pout, snit, sulkiness, grumpiness. *Why did he go off in a sulk?*

sullen *adj.* resentful, sulky, bitter, angry, glowering. *She gave us a sullen look for punishing her.* **Ant.** pleasant, cheerful, happy.

sultry *adj.* hot, humid, torrid, sweltering, steamy, muggy. *On sultry evenings I sleep with my windows open.* **Ant.** cold, freezing, frigid.

sum *n.* **1.** total, amount, value, result. *The sum of five plus six is eleven.* –*vb.* **2.** add, total, calculate, compute. *The student summed up his total points.* **3.** summarize, review, outline, close, conclude. *Please sum up your report in a few words.* **Ant. 2.** subtract.

summary *n.* **1.** review, digest, outline, breakdown, analysis. *The teacher asked us to write a summary of the book we read.* –*adj.* **2.** brief, condensed, compact, shortened, abridged. *He provided her with a summary report.* **Ant. 2.** complete, lengthy, detailed, unabridged.

summit *n.* peak, tip, pinnacle, top, crest. *The climbers rested after reaching the mountains's summit.* **Ant.** bottom, base.

summon *vb.* **1.** call, order, ask, command. *She was summoned to the principal's office for misbehaving.* –*n.* **2.** order, directive, call, notification. *The soldier received his summons to active duty.*

sun *n.* star, sphere, orb, luminary, Sol. *According to scientists, Earth's Sun has enough fuel to burn for at least another five billion years.*

WORD SEARCH

atmosphere, outer: *chromosphere, corona*
blotches,dark, circular: *sunspots*
ejected tongue of flaming gas: *solar flare, solar prominence*
obscuring of by Moon: *solar eclipse*

orbit: *ecliptic*
referring to: *helio, solar*
surface: *photosphere*
worship: *heliolatry*

sunken *adj.* submerged, submersed, immersed, drowned. *The sailors spoke of a sunken treasure lying off the coast.* **Ant.** floating, surface.

sunny *adj.* **1.** sunlit, cloudless, clear, radiant, bright. *It's fun to have a picnic on a sunny day.* **2.** cheerful, smiling, happy, joyful, jolly. *She has a very sunny outlook on life.* **Ant. 1.** cloudy, overcast, dark. **2.** gloomy, unhappy, unsmiling.

sunrise *n.* dawn, daybreak, sunup, daylight. *She woke early, to see the sunrise.* **Ant.** sunset, dusk, twilight.

sunset *n.* dusk, twilight, nightfall, sundown. *We must try to get back before sunset.* **Ant.** sunrise, dawn, daybreak.

sunscreen *n.* sunblock, sun cream, lotion, preparation, UV protection. *Be sure to slather on lots of sunscreen before going out on the beach.*

super *adj.* extraordinary, superior, great, outstanding, superb, peerless. *The bushmen were found to have super hearing and could perceive sounds citified people could not.* **Ant.** inferior, terrible, awful.

superb *adj.* excellent, admirable, praiseworthy, magnificent, fine. *The students did a superb job on this year's musical.* **Ant.** poor, bad, terrible, awful.

superficial *adj.* shallow, surface, skin-deep, external. *He suffered only superficial cuts.* **Ant.** deep, internal.

superfluous *adj.* extraneous, unnecessary, excess, inessential, expendable, surplus. *When writing, avoid using superfluous words.* **Ant.** necessary, essential, needed.

superhuman *adj.* supernatural, omnipotent, godlike, divine, otherworldly. *The weight lifter was ruggedly built and appeared to have superhuman strength.* **Ant.** subhuman.

superintendent *n.* director, administrator, chief, head, supervisor, overseer. *The blizzard convinced the superintendent to cancel school.*

superior *adj.* **1.** exceptional, unrivaled, first-rate, lofty, admirable. *She feels that Cadillacs are superior cars.* –*n.* **2.** supervisor, manager, boss. *All final decisions are made by my superior.* **Ant. 1.** inferior, poor, average. **2.** inferior, employee, subordinate.

superman *n.* superwoman, god, immortal, Olympian, super hero, ironman. *We're going to need a superman to clean this mess by the end of the day.*

supernatural *adj.* mystical, spectral, occult, spiritual, otherworldly. *Do you believe in supernatural things like ghosts?* **Ant.** natural, worldly.

supersede *vb.* replace, succeed, supplant, outmode, take the place of, override. *The word processor quickly superseded the typewriter.*

superstition *n.* irrational belief, fear, phobia, fallacy, old wives' tale, delusion. *You won't really have bad luck if you cross paths with a black cat; that's just a superstition.*

superstitious *adj.* fearful, phobic, irrational, delusional, neurotic, apprehensive. *Many superstitious people confess their fear of Friday the thirteenth.*

supervise *vb.* oversee, administer, manage, direct, govern. *Please supervise your younger sister while I go to the store.* **Ant.** neglect, ignore.

supervisor *n.* manager, boss, administrator, chief, commander. *The supervisor made sure the employees were doing their jobs.* **Ant.** underling, subordinate.

supplant *vb.* replace, displace, succeed, dethrone, oust, unseat. *Mr. Smith is planning to supplant Ms. Adams as chair of the board of directors.*

supple *adj.* soft, malleable, pliable, flexible, plastic, resilient. *The new steering wheels are supple and cause less injury in accidents.* **Ant.** hard, inflexible, rigid.

supplement *n.* **1.** addition, complement, attachment, extra, continuation. *A vitamin supplement was recommended by the doctor.* *–vb.* **2.** increase, extend, enlarge, augment, fortify. *She supplements her allowance with money from baby-sitting.*

supply *vb.* **1.** provide, equip, furnish, outfit. *The company supplies nearby hospitals with medicine.* *–n.* **2.** store, stock, reserve, hoard. *The hikers ate their entire supply of chocolate.*

support *vb.* **1.** brace, prop, uphold, sustain. *Thick concrete columns supported the bridge.* **2.** back, champion, favor, aid, assist. *Her friends supported her in the class election.* *–n.* **3.** brace, post, pillar, buttress. *The bridge collapsed when its supports gave way.* **4.** help, aid, assistance, backing, encouragement. *He received financial support from his parents while he was away at college.*

supporter *n.* proponent, advocate, champion, backer, adherent, fan. *I am a strong supporter of land conservation.* **Ant.** opponent, detractor, critic.

supportive *adj.* encouraging, helping, bolstering, boosting, upholding, championing. *She is supportive of community policing.* **Ant.** opposing, critical, discouraging.

suppose *vb.* guess, imagine, think, assume, believe. *Do you suppose we will get out of class early?*

suppress *vb.* stop, restrain, curb, smother, squelch. *They tried to suppress their laughter during the movie.* **Ant.** unleash, express, encourage.

supreme *adj.* **1.** highest, top, chief, head, primary. *The general is the supreme commander in Europe.* **2.** outstanding, prime, unequaled, superlative, matchless. *The restaurant's hamburgers are supreme.* **Ant.** **1.** lowest, secondary. **2.** poor, mediocre.

sure *adj.* **1.** certain, positive, definite, confident, convinced. *She was sure she saw something move behind the bushes.* **2.** firm, solid, steady, reliable. *The surgeon had a sure hand.* **Ant.** **1.** unsure, uncertain, doubtful. **2.** unsure, shaky, unsteady.

surely *adv.* doubtlessly, definitely, certainly, assuredly. *Surely you don't believe in Big Foot?*

surf *n.* waves, breakers, tide, swells, rollers, combers, spindrift. *The surf was roughened by the wind.*

WORD SEARCH

gray-crested waves: *graybeards*
hollow between waves: *trough*
series of waves: *train*
sound of: *lap, rote, thunder, swash*

surface *n.* **1.** top, crust, exterior, outside, skin. *The road's surface was cracked.* *–adj.* **2.** exterior, outer, outward, superficial. *The quick washing only removed the surface dirt.* *–vb.* **3.** rise, ascend, emerge, appear, materialize. *Dolphins surface to breathe.* **4.** cover, overlay, pave, blanket. *A maintenance crew surfaced the street with fresh asphalt.* **Ant.** **1.** interior, insides, depths. **2.** interior, internal, inside. **3.** submerge, descend, sink. **4.** uncover, expose.

surge *vb.* increase, flood, escalate, expand, rise, explode, swell. *The requests for tickets began to surge the day before the show.* **Ant.** decrease, wane, recede.

surgeon *n.* physician, specialist, doctor, medical professional, practitioner. *The surgeon removed my tonsils with great skill.*

surly *adj.* grouchy, grumpy, sour, ill-tempered, moody, sullen, nasty. *Don't ask your father for a bigger allowance when he is in such a surly mood.* **Ant.** cheerful, happy, friendly.

surmise *vb.* **1.** guess, imagine, conjecture, assume, conclude. *I can only surmise why she left without telling anyone.* –*n.* **2.** guess, assumption, conjecture, idea, opinion. *My surmise is that he quit because of the low pay.*

surmount *vb.* overcome, conquer, top, climb, master. *The student surmounted his reading difficulties.*

surpass *vb.* exceed, outdo, outperform, outshine, transcend. *The new spaceship surpasses all others in speed.*

surplus *n.* **1.** excess, oversupply, glut, overload. *A food surplus was kept in the warehouse.* –*adj.* **2.** extra, excess, unused, remaining, spare. *The store sold surplus army equipment.*

surprise *vb.* **1.** astonish, amaze, startle, shock, stun. *The movie's ending surprised me.* –*n.* **2.** wonder, amazement, astonishment, marvel, shock. *It was a surprise to see him after so many years.* **Ant. 1.** bore, weary.

surprising *adj.* astonishing, amazing, startling, unusual, unexpected. *There was a surprising snowstorm last summer.* **Ant.** expected, routine, predictable.

surreal *adj.* nightmarish, otherworldly, dreamlike, strange, fantastic, grotesque. *The abstract painter loved to paint surreal landscapes.*

surrealistic *adj.* nightmarish, otherworldly, dreamlike, strange, fantastic, grotesque. *Horror writers specialize in surrealistic plotlines.*

surrender *vb.* **1.** yield, release, relinquish, submit. *The defenders surrendered their castle to the victorious attackers.* –*n.* **2.** yielding, submission, resignation, relinquishment. *The losing army announced its surrender.*

surrogate *n.* stand-in, substitute, replacement, proxy, understudy, delegate. *My aunt served as a parental surrogate while my mom was away.*

surround *vb.* circle, ring, enclose, envelop, bound. *A moat surrounds the castle.*

surveillance *n.* eavesdropping, bugging, spying, stake-out, reconnaissance, observation. *The police often employ surveillance to catch crooks.*

survey *vb.* **1.** review, scan, observe, inspect, assess. *A critic surveyed the painting.* –*n.* **2.** poll, investigation, review, study, examination, assessment. *The survey said that half the town's residents were employed locally.*

survival *n.* living, continuation, continuance. *A nuclear war would threaten the survival of the entire planet.* **Ant.** death, ending.

survive *vb.* live, persist, endure, exist, withstand. *They hoped the injured horse would survive.* **Ant.** die, perish, succumb.

susceptible *adj.* vulnerable, defenseless, receptive, open, sensitive. *Malnutrition leaves people susceptible to disease.* **Ant.** unsusceptible, invulnerable, unreceptive.

suspect *vb.* **1.** mistrust, distrust, question, doubt. *I suspect his intentions.* **2.** guess, imagine, think, suppose, surmise. *I suspect it will rain tomorrow.* –*adj.* **3.** questionable, suspicious, doubtful, dubious, debatable. *The dishonest woman's story was suspect.* –*n.* **4.** accused, defendant, culprit. *The police said they had no suspects in the case.* **Ant. 1.** trust, believe. **2.** know. **3.** trustworthy, reliable.

suspend *vb.* **1.** hang, dangle, sling. *She suspended the bird feeder from her porch.* **2.** postpone, withhold, delay, defer. *Mother suspended my allowance because I told a lie.* **3.** expel, dismiss, eject, evict. *He was suspended from school for fighting.*

suspense *n.* uncertainty, tension, anticipation, apprehension, edginess. *Horror movies are filled with suspense.*

suspension *n.* stay, interruption, postponement, halt, pause. *The boy's suspension from school will last one week.* **Ant.** continuation, restoration.

suspicion *n.* **1.** mistrust, distrust, doubt. *He was under suspicion for last night's burglary.* **2.** idea, feeling, guess, hunch, notion. *I had a suspicion that she was the one who did it.* **Ant.** **1.** trust, confidence.

suspicious *adj.* **1.** suspect, questionable, (slang) fishy, peculiar, doubtful, dubious. *His alibi was suspicious.* **2.** mistrusting, distrustful, skeptical, cynical, leery, wary. *People knocking on my door at night make me suspicious.* **Ant.** **1.** trustworthy, sound, aboveboard. **2.** trusting, confident, naive.

sustain *vb.* **1.** bear, carry, endure, tolerate, continue. *The runner could not sustain the rapid pace.* **2.** nourish, nurture, feed, maintain. *The lost hiker had only candy bars to sustain himself.*

svelte *adj.* slender, lissome, lithe, thin, slight, willowy, graceful. *All the ballet dancers were remarkably svelte.* **Ant.** obese, fat, stout.

Svengali *n.* mesmerizer, charmer, spellbinder, brainwasher, hypnotist. *The serial killer was a Svengali who persuaded dozens of hapless victims into his car.*

swaddle *vb.* wrap, bind, swathe, bundle up. *Swaddle the baby in the blanket so she won't get a chill.*

swagger *vb.* strut, vaunt, parade, flaunt, stride arrogantly. *We watched the loudmouthed wrestlers swagger into the arena.*

swallow *vb.* **1.** gulp, guzzle, imbibe, swill, bolt. *The boy swallowed his aspirin with a glass of water.* *–n.* **2.** gulp, drink, sip, mouthful. *She took a swallow from the canteen.*

swamp *n.* **1.** marsh, bog, morass, quagmire, everglade. *Alligators live in Florida's coastal swamps.* *–vb.* **2.** flood, deluge, submerge, saturate, overwhelm. *The singer was swamped with fan letters.*

WORD SEARCH

floating island of decaying vegetation: *battery*
gas: *methane*
luminescence, nighttime: *foxfire*
moss: *sphagnum*
tree island: *hammock*

swanky *adj.* elegant, fashionably, showy, stylish, ostentatious, chic, dapper. *He strutted in wearing a swanky three-piece suit.* **Ant.** frumpy, unfashionable.

swan song *n.* last hurrah, last act, last song, farewell performance, goodbye, parting song. *The artist's swan song turned out to be her greatest work.*

swap *vb.* trade, exchange, switch, barter, substitute. *My friend and I swap comic books.*

swarm *n.* **1.** horde, host, cloud, multitude, throng. *A swarm of locusts darkened the sky.* *–vb.* **2.** crowd, flock, mass, throng, congregate. *People swarmed around the popular singer.* **Ant.** **2.** scatter, separate, disperse.

swat *vb.* **1.** hit, whack, slap, knock, smack. *She tried to swat the fly with her magazine.* *–n.* **2.** hit, slap, whack, smack. *He gave the tennis ball a good swat.*

swatch *n.* piece, scrap, specimen, sample, bit. *The merchant brought out a swatch of fabric for us to look at.*

swear *vb.* **1.** promise, pledge, vow, affirm, assert. *She swore she would tell the truth.* **2.** curse, cuss. *Please do not swear when you're angry.*

sweat *vb.* **1.** perspire, glow, exude, swelter, work up a lather. *Aerobics class makes me sweat.* –*n.* **2.** perspiration, excretion, diaphoresis, moisture, lather, body odor. *After gym class, the sweat was streaming down my face.*

sweater *n.* pullover, turtleneck, cardigan, jersey, garment. *Wear a sweater if it's cold outside.*

WORD SEARCH

diamond design: *argyle*
geometric or deer design on front: *jacquard*
goat hair: *cashmere*
jacket-like: *cardigan*
natural-colored with banded collar: *Icelandic*
pullover with round neck: *crew neck*
pullover with V-shaped neck: *V-neck*

sweep *vb.* **1.** brush, whisk, wipe, push, clear, dust. *Will you sweep the leaves off the patio?* –*n.* **2.** swoop, push, drive, thrust, stroke. *The police sweep resulted in the arrest of several suspected drug dealers.* **3.** stretch, span, spread, range, measure, reach. *A sweep of white beach extended down the coast.*

sweeping *adj.* broad, wide, widespread, extensive, far-reaching, comprehensive, blanket. *Avoid making sweeping generalizations about anyone or anything; they're usually inaccurate.* **Ant.** limited, restricted, partial.

sweet *adj.* **1.** sugary, candied, rich, honeyed. *Candy is much too sweet for me to eat.* **2.** kind, nice, gracious, affectionate, friendly. *It was really sweet of her to send flowers.* **Ant. 1.** sour, bitter. **2.** selfish, inconsiderate.

sweetheart *n.* lover, darling, flame, heartthrob, (slang) baby, (slang) honey. *Sally is my sweetheart for the moment, but Joan might be tomorrow.*

sweet-talk *vb.* flatter, cajole, sugar-coat, (slang) butter up, (slang) B.S. *Sorry, Kara, but you're not going to sweet-talk me into taking you to the mall.*

swell *vb.* **1.** rise, increase, inflate, bulge, puff. *His sprained ankle swelled to twice its normal size.* –*n.* **2.** wave, breaker, comber, rise, hill. *The raft rose up on an ocean swell.* **Ant. 1.** descend, shrink, lower. **2.** dip, depression.

swelling *n.* lump, inflammation, bulge, protuberance. *The boxer had a swelling under his bruised eye.* **Ant.** depression, indentation.

swelter *vb.* sweat, broil, cook, bake, roast, wilt. *We sweltered in the desert heat.*

swerve *vb.* twist, turn, veer, shift, move. *The driver swerved to miss a cat.*

swift *adj.* fast, rapid, quick, fleet, brisk, nimble. *The cheetah is a swift runner.* **Ant.** slow, sluggish.

swim *vb.* bathe, (slang) go for a dip, breaststroke, crawl, backstroke, tread water. *Swim to shore before the storm gets here.*

swimsuit *n.* bathing suit, shorts, swim trunks, swimwear, bikini, two-piece. *Swimming without a swimsuit is called skinny-dipping.*

swindle *vb.* **1.** cheat, trick, con, bilk, deceive, defraud. *She swindled me out of several hundred dollars.* –*n.* **2.** fraud, trick, deception, hoax, racket. *He was arrested for cheating people in a stock swindle.*

swindler *n.* con man, con artist, (slang) ripoff artist, fraud, chiseler, crook, (slang) sham artist. *If you're not careful you could lose your shirt to a swindler.*

swing *vb.* **1.** sway, seesaw, lurch, hurl, rock. *An ape swung through the trees.* **2.** curve, veer, twist, turn, swerve. *The road swings to the left.* –*n.* **3.** swaying, rocking, rolling, motion, vibration. *The swing of the rope bridge made it difficult to get* *across.* **4.** stroke, sweep, swat. *The batter took a swing at the ball.*

swirl *vb.* **1.** whirl, spin, twist, twirl, swish. *Water swirled down the drain.* *–n.* **2.** whirl, twist, twirl. *I would like a swirl of chocolate on my sundae.*

switch *vb.* **1.** exchange, swap, trade, change, shift. *Will you switch seats with me?* *–n.* **2.** change, alteration, shift, swap, trade. *I made a switch in my vacation plans.* **3.** branch, twig, stick, rod, whip. *The shepherd used a switch to drive the lambs forward.*

swollen *adj.* bloated, edemic, puffed-up, bulging, inflated, distended, enlarged. *A swollen finger may indicate an infection.* **Ant.** deflated, contracted, shriveled.

swoon *vb.* faint, pass out, collapse, go limp, keel over. *I declare, I am going to swoon in this heat.*

sword *n.* blade, saber, cutlass, rapier, foil. *The king's jeweled sword hung at his side.*

sycophant *n.* toady, (slang) kiss-up, flatterer, (slang) brownnose, (slang) yes-man, fawner. *The last thing any celebrity needs is a sycophant following him around and lapping at his feet.*

symbiotic *adj.* mutually beneficial, cooperative, give-and-take. *Flowers enjoy a symbiotic relationship with bees.* **Ant.** adversarial, competitive, antagonistic.

symbol *n.* figure, sign, emblem, image, representation. *The bald eagle is a symbol for America.*

symbolic *adj.* emblematic, illustrative, representative, suggestive, metaphorical. *The protester made a symbolic gesture of defiance.* **Ant.** actual, literal.

symmetrical *adj.* balanced, proportional, even, regular, parallel. *Individual snowflakes are symmetrical, but no two are alike.* **Ant.** asymmetrical, unbalanced, uneven.

symmetry *n.* uniformity, correspondence, evenness, parity, congruity, harmony, balance. *Scientists have discovered that faces with the most symmetry are the most attractive.* **Ant.** unevenness, asymmetry, imbalance.

sympathize *vb.* empathize, relate, agree, appreciate, understand. *I can really sympathize with your fear of speaking in front of crowds.* **Ant.** disagree, belittle.

sympathy *n.* understanding, empathy, concern, compassion, support. *I expressed my sympathy to the owner of the dog killed in the accident.* **Ant.** indifference, aloofness, insensitivity, disinterest.

symposium *n.* seminar, meeting, conference, panel discussion, forum, assembly. *Are you going to attend the symposium on the future of space travel?*

symptom *n.* sign, signal, indication, trait, feature. *His headache is only one symptom of his illness.*

synergy *n.* collaboration, cooperation, teamwork, symbiosis, working together. *I'm amazed at the synergy created by the opposing sides.*

synod *n.* conclave, convocation, assembly, ecclesiastical council, meeting. *A synod will be held to discuss marriage and the clergy.*

synonymous *adj.* like, similar, same, equivalent, comparable, interchangeable, corresponding. *The words "garbage," "rubbish," and "trash" are synonymous.* **Ant.** opposite, unlike, antonymous.

synthetic *adj.* artificial, manufactured, unnatural, imitation. *Polyester is a synthetic material.* **Ant.** natural, organic, genuine.

system *n.* **1.** setup, structure, layout, arrangement. *What type of computer system does she have?* **2.** method, methodology, plan, practice, procedure. *Do you understand our billing system?*

T

tab *n.* bill, tally, reckoning, account, record. *Add up my tab for the day and I'll pay you.*

table *n.* **1.** stand, counter, bench, bar. *Please set the table for dinner.* **2.** index, list, chart, tabulation, schedule, catalog, itemization. *This science book has many useful photographs, drawings, and tables.* *–vb.* **3.** delay, postpone, defer, shelve, put aside. *The city council tabled discussion of the controversial new ordinance.* **Ant. 3.** resume, continue, proceed, begin, start, initiate.

tablet *n.* **1.** pad, writing pad, notebook, sketchbook. *The university bookstore stocks a large supply of writing tablets.* **2.** pill, capsule, lozenge, drop. *Medicinal tablets come in a large variety of sizes and shapes.*

taboo *adj.* **1.** prohibited, banned, forbidden, outlawed, illicit, unacceptable. *During the Middle Ages, many scientific theories were taboo subjects.* *–n.* **2.** prohibition, ban, restriction, limitation. *Many religions have taboos against eating certain types of meat.* **Ant. 1.** permissible, acceptable, approved, allowed, permitted. **2.** acceptance, approval, endorsement, sanction.

tacit *adj.* implied, understood, assumed, acknowledged, unspoken, unstated. *The roommates had a tacit agreement to keep their apartment neat and clean.*

taciturn *adj.* quiet, uncommunicative, reticent, withdrawn, reserved, mute, silent. *He was a taciturn man who refused to waste his breath on small talk.* **Ant.** loquacious, talkative, voluble.

tack *vb.* **1.** fasten, attach, affix, pin, nail. *Tack this notice up where everyone can see it.* *–n.* **2.** strategy, course, plan, policy, approach, method. *The new chairwoman hoped to start her department off on a fresh tack.* **Ant. 1.** remove, detach, take down, take off.

tackle *vb.* **1.** undertake, take on, attack, attempt, accept, assume, embrace, begin, start. *Don't tackle a project you can't finish.* **2.** capture, catch, intercept, seize, grab, stop. *The quarterback was tackled before he could pass the ball.* *–n.* **3.** gear, equipment, apparatus, paraphernalia, materials, tools. *Since fishing was out of season, she left her tackle at home.* **4.** ropes, roping, rigging, cordage. *He used a block and tackle to extract the car's engine.* **Ant. 1.** avoid, evade, reject, forgo, hesitate, delay, postpone.

tacky *adj.* tasteless, unfashionable, cheap, gaudy, garish, loud, (slang) chintzy. *He wore a tacky suit that was thirty years out of date.* **Ant.** fashionable, tasteful, stylish.

tact *n.* discretion, diplomacy, delicacy, judgment, finesse, consideration, courtesy. *Embarrassing situations sometimes require lots of tact to avoid hurting a person's feelings.* **Ant.** tactlessness, insensitivity, indiscretion, crudeness.

tactful *adj.* considerate, sensitive, thoughtful, delicate, diplomatic, discrete, polite. *A considerate manager tries to be tactful when dealing with an employee's mistake.* **Ant.** tactless, untactful, blunt, indiscrete, indelicate, clumsy, thoughtless, insensitive.

tactic *n.* plan, strategy, policy, scheme, course, approach, method, system. *The millionaire employed questionable tactics in the pursuit of her fortune.*

tactical *adj.* strategic, tricky, cunning, skillful, clever. *We need to take tactical advantage of our enemy before they get wise to us.*

tactless *adj.* impolite, inconsiderate, insensitive, thoughtless, rude, untactful, tasteless, undiplomatic. *His tactless remarks offended everyone at the party.* **Ant.** tactful, considerate, thoughtful, diplomatic, polite.

tag *n.* **1.** label, marker, ticket, tab, slip, sticker. *Check the price tag to see how much it costs.* *–vb.* **2.** mark, label, identify, classify, ticket. *Please tag these for immediate delivery.* **3.** follow, tail, trail, accompany, shadow. *Her dog tags along wherever she goes.*

tail *n.* **1.** appendage, extension, attachment, back, rear. *He could see the comet's tail through his telescope.* *–vb.* **2.** follow, trail, shadow, pursue. *The detective tailed two suspects.* *–adj.* **3.** rearmost, hindmost, final, last, concluding. *A marching band brought up the tail end of the parade.* **Ant.** **1.** front, head. **3.** beginning, foremost, front, start.

tailor *n.* **1.** clothier, designer, garment maker, seamstress. *I must have the tailor alter these pants.* **2.** fit, suit, adapt, alter, cut, adjust. *Tammy tailors my suits to fit perfectly.*

taint *n.* **1.** stain, blot, blemish, impurity, imperfection, defilement, contamination. *The one incident made a permanent taint on his reputation.* *–vb.* **2.** spoil, rot, putrefy, decay, contaminate, ruin. *Refrigerate this meat or it will taint.* **3.** tarnish, blemish, blight, besmear, soil, stain. *Her remarks were tainted with prejudice.* **Ant.** **2.** purify, disinfect, clean. **3.** boost, enhance, elevate.

take *vb.* **1.** obtain, acquire, seize, get, gain, have. *Take a number and wait your turn.* **2.** carry, bring, move, transport, transfer, haul, fetch. *Many students take their books home every day.* **3.** escort, guide, conduct, chaperon, usher. *Take your little brother to the movies with you.* **4.** remove, appropriate, confiscate, steal, rob, misappropriate. *Who took my car?* **5.** swallow, consume, ingest, eat, drink. *Take two aspirin and get some rest.* **6.** tolerate, endure, suffer, undergo, accept, abide, go through. *Her parents couldn't take any more of her loud music.* **7.** subtract, deduct, remove, eliminate, withdraw. *Take thirty from forty to get ten.* **8.** understand, interpret, comprehend, grasp, perceive, infer. *I take your silence to mean you're unhappy with me.* **9.** accept, heed, follow, observe, obey. *Take my word for it.* **10.** demand, require, necessitate, need, entail. *This report will take three days to prepare.* **11.** cheat, defraud, swindle, trick, bilk. *The con artist took me for a hundred dollars.* **12.** attract, fascinate, enchant, charm, bewitch. *He seems to be taken with you.* **Ant.** **1.** release, relinquish, surrender, return, let go. **4.** return, restore, surrender. **7.** add, annex, affix, attach. **9.** reject, spurn, renounce, repudiate. **12.** repel, repulse, disgust.

takeover *n.* coup, coup d'état, rout, deposition, dethronement, overthrow, subjugation. *The military takeover of the tiny nation was quick and decisive.* **Ant.** relinquishment, abandonment, liberation.

tale *n.* **1.** story, narrative, anecdote, yarn, report, account. *The traveler had many fascinating tales to share.* **2.** lie, fib, fabrication, falsehood, fiction. *Mark Twain was a literary master of the tall tale.*

talent *n.* skill, ability, gift, aptitude, capability, capacity, expertise. *She has a talent for playing the pianc.*

talented *adj.* gifted, brilliant, expert, skilled, proficient. *She is a talented artist.* **Ant.** untalented, unskilled, mediocre.

talisman *n.* amulet, charm, fetish, stone, ring. *The talisman holds power only if you believe it does.*

talk *n.* **1.** conversation, chat, discussion, conference, dialogue, consultation. *The parents wanted to have a talk with their son about the late hours he'd been keeping.* **2.** lecture, speech, address, discourse, oration. *A local celebrity gave a talk to our class.* **3.** gossip, rumor, hearsay, tales, stories, comments. *There's been some talk going around about the actress and her new boyfriend.* *–vb.* **4.** speak, converse, discuss, chat, communicate, confer, consult. *We need to talk about your new proposal.*

talkative *adj.* garrulous, loquacious, long-winded, windy, verbose. *The talkative man was continuously interrupting everyone else.* **Ant.** silent, mute, quiet, taciturn.

talker *n.* (slang) chatterbox, motormouth, bigmouth, (slang) windbag, gossip, mouthpiece. *Talkers are fine, but only if they know when to be quiet.*

tall *adj.* towering, high, lofty, long, lengthy, soaring. *She gets dizzy looking up at tall buildings.* **Ant.** short, squat, low.

tally *n.* count, reckoning, sum, total, account, score. *The final tally was sixty-three "yes" votes and forty-nine "no" votes.*

tame *adj.* **1.** domesticated, broken, subdued, submissive, docile, timid, mild, obedient. *The animal trainer liked to pet his tame lion.* **2.** unexciting, bland, boring, uninteresting, dull, commonplace, tedious. *Life ashore seemed pretty tame to the veteran sailor.* *–vb.* **3.** domesticate, break, train, discipline, soften, subdue, moderate. *She likes to tame wild animals.* **Ant.** **1.** untamed, undomesticated, wild, feral, savage, fierce. **2.** exciting, stimulating, thrilling, interesting.

tamper *vb.* interfere, intrude, meddle, change, alter, mess, fool. *The writer hoped his publisher would not tamper with his manuscript.*

tang *n.* flavor, taste, quality, aroma, trace, hint, suggestion. *This spaghetti sauce has a tang of garlic.*

tangible *adj.* substantial, solid, obvious, concrete, real, physical, material. *She presented tangible proof of her innocence.* **Ant.** intangible, vague, imaginary.

tangle *vb.* **1.** twist, snarl, knot, muddle, mess, ravel, dishevel. *A strong breeze tangled the wind chime.* *–n.* **2.** snarl, knot, mess, maze, morass, muddle. *The cat turned the ball of yarn into a hopeless tangle.* **Ant.** **1.** untangle, disentangle, unravel, untwist.

tangy *adj.* zesty, biting, sharp, tart, flavorful. *This citrus salad dressing is especially tangy.*

tank *n.* vat, cistern, vessel, reservoir, receptacle, container. *The beer was poured into a large storage tank.*

tankard *n.* stein, mug, cup, pottle. *The innkeeper served tankards of grog.*

tantalize *vb.* entice, lure, seduce, tempt, titillate, bait. *The pictures of rich, gooey desserts on the menu were designed to tantalize.* **Ant.** disgust, repel, sicken.

tantamount *adj.* equal, equivalent, like, comparable, as good as, the same. *Driving while intoxi-*

cated is tantamount to threatening with a dangerous weapon. **Ant.** unlike, different, opposite.

tantrum *n.* outburst, fit, scene, snit, storm, rampage. *The spoiled child went into a tantrum whenever he didn't get what he wanted.*

tap *n.* **1.** rap, pat, knock, light blow, strike, touch. *Who wouldn't be startled by a tap at the window on a dark and stormy night?* **2.** faucet, spigot, spout, valve. *The outside tap froze last night.* –*vb.* **3.** rap, pat, drum, strike, knock. *She tapped her feet in time to the music.* **4.** use, utilize, draw on, exploit, manipulate. *The runner tapped all her reserves to finish the marathon.*

tape *n.* **1.** strip, ribbon, band, roll, reel, spool. *This measuring tape is fifty feet long.* –*vb.* **2.** wrap, bind, tie, seal, secure, fasten. *Tape the package securely before mailing it.* **3.** record. *He taped his favorite TV show.* **Ant. 2.** unwrap, untie, unfasten. **3.** delete.

taper *vb.* decrease, lessen, abate, diminish, dwindle, slacken, weaken. *The storm tapered off at sunset.* **Ant.** increase, strengthen, intensify.

tardy *adj.* late, behind, overdue, unpunctual, lagging, slow, delayed. *I was tardy because my car refused to start this morning.* **Ant.** early, on-time, punctual.

target *n.* goal, objective, object, end, aim, mark. *Their target is to complete the project by next summer.*

tarnish *n.* **1.** discoloration, stain, blemish, spot. *The unused silver bowl had accumulated a solid coat of tarnish.* –*vb.* **2.** dim, dull, darken, oxidize, discolor, corrode, stain. *The silverware has tarnished.* **3.** taint, besmear, defile, disgrace, darken, blemish, soil. *His public image was tarnished by the scandal.* **Ant. 2.** brighten, shine, sparkle, gleam. **3.** enhance, heighten, improve, strengthen.

tarry *vb.* linger, loiter, dawdle, dally, delay, procrastinate, remain, wait, stay. *Don't tarry or we'll miss the movie.* **Ant.** hurry, hasten, rush.

tart *adj.* **1.** sour, acid, sharp, tangy, bitter. *These strawberries are too tart.* **2.** biting, cutting, caustic, acerbic, sharp. *The radio announcer was known for her tart commentaries.* **Ant. 1.** sweet, sugary, honeyed, mild, flat. **2.** pleasant, gentle, kind, polite, friendly.

tart *n.* fruit pie, pastry, turnover, flan, dessert. *I prefer tarts with an apple filling.*

task *n.* assignment, obligation, responsibility, job, chore, duty, work. *His task is to wash the dishes.*

taskmaster *n.* boss, commander, slave driver, overseer, supervisor, tyrant. *The boss is a nice woman, but is she ever a taskmaster.*

taste *n.* **1.** flavor, savor, savoriness, essence, tang. *I'll never forget the taste of fresh strawberries.* **2.** judgment, discernment, propriety, discrimination, decorum. *Racist jokes are in very poor taste.* **3.** preference, inclination, penchant, fondness, liking. *She has a taste for good literature.* –*vb.* **4.** savor, sample, experience, partake of, encounter, test. *Have you ever tasted anything so good?* **Ant. 3.** distaste, dislike, objection, aversion. **4.** miss, elude.

tasteful *adj.* elegant, aesthetic, beautiful, artistic, becoming, discriminating. *The socialite always dressed in a tasteful way.* **Ant.** tasteless, unbecoming, vulgar, inelegant, ugly.

tasteless *adj.* **1.** tactless, gauche, unrefined, rude, crude, crass, coarse, vulgar, offensive, improper. *His tasteless remark offended all his co-workers.* **2.** flavorless, bland, savorless, insipid, dull, boring. *The school cafeteria is known for its tasteless food.* **Ant. 1.** tasteful, elegant, refined. **2.** tasteful, tasty, flavorful.

tasty *adj.* delicious, flavorful, delectable, (slang) yummy, (slang) scrumptious, appetizing, savory. *Ice cream is a tasty treat.* **Ant.** disgusting, bland, nauseating.

tattered *adj.* ragged, frazzled, frayed, torn, shabby, shoddy. *The accident-prone lion trainer has a tattered appearance.*

tattle *vb.* tell, inform, tattletale, betray, divulge, (slang) squeal, (slang) rat. *I hate when my little brother tattles on me for stealing cookies.*

tattletale *n.* informer, telltale, (slang) snitch, (slang) rat, blabbermouth, (slang) squealer. *My brother is such a tattletale; I can't do anything sneaky in front of him or he'll tell my mother.*

taunt *n.* **1.** jeer, gibe, scoff, insult, slur, provocation, ridicule. *The short boy dreaded the cruel taunts of his classmates.* *–vb.* **2.** deride, ridicule, insult, provoke, torment, harass. *Why is it some people taunt anyone less fortunate than themselves?* **Ant.** **1.** praise, compliment. **2.** commend, flatter, praise.

taut *adj.* tight, tense, drawn, extended, firm, rigid, stiff, stretched, strained. *Please hold this string taut.* **Ant.** slack, loose, flexible.

tavern *n.* bar, barroom, saloon, pub, inn, alehouse, roadhouse. *Jim Hawkins met Long John Silver in a tavern.*

tawdry *adj.* cheap, gaudy, tacky, showy, sleazy, tasteless. *The off-Broadway show was tawdry and poorly written.* **Ant.** classy, high class, tasteful.

tax *n.* **1.** tariff, levy, excise, assessment, duty. *Americans have to pay their income taxes on April fifteenth.* **2.** burden, strain, imposition, responsibility, duty, chore. *Putting three children through college was a severe tax on her financial resources.* *–vb.* **3.** assess, levy. *The government taxes everything we make.* **4.** burden, strain, encumber, load, saddle, exhaust, weaken. *The hyperactive child taxed his parents' patience.*

taxing *adj.* tiring, exhausting, draining, strenuous, demanding, sapping. *Shoveling snow is a taxing job.* **Ant.** invigorating, energizing, refreshing.

tea *n.* beverage, drink, brew, decoction, oolong, pekoe. *Let's have a cup of tea at four o'clock.*

teach *vb.* educate, instruct, lecture, inform, enlighten, tutor, train. *Will you teach me Spanish?* **Ant.** learn, study.

teacher *n.* instructor, educator, schoolmaster, faculty member, professor, guide, preceptor. *Ask the teacher to help you with your math.*

team *n.* **1.** group, unit, company, crew, band, squad. *She tried out for the basketball team.* *–vb.* **2.** pair, couple, unite, join, combine, mate. *Let's team up to get this project done faster.* **Ant.** **2.** unjoin, uncouple, separate.

tear *n.* **1.** teardrop, drop. *The child was no longer crying, but there were still tears in his eyes.* *–vb.* **2.** water, swim, mist. *Peeling an onion made her eyes tear.*

tear *n.* **1.** rip, split, rent, gap, break, damage, injury. *There's a tear in your jeans.* *–vb.* **2.** rip, rend, split, pull, apart, shred, divide. *Tear up this old sheet to get the rags you need.* **3.** rush, dash, bolt, race, charge, hustle, scramble. *The cat tore out of the yard with a dog in hot pursuit.* **Ant.** **2.** patch, mend, repair, sew. **3.** saunter, amble, stroll.

tease *vb.* taunt, ridicule, provoke, heckle, torment, pester, annoy, harass, bother. *Try not to tease your little sister.* **Ant.** commend, flatter, praise, compliment.

technical *adj.* technological, mechanical, high-tech, scientific, complex, specialized, industrial. *The workings of a computer are very technical.*

technicality *n.* formality, minor detail, triviality, minor point. *The defendant was let off on a minor technicality.*

technician *n.* specialist, mechanic, (slang) techie, master, expert, troubleshooter. *We need a technician down here to repair the copy machine.*

technique *n.* procedure, method, system, approach, skill, form, style. *The golfer spent considerable time perfecting her technique.*

technology *n.* mechanics, instrumentation, applied science, mechanization, industrial science, machinery, automation. *Modern technology is making the world an easier place to live in.*

tedious *adj.* dreary, irksome, weary, tiresome, boring, monotonous, uninteresting, routine. *Memorizing multiplication tables is a tedious task.* **Ant.** interesting, exciting, challenging, stimulating.

teeming *adj.* overflowing, overrun, swarming, bristling, dense, thick. *The forest was teeming with mosquitoes.* **Ant.** empty, unoccupied, vacant.

teenager *n.* adolescent, young adult, teen, minor, juvenile, sophomore, high schooler. *Teenagers mobbed the civic center to see their favorite rock musicians.*

teepee *n.* tent, wigwam, wickiup, lodge. *It's rare to see a teepee on a reservation today.*

teeter *vb.* wobble, sway, stagger, lurch, weave. *His heart pounded as he teetered on the brink of the precipice.*

teeth *n.* incisors, molars, fangs, bicuspids, (slang) choppers, (slang) pearly whites. *Brush your teeth after every meal.*

telegram *n.* wire, telegraph, message, cable, dispatch, transmission. *Send a telegram to your father and ask him to send money.*

telepathy *n.* extrasensory perception, ESP, mindreading, clairvoyance, sixth sense. *The mysterious woman claimed to use telepathy to receive messages from aliens.*

telephone *n.* phone, line, extension, transmitter, receiver, (slang) horn. *Get on the telephone and order a pepperoni pizza.*

WORD SEARCH

beeper: *pager*
centralized connection apparatus for multiple lines: *switchboard*
conference via closed-circuit TV and speakerphone: *teleconference*
eavesdrop electronically on another's call: *tap*
messaging system: *voice mail*
number identification system: *caller ID*
office-to-office communication system: *intercom, Private Branch Exchange (PBX)*
science: *telephonics, telephony*
signal of another call on the line, service or: *call waiting*

television *n.* TV, (slang) boob tube, (slang) the tube, video, set, console, entertainment center. *Last night I watched television until my eyes were bloodshot.*

WORD SEARCH

award: *Emmy*
broadcast: *air, televise*
broadcast on radio and TV simultaneously: *simulcast*
card with lines read by performers: *cue card, flip card*
comedy, slang for situation: *sitcom*
commercials, group of: *pod*
credits at end of show, rolling: *crawl*
distribution of shows to various stations: *syndication*
electrician, studio: *gaffer*
engineering and director's station: *control room*
fee, minimum standard performer's: *scale*
goofs removed from shows, performers': *bloopers, outtakes*

laughter, pre-recorded: *canned laughter, laugh track*
local station as part of a national network: *affiliate*
narrating voice: *voice-over*
optical transition effect: *dissolve, fade-in, fade-out, fade to black, wipe*
promotional piece for upcoming show: *preview, teaser, trailer*
ratings period: *sweeps*
read script while looking into camera, device that allows performer to: *prompter, TelePrompTer (trademark)*
record sound effects and music: *dub, foley*
regulating commission: *Federal Communications Commission (FCC)*
resolution, advanced sets with high picture: *high-definition television (HDTV)*
sound effects, one who records: *foley artist*
stations, affiliated: *network*
studio assistant: *grip, hammer, set carpenter*
tryout episode of new program: *pilot*
time, biggest viewing audience: *prime time (8 P.M. to 11 P.M.)*
transmission of program to local affiliate station: *feed*
video tape cutter, splicer, arranger: *editor*

tell *vb.* **1.** narrate, describe, relate, recite, speak, utter, voice, express, impart, convey, communicate. *The children love to have their grandfather tell stories.* **2.** order, direct, command, bid, require. *You'd better do what you've told.* **3.** distinguish, discern, determine, discover, perceive, ascertain. *Can you tell good apples from bad ones?* **4.** reveal, divulge, disclose, apprise, inform. *Could you tell me what time it is?* **Ant. 3.** confuse, mix up.

temerity *n.* boldness, foolhardiness, recklessness, audacity, carelessness, gall, indiscretion. *Few experienced climbers have the temerity to ascend Mt. Everest without supplemental oxygen.* **Ant.** prudence, caution, cowardice.

temper *n.* **1.** rage, anger, fury, ire, wrath, outburst, irritation, passion. *She yelled at him in a fit of temper.* **2.** mood. disposition, composure, self-control. *He loses his temper easily.* *–vb.* **3.** moderate, soften, soothe, pacify, quiet. *It is wise to temper justice with mercy.* **4.** toughen, harden, strengthen, fortify, anneal. *Her resolve was tempered by the many injustices she had endured.* **Ant. 1.** calmness, composure. **3.** intensify, increase, arouse. **4.** soften, weaken.

temperamental *adj.* moody, irritable, excitable, capricious, volatile, passionate, emotional. *Artists, poets, and musicians are among the most temperamental people I know.* **Ant.** serene, steady, calm, stable, unexcitable.

temperate *adj.* **1.** mild, pleasant, agreeable, clement, mellow, balmy. *Miami is blessed with a temperate climate.* **2.** moderate, restrained, controlled, self-controlled, composed, collected, rational, reasonable. *Temperate eating habits are rare on Thanksgiving Day.* **Ant. 1.** intemperate, inclement. **2.** excessive, extreme, unrestrained.

tempest *n.* storm, gale, commotion, turmoil, uproar, clamor, tumult. *When the teacher assigned two new books, the class erupted in a tempest of protest.* **Ant.** peace, quiet, calm, serenity.

tempestuous *adj.* stormy, wild, tumultuous, blustery, raging, violent, feverish. *They split up because their relationship was too often tempestuous.* **Ant.** calm, tranquil, serene.

temple *n.* house of worship, holy place, church, synagogue, cathedral, pagoda. *I went to the temple to pray for guidance.*

tempo *n.* pace, rate, speed, velocity, measure, beat, rhythm. *She's leading her life at too fast a tempo.*

temporary *adj.* momentary, passing, transient, fleeting, short, brief, short-lived. *She's holding a* *temporary job while searching for a career position.* **Ant.** permanent, lasting, long-lived, enduring.

tempt *vb.* attract, entice, induce, invite, lure, lead on, seduce, tantalize. *He was having so much fun that he was tempted to extend his vacation.* **Ant.** discourage, dissuade, repel, repulse.

temptation *n.* attraction, enticement, lure, allurement, pull, draw. *A chocolate sundae is a temptation that's hard to resist.*

tempting *adj.* attractive, alluring, enticing, inviting, provocative, appetizing, tantalizing. *That pizza sure looks tempting.* **Ant.** unattractive, uninviting, repulsive.

tenacious *adj.* determined, stubborn, obstinate, persistent, strong, firm, clinging, set, unyielding. *The dog had a tenacious grip on his master's slipper.* **Ant.** lax, slack, loose, yielding.

tenacity *n.* perseverance, stick-to-itiveness, persistence, resolve, doggedness, endurance. *You must have great tenacity to succeed as an Olympic athlete.*

tenant *n.* occupant, resident, inhabitant, dweller, renter, lodger, leaseholder. *Have you met the new tenants next door?*

tend *vb.* **1.** lean, incline, verge, be disposed. *She tends to spend too much time playing computer games.* **2.** protect, watch, guard, attend, look after, care for, supervise. *Will you tend my plants while I'm on vacation?* **Ant. 2.** neglect, ignore, disregard.

tendency *n.* inclination, leaning, disposition, trend, bias, bent, propensity, penchant, habit. *He has a tendency to sleep late.* **Ant.** disinclination, aversion.

tender *adj.* **1.** soft, gentle, caring, compassionate, kindhearted, warm, warmhearted, affectionate, fond, loving. *The lioness was very tender with her cubs.* **2.** delicate, frail, fragile, weak, soft, vulnerable. *Because of her dental problems, she could only eat tender foods.* **3.** sore, uncomfortable, painful, sensitive, aching, troublesome. *His sprained ankle is still tender.* *–vb.* **4.** offer, bid, present, propose, submit, advance, suggest, give. *The unhappy employee tendered her resignation.* **Ant. 1.** callous, harsh, unfeeling, heartless, insensitive. **2.** tough, strong, sturdy. **3.** painless, insensitive. **4.** retract, withdraw.

tenderness *n.* tenderheartedness, kindness, compassion, softness, mercy, sweetness. *Raising a small child requires great tenderness.* **Ant.** roughness, cruelty, brutality.

tendon *n.* sinew, connective tissue, muscle fiber. *The Red Sox Star short stop is on the disabled list due to a strained tendon.*

tenement *n.* apartment, rental property, flat, duplex, triplex, boardinghouse. *They lived in a dingy tenement in a poor part of town.*

tenet *n.* principle, truth, belief, teaching, doctrine, maxim, rule. *Sometimes it is beneficial to question some of the tenets of your religion.*

tennis *n.* racket sport, lawn tennis, game. *Let's go up to the court and have a game of tennis.*

WORD SEARCH

audience area: *gallery*
boundary lines: *baseline, service line*
four players, game played with: *doubles*
long exchange between players without a miss: *rally*
officials: *baseline judge, linesman, net judge*
racket, middle of: *sweet spot*
returning ball before it touches the ground: *volley*
rotation imparted on ball, intentional: *topspin, backspin*
score, zero: *love*
scoring unit: *fifteen*

serve, failure to deliver a legal: *fault, double fault, foot fault*
serve that opponent is unable to return: *ace*
strokes: *backhand, chop, drink, drive, forehand, lob, slice, smash*
tie-breaking game: *sudden death*
winning best of three or more sets: *match*

tense *adj.* **1.** stretched, strained, taut, tight, drawn, stiff. *His arms were tense from doing too many push-ups.* **2.** nervous, anxious, apprehensive, fearful, excited, uneasy, uptight, jittery. *She was very tense just before her math final.* **Ant. 1.** slack, loose, limp, relaxed. **2.** relaxed, calm, cool.

tent *n.* shelter, tepee, wigwam, wickiup, pavilion, yurt. *It's fun to camp out in a tent.*

tentative *adj.* conditional, unconfirmed, contingent, provisional, indefinite, temporary. *The new employee has been given a tentative work schedule.* **Ant.** confirmed, definite, settled, final.

tenuous *adj.* weak, thin, small, feeble, insubstantial, shallow, uncertain. *He has only a tenuous grip on reality.* **Ant.** strong, firm, sound, solid, substantial.

tenure *n.* **1.** term, time, residence, reign, occupancy. *We have enjoyed your tenure here, Dr. Jones.* **2.** permanency, lifetime position. *Professor Smith was finally granted tenure at the university.*

term *n.* **1.** word, name, expression, phrase, appellation. *This dictionary has an extensive listing of computer terms.* **2.** period, time, interval, duration, session, season. *She was elected for a term of two years.* **3.** condition, stipulation, provision, detail, item, limit. *What are the terms of your agreement with your parents?*

terminal *adj.* **1.** concluding, final, end, last, fatal, lethal, mortal. *His cancer was in its terminal stage.* –*n.* **2.** station, terminus, end, depot. *You'll find her at the computer terminal.* **Ant. 1.** initial, beginning, first, nonlethal.

terminate *vb.* finish, end, conclude, stop, cease, discontinue, expire, halt. *Her temporary job terminates next week.* **Ant.** begin, start, commence, inaugurate.

termination *n.* discontinuance, ending, cancellation, dismissal, firing, end. *He complained about his sudden termination, but he was one of many employees who were laid off.* **Ant.** start, commencement, beginning.

terminology *n.* vernacular, vocabulary, jargon, nomenclature, lingo, wording. *It's hard to keep track of all the new computer terminology.*

terrace *n.* patio, garden, gallery, veranda, balcony. *Let's take the telescope out on to the terrace.*

terrestrial *adj.* worldly, earthly, terrene, tellurian, mundane. *I don't think much about an afterlife because I have too many terrestrial concerns.*

terrible *adj.* horrible, horrid, horrifying, awful, dreadful, fearful, frightful, alarming. *A terrible earthquake devastated Mexico City.* **Ant.** pleasant, mild, harmless.

terrific *adj.* **1.** great, superb, magnificent, wonderful, marvelous, extraordinary, splendid. *It was a terrific movie.* **2.** terrible, horrible, awful, dreadful, severe, intense, huge. *The storm did terrific damage.* **Ant. 1.** mediocre, poor, bad, unpleasant. **2.** minor, moderate, slight.

terrify *vb.* frighten, scare, alarm, terrorize, horrify, petrify, appall, dismay. *The thought of a major earthquake terrifies many Southern Californians.* **Ant.** reassure, comfort, soothe, calm.

territorial *adj.* proprietary, defensive, protective, aggressive. *Lions and other predators tend to be fiercely territorial.*

territory *n.* domain, region, area, terrain, locale, realm, district. *A grizzly bear roams over a territory of about 100 square miles.*

terror *n.* fear, dread, horror, panic, alarm, apprehension, anxiety. *The child was filled with terror at the approach of a thunderstorm.*

terrorism *n.* extortion, coercion, arm-twisting, intimidation, bullying, hostage-taking, bomb threats. *The government has a firm policy never to give in to terrorism.*

terrorist *n.* revolutionary, subversive, extortionist, bully, radical, rebel. *Police captured a terrorist attempting to smuggle bomb-making materials.*

terse *adj.* brief, concise, short, curt, succinct, crisp. *Her terse comments indicated she was displeased.* **Ant.** lengthy, long, wordy, verbose, rambling.

test *n.* **1.** examination, exam, quiz, analysis, investigation, trial. *You have to take a test to get a driver's license.* –*vb.* **2.** examine, question, quiz, analyze, investigate assess, check. *The manufacturer thoroughly tested the new product before releasing it.*

testament *n.* testimony, testimonial, proof, evidence, affirmation, confirmation. *That fewer people are hurt in fires nowadays is testament to the efficacy of smoke alarms.*

testify *vb.* affirm, declare, swear, attest, state, confirm, substantiate. *Will there be anyone to testify on your behalf?*

testimonial *n.* endorsement, commendation, recommendation, tribute, (slang) blurb, (slang) plug. *A product touted with numerous testimonials can usually be trusted.*

testimony *n.* declaration, statement, oath, evidence, proof, affirmation. *The victim's testimony led to a conviction.*

testy *adj.* grouchy, cranky, irritable, touchy, peevish, grumpy. *I can be testy in the morning until I've had my coffee.* **Ant.** sweet, good-natured, cheerful.

text *n.* **1.** textbook, schoolbook, book, manual, tome. *The class is using the same text as last semester.* **2.** words, wording, contents, subject, topic, theme. *The local newspaper printed the full text of the mayor's speech.*

textbook *n.* text, reference book, school book, manual, tome. *Textbooks are very expensive today.*

textile *n.* woven, fabric, knitted fabric, cloth, material, fiber. *Cotton is the most commonly used textile in the garment industry.*

texture *n.* structure, composition, consistency, character quality, nature, touch, feel. *Frozen yogurt has a pleasingly smooth texture.*

thankful *adj.* grateful, appreciative, obliged, gratified, pleased. *He was very thankful for the pay raise.* **Ant.** thankless, ungrateful, unappreciative.

thankless *adj.* unappreciated, unacknowledged, unheeded, unrewarded. *Cleaning up after a party is a thankless chore.*

thatch *n.* straw, mat, roofing, rushes. *We were astonished to see that many of the houses in the village had roofs made from thatch.*

thaw *vb.* **1.** defrost, soften, warm, melt, dissolve. *Frozen hamburger should be thawed before frying.* –*n.* **2.** melting, warming, thawing. *Many animals come out of hibernation during spring's first thaw.* **Ant.** **1.** freeze, solidify, stiffen, harden, **2.** freeze, frost.

theater *n.* **1.** playhouse, cinema, stage, auditorium, hall. *When you said you were going to the theater, I didn't know if you meant a movie or a play.* **2.** site, field, setting, scene, sector, zone. *The army was prepared to cope with a widespread theater of operations.*

WORD SEARCH

advertisement at front of theater: *marquee*
afternoon show: *matinee*
anxiety suffered by actors, performance: *flop sweat, stage fright*
award: *Tony*
background scenery: *backdrop, ground row, cyclorama*
backstage area: *wings*
brochure of show, descriptive: *playbill, program*
Christ, play centered around the suffering of: *passion play*
comedy, dark: *black comedy*
comedy, physical or slapstick: *low comedy*
comedy, spoofing: *lampoon, parody, satire, send-up*
comedy, witty: *high comedy*
comedy of exaggeration: *farce*
company of performers: *repertory, troupe*
drama, exaggerated: *melodrama*
drama, sad: *tragedy*
emergency fill-in, performer's: *understudy*
financier: *angel*
furnish stage with scenery, props, etc.: *dress*
hit show: *boffo*
musicals, theater specializing in: *lyric theater*
music of show, written: *score*
object used in show: *prop*
platform or walkway for hanging lights, high: *fly*
segment of show: *act*
serious emotions or issues, show featuring: *drama*
speech to audience, actor's solo: *soliloquy*
summertime productions: *summer stock*
tryout for parts, open: *audition, cattle call*
variety show, early 20th-century: *burlesque, vaudeville*
worker, stage: *stagehand*
writer, show's: *playwright, scriptwriter*

theatrical *adj.* dramatic, melodramatic, histrionic, exaggerated, (slang) hammy, campy. *She was being rather theatrical when she screamed that the world would end if she didn't get a new pair of shoes.* **Ant.** understated, sincere, real.

theft *n.* robbery, stealing, larceny, burglary, pilfering, looting. *She was heartbroken by the theft of her wedding ring.*

theme *n.* **1.** topic, subject, point, thesis, premise, argument. *Do you understand the theme of this novel?* **2.** essay, article, composition, paper, report. *He has to write a theme for his English class.*

theology *n.* theosophy, religious study, divinity, Scripture, the gospel, study of God. *You'll have to study theology if you want to be a preacher.*

theoretical *adj.* hypothetical, conjectural, speculative, unproven, untested, presumed. *That life exists on other planets is purely theoretical.* **Ant.** proven, actual, practical.

theory *n.* hypothesis, assumption, conjecture, speculation, guess, deduction, proposition, idea, explanation. *Everyone had a theory about who had committed the crime.* **Ant.** proof, certainty, knowledge.

therapeutic *adj.* healing, medicinal, remedial, corrective, restorative, beneficial. *Massage is very therapeutic when you're stressed out.* **Ant.** deleterious, harmful, unhealthy.

therapist *n.* practitioner, healer, doctor, physician, social worker, psychologist, counselor. *If you've plagued by stress, a therapist can help you manage it.*

therapy *n.* treatment, regimen, rehabilitation, remedy, homeopathy, psychotherapy. *Therapy can help relieve your anxiety.*

therefore *adv.* consequently, accordingly, hence, thus, then, ergo. *She has a cold and therefore could not go to school.* **Ant.** but, however, nevertheless.

thesaurus *n.* lexicon, glossary, synonym finder, word treasury. *A thesaurus can often help you improve your writing.*

thesis *n.* dissertation, essay, research paper, composition, treatment, treatise. *I'm writing a thesis on human behavior during a full moon.*

thick *adj.* 1. broad, deep, hefty, bulky, thick-set, massive, large. *He improvised a bookshelf from concrete blocks and thick boards.* 2. viscous, syrupy, condensed, concentrated, heavy, solid. *She likes thick and chunky spaghetti sauce.* 3. crowded, dense, tight, swarming, teeming, crammed. *The forest was thick with hunters.* **Ant.** 1. slim, slender, thin, narrow, small. 2. diluted, watery, runny, liquid. 3. bare, barren, empty, void.

thicket *n.* underbrush, brush, scrub, tangle, bushes, shrubbery. *I crawled into the thicket to find my lost golf balls.*

thief *n.* burglar, robber, bandit, pilferer, criminal, crook, racketeer, swindler, defrauder. *A thief stole my new watch.*

thin *adj.* 1. slim, lean, slender, skinny, gaunt, narrow, flimsy, slight. *Pencil lead is very thin.* 2. watery, diluted, weak, runny, diffused, scant, sparse, spare. *This soup is too thin for my tastes.* *–vb.* 3. diminish, reduce, decrease, weaken, dilute, water down. *His hair has begun to thin on top.* **Ant.** 1. thick, fat, stout, wide, bulky. 2. heavy, thick, dense, concentrated. 3. thicken, increase, concentrate.

thing *n.* object, entity, article, being, item. *Anyone know what this thing is?* 2. matter, circumstance, condition, factor, quality, attribute, feature. *There's not a thing wrong with me.* 3. statement, utterance, thought, expression, point. *I haven't heard a single thing you've said.* 4. possession, belonging, personal effect, clothing, apparel, attire. *Will all your things fit in this closet?* 5. act, action, deed, feat, accomplishment. *A good artist can do incredible things with a blank canvas.*

think *vb.* 1. reason, reflect, ponder, meditate, contemplate, speculate, deliberate, rationalize. *Let's think about it before making a decision.* 2. believe, presume, suppose, propose, guess, assume, imagine, conclude. *Do you think it'll rain today?*

thinking *adj.* 1. thoughtful, contemplative, pensive, meditative, intelligent, smart. *Chess is a thinking person's game.* *–n.* 2. thought, reasoning, reflection, calculation, judgment. *He acted without thinking.* **Ant.** 1. unthinking, thoughtless.

thirst *n.* 1. longing, craving, yearning, desire, hunger yen, appetite. *She has a nearly insatiable thirst for knowledge.* *–vb.* 2. crave, covet, desire, want, long, ache, yearn. *The art collector thirsted for an original Van Gogh.* **Ant.** 1. aversion, distaste, revulsion, dislike.

thorough *adj.* total, complete, entire, full, perfect, absolute, exhaustive. *The doctor gave his patient a thorough physical.* **Ant.** incomplete, partial, imperfect, inadequate, careless.

thought *n.* 1. thinking, reasoning, reflection, idea, concept, notion, judgment, opinion, belief. *Do you have any thoughts on the subject being discussed.* 2. intent, intention, plan, design, purpose, aim, goal, objective. *It's his thought to take a vacation next summer.*

thoughtful *adj.* 1. kind, kindhearted, considerate, attentive, caring, concerned, courteous. *Visiting her in the hospital was a thoughtful thing for you to do.* 2. contemplative, meditative, reflecting, reflective, thinking. *She's in a thoughtful mood.* **Ant.** 1. unkind, inconsiderate, mean. 2. thoughtless, unreflective.

thoughtless *adj.* 1. careless, heedless, regardless, neglectful, inattentive, stupid, dumb. *This report reflects thoughtless and hasty writing.* 2.

loose. **3.** large, roomy, ample. **4.** empty, vacant, void, easy, light.

tighten *vb.* fasten, fix, secure, tauten, cinch, contract, constrict. *Tighten your belt before your pants fall down.* **Ant.** loosen, slacken, release.

tightwad *n.* (slang) cheapskate, (slang) pennypincher, miser, (slang) scrooge, hoarder. *The tightwad's favorite pastime was searching the ground for pennies.* **Ant.** spendthrift, free-spender.

till *prep.* **1.** until, before, prior to, up to. *He'll be at the office till nine o'clock.* –*vb.* **2.** cultivate, plow, harrow, hoe, turn. *In the springtime, farmers till their fields in preparation for planting.* –*n.* **3.** cash register, cashbox, coffer, safe, vault. *He was caught with his hand in the till.*

tilt *n.* **1.** incline, slope, slant, list, lean, cant, pitch. *The Leaning Tower of Pisa has so much tilt it looks as if it should fall.* –*vb.* **2.** tip, pitch, slope, slant, incline. *Sometimes it's hard to resist the urge to tilt a pinball machine.*

time *n.* **1.** interval, term, period, spell, span, space, stretch, while. *When the school year starts, it seems like a long time until Christmas break.* **2.** age, epoch, era, period, eon. *Life was difficult during the time of the caveman.* **3.** beat, meter, rhythm, tempo, measure, pace. *Play this song in three-four time.* –*vb.* **4.** measure, regulate, adjust, pace, gauge. *The socialite timed her appearance for maximum effect.*

timeless *adj.* neverending, infinite, everlasting, immortal, undying, eternal. *The storyteller's favorite plot of human against nature is timeless.* **Ant.** limited, finite, temporary.

timely *adj.* convenient, fitting, opportune, favorable, suitable, prompt, punctual, early. *The timely arrival of reinforcements saved the army from defeat.* **Ant.** untimely, inconvenient, inopportune, late.

timid *adj.* shy, bashful, diffident, unassertive, hesitant, cautious, unassuming, afraid, apprehensive, fearful. *He is too timid to ask her for a date.* **Ant.** bold, assertive, confident, forward, fearless.

tinge *n.* **1.** color, tint, trace, hint, touch, shade, suggestion, streak. *There was a tinge of anger in her voice.* –*vb.* **2.** color, tint, touch, season. *The document was tinged yellow with age.*

tinker *vb.* putter, fiddle, doodle, fuss, mend, fix repair. *She tinkered with the lawn mower until she got it running again.*

tint *n.* **1.** tinge, color, hint, trace, shade, suggestion. *The wallpaper has a slight pinkish tint.* **2.** dye, stain, coloring. *The local supermarket carries tints for both hair and fabrics.* –*vb.* **3.** tinge, color, tone, dye, stain. *She tinted her hair to keep the gray from showing.*

tiny *adj.* small, little, minute, miniature, dwarfish, midget, petite. *The tiny kitten could fit in the palm of her hand.* **Ant.** huge, enormous, colossal, immense, large, big.

tip *n.* **1.** top, point, peak, head, apex, extremity, end. *This pencil has a dull tip.* **2.** advice, suggestion, information, clue, hint, warning. *Do you have any good tips on how I should invest my savings?* **3.** gratuity, bonus, gift, reward. *Let's give the waitress a good tip.* –*vb.* **4.** tilt, upset, overturn, overthrow, topple. *The lamp tipped over and fell to the floor.* **5.** pay, reward, recompense, remunerate. *We should probably tip both the bellboy and the maid.* **Ant. 1.** bottom, base, foot.

tirade *n.* outburst, outpouring, harangue, diatribe, scolding, rant. *The manager delivered a tirade to the late employee.*

tire *vb.* **1.** weaken, fatigue, exhaust, weary, enervate, wear out, drain. *She was tired from playing three games of tennis.* **2.** bore, irk, bother, disgust, exasperate, annoy. *She quickly* *tired of her dog's continuous barking.* **Ant. 1.** refresh, revive, invigorate. **2.** delight, please, excite.

tired *adj.* exhausted, weary, fatigued, enervated, worn, spent, drained. *The runner was too tired to finish the marathon.* **Ant.** rested, refreshed, energetic, fresh, tireless.

tireless *adj.* untiring, inexhaustible, energetic, enduring, unceasing, determined, steady. *The senator's tireless campaign against drunk drivers resulted in a tough new law.* **Ant.** tired, unenergetic, inactive, listless.

titillate *vb.* arouse, tantalize, excite, stimulate, turn on, tease. *The movie maker's job is to titillate the audience.* **Ant.** bore, put to sleep.

title *n.* **1.** name, designation, heading, caption, legend. *What's the title of the new movie everyone's talking about?* **2.** deed, claim, right, ownership. *The mortgage bank still holds the title to my house.* **3.** crown, championship, honors. *The unknown boxer has dreams of wresting the title from the current champion.* *–vb.* **4.** name, call, designate, term, entitle. *What will you title your new play?*

toady *n.* psychophant, (slang) yes-man, flatterer, groveler, fawner, lackey. *The wealthy boxer had more than one pathetic toady in his entourage.*

toddler *n.* tot, child, preschooler, baby. *The toddler shouldn't be allowed to climb stairs alone.*

together *adv.* jointly, collectively, mutually, simultaneously. *Let's go to the party together.* **Ant.** separately, individually, singly, alone.

toil *n.* **1.** work, labor, exertion, effort, struggle, drudgery, hardship. *He was ready to retire after thirty years of toil.* *–vb.* **2.** labor, slave, sweat, work, struggle, strain, strive. *She toiled night and day to get her law degree.* **Ant. 1.** leisure, relaxation, rest. **2.** relax, rest, loll.

toilet *n.* flush, (slang) potty, commode, (slang) john, privy, bathroom, rest room, lavatory. *Toddlers wear diapers until they learn to use the toilet.*

token *n.* **1.** symbol, sign, mark, evidence, expression, indication, souvenir, memento, keepsake. *The rose was a token of her love for him.* *–adj.* **2.** superficial, perfunctory, symbolic, pretended. *The hiring of only one minority employee was merely token compliance with equal opportunity laws.* **Ant. 2.** genuine, real, actual.

tolerable *adj.* acceptable, adequate, bearable, endurable, allowable, supportable. *Tumultuous behavior is not tolerable in the classroom.* **Ant.** intolerable, unbearable, unacceptable.

tolerant *adj.* indulgent, lenient, permissive, patient, accepting, understanding, forbearing, liberal. *The parents were overly tolerant of their child's mischievousness.* **Ant.** intolerant, uncompromising, strict, harsh, rigid.

tolerate *vb.* **1.** bear, endure, suffer, take, abide. *I can't tolerate much more of this cold weather.* **2.** condone, allow, permit, approve, authorize, accept. *Most restaurants have sections where smoking is not tolerated.* **Ant. 2.** prohibit, forbid, ban, discourage.

toll *n.* **1.** expense, cost, price, tax, charge, tariff, fee. *You have to pay a toll to use that bridge.* *–vb.* **2.** ring, chime, peal, knell, strike. *The bells are tolling in honor of the new pope.*

tomb *n.* grave, crypt, vault, burial, place, mausoleum, sepulcher. *Abraham Lincoln's tomb is a national shrine.*

tombstone *n.* headstone, gravestone, marker, monument, stela. *The inscription on the tombstone had weathered and was nearly impossible to read.*

ton *n.* two thousand pounds, load, mass, pile, truckload. *We spread nearly a ton of manure on the garden and the plants grew like crazy.*

tone *n.* **1.** sound, pitch, note, noise. *Only a dog can hear the tone of this whistle.* **2.** attitude, mood, temper, spirit, manner. *Although she tried to be cheerful, the tone of her letter seemed to indicate that she was unhappy.* **3.** color, tint, tinge, hue, shade. *He dyed his shirt three tones of blue.* **4.** vigor, health, strength. *She used aerobics to maintain good muscle tone.*

tongs *n.* pincers, clamp, forceps. *You can pick up those hot coals with the tongs.*

tongue *n.* language, dialect, speech, idiom, vocabulary, jargon. *His native tongue is German.*

tongue-in-cheek *adv.* **1.** kiddingly, jokingly, facetiously, ironically, in jest. *Her comments were given totally tongue-in-cheek and weren't meant to be taken seriously.* *–adj.* **2.** facetious, ironic, insincere, waggish. *His tongue-in-cheek remarks were biting and hurtful.* **Ant. 1.** seriously, sincerely. **2.** serious, sincere.

too *adv.* **1.** also, additionally, besides, likewise, moreover, furthermore. *Let's take in dinner and a movie too.* **2.** very, excessively, extremely, overly, unduly. *This house is too small for the three of us.*

tool *n.* **1.** implement, utensil, instrument, device, apparatus, gadget. *A hammer, saw, and screwdriver are useful tools for household repairs.* **2.** pawn, puppet, agent, figurehead, hireling. *The dictator was only a tool of his country's army.*

top *n.* **1.** summit, peak, pinnacle, tip, apex, head, zenith, crest. *The view from the top was worth the difficulties of climbing the mountain.* **2.** lid, cover, cap, stopper. *Put the top back on the jar when you're through with it.* *–adj.* **3.** highest, topmost, leading, main, uppermost, foremost, chief, principal. *All the top rock stars performed at the benefit concert.* *–vb.* **4.** excel, surpass, exceed, transcend, beat, better, best. *Her new novel tops anything she's written before.* **Ant. 1.** bottom, base, foot, nadir. **3.** lowest, worst, least.

topic *n.* subject, theme, thesis, point, question, issue, matter, text. *He has to write a report on a topic related to ecology.*

topical *adj.* contemporary, current, up-to-the-minute, modern, popular, in the news. *The subjects of the debates ranged from historical to topical issues.* **Ant.** old, out-of-date, past.

topple *vb.* overturn, overthrow, upset, fall, drop, collapse. *His dream of an early retirement was toppled by the stock-market crash.*

torch *n.* light, burning, brand, flame, flare, lamp, flashlight, spotlight. *Angry villagers chased after Frankenstein with burning torches.* *–vb.* **2.** burn, set, afire, ignite, kindle, inflame. *An angry mob torched the desperado's hideout.*

torment *n.* **1.** suffering, pain, anguish, agony, misery, torture, distress, despair. *Her migraine headaches were a continuous source of torment.* *–vb.* **2.** agonize, pain, distress, torture, plague, annoy, provoke. *He was tormented with remorse for his past indiscretions.* **Ant. 1.** pleasure, joy, comfort. **2.** soothe, ease, relieve.

tornado *n.* twister, whirlwind, cyclone, windstorm, tempest, waterspout. *The safest place to be during a tornado is down in a cellar.*

torpid *adj.* lethargic, unmoving, slothful, slow-moving, sluggish, listless, hibernating. *Bears are remarkably torpid during winter months.* **Ant.** lively, active, hyperactive.

torpor *n.* inactivity, lethargy, sluggishness, listlessness, hibernation, dormancy. *In winter, bears fall into a torpor and rarely emerge from their dens.*

torrent *n.* deluge, flood, downpour, inundation, rain, stream, outburst, outpouring. *The manager faced a torrent of protests when she tried to eliminate coffee breaks.*

torrid *adj.* hot, sweltering, blistering, sultry, scorching, blazing, passionate, lustful. *Accord-*

ing to published reports, the two movie stars were carrying on a torrid love affair. **Ant.** cold, frigid, icy.

torture *n.* 1. torment, brutality, cruelty, punishment, ordeal, suffering, agony, pain, anguish. *Going to a party can be sheer torture for a shy person.* –*vb.* 2. torment, agonize, afflict, maim, mutilate, mistreat, abuse. *The soldiers tortured their prisoners to exact information.* **Ant.** 1. pleasure, joy, comfort. 2. soothe, ease, comfort.

torturous *adj.* excruciating, agonizing, tormenting, torturing, painful, anguished, distressful. *The lost hiker experienced a torturous night alone in the woods.* **Ant.** painless, pleasant, comforting.

toss *vb.* 1. throw, pitch, cast, hurl, fling, heave. *The bachelor's apartment had dirty clothes tossed everywhere.* 2. turn, stir, sway, tumble, writhe, wriggle. *The insomniac spent yet another night tossing around in bed.* 3. discuss, debate, argue, deliberate, consider. *The committee tossed around the new proposal.* –*n.* 4. throw, pitch, cast, fling. *The decision was made by a toss of a coin.*

total *n.* 1. sum, whole, entirety, totality, aggregate. *The cost of my new computer and programs came to a total of $2,000.* –*adj.* 2. entire, whole, complete, full, inclusive, absolute, outright. *She unhappily acknowledged that the evening had been far from a total success.* –*vb.* 3. add, compute, calculate, reckon, sum up. *When he totaled his bills, he realized he didn't have enough to pay them all.* **Ant.** 2. partial, limited, qualified, incomplete.

totalitarian *adj.* autocratic, dictatorial, tyrannical, despotic, authoritarian, fascist. *The totalitarian government does not allow its populace to vote.* **Ant.** democratic, free, liberal.

totally *adv.* completely, utterly, wholly, entirely, thoroughly, absolutely, perfectly. *She isn't being totally honest with you.* **Ant.** partially, incompletely.

totter *vb.* reel, falter, stagger, wobble, sway, falter, shake, flounder. *A loose rock tottered on the brink of the precipice.*

touch *n.* 1. contact, feeling, touching, handling, brush, stroke. *His injury was so sensitive that even the slightest touch was painful.* 2. feel, texture, quality, nature, character. *This blanket has a soft touch.* 3. trace, hint, shade, tinge, dash, suggestion. *This paint needs just a touch more blue to match the original color.* –*vb.* 4. finger, feel, handle, probe, stroke, manipulate. *Do not touch the wet paint.* 5. affect, move, stir, impress, influence, sway, arouse. *The old recluse was touched by a child's kindness.* 6. border, abut, meet, contact, join, converge. *During the dry season, their dock didn't even touch the water.* 7. mention, discuss, allude to, refer to, note. *The report was full of trivialities, and it didn't even touch the real issue.* **Ant.** 6. diverge, past, separate. 7. ignore, disregard, omit.

touching *adj.* moving, stirring, soul-stirring, poignant, heartwarming, heartbreaking. *The movie's most touching scene caused theatergoers to weep.* **Ant.** unemotional, inane, insipid.

touchstone *n.* standard, measure, benchmark, ideal, yardstick, gauge. Titanic *is the touchstone for all profit-seeking movie makers.*

touchy *adj.* sensitive, delicate, controversial, divisive, ticklish, risky. *Offshore drilling is a touchy issue to discuss with an environmentalist.* **Ant.** safe, uncontroversial, easy.

tough *adj.* 1. strong, hard, hardy, sturdy, durable, resilient. *Denim is a tough fabric.* 2. difficult, laborious, arduous, demanding, strenuous, rigorous. *Chinese is a tough language to learn.* **Ant.** 1. delicate, fragile, soft, weak. 2. easy, simple.

tour *n.* 1. visit, journey, excursion, trip, outing, expedition. *She took a tour of the pyramids.* 2. term, period, shift, time, turn, assignment. *He served a three-year tour in the army.* –*vb.* 3. travel, visit, journey, roam, sightsee, see, explore. *She will be touring England next year.*

tourist *n.* traveler, sightseer, visitor, tourer. *Disneyland attracts tourists from all over the world.*

tournament *n.* contest, match, competition, game, meet. *Who's favored to win this year's bowling tournament?*

tow *vb.* 1. drag, draw, pull, haul, tug. *There was so much snow in his driveway, he had to have his car towed out.* –*n.* 2. towing, drag, draw, pull, haul. *Can you give my car a tow?*

towel *n.* wipe, wash cloth, hand cloth. *I'd rather dry my hair with a towel than with a hair dryer.*

tower *n.* 1. spire, steeple, turret, minaret, column. *The church has a picturesque bell tower.* –*vb.* 2. ascend, soar, loom, dominate, overlook. *The basketball player towers above all his friends.*

towering *adj.* high, tall, skyscraping, sky-high, lofty, soaring, gigantic, gargantuan. *Tourists in New York like to gape at all the towering buildings.* **Ant.** short, stubby, low.

town *n.* municipality, community, settlement, village, metropolis, city. *Life in small towns is less hectic than in big cities.*

toxic *adj.* poisonous, noxious, harmful, injurious, unhealthy, deadly. *No one likes to live next to a toxic-waste dump.* **Ant.** nontoxic, nonpoisonous, harmless, healthy.

toxin *n.* poison, venom, pathogen, virus, lethal substance, hazardous material. *Some mushrooms contain deadly toxins.*

toy *n.* 1. plaything, pastime, trifle, trinket, bauble. *His computer is just another toy to him.* –*vb.* 2. play, trifle, tease, fiddle, sport. *Don't toy with my emotions.*

trace *n.* 1. vestige, remains, mark, sign, track, trail, evidence, proof. *The search-and-rescue team could find no trace of the lost hiker.* 2. hint, suggestion, touch, tinge, tint, streak. *There's just a trace of smog today.* –*vb.* 3. track, trail, follow, hunt, pursue, search, seek. *The police traced the stolen car and found the thief.* 4. copy, draw, sketch, outline, diagram. *The student's report included several drawings traced from a science textbook.*

track *n.* 1. trail, spoor, footprint, mark, sign, trace. *Last winter I found bear tracks near my mountain cabin.* 2. course, path, pathway, route, road, trail, way. *The new president hoped to get his administration started on the right track.* –*vb.* 3. trail, follow, hunt, pursue, search, seek, trace. *The sheriff tracked the fugitive to his hideout.* 4. carry, drag, bring, bear. *The child tracked snow into the house.*

tract *n.* region, area, district, territory, expanse, parcel, space. *The new national park contains a vast tract of tundra.*

traction *n.* grip, hold, friction, clutch, clasp, pull, drag. *Her new tires give good traction on icy roads.*

tractor trailer *n.* truck, eighteen-wheeler, semi, trailer truck. *It is rather difficult to park a tractor trailer while driving in reverse.*

trade *n.* 1. commerce, business, industry, traffic, transactions, dealings. *Japan's economy is dependent upon foreign trade.* 2. art, craft, occupation, profession, job, employment. *He hopes to learn the plumber's trade.* 3. exchange, barter, swap. *A classmate gave her two cookies in trade for her candy bar.* –*vb.* 4. exchange, barter, swap, bargain. *Let's trade sandwiches.*

trademark *n.* brand, logo, label, symbol, insignia, identification. *Don't infringe on another corporation's trademark or you'll be sued.*

trader *n.* merchant, dealer, retailer, wholesaler, vendor, peddler, monger. *A trader down the street from here sells imported works of art.*

tradition *n.* custom, convention, ritual, standard, habit, practice. *She has a tradition of making popcorn balls for Halloween.*

traditional *adj.* customary, usual, ritual, habitual, normal, routine. *It's traditional to have turkey for Thanksgiving dinner.* **Ant.** unusual, uncommon, rare.

traffic *n.* **1.** trade, sale, commerce, exchange, business, marketing. *Control of the drug traffic is a national priority.* **2.** travel, movement, transit, transport. *The freeway is congested with rush-hour traffic.* *–vb.* **3.** smuggle, bootleg, trade, barter, buy, sell. *He was arrested for trafficking in stolen art objects.*

tragedy *n.* disaster, catastrophe, calamity, misfortune, accident, adversity, unhappiness. *The tragedy could have been avoided had they not attempted to fly in bad weather.* **Ant.** fortune, happiness, success.

tragic *adj.* unfortunate, dreadful, deplorable, unhappy, sad, mournful, grievous, awful, bad. *She was killed in a tragic accident.* **Ant.** happy, fortunate, bright, cheerful.

trail *vb.* **1.** track, hunt, trace, follow, pursue, stalk. *A team of detectives trailed the suspect night and day.* **2.** follow, come, after, tail, lag. *His team trailed by seven points at halftime.* **3.** draw, pull, drag, tow, troll, trawl. *The girl trailed a string of tin cans behind her bike.* *–n.* **4.** path, footpath, track, way, route, course. *This trail leads to Yosemite Falls.* **5.** track, scent, spoor, sign, mark, trace. *Hyenas found the injured animal by following its trail.* **Ant 2.** lead, head, go before.

train *n.* **1.** chain, succession, series, sequence, line, string. *He had trouble following her train of thought.* **2.** staff, followers, retinue, entourage, suite, attendants. *The princess was accompanied by a large train.* **3.** caravan, procession, column, line, string. *Supplies had to be brought in by mule train.* *–vb.* **4.** teach, educate, instruct, drill, tutor, prepare. *How long will it take to train your new employee?*

trainee *n.* student, apprentice, pupil, novitiate, learner. *Eddy is a trainee at the cash register today, so please be patient with him.*

trainer *n.* coach, instructor, teacher, manager, mentor, handler. *The trainer had the entire team run ten laps around the track.*

trait *n.* characteristic, attribute, feature, quality, property. *Self-discipline is a trait necessary for success as a writer.*

traitor *n.* betrayer, turncoat, renegade, spy, deserter, defector, deceiver, mutineer. *A traitor told the enemy our plans.* **Ant.** supporter, defender.

traitorous *adj.* treacherous, turncoat, treasonous, two-faced, (slang) double-crossing, backstabbing. *A traitorous friend is disloyal and is no friend at all.* **Ant.** loyal, devoted, faithful.

trajectory *n.* flight path, course, track, arc, orbit. *The rocket's trajectory was nearly vertical.*

tramp *n.* **1.** vagabond, hobo, vagrant, derelict, bum. *Tramps can frequently be found near railroad yards.* **2.** hike, stroll, walk, ramble, saunter, excursion. *She's out on a tramp through the forest.* *–vb.* **3.** trek, trudge, plod, slog, hike, walk, stroll, ramble. *The mountaineers spent several days merely tramping up a glacier.* **4.** stamp, stomp, tromp, trample. *The spoiled child tramped out of the room in a fit of anger.*

trample crush, squash, flatten, stamp, stomp, tromp, tramp. *Neighborhood children trampled his new lawn.*

trance *n.* daze, daydream, reverie, spell, muse, coma, stupor. *The hypnotist put her into a deep trance.*

tranquil *adj.* quiet, peaceful, calm, serene, restful, still, unperturbed. *The arrival of unannounced visitors shattered his hopes for a tranquil weekend.* **Ant.** agitated, disturbed, tumultuous.

tranquillity *n.* peacefulness, serenity, calmness, stillness, peace, quiet, restfulness, repose. *After a hectic day at the office, she longed for the tranquillity of home.* **Ant.** commotion, disturbance, disorder.

transaction *n.* negotiation, deal, agreement, arrangement, settlement, business. *Both parties agreed to the terms of the loan transaction.*

transcend *vb.* surpass, top, exceed, go beyond, excel, outshine. *The infinity of the universe transcends logic.*

transcendental *adj.* **1.** unsurpassed, extraordinary, supreme, incomparable, unrivaled, topping. *Among human experiences, Neil Armstrong's walk on the Moon is transcendental.* **2.** supernatural, spiritual, mystical, otherworldly, metaphysical, intangible. *He used deep meditation to bring him to a transcendental state of mind.* **Ant. 1.** ordinary, common, inferior. **2.** earthly, worldly, mundane.

transcribe *vb.* transfer, record, copy, write, type, translate. *I asked the secretary to transcribe my notes with the word processor.*

transfer *vb.* **1.** move, transport, carry, shift, convey, relocate, send, ship, consign, assign, relegate. *She transferred all her files from her old computer to the new one.* –*n.* **2.** change, move, shift, transferal, assignment, relocation. *The soldier stationed overseas eagerly awaited his transfer back to the United States.*

transfix *vb.* spellbind, freeze, paralyze, rivet, fill with awe, mesmerize. *Young children are easily transfixed by parades.*

transform *vb.* change, convert, alter, turn, modify, refashion, remake, transmute. *Cinderella's fairy godmother transformed a pumpkin into a carriage.*

transformation *n.* alteration, modification, conversion, change, shift, makeover. *Taking a bath created a complete transformation in the child's appearance.*

transgress *vb.* sin, violate, break the law, overstep one's bounds, disobey, infringe. *Don't transgress and steal any more cookies.*

transgression *n.* sin, violation, crime, offense, felony, wrong, infraction. *In my house, eating cookies before dinner would be a major transgression.*

transient *adj.* temporary, brief, passing, fleeting, momentary, short-lived, ephemeral. *The actor hoped his new fame would not be a transient phenomenon.* **Ant.** permanent, enduring, lasting, perpetual.

transit *n.* passage, progress, conveyance, transport. *Rest assured, Mr. Hitchcock, your package is in transit.*

transition *n.* change, alteration, modification, transformation, shift. *New graduates sometimes have trouble coping with the transition from student to worker.*

translate *vb.* change, transform, convert, modify, alter, render. *Her job was to translate Japanese technical manuals into English.*

translation *n.* transcription, interpretation, deciphering, rewording, rephrasing, decryption. *For most French terms, I need a translation.*

translator *n.* interpreter, linguist, polyglot, transcriber. *I need a translator in order to understand Japanese.*

transmission *n.* **1.** conveyance, transfer, transference, transmittal, passage, delivery, sending. *Mosquitoes cause the transmission of* *malaria.* **2.** broadcast, signal, report, message, communication. *Because their radio batteries were weak, we were barely able to receive their transmission.*

transmit *vb.* send, convey, forward, dispatch, relay, conduct, transfer, deliver, disperse, broadcast. *Many companies use fax machines to transmit documents instantaneously.*

transmitter *n.* signal device, transceiver, conductor, radio, broadcaster. *Speak into the transmitter to send a message to the receiver.*

transparent *adj.* **1.** obvious, evident, plain, visible, apparent, unmistakable, blatant. *The defendant's testimony was full of transparent lies.* **2.** clear, lucid, translucent, see-through. *He covered his notebook with transparent plastic.* **Ant. 1.** hidden, invisible, concealed. **2.** opaque.

transpire *vb.* happen, occur, come about, materialize, come to pass, befall, ensue. *No matter how much I wish otherwise, the big math test will transpire tomorrow afternoon.*

transplant *vb.* **1.** transfer, graft, relocate, replant, move, uproot. *The surgeons are scheduled to transplant a vein from my uncle's leg to a place near his heart. –n.* **2.** donor organ, graft. *My aunt received a kidney transplant from an anonymous donor.*

transport *vb.* **1.** transfer, convey, conduct, carry, move, shift, ferry. *Coal is typically transported by railroad cars. –n.* **2.** transportation, conveyance, shipment, transfer, transference, shipping, carrying. *Many people don't like to see their local roads used for the transport of toxic wastes.*

transportation *n.* transport, transfer, transference, conveyance, movement, transit. *Many forms of transportation are available to anyone wishing to tour Europe.*

transpose *vb.* interchange, reverse, flip, flip-flop, switch, exchange. *I usually write well, but tend to transpose letters when I'm tired.*

trap *n.* **1.** snare, pitfall, pit, net, deception, ploy, ruse, trick, morass, quagmire. *The sheepherder set out traps to protect his flock from coyotes. –vb.* **2.** catch, capture, entrap, ensnare, net. *In the 19th century, mountain men trapped beaver for their pelts.* **Ant. 2.** release, free, liberate.

trash *n.* **1.** garbage, junk, waste, rubbish, refuse, litter, debris. *Whose turn is it to take the trash to the dump?* **2.** nonsense, drivel, inanity, malarkey, gibberish. *This magazine is pure trash.* **Ant. 1.** treasure, valuables. **2.** sense, substance.

trauma *n.* shock, upset, ordeal, jolt, stress, wound, injury. *The emotional trauma of a serious car accident is impossible to forget.*

traumatic *adj.* shocking, upsetting, injurious, hurtful, stressful, wounding, scarring. *Every battle fought by soldiers is emotionally traumatic.* **Ant.** soothing, tranquilizing, comforting.

traumatize *vb.* shock, upset, injure, hurt, stress, wound, scar. *A severely violent movie may traumatize a young child.* **Ant.** soothe, comfort, tranquilize.

travel *n.* **1.** tour, trek, journey, trip, touring, traveling, journeying. *Tell me about your latest travels. –vb.* **2.** tour, wander, roam, trek, journey, visit, sightsee. *Let's travel through Europe next summer.* **3.** move, proceed, advance, progress, go. *Sound waves cannot travel through a vacuum.* **Ant. 2.** stay, remain, linger.

traveler *n.* tourist, sightseer, voyager, explorer, wayfarer, globetrotter. *The foreign traveler can see more of the countryside by taking the train.*

traverse *vb.* cross, pass over, travel, bridge, span, crisscross. *We plan to traverse all of the terrain at the base of the volcano.*

travesty *n.* gross imitation, farce, caricature, burlesque, parody, mockery, joke. *The botched handling of the case by the judge was a travesty of justice.*

treacherous *adj.* **1.** dangerous, unsafe, hazardous, precarious, perilous, risky, undependable. *Snow and ice make for treacherous driving conditions.* **2.** traitorous, disloyal, treasonous, unfaithful, deceitful. *A treacherous guard let assassins into the palace.* **Ant. 1.** safe, reliable, sound. **2.** loyal, faithful, dependable.

treachery *n.* betrayal, perfidy, treason, disloyalty, backstabbing, (slang) double-cross. *Anyone involved with treachery shall be removed from office.* **Ant.** loyalty, faithfulness, fidelity.

tread *vb.* **1.** walk, step, tramp, stamp, stomp, trample. *Don't tread on the new grass.* –*n.* **2.** footstep, step, football, walk, plod. *She heard the tread of someone approaching.*

treason *n.* disloyalty, betrayal, treachery, subversion, sedition, conspiracy. *The patriot thought that treason against his country was the worst possible crime.* **Ant.** loyalty, allegiance, patriotism.

treasonous *adj.* betraying, disloyal, backstabbing, duplicitous, (slang) double-crossing, unfaithful. *By aiding the enemy, he surely will be convicted of treasonous behavior.* **Ant.** loyal, faithful, true.

treasure *n.* **1.** riches, hoard, trove, fortune, wealth, jewels, gems, gold. *Many children dream of finding a pirate's buried treasure.* –*vb.* **2.** cherish, value, prize, esteem, love, adore, revere. *She treasures her family more than anything else.*

treasury *n.* coffer, bank, depository, vault, funds, reserve, revenue, savings. *How much money do we have in the treasury?*

treat *n.* **1.** pleasure, enjoyment, joy, delight, comfort, delicacy, morsel. *Ice cream cones are a treat most people enjoy.* –*vb.* **2.** handle, manage, consider, regard, respect, use, utilize. *She is tired of being treated like a child.* **3.** doctor, medicate, remedy, relieve, cure, heal. *You'd better go to the hospital to get that burn treated properly.*

treatment *n.* handling, management, dealing, usage, application. *The new manager is known for her fair treatment of all employees.*

treaty *n.* agreement, accord, pact, compact, arrangement, understanding. *The negotiations eventually led to the signing of an arms-control treaty.*

tree *n.* plant, timber, hardwood tree, softwood tree, conifer, evergreen, sapling, shrub. *Let's climb the old apple tree.*

WORD SEARCH

covering: *bark*
cultivation of: *arborculture*
cutoff stub: *stump*
fungal growth sometimes seen growing on a side: *conk*
garden of: *arboretum*
leaf-dropping: *deciduous*
leaf-retaining: *coniferous*
rings, age: *growth rings*
root, central: *taproot*
secretion: *resin, sap*
study of: *dendrology*
top tier of leaves and branches: *canopy, crown*
trunk: *bole, stock*
tumor in which insect lives: *gall*
twisted: *gnarled*
wartlike growth: *burl*
wind, line of trees planted to stop the flow of: *windbreak*
wind, one or bunch knocked over by: *windfall, windthrow*

trek *n.* **1.** journey, trip, odyssey, expedition, hike, walk. *Their trek took them through the*

White Mountains. –*vb.* **2.** travel, journey, walk, hike, rove, slog, trudge. *We plan to trek through some very rugged mountains.*

trellis *n.* lattice, lattice work, espalier, pergola, arbor. *I love the way those roses climb the trellis.*

tremble *vb.* shake, quake, quiver, shiver, shudder, throb, pulsate. *The cornered deer trembled with fright.*

tremendous *adj.* **1.** huge, gigantic, enormous, immense, vast, great, mammoth, large. *Writing a book is a tremendous amount of work.* **2.** wonderful, marvelous, exceptional, remarkable, extraordinary, fabulous, excellent. *This new program does a tremendous job of organizing computer files.* **Ant. 1.** small, tiny, little. **2.** ordinary, average, mediocre.

tremor *n.* shake, shaking, quiver, quivering, tremble, trembling, flutter. *The nervous speaker had a slight tremor in her voice.*

trench *n.* ditch, furrow, trough, excavation, channel, gully. *We need to dig a trench for the new water pipe.*

trenchant *adj.* sharp, scathing, pointed, cutting, caustic, incisive. *The food critic made some rather trenchant comments about the poor food at Uncle Eddy's restaurant.*

trend *n.* direction, inclination, tendency, course, drift, style, fashion, vogue. *During the oil crisis, there was a trend toward the purchase of more fuel-efficient cars.*

trepidation *n.* fear, apprehension, anxiety, nervousness, fright, uneasiness, misgiving. *Going into the haunted house at night filled us with great trepidation.* **Ant.** fearlessness, confidence, composure.

trespass *vb.* enter, penetrate, intrude, encroach, infringe, invade. *He was arrested when he trespassed on private properly.*

trial *n.* **1.** test, tryout, check, examination, analysis, try, attempt. *She took the new car out for a trial before purchasing it.* **2.** lawsuit, suit, hearing, litigation, case. *Due to a backlog in the courts, his trial won't start for another month.* **3.** ordeal, trouble, misfortune, hardship, difficulty, torment, worry. *Since adopting five rowdy children, her life has been one trial after another.*

tribe *n.* clan, race, group, family, stock, kindred, sect. *The museum had trouble finding a volunteer to live with the tribe of cannibals.*

tribulation *n.* suffering, misery, affliction, distress, hardship, adversity, woe. *Fixing two flat tires in subzero weather is a tribulation I'd rather not experience again.*

tribunal *n.* court, forum, judiciary, bench. *A special tribunal will be held to hear the defendant's case.*

tribute *n.* **1.** praise, compliment, acclaim, acknowledgment, recognition. *The actress gave tribute to her director when she accepted her Oscar.* **2.** tax, levy, payment, duty, assessment, bribe. *The defeated country was forced to pay tribute to the victor.* **Ant. 1.** condemnation, disrespect, dishonor.

trick *n.* **1** deception, fraud, deceit, ruse, ploy, scheme, wile, trickery, stratagem. *Resetting the car's mileage was just one of the tricks employed by the unscrupulous dealer.* **2.** feat, stunt, accomplishment. *Rolling over is just one of the dog's many tricks.* **3.** joke, jest, prank, gag, antic, mischief. *Soaping someone's window is a Halloween trick that the victim isn't likely to find funny.* –*vb.* **4.** cheat, dupe, deceive, delude, defraud, fool, swindle. *The con artist tricked me out of $100.* **Ant. 1.** truth, sincerity, honesty.

trickery *n.* deception, sleight of hand, deceit, hocus-pocus, artifice, magic, (slang) smoke and mirrors. *The street swindler is notorious for his trickery.*

trickle *n.* **1.** dribble, drop, droplet, drip, seepage. *The old pump provided the barest trickle of water.* *–vb.* **2.** seep, leak, ooze, drop, drip, dribble. *Blood trickled from the small wound.* **Ant.** **1.** gush, flood, stream. **2.** pour, spurt, gush, stream.

trifle *n.* **1.** bauble, triviality, trinket, plaything, toy, nothing. *She likes costume jewelry and similar trifles.* **2.** little, bit, trace, touch, tinge. *My scratch hurts just a trifle.* *–vb.* **3.** fool, fiddle, play, toy. *The flirtatious man enjoyed trifling with the emotions of his female acquaintances.*

trifling *adj.* trivial, petty, unimportant, insignificant, inconsequential, slight, negligible, small. *Since both brands are virtually identical, the choice between them is a trifling matter.* **Ant.** important, significant, considerable, large.

trigger *vb.* begin, start, set off, touch off, cause, produce. *Heavy snowfall triggered a major avalanche.* **Ant.** prevent, stop, block.

trim *vb.* **1.** prune, clip, cut, crop, shorten, neaten. *He needs to have his beard trimmed.* **2.** decorate, adorn, ornament, embellish, furbish. *She trimmed her house by painting the doors and window frames a lighter color.* *–n.* **3.** order, condition, repair, shape, state, fitness. *His yacht is in fine trim.* **4.** decoration, adornment, embellishment, border. *This lace will make a nice trim for your blouse.* **5.** pruning, clip ping, cutting, cropping, shortening. *Your hair could use a trim.* *–adj.* **6.** neat, tidy, compact, lean, slim, slender. *She's looking fit and trim from doing aerobics.* **Ant.** **6.** messy, sloppy, disordered.

trinket *n.* bauble, gewgaw, knickknack, souvenir, ornament, trifle. *I won a cheap little trinket at the carnival.*

trio *n.* triad, trinity, threesome, troika, triumvirate, triplets. *The trio of musicians produced an amazingly big sound.*

trip *n.* **1.** journey, excursion, tour, jaunt, outing, voyage, cruise. *Let's take a trip to Europe next summer.* *–vb.* **2.** stagger, stumble, slip, tumble, fall. *He tripped over the dog and fell to the ground.*

trite *adj.* ordinary, routine, common, everyday, stale, dull, banal, overused. *The teacher was tired of hearing the same trite excuses.* **Ant.** fresh, original, new, unique.

triumph *n.* **1.** victory, success, conquest, win, mastery. *The boxer savored his triumph in the ring.* *–vb.* **2.** succeed, win, prevail, conquer, vanquish, defeat, outdo. *In most movies, the good guys triumph over the bad guys.* **Ant.** **1.** defeat, failure. **2.** lose, fail, succumb.

triumphant *adj.* victorious, winning, conquering, triumphal, joyful, exultant. *Napoleon made a triumphant entry into Moscow.* **Ant.** defeated, unsuccessful, humbled.

trivial *adj.* unimportant, insignificant, petty, slight, trifling, meaningless, worthless. *The new textbook is quite good, though it does contain a few trivial errors.* **Ant.** significant, important, serious, substantial.

troll *n.* creature, dwarf, bridge-dweller, ogre, beast, goblin. *Watch out for the troll who lives under the bridge.*

trolley *n.* street car, tram, conveyance, public transportation. *Let's ride the trolley uptown.*

troop *n.* **1.** group, unit, band, squad, company. *A troop of cavalry rode by.* *–vb.* **2.** march, file, step, stride, proceed, advance, parade. *A long line of inmates trooped across the prison courtyard.*

trophy *n.* prize, award, medal, citation, laurels, crown, cup. *She won a trophy for placing first in the chess contest.*

tropical *adj.* equatorial, hot, humid, steamy, sweltering, torrid, muggy. *We vacationed in a tropical village and tried desperately to stay cool.*

troubadour *n.* poet musician, minstrel, singer, balladeer, songwriter. *There isn't much call for a troubadour in the age of MTV, or is there?*

trouble *vb.* **1.** distress, bother, pester, annoy, vex, disturb, inconvenience, worry, upset, pain. *Her worried look indicated something was troubling her.* –*n.* **2.** difficulty, predicament, dilemma, problem, quandary. *Most of his troubles stem from his laziness.* **3.** inconvenience, exertion, effort, pains, care, bother, work. *He went to a lot of trouble to make this wallet for you.* **Ant. 1.** soothe, please, appease.

troublemaker *n.* mischief maker, agent provocateur, hellion, juvenile delinquent, malcontent, rebel. *Troublemakers will have to stay after school and wash the chalkboards.*

troublesome *adj.* annoying, irritating, disturbing, upsetting, exasperating, bothersome, worrisome. *Her toothache was so troublesome that she finally agreed to see a dentist.* **Ant.** calming, soothing, innocuous.

troupe *n.* company, cast, group, performers, band. *We went to see a comedy troupe in the club last night.*

truant *adj.* absent, AWOL (absent without leave), (slang) playing hooky, skipping school, shirking, neglectful. *If you're truant too often, you'll flunk out of school.*

truce *n.* cease-fire, armistice, peace, cessation, stop, halt, respite, lull, intermission. *The bickering couple agreed to a temporary truce until their visitors left.*

truck *n.* tractor, trailer, eighteen-wheeler, trailer truck, (slang) semi, (slang) big rig, vehicle, transport. *They delivered the logs on a flatbed truck.*

trudge *vb.* tramp, plod, slog, shamble, shuffle, limp, trek, hike. *He trudged through the deep snow.*

true *adj.* **1.** valid, accurate, correct, real, factual, exact, right. *She gave the jury a true account of the accident.* **2.** genuine, authentic, legitimate, actual, absolute. *The child who saved his brother from drowning is a true hero.* **3.** faithful, loyal, trustworthy, dependable, reliable, steady. *You are a true friend.* **4.** just, rightful, lawful, legitimate, legal, official. *The jury tried to determine who was the true heir to the millionaire's estate.* **Ant 1.** false, invalid, incorrect. **2.** phony, artificial, imitation. **3.** faithless, disloyal. **4.** illegal, illicit, unauthorized.

truly *adv.* really, actually honestly, truthfully, sincerely, genuinely, absolutely. *I'm truly sorry for the problems I've caused.* **Ant.** insincerely, untruthfully, uncertainty.

trump *vb.* best, surpass, beat, outwit, outscore, vanquish. *My brother can easily trump me at chess.*

trumpet *n.* horn, wind instrument, bugle, flugelhorn. *If you're going to practice your trumpet, please shut the door.*

trust *n.* **1.** confidence, faith, reliance, belief, conviction, hope, expectation. *Rock climbers need to have trust not only in their equipment but also in themselves.* **2.** care, keeping, protection, custody, guardianship. *The orphan was placed in the trust of foster parents.* –*vb.* **3.** believe in, rely on, depend on, swear by. *You can't always trust what a salesman tells you.* **4.** presume, suppose, assume, expect, anticipate. *I trust you won't be late again.* **Ant. 1.** mistrust, suspicion, doubt. **3.** mistrust, question.

trusting *n.* confident, unsuspecting, naive, gullible, credulous, unquestioning. *In a gang of thieves, it never pays to be too trusting.* **Ant.** distrustful, skeptical, wary.

trustworthy *adj.* reliable, dependable, responsible, faithful, loyal, proven. *Every manager hopes for trustworthy employees.* **Ant.** untrustworthy, unreliable, undependable, irresponsible.

truth *n.* truthfulness, facts, reality, veracity, trueness, honesty, authenticity. *The truth of the matter is that I don't like him.* **Ant.** falsehood, untruth, falseness.

truthful *adj.* honest, forthright, sincere, straightforward, candid, scrupulous, factual. *I am always truthful, except when it comes to sneaking cookies.* **Ant.** dishonest, insincere, deceitful.

try *vb.* 1. attempt, endeavor, strive, aim, struggle, aspire, undertake. *Please try to be nice tonight.* 2. test, prove, check, examine, inspect, experiment, investigate. *The new medicine was tried on animals before being released.* 3. judge, deliberate, adjudicate, consider. *The superior court tried three cases last week.* –*n.* 4. trial, test, experiment, attempt, endeavor, effort. *Let's give the car one more try before we call a tow truck.*

trying *adj.* difficult, hard, tough, arduous, troublesome, bothersome, distressing. *Everyone had a trying time during the Depression.* **Ant.** easy, comforting, simple.

tryout *n.* audition, trial, (slang) shot, (slang) cattle call, test, evaluation. *I always get nervous before an acting tryout.*

tryst *n.* engagement, appointment, meeting, rendezvous, date, assignation. *The lovers arranged a tryst by the waterfront at midnight.*

tsunami *n.* wave, tidal bore, eagre, tidal wave. *Beware of tsunamis following an earthquake.*

tube *n.* cylinder, pipe, shaft, conduit, hose, drain. *We need to insert a tube to drain the water out.*

tug *vb.* 1. pull, jerk, yank, heave, haul, drag, draw. *A fish tugged on his line.* –*n.* 2. pull, jerk, yank, heave. *Give his beard a tug and see what happens.*

tumble *vb.* 1. topple, fall, sprawl, slip, drop, plunge, stumble, trip. *She tumbled off her horse.* 2. roll, somersault, toss, bounce, pitch, reel. *We could see our clothes tumbling in the dryer.* –*n.* 3. fall, spill, sprawl, plunge, drop. *He took a tumble when he tripped on the rug.*

tumbledown *adj.* dilapidated, broken-down, ramshackle, rickety, decrepit, unstable. *We were afraid to say boo or the tumbledown shack would collapse.* **Ant.** sturdy, stable, sound.

tumult *n.* commotion, disturbance, uproar, furor, clamor, ferment, turmoil, confusion. *The classroom was in a state of tumult when the snake got out of its cage.* **Ant.** peace, quiet, serenity, tranquillity.

tumultuous *adj.* wild, turbulent, stormy, uproarious, tempestuous, clamorous. *The drunken patrons started throwing chairs and instigated the most tumultuous brawl I've ever seen.* **Ant.** calm, tranquil, serene.

tune *n.* 1. refrain, melody, song, strain, air, theme. *What's the name of that lovely tune you're singing?* 2. pitch, harmony, agreement, conformity, concord, accord. *Someone's guitar is badly out of tune.* –*vb.* 3. adjust, adapt, reconcile, conform, fix. *When was the last time you had your piano tuned?* **Ant.** 2. discord, discordance, dissonance.

tunnel *n.* 1. passage, passageway, corridor, tube, shaft. *An underground tunnel connects the two buildings.* –*vb.* 2. burrow, dig, excavate, quarry, mine. *The prisoners tunneled under the walls.*

turbulence *n.* agitation, roughness, instability, disturbance, turmoil, wind shear. *I get very nervous when flying through turbulence.* **Ant.** calm, stillness.

turbulent *adj.* tumultuous, disturbed agitated, wild, raging, stormy. *We didn't go sailing because the lake was too turbulent.* **Ant.** calm, quiet, placid, orderly.

turmoil *n.* tumult, pandemonium, chaos, uproar, commotion, ferment. *Rapidly rising interest rates threw the housing market into turmoil.* **Ant.** order, peace, quiet, tranquillity.

turn *n.* **1.** occasion, stint, shift, spell, chance, opportunity, attempt. *It's your turn to do the dishes.* **2.** rotation, revolution, spin, twist, twirl, whirl, cycle. *She gave the steering wheel a quick turn in order to avoid hitting the dog.* **3.** change, shift, deviation, alteration, turning. *Her condition has taken a turn for the better.* **4.** curve, twist, zigzag, bend, angle, corner. *This road makes a hairpin turn just ahead.* –*vb.* **5.** revolve, rotate, spin, twirl, whirl, circle. *You have to turn that handle to the left.* **6.** divert, deflect, redirect, swerve, shift. *The road turns west to follow the river.* **7.** transform, alter, change, become, reform, reshape. *The rain turned to snow when the temperature dropped.* **8.** sprain, twist, wrench. *He turned his ankle playing basketball.* **9.** sour, spoil, curdle, ferment, clabber. *Put the cream back in the refrigerator before it turns.*

turncoat *n.* traitor, Benedict Arnold, betrayer, Judas, (slang) backstabber. *If we discover any turncoats in our army, they will be shot on sight.*

turnpike *n.* toll highway, toll road, interstate, expressway, superhighway. *The turnpike is the quickest route to our destination.*

turret *n.* tower, watchtower, bartizan, lookout, structure. *We could see a damsel in distress waving from the turret window.*

turtle *n.* terrapin, chelonian, tortoise, beast, animal, reptile. *Be advised that snapping turtles may snap off a finger if given half a chance.*

tussle *n.* scuffle, conflict, clash, struggle, fight, fray, (slang) scrap. *The police broke up a minor tussle between opposing fans.*

tutelage *n.* instruction, teaching, schooling, tutoring, guidance. *Under Stephen King's tutelage, the young horror writer should do well.*

tutor *n.* **1.** teacher, instructor, educator, coach, trainer. *His parents hired a private tutor to help him prepare for the entrance examination.* –*vb.* **2.** teach, instruct, educate, inform, train, prepare. *She tutors math for a living.*

TV *n.* television, video, monitor, (slang) boob tube. *I'm sick of watching TV, let's go outside.*

tweezers *n.* nippers, pincers, tongs, forceps. *I need the tweezers in order to remove a splinter in my foot.*

twilight *n.* **1.** sundown, sunset, dusk, evening, nightfall. *Nocturnal animals become active at twilight.* **2.** finale, decline, ebb, end, close. *Her career is in its twilight, and she'll be retiring soon.* **Ant.** **1.** dawn, sunrise, daybreak. **2.** start, beginning, peak.

twine *n.* cord, string, cordage, thread, line, yarn. *We need some twine to tie these garden stakes together.*

twinkle *vb.* glitter, sparkle, shine, glimmer, glow, blink, wink, flutter. *He could see a faint light twinkling in the distance.*

twirl *vb.* whirl, turn, rotate, spin, revolve, wheel. *The cowgirl twirled her rope overhead as she prepared to lasso the calf.*

twist *n.* **1.** curve, bend, turn, zigzag, angle. *This rope is so stiff I can't get the twists out.* **2.** variation, novelty, change, development, treatment, notion, idea. *This movie has a new twist to an old plot.* –*vb.* **3.** wind, twine, encircle, entwine, coil, curl, roll, wrap. *Garbage bags have ties that you twist to close.* **4.** distort, contort, deform, distort warp. *The wrecked car was twisted beyond recognition.* **5.** squirm, writhe, wrest, yank, pull. *The child twisted out of his mother's grasp.* **6.** sprain, wrench, turn. *She twisted her ankle when she fell off the horse.* **Ant.** **3.** untwist, unwind, uncoil, unroll.

twister *n.* tornado, cyclone, whirlwind, tempest, waterspout. *The twister roared through our neighborhood and tore down several trees.*

twitch *n.* **1.** spasm, quiver, shiver, jerk, tremor, convulsion. *I could tell he was nervous by the twitch of his lip.* –*vb.* **2.** spasm, quiver, shiver, jerk, convulse, flutter, quaver. *My lip will start to twitch when I'm anxious.*

two-bit *adj.* cheap, low-budget, inferior, (slang) tinhorn, small-time. *The two-bit town had nothing for entertainment but a post office and a grocery store.* **Ant.** luxurious, extravagant, rich.

two-faced *adj.* Janus-faced, duplicitous, deceitful, treacherous, backstabbing, double-dealing. *The two-faced politician had perfected the art of speaking out of both sides of his mouth.* **Ant.** sincere, honest, loyal.

tycoon *n.* mogul, magnate, capitalist, industrialist, enterpriser, financier. *The real estate tycoon bought my neighbor's farm in order to develop the land.*

type *n.* kind, sort, class, group, variety, category, brand. *What type of music do you like?*

typical *adj.* representative, characteristic, standard, normal, average. *The magazine ran a series on the typical American family.* **Ant.** atypical, unusual, odd, unique.

tyrannical *adj.* dictatorial, autocratic, despotic, authoritarian, totalitarian, oppressive. *The tyrannical boss will have many unhappy employees to contend with.* **Ant.** democratic.

tyranny *n.* despotism, dictatorship, oppression, repression, severity, cruelty. *A popular rebellion ended the government's tyranny.* **Ant.** benevolence, humanity, kindness.

tyrant *n.* dictator, despot, autocrat, totalitarian, oppressor. *The cruel tyrant used his secret police to suppress opposition.*

U

ubiquitous *adj.* everywhere, omnipresent, widespread, universal, pervasive. *Errors were ubiquitous in his hastily typed manuscript.*

UFO *n.* unidentified flying object, flying saucer, alien spaceship, extraterrestrial spacecraft, (slang) bogey. *What we thought was a UFO from space was actually a weather balloon.*

ugly *adj.* **1.** unsightly, unattractive, repulsive, hideous, repugnant. *That purple and green tie certainly is ugly.* **2.** unpleasant, vicious, vile, nasty, mean, foul. *Because she was upset, she made some ugly comments she later regretted.* **Ant. 1.** beautiful, lovely, pretty. **2.** pleasant, agreeable, nice.

ulcer *n.* ulceration, lesion, abscess, sore, canker, perforation. *Stress can aggravate a stomach ulcer.*

ulterior *adj.* hidden, concealed, covert, unexpressed, undeclared, selfish. *He had ulterior motives for dating the wealthy girl.* **Ant.** obvious, open, plain, unselfish.

ultimate *adj.* **1.** final, last, concluding, end, highest, supreme, greatest, maximum. *The ultimate award for an athlete is an Olympic gold medal.* –*n.* **2.** summit, apex, height, peak, extreme, culmination. *He personifies the ultimate in selfishness.* **Ant. 1.** first, beginning, lowest, least.

ultimately *adv.* finally, eventually, at last, in due time. *She ultimately decided against going to graduate school.*

ultimatum *n.* threat, requirement, demand, warning, last offer, last chance. *We were given an ultimatum: to either down or stay after school.*

umbrage *n.* offense, resentment, anger, displeasure, indignation. *Eddy took umbrage at the observation that he was a poor basketball player.*

umbrella *n.* parasol, shade, canopy, bumbershoot. *Take your umbrella, it's going to rain.*

umpire *n.* official, referee, judge, arbiter, mediator. *The crowd groaned loudly when the umpire called the runner out.*

unable *adj.* incapable, ineffective, powerless, incompetent, helpless, inept. *He's unable to do his homework without help.* **Ant.** able, capable, competent.

unabridged *adj.* whole, uncut, complete, full-length, total. *An unabridged dictionary is more likely to have obscure words in it that an abridged one.* **Ant.** abridged, cut, condensed.

unaccustomed *adj.* unacquainted, inexperienced, ignorant, raw, (slang) green. *The southerner was unaccustomed to Chicago's cold winds.* **Ant.** accustomed, experienced.

unadulterated *adj.* pure, uncorrupted, unpolluted, unspoiled, untainted. *The lake is inaccessible and completely unadulterated by chemicals.* **Ant.** adulterated, tainted, spoiled.

unaffected *adj.* **1.** unmoved, unimpressed, unchanged, impassive, unruffled, impervious.

The police officer was unaffected by the thug's idle threats. **2.** genuine, real, natural, true, unpretentious, sincere, down-to-earth. *The most likable personality is one that is unaffected and honest.* **Ant. 1.** affected, moved, impressed. **2.** affected, pretentious, fake.

unanimity *n.* accord, agreement, unity, conformity, consent. *There was complete unanimity among the striking employees.* **Ant.** disagreement, discord.

unanimous *adj.* united, undivided, unified, agreed, agreeing, harmonious. *The council members were unanimous in their support of the new ordinance.* **Ant.** divided, disagreed, disagreeing, differing.

unassuming *adj.* modest, humble, reserved, retiring, unpretentious, simple, plain. *When I met the successful actor at a party, I was surprised to find him so unassuming.* **Ant.** vain, arrogant, pretentious.

unauthorized *adj.* unapproved, unsanctioned, unofficial, illegitimate, illegal. *Since the writer did not have her subject's permission, the resulting book is an unauthorized biography.* **Ant.** authorized, approved, sanctioned, official.

unavoidable *adj.* inevitable, inescapable, unpreventable, compulsory, certain, sure. *It was an unavoidable mistake.* **Ant.** avoidable, preventable.

unaware *adj.* heedless, oblivious, ignorant, unfamiliar, uninformed. *She was unaware of how much homework the course required.* **Ant.** aware, conscious, informed.

unawares *adv.* unexpectedly, abruptly, suddenly, without warning. *The rain shower caught her unawares.* **Ant.** prepared, forewarned.

unbearable *adj.* unendurable, intolerable, insufferable, agonizing, unacceptable, torturous. *Below-zero temperatures are unbearable if you're inadequately dressed.* **Ant.** bearable, tolerable, acceptable.

unbelievable *adj.* incredible, improbable, preposterous, questionable, farfetched, absurd. *He told an unbelievable story about being abducted by Martians.* **Ant.** believable, credible, convincing.

unbiased *adj.* impartial, unprejudiced, disinterested, fair, just, neutral. *Since my job is at stake, I definitely do not have an unbiased attitude toward the new proposal.* **Ant.** biased, prejudiced, slanted.

unblemished *adj.* flawless, unmarred, perfect, unmarked, clean. *The old record album was unblemished by smudges or scratches.* **Ant.** blemished, marked, spotted.

uncanny *adj.* remarkable, amazing, extraordinary, fantastic, strange, mysterious, curious. *Though the two women are not related, they bear an uncanny resemblance to each other.* **Ant.** common, ordinary, average.

uncertain *adj.* indefinite, undecided, unpredictable, unclear, unsure, obscure, doubtful, dubious. *Uncertain weather forced us to change our vacation plans.* **Ant.** definite, predictable, certain.

uncharted *adj.* unmapped, unexplored, unknown, mysterious. *It is all but impossible to find an uncharted island today.*

uncivilized *adj.* **1.** savage, barbaric, barbarous, primitive, wild. *Those cannibals certainly are uncivilized.* **2.** uncouth, coarse, uncivil, rude, vulgar. *His racist comment was uncivilized.* **Ant. 1.** civilized. **2.** civil, refined, cultured.

uncomfortable *adj.* **1.** painful, causing discomfort. *The sofa bed was lumpy and uncomfortable.* **2.** uneasy, embarrassed, awkward, troubled, distressing, nervous. *She was uncomfortable the first time she met her future mother-in-law.* **Ant. 1.** painless. **2.** comfortable, relaxed, untroubled.

uncommon *adj.* unusual, unique, rare, strange, remarkable, exceptional. *He seeded his lawn with an uncommon variety of grass.* **Ant.** common, familiar, ordinary.

uncompromising *adj.* inflexible, unyielding, immovable, set, obstinate, stubborn. *When one party is uncompromising, no agreement can be reached.* **Ant.** compromising, flexible, yielding.

unconcerned *adj.* indifferent, uninterested, uninvolved, apathetic, unperturbed, oblivious. *The failing student seemed unconcerned about her low grades.* **Ant.** concerned, interested, involved.

unconditional *adj.* absolute, unqualified, unlimited, total, full, complete. *Only an unconditional surrender was acceptable to the victorious army.* **Ant.** qualified, limited, incomplete.

unconscionable *adj.* beastly, Satanic, wicked, evil, immoral, outrageous. *Your participation in the bank robbery was unconscionable.* **Ant.** moral, upright, good.

unconscious *adj.* **1.** insensible, senseless, comatose. *He was unconscious for several hours after the accident.* **2.** unknowing, unaware, ignorant, unmindful. *She was unconscious of the effect her story was having on her listeners.* **3.** accidental, inadvertent, unintentional. *Unconscious mistakes are sometimes called "Freudian slips."* **Ant. 1.** conscious, alert, aware. **2.** conscious, familiar, knowing. **3.** deliberate, intentional.

unconstitutional *adj.* unlawful, illegal, against the law, prohibited, wrongful, proscribed. *Prohibiting citizens from bearing arms is unconstitutional.* **Ant.** legal, lawful, constitutional.

uncontrollable *adj.* wild, untamed, unmanageable, frenzied, ungovernable, intractable. *Wild animals can be both unpredictable and uncontrollable.* **Ant.** controllable, manageable, governable.

unconventional *adj.* odd eccentric, peculiar, strange, unusual, bizarre. *His unconventional behavior worried his parents.* **Ant.** conventional, ordinary, routine.

unconvincing *adj.* doubtful, questionable, unproven, weak, suspect. *Your argument that the Moon is made of green cheese is unconvincing.* **Ant.** convincing, proven.

uncoordinated *adj.* awkward, clumsy, oafish, having two left feet, bumbling, blundering. *I am too uncoordinated to be a gymnast.* **Ant.** coordinated, graceful, athletic.

uncouth *adj.* rude, impolite, discourteous, crude, coarse, crass, vulgar. *He offended everyone with his uncouth remarks.* **Ant.** polite, courteous, refined.

uncover *vb.* reveal, disclose, expose, discover, open, show. *A private detective uncovered the truth about the woman's past.* **Ant.** conceal, hide, disguise, cover.

unctuous *adj.* slick, slippery, smooth, suave, oily, insincere. *In his use of flattery, the car salesman was more unctuous than sincere.*

undaunted *adj.* undismayed, unfazed, unfaltering, courageous, brave, fearless, valorous. *The climber was undaunted by the steep cliff.* **Ant.** daunted, dismayed, fazed, meek, fearful.

undecided *adj.* undetermined, uncertain, unsure, unresolved, wavering, hesitant. *She's still undecided about which college to attend.* **Ant.** decided, determined, certain, resolved.

undependable *adj.* unreliable, irresponsible, careless, fickle, inconsistent, unpredictable. *When it comes to performing chores, young chil-*

dren are often undependable. **Ant.** dependable, reliable, responsible.

under *prep.* **1.** beneath, below, underneath. *You'll find your shoes under the bed.* **2.** subject to, according to, following. *That move is not permissible under international chess rules.* *–adv.* **3.** beneath, below, underneath, lower. *The captain watched as his ship went under.* *–adj.* **4.** subordinate inferior, lower, lesser, junior. *He is the under secretary for international affairs.* **Ant. 1–3.** above, over. **4.** superior, higher.

undercover *adj.* secret, covert, clandestine, concealed, hidden, disguised. *Her brother is an undercover police detective.* **Ant.** open, undisguised, unconcealed.

underdog *n.* dark horse, longshot, weakling, subordinate, inferior. *In sports, many people like to root for the underdog.* **Ant.** top dog, champion, favorite

underestimate *vb.* underrate, slight, belittle, discount, (slang) sell short. *Don't underestimate the ability of a small man on the basketball court.* **Ant.** overestimate.

undergo *vb.* experience, encounter, endure, bear, suffer, withstand. *She underwent considerable hardships while in the army.* **Ant.** miss, avoid, forgo.

underground *adj.* **1.** subterranean, buried, belowground, subterrestrial. *The treasure was hidden in an underground cache.* **2.** secret, covert, clandestine, undercover, concealed, hush-hush. *Few people are aware of their underground organization.* **Ant. 1.** surface, lofty. **2.** open, public, famous.

underhanded *adj.* deceitful, dishonest, treacherous, devious, sneaky, crafty. *Swindlers use many underhanded devices to separate you from your money.* **Ant.** honest, scrupulous, ethical.

underling *n.* subordinate, minion, inferior, flunky, lackey. *The boss likes to travel with an entourage of his underlings.* **Ant.** superior, boss, dominator.

undermine *vb.* weaken, undercut, erode, subvert, impair, debilitate. *The criticism from his own party tended to undermine the senator's bid for the presidency.* **Ant.** support, bolster, buttress.

underneath *prep.* **1.** below, under, beneath. *She found a worm underneath the rock.* *–adv.* **2.** below, under, beneath, lower. *When she moved the rock, she didn't know what she would find underneath.* **Ant. 1–2.** above, over.

underprivileged *adj.* disadvantaged, poor, poverty-stricken, destitute, impoverished, needy. *Underprivileged children may not have all the same educational opportunities as others.* **Ant.** privileged, advantaged, affluent.

understand *vb.* comprehend, perceive, realize, recognize, discern. *I can't understand why anyone would pay that much for a new car.* **Ant.** misunderstand, misinterpret, confuse.

understanding *n.* **1.** agreement, pact, bargain, arrangement, accord, compromise. *Management and labor have reached an understanding that should end the strike.* **2.** knowledge, comprehension, perception, grasp, appreciation. *Though he can use a computer, he has no understanding of its inner workings.* *–adj.* **3.** sympathetic, compassionate, sensitive, kind, tender. *The troubled child was fortunate to have an understanding teacher.* **Ant. 1.** misunderstanding. **2.** ignorance, incomprehension. **3.** unsympathetic, uncompassionate, insensitive.

undertake *vb.* try, attempt, venture, endeavor, assume, accept, begin, start. *Cleaning the bathroom was a chore no one wanted to undertake.* **Ant.** avoid, refuse, abstain, stop.

undertaking *n.* project, task, job, enterprise, endeavor, venture. *Climbing Mt. Everest is a serious undertaking.*

underwear *n.* underclothes, undershorts, panties, briefs, boxers, lingerie. *In the north, it's always a good idea to wear long underwear in January.*

underworld *n.* **1.** netherworld, Hades, Hell, Erebus, Sheol. *The coven of witches tried to summon the forces of the underworld.* **2.** organized crime, Mafia, black market. *A member of the underworld was gunned down by police today.*

underwrite *vb.* finance, subsidize, bankroll, fund, support, sponsor. *We need a wealthy individual to underwrite our theater program.*

underwriter *n.* financier, supporter, sponsor, insurer. *If this show is going to be expensive to put on, we'll need to find an underwriter.*

undesirable *adj.* distasteful, objectionable, offensive, unacceptable, unwelcome, unwanted. *She didn't quit her job because the alternatives were undesirable.* **Ant.** desirable, inviting, attractive, welcome.

undignified *adj.* degrading, shameful, childish, juvenile, (slang) goofy, unseemly. *The president's chicken dance was rather undignified.* **Ant.** dignified, decorous, mature.

undisciplined *adj.* lazy, slack, indolent, unregimented, irresolute, self-indulgent. *You'll never learn to play the piano if you continue to be so undisciplined.* **Ant.** disciplined, regimented, resolute.

undivided *adj.* complete, entire, whole, total, exclusive. *You have my undivided attention.* **Ant.** partial, incomplete.

undo *vb.* **1.** free, open, loosen, unfasten, disentangle, unravel, untie. *The child couldn't undo the lacings on her dress.* **2.** reverse, cancel, annul, offset, neutralize, rectify. *It will take months to undo the damage caused by the disgruntled employee.* **Ant. 1.** fasten, tie, close. **2.** do, accomplish, uphold.

undoing *n.* downfall, ruin, destruction, disgrace, fall, defeat, upset. *Bad investments proved to be the undoing of his plans for an early retirement.* **Ant.** success, victory, triumph.

undress *vb.* disrobe, strip, unclothe, doff, shuck, remove clothing, peel. *Ask the patient to undress in the examination room.*

undulate *vb.* ripple, wave, move sinuously, roll, oscillate. *The belly dancer knew how to undulate to maximum effect.*

unduly *adv.* excessively, extremely, overly, inordinately, unnecessarily, unusually. *The parents were unduly concerned with their daughter's shyness.* **Ant.** properly, appropriately, reasonably.

undying *adj.* eternal, immortal, endless, unceasing, perpetual, permanent. *He assured her of his undying love.* **Ant.** temporary, fleeting, brief, momentary.

unearth *vb.* exhume, dig up, excavate, uncover, dredge up. *Every time you go digging in the dump, you unearth something disgusting.* **Ant.** bury, inter, cover.

unearthly *adj.* otherworldly, extraterrestrial, alien, supernatural, out-of-this-world, ethereal, spiritual. *Attending a seance is an unearthly experience.* **Ant.** mundane, earthly, terrestrial.

uneasy *adj.* **1.** worried, troubled, nervous, apprehensive, disturbed, anxious. *She felt uneasy about taking on more responsibilities.* **2.** uncomfortable, disturbing, unpleasant, strained, embarrassed. *They experienced an uneasy pause in their conversation.* **Ant. 1.** easy, calm, unworried. **2.** easy, comfortable, pleasant.

uneducated *adj.* ignorant, stupid, unenlightened, dumb, unschooled, untrained. *Many criminals are uneducated.* **Ant.** educated, schooled, trained.

unemployed *adj.* jobless, out of work, unoccupied, inactive, idle. *Approximately one out of every fifteen workers is unemployed.* **Ant.** employed, working, busy.

unending *adj.* endless, ceaseless, everlasting, eternal, immortal, perpetual, constant. *Books can be an unending source of pleasure.* **Ant.** brief, fleeting, momentary.

unequal *adj.* uneven, disparate, disproportionate, different, unlike, dissimilar, biased. *The champion won the unequal match with a knockout in the first round.* **Ant.** equal, even, like, similar.

unequivocal *adj.* unambiguous, concrete, plain, clear, unmistakable, definite. *The politician's promise to lower taxes was unequivocal.* **Ant.** ambiguous, equivocal, unclear.

unethical *adj.* unscrupulous, dishonest, immoral, wrong, disreputable, unfair. *Cheating on your taxes is unethical.* **Ant.** ethical, scrupulous, honest.

uneven *adj.* **1.** irregular, rough, jagged, lopsided, unbalanced, coarse, unlevel. *Bush pilots frequently have to use uneven dirt or gravel landing strips.* **2.** unequal, disparate, different, unlike, dissimilar. *The uneven chess match had a novice playing a master.* **Ant. 1.** smooth, level, straight. **2.** even, equal, balanced.

unexpected *adj.* unforeseen, unanticipated, unpredicted, sudden, abrupt. *She was delighted when she received an unexpected promotion.* **Ant.** expected, anticipated, planned.

unfair *adj.* unjust, biased, discriminatory, partial, prejudiced. *The fired employee felt he had received unfair treatment.* **Ant.** fair, just, impartial, honest.

unfaithful *adj.* treacherous, disloyal, deceitful, faithless, false, untrue. *She was betrayed by an unfaithful friend.* **Ant.** faithful, loyal, true.

unfamiliar *adj.* **1.** strange, new, unknown, different, unusual, exotic, foreign, novel. *She couldn't understand the unfamiliar dialect.* **2.** unacquainted, inexperienced, unaware, uninformed. *He is unfamiliar with the latest computer technology.* **Ant. 1.** familiar, accustomed, common. **2.** familiar, acquainted.

unfathomable *adj.* incomprehensible, unknowable, impenetrable, deep, immeasurable. *The meaning behind the universe is unfathomable.* **Ant.** knowable, comprehensible, measurable.

unfavorable *adj.* adverse, detrimental, negative, unsuitable, inconvenient, poor, bad. *Since he has just lost his job, it is an unfavorable time to ask him for a loan.* **Ant.** favorable, positive, good.

unfinished *adj.* incomplete, uncompleted, undone, undeveloped, partial. *An unfinished manuscript was found after the author's death.* **ant.** finished, complete, whole.

unfit *adj.* **1.** unsuitable, inappropriate, inadequate, unprepared. *The shy man is unfit for a career in politics.* **2.** unhealthy, weak, debilitated, infirm. *The long illness has left her physically unfit.* **Ant. 1.** suitable, qualified, competent. **2.** fit, healthy, robust.

unflappable *adj.* unexcitable, cool, self-possessed, imperturbable, composed, level-headed. *In stressful situations, police officers are required to be unflappable.* **Ant.** temperamental, hotheaded, reactive.

unflinching *adj.* unblinking, unshrinking, unafraid, unfaltering, undaunted. *The two fighters shot unflinching stares at each other.* **Ant.** shaky, flinching, nervous.

unforeseen *adj.* unexpected, unanticipated, unpredicted, sudden, surprise, abrupt. *Unforeseen* *events made him miss his deadline.* **Ant.** foreseen, expected, anticipated.

unforgettable *adj.* memorable, notable, significant, remarkable, outstanding, exceptional. *Her first view of the ocean was an unforgettable experience.* **Ant.** ordinary, common, routine.

unforgivable *adj.* unpardonable, inexcusable, indefensible, unconscionable, abominable, heinous. *Murder is almost always an unforgivable crime.* **Ant.** forgivable, pardonable, excusable.

unfortunate *adj.* unlucky, luckless, untimely, unhappy, regrettable. *An unfortunate injury ended his athletic career.* **Ant.** fortunate, lucky, timely.

unfounded *adj.* groundless, unproven, unsubstantiated, speculative, baseless, untrue. *Reports of an imminent invasion by aliens are unfounded.* **Ant.** proven, substantiated, true.

unfriendly *adj.* **1.** unsociable, aloof, haughty, snobbish, cool, distant, remote. *Her unfriendly behavior is the main reason she's not popular.* **2.** hostile, malevolent, antagonistic, warlike. *The cold war was abetted by unfriendly actions between nations.* **Ant. 1.** friendly, sociable, warm. **2.** friendly, peaceful.

ungainly *adj.* awkward, clumsy, bungling, ungraceful, inelegant. *The shy young man was ungainly on the dance floor.* **Ant.** graceful, elegant.

ungrateful *adj.* unappreciative, thankless, unthankful, selfish, heedless. *The ungrateful boy refused to acknowledge how much his friends had done for him.* **Ant.** grateful, thankful, appreciative.

unhappy *adj.* sad, depressed, sorrowful, dejected, wretched, miserable, downcast. *She's unhappy because she can't get what she wants.* **Ant.** happy, cheerful, gay, joyful.

unhealthy *adj.* **1.** ill, unwell, sick, sickly, infirm, frail, weak. *Because of his heart condition, he's going to be unhealthy the rest of his life.* **2.** unhealthful, harmful, poisonous, virulent, noxious. *Many people fear it's unhealthy to live next to a toxic-waste dump.* **Ant. 1.** healthy, well, robust. **2.** healthy, beneficial.

unheeded *adj.* unnoticed, disregarded, unobserved, unused. *Advice that isn't asked for usually goes unheeded.* **Ant.** heeded, noticed, used.

unidentified *adj.* unknown, mysterious, unrecognized, anonymous, secret, unclassified. *An aircraft that is unidentified is not necessarily of alien origin.* **Ant.** identified, known, classified.

unification *n.* consolidation, merger, union, alliance. *The new law resulted in the unification of all the city's school districts.* **Ant.** disunification, separation, division.

unified *adj.* united, allied, joined, confederated, married, consolidated. *If we're unified in our efforts, we'll win.* **Ant.** separated, divided, fractured.

uniform *n.* **1.** outfit, attire, costume, regalia, dress. *You can tell a police officer by his or her uniform.* –*adj.* **2.** identical, alike, equal, similar. *Most paperback books are of uniform size.* **3.** even, constant, unvarying, unchanging, undeviating. *The old furnace is not capable of providing uniform heating.* **Ant. 2.** unalike, unequal, dissimilar. **3.** uneven, variable.

unify *vb.* unite, combine, consolidate, bind, connect, link, join, merge. *The American colonies were unified in their struggle against British domination.* **Ant.** separate, divide, disunite.

unimportant *adj.* inconsequential, trivial, petty, insignificant, minor, paltry, trifling. *My boss does not like to bother with unimportant details.* **Ant.** important, significant, major.

uninhabited *adj.* unoccupied, vacant, empty, deserted, abandoned. *Neighborhood kids thought* *the old uninhabited house was haunted.* **Ant.** inhabited, occupied.

uninhibited *adj.* uncontrolled, unrepressed, unrestrained, free, open, liberated. *Her uninhibited behavior shocked many of her friends.* **Ant.** inhibited, controlled, suppressed.

union *n.* **1.** combination, consolidation, incorporation, mixture, joining, merger. *Bronze is formed by the union of copper and tin.* **2.** association, alliance, partnership, league, order, society. *His sister joined a labor union.* **Ant. 1.** separation, division.

unique *adj.* distinctive, singular, unrivaled, incomparable, exceptional, extraordinary. *She has the unique ability to do her homework while talking on the phone.* **Ant.** common, ordinary, routine.

unite *vb.* unify, combine, join, connect, link, associate, merge. *The two companies united to form a big corporation.* **Ant.** disunite, divide, separate, part.

United States *n.* America, U.S., USA, Land of Liberty, the Great Melting Pot. *The United States is the second largest country in North America.*

unity *n.* unification, togetherness, union, marriage, oneness, harmony, solidarity. *We need unity to defeat our opponents.* **Ant.** division, separation, discord.

universal *adj.* boundless, unlimited, widespread, general, total, entire. *This classic children's book has universal appeal.* **Ant.** limited, local, restricted, individual.

universe *n.* cosmos, space, outer space, creation, macrocosm, infinity. *Does the universe go on forever?*

university *n.* college, school, graduate school, institute of higher learning, professional school, academy. *I plan to attend the university nearest us.*

unjust *adj.* wrongful, wrong, unfair, undeserved, biased, prejudiced. *Her reputation was hurt by an unjust accusation.* **Ant.** just, fair, right, impartial.

unkempt *adj.* slovenly, disheveled, sloppy, careless, neglected. *He has an unkempt appearance.* **Ant.** neat, tidy, well-groomed.

unkind *adj.* unfeeling, unsympathetic, inconsiderate, thoughtless, harsh, cruel, mean. *It was unkind of you to comment so bluntly on the weight he's gained.* **Ant.** kind, sympathetic, considerate, thoughtful.

unknown *adj.* unidentified, anonymous, unrecognized, nameless, mysterious, obscure. *Despite having written several books, her name is still unknown to the average reader.* **Ant.** known, recognized, identified, familiar.

unlike *adj.* different, dissimilar, unrelated, opposite. *She is completely unlike her sister.* **Ant.** like, similar, identical.

unlikely *adj.* improbable, doubtful, questionable, implausible. *It's unlikely to snow today.* **Ant.** likely, probable, certain.

unmistakable *adj.* clear, obvious, evident, distinct, plain, apparent, conspicuous. *He bears an unmistakable resemblance to his father.* **Ant.** vague, unclear, uncertain, obscure.

unmitigated *adj.* out-and-out, absolute, downright, sheer, complete. *I've never seen such unmitigated gall as when the billionaire pleaded poverty.*

unmotivated *adj.* apathetic, indifferent, unambitious, unenterprising, lazy. *Joe, alas, has always been an unmotivated student.* **Ant.** motivated, impassioned, passionate.

unnecessary *adj.* unneeded, needless, useless, superfluous, pointless. *The soldiers were cautioned not to take unnecessary risks.* **Ant.** necessary, essential, useful.

unnoticed *adj.* unobserved, unseen, undiscovered, unheeded. *He hoped that his mismatched socks would go unnoticed.* **Ant.** noticed observed, discovered.

unoccupied *adj.* uninhabited, vacant, empty, deserted, idle, open. *You may stay in our unoccupied guest room.* **Ant.** inhabited, occupied, full.

unorthodox *adj.* unconventional, unofficial, deviant, nonconforming, irregular, nonstandard. *His unorthodox style of pitching proved to be highly effective.* **Ant.** orthodox, standard, normal.

unpleasant *adj.* disagreeable, objectionable, displeasing, offensive, repulsive. *The room had an unpleasant odor.* **Ant.** pleasant, agreeable, pleasing.

unpopular *adj.* disliked, unloved, unwanted, friendless, unwelcome, undesirable. *Eliminating summer vacation is an idea that is unpopular with most schoolchildren.* **Ant.** liked, loved, wanted, desired.

unprecedented *adj.* unique, novel, singular, extraordinary, unparalleled, original. *Snowfall in July here is unprecedented.* **Ant.** precedented, usual, ordinary.

unprofessional *adj.* amateurish, inexpert, slack, nonprofessional, inadequate, sloppy. *The carpenter's handiwork was shoddy and unprofessional.* **Ant.** professional, expert, adequate.

unqualified *adj.* **1.** incompetent, incapable, inexperienced, unprepared, unsuited, unfit. *He is completely unqualified to be an astronaut.* **2.** absolute, total, complete, utter, unconditional. *Her response to the marriage proposal was an unqualified yes.* **Ant. 1.** qualified, competent, capable. **2.** conditional, limited.

unreal *adj.* imaginary, imagined, pretended, dreamlike, fictitious, false, imitation. *Though the movie was delightful, the world it portrayed is unreal.* **Ant.** real, realistic, factual, true.

unreasonable *adj.* **1.** absurd, irrational, senseless, illogical, foolish. *It's unreasonable to expect all the world's problems will be solved overnight.* **2.** excessive, extreme, exorbitant, unfair, impossible. *Don't place unreasonable demands on your friends.* **Ant. 1.** reasonable, logical, sensible. **2.** moderate, fair.

unrefined *adj.* rough, unpolished, unfinished, course, crude. *It is rather unrefined of you to burp at the table.* **Ant.** refined, polished, perfected.

unreliable *adj.* undependable, untrustworthy, irresponsible, uncertain, questionable. *His information comes from an unreliable source.* **Ant.** reliable, dependable, responsible.

unrest *n.* turmoil, turbulence, disturbance, trouble, agitation, disorder, dissatisfaction. *There is much unrest in the world today.* **Ant.** peace, quiet, calm.

unrivaled *adj.* incomparable, unequaled, peerless, matchless, greatest, finest. *He is the unrivaled chess champion of our school.*

unruly *adj.* ungovernable, uncontrollable, unmanageable, disobedient, disorderly, wild. *Police tried to control the unruly mob.* **Ant.** controllable, manageable, obedient, docile.

unsafe *adj.* hazardous, dangerous, risky, perilous, insecure, precarious, unreliable, vulnerable. *Heavy flooding undermined the bridge and made it unsafe to cross.* **Ant.** safe, secure, harmless, reliable.

unsanitary *adj.* unclean, filthy, dirty, unhealthy, germ-infested, unhygienic. *The unsanitary hospital was shut down by health officials.* **Ant.** sanitary, clean, sterile.

unsatisfactory *adj.* unacceptable, inadequate, insufficient, poor, deficient, unsuitable. *The new* *employee's output is unsatisfactory.* **Ant.** satisfactory, adequate, appropriate.

unseemly *adj.* improper, inappropriate, indecent, vulgar, crude. *Uncle's Joe's ribald jokes were unseemly, especially in mixed company.*

unselfish *adj.* altruistic, selfless, generous, considerate, magnanimous. *Her unselfish behavior earned everyone's respect.* **Ant.** selfish, greedy, egotistical.

unskilled *adj.* inexperienced, untrained, untalented, inexpert. *Since he's an unskilled worker, he is having trouble finding a job.* **Ant.** skilled, trained, experienced.

unsophisticated *adj.* naive, inexperienced, unassuming, simple, natural, plain. *A child's view of the world is usually unsophisticated.* **Ant.** sophisticated, experienced, complex.

unstable *adj.* **1.** unsteady, insecure, unsafe, precarious, shaky, infirm. *Your ladder is pretty unstable the way you've got it positioned.* **2.** fluctuating, changing, changeable, vacillating, volatile. *That chemical compound is unstable at room temperature.* **Ant. 1.** stable, steady, safe. **2.** stable, unchanging, constant.

unsubstantiated *adj.* unproven, questionable, unconfirmed, uncertified, unauthenticated. *The reports of flying saucers over Washington have been unsubstantiated.* **Ant.** confirmed, proven, substantiated.

unsuccessful *adj.* failed, abortive, fruitless, unproductive, futile, vain, unprosperous. *He was unsuccessful in his attempt to make the basketball team.* **Ant.** successful, productive, winning.

unsuitable *adj.* inappropriate, unfitting, unsatisfactory, improper, unacceptable. *He was unsuitable for the job because he had no relevant experience.* **Ant.** appropriate, satisfactory, fitting.

unsuspecting *adj.* gullible, naive, innocent, trusting, oblivious, unwary. *The swindler looks for victims who are likely to be unsuspecting.* **Ant.** suspicious, distrustful, wary.

unthinkable *adj.* inconceivable, unimaginable, incomprehensible, incredible, absurd, ridiculous, preposterous. *For dedicated students, cutting class is unthinkable.* **Ant.** conceivable, believable.

unused *adj.* **1.** new, fresh, pristine, untouched, untried, original. *Here's an unused toothbrush for you.* **2.** unutilized, unemployed, vacant, idle. *You can stay in our unused guest room.* **3.** unaccustomed, unfamiliar with, unacquainted with. *The bachelor was unused to the commotion caused by his friend's children.* **Ant. 1.** used, old, secondhand. **2.** used, utilized. **3.** accustomed.

unusual *adj.* exceptional, extraordinary, uncommon, rare, unique, strange. *It's unusual for him to turn down a second piece of cake.* **Ant.** usual, common, ordinary, typical.

unwary *adj.* incautious, careless, reckless, imprudent, unsuspecting, rash. *The accident was caused by an unwary driver.* **Ant.** wary, cautious.

unwell *adj.* sick, ill, ailing, unhealthy, indisposed, poorly, weak, frail. *Since she's feeling unwell, she decided to stay home.* **Ant.** well, healthy, fit, vigorous.

unwilling *adj.* reluctant, disinclined, opposed, loath, averse. *The bank was unwilling to lend more money to the bankrupt company.* **Ant.** willing, amenable, inclined.

unwitting *adj.* unknowing, unaware, unconscious, inadvertent, accidental, involuntary. *By telling a friend about her bank's procedures, she became an unwitting accomplice to a robbery.* **Ant.** knowing, voluntary, intentional.

unyielding *adj.* inflexible, resolute, persistent, obstinate, stubborn, firm, rigid. *The negotiations are stalled because both sides have taken unyielding stands.* **Ant.** yielding, flexible, adaptable.

up *adv.* **1.** upward, aloft, higher, above, overhead. *She looked up and saw the airplane.* –*vb.* **2.** increase, raise, lift, boost, hike. *They upped their prices.* –*adj.* **3.** awake, alert, ready, prepared, set. *He's up for tomorrow's midterm.* **Ant. 1.** down, below. **2.** lower, reduce, decrease. **3.** unprepared.

upbraid *vb.* scold, rebuke, reprimand, reproach, chastise, berate. *Please don't upbraid the kids in front of their friends.*

upchuck *vb.* vomit, puke, throw up, regurgitate (slang) barf. *Don't eat too much pizza or you may get sick and upchuck.*

upcoming *adj.* forthcoming, approaching, coming, nearing, imminent, momentary. *She's getting nervous about her upcoming wedding.* **Ant.** distant, remote.

update *vb.* revise, modernize, renew, refresh, renovate. *She updated her résumé to show her most recent work experience.*

upgrade *vb.* improve, better, advance, elevate, raise, update. *I plan to upgrade my computer with more accessories soon.* **Ant.** downgrade, degrade.

upheaval *n.* upset, eruption, explosion, blowup, catastrophe, disruption, disturbance. *The recent layoffs have caused a great upheaval within the corporation.*

uphold *vb.* support, maintain, sustain, defend, preserve, protect. *Police officers are sworn to uphold the law.*

upkeep *n.* maintenance, repair, support, overhead, backing, provision. *More money needs to be allocated for the upkeep of our roads.*

upper *adj.* higher, superior, greater, top, top most, eminent, important. *She wants to become a member of the upper class.* **Ant.** lower, inferior.

uppity *adj.* presumptuous, arrogant, haughty, conceited, snobbish, stuck-up. *To assume that she didn't have to wait in the line like the rest of us was quite uppity.* **Ant.** down-to-earth, humble, modest.

upright *adj.* **1.** vertical, perpendicular, erect, raised. *The arrow missed the target and landed in an upright position.* **2.** honest, just, virtuous, honorable, moral, trustworthy. *Since we had thought he was upright, we were surprised when he lied to us.* **Ant. 1.** horizontal, prone. **2.** dishonest, corrupt, unethical.

uprising *n.* revolt, rebellion, revolution, insurrection, mutiny, outbreak, upheaval. *The American War of Independence was a popular uprising against British rule.*

uproar *n.* commotion, turmoil, tumult, clamor, furor, stir, noise, disturbance. *People were in an uproar over the new taxes.* **Ant.** serenity, tranquillity, peace, calm.

upset *vb.* **1.** overturn, upend, topple, invert, capsize. *The inexperienced sailors upset their boat on a calm day.* **2.** disturb, distress, agitate, perturb, dismay, bother, annoy. *The news of her friend's accident upset her.* **3.** disorganize, disorder, confuse, jumble, change, cancel. *The unexpected rain upset our plans for a softball game.* **4.** sicken, turn, afflict, indispose. *Eating all that cake will upset your stomach.* –*adj.* **5.** overturned, upended, upturned, toppled, capsized. *All lanes of the freeway were blocked by an upset truck.* **6.** perturbed, distressed, disturbed, troubled, bothered, annoyed. *She was upset by my tactless remark.* **7.** sickened, turned, afflicted, indisposed. *She has an upset stomach.* **Ant. 2.** soothe, calm, pacify. **3.** organize, order, stabilize. **5.** upright, standing, erect. **6.** unperturbed, calm, quiet.

upside down *adv.* inversely, topsy-turvy, top-side down, bottom-side up, reversely. *I was embarrassed to learn that I had hung the abstract painting upside down.* **Ant.** right-side up.

upstanding *adj.* upright, good, moral, scrupulous, ethical, honorable. *She was an upstanding citizen who would do anything to help others in need.* **Ant.** unscrupulous, bad, unprincipled.

uptight *adj.* **1.** conventional, conservative, rigid, staid, stodgy, straitlaced. *The preacher was too uptight to allow himself to have any fun.* **2.** nervous, anxious, stressed, tense, uneasy, worried. *You can't enjoy yourself at a party if you're uptight.* **Ant. 1.** liberal, open-minded, broad-minded. **2.** relaxed, calm, tranquil.

urban *adj.* city, metropolitan, municipal, civic, cosmopolitan. *The small-town boy had trouble adjusting to urban living.* **Ant.** rural, rustic, pastoral.

urbane *adj.* suave, sophisticated, elegant, refined, cultivated, polished, courteous, polite. *The young man was impressed by the socialite's urbane mannerisms.* **Ant.** crude, unrefined, inelegant, tactless.

urge *vb.* **1.** plead, beg, implore, beseech, entreat, advise. *They urged me to join their club.* **2.** force, drive, push, press, prod, impel. *She urged her horse over the jump.* *–n.* **3.** impulse, yearning, longing, desire, wish. *He has an urge for pineapple pizza.* **Ant. 1.** discourage, dissuade, caution. **2.** restrain, prevent. **3.** distaste, repugnance, aversion.

urgent *adj.* pressing, compelling, crucial, essential, critical, important, immediate. *She was called out of town on urgent business.* **Ant.** unimportant, insignificant, unnecessary.

urn *n.* container, vessel, jar, receptacle, vase. *We keep our great-grandmother's remains in an urn above the mantle.*

usage *n.* use, treatment, employment, application, handling. *His skis are still in good shape despite years of hard usage.*

use *vb.* **1.** utilize, employ, operate, work, manipulate, apply. *Do you know how to use a computer?* **2.** consume, expend, spend, exhaust, deplete. *That old air conditioner uses too much electricity.* *–n.* **3.** service, application, employment, utilization, usage, work. *She's gotten a lot of use out of that old car.* **4.** benefit, utility, advantage, significance, value. *There's no use talking to him because he won't listen.* **Ant. 2.** save, conserve. **3.** disuse, unemployment. **4.** disadvantage.

useful *adj.* helpful, beneficial, advantageous, valuable, practical. *A microwave oven is useful if you don't have much time for cooking.* **Ant.** useless, worthless, unhelpful.

useless *adj.* valueless, worthless, ineffectual, unserviceable, futile, unavailing. *This old saw is so dull it's now useless.* **Ant.** useful, practical, worthwhile.

usher *n.* **1.** guide, escort, attendant, doorkeeper, page. *Let the usher guide you to your seat.* *–vb.* **2.** guide, escort, lead, direct, conduct, marshal. *The doorkeeper will usher you to your seats.*

usual *adj.* normal, customary, habitual, regular, accustomed, typical, ordinary. *She took her usual seat at the table.* **Ant.** uncommon, unusual, rare, unique.

usurp *vb.* seize, steal, grab, preempt, appropriate, assume. *I feel like he's trying to usurp my authority.* **Ant.** surrender, yield, relinquish.

utensil *n.* implement, instrument, tool, device, apparatus, gadget. *Please lay out the eating utensils.*

utilize *vb.* use, employ, exploit, handle, apply. *What kind of fuel does your camp stove utilize?*

utilitarian *adj.* practical, functional, useful, pragmatic, realistic, serviceable. *He prefers utilitarian automobiles over showy ones.* **Ant.** impractical, fanciful, indulgent.

utmost *adj.* **1.** maximum, extreme, greatest, largest, highest, most. *I have the utmost respect for his accomplishments.* *–n.* **2.** ultimate, best, maximum, peak. *She did her utmost to help him.* **Ant. 1–2.** least, minimum.

utopia *n.* paradise, heaven on earth, Shangri-la, Eden, perfect world, ideal. *A utopia could never be achieved because humans are too imperfect.*

utopian *adj.* idealistic, perfect, visionary, fanciful, grandiose, romantic. *Many science fiction writers have imagined trouble-free, utopian worlds.* **Ant.** hellish, realistic, imperfect.

utter *adj.* **1.** complete, total, entire, absolute, extreme, thorough, unqualified. *His room is an utter mess.* *–vb.* **2.** speak, say, articulate, express, pronounce, talk. *She didn't utter a single word.* **Ant. 1.** incomplete, partial, limited.

utterly *adv.* completely, thoroughly, entirely, totally, wholly, fully. *Dinner was utterly enjoyable.* **Ant.** partially, incompletely.

V

vacancy *n.* opening, space, room, gap, emptiness, vacuity, vacuum. *Our apartment building currently has a vacancy.*

vacant *adj.* unoccupied, empty, uninhabited, unfilled, void, open, clear. *The apartment next to ours is vacant.* **Ant.** occupied, full, filled.

vacate *vb.* leave, clear, empty, relinquish, give up. *Since our house has been sold, we have to vacate it in two weeks.* **Ant.** occupy, fill, possess.

vacation *n.* holiday, break, rest, leave, furlough. *She's going to Mexico on her vacation.*

vaccination *n.* inoculation, shot, injection, booster, shot, protection, immunity. *The measles vaccination was almost painless.*

vacillate *vb.* oscillate, swing, go back and forth, waver, equivocate, (slang) shilly-shally. *When asked if she would raise taxes, the congresswoman tended to vacillate.* **Ant.** commit, be decisive.

vacuous *adj.* empty, vacant, blank, stupid, dumb, empty-headed. *His vacuous facial expression told me he didn't comprehend the question.* **Ant.** intelligent, bright, comprehending.

vacuum *n.* **1.** emptiness, void, nothingness, empty space. *Sound cannot travel through the vacuum of outer space.* –*vb.* **2.** clean, sweep. *Please vacuum the rug.*

vagabond *n.* vagrant, rover, wanderer, tramp, transient, drifter. *She is a vagabond who is uncomfortable staying in any one place for longer than six months.*

vagrant *n.* wanderer, rover, vagabond, rambler, nomad, tramp. *A vagrant passed through town and only stopped long enough to beg for money.*

vague *adj.* indefinite, uncertain, intangible, confusing, indistinct, fuzzy, hazy. *The suspect gave only a vague response when questioned about his activities.* **Ant.** definite, certain, clear, specific.

vain *adj.* **1.** conceited, arrogant, proud, smug, egotistical, haughty. *The actor was so vain he assumed everyone admired him.* **2.** useless, futile, worthless, unsuccessful, ineffective. *She made a vain attempt to save the crippled bird.* **Ant.** **1.** humble, modest, unassuming. **2.** successful, effective.

valiant *adj.* courageous, valorous, brave, heroic, fearless, gallant, bold. *Valiant men and women are needed to lead the struggle against drug and alcohol abuse.* **Ant.** cowardly, timid, fearful.

valid *adj.* **1.** sound, logical, acceptable, suitable, justifiable. *The child could not offer a valid explanation for missing school.* **2.** authentic, genuine, legitimate, real, legal, lawful. *You need a valid passport to enter that country.* **Ant.** **1.** unacceptable, unconvincing. **2.** invalid, fake, illegal.

validate *vb.* substantiate, authenticate, certify, prove, verify, corroborate. *I need the teacher to validate my theories.* **Ant.** invalidate, disprove, challenge.

valise *n.* suitcase, bag, carryall, luggage. *Don't leave your valise on the train.*

valley *n.* basin, vale, dale, dell, glen. *Her dream is to have a cabin in a remote mountain valley.*

valor *n.* courage, bravery, heroism, fearlessness, gallantry. *The firefighter was decorated for valor after he saved three people from a burning home.* **Ant.** cowardice, fear.

valuable *adj.* **1.** important, worthy, worthwhile, valued, invaluable. *Though he's not getting paid much, he's gaining valuable experience.* **2.** costly, expensive, high-priced, precious. *She has a valuable collection of first-edition books.* **Ant. 1.** unimportant, worthless. **2.** inexpensive, cheap, valueless.

value *n.* **1.** importance, merit, worth, significance, use, usefulness. *Having a knowledge of computers can be of great value when looking for a job.* **2.** cost, price, expense, amount, charge. *The value of gold changes from day to day.* –*vb.* **3.** price, appraise, assess, evaluate, estimate. *My art collection has been valued at $20,000.* **4.** treasure, appreciate, prize, cherish, revere, esteem. *I truly value your friendship.* **Ant. 1.** unimportance, insignificance. **4.** disdain, disregard.

valve *n.* shutoff, spigot, regulator, governor, plug, stopper. *Turn the valve to the right to shut off the water.*

vampire *n.* bloodsucker, Dracula, ghoul, bat. *To ward off a vampire, carry garlic.*

vandal *n.* destroyer, wrecker, despoiler, plunderer, hoodlum. *Vandals did extensive damage to several of the school's classrooms.*

vandalism *n.* destruction, defacement, mutilation, sabotage, mischief. *He was charged with vandalism for tipping over tombstones.*

vanguard *n.* front, advance guard, cutting edge, trailblazers, forerunners, pioneers, fore. *The company is at the vanguard of computer innovation.* **Ant.** rear, back, followers.

vanish *vb.* disappear, fade, evaporate, dissolve, dematerialize. *The sorceress vanished into thin air.* **Ant.** appear, materialize.

vanity *n.* pride, conceit, arrogance, egotism, smugness. *She liked to flirt because the responses she got appealed to her vanity.* **Ant.** humility, humbleness, modesty.

vanquish *vb.* overcome, conquer, defeat, subdue, beat, eliminate, master. *The shy boy was able to vanquish his fear of meeting girls.* **Ant.** lose, surrender, yield, submit.

vapor *n.* mist, fog, haze, smoke, steam, moisture. *In old horror movies, the monsters frequently appear amidst clouds of vapor.*

variable *adj.* **1.** changing, changeable, shifting, fluctuating, unsteady, unstable. *In the spring, weather conditions are highly variable.* –*n.* **2.** uncertainty, contingency, possibility. *It's hard to predict the weather because there are so many variables.* **Ant. 1.** invariable, unchanging, constant. **2.** certainty, constant.

varied *adj.* assorted, diversified, motley, different, miscellaneous, diverse. *The store carried a varied assortment of penny candy.*

variegated *adj.* varicolored, parti-colored, mottled, streaked, polychromatic, dappled. *In the wild, the variegated coats of some animals serve as an effective camouflage.* **Ant.** monochromatic, uniform.

variety *n.* **1.** diversity, diverseness, variation, change, difference. *For the sake of variety, let's go camping on our next vacation.* **2.** collection, assortment, mixture, conglomeration, hodgepodge. *The mountaineer carried a large variety of climbing hardware.* **3.** type, sort, class, kind, brand, species, classification. *The local super-*

market stocks apples of many different varieties. **Ant. 1.** uniformity, similarity, monotony.

various *adj.* different, diverse, varied, varying, assorted, numerous, many. *There are various ways to deal with this problem.* **Ant.** identical, uniform, few.

varnish *n.* lacquer, shellac, enamel, veneer, stain, coat, glaze. *Put another coat of varnish on that table to protect it.*

vary *vb.* deviate, change, differ, alter, diversify, fluctuate, shift. *The price of gasoline varies almost continuously.*

vase *n.* vessel, pot, jar, pitcher, amphora, potiche. *Please put those lilacs in a vase.*

vast *adj.* immense, enormous, colossal, huge, limitless, infinite. *The starship "Enterprise" explores the vast reaches of outer space.* **Ant.** minute, small, tiny, limited.

vault *n.* **1.** tomb, crypt, sepulcher, mausoleum, grave. *The pyramid's vault contained the mummified remains of an Egyptian pharaoh.* **2.** safe, strongroom, depository, repository. *The bank's vault is sealed with a time clock.* –*vb.* **3.** leap, spring, jump, bound, hurdle, hop. *The deer vaulted gracefully over a fallen tree.*

veer *vb.* swerve, pivot, turn, shift, curve, drift. *The driver had to veer sharply to avoid a head-on collision.*

vegetarian *n.* vegan, plant-eating, herbivorous. *Are you a vegetarian or do you eat meat?* **Ant.** carnivorous, meat-eating.

vegetation *n.* flora, plant life, plants, shrubbery, foliage, growth. *Jungle travel is difficult because of the thick vegetation.*

vehemence *n.* passion, fierceness, fervor, ardor, zeal, fire. *She defended her position with great vehemence.* **Ant.** apathy, indifference.

vehement *adj.* passionate, enthusiastic, ardent, fervent, zealous, forceful, eager. *She's a vehement advocate of animal rights.* **Ant.** indifferent, unconcerned, apathetic.

vehicle *n.* **1.** conveyance, transportation, transport. *Bicycles and automobiles are two examples of commonly used vehicles.* **2.** means, medium, agency, instrument, channel, tool. *The actress hoped her small role would be a vehicle to greater recognition.*

veil *n.* **1.** cover, covering, screen, mask, curtain. *The mountaintop was hidden behind a veil of clouds.* –*vb.* **2.** hide, cover, screen, conceal, mask. *The bandit veiled his face with a bright red scarf.* **Ant. 2.** reveal, expose, show.

vein *n.* **1.** seam, streak, course, line, stratum, layer. *The prospector was overjoyed when he found a large vein of gold.* **2.** manner, style, mood, character, tone, bent. *Mark Twain typically wrote in a humorous vein.*

velocity *n.* speed, pace, rate, swiftness, quickness. *Sound waves travel at a velocity of approximately 740 miles per hour.*

venal *adj.* unscrupulous, corruptible, unprincipled, immoral, unethical. *The venal gang members were easily lead into a life of crime.* **Ant.** moral, ethical.

vendetta *n.* feud, quarrel, fight, bad blood, vengeance campaign, blood feud, retaliation campaign. *The violence could not be controlled because one tribe had a long-standing vendetta against a neighboring tribe.*

vendor *n.* peddler, seller, purveyor, merchandiser, supplier. *She has a part-time job as an ice cream vendor.* **Ant.** buyer, purchaser, customer.

venerable *adj.* honored, revered, respected, respectable, dignified, worthy. *The venerable old man took his customary place at the head of* *the table.* **Ant.** dishonorable, undeserving, unworthy.

vengeance *n.* revenge, retaliation, reprisal, retribution, avenging. *The honorable hero of* Les Miserables *did not seek vengeance against those who had wronged him.*

venom *n.* **1.** poison, toxin. *A rattlesnake can control the amount of venom it injects.* **2.** hate, hatred, bitterness, malice, spite, spitefulness. *The disillusioned critic wrote reviews that were always full of venom.* **Ant. 2.** kindness, love, charity.

venomous *adj.* **1.** poisonous, toxic, lethal, deadly. *The rattlesnake is venomous, so be careful.* **2.** malicious, malevolent, spiteful, hostile, malignant. *The venomous woman spewed insults at everyone around her.* **Ant.** kind, benevolent, sweet.

vent *n.* **1.** outlet, opening, aperture, hole, passage. *She opened the vent to let fresh air into her car.* **2.** expression, exposure, voice, utterance. *The child gave vent to her anger by kicking the door.* *–vb.* **3.** discharge, release, emit, express, air. *He vented his frustrations on his hapless employees.* **Ant. 3.** suppress, repress, restrain.

ventilate *vb.* **1.** air, aerate, refresh. *This room needs to be ventilated.* **2.** expose, divulge, examine, discuss, publicize, circulate. *The open-door policy was designed to give employees an opportunity to ventilate their grievances.* **Ant. 2.** conceal, repress, suppress.

venture *n.* **1.** risk, chance, hazard, gamble, endeavor, undertaking. *The daredevil's ventures were well publicized.* *–vb.* **2.** risk, chance, gamble, hazard, speculate. *She was unwilling to venture her money on the stock market.* **3.** journey, travel, go, advance. *A firefighter ventured into the burning building.* **Ant. 2.** save, preserve, protect.

veracity *n.* truthfulness, accuracy, honesty, credibility, authenticity, reality, integrity. *We doubted the veracity of the crook's alibi.* **Ant.** deception, inaccuracy, dishonesty.

verbal *adj.* spoken, oral, voiced, unwritten. *The witness gave police a verbal description of the suspect.* **Ant.** written, documented.

verbatim *adv.* word for word, as written, exactly, as heard, faithfully, precisely. *Don't exaggerate, just tell us what you heard verbatim.* **Ant.** roughly, approximately.

verbose *adj.* wordy, prolix, long-winded, voluble, talkative, loquacious. *The congressman's speeches tend to be verbose.* **Ant.** brief, to the point, succinct.

verdict *n.* decision, judgment, finding, ruling, conclusion. *The jury took five days to reach a verdict.*

verge *n.* **1.** edge, rim, margin, brink, threshold. *The boy was on the verge of tears when his parents scolded him.* *–vb.* **2.** approach, approximate, border, touch. *Her remark verges on heresy.*

verification *n.* substantiation, corroboration, authentication, certification, proof, affirmation. *We heard that school might be called off due to the storm, but we needed verification.*

verify *vb.* attest, confirm, affirm, authenticate, corroborate, prove, substantiate. *Her testimony verified that the suspect could not have been at the scene of the crime.* **Ant.** refute, deny, disprove.

vernacular *n.* language, native tongue, dialect, lingo, idiom, jargon, slang. *The popular vernacular of teenagers changes from decade to decade.*

versatile *adj.* **1.** multifaceted, many-sided, all-around, adaptable, talented, gifted. *The versatile ballplayer was as good in the infield as he was in the outfield.* **2.** all-purpose, practical, useful, handy, convenient. *A Swiss army knife is a versatile tool.* **Ant. 1.** specialized, limited. **2.** impractical, useless.

verse *n.* line, stanza, lyric, rhyme, poem, poetry. *I couldn't remember the last verse of the song, so I faked it.*

version *n.* **1.** account, rendition, story, report, description. *Each driver had his own version of how the accident occurred.* **2.** rendering, adaptation, portrayal, translation. *She makes her living writing modern versions of old fairy tales.*

vertical *adj.* perpendicular, upright, erect, plumb, standing. *She easily scaled the vertical rock face.* **Ant.** horizontal, flat, level.

verve *n.* energy, liveliness, enthusiasm, vitality, spirit, vigor. *The pop singer belted out her songs with great emotion and verve.* **Ant.** weariness, slothfulness, laziness.

very *adv.* **1.** extremely, especially, immensely, enormously, remarkably, exceedingly. *He's a very good tennis player.* *–adj.* **2.** exact, precise, specific, perfect, genuine, real. *This is the very thing you need to cure your cold.* **3.** mere, bare, sheer, simple. *The very idea of climbing a mountain makes most people uneasy.* **Ant. 1.** scarcely, hardly, barely. **2.** inappropriate, wrong, useless.

vessel *n.* **1.** boat, ship, craft. *The port was crowded with many types of sailing vessels.* **2.** container, receptacle, utensil, pot, jar. *This acid must be stored in a glass vessel.*

vested *adj.* fixed, set, guaranteed, absolute, inviolable. *I have a vested interest in the success of company I own.*

vestibule *n.* entrance, entranceway, foyer, lobby. *Please take your shoes off in the vestibule.*

vestige *n.* trace, hint, suggestion, remnant, remains, evidence. *A few stone implements were the only vestiges of the lost tribe.*

vestment *n.* garment, gown, robe, cassock, alb. *The priest entered the church wearing all of his vestments.*

veteran *n.* **1.** old-timer, master, expert, professional, pro. *The golf veteran had played in numerous previous tournaments.* *–adj.* **2.** experienced, practiced, seasoned, skilled, proficient, expert. *The veteran congressman was elected to a sixth term.* **Ant. 1.** novice, beginner, recruit. **2.** inexperienced, unpracticed.

veto *vb.* **1.** refuse, reject, deny, forbid, kill, void. *The president vetoed the new tax bill.* *–n.* **2.** denial, refusal, disapproval, rejection, ban. *The mayor's veto was overturned by the city council.* **Ant. 1.** approve, endorse, ratify. **2.** approval, endorsement.

vex *vb.* annoy, bother, irritate, trouble, distress, provoke, worry. *She is frequently vexed by her friend's constant complaining.*

viable *adj.* workable, practical, doable, feasible, possible, able to succeed. *We launched what we thought would be a viable plan for cleaning up our local environment.* **Ant.** unworkable, impractical, fanciful.

vial *n.* phial, ampule, container, receptacle, vessel, syringe. *The vial held a potent medicine.*

vibrant *adj.* lively, vital, vigorous, pulsing with life, radiant, energetic. *We need someone with a vibrant personality to greet customers.* **Ant.** dull, bland, dead.

vibrate *vb.* shake, tremble, quiver, quaver, quake. *Our windows vibrate whenever a plane passes overhead.*

vibration *n.* trembling, shaking, quivering, throbbing, tremor. *We could feel the vibrations caused by a big truck driving by outside.*

vicarious *adj.* indirect, imagined, secondhand, secondary, surrogate, sympathetic. *I get a* *vicarious thrill from watching skydivers jump out of airplanes.* **Ant.** direct, firsthand, personal.

vice *n.* **1.** immorality, depravity, corruption, evil, ill, sin. *The local newspaper ran a series on vice in the city.* **2.** weakness, shortcoming, frailty, fault, flaw, bad point. *Her only vice is a constant craving for sweets.* **Ant. 1.** virtue, morality. **2.** good point, strong point.

vicinity *n.* proximity, neighborhood, environs, region. *We live in the vicinity of the airport.*

vicious *adj.* **1.** savage, dangerous, ferocious, fierce, violent. *Pit bulls have a reputation for being vicious dogs.* **2.** depraved, wicked, evil, vile, terrible. *Kidnapping is a vicious crime.* **3.** spiteful, malicious, hateful, hurtful, cruel, mean. *He told a vicious lie about his sister.* **Ant. 1.** tamed, gentle, friendly. **2.** moral, decent, virtuous. **3.** kind, good-natured, complimentary.

vicissitudes *n.* changes, shifts, ups and downs, reversals, variations, peaks and valleys. *Sometimes you have to be strong in order to withstand the vicissitudes of life.*

victim *n.* **1.** casualty, injured, fatality. *There were five victims in yesterday's accident.* **2.** dupe, loser, target, prey, scapegoat, sufferer. *The con artist swindled his victims out of all their savings.*

victimize *vb.* bully, pick on, target, prey on, abuse, molest. *Don't let that bully victimize you.*

victor *n.* winner, champion, conqueror, vanquisher. *The United States and its allies were the victors of World War II.* **Ant.** loser, defeated, vanquished.

victorious *adj.* winning, triumphant, successful, conquering, champion. *The victorious team advanced to the state finals.* **Ant.** losing, defeated, beaten.

victory *n.* triumph, success, conquest, supremacy, primacy, win. *The candidate claimed victory before the polls closed.* **Ant.** defeat, loss, failure.

video *n.* TV, television, videocassette, cable, tape, movie, motion picture. *Let's make some popcorn and watch a video.*

vie *vb.* complete, contend, contest, challenge, jockey for position, lock horns. *Our football team will vie for the championship starting next Saturday.*

view *n.* **1.** vista, panorama, scene, outlook, sight, vision. *We have a lovely view of the surrounding hills from our front porch.* **2.** look, sight, glimpse, glance, peek. *As we turned up the driveway, we got our first view of our new home.* **3.** opinion, thought, conviction, sentiment, notion, judgment. *What are your views on nuclear energy?* *–vb.* **4.** see, watch, behold, witness, observe. *People come from all over the world to view the splendors of Yosemite.*

viewpoint *n.* perspective, view, opinion, outlook, feeling, point of view. *My viewpoint tends to be rather conservative.*

vigil *n.* watch, monitoring, observation, surveillance. *We held a vigil at the child's bedside while she recuperated.*

vigilant *adj.* observant, watchful, attentive, heedful, alert, wary. *A vigilant guard foiled the attempted robbery.* **Ant.** negligent, careless, heedless.

vignette *n.* bit, sketch, skit, scene, cameo. *In between main acts, the troupe performed a brief vignette on the dangers of smoking.*

vigor *n.* energy, vitality, animation, fervor, strength, force, might. *She presented her idea with great vigor.* **Ant.** indifference, apathy, weakness.

vigorous *adj.* energetic, active, robust, dynamic, strong, forceful, lively. *He was very tired after playing a vigorous set of tennis.* **Ant.** lethargic, unenergetic, feeble, weak.

vile *adj.* **1.** offensive, disgusting, objectionable, nauseating, revolting, repugnant. *Rotten eggs have a vile odor.* **2.** evil, wicked, corrupt, immoral, vicious, sinful. *Terrorism is widely considered to be one of the most vile crimes imaginable.* **Ant. 1.** agreeable, pleasant, appealing. **2.** righteous, moral.

vilify *vb.* defame, denounce, slander, smear, criticize, denigrate. *The media launched a campaign to vilify the corrupt politician.* **Ant.** honor, praise, commend.

villa *n.* country house, country estate, mansion, summerhouse, hacienda. *He was wealthy enough to own a villa in Jamaica.*

village *n.* hamlet, settlement, municipality, small town, community. *The Swiss village was nestled among the Alps.* **Ant.** city, metropolis.

villain *n.* scoundrel, rascal, rogue, knave, brute, devil, wretch. *The audience cheered when the movie's villain was defeated.* **Ant.** hero, heroine, champion.

vindicate *vb.* clear, exonerate, acquit, absolve, exculpate, prove innocent. *The new evidence will vindicate my client.* **Ant.** implicate, damn, convict.

vindictive *adj.* spiteful, revengeful, vengeful, malicious, bitter. *The fired employee spread vindictive rumors about his ex-boss.* **Ant.** forgiving, charitable.

vintage *adj.* superior, supreme, best, classic, select, prime. *The innkeeper offered his guests some vintage wine.* **Ant.** inferior, poor, second-rate.

violate *vb.* breach, break, infringe, disobey, disregard, defy. *By staying out late, she violated her parents' trust.* **Ant.** respect, uphold, obey.

violation *n.* breach, infraction, infringement, dishonoring. *He will lose his driver's license if he gets another moving violation.* **Ant.** observance, obedience, compliance.

violence *n.* **1.** force, brutality, savagery, ferociousness, roughness. *Many people think there is too much violence on television.* **2.** intensity, severity, might, power, magnitude. *We were not prepared for a storm of such violence.* **Ant. 1.** nonviolence, peacefulness. **2.** mildness, weakness.

violent *adj.* **1.** powerful, strong, forceful, intense, severe. *The sailboat was capsized by a violent wind.* **2.** brutal, cruel, destructive, murderous, savage, ferocious. *There is too much violent crime in our city.* **3.** fiery, passionate, uncontrollable, ungovernable. *He has a violent temper.* **Ant. 1.** mild, weak. **2.** nonviolent, peaceful. **3.** composed, collected.

VIP *n.* very important person, personage, dignitary, celebrity, (slang) big shot, nabob. *Our organization will be hosting a VIP from overseas.* **Ant.** nobody, (slang) lightweight.

virgin *adj.* unused, untouched, unspoiled, pristine, pure, new. *There is not much virgin wilderness left in the world today.* **Ant.** used, spoiled, contaminated.

virginity *n.* chastity, purity, celibacy, virtue, innocence, abstinence. *The conservation group purchased the remote land to protect its virginity.*

virile *adj.* potent, manly, macho, strong, masculine, powerful. *Romance novels frequently feature paintings of virile men on the cover.* **Ant.** weak, impotent, effeminate.

virility *n.* potency, manliness, strength, masculinity, power, vigor. *She was attracted only to men with great virility.* **Ant.** impotence, weakness, femininity.

virtually *adv.* practically, in effect, equal to, essentially, nearly, in substance. *In the middle of the desert, we were virtually alone.*

virtue *n.* **1.** morality, integrity, goodness, righteousness, honor, honesty. *Her virtue is unquestioned.* **2.** strength, quality, merit, advantage, value, benefit. *The fact that this computer is easy to use is just one of its many virtues.* **Ant. 1.** immorality, sinfulness, vice. **2.** disadvantage, drawback.

virtuoso *n.* master, expert, professional, ace, superstar, savant, artist. *The piano virtuoso wowed audiences all over the world.* **Ant.** amateur, bumbler, neophyte.

virtuous *adj.* moral, good, righteous, honorable, ethical, principled. *He seems so virtuous, it's hard to believe he could tell a lie.* **Ant.** immoral, bad, sinful.

virulent *adj.* infectious, contagious, poisonous, toxic, noxious, deadly. *The health center is warning of a particularly virulent strain of flu this year.* **Ant.** harmless, benign, mild.

virus *n.* germ, microorganism, microbe, pathogen, (slang) bug, infectious agent. *It's easy to pick up a cold virus from school.*

visceral *adj.* instinctive, intuitive, gut, internal, reflexive, natural, unconscious. *The desire to have children is often purely visceral.*

viscosity *n.* thickness, stickiness, viscidity, cohesiveness, pastiness. *The engine required a lubricant with a high viscosity.*

viscous *adj.* viscid, sticky, tacky, gluey, syrupy. *Oil is hard to wash off because it is so viscous.*

visible *adj.* **1.** observable, seeable, viewable, noticeable, perceptible. *Our house is not visible from the road.* **2.** apparent, evident, obvious, clear, plain. *She has made no visible progress toward her college degree.* **Ant. 1.** invisible, hidden, concealed. **2.** imperceptible, unapparent.

vision *n.* **1.** sight, eyesight, seeing. *Her vision was corrected to 20/20 with eyeglasses.* **2.** foresight, imagination, perception, intuition, wisdom. *The company's success is largely due to the vision of its founder.* **3.** dream, fantasy, fancy, idea, notion. *The young actor has visions of becoming a famous star.*

visionary *n.* dreamer, romantic, idealist, daydreamer, utopian, prophet. *He was a visionary who saw the future purely in utopian terms.*

visit *vb.* **1.** call on, see, attend, go to, drop by. *Let's visit Grandmother next weekend.* –*n.* **2.** call, stop, visitation, stopover, stay, sojourn. *Our neighbor came over for a short visit.*

visitor *n.* **1.** guest, caller, company. *I can't go out tonight because I'm expecting visitors.* **2.** tourist, traveler, vacationer, sightseer. *We're visitors in your country.*

vista *n.* view, scene, prospect, outlook, panorama. *Emerging from the forest, we were treated to a sweeping vista of rolling farmland.*

visual *adj.* visible, observable, perceptible, discernible, seeable. *The air-traffic controller does not yet have visual contact with the approaching plane.*

visualize *vb.* imagine, see, picture, fantasize, envision, conceive. *Visualize a peaceful future.*

vital *adj.* **1.** essential, crucial, critical, important, imperative, necessary. *Her contributions were vital to the project's success.* **2.** energetic, dynamic, spirited, lively, animated, active. *Despite his age, he still has a vital personality.* **Ant. 1.** unimportant, insignificant. **2.** lethargic, listless.

vitality *n.* strength, vigor, energy, life, liveliness, spirit. *Grandmother's vitality continuously amazes me.* **Ant.** weakness, lifelessness.

vitriol *adj.* venom, nastiness, maliciousness, malevolence, contempt. *The vitriol between the two enemies made our ears burn.* **Ant.** benevolence, kindness, friendliness.

vitriolic *adj.* caustic, scathing, bitter, venomous, acid, biting, nasty. *His vitriolic statements drove many from the room.* **Ant.** sweet, soothing, nice.

vivacious *adj.* lively, animated, bubbly, vital, effervescent, ebullient. *The vivacious entertainer seemed to have endless reserves of energy.* **Ant.** lifeless, dead, dull.

vivid *adj.* **1.** keen, sharp, intense, strong, acute, clear. *He has vivid recollections of his childhood.* **2.** bright, brilliant, loud, colorful, shiny. *She painted her bike a vivid green.* **Ant. 1.** average, routine. **2.** dull, drab, colorless.

vocabulary *n.* lexicon, glossary, vernacular, nomenclature, terminology, language, lingo, jargon. *I don't always understand the vocabulary of surfers.*

vocal *adj.* **1.** said, spoken, oral, uttered, voiced, vocalized. *The parrot made many vocal sounds, but it couldn't really speak.* **2.** outspoken, blunt, frank, free, candid, direct. *You shouldn't be so vocal in your criticism of others.* **Ant. 1.** unspoken, unvoiced. **2.** silent, quiet, reserved.

vocation *n.* occupation, profession, career, business, employment. *What vocation are you preparing for?*

vociferous *adj.* loud, vehement, clamorous, uproarious, vocal, thunderous. *The change in policy met with a vociferous outcry.* **Ant.** quiet, reserved, mousy.

vogue *n.* fashion, style, fad, rage, custom, practice. *Skinny ties have not been in vogue for years.*

voice *n.* **1.** speech, speaking, vocalization, verbalization, articulation, utterance. *She has temporarily lost her voice due to laryngitis.* **2.** opinion, choice, option, vote, say, role, part. *Local residents should have a voice in running their town government.* *–vb.* **3.** say, state, speak, utter, verbalize, express, proclaim. *If you have any complaints, please voice them now.*

void *adj.* **1.** empty, vacant, barren, devoid, destitute. *The movie was completely void of any redeeming qualities.* **2.** invalid, meaningless, worthless, useless, canceled. *This contest is void wherever prohibited by law.* *–n.* **3.** vacuum, emptiness, nothingness, hollow. *After he lost his job, his life seemed to be a meaningless void.* *–vb.* **4.** cancel, nullify, invalidate, revoke, annul. *Since the salesman had lied to her, she wanted to void her purchase contract.* **Ant. 1.** full, complete, occupied. **2.** valid, binding, useful. **4.** validate, enforce, uphold.

volatile *adj.* unstable, changeable, capricious, inconstant, explosive, inflammable, incendiary. *In times of economic change, the stock market can be volatile.* **Ant.** stable, steady, predictable.

volcano *n.* mountain, vent, crater. *It's unwise to build a home at the base of a volcano.*

WORD SEARCH

avalanche of superheated gas and ash: *pyroclastic flow, nuee ardente*
blob of lava, ejected: *bomb*
cavern formed by lava flow: *lava tube*
crater that eventually fills with water: *caldera*
explosion of: *eruption, cataclysm, upheaval*
glass, volcanic: *obsidian*
inactive, permanently: *extinct*
inactive, temporarily: *dormant*
molten rock before it is expelled: *magma*
molten rock expelled: *lava*
mouth: *crater*
mud and ash flow: *lahar*
science of: *volcanology*
scientist: *volcanologist, vulcanist*
vent, small gas: *fumerole, monticule*
vibration measurement apparatus: *seismograph*

volition *n.* choice, will, desire, election, willingness, determination. *He joined the marines of his own volition.*

volume *n.* **1.** book, publication, tract, treatise. *She has written several volumes of poetry.* **2.** capacity, size, bulk, dimensions. *The jar has a volume of three liters.* **3.** amount, quantity, mass, measure, extent. *The new video store did a large volume of business on its opening day.* **4.** sound, power, intensity, loudness. *Do you mind if I turn up the volume on the TV?*

voluntarily *adv.* willingly, freely, electively, of one's own free will, of one's own choice. *He washed the chalkboards voluntarily.* **Ant.** involuntarily, unwillingly, against one's will.

voluntary *adj.* optional, free, willing, unforced, volunteered. *Only voluntary confessions are admissible in a court of law.* **Ant.** involuntary, forced, coerced, compelled.

volunteer *adj.* **1.** voluntary, willing, unforced, unpaid, nonprofessional. *The Revolutionary War was won by volunteer soldiers –n.* **2.** unforced person, voluntary person, unpaid person. *The senator asked for volunteers to staff his reelection committee. –vb.* **3.** offer, give, provide, donate, contribute. *She volunteered her time to serve on the fund-raising committee.* **Ant. 1.** involuntary, forced, paid. **3.** withhold, refuse.

voluptuous *adj.* sexually attractive, curvaceous, buxom, well-built, well-endowed. *Venus is often depicted as a voluptuous woman.*

vomit *vb.* regurgitate, puke, upchuck, disgorge, (slang) barf. *If I eat one more piece of cake I'm going to vomit.*

voodoo *n.* black magic, witchcraft, sorcery, hoodoo, obeah, religion. *Voodoo can be used to manipulate some people through superstitious fears.*

voracious *adj.* ravenous, hungry, starved, greedy, insatiable, gluttonous. *Authors usually have a voracious appetite for books and reading.*

vortex *n.* whirlpool, whirlwind, gyre, eddy, maelstrom, cyclone. *The water formed a natural vortex as it ran down the drain.*

vote *n.* **1.** ballot, ticket, selection, choice, preference. *Who did you cast your vote for? –vb.* **2.** cast a ballot, elect, select, choose. *Don't forget to vote in this year's elections.*

vouch *vb.* guarantee, affirm, assure, confirm, verify, certify. *I can vouch for her honesty.* **Ant.** deny, refute, repudiate.

vow *n.* **1.** pledge, promise, oath, assurance, guarantee. *He made a vow to stop drinking. –vb.* **2.** pledge, promise, swear, resolve, declare. *She vowed to stop smoking by next week.*

voyage *n.* **1.** cruise, sail, crossing, passage, journey, excursion. *She took her new sailboat on a long voyage. –vb.* **2.** cruise, sail, navigate, boat, journey. *People will someday be able to voyage between the stars.*

voyeur *n.* peeping Tom, pervert, watcher, spy. *The police are on the lookout for a voyeur, who spies on people during the day.*

vulgar *adj.* coarse, crude, rude, impolite, unrefined, tasteless, indecent. *Vulgar language has no place in school.* **Ant.** polite, refined, tasteful.

vulnerable *adj.* defenseless, susceptible, unguarded, unprotected, exposed. *His weakened condition left him vulnerable to disease.* **Ant.** protected, guarded, invincible.

W

wacky *adj.* crazy, silly, (slang) goofy, (slang) nuts, clownish, zany, eccentric. *Inventors sometimes come up with some wacky, impractical ideas.* **Ant.** sensible, serious, rational.

wad *n.* batch, lump, mass, chunk, plug, pack. *She chewed on a huge wad of gum.*

waffle *vb.* equivocate, hedge, sidestep, evade, dodge, hem and haw. *Politicians tend to waffle on the issue of raising taxes.*

wage *n.* **1.** salary, pay, payment, fee, compensation, earnings. *His new job pays only minimum wage.* *–vb.* **2.** conduct, pursue, undertake, make, carry on. *She is waging a personal war against drunk drivers.*

wager *n.* **1.** bet, gamble, speculation, chance. *They made a wager on the outcome of the bowling tournament.* *–vb.* **2.** bet, gamble, venture, speculate, risk. *He wagered five dollars at the race track.*

wagon *n.* cart, buggy, trailer, truck, carriage, dray. *The farmer loaded the dried hay on to the wagon.*

waif *n.* orphan, stray, homeless, person, lost child, foundling, gamin. *The kindly couple took in the young waif and adopted him.*

wail *n.* **1.** moan, cry, whine, lamentation, howl. *The siren's wail could be heard throughout town.* *–vb.* **2.** moan, weep, cry, whine, howl, roar. *The wind wailed all night long.*

wait *vb.* **1.** linger, tarry, dally, remain, delay, stay. *Let's wait till next week to wash the car.* *–n.* **2.** delay, pause, holdup, postponement, lull. *We have a two-hour wait before the next bus leaves.* **Ant. 1.** begin, start, commence.

waiter *n.* server, steward, waitress, garcon, maître d', servant, host. *We gave the waiter a big tip for his excellent service.*

waive *vb.* relinquish, renounce, drop, forgo, resign, yield. *She signed an agreement that waived her right to sue.* **Ant.** demand, require, clam.

wake *vb.* **1.** arouse, rouse, stir, awaken, waken. *Please wake me at seven o'clock.* *–n.* **2.** aftermath, track, trail, course, path. *There was great damage in the wake of the hurricane.* **Ant. 1.** sleep, doze, slumber.

walk *vb.* **1.** stroll, saunter, amble, hike, march. *Let's walk to school today.* *–n.* **2.** stroll, hike, saunter, ramble, trek. *Grandfather likes to take a walk after dinner.* **3.** sidewalk, pathway, path, lane, passage. *It's your turn to shovel the front walk.* **4.** field, sphere, dominion, domain, area. *The new TV show appeals to people from all walks of life.*

wall *n.* barrier, partition, divider, barricade, fence. *The castle's walls were crumbling with age.*

wallop *vb.* punch, hit, strike, pound, thump, beat. *The irate boxer threatened to wallop everyone around him.*

wallow *vb.* **1.** roll, slosh, grovel, tumble, nestle. *On hot days, pigs keep cool by wallowing in mud.* **2.** flounder, stumble, reel, stagger, blunder. *The* *hunters wallowed through miles of swampland.* **3.** indulge, revel, bask, luxuriate, delight. *Since winning the lottery, she's been wallowing in luxury.* **Ant. 3.** abstain, refrain, forbear.

wan *adj.* pale, white, pallid, ghostly, blanched, colorless. *She was suffering from the flu and looked wan.*

wander *vb.* **1.** rove, roam, ramble, range, drift, amble, stroll. *She wandered through the store, looking for an unusual gift.* **2.** stray, deviate, swerve, veer, digress. *His attention wandered as he watched the boring movie.* **Ant. 1.** stay, remain. **2.** conform, follow.

wane *vb.* decrease, lessen, ebb, reduce, weaken, decline, fade. *As the wind died down we knew the storm was beginning to wane.* **Ant.** grow, increase, wax.

want *vb.* **1.** desire, wish, yearn, crave, covet, need, require. *She wants a computer for her birthday.* –*n.* **2.** need, requirement, necessity, desire, yearning, craving. *Since inheriting his father's fortune, he has no more material wants.* **Ant. 1.** loathe, hate, reject. **2.** abundance, sufficiency.

wanton *adj.* malicious, cruel, merciless, unrestrained, reckless, out-of-control. *The dictator's army waged a wanton campaign of terror.* **Ant.** judicious, prudent, merciful.

war *n.* **1.** warfare, combat, battle, conflict, struggle, fight, strife. *The war against drugs is an international effort.* –*vb.* **2.** fight, battle, attack, struggle, combat. *The two factions have been warring against each other for years.* **Ant. 1.** peace, harmony, alliance.

WORD SEARCH

attack: *offensive*
cease-fire, mutual: *armistice, truce, peace treaty*
games, preparatory: *maneuvers*
god of: *Mars*
holy war: *crusade, jihad*
invasion, all-out: *blitzkrieg, sweep*
military's presence in and control of a foreign nation: *occupation*
operation: *campaign*
organization and deployment of troops and supplies: *logistics*
referring to: *martial*
surrender: *capitulation*
tensions but no physical war between nations: *cold war*
threatening an opponent with potential action: *saber rattling, gunboat diplomacy*
winnings: *spoils*

ward *n.* **1.** district, precinct, borough, zone. *The city is divided into seven administrative wards.* **2.** room, section, annex, department. *She has been admitted to the hospital's intensive-care ward.* **3.** charge, dependent, client. *The juvenile delinquent has become a ward of the court.* –*vb.* **4.** avert, avoid, evade, deter, block, repel. *This repellent will ward off mosquitoes.* **Ant. 4.** permit, accept, allow.

warden *n.* custodian, guardian, keeper, superintendent, supervisor. *He has retired from his position as warden of the state prison.*

wardrobe *n.* clothes, clothing, apparel, outfits, garments, garb, fashion collection. *I have three sweatshirts and one sweater in my wardrobe.*

warehouse *n.* storehouse, depot, repository, stockroom, storage facility. *Hundreds of kitchen appliances are stored in the warehouse down the street.*

wares *n.* merchandise, goods, products, stock, supplies. *The traveling merchant sold his wares at various swap meets.*

warhead *n.* bomb, explosive charge, payload, (slang) business end, (slang) physics package.

The technicians carefully disengaged the warheads before unloading the missiles.

warlike *adj.* hostile, belligerent, bellicose, combative, militant. *A naval blockade is a warlike act.* **Ant.** peaceful, friendly, conciliatory.

warlock *n.* sorcerer, wizard, necromancer, conjurer, magician, shaman. *The warlock cast a spell over us.*

warlord *n.* tyrant, autocrat, hawk, dictator, strongman, despot, overlord. *A warlord is still the ultimate authority in some of Afghanistan.*

warm *adj.* **1.** heated, lukewarm, tepid. *He enjoys warm spring days.* **2.** sunny, sunshiny, summery, mild. *She likes to dress in warm colors.* **3.** loving, affectionate, tender, friendly, kind. *She gave him a warm smile.* **4.** enthusiastic, lively, ardent, eager, sympathetic. *He was not particularly warm to the suggestion that he retire early.* *–vb.* **5.** heat, thaw, cook, simmer. *He warmed his hands over the campfire.* **6.** cheer, please, comfort, gladden, delight. *The sight of children playing warmed the old man's heart.* **Ant.** **1.** cool, cold, chilly. **2.** dull, drab. **3.** unfriendly, uncaring. **4.** indifferent, apathetic. **5.** cool, chill. **6.** depress, sadden.

warmonger *n.* hawk, militant, militarist, jingoist. *I'm not going to vote for Congressman Jones again because he has turned out to be a warmonger.* **Ant.** pacifist, dove.

warn *vb.* forewarn, alert, caution, advise, admonish, inform. *She warned me not to eat the second pizza.*

warning *n.* notice, notification, signal, sign, omen, hint. *The police officer let me off with only a warning.*

warp *vb.* contort, twist, bend, bend out of shape, misshape, deform. *Don't leave that recording in the Sun or it will warp.*

warranty *n.* guarantee, assurance, pledge, security. *Her new car has a five-year warranty against defects.*

warrior *n.* fighter, soldier, combatant, military person. *Barbarian warriors swept down on the defenseless village.*

wary *adj.* cautious, suspicious, careful, watchful, guarded. *After losing her investment, she's wary of buying any more stocks.* **Ant.** unwary, unsuspecting, incautious.

wash *vb.* **1.** clean, cleanse, scrub, launder, bathe. *Please wash your hands before dinner.* **2.** drift, float, ride, slide, bob. *Debris from the sunken ship washed up on the beach.* **3.** carry away, remove, destroy, sweep. *Flood water washed out the local bridge.* *–n.* **4.** washing, cleaning, cleansing, laundering, bath. *Your car is in bad need of a wash.* **5.** laundry, clothes washing. *Since I have no clean clothes left, I'd better do the wash today.*

waste *vb.* **1.** squander, misuse, dissipate, throw away, deplete. *Don't waste your money buying clothes you don't need.* **2.** devastate, despoil, ravage, destroy, ruin. *The tornado wasted everything in its path.* **3.** decline, weaken, diminish, decrease, fade. *His strength wasted away during his long illness.* *–n.* **4.** garbage, rubbish, trash, debris, litter. *Toxic waste should be properly decontaminated before disposal.* **5.** extravagance, squandering, misuse, misapplication. *It's a waste of time and money trying to fix that old car.* **Ant.** **1.** save, conserve, economize. **3.** strengthen, improve, increase. **5.** saving, conservation, economy.

wasteful *adj.* extravagant, squandering, uneconomical, nonproductive. *It's wasteful to throw away plastic containers that can be recycled.* **Ant.** economical, thrifty, productive.

watch *vb.* **1.** look, observe, see, view, notice, eye. *He thought no one was watching when he ate* *the last cookie.* **2.** guard, protect, attend, tend, supervise, oversee. *She asked her neighbor to watch her dogs while she was on vacation.* –*n.* **3.** observation, attention, surveillance, notice, heed. *The lifeguard kept a close watch over the children in the pool.* **4.** guard, sentry, sentinel, vigil, patrol, shift. *The night watch comes on duty in two hours.* **5.** timepiece, wristwatch, pocket watch, clock. *Don't forget to set your watch to daylight savings time.*

watchful *adj.* attentive, alert, vigilant, aware, wary. *The bank guard kept a watchful eye on the suspicious-looking man.* **Ant.** inattentive, unobservant, unaware.

water *vb.* moisten, wet, sprinkle, irrigate, soak. *Please water the plants while I'm on vacation.* **Ant.** parch, dehydrate, dry.

waterfall *n.* falls, deluge, cascade, cataract, chute, whitewater. *Take the canoe out of the water before you get too close to the waterfall.*

waterlogged *adj.* saturated, sodden, soaked, drenched, sopping. *The chair cushions had been left in the rain and were waterlogged.*

watershed *adj.* turning point, pivotal event, landmark, milestone. *The development of the Internet was a watershed event in the history of the computer.*

wave *n.* **1.** swell, breaker, surf, roller, comber. *Most surfers prefer big waves.* **2.** curl, twist, curve, spiral, coil. *A wave of hair kept blowing into her eyes.* **3.** pulse, pulsation, vibration, undulation. *Sound travels in waves.* **4.** surge, upsurge, flood, deluge, rush. *His announcement was greeted with a wave of protest.* **5.** gesture, signal, sign, motion. *The police officer signaled us to stop with a wave of his hand.* –*vb.* **6.** sway, ripple, flutter, shake, waver. *The trees waved in the wind.* **7.** gesture, signal, motion. *She waved good-bye to her friends as they drove away.*

WORD SEARCH

colliding waves: *cross seas*
giant wave produced by earthquake: *tsunami*
giant wave produced by tidal surge: *bore, eagre*
gray-crested and frothy: *graybeard*
large wave among smaller waves, unusually: *rogue wave*
roughness of sea's surface: *chop*
series of: *train*
spray: *spindrift*
sweep up shore: *swash*
wall or line of rocks erected to block erosion of waves: *jetty, groin*
wind's distance crossed in relation to wave height: *fetch*

waver *vb.* vacillate, fluctuate, go back and forth, swing, sway, oscillate. *In unstable economic times, stock prices tend to waver.*

wax *vb.* **1.** polish, shine, buff, gloss. *It's time to wax the car.* –*n.* **2.** polish, resin, silicon. *Use this wax on the furniture.*

way *n.* **1.** method, style, manner, approach, technique. *What's the best way to solve this puzzle?* **2.** direction, route, course, path, trail. *The lost hiker couldn't find her way out of the forest.* **3.** distance, span, space, stretch. *The stranded motorist had to walk a long way to find a gas station.* **4.** wish, desire, will, fancy, choice. *That spoiled child throws a fit if he can't have his way.*

wayfarer *n.* traveler, wanderer, nomad, drifter, rover, gadabout. *He was a wayfarer, moving quickly from province to province.*

weak *adj.* **1.** feeble, frail, fragile, infirm, delicate, powerless. *After her long illness, she's too weak to walk.* **2.** thin, diluted, watery, cut, tasteless. *This tea is too weak.* **Ant.** **1.** strong, powerful, sturdy. **2.** thick, concentrated.

weaken *vb.* soften, lower, lessen, fade, fail, thin, exhaust. *Her enthusiasm for the project is* *beginning to weaken.* **Ant.** strengthen, increase, improve.

weakling *n.* (slang) wimp, Milquetoast, crybaby, namby-pamby, pushover, (slang) creampuff. *You'll see very few weaklings on a big league football team.* **Ant.** (slang) he-man, (slang) macho man, Hercules.

weakness *n.* **1.** frailty, feebleness, infirmity, debility. *His weakness is the result of not exercising properly.* **2.** shortcoming, flaw, fault, defect, blemish. *Her biggest weakness is that she doesn't like to follow directions.* **3.** fondness, passion, liking, inclination, bias. *She has a weakness for frozen yogurt.* **Ant. 1.** strength, vitality. **2.** effectiveness. **3.** dislike, aversion.

wealth *n.* **1.** fortune, money, assets, capital, riches. *The heiress is a woman of great wealth.* **2.** abundance, profusion, store, fund, bounty. *He has discovered a wealth of information on that subject.* **Ant. 1.** poverty, destitution. **2.** scarcity, lack, shortage.

wealthy *adj.* rich, affluent, prosperous, well-off. *The wealthy woman buys a new sports car every year.* **Ant.** poor, needy, destitute.

weapon *n.* arm, armament, firearm, defense, rifle, gun. *Humans have been designing weapons for tens of thousands of years.*

wear *vb.* **1.** have on, dress in, don, bear. *She wore blue jeans to the party.* **2.** use up, exhaust, consume, abrade, fray. *He's had that shirt so long it's totally worn out.* **3.** tire, fatigue, strain, drain, exhaust. *She was worn out from working seven days a week.* –*n.* **4.** apparel, clothes, clothing, garments. *Does this store sell men's wear?* **5.** use, service, utilization, employment. *She's gotten a lot of wear out of that jacket.* **Ant. 2.** save, conserve. **3.** refresh, revitalize.

weary *adj.* **1.** tired, exhausted, fatigued, drained, spent. *She was very weary after the long hike.* **2.** tiring, tiresome, fatiguing, tedious, boring, dull. *Most people consider writing a dictionary to be a weary task.* –*vb.* **3.** tire, fatigue, exhaust, wear out. *The long lecture wearied the entire audience.* **Ant. 1.** refreshed, revived, energetic. **2.** refreshing, interesting, exciting. **3.** refresh, revive.

weather *n.* **1.** climate, elements, conditions, temperature. *What's the weather like in California?* –*vb.* **2.** season, dry, bleach, age, wrinkle. *His face is weathered from the long years he has worked outside.* **3.** survive, endure, withstand, come through. *Her large yacht easily weathered the storm.* **Ant. 3.** succumb, yield, fail.

weave *vb.* **1.** knit, braid, plait, lace, spin. *A loom is used to weave cloth.* **2.** zigzag, wind, careen, wobble, stagger. *She had to weave her way through a large crowd to find an exit.*

web *n.* maze, tangle, net, network, snare, trap. *The spy was caught in the web of intrigue he had helped create.*

wed *vb.* marry, unite, bind, join, link, devote, dedicate. *He is wedded to his old-fashioned ways.* **Ant.** divorce, separate, divide.

wedding *n.* marriage, matrimony, nuptials, wedlock, ceremony, espousal. *The couple planned to have their wedding in May.*

weep *vb.* cry, sob, lament, mourn, grieve. *The sad movie made me weep.*

weight *n.* **1.** mass, poundage, heaviness. *The wrestler had to get his weight down to qualify for the tournament.* **2.** burden, strain, pressure, load, anxiety. *She's strong enough to carry the weight of her responsibilities.* **3.** importance, significance, influence, impact, authority. *Her opinion carries a lot of weight with me.* **Ant. 1.** weightlessness. **3.** unimportance, insignificance.

weird *adj.* odd, bizarre, strange, peculiar, queer, unnatural, eerie. *My car is making weird noises.* **Ant.** normal, usual, natural, ordinary.

weirdo *n.* (slang) oddball, character, freak, nonconformist, (slang) screwball. *It's perfectly acceptable to act like a weirdo on Halloween.*

welcome *vb.* **1.** receive, greet, hail, meet, accept. *She was sad because no one was there to welcome her home.* *–n.* **2.** greeting, reception, welcoming, acceptance. *He always gives his guests a warm welcome.* *–adj.* **3.** agreeable, pleasant, pleasing, delightful, enjoyable. *Hearing about your new job was welcome news.* **Ant. 1–2.** snub, rebuff. **3.** unwelcome, unwanted.

weld *vb.* braze, solder, connect, join, unite, combine. *The boy heated the piece of plastic to weld it into place.* **Ant.** detach, separate, sever.

welfare *n.* well-being, happiness, fortune, good, prosperity. *This law has been enacted for the welfare of the people.*

well *n.* **1.** hole, shaft, pit, spring, fountain. *We get our water from a well.* *–adj.* **2.** healthy, sound, robust, hale, hearty. *Though she has been sick, she's now feeling well.* *–adv.* **3.** satisfactorily, adequately, favorably, agreeably, nicely. *She hasn't slept well for the past several days.* **4.** fully, thoroughly, considerably, substantially, amply. *His new car is worth well over $20,000.* **Ant. 2.** sick, ill, infirm. **3.** badly, poorly. **4.** somewhat, scarcely.

well-being *n.* health, welfare, fitness, benefit, comfort, prosperity. *You should eat right and exercise for your own well-being.*

wet *adj.* **1.** moist, damp, soaked, soaking, drenched, soggy. *Take off those wet clothes.* **2.** rainy, stormy, showery. *The last wet spell lasted for three weeks.* *–vb.* **3.** moisten, dampen, water, soak, saturate, drench. *The directions say you should wet your hair before applying this shampoo.* **Ant. 1.** dry, waterless. **2.** arid, parched. **3.** dry, dehydrate.

wetland *n.* marsh, marshland, swamp, fen, everglade, quagmire. *Wetlands are critical habitats for many animals.*

whale *n.* cetacean, marine animal, leviathan, mammal, aquatic mammal. *The largest whale is the blue whale.*

WORD SEARCH

air hole: *blowhole, spiracle*
beaching of: *stranding*
carving made from bone or tooth: *scrimshaw*
fat: *blubber*
female: *cow*
fins, tail: *flukes*
group of: *gam, pod*
horned variety: *narwhal*
killer whale: *orca*
leaping out of the water: *breaching*
male: *bull*
strainer found in some varieties, mouth: *baleen*
study of: *cetology*
young: *calf*

wharf *n.* dock, pier, jetty, berth, landing, mooring. *This wharf is used for the unloading of cargo ships.*

wheedle *vb.* coax, cajole, persuade, charm, flatter. *He wheedled his sister into taking him to the movies.*

wheel *vb.* **1.** turn, rotate, revolve, pivot, spin, twirl. *She wheeled around when she heard someone approaching from behind.* **2.** roll, push, maneuver, shove, propel. *They used a dolly to wheel the stove out to the moving van.*

wheeze *vb.* rasp, gasp, rattle, breathe with difficulty, huff and puff. *I start to wheeze when I have an allergic reaction.*

whet *vb.* sharpen, excite, stimulate, arouse, entice. *Her brief story whet my curiosity to hear more about her travels.* **Ant.** satisfy, stifle, deaden.

whim *n.* impulse, inclination, caprice, notion, whimsy, fancy. *He bought that dreadful suit on a whim.*

whimper *vb.* cry, whine, snivel, moan, sob. *As soon as we took his toy away, the tot began to whimper.*

whimsical *adj.* erratic, unpredictable, capricious, uncertain, eccentric, impulsive. *Her decisions were just as often whimsical as they were carefully planned.* **Ant.** planned, predictable, thoughtful.

whine *vb.* cry, sob, whimper, moan, complain. *The spoiled child whined to get what he wanted.*

whip *vb.* **1.** beat, strike, lash, flog, flail. *The stern schoolmaster whipped any student who misbehaved.* **2.** whisk, flick, jerk, snatch, sweep. *He whipped his sword out of its scabbard.* **3.** defeat, vanquish, overcome, trounce, beat. *Our women's softball team whipped their opponents.* *–n.* **4.** switch, lash, strap, crop. *The animal trainer used a whip to keep the lion at a safe distance.*

whirl *vb.* **1.** twist, spin, rotate, reel, revolve, turn. *The windmill's blades whirled in the breeze.* *–n.* **2.** turn, spin, revolution, rotation, twirl. *The dancers executed a graceful whirl.* **3.** bustle, rush, flurry, tumult, uproar. *There was a whirl of last-minute activity as we prepared the house for guests.*

whirlpool *n.* vortex, gyre, eddy, maelstrom, swirl. *The water formed a natural whirlpool as it flowed into the sewer pipe.*

whisk *vb.* **1.** brush, flick, sweep, swish, swipe. *She used her beach towel to whisk the sand off her legs.* **2.** hurry, speed, rush, hasten, zip. *The jogger was startled when a car whisked by.* **Ant.** **2.** crawl, creep, drag.

whiskers *n.* stubble, beard, bristles, hair, (slang) five o'clock shadow, sideburns. *He looked terribly ungroomed with his five-day growth of whiskers.*

whisper *vb.* **1.** speak softly, mumble, mutter, murmur. *It's impolite to whisper during the minister's sermon.* **2.** rustle, drone, sigh, buzz. *She enjoys listening to the wind whisper through the trees.* *–n.* **3.** murmur, mumble, mutter, undertone. *Though she spoke in a whisper, everyone heard what she said to her friend.* **Ant.** **1–3.** shout, scream, bellow.

white *adj.* **1.** colorless, pallid, pale, blanched, bleached. *He turned white with fear.* **2.** snowy, pearly, milky, silvery, snow-white. *The bride wore a beautiful white gown.* **3.** harmless, innocent, innocuous, inoffensive. *He told a white lie when he said he liked your present.* **Ant.** **1.** flushed, florid. **2.** black, ebony. **3.** harmful, hurtful.

whole *adj.* **1.** entire, complete, undivided, full, total. *He ate the whole cake by himself.* *–n.* **2.** entirety, totality, aggregate, sum, all. *She spent the whole of her vacation in England.* **Ant.** **1.** incomplete, partial, divided. **2.** part, piece.

wholesale *adj.* sweeping, blanket, extensive, broad, comprehensive, general. *The boss warned that she would make wholesale changes in personnel if our production didn't improve.* **Ant.** limited, small-scale.

wholesome *adj.* **1.** healthy, healthful, nutritious, nourishing. *A wholesome diet is essential for good health.* **2.** moral, virtuous, decent, pure, clean. *She writes wholesome children's books.* **Ant.** **1.** unwholesome, unhealthy, harmful. **2.** immoral, sinful.

wholly *adv.* completely, entirely, totally, fully, thoroughly. *He was wholly responsible for the accident.* **Ant.** incompletely, partially, partly.

whore *n.* (slang) prostitute, (slang) ho, (slang) call girl, (slang) lady of the evening, (slang) hooker, courtesan. *"Whore" is an impolite word for prostitute.*

wicked *adj.* immoral, bad, sinful, evil, vile, foul. *You should be ashamed of yourself for saying such a wicked thing about your friend.* **Ant.** moral, good, noble.

wide *adj.* **1.** broad, large, vast, extensive, spacious. *They can park two cars side by side on their wide driveway.* **2.** far, distant, off, remote, away. *His free-throw attempt was wide of the basket.* *–adv.* **3.** fully, completely, totally, entirely. *She had to hold her mouth wide open while the doctor examined her tonsils.* **Ant. 1.** narrow, thin, small. **2.** close, near, nearby. **3.** partially, incompletely, narrowly.

widespread *adj.* pervasive, extensive, far-reaching, worldwide, prevalent, universal, common. *The flu is now widespread.* **Ant.** local, confined, regional.

widget *n.* gadget, (slang) gizmo, contraption, control, (slang) thingamajig, device. *If you want more heat, turn that little widget to the left.*

width *n.* breadth, broadness, girth, reach, range. *What is the width of your new garage?*

wield *vb.* command, exercise, manage, handle, exert, use. *The boxer's agent wields total control over his career.*

wife *n.* spouse, bride, mate, partner, companion. *My wife and I have been married for thirty years.*

wig *n.* hairpiece, toupee, fall, (slang) rug, peruke. *The witch wore a wig to hide her bald, warty head.*

wiggle *vb.* wriggle, waggle, squirm, worm, shake, quiver. *We watched the dancers wiggle and stomp across the floor.*

wild *adj.* **1.** untamed, undomesticated, uncivilized, primitive, savage. *She thinks wild animals shouldn't be caged in zoos.* **2.** unruly, undisciplined, uncontrolled, unrestrained. *A group of wild kids vandalized the school.* **3.** crazy, fantastic, foolish, silly, reckless. *That's just another of his wild schemes to get rich quick.* **4.** violent, ferocious, turbulent, raging, stormy. *A wild wind blew down the tree in our front yard.* **Ant. 1.** tamed, domesticated, civilized. **2.** disciplined, controlled. **3.** thoughtful, practical, realistic. **4.** calm, mild, gentle.

wilderness *n.* wilds, hinterland, backcountry, outback, undeveloped region, badland. *We're going camping for seven days in the wilderness.*

will *n.* **1.** resolution, determination, purpose, conviction, volition. *You'll have a hard time getting her to do anything against her will.* **2.** legacy, testament, bequest. *Were you mentioned in your late uncle's will?* *–vb.* **3.** resolve, determine, wish, desire, want. *You can do whatever you will with your life.* **4.** bequeath, endow, bestow, confer. *She willed her book collection to the local library.*

willful *adj.* deliberate, on purpose, intentional, planned, premeditated, voluntary. *He mcde a willful decision to eat the last cookie.* **Ant.** involuntary, coerced.

willing *adj.* consenting, agreeing, ready, inclined, disposed. *He was a willing accomplice to the robbery.* **Ant.** unwilling, reluctant, disinclined.

willowy *adj.* svelte, slim, slender, thin, lithe, lissome. *The models slinking down the catwalk were among the most willowy women I'd ever seen.* **Ant.** fat, obese, plump.

willpower *n.* self-control, discipline, strength, will, resolve, determination. *Smokers must have great willpower to quit.* **Ant.** weakness, lack of resolve.

wilt *vb.* droop, sag, wither, languish, fade, weaken, die. *This hot weather has wilted my house plants.* **Ant.** thrive, flourish, bloom.

wily *adj.* sly, crafty, sneaky, tricky, shrewd, cunning. *The wily fox is not easily fooled by traps.* **Ant.** dumb, dense, naive.

win *vb.* **1.** triumph, conquer, vanquish, defeat, beat, succeed. *She usually wins when we play tennis.* **2.** attain, achieve, obtain, gain, acquire. *He won a television set in last year's contest.* –*n.* **3.** victory, triumph, conquest, success. *Our team needs three wins out of the next four games.* **Ant. 1.** lose, fail, fall. **2.** lose, miss. **3.** defeat, loss, failure.

wince *vb.* grimace, cringe, flinch, blink, shrink, withdraw. *Dropping the bowling ball on my toe made me wince.*

wind *n.* **1.** breeze, gust, draft, blow, gale. *The wind blew strongly just before the storm hit.* **2.** breath, air. *The football player had the wind knocked out of him.* **3.** hint, clue, suggestion, scent, smell. *If he catches wind of our plans, all our work will be lost.*

WORD SEARCH

altitude, high-speed wind of very high: *jet stream*
burst accompanied by rain: *squall*
god of: *Aeolus*
hazard to aviation: *windshear*
hot wind of Asiatic and African deserts: *simoom*
indicator, direction: *anemoscope, sock, weather vane*
indicator, speed: *anemometer*
pertaining to: *eolian*
scale: *Beaufort*
shifting: *backing, veering*
trees, limbs and fruit knocked down by: *windfall*
windless area of sea: *doldrums*

wind *vb.* **1.** coil, wrap, twist, entwine, screw. *Please wind this string into a ball.* **2.** turn, wander, meander, weave, twist. *The trail winds its way up the mountain.*

windfall *n.* godsend, manna, gift, blessing, boon, jackpot. *Winning the lottery was a windfall for us.*

window *n.* opening, portal, deadlight, casement, dormer, glazing. *Close the window before the mosquitoes come in.*

windy *adj.* breezy, blustery, gusting, drafty, blowing, tempestuous. *It's too windy to go out on the lake with a boat.* **Ant.** calm, becalmed, still.

wine *n.* beverage, drink, alcohol, fermented grape juice, port, muscatel, vintage. *Some people like to have a little wine with their dinner.*

wing *n.* **1.** appendage, annex, addition, extension, branch, section. *The construction of a new wing doubled the hospital's size.* –*vb.* **2.** fly, soar, drift, glide, sail, speed. *In the fall, migratory birds wing their way south.*

winner *n.* victor, champion, vanquisher, conqueror. *She's the winner of our school's poetry contest.* **Ant.** loser.

wipe *vb.* **1.** rub, mop, scrub, cleanse, polish, dry. *Please wipe off the countertop.* **2.** erase, eradicate, eliminate, extinguish. *The hurricane wiped out an entire village.*

wire *n.* **1.** cable, filament, strand, cord. *I need a piece of wire to fix my pack.* **2.** telegraph, telegram, cable, cablegram. *News of the disaster arrived by wire.* –*vb.* **3.** fasten, tie, bind, lash, secure. *He wired the broken parts together.* **4.** telegraph, cable. *The traveling student wired home for more money.* **Ant. 3.** loosen, unfasten, untie.

wiry *adj.* sinewy, stringy, lean, tough, strong, athletic. *His wiry build is a result of all the running he does.* **Ant.** stout, fat, weak.

wisdom *n.* judgment, discernment, understanding, sense, sagacity. *People typically gain wisdom as they grow older and more experienced.* **Ant.** stupidity, foolishness, folly.

wise *adj.* bright, smart, intelligent, knowledgeable, educated. *She made a wise decision when* *she bought that business.* **Ant.** unwise, foolish, dumb, ignorant.

wish *n.* **1.** desire, want, hope, longing, yen, yearning. *His wish is to become a successful author.* *–vb.* **2.** desire, want, crave, covet, long for. *Everyone wishes to be healthy, wealthy, and wise.*

wishy-washy *adj.* indecisive, irresolute, spineless, weak, vacillating, equivocating. *Stop being so wishy-washy and make up your mind.* **Ant.** decisive, resolute, firm.

wistful *adj.* yearning, pensive, sad, nostalgic, wishful, heartsick, troubled. *He thought of his childhood and grew wistful.*

wit *n.* **1.** wittiness, witticism, humor, cleverness, fun. *I enjoy her books because they're full of wit.* **2.** intelligence, understanding, cleverness, reason, judgment. *He had sufficient wit to know he couldn't finish the job by himself.* **3.** comedian, comic, humorist, jester, joker. *She was known as the office wit.* **4.** mind, sanity, reason, senses. *He was frightened out of his wits.* **Ant.** **1.** dullness, solemnity. **2.** stupidity, foolishness.

witch *n.* sorceress, enchantress, enchanter, magician. *In* The Wizard of Oz, *Dorothy dissolved the Wicked Witch of the West.*

witchcraft *n.* sorcery, spellcasting, magic, black arts, necromancy, diabolism. *The old lady used witchcraft to put the children to sleep.*

withdraw *vb.* **1.** remove, extract, subtract, deduct, retract. *She withdrew her name from consideration.* **2.** retire, retreat, depart, leave, quit. *The defeated army withdrew from the battlefield.* **Ant.** **1.** submit, introduce. **2.** arrive, stand, maintain.

withdrawn *adj.* quiet, silent, reserved, shy, remote, aloof, introspective. *I tried to talk to that shy girl, but she was too withdrawn.* **Ant.** friendly, talkative, loquacious.

wither *vb.* shrivel, dry, wilt, droop, fade, fail. *His plants withered because he forgot to water them.* **Ant.** flourish, thrive, prosper.

withhold *vb.* hold, keep, retain, repress, suppress. *The teacher asked her students to withhold their questions till the end of class.* **Ant.** give, provide, reveal.

withstand *vb.* oppose, resist, defy, endure, confront, brave. *The champion boxer withstood all contenders for his title.* **Ant.** yield, capitulate, surrender to.

witness *n.* **1.** eyewitness, spectator, viewer, observer, onlooker. *Were there any witnesses to the crime?* *–vb.* **2.** see, observe, view, watch, notice. *Did you witness the accident*

witty *adj.* humorous, funny, amusing, clever, entertaining. *Everyone enjoyed her witty comments.* **Ant.** dull, witless, humorless.

wizard *n.* **1.** mage, magician, sorcerer, conjuror. *A wizard set out to slay the dragon.* **2.** expert, genius, prodigy, master, pro. *She is known for being a computer wizard.* **Ant.** **2.** duffer, amateur, imbecile.

wizardry *n.* magic, sorcery, conjuring, witchcraft, black art. *To people who lived in medieval times, television would appear to be a form of wizardry.*

wizened *adj.* withered, shriveled, wrinkled, wasted, weathered, wilted. *A wizened old man with white hair asked us to help him cross the street.*

wobble *vb.* sway, stagger, totter, shake, quake. *This chair wobbles when you sit in it.*

woe *n.* grief, distress, unhappiness, sorrow, anguish, misery. *He endured poverty, illness, and other woes.* **Ant.** joy, happiness, delight, pleasure.

woman *n.* lady, female, matron, matriarch, miss, gal, girl. *Ask that woman over there where she got her hair styled.*

womanizer *n.* Casanova, Don Juan, lecher, stud, (slang) player. *A notorious womanizer risks winding up alone.*

wonder *n.* **1.** astonishment, surprise, amazement, awe, fascination. We watched in wonder as she scaled the steep cliff. **2.** curiosity, spectacle, marvel, sensation. *Can you name the seven wonders of the ancient world?* –*vb.* **3.** speculate, conjecture, question, meditate, query. *She wondered what the world will be like in the next century.* **Ant.** **1.** apathy, indifference. **2.** triviality, banality.

wonderful *adj.* amazing, marvelous, fantastic, astonishing, magnificent, excellent. *She is a wonderful dancer.* **Ant.** ordinary, routine, unremarkable.

woo *vb.* court, persuade, coax, pursue, seek. *If you are going to woo Sarah, may I suggest offering her lots of flowers and jewelry.*

wood *n.* **1.** lumber, timber, logs, planks, boards. *He needs some more wood to finish the deck he's building.* **2.** forest, grove, trees, timberland, woodland. *Her dog loves to romp through the woods.*

woodcutter *n.* sawyer, lumberjack, millworker, logger. *We were impressed with the woodcutter's massive shoulder muscles.*

wooden *adj.* stiff, stony, tense, expressionless, awkward, formal, blank. *People who are tense on the dance floor tend to look wooden.* **Ant.** relaxed, loose, expressive.

woods *n.* forest, timberland, wilderness, bush, hinterland. *We followed the trail deep into the woods.*

word *n.* **1.** term, expression, name, designation. *What's the word that describes someone who's afraid to go outside?* **2.** chat, conversation, talk, discussion. *I'd like to have a word with you.* **3.** promise, pledge, assurance, vow. *She gave me her word that she would return the money in two weeks.* **4.** message, news, tidings, report, communication. *He received word that his mother was in the hospital.* –*vb.* **5.** term, express, phrase, formulate. *She worded the memo carefully in order to assure that no one misunderstood it.*

wording *n.* phrasing, phraseology, terminology, vocabulary, syntax. *The wording of this contract is too vague.*

wordy *adj.* verbose, rambling, long-winded, windy, redundant. *His books are so wordy that few people enjoy reading them.* **Ant.** concise, succinct, brief.

work *n.* **1.** labor, toil, effort, exertion, trouble. *He didn't want to clear the weeds from his yard because it would take too much work.* **2.** employment, profession, business, occupation. *What line of work do you plan to go into?* **3.** task, chore, assignment, job, project. *The soldier checked the duty roster to see what his work would be for the day.* **4.** creation, achievement, accomplishment, product. *That author has written numerous works.* –*vb.* **5.** labor, toil, strive, strain, endeavor. *She worked hard to finish college in just three years.* **6.** perform, function, operate, run. *My microwave does not work properly.* **Ant.** **1.** effortlessness, rest. **2.** unemployment. **3.** recreation, play, leisure. **5.** rest, play. **6.** stop, fail.

worker *n.* laborer, employee, (slang) working stiff, hand, drudge, slave. *We'll need to hire another worker to meet the holiday rush.*

workmanship *n.* craftsmanship, handiwork, proficiency, artistry, skill, technique. *The carpenter's workmanship was superb.*

world *n.* **1.** Earth, planet, globe, orb. *Overpopulation is a problem that affects everyone in the world.* **2.** humanity, humankind, the human race, everyone. *The world watched when trouble broke out in the Middle East.* **3.** group, class, system, kingdom, realm. *The blue whale is the largest mammal in the animal world.* **4.** multitude, large amount, mass, pile, lots. *Taking some time off work did her a world of good.*

worldly *adj.* experienced, sophisticated, cosmopolitan, urbane, knowing, savvy. *The diplomat's worldly charm won him great respect.* **Ant.** inexperienced, naive, unsophisticated.

worldwide *adj.* international, multinational, global, cosmopolitan, universal, pandemic. *The flu is a worldwide threat to human health.* **Ant.** local, domestic, regional.

worried *adj.* troubled, disturbed, disquieted, anxious, apprehensive, distressed. *I have to be in by midnight or my mother will be worried.* **Ant.** unconcerned, untroubled, serene.

worrisome *adj.* troubling, distressing, disquieting, disturbing, bothersome, unnerving. *Your habit of driving without a seatbelt is worrisome.* **Ant.** reassuring, comforting, encouraging.

worry *vb.* **1.** fret, agonize, chafe, grieve, dread. *It's useless to worry about the weather.* **2.** disturb, perturb, upset, distress, annoy. *His son's erratic behavior is beginning to worry him.* *–n.* **3.** anxiety, concern, apprehension, dread, trouble. *She doesn't have a worry in the world.* **Ant. 2.** soothe, relieve, comfort. **3.** relief, contentment, serenity.

worsen *vb.* deteriorate, degenerate, decline, fail, sink. *He hasn't been taking care of himself, and his health continues to worsen.* **Ant.** improve, better, recover.

worship *vb.* **1.** revere, venerate, exalt, extol, glorify. *Do you worship God?* **2.** adore, idolize, admire, love. *She worships her grandfather* *–n.* **3.** adoration, reverence, homage, devotion. *Churches, synagogues and mosques are all places of worship.* **Ant. 1.** blaspheme, dishonor. **2.** scorn, hate, detest.

worth *n.* **1.** value, usefulness, merit, importance, significance. *Her new invention may prove to be of little worth.* **2.** wealth, riches, assets, estate, holdings. *His personal worth has been estimated at several million dollars.* **Ant. 1.** worthlessness, uselessness.

worthless *adj.* valueless, useless, unimportant, insignificant. *The stocks he bought turned out to be worthless.* **Ant.** worthwhile, worthy, valuable.

worthwhile *adj.* important, useful, beneficial, valuable, helpful. *Instead of wasting your time, you ought to do something worthwhile.* **Ant.** worthless, useless, unimportant.

worthy *adj.* worthwhile, deserving, fitting, excellent, good. *She willed her entire fortune to a worthy cause.* **Ant.** worthless, undeserving, useless.

wound *n.* **1.** injury, hurt, harm, sore, damage. *His old wound still bothers him.* *–vb.* **2.** injure, hurt, harm, damage, traumatize. *Her pride was wounded by her friend's careless remark.*

wrap *vb.* enclose, cover, envelop, sheathe, enfold. *Have you had a chance to wrap your Christmas presents yet?* **Ant.** unwrap, uncover, open.

wrath *n.* anger, rage, fury, ire, vexation. *I aroused my boss's wrath when I was late three days in a row.* **Ant.** serenity, forbearance, calm.

wreak *vb.* inflict, unleash, commit, exercise, work. *Godzilla wreaked havoc on the city of Tokyo.*

wreath *n.* garland, festoon, braid, decoration. *Let's suspend a wreath from the door this Christmas.*

wreck *vb.* **1.** ruin, damage, destroy, shatter, demolish, break. *If you don't drive more carefully, you'll wreck the car.* *–n.* **2.** ruins, remains, destruction, devastation, mess. *This old jalopy is a total wreck.* **Ant. 1.** save, protect, preserve.

wreckage *n.* ruins, remains, rubble, flotsam, jetsam, debris, fragments. *The police officer examined the car's wreckage solemnly.*

wrench *vb.* **1.** strain, sprain, twist, pull, tear. *The jogger wrenched her ankle when she stumbled on a rock.* **2.** jerk, tug, wring, wrest, pull. *A young hoodlum wrenched the purse out of the woman's hands.*

wrestle *vb.* **1.** grapple, tussle, scuffle, fight. *We're not allowed to wrestle inside the house.* **2.** struggle, strive, labor, strain, toll. *She's been wrestling with her smoking problem for years.*

wretch *n.* villain, scoundrel, knave, rogue, rascal. *The movie's heroine was abducted by a heartless wretch.*

wretched *adj.* **1.** distressed, miserable, forlorn, depressed, unhappy. *She's been feeling wretched ever since she lost her puppy.* **2.** despicable, contemptible, dreadful, horrid, terrible. *He has a wretched sense of humor.* **Ant. 1.** happy, cheerful, gay. **Ant. 2.** admirable, wonderful.

wriggle *vb.* wiggle, squirm, twist, worm. *You can't wriggle out of a headlock.*

wring *vb.* force, twist, squeeze, extract, wrench. *She wrung the water out of the washcloth when she was through using it.*

wrinkle *n.* **1.** crease, furrow, ridge, line, groove. *Wrinkles at the corner of the mouth are sometimes called "smile lines."* –*vb.* **2.** crease, crumple, rumple, groove, furrow. *He wouldn't sit down because he didn't want to wrinkle his new suit.* **Ant. 2.** smooth, straighten, iron.

write *vb.* **1.** inscribe, scribe, record, mark, note. *Please use the answer sheet provided and don't write on the test.* **2.** author, pen, compose, create, produce. *He writes mystery novels.*

writer *n.* author, wordsmith, scribe, novelist, reporter, journalist, hack. *The writer's next project will be a novel.*

writhe *vb.* squirm, twist, wriggle, wiggle, weave. *The snake writhed through the grass.*

writing *n.* **1.** composition, prose, fiction, nonfiction, letters, reporting. *I admire that columnist's writing tremendously.* **2.** handwriting, penmanship, calligraphy, longhand. *Your writing is barely legible.*

wrong *adj.* **1.** incorrect, inaccurate, false, erroneous, untrue. *The game-show contestant missed winning a new car when she gave a wrong answer.* **2.** immoral, sinful, bad, wicked, unethical. *It was wrong of him to lie.* **3.** improper, unsuitable, inappropriate, unfit, unacceptable. *A bathing suit is the wrong thing to wear to a formal dinner party.* **4.** faulty, amiss, awry, out of order. *The mechanic figured out what was wrong with my car.* –*adv.* **5.** incorrectly, inaccurately, falsely, erroneously. *If you thought I stole the money, you thought wrong.* –*n.* **6.** sin, evil, wickedness, crime, vice. *Do you know the difference between right and wrong?* –*vb.* **7.** injure, hurt, harm, mistreat, abuse, victimize. *She felt she had been wronged when I didn't tell her everything.* **1.** right, true, correct. **2.** moral, good, ethical. **3.** proper, suitable, appropriate. **4.** all right. **5.** rightly, correctly, accurately. **6.** morality, goodness.

wrongful *adj.* criminal, unlawful, illegal, illicit, dishonest, immoral. *Wrongful conduct is punishable by law.* **Ant.** rightful, legal, proper.

wry *adj.* **1.** twisted, crooked, slanted, contorted, distorted. *Her wry smile means she's not happy with you.* **2.** dry, ironic, sarcastic, cynical, bitter. *She didn't appreciate his wry joke.* **Ant. 1.** straight, direct, normal.

X

Xerox (trademark) *n.* **1.** photocopy, copy, duplicate, reproduction, facsimile. *Though he lost his original manuscript, fortunately he still has his xeroxes.* –*vb.* **2.** reproduce, copy, photocopy, duplicate. *Please xerox this report for me.*

X-rated *adj.* adult, pornographic, obscene, hardcore, graphic, restricted. *Nobody under the age of eighteen was allowed into the theater because the movie was X-rated.*

X-ray *n.* diagnostic picture, medical photograph, radiograph, radiogram. *Medical technicians took X-rays of the suspected fracture.*

x-ray *vb.* photograph. *Hospital personnel x-rayed the broken ankle before the doctor set it.*

Y

yacht *n.* boat, ship, pleasure, craft, sloop, ketch. *The millionaire's yacht was her pride and joy.*

yank *vb.* **1.** wrench, jerk, pull, tug, snatch, extract. *The police officer yanked a gun from the suspect's hand.* –*n.* **2.** jerk, pull, tug, wrench, joggle. *That window needs a hearty yank to get it open.* **Ant. 1.** push, shove, replace, return. **2.** push, shove.

yard *n.* grounds, lawn, court, compound, enclosure, confine. *Our school yard has a decent playground.*

yarn *n.* **1.** fiber, thread, flax, wool. *This red yarn will make an attractive sweater.* **2.** story, tale, anecdote, account, narrative, reminiscence. *The old man has many entertaining yarns to tell.*

yawn *vb.* **1.** gape, open wide. *A deep crevasse yawned in front of the startled mountaineers.* **2.** doze, drowse, nap, snooze. *Tired students have been known to yawn off during boring lectures.*

yearn *vb.* crave, desire, want, covet, ache, hunger, thirst. *The new immigrant yearned to meet someone from her native country.* **Ant.** dread, fear, abhor, hate, loathe, despise.

yearning *n.* craving, desire, longing, wish, inclination, hunger, thirst. *Though he was a vegetarian, he still experienced an occasional yearning for a pepperoni pizza.*

years *n.* decades, centuries, millennium, age, eon, time. *We spent many years learning how to navigate space.*

yell *vb.* **1.** shout, scream, holler, bellow, howl, shriek, cry. *Don't yell at me.* –*n.* **2.** call, shout, cry, holler. *Give a yell if you need anything.*

yellow *adj.* **1.** lemon, canary, mustard, gold, ocher. *The golfer was dressed in a bright yellow jacket.* **2.** cowardly, fearful, afraid, apprehensive, craven. *Conscientious objectors don't refuse to fight because they're yellow but because it's against their beliefs.* **Ant. 2.** brave, bold, daring, courageous, fearless.

yen *vb.* **1.** yearn, crave, desire, long, pine, hunger. *The hapless dieter yenned for a banana split.* –*n.* **2.** craving, desire, longing, appetite, yearning, hunger. *Anyone have a yen for popcorn?* **Ant. 1.** abhor, disdain, scorn. **2.** revulsion, abhorrence, aversion.

yes-man *n.* sycophant, toady, fawner, groveler, kow-tower. *We don't need a yes-man in this organization, we need a leader.* **Ant.** rebel, fighter.

yield *vb.* **1.** produce, bear, supply, generate, furnish, return. *This grapefruit tree yields fruit all year long.* **2.** surrender, submit, succumb, relinquish, acquiesce, capitulate. *Sometimes it's difficult not to yield to temptation.* **3.** fail, buckle, collapse, break, give way. *The old bridge yielded under the weight of the heavy truck.* –*n.* **4.** harvest, crop, produce, return, product, output. *The farmer hoped for a bountiful yield.* **5.** interest, earnings, proceeds, gain. *Bankers are always concerned with the yields of their investments.*

Ant. **2.** resist, oppose, thwart, stop. **3.** endure, sustain, withstand.

yoga *n.* Hindu discipline, ascetic discipline, posturing, meditation. *Practicing yoga every day is a great way to reduce stress.*

WORD SEARCH

ancient language from which Yoga terms originate: *Sanskrit*
breath control or conscious breathing: *pranayama*
chant, universally-used: *aum, om*
energy centers thought to reside along spine, seven: *chakras*
female practitioner: *yogini*
hymn or excerpt of sacred text chanted for meditation purposes: *mantra*
practitioner of: *yogi*
quieting of the mind through chanting or blanking out thought: *meditation*
school or retreat where yoga is taught: *ashram*
seated position with legs crossed and feet resting on opposite thighs: *lotus position*
seated position with legs folded and ankles crossed: *half-lotus*
spiritual teacher: *guru*
trance-like state leading to path to enlightenment: *samadhi*

yoke *n.* **1.** load, strain, weight, burden, oppression, servitude, enslavement. *The yoke of poverty keeps many people from fulfilling their dreams.* **2.** pair, brace, couple, span, team. *The heavy plow was pulled by a yoke of oxen.* **3.** bond, link, attachment, collar, harness, connector. *A computer yoke connects two or more magnetic reading heads.* *–vb.* **4.** join, link, attach, combine, couple, hitch, harness. *The driver yoked his horses to the stagecoach.* **Ant.** **1.** freedom, independence, liberty. **4.** separate, unhitch.

yonder *adj.* distant, remote, farther, far-off. *The grass is greener in yonder valley.* **Ant.** close, near, nearby.

young *adj.* **1.** youthful, juvenile, adolescent, underage, immature, undeveloped, inexperienced. *He was too young to understand what was happening.* *–n.* **2.** offspring, descendants, child, baby. *It's best not to approach a mother bear when she's with her young.* **Ant.** **1.** old, mature, full-grown, experienced. **2.** parent.

youngster *n.* child, youth, juvenile, minor, adolescent, boy, girl. *The youngsters are in bed.* **Ant.** oldster, adult, grown-up.

youth *n.* **1.** child, juvenile, minor, adolescent, boy, girl, youngster. *He was still a youth when he immigrated to this country.* **2.** infancy, beginning, start, onset. *The computer age is still in its youth.* **3.** childhood, adolescence, boyhood, girlhood. *In her youth, she wanted to be an explorer.* **Ant.** **1.** adult, grown-up, oldster. **2–3.** adulthood, maturity.

youthful *adj.* **1.** young, juvenile, adolescent, boyish, girlish, immature, inexperienced. *He has a youthful appearance.* **2.** fresh, energetic, optimistic, robust, lighthearted, vigorous, dynamic. *She has a youthful outlook on life.* **Ant.** **1.** old, mature, grown-up, experienced. **2.** tired, weary.

yummy *adj.* delicious, delectable, mouth-watering, (slang) scrumptious, heavenly, ambrosial. *Chocolate swirl ice cream is yummy.* **Ant.** nauseating, stomach-turning, disgusting.

Z

zany *adj.* **1.** ludicrous, clownish, foolish, absurd, funny, comical, silly. *He has a zany sense of humor.* –*n.* **2.** jester, joker, clown, fool, comic, buffoon. *Every party seems to have its drunken zany.*

zeal *n.* enthusiasm, eagerness, zest, fervor, ardor, passion, devotion. *Her zeal for work might mean she's hoping for a promotion.* **Ant.** indifference, apathy, unconcern, disinterest.

zealot *n.* enthusiast, fanatic, fan, devotee, addict, disciple, follower. *Some religious zealots do not try to understand other people's beliefs.*

zealous *adj.* enthusiastic, ardent, fervent, eager, obsessed, fanatic, devoted. *The businesswoman was a zealous collector of Oriental art.* **Ant.** apathetic, uninterested, unenthusiastic, passionless.

Zen *n.* Buddhism, quest for enlightenment. *I practice Zen every day to keep myself centered.*

zenith *n.* peak, top, high point, crest, climax, culmination, maximum. *Winning an Olympic medal was the zenith of her athletic career.* **Ant.** low point, bottom, nadir, depths.

zeppelin *n.* dirigible, aircraft, lighter-than-air craft, flying vessel.

zero *adj.* **1.** nonexistent, nothing, insignificant, nil, naught. *His chances of making the team are zero.* –*vb.* **2.** aim, direct, point, level, train. *The basketball player zeroed in on the hoop from a distance of twenty feet.*

zest *n.* gusto, ardor, fervor, passion, zeal, delight, enthusiasm, eagerness, thrill, pleasure. *The salesman's zest for his product is so great that he set a new sales record.* **Ant.** distaste, dislike, aversion, apathy.

zestful *adj.* exciting, thrilling, delightful, stimulating, enjoyable. *Grandmother's baking fills the house with zestful aromas.* **Ant.** boring, dull, unexciting, unenjoyable.

zombie *n.* the living dead, the walking dead, corpse, cadaver, (slang) space case, oddball. *I once stayed awake for 48 hours and felt like a zombie.*

zone *n.* **1.** region, territory, area, sector, district, precinct, province, locality. *The "zone" of television's classic series. The Twilight Zone refers to a region where one's imagination runs free.* –*vb.* **2.** divide, sector, separate, allocate. *This neighborhood is zoned for residential use only.*

zoo *n.* **1.** menagerie, vivarium, animal farm. *Many people do not like to see animals caged in zoos.* **2.** madhouse, insane asylum, crush, press, throng, horde. *The shopping mall is a zoo at Christmastime.*

zoom *vb.* **1.** race, flash, streak, fly, whiz, zip, speed. *She zoomed through the book in no time at* *all.* **2.** climb, soar, rise, ascend, escalate, advance. *Real-estate values zoomed after the new factory came to town.* **Ant. 2.** plummet, drop, fall, decrease.

zydeco *n.* cajun music, Louisiana blues, French Caribbean music. *When I hear zydeco, I just want to move my feet.*